THE CAMBRIDGE HISTORY OF
LATER MEDIEVAL PHILOSOPHY

The Cambridge History of
Later Medieval Philosophy

FROM THE REDISCOVERY OF
ARISTOTLE TO THE DISINTEGRATION
OF SCHOLASTICISM
1100–1600

EDITORS
NORMAN KRETZMANN
ANTHONY KENNY   JAN PINBORG

ASSOCIATE EDITOR
ELEONORE STUMP

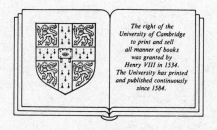

The right of the
University of Cambridge
to print and sell
all manner of books
was granted by
Henry VIII in 1534.
The University has printed
and published continuously
since 1584.

CAMBRIDGE UNIVERSITY PRESS

CAMBRIDGE
NEW YORK   PORT CHESTER
MELBOURNE   SYDNEY

Published by the Press Syndicate of the University of Cambridge
The Pitt Building, Trumpington Street, Cambridge CB2 1RP
40 West 20th Street, New York, NY 10011 USA
10 Stamford Road, Oakleigh, Melbourne 3166, Australia

First published 1982
Reprinted 1984
First paperback edition 1988
Reprinted 1989, 1990

Printed in Great Britain by Woolnough Bookbinding,
Irthlingborough, Northamptonshire

Library of Congress catalogue card number: 81-10086

British Library Cataloguing in Publication Data
The Cambridge history of later medieval philosophy.
I. Philosophy, Medieval – Historiography
I. Kretzmann, Normann II. Kenny, Anthony
III. Pinborg, Jan
189   B721

ISBN 0 521 22605 8 hard covers
ISBN 0 521 36933 9 paperback

CONTENTS

CONTRIBUTORS

PROFESSOR MARILYN ADAMS
Department of Philosophy, University of California at Los Angeles.

PROFESSOR E. J. ASHWORTH
Department of Philosophy, University of Waterloo.

DR JONATHAN BARNES
Balliol College, University of Oxford.

PROFESSOR IVAN BOH
Department of Philosophy, Ohio State University.

PROFESSOR JOHN BOLER
Department of Philosophy, University of Washington.

DR BERNARD G. DOD
189 Morrell Avenue, Oxford.

PROFESSOR ALAN DONAGAN
Department of Philosophy, University of Chicago.

MRS JEAN DUNBABIN
St Anne's College, University of Oxford.

LEKTOR STEN EBBESEN
Institut for Middelalderfilologi, University of Copenhagen.

DR P. J. FITZPATRICK
Department of Philosophy, University of Durham.

PROFESSOR EDWARD GRANT
Department of the History and Philosophy of Science, Indiana University.

DR D. P. HENRY
Department of Philosophy, University of Manchester.

DR LISA JARDINE
Jesus College, University of Cambridge.

DR ANTHONY KENNY
Balliol College, University of Oxford.

DR CHRISTIAN KNUDSEN
Ritterstrasse 3, D-4660 Gelsenkirchen-Buer, West Germany.

DR SIMO KNUUTTILA
Institute of Philosophy, University of Helsinki.

PROFESSOR J. B. KOROLEC
Polskij Akademii Nauk, Instytut Filozofii i Socjologii, Pałac Staszica, Nowy Świat 72, 00-330 Warszawa.

PROFESSOR NORMAN KRETZMANN
Sage School of Philosophy, Cornell University.

PROFESSOR ZDZISŁAW KUKSEWICZ
Polskij Akademii Nauk, Instytut Filozofii i Socjologii, Pałac Staszica, Nowy Świat 72, 00-330 Warszawa.

DR ALAIN DE LIBERA
École Pratique des Hautes Études, Section des Sciences Religieuses, Sorbonne, 45-47 rue des Écoles, Paris 5ᵉ.

DR CHARLES H. LOHR, S. J.
Raimundus-Lullus-Institut, Albert-Ludwigs-Universität, Freiburg i. Br.

PROFESSOR D. E. LUSCOMBE
Department of History, University of Sheffield.

PROFESSOR EDWARD P. MAHONEY
Department of Philosophy, Duke University.

PROFESSOR A. S. MCGRADE
Department of Philosophy, University of Connecticut.

PROFESSOR JOHN MURDOCH
Department of the History of Science, Harvard University.

PROFESSOR CALVIN NORMORE
Department of Philosophy, Princeton University.

PROFESSOR GABRIEL NUCHELMANS
Filosofisch Instituut, University of Leiden.

FR JOSEPH OWENS, C. SS. R.
Pontifical Institute of Mediaeval Studies, University of Toronto.

PROFESSOR W. KEITH PERCIVAL
Department of Linguistics, University of Kansas.

PROFESSOR JAN PINBORG
Institut for Middelalderfilologi, University of Copenhagen.

DR T. C. POTTS
Department of Philosophy, University of Leeds.

PROFESSOR L. M. DE RIJK
Filosofisch Instituut, University of Leiden.

PROFESSOR EILEEN SERENE
Department of Philosophy, Yale University.

PROFESSOR PAUL VINCENT SPADE
Department of Philosophy, Indiana University.

PROFESSOR ELEONORE STUMP
Department of Philosophy and Religion, Virginia Polytechnic Institute and State University.

PROFESSOR EDITH DUDLEY SYLLA
Department of History, North Carolina State University.

PROFESSOR JOHN TRENTMAN
Department of Philosophy, McGill University.

PROFESSOR MARTIN M. TWEEDALE
Department of Philosophy, University of Auckland.

FR JAMES A. WEISHEIPL, O. P.
Pontifical Institute of Mediaeval Studies, University of Toronto.

DR GEORG WIELAND
Philosophisches Seminar, University of Bonn.

PROFESSOR JOHN F. WIPPEL
School of Philosophy, Catholic University of America.

PREFACE

The idea of this History originated in the Cambridge University Press, and the first discussions that led directly to its publication took place in 1975. Naturally it was conceived of as one of the Cambridge Histories of philosophy. Its place in that series is described in the Introduction, where its principles of organisation and its special purposes are also discussed. Editorial decisions regarding the contents and the contributors were made in 1976, and drafts of most of the contributions were received by the end of 1978. During a two-week conference of the editorial staff in the summer of 1979 the book was given very nearly its final form, and the four editors put the finishing touches on the typescript during the following summer. Proofreading and indexing were done during the summer of 1981. The editorial work of the three last summers was alleviated by the hospitality of Cornell University's Society for the Humanities. The Directors of the Society during those years – first Professor Michael Kammen and then Professor Eric Blackall – cheerfully provided excellent offices and work-space for the staff on all those occasions. Two Cornell undergraduates served as assistants to the staff: Mary Tedeschi helped a great deal with the Bibliography, and William Haines worked with admirable efficiency and intelligence on the Index Nominum.

Editorial thanks can scarcely be offered to the contributors for the substance of their chapters; they are, after all, the authors of this book. But the editors would be remiss if they did not express their gratitude to the contributors for trying to stay within irksome limits and for acquiescing in the editing necessitated by their occasionally failing to do so. The resultant heavily edited typescript of an already complex volume posed a special problem for the typesetters, and we are pleased to offer our congratulations to the printers (the Asco Trade Typesetting company in Hong Kong) to whom the Press entrusted this project; their remarkably accurate work made the considerable task of proofreading and indexing less burdensome than we had expected it to be.

Long delays are evidently inevitable in the production of a work of this size, and the contributors, almost all of whom submitted their drafts on schedule in 1978, cannot be blamed if the Bibliography lacks references to some recent important work within the fields of their chapters. In the final phases of the book's preparation the editors did a little to bring the Bibliography up to date, but our combined expertise is not nearly broad enough to cover the range of all these chapters.

In editing the drafts we tried to reduce redundancy and inconsistency among the forty-seven chapters, but a history organised topically rather than chronologically and written by many expert authors is bound to contain differing opinions and even discrepancies. We hope those that remain prove to be stimulating.

The reader who wants to make effective use of this book should begin by reading the Introduction and the introductory notes attached to the Biographies, the Bibliography, and the Indices.

Norman Kretzmann

Ithaca, New York
August 1981

INTRODUCTION

The Cambridge History of Later Medieval Philosophy finds its natural place after *The Cambridge History of Later Greek and Early Medieval Philosophy* in the sequence that begins with Guthrie's *History of Greek Philosophy*. The sequence is not altogether smooth, however. At the beginning of *The Cambridge History of Later Greek and Early Medieval Philosophy* its editor, A. H. Armstrong, observes that although the volume 'was originally planned in connexion with W. K. C. Guthrie's *History of Greek Philosophy*, ... [it] has developed on rather different lines, and is not exactly a continuation of that work' (p. xii). Similarly, although *The Cambridge History of Later Medieval Philosophy* was conceived of as the sequel to *The Cambridge History of Later Greek and Early Medieval Philosophy*, the relationship between the two is not so simple as their titles suggest; in fact, the fit between this volume and the Armstrong volume is less exact than that between the Armstrong volume and Professor Guthrie's plan. Many reviewers noted that the Armstrong volume seems misleadingly titled since it is really a study of only the Platonist tradition in later Greek and early medieval philosophy; but in concentrating in that way it does indeed complement Professor Guthrie's plan, which includes the Stoics and Epicureans as well as Aristotle while leaving out the Neoplatonists. On the other hand, *The Cambridge History of Later Medieval Philosophy* cannot be put forward as the full realisation of Professor Armstrong's expressed hope 'that the philosophy of the thirteenth century and the later Middle Ages in the West, with later Jewish, Moslem, and Byzantine developments, will some day be dealt with in another Cambridge volume' (ibid.). We have of course undertaken to deal with the philosophy of the thirteenth century and the later Middle Ages in the West, but we have made no attempt to deal with later Jewish, Moslem, and Byzantine developments.

In deciding to restrict our attention to the Latin Christian West, we were motivated by two considerations. In the first place, we could scarcely hope to do justice to even our chosen material in a single volume of this size; if we had undertaken to deal with Arabic, Jewish, and Byzantine philosophy as well, we surely could not have dealt adequately with later medieval philosophy. And, in the second place, scholarship in those areas has not kept pace with research on medieval Christian philosophy. When a scholar with the authority of Richard Walzer acknowledges (on p. 643 of the Armstrong volume) that 'It appears premature, at the present time, to embark on a history of Islamic philosophy in the Middle Ages' because 'Too many of the basic facts are still unknown', no one else is likely to be prepared, even twelve years afterwards, to undertake the task; and the cases of medieval Jewish and Byzantine philosophy seem much the same. Of course, Arabs, Jews, and Byzantine Greeks are among the philosophers mentioned in this volume, but they figure in it only as contributors to the development of Latin philosophy during the Middle Ages.

The Cambridge History of Later Greek and Early Medieval Philosophy is described as covering the period 'from the fourth century B.C. to the beginning of the twelfth century A.D., from the Old Academy to St Anselm' (p. xii); but it encompasses those 1,500 years primarily in order to trace the development of Platonism after Plato. The sense in which that description is intended leaves ample room, of course, for Professor Guthrie's volumes on Plato and Aristotle, on the Stoics and Epicureans. Similarly, the fact that our predecessor volume reaches as far forward as the beginning of the twelfth century is explained by the facts that the philosophy of St Anselm may be thought of as the highwater mark of medieval Platonism and that Anselm died in 1109. Our volume does indeed concentrate on philosophy after Anselm, beginning with Abelard, but because it is part of our aim to present the medieval *Aristotelian* tradition and the scholastic innovations that developed in that tradition, we must reach back to consider many philosophers older than Anselm who were understandably left out of account in the Armstrong volume.

Like several other Cambridge Histories but unlike most histories of philosophy, this volume is the work of many hands; forty-one scholars from ten different countries contributed to it. We subdivided the material and assigned the subdivisions to individual contributors with the intention of providing a more faithful impression of the state of current research than could have been provided by a smaller number of contributors to whom larger areas had been assigned. Even with such a strategy we have naturally had to emphasise some subjects at the expense of others that are equally important, but we tried to make those difficult decisions in such a way that our emphasis would fall on material that had been neglected in the established literature on medieval philosophy and on material regarding which recent research had been making most progress. Thus the contributors have devoted relatively little attention to theological issues, even to the philosophically outstanding medieval achievement in rational (or natural) theology, for that side of medieval thought has not been neglected. And because the areas of concentration in contemporary philosophical scholarship on medieval thought naturally reflect the emphases in contemporary philosophy, our editorial strategy has led to a concentration on those parts of later medieval philosophy that are most readily recognisable as philosophical to a student of twentieth-century philosophy.

By combining the highest standards of medieval scholarship with a respect for the insights and interests of contemporary philosophers, particularly those working in the analytic tradition, we hope to have presented medieval philosophy in a way that will help to end the era during which it has been studied in a philosophical ghetto, with many of the major students of medieval philosophy unfamiliar or unsympathetic with twentieth-century philosophical developments, and with most contemporary work in philosophy carried out in total ignorance of the achievements of the medievals on the same topics. It is one of our aims to help make the activity of contemporary philosophy intellectually continuous with medieval philosophy to the extent to which it already is so with ancient philosophy. Such a relationship has clearly benefited both philosophical scholarship on ancient philosophy and contemporary work in philosophy, and we hope to foster a similar mutually beneficial relationship between medieval philosophy and contemporary philosophy.

The standard approach to the history of philosophy is, of course, by way of the chronological study of the doctrines of individual philosophers. That approach is not well-suited to the history of medieval philosophy, in which the identity of individuals is sometimes uncertain, the attribution of doctrines or works to individual philosophers is often disputable and sometimes impossible, and even the chronological succession of men or of works is often conjectural. We have organised our History around philosophical topics or disciplines rather than around philosophers, but not only because the standard approach is not well-suited to our period. Our principal aims in this volume are, we believe, better served by the topical approach than they would be by the standard approach. (We think of the biographical sketches supplied at the end of the volume as an important supplement to our topical approach.) In order to help the reader to discern the plan of this History, which is to a large extent not organised historically, we provide the following synopsis of the contributions.

The forty-six chapters that make up the text of this volume are arranged in eleven parts. The first and shortest of those parts is the work of two members of the editorial staff and is designed to introduce the reader to some of the distinctively medieval forms of philosophical literature. Such an introduction seems called for not only because most twentieth-century philosophical readers are likely to be unfamiliar with the presentation of philosophy in the form of *quaestiones* or *sophismata*, for instance, but also because the literary forms of scholasticism are more influential on the character of the philosophy presented or developed in those forms than are the literary forms of any other period in the history of philosophy (with the possible exception of Greek philosophy before Aristotle).

In the two chapters of Part II Bernard Dod and Charles Lohr provide accounts of the transmission of Aristotle's works to the Latin Middle Ages and of the changes effected in the form and content of thought as a result of that legacy from antiquity. None of the succeeding chapters of the book can be properly understood except against the historical background delineated in Part II.

The fact that Parts III, IV, and V all contain the word 'logic' in their titles may suggest an imbalance in the organisation of this History, and the fact that three members of the editorial staff have contributed chapters to these Parts might even suggest that editorial predilections account for the imbalance. What medieval philosophers thought of as logic does indeed figure very prominently in this book; several chapters in Parts VI, VII, and XI are also principally concerned with aspects of medieval logic. But any history of medieval philosophy which, like ours, leaves theology out of account is bound to devote more space to logic than to any other branch of philosophy. The imbalance, if there is one, is embedded in the nature of medieval scholasticism, in which the unusual importance of logic is partly a consequence of the fact that during the Middle Ages logic was conceived of more broadly than in any other period of the history of philosophy. A great deal of work that will strike a twentieth-century philosophical reader as belonging to metaphysics, philosophy of language, linguistics, natural philosophy, or philosophy of science was carried on during the Middle Ages by men who thought of themselves as working in logic. Moreover, the achievements of medieval logicians are historically more distinctive and philosophically more valuable than anything else in medieval thought, with the possible exception of rational theology; when Renaissance humanists waged their successful battle against medieval scholasticism, it was, understandably, scholastic logic against which they directed their fiercest attacks. After Christianity and Aristotelianism, the most important influence on the character of the philosophy of the Middle Ages is the medieval conception of logic.

The dominance of logic is to some extent the result of an historical accident: the fact that until the middle of the twelfth century the only ancient philosophy directly accessible to the Latin medievals was contained in two of Aristotle's works on logic, the *Categories* and *De interpretatione*. These very short and very difficult books, along with a handful of associated treatises stemming from late antiquity, constituted the secular philosophical library of the early Middle Ages and became known as the Old Logic by contrast with the New Logic – the rest of Aristotle's Organon – as it became available during the second half of the twelfth century. To the extent to which the philosophy of the later Middle Ages is a development of earlier medieval philosophy it rests on the accomplishments of men who had been working out the implications and ramifications of the Old Logic, and that essential contribution to later medieval philosophy is presented by Sten Ebbesen, D. P. Henry, and Martin Tweedale in the three chapters of Part III.

The development of medieval logic during and after the advent of the New Logic is explored in Parts IV and V. Several of the twelve chapters of these Parts will help to show how far beyond Aristotelian logic medieval logic eventually developed in various directions, but the non–Aristotelian character of later medieval logic is most striking in its semantic theories, different aspects of which are presented by L. M. de Rijk, Alain de Libera, Paul Vincent Spade, Gabriel Nuchelmans, Norman Kretzmann, and Jan Pinborg in Part IV.

The branches of medieval logic considered in Part V have not yet received as much scholarly attention as has medieval semantic theory, but, as the contributions of Eleonore Stump, Ivan Boh, Paul Vincent Spade Simo Knuuttila, and Calvin Normore help to show, they are likely to prove at least as rewarding to the further study they deserve. The first three chapters of Part V are devoted to issues associated with logic in its central role as theory of inference; the fourth and fifth chapters present medieval contributions to inquiries that lie on the border between logic and metaphysics.

Metaphysics and epistemology were very highly developed in later medieval philosophy, and there are enormous quantities of relevant textual material. The six chapters of Part VI sort out some of the more rewarding issues and explore a few of them to considerable depth, but no one is more keenly aware than the authors of these chapters that they have had to restrict themselves to merely alluding to developments that deserve detailed discussion. Fortunately, the secondary literature in these fields is more extensive than in most of the fields dealt with in this History, although a great deal of it is becoming obsolete as more texts become available and traditional interpretations are revised in the light of new evidence and changing philosophical perspectives. The first two chapters, by John Wippel and Marilyn Adams, are concerned with topics at the core of the subject-matter of metaphysics. Chapters 21 and 22, by Joseph Owens and John Boler, deal with epistemological issues that arise in different guises throughout the history of philosophy even though some of them appear here in distinctively medieval trappings. In Chapters 23 and 24 Christian Knudsen and Eileen Serene deal with epistemological issues adjacent to or included within medieval logic – semantic theory in Chapter 23, theory of inference in Chapter 24.

An important part of medieval natural philosophy, too, can be assimilated to medieval logic, as is clearly shown by Edith Sylla and John Murdoch in Chapters 27 and 28 of Part VII. Aristotle's *Physics* informed the developments in later medieval logic that look to us like speculative physical theory or proto-mathematics, but it served also as an independent source of developments in natural philosophy, especially those to be found in the many commentaries on the *Physics*. In the first chapter of Part VII James Weisheipl surveys these developments and the role of natural philosophy in the medieval university curriculum. The Condemnation of 1277, often referred to in this History because of its apparent effect on the character of later medieval thought, is summarised by Edward Grant in the second chapter of Part VII, especially with regard to its probable influence on the development of natural philosophy.

Part VIII begins with a full survey of the origins and development of philosophy of mind in the Middle Ages, carried out in a series of three co-ordinated chapters by Edward Mahoney and Z. Kuksewicz in a way that will help the reader understand not only medieval but also classical modern theories of mind. Medieval accounts of the theoretical links between philosophy of mind and moral philosophy are examined in J. B. Korolec's chapter on freedom of the will and Alan Donagan's chapter on Aquinas' theory of action.

Parts IX and X, on moral and political theory, are alike in beginning with chapters, by Georg Wieland and Jean Dunbabin respectively, that show how the reception and interpretation of Aristotle's treatises on those subjects shaped their development during the later Middle Ages. The remaining chapters in each of these Parts deal with specific ethical or political issues that were especially important to the medievals. In Part IX, on ethics, Georg Wieland examines attempts to accommodate the Aristotelian ideal of happiness within a Christian context, Timothy Potts lays out the particularly subtle medieval theory of conscience, and, in Chapter 37, D. E. Luscombe presents material that forms a natural transition between ethics and politics in his account of the natural foundations of morality and law. In Part X, on politics, Chapter 39, by A. S. McGrade, takes up the topics introduced in Part IX, Chapter 37, but in a more specifically political context. D. E. Luscombe contributes a chapter to Part X that is associated with his chapter in Part IX, this time pursuing the topic of the role of nature in the foundations of social and political institutions as the medievals saw it. Jonathan Barnes' chapter on justifications for war illuminates medieval applications of Christian principles and theories of international politics.

Because the humanist attack on medieval scholasticism aimed especially at overthrowing late medieval logic and most of the linguistic theory and educational practice associated with it, the first three chapters of Part XI, on the end of the scholastic period, are in one way or another devoted to issues of the sort that medieval logicians had concerned themselves with. In Chapter 42 E. J. Ashworth details the loss or repudiation of medieval accomplishments in logic, in Chapter 43 Lisa Jardine focuses on the educational reforms that may have constituted the primary motivation for the humanists' anti-scholasticism, and in Chapter 44 W. Keith Percival describes the new attitude towards languages and literature that saw them as subjects in their own right and not merely as instruments. In the last two chapters of Part XI and of the book John Trentman and P.J. FitzPatrick show us, first, the survival of scholasticism in the era of classical modern philosophy and, finally, the revival of scholasticism in the nineteenth century – a revival without which, as Dr FitzPatrick observes, this History would hardly have been written, however different its orientation may be from that of neoscholasticism.

One of the special virtues of a work of philosophical scholarship produced by many specialists of different sorts is to be found in the treatment of the same thinkers or closely related topics from different points of view. No system of cross-referencing could present the connections among these forty-six chapters adequately without becoming obtrusive; we urge the reader to refer frequently to the Index Nominum and Index Rerum in order to take full advantage of this History.

Limitations of space have naturally made it impossible for any of the

I
MEDIEVAL PHILOSOPHICAL LITERATURE

I
MEDIEVAL PHILOSOPHICAL LITERATURE*

Schools and universities[1]

Medieval philosophical literature is closely associated with medieval schools and universities as well as with the material and psychological conditions prevailing at these institutions. The economic prosperity of the eleventh and twelfth centuries, which is manifest in the rise of towns and the specialisation of labour, also had far-ranging repercussions in the world of learning. Learning was no longer confined to monasteries and monastic schools, but a new guild of professional intellectuals was created, which developed new intellectual aspirations. Such men were no longer satisfied with the traditional concept of Christian wisdom but wanted to pursue the whole domain of human learning, and they resolutely set out to recover and develop the intellectual heritage of antiquity.

Even in the very early Middle Ages, schools clustered around ecclesiastical centres, especially the chapters of episcopal sees, which throughout the Middle Ages provided the most important financial support for learning. Scholars shared the privileges of clergy although they were not required to take higher orders; in fact their clerical status was the best way of securing a certain amount of protection and independence against local authorities in surroundings which for the most part were hostile and brutal.

This description is especially appropriate for the situation in one of the centres of the twelfth-century intellectual expansion, the central part of France, between the Loire and the Rhine. Here schools flourished and decayed within short spans of time, often due to the presence or absence of one especially gifted teacher; Laon, Rheims, Melun, and Chartres are but a few examples of such schools. This situation calls for caution in employing

---

*Anthony Kenny is responsible for the sections *'Disputations of the theologians'*, *'The origins of disputation'*, and *'The later development of disputations'*; the other sections are the work of Jan Pinborg.

1. This chapter is a very concise survey of complex material. The most recent studies are Verger 1973 and Cobban 1975, where further references can be found. The classic in the field is Rashdall 1936. For twelfth-century schools see Delhaye 1947. Translated source material can be found in Thorndike 1944.

labels of the type 'the school of...', which often tend to confuse institutions and doctrinal trends.[2] Only at Paris was there a continuous flourishing and growth of the schools, and the best teachers from most other French schools eventually taught at one or more of the schools of Paris.

In northern Italy the situation was somewhat different. For instance, there were secular schools there from the beginning, and the interest centred more on legal training than on the liberal arts and theological studies, thus attracting students who were generally more mature. The law schools of Italy accordingly faced somewhat different problems, but even there the impact of often hostile surroundings forced the students to organise.

During the twelfth and thirteenth centuries the number of students and masters in France, England, northern Spain and Italy increased continually. This growth soon led to the demand for more secure privileges and a better way of organising, especially for means of controlling the granting of a licence to teach. Scholars began to organise into corporations, following normal medieval patterns of organisation. And so the latter decades of the twelfth century saw the emergence of universities, one of the most permanent institutions created by the Middle Ages. The oldest universities, such as those of Paris, Bologna, and Oxford, developed gradually and only later received formal recognition of their privileges from the Pope; it is therefore impossible to give a precise date for their foundation. But soon it became customary for new universities to receive their privileges from an international authority (the Pope, or in rare cases the Emperor) and from a national or local authority.

By the middle of the thirteenth century there were flourishing universities in Paris, Oxford, and Bologna and smaller ones in, e.g., Toulouse, Salamanca, and Cambridge. During the fourteenth century the university trend spread to central and eastern Europe; the first university east of the Rhine was the university of Prague, established in 1348. Before the end of the fifteenth century Europe had more than seventy universities of greatly varying size and importance. This of course does not mean that university learning was not introduced east of the Rhine till the fourteenth century. Scholars returning to their homelands from the university centres introduced a higher level of education and, as a result, the teaching and research in some town-schools of central Europe acquired almost university level. An especially well-documented case is that of the schools of Erfurt before

2. See also Southern 1970, pp. 61–85.

the foundation of the university in 1392.[3] Moreover, as early as the thirteenth century, the mendicant orders established *studia generalia* in most of their provinces, where selected friars could receive an education in philosophy and theology.[4]

The spread of universities is indicative not only of a quantitative dispersion of learning, but also of a change in the nature of universities. In principle, universities were equal, all of them having received the right to bestow the *ius ubique docendi* on their graduates; but in fact some universities could afford to be more critical than others regarding the acceptance of teachers. It is significant that the *ius ubique docendi* granted to masters from other universities did not normally gain them the right to teach in Paris. Moreover, new universities were often founded at places where the financial support was hardly adequate, which tended to make these universities smaller and more dependent on local authorities. Finally, some universities came to be no more than professional schools for those who wanted a career within civil or ecclesiastical administration, and this, too, had an effect on the recruitment of students. At the end of the Middle Ages universities were tending to become more and more aristocratic and plutocratic.[5]

Organisation of teaching

Already in the twelfth century schools tended to specialise in certain studies. Paris and central France, for example, became famous for their teaching in logic and theology, Bologna for civil and canon law. Still, the curricula were not rigidly determined but continued to change in accordance with the discovery of new material and the changing interests of the masters. Furthermore, with the emergence of universities, knowledge became organised into separable departments, differentiated and interrelated in a genre of texts called Divisions of Science.[6]

The fundamental division, which also affected the organisation of universities, was the division between faculties. The basic faculty was the faculty of Arts, which around 1250 and thereafter comprised the study of grammar and logic (which together with rhetoric made up the *Trivium*), and the whole field of Aristotelian philosophy, supplemented to some extent with a number of more technical mathematical and astronomical

3. Kleineidam 1973; Pinborg 1967a, pp. 139–50; Pinborg 1973 and 1976d.
4. See *Le Scuole Degli Ordini Mendicanti* 1978.
5. Gabriel 1977; Ijsewijn & Paquet 1978; Mornet 1978.
6. A typical example of this genre was written by John of Dacia around 1280 (ed. A. Otto, 1955).

disciplines (the *Quadrivium*). Students in the faculties of Arts were normally between 15 and 21 years old. Since there was no formal entrance examination (although of course the fact that all teaching was given in Latin restricted the number of prospective students radically), everybody who had the motivation could in principle embark upon an undergraduate career. But the often extremely difficult problems of financing studies meant that only a small fraction of the students ever completed their studies with a degree. In the fourteenth and fifteenth centuries, when statistical material is available, it can be made out that only 30–50% of the students ever attained the lowest degree possible, that of Bachelor of Arts, which presupposed between one and a half and two and a half years of study, and less that 15% the final degree of Master of Arts.

All the higher faculties of Law, Medicine, and Theology originally presupposed a basic education in Arts. In the later Middle Ages, however, this was required of theology students only, except for the friars, who had their own centres for preparatory studies (*studia particularia*) and were never required to receive a formal university training in arts. The students of the higher faculties were always more mature men; frequently they had already achieved some position or means. The number of students matriculated with the higher faculties, was, of course, much lower than the number of students studying in the Arts faculty; during the fourteenth and fifteenth centuries the Law faculties increased from about 10% to almost 20% of the total of matriculated students, Theology stayed at about 5%, and Medicine at even lower numbers (except perhaps at a few universities specialising in medicine).

It is worth emphasising that the number of law students was much higher than the number of theology students. Law studies were for the ambitious who wanted an ecclesiastical or civil career. Theology was almost a pure abstract science – its study was not required and was sometimes not even an aid to a further career.[7]

The students of these higher faculties were much more privileged than their colleagues in the faculties of Arts. Most colleges, for example, were open only to students or masters from the higher faculties. In these circumstances, the Arts course tended to be a mere preliminary, not only for theoretical reasons, because one should go on to more useful studies, but also for practical reasons, because the higher studies were also plainly more

---

7. Roger Bacon complained about this state of affairs. *Compendium studii philosophiae* c. 4 (ed. Brewer p. 418).

profitable. Thus most teachers in the faculties of Arts stayed for a few years only (two or three years of teaching were required from every person graduated as a master). Most of them were quite young, and they were often pursuing more advanced studies while carrying out their teaching.

These general remarks may give some of the background necessary to justify the following observations:

(a) The greatest quantities of medieval philosophical material as transmitted in the manuscripts are connected with the teaching in the faculties of Arts.

(b) Much of this work is of mediocre quality, even if the formal level of knowledge attained and presupposed is often astounding to us. Nevertheless, some work of high quality was done in the faculties of Arts, especially in grammar, logic, and astronomy.

(c) The most advanced scholarly research in philosophy, however, was made by students or teachers in the faculty of Theology (especially in the thirteenth and fourteenth centuries). Students of theology were more mature and better educated than the Arts students, and they had more leisure and better opportunities, whereas the 'Artists' were underpaid and relatively unprivileged. That is why so much of the study of medieval philosophy is concerned with theological texts. But this historical connection does not entail that philosophy and theology could not be studied separately, or that theological goals determined philosophy and made it unfree and unphilosophical.[8] There are large sections of pure philosophy in theological texts, often to the extent that theological authorities thought it necessary to intercede and demand a stricter limitation to theological problems.[9]

(d) Nevertheless, the Arts course, and especially the first two years of studies in grammar and logic, are of fundamental importance for the understanding of medieval philosophy. These studies provided the basic knowledge medieval intellectuals shared, and they were taken for granted in all other intellectual activity; they also formed the linguistic competence of medieval intellectuals and established their idiom of highly technical and precise Latin.[10]

---

8. Van Steenberghen 1979.
9. See the section '*Question-commentaries*' below.
10. We need a thorough study of the linguistic aspect of medieval philosophy with its important consequences for modern European (scientific) languages. A modest beginning has been made in Hubert 1949.

Teaching and books

The fact that the sources available to reconstruct the intellectual life of the Middle Ages are written records tempts us to forget that university learning was widely determined by oral teaching. That this had to be so is immediately apparent as soon as we remember the scarcity of books, a result of the great effort demanded for the production of a manuscript and its consequent costliness. Although the centralisation of book-production, beginning at the end of the thirteenth century, made book-prices much lower and books more available, private libraries remained very small. The use and the increased production of paper during the fourteenth century also made books easier to acquire, but the situation did not change radically until the invention of printed books in the late fifteenth century.[11] College libraries certainly improved the situation, but frequently only students of the higher faculties had access to them.

The pre-eminence of oral teaching as distinct from the study of books was thus an unavoidable condition, especially for the younger students. This necessity was turned into a virtue by a theory which we often find expressed in the prolegomena to the courses or the texts studied. One example will suffice (from Radulphus Brito, *ca.* 1300):

'I rightly contend that we learn more by being taught than we find through our own efforts, for one lesson heard is of more profit than ten lessons read privately. That is why Pliny says "the living voice affects the intellect much more than the reading of books". And he gives the following justification for his contention: the teacher's pronunciation, facial expressions, gestures, and whole behaviour make the pupil learn more and more effectively, and what you hear from another person is situated deeper in your mind than what you learn by yourself.'[12]

New arguments and new opinions, accordingly, did not spread only in written form. However important the study of manuscripts and the history of their availability to various medieval scholars is, we can never in this way catch the whole range of the medieval exchange of ideas. Many new thoughts spread rapidly to other universities by word of mouth,

---

11. Fink-Errera 1960. Cf. Thorndike 1944, pp. 112–18.
12. Radulphus Brito, *Prooemium in Parva mathematicalia*, MS Bruxelles, B. Royale 3540–47, f. 2ʳ: 'Bene dico quod plura scimus addiscendo ab alio quam per nosmet inveniendo, quia una lectio audita plus proficit quam si decem studeantur per se. Et ideo dicit Plinius "multo magis enim viva vox afficit intellectum quam lectio" id est quam inspectio librorum. Et reddit causam huius, quia pronuntiatio dicentis, vultus, gestus, et habitus, ista faciunt audientem plura apprehendere et magis firmiter, et altius audita ab alio in animo sedent quam si per se aliquis studeret.'

carried by traveling students and scholars. The exchange of ideas was not seriously restricted by the scarcity of books.[13]

This preponderance of the oral aspects within the medieval transmission of learning helps to elucidate the specific literary forms of medieval philosophical literature. It also helps to explain the fact that the written texts that were used for studies are often in a shockingly corrupt state. It is frequently difficult to understand how such faulty texts could be of any use to the students. But if we remember the facts associated with an oral tradition – which imply that the students had a large number of formulas, quotations, stock arguments, and standard moves stored in their memory – it becomes much easier to understand. They used the texts not as their only sources, but rather as abbreviations, reminders of what they had heard. They used written sources mainly as a source of useful arguments or distinctions, not as texts to be relied on for reconstructing the thoughts of others. The written records as we have them are only a limited reflection of a much richer oral culture.

The relations between oral and written sources changed gradually; partly because of the increasing availability of books, medieval intellectuals became more and more dependent on books. This change in the medium of communication tended to make arguments and polemics much more complex. Thus in fourteenth-century commentaries on the *Sentences* we find long and exact quotations of contemporaries which can only have been drawn from books. But, again, Sentence-commentaries were the work of privileged students who could afford books or had easy access to them. The average Arts teacher and student had to rely on memory and a few selected course-books, frequently adorned with hastily produced notes and commentaries.

Textbooks and university courses

I have just been emphasising the oral aspect of medieval philosophical literature. In another sense, however, medieval teaching was very much dependent on books. The cornerstone of any discipline was its authorita-

---

13. Maier 1964–67, II, pp. 317–34 ('Internationale Beziehungen an spätmittelalterlichen Universitäten'). The importance of personal relations is obvious – ideas spread more easily from master to students, and between masters and students of the same nation. This might to some degree account for the rapid acceptance of English ideas in fourteenth-century Germany, since both English and German masters belonged to 'the English nation' at the University of Paris.

tive course-book(s), the *littera*. Research and teaching was obliged to explain the *littera*, to show its structure and contents, to prove its inner consistency, and to harmonise any conflicting statements either in the *littera* itself or arising from comparison with other authorities. The means of doing so was a thorough reading of the textbook, explaining its arguments and presuppositions and analysing ambiguous expressions (terms or phrases). Since teaching thus proceeds in an analytical way we can detect a tendency towards ad-hoc solutions and distinctions which were sometimes quickly forgotten or dismissed, even if they could have been of further use in a more systematic approach to the discipline.

The textbooks determined the *curriculum* of the study. A student's *curriculum* consisted of the list of books required for passing a degree, together with an indication of the time required for the specific parts of the *curriculum*. This is not the place to trace the development of the curriculum in detail.[14] But an example from the end of the Middle Ages will reveal the mechanics of the system:

Greifswald, statutes of 1456:

BACHELOR'S DEGREE
Lectures:
ars vetus, 3 months (minimum)
Analytica Priora et Posteriora, 3 months
Elenchi, 2 months
parva logicalia, 4 months
Labyrinthus, $1\frac{1}{2}$ month
Physica, 6 months
De anima, 3 months
Sphaera, $1\frac{1}{2}$ month

Exercises (for this term see below):
ars vetus, $\frac{1}{2}$ year
parva logicalia, $\frac{1}{2}$ year } simultaneously

nova logica, $\frac{1}{2}$ year
Petrus Hispanus + *sophismata*
or *Sophistria* } $\frac{1}{2}$ year } simultaneously

De anima + *parva naturalia* $\frac{1}{2}$ year
Physica $\frac{1}{2}$ year } simultaneously

MASTER'S DEGREE
Lectures (without indication of duration):
Topics, De caelo et mundo, De generatione, Metheora, Parva naturalia,

14. See, e.g., Isaac 1953, pp. 61–85; Weisheipl 1964a.

Ethica Nic., Oeconomica, Politica, Theoria planetarum, Perspectiva, Arithmetica, Musica, Geometria, Metaphysica.

Exercises:
Physica, Nova logica, De caelo, De generatione, Metheora, Ethica, Metaphysica.[15]

This standard curriculum was supplemented by readings of special texts and disputations on freely chosen subjects.

In the faculty of Theology the curriculum consisted in principle of four parts. After (1) eight years of preparatory studies, (2) the student had to act for two years as a lecturer on the Bible (*baccalaureus biblicus*) and (3) two years as a lecturer on dogmatics, using (from the thirteenth century onwards) Peter Lombard's *Sentences* as the course-book (as *baccalaureus sententiarum*). Following this (4) he was supposed to attend and participate in disputations for four years. It is especially the two last phases of the study which gave rise to works of importance for the history of philosophy.

Within this general framework it was possible to put the emphasis on different parts of the text or on different problems. These special emphases tended to change with time and place. For that reason the problems and parts of the course-book treated in an otherwise anonymous text often may serve as an indication of its date and provenance.

Forms of teaching: Lectures[16]

The interplay between oral and written teaching is best seen if we briefly consider the forms of teaching. The first distinction we have to draw is between lectures (*lectiones*) and disputations.

Lectures were either ordinary, extraordinary, or cursory. Ordinary lectures were those delivered on the stipulated course-books and so were repeated regularly. When the same teacher was to repeat his course he could either repeat it *verbatim* or introduce some changes; he could even choose to deliver lectures by somebody else and modify them. (This is one cause of the vexed problem of different versions of a set of lectures, a problem we will return to shortly.) Extraordinary lectures were not restricted to the course-books but could also be on books not formally required by the statutes. They were supposed to serve as reviews or supplements of the ordinary courses. Cursory lectures were normally short reviews of the main problems connected with a standard text.

15. Kosegarten 1857, pp. 309–10, cf. Piltz 1977, pp. 23ff.
16. Glorieux 1966; Classen 1960.

The basic form of a lecture consisted of (a) the reading aloud of a section of the *littera* (in written versions of lectures this part is often omitted or just hinted at by quoting the beginning of the section of the text, the *lemma*, succeeded by an 'etc'.); (b) an account of the disposition of the text (*divisio textus*) which divides the text into always smaller parts (normally by dichotomous divisions), until we arrive at the level of single propositions (in this part of the lecture the text discussed is normally related to the preceding parts of the *littera*, so as to keep the train of thought in mind); (c) the exposition of each part, more or less extended according to the number of difficulties acknowledged. In this part the text is sometimes merely paraphrased, with an explanation of difficult words and distinctions among their various uses, but often the exposition contains a thorough and very precise interpretation of the text, occasionally summarised in the form of rules. Necessary background information is supplied, often in the form of Notabilia (rules or statements introduced by the words '*notandum*' or '*nota*'). Although such expositions can be quite tedious, they are often indispensable, since they teach us how medieval authors understood and read their sources, which is often quite different from what we think obvious. (d) The final part of the lecture was dedicated to especially important points, discussed in the form of real or fictitious disputations, normally introduced by '*dubium est*' or '*dubitandum est*'. (This entire four-part procedure could be repeated within the same lecture if there was not enough material in a single part of the text.) This form of lectures has a long history and for its main parts goes back to antiquity.[17]

Another form of lectures which is specifically medieval was apparently developed from the last section of the previously discussed form of lectures. The *dubia* or disputation part of the lectures seems to have become in-dependent from the other parts of the course,[18] and during the latter part of the thirteenth century a new type of commentary developed. From about 1260 we find commentaries consisting only of a series of *quaestiones*, each of which has the basic form of a disputation. Presumably this reflects the development of a new kind of lecture. We do not know to what extent, if any, such *quaestiones* were staged as real disputations. Certainly from the fourteenth century onwards we have testimony that they were only read

17. Peters 1968, pp. 10–17.
18. Already in the twelfth century we hear of independent disputations (see Landgraf 1935; Little & Pelster 1934, pp. 29f.; Grabmann 1911, II, pp. 497f., 535f. For the Arts courses see Hunt 1949–50, II, pp. 19, 55–6.

aloud by the master. Often he did not even have to compose his own questions, but was allowed to read questions by renowned authors in more or less rephrased forms. This was accepted explicitly in Prague (and forbidden in Paris in 1452), but certainly reflects earlier and common practice.[19] In the fourteenth and fifteenth centuries lectures of this kind were termed *exercitia,* the 'exercises' mentioned in the Greifswald statutes above.

This development is probably a result of the great interest of medieval scholars in disputations. Since disputation is an element very characteristic of medieval teaching, it will be helpful to discuss the nature of disputations more fully.

Disputations of the theologians

In the thirteenth century the principal duties of a Master in Theology were to lecture, to preach, and to dispute. The holding of academic disputations many times in the year, perhaps even weekly, formed an integral part of the academic curriculum, less frequent, but no less important, than the giving of lecture courses. The records of these disputations, in the form of *Quaestiones disputatae*, constitute a valuable part of the output of many medieval philosophers and theologians.

A formal disputation in the mid-thirteenth century fell into two parts occupying separate days. The time and topic of the disputation would be announced by the professor well in advance; all bachelors in the faculty were summoned to attend, and other masters and their students were invited as well. On the first day, after a brief introduction by a professor, one of his bachelors was appointed to receive and reply to arguments presented by members of the audience. The discussion followed the order of topics suggested by the master in his introduction; the bachelor dealt with the objections made to the master's thesis, assisted if necessary by the master himself; a secretary recorded the arguments and replies. The session continued for most of the morning, occupying perhaps three hours. On

19. *Monumenta historica Universitatis Carolo-Ferdinandeae Pragensis*, I. Prague 1830, p. 82. (Accepted, but only if the masters presented the (abridged) versions under their own name!) – *Chartularium Parisiense* IV, p. 727. Cf. Piltz 1977, pp. 30ff. The scribe of Durandus' Commentary on the Sentences, which is certainly not one of the least original medieval works, saw that large passages were *verbatim* excerpts from Peter of Auvergne. He adopted the practice of underlining such passages and added: 'Hoc oportui facere in hac quaestione ne multotiens idem scriberetur, quia ille Durandus est quidam latrunculus Petri de Alvernia, sicut sunt communiter omnes Gallici, utpote homines nullius inventionis existentes' (quoted from Decker 1967, pp. 84–5).

the next available day the company reassembled to hear the master summarise the arguments *pro* and *contra* and to give his own overall solution
(*determinatio*) to the question in dispute.[20] The proceedings of the disputation were eventually published either in the form of notes taken at the
meeting (a *reportatio*) or in a revised and expanded version by the master
himself (an *ordinatio*).

Ordinary disputations throughout the academic year would concern
topics clustering around a single theme, such as are to be found in Aquinas'
De veritate, or disputed questions on truth.[21] Twice a year, in Advent and
Lent, there were special disputations, open to a much wider public, which
could be about any topic whatever (*de quolibet*) and could be initiated by
any member of the audience (*a quolibet*). Such quodlibetal questions had to
be answered impromptu by the bachelor and determined by the master in
the same way as the questions of an ordinary disputation. It is a tribute to
the intrepidity and resourcefulness of medieval professors that so many of
them were willing to undergo such a testing public ordeal: no less than 358
sets of quodlibetal questions have come down to us.[22] If the ordinary
disputation resembled a modern seminar, the quodlibetal disputation resembled a public version of a modern professor's office hour or informal
instruction. Both types of disputation, in the words of P. Mandonnet, were
the academic equivalent of the medieval tournament-at-arms.

Quaestiones disputatae, such as Aquinas' *De veritate*, have come down to us
in texts divided into questions and articles. A question will be concerned
with a broad topic – e.g., Question Two treats of the knowledge of God –
and will be divided into articles devoted to specific problems – e.g., the
twelfth of the fifteen articles on Question Two asks whether God knows
future contingents. It is a matter of dispute whether it is the question or the
article which corresponds to a particular morning's debate: if the former,
the three hours appear to have been impossibly packed with rapid and
dense argumentation; if the latter, since the *De veritate* contains 253 disputations, the disputations of only three years, the academic calendar must
have been so full of disputations as to leave little time for lectures.[23]

20. Classic accounts of the nature of disputations in the theological faculties are to be found in
    Mandonnet 1928, Little and Pelster 1934, pp. 29–56, and in Glorieux, 1925–35.
21. Though the questions disputed by Aquinas in a single year commonly are linked fairly closely
    with each other, the traditional groupings under the headings *De veritate*, *De potentia*, *De malo*,
    include several sub-groups rather tenuously linked with each other.
22. Glorieux 1925–35.
23. The controversy between Mandonnet and Dondaine on this topic is well summarised in
    Weisheipl 1974a, pp. 123–6.

Disputations in the Arts faculties

We know less about disputations in the Arts faculties. From university statutes we can gather that Arts disputations were normal and that attendance at and participation in disputations were required before receiving a degree. But we are not told much about the actual procedures, except that it seems that some disputations were connected with the ordinary lectures, whereas others were more or less independent. These latter disputations are frequently called *sophismata*.[24]

Information on the procedures of disputation must be gathered mainly by induction. One type of evidence is the arrangement for final examinations, which included a formal disputation that was supposed to prove the candidate's ability to assume one of his main magisterial functions, that of leading a disputation, and therefore presumably proceeded according to the same rules as governed regular disputations. The structure of such disputations follows the following pattern: first, the master in charge puts a yes–no question, giving some arguments on each side. Next, the *respondens* (sometimes called the *promovendus*) gives a short solution accompanied by a refutation of the arguments leading to the opposite conclusion. Then the presiding master in his role as *opponens* argues against the respondent's solution and refutations, and the respondent is allowed to reply. Another master could then argue against the respondent's new position. It is not certain whether the respondent in his turn was obliged or at least allowed to reply. This entire procedure is not very different from the pattern of theological disputations. Also in the Arts faculties the disputation apparently was followed by a determination by the master. We have no positive evidence that the determination took place on the following day, but analogies with theological disputations would support such an inference.[25]

Further evidence can be gathered from an analysis of actually recorded disputations. The 'redacted' questions of the *exercitia* which retain only the basic structure of the actual disputation, are not so valuable as are a number of English manuscripts, which seem to be transmitted in a form closer to original disputations. Preliminary answers and solutions (presumably by the respondent) are subjected to further attacks and counter-arguments. It is often difficult to locate the final answer to the original problem, since it is mostly stated very briefly. Perhaps there was no formal determination in these cases.[26]

24. Weisheipl 1964a; Gilbert 1976.
25. Cf. Roos 1963.
26. Pinborg 1979, p. 34; Little & Pelster 1934, p. 41.

Many *sophismata*, especially from Paris in the latter half of the thirteenth century, are in the form of regular disputed questions. The formal occasion of the disputation – the sophisma proposition – is often rapidly dismissed. Then anywhere from one to four problems, with or without connection with the sophisma proposition, are stated. For each problem a few principal arguments are given on each side, followed by a brief solution by the respondent (or bachelor), who also responds to the arguments against the position he has chosen. Then numerous counter-arguments are raised against this first solution, apparently by different opponents, and the respondent replies to some or all of these. New counter-arguments are raised, sometimes concentrated on a single point of the respondent's argument, and this procedure can be repeated several times. Normally the respondent gets the last word, although the copyist sometimes does not care to report it.[27] In some sophismata we find a variant of this type of disputation. Several respondents can participate successively, each being subjected to the same treatment, but often maintaining opposed opinions.[28] In most sophismata the final, and often the largest, part is devoted to the master's determination of the problem.

That disputations were not always without danger can be seen from statutes threatening to exclude students who demonstrate by 'clamoring, hissing, making noise, stone-throwing by themselves or by their servants and accomplices, or in any other way'.[29] Even the most technical reports of medieval disputations can sometimes be relieved by glimpses of the tumult of actual disputation. Thus Matthias of Gubbio, trying to give an orderly account of his opposition against the opinions of Hervaeus Natalis concerning the nature of logical relations, is interrupted by someone: 'But before I come to the fourth point, somebody shouts against me with a loud voice: You deny such relations, I certainly deny yours.'[30] Certainly, disputations did not proceed as solemnly as the written redactions might make us believe.

The origins of disputation

Although scholars are unanimous in seeing the disputation as one of the most important and influential features of scholastic method, they are less

27. Roos 1963; Pinborg 1975b.
28. E.g., the sophismata edited in CIMAGL 24, pp. 16–34; see esp. p. 19: 'Secundo quidam alius sumpsit sibi quaestionem.' Cf. Little & Pelster 1934, p. 50.
29. Thorndike 1944, p. 237.
30. MS Erfurt 4° 276, f. 142rb.

agreed about the presuppositions and antecedents of the institution. A disputation is an institution which excellently formalises the dialectical procedure described by Aristotle: present a problem (*aporia*), set down the conflicting opinions of philosophers (*endoxa, phainomena*), resolve the difficulties and restate the *endoxa* in a muddle-free manner (e.g., *N.E.* VII 1, 1145^b2–7).[31] But it is unlikely that the disputation was designed to embody these procedures since it was in operation in medieval Europe before Aristotelian ideas and methods were fully assimilated. Some scholars regard the spread of disputations as the outcome of the study of Aristotle's *Analytics* and *Topics*; but the eristic jousts for which the Topics prescribe are a question-and-answer game quite different from the presentation of conflicting arguments in a *disputatio*.[32] Abelard's *Sic et non* was long singled out by scholars as a progenitor of scholastic dialectic, because it sets out contrasting Scriptural and theological statements in a manner which highlights conflicts of doctrines in the same way as a *Quaestio disputata*. Abelard's autobiography is one of the first records of school disputations: but it is clear that the dialectical procedures of the *Sic et non* were already practised in an earlier period.[33] Recently it has been suggested that the origin of the disputation is to be sought in the procedures adopted to reconcile conflicting legal authorities by canonists, Roman lawyers, and even Islamic jurisprudents.[34]

Perhaps the *disputatio* simply grew out of the other and older vehicle of professorial instruction: the *lectio*, or lecture. In the course of expounding a text a commentator, from time to time, is bound to encounter difficult passages which set special problems and need extended discussion. When we are dealing with a sacred or authoritative text, the difficult passages will have given rise to conflicting interpretations by different commentators, and the expositor's duty will be to set out and resolve the disagreements of previous authorities. Thus the *quaestio* arises naturally in the course of the *lectio*, and the disputation and the lecture are the institutionalised counterparts of these two facets of a method of study oriented to the interpretation of texts and the preservation of tradition.[35]

---

31. On this aspect of Aristotle's dialectic, see Owen 1967.
32. Grabmann 1911, II, p. 218, saw the influence of the *Topics* as decisive, but did not notice the difference between the type of disputation discussed by Aristotle and that found in Aquinas.
33. Grabmann 1911, I, pp. 234–6, gives Bernold of Constance and Ivo of Chartres as practitioners of the *Sic-et-non* method prior to Abelard.
34. Makdisi 1974, pp. 640–1, suggests an Islamic origin for the disputation (practised in championship style in the munāzara) and refers especially to the dialectics of Ibn Aqīl (1040–1112).
35. This account of the development of the *quaestio* from the *lectio* is given by Chenu 1954, pp. 67–77.

Whatever its origin, the *disputatio* came to have a great influence on the style of works written in other *genres*. The *Summa theologiae* of Aquinas, though designed from the outset as a manual to be read by students, is divided not into chapters but into questions and articles, and each article has the form of a miniature disputation, with three or more arguments against the position to be adopted, a brief citation of an authority in favour of the preferred view (*sed contra*), a central section (*respondeo*) corresponding to the Master's determination, and finally a set of answers to the objections. In writers such as Scotus and Ockham commentaries on the *Sentences* of Lombard follow the form of a *Quaestio disputata*.[36]

The later development of disputations

While commentaries and treatises written in and for the master's study were written in the form of disputations, the disputations themselves became more and more an exercise of dialectical skill for its own sake and less and less a method of presenting and reconciling diverse opinions on a topic of substantial import.

In post-reformation scholasticism the presentation of conflicting arguments on a substantive topic of theology or philosophy was subject to formal and codified rules analogous to those presented in an *ars obligatoria*.[37] But there was a significant difference between the medieval and the post-reformation disputations: whereas the former began with a *quaestio*, the latter began with a *thesis*. It was the respondent's duty to enunciate and explain a thesis which he was prepared to maintain against objectors. The opponent must then produce arguments to contradict this thesis; the respondent must react to each premiss of the opponent's argument by granting, denying, or distinguishing (*concedo, nego, distinguo*). If he distinguished the opponent's premiss, that meant that he granted it in one sense but denied it in another, he must then strive to show that in the sense

---

36. In Scotus in particular the *quaestio*-form can become very complicated. In the fifth part of the prologue to his commentary on the Sentences he discusses theology as a practical science. Two questions are posed, the first with five authorities on one side and three on the other, the second with three authorities on each side. There follows a definition of *praxis* argued for clause by clause through eleven paragraphs. Two further long preliminary sentences precede the solution of the questions in reverse order. The solution of the first question is preceded by a long summary of the opinions of previous thinkers, divided into five classes. This summary of previous thought, corresponding to the first part of a magisterial *determinatio*, frequently plays a dominant role in the Ordinations of Scotus and Ockham. Few *quaestiones disputatae* of Scotus have survived, and fewer have been published; but Scotus, like Ockham, left behind an important series of *Quaestiones quodlibetales*.

37. The two types of disputation are compared and contrasted in Angelelli 1970.

agreed to the premiss did not lead to the contradictory of his own original position. The opponent must then try to prove the premiss in the sense in which it is dangerous to the respondent; or he may turn to an independent argument for the contradictory of the respondent's thesis. It is the *distinguo* which is the heart of the post-reformation disputation: this means that the interest of the debate turns on the disentangling of senses of ambiguous words rather than on the more formal considerations which typically gave excitement to medieval disputations.

Disputations of this kind have been in use in scholastic institutions within living memory, and their form dictated the typical structure of neo-scholastic textbooks in which, instead of chapters, we find the material divided into *theses*.[38] Each thesis is first explained, word by word (this is the *status quaestionis*); there follows a list of *adversarii* (philosophers who have taken a position contrary to the thesis); the thesis is proved by syllogistic argument, and there follows a set of objections and replies, often with *scholia* or appendices. The structure of a medieval *quaestio disputata* is more lively: the adversaries are allowed to speak for themselves, and the arguments pro and con are presented, as in a live debate, before the magisterial resolution and not after.

The purpose of disputations

As a final consideration of medieval disputations I should like to sketch some of the ideological and methodological impetus behind the medieval preference for this method of teaching. Two texts on the problem whether the cognition of truth consists in the solution of dubitations (formally expressed doubts) may serve as a starting point.

The first text is by Siger of Brabant. It states that the goal of teaching is to find truth, and finding truth presupposes the ability to solve any objection or dubitation against the proposition accepted as true. For if you do not know how to solve objections that may arise, you are not in possession of the truth, since in that case you have not assimilated *the procedure of finding* truth and thus will not know whether or when you have arrived at truth.[39]

---

38. A typical example of such a textbook is Siwek 1948.
39. Siger of Brabant, *Quaestiones super librum De causis, Prooemium*, 1972, p. 35: 'Sicut vult Aristoteles in principio III. Metaphysicae, volentes attingere ad cognitionem veritatis in aliquibus rebus absque cognitione eorum, quae dubitationem inducunt in cognitionem veritatis illarum rerum, similes sunt incedentibus nescientibus tamen ad quem locum ire debeant. Cuius ratio est, quia absolutio dubitationis finis est tendentis ad veritatem. Et ideo sicut qui nescit locum non veniet ad ipsum nisi casu, et cum ad ipsum venerit nesciet ipsum esse locum quo tendebat, et ideo ignorabit utrum sit ibi quiescendum vel ulterius procedendum, sic non praeconcipiens dubitationes ad

The other text, probably by Henry of Brussels (*ca.* 1300), alludes directly to the three methods of teaching, stating that through lectures you arrive at truth and so should be able to solve any objections. By a lecture in the form of a (fictitious) disputation read aloud procedures for finding the truth are presented to you, and by an actual disputation you learn to find truth by actually evaluating and solving arguments.[40]

It was certainly not the case that this lofty purpose of disputations was always in the mind of the master, not to mention that of the student. Many disputations were obviously undertaken just as a means of intellectual exercise or as unreflective repetition of normal academic usage.[41] Still, medieval disputations and their written counterparts show us scholars partaking in what Chenu has aptly termed the 'recherche collective de la vérité'.[42] Medieval scholars were aware that any single disputation covered only a tiny move within this vast enterprise, and that not all disputations led to an equal degree of certainty.

There is a certain tension between the medieval ideal of 'demonstrative' science as a system of proofs deducing conclusions by ordered steps from first principles, and the actual forms of doctrinal exposition. The arguments adduced in a disputation have an almost fortuitous character and are certainly not always demonstrative. Their aim is principally to persuade

cognitionem veritatis non dirigetur nisi casu, quia si veritatem attingerit nesciet utrum ibi quiescendum vel ulterius procedendum. Et dubitans etiam similis est ligato vinculo corporali qui, si ligamentum ignoraverit, ipsum dissolvere non valebit; dubitatio enim mentem tenet ne ulterius per considerationem procedere possit, sicut vinculo corporali pedes tenentur. Et ideo dubitationes non praeconsiderans non valet absolvere dubitationes, quare nec attingere ad veritatem. Cognitio enim veritatis in aliqua rerum solutio est dubitatorum. Et sicut in iudiciis dicitur, quod melius contingit iudicare audiendo rationes utriusque partis, similiter etiam praeconsideratis rationibus ad utramque partem contradictionis dubitationem inducentibus melius contingit iudicare veritatem.'

40. Grabmann 1944, p. 82: 'Secundo prenotandum est, quod cognitio veritatis generatur in nobis dupliciter uno modo per inventionem, alio modo per doctrinam. Si per inventionem hoc fit sic, quod aliquis proponit primo sibi aliquam conclusionem (f. 91rb) quodam modo notam et per consequens arguit ad utramque partem et tunc judicat, ad quam partem rationes sunt potiores adducte illi consentiens et alias rationes dissolvens et per hoc patet, quod investigatio veritatis etc. Alio modo generatur scientia sive cognitio veritatis per doctrinam et hoc dupliciter. Uno modo, quod doctor proponat propositionem discipulo et arguat ad partem utramque et postea uni consentiat et alia, quae sunt contra ipsam partem quam tenet, dissolvit. [Alio modo] Et hoc modo patet etiam, quod cognitio veritatis est solutio dubitatorum. Alio modo per doctrinam fit cognitio veritatis sic, quod doctor simpliciter sine omni arguitione proponit discipulo veritatem et informat ipsum et sic item discipulus ista veritate cognita poterit argumenta solvere, que essent contra istam veritatem et sic patet, quod cognitio veritatis etc.'

41. An incidental remark in an anonymous series of questions on Priscian may illustrate this (MS Nürnberg, Stadtbibl., Cent. V.21 f. 37rb): 'Ista opinio tacta fuit in praecedenti quaestione et posset satis probabiliter teneri. Tamen exercitii causa aliam inquiramus.'

42. Chenu 1954, pp. 109ff.

the opponent, and because of that aim it is not necessary to start every argument from first principles. One can instead begin with commonly accepted presuppositions, either quotations from authorities or well-known maxims. One can also formally agree on some accepted presuppositions.[43] The arguments are developed in the form of syllogisms, categorical or hypothetical, consequences, or dilemmas. Overt formal errors are exceedingly rare, since such 'sophistical' moves could be detected immediately and thus defeat their author.

In most questions or disputations the introductory arguments which set up the question are almost stereotypical and transmitted from one author to another. Masters and students chose the arguments which they could remember having heard or could easily look up in accessible sources. Accordingly, questions from the same environment, raising the same problem, will tend to repeat the same stock-arguments, thus forming a kind of 'doctrinal family' which can be used with some caution for a rough sorting of texts. In rare cases we can even see how a cluster of stock-arguments arise from a specific historical situation.[44]

The literary forms: literal commentaries

Most medieval philosophical literature reflects teaching practice and its form; even writings that were never delivered as lectures or held as disputations assume the traditional forms.

Accordingly, a large proportion of medieval philosophical literature is in the form of commentaries. Commentaries range from more or less complete marginal glosses (*scholia*), which in fact are often excerpted from one or more complete commentaries, to full-scale literal commentaries, following the standard form of a lecture as sketched above. It is important to note that such commentaries do not necessarily reflect the personal views of an author on the philosophical problems involved, but only what he thinks is the correct interpretation of the *littera*. However, since new doctrines were often disguised as merely new interpretations of the authorities, it is difficult to know where the borderlines between the exposition of the authority and the author's personal philosophy may be drawn. It is known that some of the strenuously attacked 'Latin Averroists' often used as a defense that they did not develop their own opinions but only

---

43. There exists no analysis of the type of arguments which were actually used by the schoolmen. Oeing-Hahnhoff 1963 discusses some of the aspects involved.
44. Thus the arguments of John Aurifaber against the *modi significandi* soon became stock arguments of the genre; see Pinborg 1967a, pp. 167–72.

interpreted Aristotle.[45] It is also interesting to follow the fourteenth-century debate between Ockham and his followers on one side, who brought their own doctrine into harmony with Aristotle by claiming that Aristotle often spoke metaphorically, and more traditional Aristotelians on the other side, who could not concede that the philosopher ever spoke metaphorically, since he himself claimed to proceed demonstratively.[46]

Question-commentaries

Besides the literal commentaries there are commentaries in the form of a series of questions. Originally such questions formed only the latter part of lectures, but apparently they gradually became independent from the traditional lecture-form. From the latter half of the thirteenth century we find such commentaries, consisting only of questions; sometimes short paraphrases of passages of the *littera*, otherwise neglected, are still given; but often only the opening words are left from the old structure.[47]

Such questions retain the simplest possible structure of a disputation. First a problem is stated in the *titulus quaestionis* which is always formed as a question introduced by '*utrum*'. The selection of *tituli* reflects current interests, and so a mere list of questions is often indicative of the time and place of origin of the commentary. This is perhaps most striking in the case of commentaries on the Sentences.[48] Vastly different sections of the text were selected for commentary, and the questions raised in connection with the various *distinctiones* of the text varied greatly over time. Early thirteenth-century commentaries for example, often have a disproportionate amount of commentary on the first Book, and various philosophical problems are often introduced and discussed at great length in

---

45. Van Steenberghen 1977, pp. 232ff. Cf. Weisheipl 1974, p. 42, concerning Albert the Great.
46. Ockham, *Expos. Phys.* (MS Oxford Merton 293 f. 72^r, *ad* 206^{b}16): 'Verumtamen aliquando Philosophus ponit unam pro alia non curans multum de verbis et supponens quod addiscentes istam scientiam possunt esse sufficienter exercitati in logica per quam sciant discernere inter propositiones et advertere quando una ponitur pro alia et quando non. Quod tamen multi moderni ignorant . . . .' Walter Burley, *Expos. Phys.* (Venice 1524, f. 5ra): 'Non est igitur dicendum quod Philosophus et Commentator loquantur metaphorice vel singulariter ut isti exponunt, reducendo totam philosophiam ad secundum modum amphibologiae. Quia Philosophus reprehendit modum loquendi figurative vel metaphorice in doctrina demonstrativa. Sed hic (scil. in *Physicis*) procedit demonstrative. Non est ergo dicendum quod ipse loquatur metaphorice sicut loquuntur poetae in suis fabulis.'
47. Grabmann 1939, pp. 47–53.
48. The Sentence-commentaries were read, but in the fourteenth century the introduction to each book (the *principium* or the *quaestio collativa*) was presented as an actual disputation and normally published separately (Glorieux 1966, pp. 79–90). In the Arts faculties masters sometimes used material from their disputations or sophismata in their redacted questions. (An example is Boethius of Dacia; see Roos 1963, p. 379.)

connection with passages of the text which have only a very tenuous connection with the problems discussed.

Thus we find an elementary discussion of light and the multiplication of species or of the rainbow inserted into the context of creation, an examination of the problem of the motion of *gravia et levia* in a similar context, an elaborate consideration of terms of first and second intention in the context of Trinity (specifically at the discussion of *persona* in dist. 23), an extended investigation of astrology relative to the problem of whether creation occurs *de necessitate*, and even a major question *de creatione caeli* dealing with whether one can prove that there are nine spheres (for discussion of the ninth sphere, can, and does, lead to the consideration of the precession of the equinoxes, the rising and setting of the signs, the astronomy of eclipses and so on). And such phenomena can be found almost *ad infinitum*.[49]

It is hardly possible to give a catalogue of places where specific philosophical problems are discussed since it varies greatly with different authors and periods. From this one can understand that the university authorities at the end of the fourteenth century found it necessary to rule officially that Sentence-commentaries should not deal with logical and philosophical problems except to the extent justified by the text of the Sentences.[50] This ruling apparently had some effect. Late fourteenth- and fifteenth-century commentaries on the Sentences tend to be of a more purely theological nature.

After the *titulus quaestionis* follows a short series of principal arguments for one of the two possible answers to the problem stated, frequently introduced by a formula such as '*et arguitur (videtur) quod sic/non*'. These arguments normally defend the position eventually refuted. The normal number of arguments is two or three. Then follow arguments on the opposite side of the issue. They are often fewer in number (often only one), and are frequently nothing but references to authority. This is justifiable according to medieval tradition, even if an argument from authority was held to be the weakest form of argument. Real arguments were normally given in the solution of the question, where the author adopts the position he himself means to defend.

The solution (or *corpus quaestionis*) is introduced by phrases such as '*ad hoc dicendum/dico*' and states the conclusions of the author, accompanied by some arguments and the distinctions necessary to carry through the solution. These arguments are normally more carefully organised and articulated, but still may take as their major premisses propositions which have not been or are not proved 'demonstratively' but are only regarded as generally acceptable. Frequently several previous opinions on the subject are summarised and refuted, before the author states his own opinion.[51] The structure of the solution of most of the Sentence-commentaries of the fourteenth century is often very complicated along these lines. Originally these references to earlier authors were anonymous (introduced by phrases such as '*aliqui dicunt*', '*opinio cuiusdam viri*' or even '*aliquis diceret*'), either in order to retain the fiction of disputation where non-participants could not supply arguments or because nobody really cared about the authorship of the ideas discussed. From the fourteenth century onwards there is an increasing tendency to give exact references. It is interesting to note that the cluster of such opinions on a given question often varies little from one text to another, and that many authors are remembered only for their solution to one specific question. In this way, e.g., Radulphus Brito's opinion on first and second intentions is bound to appear in any discussion on this subject although he is not quoted anywhere else, and the same holds true for Peter of Auvergne on the *verbum mentis*.

Especially in earlier phases of the development, we find cases of several questions being telescoped into one: first the arguments of a number of different questions are given, then the questions are solved one after another. This may reflect the practice of discussing more than one question in the same disputation. Another way of structuring such sub-questions is to divide a question into several articles. In the fourteenth and fifteenth centuries the solution is often structured according to conclusions and corollaries, each being defended and *dubia* being solved.

The last part of a question contains the refutations of the arguments leading to the solution opposite to the one advocated by the author. They often contain some distinctions which were thought not to be necessary to the general solution of the problem but of importance only to solving one of the counter-arguments.

The whole structure of such questions should make it immediately apparent that not all parts of a question are of equal importance for

51. See, e.g., the Sophisma of Radulphus Brito edited in CIMAGL 24, p. 97: 'De ista quaestione procedendum est sicut in aliis: primo tangendae sunt opiniones aliorum; secundo tangenda est opinio probabilior; tertio tangendae sunt difficultates circa istam opinionem et solvendae sunt; quarto est solvendum rationes in oppositum.' Sometimes further complications were introduced by expressions such as 'aliquis argueret contra me', 'aliquis diceret', which may sometimes be reflections of the many-leveled disputation behind the redacted question, but often are nothing but literary devices to treat a side-issue more thoroughly.

determining the author's own argument. For such purposes, the most important part is, of course, the solution with its distinctions. The concluding responses to the counter-arguments are also important, but the distinctions introduced are often only ad-hoc distinctions never used again, and thus sometimes not equally well considered. This principle of estimating the weight of a statement within the given context was already expressed by the fifteenth-century Thomist Johannes Capreolus, but has often been sinned against.[52]

It has already been stated that some literary genres of medieval philosophical literature, such as the *sophismata*, the *quaestiones disputatae*, and the *quaestiones quodlibetales* kept closer to the original form of a disputation. This is already illustrated by small linguistic features of the text, such as the frequent use of the past instead of the present tense (*Sed contra hoc arguebatur*, etc.) or the frequent addition of '*per te*', which alludes to the opponent's presuppositions or admissions, and above all by the far greater structural complexity.

Other literary forms

Besides the commentaries with their detailed analysis of problems, a need arose for more systematic expositions of doctrine. The standard title for such expositions is *summa*, which originally meant a summary, or *tractatus* (treatise). Such expositions were generally intended for the use of beginners in order to facilitate their introduction into a discipline.[53] It is natural that such expositions tended to be shortlived. They soon lagged behind the doctrinal developments and needed to be replaced.[54]

Such manuals are often conventional in their contents. Every teacher adopting them felt free to revise his teaching manual, to change words or whole sections, to add or to remove. This accounts both for the general similarity of manuals within a given field and for their great variety in details. Accordingly, it is often very difficult to see which specific manual was used by an author, especially since we possess only a mere fraction of

---

52. Johannes Capreolus, *Defensiones* IV, d. 43, q. 1, a. 3, quoted from Grabmann 1926–56 III, p. 379: 'Tamen teneo cum sancto Thoma in Quodlibeto, unde sumptae sunt conclusiones. Qualitercumque enim sensit in Scriptis vel visus fuerit sensisse in Tertia Parte, determinatio Quodlibeti videtur mihi rationabilior, quia ibi solum tractavit istam materiam a proposito et in forma; in aliis vero locis incidenter solum et cum suppositione et respondendo magis ad hominem quam ad rem.'
53. Cf. Grabmann 1939, pp. 54–103. See also Parkes 1976.
54. Cf. John Wyclif, *De veritate Sacrae Scripturae* I, 54: 'Aliae logicae (i.e., other than his *logica scripturae*) sunt periodice et nimis multiplices; periodice quia, ut patet in Oxonia, vix durat una aliena logica per viginti annos sed saepissime variantur.'

the material that once existed. In the same way it may often be very difficult
to trace the interrelations of such manuals.

Manuals are either summaries of the formal books required for a degree
or introductions to specific disciplines or aspects of disciplines for which no
authoritative textbook had been recognised. This last type is philosophically the most interesting. Within it are to be found the various grammatical and logical manuals which will be discussed frequently in the
following chapters of the present volume.[55] Also the manuals discussing
typical medieval contributions to natural philosophy, such as treatises *De
proportionibus velocitatum*, *De intensionibus et remissionibus formarum*, and *De
primo et ultimo instanti* belong to this category, even if they are often so
intricately argued that they defy characterisation as elementary textbooks.

Subjects generally accepted into the curriculum will often be incorporated at specific sections of the formal textbooks. We have already seen
examples of this in connection with the Sentence-commentaries, but
analogous developments can be found in the Arts faculties. Thus the *modi
significandi* are treated in connection with Priscian or with Aristotle's *Peri
hermeneias*, first and second intentions with Porphyry, consequences with
Aristotle's *Sophistici elenchi* or *Prior Analytics*, restrictions and ampliations
in connection with the *Prior Analytics* or *Peri hermeneias*, proportions of
velocities in connection with the twelfth book of the *Metaphysics*, and first
instants, intension and remission of forms, and impetus theory in connection with the *Physics*. This arrangement is found, for example, in some
series of questions prepared as a help for examinations.[56]

Frequently certain manuals even came to be regarded as *de facto* authorities and accordingly were made the object of commentaries or disputations.

The nature of our sources: the channels of transmission

Since we have no direct access to the actual lectures and disputations we
have to rely on written sources. This is of course a truism, but it emphasises
the important fact that there is always an intermediary between the source
as we have it and the state of affairs we want to consider. In a technically

---

55. A survey of the types of logical manuals and the early history of their development can be found
   in De Rijk 1962–7, II. 1, pp. 593–6.
56. Pinborg 1976d. Other aids of this type can be found in Grabmann 1939, pp. 112–16 & 189–91,
   and in MSS, e.g., Erfurt 4°241: 'Puncta materiarum omnium que pro baccalariatu gradus Erfordie
   leguntur et examinatur.'

developed culture where it is possible for a large number of people to have access to the same text directly, and in a form authenticated by the author, this is less problematic, even if there is, of course, always the possibility of misunderstanding. But when we are concerned with medieval philosophical literature such relatively unproblematical lines of communication are very rare. The number of texts transmitted to us in the author's own original version or in a copy directly authenticated by him is very small. And even in these cases there are additional difficulties: the author's handwriting may be almost illegible, as is the case with Aquinas, or he may have been remiss in checking the text. But in the normal case several written intermediaries separate us from the original text of the author.

In order to gain a sketchy insight into the process of transmission let us consider briefly the route of a medieval text from its author to us.

Let us suppose that a master has just been giving a course. The students have been taking copious notes. The master has been reading either so slowly that he has actually dictated the text, or, according to the recommendations of the university, somewhat faster, so that even practised stenographers among the students may have had difficulties in getting everything straight.[57] Now we have already two types of texts: a dictated one and a reported one, both of which contain unavoidable errors: errors of the master in reading, errors of the students who may have misheard, miswritten, or misunderstood. The dictated text will of course be closer to the intentions of the master, whereas the reported text will be more or less abridged, deformed, and changed. From the students' notes other students may make copies, which are totally exempt from the control of the master.

The master may want to have his text 'published' officially. He can take either his own notes (eventually dictating from them to a secretary) or one of the dictated or reported versions as the basis for such publication.[58] In both cases he will certainly introduce some revisions such as additions, reformulations, doctrinal adjustments, or references. Some errors may still be overlooked and some may be newly introduced, e.g., if the revisions are not consistent. Such a revised manuscript is called an *ordinatio* or a text edited (*editus*) or provided for copying (*in copia datus*).[59] Frequently several

57. Thorndike 1944, p. 237f.
58. On reportations, see Pelzer 1964, pp. 422–9. On dictation: Dondaine 1956. See also Thorndike 1944, p. 58, for a modest student-copyist who excuses himself for not being competent enough to reproduce the lofty ideas of his master.
59. Fink-Errera 1960.

years pass between the course and the revision, which of course may add to the differences between the original and the 'final' text of the author.[60]

Disputations are reduced to written form along the same lines. But the complexities of the sometimes rather chaotic disputations makes the student-reporter's job much more difficult, and different *reportata* will tend to show much greater differences. Misunderstandings arising from this could sometimes be dangerous to the author, and he had a genuine interest in seeking a more authentic form of his opinions. Accordingly we find at least three different types of disputation-texts: reportations, which report only from the disputation and not from the master's ordered determination; more or less exact reportations from the determination; and the revised edition of the master.[61]

In this way we already have different versions of the 'same' text. Matters may be still more complicated if the author introduces further changes in his own copy, which is then recopied, perhaps even at different stages, or when the master in repeating his course recasts the argument, omits some problems and adds new ones. Here it is possible to talk about different redactions of a text, but it will also be apparent that the concept is somewhat fluid.[62]

The next stage in the transmission consists in the copies made from direct reportations or from authenticated texts. In the latter case the texts pass through official channels: the *stationarii* of the university, who could hire it out for copying. In both cases copies were made by copyists of varying competence and for varying purposes. Professional scribes could write beautiful manuscripts, but they often did not understand the text very well.

---

60. To give an example: Hervaeus Natalis' Commentary on the Sentences were 'published' about ten years after the course had first been given. In the meantime, reportations or private copies were circulating haphazardly. So in the published edition Hervaeus removed some discussions which he had published separately and in some other, probably more controversial, cases emphasised that he still held the same opinion (Decker 1967, p. 73). The same move can be recognised in some texts by Siger of Brabant, who says, e.g., 'quibus oretenus tunc respondimus et adhuc respondemus' (Van Steenberghen 1977, p. 193). Sometimes, however, a master just changes his opinion without notifying us (Van Steenberghen 1977, pp. 402–3). Walter Burley once even firmly rejects an opinion of 'some' (*aliqui*) without mentioning that he previously held it himself.

61. Glorieux 1925–35, I, pp. 51–5. A master defends himself by saying 'reportator meus non bene concepit' (ibid., p. 52). Discrepancies between the actual disputation and the written text are often recorded, e.g., 'Multa alia fuerunt arguta quae tamen redeunt in idem' (CIMAGL 24, p. 19). 'Hoc est sophisma nunc et alias propositum circa quod multa proponebantur inquirenda; quibusdam tamen disputatis de uno quaeratur ad praesens' (CIMAGL 26, p. 93). 'Ad quartum problema non respondebatur, propterea omitto ad praesens' (MS Worcester, 4°13, f. 33ᵛ).

62. Macken 1973; Boethius of Dacia 1969, p. xvii; Ockham *OTI*, pp. 19*–21*, 26*–31*; Scotus, *Opera omnia* I (1950) pp. 166*–75*; Pinborg 1980.

Poor students who copied texts for more fortunate colleagues often worked hurriedly. Only in some cases do we have the optimal circumstances of a copyist copying what he wants to have for himself in the best possible form.

Copyists could be interested in the text they copied simply for its own sake, which of course warrants their producing the best possible copy. But often they were interested only in some aspects of it, some of the arguments, the main trend of thought, or perhaps only in some definite sections. Thus we find manuscripts excerpting discussions from different sources, e.g., treating the same question, or having some degree of internal relationship. Sometimes copyists got disappointed or tired and just quit their work in the middle. Others might have been compiling notes which were useful for their examination, etc. The study of such miscellaneous manuscripts is still only beginning, but obviously it is important to have some general idea of what a given manuscript was intended for in order to judge its value as a source.[63]

So far we have considered only linear transmission, that is, copies made from one other copy. In the actual process of copying we meet with all sorts of cross-currents. A copyist might want to get a better text by adducing other versions for comparison. He may then substitute the readings of the 'new' source(s) for those of his archetype, or he may add alternate readings between the lines or in the margin, thus starting a contaminated version. If in this way he is combining different versions (reportations) or even different redactions of a text the resulting contamination may give very confusing results. Add to this the fact that a large number of the manuscripts are now no longer extant, and it becomes obvious that it is hardly ever possible to reconstruct precisely the history of the text which would be the necessary background for evaluating the various sources.

Even the official publication through the *stationarii*, which at first sight seems to warrant a high degree of authenticity, has been proven to introduce by its very technique new sources of error. First the actual unit for the transmission of a text is not the entire manuscript but the *pecia*, a quire normally of 16 pages; since the *stationarius* normally has at least two sets of *peciae* of a given text, more or less identical, and since the *peciae* are hired one by one, any copyist may be combining *peciae* from two different sources into his copy, thus making different parts of his text of different

63. Glorieux 1925–35, p. 54; Glorieux 1967.

critical value. Moreover, the *pecia* in itself is not a stable entity; it will suffer wear and tear, so that words or even whole sentences may have become difficult to read, corrections and marginal remarks (often totally irrelevant to the text) may have been added by less conscientious borrowers, etc. The *pecia* may even have become so worn that it had to be replaced by a new copy, which even if carefully supervised by the university is certain to introduce new errors. Thus even an official version does not offer the text authenticated by the author, but a text authenticated by the university, which might be a quite different matter. We even have indications that some texts were changed so as to offer more acceptable doctrines.[64]

The last step in the transmission is the modern edition. Here it is always important to recognise the character of the sources used and the way the editor has chosen to render his material accessible. He may be offering a mere transcript of one manuscript, or a contaminated version of his own, or a genuinely critical edition based on all available material and structured according to a specified hypothesis concerning the history of the text. In any case the modern editor has several advantages over the medieval copyist: he can make use of as much source material as he wants, thanks to the technique of microfilming manuscripts; he has technical equipment at his disposal in case the manuscript is difficult to read; he has many manuals and much secondary literature composed to help him; and above all his aim is to be faithful to the text being edited. Still in many respects his situation is akin to that of the medieval copyist: he is apt to be guilty of the same types of errors, misunderstandings and inexactitudes. As there is no manuscript without errors, so there is no faultless modern edition. Even the almost superhuman editors of the Leonine edition of Aquinas are not infallible.

Manuscripts and their errors

Manuscripts and their errors are not only a problem for the medieval user and the modern editor of a medieval text, they are also a problem for any user of modern editions. I am not referring to the fact that knowledge of the material conditions of medieval scholars can be illuminating for modern interpreters, but to the fact that any user of a critical edition must use it critically. To be able to do so, however, he must know the most important principles which inflict errors upon medieval scribes and mo-

---

64. The classical study of the pecia-system is Destrez 1935. Very important issues are considered in Fink-Errera 1962 and Brounts 1970. The prefaces of the recent volumes of the Leonine edition of Aquinas are veritable goldmines of information concerning university editions and paleographical and codicological matters generally.

dern editors. He must have a certain experience with medieval scripts in order to know which letters can be mistaken for which; in particular, he must have a working knowledge of the medieval system of abbreviations which explain many errors (see further below). This knowledge is important not only for using the critical apparatus, but also in order not to be totally at a loss whenever a text appears misleading or false.

It is not possible within the limits imposed on this chapter to provide a manual of paleography and textual criticism. Nor would it be appropriate, since a number of important and useful surveys are already in existence.[65] I propose to give a mere catalogue of typical faults with some examples found in manuscripts or in modern editions. For our purpose here, it is of little importance whether the error is medieval or modern.

All errors form, in point of principle, two different groups. In the first group, the incorrectness of the reading can be established by means of various criteria: morphological, syntactic, stylistic or contextual. (This means that a precondition for applying such criteria is a thorough knowledge of scholastic terminology and Latin usage). The second group includes cases in which the unauthentic text seems to be correct in respect to the mentioned criteria: there is a divergence from the original text, but the divergent text does not itself justify any suspicions as to its authenticity, as far as language and content are concerned.[66]

Obviously the second group is very difficult to handle without access to a great deal of primary material. But errors in the first group even the casual user of medieval texts may be able to discover. And with some grasp of the principles discussed in the following pages he may even be able to find remedies.

One group of errors is connected with the *omission* of one or more words, and the most common sort of omission occurs because of *homoioteleuta*. The copyist copies out a word, say '*syllogismus*', on line 3 and when he turns back to the manuscript his eyes fall on '*syllogismus*' on line 7, and he accidentally goes on from there. Since scholastic style always repeats the same terms for the same concepts, and since it is replete with arguments, which in order to work must repeat the same terms, this type of error is extremely common in scholastic texts. There is no medieval manuscript which does not commit this error over and over. In most cases, however, at least when the omission is not too extensive, it is possible to reconstruct the

---

65. A good introduction to the history of texts is Reynolds & Wilson 1974, although it is mainly concerned with the transmission and problems of classical authors. As an introduction to different scripts Thomson 1969 can be recommended. See also CIMAGL 5.
66. Bergh 1978, p. 5.

gist of what is missing, since the structure of the argument can be used as a control.

More difficult to deal with are omissions of one word or a few words, either because the scribe judged them superfluous or because of sheer negligence. Such omissions can in principle be detected only by comparison with other manuscripts or if the sense has become truncated or illogical as a result of the omission. However, we must always allow for the fact that both masters and students were thoroughly imbued with scholastic procedure and terminology and so did not need as much redundancy as a modern reader is likely to need.

Sometimes the scribe discovers his mistake and adds the missing words in the margin or above the line, or he just repeats the whole passage in its correct form, adding some sign such as '*va . . . cat*' (written above the words) to delete the incorrect version. This may cause the next copyist to insert the words at a wrong place or to produce a confusing duplication of material.

Deliberate changes are frequent and do not always reveal themselves. They may be due to various motives. Purely stylistic changes, which are not very serious from a philosophical point of view, are probably caused by the speed at which the copying was done and the copyist's automatic recognition of formulas. Especially noteworthy is the habit of shortening an argument by just adding an '*etc.*' when the scribe thinks the rest is obvious.

Among the more innocent changes which to a certain degree influence the sense is *the substitution of new personal or local names in examples*. The author or the copyist may substitute his own name or that of his own town or country – or in other cases he may substitute a well-known for a less well-known name. This is intriguing since such names may be a clue to the identity of the author. Unfortunately, however, it is often difficult to ascertain whether the name is the choice of the author, of an earlier copyist, or of the copyist of the extant manuscript. Sometimes, especially when the text is transmitted in more than one manuscript, it is possible to argue for what the original wording must have been. But then the names ought to be not too frequent and the context significant.[67]

Another motive for a change which is more uncomfortable for us may be the copyist's *disapproval of the wording of the original*. A rather harsh

---

67. For geographical names see De Rijk 1976a, pp. 32–6. For examples of personal names introduced by the author see, e.g., Martin of Dacia 1961, pp. 12, 53; by the copyist, De Rijk 1977b, pp. 121–2.

example of this is quoted by Anneliese Maier.[68] A copyist of a work of Burley's breaks off in the middle of a question, saying: 'From this question I would not copy anything [more], for this fellow Burley fills up a whole sheet with totally useless material, where he does nothing but give some solutions and replications which he and some other master flung against each other, and Burley presupposes many false things, so I did not copy it.'

Additions again include a whole range of more or less important errors. The trivial form is the duplication of a word or a phrase; the interesting ones are insertions of marginal material into the text, which again may vary from irrelevant material, through comments by users of the text, to afterthoughts by the master.[69]

The last class of errors consists in *substitution* of wrong words or phrases. Some are due to absentmindedness, when, e.g., the opposite term is inserted into a complex argumentation. Such errors are often to be blamed on the author himself (Aquinas is notorious for making such errors), but most instances are probably the fault of the scribe(s). It is almost impossible for anyone to avoid this type of error completely, but it is easily detectable by a close scrutiny of the argument.

Most errors of substitution are connected with the medieval system of abbreviations.[70] Because of the expensiveness of writing material and because of the hurry often imposed upon the copyist, medieval schoolmen and scribes developed a complex and effective system of abbreviations. The system is not absolutely uniform; it changes with place, time, and discipline, and even the individual scribe is not always consistent. The errors connected with abbreviations can be categorised as (a) abbreviations wrongly expanded, (b) abbreviations unrecognised as such, (c) imaginary abbreviations expanded.[71] These three types are frequently combined with misunderstandings of various sorts:[72] false reading or transposition of individual letters, misunderstanding or ignorance of technical terms, false divisions or combinations of words (reading, e.g., *'imaginationi'* for *'imaginatio i(n)'* or *'syllogismus medisanus'* for *'syllogismus in disamis'*), or in-

68. Maier 1964–7, I, 223: 'De ista quaestione nihil volui scribere quoniam ille Burleus facit usque ad finem quaestionis bene unum quaternum stationis de littera totaliter inutili, unde non ponit nisi solutiones et replicationes quas ipse et quidam alius doctor sibi invicem faciebant, et supponit Burleus multa falsa, ideo non scripsi.'
69. See Macken 1973; Dondaine 1956.
70. Capelli 1961; Pelzer 1966; Piltz 1977, pp. 315–41.
71. Bergh 1978.
72. Very instructive examples can be found in Dondaine 1967, which discusses cases where the original of the faulty copies is known.

sufficient knowledge of medieval lexical, grammatical, or orthographical idiosyncrasies.

In order to give a faint impression of what can be expected I give a short catalogue of errors actually found in modern editions or in manuscripts, structured according to the three above-mentioned types.

(a) Abbreviations wrongly expanded: *per/prae/pro*; *accidens/accentus*; *conclusio/cognitio/constructio/quaestio* (with confusion of '9' = '*con*' and '*q*'); *in/id est*; *universale/virtuale*; *proceditur/praedicatur/probatur*; *positio/ratio* (with confusion of '*p*' and long '*r*'); *dividitur/dicitur*; *homo/non* (with confusion of '*h*' and '*n*'; *conceptus/contemptus*; *sed/secundum*; *enim/autem*; *et/vel*.

(b) Abbreviations undiscovered: *poto/potero*; *praedicat/praedicatur*; *uno/numero*; *patius/paratius*; *item/in tantum*; *antecedens/antecedens probatur (ans^r)*; *sic/sicut*; *item/iterum*.

(c) Imaginary abbreviations expanded: *tamen/tu*; *opere/ope*; *partitio/positio*.

One final sort of error which is often introduced by modern editors consists in *mistaken punctuation*. Since the manuscripts normally have only a very erratic punctuation which is not taken into consideration by most modern editors, errors of this kind are the fault of modern editors, though they have sometimes been misled by the manuscript. The most frequent, and unfortunately least innocent form of this error is the separation of adverbial phrases from the proposition to which they belong. But some editors also unwittingly separate the main clause from its dependent clauses. A general rule of thumb for users of medieval texts in modern editions is simply not to trust the punctuation.

A catalogue of dangers and errors such as the one just presented might discourage the reader by destroying his confidence in all manuscripts and all editions. Fortunately, that would be an exaggerated reaction. Errors normally infect only small sections of a text, and many of them are easily recognisable. The main conclusion to be drawn is that since manuscripts and modern editions are of varying quality they cannot be used indiscriminately or uncritically. On the other hand, this is also one of the charms of the study of medieval philosophy: it is a study very much in progress and it has not yet attained the level of stability. New finds may still change the overall picture considerably, and closer scrutiny of the texts and the arguments is certain to provide new insights. The present volume is an interim report, and in no way a survey of established opinions and facts.

II

ARISTOTLE
IN THE MIDDLE AGES

2

ARISTOTELES LATINUS

Introduction to the medieval Latin Aristotle

All of Aristotle's works were translated into Latin in the Middle Ages and nearly all were intensely studied. The exceptions are the *Eudemian Ethics*, of which no complete translation survives, and the *Poetics*, which, although translated by William of Moerbeke, remained unknown. Most of the works were translated more than once, and two of them, the *Physics* and *Metaphysics*, were translated or revised no fewer than five times. The translations we are concerned with spanned a period of about 150 years; some were made from the Arabic, but the majority directly from the Greek. Some translations became popular and remained so; some became popular but were then superseded by other translations; others barely circulated at all.

An examination of the medieval Latin Aristotle cannot consider only the genuine works of Aristotle, but must also deal with works credited to Aristotle in the Middle Ages although now believed to be spurious. It is also essential to consider translations of Greek and Arabic commentators on Aristotle. (All these translations – of genuine and spurious works and of commentaries – are listed for easy reference in a single table below.)

The basic source for our knowledge of medieval Latin translations of Aristotle is a corpus of over 2,000 manuscripts dating from the ninth to the sixteenth century, most of which are distributed among the major libraries of Europe. They contain the texts of the translations and in some cases constitute the only documentation we have. Other direct documentation about translations and translators is sparse.

The scholarly study of the translations began in 1819 with the publication of Amable Jourdain's *Recherches critiques sur l'âge et l'origine des traductions latines d'Aristote*. It was continued in the burgeoning of research in the nineteenth and twentieth centuries, and culminated in 1930 when a project to edit the complete corpus of the translations was launched under the auspices of the Union Académique Internationale. The first achievement of this enterprise was a catalogue of medieval manuscripts containing

Aristotelian translations, Volume I of which appeared in 1939; Volume II and a supplementary volume appeared in 1955 and 1962 respectively, and these three volumes constitute the basic research tool for the study of the Aristotle translations. The second achievement is the continuing series of '*Aristoteles Latinus*' volumes containing critical editions of the translations.[1] As a result of all this scholarly and editorial activity, most of the basic problems about the identity and dating of the translations have been solved.[2]

The history of the translations

The basic information about the translations is summarised in the table below (pp. 74ff.). Only the more important ones are expressly considered in this discussion, which attempts to outline the stages by which the complete Aristotelian corpus slowly came into circulation.

At the beginning of our period only two of Aristotle's logical works, the *Categories* and *De interpretatione*, were known in Latin, in Boethius' translation; these two works, which together with Porphyry's *Isagoge* became known as the '*logica vetus*', had already become standard school texts in logic. One of the results of the quickening interest in logic in the early twelfth century was the recovery, from about 1120 onwards, of the rest of Boethius' translations of the logic: the *Prior Analytics*, *Topics* and *Sophistici elenchi*. How and where these translations, made some six centuries earlier, were found is not known. The logical corpus was completed by James of Venice's translation (from the Greek) of the *Posterior Analytics*; in 1159 John of Salisbury in his *Metalogicon* shows a familiarity with all these works. (He also quotes from a second translation of the *Posterior Analytics*, that of Ioannes, which otherwise remained virtually unknown.)

James of Venice also translated the *Physics*, *De anima*, *Metaphysics* (at least in part), five of the *Parva naturalia* treatises, and an anonymous introduction to the *Physics* known as the *De intelligentia*. Fragments of his translations of the *Sophistici elenchi* and of Greek commentaries on the *Posterior Analytics* and *Elenchi* have also survived. Nearly all of these translations, which were probably made before 1150, were widely circulated in the

1. The volumes of the catalogue (*Codices*) and the texts so far published are listed in the bibliography under 'Aristoteles Latinus'; the text volumes are referred to in the footnotes by 'AL', the date, and the volume number.
2. The AL catalogue and the prefaces to the published volumes of texts are the basic source both for the history outlined below and for the table. The catalogue has substantial bibliographies. Of fundamental importance also are L. Minio-Paluello's articles, which have been collected into a single volume, *Opuscula* (1972). A valuable earlier survey of the translations is in De Wulf 1934–6, I, pp. 64–80; II, pp. 28–58.

thirteenth century and played an important role in the dissemination of Aristotle's works. (The number of surviving manuscripts listed in the last column of the table can be taken as a rough but reliable indication of the popularity of the different translations.)

James of Venice's work was only part of a burst of translating activity. Before 1162 Henricus Aristippus translated Book IV of the *Meteorologica* from the Greek; whereupon Gerard of Cremona translated Books I–III from the Arabic. The two translations later circulated as one text, with a fragment translated from Avicenna (known as the *De mineralibus*) included as a sort of appendix. There were also several translations made from the Greek by unknown twelfth-century translators: one translated the *De generatione et corruptione*; another the *De sensu* and *De somno*; another, independently of James of Venice, the *Physics* (only a fragment survives)[3] and all the *Metaphysics* except Book XI (James' translation only went as far as Book IV.4); another Books II and III of the *Nicomachean Ethics* (the so-called '*Ethica vetus*');[4] another, independently of Boethius, the *Prior Analytics*[5] and *Topics*.[6] In Spain, Gerard of Cremona, who died in 1187, translated *Meteorologica* I–III, *Physics*, *De caelo*, *De generatione et corruptione* and *Posterior Analytics*, and also Themistius' paraphrase of the *Posterior Analytics* – all from Arabic versions. Of these only the *Meteorologica* and *De caelo* circulated widely.

In addition to genuine works, a number of important pseudo-Aristotelian works were translated in the twelfth century, mostly from the Arabic. These include the *De plantis* (in fact a work by the first-century-A.D. Greek philosopher Nicholas Damascenus), translated by Alfred of Sareshel before 1200; the *De proprietatibus* (an anonymous Arabic work) and *De causis* (an Arabic paraphrase of Proclus, *Elementatio theologica*) by Gerard of Cremona; the *De differentia spiritus et animae* (in fact by Costa ben Luca) by John of Seville and by an anonymous translator. All these Arabic–Latin translations were widely circulated, often under Aristotle's name. In addition to these works, sections of the philosophical encyclopedia of Avicenna, the *Kitāb al-Shifā*, were translated into Latin in Toledo in the second half of the twelfth century, as were works by Alkindi, Algazel, Alfarabi, and Avencebrol (Ibn Gabirol).[7] All more or less Aristotelian

---

3. Published in AL 1957, VII.2.
4. AL 1972–4, XXVI.1.
5. AL 1962, III.3.
6. AL 1969, V.3.
7. For these works and their translators see Lemay 1963; D'Alverny 1952, 1961–72, and Van Riet 1968, 1972 (Avicenna); Nagy 1897 (Alkindi); Lohr 1965 (Algazel); Salman 1939, Langhade and Grignaschi 1971, and Grignaschi 1972 (Alfarabi); Baeumker 1895 (Avencebrol).

in doctrine, these works made their contribution to the spread of Aristotelianism in the West. One other twelfth-century work should be mentioned, although it was not a translation at all: this is the *Liber sex principiorum*,[8] a fragment of a work by an unknown twelfth-century Latin author dealing with six of Aristotle's ten categories. Under this title it became a regular part of the logical corpus, and it was often commented on and accepted as containing genuine Aristotelian doctrine, although most medieval authors recognised that it was not by Aristotle.

Thus by the end of the twelfth century the bulk of Aristotle's works had been translated – all the logical works, all the works on natural philosophy except the *De animalibus*, and part of the *Ethics*. They do not appear to have been widely read, however; very few twelfth-century manuscripts survive, and references to Aristotle's works are sparse. The works that were studied most were the newly discovered or translated logical texts (the '*logica nova*'), particularly the *Sophistici elenchi*.[9]

By the beginning of the thirteenth century Aristotle was obviously gaining ground and being studied – as witness the edict issued in Paris in 1210 forbidding any lectures (public or private) on Aristotle's books of natural philosophy. The ban, however, was only local and did not prevent the work of translation from continuing. By 1220 Michael Scot had translated three of the five treatises of the *De animalibus* (the *Historia animalium*, *De partibus animalium*, and *De generatione animalium*). In the 1220s or 1230s (no dates are known), he accomplished the vast task of translating Averroes' Arabic commentaries into Latin. Averroes' commentaries on Aristotle were of three types: short epitomes or compendia; 'middle' commentaries made up largely of paraphrase; and 'great' commentaries consisting of very detailed sentence-by-sentence exposition. Michael translated the great commentaries on the *Physics*, *De caelo*, *De anima*, and *Metaphysics*, at the same time translating the full Arabic text of Aristotle in the form of lemmata interspersed with the sections of the commentary. In the case of the *Metaphysics* the lemmata were then transcribed as a continuous text without the commentary, and this translation (the '*Metaphysica nova*') was widely circulated as the most complete text of the *Metaphysics* available in Latin.[10] (The anonymous translation mentioned above, known as the '*Metaphysica media*', although made in the

---

8. AL 1966, I.7.
9. See, for example, De Rijk 1962–7, I; Ebbesen 1973b.
10. However, it lacked all of Books XI, XIII and XIV (i.e. K,M,N), the beginning of I (up to 987^{a}9) and the end of XII (from 1075^{b}11).

twelfth century, appears to have remained unknown until the mid-thirteenth century.) Michael also seems to be the translator of the surviving Latin versions of Averroes' middle commentaries on the *De generatione et corruptione* and Book IV of the *Meteorologica* and of his epitomes of the *De caelo, Parva naturalia* and *De animalibus*. The story of Averroes in Latin can be briefly rounded off by mentioning Hermannus Alemannus' translation of the middle commentaries on the *Nicomachean Ethics* (1240) and *Poetics* (1256), and William of Luna's translation of the middle commentaries on Porphyry's *Isagoge*, the *Categories*, *De interpretatione*, *Prior Analytics*, and *Posterior Analytics* (thirteenth century).

To return to translations from the Greek, early in the thirteenth century the whole of the *Ethics* was translated. Of this translation, however, only Book I, known as the '*Ethica nova*',[11] became known and circulated, and the existence of a complete translation has been assumed from a few surviving fragments from the other books. Between 1220 and 1230 James of Venice's translation of *Metaphysics* I–IV.4 was incompletely revised; subsequently scribes conflated the original and revised versions, so that the texts of the revision which circulated (known as the '*Metaphysica vetus*')[12] contain varying proportions of revised and unrevised text. Towards the middle of the century Robert Grosseteste translated the *Nicomachean Ethics*, along with a great corpus of Greek commentary by Eustratius and others. Grosseteste also translated at least part of *De caelo* along with Simplicius' commentary (fragments survive in one manuscript), and also the pseudo-Aristotelian *De lineis indivisibilibus* and *De laudabilibus bonis*. Between 1258 and 1266 Bartholomew of Messina, at the command of Manfred, king of Sicily, translated a sizable group of pseudo-Aristotelian works: the *Problemata, Physionomia, De mirabilibus auscultationibus, De principiis* (in fact by Aristotle's pupil Theophrastus), *De signis aquarum, De mundo, Magna moralia* and *De coloribus*. Manfred himself may have translated the *De pomo*, a work describing the death of Aristotle. The *De mundo* was also translated by Nicholas of Sicily.

The last major translator was William of Moerbeke. Between about 1260 and 1280 he translated anew or revised virtually the whole Aristotelian corpus, including two works, the *Politics* and *Poetics*, that had not been translated before. William's translations quickly established themselves as the most popular versions, except in the case of the logical works.

---

11. AL 1972, XXVI.2. According to a note in one manuscript, the '*Ethica nova*' was translated by Michael Scot; see the preface to AL 1972, XXVI, pp. cxlii–cxlvii.
12. AL 1970, XXV.1².

Although the majority of Aristotle's works had been translated in the twelfth century, the evidence of the manuscripts and other sources indicates that they were not much studied and circulated until the thirteenth century. From the early thirteenth century onwards numerous manuscripts survive containing a collection of the logical works, all in Boethius' translation except the *Posterior Analytics* (James of Venice), and almost invariably with the addition of Porphyry's *Isagoge* and the *Liber sex principiorum*. Very often two of Boethius' works, the *De topicis differentiis* and the *De divisione*, are also included, and a typical medieval manuscript of Aristotle's 'Organon' would thus contain the following ten works: Porphyry's *Isagoge*, *Categories*, *De interpretatione*, Boethius' *De divisione* and *De topicis differentiis*, *Liber sex principiorum*, *Prior Analytics*, *Posterior Analytics*, *Topics*, and *Sophistici elenchi*.

Towards the middle of the thirteenth century a similar collection containing works in natural philosophy was made, and those twelfth-century translations that were included in it now became widely circulated. The editors of the *Aristoteles Latinus* catalogue have christened this collection the '*corpus vetustius*' and describe nearly one hundred manuscripts (mostly from the thirteenth century) containing the same group of works (not always complete, almost never in the same order, and with other non-Aristotelian works often thrown in). A typical example of the '*corpus vetustius*' is found in a late thirteenth-century manuscript in the Stiftsbibliothek at Admont (no. 126) which contains the following works.

Physics (James of Venice); *De caelo* (Gerard of Cremona); *De generatione et corruptione* (anonymous); *De anima* (James of Venice); *De memoria* (James of Venice); *De sensu* (anonymous); *De somno* (anonymous); *De longitudine* (James of Venice); *De differentia spiritus et animae* (John of Seville or anonymous); *De plantis* (Alfred of Sareshel); *Meteorologica* (Gerard of Cremona and Henricus Aristippus); *Metaphysics* (James revised; Book I only); *Metaphysics* (Michael Scot); *De causis* (Gerard of Cremona); Nicholas of Amiens, *De articulis fidei*.

These then, with the logic, are the Aristotelian translations (genuine and spurious) that 'made the grade' in the thirteenth century, and in modern terms the logical collection and the '*corpus vetustius*' could be described as the standard edition of the works of Aristotle.

It can be seen from the Admont manuscript that two versions of the *Metaphysics* could appear side by side; in fact the history of the *Metaphysics* is rather complicated.[13] James of Venice's version and its anonymous

---

13. See Diem 1967.

revisions (the '*Metaphysica vetus*') covered only the first four books, while the anonymous and nearly complete twelfth-century version (the '*Metaphysica media*') seems to have remained unknown until the mid-thirteenth century; Michael Scot's version from the Arabic (the '*Metaphysica nova*') therefore represented the fullest available text and for this reason was detached from its commentary and transcribed as a plain text. The lack of a single authoritative text is reflected in the manuscripts of the '*corpus vetustius*'. About half of them have no text of the *Metaphysics* at all, while the rest have sometimes the '*vetus*', sometimes the '*nova*', sometimes both, sometimes a composite text; only a few have the '*media*'.

In the second half of the thirteenth century William of Moerbeke's versions were soon collected into a 'new edition' of the works of Aristotle. The demand for Aristotle was high and William's versions represented a more complete and in many cases obviously superior collection to the old corpus. The new collection, labelled the '*corpus recentius*' by the *Aristoteles Latinus* editors, rapidly gained ascendancy in the late thirteenth century and retained it until the Renaissance; over 170 manuscripts survive, although many of these do not contain the complete corpus. Of the manuscripts containing a reasonably full collection the majority contain the following sequence (or one very close to it):

Physics; *De caelo*; *De generatione et corruptione*; *Meteorologica*; *De anima*; *De sensu*; *De memoria*; *De somno*; *De motu animalium*; *De longitudine*; *De iuventute*; *De respiratione*; *De morte*; *Physionomia*; *De bona fortuna*.

About half of these manuscripts also contain all or most of the following works:

Metaphysics; *De nilo*; *De coloribus*; *De plantis*; *De progressu animalium*; *De pomo*; *De intelligentia*; *De causis*; *De proprietatibus*; *De lineis indivisibilibus*; *De mundo*, *Epistola ad Alexandrum*; *Vita Aristotelis*; *De differentia spiritus et animae*.

These works thus represent the new 'standard edition' of Aristotle's works on natural philosophy; it had two forms, a basic collection containing the first sequence, and a fuller collection incorporating the *Metaphysics* and many pseudo-Aristotelian works. It is not obvious why the *Metaphysics* should continue to be absent from many manuscripts of the '*corpus recentius*', as it was from the '*corpus vetustius*'; although William's translation of the *Metaphysics* is often found as the sole work in a manuscript, and so must have circulated independently. The logical collection continued to circulate unchanged in Boethius' and James' versions, and William's new translations or revisions of some of these works failed to challenge the established versions.

We may finish this account of the history of the translations with a résumé of those works that never gained a regular place in the collections mentioned above. The *De animalibus* treatises translated by Michael Scot were widely circulated, nearly always on their own, and continued to rival William's version well into the fourteenth century, to judge from the surviving manuscripts. William's version survives as a complete set in relatively few manuscripts (40 against 79 of Michael Scot's), but his *De motu* and *De progressu* achieved much wider circulation as part of the '*corpus recentius*'. The two incomplete versions of the *Ethics*, comprising the '*Ethica nova*' (Book I) and the '*Ethica vetus*' (Books II and III), achieved modest popularity in the thirteenth century, and often appear as additional texts in manuscripts of the logical collection. They were superseded by Grosseteste's complete version, which achieved immense popularity. Known as the *Liber ethicorum*, and subjected to various revisions, some of which may have been by William of Moerbeke, it survives in almost 300 manuscripts. It was often transcribed alone, but it also regularly appears along with the *Politics*, *Rhetoric*, *Oeconomica* or *Magna moralia*. One or more of these five 'ethical' treatises are often found together in manuscripts from the late thirteenth century onwards, but not in any regular combination or sequence.

Two major observations may be made on the basis of this short account of the translations. The first is the overwhelming importance of translations made directly from the Greek. There is a tenacious legend that the West learnt its Aristotle via translations from the Arabic, but the fact is that the West turned to Arabic–Latin translations only in default of the more intelligible Greek–Latin ones. The only translations from the Arabic to achieve wide circulation were the *De caelo*, *Meteorologica* I–III, *De animalibus* and *Metaphysics*, and all of these except the *De animalibus* were quickly displaced by William of Moerbeke's versions. The legend has more basis, however, when one considers Aristotelian doctrine in a vaguer sense. The twelfth-century translations of Avicenna, Alfarabi, and Algazel, for example, helped to disseminate Aristotelian doctrine, albeit in a not-very-pure form. And of course the commentaries of Averroes in the thirteenth century made a powerful impact on the West. Nevertheless, when the Latin schoolmen came to writing their own commentaries, with few exceptions they used the Greek–Latin and not the Arabic–Latin texts.

The second observation concerns the slowness with which the texts of

Aristotle came into circulation. Although much translation was done in the twelfth century, it was not until well into the thirteenth that manuscripts survive in large numbers. Many early manuscripts have undoubtedly perished, so the full story will never be known, but from the surviving evidence it seems plain that Aristotle did not become really important in the academic world until the middle of the thirteenth century.

The translators

Biographical information about most medieval authors is scarce, and this is particularly true of the translators. Even the famous figures such as Robert Grosseteste and William of Moerbeke are in fact very poorly documented, and few personal details have survived. Furthermore, for the most part the translators cannot be linked with one another; there were no schools of translators,[14] and the work was done by a handful of individuals. Seventeen translators are known by name, and about fifteen more are anonymous. Their work spans the period from about the mid-twelfth century to 1295 with the exception of Boethius, who was of course very much earlier.

Boethius

A Roman senator and minister under Theodoric, Boethius[15] falls far outside the period of this book, his translations of Aristotle being made *ca.* A.D. 510–22. He intended, apparently, to translate the whole of Aristotle, but the only works he is known to have translated are the *Categories*,[16] *De interpretatione*,[17] *Prior Analytics*,[18] *Topics*,[19] and *Sophistici elenchi*[20] – all of the 'Organon' except the *Posterior Analytics*. He also translated Porphyry's *Isagoge*,[21] a short work preparatory to the study of logic which became a regular part of the medieval 'Organon'. Boethius also wrote commentaries on the *Isagoge*, *Categories*, and *De interpretatione*[22] in addition to his independent works on arithmetic, music and logic.

14. The nearest approach to a school is the group of translators in Toledo in the second half of the twelfth century; see Lemay 1963.
15. For a good general account of Boethius with extensive bibliography, see Minio-Paluello 1970b; see also Armstrong 1967, pp. 538–64.
16. AL 1961b, I.1–2.
17. AL 1965, II.1.
18. AL 1962, III.1–2.
19. AL 1969, V.1–2.
20. AL 1975, VI.1.
21. AL 1966, I.6.
22. For a possible commentary on the *Posterior Analytics* see Ebbesen 1973a.

Boethius' authorship of the translations cannot be established with absolute certainty, but there is strong documentary and internal evidence (based on quotations in his commentaries) that the surviving translations of the *Isagoge*, *Categories*, and *De interpretatione* are by him. This being accepted, his authorship of the other three follows from a stylistic analysis, for all six are consistent among themselves in their method of translating, and different from all the other translations. Furthermore, in the oldest and best manuscript of the Latin version of the *Topics* there is a note attributing the translation to Boethius.

All the Boethian translations except the *Sophistici elenchi* have complications in their textual history indicating that the texts were revised at some stage. The revisions may be Boethius' own, or they may be the work of an unknown editor, possibly working in Constantinople where Boethius' works are known to have been transcribed (and perhaps edited) already in the sixth century.

James of Venice

The next translator, James of Venice,[23] does not appear until the second quarter of the twelfth century. He was long known to scholars through a passage in Robert of Torigny's *Chronicle*: 'James, a cleric from Venice, translated from the Greek into Latin several books of Aristotle and commented on them, viz. the *Topics*, *Prior* and *Posterior Analytics*, and *Elenchi*, although an earlier translation of these same books was already in existence.'[24] Other documentation about James is sparse and can be summed up as follows: he called himself a Venetian Greek and a philosopher; in 1136 he was present at a theological debate in Constantinople between Anselm of Havelberg and the archbishop of Nicomedia; in 1148 he presented some advice to the archbishop of Ravenna on the subject of the precedence of Ravenna over other archbishoprics; he may have been in Bologna in the 1140s, disputing with Magister Albericus over the interpretation of the *Sophistici elenchi*; his commentary (or translation of a commentary) on the *Elenchi* is mentioned in a twelfth-century grammatical '*quaestio*' and an early-thirteenth-century author mentions his commentary on the *Posterior Analytics*.[25] In addition to Robert of Torigny two other sources men-

23. For James see Minio-Paluello 1952 and the prefaces to AL 1968a, IV and AL 1975, VI.
24. 'Iacobus clericus de Venetia transtulit de Greco in Latinum quosdam libros Aristotilis et commentatus est scilicet Topica, Analiticos Priores et Posteriores, et Elencos, quamvis antiquior translatio super eosdem libros haberetur.' Minio-Paluello 1952, p. 267.
25. Ebbesen 1977b, pp. 1–3.

tion James' translation of the *Posterior Analytics*: the translator Ioannes (see below) and the author of a note in a thirteenth-century Oxford manuscript.

Robert of Torigny's note led to considerable debate among scholars as to whether the surviving translations of the '*logica nova*' (preserved anonymously in the manuscripts) should be ascribed to Boethius or to James. The debate was resolved in 1952 by L. Minio-Paluello in an important article which not only established James as an important translator but also demonstrated the validity of stylistic analysis as a means of distinguishing translators. Minio-Paluello's analysis revealed the following facts: the common versions of the *Prior Analytics*, *Topics* and *Sophistici elenchi*, surviving in numerous manuscripts, are consistent in style with each other and with the known Boethian translations of the '*logica vetus*'; the *Posterior Analytics* [26] is in a different style from the rest of the '*logica nova*' but has the same stylistic features as a passage translated from the Greek in James' advice to the archbishop of Ravenna; the twelfth-century translations of the *Physics*, *De anima*, *Metaphysics*,[27] *De memoria*, *De longitudine*, *De iuventute*, *De respiratione*, *De morte*, and *De intelligentia* reveal the same stylistic features as the *Posterior Analytics* (as do fragments of translations of the *Sophistici elenchi* and of the more recently discovered commentaries on the *Elenchi* and *Posterior Analytics*, purportedly by Alexander of Aphrodisias).[28]

The conclusion is inescapable: James translated the *Posterior Analytics*, *Sophistici elenchi*, *Metaphysics* and several important works of natural philosophy as well as most of the *Parva naturalia*. Moreover, recent research has revealed more and more of his activity as a translator. Most of his translations achieved wide circulation and make him the most important of the twelfth-century translators.

Henricus Aristippus

The opportunity and the impetus for James' translating work arose out of contact between Italy and Constantinople in the twelfth century, and in Constantinople with James in 1136 were two other distinguished translators, Burgundio of Pisa and Moses of Bergamo, neither of whom,

26. AL 1968a, IV. 1.
27. AL 1970, XXV.1. The text now ends abruptly at Book IV. 4 (1007ª31), but James possibly translated the whole work; see Minio-Paluello 1972, pp. 98–102, AL 1976, XXV.2, p. xi.
28. Minio-Paluello 1954, 1962; AL 1975, VI. 2; Ebbesen 1972.

however, translated any Aristotle.[29] Some twenty years later, in 1158, another Italian, Henricus Aristippus,[30] was in Constantinople on a diplomatic mission for the King of Sicily. At that time the Sicilian court was an important centre of translation and scholarly contact with both Arab and Byzantine worlds.[31] Henricus Aristippus was archdeacon of Catania in 1156 and became chief minister of the kingdom in 1160; in 1162, however, he was imprisoned by the king and died in prison. His only Aristotelian translation was of Book IV of the *Meteorologica*. His choice of this work reflected his interest in natural phenomena – one witness describes him investigating the marvels of Mount Etna. Henricus also translated Plato's *Phaedo*[32] and *Meno*.[33] He began work on the *Phaedo* in 1156, but the date of the *Meteorologica* translation is not known.

Ioannes

Another translator of this period is Ioannes, a shadowy figure. His translation of the *Posterior Analytics*[34] survives complete in only one manuscript, discovered in 1913 by C. H. Haskins in the cathedral library at Toledo.[35] The translation is anonymous in this manuscript, but the name 'Ioannes' is suggested by three citations in other sources: in a Paris manuscript a phrase quoted from this translation has the rubric '*translatio Ioannis*'; in another manuscript fragments of this translation bear the rubric '*translatio Io.*' ('*Io.*' being a regular abbreviation for '*Ioannes*' or '*Ioannis*'); and Albert the Great mentions a '*translatio Ioannis*' which could well be this version. Ioannes' translation has an engaging and interesting prologue:

Although hindered by many duties, my love for you compels me to translate the *Posterior Analytics* from Greek into Latin, which task I have undertaken the more readily as I know that the book contains many fruits of science. I am equally sure that knowledge of it is not widespread among the Latin-speakers of our generation, for Boethius' translation is not to be found complete among us, and what has been discovered of it is obscured by corruption. James' translation, on the other hand, is known to the masters of France, as are translations of commentaries made by the same James, but they by their silence bear witness that James' version is wrapped up in the shadows of obscurity, and do not dare to proclaim their knowledge of it. Wherefore, if Latinity is able to procure any benefit from my

29. Haskins 1927, pp. 197–209.
30. See Haskins 1927, pp. 159ff.
31. Haskins 1927, pp. 155–7.
32. *Plato Latinus* 1950, II.
33. *Plato Latinus* 1940, I.
34. AL 1968a, IV.2.
35. Haskins 1927, pp. 228ff.

translation, the credit for this is due to your request. For I undertook the task of translating not for money or empty fame but to please you and to impart something of value to Latinity. Moreover, if in any matter I shall be found to have strayed from the path of reason, I shall not be ashamed to correct it with help from you or other learned men.[36]

The references to Boethius' translation (now lost, if it ever existed), to James of Venice's translation and to the deplorable state of affairs in France are intriguing. Unfortunately the pusillanimous masters of France cannot be identified; nor can Ioannes and his learned patron.

That Ioannes' translation was made before 1159 is proved by a reference in John of Salisbury's *Metalogicon* which was completed in that year. The *Metalogicon* is the first medieval Latin work to show a knowledge of all the books of the 'Organon', and in the course of a short account of the *Posterior Analytics* John of Salisbury quotes *en passant* a phrase from what he calls the 'new translation', which is in fact Ioannes'; the rest of his quotations are from James' version.[37] Apart from Albert the Great, whose reference is uncertain, John of Salisbury is the only medieval author who is known to have quoted Ioannes' translation, and this coincidence is the basis for a conjecture. In the *Polycraticon*[38] John describes a banquet in Apulia in southern Italy where he met John Belmeis, treasurer of York, whom he describes as excelling in his knowledge of three languages. Could John Belmeis and our Ioannes be the same person? It is perhaps more likely, however, as Haskins suggests, that both the translator and his patron were south-Italian or Sicilian.[39]

James of Venice, Henricus Aristippus and Ioannes are the only twelfth-century translators of Aristotle from the Greek known by name. They do not constitute a school, but they are definitely part of a movement. To this same movement belong the five anonymous twelfth-century translators mentioned above (p. 47).

36. 'Vallatum multis occupationibus me dilectio vestra compulit ut Posteriores Analeticos Aristotelis de Greco in Latinum transferrem. Quod eo affectuosius aggressus sum quod cognoscebam librum illum multos in se sciencie fructus continere et certum erat noticiam eius nostris temporibus Latinis non patere. Nam translatio Boecii apud nos integra non invenitur, et id ipsum quod de ea reperitur vitio corruptionis obfuscatur. Translationem vero Iacobi obscuritatis tenebris involvi silentio suo peribent Francie magistri, qui quamvis illam translationem et commentarios ab eodem Iacobo translatos habeant, tamen noticiam illius libri non audent profiteri. Eapropter siquid utilitatis ex mea translatione sibi noverit Latinitas provenire, postulationi vestre debebit imputare. Non enim spe lucri aut inanis glorie ad transferendum accessi, sed ut aliquid conferens Latinitati vestre morem gererem voluntati. Ceterum si in aliquo visus fuero rationis tramitem excessisse, vestra vel aliorum ammonitione non erubescam emendare.' Haskins 1927, p. 229.
37. John of Salisbury 1929, pp. 111–12, 170–2.
38. John of Salisbury 1909, II, p. 271.
39. Haskins 1927, p. 235.

Gerard of Cremona

Translations from the Arabic constituted a second major movement. Its most important twelfth-century representative was Gerard of Cremona, who lived in Toledo and died there in 1187 at the age of 73. A brief eulogy and a catalogue of Gerard's works were produced by his pupils,[40] and among the 71 translations of Arabic texts listed are Aristotle's *Posterior Analytics*,[41] *De caelo*, *De generatione et corruptione*, *Meteorologica*, and *Physics*, and Themistius' paraphrase of the *Posterior Analytics*.[42] All of these translations have survived and two of them, the *De caelo* and *Meteorologica* (Books I–III), were widely circulated as part of the 'corpus vetustius'. Gerard's translations of the pseudo-Aristotelian *De proprietatibus* (or *De causis proprietatum elementorum*) and of the *De causis*[43] were also popular. The dates of the translations are not known.

John of Seville and Alfred of Sareshel

Two other twelfth-century translators from the Arabic were John of Seville (Iohannes Hispalensis) and Alfred of Sareshel, who were both in Spain, John around the middle of the century, Alfred towards the end. John of Seville[44] was active *ca.* 1130–40, and is credited with many translations, among them the *De differentia*, dedicated to Raymond, archbishop of Toledo, and the *De regimine sanitatis* (a fragment of the *Secretum secretorum*).[45] Alfred[46] translated the *De plantis* before about 1200 and wrote a commentary on it; he also translated the fragment of Avicenna known as the *De mineralibus*. He is best known, however, for his work *De motu cordis*,[47] written *ca.* 1210 and dedicated to Alexander Neckham, and his commentary on the *Meteorologica*.[48]

Michael Scot

Translation from the Arabic was continued in the thirteenth century by Michael Scot.[49] He is first heard of in the entourage of the bishop of Toledo

---

40. Sudhoff 1914; Sarton 1931, II.2, pp. 338–44.
41. AL 1968a, IV.3.
42. Ed. in O'Donnell 1958.
43. Ed. in Steele 1935.
44. See Thorndike 1959.
45. See Manzalaoni 1977, p. xiv.
46. See Otte 1972.
47. Baeumker 1913, 1923.
48. Otte 1976.
49. See Haskins 1927, pp. 272–98; Thorndike 1965.

in 1215,[50] and was in Toledo in 1217 when he completed his translation of the Arabic astronomer Al-bitrogi's *On the Sphere*. He appears to have been still there when he translated Aristotle's *De animalibus* from the Arabic version containing only three of the five treatises; the evidence for this is a colophon which appears in several manuscripts: 'Here ends Aristotle's book on animals, translated in Toledo from Arabic into Latin by the master Michael.'

In October 1220 Michael was in Bologna; this is known from a memorandum, signed and dated, which he wrote there and inserted into a copy of his translation of the *De animalibus*. From 1224 to 1227 there is evidence that he was under the patronage of popes Honorius III and Gregory IX, and from about 1227 he was in the service of King Frederick II of Sicily, where he was court astrologer. He died *ca.* 1236.

Michael's great achievement was his translation of many of the Arabic commentaries of Averroes: the great commentaries on the *De caelo*, *De anima*,[51] *Metaphysics*, and *Physics*, along with complete translations of the texts; the middle commentaries on the *De generatione et corruptione*[52] and Book IV of the *Meteorologica*; and the epitomes of the *De caelo*, *Parva naturalia*[53] and *De animalibus*. Of these translations only the *De caelo* is incontestably by Michael, for Michael's dedication of the work to Stephen of Provins is found in several of the manuscripts. That Michael also translated the other commentaries is a reasonable inference based on stylistic analysis and general likelihood. Further analysis, however, is needed before it can be accepted with complete confidence. The dates of these translations are not known, but scholars assume they were made in the 1220s and 1230s, probably at Frederick's court.

Hermannus Alemannus

Four minor thirteenth-century translators from the Arabic are Hermannus Alemannus, Philip of Tripoli, William of Luna and Petrus Gallegus. Hermannus ('Herman the German')[54] worked in Toledo around the middle of the thirteenth century (he was there in 1240 and 1256) and is almost certainly to be identified with the Hermannus who was bishop of Astorga in Léon from 1266 until his death in 1272. His translations have

50. Rivero Recio 1951. I am indebted to Mlle M.-T. d'Alverny for this reference.
51. Ed. Crawford 1953.
52. Ed. Fobes and Kurland 1956.
53. Ed. Shields 1949.
54. See Luquet 1901.

been identified from prologues and colophons in the manuscripts, three of which are dated. They are the *Rhetoric*, comprising the almost complete text of Aristotle interspersed with portions of Averroes' middle commentary and short fragments from Avicenna and Alfarabi; the introductory section of Alfarabi's commentary on the *Rhetoric*;[55] Averroes' middle commentary on the *Ethics*, the 'Liber Nicomachie' (Toledo, 1240); an Arabic epitome of the *Ethics* known as the *Summa Alexandrinorum* (1243 or 1244); and the middle commentary on the *Poetics* (Toledo, 1256),[56] this last being known as the 'Poetria'.

Philip of Tripoli

Philip of Tripoli,[57] a cleric in the Crusader kingdom of Syria, found at Antioch and translated into Latin an Arabic text of the *Secretum secretorum*,[58] a work on occult science and kingship allegedly written by Aristotle for Alexander the Great. Philip of Tripoli is probably identical with the Philip whose ecclesiastical career in Syria between 1227 and 1259 can partly be traced in papal and other registers. The translation was probably made *ca.* 1243 and became very popular, some 350 manuscripts surviving.

William of Luna

'Here ends the work of Averroes on the *Categories* of Aristotle translated by William of Luna at Naples.' This colophon in a fourteenth-century manuscript and a similar colophon to Averroes' epitome of the *Isagoge* in the same manuscript constitute our sole evidence of William of Luna (a town in Spain) as a translator of Averroes. That he was also responsible for translating the epitomes of the *De interpretatione* and the *Prior* and *Posterior Analytics* in the same manuscripts is a reasonable inference. Nothing else is known about him except that he may also have translated a work of algebra.[59]

Petrus Gallegus

Petrus Gallegus,[60] a Spanish Franciscan who was a confidant of Alfonso X and became Bishop of Cartagena in Spain 1250–67, translated Averroes'

55. Boggess 1971.
56. AL 1968, XXXIII.2.
57. See Haskins 1927, pp. 137–40.
58. Ed. Steele 1920. See also Manzalaoni 1977, pp. xvff.
59. Thorndike 1931, II.2, p. 563.
60. See Pelzer 1924.

epitome on the *De partibus animalium*. This version has survived in a fragmentary state in one manuscript. His only other known work is a translation of a similar compendium on household management (*Oeconomica*) which, however, was not Aristotelian.

Robert Grosseteste

After the spate of translators from the Greek in the twelfth century, the first name to figure in the thirteenth century is that of Robert Grosseteste,[61] first Chancellor of Oxford University, bishop of Lincoln from 1235 until his death in 1253, and a major political, ecclesiastical, scientific, and philosophical figure as well as a translator of Aristotelian and other works. Documentary evidence about Grosseteste's scholarly career and the chronology of his writings is almost entirely lacking. Roger Bacon says that he learnt Greek late in life, and scholars have assumed that his translating work was undertaken during his episcopate or at least after about 1230. He procured several Greek-speaking assistants, one of whom was Nicholas of Sicily (see below), and on at least one occasion he sent agents to Greece to acquire manuscripts.[62]

Grosseteste's most important Aristotelian translation was of the *Nicomachean Ethics*.[63] With characteristic thoroughness he also translated a large corpus of Greek commentaries by Eustratius and others,[64] to which he added numerous notes of his own explaining Greek terms and points of grammar. The translation of the *Ethics*, which makes use of the previously existing translations, is thought to have been made around 1246–7, and became in its original or in a revised form the standard version in the Middle Ages. Grosseteste also translated the first two books of the *De caelo*[65] along with Simplicius' commentary, and two pseudo-Aristotelian works, the *De lineis indivisibilibus* and *De laudabilibus bonis* (or *De virtute*) as well as several important non-Aristotelian works including the works of Pseudo-Dionysius.[66] The *De lineis indivisibilibus* was circulated widely as part of the '*corpus vetustius*' but the *De laudabilibus bonis* was not widely known and the *De caelo* remained unknown and survives incomplete in only one manuscript. A small fragment of Simplicius on the *Physics* found in an Oxford manuscript may have been translated by Grosseteste.

61. On Grosseteste and his works see Baur 1912, 1917; Franceschini 1933; Russell 1933; Thomson 1940; Callus 1955a.
62. Callus 1955a, p. 40.
63. AL 1972–4, XXVI.3A.
64. Ed. Mercken 1973.
65. Allan 1950.
66. See Callus 1955a, pp. 44ff.

Nicholas of Sicily

Master Nicholas the Greek[67] was a member of the household of Robert Grosseteste and was no doubt one of the 'adiutores' (helpers) who assisted him in his translating. He came from Sicily, and his name first appears in ecclesiastical documents of Grosseteste's episcopacy in 1237. He was a canon by 1246, and in 1256 he was sent to Rome to try to procure Grosseteste's canonisation. He died in 1279. Only one translation by Nicholas is known: that of the pseudo-Aristotelian *De mundo*.[68]

Bartholomew of Messina

Another Sicilian was Bartholomew of Messina. His translation of six pseudo-Aristotelian treatises – *Problemata*, *Physionomia*, *De mirabilibus auscultationibus*, *De principiis*, *De signis*, and *Magna moralia* – is testified by a series of rubrics, almost all found in a single Padua manuscript containing a collection of these and other works. A typical rubric reads as follows: 'Here begins the book by Aristotle on Physiognomy, translated from Greek into Latin by master Bartholomew of Messina, in the court and at the command of the most illustrious Manfred, most blessed king of Sicily and lover of science.'[69] From these rubrics we know that Bartholomew had some position at Manfred's court; the translations must have been made between 1258 and 1266, the dates of Manfred's reign. Bartholomew also translated from the Greek a veterinary treatise by Hierocles,[70] and two further pseudo-Aristotelian works, the *De mundo*[71] and *De coloribus*,[72] his authorship of the last two translations being established by stylistic evidence. Nothing else is known about Bartholomew.

According to some sources, Bartholomew's patron, Manfred himself, translated the *De pomo*. Scholars tend to doubt this, and it seems more likely that he was merely responsible for having it translated.

William of Moerbeke

The second half of the thirteenth century is dominated by the Dominican William of Moerbeke,[73] the most famous and most prolific of the medieval

---

67. See Callus 1955a, p. 229; Russell 1933.
68. AL 1965b, XI.2.
69. 'Incipit liber physiognomonomie [*sic*] Aris. translatus de Greco in Latinum a magistro Bartho-[lomeo] de Messana in curia illustrissimi Manfredi serenissimi regis Sicilie scientie amatoris de mandato suo. MS. Padua Ant. XVII.370, f. 72ʳ.
70. Haskins 1927, p. 269.
71. AL 1965b, XI.1.
72. AL 1965b, XI, p. xvii.
73. See Grabmann 1946; an excellent short account is in Minio-Paluello 1974, with a good bibliography.

translators of Aristotle, said to be a friend and collaborator of Thomas Aquinas. Yet very little is known of his life. He was born *ca.* 1215 or later in the village of Moerbeke, now in Belgium, and probably entered the Dominican convent at Louvain as a young man. He is known to have gone to Greece, for a manuscript colophon records that the translation of Alexander's commentary on the *Meteorologica* was completed at Nicea in April 1260, and a similar colophon records the completion of the *De animalibus* at Thebes in December of the same year; William was presumably a member of the Dominican convent established at Thebes at least since 1253. By 1271 William was at the papal court at Viterbo as chaplain and confessor to the pope, a position he had probably held for several years, for two of his translations were made in Viterbo in 1267 and 1268, as is shown by manuscript colophons. He remained at the papal court until 1278, when he was made Archbishop of Corinth in Greece. He died there in 1286. A later medieval tradition records William as translator of 'all the books of Aristotle on natural and moral philosophy' at the request of his friend Thomas Aquinas. However, there is no contemporary documentation of either friendship or collaboration, and William's relations with Thomas are a matter of conjecture.

The traditional ascription to William of all the 'new translations' dating from the second half of the thirteenth century is supported by colophons in several manuscripts. Thus the translations of the *De animalibus*, *Metaphysics*, *Meteorologica*, *Politics*, *Rhetoric*, and several of the Greek commentaries are known definitely to be by William. These and other colophons also give a place and/or a precise date for some of the translations, as noted in the table. Stylistic analysis shows that the other 'new translations' must be written by the same author, and modern research thus confirms the medieval tradition.

William was the first to translate into Latin the *De motu animalium*, *De progressu animalium*, *Politics*,[74] and *Poetics*,[75] and he made new translations of the *Categories*,[76] *De interpretatione*,[77] *De caelo*, *Meteorologica*, *Rhetoric*, and the rest of the *De animalibus*.[78] He also revised the *Posterior Analytics*,[79] *Sophistici elenchi*,[80] *Physics*, *De anima*, *Parva naturalia*, and *Metaphy-*

---

74. Ed. Susemihl 1872. William's translation is an important witness to the Greek text. What is apparently an early draft by William of Book I and part of Book II is in AL 1961, XXIX.1.
75. AL 1968b, XXXIII. 1 (2nd edn., ed. L. Minio-Paluello, 1968).
76. AL 1961b, I.3.
77. AL 1965a, II.2.
78. The *De generatione animalium* is in AL 1966b, XVII.2.
79. AL 1968a, IV.4.
80. AL 1975, VI.3. The apparent connections with a twelfth-century text noted by Ebbesen 1972, pp. 16–18, are not significant.

sics,[81] and possibly also the *De generatione et corruptione* and *Ethics*.[82] He appears to have translated one pseudo-Aristotelian work, the *De coloribus*. Of the Greek commentators he translated Simplicius on the *Categories*[83] and *De caelo*, Ammonius on the *Perihermenias*,[84] Alexander on the *Meteorologica*[85] and *De sensu*, Philoponus on the *De anima* (Book III)[86] and Themistius on the *De anima*.[87] His most important non-Aristotelian translation was of the *Elementatio theologica* of Proclus,[88] an Arabic–Latin version of which had long been circulating under the title *De causis* and was sometimes ascribed to Aristotle.

With the exception of the logical texts, where the existing translations were firmly established, all of William's revisions and new translations became the standard texts of Aristotle up to and beyond the Renaissance.

Durandus de Alvernia

The series of medieval translations of Aristotle ends with a revised version of the anonymous translation of the *Oeconomica*. Several manuscripts have a colophon recording that this translation was made at Anagni (Italy) in 1295 by 'an archbishop and a bishop from Greece and Durandus de Alvernia, a Latin-speaker, proctor of the University of Paris, at that time in the Roman Curia'.[89] Apart from his authorship of three Aristotelian commentaries, virtually nothing else is known of Durandus de Alvernia;[90] the Greek archbishop and bishop are also unknown. Durandus is the last of the medieval translators of Aristotle; the next wave of 'humanist' translations begins in the fifteenth century.[91]

The language and method of the translators

All the medieval translators of Aristotle (and medieval translators in general) adopted a literal style of translating, in which the Greek was

---

81. William was the first to translate Book XI, which was omitted in both the anonymous and Michael Scot's versions.
82. AL 1972–4, XXVI.3B.
83. Ed. Pattin 1971, 1975.
84. Ed. Verbeke 1961.
85. Ed. Smet 1968.
86. Ed. Verbeke 1966.
87. Ed. Verbeke 1957.
88. Ed. Vansteenkiste 1951.
89. '... per unum archiepiscopum et unum episcopum de Grecia, et magistrum Durandum de Alvernia latinum procuratorem Universitatis Parisiensis, tunc temporis in curia Romana ...'
90. See Lohr 1967–74, Authors A – F, p. 402.
91. For a summary of fifteenth-century translators and translations see Minio-Paluello 1970a, pp. 273–4; Garin 1951. For printed editions of the fifteenth and sixteenth centuries see the *Gesamtkatalog der Wiegendrucke* (1925ff.) and Cranz 1971 respectively; also Risse 1965.

rendered into Latin more or less word for word, with the Greek word order being retained where possible, and with conscious consistency in vocabulary. Some short examples taken at random from four of the most important translators will give the flavour of the medieval translations and show how closely they all adhere to the literal method.

1. Boethius, *Topics* 134ª5–7:

> Deinde destruentem quidem si quod naturaliter inest
> Ἔπειτ' ἀνασκευάζοντα μὲν εἰ τὸ φύσει ὑπάρχον
>
> volens assignare hoc modo ponit secundum locutionem,
> βουλόμενος ἀποδοῦναι τοῦτον τὸν τρόπον τίθησι τῇ λέξει,
>
> ut quod semper inest significet.[92]
> ὥστε τὸ ἀεὶ ὑπάρχον σημαίνειν.

1. James of Venice, *Metaphysics* 989ª26–30:

> Et omnino alterationem destrui necesse est sic
> ὅλως τε ἀλλοίωσιν ἀναιρεῖσθαι ἀνάγκη τοῖς οὕτω
>
> dicentibus; non enim ex calido frigidum neque ex
> λέγουσιν· οὐ γὰρ ἐκ θερμοῦ ψυχρὸν οὐδὲ ἐκ
>
> frigido calidum erit. Quid enim ipsa utique patietur
> ψυχροῦ θερμὸν ἔσται. τί γὰρ αὐτὰ ἂν πάσχοι
>
> contraria, et que erit una natura que fit ignis et
> τἀναντία, καὶ τίς εἴη ἂν μία φύσις ἡ γιγνομένη πῦρ καὶ
>
> aqua, quod ille non dicit.[93]
> ὕδωρ, ὃ ἐκεῖνος οὔ φησιν.

3. Grosseteste, *Ethics* 1127ª13–16:

> Circa eadem autem fere est et iactantie
> περὶ τὰ αὐτὰ δὲ σχεδόν ἐστι καὶ ἡ τῆς ἀλαζονείας
>
> medietas. Innominata autem et ipsa. Non malum autem
> μεσότης· ἀνώνυμος δὲ καὶ αὐτή. οὐ χεῖρον δὲ
>
> et tales pertransire. Magis enim utique sciemus
> καὶ τὰς τοιαύτας ἐπελθεῖν· μᾶλλόν τε γὰρ ἂν εἰδείημεν

92. 'Next, for destructive purposes, see if, while intending to render an attribute that naturally belongs, he states it in his language in such a way as to indicate one that invariably belongs.' (Oxford translation.)

93. 'And in general, change of quality is necessarily done away with for those who speak thus, for on their view cold will not come from hot nor hot from cold. For if it did there would be something that accepted the contraries themselves, and there would be some one entity that became fire and water, which Empedocles denies.' (Oxford translation.)

que circa mores singulos pertranseuntes.[94]
τὰ περὶ τὸ ἦθος καθ' ἕκαστον διελθόντες.

4. William of Moerbeke, *Politics* 1331ᵇ19–22:

Sed immorari nunc diligenter exquirentes et dicentes
Ἀλλὰ τὸ διατρίβειν νῦν ἀκριβολογουμένους καὶ λέγοντας

de talibus inutile est. Non enim difficile est
περὶ τῶν τοιούτων ἀργὸν ἐστίν· οὐ γὰρ χαλεπόν ἐστι

talia intelligere, sed facere magis. Dicere quidem
τὰ τοιαῦτα νοῆσαι ἀλλὰ ποιῆσαι μᾶλλον· τὸ μὲν γὰρ

enim voti opus est, evenire autem fortunae.[95]
λέγειν εὐχῆς ἔργον ἐστί, τὸ δὲ συμβῆναι τύχης.

This method of translating makes for somewhat stilted and occasionally very curious Latin, but one should not conclude that the translators were therefore crude and unsophisticated, or that their knowledge of either or both languages was inadequate. The method of translating was born out of respect for authority; as with sacred texts, so with Aristotle it was important to preserve the actual words of an authoritative work. Hence the ideal was to present to the reader Aristotle's actual words, put together in just the way Aristotle had put them together, with minimum 'interference' from the translator. In this respect the translator's aim matched the reader's expectation; for as the medieval scholars read and commented on the works they did not worry much about authenticity and the problems of expressing thoughts in different languages. They simply assumed that they were dealing with Aristotle's actual words – an assumption that was largely justified, even down to fine detail.

The literal method of translating was made possible by the basic similarity of the two languages, and it served its purpose well enough. On the whole the Latin of the translations is readily intelligible; at any rate it is no less intelligible than the original Greek, for awkward and odd passages in Latin often do no more than reflect faithfully the awkwardness and oddness of the original Greek. Much of Aristotle is difficult to read in Greek, and one should be careful not to blame the translators for difficulties they did not create.

94. 'The mean opposed to boastfulness is found in almost the same sphere; and this also is without a name. It will be no bad plan to describe these states as well; for we shall know the facts about character better if we go through them in detail ...' (Oxford translation.)

95. 'But it would be a waste of time for us to linger over details like these. The difficulty is not in imagining but in carrying them out. We may talk about them as much as we like, but the execution of them will depend on fortune.' (Oxford translation.)

In practice there are various reasons why the ideal of perfect literalness was never fully achieved. In the first place there are features of Greek grammar and idiom that cannot be translated literally into Latin. Take for example the phrase ἐν τῷ εἶναι ('in being'). The Greek uses a definite article (absent in Latin) and combines a preposition with an infinitive verb (not Latin idiom). One Latin translator might translate this boldly by '*in esse*', ignoring Latin grammar and the Greek article, while another might respect Latin grammar and express the article in a laborious circumlocution, '*in eo quod est esse*'. Secondly, some Greek words may have many Latin equivalents. Thus the Greek λόγος ('word', 'account', 'definition') may be expressed by different translators as '*ratio*', '*oratio*', '*definitio*', '*ratiocinatio*', '*sermo*', '*disputatio*', '*argumentatio*', '*verbum*', or '*proportio*'. In this case the different renderings reflect both systematic preferences by different translators and conscious variation to accommodate different meanings of the word. Thirdly, no translator is perfectly consistent with himself, and all make mistakes and have their idiosyncrasies.

Idiosyncrasies among the translations are of particular interest to scholars since they provide a means of distinguishing translators.[96] There are many small words (particles) in Greek, which can be translated by more than one Latin word. For example δέ ('but') can be rendered by '*autem*', '*vero*' or '*sed*'; γάρ ('for') by '*nam*', '*namque*', or '*enim*'; οὕτως ('thus') by '*sic*', '*itaque*', or '*ita*'. If one analyses the manner in which all these particles are translated, distinct patterns emerge, and it becomes plain that each translator adheres to his own preferred renderings of the particles. Each combination of preferred renderings is an unconscious signature by the author. Thus the translations now assigned to James of Venice were identified by a distinctive set of particle translations (including a strong preference for '*autem*', '*enim*' and '*sic*') which were found in those translations and no others.

Some similar clear-cut differences among the translations emerge also in choice of general vocabulary, in ways of handling grammatical and idiomatic differences between the two languages, and in some general features. Boethius, for example, exercised some ingenuity in devising Latin versions of arguments based on ambiguities or plays on words in Greek; James of Venice had a habit of leaving some untranslated words in Greek letters in his translations, to the great confusion of subsequent scribes who tried to copy them; Grosseteste was extremely literal, and helped the reader by adding explanatory notes, particularly where the Latin might be

96. See esp. Minio-Paluello 1952.

ambiguous; William of Moerbeke was also very literal, sometimes to the point of simply transcribing Greek words in Roman letters.

Translators from the Arabic adopted the same literal method as their Graeco-Latin counterparts, but the result was very different. The Arabic translations themselves were made not directly from the Greek but through intermediate Syriac versions, and so the translators into Latin were working at two removes from the original through the distorting medium of Semitic languages that did not lend themselves readily to literal translation either out of Greek or into Latin. The result is that the Arabic–Latin translations of Aristotle are much more difficult to read and understand than the Greek–Latin ones, a fact which explains why the latter were preferred when they were available.

Medieval manuscripts were of course transcribed by hand, a process that introduces a complicating factor into any assessment of the language of the translations. All the texts, and particularly the most popular ones, were subject to unintended variation at the hands of scribes, who could and did make numerous mistakes as they copied them. Errors accumulated as new copies were made, and most surviving manuscripts of Aristotle are very faulty – words and whole sentences are sometimes omitted, transposed, or garbled, similar-sounding words are interchanged, conjectures and 'improvements' are deliberately introduced, glosses are accidentally incorporated into the text, and many absurd and seemingly random errors are made simply through carelessness. Although numerous, most such mistakes are minor ones which would not have seriously impeded the reader; indeed it is surprising how often the general sense of a passage will remain clear in spite of serious errors in the text. Nevertheless, one should always bear in mind that the texts used by medieval readers were very variable, and that textual error can sometimes be a source of real misunderstanding.

For the historian of philosophy the chief interest of the language of the translations lies in its contribution to the philosophical vocabulary of medieval and later times. Aristotle became 'the Philosopher' and the study of philosophy became practically synonymous with the study of Aristotle, and in this way the Latin philosophical and technical terms chosen by the translators entered into a living philosophical tradition and became part of the language of philosophical discussion. Detailed analysis of the vocabulary of the translations is now being made possible as the full indexes of the *Aristoteles Latinus* volumes are published.

The reception of the translations[97]

The evidence on which our knowledge of the reception of Aristotle's works is based is of several kinds. First, there are the manuscripts themselves; second, there are the glosses in the manuscripts, which are direct evidence of their being read and studied; third, there are university documents, at first banning Aristotle's works but later prescribing them; fourth, there are hundreds of surviving commentaries, *quaestiones*, and other aids to study such as compendia and collections of extracts;[98] fifth, there are the numerous references to Aristotle by medieval authors.

Using all this evidence – manuscripts, university decrees, commentaries, quotations – we can sketch an outline of Aristotle's reception by the Latin West which will complement the history of the translations already given. What emerges very clearly from the evidence is the slowness of the assimilation, even of those works, such as the logic, which never came under doctrinal suspicion. Up to about the middle of the thirteenth century the surviving material with which to document Aristotle's progress is somewhat meagre; after that point it becomes a flood.

For the twelfth century,[99] evidence of interest in and study of the '*logica vetus*' and the *Sophistici elenchi*[100] is relatively abundant. The *Prior Analytics*,[101] *Posterior Analytics*,[102] and *Topics*,[103] on the other hand, appear to have been known to a few scholars, but not to have been widely studied; no commentaries on these works have survived from the twelfth century, and references to them by authors of the period are few. In particular the *Posterior Analytics* was regarded as difficult – the comment by the translator Ioannes quoted above is paralleled by John of Salisbury, who complained that the work has 'as many stumbling-blocks as it has chapters' and reported that people were inclined to blame the translator for this.[104] As for the rest of the works of Aristotle (i.e., the non-logical works, known as the 'new Aristotle'), a few twelfth-century manuscripts (some with glosses) and a handful of references are our only surviving witness to their

---

97. For general accounts see Grabmann 1939, 1950; De Wulf 1934–6; Van Steenberghen 1966; Callus 1943 (for Oxford); and many detailed studies in Grabmann 1926–56.
98. For compendia etc. see Grabmann 1939, pp. 54–104.
99. See especially Grabmann 1950.
100. De Rijk 1962–7, I; Ebbesen 1972, 1973b, 1976b.
101. AL 1962, III, pp. 429–42.
102. Dod 1970, pp. 59–80.
103. Grabmann 1938b; Green-Pedersen 1977a, pp. 41–2.
104. John of Salisbury 1929, p. 171.

study.[105] Minio-Paluello has persuasively argued that northern France, and in particular the abbey of Mont-Saint-Michel, was an important centre for the dissemination of the new Aristotle in the third quarter of the twelfth century.[106]

The oldest surviving commentaries on the new Aristotle are those by Alfred of Sareshel on the *Meteorologica* and *De plantis*, dating from around the turn of the thirteenth century, and probably written at Oxford. Alfred also wrote a commentary on the *De generatione et corruptione*, and an old catalogue of Beauvais Cathedral Library listed commentaries by him on the *De caelo*, *De anima*, *De somno* and *De morte* as well. This collection long antedates any other known commentaries on the new Aristotle.[107] Considerable knowledge of the new Aristotle is shown in the *Tractatus de anima* by John Blund, probably dating also from the turn of the century, and probably also from Oxford.[108]

Aristotle in Paris and Oxford before 1210

It seems likely that the '*logica nova*' and the new Aristotle were being lectured on in Oxford and Paris in the first decade of the thirteenth century.[109] Roger Bacon says that Saint Edmund of Canterbury was the first to lecture on the *Sophistici elenchi* at Oxford, and that a 'magister Hugo' (otherwise unknown) was the first to lecture there on the *Posterior Analytics*; both these courses probably took place *ca.* 1200–10.[110] A list of textbooks compiled by Alexander Neckham probably *ca.* 1200–10 includes all the '*logica nova*' among the books on which the student should attend lectures, and goes on to recommend that he look at (*inspiciat*) the *Metaphysics*, *De generatione et corruptione*, and *De anima*.[111] Alexander was familiar with Paris and Oxford, and one can plausibly suggest that the three last-mentioned works as well as the '*logica nova*' had some place in the curriculum at either or both universities. At any rate, we can be sure that some at least of the works on natural philosophy were being lectured on in Paris by 1210, for otherwise a ban on them would have had no point.

---

105. Grabmann 1950, pp. 159–62.
106. Minio-Paluello 1952, pp. 291–5.
107. See Otte 1972, 1976.
108. Callus 1943, pp. 241–51; Callus and Hunt 1970, p. xi.
109. See Callus 1943; Grabmann 1950, p. 162.
110. Callus 1943, pp. 238–41; Ebbesen 1977b, pp. 4–9; Lawrence 1960, pp. 112ff. It can be argued that the dates should be as late as *ca.* 1230 – an extreme example of the general uncertainty over the correct dating of many works of this period.
111. Haskins 1927, pp. 356–76.

The proscription of 1210

The proscription of Aristotle's works in Paris in 1210 is probably the most famous event in the history of Aristotle's reception by the West.[112] In that year a council of the ecclesiastical province of Sens, presided over by the archbishop, issued an edict condemning (among others) the heretics Amaury of Bène and David of Dinant and forbidding any lectures (public or private) in Paris on Aristotle's works of natural philosophy.[113] The ban appears to have been in part a move by conservative theologians against the turbulent spirits of the Arts Faculty, where Aristotle was lectured upon, and behind it was the fear that Aristotle's natural philosophy was a threat to the Christian faith. Of the two men condemned, David of Dinant is known to have been an Aristotelian, and Albert the Great attacks his materialistic and pantheistic philosophy.[114] The ban was renewed in 1215 by Robert of Courçon, the papal legate charged with reorganising studies in Paris. Of Aristotle's works Robert permitted all the logic and the *Ethics* to be lectured on, but 'the books of Aristotle on metaphysics and natural philosophy may not be lectured on, nor may any commentaries or summaries of them'.[115] (The 'commentaries and summaries', mentioned here may be the works of Avicenna and Alfarabi translated from the Arabic.)[116]

The ban remained in force for over 20 years, and seems to have been effective, for in 1229 the newly founded University of Toulouse, boasting about 'academic freedom' (*libertas scholastica*), issued a prospectus advertising lectures on 'all the books of natural philosophy proscribed in Paris'.[117] In 1231 the pope reaffirmed the ban 'until such time as the books shall be examined and purged of all errors', for which purpose he set up a three-man commission.[118] What happened to the commission is not known, and eventually the ban was forgotten.[119]

From 1210 to 1250

From around 1210 to the middle of the century the evidence regarding the study of Aristotle continues to be very thin. In Paris, for example, nothing is known about any lectures before about 1230, not even in logic, a subject

112. See Grabmann 1941; Van Steenberghen 1966, pp. 88–110.
113. Denifle and Chatelain 1889–97 (CUP), I, p. 70.
114. Van Steenberghen 1966, p. 91.
115. CUP, I, pp. 78–9.
116. The reference cannot be to Averroes, whose works did not come into circulation before the 1230s. See De Vaux 1933. See also Hunt 1977, pp. 195, 199.
117. CUP, I, p. 131.
118. CUP, I, pp. 138, 143–4.
119. For the documents apparently imposing the ban at Toulouse in 1245 and renewing it in Paris as late as 1263 (CUP, I, pp. 185, 427) see Van Steenberghen 1966, pp. 109, 146–8.

that was not banned.[120] An interesting document, probably dating from
the 1230s, throws some light on the teaching in the Arts Faculty in this
period.[121] It is a 'crib' of *quaestiones* that examination candidates would be
likely to encounter in disputations, and it gives overwhelming preponderance to logic (60 columns of the manuscript) and grammar (23 columns).
The *Ethics*[122] is definitely on the curriculum, with five columns devoted to
it, but the *Metaphysics* and natural philosophy are summarily treated in one
and a half columns. It is thus clear that the promulgations of 1215 still held
in the 1230s. However, the new Aristotle was certainly being read, for it is
quoted in works by masters in the Theological Faculty: William of
Auxerre in his *Summa aurea* (*ca.* 1215–20) quotes the *Ethics*, *De anima*, and
Physics; Philip the Chancellor in his *Summa de bono* (*ca.* 1230–6) quotes these
works and the *De animalibus*, *Metaphysics*, *De caelo*, and *De generatione et
corruptione*; William of Auvergne (writing *ca.* 1231–6) and Roland of
Cremona (*ca.* 1229–32) embrace a similar range of quotation.[123]

In Oxford (presumably) Robert Grosseteste wrote the earliest surviving
medieval Latin commentary on the *Posterior Analytics*, a work of great
intelligence and maturity; guesses about its date range from before 1209 to
the late 1220s.[124] Grosseteste also wrote glosses on the *Sophistici elenchi* and
notes on and summaries of the *Physics* and the *Ethics*,[125] the last of these
presumably dating from the time he was translating the *Ethics* (probably
1247–8). The date of the work on the *Physics* and *Elenchi* is not known, but
one may reasonably assume that, like the commentary on the *Posterior
Analytics*, it reflects his teaching career at Oxford (i.e., before 1235). One
may equally assume that Grosseteste lectured on Aristotle, although there is
no evidence to prove it. In fact, as at Paris, there is very little evidence
surviving at all about the study of Aristotle at Oxford before the mid-
thirteenth century,[126] and the same is true of other centres of learning. One
should remember that the total number of people in the whole of Europe
who had an active interest in the new Aristotle was extremely small – a
handful of masters and students in a few places.

120. Grabmann 1950, pp. 143–7. For the more general history of logic in the twelfth and thirteenth
      centuries see Grabmann 1937, 1938a; for masters in the Arts Faculty see De Wulf 1936, pp. 85–6;
      Van Steenberghen 1966, pp. 132–51.
121. Grabmann 1934a; De Wulf 1936, pp. 83–5; Van Steenberghen 1966, pp. 118–32.
122. See also Grabmann 1940b.
123. Callus 1943, p. 231; for masters in the Theological Faculty see De Wulf 1936, pp. 70–83; Van
      Steenberghen 1966, pp. 151–70.
124. See Rossi 1975.
125. Thomson 1940, pp. 81–2 (the authority of other works listed by Thomson is less assured);
      Dales 1963.
126. For a review of the known personalities see Callus 1943; Van Steenberghen 1966, pp. 171–6.

The mid-thirteenth-century flowering of the study of Aristotle

It may be partly chance that has preserved so little evidence for the study of Aristotle in the first half of the thirteenth century. There can be no doubt, however, of the burgeoning of studies around the middle of the century. This is shown by the greatly increased number of surviving manuscripts, by a plethora of commentaries, and by the statutes of the University of Paris. To take the last first: in 1252 the statutes of 'the English Nation' prescribe only the *De anima* in addition to the logic.[127] Three years later the statutes of the Arts Faculty (the oldest to survive) prescribe practically the whole corpus (and several spurious works): *Ethics, Physics, Metaphysics, De animalibus, De caelo, Meteorologica* (Books I and IV), *De anima, De generatione et corruptione, De causis, De sensu, De somno, De plantis, De memoria, De differentia, De morte*, and of course the logic.[128] Thus by 1255 Aristotle was firmly established at Paris, as he was indeed at Oxford, where documentation about commentaries and lectures becomes abundant as early as the 1240s.[129]

The importance of the glosses

It is of course no coincidence that manuscripts containing the '*corpus vetustius*' began to be written in large numbers around this time; they were written to meet a demand. Many of these manuscripts (and of course others written both earlier and later) are heavily glossed, and thus provide a rich store of material about the study of Aristotle which has so far been little explored by scholars. Often manuscripts were prepared with wide margins ruled specially for writing glosses, and glosses were copied from one manuscript to another as an aid to study, with increasing elaboration as successive masters and students transcribed sets of glosses and then added their own notes, which would then themselves be incorporated in the next round. In this way some sets of glosses eventually became so elaborate that they amounted to full-scale commentaries.

Glosses are interesting for several reasons. The very simple sets of glosses, mostly giving elementary explanations of individual words and phrases, represent the first halting attempts at interpretations by readers new to difficult texts, and enable us to see the beginnings of the assimilation of Aristotle. In the increasing elaboration of the glosses one can trace the growing self-confidence and sophistication of subsequent generations of

127. CUP, I, p. 228.
128. CUP, I, p. 278.
129. Callus 1943, pp. 255ff.; De Wulf 1936, pp. 87ff.; Van Steenberghen 1966, pp. 176–81.

readers. Many of the glosses are probably the work of humble masters and scholars and reflect the level of understanding reached by ordinary students. Many probably also represent the contents of lecture courses. The technique of the lecturer was to read the text out and expound it word for word as he went along, and one can well imagine many sets of glosses originating in lecturers' or students' notes.[130]

Glosses reflect the humble side of Aristotelian study, which has its interest and importance; of far greater importance, however, is the less humble side, represented by those teachers who felt that their contribution to the elucidation of Aristotle was sufficiently valuable to deserve publication, and whose names and works now begin to survive in large numbers. Aristotle has become established at the centre of the philosophical curriculum, and from the mid-thirteenth century onwards the roll-call of important Aristotelian commentators is identical with that of the important philosophers – to teach philosophy was to teach Aristotle. Albert the Great, Thomas Aquinas, Giles of Rome, Walter Burley, William Ockham and the other major figures all wrote commentaries or *quaestiones* on Aristotle, and for every major figure there are dozens of minor ones. Hundreds of commentators and surviving commentaries are known, providing a massive body of evidence with which to document Aristotle's domination of later medieval philosophy.[131]

A Table of Medieval Latin Translations of Aristotle's Works and of Greek and Arabic Commentaries

Work	Translator	Date	No. of surviving MSS.[132]
Categories	Boethius	*ca.* 510–22	306
	William of Moerbeke	1266	10
Simplicius	William of Moerbeke	1266	10
Averroes (middle commentary)	William of Luna	13th century	4*
De interpretatione	Boethius	*ca.* 510–22	297
	William of Moerbeke	1268	4

130. See Grabmann 1939, pp. 12–13; Callus 1943, pp. 265ff.; Dod 1970, pp. 81–97.
131. C. H. Lohr's catalogue (1967–74), with its bibliographical summaries and lists of manuscripts, provides an invaluable starting-point for the analysis of this material.
132. These statistics are taken from the AL catalogue, and are valuable as an approximate guide to the relative popularity of the translations. For pseudo-Aristotelian and spurious works the catalogue is not comprehensive and the statistics in the second section of the table are likely to be underestimates; those for the *Secretum secretorum* and the *De regimine sanitatis* are from Manzalaoni 1977. An asterisk indicates a translation from the Arabic; all the rest are from the Greek.

Table (cont.)

Work	Translator	Date	No. of surviving MSS.
Ammonius	William of Moerbeke	1268	4
Averroes (middle commentary)	William of Luna	13th century	3★
Prior Analytics	Boethius	*ca.* 510–22	275
	Anonymous	12th century	2
Averroes (middle commentary)	William of Luna	13th century	1★
Posterior Analytics	James of Venice	? 1125–50	275
	Ioannes	before 1159	1
	Gerard of Cremona	before 1187	3★
	William of Moerbeke	*ca.* 1269 or earlier	4
'Alexander'	James of Venice	? 1125–50	Fragments
Themistius	Gerard of Cremona	before 1187	3★
Averroes (middle commentary)	William of Luna	13th century	1★
Topics	Boethius	*ca.* 510–22	268
	Anonymous	12th century	1
Sophistici elenchi	Boethius	*ca.* 510–22	271
	James of Venice	*ca.* 1125–50	Fragments
	William of Moerbeke	*ca.* 1269 or earlier	1
'Alexander'	James of Venice	? 1125–50	Fragments
Physics	James of Venice	? 1125–50	139
	Anonymous ('Physica vaticana')	? mid-12th century	1 (fragment)
	Gerard of Cremona	before 1187	7★
	Michael Scot	*ca.* 1220–35	65★
	William of Moerbeke	? *ca.* 1260–70	230
Simplicius	? Robert Grosseteste	? after 1235	1 (fragment)
Averroes (great commentary)	Michael Scot	? *ca.* 1220–35	62★
De caelo	Gerard of Cremona	before 1187	101★
	Michael Scot	*ca.* 1220–35	36★
	Robert Grosseteste	? after 1247	1 (fragment)
	William of Moerbeke	? 1260–70	185
Simplicius	Robert Grosseteste	? after 1247	1 (fragment)
	William of Moerbeke	1271 (Viterbo)	4
Averroes (great commentary)	Michael Scot	*ca.* 1220–35	36★

Table (cont.)

Work	Translator	Date	No. of surviving MSS.
De generatione et corruptione	Anonymous (vetus)	12th century	118
	Gerard of Cremona	before 1187	8★
	? William of Moerbeke	before 1274	190
Averroes (middle commentary)	Michael Scot	*ca.* 1220–35	40★
Meteorologica	Henricus Aristippus (Book IV)	before 1162 ⎱	
	Gerard of Cremona (Books I–III)	before 1187 ⎰	113(★)
	William of Moerbeke	? *ca.* 1260	175
Alexander	William of Moerbeke	1260 (Nicea)	9
Averroes (middle commentary)	Michael Scot (Book IV)	*ca.* 1220–35	18★
De anima	James of Venice	? 1125–50	144
	Michael Scot	*ca.* 1220–35	62★
	William of Moerbeke	? before 1268	268
Philoponus (Book III)	William of Moerbeke	1268 (Viterbo)	3
Themistius	William of Moerbeke	1267 (Viterbo)	8
Averroes (great commentary)	Michael Scot	*ca.* 1220–35	56★
De sensu	Anonymous	12th century	94
	William of Moerbeke	? 1260–70	161
Alexander	William of Moerbeke	? 1260–70	4
Averroes (epitome)	? Michael Scot	*ca.* 1220–35	48★
De memoria	James of Venice	? 1125–50	115
	William of Moerbeke	? 1260–70	160
Averroes (epitome)	? Michael Scot	*ca.* 1220–35	46★
De somno	Anonymous	12th century	102
	William of Moerbeke	? 1260–70	162
Averroes (epitome)	? Michael Scot	*ca.* 1220–35	49★
De longitudine	James of Venice	? 1125–50	101
	William of Moerbeke	? 1260–70	158
Averroes (epitome)	? Michael Scot	*ca.* 1220–35	58★
De iuventute	James of Venice	? 1125–50	4
	William of Moerbeke	*ca.* 1260–70	157
De respiratione	James of Venice	? 1125–50	4
	William of Moerbeke	? 1260–70	149

Table (cont.)

Work	Translator	Date	No. of surviving MSS.
De morte	James of Venice	? 1125–50	5
	William of Moerbeke	? 1260–70	151
De animalibus (comprising *Historia*, *De progressu*, *De motu*, *De partibus*, *De generatione*)	Michael Scot (*Hist.*, *part.*, *gener.* only)	before 1220	69★
	William of Moerbeke	1260 (Thebes)	237[133]
	Anonymous (*part.* only)	? 13th century	1
Avicenna	Michael Scot	*ca.* 1220–35	29★
Averroes (epitome)	Petrus Gallegus	? 1250–67	1★
	? Michael Scot	*ca.* 1220–35	8★
Metaphysics	James of Venice ('vetustissima')[134]	? 1125–50	5
	Anonymous ('media')[135]	12th century	24
	Michael Scot ('nova')[136]	*ca.* 1220–35	126★
	Anonymous (revision of James; 'vetus')	*ca.* 1220–30	41
	William of Moerbeke ('novae translationis')	before 1272	217
Averroes (great commentary)	Michael Scot	*ca.* 1220–35	59★
Nicomachean Ethics	Anonymous (Books II–III; 'vetus')	12th century	48
	Anonymous (Book I and fragments of II–X; 'nova')	early 13th century	40
	Robert Grosseteste	? 1246–47	33
	Anonymous (? William of Moerbeke) revision of Grosseteste	1250–60	246
Eustratius and others	Robert Grosseteste	? 1246–47	22
Averroes (middle commentary)	Hermannus Alemannus	? 1240	9★
Eudemian Ethics (*De bona fortuna*)[137]	Anonymous	? 13th century	139
(Fragments)	Anonymous	? 13th century	3

133. Of which only 40 contain all five treatises.
134. Comprising Books I–IV.4 (1007^{a}31).
135. Lacks Book XI.
136. Comprising Books II (= α), I.5–10 (from 987^{a}9), III–X, XII.1–10 (up to 1075^{b}11).
137. The work circulating under this title consists of a single chapter of the *Eudemian Ethics* (VII.14) combined with a chapter from the *Magna moralia* (II.8).

Table (cont.)

Work	Translator	Date	No. of surviving MSS.
Politics	William of Moerbeke (Books I–II; ? early draft)	1260–4	3
	William of Moerbeke (complete)	? 1260	107
Oeconomica	Anonymous	? late 13th century	15
	Durandus de Alvernia	1295	79
Rhetoric	Anonymous	? mid 13th century	5
	Hermannus Alemannus	*ca.* 1256	3★
	William of Moerbeke	before 1270	100
Rhetorica ad Alexandrum	Anonymous	? 14th century	1
	Anonymous	? 14th century	1
Poetics	William of Moerbeke	1278	2
Averroes (middle commentary)	Hermannus Alemannus	1256	24★

Translations of Pseudo-Aristotelian and Related Works

Work	Translator	Date	No. of surviving MSS.
Problemata	Bartholomew of Messina	1258–66	55
Physionomia	Bartholomew of Messina	1258–66	119
De mirabilibus auscultationibus	Bartholomew of Messina	1258–66	1
De principiis (Theophrastus, Metaphysics)	Bartholomew of Messina	1258–66	1
De signis aquarum	Bartholomew of Messina	1258–66	10
	Anonymous	? 13th or 14th century	1
De lineis indivisibilibus	Robert Grosseteste	? *ca.* 1240–50	68
De mundo	Bartholomew of Messina	1258–66	6
	Nicholas of Sicily	? before 1240	50
Magna moralia (De bona fortuna)[137]	Bartholomew of Messina	1258–66	56

Translations of Pseudo-Aristotelian and Related Works (cont.)

Work	Translator	Date	No. of surviving MSS.
	Anonymous	? 13th century	139
De coloribus	Bartholomew of Messina	1258–66	78
	William of Moerbeke	? 1260–70	1
De inundatione Nili	Anonymous	? 13th century	82
De plantis (by Nicholaus Damascenus)	Alfred of Sareshel	before 1200	159★
De proprietatibus (or De causis proprietatum elementorum)	Gerard of Cremona	before 1187	119★
De mineralibus (Avicenna)	Alfred of Sareshel	? before 1200	32★ (+113★)
De intelligentia (anonymous introduction to the Physics)	James of Venice	? 1125–50	45
Secretum secretorum	Philip of Tripoli	? ca. 1243	350★
De regimine sanitatis (a fragment of the Secretum secretorum)	John of Seville (?)	mid-12th century	150★
De causis (Proclus)	Gerard of Cremona	before 1187	202★
De differentia spiritus et animae	John of Seville	mid-12th century	82★
	Anonymous	12th century	71★
Enigmata Aristotelis	Anonymous	12th century	2
Liber sex principiorum		12th century	231
De pomo (De morte Aristotelis)	? Manfred, King of Sicily	ca. 1258–66	70★
Vita Aristotelis	Anonymous	12th–13th century	65
Porphyry's Isagoge	Boethius	ca. 510–22	295
De laudabilibus bonis	Robert Grosseteste	? 1240–53	14
Epistola ad Alexandrum (an anonymous introduction to the Rhetorica ad Alexandrum)	Anonymous	13th century	52
Summa Alexandrinorum (an Arabic epitome of the Ethics)	Hermannus Alemannus	1243–4	14★

3

THE MEDIEVAL INTERPRETATION OF ARISTOTLE

Clerical and Aristotelian science

The question of the interpretation of Aristotle in the Middle Ages must be dealt with within the context of the medieval conception of science. Medieval learning was characterised by an attitude which was dominant – though in varying degrees and varying circumstances – from the time of Alcuin to that of Bellarmine. For the Middle Ages it was not the individual who taught, but the Church, through the clergy. Clerical science was accordingly the corporate transmission of traditional wisdom. The cleric was a 'master' chosen by God to teach his people the way of salvation, as Rhabanus Maurus put it at the beginning of his *De institutione clericorum*.[1] His authority as a teacher was guaranteed by a divine call within the ecclesiastical hierarchy; the authority of his teaching was guaranteed by Scripture and the Church Fathers. But his authority extended even beyond the sacred sciences, in a way which reveals the relationships between this clerical attitude towards knowledge and the structure of medieval society. The relationship between the clergy and the laity is clearly symbolised in Alcuin's *Dialectica*, a dialogue in which Alcuin as *magister* instructs Charlemagne himself as *discipulus*, in one of the profane sciences of the *trivium* and *quadrivium*.[2]

Within this conception of the scientific enterprise a standard method of interpretation was developed based on the presumed concordance of the fundamental authorities, and schools evolved whose function was the training of masters who should transmit traditional learning to God's people. In the thirteenth century Thomas Aquinas in his inaugural lecture as master of theology in Paris could still cite the Psalmist, 'From thy lofty abode thou waterest the mountains, and the earth is satisfied', and interpret the lofty abode as the divine wisdom which waters the minds of the masters

---

1. Rhabanus Maurus, *De institutione clericorum* I, 2: 'doceantque populum Dei omnia legitima eius et praecepta quae mandaverat ad eos' (*PL* 107, 297f.).
2. Alcuin, *Dialectica* (*PL* 101, 949–76).

(signified by the mountains), so that by their ministry that wisdom might be channelled to the laity (signified by the earth). Mixing his metaphors, Thomas tells us that the masters are, like the mountains, elevated above the earth and thus first illumined by the rays of the sun.[3]

With the introduction of the Aristotelian encyclopaedia this clerical conception encountered a radically different notion of science, a notion which would require a new method of interpretation, a new form of school, and a new type of teacher. It is clear that the gradual replacement of the clerical attitude to learning by this new conception is also related to the slow emergence of new social structures in the early modern period. But not much attention has been paid to the fact that the *way* in which the change took place was decisively conditioned by the various stages in the reception of Aristotelian science.

The reception of Aristotelian science

The works of Aristotle were made available in the Latin West in three clearly distinguishable stages. The first began in the sixth century with Boethius' translations of Aristotle's treatises on logic and his adaptations of various other works on logic and rhetoric. The second stage began in the twelfth century with the gradual translation of the entire corpus of Aristotle's works. At this stage the reception of Aristotle was part of a vast effort to absorb the philosophical, medical, astrological, and natural science not only of ancient Greece, but also of past and contemporary Judaism and Islam. The Aristotelian encyclopaedia provided the framework for all this new material. The third stage in the pre-modern study of Aristotle began in the late fifteenth century and concentrated rather on the text of Aristotle's works than on the co-ordination of the sciences. This stage produced above all new editions of the Greek text, new Latin and vernacular translations and commentaries, Greek editions and Latin translations of practically the whole corpus of the ancient Greek commentaries, and Latin versions of hitherto untranslated commentaries of Averroes.

Boethius' translations

The first wave of translations broke on the late Roman world. This world knew little of Greek philosophy and science, and, apart from some rhetorical notions transmitted by Cicero, very little of Aristotle. Boethius' translations were, so to speak, an historical accident and could have but

3. Thomas Aquinas 1954a, *Breve principium de commendatione sacrae scripturae*, I, 441–3.

little influence, not only in the final phase of classical civilisation, but also in the monastic schools of the early Middle Ages. Although the Aristotelian logic fitted neatly into the scheme of the liberal arts and although its introduction into the *trivium* would later have a profound effect on the Augustinian vision of arts and theology united in one comprehensive system of knowledge, the monastic teacher, for whom the role of *magister* was only a part-time, fugitive aspect of his existence, could find little he could use in the predicables and predicaments of the *ars vetus*. The rudimentary treatment of these subjects in the various works *De institutione clericorum* and the very fact that half the translations of Aristotle's treatises which Boethius had made were lost in this period shows that intellectual work was only one small part of the monk's concern. The monastic vocation did not regard study as an end in itself. The task of the monastic teacher was rather ordered to the service of God and centred on the understanding of God's word as recorded in the sacred writings and interpreted by the Fathers.

The twelfth-century translations and the quest of the new masters

The interest in Aristotle which appeared with a second wave of translations in the twelfth century presupposed another type of teacher, and the birthplace of this type of teacher was the medieval town. From the eleventh century knowledge was no longer confined to remote monasteries. With the rise of the towns new interests appeared and the specialisation of labour led some to concentrate on the production of goods, others on their transport, still others on financing their purchase. Within this matrix arose a new type of teacher, a new type of *magister*. Although in accordance with the traditional division of society he still belonged to the clerical class, he was no longer a teacher like Alcuin or even like Notker Labeo or Scotus Eriugena. Like the men of trade who established themselves in the towns, like the carpenters and masons who organised themselves in guilds, this new master had the consciousness of belonging to a profession. His trade was learning and teaching, personal reflection and its diffusion in the classroom. The liberal arts were his speciality.[4]

It was this type of master who turned avidly to Aristotle. From about the beginning of the eleventh century the masters of arts slowly pieced together the original fabric of the Aristotelian logic with the exception of the theory of demonstration as it is found in the *Posterior Analytics*. The vague

4. Le Goff 1957.

references to the various Aristotelian treatises on proof which we find in Alcuin's *Dialectica* were gradually replaced by a treatment of categorical and hypothetical propositions and syllogisms drawn from the works of Boethius. The Aristotelian method of the topics and the treatment of the fallacies were reconstructed from hints in the available works of Aristotle and Cicero and from the treatises surrounding them. Abelard's *Dialectica* is worlds away from Alcuin's, and it shows that the full range of the Aristotelian logic which became known in the latter half of the twelfth century was not used because the treatises were translated, but the treatises were translated because this new generation wanted to use them.[5] By the middle of the twelfth century these younger masters had come to realise that there were whole areas of knowledge of which they knew only the names. It was only natural that they should try to learn more of their subject matter.

Their seeking was already a kind of interpretation of the texts. In looking for the lost books of the Aristotelian logic they already knew what they were expecting to find. And what they were expecting to find matched their own understanding of their role in society. This is why the masters' study of the Aristotelian logic did not proceed without opposition from the representatives of the traditional conception of the cleric's task. The polemics of Peter Damian against the dialecticians, of Lanfranc against Berengarius, of Bernard of Clairvaux against Abelard represent the reaction of the older, monastic idea to the new, urban conception of the teacher's role. The new generation's search for hitherto unknown Aristotelian works is the expression of its own new self-image.

Parallel to this effort to forge a new tool for the sciences, a *novum organum*, ran an awakening interest in the subjects of the old *quadrivium*. The new interest in the study of nature which is such a prominent feature of twelfth-century thought entailed another conflict with the traditional understanding of the clerical vocation. Although in accordance with the structure of society the masters whose trade it was to teach were fitted into the clerical class, their function was no longer simply that of transmitting traditional wisdom. They could no longer simply proclaim the word of God. They themselves had to learn; they had to master the knowledge of the ancients, they had to go to school as the *discipuli* of Greeks, Arabs, and Jews, they had to confront the sayings of the Scriptures and the Fathers with the sciences of the ancient pagans and the religious teachings of infidel

5. De Rijk in Peter Abelard 1956, pp. xvi–xix.

nations, they had to concern themselves not only with the relationship between God and his people, but also with man's relationship to the world in which he finds himself. They learned the names of many new and strange sciences from the merchants who brought reports from Spain and the Orient, from the Jews whose knowledge of Hebrew and Arabic and whose international contacts had given them access to the ancient sciences of the Greeks, from scholars like the Englishmen Adelard of Bath and Daniel of Morlay whose travels in Sicily and to Toledo had brought them into direct contact with the philosophy and science which Roman civilisation had failed to hand down.

As the masters learned the names of these new sciences, they were like a modern librarian who finds a lacuna of several volumes in one of his library's periodicals; they could not rest until they had found the means to fill the gap. Thus they turned to the translators. The additions which *these* interpreters of the classical tradition made to medieval knowledge was immense: in geometry Euclid, in astronomy Ptolemy, in medicine Hippocrates and Galen, and above all – for method, for system, for wholly new and undreamt-of sciences – the works of Aristotle, the Philosopher par excellence, together with his Arabic commentators.

This quest of the twelfth-century masters of arts to regain the ancient sciences was the first step in the interpretation of the works they recovered. The works of Aristotle which were thus made available by about the year 1200 did not gain the influence they had because they were fortuitously translated, but they were translated because the masters wanted no longer simply to transmit, because they wanted to learn themselves. The spirit of reason, of curiosity, of criticism which they found in Aristotle matched their own spirit and helped to crystallise their self-image. The system, the encyclopaedia of the sciences they found gave them a sense of autonomy and freedom with respect to the traditional understanding of the clerical function. In fact, though the working out of the implications of this second wave in the reception of Aristotle would take three hundred years, the fate of the clerical conception of knowledge was already sealed with the openness of the twelfth-century *physici* to the sciences of ancient Greece.

A thirteenth-century student's guide

In Barcelona, in the Archives of the Crown of Aragon, there is a thirteenth-century manuscript which contains a manual or guidebook for students in the arts faculty in Paris.[6] This text, which was apparently based on early thirteenth-century practice, was composed about 1230–40 by an unknown master of the faculty for the benefit of students who had to prepare for examinations. This students' guide is important not only because the standard texts prescribed for each branch of the programme correspond exactly to the newly translated works in logic, mathematics, and the natural sciences, but also because it reveals the direction which the development of the arts faculty would have to take. For the author of the guide-book the arts are no longer simply the seven liberal arts of the *trivium* and *quadrivium*; they comprise rather all the philosophical and scientific disciplines newly recovered at his time. And because the author attempts to situate the plan of studies in the arts faculty within the context of a complete classification of the sciences, these arts include some disciplines as yet unknown to him.

After some reflections on the nature of philosophy, the author divides his subject into three branches: rational, natural, and practical or moral philosophy. Under rational philosophy he takes up the subjects of the *trivium*, assigning to grammar the works of Priscian and Donatus, to rhetoric Cicero's *De inventione*, and to dialectic Aristotle's Organon together with the *Isagoge* of Porphyry and the logical treatises of Boethius.

Natural philosophy he divides into metaphysics, mathematics, and physics. For metaphysics the standard texts are Aristotle's *Metaphysics* and the pseudo-Aristotelian *Liber de causis*. Under mathematics he takes up the subjects of the *quadrivium*, but assigns to some of its branches works which were unknown in the earlier Middle Ages. To astronomy he assigns Ptolemy's *Almagest*, to geometry Euclid's *Elements*, to arithmetic Boethius' *Institutio arithmetica*, and to music Boethius' *Institutio musica*. Physics, being at a lower degree of abstraction than metaphysics and mathematics, is described as *scientia naturalis inferior*. Here are taken up all the works ascribed to Aristotle on natural philosophy: *Physics*, dealing with the general principles of change; *De caelo*, dealing with the eternal motion of the celestial bodies; *De generatione et corruptione*, dealing with the four sublunary elements which explain generation and corruption; *Meteora*, dealing with a great variety of natural phenomena; *De plantis*, *De animalibus*, *De anima*, *Parva naturalia*, and *De motu cordis*, which deal with the whole range of animate nature.

6. MS Ripoll 109 f. 134^r – 158^v. See Grabmann 1936, and Van Steenberghen 1966, pp. 119–32.

Moral philosophy the author divides into the treatment of the life of the soul, first in its relation to God, then in its relation to others, and finally in itself. Here the author's assignment of texts to the different branches lacks the clarity we have found in the other sections. The study of the life of the soul in God he identifies with theology, but he indicates no standard text. The other divisions reflect Aristotle's classification of the practical sciences into those concerning the individual, the family, and the state. But the author does not yet know the *Oeconomica* and the *Politics*, and so assigns Cicero's *De officiis* to the consideration of the life of the soul in the family, and the study of Roman and canon law to the consideration of the life of the soul in the state. He assigns Aristotle's *Ethics* only to the treatment of the life of the soul in itself. After the treatment of ethics the author adds the note that two other books are also read in the faculty of arts: Plato's *Timaeus* and Boethius' *De consolatione philosophiae*.

The influence of the Aristotelian classification of the sciences

This students' guide marks a definite stage in the evolution of the medieval arts faculty, the final stage in the formation of a new type of school, a school representing the interests of the new, urban type of master and his basically unclerical conception of the scientific enterprise. Although the author attempts to assign theology a place among the practical sciences, his concern, which certainly reflects the gradual institutionalisation of instruction in Paris, is rather with the Aristotelian system of the sciences. This system will lead the masters of arts inevitably to Aristotle's division of the practical sciences. We have observed that this section is the least clear in the author's treatment, because he does not yet know the *Oeconomica* or the *Politics*. But he does know the names of the sciences, and no doubt his colleagues were searching the libraries of Europe for copies of the works to be translated. From this point the new Latin Aristotelians went beyond their Arabic forerunners. They began to turn increasingly to the Greek tradition of Aristotle's works and came eventually to regard the Arabic contribution as alien to their own self-image as the successors of the Greeks and Romans.

The Aristotelian classification of the sciences was thus instrumental in the recovery of Aristotle's own works. It also supplied the framework for the vast amount of new scientific material, for the Greek, Arabic, and Hebrew works on mathematics, astrology, medicine, and natural science which the translators of the late twelfth and early thirteenth centuries had made available. But more than this, the Aristotelian system of the sciences was decisive for the formation of the medieval university.

The arts faculty as a philosophical faculty

On 19 March 1255 Aristotelianism was officially adopted in the University of Paris as the arts faculty proclaimed a new syllabus which imposed the study of all the known works of Aristotle.[7] On that day the arts faculty became what we might call a philosophical faculty, with a new importance in its own eyes and a tendency to develop a teaching independent of the theological faculty. Such a development was bound to arouse violent reactions and a growing rivalry between the two faculties.

The conflict had broken out even earlier and concerned at first moral philosophy, the third major division of the sciences as we have found them in the students' guide. Although the author knows only *Ethics* I–III, he knows of the existence of the remaining books and assigns to the subject an importance second only to logic, if we may judge by the length of his treatment. It was certainly from this point that the conflict took its departure. The author brings the philosophical and theological conceptions of beatitude into direct opposition with each other. The resurrection of the body is a miracle which does not answer to natural laws and therefore does not belong to the subject matter of philosophy. In answer to the question whether we are the causes of our good actions as we are the causes of our bad actions our author distinguishes between the point of view of a philosopher and that of a theologian: 'To which we reply that speaking philosophically we are the entire cause of both; speaking theologically however, we are not capable of good actions, but it is necessary that God pour grace into us.'[8]

In a few decades questions concerning the eternity of the world and the immortality of the human soul were added to the questions regarding which philosophy and theology were thus expressly opposed. But far more profound than these particular differences was the difference in attitude which our master of arts here reveals. Basically the issue concerned the definition of the role of the master of arts confronted with the still dominant conception of the clerical mission. The mendicant controversy and the history of the Franciscan order bring out one side of this issue; the

7. CUP I, pp. 277–9.
8. 'Ad quod dicimus quod loquendo philosophice sumus tota causa utriusque; loquendo tamen theologice, non sumus sufficientes ad bonum, sed oportet gratiam in nobis a Deo infundi' (f. 136ᵛ; Grabmann 1936, p. 196).

view that attendance at a university and the possession of books were contrary to the practice of poverty was the allegorical expression of the anxiety aroused by the secular sciences introduced with Aristotle.

The effect of the Averroistic controversy

What came to be known as the Averroistic controversy in the 1260s and 70s led to some of the most intransigent formulations of the masters' own understanding of their role. Again Aristotle's *Ethics* furnished the arsenal. The battle was joined over the ideal of humility and its ethical antithesis, magnanimity. The victory to be won was the theoretical grounding of the dignity, the superiority of the university status. In his *Quaestiones morales* Siger of Brabant discusses the opinion that humility is not a virtue, for it is opposed to a virtue like magnanimity which tends to great things. In his own answer he makes both virtues depend on *recta ratio* and accordingly subordinates the moral to the intellectual virtues. In the same way Boethius of Dacia in his brief tract *De summo bono sive De vita philosophi* maintains that it is in the operation of the intellectual virtues that the most perfect condition possible to man is to be found. This, he proclaims, is the status of the philosopher who dedicates his life to the pursuit of wisdom.[9]

One recognises here the road which led to certain of the propositions which were condemned in 1277. Prop. 40: That there is no more excellent way of life than the philosophical way. Prop. 144: That the highest good of which man is capable consists in the intellectual virtues. Prop. 154: That the philosophers alone are the wise men of this world.[10] Throughout all of this the catchword is '*philosophus*'. The philosopher has succeeded the cleric. Abelard had already described himself as a *philosophus*. The designation was championed also by Siger of Brabant and Boethius of Dacia. For the thirteenth century Aristotle was the *philosophus* par excellence. It was in his train that the masters of arts thought of themselves as following.

Philosophical and theological discourse

The prescription of the Aristotelian corpus as the basis of instruction in the arts faculty brought with it for the masters the obligation of interpreting the texts they had so eagerly sought after. Their commentaries on the works of the Philosopher open a new epoch in the history of medieval exegesis. The masters themselves were fully conscious of the revolution

9. Siger of Brabant 1974, *Quaestiones morales* qq. 1 and 4, pp. 98f. and 102f. Boethius of Dacia 1976.
10. CUP I, pp. 543–55.

their interpretation of the newly recovered texts involved. As early as our students' guide we find the author, in the text cited above, distinguishing between philosophical and theological discourse (*loquendo secundum philosophos*; *loquendo secundum theologos et secundum veritatem*). Siger of Brabant explains his purpose even more explicitly: 'We seek what the philosophers meant in this matter, their intention rather than the truth, because we proceed philosophically.'[11]

The tradition of biblical exegesis

Medieval exegesis had been concerned with the Bible. Its premiss was that the exegete was already in possession of a truth revealed by God himself. His task was accordingly not the discovery of new truths, but rather the unveiling of the truth concealed in the words of the sacred text. In accomplishing this task he not only turned to the councils and Church Fathers as authorities to lead him, but also felt himself, as a living link in a corporate undertaking, endowed with the same authority to teach. In the twelfth century, as discrepancies among his authorities became increasingly obtrusive, his conviction that the tradition of which he was custodian was at bottom coherent guided his efforts to penetrate more deeply into the truth of God's word as a sort of *concordia discordantium*. Even the great *Summae* of the thirteenth century which arose out of this effort are in this sense exegesis. Their point of departure was the articles of faith which God had revealed in the Bible. The purpose of the summist was to try to make the *res*, the transient things of this world, shine in the light of the *voces*, the divine words as the bearers of immutable truth. That is why Thomas could say that theologians are like the mountains, elevated above the earth and first illumined by the rays of the sun.

The new philosophical exegesis

The point of departure of the masters of arts was radically different. Siger of Brabant and his fellow masters were the first to want to interpret philosophical texts 'philosophically', that is, in a way which we might perhaps call philological, or at least in the very unclerical way of abstracting from the question of the truth of the teaching. The very fact that they identified the viewpoint of the theologians with the truth shows in a paradoxical way that for them the text they had to comment upon was not a unique

---

11. Siger of Brabant 1972a, *De anima intellectiva*, cap. 7, p. 101, 'quaerendo intentionem philosophorum in hoc, magis quam veritatem, cum philosophice procedamus'.

authority, but rather one source among many. Their task was not the unveiling of a truth already possessed but hidden; it was rather the discussion of the opinion of a most distinguished colleague. For this reason Siger gave the following rule for the interpretation of Aristotle: 'It should be noted by those who undertake to comment upon the books of the Philosopher that his opinion is not to be concealed, even though it be contrary to the truth.'[12] A further consequence of this 'philosophical procedure' was that the interpreter need make no effort at a *concordia discordantium*. In rejecting Thomas Aquinas' interpretation of Aristotle's discussion of the eternity of the world one of Siger's colleagues – possibly the very Peter of Auvergne who completed so many of Aquinas' Aristotle-commentaries – explicitly opposed the method of concord:

But as is clear, Aristotle proves that motion is eternal and this is apparent from the reasons he gives. Some, however, wanting to harmonise Aristotle's intention with the teachings of faith, say that Aristotle was not for these reasons of the opinion that the world is eternal, or that he did not hold them to be demonstrations necessarily concluding what is true, but that he only adduced these reasons hypothetically and for no other purpose. But this is manifestly false, for it would follow then that Aristotle presented the greater part of his philosophy as an hypothesis.[13]

In these two rules we can see clearly the revolution which has taken place. The theologian sought to unveil a truth concealed; the philosopher need not seek to conceal the errors in his sources. Since the work of Aristotle, the primary source for a member of the arts faculty, was for him neither a new dogma nor an infallible guide, he need make no clerical attempt at harmonising science and the Bible. The interpreter, having abandoned the notion of truth possessed for the notion of truth to be sought, could approach the text of the Philosopher in a critical, questioning

12. Siger of Brabant 1948, *Quaestiones in Metaphysicam* III, q. 15 comm., p. 140: 'Propter hoc sciendum quod sententia Philosophi ab his qui eius libros suscipiunt exponendos, non est celanda, licet sit contraria veritati. Nec debet aliquis conari per rationem inquirere quae supra rationem sunt, vel rationes in contrarium dissolvere. Sed cum philosophus quantumcumque magnus in multis possit errare, non debet aliquis negare veritatem catholicam propter aliquam rationem philosophicam, licet illam dissolvere nesciat.'

13. The Pseudo-Siger of Brabant, *Quaestiones super libros Physicorum* VIII, q. 6; in Siger of Brabant 1941, p. 199: 'Aristoteles autem, ut manifestum est, probat motum esse aeternum, et hoc apparet ex rationibus quas ponit. Quidam tamen volentes concordare intentionem Aristotelis fidei dicunt quod Aristoteles non fuit opinatus ex istis rationibus mundum esse aeternum, nec tenuit eas demonstrationes concludentes verum de necessitate sed solum adduxit istas rationes propter dubitare et non propter aliquid aliud. Istud tamen est manifeste falsum, quia sic sequeretur quod Aristoteles dubitaret in maiori parte philosophiae suae, et maxime ubi loquitur de substantiis separatis: ex aeternitate enim motus probat quod sunt substantiae separatae, sicut patet *Libro "caeli et mundi"*.'

way. He could explain Aristotle's words by reducing them to their principles, confident that even where Aristotle's conclusions might conflict with the faith, Aristotle's spirit would be an invitation to go beyond himself in a search for new truths. It is this conception of truth that makes the exegesis of the masters of arts so novel in the development of medieval thought. With the distinction between philosophical and theological discourse the 'truth' has rolled out of its centre within the text to become an unknown '*x*'.

The effect of conflicts between Aristotle and Christian doctrine

Behind this revolution lay no doubt the *de facto* conflicts between Aristotle's teachings and the doctrines of faith. The masters of arts were confronted with a vast literature opposing various interpretations of Aristotle: Albert the Great, *De XV problematibus*; Thomas Aquinas, *De unitate intellectus contra Averroistas*; Giles of Rome, *De erroribus philosophorum*; the condemnations of 1270 and 1277. In the face of such opposition it was difficult to maintain that Aristotle had spoken the whole truth. But on a deeper level this revolution in the theory of interpretation represents the beginning of the end of the clerical paradigm for the scientific enterprise. The masters of arts could recognise the deficiencies in Aristotle's teaching. But in him they found a new paradigm, a new model not only for interpretation, not only for science, but also for the vocation of the university man. In Aristotle, the Philosopher, they found the researcher, the questioner, – or to use Aristotle's own words, the hunter, the discoverer, the seeker[14] – one who subjected the teachings of his predecessors to a relentless critique, who was subservient to no authority and free of all dogmatism. The masters of arts wished their commentaries also to be philosophical, seeking, hunting, critical, and in this way different from the clerical commentaries of the theologians. By their own self-image they were precluded from wanting to raise Aristotle's teaching to the level of a new dogma. They claimed an authority for Aristotle's teaching, an authority not guaranteed by a divine call or a sacred text, however, but one based solely on reason. Their 'philosophical procedure' in the interpretation of Aristotle reflected their consciousness of their own corporate position in society – an elite which owes its dignity not to privilege or hierarchical status, but to intellectual superiority.

---

14. For example, *thēreuein*, *Anal. prior.* I, 30 (46ª11); *heurēsis*, *Eth. Nic.* III, 5 (1112ᵇ19); *zētēsis*, *Metaph.* I, 2 (983ª23).

The reactions of the theologians

In the face of such an attitude the theological faculty had – since at least the time of our students' guide – been on the defensive. The theologians had traditionally attempted to solve problems arising out of divergent authorities by seeking a standpoint from which all the relevant texts could be brought into harmony. But in the thirteenth century the newly translated philosophical and scientific sources rendered questionable the simple concordances which the twelfth century had made between authorities limited to the Latin ecclesiastical tradition. In this new situation some rejected the new literature and attempted by ecclesiastical condemnations to prevent its being read; others, like Bonaventure and Olivi, saw in Aristotle the apocalyptic beast of the last days and took refuge in the historical speculations of Joachim of Fiore; still other theologians, like Albert the Great and Thomas Aquinas, showed themselves receptive to the new sources and tried in a new and very subtle way to continue the clerical enterprise of a *concordia discordantium*.

Thomas Aquinas' solution

Thomas went furthest in the attempt to answer the challenge posed by the approach of the masters of arts to the new literature. As a theologian he had to maintain the existence of truths revealed in the Bible which transcended human understanding. At the same time, the encounter with the religious teachings of Judaism and Islam had constrained Latin theologians to attempt the construction of an apologetic based on arguments acceptable to the three faiths. Because such arguments could be based only on rational demonstration, Thomas sought to justify the inclusion of philosophical questions in the subject matter of theology. Because theology is the science of revelation, he maintained that God had revealed not only strictly supernatural truths, but also some truths which are philosophically demonstrable.[15] For example, God revealed his existence, for otherwise but few men would have attained certain knowledge of this truth. Nevertheless, Thomas argued, God's existence can be also demonstrated, and he proposed five ways of doing so. The refrain which we find at the conclusion of each of them – '*Et hoc dicimus Deum*' ('And this is what we call God') – is the clearest example of Thomas' solution of the problem of the concord between philosophy and revelation. The first cause whose existence has been rationally demonstrated on the basis of the principles of the

15. Thomas Aquinas, ST, I, q. 1, a. 1. See also Lang 1962 and Lang 1964.

philosophers is that very being which the Christian by revelation knows as God.[16]

The concord between philosophy and revelation which Thomas intended involved not only the demonstration of rationally accessible truths, but also the discovery of natural analogies to transcendent truths and the ordering of both natural and supernatural truths in a scientific way.[17] Thomas' theologian had therefore to turn to nature and could employ in this effort the works of 'the master of them that know'. In the Aristotelian logic Thomas found prescriptions for the ordering of theological doctrine as a strict science. In the Aristotelian metaphysics he found the principles for the demonstration of truths such as the existence, infinity, and omnipotence of God. In the Aristotelian natural philosophy he found natural analogies to the hierarchical view of the world which the clerical tradition had handed down. This conception of the Aristotelian encyclopaedia implied, on the one hand, a reinterpretation of Aristotle's principles in the light of conclusions already known by revelation. This was the reason why the theologians could not admit the Averroist interpretation of Aristotle's doctrine. On the other hand, because the Aristotelian philosophy claimed to be an explanation of nature in all its aspects, Thomas' conception meant tying the whole of Aristotle's physics to dogma in a way which would be disastrous for both.

It was in dealing with the Aristotelian astronomy that Thomas encountered a type of discord different from that between dissenting theological authorities. In explaining the account of creation in Genesis, the Latin theologians prior to the thirteenth century had generally adopted Rhabanus Maurus' discussion of the number of the heavens, but later commentators were confronted with radically different conceptions. The translators from Arabic and Greek had made available two far more advanced, but mutually opposed discussions of this problem: Ptolemy's *Almagest* and Aristotle's *De caelo*, together with Averroes' commentary. As we have seen in the systematisation of the sciences undertaken by the author of our students' guide, the former was subsumed under the mathematical sciences, the latter under *scientia naturalis inferior*. While the professional astronomers of the period adopted Ptolemy's theory of eccentrics and epicycles and paid little attention to Aristotle's theory of homocentric spheres, the theologians, who had to treat the question in their

16. Thomas Aquinas, ST, I, q. 2, a. 3.
17. Thomas Aquinas 1948c, prooem. q. 2, a. 3.

commentaries on Book II, dist. 14 of Lombard's *Sentences*, were very disturbed by the contradiction between Ptolemy's mathematical astronomy which claimed to save the phenomena and Aristotle's physical theory which was presented as a deduction from first principles.

Thomas' attempt at a solution of this problem – a solution which we have already seen rejected by one of the colleagues of Siger of Brabant – shows clearly the difference between his theological interpretation of Aristotle and what we may call the philosophical interpretation of the masters of arts. For Thomas the harmonious order which he found in Aristotle's physical theory was based on absolutely certain, metaphysical principles. To the argument that Ptolemy's hypotheses are supported by experience, Thomas rejoined that the experimental verification of a hypothesis does not demonstrate the hypothesis:

The [mathematical] hypotheses which [Eudoxus and later astronomers] invented are not necessarily true. For even though such hypotheses should save the phenomena, it is not right to say that they are true, because the astronomical phenomena can perhaps be saved in some other way not yet understood by men.[18]

Although Thomas thus formulated explicitly one of the most important principles in the theory of science, he employed it to render harmless the objections to his theological interpretation of Aristotle's astronomy – in the hope that some day a way might be found to make Aristotle's theory agree with experience. Saving Aristotle's physics was for Thomas more important than saving the phenomena. His appeal to the principle that verification does not demonstrate an hypothesis meant only that his conception of the concordance between philosophy and revelation need not be disturbed by the contrary data of experience. Armed with Thomas' principle, the clerical world-view was able to maintain itself until the time of Bellarmine and disappeared only with the new astronomical discoveries and the new conception of science of the sixteenth and seventeenth centuries. The falsification of the Aristotelian physics then implied for many the falsification of Thomas' approach.

---

18. Thomas Aquinas 1889, II lect. 17; pp. 186f.: 'Illorum autem suppositiones quas adinvenerunt, non est necessarium esse veras; licet enim, talibus suppositionibus factis, apparentia salvarentur, non tamen oportet dicere has suppositiones esse veras, quia forte secundum aliquem alium modum, nondum ab hominibus comprehensum, apparentia circa stellas salvantur. Aristoteles tamen utitur huiusmodi suppositionibus quantum ad qualitatem motuum tamquam veris.' Cf. ST I, q. 32, a. 1, *ad* 2. See also Mittelstrass 1962, pp. 173–8.

Aristotelian demonstration and discovery

Thomas Aquinas' answer to the challenge posed by the new literature was the last speculative attempt to save the clerical conception of science as the corporate transmission of traditional wisdom. Thomas gave the clerical teacher the consciousness of belonging to a profession and remade theology on the model of an Aristotelian deductive science. But he did not alter the basic clerical notion of the scientific enterprise. In emphasising the deductive strand in science, he emphasised only one side of the Aristotelian philosophy. It is true that Aristotle himself spoke of the philosopher as the arranger, the co-ordinator,[19] but his desire for order was not directed simply toward a deductive presentation of the results of the sciences, for Aristotle was also concerned with the organisation of research. He seems to have conceived of his school as a sort of university in which research and teaching in the most diverse fields would find their place. If the method he prescribed for teaching in his *Posterior Analytics* was strictly deductive, the practice he followed in his scientific treatises ignored formalisation and concentrated on research. His practice was aimed at the acquisition of new knowledge, at discovery, at the *via inventionis*. That is what the clerical approach could not admit, and that is what the Parisian masters of arts in the thirteenth century rediscovered.

Philosophical inquiry in the thirteenth-century arts faculty

The rejection by these masters of the method of concordance, their rejection of the notion of a prior truth known by faith to which philosophical truth must conform, their conception of truth as something to be sought rather than as something possessed conformed to the image they had of themselves as the successors of the critical, curious, and searching Philosopher. Because their own status was not based on an appeal to authority, they could admit that Aristotle – whose works they had sought and made the first efforts to interpret – made mistakes. The authority of their teaching was guaranteed only by reason. Since they claimed no authority in the sacred sciences, they enjoyed a new liberty in their research, a liberty which brought with it the many new, un-Aristotelian developments of the fourteenth and fifteenth centuries.

The masters of arts regarded their work as philosophy, but in order to write a history of their contributions today it is necessary to go beyond the

19. *Metaph.* I, 2 (982ᵃ18).

standard histories of philosophy and to consult histories of logic and linguistic theory, of mathematics, mechanics, and astronomy, of ethics and political theory. We have here considered only the distinction between philosophical and theological discourse, which we first encountered in our students' guide. This distinction is usually associated with what is known as Averroism in the latter half of the thirteenth century, but in a deeper sense it laid the foundation for the great scientific achievements of the later Middle Ages. The distinction between philosophical and theological (not truth, but) discourse represents not only a break with the clerical commentatory tradition and the beginning of the end of the clerical paradigm in science, but also a new autonomy for the medieval arts faculty. No longer simply the gateway to theology, the arts faculty became an institution on an equal footing with the faculties of law, medicine, and theology. The dignity thus gained for the philosophical vocation made it possible for a Buridan to devote his entire life to the problems of logic and natural and moral philosophy. The distinction from theology also made possible the shift from the realm of the deductive *ratio* to the realm of experience and contingency, the whole new epistemological orientation which the fourteenth century itself described as a transition from *cognitio propter quid* to *cognitio quia*. The 'philosophical procedure' made it possible for the masters of arts to turn increasingly from the exposition to the question-form of commentary, to criticise the Philosopher, to ask the new logical and mathematical questions with which Ockham and the Merton school led science in the early fourteenth century into new paths; and it made it possible for Oresme to fuse Mertonian mathematics with Parisian physics in the late fourteenth century, and for Paul of Venice and others in Padua in the fifteenth century to bring these developments together with the Averroist attitude to form the secular Aristotelianism of the sixteenth-century Italian universities.

Forms of Aristotelianism from 1500 to 1650

A third wave of editions of, translations of, and commentaries on the works of Aristotle began in the late fifteenth century and lasted until about the middle of the seventeenth.[20] The Aristotelianism of the period 1500–1650 presents, however, a picture which differs radically from the university philosophy of the Middle Ages. Despite the many late medieval developments in logic and physics which would eventually contribute to

---

20. See Lohr 1974–.

the breakdown of Aristotelian science, the Aristotelianism of the earlier period remained predominantly clerical and offered an essentially unified world-view. But in the sixteenth century this unity broke down, so that we must speak not of one, but of several Aristotelianisms in the Renaissance. Within the Catholic Church the Jesuits and the other religious orders attempted to maintain Thomas' interpretation of Aristotle's *Metaphysics* in the service of Catholic theology. In Protestant Germany Melanchthon constructed a new Aristotelianism – without the *Metaphysics* – for the new schools which should serve Luther's gospel. In France scholars concerned with constitutional reform searched the logical works of the Greek Aristotle for new ways to interpret legal doctrine. In Italy humanists turned to Aristotle's moral philosophy, literary critics to the teachings of the *Poetics*, university professors to works either unknown or ignored in the Middle Ages, like the *Problemata* and the *Mechanica*, and to the Greek commentators on the natural philosophy.

This great variety of Renaissance Aristotelianisms, each concerned with a different aspect of Aristotle's encyclopaedia, certainly contributed to the disintegration of the medieval world-view. But beneath them lay a new conception of knowledge and science, a conception which was born with the Parisian masters of the thirteenth century and could still be shared by Descartes and Galileo, by Bacon and Hobbes, a conception of science no longer bound by traditional authority. The supplanting of the clerical paradigm for science is of course to be associated with the social changes which characterised this period. But the way in which the change took place was decisively conditioned by the Aristotelian philosophy. Aristotle had never really fitted into the clerical mould which formed medieval science. It was indeed the Aristotelian spirit of free research which eventually led to the breakdown of the theological syntheses of the medieval period. This was a process lasting centuries, but after some four hundred years the original fears of popes and theologians proved justified. In the thirteenth century 'the philosophical interpretation' of Aristotle appeared, in the fourteenth the arts faculty acheived institutional independence, in the fifteenth the Aristotelian encyclopaedia constrained theologians to deal with medical problems and professors of medicine to concern themselves with the problem of the immortality of the soul. In the sixteenth century new scientific interests, new classes of students, new geographical divisions led such groups of scholars to attend to various works of Aristotle without reference to his organisation of science. Although these developments took different forms in different contexts, they were all alike in discarding the

III

THE OLD LOGIC

4
ANCIENT SCHOLASTIC LOGIC AS THE SOURCE OF MEDIEVAL SCHOLASTIC . LOGIC

Scholasticism and its means of expression

Medieval logic grew out of the school (university) curriculum; consequently, one characteristic vehicle of it was the commentary on a schoolbook. Medieval philosophers were not, in general, people who believed that the authoritative authors of the text-books were infallible or had said all that could be said about the relevant subjects, but they shared some convictions that can lead to that misimpression. In general they believed that (1) the *auctores* had laid down the right principles of the several disciplines and did not normally disagree over fundamental issues; (2) they had divided logic into its sub-disciplines in a reasonable way and taken care to provide posterity with treatises on all the main subjects; (3) therefore the right way to do logic was to reach a full understanding of those books and then proceed further in the footsteps of the *auctores*, remembering never to contradict them without fully explaining the necessity of doing so or – even better – showing that their text could be interpreted so as to make them say what they ought to have said; (4) Aristotle was the greatest of the *auctores*.

'Scholastic' properly characterises philosophers who approach their task in the way men did in medieval Western Europe, but scholasticism in this sense was neither a medieval nor a Western invention. It had flourished in the Greek-speaking part of the world between *ca.* A.D. 150 and 550, and medieval Latin scholasticism is not just a phenomenon comparable with its Greek predecessor, it is directly descended from it.[1]

The ancient world had not only an Aristotelian scholasticism (in logic) but also a Platonic (in ontology). Similarly, in the Middle Ages the

---

1. As one illustration of the continuity between ancient scholasticism and that of the high Middle Ages, see the very similar arguments offered by Radulphus Brito in Paris around 1300 and by Philoponus in Alexandria around 525 to prove that Aristotle's Organon is a well-organised and exhaustive course in the essentials of logic: John Philoponus 1909, pp. 1–2; Radulphus Brito *Prooemium Quaestionum super artem veterem*, MS Bruxelles B. R. 3540–47, ff. 33ʳ–35ʳ; id., *Prooemium Quaestionum super librum Elenchorum*, same MS, ff. 480ʳ – 482ʳ.

scholastic method was not peculiar to logic, but the twelfth-century renaissance of philosophical studies concentrated on this elementary discipline rather than on any of the more advanced ones (metaphysics, physics, ethics).

Late ancient and medieval logicians had several literary forms at their disposal, but the scholastic attitude favoured the cultivation of the *scholium*, a note on some particular passage in a book. Its length may vary from a line to several pages, and long scholia often contain digressions and discussions of problems (Greek *aporiai*, Latin *dubia*) to which the text gives rise. Most scholia contain some amount of paraphrase of the text. A paraphrase of a few words is commonly called a *gloss*. In medieval times short glosses were generally written above the relevant passage of the text while the longer notes, the scholia, were placed in the margins. The typical Greek *commentary* is nothing but a collection of scholia provided with a preface in which some general aspects of the text are treated. Sometimes a certain inner structure is imposed on the commentary by means of survey paragraphs inserted into the chain of scholia. The normal way to produce a commentary was to cull earlier works and subject the excerpted scholia to some usually very superficial revision.

The Latin Middle Ages continued the tradition of writing glosses, scholia and *literal commentaries* (so called because they follow the wording of the text, the '*littera*' in medieval terminology). Twelfth-century literature of these kinds often follows the Greek patterns rather closely, even in details of phrasing, as when paraphrases are regularly introduced by the words '*quasi diceret*' = '*hōs ei elegen*' = 'as if he were to say'. Thirteenth-century university teaching produced a new kind of commentaries, the *Quaestiones* – collections of formal disputations of problems raised by the text. There is nothing quite like the *quaestiones* in the Greek tradition, although, of course, the rules of disputation were inspired and greatly influenced by the description Aristotle gives of 'the dialectical game' in the *Topics*.

Scholia and commentaries, especially the literal ones, contain a good deal of trivial material; and the fact that they follow the arrangement of Aristotle's text means that if the commentator has some theory of his own we rarely get a coherent exposition of it, but must piece it together from fragments occurring in unconnected scholia. Nevertheless, they merit close attention because they played a major role in shaping the late ancient and medieval students' conceptions of Aristotle's logic. Few, if any, would try to read the bare text of the Organon, unaided by any commentary. At the very least, they would use an annotated copy with some scholia and glosses.

A survey of the history of Greek scholasticism

The Greeks had written commentaries on classical authors before the second century A.D., but scholasticism did not really conquer philosophy till then. The fourth and third centuries B.C. were the age of the great innovative thinkers, Plato, Aristotle, Epicurus, Zeno, Chrysippus. The period from about 250 B.C to A.D. 100 was characterised by a split between higher philosophical education, which was supposed to be instruction in the dogmatic system of one of the traditional 'sects' (Epicurean, Peripatetic, etc.), and a more elementary level of instruction, where doctrines of different origin coalesced. The sects had their last days of glory in the second century when they even won a kind of official recognition through the institution of public chairs of Platonic, Peripatetic, Epicurean and Stoic philosophy.[2] But during the same period the foundations of the sects were undermined by a public demand for non-sectarian instruction in all branches of philosophy and on the basis of the classics of each branch. In practice this meant that Plato should reign in metaphysics with Aristotle providing the principles of such auxiliary disciplines as logic. Such pieces of Stoic doctrine as had become the common property of educated people were to be preserved, but the system as a whole was discarded, as was Epicureanism. Within a relatively short time the rich fathers who would pay a philosopher to read central Aristotelian and Platonic texts with their sons must have become more numerous than those who would pay for traditional courses of Hellenistic Peripateticism or Stoicism. The old sects were almost completely wiped out before the end of the third century. Whenever later writers polemicise against Stoics, for instance, they are fighting the shadows of men long since dead. Even the books of Stoic philosophers disappeared. Simplicius informs us that in the early sixth century most of them were no longer available.[3]

The logic adopted within this educational reform was Aristotelian and scholastic. Its Bible was the Organon, the received interpretation of which was masterfully developed in the commentaries of Porphyry (ca. 234–304). Porphyry had few, if any, original opinions in logic, but he knew how to combine apparently disparate pieces of commonly accepted doctrine in an intelligent way. His successors appreciated this achievement, but not the length of some of his commentaries, and so they soon boiled them down to what they thought were the essentials. No later philosopher undertook a radical revision of the Porphyrian interpretation, which still looms large in

2. Cf. Lynch 1972, pp. 170–1.
3. See Simplicius 1907, 334.1–3.

the works of Ammonius (*ca.* 440–*ca.* 520), Boethius (*ca.* 480–524), his near-contemporaries Philoponus and Simplicius, and 'Alexander' (a shadowy figure, much later than Alexander of Aphrodisias (*ca.* 200), whose name he borrowed; see below), all of whom were to influence the Latin Middle Ages.

After about 550 the study of logic suffered a decline in the East (as in the West). One of the few memorable events was external: the tradition of Aristotelian scholasticism was taken up by the Arabs, a development that was to be important for the West in later times when Arabic books could be used, because Arabic philosophy had sprung from the same Greek scholasticism as had given rise to Latin scholasticism. There were periods of revival, as in the early twelfth century when a rising interest in the Organon may have helped James of Venice find commentaries he could translate into Latin. But Byzantine 'logicians' were more nearly philologists than logicians and never rose above rehashing earlier scholia and compendia. With the possible exception of 'Alexander's' commentaries, which cannot be securely dated, no Byzantine works influenced Latin logic.

The programs of ancient courses of logic

Scholasticism had swept the old sects away but not the old traditions of elementary instruction, in which a course like the following appears to have been standard: I *1*. Theory of description: division, definition, predicables; *2*. Semantics of uncombined expressions; *3*. Structure of the proposition, quantity, quality, modality, square of opposition, conversion etc.; *4*. Syllogistic: *4.1* Categorical syllogisms; *4.2* Hypothetical syllogisms; *5*. Fallacies.[4] The commentators tried to demonstrate that the Organon provided a full course as follows: II *2. Categories, 3. De interpretatione, 4. Prior Analytics, 5. Sophistici elenchi*. It was difficult to fit the *Posterior Analytics* and the *Topics* into the programme; almost all commentaries on the Organon contain a discussion of the right 'order of reading' (*taxis tēs anagnōseōs*),[5] probably reflecting a serious uncertainty in early scholasticism about where to put those two works; however, most people agreed to

---

4. Cf. Cicero, *Brutus* 41.152; id., *De finibus* 1.7.22; id., *Orator* 32.115; id., *Tusculanae* 5.25.72; Maximus Tyrius, *Philosophumena* 1.7.8; Sextus Empiricus, *Pyrrhoneae hypotyposes* 2.213 & 229. Galen's *Institutio logica* shows that syllogistic was commonly divided into categorical and hypothetical. Albinus' *Didascalicus* (Albinus 1858, Ch. 3, p. 153, and Ch. 5, p. 156) and other sources indicate that induction was also a standard topic, though hardly an important one.
5. E.g., John Philoponus 1909, pp. 2–3.

insert them after 4. as 4.*a* and 4.*b* respectively. The instant success of Porphyry's *Isagoge* must have been partly due to the simple fact that it could (almost) fill the gap before the *Categories*. Porphyry was not the first to try to stop the gap. In the first century B.C. Andronicus of Rhodes, the first editor of the Organon, had composed a book *On Division*[6] but, for whatever reason, his work did not become a classic, and so it was still felt that something was missing until Porphyry supplied it.

Course II was for advanced students. After the second century the contents of course I became more Aristotelian, but the skeleton remained and was intact in Byzantium a thousand years later.[7] It looks as if a specifically Western variant of courses I and II arose in the fourth century, a variant which not only omitted items 4.*a–b* but also 5, while introducing Cicero's *Topica* and its doctrine as item 4.*c*.[8] The literary activity of Boethius testifies both to a will to supply the needs of this Roman course and to a wish to expand it by adding 4.*a–b* and 5.

The books that transmitted ancient logic

Boethius' efforts to expand the course met with no immediate success. With a few exceptions it was the 'Roman course' that determined which Latin books on logic were handed down to the Middle Ages. They were these:

	A Basic books	*B Commentaries*	*C Compendia and monographs*
1.	Porph. *Isagoge*	Two, by Boethius	(*a*) Marius Victorinus *De definitionibus*
			(*b*) Boethius *De divisione*
2.	Arist. *Categories*	One, by Boethius	(*a*) Augustine *De dialectica*
			(*b*) Ps.-Augustine *Decem categoriae*
3.	Arist. *De interpret.*	Two, by Boethius	Apuleius *Peri hermeneias*
4.	Arist. *Prior Analyt.*	None[9]	(*a*) Apuleius *Peri hermeneias*
			(*b*) Boethius *De syllogismis categoricis*
			(*c*) Boethius *De hypotheticis syllogismis*
4.a	None	None	None
4.b	Arist. *Topics*	None	None
4.c	Cicero *Topica*	One, by Boethius	Boethius *De topicis differentiis*
5.	Arist. *Sophistici el.*	None	None

6. Cf. Moraux 1973, pp. 120–32.

7. See Nicephorus Blemmydes' *Epitome logica* (from *ca.* 1260) in Migne's *Patrologia graeca* 142, Anonymous 1929 (from 1007), plus the remarks of Michael Psellus 1926 (eleventh century) in his *Chronographia* III.3 and of the anonymous hagiographer in *Vita beati Ioannis Psichaitae* (ninth century) (Anonymous 1902) §4.

8. Cf. Jerome *Ep.* 50 in *PL* 22 : 513 (the course he refers to may have included the *Posterior Analytics* as well). For Roman traditions cf. Hadot 1971 and Pfligersdorffer 1953.

9. Except for the Philoponean scholia (translated by Boethius?) in *Aristoteles Latinus* 1962, III.4. Cf. Ebbesen 1981a.

To make the *C*-list complete we must add Book IV of Martianus Capella's *De nuptiis Philologiae et Mercurii,* which covers 1–4.

Apuleius' *Peri hermeneias*[10] is the oldest of the *C*-books, dating from the infancy of scholasticism (second century) and containing much that smacks of Stoicism. It starts with a consideration of the kinds of utterances (orders, wishes, etc.) and picks out the indicative propositions as the one kind relevant to logic. Having divided that sort of proposition into the species *categorical* and *hypothetical,* Apuleius goes on to deal with quantity, quality, etc., and ends with a chapter on categorical syllogisms; a concluding chapter on hypothetical syllogisms may have been lost. The sources are unknown but large parts look like adaptations of a Greek text.

Victorinus' *De definitionibus*[11] is a mid-fourth-century treatise which is really more closely associated with rhetoric than with logic. The 'definitions' dealt with are all kinds of identificatory descriptions. The opuscule is studded with Greek technical terms, and other considerations also point to a Greek main source,[12] but it cannot be identified.

The Pseudo-Augustine's *Decem categoriae*[13] is a late-fourth-century (adapted) translation of some dull Greek compendium of Aristotle's *Categories* emanating from the environment of Themistius (317–88).

Augustine's *De dialectica*[14] is a fragment of an unfinished survey of the liberal arts begun in 387. It is a most interesting study of semantics with particular attention paid to ambiguity. It owes much to the Stoic tradition, which may be one reason why it ceased to be important in the twelfth century when it became clear that it was difficult to produce a synthesis of *De dialectica* and Aristotle's *Sophistici elenchi.*

Martianus Capella's *De nuptiis Philologiae et Mercurii*[15] is a compendium of the liberal arts, written in an extremely precious style and dating from the late fifth century. Book IV deals with logic, starting with the predicables, definition, and division and ending with the hypothetical syllogisms. Martianus, like Apuleius and Augustine, preserves several features of pre-scholastic systematics and terminology.

We have no Greek compendia of logic from the fourth or fifth centuries, but it can hardly be doubted that such as existed were much more similar to

---

10. About this work and its fate see Sullivan 1967.
11. For a detailed discussion of this work see Hadot 1971.
12. Thus *De definitionibus,* ed. Stangl p. 29 (= 359 Hadot) is to be compared with Blemmydes *Epitome logica, PG* 142:693D.
13. On this work and its fate, see Minio-Paluello's preface to *Aristoteles Latinus* 1961b, I.5.
14. On the work and its fate, see the introduction to the 1975 edition.
15. On this work and its fate, see Stahl 1971; Hadot 1971, p. 196 and elsewhere.

the Aristotle commentaries in systematics and terminology than are the Latin compendia. The conservative character of the latter is presumably due to the fact that most teaching of philosophy was done in Greek, even in the West. Latin treatises were composed at long intervals only, and so such old books as Varro's *Disciplinae* (first century B.C.) continued to be influential long after they had become antiquated by Greek standards.

Boethius, who was thoroughly acquainted with contemporary Greek philosophy, made an astonishing effort to bring the Latin philosophical library up to date. His works[16] all date from the first quarter of the sixth century. *De divisione* deals with various ways of drawing systematic distinctions. This short treatise is firmly rooted in the Greek tradition and is probably an adaptation of a Greek treatise on the subject.

The fragmentary *Introductio ad syllogismos categoricos* appears to be the first half of a scheduled revised and enlarged edition of *De syllogismis categoricis* which together with *De hypotheticis syllogismis* could satisfy almost any student's hunger for syllogistic. These are very thorough textbooks, starting with the elementary notions (terms, propositions, quality, quantity, conversion, etc.) and moving on to lengthy reviews of syllogistic forms, questions of validity, etc. The material is all traditional, and it is probable, though not provable, that Boethius used Porphyrian treatises as his models.

The treatise on hypothetical syllogisms is perhaps the most interesting. A hypothetical syllogism must contain at least one hypothetical premiss, a molecular proposition made up of categorical propositions. The basic connectives are '*si*' ('if'), '*cum*' ('when/since'), and '*aut*' ('or'). Hypothetical syllogisms are said to be secondary in relation to categorical syllogisms because a hypothetical premiss has categorical propositions for its constituent parts and because, if the truth of a hypothetical premiss is questioned, it must be established by means of a categorical syllogism. Thus the 'inferential power' (*vis consequentiae*) of the hypothetical major premiss and the 'power of the conclusion' (*vis conclusionis*) of the hypothetical syllogism depend on the categorical syllogism (*Hyp. Syll.* I. II. 3–5, p. 212 Obertello).

Boethius' syllogistic treatises were very influential in the twelfth century, but after the early thirteenth they were neglected. Peter of Spain and later writers of compendia do not even summarise Boethius' doctrine of the hypothetical syllogism. Hypothetical reasoning later became a subject

---

16. See Obertello 1974, which includes a rich bibliography that can be supplemented with the bibliography in Stump 1978.

of discussion in treatises on consequences (for instance, the chapter '*De consequentiis*' in Albert of Saxony's *Perutilis logica*), but the authors of such treatises did not take their cue from Boethius' work.

De topicis differentiis is a monograph on proof by means of universal axioms. It expounds the theory in the light of which Boethius had interpreted Cicero's *Topica*. Boethius' book, which, though dependent on Greek theorising (see below), is not an adaptation from the Greek, was the subject of intense study in the twelfth century and still much read in the thirteenth. A chapter on the subject matter of this treatise ('*De locis*') was a stock item of compendia of logic till the end of the Middle Ages.

As for the *B*-books, Boethius' commentary on Cicero's *Topica* contains nothing of interest to logic that is not in *De topicis differentiis*. His other commentaries follow Greek patterns quite closely without being mere translations; they depend on the same sources as their contemporary Greek counterparts, to which they are in no way inferior, and in particular on Porphyry, whose views Boethius embraces even more emphatically than many Greeks had done.

About 1130 James of Venice augmented the list of *B*-books by translating the commentaries of 'Alexander' on the *Posterior Analytics* and the *Elenchi*. His translations are not extant today, but quotations and reports of their scholia occur in many extant books.[17] The medievals thought both commentaries were by Alexander of Aphrodisias (*ca.* 200), but they were wrong. Neither of the two works can have had the Aphrodisian for its author, and they are even likely to have had two different authors. The commentary on *Posterior Analytics* I (it is uncertain if there was one on Book II) was virtually or completely identical with Philoponus'. If it was not simply his, it was a later compilation consisting mainly of extracts from his. The *Elenchi* commentary resembled most of all the one by James' contemporary (and acquaintance?) Michael of Ephesus,[18] but it was not simply identical with it, nor with any other extant Greek collection of scholia, though it had similarities with some of them.[19] It may have been James' own compilation from Michael and other sources. If not, it was

---

17. See Ebbesen 1976a, where the fragments relating to the *Posteriora* are edited. The fragments of the *Elenchi* commentary are edited in Ebbesen 1981b, vol. II.
18. The first version of Michael's commentary is contained in the MSS of Wallies' 'second class' (see *CAG* II.3, pp. XVIII–XXII); the final (revised and enlarged) version has been edited by Wallies in *CAG* II.3; extensive excerpts from the commentary on an intermediate stage occur in MSS Paris gr. 1917 ff. 539ʳ–550ᵛ and Paris gr. 2019 ff. 187ᵛ–203ᵛ. Cf. Ebbesen 1981b, vol. I, ch. V.14.
19. So in particular with *Commentarium* II, contained in MS Vat. Barb. gr. 164 ff. 235ᵛ–254ᵛ and other MSS. This collection antedates Michael, who culled many scholia from it.

probably written between about 900 and 1100. At any rate it consisted of Greek scholia, several of which had originally been extracted from commentaries on other books of Aristotle's. Thus, whichever the date of the compilation, a large part of the materials dated back to the sixth century and some items even further back. The commentaries of 'Alexander' had the important role of initiating the twelfth century into the lore of the *Posterior Analytics* and the *Elenchi*, and their influence – especially that of the *Elenchi* commentary – was great and lasting although mostly indirect. The last copies of James' translations may have been destroyed in the early fourteenth century or even earlier; in fact, most of the twelfth- or thirteenth-century people who quote, cite, paraphrase, or echo 'Alexander' betray in one way or another that they never held his books in their hands. But the works had been quarried so soon after publication of the translations that more or less precise accounts of 'Alexander's' tenets and examples, with or without indication of source, began to circulate in compendia and scholia and then to be handed down from generation to generation together with other traditional material.

The influence of ancient grammar and rhetoric

The second century A.D. wanted non-sectarian instruction on the basis of classical texts not only in logic but in other disciplines as well. Grammar (linguistics) was one of them, but since it was only a few centuries since grammar had become emancipated from its parent, Stoic logic,[20] there was no early writer qualified to become an *auctor*.[21] Consequently second-century grammarians such as Apollonius Dyscolus and Herodian themselves became classics. Apollonius was the author Priscian chose for his guide in the early sixth century when he wrote that monumental grammar of Latin that was to mean so much to medieval Latin grammar and logic.

Ancient rhetoric, too, had close ties with logic. Surviving manuals of the art and Victorinus' commentary on Cicero's *De inventione* exercised some relatively unimportant influence on twelfth-century logicians.

Ancient theories that influenced the medievals

Such mediators as Boethius, 'Alexander' and Priscian let the Middle Ages catch a glimpse of a wealth of ancient theories. Each of these theories made its contribution to the development of Latin logic and it is not possible even

---

20. Cf. Pinborg 1975d; Frede 1977 and 1978.
21. I have to except Dionysius Thrax, but his *Ars grammatica* (ed. Uhlig, *Grammatici graeci* I.1) is a very jejune work, and most of it may be spurious (cf. Pinborg 1975d).

to list them all. For the sake of illustration I select three that I consider particularly important, viz. Apollonian grammatical semantics, the proof-procedure of Galen and Themistius, and Porphyrian logical semantics.

Apollonian grammatical semantics

Priscian's grammatical theory is Apollonian, as he himself admits.[22] Like all ancient grammars, that of Apollonius Dyscolus was not historical. Of course, some historical observations would be included, but the general attitude was that the corpus of normative authors should be treated as evidence of one and the same language – Greek or Latin, as the case might be.

The elements of the discipline were ordered according to complexity. The minimal units were called elements, their symbols, letters. Elements combine to form syllables, syllables combine to form (minimal) expressions (Greek *'lexeis'*, Latin *'dictiones'*; in the following I shall use the loose rendering 'words'). Words are signs of intelligible *significata* which may combine to form complete meanings signified by grammatical sentences. Rules determined the constructional possibilities on each level of complexity, and some effort was made to make the rules on different levels conform to the same patterns. Considered as a constituent of sentences, a word is a part of speech (Greek *meros tou logou*, Latin *pars orationis*) and it belongs to a word-class (also called 'part of speech') the members of which share certain constructional 'attitudes', as it were, some of which regard the surface form of the sentences only, while others have to do with semantical components, both significates and consignificates. The Greek name for some, and perhaps all, such attitudes was *'scheseis'*; Priscian seems to have had no technical term for them. Compatibility of attitudes is required for grammatical construction. For instance, verbal forms other than the infinitive not only signify an 'activity' (Greek *'pragma'*, mistranslated into Latin as *res*) but also consignify some definite mood, number, and the like, these 'accidents' (Gk. *'parhepomena'*, Lat. *'accidentia'*) being specified by morphological devices. Grammaticality (Gk. *'katallēlotēs'*, Lat. *'congruitas'*) requires, for instance, that the subject term and the verb have compatible attitudes, which implies the same or at least compatible semantic com-

---

22. Priscian 1855–9, XVII.I.1; cf. Schneider in *Grammatici Graeci* II.3, pp. III–IV. Some crucial passages for the facets of Apollonian theory expounded below: Apollonius, *De syntaxi* I, §§1–2, pp. 1–3; III, §§24–6, pp. 290–2; §§54ff., pp. 319ff.; IV, §15, p. 448. More may be found via the index in *Gramm. Gr.* II.3 under *'sēmainō'*, *'sēmainomenon'*, *'sussēmainō'*, *'sundeloō'*, *'schēma'*, *'schēmatismos'*, and the terms mentioned in the text of this chapter. Cf. Ebbesen 1981b, vol. I, ch. IV. 4.17.

ponents. The complex of semantical components underlying a sentence is not just an intelligible duplicate of the surface sentence, for several distinct surface sentences may be equivalent, which means they share a common semantical base. For example, 'I wish that you would write' – that is, wishing mood + second person + singular number + present tense + active disposition + the activity 'write' – may be expressed by means of three different Greek sentences, namely '*euchomai se graphein*', '*graphois*' and '*eithe graphois*'. In the first sentence the wishing mood is expressed by means of the modal verb '*euchomai*' = 'I wish', the second person singular by means of the pronoun '*se*' = 'you', the remaining semantical components by means of the infinitive '*graphein*' = 'to write'. In the second and the third sentences all the information is contained in the second person singular present optative of the active voice '*graphois*'; the modal particle '*eithe*' in the last sentence does not provide any information not contained in '*graphois*', it just serves to emphasise the wishing mood. The relations between the semantical components and the surface sentences may be illustrated as follows:

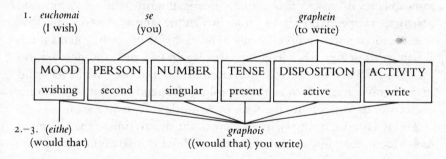

1. *euchomai*   *se*   *graphein*
   (I wish)   (you)   (to write)

MOOD	PERSON	NUMBER	TENSE	DISPOSITION	ACTIVITY
wishing	second	singular	present	active	write

2.–3. *(eithe)*   *graphois*
   (would that)   ((would that) you write)

The theory of inference in the literature on the topics

From Boethius' two works on topics the medievals inherited a theory of inference which is perhaps best called 'axiomatic topics', since in this theory the notions of *topos* and *axioma* had coalesced.

In Boethius' Latin the Greek terms *topos* and *axioma* had become *locus* and *maxima (propositio)*, respectively, but as there is no doubt which terms underlie his Latin,[23] we may retain the original nomenclature and say *topos*

---

23. That 'maxima propositio' translates *axioma* is evident, not only because Boethius adorns the 'maximae propositiones' with epithets usually given to Aristotelian axioms, but also because he actually translates *axiomata* at Arist. *Top.* VIII, c. 1, 155[b]15 as 'maximae propositiones' (see *Aristoteles Latinus* 1969, V. 1–3, p. 156). Cf. Ebbesen 1981b, vol. I, ch. IV. 3.5.

and 'axiom' (leaving '*topos*' untranslated in order to be able to reserve the term 'topics' for the discipline or theory that deals with *topoi*). Notice that in the following 'axiom' is used in the sense in which the authors discussed used it, not in any modern sense.

In the theory Boethius presents, every inference owes its cogency to an axiom. Arguments of the form 'non-axiomatic premiss(es) .˙. conclusion' are abbreviations of 'axiom. non-axiomatic premiss(es) .˙. conclusion'. Boethius describes an axiom as a self-evident, primitive, general proposition. His axioms are, in fact, laws of inference, whose only constants, besides 'if . . . then', 'and', etc., are relations (be predicated of, be the genus of, be the opposite of, etc.); the relata are variables (though there may be restrictions of domain; for instance, they may all have to be good things). The non-axiomatic premisses and the conclusion are assertions of the antecedent and the consequent, respectively, of the axiom, with proper constants substituted for the variables.

The implication of the Boethian theory would seem to be that all proof proceeds, implicitly or explicitly, by instantiation and detachment and, as some medievals saw,[24] that a categorical syllogism is not anything *sui generis*, as it depends on a law of inference of the same type as the ones that licence inferences involving other relations than plain predication. Boethius himself may not have seen that far. In fact, he turns most axioms into superficially categorical propositions by putting 'whatever' and metalinguistic terms, such as 'the opposite', 'the genus', in name-positions.

According to Boethius, the *topoi* of Aristotle's *Topics* are axioms.

This is a most startling claim in view of the description of the axioms as self-evident, etc. How do dialectical proofs differ from demonstrative ones if they have such strong backing? Boethius does distinguish between demonstrative, dialectical, rhetorical, and sophistical arguments, but he does not solve the problem of differentiation by reserving the term 'axiom' for the propositions which demonstrative proof rests on; instead he extends the notion of axiom to cover not only demonstrative axioms, which are inherently necessary, but also the propositions on which weaker proofs (or pseudo-proofs) rest; thus a *dialectical* axiom need only be generally known and inherently probable, not self-evident and inherently necessary.

Boethius further notes that the *loci* of Cicero's *Topica* are not *topoi* in the sense of axioms; they are classes or labels of groups of axioms. (This distinction between two sorts of *topoi* is reflected in medieval Latin ter-

24. See Pinborg 1969.

minology where an axiom-*topos* is called *locus maxima*, whereas a 'Ciceronian' *topos* is called *locus differentia (maximae)*.

Boethius stands at the beginning of a tradition because much medieval thought about inferences was inspired by his works on topics. But he also had a long tradition behind him. Not all stages in the development are clear, but the main ones seem to have been these: Boethius produced a compromise between Cicero's and Themistius' conceptions of topics. The axiomatic topics came from Themistius, who had produced (or inherited) a combination of Galenic ideas about axiomatic proof with a Theophrastean conception of what an Aristotelian *topos* is. Galen had identified axioms in the sense intended by the Stoic Posidonius with Aristotelian axioms.

But Aristotle left no clear definition of a *topos*, and his statements about axioms create difficulties of interpretation. One of the most serious is, to borrow Jonathan Barnes' words,[25] that 'Aristotle is clear that principles' – including axioms – 'function as premises of demonstrations; but it is not easy to see how they can do so. A typical axiom is the Law of Excluded Middle; and that is not expressible in syllogistic form.' Aristotle never compares the functions of *topoi* and axioms so as to make similarities (if there were any in his view) and differences clear.

Theophrastus, Aristotle's successor as head of the Lyceum, made an effort to clarify some aspects of his predecessor's doctrine. He provided a quasi-definition of an axiom: 'An axiom is a tenet, either about things in related domains, such as "if equals [are subtracted] from equals, [the remainders will be equals]", or about everything without restrictions, such as "the affirmation or the negation".'[26]

He identified the *topoi* of Aristotle's *Topics* as those propositions that state laws of inference, and defined a *topos* as a 'starting point (*archē*) or element from which we get the particular starting points [i.e., which suggests to us the premises we need], definite in outline [because it states certain relations], indefinite as far as the particulars are concerned [because it does not identify the relata]'.[27]

He simplified Aristotle's classification of topical problems and showed how Aristotle's arrangement of the *topoi* could in some places be made more systematic.[28]

Alexander of Aphrodisias (*ca.* A.D. 200) has an explanation of the func-

25. Barnes 1975, p. 104.
26. Theophrastus 1973, frgm. 33.
27. Theophrastus 1973, frgm. 38.
28. Theophrastus 1973, frgm. 40; Theophr. *apud* Themistius *Top.* in Averroes 1562–74c, ff. 101–13.

tion of a *topos* that is probably Theophrastean. If, he says,[29] you are inquiring whether the good is beneficial, the *topos* 'if something has a property, its opposite will have the opposite property' gives you the premiss 'if evil is harmful, the good is beneficial', which is potentially included in the *topos* and derives its credibility from it. But Alexander is clear that the *topos* itself is not part of the dialectical argument, which consists of the premiss 'if evil etc.', an assertion of its antecedent, and has its consequent for its conclusion.

There is no evidence that Theophrastus called any *topos* an axiom or any axiom a *topos*. There is good reason to believe he never did so.[30]

Theophrastus was succeeded by Strato (d. 269/8). He too wrote treatises connected with topics, but the extant remains are negligible.[31] To all appearances he was the last philosopher to show any interest in the subject before the first-century B.C. revival of Aristotelian studies. Aristotle's *Topics* was completely or almost completely forgotten for a couple of centuries.[32] One of the first to have a look at it after the interval was Cicero. He wrote a *Topica* which pretends to be a sketch of the Aristotelian discipline. In Cicero there is no trace of the Theophrastean conception of a *topos*. To Cicero a *topos* is a notion with which certain standard methods of inference are connected; the study of the topics is useful, because consideration of the proposition one wants to prove may suggest such a notion and hence the way to prove the proposition, but Cicero does not state the methods of inference in propositions; they are implicit in examples of arguments depending on each *topos*.

Cicero also presents a systematic list of *topoi*. The fact that the list, in spite of similarities with the one in Aristotle's *Rhetoric* II.23, cannot have been simply extracted from the *Rhetoric*, or from the *Topics*, suggests a Hellenistic origin. The idea is supported by the occurrence of a similar list in Themistius' paraphrase of the *Topics* (see below), and by its structure. The list may have had some sort of precursor in Theophrastus' works, but

29. Alexander of Aphrodisias 1891, pp. 126–7.
30. Alexander of Aphrodisias seems to have had first-hand acquaintance with Theophrastus' works. Yet, he never mentions the idea that *topoi* are axioms. It is scarcely credible that he would have passed over such a remarkable doctrine in silence. Galen also had first-hand acquaintance with Theophrastus' works; but he never suggests an elevation of topical propositions to the rank of scientific axioms. Averroes 1562–74c, ff. 27–8, explicitly contrasts Themistius' axiomatic interpretation of the *topoi* with Alexander's and Theophrastus'. Hence, at least, Themistius did not invoke the authority of Theophrastus for his interpretation.
31. Strato, 1967–9, frgm. 20–31.
32. Of course, much is unknown about the period 250–50 B.C., but it is indicative that Sextus Empiricus, who is usually a copious source for philosophical discussions in that period, does not waste words on *topoi*.

Theophrastus was hardly Cicero's direct source. One possibility is that Cicero had his list and his conception of topics from his rhetorical training (Themistius was also a rhetor). A superficial inspection of Aristotle's *Topics* then gave him the impression it was a longer treatise on the sort of topics he knew from rhetoric. Another possibility is that Andronicus of Rhodes, the first-century editor of Aristotle, had written a kind of companion or introduction to his edition of the *Topics*, giving in it a systematic list of the *topoi* inspired, perhaps, by early Peripatetic treatises and/or rhetorical tradition. Cicero then took Andronicus' opuscule to be a summary of Aristotle's *Topics*. Wallies suggested in 1878 that Cicero's source was his old teacher Antiochus of Ascalon. None of the three hypotheses has any real support in the sources.[33] In any event, Cicero's *Topica* is not the sketch of the doctrine of Aristotle's *Topics* it purports to be.

Aristotle probably took his term 'axiom' from geometry, and it continued to be used in geometry. The propositions which in modern editions of Euclid are called 'common notions' were generally referred to as axioms. Geometry was the science *par excellence* in antiquity, the one all dogmatic philosophers admired for its strict methodology and which sceptically inclined thinkers were fond of attacking (for if geometry was a fraud, then surely all dogmatic teaching was so). The Stoic Posidonius (*ca.*

---

33. Cicero sketches the doctrine of *loci* (= *topoi*) both in *De oratore* II.38.160sqq. and in his *Topica*. His division into technical and non-technical *loci* comes from rhetoric. But much smacks of Peripatetic logic, such as the division of the technical *loci* into (1) such as are derived from the thing itself, and (2) such as are derived from its concomitants (cf. Theophrastus' classification of topical problems into definitional and accidental in Theophrastus 1973, frgm. 40). The subdivision of (1) into *loci a definitione*, *a partium enumeratione*, *a notatione*, makes the general scheme similar to the Peripatetic classification of division known from Boethius' *De divis.*; John Damascene (see Moraux 1973, pp. 129–30); and Blemmydes' *Epitome logica*, Ch. II, *PG* vol. 142, coll. 701–8 (cf. Sextus Empiricus, *Pyrrhoneae hypotyposes* 2.213). Themistius' classification of *topoi* is known from Boethius, *De top. diff.*, II–III. The common source of Cicero and Themistius might be Theophrastus whose works on topics Themistius certainly drew on, directly or indirectly, as is evident from the frequent collocation of the two men's names in Averroes' *Expositio media Topicorum* (see, in particular, Averroes 1562–74c, ff. 101–13). But then the silence of Alexander of Aphrodisias about such a salient feature of Theophrastus' topics is hard to explain. The theory of a rhetorical source receives little support from extant manuals of the art. There is no evidence that Andronicus wrote any companion to the *Topics*, and Alexander of Aphrodisias' silence is a weighty argument against assuming he did so. Wallies' proposal is, in my estimation, the least probable of all. He considered Cicero's system a concoction of Arist. *Rhet.* II.23 and Stoic doctrine, and thought such a mixture could only stem from Antiochus. But (1) he ignored Themistius; (2) his reasons for saying that the system underlying Cicero's list is Stoic are, in my opinion, insufficient; (3) there is no need to postulate with Wallies that all the logical matter in Cicero has one source; if Cicero had the systematic list of *topoi*, he could easily supply comments on various logical questions drawing on his own knowledge of the subjects, and what he knew would often be of Stoic origin; (4) there is no independent evidence that Antiochus ever discussed topics.

135–50 B.C.) seems to have been worried about the fact that neither traditional Stoic nor Peripatetic syllogistic could be used to explain the validity of proof procedures characteristic of geometry. To defend them he proposed that relational syllogisms, i.e., such as contain propositions with polyadic predicates, are valid 'by the force of an [implicit] axiom'; thus 'A and C are each equal to B; therefore A and C are equal to each other' is valid by force of the axiom 'those that are equal to the same are equal to each other'. He probably also held that Peripatetic categorical syllogisms are elliptic arguments because they do not state the principle which permits the move from premisses to conclusion.[34]

Admiration for geometry and inspiration from Posidonius and Aristotle met in Galen, who was convinced that traditional Hellenistic syllogistic, Stoic and Peripatetic alike, was an insufficient and largely useless tool for practical men. He concluded that the thing to do was to elaborate a general theory of proof modelled on the practice of geometers and meeting, in general, the requirements for scientific procedures set forth in Aristotle's *Posterior Analytics*. He therefore stressed the importance of having explicit scientific and demonstrative axioms, capable of serving as premisses in arguments, and having the quality of self-evidence; and he insisted that such axioms be strictly separated from the similarly functioning, but less reliable (or even deceptive) propositions that belong to the spheres of dialectic, rhetoric, and sophistic. He also stressed the importance of having a method by which to discover the premisses needed to prove a conclusion, a method analogous to the 'analysis' of geometry. If a geometer wanted to prove the equality of A and C, he would take from his stock of axioms one about equality, viz. 'those that are equal to the same are equal to each other'; he would see that he needed a magnitude to which both A and C are equal; he would find it and reason, 'Those that are equal etc.; A and C are each equal to B; therefore A and C are equal to each other.' Galen all his life wanted a method of proof along these lines, an axiomatic super-syllogistic embracing the best of traditional Peripatetic and Stoic syllogistic, relational syllogistic and all. He propounded his ideas in a large number of treatises, but apparently it was only near the end of his life that he found a pregnant formulation of his own solution. While writing a short manual of logic for some friend (the *Institutio logica*) he consulted some work of Posidonius',

---

34. For Posidonius' views, see Kidd 1978. The attack on Peripatetic syllogistic which I tentatively connect with the name of Posidonius is evidenced by the defence and counter-attacks of Alexander of Aphrodisias 1883, pp. 21–2 and 334–5; and 1891, p. 14. For ancient polemics about syllogistic, cf. Frede 1974.

which suggested to him the idea that the principle justifying relational syllogisms could be extended, so that all syllogistic validity might be said to derive from the force of an axiom (implied or stated).[35]

Galen's theory had qualities the second century could appreciate: comprehensiveness, explicitness, simplicity. It was a unifying theory, not one that would force people to discard procedures that had won general approval. But for the theory to survive in a scholastic age one more thing was needed; a place must be found for it in the Aristotelian curriculum. The solution was to develop it in commentaries on the *Topics*. Galen had not thought of his axioms as *topoi* or vice versa (nor of his discovery procedure as topical); yet, it was fairly obvious that his axioms resembled *topoi* in the Theophrastean sense; somebody must have seen this, and he may even have been guided by Galen himself, for in the *Institutio logica* Galen has a remark to the effect that comparative syllogisms (*hoi kata to mallon*) are not really different from the ones he calls relational.[36] Reasoning about comparisons is treated in Aristotle's *Topics*.

It is not known who first described the *topoi* as Galenic axioms. There is still no trace of the doctrine in Alexander of Aphrodisias' commentary on the *Topics*, written while Galen was still alive or shortly afterwards. But Themistius (317–88), probably following an older commentator, propounded it in the initial chapter of his paraphrase of *Topics* II, though apparently without acknowledging any debt to Galen. Themistius also introduced the Hellenistic classification of *topoi*.[37]

---

35. Galen's logical works were many and some, in particular the monumental *On Proof*, continued to be read for centuries. Now they are all lost except *De captionibus* (which contains an interesting demonstration of Galen's discovery procedure) and *Institutio logica*. The information they give about his views must be supplemented with casual statements about logical matters in his nonlogical treatises. Much of the material has been gathered by Müller 1897. Important sources are: *De animi passionibus* II; *De placitis Hippocratis et Platonis*, ed. Müller, II & VII, pp. 588f.; *De propriis libris* Ch. XI. The following titles of lost writings are revealing of his interests: 'On Proof-discovery'; 'On the Premisses that are Omitted in the Verbal Formulations of the Proofs'. In the *Institutio*, chh. 16–18 are particularly important. For Galen's dependence on Posidonius, see Kidd 1978. I think, however, that Kidd tends to overrate Posidonius' influence on the early Galen. It is evident from the earlier works that the thoughts developed in chh. 16–18 of the *Institutio* mark no radical change of attitude on Galen's part, but it looks as if he got a bright idea while writing the work. He starts with a fairly traditional exposition of traditional doctrines; then, in Ch. 16, he adds as an afterthought that there are also relational syllogisms and goes on to deal with them; in Ch. 17 he announces it as a recent discovery of his that all demonstrative syllogisms depend on axioms in the same way as the relational syllogism (notice that in 17.7 he is careful to point out that he uses 'axiom' in the sense of 'self-evident proposition') and starts to show that this is so; at the end of Ch. 18 he reveals that he owes the inspiration to Posidonius.
36. Galen 1896, Ch. 16.12, p. 41; Ch. 18.1, p. 45.
37. Themistius' paraphrase of the *Topics* is not extant, but Boethius and Averroes refer to and echo it (see Stump 1974, pp. 89–91). It is particularly important that Boethius' definition of the *topoi* as

Boethius saw it as his task to update the Latin philosophical library. Cicero's *Topica* was already a classic and Boethius would not try to replace it. It could be modernised through interpretation. Accepting the view that Cicero reviews the doctrine of Aristotle's *Topics*, but realising that Cicero's *topoi* were not axioms (in any sense), he introduced the Themistean conception of a *topos* and established harmony between Cicero and the Aristotle of Themistius by viewing Ciceronian *topoi* as notions that group related axioms (*topoi* in the sense he attributed to Aristotle) together. He then supplemented Cicero by stating explicitly which axioms Cicero implicitly referred to. Finally, he endeavoured, not without success, to show that there is not a world of difference between Cicero's and Themistius' lists of *topoi*. He did not however, manage to conceal the fact that the axiomatic proof-procedure had no original connection with dialectic. When he introduces the notion of an axiom, it gets the epithets of an Aristotelian–Galenic demonstrative axiom; only secondarily does he make clear that not all dialectical axioms are that strong.

Thanks to Boethius, the doctrine of axiomatic topics had a future in the West. In the Greek world it did not survive the end of antiquity. Even Themistius' paraphrase of the *Topics* disappeared.

Porphyrian logical semantics

Everyone agrees that Porphyry influenced posterity very much, but little has been done in modern times by way of reconstructing Porphyry the logician. The work of Lloyd (1956) is a notable exception. My reconstruction, which is in many ways similar to his, is based on the assumption that Porphyry was a coherent thinker; on that assumption we may supplement statements in his extant concise *Isagoge* (*Introduction to the Categories*) and his equally concise commentary on the *Categories* (extant except for the last part, on Chapters 10–15) with doctrines he expounded in his lost major works insofar as they can be recovered from later authors. The lost works had a decisive influence on later interpretations of Aristotle, although

axioms and his description of their function in argumentation can be seen to stem from Themistius (*In Cic. Top.* I, PL 64 : 1051C–1052A, cf. Themistius in Averroes 1562–74c, f. 28A). Boethius' examples of arguments with explicit and implicit axioms also stem from Themistius (they are elaborations of Arist. *Top.* III, c. 1, 116ᵃ13–14 and II, c. 2, 109ᵇ35–8). Given that Themistius said the *topoi* are axioms, one should expect him to say that some axioms, at least, are *topoi*. In Themistius 1900 (pp. 18–19, cf. pp. 24–5) he does, in fact, seem to say that the most general axioms ('common axioms', which can serve as axioms of an Aristotelian science only when restrictions of domain are added) are *topoi*; but his text is not very clear.

people soon ceased to read any but the ones we still have, and few would know how much of what they read in later authors had a Porphyrian origin. Thus when late ancient and medieval scholars asked 'What does Porphyry think?' they would often disagree because they sought the answer in the concise works only, where he had deliberately simplified matters. To mention just one important case, he had avoided introducing the word 'concept' ('*noēma*') because he could drive home his main point (that the *Categories* is not a treatise 'On What There Is') without enlarging on the role of concepts.

Porphyry clearly viewed the Organon as a systematic course of logic,[38] moving from simple expressions in the *Categories* to compound expressions (propositions) in *De interpretatione* and to compounds of propositions (syllogisms) in the *Prior Analytics*, and thence to the several kinds of syllogisms in the *Posterior Analytics*, the *Topics*, and the *Elenchi*. He held that the *Categories* is about simple expressions *qua* significative,[39] i.e., about the structure of reality our language presupposes, which may not be the structure we would posit as metaphysicians. Language is fundamentally a tool for communication about the world of experience, logic studies the way this communication functions and it would be wrong to blame Aristotelian logic for being bad metaphysics as it was never intended to be metaphysics at all. Therefore, Porphyry holds,[40] Aristotle was right in considering individuals prior to universals when he established the category of substance, though a metaphysician would have to reverse the order. Similarly, it is irrelevant whether or not there are metaphysical realities corresponding to the universals of logic. Porphyry believed there are, but he also thought that logic works in either case. This radical separation of logic and ontology was not always completely grasped or accepted by later scholastic authors. Ironically, the medieval preoccupation with the ontological status of universals arose out of Boethius' comments (*In Isagogen, ed. 1ᵃ*, ed. Brandt, I, c. 10, pp. 23ff., *ed. 2ᵃ* I, c. 10, pp. 159ff.) on a passage (*Isagoge*, ed. Busse, 1.9ff.) where Porphyry discards the question as unimportant in a logical context.

A public language presupposes the identifiability of the concepts one individual has with the concepts other individuals have,[41] and the forma-

---

38. Cf. Porphyry 1887, pp. 56–8.
39. Porphyry 1887, 58.3ff. & 91.7ff.; Porphyry, *Cat. ad Gedalium*, in Simplicius 1907, 10.20–13.18. I believe that Simplicius' interpretation of Porphyry is substantially correct.
40. Porphyry 1887, p. 91.
41. Porphyry, *In De int.* in Boethius 1880, I, c. 1, pp. 39–40.

tion of concepts ultimately presupposes sensation.[42] Porphyry accounted for the relation between sensation, concepts, and language as follows: Men perceive the sensible world. The perceptions give rise to structured concepts, such as one with the ordered components +*corporeal*, +*animate*, +*sensitive*, −*rational*, +*quadrupedal*, +*able to bark*. It starts as a concept of an individual but becomes universal when men discover that several individuals give rise to it. Somehow the convention is established that to externalise the concept and cause it to be present in another man's mind you just have to say 'dog'. And as surely as people will have a *dog*-concept, they will also acquire one unmarked for the last three features (rationality, means of moving, way of making sound – in short, the concept *animal* – and they will associate a name with it. Marking for certain secondary (accidental) features, such as having floppy ears or a protruding stomach, creates fully individualised concepts with which names like 'Snuffy' are associated. Dogs happen to be conceptualised as substances, but concepts of and words for qualities, quantities, etc., are arrived at in the same way; in short, people acquire the vocabulary Aristotle treats of in his *Categories*. The words of this vocabulary are called 'names of first imposition'.

Some concepts overlap, and some are temporarily combined. To express such facts people create a new kind of words which are not names and do not externalise concepts but convey information about their 'syntax'. Armed with these 'consignificative' words (copula, prepositions, etc.) people can frame such sentences as 'The dog is an animal' and 'This dog is barking down a hole.' But men also reflect on and want to be able to talk about their own words and concepts and their 'syntactical' properties. For this purpose they create a new series of names by a second 'imposition' – names such as 'noun', 'disyllabic', 'species'.

The fact that language arises from an occupation with particulars is responsible for an inherent ambiguity: names of individuals and universals

---

42. Full documentation of the following would require extensive discussions of philological details. I list here some important passages: *Imposition*: Porphyry 1887, pp. 57–8; Dexippus 1888, pp. 11–16; Ammonius 1895, p. 11; Simplicius 1907, p. 15; Boethius 1860g, col. 159. *Concepts, internal and external discourse, truth, falsity, and ambiguity*: Porphyry 1887, 64.29, 101.24ff.–106.11ff.; Porphyry, *In De int.* in Boethius 1880, I, c. 1, pp. 26–40, and II, c. 5, pp. 106ff.; Porphyry 1886, III.3; Dexippus 1888, pp. 7–10; Ammonius 1897, pp. 18, 21, 72–5; Boethius 1880, I, c. 1, pp. 20–1 (notice how close 21.1 is to Porphyry 1887, 57.20) and p. 49. *Abstraction and predication*: Porphyry, *Isagoge* passim; Porphyry 1887, pp. 90–1; Porphyry, *Cat. ad Gedalium* in Simplicius 1907, pp. 53 and 79. *(Concepts of) individuals, proper names*: Porphyry 1887. p. 7; Dexippus 1888, 15.27; Boethius 1880, I, c. 1, 28.18ff. *Consignificative words*: Porphyry, *In De int.* in Boethius 1880, I, c. 3, p. 77; Dexippus 1888, pp. 32–3; Pseudo-Augustinus 1961, §2; Ammonius 1897, pp. 12–13; Boethius 1880, I, c. 1, p. 6; Simplicius 1907, pp. 64–5. For a more thorough discussion of Porphyrian semantics see Ebbesen 1981b, vol. I, ch. IV. 4.

on various levels are morphologically indiscernible, and no special kind of names exists to signify the concept of a particular name or of a particular concept. It is this fact that makes sentences like 'Socrates is (a) man', 'man is (an) animal', 'man is (a) species' and 'man is monosyllabic' potentially deceptive. The Stoics had dealt profusely with such problems, often as a means of combatting Platonist and Aristotelian ontology, and it is characteristic of Porphyry's writings that he incorporated many of the Stoic examples and some of their discussion of those examples.

Rational 'activity' takes place in that 'part' of the mind that is called *dianoia* and is reflected primarily in speech, secondarily in writing. Dianoetic 'activities' and their externalised reflections in speech and writing are referred to by the same names, viz. 'proposition,' 'argument', 'syllogism', etc. When the need arises, one can distinguish by saying 'vocalised discourse signifies (carries messages about) dianoetic discourse, which in turn signifies (carries messages about) things'. In normal circumstances this may be shortened to 'expresssions (vocalised discourse) signify (carry messages about) things'. Truth and falsity are primarily properties of dianoetic propositions, ambiguity is exclusively a property of external propositions.

Porphyry's account of the genesis of concepts and language can be read as an historical account implying that at some definite time men introduced all names of the first imposition and at some later time they decided to add the names of the second imposition. Post-Porphyrian commentators (Greeks and Westerners alike) sometimes took this to be the idea, and some of them would even have people believe in two different congresses at which the convened wise men created the respective vocabularies. But this was hardly what Porphyry had intended. What he meant was rather that there are certain natural steps in the development of our stock of concepts and words. Roughly speaking, it may be true that the first-imposition vocabulary of Greek is older than the second-imposition vocabulary, but what is important is that anybody must develop his stock of concepts and words in the order indicated. You simply cannot use a meta-language if you have no object-language, and you cannot master an object-language unless you have sensed and conceptualised objects.

Stages in the reception of ancient thought

The ancient materials were of great importance for the Middle Ages, but they were not received and assimilated all at once. Boethius had presented the West with an almost complete series of the *A-* and *B-*books (see above), but the fruits of his labour were not reaped till centuries after his death. In the early Middle Ages when higher education was virtually extinct most people read the C-books only. Until the twelfth century the *Analytics*, the *Topics*, and the *Elenchi* (*4–4.b.A* and *5.A*) were neglected. This neglect may have caused the irrevocable loss of Boethius' commentary on the *Topics*; references to it in medieval authors are so rare that it is very doubtful if they can be trusted;[43] to all appearances it disappeared before the twelfth century. In the course of the ninth to eleventh centuries *1–3.A + B* (*Isagoge, Categories*, and *De interpretatione* with Boethius' commentaries) took precedence over *1–3.C*, only *De divisione* retaining some importance. In the twelfth century *4.A* and *4.b.A* (*Prior Analytics* and *Topics*) began to be studied again, and they gradually replaced all other books in group *4* except *De topicis differentiis*, but the process was a slow one because of the lack of commentaries. Before 1150 James of Venice supplied the missing *4.a.A + B* – viz. the *Posterior Analytics* with 'Alexander's' commentary – and the forgotten *5.A* (*Elenchi*) became at once a central book when James provided *5.B* by translating 'Alexander's' commentary. The immediate effects of late arrivals such as Themistius' paraphrase of the *Posterior Analytics* (1180s), Simplicius on the *Categories* (1266), and Ammonius on *De interpretatione* (1268) were less important because they arrived at a time when Latin scholasticism was finding or had already found its own way of doing things.

In the early twelfth century, then, half of the C-books had ceased to be important. A century later all of them except Boethius' *De divisione* and *De topicis differentiis* had been superseded. The most surprising feature of this development is the completeness of the oblivion into which the C-books fell. It is doubtful if any important feature of later medieval logic can be traced back to the use of them during the early phases, even if the idiosyncratic Roger Bacon did dig up Augustine's *Dialectica* and find some inspiration in it. The role of these books had been to keep the ancient tradition alive and to prepare the way for a teaching based on *A + B*.

Medieval theorising on ancient foundations

The medieval schoolmen did not only read about the ancient theories, they also used them and developed them. They read about proof-procedure in Boethius' *De topicis differentiis* and were led to inquire into the foundations

---

43. Cf. Green-Pedersen 1973, p. 28.

of syllogistic and other proof. They read fragmentary accounts of Porphyrian semantics in Porphyry's own *Isagoge*, in the commentaries of Boethius and 'Alexander', and from the second half of the thirteenth century also in Ammonius and Simplicius. They did not always know how much of the material in the secondary sources had a Porphyrian origin, but they were impressed by what they read. The question of universals became the subject of a lively debate; the theory of the imposition of names came to hold a central position in thirteenth-century modistic semantics; consideration of passages about metalinguistic statements and the like contributed decisively to the formulation of the theory of supposition; and Porphyrian passages in Ammonius encouraged the fourteenth-century creators of 'nominalist' semantics.

The medievals read Greek grammatical theory in Priscian. It was tempting to combine grammar and logic, and, in fact, the two had a common origin. But – partly because logic was Aristotelian and grammar owed more to the Stoa – the same terms were not always used in the same way in the two disciplines. Thus both logic and grammar deal with 'parts of speech', but the logician operates with two parts only, viz. the name and the verb as the signifiers of the subject and the predicate concepts (*'noēmata'*) of his dianoetic propositions. The grammarian has eight parts of speech and must posit some intelligible content (*'noēton'*) even of consignificative words such as prepositions because otherwise he cannot formulate rules of syntax. Ancient writers were well aware of the differences between logical and grammatical analysis, so grammatical theory was only rarely imported into works on logic. In the Middle Ages much was done to bridge the gap between the two disciplines. The Apollonian grammar inherited via Priscian was developed into the theory of *modi significandi*; it was joined to a developed version of Porphyry's theory of imposition, and it was thought applicable to logical questions, particularly in the thirteenth century. At first blush it seemed an immense advance, for now it became possible to discuss many problems, such as syntactical ambiguity of sentences (amphiboly), which had been very difficult to formulate precisely in ancient logical terminology. But when the weaknesses of this approach became apparent and a more truly Porphyrian logic came to the fore, the gap between logic and grammar widened again, as we see in the writings of John Buridan.[44]

44. See, e.g. Buridan, *Summulae* 7.3.10, in Ebbesen 1976b, pp. 157–8.

An example of the ubiquity of ancient doctrine in medieval books

The penetrating influence of the Greeks and Boethius on the Latin Middle Ages may perhaps best be illustrated by examining some quite trivial books that a late thirteenth-century student at Paris might read to learn about fallacies. Perhaps the first thing the student would read would be a compendium such as (?Pseudo-) Aquinas' *De fallaciis*, Chapters 3–4 of which would teach him that (1) just as a dialectical argument derives its strength from a true *locus*, so a sophistical argument derives its semblance of strength from an apparent *locus* and is based on a false maximal proposition such as 'whatever is true of the accident is true of the subject'; (2) a sophistical *locus* requires a 'reason for the semblance' (*causa apparentiae*), the plausible appearance that makes people assent to the argument, and a 'reason for the failure' (*causa defectus*); (3) there are six sophistical *loci* or fallacies 'in speech', and seven 'outside speech'; (4) 'in speech' means 'having a linguistic reason for the semblance', 'outside speech' means 'having a real [extra-linguistic] reason for the semblance'; (5) fallacies in speech depend on actual, potential, or fantastical ambiguity (*multiplicitas*).

We may stop with these. Only (3) derives from Aristotle's *Sophistici elenchi*. (1) stems from Boethius' doctrine of *loci*, applied to fallacies. Boethius had indicated that such an application is possible (*De top. diff.* I, PL 64:1182C) without elaborating the point. (2), the theory of *causae apparentiae et defectus*, is a medieval invention, though with some foundation in Aristotle's text. (4) is an adaptation of 'Alexander's' adaptation of an ancient, and probably Stoic, classification of fallacies.[45] (5) stems from 'Alexander's' report of Galen's proof (in *On the Sophisms in Speech*) that Aristotle's list of fallacies 'in speech' in exhaustive.[46]

After *De fallaciis* the student might try to read Aristotle's *Sophistici elenchi*. He would use the standard translation, by Boethius, and his copy would contain interlinear glosses and marginal scholia. The book begins: '*De sophisticis autem elenchis et de his qui videntur quidem elenchi, sunt autem paralogismi sed non elenchi, dicemus.*' One of the first glosses he might find would be '*id est*' or '*pro id est*' written above '*et*' to indicate that the sense is: 'We shall speak about sophistical refutations, though in reality they are paralogisms and not refutations.'[47] He might also find a marginal scholium

---

45. Cf. Ebbesen 1976a, p. 108; Anon. *Summa SE* in De Rijk 1962–7, I, p. 353; Michael of Ephesus 1898, pp. 20–1 (shows awareness of Stoic origin; cf. Philoponus 1905, 241.1–4; Diogenes Laertius 1925, 7.43; Albinus 1858, Ch. 6, p. 159).

46. Cf., e.g., Peter of Spain, 1972, VII.24–5; Michael of Ephesus 1898, pp. 22–3.

47. E.g., in these MSS of various origins and dates: Assisi B. Com. 286: 98ʳ; Clermont-Ferrand B. M.

explaining that some hold the view that this is the sense of the passage, while others think it means 'We shall speak of sophistical refutations, that is, syllogisms that are materially defective (having a false premiss), and of apparent refutations, that is, formally defective syllogisms.'[48] Both interpretations can be traced back to 'Alexander's' commentary,[49] and the distinction between materially and formally defective syllogisms goes back further, at least to the second century A.D., since it appears in Alexander of Aphrodisias' commentary on the *Topics* (ed. Wallies, pp. 20–1). It is almost certainly an 'Aristotelianising' of a Stoic distinction between false arguments (*pseudeis logoi*) that are valid but contain a false premiss, and false arguments that are so because they are invalid, not being reducible to any of the Stoic syllogistic figures.

A few lines later, the student might find an explanation of the strange phrase '*tribualiter inflantes*' (164^{a}27, literally 'tribally inflating') to the effect that in days of old the Athenian tribes competed to see which could supply the fattest animal for sacrifice at the great festivals, and some would fraudulently try to make a meagre victim appear fat by blowing air into it.[50] The scholium might also contain the information that the source of this explanation was 'Alexander', as indeed it was.[51]

Thus, in small matters and in great ones, the student would be offered an interpretation that reflected 'Alexander's' and through him the work of earlier Greek logicians and scholars. He might also read a literal commentary, which would contain much the same material plus some *dubia*,

169:3^r; Erlangen U. B. 194:1^r; Escorial g. III.28:156^v; Napoli B. N. C. VIII.E.14:77^r; Oxford Balliol 253:245^r: Oxford Bodl. Canon. Class. lat. 188:87^r; Paris Maz. 3470:66^r; Paris B. N. lat. 7766:63^r; Vat. Pal.lat. 992:4^r; Vendôme B. M. 171:91^r; Wien VPL 2377:49^r.

48. E.g., in MS London B.L. Harley 3272:121^r (cf Firenze Laur. St. Croce 2 sin., 9:86^r): 'Nota quod ista littera secundum quosdam diversas habet expositiones. Quidam enim legunt li "et" expositive, sic: "*De sophisticis elenchis et* – pro 'id est' – ". Alii sic: "*De sophisticis etc.*, id est de elenchis peccantibus in materia, *et de his* etc., id est de peccantibus in forma".' Similar scholia occur in numerous other MSS of various dates and origins. In MS Vendôme 171:91^r an early fourteenth-century hand writes: '*De sophisticis autem* etc. Ista autem pars posset sic exponi: Uno modo: "*De sophisticis* etc., i.e. de locis peccantibus in materia, *et de his* etc., i.e. de peccantibus in forma". Vel aliter: "*De sophisticis* etc., i.e. de fallaciis in dictione, *et de his* etc., i.e. de fallaciis extra dictionem". Vel aliter, secundum Alexandrum, quod li *et* teneatur expositive.'

49. Cf. Michael of Ephesus 1898, 5.4–7; 5.24–7; 7.4–11; Ebbesen 1972, p. 25.

50. E.g., MS Paris, B. N. lat. 6289:84^r: 'Dicit tamen Alexander quod hoc dictum *tribualiter inflantes* tract[at]um est a consuetudine Atheniensium, qui solebant sacrificare diis secundum differentiam tribuum. Illi enim qui divites erant opimas adducebant victimas et pinguissimas, illi vero qui pauperes erant, quod divitiis suis non potuerunt facere arte voluerunt, scilicet macras victimas inflantes calamis, et apparebant pinguissimae.' The same scholium with minor variations appears in MSS Avignon 1018:,1^r; Cambridge Gonv. & Caius 468/575:113; Cambridge Pembroke 193:78^r; Paris B. N. lat. 17806:69^r. Similar scholia may be found in many other MSS.

51. Cf. Michael of Ephesus 1898, 8.28ff.; Ebbesen 1972, p. 28.

i.e. discussions of problems to which the text gave rise. For a fuller elucidation of such problems he would read or take part in class-room disputations of *Quaestiones super librum Elenchorum* ('Questions on the *Elenchi*'). The questions would be roughly the same, whoever directed the course. The following all stem from an anonymous work from the 1270s (edited in Ebbesen 1977):

(1) Is a materially defective syllogism a dialectical syllogism? (*op. cit.* qu. 14)

(2) Does a sophistical argument derive strength from a *locus*? (*op. cit.* qu. 33)

(3) Is the essential form of any *dictio* its capacity to signify (its *ratio significandi*)? (*op. cit.* qu. 40 (+ 41−42))

(4) Do different conditions of verification (*causae veritatis*) cause a term to be equivocal? (*op. cit.* qu. 48)

(5) Which sort of ambiguity (*multiplicitas*) is most genuinely so, the actual, the potential, or the fantastical? (*op. cit.* qu. 50)

(6) Is an equivocal term such as 'dog' one or more than one constituent of a sentence (*partes orationis*), and which construction is grammatical: 'The dog runs' or 'The dog run'? (*op. cit.* qu. 54, cf. qu. 817)

The Greek and Boethian background for asking (1), (2) and (5) should be clear from what has already been said. The discussion of (3) may have originated in an analysis of the Galenic proof of exhaustiveness mentioned above, because the proof proceeds from a search for the essential virtue or perfection of a *dictio* ('*lexis*'). Galen considers the possibility that it is to signify, but decides that it is to signify well, i.e., precisely, wherefore the gravest vice in a *dictio* is for it to signify badly, i.e. ambiguously. However the *quaestio* first arose, in the 1270s it had grown into an inquiry into the foundations of semantics, involving the whole machinery of imposition, *rationes significandi*, etc., that had developed from Priscian's version of Apollonius' semantics combined with Boethius' version of Porphyry's version of what seems to have been originally a Stoic model of the rise and acquisition of language.[52] (4) deals with the difference between 'man' in '(A) man is running' and 'man' in 'Man is a species'. The medieval discussion of such problems, which the theory of supposition was used to solve, was sparked off by passages in Boethius' and 'Alexander's' commentaries. They in turn depended on Porphyry, whose ultimate sources were Stoic. The reason why the question is raised in this particular place, in

---

52. Cf. Frede 1978, p. 69.

a commentary on the *Elenchi*, appears to be that 'Alexander' used 'Disyllabic is tetrasyllabic, Dio is disyllabic, therefore Dio is tetrasyllabic' to exemplify a sophism resulting from equivocation.[53] The example can be traced back to an ancient scholium (probably by Porphyry) on *Categories* c. 1,[54] and it may be of ultimately Stoic origin. (6) became a problem because 'Alexander', quoting Galen's *On the Sophisms in Speech*, had taught the West that an equivocal term 'actually' signifies two things, and in the framework of Priscian's Apollonian grammar this might seem to imply that construing such a term with a verb in the singular would produce an ungrammatical result.

Many more examples could be added, but these should suffice to show that ancient scholasticism meant much to its medieval heir. One should not, however, infer that the medievals just repeated what their predecessors had said and thought. The ancients were a source of inspiration. Often a casual remark or an example used by an ancient author would start a long debate that could lead to rediscovery of forgotten insights, but also to new discoveries and new theories. As often as not the result would be that the medieval pupils surpassed their ancient teachers.

---

53. Cf. Anonymus Aurelianensis I (twelfth century), *Comment. in SE*, MS Orléans B. M. 283 : 114A (*ad* 165ᵃ4–6): 'Referendum est ergo quod dicit *unus locus* ad aequivocationem. Alexander tamen hic exemplum ponit de illo vilissimo univocationis genere, quando scilicet modo agitur de nomine per nomen ipsum, modo de re, ut "homo est nomen, omne risibile est homo, ergo quoddam risibile est nomen". [. . .] *Vel arbitramur accidere in rebus quod accidit in nominibus*, nam transferimus a nominibus ad res, ut hic: "disyllabum est tetrasyllabum, sed musca (?) est disyllabum, ergo est tetrasyllabum".' Cf. also Anonymus Pragensis, *Quaestiones super SE*, qu. 9 (late thirteenth century), MS Praha M. K. L. 66:82ᵛA: 'Consequenter quaeritur utrum terminus significans se et suum significatum sit aequivocus ad illa quae significat, verbi gratia "homo" significat se cum dicimus "homo est disyllabum", sed significat suum significatum cum dicimus "homo est substantia".' – For the Greek counterpart see, e.g., Michael of Ephesus 1898, 12.32–3.
54. Cf. Simplicius 1907, 31.3–4.

5
PREDICABLES AND CATEGORIES

Aristotle, Porphyry, and the old logic

Prominent among the antecedents of medieval philosophy, particularly of logic and philosophy of language, are two logical works of Aristotle's. His *De interpretatione* and *Categories*, as transmitted by Boethius[1] and coloured by Porphyry's[2] introduction (*Isagoge*) to the *Categories*,[3] endowed the *logica vetus* with a substantial inheritance of technical terms and the metaphysical puzzles that go with them. An explanation of this inheritance requires a brief excursion into the history of the terminology central to the *Isagoge* and the *Categories*.

The terminology of the Isagoge and the Categories

Aristotle developed two loosely linked doctrines regarding the structure of propositions;[4] one is that of the predicables, the other that of the categories (or predicaments). Chapters 4, 5, and 8 of Book I of Aristotle's *Topics* contain an account of the predicables *definition, property, genus, differentia*, and *accident*. A *definition* is a phrase signifying a thing's essence. A *property* is a predicate not indicating a thing's essence but predicable convertibly of it since it belongs to that thing alone; e.g., the capacity for literacy belongs exclusively to man, so that anything that has that capacity is a man, and only a man has that capacity. A *genus* is predicated essentially of diverse sorts of things; e.g., *animal* of *man, ox, horse*, and so forth. A *differentia* in combination with the *genus* produces the *definition*, as when *mortal rational* is added to *animal* to produce the definition of *man*. Finally, an *accident* may be specified either as any predicate other than any of the predicates mentioned above or as that which may or may not belong to a given individual; e.g., the predicate *being seated* with respect to the individual

1. Liebschütz 1967, pp. 538–43. The originals, in translation, and with commentary, are available in Ackrill 1963.
2. Pinborg 1972, pp. 32–42.
3. Lloyd 1967, pp. 283–93, cf. pp. 319–22.
4. Bocheński 1961, p. 51; cf. Kneale 1962, pp. 25–32.

Socrates. By the time of the *Isagoge*, *definition* had been replaced by *species*, so that the Porphyrian list of predicables runs: *species, property, genus, differentia*, and *accident*.[5]

The *Categories*, to which the *Isagoge* purports to be an introduction, reveals certain connections with the scheme described above. Apart from some allusions to *genus* and *differentia* in Chapter 3, the significant links occur after Aristotle has listed and exemplified, in Chapter 4, his ten categories: substance (e.g., man), quantity (e.g., two cubits long), quality (e.g., literate), relation (e.g., bigger), place (e.g., in the Lyceum), time (e.g., yesterday), position (e.g., sitting), state (e.g., armed), action (e.g., cutting), and undergoing (e.g., being cut). In Chapter 5, after exemplifying *primary* substances as the individual man, the individual horse, and so on, he identifies *species* and *genera*, within which such primary substances are contained, as *secondary* substances. This link is one of several seen as significant by Boethius.[6]

The Porphyrian tree

In his commentary on Porphyry, Boethius discusses the Porphyrian 'tree'[7] which takes the category substance as *genus generalissimum* (most general sort) and uses the predicables to divide substance into a hierarchically ordered series of genera and species. These genera and species, then, may be viewed as secondary substances. For example, when one obtains the species *man* in the development of the tree by the addition of the differentiae *rational* and *mortal* to the genus *animal*, the terms 'animal' and 'man' may be seen as lying at that secondary substance level, the precise semantic status of which is problematical. Categories other than substance constitute further *genera generalissima* beneath which schemes of classification may also be constructed in accordance with the predicables. For instance, the proposition '*White* is a *colour*' is an example drawn from the classifications under the category of quality used as a *genus generalissimum*, and it displays a semantic complexity analogous to that of '*Man is animal*'[8] in which the genus (i.e., *animal*) is predicated of the species (i.e., *man*).[9]

---

5. On the consequent medieval distinction between the Aristotelian and Porphyrian treatments, see Green-Pedersen 1973, pp. 9–11. Kluge 1973–4 gives Ockham's interpretation of the predicables in translation.
6. PL 64, col. 16B.
7. PL 64, cols. 42, 103.
8. PL 64, col. 28C.
9. Henry 1974, pp. 30–1; p. 241.

The semantic source of the problem of universals

In the absence of any competent logical analysis of propositions such as those just mentioned, pre-medieval authors were still at the comparatively naive stage of searching for referents of the names occurring in such propositions. This search, and the assumption that words, things, or quasi-things must be the referents to be found, led to the formulation of the problem of universals. For instance, Boethius opts for words as the referents when he claims that 'species' and 'genus' are names of names (*nominum nomina*):[10] they name the subject terms of the sentences in question and indicate something about those terms. Thus in '*Man* is a *species*', the word 'species' names the word 'man' and indicates that that word is predicated only of individuals belonging to that species. Likewise 'genus' in '*Animal* is a *genus*' names the word 'animal' and indicates that it is predicated of its various species.[11] The full force of such semantic naiveté is plainly visible in the often-quoted Porphyrian passage which sets out a purportedly exhaustive list of possible referents of terms for species and genera: do they subsist outside the mind or are they merely mental? If outside the mind, are they corporeal or incorporeal; and are they joined to things perceptible by the senses or not thus joined?[12] Answers to these questions were taken to settle the question of the status of the universal – that which, in Aristotle's terms, is naturally fitted to be predicated of many things.[13] Since the five predicables fall under this Aristotelian description, they were sometimes known as 'the five universals'. Furthermore, since some of the alternatives in the Porphyrian passage carry implications regarding what things there are, we are here thrown into the area of metaphysics, the science of being.

Important ambiguities in the doctrine of the predicables and categories

The ambiguities and obscurities[14] permeating the predicables and categories have been deliberately maintained in the account given above; they may be heightened by considering at least two further factors. First, a term such as 'rational' is classified as a differentia and hence excluded from being an accident according to the five-fold Porphyrian classification of predicables; nevertheless, it is predicated as a quality (*in eo quod quale*).[15] But

---

10. PL 64, col. 176D; cf. also cols. 159–60.
11. Cf. Green-Pedersen 1977a, pp. 51–3 and 71–2 on some later medieval developments.
12. PL 64, col. 82; cf. Tweedale 1976, pp. 63–88 for detailed discussion.
13. PL 64, col. 170B.
14. Cf. Tweedale 1976, p. 59.
15. PL 64, col. 52.

the categories other than that of substance, including the category of quality, are collectively classified as 'accidents'. So it seems that the differentia *rational* should after all be categorised as an accident. Boethius' answer to this puzzle involves separating the qualities that are differentiae for the category substance from the qualities that are accidents in one of the other categories. To accomplish this he uses various criteria that push the former sort of qualities in the direction of secondary substances rather than accidents. Differentiae are not merely otherwise-making (*alteratum facientes*) but also other-making (*alterum facientes*); i.e., they affect the species and not merely the accidents of their subjects.[16] They are not susceptible of degree, a feature which they have in common with (secondary) substances,[17] and which distinguishes them from accidents that do admit of degree.

It is here that the second of the two complicating factors intervenes. In his commentary on the *Categories* Boethius associates the problem of differentiae with Aristotle's contrast between *being predicated of a subject* and *being in a subject*. Since the contrast between the linguistic (being predicated of ...) and the ontological (being in ...) which is apparently being developed here is in fact misleading, it will be convenient to discuss this contrast in terms of two sorts of predication, i.e., *de subiecto* (of a subject) and *in subiecto* (in a subject), respectively.[18] Roughly speaking, *de subiecto* predications are those that would be embraced by a theory or science of the subject of the predication: the theory of man, for example, would contain '*Man* is *animal*' as a thesis. It is in this sense that *de subiecto* predications may be termed substantial or essential relative to their subjects. The connection of *de subiecto* predication with definition[19] emphasises this sort of alignment.[20] *In subiecto* predications, on the other hand, do not constitute theses belonging to the theory of their subjects. As far as the problem of distinguishing between a quality that is a differentia and a quality that is an accident is concerned, it turns out that a differentia is predicated *de subiecto* and is hence akin to (secondary) substance; predications of qualities that are accidents, on the other hand, are *in subiecto* predications. So a differentia is a kind of half-way (*quoddam medium*) between substance and quality, having some of the nature of each.[21]

16. Cf. Tweedale 1976, p. 61; PL 64, col. 49A–B; Henry 1974, pp. 190–1.
17. PL 64, col. 50.
18. Ackrill 1963, pp. 75–6; Henry 1974, n. 4.101a; Henry 1967, §3.122.
19. PL 64, cols. 176A, 185B.
20. Henry 1967, pp. 43–50.
21. PL 64, col. 191–2; Ackrill 1963, pp. 85–7; De Rijk 1956, p. 51.

A final distinction which must be added in order to understand Boethius' own summary of the predicables is that between predications that are *in eo quod quid* (in respect of what-ness), which answer the question 'What is it?' (*'Quid sit?'*), and those that are *in eo quod quale*, or qualifying, predications:

> A *genus* is that which is predicated in respect of what-ness of many things different in species. A *species* is that which is predicated in respect of what-ness of many things not different in species. A *differentia* is that which is predicated substantially and in respect of quality of many things different in species. A *property* is that which is predicated of one species only in respect of quality and not substantially. An *accident* is that which is predicated in respect of quality and not substantially of many things different in species.[22]

Both genus and species are predicated *in eo quod quid*, and hence both those predications are called quidditative. In that respect they differ most from accident, the common definition of which (drawn from Porphyry) is 'that which comes and goes without the subject's perishing' (*quod adest et abest praeter subiecti corruptionem*).[23]

It is difficult to distinguish the various topical threads running through the predicables and the categories. One way to trace those threads lies in seeing as central the distinction between theory-relevant ('substantial') and theory-irrelevant ('accidental') predicates which Boethius stresses both in his *Dialogue on Porphyry*[24] and when he explains the distinction between *de subiecto* and *in subiecto* predications in his commentary on the *Categories*.[25] Hence the predicables may be construed as providing a general rationale for the construction of theoretical descriptions, which naturally calls forth questions of classification, class-inclusion (genus, species), and class-exclusion (differentia); these are sometimes expressed in terms of class-extensions in Boethius' commentaries both on the *Isagoge*[26] and on the *Categories*.[27] A full and satisfactory expression of these class-relations and

---

22. 'Genus est quod de pluribus specie differentibus in eo quod quid sit praedicatur. Species est quod de pluribus minime specie differentibus in eo quod quid sit praedicatur. Differentia est quod de pluribus specie differentibus in eo quod quale sit in substantia praedicatur. Proprium est quod de una tantum specie in eo quod quale sit non in substantia praedicatur. Accidens est quod de pluribus specie differentibus in eo quod quale sit non in substantia praedicatur.' PL 64, col. 94C; Henry 1974, pp. 231 and 236.
23. PL 64, col. 132C; cf. Henry 1974, p. 231, Pinborg 1973a, pp. 59–60, 63–4 for examples and discussions.
24. PL 64, 12B–C.
25. PL 64, col. 176A.
26. PL 64, col. 29B.
27. PL 64, cols. 177–8.

their counterparts in the theory of collective classes sometimes adumbrated here[28] requires an exact modern artificial language, incorporating all the apparatus of quantifiers, variables, and many-link functors.[29] The same applies to some of the examples, with their recondite sentential structures, used to illustrate the various categories: '*Man* is a substance', '*Literate* is a quality', and so on. The concentration of discourse at the level of 'secondary substances' (i.e., of genera and species), is a device enabling semantically complex material to be expressed in comparatively simple forms of speech such as '*Man* is a *species*', '*Animal* is a *genus*', '*Man* is *animal*'.[30] It is from lack of appreciation of the complex deep structures underlying these forms that the metaphysical disputes concerning universals can all too naturally arise. Both the problems and the disputes concerning universals are symptomatic of struggles to unravel that complexity, which was to have a part in inspiring the development of the medieval linguistic doctrine of *suppositio*.[31]

Meaning, logic, and grammar

It has long been customary[32] to allocate words to diverse 'parts of speech' or 'semantic categories', e.g., noun, verb, preposition, participle, and so on. By the eleventh and twelfth centuries the divergence between the logical and the grammatical traditions regarding the nature and number of parts of speech was already of long standing. Boethius was of the party of the logicians who, following Aristotle, held that the parts of speech important to the logician were merely two in number, these being the name (comprising nouns and adjectives) and the verb; the alleged other parts were said to be completions of, or connections between, these two, much in the same way as the brakes of a chariot supplement its main parts.[33] In contrast, the grammarian Priscian admits as essential for his purposes parts other than the name and verb, i.e., participle, pronoun, preposition, adverb, interjection, and conjunction.[34] The differences between these two opposing views were prolonged into points of detail. The most fruitful difference in the period before Abelard arises from the fact that Priscian assigned to

28. PL 64, cols. 44–5, 112 elaborated in the *De divisione* of PL 64; cf. Henry 1972, pp. 121–2.
29. Cf. Henry 1972, pp. 42, 53.
30. Henry 1974, pp. 30–1; Henry 1972, p. 43.
31. Detailed in De Rijk 1962–7; see De Rijk 1962–7, II(1), pp. 27, 51, 139, 357; Fredborg 1973, p. 20; and Nielsen 1976, pp. 51, 66 for recognition of the equivocation of '*homo*' ('man') when 'Man is a species' is introduced.
32. Robins 1951.
33. PL 64, cols. 796C–797A; cf. 766A–B.
34. Keil 1855, II, pp. 551.18–552.14; cf. p. 54.5–26; and Henry 1974, pp. 262–3.

names the specific function of signifying substance and quality,[35] whereas Aristotle had claimed that paronyms (a sub-class of names) signify a quality and only a quality.[36] Superficially, of course, there need be no incompatibility here if Priscian is understood to be saying that some names signify substances and others signify qualities, a natural interpretation of his doctrine. But twelfth- and thirteenth-century versions of Priscian's doctrine prefer the use of '*cum*' (substance *along with* quality) instead of the mere '*et*' ('and') that Priscian himself used, thereby allocating to names the signification of substance *along with* quality.[37] Examples on both sides of this dispute will serve to fill out this rather abstract description.

Paronyms or denominative names

On the logicians' side there are the well-known illustrations of the various categories provided by Aristotle in *Categories* 4. There *literate* is given as an example of a quality, and that example was to be used as a ground not only for saying that 'literate' signifies quality (rather than substance) but also that *literate* is a quality, i.e., literacy. Again, the name 'white', categorised as a quality-word, signifies a quality and nothing but a quality, according to Aristotle.[38] Both 'literate' and 'white' were classified as paronyms, or denominative names – i.e., alleged derivatives from the corresponding abstract forms: 'white' from 'whiteness', 'literate' from 'literacy', 'just' from 'justice', and so on.[39] Anselm's practice in his *De grammatico* indicates that he used the term 'denominative (name)' to cover only accidental qualitative derivatives, hence preserving not only the contrast (mentioned in the foregoing section) between the qualities that are accidents and the qualities that are differentiae but also that between accident and substance. The fact of being thus 'derived' can distinguish quality-names from substance-names only if the language in which the terms in question are embedded lacks abstract nouns corresponding to substance-names such as the 'man' and 'horse' used as examples in Aristotle's list of categories. Although that prerequisite was already not fulfilled in Boethius' logical language,[40] Anselm still presupposes it;[41] and the problem of explaining

---

35. Keil 1855, II, p. 55.6.
36. PL 64, col. 194C.
37. E.g. De Rijk 1956, p. 113. 15–24; Henry 1974, pp. 146–7, 213; Henry 1958, p. 176; Fredborg 1973, p. 47; Nielsen 1976, p. 53; Fredborg *et al.* 1975, p. 111. See also note 45 below.
38. PL 64, col. 194C.
39. *Categories* 1; cf. PL 64, cols. 167–8.
40. Henry 1964, p. 87; Henry 1958, p. 174.
41. Henry 1967, §3.131.

the meaning of such paronyms or denominative names is a persistent theme of medieval[42] and modern[43] logic. Their separation as names signifying only a quality remains a standing challenge to the grammarians' generalisation that *all* names signify both substance and quality.

Adjectives and other non-proper names

On the grammarians' side a concrete example which served to exacerbate the rift between them and the logicians may be seen in Priscian's attempt to sort out adjectives from other non-proper names. For him *name* is a genus having the proper and the common names as its species. The common name (*nomen appellativum*) in its turn has the *nomen adiectivum* or adjectival name as a further sub-species. Such adjectives, Priscian explains, are customarily joined to proper or common names, both of which signify substance, in order to make clear the quality or quantity of their referents. Among the examples he gives of such substance-signifying names is that very 'literate' ('*grammaticus*') that had been enshrined in the master-logician's *Categories* as a quality-word.[44] Hence to the general counter-logical doctrine that *all* names signify both substance and quality, Priscian adds what could be seen as a provocatively counter-logical example. And that example could (but of course need not) have inspired Anselm's choice of '*grammaticus*' as the central example in his dialogue on paronymous meaning (*De grammatico*).

Grammarians' and logicians' approaches to meaning

The resultant clash is well in evidence in the early medieval period.[45] And in spite of the ancient terminology used for its presentation the problem here at issue still has implications that reflect two possible approaches to studies of meaning. On the one hand, one may base such studies on an inspection of the way in which an approved group of users of a given language actually use that language. Priscian's refusal to deviate from the usage of those whom he regards as the best authors is an index of this adherence to a descriptive basis for his account of language.[46] On the other hand, a way of accounting for the meaning of words which need not wait upon usage came from logic, in connection with the discussion of par-

---

42. Jolivet 1975.
43. Henry 1967, pp. 68–9; Henry 1958, pp. 169, 173; Henry 1964, pp. 83, 86.
44. Keil 1855, II, p. 58.20–4; Henry 1967, pp. 66–71; Pinborg 1974, pp. 43–4.
45. De Rijk 1962–7, II(1), pp. 98, 183–6, 222–3, 226, 230–4, 241–3, 259–60, 521–2; Colish 1968, pp. 93–108 and note 37 above.
46. Keil 1855, II, p. 371.18–22; cf. Henry 1967, pp. 16–17; Robins 1951, p. 71.

onymy. Thus, to take an example from Chapter 14 of Anselm's *De grammatico*, suppose some white horses are concealed within a building, and suppose a speaker truly asserts that some *whites* are within that building. The hearer, who knows nothing of the horses' presence in the building, would still be at a loss to know the denotation of the paronymous subject term of the assertion. The openness of the range of possible denotata arises simply because, other things being equal – e.g., there are no race-riots in the vicinity – any of Aristotle's physical substances might be assumed to be the referents. (This range of possible referents would not, according to Anselm, be strictly comprised within the meaning of 'white', but would be contingently connected with 'white' because of an association grounded in experience.) Both in their use as subjects of declarative sentences and in the role of denoters of the objects of commands, such paronyms must be seen as theoretically available for novel applications. Anselm goes on to exemplify this availability by turning to a command situation in which a hearer is faced with a white horse and a black bull and receives the order to strike; in reply to his question 'Which one?' he is told '(The) white'. In the context he can see that the horse rather than the bull (both of them substances, however) has been indeterminately referred to by means of the paronym 'white'. By claiming that the strict meaning of the paronym 'white' is merely '... having whiteness' (and similarly with other paronyms), he shows, in opposition to Priscian's general claim that a name signifies *both* substance and quality, that some names at least (i.e., paronymous adjectival names) signify 'a quality and only a quality', exactly as Aristotle had claimed.[47]

Anselm recognises that pressure from the side of common usage (*usus loquendi*), on which grammar bases its descriptive account, can push one in the direction of Priscian's claim. Inspection of usage shows that at least certain paronyms, such as the already-noted 'literate', have always been used to refer to the same sort of object (i.e., human beings), a fact that seems to confirm the grammarians' claim that reference to a substance should be incorporated in any account of the meaning of 'literate'. Thus 'man displaying literacy' (substance *and* quality) rather than just the indeterminate '... displaying literacy' (quality only) would be the appropriate account. Anselm resists this grammarians' claim by means of arguments[48]

---

47. *De grammatico* Ch. 12, 18; PL 64, col. 194C; Henry 1967, pp. 86–91; Pinborg 1972, pp. 43–7.
48. *De grammatico* Ch. 12–14.

that chisel away the proposed 'man' component of the meaning of 'literate'. These involve a terminology which, while not novel, was to become widespread in the next century.

Appellatio and significatio

Appellatio (calling) is for Anselm that facet of meaning whereby a name in actual use points to its referents; in the case of paronyms these may be constant in kind (as with 'literate') or varied (as with 'white'). In contrast *significatio* (meaning) strictly or properly (*per se*) so-called conveys only the understanding or concept (*intellectus*) in the definition associated with a name; for paronyms the definition must leave place for changes in future applications by remaining open to referents not hitherto encountered in actual usage. In this sense 'literate' no more signifies *man* than does 'white',[49] and hence must, like 'white', be said to signify *per se* just the appropriate quality, i.e., literacy. Thus is justice done to the logician's contention and the methodological presuppositions which support it. At the same time, and so as to do justice to the grammarian's view, it can be said that 'literate' also signifies in an improper or oblique sense (*per aliud*) its referents; or, in the terminology mentioned above, 'literate' is *appellative* of those referents.[50] The distinction between *significatio* (meaning) and *appellatio* (calling) or *impositio* (denoting) was henceforth to be the subject of extensive discussion.[51] Thus the twelfth-century *Ars Meliduna* persists in maintaining the distinction, while also continuing to stress the connection between *appellatio* and the actual history of speech usage.[52] Abelard is alluding to the same distinction when he insists that the intellectual import rather than the denotation (*omnia quibus est impositum*) is the proper Aristotelian sense of 'signify'.[53]

This association of *significatio* with understanding served to separate the abstract account of meaning given by the logician from the descriptive

49. *De grammatico* Ch. 13.
50. *De grammatico* Ch. 12; cf. Kretzmann 1967, pp. 368–9.
51. De Rijk 1962–7, II(1), pp. 213, 228–9, 536–48; Nielsen 1976, pp. 42–3; Fredborg 1973, pp. 14, 16, 20–3, 31.
52. 'Notandum tamen quod instiucio vocum non fuit facta ad significandum, sed tantum ad appellandum, quippe cum appellacio vocum magis sit necessaria ad loquendum de rebus subiectis quam significacio'; De Rijk 1962–7, II(1), p. 294; cf. Pinborg 1972, pp. 55–8.
53. De Rijk 1956, p. 562.20–5: 'est attendendum quare "significare" diversis modis accipitur. Modo enim circa ea tantum de quibus intellectum generat, modo vero circa omnia quibus est impositum, solet accipi et secundum quidem primam et propriam significationem ita Aristoteles in *Libro Periermenias* "significare" descripsit. . . .'.

account given by the grammarian. Aristotle had spoken of a word's 'settling the understanding' (*constituere intellectum*),[54] and the whole early medieval tradition habitually used that expression for indicating exactly what a word conveys.[55] 'Understanding' thereby has its sense linked with meaning, so that William of Conches' maxim 'Even as it can be understood, so also can it be signified' (*ita ut potest intelligi potest significari*)[56] could well stand as the motto of those complex inferences based on '*intelligere*' (to understand) which adorn the early chapters of Anselm's *De grammatico*. His countenancing of the ungrammatical '*grammaticus est grammatica*' (*literate* is literacy) as the *de re* (thing-centred) correlate of the *de voce* (word-centred) assertion that 'literate' strictly signifies literacy[57] hence corresponds exactly to William of Conches' later assertion that the two names '*album*' ('white') and '*albedo*' ('whiteness') do not differ in respect of what is signified ('*in re significata*').[58] William also appreciates that when we talk of a name's signifying substance or quality, or of its content (*intelligibile*), we are working at the same level as that of the semantically complex talk of species alluded to above,[59] which was later to be subsumed under the umbrella of *suppositio simplex*.[60]

The usefulness of linguistic reformulation

The work of Anselm in logical and linguistic theory has, until recently, been completely overshadowed by his acknowledged accomplishments in theology and metaphysics (which have been discussed in *The Cambridge History of Later Greek and Early Medieval Philosophy*).[61] His concern with questions of nominal meaning was all of a piece with that of his later contemporaries, however. He is likewise at one with them in observing that for logical purposes, such as the statement of the *de re* counterparts of *de voce*[62] meaning-statements, violation of the rules of the grammar of cur-

54. PL 64, col. 309B–C, 430C; cf. Henry 1974, p. 275.
55. E.g. *De grammatico* Ch. 11, 14; cf. Henry 1974, pp. 93–7; William of Conches (De Rijk 1962–7, I, p. 222); Abelard (De Rijk 1962–7, II(1), p. 195; De Rijk 1956, p. 112.6–8, p. 128. 9–16, p. 147.30, p. 153.33, p. 155.38, p. 562.25).
56. De Rijk 1962–7 II(1), p. 223.
57. *De grammatico* Ch. 5, 12, 16, 18.
58. De Rijk 1962–7, II(1), p. 224. Cf. Gilbert of Poitiers as mentioned in Nielsen 1976, p. 65 and, in general, Pinborg 1972, pp. 43–50.
59. De Rijk 1962–7, II(1), p. 224.
60. Henry 1967, §3.4.
61. Liebschütz 1967, pp. 611–39.
62. See *De grammatico*, Ch. 18, for this distinction. Anselm's triple sense of the word 'word' is given in *Monologion*, Ch. 10. Evans 1978 and Liebschütz 1967 deal with the theological applications thereof, and Fredborg *et al.* 1975, pp. 52–3 may be consulted as an example of the use of such a

rent speech may be a useful reminder of semantic profundities. Thus technical considerations[63] relating to precisive (*per se*) meaning may call forth deviations from the norms of that ordinary usage (*usus loquendi*) which is the province of the descriptive grammarian. The latter is in no better position when it comes to the relation between his technical assertions and the way things are: his grammatical classifications of certain verbs as active or passive and of names as masculine, feminine, or neuter, may well be at odds with the nature of things.[64]

Anselm goes beyond his contemporaries, however, in claiming that a like deviation is sometimes apparent when verbs (as distinct from the names with which *De grammatico* is concerned) are in question. For example, usage allows one to assume that a correct sense of the verb 'can' is embodied in 'The universe, before it actually exists, can exist.' In a stricter language embodying the precisive (*per se*) sense of that verb, however, sentences of the form 'X can . . .' require, according to Anselm, that the object named by the subject term 'X' in this context should in fact possess the capacity which the use of this sentence-form properly implies. A nonexistent object has no capacities,[65] and the form of the sentence concerning the universe is hence incorrect. It should be reformulated with the correct subject term 'God', since it is God who, before the universe is, can make it to be.[66] Similarly, 'Hector can be conquered by Achilles' fails to display the proper, precisive sense of 'can', and rewriting it as 'Achilles can conquer Hector' reveals Achilles as the one who truly possesses the capacity implied by 'can'.[67] In *De grammatico* 15 the distinction between the precisive (*per se*) and improper (*per aliud*) senses of 'meaning' is said to be thus generally extendable to verbs as well as to names.

Anselm's general scheme of linguistic analysis

Before 1936 the exact import of this extension would have been rather mysterious. Research on the many examples of sentence-analysis that are scattered throughout Anselm's works could have produced a hypothesis

triple sense in speculative grammar. The 'mental' sense of 'word' was to become the 'mental word' prominent in later medieval logic.
63. On Anselm's attitude to technical language in general see Henry 1967, §2; Evans 1977; Hopkins 1976, Ch. 1 and pp. 66 and 92.
64. *De grammatico*, Ch. 18.
65. For Anselm's development of the consequences of this principle in modal logic see Schmitt 1936, pp. 23–4; cf. Henry 1967, pp. 158–64.
66. *De casu diaboli*, Ch. 12.
67. *De veritate*; Ch. 8, *De libertate arbitrii*, Ch. 5; *Cur Deus homo* II, Ch. 10; cf. Henry 1967, pp. 154–5, 166–73.

that the allusion was to cases such as those just described; but one might also
have formed the further, bolder conjecture that a unified systematic procedure lay behind such analyses. That such a conjecture may well be
justified is suggested by Anselm's 'Philosophical Fragments', first brought
to light by F. S. Schmitt in 1936.[68] The Fragments constitute an incomplete
draft of what could be construed as a general scheme for sentence-analysis,
designed to bring out the contrast between the looseness of ordinary usage
and the strictness of logically precise language.

In order to assemble a set of general sentence-forms Anselm argues in the
Fragments that the Latin verb *'facere'* ('to do', 'to make', 'to bring about')
can stand in the place of any verb (including even 'not to do').[69] He
concentrates on the four general forms *'facere esse . . .'* ('to do so that . . .'),
'facere non esse . . .' ('to do so that not . . .'), *'non facere esse . . .'* ('not to do so
that . . .'), and *'non facere non esse . . .'* ('not to do so that not . . .'). The
relations of contrariety and contradiction described as holding among
these general forms parallel those holding among the modal expressions
'posse esse . . .' ('to be possible to be . . .'), *'posse non esse . . .'* ('to be possible
not to be . . .'), *'non posse esse . . .'* ('to be not possible to be . . .'), and *'non
posse non esse . . .'* ('to be not possible not to be . . .', i.e., to be necessary), as
described by Aristotle in *De interpretatione* and by Boethius in his commentaries on it.[70]

Anselm claims that the first of the four general sentential forms (i.e.,
'facere esse . . .', 'to do so that . . .') has a proper sense of its own. In that sense,
one *does so that* so-and-so if one does so that so-and-so, which was not the
case, becomes the case.[71] But it is sometimes used improperly in a context
that is strictly a case of *not* doing so that not-*p* (using '*p*' as a propositional
variable instead of the 'so-and-so' of the preceding sentence). For example,
the looseness of ordinary usage allows us to say that one does so that (brings
it about that) someone is dead when in fact the context is such that one has
not done so that it is *not* the case that the person is dead, as when one refrains
from using one's (perhaps miraculous) power to restore the dead to life.[72]
And Anselm carefully distinguishes other contexts in which the same
general form 'one does so that *p*' is improperly used.[73]

68. Schmitt 1936; Southern and Schmitt 1969, pp. 334–51; translated Hopkins 1972, pp. 215–42.
69. Schmitt 1936, pp. 25–7; Southern and Schmitt 1969, pp. 337–8, cf. Henry 1967, pp. 121–3.
70. Henry 1967, pp. 136–8, 124–5.
71. Schmitt 1936, p. 32; Henry 1967, p. 126.
72. Schmitt 1936, pp. 29, 31; Henry 1967, p. 126.
73. Schmitt 1936, pp. 29–32; Henry 1967, pp. 126–7.

Anselm's Fragments attain a high degree of systematic generality.[74] His many examples suggest that while his general project demands exploitation of the widest sense of '*facere*', he is trading on the fact that this verb has 'to bring about' as one of its particular senses. It is this which has led contemporary commentators to credit Anselm with having in the Fragments the foundation of action theory (praxiology).[75] He provides complex rules of transformation by means of which modes and examples relating to the negative forms ('not to do so that . . .' and 'not to do so that not . . .') may be generated from those relating to the affirmative forms ('to do so that . . .' and 'to do so that not . . .').[76] He also discusses the extent to which the patterns thus evolved apply to other verbs considered as instances of '*facere*' in its most general sense ('to do'),[77] and he stresses his awareness that further research and elaboration of his proposals are needed.[78] Perhaps the best example of such possible developments is to be found in his extended remarks on '*velle*' ('to will'), which he assimilates to '*facere*' in several respects.[79]

The utilisation of this architectonic draft for an analytic scheme (if that is really what it is) extends into nearly all of Anselm's works. Some of the material on '*facere*' recurs elsewhere,[80] and the system is used to solve puzzles concerning verbs of capacity and liability, as well as some involving the verbs 'to give'[81] and 'to be obliged to . . .'.[82]

Anselm on 'nothing'

A final example of the all-pervasive distinction between the proper (logical) and improper (merely usage-approved) forms of an utterance may be drawn from Anselm's treatment of the pseudo-name 'nothing'. The linguistic puzzles centring around this and kindred words are manifest and numerous. Lewis Carroll's 'Nobody walks much faster than I do' requires (if inferential oddities are to be avoided) that the 'nobody' be recognised as

---

74. E.g., 'Dicimus namque rem quamlibet facere aliquid esse aut quia facit idipsum esse, quod facere dicitur, aut quia non facit idipsum non esse, aut quia facit aliud esse, aut quia non facit aliud esse, aut quia facit aliud non esse, aut quia non facit aliud non esse' (Schmitt 1936, pp. 29, 30).
75. Danto 1973; Walton 1976.
76. Schmitt 1936, pp. 30–3; Henry 1967, pp. 126 and 128–9.
77. Schmitt 1936, pp. 33–7; Henry 1967, p. 129.
78. Schmitt 1936, p. 29; Henry 1967, p. 124.
79. Schmitt 1936, pp. 37–9; Henry 1967, pp. 130–3.
80. *De veritate*, Ch. 5; *De casu diaboli*, Ch. 1; cf. Henry 1967, pp. 181–5.
81. *De casu diaboli*, Ch. 18, 20; *Cur Deus homo*, II, Ch. 10; cf. Henry 1967, pp. 185–91.
82. Schmitt 1936, pp. 35–7; *Cur Deus homo* II 18; *De veritate* 8; cf. Henry 1967, pp. 191–201.

its merely grammatical (but not logical) subject; it has its medieval counter-part in Anselm's 'Nothing taught me to fly' ('*Nihil me docuit volare*'). This too could lead to odd inferences (e.g., that I have been taught to fly), were 'nothing' taken to be a name. Modern logicians would analyse 'nobody' or 'nothing' out of the proposition by recourse to propositional negation and the quantifier 'there exists an *x* such that . . .'. Thus Anselm's sentence would become 'It is not the case that there exists an *x* such that *x* taught me to fly', i.e., 'It is not the case that something taught me to fly.' This is the counterpart of Anselm's Latin analysis '*Non me docuit aliquid volare*', in which the initial '*non*' plainly performs the office of propositional nega-tion.[83] By means of various examples Anselm underlines the analogy of grammatically permissible structure holding between sentences in which the nominal positions are occupied by empty and negative names, and those in which such positions are occupied by names that do refer. The name '*nihil*' is then seen as signifying something '*secundum formam loquendi*' (i.e., from the viewpoint of grammatical structure) but not '*secundum rem*' (i.e., from the viewpoint of reality).[84]

Apparent form and real form of propositions

These developments may be construed as further natural consequences of that rivalry between logic and grammar which was a pervasive feature of Anselm's intellectual context, a rivalry that helps to account for the sometimes striking resemblance between his theses and the present-day contrast between the 'real' (or 'logical') form of an utterance and its 'apparent logical' (or 'merely grammatical') form. It is not only 'Russell's merit' (as Wittgenstein put it) but also Anselm's 'to have shown that the apparent logical form of the proposition need not be its real form'. As far as the medievals were concerned, this was by no means the end of the matter. Equally trenchant obverse statements of this same contrast were to emerge from the side of autonomy-seeking grammarians.[85]

---

83. *Monologion*, Ch. 19; Henry 1967, pp. 218–19.
84. *De casu diaboli*, Ch. 11; Henry 1967, pp. 211–18.
85. Pinborg 1972, pp. 111–12.

6
ABELARD AND THE CULMINATION OF THE OLD LOGIC

Abelard's conception of logic

Of all the scholastic logicians writing while the old logic (*logica vetus*) was still virtually the whole of the logical curriculum in the schools, Abelard is generally conceded to have been the most profound and original.[1] He himself was keenly aware of the subtlety required of the logician and in one place says it depends on a divinely bestowed talent, rather than anything that can be developed by mere practice.[2] Abelard treats dialectic (= logic) as an *ars sermocinalis*, i.e., like grammar a linguistic science. Its peculiar subject matter is arguments as expressed in language, whose validity it tries to judge in a scientific way.[3] This linguistically oriented conception of the subject means that dialectic will overlap to some extent with grammar. In the first section below I shall selectively explore this overlap; in the second section I shall consider some of Abelard's views on more purely logical topics.

For Abelard logic also had a close relation to *physica*,[4] i.e., the sciences of nature, since in explaining the 'uses of words' the logician must investigate in a general way the 'properties of things' which the mind uses words to signify. This relationship leads to a concern with the psychology of signification, to be explored in the third section below, and with ontology, the topic of the fourth section. This discussion is necessarily very selective and must omit consideration of many of Abelard's philosophical insights on relevant topics.

Dialectic and grammar

Throughout his logical works Abelard frequently deploys terms and analyses borrowed from grammar and generally views his own dialectical

---

1. For example, Jolivet 1969, p. 338: 'Logicien, Abélard doit être mis très haut. On ne connaît avant lui aucun médiéval qui soit de sa taille.'
2. See Abelard 1956, p. 471.4–9.
3. See Abelard 1954, p. 209.
4. See Abelard 1956, pp. 286.31–287.1.

enterprise as deepening and to some extent correcting what grammar has already begun. The main contribution of dialectic is its subtler inquiry into what and how words signify, a study that sheds much light on many grammatical categories and constructions. It is clearly Abelard's assumption that the two disciplines should work hand in hand, composing what would in effect be a single science of language.[5] This is illustrated in the following summary of Abelard's work on a few crucial questions.

The distinction of nouns or names (a category that includes adjectives) from verbs was as much argued over in Abelard's day as in ancient times, and it provided Abelard with an entry to matters that lie at the heart of his philosophy. He rejects Aristotle's view that verbs differ from nouns in having a consignification of time, for he sees no reason not to ascribe a similar consignification to nouns:

For just as 'run' or 'running' indicate running in connection with a person as presently inhering in him, so 'white' determines whiteness in connection with a substance as presently inhering, for it is called white only because of present whiteness.[6]

Abelard is equally unhappy with the idea that verbs, as distinct from other parts of speech, signify only actions and passions, or what might better be called 'receptions' (*passiones*, i.e. the passive correlates of actions). This view runs afoul of the copula which although accepted as a verb can be used to 'join' (*copulare*) to its subject any sort of entity whatsoever.[7]

What distinguishes verbs, in Abelard's view, is that they provide the 'completeness of sense' (*sensus perfectio*) characteristic of whole sentences (*orationes perfectae*) as distinct from mere phrases (*orationes imperfectae*). What is the difference, he asks, between 'A man runs' and 'a running man'? Of constructions such as the latter he remarks:

But a completeness of sense has not yet been brought about in them; for when this expression has been uttered the mind of the hearer is suspended and desires to hear more in order to arrive at completeness of sense, for example, 'is' or some other acceptable verb. For without a verb there is no completeness of sense.[8]

---

5. Jolivet 1969, p. 55: '... préparée par les *Gloses*, une science unifiée du langage sous-tend les traites de la Dialectique ... il a fondu en un seul corps deux arts qu'il avait reçus séparés.' Abelard did compose a grammatical treatise, but it is lost. See Van den Eynde 1962, pp. 473–6.
6. Abelard 1956, p. 122.22–5: 'Sicut enim "*curre*" vel "*currens*" cursum circa personam tamquam ei praesentialiter inhaerentem demonstrat, ita "*album*" circa substantiam albedinem tamquam praesentialiter inhaerentem determinat; non enim album nisi ex praesenti albedine dicitur.'
7. *Ibid.*, pp. 130.32–131.7.
8. *Ibid.*, p. 148.26–30: 'Sed nondum in eis completa est sensus perfectio. Adhuc enim praemissa oratione prolata suspensus audientis animus aliquid amplius audire desiderat, ut ad perfectionem

Verbs can perform this function because they propose the 'inherence' of what they signify in the subject.

Thus we see that this completeness of sense depends mainly on verbs, since only by them is inherence of something in something indicated in a manner expressive of different mental states; without this inherence there is no completeness of sense. When I say 'Come to me' or 'If only you would come to me', in a way I propound the inherence of coming to me in a manner expressive of my order or my desire; in the one case I order that coming should belong to him, in the other I have a desire, namely, that he come.[9]

The talk of 'inherence', however, must be treated delicately, for it is not Abelard's view that any verb, even the copula, signifies some relational property of inherence. Rather verbs generally signify that which 'inheres', while the copula, according to one of Abelard's accounts of it, signifies nothing at all. If any verb were to signify 'inherence', then it would be unable to perform the 'linking' function, i.e., the function of the copula, which is to 'link' what the predicate signifies to the subject. 'Runs' signifies running and 'links' it as well. The copula 'is' really expresses just this linking function implicit in all verbs; if it were to signify anything on its own it could no more take a predicate noun or adjective and link its significate to a subject than can 'runs'.[10]

This view is taken still further when Abelard separates 'to be' used as a copula from 'to be' used to mean 'to exist'. If the separation is not made we have problems with sentences such as 'Homer is a poet' and 'A chimera is conceivable', where the subjects are non-existent or even impossible. Abelard's solution is to treat the whole phrase consisting of copula plus predicate noun or adjective as a single verb-phrase and in this way eliminate any idea that 'to be' on its own is predicated of the subject.

Thus it seems to me if I may dare to speak freely, that it would be more rational and satisfying to reason that . . . we understand as a single verb 'to be a man' or 'to be white' or 'to be conceivable'. Aristotle indeed says that in 'Homer is a poet' 'to be' is predicated *per accidens*, i.e., 'to be' is predicated accidentally of Homer in that the

---

sensus perveniat, veluti "*est*", aut aliquod aliud competens verbum. Praeter verbum namque nulla est sensus perfectio.'

9. *Ibid.*, p. 149.20–6: 'Perfectio itaque sensus maxime pendere dinoscitur in verbis, quibus solis alicuius ad aliquid inhaerentia secundum varios affectus animi demonstratur; praeter quam quidem inhaerentiam orationis perfectio non subsistit. Cum enim dico: "*Veni ad me*" vel "*utinam venires ad me*", quodammodo inhaerentiam veniendi ad me propono secundum iussum meum vel desiderium meum, in eo scilicet quod iubeo illi ut venire ei cohaereat, vel desidero, idest ut ipse veniat.'

10. See Abelard 1919–27, p. 362.25–9.

poem belongs to him, but it is not predicated *per se* of Homer that he is. But since 'to be', as was said, is not a verbal unit, to be predicated *per accidens* is not to be predicated; rather 'to be' is part of the predicate.[11]

Abelard in effect wants us to treat the copula as what a modern grammarian would call an auxiliary, and indeed Abelard draws support for his view from the implausibility of dividing up *'erit sedens'* (will be sitting) into two parts, because of the conflict of tenses between auxiliary and participle.[12]

The copula, then, turns out to be a verb-phrase-maker, taking as complements nouns, participles, and whole clauses and turning them into verb-phrases. But the process should not be thought to leave the complement with the same meaning it has in isolation, for this leads to logical absurdities. As we have seen, the noun following the copula has in isolation a tense of its own (generally the present), and this can conflict with the tense of the copula. For example, 'This old man was a boy' will be necessarily false if we treat 'boy' as retaining its signification of present time, for then the sentence is equivalent to 'This old man was one of those who is presently a boy.'[13] What we must do, Abelard says, is treat the whole copula plus predicate noun as a single verb having the tense of the copula. He shows how only in this way can the rules of conversion and syllogistic inference be made to apply to sentences with verbs in tenses other than the present.[14]

Having gone this far, Abelard sees that nouns in isolation really have the same signification as verb phrases, but just lack the ability to 'link'. He puts it this way:

It seems that the signification of a substantive verb [i.e. a copula], to which time is joined as well, is associated with nouns just as it is with verbs. For just as 'runs' amounts to saying 'is running', so 'man' amounts to 'is a mortal rational animal'.[15]

---

11. Abelard 1956, p. 138.11–22: 'Unde mihi, si profiteri audeam, illud rationabilius videtur ut rationi sufficere valeamus, ut scilicet, quemadmodum oppositionem in adiecto secundum oppositionem magis quam secundum appositionem sumimus, ita accidentalem praedicationem accipiamus, ac cum dicitur: "est homo" vel "est opinabile" vel "est album" pro uno verbo "esse hominem" vel "esse album" vel "esse opinabile" intelligamus. Quod vero Aristoteles, cum dicitur: "Homerus est poeta", dicit per accidens "esse" praedicari hoc modo: "secundum accidens enim praedicatur 'esse' de Homero, quoniam inest ei poema, sed non secundum se praedicatur de Homero quoniam est", cum non sit "esse", ut dictum est, una dictio, praedicari per accidens non est praedicari, immo pars est "esse" praedicati.'

12. *Ibid.*, pp. 138.26–139.11.

13. See Abelard 1919–27, pp. 348.28–349.17.

14. See Abelard 1956, pp. 139.12–140.22.

15. *Ibid.*, p. 122.28–31 with the correction suggested by Tweedale 1976, p. 288: 'Sicut enim substantivi verbi significatio, cui quoque tempus adiunctum est, verbis adiungitur, sic et nominibus videtur. Sicut enim "currit" quantum "est currens" dicit, ita "homo" tantumdem quantum "est animal rationale mortale".'

It is not, then, that what is basic from a logical point of view is two items, the copula and the noun, and that the verb phrase which grammatically combines these is logically derivative from them. Rather the noun in isolation, or whenever it is used to denote things (i.e. *appellative*), derives its meaning from the verb phrase. What is logically basic, i.e. basic for the analysis of meaning, is the combination of copula and predicate noun considered as an indivisible unit.

Abelard is not unaware that his inquiry has led him to treat lightly many canons of the grammarians, but he urges his reader to consider dialectic the subtler discipline:

Do not recoil in horror when in order to open up the correct meanings of sentences we put together many verbs or substantives, such as 'to be a man', or verbs derived from things other than actions or passions, such as 'to be white', and thus seem to go against the rules of grammarians. For those who are in the first rank of the discipline, out of a consideration for the capacities of beginners, have left to the advanced the inquiry into and correction of many matters in which the subtlety of dialectic must be employed.[16]

Abelard's logical inquiries have led him to find an underlying similarity where the mere grammarian sees only basic divergence. The implication is that the grammarian, at least in large part, sets out on an inquiry which can really be completed only by the more difficult art of dialectic. And this in turn implies that the study of meaning, or semantics is more fundamental to the study of language than mere syntax.

On the other hand, Abelard is fond of showing how certain grammatical constructions do *not* admit of logical analysis in any straightforward way. He does this in order to correct pseudo-dialecticians who naively apply standard Aristotelian logic where it is in fact quite out of place.

A very important instance of this use of grammar concerns the notion of an 'impersonal' construction, an idea central to some of Abelard's most puzzling remarks in ontology. Impersonal constructions in grammar are sentences without any subject, such as 'It is raining' or 'It is going well'. In such cases English supplies the grammatical subject 'it', but from a logical point of view the sentence lacks a subject altogether.

This phenomenon of language encourages Abelard to treat sentences

16. *Ibid.*, p. 140.23–9: 'Quod autem grammaticorum regulis contrarii videmur, quod multa componimus verba vel substantiva, ut "esse hominem", vel ab aliis quam ab actionibus vel passionibus sumpta, ut "esse album", propter rectam enuntiationum sententiam aperiendam, non abhorreas. Illi enim qui primum disciplinae gradum tenent, pro capacitate tenerorum multa provectis inquirere aut corrigenda reliquerunt in quibus dialecticae subtilitatem opertet laborare.'

whose grammatical subjects are nominalisations of sentences or verb phrases as logically subjectless.[17] Thus modal propositions such as 'That a chimera does not exist is true' or 'It is impossible that a chimera exist' can be treated as subjectless. Consequently, Aristotelian term logic is utterly inapplicable to these sentences. Abelard says bluntly of modal words such as 'true' or 'possible':

> But where impersonal nouns are predicated impersonally no conversion is admitted ... and neither can they properly be called universals when they do not cover anything personally [i.e. do not denote]. Nor can they be used universally or particularly ...[18]

For the moment it suffices to note that in these cases Abelard does not find the grammatical fact of impersonality just another occasion on which dialectic can correct the grammarian. Rather he turns this point of grammar into a weapon against a pseudo-dialectic that feels impelled to confine all of language to the standard term logic that the *logica vetus* took over from Aristotle.

Pure dialectic

The conception of dialectic and grammar as overlapping in interests would be difficult if not impossible had Abelard not taken words to be the subject matter of logic. But Abelard is very aware that this approach, one shared by most of his immediate precursors, is easily misunderstood. He reminds us that words are of interest to the logician because they signify, not because of their physical characteristics. Dialectic is not interested in phonology. And yet Abelard does not allow this obvious point to draw him into postulating words (*sermones*) as an entirely separate class of things from physical vocal utterances (*voces*).

The problem is to allow that the logician uses many predicates such as 'is a universal' or 'is a genus' which apply only to words and not to utterances, while maintaining that words and utterances are the same things. In *Logica 'Nostrorum petitioni sociorum'*[19] Abelard tentatively suggests a solution. It requires treating these predicates of logic much like the predicate 'was made by Socrates', which could be true of a statue but not of a piece of

---

17. See Abelard 1919–27, p. 361.26–36. Also discussion in Tweedale 1976, pp. 244–72.
18. Minio-Paluello 1956–8, II, p. 19.17–21: 'At vero, ubi inpersonalia nomina predicantur inpersonaliter, nulla (ut dictum est) conversio fit, nec ipsa, (cum aliquid personaliter non contineant), universalia proprie dici possunt, nec universaliter nec particulariter proferri possunt, sed semper ad infinitivum modum construuntur.'
19. See Abelard 1919–27, pp. 522.10–524.24. Also discussion in Tweedale 1976, pp. 142–62.

stone even when the statue is the piece of stone. This can happen because 'This statue was made by Socrates' really means 'This statue was made by Socrates *to be a statue*', and likewise 'This piece of stone was made by Socrates' means 'This piece of stone was made by Socrates *to be a piece of stone*'.[20] Now, the predicates of logic, e.g. 'is a universal', can similarly be affected by their subjects, if we allow that they implicitly assert of something that it is made or 'established' by the conventions of language. Then since a word is made to be a word by linguistic conventions but an utterance is not made to be an utterance by linguistic conventions (it is an utterance by nature), we can explain why words but not utterances are universals, although words and utterances are not different things.

When we turn to the meanings of words, we find that in the case of nouns Abelard distinguishes *significatio* (signification) from *appellatio* (denoting) or *nominatio* (naming). A noun *appellat* or *nominat* the things a modern logician would say it denotes or is true of, while it signifies (*significat*) some property belonging to whatever it denotes. Abelard is keen to distinguish denotative from non-denotative uses of nouns. The former, it seems, can be replaced by an indefinite pronoun plus relative clause without changing the meaning of the whole sentence.[21] For example, 'A boy is running' means 'Something which is a boy is running'. Furthermore, in this latter sentence the occurrence of 'a boy' is *not* denotative since, according to Abelard, no predicate noun is denotative. His reasons here are closely allied to his arguments for treating copula plus predicate noun as a single verb.[22] If 'a boy' in 'This old man was a boy' were denotative, the whole sentence would mean 'This old man was something which is a boy' and would consequently be absurd. We see then that Abelard has provided himself with a way of replacing all denotative occurrences of nouns with quantifier pronouns, such as 'something' or 'anything', accompanied by a relative clause with a verb constructed from the copula plus the noun in question used non-denotatively, as when 'something which is a boy' was substituted above for 'a boy'.

This idea is closely related to a remark Abelard makes about 'is' or 'exists' (i.e., '*est*') in his *Theologia Christiana*. What he proposes there is that we *not* treat it as a predicate taking a denotative noun as subject. For example, in the sentence 'A father exists' we are not saying 'Something which is a father

20. See the account of Abelard's view in *Introductiones Montane minores* as edited in De Rijk 1962–7, II(2), pp. 15–16.
21. See Tweedale 1976, pp. 166–9.
22. See nn. 13 and 14 above.

exists' but simply 'Something is a father'. In other words, 'exists' disappears as a predicate on its own to be replaced by a quantifier plus a verb constructed from a copula plus the noun which was the subject in the original.[23] Abelard is innovating here, and he has moved very far in the direction of letting quantificational pronouns operating on verbs carry the burden of both reference and existential import, a move whose full possibilities were not realised until Frege formulated it mathematically in the nineteenth century.

Central to dialectic is the notion of validity as applied to arguments and inferences. Abelard says of inference that it 'consists in a necessity of entailment – namely, in the fact that the meaning of the consequent is demanded by the sense of the antecedent.'[24] The antecedent and consequent must be so related that: 'It cannot happen that it is as the first says but it is not as the second says.'[25] In other words, the truth of the antecedent requires the truth of the consequent. Abelard asks on what this 'necessity of entailment' rests. Obviously it is dependent not on the physical character of the sentences as utterances but on their meanings. Abelard rejects the view which would treat psychological realities, i.e. thoughts (*intellectus*), as meanings, and then claim the entailment here is one between these thoughts. The thought expressed by the antecedent, he says, can exist entirely without that expressed by the consequent.[26] Nor is it possible, on his view, to see the entailment as one between extra-mental things, for then there would be no entailment when the things in question were non-existent. But there can be true conditionals (or consequences: *consequentiae*) about the non-existent:

For example, since we admit that the consequence 'If there is a rose, there is a flower' is always true and necessary, even when the things are destroyed, we have to see why the signification is judged to be necessary. None of the necessity is in the things, however, since even when they have been completely destroyed, that which is said by the consequence – i.e., that if this is that is – is no less necessary.[27]

23. See *Theologia Christiana* (PL vol. 178), 1312D–1313B; Abelard 1956, pp. 132.36–133.23; and Tweedale 1976, pp. 195–9.
24. Abelard 1956, p. 253.28–9: 'Inferentia itaque in necessitate consecutionis consistit, in eo scilicet quod ex sensu antecedentis sententia exigitur consequentis...' See discussion in Jolivet 1969, pp. 148–66.
25. Abelard 1919–27, p. 367.8–9: 'Sed non potest contingere ita ut prior dicit quin sit ita ut dicit posterior.'
26. See Abelard 1956, p. 154.30–8.
27. Abelard 1919–27, p. 366.6–12: '... veluti cum istam consequentiam "Si est rosa, est flos", veram semper etiam destructis rebus et necessariam concedamus, oportet videri, pro quo significatio necessaria iudicetur. At vero in rebus nihil est necessitatis, quibus etiam omnino destructis non minus necessarium est, quod a consequentia dicitur, id est, si hoc est, illud esse.'

Rather it is from what the sentences say, their *dicta*, that we judge whether or not the necessity of connection is present. But these *dicta*, or significates of propositions, are neither mental nor extra-mental things.

Abelard is very aware that the necessity of entailment may arise from the very form of the sentences involved, as with standard syllogisms.[28] On the other hand, this necessity may rest on the significates of the terms, as in the inference 'This is a man, therefore it is an animal.' These latter give rise to the doctrine of *loci* (topics) and the development of certain rules, *maximae*, that express the principles involved.[29] For example, the cited consequence holds because whatever a species is predicable of, the genus of that species is also predicable of.

In general Abelard will not allow that affirmative categorical propositions can be necessarily true, for their truth requires that the subject term denote some existent thing, but all things other than God have a contingent existence. Natural science, of course, asserts many categorical propositions which must be true as long as there do exist the things it is talking about, but this qualified necessity always rests on a 'law of nature' (*lex naturae*), i.e. a hypothetical that expresses a necessity of entailment. 'A man is an animal' must be true as long as there are men, and this conditional necessity depends on the 'law of nature' that the nature of man cannot exist without the nature of animal being in it,[30] i.e., the law that finds expression in 'If there is a man, there is an animal.' Science, for Abelard, is the search for these necessary entailments holding between the natures of the things that actually exist.

These entailments, or their absence, also determine the truth of modal propositions – i.e., those that use the terms 'necessary', 'possible', 'impossible', or expressions equivalent to these. Here Abelard nicely distinguishes two senses of modal propositions, one *per divisionem* and one *per compositionem*.[31] If we say it is possible for one standing to be sitting, we may mean to attribute, so to speak, possible truth to the proposition 'One standing is sitting', and the result is absurd since that proposition cannot be true. This is the sense *per compositionem* or *de sensu propositionis*. On the other hand we may mean to attribute to someone standing the possibility of sitting, and then the assertion is very likely true. This is the sense *per*

28. See Abelard 1956, p. 256.20–4.
29. See Jolivet 1969, pp. 153–68, and Bird 1959.
30. See Abelard 1956, p. 280.12–4.
31. See Minio-Paluello 1956–8, II, pp. 13.15–14.4. Abelard says he draws the distinction from Aristotle's *Sophistici elenchi* (165ᵇ26, 166ᵃ23–8); which shows he had some acquaintance with at least that portion of the *logica nova*.

divisionem or *de re*. Under this latter interpretation Abelard can treat the
modal proposition as really categorical with a modal predicate, and all the
rules of Aristotelian term-logic apply. But when the modal proposition is
interpreted *de sensu propositionis*, Abelard prefers *not* to treat the nominalisation of the sentence as a logical subject naming something of which a
modal property is predicated. Consequently it falls totally outside the
categories of Aristotelian term-logic,[32] and is, as noted above, to be treated
as impersonal, i.e., subjectless.

The psychology of signification

Abelard seems to take the view that the basic role of language is to express
overtly certain activities of the mind of the speaker which are prior to and
independent of language itself.[33] But while allowing that language makes
thoughts overt, Abelard is very keen to deny that language is used solely or
even primarily to *describe* thoughts. Words are not used, except when we
do psychology, to talk about the thoughts themselves; rather they are used
to talk about the same things the thoughts are about. In the following
passage Abelard talks of words signifying both ideas and things, but it is
clear that this amounts to noting two quite different kinds of signifying.

For just as nouns and verbs have two significations, one of a thing, another of an
idea, so also the propositions which are made out of them draw from them two
significations, one of ideas, the other of things. Like nouns and verbs, propositions
also deal with things, and like them they generate certain ideas. When we say, 'A
man runs', we deal with the very things, a man and running, and we join running
to a man; we do not link the ideas of them to each other. We are not saying
anything about ideas; we simply put them in the mind of the hearer while dealing
solely with things.[34]

Words signify ideas in the sense that they produce them in the minds of
hearers; they signify things in that they are used to talk about them.

It is easy to misunderstand Abelard here as saying that for each word
there is some thing it signifies. But that interpretation directly contradicts
what he says about how universals, i.e. common nouns, signify.

---

32. Minio-Paluello 1956–8, II, p. 14.14–7.
33. He even says that in some cases 'the soul grasps an idea better than language can express it'. See
    Abelard 1956, pp. 118.29–119.2.
34. *Ibid.*, p. 154.20–9: 'Sicut enim nominum et verborum duplex ad rem et ad intellectum signi-
    ficatio, ita etiam propositiones quae ex ipsis componuntur, duplicem ex ipsis significationem
    contrahunt, unam quidem de intellectibus, aliam vero de rebus. De rebus enim, sicut illa,
    propositiones quoque agunt ac de ipsis quoque, sicut illa, quosdam intellectus generant. Cum
    enim dicimus: "homo currit", de homine ac cursu rebus ipsis agimus cursumque homini
    coniungimus, non intellectus eorum ad invicem copulamus; nec quicquam de intellectibus
    dicimus, sed de rebus solis agentes eos in animo audientis constituimus.'

In a common noun such as 'man' neither Socrates nor some other man nor the whole collection of men is rationally understood via the force of the utterance .... Thus it seems that neither 'man' nor any other universal word signifies anything, since there is no thing the idea of which it introduces.[35]

This leads directly to one formulation of the problem of universals: what is the idea expressed by a universal noun an idea of? Abelard notes the close association of ideas with mental images or likenesses made up in our imaginations. It is clear he does not identify the idea, which is an act of thinking of something, with its associated image, for there can be ideas without images,[36] and in any event the image is not a thing at all, not even a mental thing, whereas an idea clearly is.[37] Might it be, though, that the image is what the idea is an idea of? Certainly Abelard says the idea 'grasps' (*concipit*) an image,[38] but in the end it is clear that his view is more subtle than this, for he allows that ideas of different things might be associated with the same image:

With one and the same image before the mind's eye I can consider both the nature of quality and the nature of whiteness. Although the image is the same, there are many ways of conceiving it, as, for example, when I consider it at one time as being a quality and at another as being white. Thus the force of an idea does not consist in that mode of signifying which even the beasts bring about with images; rather it consists in the distinction of attention, which pertains only to reason and which the beasts lack entirely.[39]

Human reason uses images to think of any of the characteristics they exhibit, and indeed it is this ability to vary what the mind is attending to without necessarily changing the contents of the imagination that Abelard thinks distinguishes human from sub-human intelligence.

Must we then say that the things we have ideas of are these natures or properties Abelard speaks of? We shall see in the next section that this too is a partial misunderstanding of his view. Here we may simply note that in

35. Abelard 1919–27, pp. 18.23–19.6: 'In nomine vero communi, quod "homo" est, nec ipse Socrates nec alius nec tota hominum collectio rationabiliter ex vi vocis intelligitur nec etiam in quantum homo est, ipse Socrates per hoc nomen, ut quidam volunt, certificatur ... Nullum itaque significare videtur vel "homo" vel aliud universale vocabulum, cum de nulla re constituat intellectum.'
36. *Ibid.*, p. 21.18–22.
37. *Ibid.*, pp. 314.25–315.17.
38. *Ibid.*, p. 21.27–36.
39. *Ibid.*, p. 329.14–22: 'Similiter eadem imagine ante mentis oculos constituta in ipsa et qualitatis et albedinis naturam considero et licet sit eadem imago, plures sunt de ea concipiendi modi, quod modo in eo quod qualitas est, modo in eo quod est album. Vis itaque intellectus non in modo significandi consistit, quod et bestiae faciunt per imaginem, sed in discretione attendendi, quod ad rationem solum pertinet, cuius omnino bestiae expertes sunt.'

Logica 'Nostrorum petitioni sociorum' Abelard suggests that the whole search
for things our ideas are of is misguided. There he compares the question
'What are you thinking of?' with 'What do you want?', in order to note
that just as 'I want a hood' does not entail that there is some hood I want, so
'I am thinking of a man' may not entail there is some man I am thinking
of.[40] The careful logician, then, can note that some nouns serving as direct
objects of verbs of mental attitude are non-denoting, i.e. not logical objects
at all. He can then allow that an idea is of something while denying that
there is something which it is an idea of. Basically it is the same point
Abelard made about impersonal sentences, only where they were subjectless these are objectless.

Ontology

What most associate Abelard with nominalists of the later Middle Ages
such as Ockham, and even of our own time, such as N. Goodman and
W. V. O. Quine, are his incessant efforts to show that dialectic and the *artes
sermocinales* in general can be developed without their requiring us to
believe in the existence of things other than those more or less ordinary
ones described by *physica*. This comes out most clearly in his lengthy
remarks on *status* and *dicta*, i.e. the significates of verb phrases (and hence of
nouns, see above) and sentences respectively. Two similar passages establish this line of approach clearly enough:

But it seems absurd for us to understand the agreement of things in such a way that
it is not some thing, as though we were uniting in nothing things which exist when
we say that they agree in the *status* of man, that is in this: that they are men. But we
mean merely that they are men and do not differ at all in this regard, i.e. not in as
much as they are men, although we call on no essence.[41] We call the *status* of man
his being a man, which is not a thing. We also say that this is the common cause of
the application of the noun to singulars in as much as they agree with each other.[42]
But it is objected: Since the *dicta* of propositions are nothing, how is it that
propositions happen to be true on account of them, for how can that be called a
cause which is completely nothing and which cannot be? But a man is hanged on

---

40. Abelard 1919–27, pp. 532.30–533.9.
41. 'Essence' (= *essentia*) has for Abelard, in contrast to later scholastics influenced by Avicenna, the
same meaning as 'thing' (= *res*).
42. Abelard 1919–27, p. 20.1–9: 'Abhorrendum autem videtur, quod convenientiam rerum
secundum id accipiamus, quod non est res aliqua, tamquam in nihilo ea quae sunt, uniamus, cum
scilicet hunc et illum in statu hominis, id est in eo quod sunt homines convenire dicimus. Sed nihil
aliud sentimus, nisi eos homines esse, et secundum hoc nullatenus differre, secundum hoc,
inquam, quod homines sunt, licet ad nullam vocemus essentiam. Statum autem hominis ipsum
esse hominem, quod non est res, vocamus quod etiam diximus communem causam impositionis
nominis ad singulos, secundum quod ipsi ad invicem conveniunt.'

account of a theft he performed which is now nothing; and a man dies because he does not eat and is damned because he does not act rightly, yet not eating and not acting rightly are not things.[43]

This 'dereification'[44] of *status* and *dicta* is not to be confused with treating them either as unreal or subjective. This emerges most clearly in Abelard's ill-received effort to explain the doctrine of the Holy Trinity. Here he says we should treat the distinction of the Father, Son, and Holy Spirit not as a difference *in essentia*, i.e. as among three distinct things, but as a difference of three properties or *status*.[45]

The Persons, i.e. the Father, Son, and Holy Spirit, are different from each other in something like the way that things different by definition or property are different, i.e., although the very same essence which is God the Son is God the Father or God the Holy Spirit, nevertheless the property distinctive of God the Father inasmuch as He is the Father is other than that distinctive of the Son and that distinctive of the Holy Spirit.[46]

Abelard certainly did not want either to deny the objective reality of the divine persons or treat those persons as some sort of 'forms' existing in God yet distinct in essence from him. Both he considered obvious heresies. The latter in particular destroys the divine simplicity:

For if the paternity which is in God is an essence other than God, is it not true that God the Father consists of two things, i.e. of God and paternity, and that He relates as a whole to these two from which He is made up?[47]

Various lines of thought reviewed in the preceding sections meet when Abelard tries to disentangle logic from its supposed ontological implications. We recall that verbs must signify in such a way that the whole sentence *says* something, rather than just being a name of something. But

---

43. *Ibid.*, pp. 368.40–369.6: 'Sed opponitur, cum dicta propositionum nil sint, quomodo propter ea contingat propositiones esse veras, quia haec quae nil omnino sunt vel esse possunt, quomodo dici causa possunt? Sed propter patratum furtum homo suspenditur, quod tamen furtum iam nil est, et moritur homo quid non comedit, et damnatur quia non bene agit. Non comedere tamen vel non bene agere non sunt essentiae aliquae.'
44. I have taken this term from Jolivet 1969, p. 355.
45. See Jolivet 1969, pp. 286–96.
46. *Theologia Christiana* (PL, vol. 178), 1253D–1254A: 'Sunt autem ab invicem diversae personae, id est Pater, et Filius, et Spiritus Sanctus ad similitudinem eorum quae diffinitione diversa sunt seu proprietate, eo videlicet quod quamvis eadem penitus essentia sit Deus Pater quae est Deus Filius, seu Deus Spiritus Sanctus, aliud tamen proprium est Dei Patris, in eo scilicet quod Pater est, et aliud Filii et aliud Spiritus Sancti.'
47. *Ibid.*, 1255B: 'Nunquid enim si paternitas, quae inest Deo, alia essentia sit ab ipso Deo, verum est Deum Patrem ex duobus consistere, hoc est ex Deo et paternitate, ipsumque esse totum ad haec duo ex quibus consistit?'

this is just what prevents the verb from being itself a name and signifying some thing as does a name. Also, common nouns really have the same signification as verbs, so they too are not to be conceived as signifying by naming what they signify. And whole sentences, of course, do not signify by naming either, because they contain the verb which imports the force of saying. Where we do have apparent names of what verbs and sentences signify, as with nominalisations, we can treat these as 'impersonal' and the sentences in which they appear as 'subjectless'. And just as we find no necessity either in ordinary discourse or in logic to employ names of what verbs and sentences signify, so in talking of the objects of thought (i.e. what our ideas are ideas of) we discover that there is no need to treat psychological discourse as containing names of things which are these objects. In the end all uses of noun phrases apparently denoting these *status* and *dicta* can be seen as non-denoting occurrences of nouns, or as parts of sentences whose assertion is quite unnecessary to any legitimate inquiry.[48]

Further we see that the 'necessity of entailment' which Abelard claims is involved in all valid inference and in the 'laws of nature' on which science relies, really concerns connections between these natures or *status* and the *dicta* of whole propositions. If we were to treat the *status* and *dicta* as things, they would be the eternal, necessary realities beloved by all Platonists, which provide whatever intelligibility the world may have. Abelard is not entirely repelled by such a vision.[49] He takes note of Priscian's view that the world is constructed on the basis of forms in the mind of God, and these forms are what we think of and what our words signify, albeit in a very confused fashion. Certainly Abelard is quite willing to acknowledge that we do not have correct conceptions of the very natures our ideas are of.[50] But in the end he avoids any commitment to this sort of realism. It was left to logicians at Melun, a school where Abelard had taught, to carry the master's ideas in this Platonist direction.[51]

Abelard's program of 'dereification' is directly connected with his effort to unify grammar and dialectic in such a way that while the latter elucidates at a deeper level much of what the former treats, grammar forces dialectic out of a simplistic reliance on Aristotle's term-logic as it is handed down by the *logica vetus*. Abelard had rethought the contents of the *logica vetus*, and in his analyses he frequently moved far beyond anything that

48. See Tweedale 1976, pp. 273–8.
49. See Jolivet 1969, p. 353, where Abelard is described as a sort of Platonist.
50. See Abelard 1919–27, p. 23.18–24.
51. See excerpts from the *Ars Meliduna*, in De Rijk 1962–7, II(1), pp. 264–390.

could be extracted from that limited heritage. Yet his style is often tentative, rarely claiming to say the last word and frequently inviting further reflection. His work should have formed the basis of a highly original development of the *artes sermocinales* and of philosophy in general in Western Europe. But this was not to be. Partly because of Abelard's poor reputation with the church authorities, but mostly because of the influx of hitherto unavailable works by Aristotle and his Islamic commentators, Abelard's work was to be largely ignored in favour of the more comprehensive and systematic philosophy these new texts provided.

IV
LOGIC IN THE
HIGH MIDDLE AGES: SEMANTIC
THEORY

7
THE ORIGINS OF THE
THEORY OF
THE PROPERTIES OF TERMS

Language, thought, and reality

Beginning as early as the eleventh century, the relationship between thought and language was a focal point of medieval thought. This does not amount to saying that the basic nature of that relationship was being studied; rather it was accepted without discussion, as it had been in antiquity. Thought was considered to be linguistically constrained by its very nature; thought and language were taken to be related both to each other and to reality in their elements and their structure. In the final analysis, language, thought, and reality were considered to be of the same logical coherence. Language was taken to be not only an instrument of thought, expression, and communication but also in itself an important source of information regarding the nature of reality. In medieval thought, logico-semantic and metaphysical points of view are, as a result of their perceived interdependence, entirely interwoven.

The first medieval scholars to have a professional interest in language as such were the grammarians. Their interest was focused on what we would call logico-semantical and syntactical questions; this is especially true of the School of Chartres as early as the 1030s. No longer were words studied as separate units quite apart from their linguistic context; rather it was that context itself that attracted the most intense interest. I have labelled this concentration of attention the 'contextual approach' (De Rijk 1967, pp. 113–17; 123–5). The statement (*propositio*), not isolated words, was taken to be the fundamental unit of meaning. The meaning of a word in its actual use in a propositional context was considered so important, indeed, as to lead to the introduction of a special terminology, centred around terms (i.e., words as parts of actual propositions) and their properties.

The development of the doctrine of the properties of terms was in fact nothing but the growing dominance of just one of the properties of terms, *suppositio*, i.e., actually 'standing for'. On the other hand, throughout that development, there remained some basic presuppositions which not only established the framework of the development but were, unfortunately, to determine later developments as well. Among them the most obstinate was the doctrine of *significatio*.

Signification and the contextual approach

In spite of the fact that the medieval logicians were aware that the actual context in which a term occurs is of paramount importance to its actual meaning, and that, accordingly, in investigating the meaning(s) of a term they practiced the contextual approach, all their investigations kept on being mortgaged by the ineradicable doctrine of *significatio* as upheld in ancient and medieval philosophy. This doctrine may be best expressed this way: a word's actual meaning (its meaning on a particular occasion of its use) ultimately is, or can be reduced to, its fundamental 'significance' (*significatio*), which as the word's natural property constitutes its essence or form (*essentia, forma*), in virtue of which it is at the root of every actual meaning of that word.

If we distinguish the contextual approach and the basic doctrine of signification as the two focal points of the theory of the properties of terms, the different aspects of the theory seem to be in close correspondence with the preponderance either of the contextual approach or of the doctrine of signification.

Medieval logicians regularly classified meaningful words into such as have meaning in their own right (*termini significativi* or *significantes*) and such as are meaningful only when joined to words of the first kind (*termini consignificativi* or *consignificantes*). The former are also called categorematic terms (*termini categorematici* or *categoremata*), the latter, syncategorematic terms (*termini syncategorematici* or *syncategoremata*). The quasi-physical character ascribed to those words by medieval logicians clearly appears from a thirteenth-century treatise (called *Syncategoreumata*) by master Nicholas (of Paris?), which opens as follows:

As the Philosopher remarks, the things that belong to art and reason are considered in relation to and in imitation of things that belong to nature. Now as regards natural things, we see that there are some that are naturally suited to accomplish something without the assistance of anything else, but others that are not suited to move unless they have been moved ... The situation is similar as regards things belonging to reason, especially as regards words, because some perform their function – i.e. they signify – without the aid of anything else ..., and words of that sort are called *categoremata* – i.e. significant. There are others that are not significant in themselves, but in conjunction with the others, and those are called *syncategoremata*.[1]

The syncategorematic words are dealt with elsewhere in this volume. Here the categorematic words are under discussion, the only words that have meaning in the strict sense (*significatio*).

Medieval semantics is focused on the meaning of the noun (*nomen*). The function or property of the noun is commonly defined in the Middle Ages (following Priscian) as signifying substance (*substantia*) together with quality (*qualitas*).[2] *Substantia*, according to the medieval interpretation, is nothing but the individual thing, and the *qualitas* meant here is the universal nature in which the particular thing participates. The anonymous author of the grammatical gloss *Promisimus* (not later than the last quarter of the twelfth century) explicitly says that, seeing that all things have existence in common, the older grammarians (*antiqui*) used '*substantia*' as a word with which to speak about things generally. So to be a *substantia* is to have the property of being subsistent (*proprietas subsistendi*), to be that which receives a thing's essential, specific nature (*quod suscipit formam*). The same author explains *qualitas* as the property which is designated by a common or appellative noun such as 'man' or the one designated by a proper noun such as 'John'.[3] An anonymous commentary on Priscian dating from about the same time says that to signify the *qualitas* is to designate to what class of things something belongs or of what nature a thing is.[4] Indeed, the prevailing view in twelfth- and thirteenth-century grammar and logic is that a *substantia* is an individual and *qualitas* its nature, picking out the class of things to which the individual belongs. As early as the second half of the twelfth century *substantia* is further identified with the subject of discourse (*id de quo sermo habetur*). In the *Quaestiones Victorinae*

---

1. 'Ut dicit Philosophus [*Physics* II, 2; 194a 21–27], ea que sunt in arte et ratione sumuntur ad proportionem et imitationem eorum que sunt in natura. In naturalibus vero ita videmus quod sunt quedam que per naturam nata sunt in se aliquid agere sine alieno suffragio, alia vero sunt que non sunt nata movere nisi mota, sicut homo a se motus et non ab alio protrahit litteras, calamus vero non a se sed ab homine motus. Similiter se habet in rebus rationis, maxime in vocibus, quod quedam faciunt id ad quod sunt sine auxilio alterius, scilicet significant, quia omnis vox est ad significandum, quoniam, ut dicit Aristotiles [*De interpretatione* 1; 16a 3–4], voces sunt notae earum que sunt in anima passionum, idest significant intellectus, qui sunt signa rerum; et ita voces significant res; et tales voces dicuntur *categoreumata*, idest: *significantes*; alie sunt que per se non significant sed in coniunctione ad alias; et tales dicuntur *sincategoreumata*' (Braakhuis 1979, 1.2–15).
2. Priscian 1855, II, 18, 55.6: 'proprium est nominis significare substantiam cum qualitate'.
3. MS Oxford, Bodleian, Laud Lat. 67, f. 49vb.
4. MS Vienna, *V. P. L.* 2486, f. 24vb: '... de quo genere rerum aliquid sit vel de qua manerie'.

(presumably written in the school of William of Champeaux) an interesting note is found on the signification of a noun. The author paraphrases Priscian's definition of the noun ('The noun signifies substance together with quality'), that is, supposits (*supponit*) a thing together with the thing's *status*, the latter term being in common use to designate a thing's universal nature. So we find as early as the twelfth century '*supponere*' (to supposit) as an equivalent for '*significare substantiam*', i.e. to signify the individual thing.[5]

Signification, univocation, and appellation

As we have seen, signification was taken by medieval logicians to be a word's natural property, the formal constituent of every kind of meaning. From the viewpoint of the interpreter of the word, it is the presentation of some universal nature to the mind, to use William of Sherwood's definition.[6] A word's signification depends on its imposition (*impositio*), that is, the word's original application. A single imposition implies a single signification. Whenever a word is used two or more times with the same signification (that is, signifying the same universal nature), the use is called univocation and the word is called univocal. (A univocal word is contrasted with an equivocal word, one that has had more than one imposition and so has different significations on different occasions of its use.) But although a univocal word retains a single signification, it stands for different things when used in different propositions. That is, appellative nouns such as 'man' or 'horse' used univocally may stand for different things. This standing for ('suppositing for') is taken to be the result of different *nominationes* or *appellationes*. Consequently, a fundamental distinction between signification and appellation arose as early as the first half of the twelfth century. Indeed, when appellative nouns are used in a proposition, they sometimes stand for the universal nature (as in 'Man is a species'), and sometimes for themselves (as in 'Man is a noun'); more importantly, their actual meanings are specified by the tenses of the verbs of the propositions of which they are subject terms. In this context appellation is taken to be the reference of the noun to some existent particular thing or things, regardless of whether it or they exist in the present or in the past or in the future.

When taken in its primary sense, however, the notion of appellation is

5. De Rijk 1962–7, II(1), pp. 261–2 and 242; II(2), p. 739. 31 ff.
6. William of Sherwood 1937, p. 74. 16–17.

always connected with the present tense of the substantive verb '*est*' ('is') or some other word implicitly containing it. So we find appellation defined by William of Sherwood as 'the present correct application of a term'.[7] But an appellation may be 'ampliated' or 'restricted' within the proposition for some reason, e.g., because of the past or future tense of the verb of that proposition, or as a result of the use of such words as '*potest*' ('can') which ampliate the appellation to include merely possible individuals. The notion of appellation certainly derives from the grammatical term '*nomen appellativum*' (appellative noun). The anonymous *Fallacie Parvipontane* says that the appellative noun was invented in order to bring together all the things denoted by it (its *appellata*) under one and the same name.[8] However, which *appellata* are actually referred to in a proposition depends upon the verb of that proposition.

So the first stage of the development of the theory of the properties of terms is characterised by the central position of appellation, not supposition, as was to be the case in later stages. During this first period the word '*suppositio*' is found principally as an equivalent for *subiectio* ('putting as a grammatical subject'). Likewise the word '*suppositum*' does not yet mean the thing supposited for (or referred to) but primarily means the grammatical subject of the proposition, as may appear from such phrases as '*res designata per suppositum*' (the thing designated by the *suppositum*).[9]

At this stage univocation is regularly defined as 'the altered appellation of a name' (*variata nominis appellatio*) rather than as 'the altered supposition'.[10] Another striking fact is that ampliation and restriction are of appellations, not of suppositions, as became standard in the fully developed form of the theory of the properties of terms. Appellation seems to have primacy even over signification. So in the two 'modern views' mentioned by the anonymous author of the *Ars Meliduna*, a work on logic of the utmost importance dating from about the middle of the twelfth century, appellation turns out to play the central role. The first view holds that the appellative noun 'appellates' (*appellat*) each thing comprehended under it but signifies (*significat*) it only in an indeterminate way; thus the word 'man' signifies the species (universal nature) *man* indeterminately, not as *this* or *that* man, and it may appellate a man who actually exists as well as one who does not exist. The other view is closely connected with the *status*-

7. William of Sherwood 1937, p. 74. 26–8.
8. De Rijk 1962–67, I, p. 563. 27–8.
9. *Fallacie Parvipontane* in De Rijk 1962–67, I, p. 566. 36.
10. E.g., *Tractatus de univocatione Monacensis* in De Rijk 1962–7, II(2), p. 337. 4–7.

doctrine concerning universals, which was prominent as early as in the days of Peter Abelard: all appellative nouns 'signify' either a common or a proper *status*. Again, not a single word about supposition.[11]

The introduction of supposition

The second stage of the development of the theory is characterised by the fact that the notion of the significative use of the appellative noun was supplemented without losing its pre-eminence. To catch the non-significative uses of nouns, too, (such as are found in 'man is a noun' or 'man is a species') the appellation theory had to be extended into a more general theory of the use of a noun as the subject term in a proposition. Thus arose a general theory of the properties of terms in which all the uses of terms in propositions were brought under the general viewpoint of *suppositio* (or *subiectio*), i.e., the way in which a word is put as the subject of a proposition, and, accordingly, as the subject of discourse (*id de quo sermo fit*). Although at this stage the different kinds of supposition do not yet appear under their later technical labels, the first beginnings of the technical terminology can already be found.

The climax of the development

The third stage of the development shows the theory of the properties of terms clearly focused on the notion of supposition, while the notions of the other, already recognised properties of terms (*appellatio, ampliatio, restrictio*) are subordinated to it. All the uses of a term in a proposition are covered by the doctrine of supposition, and the different kinds of supposition have received their own technical labels. Some authors of logical treatises (e.g., the anonymous author of the *Introductiones Parisienses*) attribute supposition to both the subject and the predicate term.[12]

The contextual approach plays a most fundamental role in all three stages of the development, sometimes to such an extent that it is no longer the appellative noun but the '*terminus*' (defined as a part of speech which may be used as the subject term or the predicate term of a proposition) that has become the special linguistic element in the focus of the theory. Accordingly, it is commonly spoken of as a theory of the properties of *terms* (rather than of appellative nouns or words).

---

11. *Ars Meliduna* in De Rijk 1962–7, II(1), p. 537.
12. In De Rijk 1962–7, II(2), 372. 15–24.

The pre-eminence of reference over signification

From the preceding sketch of the development of the theory of the properties of terms it will be apparent that both in the earliest stage, where appellation was the prevailing notion, and in the later stages a term's actual meaning was the focus of interest and reference or denotation was far more important than the more abstract notion of signification. What is primarily meant by a term is the concrete individual objects the term can be correctly applied to; that the term may also be taken to mean what those things have in common is of interest in a secondary way only.

I offer just two examples of this situation. First, the *Tractatus Anagnini* holds that the signification of a noun is its *propria confusio*, that is, the wide and often vague meaning proper to a word, by means of which the whole range of individuals covered by that word is designated.[13] Secondly, as has already been remarked, the *Ars Meliduna* mentions the view that an appellative noun appellates concrete individual things, but presents its significate only in an indeterminate way. So the species (universal nature) *man* that is the significate of the word 'man' is taken to be presented by the word in a way that involves no existential commitment (*nullam recipiunt relationem pertinentem ad essentiam*).[14]

No doubt the impulse to this development of the theory came from the practice of dialectical disputation. It is not surprising at all that many a treatise begins its exposition by stressing the basic importance of the theory of meaning for logical dispute. The grammatical-logical subject of a proposition (*id de quo*, that about which) is, at the same time, the subject matter of discussion or disputation (*id de quo sermo fit*, that which the talk is about), and, furthermore, 'that for which speech is true' (*id pro quo vera est locutio*). From this time onwards '*supponere pro*' has the broad sense of 'stand for'.

The persistent importance of the doctrine of signification

What has been said above about the preponderance of the contextual approach over the doctrine of signification is, however, only one side of the development of the theory of the properties of terms. As a matter of fact, throughout the whole of the Middle Ages the theory betrayed a radical inconsistency, which can probably be best characterised as a persistent

13. In De Rijk 1962–7, II(2), 274. 26–9.
14. De Rijk, 1962–7, II(1), p. 295.

hesitation of medieval logicians between the domains of connotation (universals) and denotation (individuals). We have seen that they were committed to the individual thing as that which is primarily meant by a term; we shall now see how important a role was assigned to signification by some authors, especially those who were somehow influenced by Neoplatonic views.

William of Conches gives as his view of the meaning of substantive nouns that they do not signify *substantia* and *qualitas*, as Priscian had thought,[15] but only that which is intelligible, the universal nature (*intelligibile*), not this or that existing thing (*actuale*). For it is the specific function of the intellect to signify things as universal natures: 'We say that it signifies the species and not the individual, for it signifies man in such a way as not to signify any [particular man], and man understood in this way is the species and not the individual.' Therefore he accepts all such phrases as 'signifies substance', 'signifies quality', 'signifies that which is intelligible', and 'signifies species' as if they meant the same. The picking out of extra-mental individual things he assigns to 'nomination' or 'appellation'.[16]

This aspect of the theory of the properties of terms may be clarified by the history of one specific type of supposition, viz. natural supposition (*suppositio naturalis*).

Signification and natural supposition

For Peter of Spain natural supposition is the acceptance of a common substantival term for all those individuals that are of such a nature as to participate in the universal form signified by it. So the term 'man' when it is taken by itself (*per se sumptus*) naturally supposits for all men, those who exist, those who have existed, and those who (possibly) will exist.[17]

Accidental supposition, the complement of natural supposition, is the acceptance of the same common term for only those individuals determined by what is adjoined to the term. So in the proposition 'man is' (*homo est*) the term 'man' accidentally supposits for (denotes) all men who exist at the present time (at the time of speaking), whereas in 'man has been' (*homo fuit*) it accidentally supposits for all men who have existed in the past, and in 'man will be' (*homo erit*) for all men who will ever exist.[18]

15. See n. 2 above.
16. See De Rijk 1962–7, II(1), pp. 223–4.
17. Peter of Spain 1972, p. 81. 2–5.
18. Peter of Spain 1972, p. 81. 5–10.

But how is natural supposition related to signification? For Peter signification is merely the conventional representation of a *res* by a word, the *res* being either a universal nature or any individual partaking in this universal nature. So for Peter the notion of signification covers both connotation (of the universal nature) and denotation (of the individuals participating in this universal nature). But the introduction of natural supposition seems to blur the clear-cut distinction commonly made between signification and supposition: signification arises by imposing a vocal sound (*vox*) on something, while supposition is the acceptance of a term already significant as standing for something or other.[19] Natural supposition, however, being defined in contradistinction with accidental supposition, which is determined by a propositional context, seems to occur apart from such context, since it is said to be the supposition of a term taken by itself.

Different interpretations have been given of Peter's natural supposition.[20] A careful exegesis of the texts involved seems to lead to the conclusion that, for Peter of Spain, natural supposition is the natural capacity of a significative word for supposition, whether within or without a proposition. When a vocal sound is endowed with signification in such a way as to become a term, it signifies a universal nature or essence (its significate), and it acquires a natural capacity to stand for (*supponere pro*) all actual and possible individuals partaking in this universal nature; it is said, then, to have natural supposition. This natural capacity, which the term has in virtue of its signification alone, may be limited in its function by another word adjoined to the first one. This adjunct may be the predicate term of the proposition of which the first term is the subject term; and in such a case the propositional context is an essential condition of the resultant accidental supposition. But the limitation, or restriction, can also come from a non-propositional adjunct, such as an adjective (e.g., 'white man'); whenever in such cases the actual context is left out of account for a moment and the term involved is taken by itself, the term has its whole, unrestricted extension: *all* particular men, present, past, and future.

So Peter's natural supposition is really the denotative counterpart of signification. Its resemblance to signification lies in the fact that in natural supposition the capacity of standing for *all* particulars involved, a capacity which the significative term has by its very nature, is completely exploited – that is, its extension is taken exhaustively – by leaving aside the actual

19. Peter of Spain 1972, p. 80. 8–11.
20. See De Rijk 1971, pp. 74–6.

context in which the term occurs. But natural supposition is unlike signification in that there *is* a context, an actual linguistic framework, which is
left out of account for a moment.

Signification and 'habitual' (dispositional) supposition

William of Sherwood's 'habitual' (dispositional) or 'virtual' supposition
bears some resemblance to Peter's natural supposition. However, what is
striking in William's defintion of it is that he considers it to be a kind of
signification. In doing so he goes even further than Peter seems to do in
distinguishing between signification and supposition. It should be noticed,
further, that for William signification, as well as supposition, is a property
of a term.[21] As a matter of fact, William's habitual supposition is the
signification of subsistent things (forms), that is, those things or forms that
are suited to be underlying (*hypokeimena: subiecta* or *supposita*), i.e., entities
that serve as substrata for adjacent entities and are signified by substantival
terms. For William, too, the context required for supposition is not
necessarily propositional; but how shall we imagine a context as required
for habitual supposition, which is really a kind of signification? That
question leads us to an important side of Sherwood's semantics. On the level
of signification there is no distinction among the species *man*, an individual
man, humanness, etc., no more than among running, the running,
runner(s), running as such, etc.: the significate of such terms is always the
same. It is the actual context in which the term occurs that divides
signification into substantival signification (which he calls habitual supposition) and adjectival or verbal signification (which he calls *copulatio*). It
is only after that division has been established that we get the further
division into the different kinds of supposition.

So Sherwood's signification seems to be a depth-structure, whereas
habitual supposition is found in the surface-structure where functions are
determinant not only of the way of suppositing, but, more fundamentally,
of the linguistic differentiation into substantival, adjectival, or verbal
forms. The functions realised in the surface-structure, including habitual
supposition, are all determined by some sort of context. William's habitual
supposition is not different from Peter's natural supposition in that respect.
The real dissimilarity occurs at a far more fundamental level, viz. in their
different views of signification. Unlike Peter and the majority of
thirteenth-century logicians, Sherwood (along with Roger Bacon)[22]

21. William of Sherwood 1937, p. 74.
22. See Braakhuis 1977.

identifies a term's significative character with its referring solely to actually existing things. For Sherwood and Bacon signification is denotative in character, and a term's extension can cover only presently existent particulars.

So with Sherwood, too, this peculiar dispositional or habitual supposition, so closely related to signification, gives us some insight into what signification meant to these thirteenth-century terminist logicians, and, especially, how central the notion of signification continued to be in the theory of supposition.[23]

Copulation, appellation, ampliation, and restriction

As we have seen already, in considering Sherwood's position, the counterpart of supposition in his theory is copulation. Copulation (or linkage) arises from the fact that an adjective is linked with a substantive (e.g. in 'white man' or 'the man is white'). It concerns the significative function not only of predicates (that is, all those terms that are not subject terms in a proposition) including verbs and participles, but also of adjectives when joined attributively to substantives. Copulation therefore is the kind of signification modifiers have. Most authors do not discuss copulation as extensively as Sherwood does.[24]

The notions of appellation, ampliation, and restriction are of major importance. In treatises dating from the thirteenth century onwards appellation is taken as a counterpart of supposition. The divergencies of the views regarding it run parallel with those concerning signification. The common view holds that the difference between supposition and appellation is that appellation concerns only things actually existing at the time of the utterance, whereas supposition, like signification, may concern non-existing things as well.[25] According to this view, then, a term has by itself (*de se*) the power of referring to all the things covered by the term, regardless of whether they are present, past, or future. For a term to denote in fact only present things, special conditions are required which are laid down in the well-known rule of appellation found already in the twelfth-century treatises: an unrestricted common term, having sufficient appellata and being the subject of a present-tense verb that has no ampliating force,

---

23. Another specimen of what is here meant by the preponderant role of signification as compared with the denotation of individual things can be found in the controversy over whether a word can lose its signification (*utrum vox possit cadere a sua significatione*). See Braakhuis 1977, pp. 133ff.
24. See, e.g., Peter of Spain 1972, p. 197. 4–14.
25. See, e.g., Peter of Spain 1972, p. 209. 4–10.

stands only for those things that do exist. On this view, then, the range of supposition is to be narrowed (restricted) in order to become the range of appellation, referring to actual things only.

Restriction accordingly is defined as the contraction (*coartatio*) of a common term from its wider supposition to a narrower one. Ampliation is defined reciprocally as an extension of a common term from a narrower supposition to a wider one. It is effected by such words as '*potest*' (can), which cause the terms to which they are adjoined to stand for things that exist possibly but not actually.

William of Sherwood and Roger Bacon defend a view contrary to this. They say that a term stands on its own (*de se*) for present things only, and whenever it stands for other things, it will do so because of what is adjoined to it, that is an ampliating verb. Sherwood provides an example: 'Thus, when I say "a man is running" "man" stands on its own for present men and is not drawn away from that supposition by the predicate. But if I say "a man ran or can run" the supposition of "man" is actually drawn away to men who do not exist.'[26] Thus, on this view the proper range of supposition basically coincides with that of appellation, with the result that supposition must be ampliated to reach beyond appellation, and no possibility is left for restriction to be effected by the verb (as is the case in the former view).

In his *Summule dialectices* Roger Bacon clearly distinguishes between the two views of appellation and is eager to defend the view that a term on its own stands only for existing things and that only as a result of some special predicates can a term stand for non-existing things.[27] The reason is that a noun is given or imposed upon *present* things. It is not surprising that the adherents of this second view, including those later logicians who were influenced by them, do not pay much attention to the notions of ampliation and restriction.

Conclusion

Concluding this sketch of the early development of the theory of the properties of terms, it may be said that in the very beginning of the

---

26. See William of Sherwood 1937, p. 85. 15–24. Revised text (see Braakhuis 1977, p. 166): 'Vel aliter, si proprie velimus loqui, dicamus quod terminus de se supponit pro presentibus; et si supponat pro aliis, hoc erit ratione sui adiuncti, scilicet verbi ampliandi vel verbi preteriti vel futuri temporis. Et erit hec ampliatio non solum ratione significati nec consignificati, sed per virtutem amborum. Unde cum dico "homo currit", supponit ly "homo" de se pro presentibus et ab hac suppositione non trahitur per predicatum. Si autem dicam "homo cucurrit" vel "potest currere", iam trahitur hec suppositio ad non existentes.'

27. See Roger Bacon 1940, pp. 277.28–283.19.

development some confusion is found regarding the relative status and function of signification in this semantic theory. The sound basis of the contextual approach seems to be undermined (more or less with various authors) by the implicit presupposition of the natural priority of signification. Even the most sagacious among medieval logicians, such as William Ockham, were not able to trace that troublesome presupposition, let alone to expose and to cut it out. They would have done a better job, if, instead of rejecting such notions as natural or simple supposition, they had abandoned their notion of signification itself. The most critical logicians of the Middle Ages used a sharp knife, but amputated the wrong leg.

8
THE OXFORD AND PARIS
TRADITIONS IN LOGIC

The hypothesis of an Oxford–Paris split

Terminist logic grew to maturity in the period 1175–1250, a period that
was also crucially important in the development of the universities of Paris
and of Oxford. Scholars have recently focused their attention on divergences in the early development of the logical and semantic theories that
constitute terminist logic, divergences suggesting that one cluster of doctrines is to be associated with Oxford, another with Paris.[1] In view of the
very marked differences between British and continental logic in the early
fourteenth century, it seems important to investigate whether such differences can be traced backwards into the thirteenth and late twelfth
centuries. As I hope to show, such divergences do in fact exist even if they
are not so great as to make the traditions of Oxford and of Paris entirely
independent.

Although by the turn of the thirteenth century terminist logic was
acknowledged by all logicians as a common frame of reference, various
interpretations of important issues were still being put forward. If divergences between the traditions of Oxford and Paris are to be established, the
evidence is likely to be found in the discussions concerning the various
properties of terms, such as supposition, appellation, ampliation, and
restriction.

The school of the Parvipontani

Twelfth-century logicians seem to have basically agreed in claiming that
an appellative (or common) name may vary its reference (*appellatio*)
according to changes in the tense of the main verb of the proposition; they
agreed further in describing this variation as either 'restriction' or 'ampliation' of the reference or appellation,[2] and in providing rules associated

---

1. De Rijk 1972, pp. LXIX–LXXX; Kretzmann et al. 1975, pp. 563–5; Braakhuis 1977; Kretzmann
   et al., 1978; Murdoch 1978b; Pinborg 1979; Ebbesen 1979.
2. Roger Bacon's later interpretation of this variation as a case of equivocation is also evidenced as
   early as in the twelfth-century *Summa Soph. Elench.*; see De Rijk 1962–7, 1, p. 365.21–4: 'sunt
   tamen alii qui dicunt quod hoc nomen "homo" habet plura significare, quia accipitur "homo" *qui*

with the three main tenses of the verb: present, past, and future. They did, however, differ over, for instance, the question whether accidental (or adjectival) names, too, may vary their appellation,[3] or whether a name loses its signification rather than its appellation when every thing it denotes has ceased to exist.[4] The antagonists of the twelfth century belonged to various (French) schools – those, for example, of Melun or of the Petit-Pont – and their divergences are thus not yet evidence of any doctrinal differences between the universities.[5] It has been argued, however, that the early Oxford tradition of logic should be traced back to the Parisian school of the Petit-Pont, the school of the *Parvipontani*,[6] and so it will prove helpful to say a few words about the most characteristic claims in semantic theory developed within this school.

In the works which have been preserved, appellation (or supposition – no clear distinction was yet drawn between these two terms) is defined against the background of the doctrine of univocation. The *Fallacie Parvipontane* offers a division of univocation that obviously underlies the division of supposition which was subsequently introduced in the early treatises from Oxford.[7] Univocation is defined as a 'variation in the supposition of a name the signification of which remains the same',[8] a variation which must therefore be effected in different contexts. This definition is followed by a set of rules designed to exhibit cases in which the range of reference of the terms is either narrowed (restriction) or extended (ampliation).[9] In the Parvipontanean tradition 'restriction' and 'ampliation' are considered as relative and reciprocal terms, without either notion being more emphasized than the other; but the roles of restriction and ampliation became the focus of some significant divergences to be observed in Oxford and Paris thirteenth-century logic.

The early Oxford treatises

In the early Oxford treatises[10] supposition is clearly distinguished from appellation (the reference to none but present, existent individuals), but the

fuit homo vel *qui est homo* vel *qui erit homo*, unde secundum hoc erit in predicto paralogismo sophisma secundum equivocationem'.

3. *Ars Meliduna* (1170s, see Hunt 1975, pp. 18–19, n. 8), quoted by De Rijk 1962–7, II(1), p. 302.
4. De Rijk 1962–7, II(1), p. 316.
5. De Rijk 1962–7, II(1), pp. 288–9.
6. De Rijk 1976a, p. 35, n. 47.
7. De Rijk 1962–7, I, pp. 562–71, especially pp. 562–3.
8. De Rijk 1962–7, I, pp. 561–2.
9. De Rijk 1962–7, I, pp. 563–4.
10. *Logica 'Cum sit nostra'* in De Rijk 1962–7, II(2), pp. 418–51, *Logica 'Ut dicit'* ibid. pp. 379–411, *Introductiones Parisienses* ibid. pp. 357–73.

general lines of the Parvipontanean doctrine are preserved. In the *Cum sit nostra* (which probably originated in the late twelfth century but was variously adapted during the whole thirteenth century)[11] restricted and ampliated suppositions are significantly presented as subdivisions of univocal supposition.[12] In addition, a variety of univocal supposition is acknowledged that introduces the divisions of metaphorical supposition (gemination, metonymy, antonomasia, synecdoche) that became standard in Oxford logic of the fourteenth century.[13] A striking difference between the two groups of texts is that the Oxford treatises ascribe supposition to subject and predicate terms alike, while the *Fallacie Parvipontane* provides rules of appellation for subject terms alone.[14] Nevertheless, the Oxford texts present restricted and ampliated suppositions in a set of rules that do not differ significantly (as regards subject terms) from the Parvipontanean rules of appellation. The Oxford rules specify the kinds of propositions in which terms may have univocal supposition either for existent entities only (by restriction through a present-tense verb) or for existent or non-existent entities (by ampliation through a past- or future-tense verb), as a consequence of the syntactical definition of supposition as 'the positioning of the referent (*res*) of the subject under the predicate' by means of the verb.[15] The Oxford theory of appellation is significantly connected with the doctrine and division of suppositions, ampliation being associated with distributive confused supposition and restriction with merely confused supposition – in a way reminiscent of the Parvipontanean texts.[16]

One might sum up the early Oxford doctrine by saying that the Oxford logicians consider supposition as a general property of terms – whether subject or predicate – occurring in propositions; that they view all the different kinds of supposition as varieties of univocal supposition; that they

---

11. De Rijk 1962–7, II(1), pp. 442–6.
12. De Rijk 1962–7, II(2), pp. 446.34–447.32.
13. De Rijk 1962–7, II(2), pp. 447.33–448.3; Roger Bacon 1940, pp. 287.33–288.36. It should be noted, however, that Buridan has a division quite different from the one used by the English logicians Ockham, Burley, and Lavenham.
14. *Cum sit nostra* in De Rijk 1962–7, II(2), p. 451.11–13: 'Terminus non restrictus ad presentes appositus verbo de preterito vel de futuro, vel verbo habenti vim ampliandi supponit confuse tantum'; *Introductiones Parisienses* in De Rijk ibid. p. 372.15–24: 'Terminus communis positus ex parte subiecti eque supponit pro presentibus et pro preteritis . . . si sit positus ex parte predicati, solummodo supponit pro preteritis . . . Similiter si supponat verbo de futuro (De Rijk: preterito) eque supponit pro presentibus et pro futuris; si autem predicat, pro futuris solum.'
15. De Rijk 1962–7 II(2), p. 446.29–33: 'Supponere est rem suam sub apposito ponere . . . . Terminus supponit quando ponitur in oratione.'
16. Compare *Fallacie Parvipontane*, De Rijk 1962–7, I, pp. 565.28, 566.28, 569.7–9, and *Cum sit nostra*, De Rijk 1962–7 II(2), p. 451.11–13.

maintain that no term is univocal by itself but only in context; and that they acknowledge that in virtue of the tensed forms of propositions terms may stand univocally either for present things (restriction) or for present or past (or present or future) things (ampliation).

Contemporary developments on the Continent

The situation on the Continent during the same period is quite different. Instead of the syntactically determined univocal supposition, Parisian logicians in the early thirteenth century[17] consider 'natural supposition', defined as the acceptance of a term taken by itself for all of its possible referents, classifying as 'accidental' all sorts of supposition affected by context.[18] This doctrine is not only concerned with the question of whether or not terms supposit only in propositions; it is further connected with a doctrine of appellation that does not consider restriction and ampliation as reciprocal in the description of the variations of the truth-value of a proposition over time. In fact, Parisian texts explain all problems connected with this variation by restriction from the original omnitemporal supposition of the term, and relegate ampliation to the solution of modal problems. Both the *Fallacie Parvipontane* and the early Oxford texts, on the other hand, seem to have viewed the influence of past- and future-tense verbs as quite similar to that of ampliating verbs such as 'can' – i.e., they seem to have assimilated tense and modality.[19]

The Paris tradition in Peter of Spain

During the Summulist period (1230–45), the contrast between Oxford and Continental doctrines increased. The Parisian doctrine essentially represented by Peter of Spain's *Tractatus* (written probably during the 1230s) definitely sets the notion of natural supposition in the forefront,[20] while that of appellation is relegated to the background. Peter focuses on supposition and restriction, treating appellation as no more than the particular kind of restricted supposition effected by a present-tense verb. All the rules of appellation are presented as rules of restriction, basically designed to

---

17. *Summule antiquorum* in De Rijk 1968, pp. 9–24, *Introductiones antique*, ibid. pp. 24–33. For some parallel doctrines in the *Dialectica Monacensis* see De Rijk 1962–7, II(2), pp. 616.31–617.8; 619.6–7; 623.24–7; 626.5–8.

18. De Rijk 1968, p. 9, ibid. p. 30. The *Introductiones antique* do not provide rules of appellation.

19. In the later summulist period William of Sherwood seems to have focused on the syntactical resemblance between tensed and modal propositions by means of the doctrine of the compounded and divided senses of propositions (*Introductiones*, p. 84.14–30; cf. p. 90.13–31).

20. Peter of Spain 1972, p. 81.1–10.

accommodate natural supposition to the actual use of words in propositions with differently tensed forms in the predicate.[21] Accordingly, ampliation becomes a notion of distinctly secondary importance, quickly disposed of in a separate, very short treatise in Peter's *Tractatus*.[22] Peter's rules of restriction are the same as those of the early Parisian textbooks.

The Oxford tradition in William of Sherwood

At the same time, in Oxford,[23] William of Sherwood was developing a doctrine of supposition and appellation founded on a syntactical definition of supposition as 'the ordering of some thought under some other thought'.[24] Sherwood provides two different accounts of the doctrine of appellation: one based on restriction and one based on ampliation, and he calls the latter the 'proper' interpretation.[25] The 'ampliative' interpretation is based on the two notions of dispositional supposition (*suppositio habitualis*, defined as the 'signification of something as subsisting')[26] and dispositional copulation (*copulatio habitualis*, defined as the 'signification of something as adjoining')[27] that designate the semantic nature of words that may actually be used in propositions as subject or as predicate terms respectively. Against that background, Sherwood's basic claim is that the appellation of substantive terms is entailed by their dispositional supposition.[28] The effect of this is that a substantive term occurring as the subject of a present-tense verb by itself (*de se*) supposits and appellates for present things only, since 'signification of something as subsisting' entails 'standing for present things'. When a substantive word occurs as a predicate term it appellates only insofar as the significate of the predicate is

21. Peter of Spain 1972, pp. 202–4.
22. Peter of Spain 1972, pp. 194–6.
23. There is unequivocal documentary evidence that Sherwood was a master at Oxford; there is a now discounted tradition and no comparable evidence that Sherwood was at Paris also. See Kretzmann 1966, pp. 8–12, and De Rijk 1976, pp. 31–42.
24. Sherwood 1937, p. 74.17–18.
25. The restrictive doctrine is found on pp. 82.20–85.15 of Sherwood 1937, the ampliative on p. 85.15–31. Though it is difficult to unravel the thought in the whole passage, it may be assumed that from pp. 82.23 to 85.15 Sherwood presents a very basic and simple doctrine which he supplements with more complicated considerations on p. 84.14–30. This last passage is no doubt a restrictive interpretation of the set of rules provided by *Cum sit nostra*. Compare especially De Rijk 1962–7, II(2), p. 451.11–13, or p. 372.15–24, with Sherwood 1937, p. 84.27–30: 'Et sic intelligendum est de verbo de futuro scilicet quod terminus communis ex parte ante supponit pro presentibus vel futuris per compositionem et divisionem, ex parte autem post solum pro futuris.' See also Braakhuis 1977, pp. 114ff.
26. William of Sherwood 1937, p. 74.22–3.
27. Ibid., p. 74.24–5.
28. See Maierù 1972, p. 91 and Braakhuis 1977, especially p. 130 n. 57; Braakhuis' interpretation is opposed both to Maierù's and to mine.

actually related to the subject's significate through the subsistent thing(s). Adjectives obviously appellate only as predicates. On the one hand, having dispositional copulation they signify an accidental form which intrinsically requires the existence of a subject; on the other hand, being predicated, their form is extrinsically taken in a syntactical relationship with that of the subject. Hence adjectives cannot appellate without having actual copulation, defined as the 'ordering of some thought above another thought'.[29]

In presenting this theory, Sherwood undoubtedly offers a more sophisticated interpretation of appellation than that provided by the earlier Oxford treatises. But I think he significantly agrees with *Cum sit nostra* in developing the theory of the entailment of appellation by dispositional supposition, insofar as this particular claim seems to be primarily meant to preserve both the old syntactical definition of supposition (in cases where the supposition of a term has a more extended range than its appellation) and the new characterisation of signification as the persisting factor that underlies appellation (in cases where the range of supposition and appellation coincides).

But even in his 'improper' account of appellation, based on restriction, Sherwood's views are much closer to the doctrine found in *Cum sit nostra* than to any text associated with Paris. For instance, Sherwood's presentation of the 'improper' account is in substantial agreement with *Cum sit nostra* on the question of the supposition of predicate terms in propositions about past and future events (except for Sherwood's concern with compounded and divided senses of propositions, an innovation that partially develops from his treatment of modalities). In both doctrines the temporal reference of the predicate is the same as that indicated by the verb, whereas the Parisian texts apply the same rules to subject and predicate terms, thus allowing predicate terms after a past-tense verb to stand for present or past things, rather than for past things only.[30]

It is surprising that Sherwood's account based on restriction may be said to be closer to the Oxford tradition in which restriction and ampliation were considered as reciprocal to each other, and less close to the Paris tradition which shows the same emphasis on restriction as Sherwood's improper account. But perhaps the approach based on restriction had been

---

29. William of Sherwood 1937, p. 74.18.

30. *Summule Antiquorum* in De Rijk 1968, p. 15; Peter of Spain 1972, pp. 203–4, especially p. 203.24–7: 'Ut cum dicitur "homo fuit animal", iste terminus "homo" supponit pro hiis qui sunt vel fuerunt homines, si illi qui sunt homines fuerunt in preterito, et "animal" pro hiis qui sunt vel fuerunt animalia.'

filtered through the Oxford tradition before finding the form presented by Sherwood. The 'proper' account may then be seen as an attempt to re-instate the genuine Oxford theory of univocally ampliated and restricted supposition and re-establish it on a more solid semantic basis. But even if this guess is incorrect, it is safe to say that before the 1250s the Oxford and Paris traditions of logic followed divergent lines of development, their characteristic disagreements being concerned with the very fundamentals of terminist logic, that is: the syntactical definition of supposition, the role and significance of restriction and ampliation, the definition of appellation as an instance of restricted supposition (Paris) or as a basic feature of terms having dispositional supposition (Oxford). From about 1250 onwards those divergences changed their character to a certain degree.

Opposition between the two traditions in Roger Bacon

In his Oxford treatise *Summule dialectices* (*ca.* 1250) Roger Bacon mentions two opposed views on the nature of appellation:

> But there are two theories of appellation, since some people say that a term appellates by itself present, past, and future *appellata*, and that it is common to beings and non-beings. Other people say that a term is only the name of present things and that nothing is common to being and non-being, or to past, present, and future, in keeping with what Aristotle says in the first book of the *Metaphysics*.[31]

The second opinion, which he favours, sounds very much like Sherwood's 'proper' account. The first one, which he rejects, is accompanied by a set of rules that are closer to those in *Cum sit nostra* or to Sherwood's 'improper' account of appellation than to Peter of Spain's.[32]

That Bacon was digging in the Oxford tradition of logic is well attested by his borrowing from *Cum sit nostra* the divisions of metaphorical sup-position (which are not found in any other thirteenth-century textbook of logic) and in his upholding a strictly syntactical definition of supposition.[33] When he calls the first account of appellation, based on restriction, 'the Common Doctrine' it is accordingly tempting to think of *Cum sit nostra* and Sherwood's 'improper' account. But there are special features in

---

31. Roger Bacon 1940, p. 277.28–34: 'duplex tamen est sentencia de appellacionibus, quia quidam dicunt quod terminus appellat de se appellata presencia, preterita et futura, et est communis entibus et non-entibus. Alii dicunt quod terminus est solum nomen presencium et nichil est commune enti et non enti, sive preterito, presenti et futuro, secundum quod dicit Aristoteles in primo Metaphysice.'
32. Ibid., pp. 277.35–278.13 and 279.8–15 (for the predicate terms).
33. Ibid., p. 268.33–4: 'suppositio non est proprietas nisi termini actualiter ordinati in oratione'.

Bacon's presentation of the Common Doctrine that do not tally with such an assumption. As a matter of fact, Bacon not only discusses such familiar notions as that of verbal restriction in the way Sherwood had done, but he also discusses doctrines that are not found in Sherwood, such as the unusual notion of the appellation of a term taken by itself for all its possible referents. Moreover, the various arguments adduced in Bacon's text both against the Common Doctrine and in support of his own doctrine are quite different from those that are found in the usual discussions concerning supposition and appellation before the 1250s.[34] In this respect the use of the word '*appellare*' deserves special consideration. Since Bacon's most basic claims are that a term cannot be common to being and non-being without ampliation, and that when it is ampliated it has equivocal appellation,[35] he is not only criticising the doctrine of univocal supposition as found for instance in the *Cum sit nostra*, but he also attacks the concept of 'appellation for all possible referents', which is associated with the Parisian notion of 'natural supposition'. In doing so, he is engaged in 'modern' controversies. In his last work, the *Compendium studii theologiae* (1292), dealing with the two much-debated questions whether a word can signify anything that is univocally common to being and non-being, and whether it can lose its meaning,[36] Bacon tells us that as early as the 1250s some people in Oxford began to answer the former question affirmatively, including Richard Rufus of Cornwall.[37] This suggests that the Common Doctrine as described in the *Summule* is already influenced by these new tendencies, which first developed within the Paris tradition.

In his later works, the *De signis* (1267) and the *Compendium studii theologiae* (1292), Bacon restates the whole doctrine of supposition, explicitly discarding univocal supposition and re-introducing the twelfth-

---

34. Arguments (in Roger Bacon 1940) supporting the restrictive doctrine of appellation (*Sentencia communis*): (1) 285.5–9 (Nomen significat sine tempore), (2) 283.20–283.37 (Terminus in negativa stat pro ente et non ente), (3) 284.1–5 (Ad propositionem de predicato privato vel infinito sequitur propositio de predicato negato et non convertitur), (4) 284.6–13 (Propositiones indefinitae possunt esse simul verae). Bacon's reply: ad(1) 283.9–19; general determination of (2), (3), (4) 284.15–24; ad(2) 284.25–37; ad(3) 285.1–286.16; ad(4) 286.17–287.10. Arguments supporting Bacon's own ampliative doctrine of appellation: (a) 279.19–279.28 (Homo mortuus–homo vivus); (b) 279.29–34 (Positio–privatio); (c) 279.34–280.1 (In omni nomine intelligitur ens), 280.2–9: Objection (ens nomen, ens participium) and its solution; (d) 280.10–15 (Nature of ampliation), 280.16–281.14 Determination, general exposition of the ampliative doctrine of appellation including the discussion of the Ps.-Boethian: 'Talia sunt subiecta qualia permiserunt predicata' and an important passage on the *Determinatio equivocationis* pp. 281.5–283.4.
35. Roger Bacon 1940, pp. 275.5–10, 287.5–10, 332.28–334.19.
36. Roger Bacon 1911, pp. 52–64.
37. Ibid., pp. 52–3.

century notions of equivocation and transumption, as if he wanted to make a new start.[38] In order to understand what kind of doctrines he was facing in 1250, it may help to examine the way in which he presented the Common Doctrine more than forty years later. In the *Compendium* the precise wording is that 'a name may signify something that is univocally common to being and non-being, or to present, past, and future'.[39] Thus I infer that already in the *Summule* he is thinking of a doctrine that holds that a term may appellate or supposit for present, past, and future things, insofar as it signifies something common to being and non-being. Now, whoever may have been the actual proponents of the Common Doctrine, those words do not tally with the doctrine of natural supposition as formulated by the early thirteenth-century Parisian terminist logicians. The use of '*appellare*' instead of '*supponere pro*' is not found in Peter of Spain's *Tractatus*, where appellation is introduced only as a kind of restricted supposition. Moreover, there is no Paris logician of the period before 1250 who maintains that positive terms like 'man' signify something that is common to being and non-being: Peter of Spain clearly states that substantive terms like 'man' are *not* common to the existent and the non-existent.[40] Hence, the Common Doctrine was probably influenced by new theories that are first found in texts from about 1250 onwards. A text representative of this new approach, accepting the kind of signification attacked by Bacon, is the *Lectura Tractatuum*, one of the earliest commentaries on Peter of Spain, by William Arnaud, master of arts at Toulouse.[41]

From this I infer that from about 1250 onwards the dispute which took place in Oxford concerning the nature of supposition and appellation had to some degree shifted ground. It can no longer be described alone in terms of two conflicting interpretations of univocal supposition; new doctrines made themselves felt, doctrines that derive from a new approach to the problem of meaning, connected with Aristotle's more sophisticated discussion on equivocation, univocation, and analogy as found in his *Metaphysics*. This new approach may safely be described as Parisian, and its

38. See Roger Bacon 1978, III.3, §81–8; pp. 109–10 (theory of equivocal and metaphorical supposition); III.4 §89–99; pp. 110–15 (ampliation and restriction); and IV.1, §134–42; pp. 125–7 (exposition of the main arguments supporting Bacon's doctrine).
39. Roger Bacon 1911, p. 53.
40. Peter of Spain 1972, p. 207.9ff.
41. De Rijk 1969b, pp. 120–62. For example p. 146: 'Sic igitur patet quod quilibet terminus communis, ut "homo", subponit de natura in subpositione pro forma communi que salvatur in suis subpositis, *sive illa subposita sunt actu existentia sive non*, solum quod in significando existat' (italics added).

principal opponent at Oxford was the former Parisian master and regent of arts, Roger Bacon.

The influence of modism in the Paris tradition

In the second half of the thirteenth century, logic at Paris was dominated by the 'Modist' approach.[42] The basic claims of Modist logicians – most of which were already to be found in William Arnaud's work[43] – are these: the new division of logic according to the three operations of the soul taken over from Aristotle's *De anima*, the reformulation of the terminists' 'natural' and 'accidental' suppositions as respectively 'supposition by virtue of discourse' (*de virtute sermonis* or *locutionis*) and 'supposition for truth's sake', the gradual accentuation of the problem of empty classes, the generalisation of the question whether terms may lose their signification, the elaboration of a doctrine of univocation firmly rooted in ontology and epistemology, and the logical use of the so-called 'modes of intellection, signification, and being' (*modi intelligendi, significandi, essendi*).[44]

A novel theory of univocal signification and supposition

The problem of univocation seems to have evoked a number of controversies between Modist logicians of the late thirteenth century such as Siger of Brabant and Peter of Auvergne.[45] But the prevailing opinion was that a term, insofar as it signified something univocally common to being and non-being, could supposit (or appellate) for present, past, and future things by virtue of discourse – i.e., in any proposition as well as taken by itself (outside of any context). Against such a background the notions of restriction and ampliation no longer played a prominent role. Once subject terms of propositions were said to supposit by virtue of discourse for all their possible referents, their standing for only present *appellata* or *supposita* was explained by referring not to the requirement of the verb but to the verification-procedure for the proposition. Thus, in the second half of the thirteenth century some Parisian masters begin to discard the notion of

---

42. Pinborg 1975a, esp. p. 69, n. 105; pp. 70–1; p. 70, n. 110.
43. De Rijk 1969b, pp. 143–6. Some of the characteristics of 'Modistic' logic are prefigured in the earlier Parisian terminist tradition. One might think, for instance, of Peter of Spain's concept of 'acceptance' (as the *definiens* of 'supposition') or of his distinction between *supponere* and *reddere locutionem veram* (Peter of Spain 1972, p. 82; cf. esp. Robert Anglicus' Modist presentation of the supposition of subject-terms *indefinite sumpti* in De Rijk 1969a, pp. 55–6).
44. Jolivet 1969.
45. Siger of Brabant 1974, pp. 44–52 (esp. p. 49.4–11) and pp. 53–9 (esp. p. 56.15–24, where a 'Baconian' doctrine of appellation is discussed); see also Siger of Brabant 1948, pp. 225–7. For Peter of Auvergne see Ebbesen & Pinborg 1970 and Pinborg 1973a; 1975a.

restriction, at least insofar as it is executed by predicate terms (leaving only to modifiers the possibility of restricting the reference of terms).[46] In doing so, they use a new terminology that shows the point of this new doctrine of reference: they prefer to speak of the various acceptations (*acceptiones*) of a word rather than of its various 'suppositions' or 'appellations', and they focus on the various causes of truth for propositions (*causae veritatis*), since these causes determine the various acceptations of the subject terms. For example, the two propositions 'Man is an animal' and 'Man is a species' have different verification – procedures or different 'causes of truth', which in turn influence the acceptation of the term 'man' in the two propositions. Of course, those different acceptations of the subject terms correspond to the basic varieties of suppositions, but against a differently interpreted background.

One of the characteristic features of logic at Paris from 1250 to 1300 is that this new doctrine of univocal signification and reference embraces the semantic question of whether or not the different contextual acceptations (the former 'accidental suppositions') constitute equivocation. This use of the concepts of equivocation and univocation is different from that of early Oxford terminism; it is linked with the discussions on equivocation, univocation, and analogy that derive from reflexions on Aristotle's theory of being as found in his *Metaphysics* and developed by the Arabic commentators.

Roger Bacon's later views on supposition and equivocation

At the same time in Oxford, Roger Bacon was deepening his criticism of the Common Doctrine. In the *De signis* he is obviously grappling with the Parisian question of whether or not the various acceptations of a term in different propositions are equivocal. And his answer – contrary to the usual Parisian one – is clearly affirmative. Furthermore, he states that all divisions of supposition, not only those of restricted and ampliated suppositions, reflect various cases of equivocation. In doing so, he generalises to all kinds of supposition the doctrine he had outlined in 1250 solely for the variations brought about by the change of tense in the verb of the proposition. He still

---

46. Radulphus Brito, *Anal. priora* I. qu. 46; in Pinborg 1976a, pp. 272–5.
47. For a general survey of Bacon's argumentation throughout the late thirteenth century, compare (1) Bacon 1940, 283.5–19; Bacon 1978 §139; Bacon 1911, p. 57.11–19; (3) 1940, 285.1–286.16; 1978, §141; 1911, pp. 57.19–58.17; (4) 1940, 284.6–14 and 286.17–287.10; 1911, pp. 58ff. Further: (a) 1940, 279.20–8; 1978, §140. (The numeration of the arguments is that of note 34 above.) For the *determinatio equivocationis* compare 1940, 281.34–282.22; and 1978, §93; for the Ps.-Boethian adage see 1940, 281.15–283.4; and 1978, §§ 95 & 99.

lays particular emphasis on the problems of time and tense, but his argumentation is from now on unmistakably linked with Parisian claims and concerns. The fact that he still speaks of supposition, restriction, and ampliation – against the Parisian fashion – indicates that his Oxford contemporaries are probably remaining closer to terminist logic than the Parisian masters. But his treatment of the material is nevertheless rejuvenated if compared to his earlier *Summule dialectices*. His basic claims are that a name does not name present, past, and future things except equivocally, since nothing is common to being and non-being (in opposition to the prevalent premodistic and modistic doctrine in Paris); all the divisions of supposition must be referred to a specific sort of equivocation (contrary to Oxford's doctrine of univocal supposition and Paris' doctrine of the various acceptations). In short, terms are imposed on existing things only, they signify only what is common to beings, and they cannot stand for other things except equivocally, ampliation being an instance of equivocal supposition. Significantly, all the main arguments of the *Summule* are adapted for use in the *De signis*, but recast in a Parisian mould. But it is striking that the role he now assigns to restriction and ampliation remains Oxonian in character: ampliation is associated with the problem of tense and modality, while restriction is confined to what was earlier described as the univocation of simple and personal suppositions.

Opposition and influence between Paris and Oxford

How do these facts tally with the hypothesis of divergent traditions of logical doctrine at Paris and Oxford universities? Since what Bacon describes as the Common Doctrine at Oxford is mainly known from Parisian sources, and since even some of Bacon's own theses are also found in a Parisian scholar such as Radulphus Brito, it is obviously not possible to talk about two independent traditions. The very persistence of Bacon's attacks throughout the second half of the thirteenth century seems to indicate a steady influence of Parisian doctrines at Oxford. At present there is not much textual evidence of such an influence, but it has been argued convincingly that the various theses considered as 'foolish' by Bacon in his *Compendium* could not lead one to think only of Richard of Cornwall as a promoter of the Parisian 'invasion'.[48] Further evidence of the Parisian influence might be drawn from the anonymous commentary on Sherwood's treatise on suppositions preserved in the Worcester manu-

48. Ebbesen and Pinborg 1970, p. 43.

script Cath. Q 13 (f. 59vb–62va). As a matter of fact, this work, probably to be dated about 1270[49] uses the doctrine of modes of conceiving and of signifying in redefining Sherwood's four properties of terms, and it restates Sherwood's claims in typical Parisian style. But most obvious, it mentions a solution to the problem of the persistence of signification after the thing signified has ceased to exist, a solution that had been eagerly discussed in Parisian circles since William Arnauld. This solution – significantly opposed to Bacon's – is ascribed to Geoffrey of Hasphall, a prominent figure at Oxford around 1270, but a master and regent of arts at Paris before 1265.[50] Thus, whoever was the anonymous commentator on Sherwood, I think that he, together with Geoffrey of Hasphall, was among the contemporary Oxford logicians criticised by Bacon. In this respect Bacon's praise of Sherwood in 1267 in comparison with Albert the Great (whose doctrine of appellation is typically Parisian)[51] and his mentioning Sherwood as an *antiquus* in 1271 could take on a particular significance,[52] as if Bacon wanted to draw a line between the old Oxford way of doing logic and the new one, markedly influenced by contemporary Parisian masters, that had begun to 'invade' Oxford after 1250. In any case, when in 1292 Bacon returns for the last time to the problem of appellation, he no longer uses the terminists' terminology of supposition. This does not necessarily mean that at that time terminism had been superseded by modistic logic in Oxford – as a matter of fact the premodistic and modistic theory of meaning never attained the dominant position in Oxford which it held in Paris, and terminism was never entirely neglected[53] – but it might mean that Bacon could not find anything in later Oxford terminism that would help avoid the Parisian errors. It seems that Bacon no longer trusted the terminist approach, but thought that the opposition between Oxford terminism (univocal supposition) and Parisian modistic logic (doctrine of univocal meaning) was actually too imprecise to prevent what Bacon

---

49. See Pinborg 1979, p. 26.
50. On Hasphall see Bazán, in Siger of Brabant 1974, p. 38. The text is found on f. 62va of the MS quoted: 'Alia opinio est magistri G. Haspale et est satis bona. Ponit quod diversimode ad representandum significatum suum imponitur terminus communis et terminus discretus, quoniam terminus communis imponitur preter omnem differentiam temporis, terminus discretus imponitur ad tempus. Et quia in termino discreto idem est suppositum et significatum, corrupto supposito corrumpitur et significatum. Tamen suppositum et significatum in termino discreto sunt diversa secundum rationem quia significatum dicitur unde intellectui representatur, suppositum unde actui substat.'
51. Albert the Great 1890–9a, I. 10, p. 474 a–b.
52. Kretzmann 1966, pp. 5–7.
53. For some evidence of the continuation of terminist logic in England, see Lewry (forthcoming); Pinborg 1979; Ebbesen 1979.

considered misunderstandings and misleading claims. He preferred to attempt a new start, based on his doctrine of signs and of equivocation.

Conclusion

I hope to have shown that there is evidence of substantial divergences between Oxford and Paris logic during the whole of the thirteenth century. Of course, these divergences changed character during that period, especially when, after about 1250, logicians shifted their attention from explaining the variations of the truth-value of a proposition over time to justifying predication regarding non-existent individuals and empty classes. This does not mean, however, that the two traditions are uniform: each tradition experienced strong internal disputes. After 1250 at the latest, a strong Parisian influence was felt in Oxford, associated with premodistic and modistic semantic theories. But Oxford, perhaps partly due to the zeal of Roger Bacon, never succumbed entirely to the Parisian doctrine.

9

THE SEMANTICS OF TERMS

Two senses of 'term'

Medieval philosophers and logicians used the word 'term' (*terminus*) in several senses, two of which are especially pertinent to this discussion. Strictly speaking, a term is what is subjected to the predicate or predicated of the subject in an ordinary categorical proposition – the subject term or the predicate term, the two ends (*termini*) of the proposition. In this sense whole phrases may be terms, but only certain sorts of words – nouns, adjectives, and verbs – can serve by themselves as terms. Less strictly, and in the later Middle Ages more prevalently, a term is any word at all, regardless of propositional context. In this discussion 'term' will be used in the less strict sense unless otherwise noted.

Signification as a psychological and causal property of terms

There are two basic properties for the medieval semantics of terms: signification and supposition. Signification is a psychologico-causal property of terms – a fact responsible for many disagreements and tensions in medieval semantics. The main source for the notion of signification was Boethius' translation of *De interpretatione* 3, 16^b 19: '[Verbs] spoken in isolation are names and signify something. For he who speaks [them] establishes an understanding and he who hears [them] rests'.[1] Hence 'to signify' something was 'to establish an understanding' of it.[2] The psychological overtones of 'to signify' are similar to those of the modern 'to mean'. Nevertheless, signification is not meaning. A term signifies that of which it makes a person think, so that, unlike meaning, signification is a species of the causal relation. Some authors explicitly drew the conclusion that the relation of signification is transitive. Thus Lambert of Auxerre argued 'For just as it is said that whatever is the cause of a cause is a cause of the caused, so

---

1. 'Ipsa quidem secundum se dicta nomina sunt et significant aliquid. Constituit enim qui dicit intellectum et qui audit quiescit.' Boethius 1877, p. 5.5–7.
2. See De Rijk 1962–7, I, Ch. 4. For the role of Augustine and for further texts, see Spade 1975c, pp. 214–17.

it can be said in its own way that whatever is the sign of a sign is a sign of the significate.'[3]

Signification in written, spoken, and mental terms

Taking their cue from *De interpretatione* 1, 16ᵃ 3–8 and from Augustine's *De trinitate*, XV, 10–11, most logicians held that there are three kinds of terms: written, spoken, and mental (or conceptual). Concepts or mental terms are the most basic; they signify 'naturally'. Spoken terms signify only derivatively, by a conventional (*ad placitum*) correlation with concepts; written terms are related to spoken terms in the same way.[4]

On the authority of Boethius, many authors held that these conventional correlations are signification relations. Hence written terms directly or immediately signify spoken ones, which in turn directly signify concepts. Only by the transitivity of signification – ultimately by means of the signification of concepts – do written or spoken terms signify anything further.[5] Hence the terminology of 'immediate' and 'ultimate' signification in some authors.[6]

This theory fits the view that language is for social communication, to make others understand our thoughts. But it conflicts with the view that language, whether spoken or written, is thoroughly conventional, so that we can 'impose' terms to signify immediately whatever we want to discuss, not just our own thoughts. Some logicians, therefore, rejected the view that the conventional correlations among the three kinds of terms are signification relations; Ockham, for instance, called them relations of 'subordination'.[7]

3. 'Sicut enim dicitur quod quidquid est causa cause est causa causate, sic potest dici suo modo quod quidquid est signum signi est signum significati.' (Lambert of Auxerre 1971, pp. 205–6.) See also Duns Scotus 1639, *In I Perihermeneias quaestiones*, q. 2, Vol. 1, pp. 186–9; and Walter Burley in Brown 1973, p. 55 par. 1.15 and in Brown 1974, p. 208 par. 1.3. (Burley is not speaking for himself in these places.)

4. Peter of Ailly is the only author I know to have held that written language is not inferior to spoken language. He says this explicitly only for sentences, but seems to have held it for terms too. Peter of Ailly 1980, par. 93: 'Hence the spoken sentence and the written [sentence] are subordinated to the mental one. But it is not necessary that the spoken [sentence] and the written one be subordinated among themselves, as many put it.' ('Unde propositio vocalis et scripta subordinantur mentali. Sed non oportet quod vocalis et scripta subordinentur sibi invicem inter se sicut multi ponunt.')

5. Boethius 1877, p. 40.15–22, and Boethius 1880, p. 25.15–p. 29.29; Lambert of Auxerre 1971, pp. 205–6; Aquinas *In Peri Hermeneias*, 1, lect. 2, §5; Aquinas *Summa theologiae*, I, q. 13, a. 1, resp.; Aquinas *De potentia*, q. 8, a. 1, resp.; Duns Scotus 1639, *In I Perihermenias quaestiones*, q. 2, Vol. 1, pp. 186–9; John Buridan 1977, 1, concls. 1–2; translated in John Buridan 1966, pp. 70–1.

6. Duns Scotus 1639, *In I Perihermenias quaestiones*, q. 2, §4, Vol. 1, p. 188; Buridan 1977, 1, concls. 8–9; translated in Buridan 1966, pp. 74–5. See also John Buridan 1957, p. 20.34–41.

7. Ockham 1974a, I, 3; *Commentarium in Perihermeneias ca. 1 (16 a 3–4)*, ed. in Boehner 1946, p. 320.

It seems to follow also from the psychologico-causal notion of signification that a speaker's or writer's terms are not significant to him but only to others. If they were significant to him, their signification would consist of 'establishing' the very concepts from which they derive their signification, which seems circular. This feature, too, fits the view that language is for social communication although, as far as I know, no medieval logician explicitly recognized the consequence.

There was another problem. The standard notion of signification did not fit mental terms. They do not causally 'establish' an act of understanding; they are concepts, and so are either themselves such an act or else, on another theory, the intentional objects of such an act,[8] but in any case they do not cause it. Some authors, therefore, refused altogether to accept the notion of a naturally significant mental language.[9]

Signification in syncategorematic and categorematic terms

Terms were divided into categorematic words – those that can serve by themselves as terms in the strictest sense – and syncategorematic words – those, such as conjunctions and prepositions, that enter into propositions only along with categorematic words.[10] There were several theories, not always clearly distinguished, of the signification of syncategorematic words:

(1) They have an 'indefinite' or 'unfixed' signification, whereas categorematic words signify definitely.[11]
(2) They 'consignify' – i.e., signify only when properly combined with categorematic words.[12]
(3) They do not signify at all, but only determine truth conditions.[13]
(4) They signify mental attitudes.[14] (Recall the claim that language is for talking

See also Duns Scotus 1639, *Opus oxoniense*, 1, d. 27, a. 1, §§1 & 19, Vol. 5.2, pp. 1135 and 1146 (contrast the text from Scotus cited in n. 5 above); Albert of Saxony 1522 *Perutilis logica*, 1, *ca.* 2, f. 2[rb]; Albert of Saxony 1496, *Quaestiones in Perihermeneias*, q. unica in proem.
8. See Boehner 1946 and Adams 1977.
9. See William of Crathorn in Schepers 1972, pp. 115–18, discussed in Nuchelmans 1973, p. 212. Buridan too tends not to speak of concepts as 'signifying' but rather as 'conceiving' their objects. (Reina 1959, pp. 382–7.) Nevertheless, contrary to Nuchelmans 1973, p. 243, Buridan does sometimes speak of concepts as signifying. (Buridan 1977, 1, concls. 2 and 7; translated in Buridan 1966, pp. 70–1 and 74.)
10. Priscian 1855–9, *Institutiones grammaticae*, ii, iv, 15. See Nuchelmans 1973, p. 124.
11. Abelard 1919–27, *Logica 'Ingredientibus'*, p. 337.11–32; Abelard 1970a, *Dialectica*, p. 118.4–25; Ockham 1974a, I, 4; Burley 1955, *De puritate*, p. 220.10–11.
12. Boethius 1880, p. 14.30–2; Abelard 1919–27, p. 337.33–40; Burley 1955, p. 220.8–11; Buridan 1957, p. 188.111–14.
13. Ockham 1974a, I, 4.
14. Augustine 1877, *De magistro*, 2, 3, *PL* 32, col. 1196. See Priscian 1855–9, 18, 9, 76.

about our thoughts, and that the relation of spoken terms to thoughts is a kind of signification.)

(5) They 'generate an understanding' but 'have no subject thing'.[15] That is, they do not produce an understanding 'of something'. In effect, 'to signify' is being used without a direct object. The objection that every understanding is 'of something'[16] is in part a terminological matter and in part depends on one's theory of mental acts.[17]

(6) They signify ways of conceiving things.[18]

(7) They do not signify 'things' but rather 'modes' or 'characteristics' of things.[19]

There was general agreement that categorematic words (except for such as 'concept' or 'knowledge') signify something extramental – 'ultimately' if not 'immediately' – and that a proper name so signifies its bearer. Signification here coincides with 'being truly predicable of'.[20] But there was controversy over the extramental significate of a general term. Realists of various degrees said it is a universal or common nature; when I hear 'man' I think only of man in general.[21] For nominalists, there are no universals or common natures in the realists' sense; they did, however, recognise universal concepts. But one cannot hold that general terms are as a rule imposed to signify concepts without committing oneself to the view that language is for talking only, or very largely, about thoughts. The only plausible alternative was to make 'man' signify individual men, and since it would be arbitrary to single out some at the expense of others, it must on that alternative be said to signify *each man*. For the nominalists signification and predication are thus linked not just for proper names but for all categorematic words.[22]

The realist theory has the disadvantage that the sentence 'Some man is a philosopher', for instance, cannot be said to make one think of individual men or philosophers, but of the universal natures 'man' and 'philosopher'; the hearer of the sentence is thus left ignorant of what it is about. The nominalist theory, however, entails that that same sentence makes the

15. Abelard 1970a, p. 119.3–16.
16. *Ibid.*
17. Buridan likewise considers and rejects the claim that the verb 'to signify' need not take a direct object (Buridan 1977, 1, sophisma 4 and concl. 3; translated in Buridan 1966, pp. 67 and 71–2).
18. Buridan 1977, 4, translated in Buridan 1966, p. 116.
19. Abelard 1970a, p. 120.3–20; Nicholas of Paris, *Summe Metenses*, quoted in De Rijk 1962–7, I, p. 481; Albert of Saxony 1496, *Quaestiones in Perihermeneias*, q. 2 de nomine, concl. 3.
20. See the discussion in Abelard 1919–27, *Logica 'Ingredientibus,'* pp. 21.27–22.6.
21. Bacon 1940, *Sumule dialectices*, p. 272.4–8; Duns Scotus 1639, *Opus secundum in Perihermenias*, q. 1, §§4–5, Vol. 1, pp. 212–13; Burley 1955, pp. 7.26–8.33; Ferrer 1909, *De suppositionibus*, p. 3; also 1977, p. 87.
22. Ockham 1974a, I, 33.

hearer think of all men and all philosophers, even those unknown to him –
which is just as great a disadvantage.[23]

Connotation

The theory of categorematic words was complicated by the notion of
'secondary signification' or 'connotation', a notion closely related to
Anselm's theory of paronymy.[24] Briefly, connotation-theory attempted
to account for the fact that words such as 'blind' in an oblique way make
one think of, and so signify, *sight*. The theory is too rich and complex to
rehearse in detail here. But it should be mentioned that it bears directly on
the notion of 'nominal definition',[25] on the theory of demonstration,[26]
and on the program of reducing the number of ontological categories.[27]

Supposition proper and 'descent to singulars'

Supposition is a property of categorematic words only when they serve as
terms (in the strict sense), or extremes, of sentences.[28] (Disputed portions of
this claim will be discussed below.) Supposition-theory is best viewed as
two theories: the theory of supposition proper and the theory of 'descent to
singulars'.[29]

Divisions of supposition proper

The theory of supposition proper is a theory of reference. Normally an
extreme of a sentence refers to or 'supposits for' everything of which it is
truly predicable;[30] in that case it was said to have 'personal' supposition.
But there are other cases. Some of them – figurative or metaphorical uses –
were classed as 'improper supposition'.[31] Others were given intermediate
status as proper but not personal. We may distinguish two classes of such

23. See Spade 1975c.
24. See Henry 1964, 1967, 1974.
25. See Spade 1975b and Loux's introduction to Ockham 1974e, pp. 1–24.
26. Moody 1935, Ch. 6.
27. Moody 1935, Ch. 4, and Loux's introduction to Ockham 1974e, pp. 1–24.
28. Ockham 1974a, I, 63; Buridan 1977, *Sophismata*, 2, remark 1; translated in Buridan 1966, pp. 99–
    100; Buridan 1957, *De suppositionibus*, p. 180.10–11; Burley *De suppositionibus* in Brown 1972,
    p. 34, par. 2.01; Lavenham *Suppositiones* in Spade 1974a, p. 93. This claim was fairly standard in
    the fourteenth century. For the earlier period see De Rijk 1962–7 and the discussion in Brown
    1972, pp. 19–21.
29. See Scott's introduction to Buridan 1966, pp. 29–42.
30. Ockham 1974a, I, 63; Buridan 1977, *Sophismata*, 4; translated in Buridan 1966, pp. 99–
    100.
31. Ockham 1974a, I, 77; Burley 1955, *De puritate*, pp. 46–7; Buridan 1957, *De suppositionibus*,
    pp. 200–1; Lavenham *Suppositiones* in Spade 1974a, pp. 93–4.

cases, although some theories combined them:[32] 'material' supposition, in which an extreme that does not have personal supposition supposits for a spoken or written expression, e.g., 'man' in 'Man is a monosyllable', and 'simple' supposition, in which an extreme that lacks personal supposition supposits for a universal, e.g., 'man' in 'Man is a species' – whether it is a universal of the realists' variety or the nominalists' universal concept.[33]

Predication and the divisions of supposition

Reversing a remark in Boethius' *De trinitate*,[34] many authors held that the predicate of a sentence determines which of the three kinds of supposition the subject may have. Most held that a subject can always have personal supposition, but one of the other kinds only if the predicate is semantically appropriate. Such 'rules of supposition' suggest that predicates always have personal supposition.[35] If so, the laws of 'conversion' must be restricted to sentences with subjects in personal supposition; otherwise the conversion 'Man is a monosyllable; therefore, a monosyllable is a man' would be sanctioned.[36]

Truth-conditions and supposition

On the basis of the theory of supposition proper, some authors constructed a theory of truth-conditions for categorical sentences. Thus a universal affirmative is true if and only if its predicate supposits for everything for which the subject supposits; other cases were handled analogously.[37] Affirmative categoricals have 'existential import'; negatives do not. Thus 'Some man is not a Greek' – read as the contradictory of 'Every man is a Greek' – is true if and only if either there is a man who is not a Greek or else there are no men at all. This odd reading is required in order to preserve traditional relations of opposition.[38]

32. Buridan 1977, *Sophismata*, 3, remark 2; translated in Buridan 1966, p. 100; Buridan 1957, *De suppositionibus*, p. 201.34–41; Paul of Pergula 1961, *Logica*, 2.1, pp. 24–6.
33. On these divisions see Boehner 1952, Pt. 2, Ch. 2; Kneale 1962, pp. 246–74.
34. Boethius 1918, §4, lines 4–5. See Spade 1974c.
35. Spade 1974c, p. 72 n. 38.
36. Swiniarski 1970, pp. 189–91.
37. Ockham 1974a, 2, 1–4; Buridan 1977, 2, concls. 10–14; translated in Buridan 1966, pp. 90–4. Such an account is by no means a regular part of supposition theory. It is not to be found, for instance, in William of Sherwood *Introductiones in logicam*, ed. Grabmann 1937 and tr. Kretzmann 1966, Peter of Spain *Tractatus* (*Summule logicales*), ed. De Rijk 1972, Burley *De puritate*, ed. Boehner 1955, Burley *De suppositionibus* in Brown 1972, or Lavenham *Suppositiones* in Spade 1974a.
38. Moody 1953, pp. 51–2.

Ampliation

In order to accommodate tense and modality, the theory of supposition proper included a theory of 'ampliation'. This theory explains how the supposition of a subject is extended or 'ampliated' by past- and future-tensed or modal copulas, and how the semantics of predicates, too, must be adjusted in those cases. Details varied, but the doctrine was relatively settled by the fourteenth century.[39] Some authors conjoined this with a theory of 'restriction' to explain how the supposition of a term may be narrowed by, for instance, an adjective ('tall man') or a relative clause ('man who runs').[40]

Descent to singulars or modes of personal supposition

The second main part of supposition theory is the theory of descent to singulars or 'modes of personal supposition'.[41] The standard modes are: 'discrete', 'confused and distributive', 'determinate', and 'merely confused'. Discrete supposition is the supposition of proper names, demonstratives, and demonstrative phrases. There was wide divergence regarding the definitions of the other modes. Ockham's definitions in *Summa logicae*, 1, 70, are perhaps the most complete. They may be put thus:

Let $\phi(T)$ be a noncompound sentence containing an occurrence T of a general term in personal supposition, and let $t_1, t_2, \ldots, t_i \ldots$ be all the singular terms that supposit for a suppositum of T. Then T is

(a) confused and distributive if and only if $\phi(T)$ implies $\phi(t_1)$ *and* $\phi(t_2)$ *and* ..., and no $\phi(t_i)$ implies $\phi(T)$;

(b) determinate if and only if $\phi(T)$ implies $\phi(t_1)$ *or* $\phi(t_2)$ *or* ..., and each $\phi(t_i)$ implies $\phi(T)$;

(c) merely confused if and only if $\phi(T)$ does not imply $\phi(t_1)$ *or* $\phi(t_2)$ *or* ..., but does imply $\phi(t_1 \text{ } or \text{ } t_2 \text{ } or \ldots)$, and each $\phi(t_i)$ implies $\phi(T)$.

Although many scholars treat descent to singulars as a theory of analysis or of truth-conditions, there are reasons to doubt this. First, no medieval author seems to have made such a claim. Second, some authors, as noted above, did have an explicit theory of truth-conditions based on sup-

---

39. Moody 1953, pp. 53–63; Scott's introduction to Buridan 1966, pp. 32–4; Loux's introduction to Ockham 1974e, pp. 37–44.

40. See Maierù 1972, Ch. 2.

41. Boehner 1952, Pt. 2, Ch. 2; Moody 1953, pp. 43–53; Kneale 1962, pp. 246–74; Scott's introduction to Buridan 1966, pp. 35–42; Swiniarski 1970; Loux's introduction to Ockham 1974e, pp. 23–37.

position, and it is quite different. Third, if descent to singulars was intended to provide such a theory, it will not work, as has been pointed out by Swiniarski 1970, pp. 210–13, and Matthews 1973.

It is not clear, therefore, what the doctrine was intended to accomplish. One possibility is that it was meant to provide a technique for checking inferences. Some authors gave syntactic criteria for deciding which mode of supposition a term has,[42] and bridge-rules to link the modes to the theory of consequences.[43] As a result, the theory of modes of personal supposition could in principle be applied to the evaluation of a wide range of inferences. Thus the inference from 'Twice you ate some bread' to 'Some bread you ate twice' is rejected because on the syntactic criteria 'bread' is merely confused in the former and determinate in the latter (as the definitions will verify), and there is a rule 'Whenever one argues from a term suppositing merely confusedly to the term suppositing determinately with respect to the same multitude, there is a fallacy of figure of speech.'[44] This technique has an advantage over modern quantification theory in that it handles inferences in natural language directly, and does not require them to be first translated, more or less by feel, into symbolic notation. On the other hand, if this was the purpose of the doctrine, it must be said that the medievals never succeeded in formulating adequate criteria and rules to accomplish this purpose.

Some controversial points

Finally, some controversial points should be mentioned briefly. First, some authors held that only subjects supposit, not predicates.[45] Again, although in order to simplify certain rules many authors held that only whole extremes supposit, not their parts,[46] few observed this principle consistently. The theory of restriction violates this principle, as does the analysis of 'Twice you ate some bread' by which 'bread' supposits although 'ate some bread' is the predicate. Again, although most authors held that terms supposit only in sentences, a few explicitly allowed them to have

42. E.g., Ockham 1974a, I, 71–4.
43. E.g., the rules in William of Sherwood 1937, *Introductiones in logicam*, pp. 80–1; 1966, pp. 118–19.
44. Burley 1955, *De puritate*, pp. 21.30–23.35.
45. Ferrer 1909, pp. 10–12; 1977, pp. 95–7.
46. Ockham 1974a, I, 69 and 72 ad 3; Burley *De suppositionibus* in Brown 1972, pp. 31–4 pars. 1.2–1.22; Ferrer 1909, p. 12; 1977, pp. 97–8. See Buridan 1977, 2, remark 1; translated in Buridan 1966, p. 100.

natural supposition outside sentences.[47] But the phrase 'natural supposition' does not always refer to this obscure doctrine.[48]

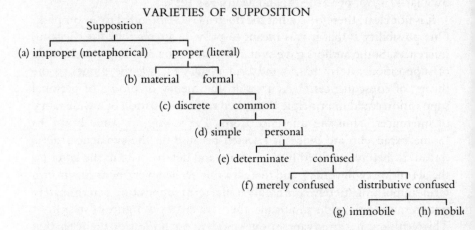

VARIETIES OF SUPPOSITION

Supposition
(a) improper (metaphorical)   proper (literal)
(b) material   formal
(c) discrete   common
(d) simple   personal
(e) determinate   confused
(f) merely confused   distributive confused
(g) immobile   (h) mobile

EXAMPLES

Each variety of supposition is exemplified by the occurrence of the word 'man' in each of these propositions. (a) After six moves the Russian chess player was a man down. (b) Man is a monosyllable. (c) That man is my brother. (d) Man is a species. (e) A man is at the door. (f) Every masseur is a man. (g) Every man other than an employee is eligible. [Immobile because the logical descent under 'man' is blocked by 'other than an employee'; one cannot infer, e.g., 'John other than an employee is eligible' or even (without further information) 'John is eligible'.] (h) Every man is an animal.

NOTE. The schema presented above is intended to include all the most important varieties of supposition recognised by medieval logicians, but neither this particular set of varieties nor their organisation can be attributed to a particular logician.

47. E.g., Lambert of Auxerre 1971, p. 206, and Robertus Anglicus quoted in Brown 1972, p. 21 n. 25. See the discussion *ibid.*
48. See Buridan 1957, pp. 206–8, and Ferrer 1909, pp. 14–43; 1977, pp. 100–34. On the notion of natural supposition, see De Rijk 1971–73.

10

THE SEMANTICS OF PROPOSITIONS

Terms and propositions

Separate treatments of the semantics of terms and the semantics of propositions are justified by the Aristotelian distinction between two levels of speech and thought (*Categories* 1ª16, 2ª4; *De interpretatione* 16ª10): the level of names and verbs and the thoughts corresponding to them, which do not yet involve any combination (*symplokē, complexio*) that makes the notions of truth and falsity applicable, and the level of expressions and thoughts formed by a kind of combination that has to do with truth and falsity. Just as Aristotle had made the applicability of the notions of truth and falsity the criterion for the relevant kind of combination, the medieval semantics of complex units of speech and thought (*complexa*) concentrated on sentences that are used for making statements and are thus either true or false – the sort of sentences with which logic is primarily concerned. A combination of words that is used to make known something that is either true or false (*oratio verum falsumve significans*)[1] was called an *enuntiatio* or *propositio*. The Latin word '*propositio*' practically always designates a declarative sentence; accordingly, in this chapter 'proposition' is used in this medieval sense and never in the modern sense of that which is expressed by a declarative sentence. Most medievals were aware of a distinction between a *complexio* in the sense of mere predication, without any assertive (or other) force, and a *complexio* which is accompanied by an act of judging or asserting that it is so. Abelard considered mere predication as the common element in different speech acts;[2] and from the beginning of the twelfth century it was customary to distinguish between an act of merely putting a predicative combination before the mind and an act of judging that that combination is the case in reality. The author of the *Ars Meliduna*[3] (between 1154 and 1180) even employed a terminological distinction to mark the difference in

---

1. Cf. Boethius, *De topicis differentiis*, PL 64, 1174B, 1177C.
2. Peter Abelard 1970a, *Dialectica*, pp. 148–53.
3. De Rijk 1962–7, II(1), p. 342.

assertive force between propositions uttered by themselves and propositions in so far as they are part of compound statements. Uttered by itself, a categorical proposition both signifies an inherence and asserts that the predicate inheres in the subject (*significat et enuntiat*); as part of a compound statement it only signifies an inherence (*tantum significat*), without asserting that it is so. For many purposes, however, the words '*complexio*' and '*complexum*' could be used in such a way that they included both the predicative and the assertive aspects.

Written, spoken, and mental propositions

As in the case of *incomplexa*, or terms, it was held that there are three kinds of propositions: written, spoken, and mental. Written and spoken declarative sentences and their mental images were contrasted with the corresponding thoughts, which were seen as belonging to a sort of universal mental language. Now the first question of the semantics of propositions concerns the relation between conventionally signifying written and spoken propositions and their mental counterparts. This question, which we might call the problem of the meaning of a declarative sentence, received a relatively uncontroversial answer.

The meaning of a declarative sentence

In accordance with Aristotle's conception in *De interpretatione* 16ᵃ3, it was held that a written proposition or its mental image conventionally signifies the corresponding spoken proposition and that a spoken proposition or its mental image conventionally signifies the corresponding mental proposition or act of thought. Some authors, for instance Ockham[4] and Gregory of Rimini,[5] were of the opinion that written and spoken propositions have the same significate as the mental propositions, the first two as conventional signs and the latter as natural signs, but even they restored something of the Aristotelian hierarchy by considering the written proposition as a secondary conventional sign compared to the spoken proposition, and the spoken proposition, in its turn, as secondary and subordinate to the mental proposition. The written and spoken propositions discharge their signifying function in subordination to the mental acts of apprehending and judging which always precede them. In the last instance, therefore, it is the mental proposition which is immediately directed towards the outside world.

4. William Ockham 1974a, *Summa logicae*, I, 12.
5. Gregory of Rimini 1522, *Prologus*, q. 1, art. 3; cf. II, Dist. 9–10, q. 2, art. 1.

The mental proposition

The mental proposition is an act of thought which consists of an act of combining the predicate with the subject in an affirmative or negative way and of an act of judging that what is thereby conceived is so in reality. Considered as a unit of a universal mental language, it is said to signify in a natural manner; at the same time – and this, as will appear, is a point of crucial importance – it contains a mental copula, and its total signification is thus determined by a syncategorematic element.

The significate of a mental proposition

In order to understand clearly the second and most controversial question of the medieval semantics of propositions, namely the problem of the significate of a mental proposition, one should realise that the word '*significare*' has a special sense in this context. On the one hand, it is used of a person who performs an act of expressing a belief or making known an opinion, and of the expression involved in that act; in such cases it has the same meaning as the verbs '*enuntiare*', '*dicere*', '*proponere*'. On the other hand, in keeping with the interpretation of thought as mental speech the terminology of the speech act of asserting could easily be transferred to the purely mental acts of judging, assenting, dissenting, believing, and knowing; judging is then conceived of as a kind of asserting in the mind (*enuntiare mentaliter quod sic est*). The question of the total or adequate significate of a mental proposition, as contrasted with the significates of written and spoken propositions and with the significates of the categorematic terms, thus becomes the problem of the specific object of an act of judging or an act of asserting, or, in other words, the question of the nature of 'the thing' (*pragma, res*) which, according to Aristotle, underlies an affirmation or negation (*Categories* 12^{b}6–15). In so far as such an object is postulated for both true and false assertions or judgements, it must have the character of something intermediate between the acts of asserting or judging and the outside world; if only true assertions and judgements are considered, it may be asked what kind of place such an object occupies in the actual world. This problem concerning the nature of the object of what we would call the propositional attitudes naturally leads to the further question of what are the primary bearers of truth values, the modalities, and the logical relations. Again, part of this further question may be seen as the problem of deciding what Aristotle meant by 'the thing' in his formula 'It is because the thing is or is not that the statement is said to be true or false' (*Categories* 4^{b}8, 14^{b}21).

The breadth of medieval semantics

From the foregoing it will be clear that the medieval semantics of propositions included, apart from problems which we would call semantic in a
strict sense, certain issues which are at least very closely connected with
such disciplines as philosophical psychology, epistemology, and ontology.
The questions treated, which still belong to the core of what is now called
philosophy of language, were often conditioned by such typically medieval interests as God's knowledge, the articles of faith, and the object of
theology. But the ways in which those questions were asked and answered
can usually be sufficiently dissociated from these narrow contexts to remain
instructive for the modern philosopher of language.

From Abelard through the thirteenth century

Both in the *Logica 'Ingredientibus'* and in the *Dialectica* Abelard draws a
sharp distinction between mere predication and the act of asserting. Since
the copula is a syncategorematic sign, predication is essentially a manner of
conceiving (*modus concipiendi*), an operation of linking subject and predicate in an affirmative or negative way. In order to get a full statement-
making utterance, however, it is not enough to perform such a formal act
of compounding or dividing; one must also assert, by means of a finite
verb, that the constructed inherence is as a matter of fact the case. Now the
dictum, or that which is asserted to be the case, although it is about things
and not about ideas or words, cannot itself be a thing in the sense of things
which are denoted by nouns; it is rather an asserted state of affairs or
manner in which the things denoted by the categorematic subject-term
and predicate-term are related (*rerum modus habendi se*).[6] Because of the
syncategorematic character of the copula a proposition can signify or assert
only the way in which things are connected; the significate of the proposition, therefore, does not belong to the category of things, but is a way
of being which can be made more explicit by such impersonal or non-
denoting expressions as '*ita* (or *sic*) *est*', '*accidit*', '*contingit*', '*evenit*' when
they are combined with an expression in indirect discourse (accusative plus
infinitive). This way of being can be signified only in a complex manner,
namely by adding a certain mode of conceiving to the conceptions of the
things which by this very *complexio* become the subject and the predicate of
the proposition. Abelard considers the *dictum*, or asserted predicative connection, as the primary bearer of the truth values; the written or spoken

6. Peter Abelard 1970a, p. 160.

propositions and their mental counterparts are true or false in a derivative sense. As a *dictum* can be true or false, it must be something intermediate between the act of asserting and the actual world, but apart from the emphatic categorisation as a non-thing its ontological status is left very much in the dark.

Some of the treatises on logic which date from the period between the middle of the twelfth century and the beginning of the thirteenth century clearly show the influence of Abelard's *dictum* theory. Besides '*dictum*' and '*significatum propositionis*' they often use the word '*enuntiabile*' for that which is asserted to be the case; in accordance with its form, this term also occasionally stands for an assertible, in the sense of that which can be asserted although it is not actually asserted. The author of the *Ars Meliduna*[7] mentions several opinions concerning the nature of assertibles and prefers the view adhered to by his teacher, according to which *enuntiabilia* are neither substances nor qualities but have a peculiar being of their own: they are grasped only by reason and thought and are inaccessible to the senses. This Platonising doctrine is also found in the *Ars Burana*,[8] where an assertible is called an *extrapraedicamentale*, not, however, because it does not belong to any category at all, but because it belongs to a separate category of being which is not one of the ten distinguished by Aristotle.

Whereas Abelard and his followers limited their attention almost exclusively to the object of an act of asserting, theologians of the same period saw themselves forced to deal with the object of acts of believing and knowing (the *creditum*, the *scitum*) by certain difficulties concerning the identity of the articles of faith and the immutability of God's knowledge. The problem of the identity of the object of faith arose from some remarks made by Augustine in his exegesis of the Gospel according to Saint John 10. 8,[9] and in his *De nuptiis et concupiscentia*:[10] although what is believed about the events in Christ's life is worded in different ways, notably by different tenses of the verbs, by those who express their belief before and after his coming, the content must remain exactly the same.

One answer to the question of what the object of faith actually is came to be called the *res* theory: the object of faith which in spite of different ways of expressing it remains the same is the actual thing or event, for instance Christ's birth (*nativitas Christi*), considered as an *incomplexum*, as something

7. De Rijk 1962–7, II(1), pp. 357–9.
8. De Rijk 1962–7, II(2), p. 208.
9. *In Johannis Evangelium tractatus*, XLV, 9, *PL* 35, 1722.
10. II, 11, *PL* 44, 450.

which in any case does not have the complexity of a proposition. This view was supported by pointing to the fact that God, the prime object of faith, is absolutely simple. Moreover, the faith of the believers who live in this world has the same object as the future vision which they will enjoy in heaven; and the object of that vision, which is a simple intuition of the highest light, is certainly not complex or determined by qualifications of time.[11]

Against this *res* theory it was urged by others that the object of an act of believing is something to which the notions of truth and falsity are applicable and which must therefore be the product of a *complexio*: a *complexum* or proposition. The adherents of this *complexum* theory often use the word '*enuntiabile*' for the proposition which is the object of belief; it should be noted that in this context '*enuntiabile*' has practically the same meaning as '*enuntiatio*' and designates a declarative sentence or the accusative-plus-infinitive expression corresponding to it. Now in order to save the sameness of the object of faith which they identified with a proposition, the *complexum* theorists tried to replace the declarative sentences which have an indexical character because of the different tenses of verbs by some kind of eternal sentence in which the indexical elements have been neutralised or eliminated and whose truth value cannot change. The simplest device was to make the proposition which is the object of faith consist of the disjunction of three differently tensed verbs, for example: 'that Christ was born or is born or will be born' ('*Christum esse natum, vel nasci, vel nasciturum esse*').[12] Another solution was suggested by the so-called *nominales*, who made a distinction between the principal signification and the accidental signification of words. Words which belong to different word-classes, such as '*albedo*', '*albet*', '*album*', have a common principal signification and different accidental significations, just as '*albus*', '*alba*', '*album*', are one and the same *nomen*, with the same principal signification and different accidental significations. In the same way, it was argued, declarative sentences with different tenses of the verbs and consequently different accidental significations may be taken as varying forms of one and the same proposition, whose identity is determined, not by the sounds or the accidental modes of signifying, but by the unity of the thing signified.[13] Others, for instance Bonaventure[14] and Peter of Tarantasia,[15]

---

11. Cf. Bonaventure 1882–1902a, Dist. 24, art. 1, q. 3; Peter of Tarantasia 1652, Dist. 24, art. 3.
12. Cf. Chenu 1934, p. 131.
13. Some of the relevant texts are quoted in Chenu 1934.
14. Bonaventure 1882–1902a, Dist. 24, art. 1, q. 3.
15. Peter of Tarantasia 1652, Dist. 24, art. 3.

who had objections against certain aspects of the theory of the *nominales*, distinguished two kinds of propositions, one with tenses of the verb which are in accordance with the contingent position occupied by the believer in the course of time, and one that is neutral and indifferent to all time, with a verb that has been made tenseless. The substance of faith does not depend upon superficial changes in the position of the believer and may thus be best expressed by means of tenseless propositions. Finally, there were also mixed views. Thomas Aquinas,[16] for example, was of the opinion that according as the question is considered from the standpoint of the believer or from the standpoint of that which is believed both the *complexum* theory and the *res* theory may claim relative truth.

Indexical expressions were also discussed in connection with the immutability of God's knowledge. Peter Lombard[17] mentions the following objection against the doctrine that if God knows something at a certain time, he has always known it and will always know it. God formerly knew that the world would be created; but he does not know now that the world will be created; therefore he knew something which he does not know now. From a consideration of the proper function of such indexical expressions as 'yesterday', 'today', 'tomorrow' and the tenses of the verb, Peter concludes, however, that in the same way as those who believed that Christ would be born and those who believe that he was born have the same faith in spite of the differences in the wording, God, who knew before the creation of the world that it would be created and who now knows that it has been created, has exactly the same knowledge about the creation of the world.

The fourteenth century

The theories concerning the significate of a proposition which were put forward in the course of the fourteenth century show a marked continuity with the views that had been developed in the past. But while one gets the impression that Abelard's *dictum* theory and, on the other hand, the *res* theory and the *complexum* theory were not really rivals, in the later period theories of all three types were commonly seen as in sharp conflict with each other. The theory which comes closest to Abelard's *dictum* theory is the theory of the *complexe significabile*, usually associated with Gregory of Rimini. It is not unlikely that a similar view had already been defended by William of Crathorn, but from the few sources which are available at

16. ST, IIaIIae, q. 1, art. 2.
17. *Sent.*, I, Dist. 41.

present it is hard to tell exactly what William's doctrine was.[18] According to Gregory, then, a mental proposition in the proper sense is either an act of assenting or an act of knowing. At the very beginning of his commentary on the *Sentences*, which he completed shortly before 1345 in Paris (*Prologus*, q. 1, art. 1), he raises the question of what exactly the object of theology is and in that connection discusses the more general problem of the nature of the object of knowledge that is acquired by scientific proof. Rejecting the view that the object of knowledge is a proposition or *complexum* and also the view that it is a *res* in the outside world, he defends the thesis that what is known and assented to or believed is that of which the mental proposition is a natural sign and of which the written and spoken propositions or their mental images are conventional signs. This total and adequate significate of the proposition he also calls the *enuntiabile* (in the sense in which that word was used in such treatises as the *Ars Meliduna* and the *Ars Burana*) and the *complexe significabile*: something that can be signified only by a proposition which contains an act of *complexio* and never by a single word or a combination of words that lacks affirmative or negative force. It should be noted that Gregory does not use '*dictum*' in Abelard's sense; when he makes use of that term, it means the words uttered and not that which is asserted by those words. In trying to answer the question of the ontological status of this object of assent and knowledge Gregory distinguishes three nuances of meaning in such words as '*aliquid*', '*res*', '*ens*'. Although it cannot be held that an assertible is something in the sense of a substance or accident as denoted by categorematic terms, it is a thing in the sense in which Aristotle speaks of the thing which underlies an affirmation or negation and in which he says that a statement is true or false because the thing is or is not; and it may also be called a thing, in case the proposition is true, in so far as it is part of the actual world. In other words, it is either that which is asserted or believed (or could be asserted or believed) to be the case and can thus be true or false, or that which is actually the case, but never a thing in the narrowest sense. For Gregory the bearers of truth and falsity (and of the modalities) are not only actually existing propositions and the significates of actually existing propositions, but also states of affairs that are capable of being signified by true or false propositions even if these corresponding propositions do not in fact exist. In that case the true assertibles are always actually signified by God as the uncreated sign of all truth.[19]

18. Cf. Nuchelmans 1973, pp. 212–9. Recent research seems to prove that Adam Wodeham held a
    similar theory before Gregory of Rimini; see Gál 1977.
19. Gregory of Rimini 1522, I, Dist. 39, q. 1, art. 2.

Among those who followed Gregory in postulating some kind of *complexe significabile* – Bonsembiante Beduarius of Padua,[20] John of Ripa,[21] and Albert of Saxony[22] – there were also some, notably Ugolino of Orvieto[23] and perhaps Paul of Venice,[24] who held that in certain cases the *complexe significabile* may be identified with a thing in the strictest sense. If, for example, the *complexe significabile* is the content of a proposition that asserts the existence of one actual thing, such as that there is a God (*deum esse*), then the significate is nothing but the thing in so far as it actually exists. The only difference between the significate that God exists and the incomplex thing, the existing God, is that they are signified and understood in different ways: in a verbal way (*deum esse*) and in a nominal way (*deus ens*). Only if an actually existing thing is signified in a verbal way, by means of a *complexio* which makes the notions of truth and falsity applicable, is it a proper object of acts of assenting and knowing.

The *Ars Meliduna*[25] had already mentioned a theory according to which an assertible is nothing but an act of thinking that something is the case. If '*complexum*' is taken in the sense of a mental proposition as a particular act of apprehending things in a manner characteristic of a *complexio*, then such an act theory of the assertible may also be called a *complexum* theory. In the fourteenth century this type of theory was put forward by William Ockham[26] and Robert Holkot.[27] In their view the immediate object of an act of believing or knowing is nothing but that act itself; the act of naturally signifying and the thing signified are one and the same. The mental propositions or particular acts of believing and knowing are also the primary bearers of the truth values; truth and falsity are not qualities of such propositions, but those propositions themselves. More or less the same thesis was maintained by John Buridan and Marsilius of Inghen.[28] Buridan[29] holds that such accusative-plus-infinitive expressions as '*Socratem currere*' ('that Socrates runs') can often be interpreted according

20. *Quattuor principia*; cf. Élie 1937, pp. 140–5.
21. Cf. Vignaux 1977, pp. 327–9.
22. Albert of Saxony 1497b, *Quaestiones super Analytica posteriora*, I, q. 2, q. 7, q. 33.
23. *Prologus* to the commentary on the *Sentences*, q. 1, art. 2 (Zumkeller 1941, pp. 290–301). Cf. also Eckermann 1972.
24. Cf. Nuchelmans 1973, pp. 268–9.
25. De Rijk 1962–7, II(1), p. 357.
26. William Ockham 1967, *Prologus*; William Ockham 1491, *Quodlibeta septem*, especially III, 6; IV, 17; V, 6; V, 24.
27. Robert Holkot 1510b, I; also *Quodlibeta* I, 6, in Courtenay 1971.
28. Marsilius of Inghen 1501, Prooemium to Book I, q. 2, art. 3; Marsilius of Inghen 1516, I, q. 1.
29. John Buridan 1588, esp. IV, q. 10, q. 14; V, q. 7; VI, q. 10., q. 11.

to material supposition, in such a way that they stand for the proposition *'Socrates currit'*. If, on the other hand, they have to be taken in a signifying function (*significative* or *personaliter*), then they refer to exactly the same thing in the outside world as does a combination of words or concepts which does not contain a copula. Just as the phrase *'Socrates currens'* ('running Socrates') has an application if in the outside world there is an individual named 'Socrates' in the state indicated, the expression *'Socratem currere'* is true if the same individual in that state exists. If there is any one significate of a *complexum* as such, it is a thing in a certain state (*res sic se habens*); but exactly the same thing can also be signified in a nominal way. Peter of Ailly,[30] on the other hand, who was also an adherent of the *complexum* theory, rejected the doctrine that basic affirmative propositions, if true, name one entity in a certain state as determined by the categorematic and syncategorematic parts of the proposition. According to him such propositions refer to all the entities referred to by the categorematic parts and they do so in a certain way (*aliqualiter*), but asking what kind of thing the significate of the proposition as a whole is betrays a lack of insight into the proper workings of language.

Finally, mention should be made of some variants of a *res* theory. In the first place, some authors agreed with the *complexum* theorists that the mental proposition is the primary bearer of truth and falsity, but at the same time rejected the view that the proposition is the object of acts of assenting or knowing. A *res* theory in this sense was probably held by Walter Chatton[31] and quite clearly by André de Neufchâteau.[32] According to the latter it is not the proposition 'God is three and one' that is the object of assent, but rather that which is signified by the proposition, namely that God is three and one. Before we judge that the proposition is true, we must give our assent to this significate. But when he comes to explain what this significate is, André does not follow Gregory of Rimini, but sides with Buridan: that God is three and one is nothing but God being three and one, the thing that is such and is in such a state as is required for the truth of the judgement. To a certain extent this theory resembles the view taken by the Thomistic school in the debate concerning the object of assent and knowledge. John Capreolus,[33] for instance, is of the opinion that the proximate object of belief and knowledge is the proposition

30. Peter of Ailly 1490–5b, esp, the first part of the *Insolubilia*.
31. Cf. Nuchelmans 1973, pp. 210–12, 217–18.
32. André de Neufchâteau 1514, *Prologus*, q. 1–3; Dist. 2, q. 1–2; Dist. 33–4.
33. John Capreolus 1900–8, I, pp. 51–7.

formed by the mind; this mental proposition is the product of an act of compounding or dividing and is the matter to which the act of judging is related. This internal object, however, is not that to which the act of believing or knowing is actually directed, but only the medium through which the mind tries to establish contact with the outside world. The ultimate object of belief and knowledge is, therefore, the thing in the outside world or rather the way in which things in the outside world may be connected, namely either as a combination of matter and form or as a combination of substance and accident. Such a proposition as 'Socrates is white' does not, according to Capreolus, have any one significate, but rather has many significates: it signifies Socrates, whiteness, that Socrates falls under the concept of whiteness, and the present. All these things, however, do not constitute a genuine unity. The Thomistic view thus seems to differ from the extreme realism maintained by Walter Burley,[34] who argued for the existence of *propositiones in re* which are compounded of things outside the mind and form the adequate and ultimate significate of true mental propositions, which consist of concepts. In a proposition which exists in the world the things that serve as subject and predicate are the matter, and the copula, which consists in the compounding or separating activity of the mind, is the form. Just as an act of attention unites the seeing in the eye and the visible object outside the eye so that we can speak of an object seen, the intellectual act of compounding or separating together with the subject-thing and the predicate-thing forms a unity which is a copulated entity (*ens copulatum*). This copulated entity presumably consists of the subject-thing and the predicate-thing in so far as they are truly judged to be identical or separate.

Sentence-tokens and sentence-types

This survey of the main currents in the medieval semantics of propositions may be concluded by briefly describing at least one further important issue connected with determining the nature of the proposition and its significate. When the proposition was considered as a bearer of truth values, either primary or secondary, it was generally taken to be a sentence-token. That at least some medievals were aware of a distinction between sentence-tokens and sentence-types is evident from Abelard,[35] who maintained that one cannot make sense of the objection that the same utterance, for

---

34. Walter Burley 1497, esp. the prooemium; cf. Peter Tartaretus 1514a, f. 5 R; 1514b, f. 41 R; Domingo de Soto 1587, *Prologus Praedicamentorum*, pp. 108–9.
35. Peter Abelard 1970a, p. 54; cf. also p. 71.

instance 'Socrates is seated', seems to be both true and false, unless the utterance is taken in the not unusual acceptation of those who call different utterances the same sentence on account of a similarity in form. This notion of a sentence-type is, however, mentioned only to be rejected. The interpretation of a proposition as a sentence-token was supported by the Boethian definition of a proposition as a combination of words which signifies (*significans*) something true or false. This definition was held not to apply to an ambiguous sentence (*multiplex propositio*). In the same vein sentences containing such indexical expressions as demonstrative or personal pronouns were thought to signify nothing if they are uttered without reference to a thing present. By themselves, without context or situation, they are not sufficient to assert something, although they are capable of being used to make a statement which is either true or false.[36] When Paul of Venice[37] felt that not only sentence-tokens but also sentence-types should be counted as propositions, he accordingly changed the Boethian definition and spoke of a combination of words which is capable of signifying (*significativa*) something true or false. That sentence-types were occasionally taken as signifying the true or the false is obvious from those cases in which the truth value is said to change. Bonaventure,[38] for example, thinks it wrong to hold – as the *nominales* did – that a verb in the present tense signifies different present things at different times. Just as the noun 'man' has exactly the same signification when it is used to refer to Peter and when it is used to refer to Paul, so a verb in the present tense has exactly the same signification whether it is uttered today or tomorrow; it signifies the present in general. Similarly, a sentence to the effect that you will be born remains the same at whatever time it is uttered; consequently, the same sentence which was formerly true is now false. And Peter of Ailly[39] says that such a proposition as 'The Antichrist will exist at the future moment c' is true before c if the Antichrist exists at c, but false (rather than inapplicable) after c. It may cease to be true and is therefore mutably true; but once it has become false it remains immutably false. In this connection it is worth mentioning that the author of the *Ars Meliduna*[40] considers the assertible which belongs to the sentence 'Socrates loves his son' as nugatory (*nugatorium*) when Socrates ceases to have a son. The context makes it clear that

36. *Introductiones Montanae minores*, in De Rijk 1962–7, II(2), p. 19.
37. Paul of Venice 1499, *Logica magna*, f. 101.
38. Bonaventure 1882–1902a, Dist. 41, art. 2, q. 2.
39. Peter of Ailly 1490, q. 11, art. 1, C–D.
40. In De Rijk 1962–7, II(1), pp. 362–3.

'nugatory' means the same as 'neither-true-nor-false'. There are, therefore, assertibles which, according to the circumstances in which they are asserted (*iuxta rei variationem*), can repeatedly begin and cease to be either-true-or-false. Apparently the assertible is here taken as belonging to the sentence-type.

The bearers of logical relations

As to the question of the bearers of logical relations, an interesting distinction is found in the *Tractatus Anagnini*.[41] Such a logical law as the law of the conversion of negative universal statements may be formulated about things (No man is a stone; therefore no stone is a man), about propositions (The proposition 'No man is a stone' is true; therefore the proposition 'No stone is a man' is true) or about assertibles (It is true that no man is a stone; therefore it is true that no stone is a man). In practice, though, logic was done mainly in the first way. The relevance to logic of the question of the nature of the bearers of truth and falsity becomes clear when one considers the consequences of such a *complexum* theory as was held by Robert Holkot.[42] According to him a proposition which is not actually formed cannot be true or false. Consequently, such logical rules as 'Some proposition is true; therefore its contradictory is false' apply only to those cases in which the proposition concerned really exists. Without this presupposition of existence the rules do not hold, for it is quite conceivable that, for example, the true proposition 'You run' is the only proposition in existence, and then it does not follow that its contradictory is false, since that contradictory has not been formulated. Walter Burley[43] pointed out that if this view were correct, it would be impossible for a debater to get involved in a contradiction. For given that the affirmative proposition and the negative proposition do not exist at the same time, the first is not true when the second is false and the second is not false when the first is true. Moreover, every disputation becomes pointless, since the respondent cannot react to the propositions that are propounded by his opponent. As an answer to this difficulty Burley maintains that the mind can understand a proposition which is abstracted from particular utterances, just as it can think of a lion or an elephant in general without conceiving of a particular lion or elephant. In the same way as the word '*homo*' uttered by me and the word '*homo*' uttered by you have something in common – the universal

41. In De Rijk 1962–7, II(2), p. 236.
42. Courtenay 1971, p. 15.
43. Walter Burley 1497, ad *Cat.* 14^b12.

nature of the word that exists in both particular utterances and is distinguishable from them – so the mind can understand a proposition which is the universal nature common to different particular utterances. It is this kind of abstract proposition which both the respondent and the opponent in a disputation have before their minds; by means of this universal it can be explained that a debater contradicts himself, because the universal is something that remains the same throughout the debate and can be first conceded and then denied.

II

SYNCATEGOREMATA, EXPONIBILIA, SOPHISMATA

A grammatical distinction between categoremata and syncategoremata

The paradigm of the categorical proposition with which medieval logicians were primarily concerned is a sentence of two words that serve as the subject term and the predicate term – e.g., '*Socrates currit.*' [1] Any word that can be used alone as a subject term or as a predicate term is classifiable as a categorematic word; all other words are classifiable as syncategorematic words, those that can occur in a proposition, whether categorical or hypothetical, [2] only along with at least one properly matched pair of categorematic words – e.g., '*Solus Socrates currit*', '*Socrates currit contingenter*', '*Socrates non currit*', '*Si Socrates currit, Socrates movetur.*' Drawing the distinction between categoremata and syncategoremata along this line, which seems to have been the original line of distinction, [3] produces mutually exclusive and jointly exhaustive classes that coincide almost

---

1. In standard twentieth-century philosophical usage a proposition is not a sentence but the content of a sentence, so that the two sentences '*Socrates currit*' and 'Socrates is running' express one and the same proposition. But when the medievals spoke of a *propositio* they were speaking not of the content of a sentence but of a sentence, a propositional vehicle or sign, written or spoken or mental. The medieval logicians' *enuntiabile* or *dictum* of a *propositio* corresponds most closely to a proposition considered as the content of a sentence. (See Kretzmann 1970 and esp. Nuchelmans 1973.) Nevertheless, in this discussion I will use 'proposition' as the English equivalent of the medieval '*propositio*'.

   In Latin a complete subject-predicate proposition may consist of only one word – e.g., '*Curro*' ('I am running', 'I run') – and Latin, like English, has impersonal verbs, such as '*pluere*' ('to rain'), which take only dummy subjects in order to form complete propositions. For purposes of this analysis, however, such understood personal pronouns and dummy subjects also count as subject terms.

2. The medieval categorical/hypothetical distinction is broader than the twentieth-century use of 'hypothetical' might suggest, closely approximating the modern distinction between atomic and molecular propositions (or sentences). Thus both these propositions are hypothetical in the relevant sense: 'If Socrates is running, he is moving'; 'Socrates is running, and Plato is walking.'

3. The source of the medieval distinction seems to have been this well-known passage from Priscian's *Institutiones grammaticae*: 'Partes igitur orationis sunt secundum dialecticos duae, nomen et verbum, quia hae solae per se coniunctae plenam faciunt orationem; alias autem partes "syncategoremata", hoc est, consignificantia, appellabant' (Priscian 1855–9, 2, 54.5). The distinction as Priscian presents it is grammatical in character despite his attribution of it to 'the dialecticians'. (On the identity of these dialecticians, see Nuchelmans 1973, p. 124.)

perfectly with certain groupings of the parts of speech (*partes orationis*) recognised by medieval grammarians: the categoremata are the names (both substantival and adjectival),[4] the personal and demonstrative pronouns, and the verbs (excluding auxiliary verbs);[5] the syncategoremata are all the others – e.g., the conjunctions, adverbs, and prepositions.

The logicians' notion of syncategoremata

The notion of syncategoremata that became important in medieval logic was, however, both narrower and broader than that comparatively orderly classification in terms of the parts of speech. Although more than fifty different words were considered in one or another medieval logician's treatment of syncategoremata, by no means all non-categorematic words in even the relatively small classes, such as conjunctions, were of enough interest to the logicians to be treated expressly among their syncategoremata. On the other hand, several words that might have been classified as categorematic on grammatical grounds became prominent members of the logicians' syncategoremata. The inclusion of certain grammatically categorematic adjectives, for instance, such as '*omnis*' and '*infinita*', may be among the reasons that led to a further distinction between categorematic and syncategorematic *uses* of a single word.[6] Certain pronouns, such as '*quicquid*' and '*uterque*',[7] and at least four verbs – '*differt*', '*vult*', and especially

---

4. Substantival names are either common ('*homo*') or proper ('*Socrates*'), either concrete ('*homo*') or abstract ('*humanitas*'). Adjectival names are adjectives, but a Latin adjective in the neuter case can be used as a substantival name – e.g., '*Album currit*' ('What is white is running', 'A white thing is running').

5. The verb '*esse*' is a special case. While it is not uncommon for medieval logicians to distinguish categorematic and syncategorematic uses of a single word, such uses are particularly obvious and important in the case of '*esse*', which can be used either existentially, and hence categorematically, as in '*Socrates est*', or copulatively, and hence syncategorematically, as in '*Socrates est homo*', '*Socrates est albus*', '*Socrates est currens*'. (For William of Sherwood's treatment of this distinction see Kretzmann 1968, pp. 90–3.) The distinction (and close relationship) between these two uses of '*esse*' was recognised and made much of in Abelard's logic, before the development of a branch of logic devoted to syncategorematic words (see Kretzmann forthcoming). Obviously, intransitive verbs such as '*currere*' ('to run') constitute the paradigm of verbs considered as categorematic words in this classification, but even such clearly transitive verbs as '*amare*' can occur in a complete two-word proposition – as in '*Socrates amat*' ('Socrates loves') – without taking an object.

6. For example, in '*Omnes currunt*' ('All are running'), '*omnes*' is used pronominally and hence categorematically; and in '*Mundus est omne*' ('The world is everything') '*omne*' is used nominally and hence categorematically. But in '*Omnis homo currit*' ('Every man is running') '*omnis*' is, despite its grammatical character as an adjective, being used as a quantifier, a *signum* (sign [of distribution]), and hence syncategorematically. (See Kretzmann 1968, pp. 17–18.) For distinctions between the categorematic and syncategorematic uses of '*infinita*' ('infinitely many'), see Kretzmann 1968, pp. 41–3.

7. '*Quicquid*' ('whatever') and '*uterque*' ('both') can and frequently do stand alone as subject terms, just as their English counterparts do, but they are also signs of distribution.

'*incipit*' and '*desinit*'[8] – were also discussed more or less regularly as syncategoremata. But those pronouns and verbs found places among the syncategoremata not so much because of their syntactic roles or in virtue of special syncategorematic uses to which they can be put as because of the meanings they have in their standard uses.[9] The logicians' notion of syncategoremata, then, was less precisely defined than the grammatical notion from which it had been derived. Most logicians who dealt with syncategoremata explicitly offered some sort of general account of them, and a few attempted to order them systematically,[10] but the notion persisted and evolved because of its usefulness and not because it picked out a clearly recognisable category of linguistic or logical entities. Perhaps the most persistent theme in general accounts of the nature of the syncategoremata is that they are words whose signification is incomplete in a special respect, different from the respect in which, as Aristotle had pointed out, the signification of (categorematic) verbs is incomplete.[11] Here, for instance, is the account offered by Henry of Ghent: 'And they are called syncategorematic as if to say "consignificant" – i.e., significant together with others, namely, with categoremata – not because they signify *nothing* on their own, but because they have a signification that is not definite but indefinite, a signification whose definiteness they derive from those [words] that are adjoined to them. For they do not signify any *thing*, but

8. All these verbs ordinarily call for complements, either infinitive or prepositional phrases. They can, however, stand alone as predicate terms, as in the crusaders' motto '*Deus vult*'. ('*Vult*', by the way, seems very rare as a syncategorematic word; I have found it treated explicitly as such only by Nicholas of Paris.) '*Differt*', '*incipit*', and '*desinit*' are likely to have found their way into the syncategoremata originally because each of them involves covert negation (brought out explicitly in the analyses (*expositiones*) of propositions in which they occur), and negating devices are among the most important and universally recognised syncategoremata. (See Kretzmann 1976.)

9. See, however, William of Sherwood's attempt to distinguish categorematic and syncategorematic uses of '*incipit*' (Kretzmann 1968, pp. 106–8).

10. See, for example, the reasonably systematic organisation of William of Sherwood's treatment of syncategoremata (Kretzmann 1968, p. 8). The notion of syncategoremata might be sorted less systematically, but perhaps more recognisably from a twentieth-century point of view, into the following topics, each of which is associated with one or more than one logical or semantic relationship: Distribution (or quantification), e.g., '*omnis*', '*totus*'; Negation, e.g., '*non*', '*nihil*'; Exclusion, e.g., '*solus*', '*tantum*'; Exception, e.g., '*praeter*', '*nisi*'; Composition (or predication), e.g., '*est*', '*incipit*'; Modality, e.g., '*necessario*', '*contingenter*'; Conditionality, e.g., '*si*', '*quin*'; Copulation (or conjunction), e.g., '*et*'; Disjunction, e.g., '*vel*', '*utrum*'; Comparison, e.g., '*quam*'; Reduplication, e.g., '*inquantum*', '*secundum quod*'.

11. *De interpretatione*, Ch. 3: 'A verb ... is a sign of things said of something else ... And it is always a sign of what holds, that is, holds of a subject ... When uttered just by itself a verb is a name and signifies something – the speaker arrests his thought and the hearer pauses – but it does not yet signify whether it is or not. For not even "to be" or "not to be" is a sign of the actual thing (nor if you say simply "that which is"); for by itself it is nothing, but it additionally signifies some combination, which cannot be thought of without the components.' (Ackrill translation.)

they signify rather in the manner of a disposition of a thing and of terms signifying things. Every disposition, however, is indefinite in itself and is made definite by that which it disposes.'[12]

Syncategoremata in the logica moderna

The logicians' interest in syncategoremata began to flourish, naturally enough, in the rise of the *logica moderna*, stimulated by the recovery of Aristotle's treatise on fallacies around the middle of the twelfth century.[13] The analysis of linguistic fallacies seems to have alerted the early terminist logicians to the possibility that the logical relationships central to syllogistic theory can be altered or blocked when certain expressions (common in ordinary discourse but excluded from the standard forms of Aristotelian logic) occur in the propositions whose logical relationships are in question. Some of the words that were later to be treated systematically as the syncategoremata are cited more or less casually in the early literature of the *logica moderna* just because of their disruptive effect on standard logical relationships or operations,[14] or because of the changes they bring about in the standard interpretation of other expressions important to logicians.[15]

---

12. 'Et dicuntur sincathegoreumatice, quasi: consignificative, idest: *cum aliis significative*, scilicet cum cathegoreumaticis; non quia de se nichil significant, sed quia habent significationem non finitam sed infinitam, cuius finitationem trahunt ab adjunctis. Non enim significant aliquam rem, sed significant per modum dispositionis rei et terminorum significantium res. Dispositio autem omnis est in se infinita et finitatur per illud quod disponit' (ed. Braakhuis 1978, 1.7–2.2).

13. On this development see especially L. M. de Rijk's indispensable *Logica Modernorum* (De Rijk 1962–7).

14. An example from the anonymous *Ars Emmerana*: 'It must also be noted that there are sophistical terms by means of which the conversion of propositions is blocked. Such terms are "alone", "only", "besides", "except". Thus this proposition does not convert: "Something is one alone"; "Something is only an animal"; "Something besides Socrates is a man"' (although without 'alone', 'only', and 'besides Socrates' each of those particular affirmative propositions would convert). 'Hoc etiam notandum est quod sunt sophistici termini quibus propositionum impeditur conversio. Tales sunt: "*solum*", "*tantum*", "*praeter*", "*nisi*". Unde haec propositio non convertitur: "*aliquid est unum solum*", "*aliquid est tantum animal*", "*aliquid praeter Socratem est homo*"' (ed. De Rijk 1962–7, II(2), 157.30–158.2).

15. An example from the anonymous *Tractatus de univocatione Monacensis*: 'Again, there are people who say that when the word "besides" or the word "other" are placed between the name of an existent thing and the name of a non-existent thing, the reference of the name is expanded, even though a present-tense verb is used in [the proposition]. Thus they say that these are true and grammatically correct: "Something besides Antichrist is not other than Caesar." It is better, however, that these be called worthless, because they say falsely that something is not, and every assertion of what is false is worthless.' 'Item sunt qui dicunt quod quando hec dictio "*praeter*" sive hec dictio "*aliud*" ponuntur inter nomen rei existentis et ... nomen rei non existentis, nominis appellatio ampliatur, licet in ea ponatur verbum presentis temporis. Unde dicunt has esse veras et congruas: "*aliquid preter Antichristum non est aliud quam Cesar*". Melius tamen est ut hec dicantur nugatorie, quia ⟨dicunt⟩ aliquid non esse quod falsum est, et omnis positio falsi nugatoria est' (ed. De Rijk 1962–7, II(2), 340.23–30).

Presumably as a result of being noticed in such connections, the syn-categoremata emerged as occasions for refinements and extensions of logical or semantic theory, the role in which they naturally became and remained important for medieval logicians.

With all the warnings and disclaimers appropriate to historical generalis-ations of vast scope and meagre detail, I suggest that the career of the syncategoremata within the *logica moderna* falls into three stages, the third of which is divided into two contemporaneous lines of development:

[1] their emergence as the focal points of certain logical or semantic relationships or special problems of interpretation (in the twelfth century, especially the latter half);

[2] their identification as a distinguishable set of topics worthy of development in separate treatises called, typically, *Syncategoremata* (from the last quarter of the twelfth century to the last quarter of the thirteenth);

[3a] their assimilation into general treatises on logic, sometimes as a group, but sometimes dispersed in ways designed to associate particular syncategoremata with more general topics in logic to which they are appropriate; and

[3b] their absorption into the sophisma-literature, where a particular syncate-gorema may serve as the germ of a paradox the interest of which is often associated with metaphysics or natural philosophy more than with logic or semantics proper (from the first quarter of the fourteenth century to the disintegration of scholastic logic).[16]

It might be an exaggeration to say that concern with the syncategoremata constituted the stimulus for the development of medieval techniques of linguistic analysis (of which *expositio* is the most important)[17] and the basis for the development of the sophisma-literature, but there can be no doubt

16. These historical stages may be exemplified by texts drawn from the list of relevant texts in Appendix I as follows. Stage [1]: Texts (2/3), (3/2), (7); Stage [2]: Texts (5), (9), (21); Stage [3a]: Texts (22), (23), (29); Stage [3b]: Texts (24), (25/26), (28). For an earlier development in the sophisma-literature, much less closely associated with the syncategoremata, see Pinborg 1975a, pp. 44–5.

17. The *Tractatus exponibilium* formerly attributed to Peter of Spain but certainly later (see De Rijk 1972, pp. LIV–LV) defines an exponible proposition in terms of syncategoremata: 'An exponible proposition is a proposition that has an obscure sense requiring exposition in virtue of some syncategorema occurring either explicitly or included within some word.' 'Propositio ex-ponibilis est propositio habens obscurum sensum expositione indigentem propter aliquod syn-categorema explicite positum vel in aliqua dictione inclusum' (Pseudo-Petrus 1489, f. 35vb). Perhaps the systematic classification and organized explicit discussion of exponible propositions (*exponibilia*) in treatises devoted to them as such (which seem to have begun around the middle of the fourteenth century and to have flourished in the fifteenth and sixteenth centuries) should be considered a fourth stage in the career of the syncategoremata. See Ashworth 1973. Professor Ashworth's article has more than a general relevance to the topics of this investigation: Section Three (pp. 153–9) is devoted to exceptive propositions (which she inadvertently calls 'exclusive propositions' several times in the Section) and thus constitutes a historical extension of the study of medieval treatments of exception that will be presented in this discussion.

that both those developments owed a great deal of their form and content to problems associated with syncategoremata and to techniques developed first in order to cope with those problems. Without too much distortion it can be said that the inclusion of at least one syncategorematic word is the defining characteristic of an exponible proposition, and that the vast majority of sophismata focus on exponible propositions.[18]

The strategy of this investigation

At the present stage of the scholarly investigation of syncategoremata, any study such as this that attempts to present the topic in a strictly limited format can only scratch the surface in one way or another.[19] Tracing the treatment of one or two of the standard syncategoremata through many texts[20] reveals historical connections and doctrinal developments in more detail than would be accessible in a broad encyclopedic survey of comparable length. The remainder of this discussion is therefore based on a fairly detailed examination of two of the most frequently discussed syncategorematic words, *'praeter'* ('but', 'besides', 'except') and *'totus'* ('whole'). representing exception and distribution, respectively.[21]

18. On the development of the techniques of linguistic analysis, see Pinborg 1972. On the development of the sophisma-literature, see Grabmann 1940.
19. Research in this area will be stimulated and aided by the publication of H. A. G. Braakhuis' monumental study of the treatment of the syncategoremata in the thirteenth century, accompanied by his editions of the central texts. Braakhuis 1979, the only portion of his work published to date, has appeared in two volumes: Deel I, *Inleidende Studie* (Hoofdstuk I, *De ontwikkeling van de theorie van de syncategoremata tot aan de 13de eeuw*; Hoofdstuk II, *De 13de eeuwse syncategoremata-tractaten*; Hoofdstuk III, *Enkele aspecten van de ontwikkeling van de theorie van de syncategoremata in de 13de eeuw*); Deel II, *Uitgave van Nicolaas van Parijs' Sincategoreumata*. Eventually Dr Braakhuis plans to publish his historical and critical studies in English. I am grateful to Dr Braakhuis for his extraordinary generosity in allowing me to make use of everything he had completed as of November 1978 (Braakhuis 1978 and 1978a): Deel I (Hoofdstuk I and parts of Hoofdstuk II), Deel II (preliminary version), and preliminary editions of Robert Bacon (?) and Henry of Ghent, with excerpts from John le Page and Peter of Spain. This study could never have been attempted without his help. Braakhuis 1979 appeared too late for me to take full account of it, but my references to Nicholas of Paris are to Braakhuis 1979, Deel II.
20. In one way or another I have made use of thirty-three texts, dating from the first half of the twelfth century to the first half of the fifteenth. The texts are listed in Appendix I attached to this discussion. Some of those texts are not treatises independent of one another, and in a few cases the relationships among them are not yet clear. The confusion surrounding Peter of Spain's treatise on syncategoremata is particularly great, partly because of the misleading impression made by J. P. Mullally's translation (Mullally 1964), the only form in which this work has been available to non-specialists, and partly because 'the text of the *Syncategoremata* as presented in the Cologne incunabular editions ... is quite different from Peter's own text' (Braakhuis 1977, p. 122, n. 33). (Mullally's translation is based on the Cologne editions. The relationship of the text of the Cologne editions to the genuine text of Peter's *Syncategoremata* may be determinable after the publication of Braakhuis' edition based on the manuscripts. Meanwhile it is safe to say that neither Mullally's translation nor the Cologne editions of 1489 and 1494 can be considered reliable witnesses to Peter's views on syncategoremata. See n. 48 below.)
21. Other syncategorematic words are likely to seem better choices for such single-track explor-

Standard elements in the treatment of a syncategorema

For all the variation in the ways in which different authors treated a single syncategorema, there is a marked tendency to organise the discussion around certain common expository and critical elements which thus provide the most promising lines along which to pursue an investigation of this sort. In tracing the treatments of *'praeter'* and *'totus'* it is useful to sort the material in terms of these seven elements:

I.   Definitions and analyses (of exception or of the sort of distribution effected by *'totus'*),
II. Classifications of the uses of the words (*'praeter'* and *'totus'*),
III. Grammatical, semantic, and logical rules governing propositions (involving *'praeter'* or *'totus'*),
IV. Examples (associated with II or III),
V.   Sophismata (involving *'praeter'* or *'totus'*),
VI. Expositions of propositions (involving *'praeter'* or *'totus'*),
VII. Questions (arising from I–VI).[22]

Focusing on any one of these elements through all the texts that contain it is instructive,[23] but the fullest development of the most interesting material is to be found in the sophismata.[24] It is there that the rules are applied in order to resolve apparent paradoxes or tested by being confronted with apparent counter-instances. And because different medieval logicians tend to take up the same logical or semantic issues in connection with the same sophismata, their discussions of those puzzles can provide a rich, historically continuous

ations. From the standpoint of the history of logic, *'omnis'* ('every') or *'si'* ('if'), for instance, look more promising; they are however, likely to receive more elaborate treatments than *'praeter'* or *'totus'*, which makes them less manageable for present purposes, and just because of their wider logical interest they are less distinctive of the medieval literature on syncategoremata. Similarly, the pairs *'necessario'/'contingenter'* ('necessarily'/'contingently') and *'incipit'/'desinit'* ('begins'/ 'ceases') have many more points of connection with other philosophical inquiries than do *'praeter'* and *'totus'*, but for just that reason they would give rise to issues that would be distracting in this context. Obviously there is a great deal of interesting work to be done in this area.

22. For samples of all these elements drawn from various texts, see Appendix II attached to this discussion.
23. It would be natural to suppose that the most philosophically interesting material would be found in VII, the questions; but VII is the rarest of these elements in the literature I have examined. Although any author may occasionally organise some of his discussion of a syncategorema in the form of a scholastic question, I have found only Nicholas of Paris making regular and extensive use of this form of exposition and criticism in connection with *'praeter'* and *'totus'*.
24. On sophismata generally, see Kretzmann 1977, esp. p. 6: '[A sophisma is] a sentence puzzling in its own right or on the basis of a certain assumption, designed to bring some abstract issue into sharper focus – the medieval ancestor of "The morning star is the evening star" or "George IV wished to know whether Scott was the author of *Waverley*"'; also n. 9: 'Because sophismata are sentences rather than arguments and intended to be illuminating and instructive rather than specious and misleading, it is misleading to call them sophisms', as many writers on this material still do.

line of doctrinal development or dispute. Accordingly, a consideration of a few of the relevant sophismata is perhaps the most efficient means of acquiring an initial understanding of philosophical and historical aspects of the medieval treatment of the syncategoremata.

A typical analysis of exception

I will present two sophismata involving '*praeter*', which it will be helpful to view against the background of this fairly typical analysis of exception: 'It must be noted that four things are required for exception: [1] the part that is excepted, [2] the whole from which the exception is made, [3] something in respect of which the exception is made, and [4] the act of excepting, which is conveyed by means of the exceptive word as by an instrument.'[25] Thus in the standard example 'Every man besides Socrates is running', Socrates is [1], all men constitute [2], the act of running is [3], and 'besides' ('*praeter*') is the instrument of the act of excepting.

The sophisma 'Socrates bis videt omnem hominem praeter Platonem'

The first of these two sophismata is treated in nine of the texts listed in Appendix I, and I have had access to the full text of eight of those treatments.[26] The interesting differences among those treatments occur not in the presentation of the problem but in its resolution, and so I will present the problem in a homogenised version of the sophisma sentence, the hypothesis, the proof, and the disproof before considering the various resolutions.

SOCRATES TWICE SEES EVERY MAN BESIDES PLATO[27]

Suppose that on one occasion Socrates sees every man and that on another occasion he sees every man other than Plato and does not see Plato.[28]

---

25. Walter Burley (ed. Boehner 1955, 165.16–22): 'Notandum, quod ad exceptionem requiruntur quatuor: Pars quae excipitur; totum, a quo fit exceptio; et aliquid, respectu cuius fiat exceptio; et actus excipiendi, qui importatur per dictionem exceptivam sicut per instrumentum. Verbi gratia sic dicendo: "Omnis homo praeter Sortem currit", Sortes est pars, quae excipitur, omnis homo est totum, a quo fit exceptio, currere est illud, respectu cuius fit exceptio, "praeter" est dictio exceptiva.' (I have made some changes in Boehner's punctuation.) See Appendix II, I, Definitions and Analyses, for other examples of such analyses of exception.
26. It is found in texts (7), (9), (11/10), ★(13), (15), (18), ★(20/19), (25/26), and (33/32).
27. This present-tense form is found in texts (7), ★(13), (18), and ★(20/19); texts (9), (11/10), and (15) have it in the future tense; (25/26) and (33/32) in the perfect.
28. Text (7) has no hypothesis – indeed, nothing but the sophisma sentence and the resolution (see n. 31 below). Text (11/10) also lacks a hypothesis, but in rather different circumstances, as the

Proof: The proposition 'Socrates twice sees every man' is false, and Plato is the only counter-instance; therefore when Plato is excepted, the resultant proposition is true.[29]

Disproof: Socrates twice sees every man besides Plato; therefore on one occasion he sees every man besides Plato, and on another occasion he sees every man besides Plato – which is false *ex hypothesi*.[30]

With one possible exception to be noted later, each of the eight texts under consideration offers the same basic appraisal of the sophisma sentence: it is ambiguous, being true in one of its senses and false in the other. But there are significant differences among the ways in which the ambiguity is characterised and resolved.

In *Dialectica Monacensis*, where the sophisma is introduced in connection with the fallacy of division, the entire resolution consists in this one, highly compressed observation: 'For it can be judged on the basis of "twice" or on the basis of "besides".'[31] The point of that observation and the theory that may be implicit in it can be understood most easily in the light of the fuller treatments to be discussed below.

Bacon clearly sees the sophisma as presenting a scope-ambiguity: is the logical operation of distribution (over two occasions) performed by 'twice' included by or inclusive of the logical operation of exception performed by 'besides'? That is, is the sophisma sentence to be read in this way '(Twice Socrates sees every every man) but Plato' or in this way 'Twice (Socrates sees every man but Plato)'? In the first way it is true; in the second, false. Bacon thinks that the ambiguity might also be expressed in terms of a choice between predicates in respect of which the exception is made – either 'twice sees' or 'sees' – but he prefers the resolution in terms of the inclusion of one operation by another as more generally applicable.[32]

discussion of it will show. In the other seven texts the hypothesis is virtually the same, but for purposes of tracing historical associations it may be worth noting that in texts (9), (15), and ★(20/19) the situation is presented in terms of two times, designated 'A' and 'B', while in texts ★(13), (18), (25/26), and (33/32) the presentation is in terms of 'one occasion' (*una vice*) and another, with no special designation for either occasion.

29. Text (7) has no proof, and (9) has merely '*Probatio, etc.*'. I have not seen anything beyond the hypothesis in ★(20/19), and so it will not figure in the rest of this discussion. In the other six texts the proof is essentially the one presented here.

30. Text (7) has no disproof. In the other seven texts the disproof is essentially the one presented here, but it is given most succinctly in (9) and most elaborately in (25/26).

31. 'Item. Secundum has fallacias accidit multiplicitas in omni oratione in qua sunt duo sincategoreumata sic se habentia quod locutio potest iudicari penes unum illorum vel penes reliquum ... Eodem modo solvitur hoc sophisma: "*Sor bis videt omnem hominem preter Platonem.*" Potest enim iudicari per "*bis*" vel per "*preter*"' (ed. De Rijk 1962–7, II(2), 572.38–573.2; 573.7–8).

32. 'Similiter contingit aptare omne sophisma quod contingit in exceptivis ex *includere vel includi* ... Solutio: prima duplex est ex eo quod potest fieri exceptio respectu eius quod est "*videre bis*" vel

The author of the *Abstractiones*[33] takes a position that is at least superficially quite different from the positions taken by the other seven authors.
Having provided no hypothesis at all,[34] he appraises the sophisma sentence
as 'unconditionally true' (*vera simpliciter*). But he shows that he recognises
its ambiguity when he rejects the disproof because it requires one to derive
from the hypothesis the premiss that on neither occasion does Socrates see
Plato, and 'we know that from a proposition that can have more than one
cause of its truth we cannot infer one of those causes'.[35] In the absence of a
hypothesis stipulating one cause of the truth of the sophisma sentence the
author cannot say in which sense the sentence is true, and his observation
regarding the invalid inference implicit in the disproof depends on his
preserving the ambiguity of the sophisma sentence – an intelligent resolution but one that suggests a lack of interest or of sophistication regarding
the peculiar properties of the syncategoremata.[36]

Peter of Spain locates the ambiguity in the possibility of assigning two
different scopes (or determinations) to 'twice': either it determines the
entire expression 'sees every man besides Plato' – in which case the
sophisma sentence is false – or it determines only 'sees every man' – in
which case the sophisma sentence is true. But Peter presents this basically

respectu eius quod est "*videre*". Primo modo vera, quia tunc significat vere (?) quod Sortes non
videbit Platonem bis, sed omnes alios; secundo modo falsa; non enim erit vera hec bis "*Sortes
videbit omnem hominem preter Platonem*", sed tantum in B. Hoc autem nichil aliud est quam quod
exceptio potest includere distributionem de li "*bis*" vel econverso. Si enim includat: excipit
respectu eius quod est "*videre bis*"; si includatur: excipit ab eo quod est "*videre*". Et multiplicatur
illa exceptio per distributionem de li "*bis*"' (ed. Braakhuis 1978, 171.12–13; 171.18–172.2). I have
made one significant change in Braakhuis' punctuation. On the uncertain authorship and
relative dating of this treatise, see n. 41 below.

33. The author is identified in MSS Digby 24 and Bruges 497 as a master Richard, sometimes referred
to as '*Ricardus sophista*'. De Rijk has suggested that he may be Richard Fishacre, a student of
Robert Bacon's, who died in 1248, when Bacon also died (De Rijk 1962–7, II(1), pp. 71–2). More
recently Pinborg has suggested Richard Rufus of Cornwall, a slightly younger contemporary of
Richard Fishacre's (Pinborg 1976c). The editors of the forthcoming edition of the *Abstractiones*
(Calvin Normore, Mary Sirridge, Paul Streveler, and Katherine Tachau) have so far not
committed themselves on the question of authorship. I am grateful to those editors, and to Tachau
in particular, for allowing me to see rough drafts of their transcriptions.

34. The text is obviously defective at this point (f. 83ra–b in MS Digby 24, transcribed Tachau *et al.*),
and it is conceivable that the hypothesis has simply dropped out; but the structure of the resolution
leads me to think that the author deliberately omitted any hypothesis.

35. 'Et scimus quod ex propositione quae potest habere plures causas veritatis non sequitur una
illarum' (MS Digby 24, f. 83rb; transcribed Tachau *et al.*).

36. The treatment of this sophisma and the nature of the *Abstractiones* generally suggest, however
weakly, that the treatise is somewhat anachronistic if it is indeed to be located chronologically
between the treatise attributed to Robert Bacon and Peter of Spain's *Syncategoremata*; it seems
earlier than either of those. I think that the source of the apparent anachronism is more likely to be
in the proposed dating (and authorship) of the Bacon treatise, however, about which I will say
more in n. 41 below.

simple, sensible analysis in a way that suggests that it was still inchoate when he wrote. His exposition of it is labored and unduly complex, he confuses that in respect of which the exception is made with that from which it is made,[37] and he introduces the peculiar doctrine of different arrival times of expressions in a proposition in order to explain the two possible determinations ascribable to 'twice':[38] in the formation of the first sense 'besides' arrives before (*prius advenit*) 'twice'; in the formation of the second (true) sense that order of arrival is reversed.[39]

William of Sherwood uses this sophisma to conclude his development of the rule that 'If there is more than one division [i.e., distribution] and an exception is made from one in respect of another, then the one in respect of which the exception is made is immobilised'.[40] The two distributions are those effected by 'twice' and by 'every', and since Plato is excepted *from* all the men *in respect of* the two occasions, the distribution effected by 'twice' is 'immobilised'; that is, the inference from 'twice' to 'on the one occasion . . . and on the other occasion . . .' is blocked. In presenting his resolution, however, William leaves the application of the rule implicit and sorts out the ambiguity as we have seen it done in the treatise attributed to Robert Bacon,[41] in terms of the one operation's including or being included by the

37. For Peter's confusion, see n. 39 below. This particular confusion is not uncommon among writers on the syncategoremata, however.

38. William of Sherwood also uses this doctrine in connection with his discussion of exposition, although not in his discussion of this sophisma. See Kretzmann 1968, p. 62, p. 62 n. 22, pp. 66–7, p. 67 n. 34; also Geach 1962, pp. 102–4.

39. 'Solutio. Prima est duplex, eoquod hec dictio "*bis*" potest determinare hoc verbum "*videre*" prout transit supra accusativum sequentem cum sua determinatione facta per exceptionem. Et tunc est sensus "*Sortes videt omnem hominem preter Platonem et hoc bis*"; et tunc sequitur quod nulla vice viderit Platonem, et sic est falsa. Et sic haec dictio "*preter*" excipit ab hoc quod est "*videre omnem hominem*", et sic prius advenit hec dictio "*preter*" in oratione. Alio autem modo hec dictio "*bis*" potest determinare tantum hoc quod est "*videre omnem hominem*". Et tunc hec dictio "*preter*" excipit ab eo quod est "*bis videre omnem hominem*". Et sic est vera, quia non bis videt Platonem. Et sic hec dictio "*bis*" prius intelligitur advenire in oratione quam hec dictio "*preter*"' (ed. in Braakhuis 1978, pp. 162–3). (I have made some changes in Braakhuis' punctuation.)

40. 'Si fuerint plures divisiones et excipiatur ab una et respectu alterius, etiam illa respectu cujus fit exceptio immobilitatur' (ed. O'Donnell 1941, 62.38–40; cf. Kretzmann 1968, p. 66).

41. On grounds that deserve careful consideration of a sort they cannot be given here, Braakhuis argues that it is Robert Bacon to whom we ought to attribute the *Syncategoremata* that has been attributed to Roger Bacon, and that it should be dated as early as the first decade of the thirteenth century. Robert certainly wrote earlier than William of Sherwood; Roger was William's younger contemporary and outspoken admirer (see Kretzmann 1966, pp. 5–7). Everything I have seen in the Bacon treatise and in the others I have consulted leads me to think that it belongs after William of Sherwood and Peter of Spain rather than before them or, even harder to credit, before the *Abstractiones*. Its advanced level of sophistication, its casual treatment of proofs and disproofs, and its casual treatment of other resolutions are strongly suggestive of the middle rather than the first decades of the thirteenth century; and in this particular instance Bacon's use of the letter-designations in the hypothesis, his casual introduction of inclusion as the leading idea in his

other. But he adds the observation that the familiar distinction between the compounded and divided senses is involved in the resolution in terms of inclusion.[42]

Nicholas of Paris, having put forward his rule that 'An argument from an inferior to its superior with an exceptive word is unacceptable',[43] takes up two apparent counter-instances. It is easy to see how the first of them serves his purpose,[44] but the second counter-instance is supposed to be this sophisma, and I have not seen any good reason for his treating it in that way.[45] Nicholas' resolution of the sophisma consists first in an observation strikingly like the one made in *Dialectica Monacensis*: the proposition 'can be judged on the basis of the numerical adverb', in which case it is false. He notes, on the other hand, that the disproof may be considered unacceptable because of treating 'Socrates twice sees' as if it were compounded rather than divided. On this particular sophisma Nicholas is less good than his English predecessors.[46]

Albert of Saxony, after quickly sorting out the ambiguity, focuses on the semantic issue in the sophisma: 'But which of those senses is more proper?' His analysis of the issue makes intelligent use of the concepts of the

resolution, and his restatement of the type of resolution employed by Peter of Spain in his own preferred terms of inclusion could even be taken to suggest that the author was aware of William's work. Braakhuis' formidable considerations to the contrary notwithstanding, I am still inclined to think that this Bacon is Roger, not Robert, or at any rate that the treatise was written later than 1200–10.

42. 'Et dicendum quod exceptio potest includere ly bis vel e converso. Si ly bis includat, significat quod "videre omnem hominem praeter Platonem" conveniat Sorti bis et falsa est; si ly bis includatur, significat quod "videre omnem alium" conveniat Sorti bis; sed "videre Platonem" non, et est vera et sic probatur. Primo modo debet hoc totum "videre omnem hominem praeter Platonem" componi, ut significetur quod hoc totum multiplicatur per ly bis; secundo modo debet ly praeter dividi a residuo, ut significetur quod ly bis non extendit se ad ly praeter, sed e converso' (ed. O'Donnell 1941, 63.33–40; cf. Kretzmann 1968, pp. 68–9).

43. 'Regula est quod *non valet argumentatio ab inferiori ad superius cum dictione exceptiva*' (ed. Braakhuis 1979, II, 167.5–7).

44. 'Sed quod hoc sit falsum videtur, quia sequitur: "omnis homo preter Sortem currit; ergo omnis homo preter unum currit"; sed *unum* superius est ad *Sortem*; ergo' (ed. Braakhuis 1979, II, 167.16–18).

45. The only relevant unacceptable inference is the one that derives 'on the one occasion ... and on the other occasion' from 'twice', and, as is clear in William of Sherwood's treatment of this sophisma, that inference is a case of logical *descent* (*from* what is logically *superior to* what is logically *inferior*).

46. 'Ad illud vero "*Sortes bis videt omnem hominem preter Platonem*", dicendum quod est duplex secundum regulam generalem: quia potest iudicari per adverbium numeri, et sic falsa, et sic improbat et sensus patet ⟨in⟩ improbatione; vel potest iudicari per dictionem exceptivam, et sic vera et patet sensus in probatione et est instantia huius "*Sortes ⟨bis⟩ videt omnem*". Vel potest dici quod non sequitur: "Sortes bis videt omnem hominem preter Platonem; ergo una vice videt omnem hominem preter Platonem et alia", quia fit exceptio ab hoc toto "*Sortes bis videt*" coniunctim, et arguitur ac si fieret divisim, unde est ibi fallacia *consequentis*" (ed. Braakhuis 1979, II, 168.8–17).

exposition of propositions and the supposition of terms: 'Now in "Socrates did not see Plato twice" the whole predicate ["did see Plato twice"] is denied of the whole subject; but in "Socrates twice did not see Plato" not the whole predicate but a part of it is denied of the subject, because the term "twice" remains affirmed.' [47]

The Pseudo-Petrus[48] uses the sophisma to illustrate the widely recognised rule that 'If a proposition is in part false, it can be made true by means of an exception, but not if it is completely false.' [49] The proposition 'Socrates twice saw every man' is in part false because it is false only as regards Plato on one occasion, not completely false as it would be if Socrates had never seen any man. The Pseudo-Petrus is like Peter himself in developing the resolution in terms of different determinations, but here 'twice' is said to determine 'besides' in the false sense of the proposition,

47. 'Ad sophisma respondetur quod in ipso exceptio potest denotare vel quod Socrates non vidit bis Platonem – et sic sophisma est verum – vel quod Socrates bis non vidit Platonem – et sic est falsum. Sed quis istorum sensuum sit magis proprius? Dico quod primus videtur esse magis proprius quam secundus, ex eo quod dictae propositionis exceptivae expositio est magis propria secundum quam totum praedicatum affirmatur de subiecto toto quantum ad supposita non excepta et negatur totum de toto quantum ad suppositum exceptum quam in qua non totum sed pars negatur de toto. Modo in ista "Socrates non vidit bis Platonem" negatur totum praedicatum de toto subiecto; sed in ista "Socrates bis non vidit Platonem" negatur non totum praedicatum sed pars eius de subiecto, quia iste terminus "bis" remanet affirmatus' (Albert of Saxony 1502, Part II, Sophisma lxvii [actually lxv], f. 57ra).

48. I am using this designation to refer to the author or authors of the presumably fifteenth-century material included in the Cologne 1489 edition of the logical works of Peter of Spain in such a way that it has been or can be confused with the genuine text of Peter's *Syncategoremata*. The Cologne Dominicans brought out their edition of Peter's logical works '*cum copulatis secundum doctrinam divi Thomae Aquinatis, iuxta processum magistrorum Coloniae in bursa Montis regentium*' (from the title-page of the 1489 edition). In the 1489 edition the text of what purports to be Peter's treatise on the syncategoremata (there entitled *Tractatus syncategorematum*) is printed in larger type; that text has been designated (14) in Appendix I attaching to this study. In the same edition smaller type is regularly used for the commentary on Peter's text. The material in smaller type printed with the *Tractatus syncategorematum* is not a commentary, but it is explicitly distinguished from the text put forward as Peter's; for instance, at the end of the material in smaller type concerned with exception and before the beginning of the next section of larger type the words '*Sequitur textus*' appear (f. 46vb). This material contains sophismata that occur also in Peter's genuine *Syncategoremata*, but they are treated differently here. The resolution of this tangled textual relationship must await the publication of Braakhuis' edition. Meanwhile I am considering the smaller-type material accompanying the *Tractatus syncategorematum* as a fifteenth-century supplement to Peter's treatment of syncategoremata; this material is designated as text (33/32) in Appendix I.

The presentation of this sophisma through the disproof is very much the same in texts ⋆ (13) and (33/32) – it does not appear at all in (14) – but the resolutions are too divergent to be considered merely two versions of the same text (compare nn. 39 and 50), and the divergence between resolutions is even more marked in other sophismata, as we shall see. Moreover, the contexts in which the same sophismata are introduced are quite different in texts ⋆ (13) and (33/32). (See n. 20 above.)

49. 'Si enim aliqua propositio exceptiva [!] est in parte falsa, potest per exceptionem fieri vera, non autem si fuerit in tota falsa, ut prius visum est' (Pseudo-Petrus 1489, f. 46rb). Versions of this rule are found also in texts (15), (18), (21), (23), (25/26), and (26/25).

while 'besides' is said to determine 'twice' in the true sense 'in such a way that the adverb "twice" determines the verb itself and not everything following it'. There is nothing novel in this resolution except, perhaps, for the characterisations of the two senses as 'a duality of exception . . . [and] an exception from duality'.[50]

The sophisma 'Omnis homo praeter Socratem excipitur'

Of the many explicit rules governing exceptives,[51] the one perhaps most widely recognised was the rule that the universal proposition on which a true exceptive proposition is founded – the 'prejacent' of the exceptive – is false without the exception.[52] The second sophisma I will present to illustrate the treatment of exception was designed primarily to challenge that fundamental rule and is, accordingly, more important and more complicated than the previous example. This sophisma is found in nine of the texts listed in Appendix I, two of which are by a single author.[53] I will again present the problem portion of the sophisma in a homogenised (and in this case modernised) version.

(S) EVERY MAN BESIDES SOCRATES IS EXCEPTED

Suppose that every man other than Socrates is excepted from the provisions of some law – i.e., every man is subject to this law except for those whose names are other than 'Socrates'.[54]

Proof 1: The universal proposition 'Every man is excepted' is false, and the only counter-instance to it is Socrates; therefore (S) is true.[55]

---

50. 'Solutio. Prima est duplex eo quod haec determinatio "bis" potest determinare hanc dictionem "praeter" et praesupponere eam. Et sic est falsa, quia sensus est "Socrates vidit omnem hominem praeter Platonem et hoc bis"; et tunc sequitur quod nulla vice viderit Platonem. Alio modo illa determinatio "praeter" potest determinare illud adverbium "bis" ita quod illud adverbium "bis" determinet verbum secundum se et non totum sequens. Et sic est vera, quia sensus est quod Socrates bis vidit ⟨omnem⟩ hominem alium a Platone sed non bis Platonem. Ideo communiter fit exceptio pro Platone. Primo modo ponitur dualitas exceptionis; secundo modo ponitur exceptio a dualitate' (Pseudo-Petrus 1489, ff. 46^{rb-va}).

51. I have picked out more than fifty in the texts I have consulted.

52. Some version of this rule is found in texts (5), (9), (15), (18), (21), (22), (23), (25/26), (26/25), (29), and (33/32).

53. The sophisma is found in texts (11/10), ⋆(13), (18), (21), (23), (25/26), (26/25), (27), and (33/32).

54. Text (18) mentions four men, texts (25/26) and (26/25) mention three men and provide them with names, and all the other texts refer to all men. In (11/10), (18), (23), (25/26), and (26/25) the exception is said to be in respect of (or, mistakenly, from) some action; in (23) Walter Burley uses the (unfortunate) example of the act of being; in both (25/26) and (26/25) Albert of Saxony uses running. In ⋆(13) and (33/32) the exception is in respect of some (unspecified) predicate, and in (21) it is simply 'from something'. My example of a law is simply intended to render the notion of being excepted less unnatural in English.

55. Some version of this first proof is found in seven of the nine texts under consideration; notice that it is structurally just like the proof in the previously considered sophisma. Neither (11/10) nor (27)

Proof 2: The correct exposition of a proposition of the form 'Every *x* besides A is *F*' is (i) 'There is at least and at most one *x* such that *x* = A' and (ii) 'Every *x* such that *x* ≠ A is *F*' and (iii) 'A is not *F*'. The instances of the exponents (i), (ii), and (iii) are all true in this case *ex hypothesi*; therefore (S) is true.[56]

Disproof 1: If Socrates is running and all the other men are running, then 'Every man besides Socrates is running' is false. In that case 'Every man is running' is true, and a universal proposition that is true without an exception is false with one. Analogously, (S) is false if Socrates is excepted and all the other men are excepted. But Socrates is excepted in (S). Therefore 'Every man is excepted' is true; therefore (S) is false.[57]

Disproof 2: If (S) is true, then Socrates is not excepted. But Socrates is excepted in (S). Therefore if (S) is true, (S) is false.[58]

The resolutions can be understood best as attempts to deal with the apparent paradox (brought out most clearly in Disproof 2) that the exceptive proposition 'Every man besides Socrates is excepted' and its prejacent 'Every man is excepted' are true together. Seven of the eight authors under consideration are out to dispel the paradox and to accept the exceptive (S) as true; only Albert of Saxony thinks (S) is 'false and impossible'. Almost all the resolutions offered or mentioned fall into one or another of three types.[59]

The first and most important type of resolution seems to grow out of a fundamental observation to be found in the *Abstractiones*: to be excepted in respect of being excepted is not to be excepted at all; and so even though Socrates is excepted in that respect, he is not excepted; therefore it is not

---

has this proof explicitly, but those two texts differ from the others in their non-standard presentations of the sophisma, and the omission has no discernible historical or doctrinal significance.

56. Proof 2 is a modernised version of the proof from the exponents offered in texts (23), (25/26), and (26/25); a proof from the standard exponents is expressly rejected by Paul of Venice in (27), as we shall see. Walter Burley presents it schematically: 'the exponents are true; therefore the exceptive is true'; Albert of Saxony spells it out a little more fully: 'Socrates is not excepted from the act of running, and every man other than Socrates is excepted from the act of running; therefore every man other than Socrates is excepted from the act of running', omitting the conclusion in (25/26). Albert also offers a third proof in each of his texts: 'Every man besides Socrates is excepted from the act of running; therefore every man besides Socrates is excepted', but it is only technical reasons of his own that prompt him to present what is in any case an obviously trivial proof.

57. Some version of Disproof 1 is found in (11/10) (18), (23), (25/26), and (26/25); the version presented here is most like the one in (18).

58. Only Albert of Saxony offers Disproof 2 in this form (the versions of the disproofs in (26/25) are more succinct than those in (25/26)). But *(13), (21), and (33/32) offer as their only disproof a very simple argument that seems intended to take the same line as this Disproof 2. As Peter of Spain puts it, 'In this proposition the exceptive word is adjoined to "Socrates"; therefore it excepts him in respect of the predicate. Therefore Socrates is excepted; therefore the first [i.e., (S)] is false.'

59. The unusual resolutions offered by the Pseudo-Petrus and by Paul of Venice will be considered after the consideration of the three main types.

true in general that if Socrates is excepted in this or that respect, he is excepted.[60] Albert of Saxony, acknowledging that others base an *affirmative* reply on this observation, interprets it as an instance of the even more fundamental observation that an inference from an inferior to its superior with negation is invalid. Thus just as 'Socrates is not running; therefore Socrates is not moving' is invalid, so 'Every man besides Socrates is excepted in respect of some action; therefore every man besides Socrates is excepted' is invalid; and so (S) is not supported by the hypothesis, for 'is excepted' includes negation.[61] But the more usual development of the observation regarding exception in respect of being excepted lies in the direction of accepting (S) and rejecting the negative side of the sophisma as an instance of the fallacy of *secundum quid et simpliciter*. Peter of Spain provides a full version of this type of resolution: 'The first [(S)] is true unconditionally (*simpliciter*), and the disproof commits the fallacy of *secundum quid et simpliciter*; for to except from exception is not to except unconditionally but in a certain respect, just as to be deprived of a privation is not to be deprived unconditionally but in a certain respect. Indeed, it is rather to give possession, as to deprive of blindness is to give

60. '...Socrates non excipitur, quamvis excipiatur respectu eius quod est exceptum, quia excipi respectu istius non est ⟨esse⟩ exceptum... Et non valet "Socrates excipitur in hac; igitur excipitur", sed sequitur eius oppositum' (MS Digby 24, f. 83ᵛᵃ; transcribed Tachau *et al.*).

61. 'Ad sophisma respondetur quod ipsum est falsum et impossibile, sicut probatum est. Ad rationes. Ad primam, quando dicitur "Omnis homo praeter Socratem [ab actu currendi excipitur; ergo omnis homo praeter Socratem excipitur]", negatur consequentia propter negationem inclusam in hoc verbo "excipitur". Unde sicut non sequitur ab inferiori ad superius cum negatione, ita nec cum termino includente negationem. Et ideo non sequitur "Hoc excipitur a currere; ergo excipitur ab agere"; nec sequitur "Omnis homo praeter Socratem ab agere excipitur; ergo omnis homo praeter Socratem excipitur." Ex hoc patet ad alias duas rationes sequentes. / Aliter alii dicunt ad sophisma quod ipsum est verum. Et Socrates non excipitur, quia excipi ab exceptione non est excipi; modo in proposito Socrates excipitur ab exceptione' (Albert of Saxony 1502, f. 56ʳᵇ). The version found in Albert's *Perutilis logica* differs in some interesting details: 'Respondetur quod sophisma est falsum et impossibile, sicut patet per improbationem. / Sed contra sic breviter. Ista propositio sit A: "Omnis homo praeter Platonem et Ciceronem currit." [He is supposing that Socrates, Plato, and Cicero constitute all men.] Tunc sic: "Omnis homo praeter Socratem ab actu currendi excipitur; ergo omnis homo praeter Socratem excipitur." / Breviter respondetur negando consequentiam; immo, ratione negationis inclusae in hoc verbo "excipitur" est fallacia consequentis – ab inferiori ad superius negative. Unde non sequitur "Socrates excipitur a currere; ergo Socrates excipitur ab agere"; sic etiam non sequitur "Omnis homo excipitur praeter Socratem in B; ergo omnis homo praeter Socratem excipitur." / Ad rationes dico quod non sequitur "Omnis homo praeter Socratem excipitur ab illo actu – scilicet, ab actu currendi; ergo omnis homo praeter Socratem excipitur." / Ad secundam dico quod haec est vera: "Omnis homo excipitur", quia quilibet homo excipitur in sophismate vel in A propositione. Et propter hoc dico quod exponentes non sunt verae, quia ista est falsa: "Socrates non excipitur." / Tertiam [!] soluta est per primam solutionem' (Albert of Saxony 1522, f. 22ʳᵃ). The fact that the differences between Albert's *Sophismata* and his *Perutilis logica* in this case and others leave *Perutilis logica* looking generally like an amplification or improvement of *Sophismata* has led me to think, contrary to my original assumption, that his *Sophismata* is earlier than his *Perutilis logica*; but see n. 94 below.

sight ...'[62] Henry of Ghent offers a version very like Peter's as one of his two alternate resolutions,[63] and Walter Burley offers it as his preferred resolution.[64] Nicholas of Paris mentions it, attributing it to others and oddly reversing the assignments of *secundum quid* and *simpliciter*.[65] The Pseudo-Petrus mentions Peter's only resolution merely as one that *might* be offered.[66]

The type of resolution evidently preferred by Nicholas of Paris is based on a distinction that was frequently drawn between actually effecting exception and merely signifying it,[67] for he introduces this sophisma as pertaining to the rule that 'an argument from a word signifying the operation [of exception – e.g., "besides"] to one that signifies the concept [of exception – e.g., "is excepted"] is not acceptable'.[68] Nicholas leaves the application of the rule tacit; the type of resolution thought to be available under it is more accessible in the version offered later by Henry of Ghent as the second of his two alternate resolutions.[69]

62. 'Solutio. Prima est vera simpliciter, et improbatio peccat *secundum quid et simpliciter*, quia excipere ab exceptione non est excipere *simpliciter*, sed *secundum quid*, sicut privari a privatione non est privari *simpliciter*, sed *secundum quid*, immo potius est dare habitum, ut privare a cecitate est dare visum; ergo excipi ab exceptione non est excipi *simpliciter*, sed *secundum quid*. Et ideo, licet Sortes excipiatur respectu huius predicati *"excipi"*, sicut est in prima, non tamen excipitur; et ideo est ibi fallacia *secundum quid et simpliciter*' (ed. Braakhuis 1978a, p. 153).

63. 'Solutio: dicendum quod prima est vera simpliciter. Et inprobatio peccat per fallaciam secundum quid et simpliciter, quia excipi ab exceptione est excipi secundum quid, sicut privari a privatione, ut a cecitate, est privari secundum quid' (ed. Braakhuis 1978a, 47.19–22).

64. 'Posset tamen probabiliter dici, quod illo casu supposito haec est falsa: "Omnis homo excipitur." Et cum dicitur: Sortes excipitur in ista: "Omnis homo praeter Sortem excipitur", dico, quod Sortem excipi in ista: "Omnis homo praeter Sortem excipitur", est Sortem excipi ab exceptione, et Sortem excipi ab exceptione est Sortem non excipi, et ideo Sortem excipi respectu excipi est Sortem non excipi. Et ideo dicitur, quod haec est fallacia secundum quid et simpliciter, quia Sortes excipitur in ista: "Omnis homo praeter Sortem excipitur", quia Sortem excipi in ista est Sortem excipi secundum quid, et simpliciter non excipi' (ed. Boehner 1955, 170.13–22).

65. 'Aliter dicunt alii quod hic est fallacia *secundum quid et simpliciter*, quia excipi ab hac actione est excipi secundum quid; sed, cum dicitur "Sortes excipitur", est ibi excipi simpliciter; unde proceditur ab eo quod est secundum quid ad id quod est simpliciter' (ed. Braakhuis 1979, II, 170.6–9).

66. 'Vel potest dici quod ibi Socrates excipitur ab exceptione, sed excipi ab exceptione solum est excipi secundum quid et non simpliciter, sicut privari ⟨a⟩ privatione est privari secundum quid et non simpliciter, etc.' (Pseudo-Petrus 1489, f. 46ra).

67. See, for example, Bacon's introductory remark that 'praeter' 'significat exceptionem, sed non per modum conceptus, sicut hoc nomen *"exceptio"* et hoc verbum *"excipio"*, sed per modum affectus' (ed. Braakhuis 1978a; 163.18–20); and compare this passage from *Abstractiones*: 'Et solet dici quod non valet "Omnis homo excipitur praeter Socratem; ergo omnis homo excipitur, Socrate excepto" eo ⟨quod⟩ per hanc dictionem "excepto" non exerceretur exceptio sed significatur; per hanc dictionem "praeter" ⟨autem⟩ exerceretur et non significatur' (MS Digby 24, f. 83va; transcribed Tachau *et al.*).

68. 'Regula est quod non valet argumentatio a dictione significante affectum ad eam que significat conceptum.' And Nicholas goes on at once to exemplify this rule in a way strongly reminiscent of the *Abstractiones*: 'Secundum hoc dicitur quod non sequitur: "omnis homo preter Sortem currit; ergo omnis homo Sorte excepto currit"' (ed. Braakhuis 1979, II, 168.19–169.1).

69. 'Vel: prima potest solvi per equivocationem exceptionis, quod quedam est exercita, quedam

Three authors – *Ricardus sophista*, Nicholas of Paris, and Walter Burley – allude to a type of resolution that none of them prefers. It seems right to describe this type generally as based on the concept of *transcasus* even though only Nicholas uses that technical term in this connection: '*Transcasus* is the change of the truth of a statement in accordance with the change of time. For example, if with my hand closed I say "My hand is closed" and go on to say "therefore my hand is not open", it is said that this does not follow in virtue of *transcasus*.'[70] But how is *transcasus* supposed to apply in the resolution of this sophisma? Nicholas offers very little help: 'Likewise this does not follow: "Every man besides Socrates is excepted; therefore Socrates is excepted".' Drawing on hints in the other two discussions, we can, however, fill in at least the essential details. If all one knows is that every man other than Socrates and not Socrates is excepted in respect of some predicate, on that basis alone the prejacent (P) 'Every man is excepted' seems clearly false. And just because (P) is false on that basis, one would be led to affirm (S) 'Every man besides Socrates is excepted' and to prove it as in Proof 1. But then, realising that if (S) is true, Socrates, too, is excepted, one would feel entitled to affirm (P). Thus *before* (S) is affirmed and proved, (P) seems false and (S) seems true; but *after* the affirmation and proof of (S), (P) seems true and (S) seems false. *Ricardus sophista* flatly rejects a resolution of this type: 'But ... I say that the prejacent is false and the exceptive true *after* the proof just as *before* it', because to be excepted in respect of being excepted is not to be excepted at all.[71]

The resolution based on *transcasus* suggests that this sophisma might be

significata. Et loquendo de exceptione significata: sic prima est vera, ut probatur; loquendo autem de exceptione exercita: sic est falsa, ut inprobatur. Et sic loquendo de eadem exceptione, non sunt simul vere cum exceptione et sine exceptione' (ed. Braakhuis 1978a; 47.22–48.4).

70. 'Ad hoc sophisma solvunt quidam per *transcasum*. Est autem transcasus transmutatio veritatis enuntiationis secundum transmutationem temporis, ut manu mea existente clausa si dicam "manus mea est clausa", et proferendo hanc "*ergo manus mea non est aperta*", dicitur quod non sequitur propter transcasum. Similiter non sequitur: "omnis homo preter Sortem excipitur; ergo Sortes excipitur"' (ed. Braakhuis 1979, II, 169.22–170.5).

71. *Ricardus sophista* introduces this type of resolution as one likely to be familiar to his readers: 'Et solet dici ...'. The portion of the text in which he presents this resolution is obviously corrupt in the transcription from which I have worked, but his rejoinder is clear enough: 'sed quia Socrates non excipitur, quamvis excipiatur respectu eius quod est exceptum, quia excipi respectu istius non est ⟨esse⟩ exceptum, dico quod praeiacens est falsa et exceptiva vera post probationem sicut et ante' (MS Digby 24, f. 83va; transcribed Tachau *et al.*; cf. n. 60 above). Walter Burley's presentation of a resolution of this type: 'Solutio huius sophismatis secundum aliquos est, quod ante pro-lationem huius: "Omnis homo praeter Sortem excipitur" est praeiacens falsa et exceptiva vera, et post prolationem huius accidit econtrario, et ita non sunt simul verae' (ed. Boehner 1955, 170.9–12). Four of the six MSS on which Boehner based his edition have 'probationem' where his edition has 'prolationem'.

viewed as presenting a special problem of self-reference. The Pseudo-Petrus seems to have taken such a view of it, although the resolution as he offers it is too succinct to be altogether clear: 'The first [i.e., (S)] is true on the hypothesis, as is evident from the proof. And the reply to the disproof is that although in "Every man besides Socrates is excepted" Socrates is excepted in respect of the predicate "is excepted", in another proposition only those other than Socrates are excepted in respect of that predicate and not Socrates, and it is of that [proposition] that [this] proposition is speaking, and not of itself.'[72]

Paul of Venice's treatment of this sophisma is very different from that of the other seven authors, but to a large extent the unusual features of his discussion are a function of the rigid, artificial structure of his *Quadratura*.[73] As one of the fifty *principalia* of the first of the four *dubia* that comprise the treatise, Paul's discussion of the sophisma centres around that first *dubium*: whether one and the same inference can be both acceptable and unacceptable at once. Accordingly he presents the sophisma as the conclusion of an inference regarding which that question might be raised: 'Socrates is not excepted, and every man other than Socrates is excepted; therefore every man besides Socrates is excepted.' The acceptability of the inference seems obvious since its premisses appear to be the standard exponents of the exceptive proposition that is its conclusion. And yet it is easy to lay down a hypothesis on which those premisses are true even though the conclusion appears to entail a contradiction – both that Socrates is not excepted and that Socrates is excepted.[74] After developing the obligatory four *conclusiones* relevant to this issue, in which he raises putative counter-instances

---

72. 'Solutio. Prima est vera in casu posito, ut patet per probationem. Et ad improbationem dicitur quod licet in ista "Omnis homo praeter Socratem excipitur" Socrates excipiatur respectu illius praedicati "excipitur", tamen in alia propositione solum alii a Socrate excipiuntur respectu illius praedicati et Socrates non; et de illa loquitur propositio, et non de se ipsa' (Pseudo-Petrus 1489, f. 46ʳᵃ). Conceivably the reference to 'another proposition' is based on considerations like those raised in text (26/25); see n. 61.

73. Each of the four *dubia* has fifty *principalia* (or chapters), and in the course of developing each of those *principalia* he defends four *conclusiones*. A printed marginal note in the 1522 edition of Albert of Saxony's *Perutilis logica* alongside Albert's discussion of this sophisma reads: 'Vide de hoc sophismate Petrum Mantuam, capitulo proprio, et Paulum Venetum, octavo principali primi dubii *Quadraturae*' (f. 22ʳᵃ marg.). I am grateful to Edith Sylla for lending me her photocopy of the Venice 1493 edition of the *Quadratura* and *Sophismata*.

74. 'Consequentia tenet cum prima parte antecedentis, quia arguitur ab exponentibus ad expositum. Et secundam partem [i.e., quod eadem non valet] probo: casu possibili posito, est antecedens verum et consequens falsum; igitur consequentia non valet ... Et quod consequens sit falsum probatur: ex ipso enim sequitur quod Socrates non excipitur et quod Socrates excipitur; igitur ipsum est falsum et implicans contradictionem' (Paul of Venice 1493a, f. 5ʳᵃ).

to the standard exposition of exceptives,[75] Paul offers new exponents for (S): 'No Socrates is excepted, and every man not Socrates is excepted.' And on that basis he can reject the original grounds for accepting the inference: its premisses were, after all, not the genuine exponents of its conclusion. As he admits, however, that move does not resolve the difficulty, since we can simply reformulate the inference with those refurbished premisses. His final resolution of the sophisma consists in claiming that it involves a confusion between Socrates and the name 'Socrates'; from the fact that Socrates is a part extracted from the quantitative whole that is all men we can rightly infer only that 'Socrates' is excepted, and not that Socrates is excepted[76] – a resolution that is neither credible nor creditable.

Wholes and parts

Exception as conceived of by medieval logicians is invariably the exception of some sort of part from the appropriate whole; thus the familiar exception of Socrates from all men is the exception of a 'subjective' part from its 'universal' whole. But other sorts of parts and wholes provide different contexts for exception. The most important of those contexts after the universal/subjective context in which we have been considering exception

75. In the first *conclusio*, which turns out to be most important for his purposes, he makes this implausible and, as far as I know, idiosyncratic claim: 'Unde hic notandum quod iste terminus "pars extracapta" est terminus secundae intentionis vel impositionis limitans ad suppositionem materialem, et iste terminus "excipitur" est terminus primae intentionis vel impositionis. Et ideo non mirum si illa consequentia non valet: "Socrates est pars extracapta; igitur Socrates excipitur", quia ly "Socrates" in antecedente supponit materialiter et in consequente personaliter. Sed deberet inferri illa: ly "Socrates" excipitur – quod est verum' (Paul of Venice 1493a, f. 5ra). The second *conclusio* raises the possibility that women as well as men are referred to in the conclusion, which contains no inflectional barrier to such an interpretation, but only men in the second premiss, where '*homo*' is restricted to such an interpretation by the masculine ending of '*alius*'. The third *conclusio* presents a variation on that theme, and the fourth proceeds on the possibility that there are two men named 'Socrates', so that 'Socrates non currit, et omnis homo non Socrates currit, et tamen non omnis homo praeter Socratem currit' (Paul of Venice 1493a, f. 5rb).

76. 'Pro tanto igitur dico quod illa "Omnis homo praeter Socratem currit" sic exponitur: "Nullus Socrates currit, et omnis homo non Socrates currit"; et ita illa "Omnis homo praeter Socratem excipitur: 'Nullus Socrates excipitur, et omnis homo non Socrates excipitur'. Ergo, etc." Ex quibus sequitur manifeste responsio ad rationem principalem, negando consequentiam. Nec arguitur ab exponentibus ad expositum, quia illae non sunt suae exponentes, ut dictum est. Sed quoniam per hoc non solvitur difficultas argumenti, ideo proponatur consequentia illa sub hac forma: "Nullus Socrates excipitur, et omnis homo non Socrates excipitur; igitur omnis homo praeter Socratem excipitur", et redit eadem difficultas. Propterea dico quod consequentia est bona. Et admisso casu illo, dico quod consequens est verum, sicut et antecedens. Et ad improbationem nego quod sequitur quod Socrates excipitur. Et cum dicitur "Socrates est pars extracapta; igitur Socrates excipitur", negatur consequentia, ut docuit prima conclusio. Sed bene sequitur quod ly "Socrates" excipitur – sicut etiam non sequitur "Chimaera est terminus; ergo chimaera est", sed bene sequitur "igitur ly 'chimaera' est", reservando continue eandem suppositionem. Quare, etc.' (Paul of Venice 1493a, f. 5rb).

is that provided by the notion of 'integral' wholes and parts,[77] and '*totus*', the second syncategorema to be presented in this sampler, is associated primarily with an integral whole as '*omnis*' is with a universal whole. There is, therefore, a special connection between the two syncategorematic words '*praeter*' and '*totus*',[78] one that is brought out in the fact that the same examples can sometimes be found associated with either or with both – e.g., '*Tota domus est alba praeter parietem*' ('The whole house is white except the wall'), '*Totus Socrates est albus praeter pedem*' ('All of Socrates is white except his foot').[79] Grammatically the preposition '*praeter*' and the adjective '*totus*' are quite distinct, and that distinction is worth mentioning because it means that '*totus*', unlike '*praeter*', can be used categorematically as well as syncategorematically,[80] an ambiguity made much of in the discussions of '*totus*', as we shall see.

Distribution effected by 'totus'

'*Totus*' typically finds its place among the syncategoremata just after '*omnis*' since it seems clear that it is like '*omnis*' in being adjoined to names and

77. Broadly speaking, it is only composite entities that are integral wholes, and integral parts are those that can be produced by the physical division of such a whole. The development of the discussions of '*totus*' revealed difficulties in that simple notion, however, and eventually a more refined account was called for. The one offered by Albert of Saxony is a good example: 'pars integralis dicitur pars quantitativa – id est, habens quantitatem quae cum alia parte quantitativa constituit aliquod totum quantum, nec una illarum est potentia ad aliam, nec perfectibilis per eam' (Albert of Saxony 1502, f. 25[rb]). The reasons for Albert's final restrictions will become clear in the remainder of this discussion.

78. Because the notion of exception depends on the notion of a whole, there is also a general connection in the use of '*totus*' in definitions of exception – e.g., in texts (5): 'Exceptio vero nichil aliud est quam captatio partis a toto' (ed. Braakhuis 1979, I, 97.3), and (9): 'Quoniam autem illud a quo fit exceptio non solum est totum sed sumptum per modum totius, si deficiat in modo totius, tunc tenebitur hec dictio "*preter*" additive vel remotive, ut: "*homo currit preter Sortem*", idest: *aliquis homo et Sortes*, et: *homo currit sine Sorte*' (ed. Braakhuis 1978, 164.19–23).

79. The first example is found in both (18) and (33/32) associated with '*praeter*'; the second is found in (18) associated with '*totus*', and several highly similar examples are associated with '*praeter*' in other texts. But the most interesting link of this sort is the sophisma '*Animal est pars animalis*', which occurs in texts (15) and *(20/19) associated with '*praeter*' and in texts (9) and (11/10) associated with '*totus*'. The sophisma deserves separate study, but its problem, briefly, is this. Suppose that we designate a whole man 'A' and the same man except for his foot 'B'. In that case B is now a part of an animal. But if the foot in question were amputated tomorrow, B would be an animal. Now if B will be an animal tomorrow, surely it is also an animal today; therefore an animal is a part of an animal. And since there are infinitely many parts of the B-type in any whole animal, every animal contains infinitely many animals. (Problems of this sort eventually became associated with the sophisma '*Totus Socrates est minor Socrate*', as we shall see.)

80. See p. 212 above. In text (29) Paul of Venice devotes an entire treatise to the categorematic and syncategorematic uses of '*totus*' (Part I, Tr. 14), which he introduces as the first of a group of words 'qui quandoque categorematice, quandoque syncategorematice tenentur – ut sunt hi: "totus"/"tota"/"totum", "semper" et "ab aeterno", quibus annectitur "infinitus"/"infinita"/ "infinitum"' (Paul of Venice 1499, f. 56[ra]).

thereby effecting distribution; but it is equally clear that '*totus*' and '*omnis*' operate differently.[81] The significations of '*omnis homo*' ('every man') and '*totus homo*' ('the whole man') are so different that some authors suggest that '*totus*' is suited only to uniquely referring expressions as '*omnis*' is suited to common names,[82] and others think that at any rate some syntactic refinement is called for when '*totus*' is adjoined to a common name.[83] Their apparently grammatical scruples were no doubt inspired by logical considerations: one cannot infer from '*totus homo*' as from '*omnis homo*', and even if the logical descent under the former is restricted to integral (rather than subjective) parts, one is obviously in danger of committing the fallacy of division. Thus if the whole house is white, its wall is white; but it is not the case that if the whole house is worth one hundred pounds its wall is worth one hundred pounds.[84] 'Whole' is distributive in the antecedent of the first conditional, but not in the antecedent of the second; and the standard way of registering that difference is to say that in the first case 'whole' ('*totus*') is being used syncategorematically and in the second categorematically.

But there are special problems of interpretation surrounding '*totus*' even in its syncategorematic use alone. Since '*totus*' does not distribute the term to which it is adjoined as '*omnis*' does – compare 'whole man' and 'every

---

81. For instance, adjoining '*omnis*' to the indefinite proposition '*Homo est albus*' transforms it into a universal proposition; but what is the corresponding effect of adjoining '*totus*' to that proposition, or to any other? This difference between the distributive signs was recognised very early in the discussion of '*totus*' and led the author of *Ars Emmerana* to say that '*Totus lapis est substantia*' is a 'mixed proposition' that, like '*Omnis homo et quidam asinus currunt*', is not of any quantity at all (ed. De Rijk 1962–7, II(2), 154.23–30).

82. E.g., text (9): '*Totus* 'distribuit enim inter partes integrales per se et non per accidens; ergo non potest distribuere in termino communi. Ergo terminus subiectus [cui "totus" adiungitur] aut erit discretus aut equipollens discreto, ut "*totus Sortes*" ... Omnia autem que predicta sunt intelligenda sunt de "*toto*" quando tenetur proprie. Improprie enim potest adiungi termino communi, secundum quod est commune, eo modo quo dicit Boethius in libro *Divisionum* quod particulares homines sunt partes integrales hominis simpliciter ...' (ed. Braakhuis 1978, 14.10–13; 15.3–6).

83. E.g., text (8): 'Quando ["totus"] determinat dictionem confuse significantem et non articulariter, tantum potest postponi, ut "*homo totus est albus*". Si autem preponatur, incongrua est locutio, ut "*totus homo est albus*". ... Si autem determinet dictionem discrete significantem vel articulariter, indifferenter potest preponi et postponi, ut "*Socrates totus*", "*totus Socrates*", "*rex totus*", "*totus rex*"' (ed. De Rijk 1962–7, II(2), 305.25–7; 29–32).

84. Discussions of examples of this sort are easy to find. In text (5) such a discussion constitutes almost the entire treatment of '*totus*': 'Sequitur de hac dictione "*totus*". Que quandoque tenetur collective, quandoque distributive. Quando tenetur collective, tunc non exigit predicatum convenire cuilibet sue parti divisim sed coniunctim. Et secundum hoc hec est vera "*tota domus valet centum libras*", sensus enim est: *domus valet centum libras et non quelibet eius pars valet centum libras*. Quando tenetur distributive, tunc exigitur quod predicatum conveniat cuilibet sue parti divisim. Unde hec est falsa: "*tota domus ista valet centum libras; ergo quelibet eius pars valet centum libras*"' (ed. Braakhuis 1979, I, 102.14–22).

man' – what does it distribute and how does it do so? The short, standard answer to the first question is that it distributes the integral parts of the whole named by the term to which it is adjoined, but, as we shall see, that standard answer ran into difficulties as the literature on '*totus*' developed. There seems to be no standard answer to the second question, and some of the earlier answers are best applied to the two questions taken together – e.g., '*totus*' 'distributes for the integral parts', 'divides the whole adjoined to it into integral parts', 'indicates the distribution of the integral parts of the term to which it is adjoined'.[85] But the long-term tendency of these answers seems to point in the direction of Albert of Saxony's careful formulation: 'There are some syncategoremata that do not distribute the term outside themselves to which they are added – i.e., a term that is not part of the expression to which that syncategorema is equivalent in signification – but do nevertheless distribute a term within themselves – i.e., a term that is part of the expression to which they are equivalent in signification – if that term is distributable. For example, the syncategorema "*totus*" does not distribute the term outside itself to which it is added, such as the term "Socrates", but rather the term within itself, such as the term "part".'[86]

A typical analysis of 'whole'

As Albert's account of the distribution effected by '*totus*' indicates, much of what a medieval logician maintains regarding '*totus*' depends on his initial analysis of it, his choice of 'the expression to which that syncategorema is equivalent in signification'. The most common analysis of 'whole' in its syncategorematic use is simply 'each part', so that 'the whole man' ('*totus homo*') is typically said to be equipollent to 'each part of the man' ('*quaelibet pars hominis*'). Obviously the categorematic use of 'whole' calls for a different analysis, and in this case the standard equipollent expression is 'made up of its parts', so that 'the whole man' is equipollent to 'the man made up of his parts' ('*homo perfectus ex partibus*'). Neither of these common

85. 'Totus' 'distribuit pro partibus integralibus' (text (5), ed. Braakhuis 1979, I, 102.25); 'totus' et 'singuli' sunt signa universalia 'que totum sibi adiunctum dividunt in partes integrales' (text (7), ed. De Rijk 1962–7, II(2), 469.32–470.2); 'totus' 'notat distributionem partium integralium termini cui adiungitur, et non appellatorum' (text (8), ed. De Rijk 1962–7, II(2), 305.16–18).
86. '. . . aliqua sunt syncategoremata quae non distribuunt terminum extra se cui adduntur – id est, terminum qui non est pars orationis cui illa syncategoremata aequivalent in significando – sed tamen distribuunt terminum intra se – hoc est, terminum qui est pars orationis cui aequivalent in significando – et hoc si ille terminus sit distribuibilis. Verbi gratia, hoc syncategorema "totus" non distribuit terminum extra se cui additur, sicut est iste terminus "Socrates", sed bene intra se, sicut iste terminus "pars"' (Albert of Saxony 1502, f. 25$^{\text{ra–b}}$).

analyses is entirely unproblematic, but the first is both more important and more troublesome, as can best be seen in connection with a final sophisma. Like the two sophismata considered above in connection with '*praeter*', this one will be presented in a homogenised version up to the resolution.[87]

The sophisma 'Totus Socrates est minor Socrate'

THE WHOLE SOCRATES IS LESS THAN SOCRATES[88]

Proof. Socrates's foot is less than Socrates, Socrates's head is less than Socrates, and so on as regards his integral parts; therefore each part of Socrates is less than Socrates, and so the whole Socrates is less than Socrates.[89]

Disproof. The whole Socrates is less than Socrates, but the whole Socrates is Socrates; therefore Socrates is less than Socrates – which is absurd.[90]

Despite its unpromising appearance, this sophisma generated resolutions of at least three basic types, and those of the third type show that it contains hidden depths. But the resolutions of the first type are just what we might expect: they take the sophisma sentence to be ambiguous and resolve its ambiguity in terms of two uses of '*totus*'. Full versions of this first type of resolution are offered by *Ricardus sophista*, Henry of Ghent, and Walter Burley. Burley's resolution is representative of the type: 'The first [i.e., the sophisma sentence] is ambiguous in respect of equivocation, because "whole" can be taken categorematically; and in that case it is false, because it denotes that Socrates made up of his parts is less than Socrates. But if it is understood syncategorematically, it is true, because it denotes that each part of Socrates is less than Socrates.'[91]

---

87. In connection with '*praeter*' the treatises I have taken into account provide many sophismata of several different types; in connection with '*totus*' they provide very few, and of those the only one that receives a great deal of attention and provides historical continuity is '*Totus Socrates est minor Socrate*', which is discussed more or less thoroughly in sixteen of the texts: (11/10), (12), (15), *(16), (21), (22), (23), (24), (25/26), (26/25), (27), (28), (29), (30), (31), and (32/33).

88 The problem this sophisma presents, at least initially, is the fundamental issue of the correct analysis of '*totus*', and the sophisma sentence raises that issue clearly without any specified context. Consequently this sophisma needs no hypothesis.

89. Most authors use the proposition appearing as the subconclusion in this version of the proof as its only premiss. This slightly more elaborate, inductive version is employed by Henry of Ghent, Walter Burley, and Albert of Saxony (25/26).

90. Although the proof and disproof offered here are to be found in most presentations of this sophisma, texts (24), (25/26), (28), and (29) involve more elaborate arguments in addition to these.

91. 'Solutio. Prima est multiplex secundum aequivocationem, eo quod li "totus" potest teneri categorematice, et sic est falsa, quia denotatur, quod perfectus Sortes ex suis partibus est minor Sorte. Si autem intelligatur syncategorematice, sic est verum, quia denotatur, quod quaelibet pars Sortis est minor Sorte' (ed. Boehner 1955, 256.23–7). (The '*totus*' in line 21 of Boehner's edition of this sophisma should be deleted.) *Ricardus sophista* offers a slightly more primitive resolution of this type: 'Solutio. "Totus Socrates" est aequivocum, sicut dixi; et illo sumpto pro eo quod est

The simple strategy of resolutions such as Burley's is what leads me to group them as a type, but they are alike also in their use of '*quaelibet pars Socratis*' as the analysis of '*totus Socrates*' in its syncategorematic use.[92] Three further texts also use that analysis in dealing with the sophisma sentence although they do not develop the sophisma fully, and on that basis they may be loosely associated with texts of the first type.[93] Albert of Saxony's *Perutilis logica* illustrates such partial resolutions: 'Thus when ["*whole*"] is taken syncategorematically it is equivalent to "each part." And it is on that basis that the sophisma "The whole Socrates is less than Socrates" is usually resolved; for it is equivalent to "Each part of Socrates is less than Socrates", and that is true.'[94]

A second type of resolution of this sophisma is identifiable by its centering around a non-standard analysis of the syncategorematic use of '*totus*'. Peter of Spain and William of Sherwood are the principal proponents of resolutions of the second type, but in their rejection of the

"quaelibet pars", maior vera et minor falsa. Si dicatur "totus" "perfectum ex partibus", accidit econverso' (MS Digby 24, f. 68[vb]; transcribed Tachau *et al.*). The version offered by Henry is somewhat more refined than Walter's: '*Solutio*: dicendum quod prima est duplex ex eo quod hoc signum "*totus*" teneri potest collective vel distributive. Si teneatur collective: sic est falsa, ut inprobatur; et est sensus: "*totus Sortes est minor Sorte*", idest: *Sortes ex omnibus suis partibus conpositus simul sumptis est minor Sorte*. Si teneatur distributive: sic est vera, ut probatur; et est sensus: "*totus Sortes etc.*", idest: *quelibet pars Sortis per se sumpta est minor Sorte*' (ed. Braakhuis 1978, 9.23–10.6). Henry also offers an alternate resolution; see n. 97 below.

92. Henry of Ghent refines the categorematic and syncategorematic analyses in order to bring out more clearly their collective and distributive functions respectively, adding 'taken together' ('*simul sumptis*') to the former and 'taken individually' ('*per se sumpta*') to the latter; but for reasons to be brought out in connection with resolutions of the second type, these refinements do not affect the essential characteristics of the analyses.

93. In his *Summa logicae* William Ockham uses the '*quaelibet pars*' analysis in this way at least twice: 'Sic enim concedunt in logica eruditi quod hoc signum 'totus' includit suum distribuibile, ut aequivaleat isti "quaelibet pars", quando sumitur syncategorematice. Unde ista "totus Sortes est minor Sorte" aequivalet isti "quaelibet pars Sortis est minor Sorte"' (William Ockham 1974a, *OP* I, 32.95–8). (Gedeon Gál, the principal editor of *OP* I, suggests William of Sherwood and Peter of Spain as the 'eruditi' Ockham refers to (p. 32, n. 5), but they both reject this analysis, as we shall see.) See also *Summa logicae*, Pars II, cap. 6 (*Ibid.*, 267.1–269.50, esp. 268.22–7, where Ockham's uniform application of the '*quaelibet pars*' analysis leads him to accept '*Totus Sortes est minor Sorte*' as true and to reject '*Totus Sortes currit*' as false on the syncategorematic interpretation). Paul of Venice treats this sophisma quite fully in other works, and with different results, as we shall see, but in his *Quadratura* he says simply 'non totus Socrates est minor Socrate, ... quia non quaelibet pars Socratis est minor Socrate, ut patet de anima sua ...' (Paul of Venice 1493a, f. 27 (bis)[vb]).

94. 'Unde cum tenetur synactegorematice valet istam "quaelibet pars". Et secundum hoc solet concedi hoc sophisma "Totus Socrates est minor Socrate"; valet enim istam "Quaelibet pars Socratis est minor Socrate", et hoc verum est' (Albert of Saxony 1522, f. 17[vb]). The contrast between this treatment of '*Totus Socrates est minor Socrate*' and the treatment Albert gives it in his *Sophismata* is so great and of such a nature as to suggest that the *Sophismata* is the later work, just as other comparisons suggest the converse (see n. 61 above). Albert's other treatment of the sophisma will be considered below along with other resolutions of the third type.

standard analysis they are joined by Nicholas of Paris (who happens not to have considered this sophisma).[95] The standard 'each part' analysis has the advantages of simplicity and of making explicit the distribution implicit in 'whole', but it achieves those advantages at the cost of changing the subject term of the proposition from 'Socrates' to 'part of Socrates'. Peter's analysis brings out the distribution while retaining the original subject term, and he explains the importance of doing so: 'For in the original proposition "The whole Socrates is white", Socrates is subjected to whiteness in respect of himself, and the parts not in respect of themselves but insofar as they are in the whole of him. But insofar as they are in the whole of him, they are under the form of the whole. Therefore they are subjected to whiteness only in virtue of the whole. Therefore what follows first is "Socrates in respect of each part of him is white", and afterwards "Each part of Socrates is white".'[96] On the basis of that analysis Peter feels entitled to take the position that the sophisma sentence is true and that the disproof is guilty of the fallacy of *secundum quid et simpliciter*; inferring the unconditional 'Socrates is less than Socrates' from 'The whole Socrates (i.e., Socrates in respect of each part of him) is less than Socrates' is as illegitimate as inferring it from 'Socrates in respect of his foot is less than Socrates.'[97]

95. At least three other texts, all of them from the fifteenth century, use Peter of Spain's analysis of '*totus*' in resolving this sophisma, and so their resolutions are of the second type. But one of those texts is (31), a commentary on Peter's resolution (Peter of Spain 1489, f. 32^{va-b}), and the other two are at least strongly influenced by Peter of Spain: (30) (*Ibid.*, f. 40^{ra-b}) and (32/33) (*Ibid.*, f. 40rb). Furthermore, texts (30) and (32/33) offer only partial treatments of the sophisma.

96. 'In hac enim propositione: "*totus Sortes est albus*" Sortes subicitur albedini secundum se, et partes non secundum se, sed prout sunt in suo toto. Sed prout sunt in suo toto, sunt sub forma totius. Ergo non subiciuntur albedini nisi per totum. Ergo per prius sequitur hec: "*Sortes secundum quamlibet sui partem est albus*", et per posterius illa: "*quelibet pars Sortis est alba*"' (*Tractatus*, ed. De Rijk 1972, 226.12–17). William is more emphatic in his rejection of the standard analysis, but his preferred analysis is more awkward than Peter's (I have not seen it in any other text), and his explanation is cryptic: 'Et dicendum quod "totus Sortes" non aequipollet huic "quaelibet pars Sortis", sed huic "Sortes, ita quod quaelibet pars". Cum enim sit signum universale affirmativum, supponit praedicatum inesse subiecto, et est in probatione fallacia consequentis. Ad contra [i.e., ad improbationem] sciendum quod ipsum procedit secundum quod ly "totus" est syncategorema' (ed. O'Donnell 1941, 54.23–6; some punctuation added). Nicholas, like William, flatly rejects the '*quaelibet pars*' analysis, offering an explanation different from Peter's and much fuller than William's: 'Primo videndum est utrum hec dictio "*totus*" aliquid significet aut nichil . . . Si aliquid: sed nonnisi totalitatem. / Ex hoc videtur quod non sequatur: "totus Sortes est albus; ergo quelibet pars Sortis est alba", quia Sortes non est aliqua pars sui; unde ille terminus "*totus Sortes*" non supponit pro aliqua parte Sortis; ergo illa "*totus Sortes est albus*" non debet sic exponi: *quelibet pars Sortis est alba* . . . *unde sicut* "*partim*" sic se habet resolvi: "*partim*" idest: *secundum partem*, eodem modo "*totaliter*", idest: *secundum quamlibet partem*. Eodem modo dicimus de hac dictione "*totus*", quia "*totus*" et "*totaliter*" non differunt nisi in casu' (ed. Braakhuis 1979, II, 432.7–8; 432.11–433.1; 434.15–18).

97. 'Peccat etiam improbatio secundum quid et simpliciter, quia ista "*totus Sortes est minor Sorte*" non ponit Sortem esse minorem Sorte simpliciter sed secundum suas partes; et ita ponit Sortem

It seems fair to say that resolutions of the second type mark an advance over those of the first type, but the qualitative difference between those first two types is negligible compared with the difference between the third type and either of those first two; for what I am designating resolutions of the third type are characterised by a radically new approach to the sophisma. '*Totus Socrates est minor Socrate*', which had seemed moribund in Ockham's and Burley's discussions, became the occasion for considering new and more important issues in William Heytesbury's complicated, impressive treatment of it. Heytesbury's work may well have been what inspired Albert of Saxony and Paul of Venice to develop philosophically interesting discussions of a sophisma that for a hundred years had been the occasion for only a few relatively simple observations; at any rate, it is in works of those three authors that I have found resolutions of the third type.[98] Of course, Heytesbury may not have been the first to discern the greater potential in this sophisma, but until another candidate for the honour emerges we may think of most of the distinguishing characteristics of this third type of resolution as Heytesbury's innovations. First, he supplements the standard proof with another, in which '*Totus Socrates est minor Socrate*' is justifiably assimilated to the subtler '*Animal est pars animalis*',[99] thereby enhancing the philosophical interest of this sophisma.[100] Second, after beginning his reply to the sophisma with the standard observation regarding the two interpretations of '*totus*', he points out that there is a further and equally important ambiguity in the '*pars*' of the

secundum quid esse minorem Sorte. Et ita, cum simpliciter infert sic: "*ergo Sortes est minor Sorte*", peccat secundum quid et simpliciter. Sicut hic: "*Sortes est minor Sorte secundum pedem; ergo Sortes est minor Sorte*"' (*Tractatus*, ed. De Rijk 1972, 227.15–21). Peter also attacks the disproof as an instance of the fallacy of accident (227.8–15), a line taken up by Henry of Ghent as an alternative to his preferred resolution (ed. Braakhuis 1978, 10.7–13; see n. 91 above).

98. The relevant texts are (24), (25/26), (28), and (29). This sophisma is treated in Heytesbury's *Sophismata* on ff. 147rb–148va, in Albert's *Sophismata* on ff. 24vb–25va, in Paul's *Sophismata* on ff. 40va–41rb, and in Paul's *Logica magna* on f. 56^{ra-va}. I am grateful to Edith Sylla for calling my attention to the fact that Heytesbury treats this sophisma. In his list of Heytesbury's sophismata, Curtis Wilson mentions Albert's and Paul's *Sophismata* as containing treatments of this sophisma (Wilson 1956, p. 162).

99. See n. 79 above.

100. The material Heytesbury introduces in the second proof and his rejoinder to it seems clearly to have been drawn from discussions of '*Animal est pars animalis*', but Heytesbury does not explicitly allude to it: 'Antecedens probatur in casu communi signando totum residuum Socratis praeter digitum illius; et ponatur quod ille digitus incipiat non esse pars Socratis, ita quod totum residuum maneat continue secundum quamlibet sui partem. Quo posito, sit A illud residuum. Tunc arguitur sic. A incipit esse Socrates, et A est pars Socratis; ergo pars Socratis incipit esse Socrates … Si enim A foret compositum huiusmodi, sequitur quod A foret homo; quia omne compositum ex materia et forma ultima quae est anima intellectiva est homo. Et sic sequitur quod unus homo foret infiniti homines – quod est impossibile' (William Heytesbury 1494c, f. 147rb; f. 147vb).

'*quaelibet pars*' analysis; for not only quantitative parts may be at issue, but also qualitative parts, such as form and matter.[101] Third, after completing an admirably thorough discussion of the sophisma as enhanced by those first two innovations, concluding that the sophisma sentence is false on any legitimate interpretation, he undertakes a second consideration of it, taking '*Socrates est minor Socrate*', the putative absurdity to which the sophisma sentence is reduced in the standard disproof, as a premiss from which to infer '*Totus Socrates est minor Socrate*' on radically different grounds.[102] Finally, and most significantly, he organises this second, even fuller consideration of the sophisma around the concepts and lines of argument that are characteristic of the kind of work for which he and the other Oxford Calculators are most famous.[103]

Albert of Saxony offers some arguments that may be innovations of his

101. 'Ibidem etiam distinguitur de isto termino "pars", quoniam "pars" dicitur dupliciter. Quaedam enim est pars quantitativa, quaedam est pars qualitativa. Pars quantitativa est talis quae est in actu quantam minorem habens magnitudinem quam totum cuius est pars; qualitativa est maxime [reading 'maxime' for 'maxima'] materia rei, propinqua vel remota, sive sit quanta in actu sive in potentia, et forma, sive quanta sive non quanta' (f. 147rb). Conceivably Heytesbury could in this case be taking his cue from Ockham: 'Verumtamen sciendum quod aliquando, sive de virtute sermonis sive ex usu vel placito alicuius utentis, non curo, "totus" tantum distribuit pro partibus integralibus, non pro partibus essentialibus, cuiusmodi vocantur materia et forma, quandoque autem distribuit pro omnibus partibus, sive sint integrales sive essentiales sive qualescumque' (William Ockham 1974a, *OP* I, 269.37–41). Albert of Saxony later expressly identified qualitative and essential parts; see n. 105 below.

102. 'Ad sophisma arguitur adhuc sic. Socrates est minor Socrate; ergo etc.' (William Heytesbury 1494c, f. 147vb). Heytesbury's second consideration of the sophisma, stemming from this first, novel proof of it, is about three times as long as and far more complex than his first consideration of it. Paul of Venice's second, third, and fourth proofs appear to be drawn from Heytesbury's second consideration of this sophisma as his first appears to derive from the first consideration (Paul of Venice 1493b, f. 40^{va–b}).

103. See, e.g., the passage immediately following the one quoted in n. 102: 'Antecedens arguitur. Socrates erit minor Platone ante A instans, et continue ante A instans Socrates erit aequalis Platoni; ergo, etc. Assumptum arguitur sic. Ponatur quod Socrates et Plato iam sint aequales, et quod quandocumque erunt, erunt aequales, et augeatur uterque illorum aequevelociter usque ad A instans. Et ponatur quod Plato erit in A instanti, et quod Socrates tunc primo erit corruptus. Quo posito, probatur quod Socrates erit minor Platone ante A instans; quia Socrates erit minor quam erit Plato, quia Plato erit maior quam erit Socrates. Ergo Socrates erit minor quam erit Plato, sed numquam nisi ante A instans; ergo Socrates erit minor Platone ante A instans, casus enim ponit quod Socrates numquam erit nisi ante A instans" (William Heytesbury 1494c, f. 147vb). This hypothesis and the lines of argument that derive from it are so typical of the concerns of the Calculators and so indirectly attached to the original problems of the sophisma that in the intricacies of this second consideration Heytesbury seems sometimes to be addressing only the concerns of the Calculators. For example, he refers at one point to views held by others, and they are surely views that can be found among the earlier Calculators, such as Thomas Bradwardine and Richard Kilvington, but they are very unlikely to have had anything to do with the sophisma that is ostensibly still at issue: 'Ideo dicitur a multis quod Plato habebit ante A quamcumque quantitatem sibi acquiret ante A et etiam ipse Socrates, sed ipse in nullo instanti habebit maximam quantitatem quam habebit vel acquiret sibi ante A. Unde dicunt ipsi quod A erit primum instans in quo Plato habebit maximam quantitatem quam ipse acquiret ante A, tamen Plato tunc non primo habebit totam quantitatem quam acquiret ante A; in toto enim illo

own,[104] but the most valuable features of his treatment of the sophisma are to be found in the three notes in which he lays the foundation for his resolution of it; and in the third note he provides a detailed account of the notion of an integral part in order to set aside the sort of ambiguity pointed out in Heytesbury's second innovation.[105]

In his *Sophismata* Paul of Venice apparently borrows heavily from Heytesbury and perhaps also from Albert, but his use of the material is intelligent, and he seems to make some contributions of his own in his rejoinders to the four proofs he offers.[106] In his *Logica magna*, however, Paul seems to present the sophisma in a way designed to avoid some of the problems to which he devotes his attention in the *Sophismata*; here again he

tempore terminato ad illud A instans Plato habebit totam quantitatem quam habebit in A, sed in nullo instanti illius temporis habebit illam. Et dicunt quod illa quantitas prius erit acquisita vel habita a Platone, sed in nullo instanti prius erit acquisita alicui' (*Ibid.*, f. 148[ra]).

104. E.g., his second disproof and his rejoinder to it: 'Si totus Socrates est minor Socrate, tunc totus homo est minor Socrate – quod est falsum. Consequentia videtur valere eo quod arguitur ab inferiori ad superius. Falsitas consequentis probatur, nam si totus homo est minor Socrate, tunc quaelibet pars hominis est minor Socrate. Modo hoc est falsum, posito quod Socrates sit parvus et Plato sit magnus; tunc non quaelibet pars hominis est minor Socrate. Nam sequitur "Quaelibet pars hominis est minor Socrate; ergo quaelibet pars Platonis est minor Socrate"; sed hoc est falsum ex casu. Consequentia tenet: a superiori distributo ad inferius distributum; nam in ista "Quaelibet pars hominis est minor Socrate" hoc aggregatum "pars hominis" distribuitur per unam regulam prius dictam – scilicet, *Quotienscumque signum distributivum additur aggregato ex recto et obliquo, recto praecedente obliquum, tunc aggregatum ex recto et obliquo distribuitur*. Et ideo ly "hominis" ita bene distribuitur sicut ly "pars"' (Albert of Saxony 1502, f. 25[ra]). Albert's rejoinder consists essentially in rejecting the main inference: 'Unde sicut non sequitur "Quelibet pars integralis Socratis est minor Socrate; ergo quaelibet pars integralis hominis est minor Socrate", ita non sequitur "Totus Socrates est minor Socrate; ergo totus homo est minor Socrate" ... in ista oratione "Quaelibet pars integralis hominis est minor Socrate" non solum distribuitur ibi "pars integralis" sed hoc aggregatum "pars integralis hominis"' (*Ibid.*, f. 25[va]).

105. 'Tertio notandum est quod pars integralis dicitur pars quantitativa – id est, habens quantitatem quae cum alia parte quantitativa constituit aliquod totum quantum, nec una illarum est potentia ad aliam, nec perfectibilis per eam. Ex hoc patet quod anima Socratis vel corpus Socratis non dicitur pars integralis Socratis, quia licet anima Socratis constituat Socratem quantum, et etiam corpus Socratis sic habens quantitatem, tamen anima Socratis non est pars quantitativa; et etiam materia Socratis est perfectibilis per animam Socratis ... Et tales partes quarum una est sic perfectibilis per aliam non dicuntur partes integrales sed essentiales vel qualitativae' (Albert of Saxony 1502, f. 25[rb]).

106. Here, for instance, is a passage in which Paul again shows his concern with the details of exposition as a means of resolving difficulties involving syncategoremata (see also n. 76 above): 'Non est ergo aliqua propositio exponibilis ratione alicuius syncategorematis praecedentis totam propositionem quin ab illa ad suum praeiacens sit bonum argumentum. Sed ly "Socrates est pars Socratis" est praeiacens illius "Totus Socrates est pars Socratis", quia praeiacens est illud quod remanet, dempto signo. Ergo illa consequentia est bona: "Totus Socrates est pars Socratis; ergo Socrates est pars Socratis." / Dicatur quod illa propositio "Totus Socrates est pars Socratis" sic exponitur: "Socrates est pars Socratis, et quaelibet pars Socratis est pars Socratis"; ergo, etc. Et hoc patet secundum communem modum loquendi; si enim totus Socrates est albus, intelligitur quod Socrates secundum se et quamlibet sui partem est albus. Et notanter dico secundam exponentem universalem affirmativam et non illam universalem negativam: "et nulla est pars Socratis quin illa sit pars Socratis", quia aliter illae essent verae: "Totus punctus est punctus", "Tota anima intellectiva est anima", quia ambae exponentes essent verae. Sed consequens est falsum, quia ly

seems to have learned from Heytesbury and perhaps even more markedly from Albert.[107]

Conclusion

As I have indicated at several points in this discussion, my historical and philosophical sampling has turned up doctrinal or methodological similarities among some of the texts considered in this exploration, but the historically significant groupings of texts that may eventually emerge from comparative studies of this sort are not yet clear enough to be presented definitively. At the conclusion of this necessarily restricted exploration of the medieval literature on the syncategoremata it is essential to remember that it has been no more than the shallow, narrow trenching of an immeasurably rich site, intended primarily to stimulate and orient further exploration.[108]

APPENDIX I

A SELECTION OF TEXTS IN APPROXIMATE
CHRONOLOGICAL ORDER

The numerical order of this list indicates either the received opinion or my best guess regarding the chronological order of the texts listed. Divided numerical designations, such as '(2/3)' and '(3/2)', indicate particular un-

---

"totum" syncategorematice tantum distribuit implicite pro partibus et importat significatum subiecti habere partes' (Paul of Venice 1493b, f. 40vb). Paul's concern about such expressions as '*totus punctus*' was also felt by several earlier authors; see, e.g., Nicholas of Paris in *Sum:ne Metenses*, exc. De Rijk 1962–7, II(1), 488.16–21. The account of the distributive effect of '*totus*' offered by Paul at the end of the passage quoted above is reminiscent of the one developed by Albert of Saxony; see n. 86 above.

107. See, e.g., his disproof and his rejoinder to it: '... arguitur probando illam esse falsam: "Totus Socrates est minor Socrate", quia non quaelibet pars quantitativa Socratis est minor Socrate ... nam materia Socratis, quae est altera pars compositi, est pars quantitativa ... et tamen non est minor Socrati; igitur, etc. / ... nego quod quaelibet pars quantitativa Socratis est minor Socrate, et etiam nego quod materia quae est altera pars compositi est pars quantitativa, ut huiusmodi responsio intelligatur. Est notandum quod in Socrates est duplex pars – scilicet, qualitativa, quae est altera pars compositi, ut patet tota illa materia cum qua componitur anima, et quantitativa, quae est minor toto minorem continens materiam quam totum, quae cum alia quantitate constituit aliquod totum quantum, quarum nulla est in potentia ad aliam. Ex hoc patet quod materia Socratis vel eius corpus non dicitur pars quantitativa vel integralis, quia perfectibilis est per animam et in potentia respectu eiusdem, non obstante quod ambo constituant corpus habens quantitatem' (Paul of Venice 1499, f. 56rb; ff. 56rb–56va). Compare Albert of Saxony on quantitative and qualitative parts, n. 105 above.

108. I am very grateful to Eleonore Stump for her helpful criticisms of an earlier draft and to Jan Pinborg and Barbara Ensign Kretzmann for many suggestions that enabled me to improve my presentation of this material.

certainty on my part regarding the order of the two texts thus designated relative to each other; my best guess is represented by the first numeral in such divided designations. Designations preceded by asterisks indicate texts that I have seen only in excerpts. Titles in brackets have been supplied by me.

(1)	*Quaestiones Victorinae* [ed. De Rijk]	1st half XII
(2/3)	*Tractatus de univocatione Monacensis* [ed. De Rijk]	3rd qu. XII
(3/2)	*Ars Emmerana* [ed. De Rijk]	3rd qu. XII
*(4)	*Ars Meliduna* [exc. De Rijk]	1170/1180
(5)	*Sincategoreumata Monacensia* [ed. Braakhuis]	4th qu. XII
(6)	*Tractatus implicitarum* [ed. Giusberti]	turn of century
(7)	*Dialectica Monacensis* [ed. De Rijk]	4th qu. XII
(8)	*Tractatus Anagnini* [ed. De Rijk]	1st decades XIII
(9)	Robert Bacon (?): *Sincategoreumata* [ed. Braakhuis]	1200/1210
*(10/11)	John le Page: *Syncategoremata* [exc. Braakhuis]	1220/1230
(11/10)	*Ricardus sophista*: *Abstractiones* [ed. Tachau *et al.*]	1220/1230 (?)
(12)	Peter of Spain: *Tractatus* [ed. De Rijk]	1230/1240
*(13)	Peter of Spain: *Syncategoremata* [exc. Braakhuis]	1230/1240
(14)	Pseudo-Petrus: *Tractatus syncategorematum* [1489 edn.]	1230/1240 (?)
(15)	William of Sherwood: *Syncategoremata* [ed. O'Donnell]	1230/1240
*(16)	['*Sophismata logicalia*'] [exc. Grabmann]	after 1230
*(17)	Nicholas of Paris: *Summe Metenses* [exc. De Rijk]	ca. 1250
(18)	Nicholas of Paris: *Sincategoreumata* [ed. Braakhuis]	ca. 1250
*(19/20)	'*Quoniam ignoratis communibus*' [exc. Grabmann]	mid-XIII
*(20/19)	['*Sophismata Parisius determinata*'] [exc. Grabmann/Braakhuis]	mid-XIII
(21)	Henry of Ghent: *Sincathegoreumata* [ed. Braakhuis]	3rd qu. XIII
(22)	William Ockham: *Summa logicae* [ed. Boehner/Gál]	1323
(23)	Walter Burley: *De puritate artis logicae* [ed. Boehner]	before 1329
(24)	William Heytesbury: *Sophismata* [1494 edn.]	ca. 1340 (?)
(25/26)	Albert of Saxony: *Sophismata* [1502 edn.]	ca. 1350 (?)
(26/25)	Albert of Saxony: *Perutilis logica* [1522 edn.]	ca. 1350 (?)
(27)	Paul of Venice: *Quadratura* [1493 edn.]	after 1390 (?)
(28)	Paul of Venice: *Sophismata* [1493 edn.]	after 1390 (?)
(29)	Paul of Venice: *Logica magna* [1499 edn.]	after 1393
(30)	Pseudo-Petrus: *Tractatus exponibilium* [1489 edn.]	XV (?)
(31)	Cologne Dominicans: *Comm. on Tractatus* (12)	XV
(32/33)	Cologne Domincans: *Comm. on Tr. exponibilium* (30)	XV
(33/32)	Pseudo-Petrus: *Tr. syncategorematum* (supp.) [1489 edn.]	XV

APPENDIX II

EXAMPLES OF ELEMENTS IN THE TREATMENT OF 'PRAETER'
('BESIDES') AND 'TOTUS' ('WHOLE')

*I. Definitions and analyses (of exception or of the sort of
distribution effected by 'totus')*

'Exception is nothing other than the taking of a part from a whole.' (5)
'To except is to take one thing from another in respect of a third.' (18)
'For exception, properly so-called, four things are required – namely, that
by which it is excepted, and that in respect of which, and that which is
excepted, and that from which it is excepted.' (9)
'Five things are required for exception. One is the excepting thing, and that
is the soul; and another is the instrument of excepting, and that is an
exceptive word, such as "besides" and the like. Moreover, these three,
regarding which it occurred, are required – namely, that which is excepted,
and that from which it is excepted, and that in respect of which it is
excepted.'★(13)

'Notice that the signs "every" and "whole" are different, for the sign
"every" distributes for subjective parts, and the word "whole" distributes
for integral parts.' (5)
'Its signification is evident in this way. "Whole" is either a categorema or a
syncategorema. If it is a categorema, it signifies the wholeness of a thing;
and in that case one usually speaks of a formal, or collective, or integral
whole, and "whole" is the same as "complete" and is explained in this way:
a whole is that outside of which there is nothing [belonging to itself]. If it is
a syncategorema, it signifies the wholeness of the subject insofar as it is the
subject; and in that case it is distributive and one usually speaks of a material
whole.' (9)

II. Classifications of the uses of the words ('praeter' *and* 'totus')

'Exceptively, Inclusively, Exclusively, Distributively, Collectively' (6)
'Additively, Exceptively: Diminutionally, Counter-instantively' (15)
'Exceptively, Diminutionally' (22)
'Properly, Improperly: Negatively, Additively, Subtractively (or Diminu-
tionally)' (25/26)

'Collectively, Distributively' (5)
'It sometimes determines a word signifying confusedly and not articulately, sometimes [a word signifying] discretely or articulately.' (8)

'It is, however, equivocal relative to these two: "each part" and "made up of parts". (11/10)
'The name "whole" can be considered in two ways: one in which it is a distributive sign and one in which it is the same as "complete".'*(17)
'The word "whole" is sometimes taken distributively, sometimes collectively; thus sometimes it signifies universally and divisively, sometimes universally and conjunctively.' (18)

III. Grammatical, semantic, and logical rules governing propositions (involving 'praeter' and 'totus')

'If a sentence in which the word "besides" occurs is true, it is false without it.' (5)
'Even though [a proposition involving] exception has a copulative proposition within itself implicitly [i.e., the conjunction of its exponents], it is called not hypothetical but categorical.' (9)
'Whenever as many things are excepted in a given expression as are supposited, the sentence is false or ungrammatical.' (21)
'One must not make a logical descent together with exception under the subject of an exceptive proposition.' (25/26)

'When ["whole"] is taken distributively, it is required that the predicate go together with each part of the subject dividedly.' (5)
'The word "whole" cannot determine a word that discretely signifies something that is not composite.' (8)
'The sign "whole" can be added to a term to which the sign "every" cannot be added, because something can be divided into integral parts that cannot be divided into subjective parts.' *(17)
'An inference from a term taken together with "whole" to the term taken without it does not follow.' (22)

IV. Examples (associated with II or III)

'Every man besides Socrates is running.' (5)
'Ten besides five are five.' *(10/11)
'The whole house besides the wall is white.' (18)
'Every animal besides man is irrational.' (22)

'The whole stone is a substance.' (3/2)
'A genus is a whole relative to its species.' (18)
'If the whole man is an animal, the man is an animal.' (22)
'A whole [or the whole] that is in the world is in your eye or in your purse.' (29)

V. Sophismata (*involving* 'praeter' *or* 'totus')

'Every animal is rational besides the irrational.' (1)
'Everything is everything with the exception of everything besides everything.' (9)
'Ten besides one know themselves to be nine.' *(10/11)
'Every man sees every man besides himself.' (11/10)
'Nothing is true except (*nisi*) at this instant.' (18)

'A whole disjunctive proposition is true of which either part is true.' (11/10)
'Every whole is greater than its part.' (25/26)

VI. Expositions of propositions (*involving* 'praeter' *or* 'totus')

'No man besides Socrates is running – i.e., Socrates is running, and no one else is running.' (6)
'No man besides Socrates is running – i.e., Socrates is running, and no man other than Socrates is running.' (22)
'No man besides Socrates is running – i.e., Socrates is running, and every man other than Socrates is not running.' (25/26)
'Some man besides Socrates is risible – i.e., Not only Socrates is risible, but also some other man.' (23)
'Ten besides five are five – i.e., If from ten five are taken away, five remain.' (29)

'The whole house is worth one hundred pounds – i.e., The house is worth one hundred pounds, and not each part of it is worth one hundred pounds.' (5)
'The whole man is white – i.e., The man is white, and each part of him is white.' (8)
'This whole proposition is true – i.e, Each quantitative part of this proposition is true.' (29)

VII. Questions (*arising from* I–VI)

'Can an exception be made from the predicate as from the subject?' (18)
'Can an exception be made from a relative pronoun related to a distributed term?' (18)
'Since everything that signifies signifies either by way of a concept or by way of an operation, in which of those ways does the word "besides" signify exception?' (18)

'In some cases this follows: "the whole Socrates; therefore Socrates' – e.g., "The whole Socrates is white; therefore Socrates is white" – and in some cases it does not follow; therefore in which does it follow?' (13)

'Can the sign "whole" be added to a term signifying something that is not divisible into integral parts – i.e., can one say "whole God", "whole soul", "whole point", "whole unity"?' ★ (17)

12
INSOLUBILIA

The nature and history of insolubilia

Medieval literature on 'insolubles' began to appear by the early thirteenth century at the latest and continued to the end of the Middle Ages.[1] Insolubles were primarily certain sorts of self-referential sentences, semantic paradoxes like the 'liar paradox' ('What I am now saying is false'). But few authors tried to give a rigorous definition,[2] so that other more or less unrelated kinds of paradoxes were also treated under this heading.[3]

Three periods may be distinguished in the medieval *insolubilia* literature: (1) from the beginnings to *ca.* 1320; (2) the period of the most original work, from *ca.* 1320 to the time of the Black Death (1347–50); (3) after *ca.* 1350, a period of refinement and elaboration but, with a few exceptions, little that was new.

Resolutions in terms of cassation

Several approaches may be distinguished during the first period. One was called 'cassation' – i.e., nullification. On this theory, he who utters an insoluble 'says nothing'.[4] The earliest known text[5] adopts this view, and by *ca.* 1225 it was said to be 'according to the common judgement'.[6] Nevertheless, it soon died out and seems not to have been revived until David Derodon in the seventeenth century.[7] It is not clear how the theory is to be taken. In the middle thirteenth century a text attributed to William

---

1. Spade 1973 and Spade 1975a, Bottin 1976. For the later period see Ashworth 1972, Ashworth 1974, Ch. 2, §4, Prantl 1855–67, Vol. 4, §22, and Roure 1962.
2. William Heytesbury did. See the texts in Spade 1975a, pp. 117–18.
3. E.g., Buridan 1977, *Sophismata*, 8, sophismata 1–2 and 17–20, translated in Buridan 1966, pp. 180–5 and 219–23.
4. Spade 1975a, pp. 32 and 44.
5. Edited in De Rijk 1966b. See the discussion in Spade 1975a, p. 32, and Bottin 1976, pp. 47–54.
6. Spade 1975a, p. 43. This might mean only that it is the way the common man would respond to insolubles, not that it was the general view of those who had considered the question theoretically. See the anonymous author's remarks in Spade 1975a, p. 44.
7. Ashworth 1974, p. 115.

of Sherwood[8] discussed several views that might be considered versions of cassation, including one theory that insolubles for semantic reasons fail to be sentences, so that he who utters them 'says nothing'.[9] This theory has modern parallels, e.g., in Fitch 1970. Nevertheless, the author of the text reserved the word 'cassation' for only one of those views,[10] which he refuted merely by observing that it 'denies the senses'.[11] Thomas Bradwardine made the same point *ca.* 1324[12]: he who says the words 'I am saying a falsehood' is saying at least those words, and so not 'nothing'.[13] Through Bradwardine, this argument became standard.[14] The theory was not so facile as this refutation implies, however. In the earliest known version of the theory, distinctions were already made that suffice to disarm this refutation.[15] Nevertheless, those who later held the theory seem to have been remarkably unable to defend themselves against such objections, so that their view soon died out.

Resolutions in terms of 'secundum quid et simpliciter'

A second approach, the most common early one, tried to treat insolubles as fallacies of confusing what is true only in a certain respect with what is true absolutely (*secundum quid et simpliciter*). Aristotle discussed such fallacies in *Sophistici elenchi*, 25, 180[a]27–[b]7, and briefly alluded to 'the problem whether the same man can at the same time say what is both false and true' (Oxford translation). The almost universal testimony of the extant thirteenth-century treatises indicates that the medieval literature arose out of speculation on this passage.[16] All but two of those treatises[17] adopt variants of this approach, sometimes combining it with other views. Nevertheless, insolubles do not fit very well the pattern of the fallacy *secundum quid et simpliciter*, so that such approaches were always strained.[18]

---

8. Edited in Roure 1970. See Spade 1975a, pp. 26–8. On the doubtful attribution, see De Rijk 1966b, p. 93.
9. Roure 1970, pp. 257–60, pars. 8.01–11.01. Note the phrase 'says nothing' – '*nihil dicit*' – in 11.01.
10. Roure 1970, pp. 249–50, pars. 1.01–2.06.
11. *Ibid.*, p. 259, par. 2.01. At least two other thirteenth-century authors discussed cassation. See Spade 1975a, pp. 43–4 (anonymous) and pp. 94–5 (Richard of Sherwood).
12. On the date see Weisheipl 1968, p. 190.
13. *Insolubilia*, edited in Roure 1970, p. 295, pars. 5.05–5.06.
14. E.g., Paul of Venice 1499, *Logica magna*, 2, 15, 4th and 5th previous opinions, f. 192[va]; also Ralph Strode cited in Spade 1975a, p. 87.
15. See the discussion in Bottin 1976, pp. 51–2.
16. Spade 1973.
17. Edited in De Rijk 1966b and Braakhuis 1967.
18. Spade 1973.

They seem to have died out around 1330 with Richard Kilvington,[19] although a certain Henry of England held this view, perhaps much later.[20]

Resolutions in terms of transcasus

A third early theory perhaps arose out of attempts to make insolubles fit what Aristotle says about fallacies *secundum quid et simpliciter.*[21] According to this view, present-tensed verbs in insolubles refer to the time just before the insoluble utterance, so that 'I am speaking a falsehood', despite its grammar, means 'I spoke a falsehood a moment ago'. Insolubles are true or false depending on whether one did in fact utter a falsehood at that earlier time. Walter Burley refers to such a view as '*transcasus*', and rejects it.[22]

The anonymous text in Braakhuis 1967 adopts this position and links it with a rejection of self-reference. Bradwardine, too,[23] treats the view as a variant of the theory of the 'restricters' (*restringentes*), who denied self-reference. The restricters argued that 'a part cannot supposit for the whole of which it is a part' – e.g., a term for the sentence in which it occurs. Some ruled out more general kinds of referential cycles as well. Two groups of restricters may be distinguished. Some ruled out self-reference in all cases, mostly on the basis of very bad arguments.[24] It was quickly realised that this strong view prevented innocuous as well as vicious self-reference.[25] Others allowed self-reference in some cases, but not in insolubles;[26] they did not provide any very informative way to distinguish such cases.[27]

---

19. See Spade 1975a, pp. 92–3, and the anonymous text, probably from the fourteenth century, discussed *ibid.*, pp. 41–2.
20. Spade 1975a, pp. 55–6.
21. Spade 1973, p. 307, n. 64.
22. *Insolubilia*, edited in Roure 1970, pp. 270–1, pars. 2.07–2.08. The exact sense of the word '*transcasus*' in this context is obscure, and Burley's own explanation is of little help: 'And there is a *transcasus* when some sentence is changed from truth to falsehood, or conversely' ('*Et est transcasus quando aliqua propositio mutatur a veritate in falsitatem vel e converso*'; *ibid.*, p. 270 par. 2.07). Perhaps the best translation is 'passage of time', i.e., the time between the occurrence of the events described and the description of them. Thus 'The time in which I say something is other than the time for which I say something' ('[*aliud*] *est tempus in quo dico aliquid et pro quo dico aliquid*'; ibid.). Perhaps '*transcasus*' is a corruption of '*transcursus*', which had the sense 'passage of time' in the late Middle Ages; see Latham 1965.
23. In Roure 1970, pp. 294–5, pars. 5.04–5.042.
24. E.g., the text in Braakhuis 1967 and the anonymous text discussed in Spade 1975a, pp. 33–4.
25. Thus Pseudo-Sherwood in Roure 1970, p. 252, par. 4.02.
26. E.g., Burley in Roure 1970; Ockham 1974a, 3–3, 46, discussed in Spade 1974b; Walter Sexgrave, discussed in Spade 1975a, pp. 113–16; Roger Roseth, discussed in Spade 1975a, pp. 101–2.
27. See Spade 1974b.

Resolutions in terms of truth-conditions

Bradwardine presents a survey of these and other early views.[28] With him, the *insolubilia*-literature entered its second and most productive phase.[29] Bradwardine seems to have been the first to formulate carefully and take seriously the theory that insolubles not only 'signify' or 'imply' that they are false, but also that they are true.[30] Some went further and said that *all* sentences signify or imply that they are true.[31] Since in order that a sentence be true, everything that it signifies or implies must be so, it follows that insolubles are true only if they are both true and false. On this approach insolubles are false and no paradox can be derived. Variations of this approach were adopted by many authors; indeed, it became one of the main traditions in the fourteenth century.[32] The phrases 'direct' and 'consecutive signification' that one sometimes sees in the *insolubilia*-literature belong to this tradition.[33] Although the claim that sentences signify or imply that they are true may be traced back at least to Bonaventure,[34] Bradwardine was among the first to apply it to insolubles. Note that if only insolubles signify or imply their own truth, the theory seems *ad hoc*. But if all sentences do so, then the theory amounts to a wholesale abandonment of half the so-called 'Tarski biconditionals',[35] which seems too heavy a price.

28. Roure 1970, pp. 286–96, pars. 2.01–5.08.
29. Ralph Strode, after paraphrasing Bradwardine's survey, says, 'After them there arose the prince of modern natural philosophers, namely, Master Thomas Bradwardine, who first came upon something of value concerning insolubles.' ('Post quos surrexit princeps modernorum physicorum, videlicet, magister Thomas Bradwardine, qui aliquid quod valuerit de insolubilibus primitus adinvenit.' Quoted in Spade 1975a, p. 88.)
30. In Roure 1970, p. 298, par. 6.05, conclusion 2. See Spade 1975a, p. 109, n. 200 for an importantly different reading of this passage. Not all who held this view were willing to put it in terms of signification. E.g., Buridan 1977, 8, sophisma 7, translated in Buridan 1966, pp. 194–6. The theory is mentioned very briefly, before Bradwardine, in Burley's *Insolubilia*, ed. Roure 1970, p. 272, par. 3.02.
31. Burley 1955, p. 25.37–8; Burley in Roure 1970, p. 272, par. 3.02; Buridan 1977, 8, sophisma 7, translated in Buridan 1966, pp. 195–6; Albert of Saxony 1518, *Perutilis logica*, 6, 1, concls. 1–3, f. 43rb.
32. See, besides Bradwardine, the texts cited in Spade 1975a as items IV, VIII, XII (all anonymous), XXIV (Albert of Saxony), XXXI (Henry Hopton), XXXIV (John Buridan), XXXVIII (John of Holland), XXXIX (John Hunter), XLIX (Paul of Pergula), LIII (Ralph Strode), LVI (Richard Lavenham), LVIII (Robert Fland).
33. See Spade 1975a, pp. 47 and 60.
34. *Quaestiones disputatae de mysterio trinitatis*, q. 1, a. 1, *ad* 5; in Bonaventure 1882–1902, Vol. 5, p. 50. See Spade 1975a, p. 53.
35. See Spade 1971, pp. 1–3.

Resolutions in terms of self-falsification

Roger Swineshead, writing probably shortly after Bradwardine, took a different approach. For him, a true sentence is one that not only corresponds to reality ('signifies principally as is the case') but also does not 'falsify itself'.[36] Conversely, a false sentence is one that either misrepresents reality ('signifies principally otherwise than is the case') or else 'falsifies itself'.[37] A sentence 'falsifies itself' just in case it is 'relevant' (*pertinens*) to inferring that it is false.[38] This notion of 'relevance' is a complex one, and needs further study.[39] Insolubles, in any case, turn out to 'falsify themselves'.[40] Thus the insoluble 'This sentence is false' is simply false, and no paradox arises. One cannot argue that, since that is exactly what the sentence signifies, it must be true after all. For Swineshead, truth requires more than that.

Swineshead's conclusions

Swineshead drew three famous conclusions from his approach; they were the topic of much controversy after him.[41] First, 'some false sentence signifies principally as is the case';[42] we have just seen one. Second, 'in some good formal consequence, the false follows from the true'.[43] For example,

36. 'Propositio vera est propositio non falsificans se principaliter sicut est significans naturaliter aut ex impositione vel impositionibus qua vel quibus ultimo fuit imposita ad significandum.' (*Insolubilia*, ed. Spade 1979a, par. 14.) See also Spade 1975a, pp. 102–5.

37. 'Tertia definitio: Propositio falsa est oratio falsificans se vel oratio non falsificans se principaliter aliter quam est significans naturaliter, ex impositione, vel impositionibus qua vel quibus ultimo fuit imposita ad significandum.' (Ed. Spade 1979a, par. 15.)

38. 'Omnis propositio pertinens ad inferendum se ipsam fore falsam est falsificans se.' (Ed. Spade 1979a, par. 17.)

39 It is not the same as the notion of relevance in the *obligationes*-literature, where a sentence *S* is said to be 'relevant' (*pertinens*) to another sentence *S'* if and only if *S* either follows from or is inconsistent with *S'*. See Swineshead's *Obligationes*, ed. Spade 1977, par. 4; 'Tertia divisio est haec: Propositionum alia est pertinens obligato, alia est impertinens obligato. Et pertinentium obligato alia est sequens ex obligato, alia repugnans obligato.' See also n. 43 below.

40. Strictly speaking, Swineshead includes certain epistemic paradoxes under the heading 'insoluble', so that his official definition provides for them too: 'Insolubile ad propositum est propositio significans principaliter sicut est vel aliter quam est pertinens ad inferendum se ipsam fore falsam vel nescitam vel creditam, et sic de singulis.' (*Insolubilia*, ed. Spade 1979a, par. 16.)

41. See e.g., Spade 1975a, items III (anonymous), XXVI (Anthony de Monte), XLII (John of Wesel), XLIX (Paul of Pergula), L (Paul of Venice), LVIII (Robert Fland), LXII (Roger Roseth), and LXIX (William Heytesbury).

42. 'Aliqua propositio falsa significat principaliter sicut est.' (Ed. Spade 1979a, par. 25.)

43. 'In aliqua consequentia bona formali ex vero sequitur falsum.' (Ed. Spade 1979a, par. 26.) For the example, see *ibid*. Perhaps this feature of Swineshead's position was prompted by reflection on the end of Sophisma 48 in Richard Kilvington's *Sophismata*. Kilvington allows that 'in some good consequence, some sentence that is false in a certain respect follows from [ones that are] true

'The consequent of this consequence is false; therefore, the consequent of this consequence is false'; although both antecedent and consequent correspond to reality, the latter falsifies itself and the former does not. (For many medievals, it was the sentence token that was the bearer of truth-value.) Swineshead explicitly says that although valid consequences need not preserve truth, they do preserve the property of corresponding to reality.[44] Third, in the case of insolubles, 'two mutual contradictories are false at the same time'.[45] Thus the insoluble 'This sentence is false', although false, corresponds to reality. Its contradictory, 'That sentence is not false', fails to correspond and so is likewise false.

Swineshead distinguished the notion of truth from the notion of corresponding to reality. If, when the two were identified, there were paradoxes involving truth and falsehood, one may well suspect that the paradoxes are still there in the notion of correspondence, even though they will no longer be expressed in terms of truth and falsehood. Thus, consider the sentence 'This sentence signifies principally otherwise than is the case.' Swineshead discusses these paradoxes too,[46] and seems to say that they are neither true nor false.[47] But the details are obscure and it is not clear that he can handle them adequately. Swineshead's view was sharply attacked by William Heytesbury in his *Regulae solvendi sophismata*, c. 1. Nevertheless it was adopted in an amplified and sometimes modified form by Paul of Venice[48] and John of Celaya,[49] and by several authors in the sixteenth century.[50]

---

absolutely' ('in aliqua consequentia bona aliqua propositio quae est falsa secundum quid sequitur ex veris simpliciter'). In Swineshead, of course, the distinction between truth or falsehood 'in a certain respect' and truth or falsehood 'absolutely' is dropped. This possible source for Swineshead's conclusion is all the more interesting because in the immediately following lines Kilvington goes on to say, 'But nevertheless this sentence [that is] false in a certain respect is not false because it follows from truths, but because from it, together with some truth or other truths, there follows its contradictory' ('Sed tamen ista propositio falsa secundum quid non est falsa quia sequitur ex veris, sed quia ex ea cum aliquo vero vel aliis veris sequitur suum contradictorium'). This looks suggestively like Swineshead's notion of a 'sentence relevant to inferring that it is false'.

44. 'Si ex aliquibus propositionibus quarum quaelibet significat principaliter sicut est sequitur aliqua propositio, ipsa significat sicut est.' (Ed. Spade 1979a, par. 35.)
45. 'Duo contradictoria sibi mutuo contradicentia sunt simul falsa.' (Ed. Spade 1979a, par. 27.) For the example below see *ibid.*
46. Ed. Spade 1979a, pars. 2–3, 93, 99.
47. This is explicit in MS Vat. lat. 2154, f. 6[va]. Other MSS omit the claim, but it seems to follow from Swineshead's doctrine.
48. *Logica magna*, 2, 15. See Spade 1975a, pp. 82–4.
49. Edited in Roure 1962.
50. Ashworth 1974, pp. 112–13.

Resolutions in terms of obligationes

Heytesbury's own theory was even more influential.[51] According to him, insolubles should be treated within the context of *obligationes*, the codified conditions of formal scholastic disputation. The upshot of his approach is that no sentence, under a set of circumstances or hypothesis (*casus*) that makes it insoluble, can signify *exactly* as it ordinarily does; the assumption that it can do so is what is responsible for the paradoxes. If in such a case the sentence signifies as it ordinarily does, it must signify more as well. Depending on what that additional signification is, and how it is related to the ordinary one, different responses to the insoluble are appropriate. Heytesbury formulates his position in five rules governing a respondent's replies when insolubles emerge in a disputation *de obligationibus*.[52]

One of Heytesbury's claims proved to be especially controversial: when the opponent in a disputation does not specify an insoluble's additional signification, the respondent does not have to specify it either. Heytesbury was in effect refusing to say how the signification of a sentence in insoluble circumstances differs from its ordinary signification. While by the strict rules of *obligationes*, his silence is justified, many authors felt Heytesbury had simply failed to answer the most obvious question his theory raised.[53] Some tried to answer it for him by saying that insolubles, in addition to their ordinary signification, signify that they are true.[54] This move brings together the two traditions stemming from Heytesbury and Bradwardine.

Heytesbury's claim, that sentences in insoluble circumstances do not signify what they ordinarily do, has important consequences. For the signification of spoken and written sentences, like that of terms, depends on the voluntary adoption of conventions. If sentences signify differently in insoluble circumstances, then it must be because a new convention has been voluntarily adopted. But in fact that seems rarely if ever to be what happens. Heytesbury considers this objection, and admits he has no satisfactory answer.[55] Again, for most authors, mental language signifies by

---

51. See e.g., Spade 1975a, items V, VII, VIII, XII, XIII, XXIII (all anonymous), XXV (Angelo of Fossombrone), XXVIII (Gaetano di Thiene), XXXV (John of Constance), XXXVI (John Dumbleton), XXXVIII (John of Holland), XXXIX (John Hunter), XLII, (John of Wesel), XLIII (John Wyclif), XLVIII (Paul of Pergula), L (Paul of Venice), LIII (Ralph Strode), LVIII (Robert Fland).
52. See Spade 1975a, p. 118.
53. See. e.g., Spade 1975a, pp. 24–5.
54. See, e.g., Spade 1971 and Spade 1975a, items XII (anonymous), XXXVIII (John of Holland), and XXXIX (John Hunter).
55. Heytesbury 1494b, *Regulae*, f. 6rb: 'Multae possent fieri hujusmodi objectiones contra istam responsionem quibus esset difficile vel impossibile in toto satisfacere.'

nature, not by convention. Hence mental sentences always signify the same way, never other than as they 'ordinarily' do. It follows from Heytesbury's theory, then, that there are no insolubles in mental language.

Resolutions in terms of the notion of mental language

It was perhaps by speculating on this fact that Gregory of Rimini and Peter of Ailly were led to base their own theories of insolubles on the notion of mental language. Little is known of Gregory's view,[56] but Peter in his *Conceptus et insolubilia* held that there are no insolubles in mental language, and that spoken or written insolubles are ambiguous sentences insofar as they correspond not to one but to two distinct mental sentences, one true and the other false.[57] Peter's view was subtle and complex; it had some influence in the sixteenth century.[58]

With the exception of Peter of Ailly's and related views, the major theories of insolubles after *ca.* 1350 were elaborations or modified forms of the theories of Bradwardine, Swineshead, and Heytesbury. There were other views, of course, throughout the history of the *insolubilia*-literature; but these were the main ones.

Conclusion

Certain general features characterised this literature. First, there was a tendency to multiply examples. Albert of Saxony, for instance, in *Perutilis logica*, 6, 1, discusses no fewer than nineteen insolubles. Contrast the modern tendency to look for a paradigm case that shows the structure of the paradox with a minimum of inessentials. Second, the medievals did not seem to have had any 'crisis mentality' about these paradoxes. Although they wrote a great deal about them, there is no hint that they thought the paradoxes were crucial test cases against which their whole logic and semantics might fail. Again, contrast the modern attitude. Third, the medievals did not draw great theoretical lessons from the insolubles. They did not seem to think the paradoxes showed anything very deep or important about the nature of language or its expressive capacity. Once again, contrast modern attitudes. One might do well to speculate on the reasons for these differences between medieval and modern semantic theory.

56. Spade 1975a, pp. 54–5. But see Peter of Ailly 1980, pp. 6–7 and 11–12 for a tentative reconstruction.
57. See Spade 1975a, pp. 84–5 and Peter of Ailly 1980, pp. 11–12 and Chs. 3–4.
58. Ashworth 1974, pp. 108–10.

13
SPECULATIVE GRAMMAR

Grammar in the early Middle Ages

Medieval speculative grammar grew out of the schoolmens' work with ancient Latin grammar as it had been transmitted in the canonical works of Donatus and Priscian. The efforts of early medieval glossators were directed towards explaining the authoritative texts, towards systematising the descriptional apparatus used by the authors, and towards harmonising the apparent or real contradictions which arose in a comparison of the grammatical and logical traditions.[1] The results of their combined efforts were summarised in the famous *Summa super Priscianum* compiled about 1140 by Peter Helias.[2] The grammarians' discussions, which had been influenced by the logicians, in their turn influenced and refined logical doctrine and played an important role in the emergence of the specifically medieval logical doctrines known collectively as terminist logic. The grammatical discussions about the meaning of substantive words, for instance, were crucial to the development of the theory of supposition.[3] The twelfth-century grammarians emphasised the importance of explaining linguistic features causally, instead of just describing them as Priscian had done,[4] and in this way attained a high degree of linguistic sophistication. But it would perhaps be too much to say that their efforts already inaugurated a new paradigm of linguistic description.

The general nature of 'modistic' grammar

Around 1270, however, a new theoretical framework was established. The phases of the development which brought this about are not yet known in

---

1. See Ebbesen's and Henry's contributions to this volume.
2. For further discussion of the early glosses see Thurot 1868; Hunt 1949–50; De Rijk 1962–7, II(1), pp. 95–125; Fredborg 1973; Kneepkens 1977 and 1978.
3. See De Rijk 1962–7.
4. See William of Conches, *De philosophia mundi* (Thurot 1868, p. 17): 'Quoniam in omni doctrina grammatica praecedit, de ea dicere proposuimus, quoniam, etsi Priscianus inde satis dicat, tamen obscuras dat definitiones nec exponit, causas vero inventionis diversarum partium et diversorum accidentium in unaquaque pretermittit.'

detail, but the first representatives of the new doctrine seem to be Boethius of Dacia and Martin of Dacia.[5] In their works we find a coherent linguistic theory, in which every grammatical feature treated is fitted into a single descriptive framework, based on expressly formulated premisses. The attitude governing this endeavour has several points of resemblance with later types of rationalistic or universal grammar, including some twentieth-century developments, but it is often more explicit.[6] The medieval theory is based on the concept of meaning (*significatio*), inherited from ancient tradition, and develops its consequences in a comprehensive and pertinent way. The theory has been labelled 'modistic' grammar from the concept of *modus significandi*, which is a central concept of the theory since it is the very term used to describe the changes of meaning imported by grammatical features. The term 'Modistae' is used accordingly to denote the (mostly Parisian) masters of the late thirteenth and early fourteenth century who wrote on grammar, logic, and metaphysics within this tradition.[7]

The influence of the new Aristotle and the Arabic commentators

The most important factor for the development of modistic theory is the recovery of the whole Aristotelian corpus, especially the *Posterior Analytics*, the *Metaphysics*, and the *De anima*, with their strong requirements for the construction of a scientific theory and their more complex semantic doctrines based on an elaborate epistemological foundation. These features of the Aristotelian writings were emphasised by the Arabic commentators, and it is no accident that the writings of the Modistae are filled with quotations from Avicenna and Averroes. The claim – read out of Aristotle's *Posterior Analytics* – that any discipline worthy to be called a science would have to treat features of reality which are universal and immutable had especially far-ranging repercussions.

Grammar as a speculative and auxiliary science

Such reflections determined the course of grammar when grammarians wanted to raise it to the status of a science and situate it within the medieval system of sciences. It was accordingly determined to be a speculative and auxiliary science: 'speculative' (i.e., theoretical) because its goal was not to teach language but to describe and explain the nature and organisation of

5. Pinborg 1967a, pp. 19–21 and 60ff.
6. See Trentman 1975.
7. For a list of authors and information on MSS see Pinborg 1975a.

language (in this case Latin) as the most important and convenient vehicle of communication;[8] 'auxiliary' because grammar, like logic, was not directly concerned with the world, but with the reflection of it in our descriptions.[9]

The modi significandi

Since vocal expressions obviously differ from one language to another, they cannot constitute the true objects of grammar. The obvious place to look for universal features of language is in the semantic component, but it is not the meanings of individual words which prove to be relevant to the grammarian. Grammar is traditionally concerned with more general matters, namely, types of words and their constructions. Accordingly, the interest of the Modistae was concentrated on what was sometimes called the general meanings of words (*significata generalia*). These comprise all such components of meaning as constitute grammatical categories – e.g., nouns, verbs, cases, or tenses. All such components were described as *modi significandi*.

The career of speculative grammar

Among the later authors of modistic grammar the most important is perhaps Radulphus Brito, who provided the most comprehensive discussion on the principles of speculative grammar after Boethius of Dacia, one which took into account all the doctrinal refinements introduced in the meantime. Shortly after 1300 Thomas of Erfurt wrote a manual that included the new theoretical developments and replaced the work of Martin of Dacia. This text, long attributed to Duns Scotus, remains the best known treatise of modistic grammar.

After 1300 no original contribution to modistic theory was made, although modistic terminology continued to govern grammatical description. The theoretical framework of the theory was made the target of sharp attacks, directed especially against the epistemological presuppositions of the theory, the proliferating subtleties of which could not conceal the theory's serious intrinsic difficulties, particularly in connection with the analysis of the relationship between language and reality. The critics included both nominalists like Ockham and Buridan and conservative

---

8. Martin of Dacia, *Modi significandi*, 10 (1961, p. 7): 'Et sciendum quod vox per accidens consideratur a grammatico. Quia omne quod potest esse signum rei significatae etiam potest esse de consideratione grammatici. Sed quia vox est habilius signum quam aliquid aliud, utpote nutus corporeus et conniventia oculorum et huiusmodi, ideo plus consideratur a grammatico; et intelligendum quod hoc est per accidens.'

9. John of Dacia, *Divisio scientiae* (1955, pp. 34–5).

Averroists like John of Jandun and John Aurifaber; their fundamental charge against the Modistae was that they had confused linguistic distinctions with real ones. So medieval speculative grammar gradually lost its position of dominance, even if parts of the theory were never wholly abandoned, even by the Humanists.[10]

The linguistic doctrine of the Modistae[11]

According to modistic analysis words consist of a phonological element (*vox*) and two levels of semantic components, one concerned with specific or lexical meanings (*significata specialia*), the other with more general meanings, called *modi significandi*, on which in turn the syntactical component depends. Since the coupling of expression and meaning is arbitrary, it presupposes a deliberate act by which it is brought about, an *impositio* associating an expression with an object or content. A distinct act corresponds to each level of meaning. By a first imposition the expression is connected with a referent, insofar as a name is instituted to refer to a definite object or attribute of an object. How this happens is almost never discussed in any detail.[12] The relation holding between the expression and the object referred to is called the *ratio significandi*. It is often described as the 'form' which turns a mere sound into a lexeme (*dictio*). (The term 'lexeme' seems to be the nearest modern equivalent to the modistic *dictio*, which is a highly abstract term, including under one head not only all flexional forms and all occurrences of a word but even derivational forms.)

In a secondary imposition the lexeme receives a number of *modi significandi* which determine the grammatical categories of the word.[13] They are not bound to any specific phonological element. The *modus significandi* of grammatical case can be expressed by different terminations, and the same termination can express more than one *modus* (e.g., in the second declension '*-us*' represents nominative case, singular number, and masculine gender). The relation of the *modi* to the lexical meaning is not wholly overt. A given lexeme can be associated with different *modi*, so that the same lexeme may be realised as different parts of speech and as different grammatical forms. A favorite example of the Modistae is the lexeme connected with pain, which according to the general feature consignified may be realised as a noun

---

10. See Percival's contribution to this volume.
11. For further particulars see Pinborg 1967a and 1972; also Bursill-Hall 1971. In the following sections I have tried to use a terminology fairly consistent with the one advocated in Lyons 1977.
12. A notable exception is John of Dacia 1955, pp. 177ff., who is, however, dependent on a pre-modistic source, viz. Robert Kilwardby 1975.
13. See Boethius of Dacia, *Modi sign.*, (1969) qu. 114

(*dolor*) – this again in various cases and numbers – as a verb (*doleo*), a participle (*dolens*), an adverb (*dolenter*), or even as an interjection (*heu*).[14] Obviously then, the *modi* are a kind of semantical modifiers, further determining the lexical meaning of the *dictio*, thus preparing it for various syntactical functions. The ontological counterparts of the *modi* are some general features of the object signified, which do not belong to the definitional properties of the object, and accordingly are not signified directly, but only implied. Thus when I use the form '*homo*' to talk about man I signify a human being and imply that he is an agent (because of the nominative case). According to modistic terminology the general features are 'consignified', i.e., signified along with the specific, lexical meaning. Therefore, the relation between the expression and the ontological counterparts of the *modi* is called the *ratio consignificandi*, a term which is used synonymously with *modus significandi*; it is described as the 'form' which turns a lexeme into a part of speech (*pars orationis*), i.e., prepares it to perform a particular function as a segment of a linguistic string.

Of the *modi significandi* attributed to a lexeme one is essential (*essentialis*), namely the mode which determines the subsumption of the word under the most fundamental grammatical categories: the eight parts of speech taken over from ancient grammar. Some Modistae divide this mode further into a *modus generalis* which is common to several parts of speech and a *modus specificus* which defines one and only one part of speech. Thus they arrive at a paradigm like the following, where Roman numerals indicate general modes, Arabic numerals specific modes:

I. + stability (*modus habitus et quietis* or *modus substantiae*)
   1. + definite reference (*modus determinatae apprehensionis* or *modus qualitatis*) NOUN (substantival and adjectival)
   2. − definite reference (*modus indeterminatae apprehensionis*) PRONOUN
II. + change (*modus fluxus et fieri*)
   3. + predicability or separability (*modus distantis*) VERB
   4. − predicability or separability (*modus indistantis*) PARTICIPLE
III. + modification (*modus disponentis*)
   5. + act-determinant (*modus determinantis actum*) ADVERB
   6. + referring object to an act (*modus retorquendi substantiam ad actum*) PREPOSITION
   7. + uniting (*modus uniendi*) CONJUNCTION
   8. + emotionally affecting the mind (*modus afficientis animam*) INTERJECTION[15]

---

14. See *ibid*. qu. 14.
15. See Pinborg 1967a, pp. 125–6.

Besides the essential mode, lexemes are endowed with a variant number of further modes. Some of them (the *modi speciales*) sort the part of speech into semantic subcategories (e.g., proper names), others endow it with less basic grammatical features, such as case, number, or tense. These are called *modi accidentales*, and their number and to some extent their definitions correspond to the accidents of traditional grammar.[16]

Thus each wordform is a bundle of semantic and syntactical features. Two forms can be combined in speech only when at least one feature or mode of one form (now called a *constructibile*) is related to a mode of the other form in either of two ways: The two forms may have identical modes, but such that the one possesses it only because of the other, as e.g. the adjective receives gender, case, and number from the noun to which it is attributed (this case corresponds to 'concord' in traditional grammar); or the mode of one may be proportional (*proportionalis*) to a mode of the other, such that the one specifies a relation, by which the other is specified (this case corresponds roughly to 'government' in traditional grammar).[17]

In both cases, however, the relation between the two forms is one of dependency. One form has a semantic feature which depends on or presupposes a feature in the other form, which is thus viewed as completing the dependency (being the 'terminant').[18] Unfortunately, the notion of dependency seems to have been intuitional for the Modistae: no purely linguistic rules are formulated in modistic grammar which help in deciding which of two semantic features is dependent on the other. A look at the examples of dependency which we actually find stated may help to elucidate the nature of modistic 'dependency': (the arrows denote dependency and its direction) *Socrates* ← *currit* (Socrates ← runs); *percutit* → *Platonem* ([he] strikes → Plato); *Socrates* ← *albus* (the white → Socrates); *misereor* → *Socratis* (I pity → Socrates); *currit* ← *bene* ([he] runs ← well); *est* ← *homo* ([he] is ← [a] man); *cappa* ← *Socratis* (Socrates' → cape). It may be difficult for us to discover one and the same relation in all instances, but the main intuition seems to have been that of an accident or a relation dependent on or being predicated of a substance (something *per se stans*). This interpretation covers the first four examples without difficulty; for

16. For details see Bursill-Hall 1971, pp. 133ff. and 391.
17. For further discussion of the syntactical theory of the Modistae see Pinborg 1972, pp. 120–6; Pinborg 1973a and 1973b; Siger of Courtrai 1978, pp. xxixff. – For an interesting comparison of modistic doctrine with the extended standard model of transformational grammar, especially based on the analogous role of 'syntactical features', see Coleman 1971, pp. 105ff.
18. See Martin of Dacia, *Modi significandi* 203–11 (1961, pp. 90–4); Anon., *Quaest. in Prisc. minor.* (MS Nürnberg, Stadtbibl. Cent.V.21, f. 36ᵛ): 'Omne determinans sive specificans praesupponit suum determinabile sive specificabile et dependet ad ipsum.'

the last three further explanation is required. *Currit* ← *bene* is anomalous in the sense that both forms signify an accident; the adverb, however, determines the action signified by the verb and can thus be said to be dependent on it. In the same way *homo* in *est homo* specifies the kind of being signified by *est*. *Cappa* ← *Socratis* is difficult since both wordforms signify a substance and since *Socratis* would seem to determine *cappa* rather than the other way around. However the construction is interpreted in the same way as *misereor Socratis* and the genitive is seen as completing one semantic feature of *cappa*, viz., the feature of belonging-to.

This model of description as presented so far does not permit us to distinguish different types of constructions. Medieval grammarians, however, did distinguish two main types of constructions: transitive (e.g., the Latin examples above in which the arrow points to the right) and intransitive (e.g., the examples in which the arrow points to the left). In order to establish this distinction the Modistae had to introduce a further syntactic relation. They came to distinguish a dependency *ex parte ante* from a dependency *ex parte post*. This distinction implies a relation of priority within the sentence. If the dependent wordform is prior to the terminant we have a transitive construction; if the terminant is prior we have an intransitive one. But what does 'prior' mean here? Obviously it has something to do with word-order, but not necessarily with the arbitrary word-order of the surface-structure of a Latin sentence. Radulphus Brito makes this point explicitly when discussing the construction *quem video*: Even if *quem* is expressed first in the surface structure, it is nevertheless posterior when we consider the nature of its *modus significandi* (the accusative case).[19] Here a natural (or logical) word-order seems to be presupposed which somehow reflects the order of nature: in this order the agent must precede the action, the substance its accidents, the action its objects, etc.[20]

By means of the two concepts of dependency and natural word-order the Modistae succeed in deducing the whole system of possible Latin constructions. It is fundamentally a system based on wordforms and their potential constructions, not an analysis of constituent structures of sentences, and accordingly it is not very efficient in analysing propositional relations.[21] But despite these shortcomings it is a major achievement: the first systematic syntax developed in Western linguistics.

19. See Radulphus Brito 1980, I, qu. 44: 'Dico quod [quem] construitur cum verbo a parte post realiter, tamen vocetenus construitur a parte ante.'
20. See Priscian, *Inst. gramm.* XVII, 105 (1855, III, p. 164.16ff.). Here as in the Modistae the *ordo naturalis* is presupposed and exemplified, but not described exhaustively.
21. According to Boethius of Dacia 1969, qu. 132, propositions as such have no *modi significandi* and accordingly cannot be construed in the strict sense. This conclusion is modified by Radulphus

We have seen that logical and ontological considerations play a considerable role for the grammatical analysis of the Modistae. But they did not forget that they were dealing with language, not reality. They were not so naive as to think that every sentence corresponded to the structure of reality. They recognised for instance that the subject of the process described and the subject intimated by the proposition describing it could very well be different.[22] What mattered to the grammarian was the way reality was described, not reality itself. Or in the terminology of the Modistae: the grammarian was concerned with congruity of speech, not with truth.

The discovery-procedures of the Modistae

How, according to the Modistae, do we discover the existence of semantic features in speech? Since the answer to this question may help us in assessing the nature of speculative grammar, it deserves closer scrutiny. Radulphus Brito distinguishes four discovery-procedures:

(a) *a priori* from the nature of the object signified: if the object has a certain *modus essendi* the word may have the corresponding *modus significandi*.
(b) *a posteriori* from the constructions into which the word actually enters: the wordform must possess the *modus significandi* necessary for the construction.
(c) from the *modi significandi* of the wordform with which it is construed: if the one wordform has certain modes, the other form must have proportional modes.
(d) by the authority of the classical grammarians.[23]

These discovery procedures tell us something about the nature of modistic theory. It was based on observation of linguistic facts, often as interpreted in the grammatical tradition, which were then fitted into a descriptive framework of great consistency. The observations were not limited to the surface-structure of words and sentences, but involved consideration of 'deeper' semantic features. The aim of speculative grammar was to describe intra-linguistic relationships, but the Modistae could not accomplish what they wanted without invoking to some degree the structure of reality. This actually was their warrant for believing that their results were scientific and universal. Accordingly it becomes crucial to investigate the epistemological presuppositions of their doctrine.

Brito 1980, I, qu. 70, and Siger of Courtrai 1978, pp. 60–1. But in their view, too, propositions are connected only in virtue of the semantical relations holding between their terms. This view makes problems for the theory of consequences, and especially for the development of a propositional logic.
22. See Radulphus Brito 1980, II, qu. 4; Pinborg 1972, pp. 11–12.
23. See Radulphus Brito 1980, I, qu. 30.

The semantics of the Modistae

The semantic status of the *modi significandi* was described within a triadic system: the *modi significandi* correspond to *modi intelligendi*, which in turn correspond to *modi essendi*. This is consonant with the traditional interpretation of Aristotelian semantics – to be found, e.g., in Boethius, Avicenna, Averroes, Albert the Great, and Thomas Aquinas – according to which words signify concepts which in turn represent the objects signified.

We find no definition of *modus essendi* in modistic literature, although it obviously is a term essential to their doctrine. This may result from the fact that the theory was centred around the modes of signifying, whereas the *modi essendi* were simply introduced as the necessary ontological counterparts of the former. A description can, however, be constructed from stray remarks in the logical writings of the Modistae.[24] The *modi essendi* (or *proprietates rerum*) are accidental properties of the objects, as distinct from their substantial forms. It is, however, such properties which give rise to our concepts. The Modistae agreed with Aquinas in assuming that we can attain knowledge even of the essence of objects through their accidental properties – a doctrine which was to be challenged by Peter Aureoli and John of Jandun.[25]

According to the Modistae two kinds of *modi essendi* must be taken into account: proper and common modes. Proper modes are those which belong to the object considered in itself and give rise to first-order descriptions; common modes are those which serve as the source of a description in terms that are general and sometimes are second-order predicates: the properties involved are all such that they do not characterise items of one category only, but can be used indiscriminately of items of all categories. From such common properties the logicians derive their second intentions and the grammarians their modes of signifying. It is tempting, then, to identify these properties with second-order features, but this interpretation is too narrow: according to the logician *genus* and *species* are not to be explained only as concepts of concepts (and thus as second-order terms): they reflect features of the object to which they refer. Not every item in the world can be described as a genus, but only such items the nature of which can be

---

24. Most logical texts of the Modistae are so far unpublished, the only exceptions being the commentaries on the Organon by John Duns Scotus, Boethius of Dacia's questions on the *Topics* (1976), the questions on *Logica vetus* by Simon of Faversham (1957), and two sets of anonymous questions on the *Sophistici elenchi* (Ebbesen 1977a). Further fragments of texts are to be found scattered in various publications, especially Ebbesen & Pinborg 1970; Ebbesen 1977c, 1979; Pinborg 1971, 1973a, 1973b, 1975a, 1975b, 1976a; Roos 1977.

25. See Pinborg 1975c.

predicated of different species.[26] In a similar way the modes of signifying are not purely arbitrary; their relation to the objects is nevertheless less precise than that of the second intentions. Speaking in terms of the *modi significandi*, one may even be allowed to describe objects as having properties which they do not, strictly speaking, possess. Even non-existent objects may be denoted by *modi significandi*, which of course only reflect our way of imagining such objects. Hence we can draw an important corollary: the fact that an object is signified by a noun does not imply that the object signified belongs to the category of substance; it does, however, imply that we conceive of it as if it were a distinct object, somehow analogous to a primary substance. Thus a mode of signifying need not have an ontological counterpart in the object signified, as long as the combination of the object and the general feature signified by the mode is not inconceivable.[27]

This association of the modes of signifying with modes of conceiving of things explains the necessity of positing *modi intelligendi* between the *modi essendi* and *significandi*. Even if words are taken to signify extramental objects they do so *sub modo intelligendi*. The following example may help to make this more precise. Conceiving of man we conceive of something which possesses the proper mode of being human (*humanitas*), which can in turn be analysed into being alive and self-moving (*animalitas*) and being rational (*rationalitas*); besides we find in man some common properties, e.g., that of being predicable of different individuals (*specialitas*) and that of being an autonomous entity (*persestantia*). Each of these modes can of course be conceived of separately and abstractly; they can also be conceived of and signified concretely, giving rise to concrete first-order concepts and terms such as 'man', 'animal' (or 'living being'), 'rational', and – relative to the common modes – such second-order concepts and terms as 'species' and 'noun'.[28] The mode which is directly signified is said to be the mode under which the term is imposed to signify. A first-order term such as 'man' thus signifies under the mode of 'being human' (*humanitas*) and refers to (*denominat*) all human beings who participate in this nature. The common modes observed in man are not signified directly, but they are nevertheless modes under which the object is also understood or consignified. In this way the term has both a direct signification 'under' which it is

---

26. See Pinborg 1975b; Boethius of Dacia 1976, pp. 10 and 183–95.
27. See Boethius of Dacia 1969, 17–20; Radulphus Brito 1980, I, qu. 21.
28. See Radulphus Brito's sophisma 'Aliquis homo est species' in Pinborg 1975b; see also Pinborg 1975a.

imposed (*ratio significandi*), implied meaning (*ratio consignificandi*), and reference (*denominatio*).[29]

The status of meanings is, however, still not exactly determined. Even if they are obviously bound to words since they are what make words signify what and as they do, and thus are not properties of the objects, they can nevertheless not be identified with any specific part of the vocal expression. Neither can they be said to be a property of the intellect; for the expressions as such are real entities, and how could something existing in the intellect determine real entities? The later modistic solution to this problem was to distinguish between active and passive aspects of meaning. The active aspect consisted of properties of words, imposed by the intellect, whereas the passive aspect consisted of properties of the objects as conceived of or signified (i.e., *sub modo*). Hence, according to Radulphus Brito the active and passive aspects are formally identical, since they are distinguished from all other beings by the same relational form, namely, the relation holding between the word and the property actually signified or consignified. But they differ materially since the active aspect concerns attributes of words, while the passive aspect is concerned with properties of objects referred to (denominated) by words. Sometimes Radulphus even talks about 'aggregates' of the extramental property and the *ratio significandi*.[30]

The entire modistic theory of semantics obviously belongs to a type of semantics in which sense, not reference, is the focal point. This distinction is described as the distinction between 'formal' and 'material meaning'. 'Formal meaning', often also called *virtus sermonis*, is associated with imposition and comprises all that belongs to the word in virtue of its *ratio significandi* and *modi significandi*; 'material meaning' covers also the denoted or implied referents (the passive aspect), and unlike formal meaning introduces questions of applicability, and, in propositional contexts, of truth and falsity.[31] Such questions are considered accidental to the study of formal

---

29. See Radulphus Brito, *Quaest. Peri hermeneias* in Pinborg 1971, p. 276: 'Essentia rei est quod intelligitur et per consequens est illud quod significatur per vocem primae impositionis. Est tamen notandum quod istae voces significant illas res sub aliquibus conceptibus, sicut "homo" et "animal" significant sub aliqua ratione intelligendi. Et illae rationes intelligendi sunt conceptus quidam existentes in anima. Et ex hoc sequitur quod consignificant istos conceptus. Unde dato quod non significantur per istas voces, tamen dantur intelligi.'

30. See Pinborg 1967a, pp. 85ff., 109ff.; 1975a. In his logical writings Radulphus Brito talks in terms of abstract and concrete intentions instead of active and passive *modi intelligendi*. In both cases, however, a *modus essendi* conceived under a concept (active or abstract) is called a passive mode or a concrete intention.

31. The terms 'formal' and 'material meaning' are used by Peter of Auvergne (Pinborg 1973a, p. 52). '*Virtus sermonis*' is common in all texts. Cf., e.g., Simon of Faversham (Pinborg 1975a, p. 69): 'In locutione sunt duo consideranda, scilicet virtus et veritas locutionis' or the anonymous author of the questions on the *Elenchi* (Ebbesen 1977a, p. 107): 'Illa autem quae de virtute sermonis sunt in termino sunt sua significata et modi significandi.'

meaning. This of course reflects the correct assumption that the meaning (or sense) of a term determines its range of application (or reference).[32] Endeavouring to find invariables of language, the Modistae tended to establish a rather static interpretation of formal meaning. Even if the imposition through which words originally receive their meaning is arbitrary, once this imposition has occurred the meaning cannot change. This holds true also for the accessory meanings conveyed by the modes of signifying. As a result, terms and clauses which may be interchanged without affecting the truth-value of a proposition, such as 'Brunellus' and 'this donkey', assuming 'Brunellus' to be the name of the donkey in question, may nevertheless have different formal meanings.[33]

This notion of meaning has some obvious advantages for the construction of a linguistic theory. For this reason the speculative grammar of the Modistae is a valuable attempt to systematise a universal semantic approach to language, leading to a high degree of sophistication and adequacy in linguistic description. The success of this doctrine as regards problems of logical analysis depends very much upon its ability to account for 'material meaning' and the various acceptations of words in different contexts. In a manner not easily describable in modistic terms, the material meaning of the term, or its reference in a specific context, can influence the acceptation of the term in a way which changes the conditions for the verification of the proposition. Thus even if 'man' retains the same formal meaning in the two propositions 'man is a species' and 'every man is an animal', the propositions nevertheless have generically different presuppositions or *causae veritatis*. The type and range of referents to be investigated before the truth or falsity of the proposition is determined are accordingly restricted or ampliated in comparison with the normal range of the term. In this way potential acceptations or functions of the term, included somehow in its formal meaning, become actualised. This actualisation is effected by the addition of attributes, or even to a certain degree, by the addition of predicates.[34]

Curiously enough, the Modistae found no use for the terminists' theory

32. The usual way of phrasing this assumption is: 'Terminus communis suppoint significatum pro suppositis' (See Pinborg 1975a).

33. See e.g. the anonymous *Quaest. in Prisc. minor.* (MS Nürnberg, Stadtbibl., Cent.V.21, f. 39ᵛ): 'Dico quod possunt aequipollere [sc. Brunellus et iste asinus] quo ad significatum [used in a loose way, probably equivalent to *significatum materiale*], sed non quo ad modum significandi. Quantumcumque enim pronomen demonstrativum contrahat ly "asinus" ad determinatum suppositum, hoc tamen non aufert sibi modum significandi. Voces enim non cadunt a suis significatis nec consignificatis.' See also Pinborg 1972, pp. 111–12.

34. See Boethius of Dacia 1976, II, qu. 11. Radulphus Brito, *Quaest. Priora analyt.* I, qu. 46 in Pinborg 1976a, pp. 272–5; Anon., *Quaest. Soph. elenchi*, qu. 48, in Ebbesen 1977a.

of supposition to solve problems of this type. The fourteenth century would prove the superiority of the terminists' approach, especially when it was combined with the doctrine of exposition, which could handle presupposition and explicate the *causae veritatis* with a detailed terminology and within a system of rules. It is difficult to explain why the terminist approach was neglected by the Modistae, since it does not necessarily contradict modistic doctrine. Perhaps the elaborate semantic system inherited from Aristotle and the Arabs at first looked so impressive in itself that the previous form of logical interpretation was thought to be dispensable.

The fundamental epistemological difficulty of modistic semantics is the same encountered by any picture theory of cognition or of meaning, namely: how can properties of spoken words 'correspond' to mental acts and through them to external objects? No division into active and passive aspects will ever provide the necessary *tertium comparationis*. At the high price of accepting as mediators the curious aggregates of real and mental properties termed the passive aspect, the Modistae avoid committing themselves to a third and independent 'level' of meaning. Others (e.g. Walter Burley, Hervaeus Natalis and Peter Aureoli) were more prone to accept the existence of 'objectively' existing conceptual contents, to be distinguished both from the objects and from actual mental acts. To them this assumption was the only means of warranting intersubjective knowledge. But apparently this departure did not meet with any greater success, except within the discussions of propositional meaning.[35]

Alternative approaches: Roger Bacon

Modistic grammar and semantics did not meet with unanimous approval. Roger Bacon is often alluded to as a proponent of speculative grammar, and we owe to him one of the best known formulations of the basic principle of universal grammar.[36] Nevertheless, he was not influenced by the fully developed modistic doctrine and actually he reacted strongly against some of its main tenets. He had a strong predilection for empirical grammar, as is well known, but he also supplied a theoretical framework for language studies, partly adapted from Augustine's doctrine of signs. This is best known from his *Compendium studii theologiae* (1292), but it was already developed in 1267 when he wrote the treatise *De signis*.[37]

---

35. See Kretzmann 1970; Nuchelmans 1973; see also Nuchelmans' contribution to this volume.
36. See Roger Bacon 1902, p. 27: 'Grammatica una et eadem est secundum substantiam in omnibus linguis, licet accidentaliter varietur.'
37. See Fredborg *et al.* 1978. See also A. de Libera, forthcoming.

Bacon emphasises that human utterances always belong to a context. The meaning of words is not unchanging; a new imposition can always supersede earlier ones. If all new impositions were explicit, there would be no difficulty; but most of them are tacit and not even the result of a conscious act on the part of the speaker. Moreover, they are often concealed by the fact that the new sense of a word is related to an earlier sense. These facts emphasise the necessity of determining the particular sense in which a word is used in a particular context. In consequence of this theory of new impositions, Bacon can explain all meaning-differences which influence the truth-conditions of statements as cases of homonymy (equivocation), without involving himself in any of the trouble arising from the rigidity of 'formal meaning'.[38]

John of Jandun and John Aurifaber

Bacon's approach differs significantly from the standard modistic approach, but the first direct attack on the theoretical foundations of modistic theory was launched from another direction. Sometime around 1330 John Aurifaber, an Averroist master at Erfurt, gave a public determination in which he undertook to prove the non-existence of the *modi significandi*.[39] Drawing his inspiration from the Parisian master John of Jandun, he propagated a purified Aristotelianism which defied all superfluous innovations of the schoolmen. According to Aurifaber, it suffices to know the distinctions of objects and concepts in order to describe how language works. Words are just secondary signs used by the intellect to communicate its concepts and express the distinctions already formed. There is no need to posit any intermediate entities such as the modes of signifying in order to explain the different ways in which words signify. Nouns and verbs are distinguished, not in virtue of any inherent semantical features, but because they are used to signify different classes of objects. Some changes in the vocal *substratum* may occur (such as inflection and derivation), but either they have no semantical relevance, or they substitute a different, though related concept. Similarly, words are construed with other words because they are subordinated to relational concepts. On this view every conceptual distinction has an ontological counterpart, a doctrine that would seem to commit Aurifaber to a great many real, abstract

---

38. Roger Bacon, *De signis* (ed. Fredborg *et al.* 1978), especially §§143–61.
39. Aurifaber's text is edited in Pinborg 1967a, pp. 215–32. For the interpretation of Aurifaber as an Averroist see Pinborg 1975a, 1975c.

entities; but, like John of Jandun, he would probably not be deterred by such a consideration.

An important corollary of this approach to language is that any speculative grammar founded on inherent semantic features is made impossible. Only one task remains for the grammarian: to assert the positive rules of actual usage in the different languages; the task of constructing a universal grammar is reserved for the logician or metaphysician.[40]

Walter Burley and William Ockham

A similar evaluation of the *modi significandi* is hinted at by Walter Burley.[41] The nominalists also agreed with Aurifaber in an interesting way, although of course without committing themselves to his strong realist assumptions. To William Ockham the term '*modus significandi*' is nothing but a metaphor, the literal basis of which is the fact that words signify or connote different classes of objects.[42] Since words in signifying and connoting objects are subordinated to concepts, we need not bother with the *modi* at all; it is enough to know the objects and the mental language of concepts used in describing them. The *use* of language, emphasised in Ockham's account, differs from the *modi* in that it does not change the properties of the objects signified.[43] Language, in his view, establishes many distinctions which have no semantic relevance at all. Such distinctions are not reflected in mental language. But the disparity between language and concepts goes even deeper: Where spoken or written language uses one word – e.g. a verbal noun – mental language sometimes has to use a proposition. The true interpretation of a spoken or written proposition consists in reducing it to the mental proposition or set of propositions which explicates the conditions for verifying it.[44]

Peter of Ailly

Peter of Ailly applied this approach to language in an efficient attack on the grammar of the Modistae, in which he tried to reduce all grammatical

---

40. See Aurifaber (Pinborg 1967a, p. 231.27ff.): 'Unde nunc dico quod [grammaticus et logicus] considerant easdem partes diversimode: logicus quidem ut illa consideratio videtur esse communis omni linguae; grammaticus autem non sic universaliter, quia non considerat ut sint communia omni linguae, cum aliqua considerat grammaticus ⟨congruentia quae⟩ lingua latina tantum invenitur, et iste grammaticus graecus congruentia linguae graecae.'
41. See Pinborg 1975a, p. 60 (Burley, *In Peri herm. ad* 16ᵃ28); Brown 1973, p. 254.
42. William Ockham 1974a, *OP* I, III, 4, 10.
43. William Ockham 1957b, pp. 14–15; 1977a, *OT* III, I, d. 4, q. 1, pp. 9–11.
44. William Ockham 1974a, *OP* I, I.3, *et passim*.

distinctions to the relevant distinctions within mental language.[45] But even if the nominalists in this way renounced the theoretical framework of modistic grammar, they accepted the fact that grammatical analysis was carried on with modistic terminology, except for the proviso that '*modus significandi*' had to be understood in the right way, i.e. as a metaphor that had to be interpreted in terms of mental language.[46]

Modistic theory in the revived via antiqua

The revival of the *via antiqua* (the revived Thomist, Albertist, and Scotist schools) in the late fourteenth and the fifteenth century also entailed an increased interest in modistic theory, even if no theoretical innovations have been recorded. Thus central parts of the linguistic theory of modistic grammar remained in use and could be repossessed by later universalist grammarians, even if the new approach to grammar advocated by the humanists dislodged the doctrines from their context within medieval philosophy.[47]

45. See Pinborg 1967a, pp. 202–7.
46. See Pinborg 1967a, pp. 208–9; Heath 1971, pp. 56–7.
47. See Heath 1971, pp. 40–1.

V

LOGIC IN THE
HIGH MIDDLE AGES:
PROPOSITIONS AND MODALITIES

14
TOPICS: THEIR DEVELOPMENT AND ABSORPTION INTO CONSEQUENCES

From Aristotle through Boethius to scholasticism

'Topic' is the infelicitous but by now standard translation for the Latin technical term '*locus*', designating a logical concept variously understood throughout ancient and medieval philosophy. The medieval tradition of the Topics has its roots in Aristotle's *Topics*.[1] In that book, Aristotle's purpose is to present an art of arguing, more precisely the art of dialectical disputation or Socratic arguing; and most of the book is devoted to a method for the discovery of arguments. The main instrument of this method is a Topic, by which Aristotle understands primarily a strategy of argumentation (such as, 'If the species is a relative, [one must] examine whether the genus is also a relative') and secondarily a principle confirming the line of argument produced by the strategy (for example, 'If the species is a relative, the genus is also').[2] Six of the eight books of the *Topics* consist largely in a loosely ordered compilation of such strategies and principles. Aristotle considers these Topics part of dialectic and distinguishes them from two different but analogous sorts of Topics, rhetorical Topics (which aid in the construction of rhetorical arguments)[3] and mnemonic Topics (which aid in recalling things committed to memory).[4]

Topics received considerable attention in later antiquity from the Greek commentators on Aristotle[5] and from Latin rhetoricians,[6] including Cicero, who wrote his own treatise (*Topica*) on dialectical Topics.[7] In the

1. For discussion of Aristotle's *Topics*, see, for example, De Pater 1965 and 1968, pp. 164–88, and Stump 1978, pp. 159–78.
2. *Topics* 124^{b}15–16.
3. See Stump 1978, pp. 170–2.
4. Cf. Yates 1966 and Sorabji 1972. For mnemonic topics in the Latin rhetorical tradition, see, e.g., the anonymous *Rhetorica ad Herennium* 1954, III, xvii–xxiv, pp. 208–24.
5. See esp. Alexander of Aphrodisias 1891.
6. See, e.g., the following: Tacitus 1949, p. 31; Quintilian 1920–2, V. x. 20ff., V. x. 100ff., V. xii. 15ff.; Victorinus, *Explanationum in Ciceronis rhetoricam libri II*, in Halm 1863, pp. 213ff.; Martianus Capella, *Liber de arte rhetorica*, in Halm 1863, pp. 465ff.; Fortunatianus, *Artis rhetoricae libri III*, in Halm 1863, pp. 105ff.; Cassiodorus 1937, pp. 125ff.
7. For a brief historical survey of Cicero's *Topica* and the literature on it, see Stump 1978, pp. 20–3.

course of their work, the discipline of the Topics changed until by Boethius' time it had become very different from Aristotle's art of Topics, particularly in its understanding of the nature of a Topic. Boethius himself wrote two treatises on Topics, one a commentary on Cicero's *Topica*, *In Ciceronis Topica*, and one a definitive summary of dialectical and rhetorical Topics, *De topicis differentiis*. His work on the Topics, especially Book II of *De topicis differentiis*, is the most important (though by no means the sole) source for the scholastic discussion of the Topics.

According to Boethius, who is dependent on both the Greek and Latin traditions,[8] two different sorts of things are Topics: a Topic is both a maximal proposition and the Differentia[9] of a maximal proposition. On Boethius' view, a maximal proposition is a self-evidently true, universal generalisation, such as 'Things whose definitions are different are themselves also different.' Boethian Topics of this sort probably have as their ancestors the Aristotelian Topics that are principles. Their official function, on Boethius' account, is to aid in the discovery of arguments; but in practice Boethius tends to use them to confirm arguments.[10] Differentiae are theoretically the differentiae dividing the genus *maximal proposition* into its subaltern genera and species, and in that capacity they do serve to classify maximal propositions into groups. Some maximal propositions have to do with definition, for example, and others with genus; so *from definition* and *from genus* are Differentiae. Much more important, however, is the role Differentiae play in Boethius's method for the discovery of dialectical arguments. For the most part, Boethius thinks of dialectical arguments as having categorical rather than conditional conclusions, and he conceives of the discovery of an argument as the discovery of a middle term capable of linking the two terms of the desired conclusion. Boethian Differentiae are, for the most part, the genera of such middle terms. To find an argument, using Boethius' method, one first chooses an appropriate Differentia (criteria for appropriateness are left to the arguer's intuition). The genus of middle terms, determined by the Differentia chosen, and the two terms of the desired conclusion then indicate the specific middle term of the argument and so indicate a dialectical argument supporting the conclusion. In Book II of *De topicis differentiis*, Boethius gives what he claims is an

---

8. For a summary of the controversy over Boethius' sources, see Stump 1974.
9. I am capitalising 'Differentia' here to distinguish this technical use of the word from its more ordinary use designating one of the predicables.
10. For a detailed analysis of Boethius' use and understanding of Topics, see Stump 1978, especially pp. 179–204.

exhaustive list of Differentiae, taken from Themistius. These Themistian Differentiae or some subset of them constitute the core of most scholastic discussion of the Topics (except, of course, for scholastic commentaries on Aristotle's *Topics*).

In one form or another, Topics were treated by Isidore of Seville[11] and various writers in the Carolingian Renaissance,[12] and they were discussed continuously throughout the scholastic period, beginning in the first half of the eleventh century. The culmination of the scholastic tradition of the Topics is the absorption of the Topics into the theories of consequences, or conditional inferences, in the fourteenth century.[13] A definitive history of the scholastic treatment and transformation of the Topics cannot yet be written; much of the important material is unresearched, and many of the relevant treatises are unedited. What follows is no more than a preliminary, tentative sketch of the development of the Topics in the scholastic period.

From Garlandus Compotista through the early logica moderna

The earliest known scholastic discussion of Topics which is still extant occurs in Garlandus Compotista's *Dialectica*,[14] one chapter of which is devoted to Topics. It is plain from Garlandus' references to other discussions of Topics[15] and from the considerable but apparently not original divergence between his work on Topics and Boethius' that scholastics contemporary with and immediately preceding Garlandus also discussed the Topics, but as yet we know too little about this early period to say anything definite about Garlandus' sources for his treatment of the Topics. In many respects – in language, subject matter, order of material presented – Garlandus' discussion of the Topics resembles Boethius' closely, but his conception of the function and purpose of a Topic is very different from that of Boethius.

On Garlandus' account, Topics provide and confirm the conditional premiss of a simple hypothetical syllogism (consisting in a conditional premiss, a categorical premiss, and categorical conclusion), in roughly this way.[16] Garlandus lists and discusses almost all the Boethian Differentiae,

---

11. Isidore 1911, II. xxx.
12. See e.g., Alcuin 1941, pp. 112ff. and 120 ff.; Rhabanus Maurus 1901, pp. 227–30; for Notker's later work, see also Piper 1882, vol. 1, pp. 593ff., 618ff., and 623ff. (esp. pp. 632–3).
13. This view is now well established. See e.g., Boehner 1952, p. 54, Bird 1960, 1961, and 1962a; Pinborg 1969, p. 157, and 1972, pp. 168–9.
14. Garlandus Compotista 1959.
15. Garlandus Compotista 1959; see, e.g., pp. 87.16ff., 88.10–21, and 88.28–36.
16. For a detailed analysis of Garlandus' treatment of the Topics, see Stump 1980a.

and for a number of these he gives modes of arguing. For example, one mode of arguing given for the Differentia *from an integral whole* is 'universally attributing something to an integral whole'.[17] This mode and its Differentia together spell out a certain kind of true conditional proposition. The mode gives the quantity and quality of the antecedent and, implicitly, of the consequent as well (though frequently the quantity of the consequent is simply indefinite). Furthermore, the mode indicates whether the term specified by the Differentia *from an integral whole* will be subject or predicate in the antecedent, and implicitly determines the subject or predicate of the consequent also. Suppose, for example, that the integral whole under discussion is *house* and that we attribute, say, *whiteness* to this integral whole. Following the suggestions of the mode gives us a conditional in which *whiteness* is universally attributed to the integral whole in the antecedent and indefinitely attributed to the integral part in the consequent: 'If the whole house is white, the wall also is white.'[18] The function of the Differentiae on Garlandus' account, then, is to aid in the discovery or construction of true conditionals. The function of the maximal propositions is to demonstrate or confirm the truth of these conditionals, which turn out to be instances covered by the generalisations that are the maximal propositions.

Garlandus is interested in the Topics because he thinks they are useful in the study of hypothetical syllogisms, which appear to be his main interest in the *Dialectica*. His chapter on hypothetical syllogisms is more than five times as long as his chapter on categorical syllogisms and more than twice as long as the next longest chapter in the book. Garlandus considers the study of Topics propaedeutic to the study of hypothetical syllogisms,[19] and he says that all Topics, not just some subset of them, are an aid to hypothetical syllogisms.[20] He holds this view of the Topics apparently because he conceives of the study of hypothetical syllogisms almost exclusively as the investigation of the acceptable forms of hypothetical syllogisms; but the discovery and confirmation of true conditional premises used in hypothetical syllogisms are provided, on his account, by the Topics.

Garlandus ranks the various Differentiae and maximal propositions in two historically and philosophically important ways. First, he says that

17. Garlandus 1959, p. 103.10–11.
18. Garlandus 1959, p. 103.11.
19. Garlandus 1959, p. 86.18–23.
20. Garlandus 1959, p. 114.17.

categorical syllogisms are aided *only* by the Topics *from a whole, from a part,* and *from an equal.*[21] And he uses two of the maximal propositions from the Topic *from a whole* – 'What is universally attributed to the whole is attributed also to the part'[22] and 'What is universally removed from the whole is removed also from the part'[23] – as if they were rules governing the first-figure syllogistic moods *Barbara* and *Celarent*, on which the other moods of the syllogism depend.[24] Secondly, he says that all Topics can be subsumed under the Topics *from the antecedent* and *from the consequent.* The maximal propositions Garlandus gives for these Differentiae amount to the rules for *modus ponendo ponens* and *modus tollendo tollens* respectively; and these are, of course, basic principles for all hypothetical syllogisms. These two claims Garlandus makes strongly suggest that on his view all inferences are dependent on the Topics.

There is a marked divergence between Garlandus' treatment of the Topics and that provided by the major terminist logicians in the first half of the thirteenth century; and Garlandus in the eleventh century and the terminists in the thirteenth mark the poles between which the abundant twelfth-century work on the Topics lies. Much of this work, mostly from the second and third quarters of the twelfth century, bears some resemblance to the *sort* of Topical theory represented by Garlandus' work, though whether and to what extent Garlandus' own treatment of the Topics was itself a source for this twelfth-century material is not clear.

An early twelfth-century example of Topical treatment resembling Garlandus' occurs in an *Introductiones dialectice* which may come from the school of William of Champeaux.[25] There, in connection with inferences in which one categorical is inferred from another, the author singles out the three Topics which Garlandus described as aids to categorical syllogisms: *from a whole, from a part,* and *from an equal.* (When the Differentia or its instance is a predicate in the inference, the anonymous author also adduces

21. Garlandus 1959, p. 114.18.
22. Garlandus 1959, p. 88.18.
23. Garlandus 1959, p. 103.1–6.
24. Garlandus 1959, pp. 118.35ff. What connection Garlandus thinks there is among the Topics *from a whole, from a part,* and *from an equal* is not clear; but in twelfth-century treatises the Topic *from an equal* is frequently cited as confirming a logical conversion. See, e.g., De Rijk 1962–7, II(1), p. 143, where this Topic is cited as support for contraposition; and in *Introductiones Montane minores, Abbreviatio Montana,* and *Tractatus Anagnini,* conversion of all sorts is associated with this Topic (De Rijk 1962–7, II(2), pp. 34, 96–7, and 235; cf. also II(1), pp. 393–4). Cf. also *Logica 'Ut dicit'* in De Rijk 1962–7, II(2), p. 402.12–14.
25. *Introductiones dialectice secundum Wilgelmum* in De Rijk 1962–7, II(1), pp. 135–6. For further information on William of Champeaux's theories of Topics, see Green-Pedersen 1974.

the Topics *from opposites* and *from immediates*.) At least thirteen twelfth-century commentaries on Boethius' *De topicis differentiis* have survived,[26] including one by Abelard;[27] and several of these also show points of contact with the views represented in Garlandus' work, for example, in their concern over the nature and ontological status of Topics and in their emphasis on the two Topics governing hypothetical syllogisms, the Topics *from the antecedent* and *from the consequent*.[28]

A large number of the (mostly twelfth-century) treatises edited or partially transcribed by De Rijk in *Logica Modernorum* discuss Topics: *Introductiones Montane minores, Abbreviatio Montana, Excerpta Norimbergensia, Tractatus Anagnini, Ars Meliduna, Introductiones Parisienses, Logica 'Ut dicit', Logica 'Cum sit nostra', Dialectica Monacensis,* and *Summe Metenses.* These tend to fall into two groups, each of which has its own pattern of contents and particular handling of the Topics. *Introductiones Montane minores* and *Abbreviatio Montana* belong to one group, which is represented also by the *Ars Emmerana* and the *Ars Burana.* All four of these treatises show, *very roughly,* this pattern in the table of contents: *De sono, de voce, de oratione, de propositione, de propositione categorica* (including a section on conversion), *de propositione hypothetica,* Topics (*de locis*), and hypothetical and categorical syllogisms (usually in that order). (Both *Ars Emmerana* and *Ars Burana* have a section on dialectical questions in place of the section on Topics in the other two treatises. *Introductiones Montane minores* lacks the section on categorical and *Ars Burana* the section on hypothetical syllogisms, and *Ars Emmerana* concludes with a section on the properties of terms.) The *Tractatus Anagnini* seem idiosyncratic; but the treatment of Topics found there places them in this group, and the order of materials in the second tractate shows some resemblance to the order of the contents of the treatises of this group: conversion, Topics, categorical syllogisms, and hypothetical syllogisms. It is worth noticing that the order of subjects in Garlandus' *Dialectica* also resembles this pattern. After a first Book on the predicables and categories, Garlandus' work is arranged, roughly, in this way: *de oratione, de propositione, de categorica propositione* (including a section on conversion), single and composite propositions, Topics, categorical syllogisms, and hypothetical syllogisms.

The treatments of Topics in the three treatises of this group that discuss

26. See Green-Pedersen 1977b.
27. Peter Abelard 1969, pp. 205–330.
28. For a very brief but detailed comparison of these commentaries with Garlandus' views, see Stump (forthcoming).

Topics at any length – *Introductiones Montane minores, Abbreviatio Montana,* and *Tractatus Anagnini* – resemble the views in Garlandus' work much more than the views of a terminist such as Peter of Spain. All three treatises devote considerable attention to hypothetical propositions or hypothetical syllogisms or both; and *Introductiones Montane minores* and *Abbreviatio Montana* include their treatment of Topics in their sections on hypothetical propositions. All three concentrate almost exclusively on the three Topics Garlandus associated with categorical syllogisms, *from a whole, from a part,* and *from an equal* (*from opposites* and *from similars* also receive attention).[29] Finally, like Garlandus, all three have detailed discussions of conversion, which they associate with the Topics.[30] All these treatises date from the second or third quarter of the twelfth century, except the *Tractatus Anagnini*, which stems from the end of the century.[31]

In contrast with these are the treatises of the second group: *Introductiones Parisienses, Logica 'Ut dicit', Logica 'Cum sit nostra',* and *Dialectica Monacensis.* These, too, tend to show a rough pattern in the order of their contents: introduction, propositions, syllogisms, Topics, and properties of terms (supposition and sometimes others as well). All but *Introductiones Parisienses* have a section on categories or predicables or both, variously placed, and *Dialectica Monacensis* includes a section on sophistical arguments between the chapters on Topics and properties of terms. These treatises tend to have little or nothing on hypothetical propositions and syllogisms; with the exception of *Dialectica Monacensis*, they also have little or nothing on conversion. They all have lengthy discussions of categorical syllogisms, however. Furthermore, all of them discuss the entire list of Boethian (Themistian) Differentiae;[32] and all tend to present the Topics in the same

29. In emphasising the Topics *from a whole, from a part,* and *from an equal, Excerpta Norimbergensia* and *Ars Meliduna* are like these treatises, and both discuss Topics in their section on hypothetical propositions; see De Rijk 1962–7 II(2), p. 116ff., and II(1), pp. 272–3 and 347ff.
30. See n. 24 above.
31. Braakhuis 1979, I, pp. 407–8, n. 89.
32. And in this respect *Summe Metenses* (now believed to be by Nicholas of Paris, *ca.* 1250; see Braakhuis 1979, pp. 317–26) apparently resembles them; see De Rijk 1962–7, II(1), pp. 472–3. In their discussion of Topics that Boethius classifies as intrinsic and intermediate, all the treatises discussed in this paragraph of the text follow the Boethian order as we now have it in the *PL* edition, except for *Dialectica Monacensis*, which misplaces the Differentia *from uses.* For the extrinsic Differentiae, however, each treatise has its own particular order not reflected in any of the others. The order in the *Dialectica Monacensis* is the same as the Boethian order in the *PL* edition; it is identical with the order in Roger Bacon's *Sumule dialectices* and very similar to that in William of Sherwood's *Introductiones in logicam* (only the Topic *from opposites* is in a different place in the list). The order in *Introductiones Parisienses* is very similar to the order in Peter of Spain's *Tractatus*; again only the Topic *from opposites* occurs in a different place. And the order in *Logica 'Ut dicit'* is the same as the order in Lambert of Auxerre's *Logica.* The orders of the extrinsic Topics

way: one Differentia, for which generally more than one maximal proposition (each with corresponding example) is given. In all these respects, and others as well,[33] these treatises are like terminist treatises, such as Peter of Spain's *Tractatus*, and unlike Garlandus' *Dialectica*. For present purposes their theories of the Topics can be considered to be represented by those of the terminists, discussed below. The twelfth-century treatises in this group stem from the last decade of the century, except for *Dialectica Monacensis* (whose account of Topics is in certain respects more sophisticated than even Peter of Spain's), which De Rijk thinks may be as early as 1160–70.[34]

Abelard's treatment of the Topics is voluminous and cannot be handled in detail here.[35] In general, it is highly original and represents (or, perhaps, introduces) a transitional stage in twelfth-century discussions of Topics and syllogisms. He distinguishes inferences into those that are perfect and those that are imperfect. The former he identifies with syllogisms, whose form alone guarantees their validity. Imperfect inferences he identifies with Topical arguments, which need to be confirmed by a Differentia and maximal proposition.[36] In these respects, his work resembles thirteenth-century discussions of Topics, such as Peter of Spain's. On the other hand, he claims that the truth or falsity of hypothetical propositions is known by means of Topics, and he identifies Topical inferences with hypothetical propositions.[37] And in this respect, his work is remniscent of treatises from

in Roger, William, and Lambert resemble one another much more than they resemble that in Peter of Spain:

Peter	William	Roger	Lambert
opposites	authority	authority	authority
greater	similars	similars	greater
lesser	greater	greater	lesser
similars	lesser	lesser	similars
proportion	opposites	proportion	proportion
transumption	proportion	opposites	opposites
authority	transumption	transumption	transumption

33. To take just one example, *Introductiones Parisienses* and *Dialectica Monacensis* define a Differentia as Peter of Spain does, as a relationship of a certain sort.
34. De Rijk 1962–7, II (1), pp. 410–14. Grabmann had suggested a date later than Peter of Spain's *Tractatus* for it (Grabmann 1937, pp. 48–51), but De Rijk argues at length against Grabmann's dating.
35. *Dialectica*, ed. De Rijk 1970, pp. 253–466 and *Super Topica glossae* in *Scritti di Logica*, ed. Dal Pra 1969, pp. 205–330. For analyses of Abelard's account of Topics, see Bird 1959, pp. 53–7, and 1960, pp. 141–5; Pinborg 1969, pp. 160–2, and 1972, pp. 69–71. For a detailed discussion of the originality of Abelard's work on Topics and its place in twelfth-century logic, see 'Abelard on Topics' and 'Topics and Formal Logic in the Twelfth Century' in Stump forthcoming c.
36. *Dialectica*, pp. 253 and 256–7.
37. *Ibid.*, p. 253.

the earlier part of the twelfth century. The extent to which Abelard's treatment of Topics influenced subsequent discussion of the subject is not clear, but it is not unlikely that he is responsible for turning twelfth-century treatments of Topics away from the tradition represented by Garlandus Compotista and towards the approach taken by the terminists.

Terminist logicians

Peter of Spain, William of Sherwood, and Lambert of Auxerre all included a chapter on the Topics in their logic texts.[38] Their treatments of the Topics differ from one another in significant ways: Peter's treatise is straightforward and rather elementary, William's includes a laborious effort to show that Topical arguments can be reduced to syllogisms, and Lambert's is more detailed and sophisticated than either of the other two. They are enough alike, however, that for present purposes they can be treated together; Peter of Spain may be taken as representative of the group.

In contrast with the first group of twelfth-century logic texts discussed above, Peter's *Tractatus* has very little or nothing on hypothetical propositions and syllogisms and only a short section on conversion. (The same can be said of William and Lambert with this exception, that Lambert has a lengthy section on conversion, especially the conversion of modal propositions.) Instead, the *Tractatus* has a long exposition of the categorical syllogism, and Topical (as well as sophistical)[39] arguments are explained in terms of the categorical syllogism. On Peter's view, Topical arguments are dialectical syllogisms, and he makes a sharp distinction between dialectical and demonstrative syllogisms. The premisses of dialectical syllogisms are not necessary but probable.[40] Consequently, they produce only opinion, not knowledge, and the study of Topics is just an art, not a science.[41] So

---

38. Cf. Peter of Spain 1972, *Tractatus*, pp. 55–77; Lambert of Auxerre 1971, *Logica*, pp. 121–40; and William of Sherwood 1937, *Introductiones in logicam*, pp. 56–74.
39. Cf. Peter of Spain, op. cit., pp. 90–3.
40. See Peter of Spain 1972, p. 90.18–24; cf. William of Sherwood 1937, p. 56; and Lambert of Auxerre 1971, pp. 105ff. and 141ff.
41. There is a sense in which dialectic is a science. Dialectic can be thought of as the use of Topics to construct and evaluate probable arguments (this is *dialectica utens*), or it can be thought of as reflection on and analysis of such use of Topics (*dialectica docens*). *Dialectica utens* is only an art, not a science; its arguments are Topical and its conclusions only probable. *Dialectica docens* may be thought of as the study of *dialectica utens*. It uses demonstrative arguments about *dialectica utens*; it produces knowledge, rather than opinion, and it is a science. For examples of this distinction, widespread among scholastics, see, for example, Lambert of Auxerre 1971, pp. 5–6; Simon of Faversham's commentary on Peter of Spain's *Tractatus* (De Rijk 1968b, p. 81); Boethius of Dacia 1976, pp. 12–13. For the distinction in the unedited commentaries on Aristotle's *Topics* by Kilwardby, Albert the Great, Adenulph of Anagni, Simon of Faversham, Radulphus Brito, and Angelo of Camerino, see Green-Pedersen 1973, pp. 14–15. Green-Pedersen suggests that the distinction may go back to Abelard; see Abelard 1969, p. 315.

dialectical or Topical arguments are plainly given a subsidiary status, secondary to demonstration and demonstrative syllogisms.

According to Peter, a Topical argument is theoretically an enthymeme, an incomplete syllogism missing a premiss,[42] and all enthymemes can be reduced to syllogisms by supplying the missing premiss.[43] But the validity of an enthymeme that is a Topical argument is also shown and confirmed by a Differentia and a maxim (*'maxima'*, Peter's abbreviated version of *'propositio maxima'*). On Peter's view, a Differentia is a relationship of a certain sort[44] (for example, the relationship of a definition to its *definitum*) and a maxim is a rule governing inferences dependent on that relationship (for example, 'What is predicated of a definition is predicated also of its *definitum*').[45] Any Differentia may (and usually does) have more than one maxim corresponding to it; the Differentia *from definition*, for example, has three maxims besides the one just given. Together, a Differentia and a maxim confirm an enthymeme in this way. Take the enthymeme 'A mortal rational animal is running; therefore a man is running.' The relationship of the subject in the premiss to the subject in the conclusion is that of the Differentia *from definition*; that is, *mortal rational animal* is the definition of *man*, the *definitum*. The maxim quoted above gives us an inference rule for such a relationship; and the maxim, the statement of the relationship between *mortal rational animal* and *man*, and the enthymeme's premiss together entail the enthymeme's conclusion. Peter gives twenty-five Differentiae and fifty-seven maxims, which are meant to cover all the kinds of Topical enthymemes.[46]

This special method for coping with a special group of enthymemes is an odd excrescence on the logical theory of the terminists. First, Topical arguments are taken to be enthymemes, which are simply incomplete syllogisms, and the syllogism is taken as the foundation for and the guarantor of valid inferences; but in practice the validity of a Topical argument is shown and confirmed *not* by reducing it to a syllogism but by

42. See Stump 1978, pp. 218–21; cf. Lambert of Auxerre 1971, pp. 139–40.
43. See Peter of Spain 1972, pp. 57–8.
44. The character of the relata, as well as the nature and ontological status of a Differentia, were the subject of dispute among scholastics. See Green-Pedersen 1977a and 1977b. Peter's views on the subject are not unambiguous, but he seems to understand a Differentia as a relationship between two terms; see Peter of Spain 1972, p. 59.11–16 and p. 61.21–5. This was a popular view in the thirteenth century. See, for example, Radulphus Brito 1978a, pp. 25–6.
45. Peter of Spain 1972, p. 60.17–19.
46. The numbers depend on what is counted as *one* Differentia or *one* maxim. For instance, I have counted the Topic *from definition* and *from the definitum* as one Topic, and I have counted all four varieties of opposites as one Topic *from opposites*.

adducing for it a Differentia and a maxim. Secondly, no reason is given to explain why just these kinds of enthymemes can be confirmed without reduction to syllogism or why just twenty-five relationships indicated by the Differentiae should confirm arguments. And thirdly, all Topical arguments are said to be dialectical, but the reasons why Topical enthymemes should always reduce only to dialectical and never to demonstrative syllogisms are obscure. That the first of these perplexities, at least, was something of an embarrassment to the terminists themselves can be seen most clearly in William of Sherwood's case. He treats Topical confirmation of enthymemes as if it were only a kind of abbreviated alternative to real confirmation by reduction to syllogism.[47] For many of the Topics, he gives a Topical confirmation of a particular enthymeme and then immediately appends a syllogistic reduction, which often appears laboured and contrived. For example, William reduces the enthymeme 'Socrates is not running; therefore he is not running well' to this syllogism, which he claims is a syllogism in *Ferio*: 'Not running is Socrates, running well is running; therefore not running well is Socrates.'[48]

In the work of the terminists there are occasional hints of metaphysical theories which might go some way towards resolving these perplexities, but the hints are slight. Peter says, for example, that a good dialectical argument occurs where something is naturally suited to be proved in one way of knowing (by means of the intellect or by means of the senses) and is proved by what is prior to it in that way (that is, intellectually prior or prior in sense experience).[49] And Lambert says that the relationships indicated by the Differentiae are natural relationships between a term in the premiss of an enthymeme and a term in the conclusion. He explains the relationship of a Topic such as *from definition* by saying that a definition and its *definitum* are convertible terms because each expresses the whole substance of the other.[50] But the meagreness of such suggestions and the labored attempt to force Topical arguments into syllogistic moods indicate that the terminists took up the Topics as a part of logic inherited from antiquity without being altogether sure, and perhaps without being much concerned, about the way in which the Topics fit into the rest of their logical theory.

---

47. Cf. also Roger Bacon 1940, p. 315.7–13.
48. William of Sherwood 1937, p. 63; cf. Kretzmann 1966, p. 83.
49. Peter of Spain 1972, p. 169.1–4.
50. Lambert of Auxerre 1971, pp. 123–4.

The shift towards the consequences exemplified in
Robert Kilwardby and Boethius of Dacia

The sort of metaphysical theory suggested in the terminists can be found more fully developed in other thirteenth-century logicians, particularly in the modists but also, for example, in Robert Kilwardby. Kilwardby takes this not uncommon thirteenth-century view of logic. The subject of logic is reasoning, and all reasoning derives its force from the syllogism and is reducible to the syllogism.[51] A syllogism has both form and matter; the form consists in the arrangement of the three terms comprised in two premisses according to the various syllogistic moods and figures, and the matter is the necessity or probability of the premisses (which depends on the actual terms employed in the premisses).[52] Both dialectical and demonstrative arguments are syllogisms. The two sorts of arguments do not differ from one another with respect to the form of the syllogism but only with respect to its matter; the matter of demonstrative syllogisms consists in necessary premisses, that of dialectical syllogisms in probable premisses.[53] Furthermore, a demonstrative syllogism takes as its middle term only the cause or the definition of one of the terms in the conclusion, but a dialectical syllogism uses a great variety of middle terms. Although the Topics *from definition* and *from cause* may produce a dialectical syllogism with a cause or definition as middle term, these middle terms are not the same in dialectical and demonstrative syllogisms because they are used in dialectic only insofar as they are considered probable and contingently related to a term in the conclusion, while in demonstration they are always essentially and necessarily related to a term in the conclusion. Consequently, a dialectical syllogism can produce only opinion, while a demonstrative one produces knowledge;[54] and dialectical syllogisms, unlike demonstrative ones, depend on Topics to confirm them.[55] The metaphysical theory Kilwardby gives to support the status and function of the Topics in this account is only briefly sketched. Individual things have certain common characteristics (*communes rationes*) which we can in

---

51. Robert Kilwardby 1976, LIII.523.
52. Robert Kilwardby 1976, LIII.500–2.
53. Robert Kilwardby 1976, LIII.503 and 506. For discussion of this view of Kilwardby's and comparison with other thirteenth-century views, see Pinborg 1969, pp. 164–74, and Green-Pedersen 1977a, pp. 55–60.
54. Robert Kilwardby 1976, LIII.557, 558, and 561.
55. Cf. Thomas 1953, also 1954, pp. 132–3; and Pinborg 1969, p. 167. Kilwardby's commentary was printed in Venice in 1516 under the name of Giles of Rome (Aegidius Romanus). This edition was reprinted by Minerva in 1968 but was not available to me during the writing of this chapter.

thought abstract from them – e.g., whole, part, genus, species, and similars – and the Topics are drawn from these common characteristics of things.[56]

A more fully developed metaphysical theory along these lines can be found in Boethius of Dacia. According to him, things have certain modes of being; and from these modes of being, common concepts (*intentiones communes*) are drawn. For example, a thing may have a mode of being according to which it can be divided by several differentiae into various species. From this mode of being, the common concept of genus is drawn;[57] and from the common concepts, the Topics are drawn.[58] Common concepts are relatives (*respectivae*) because they are concepts not of a thing considered absolutely and by itself but of a thing considered in relation to something else. A thing is thought of as a genus, for instance, only when considered in relation to the things that are its species. Consequently, the Topics, which are based on common concepts, are also relatives and consist in the relation of one thing to another. Hence, a dialectical argument, which is confirmed by a Topic, depends on a relationship.[59]

Because the common concepts are relatives, however, they are only accidents[60] of the things of which they are concepts, and not part of their substance.[61] And apparently because a common concept is only accidentally related to the thing of which it is a concept, the Topic drawn from it is not a cause of the conclusion of a dialectical syllogism. But a Topic is a sign of various dialectical consequences,[62] because (since it is founded on a relative concept of a thing) it is a sign of a thing's following from something else or of something else's following from that thing. For example, 'this thing which is signified by the word "colour", by means of the relation which it has to the thing which is signified by the word

56. Robert Kilwardby 1976, XLVIII.454 and LIII.498.
57. Second intentions, which are similar to but not identical with Boethius' common concepts (*communes intentiones*), receive a great deal of attention in connection with the Topics. See, for example, Simon of Faversham's commentary on Peter of Spain's *Tractatus* (De Rijk 1968b, pp. 94–5); Buridan's commentary on the same work (Green-Pedersen 1976, p. 137); and Albert of Saxony 1522, f. 33ra. They receive especially detailed treatment by Radulphus Brito; cf., e.g., Radulphus Brito 1978, pp. 100–1, and 'Aliquis homo est species' in Pinborg 1975b. See also Green-Pedersen 1977a, pp. 51–5 and 58–9; and Pinborg 1974, pp. 49–59, especially p. 54.
58. For the connection between Topics and modes of being and the properties of things, cf. also Radulphus Brito 1978a, pp. 58–9; 1978b, pp. 93ff.
59. Boethius of Dacia 1976, pp. 10–11; cf. also pp. 209–10. For the difference between a common concept and a Topic, see pp. 217–18.
60. Relatives are, of course, one of the nine categories that are accidents with respect to the subjects they are predicated of.
61. Boethius of Dacia 1976, p. 14.
62. Boethius of Dacia 1976, p. 15.

"whiteness", has the characteristic (*ratio*) of genus and the Topical relationship of genus to species'.[63] A dialectical inference such as 'Socrates is a man; therefore Socrates is an animal' holds by means of the Topical relationship of species to genus. It is a good inference because of the nature of the *things* signified by the words 'man' and 'animal': *man* includes *animal* in its substance, name, and definition, so that whatever 'man' is predicated of, 'animal' is predicated of also. The Topical *relationship* of species to genus is not the *cause* of this connection between man and animal, and so it is not a cause of the validity of the inference either; but it is a *sign* of both the connection between the things and the validity of the inference. All dialectical inferences (considered as such) hold by means of such signs, rather than by means of causes of the conclusion; and so dialectical arguments, in contrast with demonstrative ones, produce only opinion, not knowledge.[64]

Seen apart from metaphysical theories, the logical strand of the accounts of Topics found in Kilwardby and Boethius of Dacia represents a kind of Aristotelianism[65] in the tradition of the Topics, characterised by emphasis on the categorical syllogism as the foundation of all inference, a sharp distinction between dialectic and demonstration, and relegation of dialectical or Topical arguments to a secondary epistemological status.[66] The transformation of the Topics into the consequences seems to have been accomplished by the convergence of two lines of development: a gradual erosion of this Aristotelianism, and an increasing concentration on the nature of and the rules for consequences. In what follows, I will concentrate on the first line of development, the change in attitudes towards dialectic and the Topics, but I will also say a little about the rise of interest in the consequences. Plainly, the two lines of development are not unconnected. As long as the categorical syllogism is conceived of as the ultimate guarantor of validity, interest in non-syllogistic inferences will focus on attempts to reduce them to syllogisms; and study of non-syllogistic in-

63. Boethius of Dacia 1976, p. 28: 'haec res, quae significatur per hoc nomen "color", per relationem, quam habet ad rem, quae significatur per hoc nomen "albedo", habet rationem generis et habitudinem localem generis ad speciem'.
64. Boethius of Dacia 1976, pp. 20–3.
65. By 'Aristotelianism' I mean to suggest only that their views were heavily influenced by their understanding of Aristotle's writings, not that these views represent Aristotle's own theories, which are very unlike anything that can be found in scholastic treatments of the Topics.
66. Cf. Roger Bacon 1940, pp. 303–5; Simon of Faversham's commentary on Peter of Spain (De Rijk 1968b), p. 80; Boethius of Dacia 1976, pp. 30–9, esp. pp. 32.55–33.59; and Simon of Faversham (forthcoming), *Quaestiones novae super librum Elenchorum*; cf. Question 6, 'Utrum sit ponere syllogismum peccantem in materia absque syllogismo peccante in forma', and Question 30, 'Utrum locus sophisticus accidat in demonstrativis'.

ferences will not be a central concern as long as all knowledge is thought to be produced only by demonstrative syllogisms. When the distinction between dialectic and demonstration weakens and the special status of the categorical syllogism is undermined, interest in consequences is free to develop.

The decline in the status of the syllogism

The undermining of Aristotelianism in the treatment of the Topics can itself be seen as a two-pronged development: first, a growing inclination to see all syllogisms as dependent on Topics, and, second, a tendency to consider not only demonstrative but also Topical arguments necessary. Both developments at least blur the distinction between dialectic and demonstration, and the first drastically undermines the special status of the syllogism as well.

A sign of the coming decline in the status of the syllogism can be found in the work of the terminist logicians themselves, in their account of the Topic *from a quantitative whole*,[67] which they take in a way not intended, I think, by Boethius.[68] Lambert of Auxerre's account is the most suggestive.[69] On his view, a quantitative whole is a common term with a universal sign, and the Topical relationship is that of a quantitative whole to its part. It validates two sorts of inferences, represented by these examples: 'Every man is running; therefore Socrates is running', and 'No man is running; therefore Socrates is not running'. The description of the Topic and the examples given are reminiscent of first-figure syllogisms in *Barbara* and *Celarent*; and the maxims for this Topic – 'Whatever is posited of a quantitative whole is posited also of its part' and 'Whatever is denied of a quantitative whole is denied also of its part' – resemble the principles *dici de omni* and *dici de nullo*, associated with the foundation of the syllogism. Discussion of this Topic must have provoked inquiry into the relation between this Topic and the principles *dici de omni et nullo* and given impetus to the notion that syllogisms are Topically dependent, as will be more apparent after a brief discussion of *dici de omni et nullo*.

The connection between the principles *dici de omni et nullo* and the syllogism is variously expressed by thirteenth- and fourteenth-century logicians. For instance, Roger Bacon says simply that every syllogism

---

67. Peter of Spain 1972, pp. 64–5; William of Sherwood 1937, p. 61; and Lambert of Auxerre 1971, p. 127.
68. *De topicis differentiis*, 1189B–C.
69. See also Roger Bacon 1940, p. 319.

depends on (*decurrit super*) these principles.[70] Siger of Courtrai and the Pseudo-Scotus claim that every first-figure syllogism (to which all the other syllogistic moods can be reduced) holds by means of these principles;[71] by this, the Pseudo-Scotus apparently means that the validity of the syllogism depends on these principles. And Giles of Rome goes so far as to say that the principles *dici de omni et nullo* prove the form of the syllogism and include within themselves the syllogistic order.[72] These views are all consistent with the scholastic conception of these principles. The abbreviated phrase '*dici de omni*' is generally said to mean that in a universal proposition nothing is to be subsumed under the subject which is not also subsumed under the predicate,[73] so that this principle amounts to a description or explanation of the nature of a universal proposition. Its connection with the syllogism derives from its connection with the first-figure syllogism in *Barbara*. This syllogistic mood has a universal affirmative proposition for the major premiss ('Every B is C'), and the minor premiss ('Every A is B') in effect indicates that a certain group is to be subsumed under the subject of the major premiss. By the nature of a universal proposition, that is, by the principle *dici de omni*, the conclusion of this mood ('Every A is C') follows: every B is C (the major premiss); a universal proposition is one in which nothing is to be subsumed under the subject which is not subsumed under the predicate (*dici de omni*); every A is subsumed under the subject of the universal proposition 'Every B is C' (minor premiss); so every A is also subsumed under the predicate of that universal proposition, and hence every A is C (conclusion). So the validity of the first-figure syllogism in *Barbara* appears to be dependent on the nature of a universal (affirmative) proposition, expressed in the principle *dici de omni*; and, *mutatis mutandis*, the same things can be said about the principle *dici de nullo* and the first-figure syllogism in *Celarent*.

This explanation makes plainer the resemblance between the principles *dici de omni et nullo* and the Topic *from the whole*.[74] The subject of the minor premiss in a first-figure syllogism in *Barbara* is included in the subject of the universal major premiss; and so it appears that the subject of the minor premiss is a quantitative part of the subject in the major premiss, which is its

70. Roger Bacon 1940, p. 290.
71. Cf. Siger of Courtrai 1913, *Ars Priorum*, pp. 10 and 22; cf. also the Pseudo-Scotus 1891, qu. VII, p. 97.
72. Giles of Rome, *In 'Rhetoricam Aristotelis'*, in Pinborg 1972, pp. 200–3.
73. Cf., e.g., Peter of Spain 1972, p. 43.6–12.
74. The connection may have been made easier by Aristotle's identification of *dici de omni* and being in the whole (*esse in toto*), *Prior Analytics* 24[b]26–30, and Boethius' *De syll. cat.* 809C10–810C4. Cf. also *Dialectica Monacensis*, De Rijk 1962–7, II(2), p. 490, and Lambert of Auxerre 1971, pp. 112–13.

quantitative whole. It is reasonable, then, to ask whether the first-figure syllogism in *Barbara* is dependent on a Topical relationship between its terms and whether the principles *dici de omni et nullo* are equivalent to the maxims for this Topic.

That the scholastics did ask these questions and frequently enough answered them affirmatively is evident from a number of texts. An anonymous commentary on the *Prior Analytics* from around 1270 attacks the view that every syllogism considered apart from any particular material proves its conclusion, and in doing so it has to argue against the objection that every syllogism holds by the Topical relationship *from a quantitative whole*, whose maxims are in every syllogism constituted by the principles *dici de omni et nullo*, and that every Topical relationship proves something.[75] Radulphus Brito in his commentary on Boethius' *De topicis differentiis* devotes a question to the issue whether there is such a Topic as *from a quantitative whole* and if so, whether it is a good one. He answers both questions affirmatively. On his view, this Topic is good whenever a predicate is more known to inhere in a term taken universally than in any of the supposita for that term, and he identifies predicates (*per se*) in the first and second moods of the syllogism as of this type.[76] Simon of Faversham, commenting on the *Sophistici elenchi*, specifies as one of the general conditions for all syllogisms that one of the two premisses is related to the other as whole to part.[77] And in an anonymous commentary on the *Sophistici elenchi* from the 1270s it is said that 'Every syllogism holds by means of a Topical relationship, for every syllogism holds by means of the Topic *from a quantitative whole to its part*, because the minor is a part of the major . . .'[78]

What results from such considerations, and no doubt from other, very different ones as well, is the view that all syllogisms are dependent on the Topics for their validity. In addition to its implicit or explicit occurrence in the passages just discussed, mention of this view or something very similar can be found, for example, in Boethius of Dacia's commentary on Aristotle's *Topics* where he apparently accepts the view that there is a Topical relationship in every demonstrative syllogism,[79] or in Simon of Faversham's commentary on the *Sophistici elenchi*, where he says that every

---

75. Pinborg 1969, pp. 166–7.

76. Radulphus Brito 1978a, p. 47; 'in toto in quantitate universalis distribuitur in omnia sua inferiora, et quodlibet eius suppositum suscipit eius praedicationem . . .'

77. Simon of Faversham (forthcoming), *Quaestiones novae super librum Elenchorum*, Question 5, 'Utrum syllogismus peccans in forma sit syllogismus'.

78. Ebbesen 1977a, pp. 34–5 (qu. 16, lines 21–3): 'Omnis syllogismus est tenens per habitudinem localem; omnis enim syllogismus tenet per locum a toto in quantitate ad partem suam, quia minor est pars maioris . . .'

79. Boethius of Dacia 1976, pp. 39–40.

good consequence is founded on a Topical relationship, and the ensuing explanation strongly suggests that syllogisms in general are included under the heading of 'consequence'.[80]

The acceptance of Topical inferences as necessary

A second change in the treatment of the Topics, which is complementary to the view of syllogisms as Topically dependent, is the increased acceptance of the claim that Topical inferences are necessary. This claim is not unconnected to metaphysical theories about the ontological status of Topics and their relations to real things, and it is well represented in Boethius of Dacia. He retains the traditional view that dialectical inferences produce only probable conclusions and opinion rather than knowledge, but he makes a subtle distinction which in effect demolishes the traditional view. In the case of the dialectical argument 'Socrates is a man; therefore Socrates is an animal', the *things* signified by 'man' and 'animal' are the causes of the inference. Because *man* includes *animal* in its substance, name, and definition, the connection between these two things is necessary, and consequently the argument is necessary too. But considered in this way, in respect of its relation to a necessary connection between two things, the argument is not dialectical. If we think of the argument as based on the Topical relation of species to genus, however, it is a dialectical argument; and in that case, its conclusion is only probable. And similarly in all other cases: the very same argument considered in respect of its relation to the natures of things, which are the causes of consequences, is a necessary argument; considered as based on a Topical relationship, it is a dialectical argument and its conclusion is only probable.[81]

Finally, it is worth pointing out in connection with changes in the tradition of the Topics that Topical arguments are increasingly referred to as consequences in the thirteenth century. Use of the term '*consequentia*' to refer to dialectical inferences can be found, for example, in Kilwardby and Bacon,[82] and it is very evident in scholastics such as Radulphus Brito and Simon of Faversham.[83]

---

80. Simon of Faversham (forthcoming), Question 32, 'Utrum ista consequentia sit bona: omnis homo currit; ergo omnis homo currit'.
81. Boethius of Dacia 1976, pp. 20–3. Cf. also Radulphus Brito 1978a, pp. 58–60.
82. Cf. Robert Kilwardby 1976, pp. 174 and 185, and Roger Bacon 1940, p. 323.
83. Cf., e.g., Radulphus Brito 1978a, pp. 25, 26, 28–9, 33, 40, and 42ff.; and Simon of Faversham, *Commentary on Peter of Spain's Tractatus* in De Rijk 1968b, p. 98, and *Quaestiones novae super librum Elenchorum* (forthcoming), Question 29, 'Utrum petitio principii sit locus sophisticus' and Question 32, 'Utrum ista consequentia sit bona: omnis homo currit; ergo omnis homo currit'.

Discussions of consequences in connection with 'si'

Apart from the commentaries on Aristotle's and Boethius' works on Topics,[84] there are three other places in thirteenth-century logic, relevant to the purposes of this chapter, where consequences are discussed.[85] The first is in the treatment of the syncategorematic word '*si*'. In their treatises on syncategorematic words, William of Sherwood and Peter of Spain include some detailed discussion of consequences in the section on'*si*'.[86] William distinguishes absolute and as-of-now (*ut nunc*) consequences and natural and accidental consequences. The first is a basic distinction occurring very frequently in fourteenth-century accounts of consequences, and something like the second can be found in Walter Burley's work.[87] William also discusses very briefly different sorts of difficult consequences, such as those involving exclusives and modal operators, the sorts of consequences typically discussed at length in the fourteenth century. Peter's basic division of consequences into simple and composite can also be found in Burley's work,[88] and four of the six rules of consequences Peter discusses occur frequently in one form or another in fourteenth-century accounts of consequences. Two other rules of consequences which Peter considers and rejects – 'From the impossible anything follows' and 'The necessary follows from anything' – are widely accepted in the fourteenth century. Many of the consequences Peter discusses in connection with the syncategorematic word '*si*' are standard Topical arguments, as he himself points out. In Burley's own discussion of '*si*', he says that since the rules for consequences have already been given in the section on consequences, there is not much left to be said about '*si*'.[89]

Discussions of consequences in connection with the fallacy of the consequent

The second place in which consequences tend to be discussed at some length is in analyses of the fallacy of the consequent. As early as the twelfth-century treatises *Dialectica Monacensis*, *Fallacie Londinenses*, and *Fallacie Magistri Willelmi*,[90] there is some work on consequences in connection with this fallacy, for which *Fallacie Londinenses* makes use of the Topics *from*

---

84. Cf., e.g., Boethius of Dacia 1976, pp. 220ff. and Radulphus Brito 1978a, pp. 38ff.
85. For a fuller discussion of the following material, see the contributions to this volume by Boh, Kretzmann, and De Rijk.
86. See William of Sherwood 1941, pp. 78–82; and Peter of Spain 1489, ff. 47rb–48rb.
87. Walter Burley 1955, *Tractatus longior* p. 61.
88. *Ibid.*
89. Walter Burley 1955, *Tractatus brevior* p. 248.
90. De Rijk 1962–7, II(2), pp. 588–92, 675–6, and 699–700 respectively.

a similar and *from proportion*. Peter of Spain and Lambert of Auxerre in their discussions of this fallacy give detailed accounts of certain kinds of consequences, including Topical inferences, in which the fallacy of the consequent can or does occur.[91] Peter begins his account by describing basic sorts of consequences, in a discussion similar to that in his treatment of the syncategorematic word '*si*'. Some of the rules of consequences Peter and Lambert give in their discussions can also be found in fourteenth-century treatises on consequences; for example, Lambert's rule that an inference from a proposition having many causes of truth to one having only one of those causes of truth is fallacious is one of the ten basic rules of consequences in Burley's *Tractatus brevior*.[92] Peter, Lambert, William of Sherwood, and Roger Bacon all give, in one form or another, Aristotle's explanation for the origin of the fallacy of the consequent: the fallacy of the consequent occurs when we are deceived and think that a consequence converts when it does not.[93] The same view is represented also in Simon of Faversham's commentary on the *Sophistici elenchi*, for example, where three questions are devoted to detailed discussion of consequences and rules for consequences.[94] It is not unreasonable to suppose that this explanation of the origin of the fallacy gave impetus to the investigation of rules distinguishing valid from invalid consequences.

Discussions of consequences in connection with conversion

The third and most important place, however, is the discussion of conversion in commentaries on the *Prior Analytics*. Concern about the logical status of conversion can be found, for example, in Albert the Great, Robert Kilwardby, Lambert of Auxerre, and texts associated with Boethius of Dacia.[95] A common response, found in one form or another in all these authors, is to say that conversion is an inference (sometimes, a consequence) but not an argument. The concern generated by the problem of conversion and the importance of this solution to it both stem from the fact

91. Peter of Spain 1972, pp. 160–73; and Lambert of Auxerre 1971, pp. 195–9.
92. Lambert of Auxerre 1971, p. 197 and Burley 1955, *Tractatus brevior*, p. 212.29–31.
93. *Soph. el.* 167^{b}1–2, Peter of Spain 1972, p. 170.15–17; Lambert of Auxerre 1971, p. 195; William of Sherwood 1937, p. 100; and Roger Bacon 1940, p. 350.15–19. Cf. also *Dialectica Monacensis*, De Rijk 1962–7, II(2), p. 589.
94. Simon of Faversham (forthcoming), *Quaestiones novae super librum Elenchorum*, Questions 35–7, 'Utrum ubicumque est fallacia consequentis necesse sit consequentiam conversam esse bonam', 'Utrum arguendo a positione consequentis ad positionem antecedentis sit bona consequentia', and 'Utrum arguendo a destructione antecedentis ad destructionem consequentis sit bona consequentia'.
95. Cf. Pinborg 1972, pp. 86–7; Kilwardby's commentary on the *Prior Analytics* in Thomas 1953, pp. 65ff.; and Lambert of Auxerre 1971, pp. 24ff.

that syllogisms in the second and third figures are reduced to (and so confirmed by) first-figure syllogisms by conversion. When conversion is explicitly referred to as a consequence, the implication is that second- and third-figure syllogisms are at least partially dependent on certain sorts of consequences for their validity. This notion works together with the contemporaneous discussion of the principles *dici de omni et nullo* to undermine the primacy of the syllogism: second- and third-figure syllogisms depend on consequences (conversion) and first-figure syllogisms; first-figure syllogisms depend on the principles *dici de omni et nullo*, which look very much like Topical maxims. Lambert adds, with some justice,[96] that reduction to the impossible, also used to reduce second- and third-figure syllogisms to those of the first figure, is equivalent to or dependent on (his views are not quite clear) the Topic *from division*.[97] In effect, such views shift the emphasis from the syllogism to consequences as the ultimate guarantor of validity, and they must have stimulated study of the nature and kinds of valid consequences. Detailed work on assertoric and modal consequences can be found in the treatments of conversion by, for example, Roger Bacon, Siger of Courtrai, Richard of Campsall, and the Pseudo-Scotus;[98] in fact, Richard of Campsall's *Questiones super librum Priorum analeticorum* is devoted mostly to conversion and consequences. The logical culmination of such treatment of conversion can be seen, for instance, in Albert of Saxony's *Perutilis logica* where conversion, as well as syllogism, is among the various subjects contained within his account of consequences.[99]

The incorporation of the Topics into the consequences

Among the earliest full-fledged accounts of consequences now known to be extant are those by Walter Burley in his *De consequentiis, De puritate artis logicae* (*Tractatus brevior* and *Tractatus longior*) and by William Ockham in his *Summa logicae*. The relation between Burley's *Tractatus brevior* and *Tractatus longior*, as well as the relation between either of these and Ockham's *Summa logicae* is not clear, but the currently prevailing view is

---

96. Cf. Boethius, *De topicis differentiis* 1193A–C and Stump 1978, p. 125, notes 112 and 113.
97. Lambert of Auxerre 1971, pp. 138–9.
98. Cf. Robert Kilwardby's commentary on the *Prior Analytics* in Thomas 1953, pp. 56ff. and see also Thomas 1954, pp. 129ff. Roger Bacon 1940, pp. 290–7, cf. also pp. 322–3. Siger of Courtrai 1913, pp. 10–20, cf. also pp. 25ff. Richard of Campsall 1968, pp. 69ff. The Pseudo-Scotus 1891, qu. 10, pp. 103ff. De Rijk mentions Simon of Faversham's discussion of conversion in his commentary on Peter of Spain's *Tractatus* as another example; De Rijk 1968b, p. 89.
99. Albert of Saxony 1522, f. 26ra ff.

that the *Tractatus brevior* was written before Ockham's *Summa logicae* and that the *Tractatus longior* is an expanded revision of the *Tractatus brevior*, written in answer to Ockham's work.[100]

Topics and consequences in Burley's Tractatus brevior

We know very little about Burley's immediate sources for his work on consequences. The section on consequences in the *Tractatus brevior* gives the impression of being a summary compilation, for pedagogical purposes, of already existing material.[101] It consists in the presentation and discussion of ten principal rules of consequences (with some corollaries), very few of which, if any, originate with Burley even in their formulation. If there is anything new here, it is the facile, unexplained but explicit inclusion of syllogisms and rules for syllogisms within a treatment of consequences. There is very little discussion of Topics in the *Tractatus brevior*. The most notable discussion occurs not in the section on consequences but in the section on the syncategorematic word '*si*'. There Burley cites the Topic *from the lesser* as support for two rules for consequences: the necessary follows from anything, and from the impossible anything follows.[102]

Topics and consequences in Ockham's Summa logicae

The third treatise of Ockham's *Summa logicae* is devoted to arguments, and the first chapter of the treatise is given over to the syllogism because of the syllogism's special status among arguments, as Ockham explains. On his view, all syllogisms are divided into those that are demonstrative, those that are Topical, and those that are neither (this group seems at least to include and perhaps to coincide with sophistical syllogisms).[103] Demonstrative syllogisms are those whose premisses are necessary propositions; Topical syllogisms, on the other hand, consist of probable propositions.[104] This account of Ockham's is reminiscent of views from the first half of the thirteenth century, but what Ockham goes on to say is a repudiation of the spirit of those views. First of all, he takes the probable to be what is true, readily believable, *and necessary*, only not self-evident or derivable from

---

100. See Boehner 1955, pp. VI–XIV.
101. Walter Burley 1955, p. 199, 'Ut iuvenes in quolibet problemate disputantes possint esse exercitati et velociter obviantes, quemdam tractatum de puritate artis logicae propono, concedente Deo, compilare.'
102. Walter Burley 1955, pp. 248.24–249.3.
103. William Ockham 1974a, p. 360.43–6.
104. William Ockham 1974a, p. 359.

what is self-evident. So a Topical syllogism, consisting of probable pre-misses, is deficient in neither the matter nor the form of a syllogism.[105] Secondly, he says that all the syllogistic moods of the first figure are directly dependent on (*regulari per*) the principles *dici de omni et nullo* for their validity. The other syllogistic moods are reducible to those of the first figure by conversion, reduction to the impossible, or transposition of premisses;[106] and he thinks of cases of conversion (at least) as conse-quences.[107] Furthermore, in his chapter on demonstrative syllogisms, he says that maxims are necessary for all demonstration, because it is in virtue of such maximal propositions that the premisses of a demonstration are known in some way or other (*aliquo modo*).[108] And finally, in the section on consequences, he claims that all syllogisms hold in virtue of extrinsic means, by which he understands a general rule of consequences, and the extrinsic means he gives are often traditional Topical maxims.[109] So though Ockham casts his discussion of arguments and inferences in Aris-totelian terminology, his views differ widely from the scholastic Aristote-lianism found in the earlier part of the thirteenth century.

After the chapters on the syllogism in general and on the demonstrative syllogism comes Ockham's first chapter on Topics and consequences. He introduces it as his chapter on enthymemes and claims that what follows will teach the diligent student correct views about all non-demonstrative (i.e., Topical and sophistical) syllogisms.[110] The chapter begins with three basic and overlapping divisions of consequences. (1) Some consequences are absolute and some are as-of-now (*ut nunc*). For those of the first sort, there is no time at which the antecedent can be true without the con-sequent; but for those of the second sort, there is some time, only not *this* time, at which the antecedent can be true without the consequent. (2) Some consequences hold by an intrinsic and some by an extrinsic means. The former are consequences valid in virtue of a proposition composed of the same terms as the consequence, while the latter are those valid in virtue of a general proposition not composed of the same terms as the consequence. 'Socrates is not running; therefore a man is not running' is a consequence holding by an intrinsic means, because it is validated by the addition of the

---

105. William Ockham 1974a, p. 360.20–4, 360.35–6.
106. William Ockham 1974a, pp. 362–4.
107. William Ockham 1974a, pp. 322.18–23, 323.40–50, and 323.67–324.86. The following twenty pages contain many such examples.
108. William Ockham 1974a, pp. 509.3–510.10.
109. William Ockham 1974a, p. 588.23–35.
110. William Ockham 1974a, p. 587.4–9.

proposition 'Socrates is a man'. 'Only a man is a donkey; therefore every donkey is a man' holds through an extrinsic means, because it is validated by the rule 'An exclusive and a universal, with the terms transposed, signify the same thing and convert.' (3) Some consequences are formal and some material. A formal consequence is one holding by an extrinsic or intrinsic means. A material consequence is one holding just in virtue of the terms composing it; by this Ockham apparently intends a consequence whose antecedent is impossible or whose consequent is necessary.[111]

Most of the rest of Ockham's treatise on arguments is devoted to presenting and discussing rules of consequences, and the succeeding chapters are divided roughly in this way. First he deals with assertoric consequences, beginning with those that hold in virtue of an intrinsic means, whose terms supposit significatively and personally. Then he turns to assertoric consequences that hold by an extrinsic means. Though Ockham does not use the technical terminology generally associated with the Topics, Topical maxims and arguments traditionally associated with one of the Differentiae are scattered throughout these parts of his treatise. Consequences depending on definition, description, interpretation of a name, genus and species (superior and inferior), integral whole and part, whole in mode, and relative opposites, for example, can be found recurrently throughout these chapters (chapters 2–9). Chapters 10–16 deal with modal consequences; if there is Topical lore in these chapters, it is much less evident than in the preceding chapters. All the consequences in chapters 2–16 are those in which the terms supposit significatively and personally;[112] beginning in chapter 17, Ockham discusses consequences whose terms supposit materially. Under this heading, he deals in detail with Aristotelian Topics in roughly the order in which they occur in Aristotle's *Topics* (consequences dealing with accident, genus, property, and definition), and then he discusses the things annexed to one of these four, such as questions of sameness and difference, annexed to definition. After several chapters on induction and equivocation, Ockham concludes the material on consequences with a brief chapter on eight general rules (and some corollaries) of consequences; Topics play no part in this chapter. Numerous Boethian as well as Aristotelian Topics are woven throughout Ockham's chapters on consequences, then; and the Boethian Topics are most in

111. William Ockham 1974a, pp. 587–9. For discussion of Ockham's material consequences and the relation between his views of consequences and contemporary logic, see, e.g., Boehner 1952, pp. 53–70, Moody 1953, pp. 64–80, Mullick 1971, pp. 117–24, and Adams 1973, pp. 5–37.
112. William Ockham 1974a, pp. 649.4–650.6.

evidence in the analyses of consequences holding by intrinsic or extrinsic means, that is, the formal consequences.[113]

Topics and consequences in Burley's Tractatus longior

There is not so much theorising about logic in the *Tractatus longior* as there is in the *Summa logicae*. Burley divides the section of his book on consequences into three main parts. The first deals with enthymematic consequences, and the second concerns conditional syllogistic consequences. The third – which is fully half the entire book – investigates hypothetical consequences which do not involve conditionals (i.e., those involving conjunctions, disjunctions, exclusives, exceptives, reduplicatives, or the verbs '*incipit*' and '*desinit*'); syllogistic consequences having such hypotheticals among the premisses are also discussed in this section. According to Burley, every good consequence holds by a Topic, and a Topical maxim is nothing other than a rule in virtue of which certain consequences hold. He distinguishes, however, between logical and dialectical Topics. Although every good consequence holds in virtue of a *logical* Topic which is a maxim, it is not the case that every good consequence holds in virtue of a *dialectical* maxim. By 'logical Topic' or 'logical maxim', he seems to understand simply a rule of logic; he says that Aristotle presents his logical Topics in the *Prior Analytics*.[114]

In the *Tractatus brevior*, Burley divided consequences just into absolute and as-of-now consequences. In the *Tractatus longior*, he gives a much more elaborate division, reminiscent of Ockham's, though cast in different terms and differently ordered. Like Ockham, he begins with the division into absolute and as-of-now consequences, though his explanation of these divisions is slightly different from Ockham's. Absolute consequences he divides into two sorts; natural and accidental. Natural consequences are those in which the antecedent includes the consequent, and these hold by an intrinsic Topic; accidental consequences are those in which the antecedent does not include the consequent, and these hold by an extrinsic Topic. He makes three other divisions of consequences, ambiguously related to the preceding ones. First, he says that all consequences are either simple (*simplex*) or composite; the former consists of two categoricals, the

---

113. For Ockham's theory of Topics, see Bird 1961, pp. 65–78 and 1962a, pp. 307–23.
114. Walter Burley 1955, pp. 75–7. 'Dico quod omnis consequentia bona tenet per aliquem locum logicum, non tamen oportet quod omnis consequentia bona tenet per aliquem locum dialecticum, nisi extendo dialecticam ad totam logicam' (p. 75.35–8).

latter of two hypotheticals or of a hypothetical and a categorical.[115] And secondly, some consequences hold by reason of a whole complex (conversion and syllogism are examples); some hold by reason of the terms. This second distinction overlaps with the third. Some consequences that hold by reason of the terms hold materially or accidentally; these are not formal consequences. Formal consequences are those that hold formally by reason of the terms and those that hold by reason of a whole complex.[116] He says little to explain this complicated division, but the distinction between consequences that hold by reason of the terms materially, on the one hand, and both sorts of formal consequences, on the other, bears some resemblance to Ockham's distinction between material and formal consequences.

Topics, as either logical or dialectical maxims, occur throughout all three parts of the section on consequences in the *Tractatus longior*. Burley explicitly identifies two of his general rules for consequences as logical maxims,[117] and he shows how the use of logical Topics can be cast in the traditional form for the presentation of dialectical Topics.[118] He cites the Topics *from the antecedent* and *from the destruction of the consequent* as support for inferences of *modus ponendo ponens* and *modus tollendo tollens*.[119] And he gives the Topic *from division* as the warrant for the principle of the disjunctive syllogism.[120] Theoretically, then, Topics are basic to Burley's theory of consequences, but there are very few recognisable dialectical Topics in his treatise, far fewer than in Ockham's *Summa logicae*.[121]

Conclusion

In Ockham's and Burley's work, the slow process of the absorption of the Topics into theories of consequences has been completed. Throughout the fourteenth century, Topics continue to be discussed, in treatises on consequences but also (and frequently more fully) in, for example, commentaries on Peter of Spain's *Tractatus* and on Aristotle's *Topics*.[122] Certain of the fourteenth-century logicians writing on consequences understand

115. Walter Burley 1955, p. 61.
116. Walter Burley 1955, pp. 84, 86.
117. Walter Burley 1955, cf. p. 76.7–10 and p. 62.9–13.
118. Walter Burley 1955, pp. 76.33–77.23.
119. Walter Burley 1955, pp. 103.24–104.7.
120. Walter Burley 1955, pp. 119.32–121.18.
121. For a detailed discussion of Burley's treatment of consequences, see, for example, Prior 1953; Boh 1962, 1963a, 1963b, and 1964.
122. For example, John Buridan, whose work on consequences was very influential, wrote commentaries on both works and discussed Topics in both commentaries. Cf. Markowski 1968, pp. 3–7, and Green-Pedersen 1976, pp. 121–38.

material consequences as Ockham does, namely, as those in which the antecedent is impossible or the consequent necessary. Robert Fland, Ralph Strode, Richard Lavenham, Paul of Venice, and Paul of Pergula appear to fall into this group.[123] Whether they, like Ockham, include Topical inferences among the formal consequences or even whether Topics play any part at all in their theories of consequences is as yet uninvestigated. Buridan, Albert of Saxony, and the Pseudo-Scotus, on the other hand, are examples of logicians who take material consequences in a different way.[124] For them, a formal consequence is one which holds solely in virtue of the form of the consequence, and a material consequence is a good consequence that does not hold in this way.[125] In the work of these logicians, Topical inferences are equated with a subdivision of material consequences, sometimes labeled 'simple material consequences'.[126] In these authors, (simple) material consequences tend to be taken as enthymematic consequences, reducible to formal consequences by the addition of a premiss.[127] Very little of the theories of Topics among these authors has been investigated.[128] But as far as we now know, Topics continue in this way to eke out a meagre existence throughout the fourteenth and early fifteenth centuries until they experience their own rebirth in the Renaissance in the work of logicians such as Lorenzo Valla and Rudolph Agricola,[129] who elevate Cicero's *Topica* and Boethius' two treatises on the Topics to the very centre of logical studies.[130]

123. Robert Fland, *Consequentiae*, in Spade 1976, cf. pp. 63–4. Ralph Strode 1493, *Consequentiae*, f.2[va]. Richard Lavenham, *Consequentiae*, in Spade 1974a, pp. 76–81 and 99–101. Paul of Pergula 1961, *Logica*, pp. 87–8. Cf. Pinborg 1972, p. 176, Boh 1965, pp. 33–4, and Bottin 1976, pp. 305ff.

124. For a thorough examination of Albert's theories of consequences with some useful comparisons with Ockham and Buridan, see González 1958 and 1959. For a study of consequences in the Pseudo-Scotus, see McDermott 1972.

125. Cf. Buridan 1976, *Tractatus de consequentiis*, pp. 22–3; Albert of Saxony 1522, ff. 24[ra–rb]; the Pseudo-Scotus 1891, pp. 105 and 184. Cf. also Bos 1976, pp. 62–9, and Pinborg 1972, pp. 174–6, and 1969, pp. 176–7.

126. Cf. Green-Pedersen 1976, pp. 125–6 and pp. 136–7. Albert of Saxony 1522, ff. 36[vb]–37[ra] and 37[rb] and the Pseudo-Scotus 1891, p. 105. Cf. also Bendiek 1952, p. 220. This division may explain why Buridan, for example, has little if anything to say about Topics in his treatise on consequences, because in that book he concentrates on formal consequences; cf. Pinborg 1969, pp. 175–6.

127. See, e.g., Buridan 1976, p. 23.10–23, and Bendiek 1952.

128. Cf. Green-Pedersen 1976, pp. 121–8.

129. See Jardine 1977, pp. 143–64.

130. I am glad to acknowledge my debt to John Crossett, whose excellence at the theory and practice of dialectic first aroused my interest in the subject, and I am grateful to Norman Kretzmann and Jan Pinborg for their numerous helpful comments and suggestions.

15

CONSEQUENCES

The notion of consequentia

Etymologically, '*consequentia*' suggests a following along. In medieval philosophical literature it was apparently quite proper to say that one concept follows another – e.g., that *animal* follows *man* – but more generally consequence was thought of as involving entire propositions.

There are, of course, many different relationships in which propositions can stand to each other. For instance, in a conditional proposition of the form 'if *p* then *q*' the proposition taking the place of '*p*' is the antecedent of the conditional proposition, and the proposition taking the place of '*q*' is the consequent. The relationship between that antecedent and the consequent in a true conditional is called *implication* by modern logicians. Again, two propositions may be related to each other in such a way that the first cannot be true unless the second is true also; and the relationship between the two propositions in that case is called *entailment*. Again, two propositions may constitute an argument. In the argument-form '*p*; therefore *q*' the proposition taking the place of '*p*' is the premiss and the proposition taking the place of '*q*' is the conclusion. To employ an argument is to derive or infer the conclusion from the premiss (or premisses), and so the relationship between those two propositions is called *derivation* or *inference*.

Implication, entailment, and inference are all distinct from one another. For instance, a conditional proposition, like other propositions, is accepted or rejected by being classified as true or as false; an argument is neither true nor false but is accepted or rejected as valid or as invalid. Again, to assert '*p*; therefore *q*' is to assert both '*p*' and '*q*', but to assert 'if *p* then *q*' is to assert neither '*p*' nor '*q*'. Nevertheless, medieval logicians disconcertingly use the single notion of consequence to cover all three of these relationships between propositions. A *consequentia* may be a conditional proposition or the relationship between the antecedent and the consequent in a conditional proposition. It may be an argument or the relationship between the premiss and conclusion of an argument, which may be called, confusingly, 'a rational proposition'. A *consequentia* may be an immediate inference – e.g., 'No S is P; therefore no P is S' – or an enthymeme – e.g., 'Socrates is a man; therefore Socrates is an animal' – or a fully expressed syllogism in the object language – e.g., 'If every M is P and every S is M, then every S is P' – or, finally, as a disconnected series of propositions arranged as premisses and conclusion expressed in the meta-language – e.g., 'A, B; therefore C'.

The relationship between propositions in a consequence is a second intention,[1] is in fact the second intention of most interest to logicians of the Middle Ages (or, indeed, of any other period). The terms 'antecedent', 'consequent', and 'consequence' are terms of second intention, which stand for such expressions of first intention as 'Socrates is a man', 'Socrates is an animal', and 'If Socrates is a man, then Socrates is an animal.'

Consequences, conditional propositions, and rational propositions

When reading the medievals it is frequently most natural to think of a *consequentia* as a conditional proposition, though it often becomes clear from the context that what is being discussed is an argument. This circumstance leads to difficulties: is the consequence to be evaluated as true or false or as valid or invalid?[2] If medieval logicians wanted to classify consequences as propositions, why should they not have classified them as *rational* rather than as *conditional* propositions?[3] Logic, on the medieval view of it, was supposed to teach men to speak truly, and so it is perhaps understandable that arguments were often evaluated as true; but the parallel use of such expressions as '*consequentia est bona*' or '*consequentia valet*', or simply '[*consequentia*] *bene sequitur*' indicates also a recognition that the transition from the one proposition in the consequence to the other is to be evaluated in terms other than those appropriate to affirmations and denials.

1. See Knudsen's contribution to this volume.
2. Both *consequentia est vera* (*falsa*) and *consequentia valet* (*non valet*) were considered proper characterisations by authors who flatly stated that a *consequentia* is a hypothetical proposition (Buridan 1976, I, 3), by those who said that it is an inference or *illatio* (Strode 1484, f. l^v and by those who wavered (cf. Burley 1955, pp. 65 and 208).
3. The rational proposition – '*p*; therefore *q*' – was counted among the six or seven basic hypothetical propositions (conjunctive, disjunctive, conditional; causal, local, temporal, rational). Buridan treats it as an alternative to the conditional proposition: 'if' and 'therefore' both designate that one of the two propositions connected by them follows from the other; they differ in that 'if' designates the proposition immediately following it as the antecedent while 'therefore' designates just the opposite. Cf. Buridan 1976, I, 3.

There is, of course, a connection between the validity of an argument and the truth of a corresponding conditional proposition. Whenever 'A; therefore B' is a valid argument, there is a true conditional proposition of the form 'if A, then B'. It is this connection that is exploited in the medieval notion of *consequentia*: the aim is to use the truth of the conditional proposition as a criterion for the validity of the corresponding argument. But the matter is not simple, because the connection is not a symmetric relationship. We cannot correctly say that whenever 'if A, then B' is true there is a valid argument of the form 'A; therefore B'. It is only if the 'if . . . then . . .' is taken as representing entailment that this is so.

This fact about the relationship between arguments and conditional propositions seems to have been recognised by the medievals in their insistence that the conditional corresponding to an argument is to be understood in a strong sense, as a hypothetical proposition that expresses a close tie between its antecedent and its consequent. Thus we find in the early twelfth century Abelard's clear predilection for a consequence which is based on the 'necessity of consecution'.[4] Peter of Spain in the middle of the thirteenth century states that the antecedent in a true conditional cannot be true without the consequent being true also, adding that 'every true conditional is necessary and every false conditional impossible', a view reaffirmed in the fourteenth century by Albert of Saxony and in the fifteenth by Paul of Pergula.[5] There was occasionally even some reluctance to accept as a consequence a consequence which does not hold. The distinction in question here is that between a genuine consequence, in which the appropriate consequential connections are present, and a counterfeit consequence, in which we have merely an external semblance of consequence. While Buridan recognises that the issue is basically a terminological one, he says that he will understand by 'consequence' a

---

4. See Abelard 1970a, pp. 283.37–284.3: note that even the broader sense of the necessity of consecution is expressed by him in modal terms: 'Videntur autem due consecutionis necessitates: una quidem *largior*, cum videlicet id quod dicit antecedens non potest esse absque eo quod dicit consequens; altera vero *strictior*, cum scilicet non solum antecedens absque consequenti non potest esse verum, ⟨sed etiam⟩ ex se ipsum exigit; que quidem necessitas in propria consecutionis sententia consistit et veritatem tenet incommutabilem . . .'

5. See Peter of Spain 1972, p. 9.15–18: 'Ad veritatem conditionalis exigitur quod antecedens non possit esse verum sine consequenti, ut "*si homo est, animal est*". Unde omnis conditionalis vera est necessaria, et omnis conditionalis falsa est impossibilis.' Cf. González 1958, p. 333, n. 48, where he quotes from Albert's *Perutilis logica*, t. 3, c. 5, f. 19ᵛ: 'Omnis conditionalis vera est necessaria, et omnis falsa est impossibilis'. Cf. Paul of Pergula 1961, p. 17: 'Nota quod omnis conditionalis vera est possibilis et necessaria, et omnis falsa est impossibilis et nulla est quae sit contingens.'

hypothetical proposition which is true,[6] even though in the course of his discussion he shows no hesitation to use the notion of a consequence that does not hold, is invalid, is bad, etc.

The origins of the theory of consequences

Scholars disagree about the origins of the theory of consequences. The word '*consequentia*' can be found in Boethius, who found its Greek equivalent ('*akolouthēsis*') in Aristotle, even though it does not there have the technical sense of a relation among propositions.[7] If we understand the theory of consequences as basically a theory of propositions, and if we accept the view that Megaric-Stoic logic was the first systematic logic of unanalysed propositions,[8] we might expect to find some influence, direct or indirect, of Stoic logic upon the medieval theories of consequences.[9] We do in fact find Stoic elements in Boethius' hypothetical syllogistic, even if they are not the result of direct influence,[10] and Boethius' work on the subject made a significant contribution to scholastic logic. He introduced the notion of *consequentia* into medieval logical discussion, he distinguished the temporally-conditioned accidental connection from the natural connection between an antecedent and its consequent, and he classified and discussed the Topics, which were influential in the development of scholastic theories of consequences.[11]

Consequences in Garlandus Compotista

Garlandus Compotista and Peter Abelard inherited much from Boethius, yet in many ways the two were rethinking his doctrine very carefully. In his *Dialectica* Garlandus is fairly detailed in his discussion of Boethian

---

6. Buridan 1976, p. 21: 'Alii dicunt si [consequentia] sit falsa non debet dici "consequentia", sed solum si sit uera. Et de hoc non est disputandum, quia nomina significant ad placitum; et siue sic siue non sic, ergo in hoc tractatu per hoc nomen "consequentia" uolo intelligere consequentiam ueram, et per "antecedens" et "consequens" uolo intelligere propositiones quarum una sequitur ad aliam uera seu bona consequentia.'

7. See Bocheński 1961, p. 189.

8. The agreement here is unanimous. Cf. Łukasiewicz 1935, Boehner 1952, Bocheński 1961, Dumitriu 1977.

9. Everyone agrees that there are striking resemblances between the theory of *consequentiae* and the Megaric-Stoic propositional logic; e.g. Łukasiewicz 1935, Bocheński 1938, 1961, Dumitriu 1977, Mates 1965b, Moody 1953. However, the actual historical influence, if it indeed took place, has not been demonstrated and the opinions of the foremost scholars differ. Cf., e.g., Moody 1953, 1967; Dürr 1951.

10. An extensive study of Boethius' sources is available in Obertello 1969.

11. See Stump's preceding contribution to this volume.

hypothetical syllogistic and, interestingly enough, he places the chapter on Topics just before the one on syllogisms. What is interesting from our point of view here is that Garlandus finds himself discussing not only Topics but also the four Aristotelian types of argument – categorical syllogism, induction, enthymeme, and example – within the chapter on Topics; furthermore, some Topical maxims are so general as to pass for rules of consequences – for example, 'If the antecedent is posited [i.e., affirmed], so is the consequent'; 'If the consequent is removed [i.e., denied], so is the antecedent.' [12]

Much of what Garlandus says about hypothetical syllogism obviously has its roots in Boethius, both in content and in terminology. He discusses negation and allows for contradictory opposition between 'P' and '$\sim P$' and also, at least implicitly, for the equipollence of 'P' and '$\sim \sim P$'. Although he seems to recognise both term-conjunction and propositional conjunction, he does not have much to say about either. He compares 'If (si) a man is, an animal is' and 'When (cum) a man is, an animal is'. If both imply 'Because ($quia$) a man is, an animal is', then 'cum' is not significantly different from 'si'. But he finds that there is a great difference between these two conjunctions, as indicated by the following example: 'When (cum) fire is hot, the sky is round.' Here, he says, 'I say not that *because* fire is hot, the sky is round, but rather that the sky is round *at a time when* fire is hot.' [13] He even goes so far as to suggest a division of consequences based on this distinction, into consequences *per accidens* and natural consequences. The recognition of the difference between 'si' and 'cum' is echoed in the later distinction between consequences that are absolute and those that hold as of now ($ut\ nunc$). [14]

Of the remaining hypothetical propositions Garlandus recognises dis-

---

12. Garlandus 1959, p. 114. He ends his chapter 'De topicis differentiis' with the remark that: 'While all the Topics are in the service of hypothetical syllogisms, only the Topics from the whole and part and from the equals are of service to categorical syllogisms.' ('Sciendum est quod omnes loci serviunt hipoteticis sillogismis; cathegoricis vero tantum serviunt locus a toto et a parte et a pari.')

13. Garlandus 1959, p. 141: 'Propositio hipotetica connexa in qua preponitur "*cum*", aliquando eandem vim optinet cum ea in qua preponitur "*si*", ut cum dico: "*si homo est, animal est*": utraque enim dicit: "*quia homo est, animal est*". Aliquando autem aliam vim optinet, ut hic "*cum ignis calidus est, celum rotundum est*": non enim hic dico quia ignis calidus sit, celum rotundum esse, sed dico celum esse rotundum *ex tempore quo* ignis calidus est.' Similar remarks on the ambiguity of '*cum*' are found in Boethius, although the latter does not explicitly stress the causal connection between the antecedent and the consequent, but rather the omnitemporal character of '*si*' and the temporally-restrictive character of '*cum*'. Sometimes the logical force of '*cum*' is that of '*et*'. Cf. Dürr 1951, pp. 56f. in conjunction with Prantl 1855–70, I, p. 715, n. 162.

14. Garlandus 1959, p. 141. This division of *consequentia* was adopted but greatly refined by Abelard 1970a, pp. 473ff., and accepted by most later medieval writers on *consequentiae*; see, for example, Ockham 1974a, III, 3, 1.

junctions, but he undermines the role of disjunctions in syllogisms. In fact, he reduces the disjunctive proposition formed by '*aut*. . . . *aut*' to a conditional; conversely, he equates 'Either it is not a man or it is an animal' with 'If it is a man, it is an animal.'[15] The questions whether or not '*aut*' is truth-functional and if it is, whether it is inclusive or exclusive, are undetermined then, unless we know what the truth-conditions of the associated conditional proposition are. Garlandus says that a conditional proposition is a sentence composed of 'if' ('*si*') and two or more categorical propositions. He recognises that the component categorical propositions can be both true, both false, one true and one false, or – surprisingly – both neither true nor false. By the last kind we should, it seems, understand a conditional composed of subjunctive propositions. It is the indeterminacy of subjunctive propositions that makes him talk about four ways in which a consequence can be true and five ways in which it can be false.[16] (The examples of both true and false consequences given by Garlandus make it implausible that he considered Philonian implication at all.) The basis for the connection between the antecedent and the consequent is provided by the Topical maxims that serve as the foundation for natural consequences in which '*si*' has more than a temporal force. In fact, Garlandus' talk about propositions which are neither true nor false suggests that his natural consequences are supportable by counterfactual conditionals.

Consequences in Peter Abelard

Although Abelard does not define '*consequentia*', he does characterise '*inferentia*', of which *consequentia* is, in his view a sub-species.[17] Inference consists, he says, 'in the necessity of the consecution, that is, in the fact that from the meaning of the antecedent the thought of the consequent fol-

---

15. See Garlandus 1959, pp. 131f., where he not only considers the equivalence of disjunctives and conjunctives but also relates both of them to a universal affirmative proposition: 'Equipollent etiam quedam cathegorice quibusdam hipoteticis propositionibus tam connexis quam disiunctis. Ut hic patet: "*si est homo, est animal*", "*aut non est homo, aut est animal*", "*omnis homo est animal*"; he enim eandem veritatem tenent et per unam alie probantur. Ideoque notandum est quod coniuncte atque disiuncte simplices per universales cathegoricas sibi equipollentes probantur: "*si est homo, est animal*", "*aut non est homo, aut est animal*" verificantur per istam in veritate eis consimilem: "*omnis homo est animal*".'

16. Garlandus 1959, pp. 136f.: 'Nunc sciendum est item quod consequentia quatuor modis fit vera, alia ex utrisque veris . . . , alia ex utrisque falsis . . . , alia ex falso antecedenti et vero consequenti . . . , alia ex utrisque terminis neque veris neque falsis, quemadmodum in ista potest dinosci: "*si esset homo, esset animal*": neuter namque verus est neque falsus. / Verum etiam quinque modis fit falsa consequentia: alia ex utrisque veris . . . , alia ex utrisque falsis . . . , alia ex falso antecedenti et vero consequenti . . . , alia ex utrisque neque veris neque falsis, ut hic: "*si Socrates esset animal, esset homo*", alia iterum fit falsa ex vero antecedenti et falso consequenti.'

17. De Rijk in Abelard 1970a, p. XXXIV.

lows'.[18] It is *perfect* if the necessity of the consecution is based on the arrangement of terms regardless of their meaning; it is *imperfect* if the meaning of terms must be taken into account in order to have the necessary connection. This is the most general division, which comprises all the traditional forms of argumentation. Abelard understands a consequence as fundamentally a *coniunctio* between antecedent and consequent, and the basic division of such a conjunctive implication which he rightly attributes to Boethius, is into natural and temporal.[19] The difference between the two is perhaps best seen in Abelard's examples: 'If a man is, an animal is' and 'When it rains, it thunders.' In the former, we have a natural *consecutio*, in the latter we have only a temporal *comitatio*. For the most part Abelard uses something like modern strict implication as the paradigm of implication,[20] but he is also aware of implications of a weaker sort.[21]

Since Abelard follows Boethius in associating disjunction with something like strict implication, it is obvious that disjunction in his view is not a mere truth-function. But while Abelard would reject the view that for the truth of a disjunction it is sufficient that one of its components be true, he also wanted to relax the (Stoic) requirement that the disjuncts must be incompatible; in this way he left room for further developments which led eventually to the medieval discovery of inclusive truth-functional disjunction, the so-called De Morgan's Laws.[22]

The period immediately following Abelard is still not adequately explored, although recent scholarship has shown that there was intense logical activity during that time.[23]

Consequences in the terminist logicians

As for the terminists, it is significant that in none of the three best-known textbooks of the thirteenth century[24] – viz., those of Peter of Spain,

---

18. Abelard 1970a, p. 253.28–31: 'Inferentia itaque in necessitate consecutionis consistit, in eo scilicet quod ex sensu antecedentis sententia exigitur consequentis, sicut in ipotetica propositione dicitur, ut in sequentibus monstrabitur. Hec autem inferentia alias *perfecta* est, alias *imperfecta*.'
19. Abelard 1970a, p. 472.
20. Abelard 1970a, pp. 283f. (Cf. n. 4 above.)
21. Abelard 1970a, p. 293.13–17. '[Aliquae consequentiae] liberius expediuntur et assignantur secundum sensus totarum enuntiationum et laxius accipiuntur, ut videlicet ita exponantur: posito antecedenti, idest existente eo quod dicit antecedens propositio, existit illud quoque quod consequens proponit'; p. 330.28–30 'Nichil itaque ⟨aliud⟩ in "*antecedere hoc ad aliud*" vel "*inferre hoc illud*" accipimus, quam "*si hoc est, illud esse*".'
22. For the scholastic origins and tradition of these laws see Boehner 1951a.
23. See, e.g., Minio-Paluello 1956, De Rijk 1962–7, and Giusberti 1977. The survey in Pinborg 1972 gives an impression of a very lively interest in logic, semantics, and language generally during this period. Grabmann 1937 is still worth reading in this connection.
24. I.e., William of Sherwood 1937, 1966; Lambert of Auxerre 1971; and Peter of Spain 1972.

William of Sherwood, and Lambert of Auxerre – do we find a special chapter or treatise on consequences. But even in these introductory texts the authors supply us with information on the notion of consequence generally in the chapters on propositions, on Topics, and on fallacies.[25] And further details are provided in the treatises on *syncategoremata* by William and by Peter.[26]

Consequences in the Pseudo-Scotus

We can consider only a few features of the theory of consequences and its rise to prominence during the late thirteenth, fourteenth, and early fifteenth centuries.[27] For a sample of the difficulties encountered in later medieval attempts to formulate a satisfactory definition of a consequence, we can turn to the Pseudo-Scotus. In his commentary on the *Prior Analytics*, he proposes the following definition: 'A consequence is a hypothetical proposition composed of an antecedent and a consequent by means of a conditional or rational conjunction, which denotes that it is impossible for them – namely, for the antecedent and the consequent – that the antecedent be true and the consequent false when they are formed at the same time.'[28] The apparently undiscriminating acceptance of two ways of

25. Cf. William of Sherwood 1966, Ch. IV, esp. pp. 34f. where he speaks of consecutive conjunction which he equates with conditional proposition, and where he states the truth conditions of a conditional: 'In order that a conditional be true the truth of its parts is not required, but only that whenever the antecedent is [true] the consequent is [true].' Cf. *ibid.*, Ch. VI, esp. the sections on the Fallacy of Begging the Original Issue (pp. 157f.) and the section on the Fallacy of Consequent (p. 160). Cf. Lambert of Auxerre 1971, p. 16, for his definition of conditional; p. 120 for his recognition of *locus maxima* as an inferential rule, and esp. pp. 195f. where he explicitly uses '*consequentia*' in a technical sense and distinguishes two types: 'Duplex est consequentia: una scilicet in qua, posito antecedente, de necessitate ponitur consequens, et hec potest dici naturalis vel necessaria; alia vero est consequentia in qua, posito antecedente, non propter hoc de necessitate ponitur consequens, sed ut frequentius concomitatur antecedens consequens et hoc potest dici consequentia probabilis vel consequentia ut in pluribus.' Cf. Peter of Spain 1972, pp. 8f. and esp. pp. 169f. where he devotes several brief paragraphs to the notion of consequence and its several types before discussing the Fallacy of the Consequent.
26. See William of Sherwood 1968, Chapter XVII on '*IF*' (*SI*) and also the following chapter on '*UNLESS*' (*NISI*), which present a meticulous discussion of basic consecutive conjunctions. In Peter of Spain 1964, pp. 50–65 on 'consecutive words' are instructive.
27. The most important texts from the early fourteenth century are by Burley (written in the 1320s ed. Boehner 1955), Ockham (written in the late 1320s, ed. Boehner and Gál 1974). Buridan (written in the 1330s, ed. Hubien 1976), and the Pseudo-Scotus (written around 1350, in Duns Scotus ed. Vives 1891).
28. Pseudo-Scotus 1891, I. 287B: 'Consequentia est propositio hypothetica, composita ex antecedente, et consequente, mediante coniunctione conditionali, vel rationali, quae denotat, quod impossibile est ipsis, scilicet antecedente, et consequente simul formatis, quod antecedens sit verum, et consequens falsum'. The reconstruction of the difficulties connected with formulating conditions of the truth or validity of consequences is based on q. 10 of the Pseudo-Scotus' commentary on Book I of the *Prior Analytics*, but it also takes into account the discussions by Bendiek 1952, Mates 1965b, Kneale 1962, pp. 286–8, and McDermott 1972.

forming a consequence – 'if *p*, then *q*', and '*p*; therefore *q*' – is typical of the medievals and does not present an important difficulty. Much more interesting is the fact that plausible counter-examples can be offered to the definitions typically given. The Pseudo-Scotus, among others,[29] reviews and criticises accepted or possible formulations of a definition.

(i) 'For the validity of a consequence it is necessary and sufficient that it be impossible for the antecedent to be true and the consequent false.'[30] To this, according to the Pseudo-Scotus, there is the following counter-example: 'Every proposition is affirmative, therefore no proposition is negative.' The objector points out that 'Every proposition is affirmative' would be true if all negative propositions were destroyed, while 'No proposition is negative' could not possibly be true since it falsifies itself by its very existence. Thus the intuitively acceptable consequence. 'Every proposition is affirmative, therefore no proposition is negative' turns out to be unacceptable if we apply definition (i).[31] To avoid such undesirable results, the proponent offers two other criteria, but they also are subjected to powerful objections.

(ii) 'For the validity of a consequence it is necessary and sufficient that it be impossible for things to be as signified by the antecedent without also being as signified by the consequent.'[32] The Pseudo-Scotus' counter-example here is: 'No chimaera is a goat-stag; therefore a man is a jack-ass.' To appreciate the force of this, one should note that for the Pseudo-Scotus negative propositions require for their truth only that things should not be as signified by the corresponding affirmative proposition; on that assumption, the antecedent is clearly true and the consequent false. Hence, since formulation (ii) does not rule out such counter-examples, it is inadequate. The Pseudo-Scotus therefore considers another definition.

(iii) 'For a consequence to be valid it is necessary and sufficient that it be impossible that if the antecedent and the consequent are formed at the same time, the antecedent be true and the consequent false.'[33] But again there is a troublesome counter-example: 'God exists; therefore this consequence is not valid.' Although the counter-example fulfills the conditions of (iii), it is not valid. For if it were a valid consequence, its consequent would be false,

29. E.g., Buridan 1976, I, 3.
30. Pseudo-Scotus 1891, p. 286B: 'Ad bonitatem consequentiae requiritur, et sufficit, quod impossibile est antecedens esse verum, et consequens falsum.'
31. Pseudo-Scotus 1891, p. 287A.
32. Pseudo-Scotus 1891, p. 287A: 'Ad bonitatem consequentiae requiritur, et sufficit, quod impossibile est sic esse, sicut significatur per antecedens, quin sic sit, sicut significatur per consequens.'
33. Pseudo-Scotus 1891, p. 287A: 'Ad bonitatem consequentiae requiritur, et sufficit, quod impossibile est antecedente, et consequente simul formatis, antecedens esse verum, et consequens falsum.'

since it asserts precisely that the consequence is not valid. But since the antecedent, 'God exists', is true if the consequent, 'this consequence is not valid', is false, the consequence could *not* be valid. Thus the assumption that this consequence is valid refutes itself. Yet the conditions of (iii) are fulfilled, since the antecedent and the consequent are both necessary and so the case of the antecedent being true while the consequent is false could never arise. That the consequent is necessary is shown by the fact that the consequence 'God exists; therefore this consequence is not valid' could not possibly be valid.

In spite of the difficulty encountered by such an unusual counter-example, the Pseudo-Scotus endorses (iii) but allows for an exception of the case 'where the meaning of the consequent is incompatible with the meaning of the sign of consequence as the very connective which specifies that there is a consequence'.[34]

According to the Pseudo-Scotus, the principles 'From the impossible anything follows' and 'The necessary follows from anything' are generally accepted but need explication. First, one should determine what is meant by 'impossible'. Everyone will agree that a formal contradiction, '$p. \sim p$', is a paradigm case of impossibility. The Pseudo-Scotus easily proves 'q' – any proposition at all – from the conjunction of 'p' and its denial by an appeal to the intuitively obvious formal rules of simplification-of-conjunction, logical addition, and disjunctive syllogism.[35] (John Buridan had already offered much the same proof.)[36]

Attempts were made to provide an adequate classification of consequences. One important step in this direction was the general division into formal and material consequences.[37] In the Pseudo-Scotus' theory, formal consequences comprise all the logical principles of traditional syllogism, the laws of conversion of propositions, the laws of the square of opposition, and other principles of Aristotelian logic; but they also include the laws of propositional logic determined by the most general rules of consequences governing propositions taken as unanalysed units. Material consequences are subdivided into those that hold *absolutely* (*simpliciter*) and those that hold only *as-of-now* (*ut nunc*). Both are enthymematic as they

---

34. Pseudo-Scotus 1891, p. 287A–B: 'Dico igitur, quod ad bonitatem consequentiae, requiritur et sufficit vltimus modus, scilicet impossibile est, antecedente, et consequente simul formatis, quod antecedens sit verum, et consequens falsum, excepto vno casu, scilicet vbi significatum consequentis repugnat significationi notae consequentiae, sicut coniunctionis, quae denotat consequentiam esse . . .'
35. Pseudo-Scotus 1891, p. 288A–B.
36. Buridan 1976, I, 8, 7ª conclusio: 'Ad omnem propositionem copulativam ex duabus inuicem contradictoriis constitutam sequi quamlibet aliam . . . consequentia formali.'
37. Pseudo-Scotus 1891, p. 287B. On this division cf. Stump's preceding contribution to this volume.

stand, but a material consequence is said to be *absolute* if it is reducible to a formal consequence by addition of a necessary premiss; and it is said to be *as-of-now* if it is reducible to a formal consequence by the addition of a factually true premise which could conceivably be false at some time. Both absolute and as-of-now consequences are such that if they do hold at all, it is impossible for the antecedent to be true and the consequent false. The apparently paradoxical principles 'From the impossible anything follows' and 'The necessary follows from anything' in the sense of '$\sim \Diamond\ p \rightarrow (p \rightarrow q)$' and '$\sim \Diamond \sim q \rightarrow (p \rightarrow q)$' were considered to be 'merely material' consequences, presumably on the ground that it is their content, their modality, rather than their propositional form which determines their validity.

Consequences in William Ockham

William Ockham presents a somewhat different, threefold division.[38] (1) A consequence is valid either *absolutely* or *as-of-now*. (2) A consequence holds *per medium extrinsecum* or *per medium intrinsecum*. A consequence of the former kind – one that holds in virtue of an extrinsic medium – is valid in virtue of a logical rule. For example, 'Only an animal is a man; therefore every man is an animal' holds in virtue of the rule 'From an affirmative exclusive proposition to the universal affirmative proposition with the terms transposed there is a valid consequence (and conversely).' Consequences that hold in virtue of an intrinsic medium are valid in virtue of an additional premiss which transforms the original enthymeme into a fully stated argument. For example, 'Every man is an animal; therefore every man is mortal' is turned into an explicit argument by the addition of the premiss 'Every animal is mortal'. The added premiss may, of course, be either necessary or contingent. (3) A consequence is either *formal* or *material*. A *formal* consequence can be one of two sorts: either it holds (i) by an extrinsic medium, that is, by some meta-rule such as is operative in the above example of logical relation between an exclusive and a universal affirmative proposition; or (ii) if it holds directly by an intrinsic medium and indirectly by an extrinsic medium or a rule 'which concerns general features of propositions and not their truth and falsity or possibility and impossibility' – as in the case of 'Socrates is not running, therefore a man is not running' (which holds directly by the additional premisses 'Socrates is a man' and indirectly by some syllogistic or Topical rule).

38. Ockham 1974a, III, 3, 1.

A consequence is *material*[39] if it holds precisely in virtue of the meanings of its terms – that is, not in virtue of some extrinsic principle determining the inferential connection on the basis of the general conditions of propositions but on the basis of special conditions such as their truth-value or modal status. The examples given are the two paradoxical consequences: 'A man is running; therefore God exists' and 'A man is a jack-ass; therefore God does not exist.'

Consequences in Walter Burley

For a good sample of a medieval theory of consequences we can turn to Walter Burley.[40] He was perhaps the earliest medieval logician who fully understood the logical priority of propositional logic and also developed it to a considerable degree. Although his contemporary William Ockham also wrote lengthy sections on consequences and on hypothetical propositions, Ockham's *Summa logicae* is organised around terms, propositions, and arguments. Burley on the other hand, in his two versions of *De puritate artis logicae*,[41] starts with the most general rules of consequences and then subsumes hypothetical and categorical syllogistics under that primary logic. Furthermore, his treatment of the properties of terms and of various *sophismata* throughout his work presupposes an understanding of consequential rules.

Of the two versions of the chapter '*De regulis generalibus consequentiarum*', the one contained in the *Tractatus brevior* is the more revealing. I will base my presentation on it and invoke the other version only for comparison. In the prologue Burley remarks that he will state 'certain general rules which will have to be used in what follows'. Then, without offering any general definition of a consequence, he draws a distinction between absolute and

---

39. There is still disagreement about whether medieval logicians, and Ockham in particular, recognised material implication. 'Material' in the sense in question precludes any modal notions or any semantic connection between the antecedent and the consequent. *P* materially implies *Q* if and only if it is not the case that *P* is true and *Q* false. Boehner 1951b argued with some force on the basis of selected textual evidence that Ockham indeed recognised material implication of a purely truth-functional sense. Adams 1973, on the other hand, makes so many careful distinctions regarding what could be meant by knowing material (and strict) implication that one prefers to stay within Ockham's own conceptual framework and try to do one's best to determine precisely how his three divisions of *consequentiae* organise the whole field.

40. See n. 54 below.

41. Boehner argued persuasively that the first version (the *Tractatus brevior*) was begun independently of Ockham's *Summa logicae*. But when Ockham's treatise appeared, Burley wrote his second version, the *Tractatus longior*, starting with the tract on supposition in which Burley argues against Ockham's nominalistic interpretation of *suppositio simplex*. This second version was finished before 1329. All the references are to Boehner's edition of both versions; the sections on *consequentiae* are on pp. 60–6 and 199–219.

as-of-now consequences. 'A consequence is absolute', he says, 'if it holds always; for example, "A man is running, therefore an animal is running." A consequence is as-of-now if it holds for a certain time and not always; for example, "Every man is running, therefore Socrates is running"; for this consequence does not hold always but only while there is a man Socrates.'[42] Then he states his ten principal rules, discussing each of them as he goes along.

Using the schematic letters P, Q, R, etc., the symbol '→' as a sign of a consequence, and the usual symbols for logical constants, we can schematise Burley's rules and proofs, preserving as much as possible of his natural deduction technique. (PR = Principal Rule, DR = derived rule.) Only those rules which can reasonably be considered as propositional rules are given.

PR 1 $P \to Q \,/\, \therefore \, \sim \Diamond (P . \sim Q)$, and the corollary:

       $\Diamond (P . \sim Q) \,/\, \therefore \, \sim (P \to Q)$[43]

DR 1.1 $\Diamond P, \, \sim \Diamond Q \,/\, \therefore \, \sim (P \to Q)$

DR 1.2 $\sim \Diamond \sim P, \, \Diamond \sim Q \,/\, \therefore \, \sim (P \to Q)$[44]

PR 2 $P \to Q \,/\, \therefore \, (Q \to R) \to (P \to R)$ and the corollary

       $P \to Q \,/\, \therefore \, (R \to P) \to (R \to Q)$[45]

DR 2.1 $P \to Q, Q \to R \dots T \to U \,/\, \therefore \, P \to U$[46]

DR 2.2 $P \to Q, (P.Q) \to R \,/\, \therefore \, P \to R$

DR 2.3 $P \to Q, (Q.R) \to S \,/\, \therefore \, (P.R) \to S$[47]

PR 3 $P \to Q \,/\, \therefore \, \sim Q \to \sim P$[48]

42. Burley 1955, p. 199: 'Consequentiarum quaedam est simplex, quaedam est ut nunc. Consequentia simplex est ista, quae tenet pro omni tempore, ut: "Homo currit, igitur animal currit." Consequentia ut nunc tenet pro tempore determinato et non semper, ut: "Omnis homo currit, igitur Sortes currit"; illa enim consequentia non tenet semper, sed solum dum Sortes est homo.'

43. Burley 1955, pp. 199f.: 'In omni consequentia bona simplici antecedens non potest esse verum sine consequente. Et ideo, si in aliquo casu possibili posito posset antecedens esse verum sine consequente, tunc non fuit consequentia bona. In consequentia autem ut nunc non potest antecedens ut nunc, scilicet pro tempore, pro quo consequentia tenet, esse verum sine consequente.'

44. Burley 1955, p. 200: 'Ex contingenti non sequitur impossibile in consequentia simplici ... Ex necessario non sequitur contingens.'

45. Burley 1955, p. 200: 'Quidquid sequitur ad consequens, sequitur ad antecedens ... Quidquid antecedit ad antecedens, antecedit ad consequens.'

46. Burley 1955, p. 200: 'Per hanc regulam: Quidquid sequitur ad consequens, sequitur ad antecedens, tenet consequentia a primo ad ultimum, quando arguitur per multas consequentias intermedias.'

47. Burley 1955. p. 203: 'Quidquid sequitur ex consequente et antecedente, sequitur ex antecedente per se ... Quidquid sequitur ad consequens cum aliquo addito, sequitur ad antecedens cum eodem addito.'

48. Burley 1955, p. 207: 'In omni consequentia bona, quae non est syllogistica, ex opposito consequentis contradictorie sequitur oppositum antecedentis.'

For syllogistic consequence Burley states the following important rule(s):

DR 3.1 $(P, Q) \rightarrow R / \therefore (\sim R, P) \rightarrow \sim Q$

DR 3.2 $(P, Q) \rightarrow R / \therefore (\sim R, Q) \rightarrow \sim P$[49]

This insight into the link between the indirect syllogistic reductions and the principles of propositional logic is remarkable.

To clarify the nature of the denial of propositions, especially of compound propositions, Burley gives the following rule:

PR 4   'The basic formal element (*formale*) affirmed in one of the contradictories must be denied in the other.'[50]

Among particular instances we find

DR 4.1 $\sim(P.Q) \leftrightarrow (\sim P \vee \sim Q)$

DR 4.2 $\sim(P \vee Q) \leftrightarrow (\sim P . \sim Q)$

DR 4.3 $\sim(P \rightarrow Q) \leftrightarrow (P . \sim Q)$[51]

PR 5–10 go beyond propositional logic, since they govern propositions whose internal structure needs to be taken into account.

To illustrate Burley's method of deriving a rule from other rules, we can present his proofs for the two rules DR 2.2 and DR 2.3 in a schematic way, justifying each step on the basis of Burley's text.

Proof (*ratio*) for DR 2.2 'Every proposition implies itself along with its consequent ... Since, then, the antecedent implies both the antecedent and the consequent, and since whatever follows from the consequent follows from the antecedent, it follows that whatever is implied by the antecedent and the consequent follows from the antecedent alone.'[52]

1. $P \rightarrow Q$ Assumption of a consequence

2. $(P.Q) \rightarrow R$ Assumption that something follows from the consequent and the antecedent conjoined

3. $(P \rightarrow Q) \rightarrow [P \rightarrow (P.Q)]$ A rule tacitly assumed by Burley (see the first sentence of his proof)

4. $P \rightarrow (P.Q)$ From (3) and (1) by *modus ponens* (stated by Burley in his hypothetical syllogistic, but apparently too obvious to be explicitly stated here)

49. Burley 1955, p. 208: 'In consequentia syllogistica ex opposito conclusionis cum altera praemissarum sequitur oppositum alterius praemissae.'

50. Burley 1955, p. 208: 'Formale affirmatum in uno contradictorio debet negari in reliquo ...'

51. Burley 1955, p. 209: 'Contradictorium copulativae valet unam disiunctivam habentem partes contradicentes partibus copulativae ... Contradictorium disiunctivae aequipollet copulativae factae ex contradictoriis partium disiunctivae. Contradictorium conditionis valet unam propositionem, quae significat oppositum sui consequentis stare cum suo antecedente ...'

52. Burley 1955, p. 203: 'Quaelibet propositio infert seipsam cum suo consequente ... Cum igitur antecedens inferat antecedens et consequens, et quidquid sequitur ad consequens, sequitur ad antecedens, sequitur quod quidquid sequitur ex antecedente et consequente, sequitur ex antecedente per se.'

5. P → R   From (4) and (2) by PR 2
6. {(P → Q). [(P.Q) → R]} → (P → R) From the conjunction of as-
                                        sumptions (1) and (2) the con-
                                        sequent (5) has been shown to
                                        follow.

Proof for DR 2.3 'An antecedent with something added implies the
consequent with the same thing added ... Since, therefore, whatever is
implied by the consequent is implied by the antecedent, it follows that
whatever is implied by the consequent with a proposition added is
implied by the antecedent with the same proposition added.'[53]

1. P → Q   }
2. (Q.R) → S   } Assumptions

3. (P → Q) → [(P.R) → (Q.R)]   A rule expressed by Burley's first
                                sentence
4. (P.R) → (Q.R)   From (3) and (1) by *modus ponens*
5. (P.R) → S   From (4) and (2) by PR 2
6. {(P → Q). [(Q.R) → S]} → [(P.R) → S]   From (1) and (2) and (5)
                                              Q.E.D.

The main shortcoming of these and similar proofs is obvious: Burley
ought to have stated *all* the rules he needs before constructing the proof. In
any case his fundamental idea of proof is sound, and his work paved the
way for the subsequent logical treatises on consequences.[54]

Conclusion

The century of Burley, Ockham, Buridan, and others was indeed a golden
age of logic, in which the theory of consequences attained its mature form.
It was followed by a slow but steady decline. While the theory of consequences continued to be cultivated, it grew by way of commentaries and
extensive discussions of details, rather than by strikingly new discoveries.
However, the post-fourteenth century period is certainly not uninteresting.[55] Examinations of the immense literature which came to be available
in printed form might be very revealing regarding the cause of the eventual
eclipse of medieval logic in general and the theory of consequences in
particular.

53. Burley 1955, p. 203: 'Antecedens cum aliquo addito infert consequens cum eodem
    addito ... Cum igitur, quidquid sequitur ad consequens, sequitur ad antecedens, oportet quod
    quidquid sequitur ad consequens cum aliquo addito, sequitur ad antecedens cum eodem addito.'
54. For a comprehensive study of Burley see Uña Juárez 1978.
55. Cf. Ashworth 1974, esp. pp. 118–186. For activities in this field in Spain see Muñoz Delgado 1964
    and his numerous other works. See also Ashworth's contribution to this volume.

16

OBLIGATIONS:
A. FROM THE BEGINNING TO
THE EARLY FOURTEENTH CENTURY

Introduction

Perhaps one of the last really obscure areas of medieval logic is contained in the scholastic work on 'obligations'. We know something about the authors and the contents of scholastic treatises on obligations (De obligationibus), and we think that these treatises came to be a standard, perhaps even an important part of medieval logic; but we do not yet fully understand the nature of the material contained in them. We are unclear about the function and purpose of obligations and its significance for other parts of medieval logic; and we have only a sketchy notion of the rich and complicated development of obligations from its beginnings in the late twelfth or early thirteenth centuries to the end of the scholastic period. There are as many guesses about the purpose and function of obligations as there are scholars who have written on the subject: it has been described variously as anything from ingenious schoolboy exercises[1] to primitive axiomatised logic.[2] My own account of obligations will emerge in the course of this chapter.

Historical survey

Even in the twelfth century, there is some use of terminology associated with obligations in discussion of disputation,[3] and in some treatises from this period either disputation or obligations themselves are connected with fallacies or sophismata.[4] In the first half of the thirteenth century, in the

---

1. Weisheipl 1956, p. 150. For a brief survey of contemporary literature on obligations, see Spade 1977.
2. Boehner 1952, pp. 14–15.
3. *Excerpta Norimbergensia*, for example, says that a disputation consists of opposition and response (De Rijk 1962–7, II.2, p. 127; cf. also pp. 125–6 and II. 1, pp. 155–60); and *Ars Emmerana* explains that disputation has three parts: *positio*, opposition, and response (De Rijk 1962–7, II.2, p. 148). The thirteenth-century treatises edited by De Rijk tend to make the same point (cf. De Rijk 1974, p. 117.8–9 and 1975, pp. 26.1–27.26).
4. *Excerpta Norimbergensia* discusses disputation in its section on the sophistical art, where fallacies are also discussed. It divides disputation into two kinds, the science of argument and the science of *redargutio*, which is opposing and responding; and it claims that all species of sophismata fall under

work of the terminists,[5] the investigation of fallacies tends to contain a long discussion of disputation, and one of the species of disputation discussed there has as its goal *redargutio*: the forced denial of something previously granted or the granting of something previously denied in one and the same disputation – very similar to the stated goal of obligations in, for example, Walter Burley.[6] So there seems to have been some early connection between interest in fallacies or sophismata and interest in obligations; but we are not yet in a position to trace the early history of this material, and anything definite about the origin of treatises on obligations must await further identification and analysis of the relevant early texts.

It is clear that obligations existed in some form in the thirteenth century. For the second half of the thirteenth century, L. M. de Rijk mentions three authors in whose work we find evidence of obligations: Godfrey of Fontaines, John Duns Scotus, and Roger Marston;[7] and we can add Boethius of Dacia to this list.[8] With some reservations, Romuald Green has argued that one of the treatises on obligations edited in his dissertation *An Introduction to the Logical Treatise "De Obligationibus"* [9] should be attributed to William of Sherwood;[10] De Rijk, dismissing Green's reservations, has claimed that the treatise in question is indisputably by Sherwood.[11] If this attribution is correct, then we have at least one complete, interesting treatise on obligations from the first half of the thirteenth century. But apart from Green's own reservations, which De Rijk seems correct to set aside, there are other serious worries about the attribution of this treatise to Sherwood, worries to which De Rijk has not addressed himself in claiming that the treatise is definitely by Sherwood. Careful consideration of these

this science of opposing (De Rijk 1962–7, II.2, pp. 130–2). *Tractatus Sorbonnensis de petitionibus contrariorum* divides all sophismata into those which depend on a sophistical *locus* (fallacies proper) and those that depend on a hidden incompatiblity, which is how this treatise seems to understand obligations (De Rijk 1976, p. 43).

5. See Peter of Spain's *Tractatus* (De Rijk 1972, pp. 94ff.) and Lambert of Auxerre's *Logica* (1971, pp. 142ff.); cf. also William of Sherwood's *Introductiones in logicam* (1937, p. 86).

6. Walter Burley, *Tractatus de obligationibus* (Green forthcoming), 0.01. Because the published version of Green's work will not be available until sometime in 1981, I have based my citations on the texts as edited in the revised version of Green's dissertation, made available by the Franciscan Institute. References to the introductory chapters of Green's book are given as 'Intro.: [plus chapter number]'; references to the edition of Burley use Green's paragraph numbers. I am grateful to Father Gedeon Gál and to Professor Paul Spade for helping me obtain a copy of the typescript.

7. De Rijk 1974, p. 95, n. 11.

8. Cf. Boethius of Dacia 1976, pp. 329.4–331.46.

9. Green forthcoming; see n. 6 above.

10. Green forthcoming, Intro.: Chapter V.

11. De Rijk 1976.

worries, together with the manuscript evidence, makes it seem altogether possible that what we really have in the putative Sherwood treatise is an early treatise on obligations by Walter Burley.[12] If that is so, then Burley wrote two treatises on obligations, just as he wrote two versions of *De puritate artis logicae*: a first, brief treatise, which is now associated with Sherwood in the literature, and a second, more developed treatise, probably written around 1302.[13]

De Rijk has edited four short anonymous treatises on obligations from the thirteenth century: (a) *Tractatus Emmeranus de falsi positione*, (b) *Tractatus Emmeranus de impossibili positione*,[14] (c) *Obligationes Parisienses*,[15] and (d) *Tractatus Sorbonnensis de petitionibus contrariorum*.[16] De Rijk ventures no guess concerning the date of treatise (d); it may stem from any time in the thirteenth century. Treatise (c) De Rijk dates by internal evidence, on the basis of a comparison with the putative Sherwood obligations; because it is considerably more primitive than the work ascribed to Sherwood, he assigns (c) to the beginning of the thirteenth century.[17] If the treatise ascribed to Sherwood is not in fact his, however, then the dating of treatise (c) will have to be reconsidered also. Treatises (a) and (b) De Rijk dates on the basis of the similarity in content between the two and a reference in (b) to a thesis of the 'Adamites' (namely, that from the impossible anything follows). De Rijk identifies the Adamites as followers of Adam Parvipontanus; and he claims that since their thesis was still in dispute in treatise (b), that treatise could not have been written later than the 1220s.[18] He is mistaken in thinking that the thesis is in dispute in treatise (b);[19] but perhaps all he needs for his claim is the attribution in treatise (b) of this thesis to the Adamites (provided, of course, that his identification of the Adamites as followers of Adam Parvipontanus is correct). The content of treatises (a), (b), and (c) is much less advanced than that of the putative Sherwood obligations; but none of these anonymous treatises has been carefully studied yet.

From the fourteenth century onwards, scholastic work on obligations proliferates and diversifies. In what follows, I will concentrate on the first

---

12. Spade and Stump forthcoming.
13. Green forthcoming, Intro.: Chapter V.
14. De Rijk 1974.
15. De Rijk 1975.
16. De Rijk 1976.
17. De Rijk 1975, p. 26.
18. De Rijk 1974, p. 102.
19. Stump 1980, n. 12.

decades of the fourteenth century; a discussion of obligations in the succeeding period is contained in Part B of this chapter.

Walter Burley

The putative Sherwood and the authentic Burley treatises on obligations
differ only in the fulness of discussion, in the number of species of obligations considered, and in minor details of organisation or of content. In
general, the organisation, the approach taken, and the theory of obligations are the same in the two treatises; and even the wording, the
examples, and the order of their discussion are in many cases the same. I will
look in detail at Burley's treatise, then, leaving the putative Sherwood
obligations to one side; but much of what is said here about Burley applies
to the putative Sherwood also. Burley's treatise, stemming from the
beginning of the fourteenth century, constitutes a representative account
of obligations in an early stage of their development, before the subtle shifts
of emphasis in the work of Richard Kilvington,[20] one of the earliest of the
Oxford Calculators, and before the enormous changes in obligations
introduced by or represented in later Oxford Calculators such as Roger
Swineshead[21] and other later fourteenth-century logicians. Consequently,
Burley's treatise is fundamental for an understanding of obligations in the
fourteenth century.

As is true in general of obligations treatises, Burley's work is set in the
context of dialectical disputation, in the highly structured and stylised form
the scholastics inherited from Aristotle's *Topics* via Boethius.[22] The scholastics themselves tend to attribute the source for their work on the
obligations to one or another or both of two Aristotelian passages.[23] The
first, from Topics VIII 3 (159ª15–24), says that the primary job of the
respondent in a disputation is to answer in such a way that anything
impossible which the respondent is compelled to defend is the fault of the
position he maintains rather than the fault of his defence of that position.
The second, from *Prior Analytics* I 13 (32ª18–20), says that from the possible
nothing impossible follows. These two quotations together provide the
theoretical foundation for obligations. If the respondent in a disputation

20. Richard Kilvington forthcoming. I am grateful to Norman Kretzmann for calling my attention
    to the material on obligations in Kilvington's *Sophismata*.
21. Spade 1977; see also Part B of this Chapter.
22. Cf. Stump 1978, pp. 159–204.
23. Green forthcoming, Intro.: Chapter II.

adopts a position which is possible and is subsequently compelled to maintain something impossible (something logically incompatible with the position adopted or something impossible in its own right), then he has failed in his job as respondent. Nothing impossible follows from the possible; so, because it is possible, the position adopted by the respondent does not entail anything impossible. If the repondent is then logically compelled to maintain contradictory propositions, it must be because he has made logical mistakes in responding, so that the impossible, which is not entailed by the original position the respondent adopts, is entailed by the respondent's faulty defence of that position. The job of the interlocutor, called the 'opponent' in obligations disputations, is to trap a respondent into maintaining contradictories, and the job of the respondent is to avoid such traps. Burley's own main interest is in what might be called paradoxes of disputation. A paradox of disputation occurs when, after a seemingly unimpeachable exchange between an opponent and his respondent, the opponent proposes a proposition which the respondent can neither grant nor deny because either the granting or the denial leads immediately to a contradiction. The heart of Burley's treatise is a long series of such paradoxes, each accompanied by his solution to it.

Burley's treatise begins with an ordered division of obligations into six species.[24] In every obligations disputation, the disputation opens with something put forward by the opponent, which the respondent obligates himself to take a certain attitude towards. The variations on what the opponent can propose and on the attitudes the respondent can adopt constitute the species of obligations. One is obligated to an act or to a disposition, Burley says;[25] and in either case, the obligation covers either what is complex (that is, a proposition), or what is non-complex. If one is obligated to an act and the obligation covers what is non-complex, the species of obligation is *petitio*. If one is obligated to an act and the obligation covers what is complex, we have the species *sit verum*. If one is obligated to a disposition with respect to what is non-complex, we have *institutio*. And if one is obligated to a disposition with respect to what is complex, there are three possibilities: one can maintain the proposition at issue as true, as false, or as uncertain. These three give us the last three species of obligation, namely, *positio*, *depositio*, and *dubitatio*. We can represent Burley's schema in the following way, then:

24. Green forthcoming, Burley 0.02.
25. 'Obligatio sic dividitur: aut obligat ad actum aut ad habitum' (*ibid.*).

	Act	Disposition
Non-complex	*petitio*	*institutio*
Complex	*sit verum*	*positio* *depositio* *dubitatio*

Burley discusses these six species of obligations one by one, beginning with the two types in which the obligation covers what is non-complex, and taking first each time the case in which one is obligated to a disposition. So he considers first *institutio*, then *petitio*, then *positio*, *depositio*, and *dubitatio*, and finally *sit verum*. His main interest, however, is clearly in *positio*, and his examination of *positio* alone constitutes more than three-fifths of the entire treatise. I will say something briefly about these various species of obligations and then follow Burley in concentrating on *positio*.

Institutio is a new imposition for some utterance, giving it a new signification.[26] Burley's first example is this: 'let "A" signify a donkey in a true proposition, a man in a false proposition, and the disjunction a-man-or-not-a-man in an uncertain proposition [i.e., a proposition whose truth-value is not known to the respondent].'[27] Many cases of *institutio*, like this one, resemble or just are *insolubilia*. *Petitio* is the species of obligation in which the opponent asks or obligates the respondent to *do* something.[28] The first proposition an opponent in *petitio* puts forward and obligates his respondent to grant is not an ordinary third-person proposition such as 'Socrates is running', but rather a second-person proposition regarding an ordinary proposition – for example, 'You respond affirmatively to the proposition "Socrates is running"' or 'You deny that Socrates is running', or something of the sort which makes reference to an *action* on the part of the respondent with a proposition as its object. *Sit verum*, on the other hand, is the species of obligations in which the main proposition at issue always includes mention of the respondent's knowing, his not knowing, or his being in doubt.[29] So, for example, the first proposition put forward by the opponent in a case of *sit verum* is not 'Socrates is running' or even 'You grant that Socrates is running', but 'You know that Socrates is running', or 'You do not know that Socrates is running', or 'You are in doubt whether

---

26. *Ibid.*, Burley 0.02 and 1.01.
27. *Ibid.*, Burley 1.03.
28. *Ibid.*, Burley 2.01 and 2.02.
29. *Ibid.*, Burley 6.01–6.03.

Socrates is running'. Burley gives this variety of obligations short shrift. But it may be that it played an important role in stimulating the investigation of epistemic verbs in the later fourteenth-century treatises *De scire et dubitare* and in the sections of the treatises *De sensu composito et diviso* that deal with epistemic verbs, where there are sometimes strong, explicit connections with obligations. For example, Paul of Pergula in his treatise on the compounded and divided sense concludes with a discussion of epistemic verbs, which he ends by saying that this material cannot be perfectly understood except after a study of obligations, which is a necessary prerequisite, for 'otherwise no one will understand what is said in this material [on the compounded and divided sense in the context of epistemic verbs]'.[30] *Depositio* and *dubitatio* are just like *positio*, except that while the respondent is obligated to maintain the proposition that is the *positum* as true, he is obligated to maintain the *depositum* as false and the *dubitatum* as uncertain (of unknown truth-value).[31] Consequently, the basic rules of obligations for *positio*, which apply to *petitio*, *institutio*, and *sit verum* as well, do not apply to *depositio* and *dubitatio*, each of which has its own set of basic rules.[32]

Burley begins his discussion of *positio*, as he does his discussion of obligations at the opening of the treatise, with a division into species.[33] The various species of *positio* are determined by considering the sorts of propositions which can be the *positum*. Such propositions can be possible or impossible, simple or composite. Those that are composite can consist in two propositions joined by a conjunction (conjoined *positio*) or a disjunction (indeterminate *positio*), or they can consist in propositions with attached conditions – for example, 'If you respond affirmatively to the first *propositum*, let the *positum* be "You run", and otherwise not'[34] (dependent *positio*). This last species of *positio* is divided into two further sub-groups, depending on the nature of the condition attached to the *positum*. If the condition specifies that after a certain time or a certain point in the disputation, the *positum* ceases to be the *positum*, we have *positio cadens*; and if the condition specifies that after an interval or at a certain point it

30. Paul of Pergula 1961, p. 158.307–15. I am grateful to Norman Kretzmann for calling my attention to this material.

31. The rules for *dubitatio* bear at least some resemblance to three-valued logic; and scholastic attempts to solve the problem of foreknowledge and free will by using three-valued logic are sometimes couched in obligations-terminology. See, for example, Ferdinand of Cordoba, in Baudry 1950, p. 145. I am grateful to Anthony Kenny for the reference.

32. Green forthcoming, Burley 4.01ff. and 5.01ff.

33. *Ibid.*, Burley 3.01.

34. *Ibid.*, Burley 3.148.

becomes the *positum* again, then we have *positio renascens*. So Burley has in mind something like this division of *positio*:

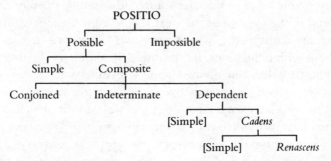

For *positio*, Burley gives three fundamental rules of obligations:[35]

(1) Everything which follows from (a) the *positum*, with (b) a granted proposition or propositions, or with (c) the opposite(s) of a correctly denied proposition or propositions, known to be such, must be granted.
(2) Everything which is incompatible with (a) the *positum*, with (b) a granted proposition or propositions, or with (c) the opposite(s) of a correctly denied proposition or propositions, known to be such, must be denied.
(3) Everything which is irrelevant (*impertinens*) [that is, every proposition to which neither rule (1) nor rule (2) applies] must be granted or denied or doubted according to its own quality, that is, according to the quality it has in relation to us [i.e., if we *know* it to be true, we grant it; if we *know* it to be false, we deny it; if we *do not know* it to be true or *do not know* it to be false, we doubt it].

These rules, together with the original definitions of the basic species of obligations, are to obligations what the rules of tennis are to tennis: they constitute the enterprise, making it what it is and differentiating it from its near relatives. The way in which the rules and definitions give structure to obligations can be seen in the examples which follow.

In general, in discussing *positio*, Burley proceeds by a successive consideration of paradoxes. A paradox begins with what Burley calls a *casus*,[36] which is a stipulation (frequently altogether fictional) about the nature of reality outside the obligational disputation. The *casus* is followed by the *positum*, which is in some way or other at odds with the *casus*. For example, a typical *casus* might stipulate that Socrates and Plato are black, and the *positum* will be that Socrates is white. After the *positum* a series of propositions are put forward by the opponent (the *proposita*), to each of which the respondent must respond in a way governed by the three basic rules of

35. *Ibid.*, Burley 3.14–16.
36. *Ibid.*, Burley 3.03.

obligations. At some point, the opponent puts forward a *propositum* to which the respondent can give no correct answer, because any answer he gives involves him in contradiction, because it commits him either to assigning contradictory truth-values to the same proposition or to assigning the same truth-value to contradictory propositions. At that point the disputation is over; the respondent has lost. Burley then offers a solution to the respondent's difficulty.

With that background, I want to look at some typical examples of *positio*. Consider the following case:

And let this be posited: 'You are in Rome or that you are in Rome is to be granted.' Then let this be put forward: 'That you are in Rome is to be granted.' This is false and irrelevant, and therefore it must be denied. Then let this be put forward: 'That you are in Rome follows from the *positum* and the opposite of something correctly denied.' This is necessary because this conditional is necessary: 'If it is the case either that you are in Rome or that that you are in Rome is to be granted, and that you are in Rome is not to be granted, then you are in Rome.' Once this is granted, [namely], 'That you are in Rome follows from the *positum* and the opposite of something correctly denied', then let this be put forward: 'That you are in Rome is to be granted.' If you grant [this], you have granted and denied the same thing, and therefore [you have responded] badly. If you deny it, the disputation is over; you have denied something which follows by a rule [of obligations]. Because if the rule is good, then this follows: 'That you are in Rome follows from the *positum* and the opposite of something correctly denied; therefore, that you are in Rome is to be granted.'[37]

We can show the structure of this example in this way.

	Opponent		Respondent	Reason
(1)	You are in Rome or that you are in Rome is to be granted.	(1a) T	(1b)	(1) is the *positum*
(2)	That you are in Rome is to be granted.	(2a) F	(2b)	(2) is irrelevant and false
(3)	That you are in Rome follows from the *positum* and the opposite of something correctly denied.	(3a) T	(3b)	(3) follows from the truth of (1) and the falsity of (2)
(4)	That you are in Rome is to be granted.	(4a) —		

37. 'Item, probatur quod non omne sequens ex posito et opposito bene negati sit concedendum. Et ponatur ista: tu es Romae vel "te esse Romae" est concedendum. Deinde, proponatur: "te esse Romae" est concedendum. Haec est falsa et impertinens, igitur neganda. Deinde, proponatur: "te esse Romae" sequitur ex posito et opposito bene negati. Haec est necessaria, quia haec conditionalis est necessaria: si tu es Romae vel "te esse Romae" est concedendum, sed "te esse Romae" non est concedendum, igitur tu es Romae. Concessa ista '"te esse Romae" sequitur ex posito et opposito bene negati', proponatur ista: "te esse Romae" est concedendum. Si concedas, idem concessisti et negasti, igitur male. Si neges, cedat tempus, negasti sequens per regulam. Quia, si regula sit bona, tunc sequitur: "te esse Romae" sequitur ex posito et opposito bene negati, igitur "te esse Romae" est concedendum.' *Ibid.*, Burley 3.21.

Trouble arises for the respondent at (4a), on Burley's view, in this way. The respondent cannot grant (4) since he has already denied the same proposition at (2a). On the other hand, he cannot deny (4) either. From (3) it follows that you are in Rome; and if it follows, it must be granted, and so (4) is true.

Burley's solution to this paradox looks bizarre. On his view,[38]

It is said that this should be denied: 'That you are in Rome follows from the *positum* and the opposite of something correctly denied.' Nor is this [(3)] necessary. Even if it were necessary that it follows from the posited disjunction with the opposite of one of the disjuncts that you are in Rome, nonetheless it is not necessary that this disjunction be posited.

On the face of it, then, Burley is saying that (3) is to be denied because it is not necessary, and his reason for claiming that (3) is not necessary is that one of the premisses it is derived from, namely, (1), is not necessary. But in the first place, there is no obligations rule to the effect that we must deny any propositions which are not necessary. And in the second place, if we had to deny as not necessary any proposition which followed from the *positum* on the fallacious grounds that it was not necessary to posit this particular *positum* and therefore the *positum* was not necessary, we would have demolished rule (1) of obligations and with it the whole precarious structure of obligations.

But I think we do not have to read Burley's solution as quite so bizarre. If we look again at (3) and the reasons given for granting (3), we should see that there is an important confusion there. Let p stand for 'You are in Rome' and q for 'That you are in Rome is to be granted'. Then what we have in steps (1)–(3) of this argument is this:

Opponent	Respondent	Reason
(1′) p ∨ q	(1′a) T	
(2′) q	(2′a) F	
(3′) p follows from the *positum* and the opposite of something correctly denied.	(3′a) T	(3′b) (3) follows from the truth of (1) and the falsity of (2)

Now (3′) does *not* follow from the truth of (1′) and the falsity of (2′), as (3′b) alleges; p follows (as Burley acknowledges), but (3′) does not. Suppose we then consider (3) irrelevant and judge it on its own merits.

38. 'Dicitur quod haec est neganda: ' "te esse Romae" sequitur ex posito et opposito bene negati'. Nec haec est necessaria. Et, si sit necessarium "te esse Romae" sequi ex disiunctiva, quae ponitur, cum opposito alterius partis, tamen non est necessarium istam disiunctivam poni.' *Ibid.*, Burley 3.22.

According to Burley, we ought to judge it false. If (3) had read 'That you are in Rome follows from the conjunction of this disjunction – namely, "You are in Rome or that you are in Rome is to be granted" with the denial of the second disjunct', then Burley would, I think, agree that (3) had to be granted. But (3) does not read that way; and if we are considering (3) as it stands, on its own merits, then Burley seems to think we should deny it because the phrase 'from the *positum*' *need* not refer to the particular disjunction which just happens to be the *positum* in this particular case of obligations. It *could* refer to some other *positum*; but unless it refers to *this* one, (3) is false. Therefore, on Burley's view, it is a mistake to grant (3).

This second and, I hope, more charitable reading of Burley turns what was an unintelligible solution into an intelligible red herring, I think. Because suppose that we deny (3), on the rather dubious grounds that it is irrelevant and false in virtue of the ambiguous phrase 'from the *positum*'. Then let (4) be put forward again. Remember that the reasoning for *granting* (4) in the paradox went like this: (a) that you are in Rome follows from the *positum* and the opposite of something correctly denied; therefore (c) that you are in Rome is to be granted. And what Burley attacks is *not* the inference from (a) to (c), but the truth of premiss (a). He seems to have in mind the mistaken notion that if (a) is false, (c) is false – hence we can deny (4) and the paradox is solved. But, of course, he has not solved the paradox by such means since (c) can be true even if (a) is false. Furthermore, if Burley is willing to accept the *inference* from (a) to (c), we can show him that on his own views (c) must be true. The inference from (a) to (c) depends on accepting as valid the inference from (b) 'You are in Rome' to (c) 'That you are in Rome must be granted'; and there is some reason for accepting the inference from (b) to (c) in an obligations disputation. If the proposition 'You are in Rome' is true in an obligations disputation, it is to be granted. And so in an obligations disputation, the inference from p to 'p is to be granted' is a good one. Or, to put it another way, if the respondent must grant p, he must also grant that he must grant p.

Now consider step (4) of the argument, supposing for the moment that we have accepted Burley's argument and have denied (3) for the reasons he gives. Even with the denial of (3), however, from the truth of (1) and the falsity of (2), it follows that you are in Rome. And so, given the validity of the inference from (b) to (c), from 'You are in Rome' it follows that 'You are in Rome' is to be granted. Hence even with the denial of (3), we are committed, on Burley's own views, to the truth of (4). And so, even if we give Burley all he wants, the falsity of (3) and the validity of the inference from (a) to (c), we can demonstrate that the paradox remains. The respondent is committed to the truth of (4) although he has correctly denied the same proposition at (2a).

The real solution to this paradox depends on considering at the outset the relations between the two propositions 'p', 'You are in Rome', and 'q', 'That you are in Rome is to be granted'. It will help in this discussion to take 'is true' as meaning 'is true in an obligational disputation' or 'must be granted by a respondent', and analogously for 'is false'. If p is true, q is true, as I have already argued. And we can also show the converse, that if q is true, p is true. If you grant q, you are granting that p is to be granted. But if you grant that p must be granted, you cannot consistently deny p, and so you must also grant p. Hence, if q is true, so is p. Consequently, p and q are logically equivalent. Now in the obligations paradox we are considering, the *positum*, which we are obligated to maintain as true, is a disjunction of p and q. But since p and q are equivalent, the disjunction can be true only in case both p and q are true, because

$$[(p \leftrightarrow q) \land (p \lor q)] \to (p \land q)$$

Hence, in this case, it is a mistake to consider (2) in the schematisation as irrelevant. In fact, it follows from the *positum* and the implicit logical relationship between p and q. And so (2) ought to be granted. In this way, I think, the paradox is really solved; or, more accurately, in this way the paradox fails to arise in the first place.

Finally, for historical purposes,[39] it is worthwhile considering again Burley's solution to the paradox on my second interpretation of his

---

39. It is also worth pointing out that Green takes this paradox to be an example of disagreement between Burley's obligations and the putative Sherwood obligations because, he says. (Intro.: Chapter V), Burley denies what 'Sherwood' concedes, namely, that the proposition 'You must grant that you are in Rome' entails the proposition 'You are in Rome'. 'Sherwood' in the passage Green has in mind (*Ibid.*, Sherwood 1.56 and 1.58) does address just that issue, and he does grant the validity of that inference. Burley is, of course, not addressing that issue at all in this paradox of his. He is, as we have seen, concerned instead with the proposition 'That you are in Rome follows from the *positum* and the opposite of something correctly denied.' And his concern with this proposition and his overall purpose in considering this paradox stem from a worry over the acceptability of the obligations rule that whatever follows from the *positum* with the opposite of something correctly denied must be granted (cf. Burley 3.21). But in so far as we have any evidence at all from this paradox about Burley's attitude toward the inference from (c) to (b) – '(c) That you are in Rome is to be granted; therefore, (b) you are in Rome' – it seems plain that he would accept it, because the sorts of reasons for accepting the converse inference from (b) to (c) – '(b) You are in Rome; therefore, (c) that you are in Rome is to be granted' – also support the inference from (c) to (b). And, as we saw, Burley clearly does accept the inference from (b) to (c). So this paradox of Burley's in fact shows us a *similarity* between the two treatises, rather than a difference, as Green thinks.

solution. On that interpretation, Burley is taking (3) as irrelevant; and so, by the obligations rule for irrelevant premisses, he considers (3) on its own merits. But the way in which he does so suggests that he is giving the rule for irrelevant premisses an extreme interpretation (although his interpretation of it may well have been typical for the period). Burley's decision to judge (3) false stems apparently from his feeling that, after all, the phrase 'from the *positum*' which occurs in (3) could refer to just any *positum*. But, of course, it cannot be taken to refer indifferently in that way if we remember that (3) is occurring within *this* obligations disputation. To feel the force of the ambiguity of the phrase 'from the *positum*', it is necessary to wrench (3) out of its context in this disputation and to consider it altogether apart from the disputation in which it occurs. It is as if Burley took the obligations rule for irrelevant premisses to read in this way: If a proposition does not follow from or is not compatible with what has been previously maintained, it is irrelevant; and if it is irrelevant, then ignore everything said in the disputation so far — in fact, ignore the fact that you are in an obligations disputation — and judge the irrelevant proposition as you would if you had never even heard of obligations disputation. That extreme interpretation of the rule for irrelevant propositions has significant implications for the whole function of obligations, as we will see more clearly when we consider the changes Richard Kilvington makes in this rule.

But as for Burley, the function of obligations at the stage of development represented by his treatise and that attributed to Sherwood can be summarised in this way.[40] Obligations in these treatises is a complicated set of rules for consequences or inferences which are set in a disputational context, where the disputational context makes a difference to the evaluation of the inferences. Frequently, complications for the evaluation of an obligations consequence arise because there is a reference in the premisses themselves to the evaluator of those premisses or to an action by the evaluator (such as granting or denying something) within the disputation. In the example above, for instance, the validity of the crucial inference from (b) 'You are in Rome' to (c) 'That you are in Rome must be granted [by you]' depends on the disputational context and the references in the inference to the evaluator of it. The inference 'p; therefore, Socrates must grant p', or even 'Socrates is in Rome; therefore Socrates must grant that

---

40. For detailed argument for this conclusion, see Stump 1980 and 'Obligations according to Walter Burley' in Stump forthcoming c.

he is in Rome' is invalid. Socrates may have been brought to Rome while he was in a coma, for example, or while in the hands of kidnappers who deceive him about his location, and so on; and so it can be true that Socrates is in Rome without its being true that Socrates must grant that he is in Rome. But we need not have a reference in the premises to the evaluator of those premises in order to generate the sort of difficulties of interest to medieval logicians working on obligations. Other characteristics of disputation, such as the passage of time, will do just as well. Consider, for example, this very simple disputation argument, which Burley presents in connection with a different issue (namely, to show that we must sometimes and without penalty grant an impossible proposition if it has *become* impossible in the course of the disputation):[41]

'For example, let A be the instant at which the *positum* is posited. And let it be posited that it is A. Then let [this] be put forward: "It is A". This should be granted since it is the *positum* and yet it is impossible *per accidens. ...*'

Because A designates the instant at which the *positum* is posited, the proposition 'It is A' is true only at the instant at which the *positum* is posited. At any step of the argument after the first, the proposition 'It is A' is not only false but impossible, since it maintains in effect that an instant which is past (namely, instant A at any time after step (1) of the argument) is present. Nonetheless, the proposition 'It is A' is the *positum*, and so by the basic rules of obligations it must be granted whenever it is put forward in the disputation. And so this paradox arises solely in virtue of the passage of time, which must be taken serious account of in an obligations disputation, as it need not be or even should not be in a straightforward evaluation of inferences outside the context of disputation.

What we have in Burley's obligations, then, as in the putative Sherwood obligations, is a concern with special sorts of difficulties in evaluating consequences or inferences as a result of the disputational context in which the inferences occur. Given the enormous scholastic emphasis on disputation, it is not surprising that scholastics would develop an interest in coping with inferences made tricky by the peculiarities of the disputational context. But any practical concerns they may have had in connection with obligations seem to have been quickly swamped by theoretical interest in the complexities of obligations inferences for their own sake.

---

41. 'Verbi gratia: sit A: instans in quo ponitur positum. Et ponatur A esse. Et proponatur: A est. Hoc debet concedi, quia est positum. Et tamen est impossibile per accidens, nec est hoc inconveniens.' *Ibid.*, Burley 3.59.

Richard Kilvington

A clear and historically significant example of theoretical, philosophical interest in obligations can be seen in the forty-seventh of Richard Kilvington's *Sophismata*,[42] written around 1325, more than twenty years after Burley's obligations. Kilvington's S47 is a sophisma and not a standard paradox of disputation, and so it has a somewhat different form from the problems presented by Burley. It consists of a hypothesis and the sophisma sentence, which is to be proved or disproved. The hypothesis is a conjunction of conditionals:[43]

(H)   If the king is seated, you know that the king is seated; if the king is not seated, you know that the king is not seated.

The sophisma sentence is 'You know that the king is seated'. The hypothesis, together with the tautologous premiss 'Either the king is seated or the king is not seated' entails this disjunction:

(HD)   (i) You know that the king is seated, or (ii) you know that the king is not seated.

Now *in fact*, because you are in Oxford and the King is in Westminster, this conjunction is true:

(C)   (i) You do not know that the king is seated, and (ii) you do not know that the king is not seated.

The entire conjunction (C) is plainly incompatible with (HD), the disjunction entailed by the stipulated hypothesis in S47 (the hypothesis here plays the same role as the *positum* in Burley's obligations). But neither conjunct of (C) taken separately is incompatible with (HD); each conjunct is in fact irrelevant in respect of (HD). And the basic problem of the sophisma arises from these relationships between (C) and its conjuncts, on the one hand, and (HD), on the other. (HD) entails that (C) cannot be true and, consequently, that one or another of the conjuncts of (C) must be false; but it does not entail that one particular conjunct must be false. Both the Proof and the Disproof for this sophisma depend on that fact.

The Proof proceeds in this way. We posit (HD), which must be accepted. Then we put forward (C) (ii); this is irrelevant, and judged on its

---

42. For a full exposition of this sophisma of Kilvington's, see Kretzmann's commentary on it in *Richard Kilvington* forthcoming.

43. 'Supposito isto casu, quod si rex sedeat, tu scias regem sedere; et si rex non sedeat, tu scias regem non sedere.' All citations of Kilvington's text are from Kretzmann's edition in *Richard Kilvington* forthcoming.

own merits, outside the context of the sophisma, it is true. But (HD) and (C) (ii) together entail (HD) (i), the sophisma sentence; and so the sophisma sentence is proved. The Disproof works in precisely the same way, except that the second step is (C) (i), instead of (C) (ii). The conclusion derived is (HD) (ii), and this entails the denial of (HD) (i), which is the sophisma sentence.[44] From a possible proposition (namely, (HD)), then, Kilvington has by the rules of obligations derived contradictory propositions. He considers a variety of attempts to solve this problem, and he shows effectively that none of them succeeds. Consequently, what his Proof and Disproof show us is an incoherence in the basic rules of obligations, an incoherence apparently unrecognised during the stage of obligations represented by Burley. The trouble in Kilvington's example is brought about by the basic rule of obligations which has to do with irrelevant propositions. The rule brings it about that a second and different set of criteria for determining the truth-value of propositions is sometimes brought into play in assessing the premisses of obligations arguments. In general, in obligations disputations we assess the truth or falsity of propositions proposed by considering them with regard to the false *positum* and other previously granted or denied propositions, if there are any. But when a proposition is irrelevant, we assess it instead by considering only the state of affairs actually obtaining in the world as it now is (or the state of affairs stipulated in the *casus*). If we construct a conjunction (or disjunction) in just the right way, we can ensure that the individual conjuncts (or disjuncts) are assessed by criteria different from those used to assess the truth-value of the whole conjunction (or disjunction) if the conjuncts (or disjuncts) are put forward separately at the same step of the argument as the conjunction (or disjunction). So, in S47, for example, either conjunct of (C), put forward as the second step of the argument, is irrelevant; consequently, assessed outside the sophisma context, either conjunct is true. But the whole conjunction, put forward at step (2), is not irrelevant; consequently, assessed within the sophisma context, it is false, which entails that at least one of the conjuncts is false.

---

44. 'Tunc probatur sophisma sic. Tu scis regem sedere vel tu scis regem non sedere, sed tu non scis regem non sedere; igitur tu scis regem sedere. Maior patet per casum, et minor patet quia est vera non repugnans. Quod patet, nam ista non repugnant: "Si rex sedet, tu scis regem sedere; et si rex non sedet, tu scis regem non sedere" et "Tu non scis regem non sedere".

Ad oppositum arguitur sic. Tu scis regem non sedere; igitur tu non scis regem sedere. Antecedens patet, quia tu scis regem sedere vel tu scis regem non sedere, sed tu non scis regem sedere; igitur tu scis regem non sedere. Et per consequens sophisma est falsum. Et minor patet ut prius, quia est vera et impertinens.'

Faced with the apparently insoluble paradox of S47, and the incoherence in the rules for obligations which S47 brings to light, Kilvington revises the rule for irrelevant propositions. The Kilvingtonian revision in effect transforms the traditional rule into this:

(K) If a proposition is neither entailed by nor incompatible with what has been previously maintained in the disputation, it is irrelevant; and an irrelevant proposition is to be replied to on the basis of the way the world would be if things were the way the *positum* says they are.[45]

The traditional rule for irrelevant propositions found in Burley's treatise interrupted the obligations disputation and obliterated all its preceding steps every time an irrelevant proposition was to be evaluated. (K) forbids such a disconnected train of reasoning and ensures that the *positum* will exert its influence over all succeeding propositions, including those propositions neither entailed by nor incompatible with the *positum*.

By using this new rule for irrelevant propositions, Kilvington solves the original difficulty of S47. In accordance with (K), the second step of both the Proof and the Disproof must now be evaluated on the supposition that the hypothesis is true. On this supposition, what we must conclude is not that the proposition (C) (ii) 'You do not know that the king is not seated' (the second step of the Proof) is plainly true. Rather, if the world were the way the hypothesis says it is, you would not know whether (C) (ii) is true or false; that is, you would not know whether or not you know that the king is not seated. By the same token, it is not the case that the second step of the Disproof, (C) (i) 'You do not know that the king is seated', is plainly true; given the hypothesis, by (K), you do not know whether or not you know that the king is seated. Kilvington here is apparently reasoning in this way:

(1) If the king is seated, you know that the king is seated; if the king is not seated, you know that the king is not seated. [This is the hypothesis (H).]
(2) You do not know that the king is seated, and you do not know that the king is not seated.
(3) Therefore, you do not know whether you know that the king is seated or whether you know that the king is not seated.

45. Kilvington's formulation of the rule in fact takes into account only those irrelevant propositions which are true outside the context of the sophisma or obligations disputation, but there is no reason to suppose that he would object to spelling out the rule for irrelevant propositions which are false outside the context of the sophisma. 'Si tamen accipiatur iste terminus "impertinens" pro propositione quae nunc est vera et quae non foret vera ex hoc quod ita foret ex parte rei sicut significatur per positum, tunc dico quod ista propositio ' "Tu es Romae" et "Tu es episcopus" sunt similia' est impertinens huic posito, quod est "Tu es Romae". Quia si tu esses Romae et non esses episcopus, haec foret neganda: ' "Tu es Romae" et "Tu es episcopus" sunt similia.' '

Since the hypothesis ascribes to you infallibility regarding the king's position, it must be the case that you know he is seated or you know he is not seated. In view of premiss (2) above, then, what we must conclude is that you do not know which of those alternatives you know; that is, it is possible to know something and yet not know that you know it. The disjunction (HD) can be true, and you can grant it as true, without your thereby being in a position to grant or deny either of the disjuncts; and that is the case the example in S47 illustrates. Consequently, for both the Proof and the Disproof of S47, instead of granting the second step of the argument as irrelevant and true, the respondent should take it as irrelevant in Kilvington's sense and doubt it.[46] Hence, we can neither prove nor disprove the sophisma sentence; and the original paradox is resolved.

What Kilvington has done in his work on S47, by his change in the rule for irrelevant propositions, is to shift the whole purpose of obligations. The new rule (K), when added to the rest of the traditional structure of obligations, shifts the emphasis of obligations away from a consideration of scattered paradoxes arising from difficulties in evaluating certain inferences in disputational contexts and towards a logic of counterfactuals.[47]

William Ockham

Something of the same shift of emphasis, though much less dramatic or historically significant, I think, can be seen in Ockham's work on obligations in his *Summa logicae*, written only a year or so before Kilvington's *Sophismata*.[48] One of the things that apparently interested Ockham most in the study of obligations is the case when the proposition that is the *positum* is an impossible proposition.

Ockham begins his discussion of an impossible proposition in the *positum* in a way that seems puzzling at first glance, by claiming that there is a great difference between an impossible proposition in the *positum* and a consequence composed of impossible propositions.[49] The consequence 'God is

---

46. 'Ad argumentum concedendum est quod tu scis regem sedere vel tu scis regem non sedere. Sed minor coassumpta est dubitanda – scilicet, haec: "Tu non scis regem non sedere". Quia si rex sedet, tu non scis regem non sedere – per casum – et antecedens est dubitandum; igitur consequens est dubitandum.'

47. For a discussion of counterfactual reasoning in connection with this sophisma, see Kretzmann's commentary on it in Richard Kilvington forthcoming.

48. For a fuller discussion of Ockham on obligations, see 'Topics, Consequences, and Obligations in Ockham's *Summa logicae*' in Stump forthcoming c.

49. Ockham 1974a, pp. 739ff. 'Similiter multum refert ponere istam propositionem "Deus non est Deus" et inferre istam consequentiam "si Deus non est, Deus non est Deus"; propter quod ista condicionalis sive consequentia concedenda est et positio non est recipienda, et quandoque positio est recipienda tamquam impossibilis et sustinenda est in positione impossibili. Et tamen

not three persons; therefore God is not God' is a good one, on Ockham's view; it is, in fact, a material consequence, warranted by the seventh of Ockham's general rules of consequences, namely, that anything follows from an impossible proposition. Nonetheless, according to Ockham, if the antecedent of this consequence – 'God is not three persons' – is put in the *positum* a respondent ought to deny the consequent, 'God is not God'.

On the basis of this puzzling claim, Ockham makes two further sets of stipulations about the *positum* when the proposition posited is impossible. In the first place, he maintains that not every impossible proposition can be posited, but only those which do not *manifestly* or *obviously* entail a contradiction. In the second place, not all the rules for *positio* where the proposition posited is possible hold for the positing of an impossible proposition; in particular, not all the rules of consequences hold for cases in which the proposition posited is impossible. No as-of-now consequences or material consequences are acceptable in any obligations disputation where the *positum* is impossible.

This second stipulation makes sense out of the original claim, namely, that although the consequence 'God is not three persons; therefore God is not God' is a good consequence, the consequent is to be denied if the antecedent is posited. The consequence in this case is a material consequence; and if all such consequences are to be rejected in cases where the proposition posited is impossible, then, of course, the respondent cannot maintain that 'God is not God' *follows from* 'God is not three persons'. But why would Ockham stipulate that material consequences are to be rejected in such cases? There are, I think, two reasons – the first practical and the second philosophical – for his stipulation. If we accept the rule that anything follows from an impossible proposition in an obligations disputation where the *positum* is impossible, it will not be possible to have anything but a trivial disputation, because no matter *what* proposition is put to the respondent, it is clear from the outset that the respondent will have to grant it as following from the proposition posited. Hence if we accept this rule of consequences in the context of an obligations disputation, we cannot have a disputation which is of any philosophical interest. Secondly, if we reject this rule of consequences in such obligations and allow only simple, formal consequences, the result *will* be philosophically interesting, because what we will have in such cases then is something very

consequentia seu condicionalis bona est; sicut ista consequentia bona est "Deus non est tres personae, igitur Deus non est Deus"; et tamen antecedens potest recipi in positione impossibili et debet negari consequens' (p. 739.9–15).

roughly similar to a logic of counterfactuals for a restricted class of propositions. The purpose of obligations disputations where the *positum* is impossible is apparently to see what is entailed if one takes as true such propositions as 'God does not exist', 'The Holy Spirit does not proceed from the Son', or 'Man is not capable of laughter'. This enables us to understand Ockham's other stipulation, namely, that impossible propositions which can be used in the *positum* must not manifestly and obviously entail a contradiction. If they did obviously entail a contradiction, the disputation would end quickly in an uninteresting way. The opponent would derive the contradictory propositions entailed by the posited proposition, which the respondent would be forced to grant; and the disputation would be over because the respondent has granted contradictory propositions. Furthermore, even if the opponent agreed to forego such a cheap victory, interesting and rational results are still not likely to follow since all sorts of incompatible propositions are quickly derivable from the impossible proposition in virtue of its obviously entailing contradictories.

Conclusion

We are not yet in a position to assess either the significance of this shift of emphasis in the work of Ockham and Kilvington for later developments in obligations or the historical importance and influence of Kilvington's treatment on subsequent discussions of obligations, though there is some reason to suppose that both were great.[50] But an understanding of Kilvington's influence, as well as of the subsequent changes in scholastic theories of obligations, must wait until a good deal more work has been done on obligations in the fourteenth century.[51]

50. It seems likely that Kilvington's work had some influence on Roger Swineshead's obligations, which was an important source for subsequent changes and developments in obligations (see Part B of this Chapter). I hope to investigate Swineshead's obligations in detail in a forthcoming paper.
51. I am grateful to Norman Kretzmann for numerous helpful comments and suggestions on an earlier draft of this chapter and to John Crossett, whose efforts on my behalf made this work possible.

OBLIGATIONS:
B. DEVELOPMENTS IN
THE FOURTEENTH CENTURY

The old and the new responses

The obligations-literature appears to have entered a new phase with the Oxford Calculators, centred at Merton College in the 1320s and 1330s. Although the Mertonian Thomas Bradwardine seems to have contributed little to the development of obligations,[1] his contemporary Richard Kilvington was more innovative in this regard, in ways described in Part A of this Chapter.

We are in a somewhat better position to assess the contribution of Roger Swineshead to obligations. Swineshead certainly appears to have been part of the intellectual circle with which Kilvington and Bradwardine are associated, and he may well have studied with them.[2] Probably sometime after 1330 and before 1335,[3] Swineshead wrote his pair of treatises on obligations and insolubles.[4] There is reason to speculate that some of the most characteristic features of Swineshead's *Insolubilia* grew out of reflection on Kilvington's *Sophismata*.[5] It is possible that this is true of Swineshead's *Obligationes* as well, but that remains to be established.

Swineshead's *Obligationes* is markedly different from earlier treatises in the genre. So true is this that Robert Fland, writing some time between 1335 and 1370,[6] distinguishes two separate traditions in the obligations-literature. One of these traditions he calls the 'old response' (*antiqua responsio*)[7]; it conforms to the views of Burley, to those of the treatise attributed to William of Sherwood, and to those found in most if not all of the other early treatises.[8] The second tradition Fland calls the 'new re-

---

1. See the list of his works in Weisheipl 1969, pp. 177–83.
2. See Weisheipl 1964, especially p. 237. Roger Swineshead is not to be confused with Richard Swineshead, another of the Oxford calculators.
3. *Ibid.*, pp. 244–7.
4. Edited in Spade 1977 and Spade 1979a.
5. See Chapter 12 above, n. 43.
6. See Spade 1978c, pp. 56–62.
7. Ed. Spade 1980, pars. 13 and 20.
8. See the texts edited in De Rijk 1974–6, and in Green forthcoming.

sponse' (*nova responsio*)[9]; it appears to have originated with Swineshead.

Fland lists two rules as characteristic of the new response.[10] First, it is possible that a copulative (conjunctive) sentence is to be denied, even though both conjuncts have been granted. Second, it is possible that a disjunctive sentence is to be granted, even though both disjuncts have been denied. These rules are in fact to be found combined in Swineshead's second 'conclusion'.[11]

The basis for this remarkable conclusion was a fundamental change in the rules governing a respondent's replies to proposed sentences. The change centred on the notion of relevance (*pertinentia*). For simplicity, let us confine our remarks to the species of obligation called *positio*.[12] According to the old response, a relevant sentence was one that either followed from (*pertinens sequens*) or was inconsistent with (*pertinens repugnans*) the conjunction of (a) the posited sentence, together with (b) all subsequently proposed sentences that had been granted by the respondent, and together with (c) the contradictory opposites of all subsequently proposed sentences that had been correctly denied by the respondent.[13] For the new response, however, a relevant sentence was one that either followed from or was inconsistent with the posited sentence alone. The subsequent steps of the disputation played no role in assessing relevance or irrelevance.[14]

Hence if the false sentence P is posited, it must be granted whenever it is subsequently proposed, since it (trivially) follows from the posited sentence, namely from itself. And if the true but irrelevant sentence Q is proposed anywhere in the same disputation, it must likewise be granted. But if the conjunction $P \& Q$ is proposed anywhere in the disputation, it must be denied, according to the new response, because that conjunction as a whole neither follows from nor is inconsistent with P, and is moreover false since P is false. Similarly, if *not-P* is proposed anywhere in the disputation, it is to be denied since it is inconsistent with the posited

---

9. Ed. Spade 1980, pars. 14 and 20.
10. *Ibid.*, par. 17.
11. Ed. Spade 1977, p. 257, par. 32: 'Secunda conclusio: Propter concessionem partium copulativae non est copulativa concedenda, nec propter concessionem disjunctivae est aliqua pars ejus concedenda.'
12. For a description of this species and its relations with the others, see the discussion in Part A of this Chapter.
13. See, for example, the treatise attributed to William of Sherwood, ed. Green forthcoming, par. 1.04.
14. See Swineshead in Spade 1977, especially pars. 4 and 32, and Fland in Spade 1980, especially pars. 10–20.

sentence *P*. And if *not-Q* is proposed anywhere in the disputation, it is to be denied since it is irrelevant and false. But if *not-P or not-Q* is proposed anywhere in the disputation, it is to be granted since it neither follows from nor is inconsistent with *P* and is moreover true since *not-P* is true. Hence, Swineshead's second 'conclusion'.[15]

One of the most characteristic features of the old tradition of obligations was lost in this new response. For according to the old tradition, the order in which the opponent proposed his sentences in the subsequent steps of the disputation was an important factor in determining the respondent's correct reply.[16] This fact was the basis for many complicated and tricky examples in the old tradition.[17] But, according to the new response, the order of the proposed sentences is not a factor, since relevance or irrelevance is not affected by any steps of the disputation after the initial 'positing'.

The rationale behind Swineshead's new response is not at all clear. Certainly, if the purpose of the obligations was to provide students with logical exercises to sharpen their skills, the old response was much better suited to that purpose than was the new response. (Nevertheless, perhaps students were exercised by shifting from the one style of disputation to the other.) It is possible that Swineshead's innovations were meant to take account of the fact that a disputation *de obligationibus* takes place in practice during an interval of time, and that during that interval there may be changes in the world that are irrelevant to the posited sentence.[18] Given the present state of research on obligations, this is no more than speculation. But if it is true, it means that Swineshead also departed from his predecessors insofar as the earlier treatises maintained that all the steps in a disputation *de obligationibus* are to be taken to refer to the same moment of time.[19]

Swineshead's new response generated a certain amount of controversy. His view was accepted by Richard Lavenham[20] in the second half of the

15. See Spade 1977, par. 32.
16. See, for example, Burley in Green forthcoming, par. 3.34: 'Una regula de arte obligatoria est ista: ordo est maxime attendendus. Et ratio hujus regulae est ista: quod uno loco est concedendum, alio loco non est concedendum. Et ideo, quando aliquid proponitur, videndum est quem ordinem illud habeat ad praeconcessa.'
17. See, for example, the texts edited in Green forthcoming, and some of the examples excerpted from those texts and discussed in Part A of this Chapter.
18. See Spade 1977, p. 274 n. 97.
19. See, for example, the text attributed to William of Sherwood in Green forthcoming, par. 1.36, and Burley in Green forthcoming, par. 3.84.
20. Ed. Spade 1978b.

fourteenth century, and was discussed by Robert Fland as apparently no less plausible than the old response. Indeed, Fland appears generally favourable to the new response. Ralph Strode, on the other hand, a contemporary of John Wyclif, rejected Swineshead's second conclusion, but observed that 'not a few sophisters' held it.[21] 'Many people', he says,[22]

thought that they demonstrated conclusively from the common rules that a copulative was to be denied, such as the one just proposed, each part of which was nevertheless to be granted. And likewise they grant the disjunctive opposite of such a copulative, while denying each of its parts. By this means not a few sophisters are given courage to admit cases like 'Everything standing in this house is a donkey'. Along with this, when 'You are standing in this house' is proposed, they grant it. But when from these things it is concluded that you are a donkey, they grant the consequence and deny the antecedent. And when it is asked 'In virtue of which part?', they say that it is neither in virtue of the major nor in virtue of the minor, but in virtue of the whole copulative composed of them, which is the antecedent. They say that this is false and irrelevant since it is composed of a posited falsehood and an irrelevant truth, as was said in the beginning. Therefore, although this view is now upheld by many people, it could deservedly be called sophistical, since it appears to be valid but is not valid.

Peter of Candia also rejected Swineshead's second conclusion in the later fourteenth century,[23] as did Paul of Venice in the early fifteenth century.[24] By the time Paul wrote, he was able to say that those who held Swines-

---

21. Strode 1493, f. 95vb. See n. 22 below. Bodleian MS Canon. Misc. 219, f. 37vb, explicitly mentions the 'opinio Suyset' in this context. ('Suyset' is a common medieval spelling of Swineshead's name.)

22. Strode 1493, f. 95vb (corrected in a few places according to the Bodleian MS Canon. Misc. 219, f. 39ra): '... putaverunt se multi velut inevitabiliter ex regulis communibus [omnibus *ed. 1493*] demonstrare quod copulativa esset neganda cujus tamen quaelibet pars esset concedenda. Et consimiliter concedunt disjunctivam oppositam tali copulativae negantes quamlibet ejus partem. Per quod medium non pauci sophistae sunt animosi facti ad admittendum tales casus "Omnes stans in ista domo est asinus". Et cum hoc cum proponitur "Tu stas in ista domo" concedunt. Sed cum concluditur ex illis quod tu es asinus concedunt consequentiam et negant antecedens. Et quando quaeritur pro qua parte dicunt quod [*om. ed. 1493*] nec pro majori nec pro minori sed pro tota copulativa quae est antecedens ex illis composita. Quam dicunt esse falsam et impertinentem cum sit ex posito falso et impertinenti vero, sicut primo dicebatur. Licet ergo modo a multis sustineatur illa via, merito tamen sophistica poterit appellari cum sit apparens valida sed non valet.'

23. Peter of Candia, *Obligationes*: 'Decima tertia regula est haec: Quod concessa qualibet parte copulativae copulativa est concedenda ... Et quia aliqui ponunt oppositum istius regulae pro regula summa, ideo pro regula maiori declaratione arguo contra ipsos.' (I am grateful to Stephen F. Brown for allowing me to see his partially completed edition of this work.) On Peter of Candia, see Ehrle 1925 and Gray 1967.

24. Paul of Venice 1499, II, 14, f. 179vb (on 'positio'): 'Ultima regula est ista: qualibet parte copulativa concessa, concedenda est copulativa cujus illae vel consimiles sunt partes principales ... Sed quia aliqui tenent oppositum hujus regulae quasi omnes antiqui, pro majori declaratione arguo contra eos.'

head's view were '*quasi omnes antiqui*'.[25] Swineshead's new response, which Strode in the above passage regarded as rather widespread in his own day, appears to have been only a historical reference by the time of Paul of Venice; it seems never to have been the dominant view. The old response was apparently the norm throughout the history of the obligations-literature, as far as present research has determined.[26]

There were several other features of Swineshead's view that were also disputed. At present, it is impossible to say whether these features orig-inated with Swineshead or came from some other source. Indeed, until further research is done, it would be premature to think that there were only two 'responses' in the obligations-literature, the standard one and Swineshead's. The situation was almost surely much more complex.

Nevertheless, Swineshead did maintain, as the eighth assumption or 'supposition' in his treatise, the characteristic thesis that 'the response to a sentence is not to be varied because of an imposition'.[27] The idea seems to have been to regard 'imposition', one of the main species of obligation, as a kind of metalinguistic positing, so that once the respondent admits, for instance, that the sentence 'God exists' is newly imposed to signify that man is a donkey, he has to grant the sentence '"God exists" is false' whenever it is proposed in the disputation, since it follows from the admitted imposition. And yet the respondent must also grant the sentence 'God exists' whenever it is proposed in the disputation. To think that he has to deny the latter sentence on the basis of the admitted new imposition is to make an illegitimate move from metalanguage to object-language.

Not everyone accepted this thesis. Fland felt the need to discuss it at some length,[28] although he did not reject it. Richard Brinkley, however, did reject it sometime during the second half of the fourteenth century.[29] And

25. See n. 24 above. The most natural reading of this phrase is 'almost all the ancients', implying that at one time Swineshead's view was almost universally held. No other evidence has been found so far that Swineshead's new response was ever widely accepted. On the other hand, the phrase might also be read 'almost all [of them were] ancients'. This admittedly less natural reading would not imply that Swineshead's view was ever the dominant one, but it would suggest what in any case appears to be true, that the view had died out by the time Paul of Venice was writing.

26. In addition to the texts before Swineshead, in De Rijk 1974–6 and Green forthcoming, see Albert of Saxony 1522, VI, 2, ff. 46va–51vb; the *Tractatus de arte obligandi* attributed to Peter of Ailly in Peter of Ailly 1489 (this tract is perhaps in fact by Marsilius of Inghen); Paul of Venice 1472, tract. V; Paul of Venice 1499, II, 14, ff. 177ra–192rb; and Paul of Pergula 1961, tract. V.

27. Ed. Spade 1977, p. 254, par. 21: 'Propter impositionem alicujus propositionis ad illam non est responsio varianda.'

28. Ed. Spade 1980, pars. 69–86.

29. Richard Brinkley, *Obligationes*, Prague, Bibl. univ., MS 396, f. 98ra: 'Octava suppositio: Propter impositionem novam factam circa propositionem est responsio ad eam varianda. Nam propter impositionem significat propositio aliquid, aliqua vel aliqualiter, quod, quae vel qualiter prius non significavit; igitur.'

John Buridan remarks,[30]

Still another case frequently occurs in obligational disputations, namely, that in the schools the master posits that for the time of those disputations the term 'donkey' signifies to them precisely the same as the term 'animal' signifies to us according to its usual signification. And the respondent and the others agree. Then the sentence 'A man is a donkey' is true for them, and to be granted. Yet a vocally similar one would be false and impossible if, without such an obligation, it should be posited in the church of the Blessed Mary to those who were there.

This violates Swineshead's eighth assumption. Note that Buridan seems to suggest that what he says here agrees with more or less standard practice in the schools.

Fland points to yet another rule that he calls 'new' and seems to associate with Swineshead.[31] His formulation of the rule is slightly different from Swineshead's[32] and also from Lavenham's, whose own text is based on Swineshead's.[33] But the idea is this. If a posited sentence is inconsistent with the claim that it is posited, the respondent must reply to it, if it is proposed, as though it were irrelevant. For instance, if the opponent says, 'I posit that nothing is posited to you', the respondent must admit the position since the posited sentence 'Nothing is posited to you' is a possible one. But if that posited sentence should be proposed at a later step of the disputation, the respondent must respond as though it were irrelevant. For although 'Nothing is posited to you' is quite possible in itself, it is inconsistent with the claim 'I posit that nothing is posited to you', since if nothing is posited to you, then in particular, 'Nothing is posited to you' is not posited to you.

The exact purpose of this suggestive rule and the details of how it works are not yet well understood. Neither are its possible antecedents in the earlier literature or its subsequent history in the later. Fland treats the rule as a novelty. The rule is obviously meant to avoid certain kinds of paradoxes. But exactly how those paradoxes would otherwise arise and exactly how this rule disarms them are not yet clear.

30. Buridan 1977, VI, soph. 1, p. 105: 'Adhuc alius casus accidit communiter in disputationibus obligatoriis, videlicet quod in scholis magister ponit quod tempore illarum disputationum iste terminus "asinus" significet eis praecise idem quod significat iste terminus "animal" nobis, secundum communem eius significationem. Et respondens et alii consentiunt. Tunc ista propositio "Homo est asinus" est illis vera et concedenda. Et tamen similis secundum vocem esset falsa et impossibilis, si sine tali obligatione poneretur in ecclesia beatae Mariae illis qui ibi essent.'
31. Ed. Spade 1980, par. 23: 'Alia regula est nova, scilicet, eodem modo respondendum est ad positum et propter repugnans posito infra tempus obligationis sicut extra.'
32. Ed. Spade 1977, p. 265, par. 64: 'Si tamen positum repugnat positioni respondendum est ad illud sicut ad impertinens.'
33. Ed. Spade 1978b, p. 229, par. 8: 'Unde quandocumque propositio ponitur cum pertinentia obligationis vel cum repugnantia positionis homo non tenetur concedere propositionem obligatam in eo quod est obligata, sed si est vera debet concedere eam, si est falsa debet negare eam.'

Conclusion

The study of the obligations-literature is only just beginning to get under way in earnest. But already it is obvious that such common and seemingly innocuous expressions as 'I grant' (*Concedo*), 'I deny' (*Nego*) and 'when the case has been admitted' (*admisso casu*) are highly rule-governed expressions, rule-governed in ways that are codified in the obligations-literature itself, but that spill over into other, more concretely philosophical contexts as well. This had happened already by the time of Richard Kilvington's *Sophismata*, and it became increasingly obvious in later literature, for instance, in treatises *De scire et dubitare*.[34] As the study of obligations progresses, it may be expected to shed light on many now obscure arguments in such texts.

34. See, for instance, the influential Ch. 2 ('De scire et dubitare') of William Heytesbury's *Regulae solvendi sophismata*, in Heytesbury 1494, ff. 12va-16va.

17

MODAL LOGIC

Two notions of possibility

For Aristotle the term 'possibility' is homonymous (*Pr. An.* I, 3, 25ᵃ37–40): on some occasions the possible and the impossible are contradictories (e.g., *De int.* 12, 22ᵃ11–13; 13, 22ᵃ32–38), while on others possibility is incompatible not only with impossibility but also with necessity (e.g., *An. pr.* I, 13, 32ᵃ18–21).[1] Whenever the distinction is relevant, I shall call possibility in the first sense 'possibility proper' and possibility in the second sense 'contingency'.

In the Latin translation of *De interpretatione* by Marius Victorinus which was used by Boethius Aristotle's two terms for 'possible' were translated by the Latin terms '*possibile*' and '*contingens*',[2] which Boethius understood to be synonyms.[3] This was the usual view in early medieval logic,[4] and it can still be found in the squares of opposition for modalities presented by William of Sherwood and Peter of Spain in the middle of the thirteenth century.[5] Already in the twelfth century, however, there were attempts to give separate meanings to the two words. For instance, John of Salisbury criticised those who used the terms as synonyms; according to usage in his time a mere absence of impossibility did not warrant calling something contingent.[6] Even in those works in which the terms are used as synonyms there often is a remark referring to a related distinction, according to which '*contingens*' is opposed to '*necessarium*' in the sense that some possible sentences are necessary and others contingent.[7] This became the dominant

---

1. For Aristotle's different sorts of possibility see Hintikka 1973, pp. 27–40.
2. Although Aristotle has two words for 'possible' – '*dunaton*' and '*endechomenon*' – he appears not to use them systematically in order to mark a distinction. See Becker-Freyseng 1938, pp. 20–4.
3. Boethius 1880, II, 382.17–18; 383.4–5; 384.6–7 *et passim*. See, however, II, 392.17–393.9, where Boethius draws a distinction between *enuntiatio possibilis* and *enuntiatio contingens*.
4. See, e.g., Abelard 1970a, p. 193.31; De Rijk 1962–7 II(2), 390.35–6; 391.17–18; 393–4; 430–1; 481.14–17.
5. William of Sherwood 1937, p. 45; Peter of Spain 1972, p. 16.
6. John of Salisbury 1929, III, 4.
7. De Rijk 1962–7, II(2), 481.9–13. For the whole question see Schepers 1963.

use of the words in later medieval logic. It was further encouraged by the need of having available different terms for possibility proper and contingency in dealing with the Aristotelian modal syllogistic.[8] *'Possibile'* is then reserved for possibility proper. Sometimes a subdivision is made within the field of what we are calling contingency so that *'contingens'* describes what is true but can be false and *'possibile'* describes what is false but can be true.[9]

Because of the two senses of 'possibility' and the different fields of application of possibility proper, Aristotle's treatments of the equipollence and opposition of various modalities are rather complicated. His accounts of them in *De interpretatione*, Chapters 12 and 13, are in fact incompatible because different senses of 'possibility' are presupposed in them.[10]

In order to present a square of opposition for modal sentences (analogous to that for sentences *de inesse*) early medieval logicians took possibility proper as the basic notion.[11] The rules of equipollence and opposition were accordingly presented by many authors as in the following square:[12]

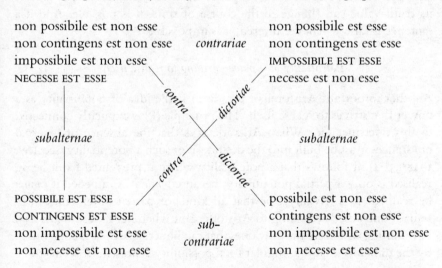

non possibile est non esse
non contingens est non esse   *contrariae*   non possibile est esse
impossibile est non esse   non contingens est esse
NECESSE EST ESSE   IMPOSSIBILE EST ESSE
                                            necesse est non esse

contra   dictoriae

subalternae   *subalternae*

contra   dictoriae

POSSIBILE EST ESSE   possibile est non esse
CONTINGENS EST ESSE   contingens est non esse
non impossibile est esse   *sub-*   non impossibile est non esse
non necesse est non esse *contrariae*   non necesse est esse

8. So Albert the Great in commenting on Aristotle's modal syllogistic uses the term *'contingens pro possibili'* for possibility proper; see Albert the Great 1890–9a, tr. IV, cap. 4, 5, pp. 545–9.
9. See De Rijk 1962–7, II(2), 391.18–19; Roger Bacon 1940, p. 267.
10. Jaakko Hintikka has described and diagrammed the different patterns of analysis used in *De interpretatione*; see Hintikka 1973, p. 48.
11. In this respect they were following the Theophrastian and Eudemian modal logic rather than Aristotle's, in which contingency is basic. See Bocheński 1947, pp. 73–87; 1951, pp. 73–5; 1956, pp. 116–18; Graeser 1973, pp. 72–5.
12. De Rijk 1962–7, II(2), 393.6–394.5; 431.19–26; 484.5–6; William of Sherwood 1937, p. 45.11; Peter of Spain 1972, I, 25; p. 16.12–13.

The principle of plenitude

Aristotle's modal theory evidently implies the so-called Principle of Plenitude:[13]

(P)   No genuine possibility can remain forever unrealised.

Although Aristotle does not directly define modal terms with the help of (P), it seems that (P) was in some way natural for him. The principle can be found in its most explicit form in that part of Aristotle's modal theory which has been described as the 'statistical' interpretation of modal concepts as applied to temporally indefinite sentences.[14] Aristotle regarded a temporally unqualified sentence as the typical form of a singular declarative statement (see, e.g., *Cat.* 4^{a}23–^{b}2, *Met.* 1051^{b}13–18). Such sentences contain implicitly or explicitly a reference to the time of utterance as a part of their meaning. On the statistical interpretation of modal statements the use of such sentences is connected by Aristotle with the principle (P): if a sentence which is true now is true whenever uttered, it is necessarily true. If its truth-value can change in the course of time, it is possible. And if a sentence is false whenever uttered, it is impossible.[15]

Potentiality as a power striving to realise itself

Another important Aristotelian paradigm is the idea of potentiality as a power that strives to realise itself. The principle (P) is explicitly connected to this doctrine, too. When Aristotle says that the absence of external hindrances must be built into the definition of such a potentiality (see *Met.* 1048^{a}23–4), it follows that a potentiality which is prevented from being realised is only a partial potentiality, because *while* it is impeded it *cannot* be realised. It is trivially true that all kinds of partial potentialities can remain unrealised according to Aristotle. But when he is speaking of *total* possibilities, which are the only ones that can be actualised, he is confronted by the difficulty that if a singular total possibility is present, it seems to be

13. For the history of the principle in general see Lovejoy 1936. According to Lovejoy, the principle originated in the ancient Platonic tradition and was not adopted by Aristotle. Hintikka has disproved the second part of that view in Hintikka 1973, pp. 93–113.
14. Hintikka 1973, pp. 63–70, 84–6, 102–3, 149–51. See also Becker 1952, pp. 16–19.
15. For the link between time and necessity see, e.g., *Nic. Eth.* 1139^{b}18–25, time and possibility *Met.* 1047^{b}3–9 and *De caelo* 281^{b}15–21, and time and impossibility *Met.* 1047^{a}12–14; cf. also Hintikka, Remes, and Knuuttila 1977, pp. 15–22, 31–2, 43–5. See also Bosley 1978, pp. 29–40.

realised immediately (see, e.g., *Met.* 1048ª6–21, 1049ª5–14, *Phys.* VIII, 4, 255ᵇ3–12).[16]

Aristotle's 'logical' definition of possibility

Aristotle's 'logical' definition of possibility might be recognised as another important element of his modal theory. According to it, what is possible can be assumed to be actual without any impossibility resulting from this assumption (*Pr. An.* I, 13, 32ª18–21). In many places he relies on the definition outside strictly logical contexts, and in *De caelo* 281ᵇ15–21 he explicitly says that if a possibility is never realised, something impossible will follow from supposing it to be realised.[17]

The medieval use of the statistical interpretation of modality

Several of the concepts and principles characteristic of Aristotle's modal theory remained important in post-Aristotelian philosophy,[18] which is marked by an implicit or explicit acceptance of the principle (P). The same is true, with qualifications, of medieval thought until the late thirteenth century. I shall first give some examples of the medieval use of the statistical interpretation of modality, because it seems to have been the dominant model in logical contexts.

According to the twelfth-century *Dialectica Monacensis*,[19] an assertoric statement is changed into a modal statement by increasing or decreasing

---

16. Hintikka, Remes, and Knuuttila 1977, pp. 25–8, 35–9, 50–6. There is in Aristotle a more promising way to find room for unactualised potentialities *qua* potentialities. It is based on a distinction between potentialities of *energeiai* instantaneously realised through *energeiai* and potential outcomes of *kinesis* realised gradually through a *kinesis*. See Hintikka, Remes, and Knuuttila 1977, pp. 59–76.

17. Hintikka, Remes, and Knuuttila 1977, pp. 22–5, 32–3; Pape 1965, pp. 39–43.

18. The modal paradigms of later antiquity seem to be related to those employed by Aristotle. The Master Argument of Diodorus Kronos is designed to establish the statistical interpretation of modality; see Epictetus 1898, II, 19, 1; for literature concerning the argument see Döring 1972, pp. 132–5. Philo of Megara's idea of possibility seems to have resembled Aristotelian partial possibility (Boethius 1880, II, 234.10–22; 235.6–9; John Philoponus 1905, 169.19–21; Alexander of Aphrodisias 1883, 184.6–10). According to Alexander of Aphrodisias 1892, 177.7ff., the Stoics said that the statement 'There will be a sea-battle tomorrow' is possible and not necessary because, even if it is true, it does not remain true after the battle has taken place (for the Stoic doctrine of changing truth-values see Kneale and Kneale 1962, pp. 144–6, 153–4; Frede 1974, pp. 44–8; cf. the rather cryptic characterisation of Stoic modal theory in Diogenes Laertius VII, 75). On modalities in the Stoic system of causal determinism see Sambursky 1959, pp. 76–9. In Neoplatonism, Plotinus is the principal witness for the metaphysical form of the Principle of Plenitude discussed in Lovejoy 1936; for Plotinus' modal notions see also Buchner 1968.

19. For an introduction to the work see De Rijk 1962–7 II(1), 408–15; the text is edited in II(2), 435–638.

(*addendo vel diminuendo*), as in 'It is necessary that Socrates is running' or 'It is impossible that Socrates is running.' *True* and *false* are not modal concepts because they do not change the assertoric statement in a similar way.[20] Modal concepts are evidently thought of as qualifying the temporal domain of a token-reflexive assertoric statement, a view that involves an acceptance of the statistical interpretation of modal statements as applied to temporally indefinite sentences. The same treatise states that what is *necessarium per se* is infallibly true in all times – i.e., in the past, present, and future – and what is *necessarium per accidens* cannot be false either now or in the future, although it might have been false in the past – e.g., 'This man has studied in Paris.'[21] If the criterion of the necessity of a sentence is the immutability of its truth-value, it follows that every true sentence is necessarily true *when it is uttered*, although not necessarily *per se*. This is in effect precisely the Aristotelian principle that 'what is, *necessarily* is *when* it is'. It follows, of course, that a possible sentence must be true at some time, because otherwise its negation would be immutably true and the sentence itself impossible.

These ideas are repeated in identical terms in many logical treatises from the twelfth and thirteenth centuries.[22] Boethius' commentaries on *De interpretatione* present them in an early form. He makes a distinction between *necessarium temporale* and *necessarium simplex*. The former refers to the necessary truth of a temporally definite true sentence. This necessity disappears, however, when the sentence is taken in a temporally indefinite sense, *sine temporis praesentis descriptione*.[23] In the fifth book of his *Consolation of Philosophy* Boethius tries to use the distinction mentioned above to show that the purported inference from divine providence to determinism is fallacious.[24] It is easy to collect other examples in which this solution is offered to the problems of divine foreknowledge, determinism, and related questions;[25] it, too, is based on the statistical interpretation of modal notions.

20. De Rijk 1962–7, II(2), 478.27–479.2.
21. De Rijk 1962–7, II(2), 481.22–482.9.
22. See De Rijk 1962–7, II(2), 390.18–31; 429.1–10; William of Sherwood 1937, p. 41.13–16.
23. Boethius 1877, I, 121.25–122.4; 1880, II, 241.29–242.4.
24. Boethius, *Philos. cons.*, V, 6. There is another example of an analogous change of viewpoint in Boethius 1880, II, 387.2–4.
25. See Peter Abelard 1859, pp. 142–3, 146; 1970a, 221.3–13; 1919–27, 229.34–6; 274.10–12; 429.18–25; Thomas Aquinas, 1949b, I, q. 2, a. 12, *ad* 4; *In quatuor libros Sententiarum*, I, d. 38, q. 1, a. 5, *ad* 3. In thirteenth-century physics every effect, when it occurs, is necessary with respect to its cause, but the same effect can be taken to be contingent if at another time the corresponding cause is impeded; see Maier 1949, pp. 226–34. This interpretation of the Avicennian principle of causation was first presented by Averroes, who is one of the most explicit adherents of the

Modal sentences in the compounded or the divided sense

Medieval Aristotelian solutions to certain kinds of problems containing modal notions are often based on an analysis according to which modal sentences can be taken either in the compounded or in the divided sense (*in sensu composito* or *in sensu diviso*). This was also called the distinction between readings *de dicto* (or *de sensu*) and *de re*.[26] It owes its origin to Aristotle's *Sophistici elenchi*, 166ª22–30. There Aristotle shows how the meaning of a statement changes according to whether its elements are understood in a conjoined or a divided meaning. The sentences 'a man who is not writing can write' and 'a sitting man can walk' are false when the possibility is understood to qualify the conjunction of two mutually exclusive predicates with the same subject at the same time. But although it is true that a man who is not writing cannot write while not writing, and that while not writing he is necessarily not writing, the same proposition can also be taken in the divided sense. It is then true that someone-not-writing can write. In Aristotle's opinion a temporally unqualified modal sentence which includes mutually exclusive predicates is structurally ambiguous, because the possibility can refer to a supposed actualisation of predicates at the same time (*in sensu composito*) or at different times (*in sensu diviso*). The distinction is, in the last analysis, reduced to a temporal distinction between the simultaneity and non-simultaneity of the actualisation of two predicates. In fact Aristotle says that in the divided sense the possibility must be actual at some time, because otherwise the distinction cannot be made (*De caelo* 281ᵇ15–21).

This analysis of modal sentences was widely accepted in the Middle Ages. While discussing the fallacy *secundum diversum tempus* Boethius maintains that both of two apparently contradictory sentences can be true if they refer to different points of time. He is thus articulating precisely the semantical principle by means of which Aristotle tried to overcome the difficulties of statistical modalities in connection with temporally qualified sentences.[27] Abelard seems to have been the first medieval author to use the crucial passage from the *Sophistici elenchi* quoted above in connection with the strategy of moving from temporally definite to temporally indefinite sentences.[28] After Abelard, this analysis of modal statements by means of

statistical interpretation of modal notions. See, e.g., his *Quaesitum II in Pr. an.*, pp. 78–80; Rescher 1963, pp. 91–105; Jalbert 1961, pp. 37–40; Knuuttila 1978, pp. 79–87.

26. Abelard 1919–27, 489.1–14; Peter of Spain 1972, VII, 68, 71, pp. 122–4.
27. Boethius 1880, II, 133.9–29; 1860e, *PL* 64, 778–9.
28. Abelard 1919–27, 489.1–14.

the *compositio/divisio* distinction became a commonplace in logical text-books.[29] The sophism *stans potest sedere* (or *nigrum possibile est esse album*) was solved in the Aristotelian manner by saying that it is false *in sensu composito* but true *in sensu diviso*, because things can be otherwise at another time. The usual formulation of the sophism is as follows:

What is possible will be true
A black thing can be white
Thus it will be true that a black thing is white.

According to the solution proposed in very similar terms by William of Sherwood, Peter of Spain, Lambert of Auxerre, and others, the first premiss (which entails (P)) is not taken to be problematic. In the second premiss the compounded and the divided senses are to be distinguished from each other, and the distinction is typically interpreted in the texts as a temporal distinction between the possibilities of simultaneous actuality and actuality at different times. The problematic conclusion is said to rely only on the composite meaning.[30] Thomas Aquinas believed that by means of this strategy he could defend indeterminism in the world while accepting (P), without resorting to the concept of the absolute power of God.[31]

Modality and consequences

In their doctrine of *consequentiae ut nunc* some writers explicitly used the interrelated ideas of statistically interpreted modal concepts and changing truth-values.[32] The distinction between as-of-now consequences and absolute consequences is then characterised so that as-of-now consequences do not hold at every time but only at a determinate time, and absolute

---

29. In the oldest extant medieval commentary on Aristotle's *Soph. el.* the following gloss is made upon the passage 166ª22–30: 'Secundum conpositionem autem huiusmodi, ut posse sedentem anbulare, idest possibile est quod sedens simul anbulet, vel possibile est quod sedens alio tempore anbulet. Si quis didicit litteras, possibile est nunc discere litteras quos scit. Hec oratio significat aliquem didicisse litteras et eum nunc posse illas litteras discere, que coniunctim sunt falsa, quia aliquis non potest didicisse litteras et simul discere; sed divisim potest aliquis didicisse et discere. Sicut si Deus providit Socratem legere, possibile est Socratem ⟨legere⟩.' See De Rijk 1962–7, 1, 210.10–17. I shall supply '*non legere*' instead of De Rijk's '⟨*legere*⟩' in the last line; for '*didicisse*' and '*discere*', like '*sedere*' and '*ambulare*', are mutually exclusive predicates. For similar analyses, see De Rijk 1962–7, 1, 311.6–15; 316.1–7; 613.23–8; II(2), 687.28–688.1; 570.18–29. In the last-mentioned text the writer does not interpret the possibility as an alternative state of affairs, because he believes that every true statement about the present is necessarily true: 'omne dictum de praesenti verum et affirmativum est necessarium'. II(2), 481.32–3.
30. William of Sherwood 1937, 90.11–24; Peter of Spain 1972, VII, 68, 70–1; Lambert of Auxerre 1971, p. 158.
31. See especially *De veritate* I, q. 2, a. 12, *ad* 4.
32. William of Sherwood 1941, pp. 79–80; Walter Burley 1955, p. 61; William Ockham (?) 1964, p. 77.

consequences hold at every time. When the validity of the absolute material consequence is based on the impossibility of the conjunction of the antecedent and the denial of the consequent, it seems that the modalities are to be interpreted in terms of time, so that a proposition is necessary if and only if it is always true, impossible if and only if it is never true, and possible if and only if it is true at some time.[33] The necessity of an 'as-of-now' consequence is then a kind of temporal necessity – the truth-value cannot change at the time when a contingent condition is actual.

Medieval acceptance of the Aristotelian conception of potentiality

The Aristotelian paradigm of potentiality as a power which strives to manifest itself was unqualifiedly accepted in Aristotelian scholasticism as a characterisation of natural reality.[34] Although according to this model there can be potentialities which are unrealised for some time, as partial ingredients of genuine possibilities they must be actualised at some time. So Moses Maimonides formulates the following principle, which he describes as Aristotelian: 'It is possible for whatever is *in potentia* and in whose essence there is a certain possibility, not to exist *in actu* at a certain time.' According to Maimonides, it follows from this that if there were anything potential in the essence of a perpetually existing being, that being would at some time become nonexistent. This is the basis for a proof of God's existence: if there were only beings which have a possibility of not being, all things would have ceased to exist and there would be no world.[35] The same idea, based on (P), is used in Thomas Aquinas' Third Way, and in other contexts, too.[36]

Medieval attitudes towards the principle of plenitude

Modal paradigms containing (P) were not accepted by most schoolmen without qualification because the principle was thought to restrict God's freedom and power. In the twelfth century it was usual to make a distinction between natural possibilities and God's possibilities. By this distinction the schoolmen wanted to show that possibilities according to the superior cause (God) may be impossibilities according to inferior (natural) causes. The criterion of natural possibility and impossibility was the accustomed

---

33. Adams 1973, pp. 13–14; see also Moody 1953, pp. 73–4.
34. See, for example, Thomas Aquinas, *In De caelo* I, *cap.* 12, *lect.* 26, 6. In John of Jandun's question *Utrum omne generabile de necessitate generabitur* (MS Firenze BN, Conv. Soppr. I III 6, ff. 109ra–110vb) John disproves fifteen different counterexamples to the Principle of Plenitude.
35. Moses Maimonides 1974, introduction to the second part, premiss 23, and Ch. 1, pp. 238–9, 249.
36. Thomas Aquinas, *ST*, I, q. 2, a. 3c; see also *In IX Metaph.*, *lect.* 9; n. 1870. *ST*, I, q. 48, a. 2c.

course of nature (*consuetudo*).[37] God's possibilities were sometimes taken to be an exception to this criterion, such that (P) does not hold of them although it holds with respect to natural possibilities.

Thomas Aquinas put the theological denial of (P) on a firmer theoretical basis. Accepting (P) as far as natural possibilities are concerned, he denied it for God's possibilities. But, following Aristotelian epistemology, Aquinas thought that, although we can prove that there are unrealised Divine possibilities, all knowledge of what they are is beyond human capacity.[38] Divine possibilities are characterised simply by the absence of contradiction, a characterisation that Thomas also gives to Aristotle's possibilities *ou kata dynamin*.[39] In spite of its epistemic limitations, this theory was a big step towards a logical interpretation of modality in which (P) is explicitly denied.

Problems in the interpretation of Aristotelian modal syllogistic

In Book I, Chapters 8–22 of his *Prior Analytics* Aristotle presents his modal syllogistic in which the following combinations of modal premisses are considered: □–□, □–A, A–□, ◇–◇, ◇–A, A–◇, ◇–□, □–◇ ('□' stands for a necessary premiss, '◇' for a possible premiss, and 'A' for an assertoric premiss). It has offered frustrating difficulties to commentators beginning with Aristotle's immediate Peripatetic followers. After Albert Becker's dissertation *Die Aristotelische Theorie der Möglichkeitsschlüsse* (1933) many attempts have been made to reconstruct it as a system in terms of modern symbolic logic.[40] The results have been scanty, and the reason for this lack of success is almost certainly the fact that Aristotle's modal syllogistic is put together from elements which contain different and partially independent insights into the logic of modal notions.[41] It is therefore not surprising that the first medieval comments on Aristotle's modal syllogistic are often confused.

Aristotle's choice of the two-edged possibility (incompatible with both impossibility and necessity) as the principal notion of possibility in his modal syllogistic suggests that he understood it to be a theory about the structure of the actual world – it discusses the logic of necessary and

---

37. See for example Alan of Lille, *Regulae de sacra theologia*, 57–8; *PL* 210, 648; Simon of Tournai, *Expositio super Simbolum*, ed. prima, 36–43; ed. secunda, 48–54.
38. Thomas Aquinas, *ST*, I, q. 12, a. 8, *ad* 4; *De unione verbi incarnati*, q. un., a. 1c; cf. *In Post. an.* II, 6, n. 461.
39. *ST*, I, q. 25, a. 3c; Pape 1966, pp. 45–9.
40. See, e.g., McCall 1963; Łukasiewicz 1957, Chs. 6–8; Rescher 1963, pp. 152–77.
41. Hintikka 1973, pp. 135–46.

accidental properties.[42] This assumption may solve a general difficulty in the interpretation of Aristotle's theory. Since Becker it has often been pointed out that the premisses of Aristotle's modal syllogisms are usually to be read *de re*, but the Aristotelian rules of conversion essential to his theory in many cases seem to imply that modal premisses are to be interpreted *de dicto*.[43] Now, according to Aristotle, natural kinds are eternal. If necessity is interpreted as expressing a genus–species relationship between eternal and hence necessary kinds, then the rules of conversion are similar no matter whether the statements are read *de dicto* or *de re*. In the conversion of the contingent premisses interpreted *de re* the statistical interpretation of modality is accepted, but this was natural for Aristotle, as we have seen.[44]

Since the premisses of modal syllogisms are read *de re* by the author of *Dialectica Monacensis*, Averroes, and Albert the Great,[45] but no separate treatments are offered for the conversion of modal statements interpreted *de dicto* or *de re*,[46] it seems that philosophical assumptions similar to those just mentioned were held by them. The acceptance of the statistical interpretation of modality was quite natural for Averroes and the author of *Dialectica Monacensis*; the same holds good of Albert the Great as well. He proves, e.g., the rule 'if q follows from p, then possibly-q follows from possibly-p' by stating that what is possible is at some time actual. If q were impossible it would follow that p is at some time true without q.[47]

The problems caused by the philosophical assumptions may be illustrated by the difficulties in the mixed apodictic and assertoric syllogisms. According to the statistical interpretation of modality, what is always true is necessarily true. In *Pr. An.* I, 15, 34^{b}7–18 Aristotle seems to say that the premisses in syllogisms must be taken without any limitations with respect to time. What happens then to the distinction between apodictic and assertoric premisses? On the other hand, Aristotle says in *Pr. An.* 30^{b}31–40 that if the conclusion is necessary in a valid mixed syllogism, it must be necessary *haplōs* and not only *toutōn ontōn*, i.e., when the assertoric premiss is true. It thus seems that according to Aristotle the truth value of an assertoric premiss can be changed and the conclusion may nevertheless be

42. Ross 1949, pp. 43, 46.
43. See Becker 1933, pp. 19, 39; Bocheński 1956, pp. 98–101; Hintikka 1973, p. 139.
44. In *Prior Analytics* I, 39^{a}31–5 it is explicitly stated that if some X is possibly Y, then some Y is possibly X. The rule is often applied in the succeeding chapters; cf. also Becker 1933, pp. 60, 64.
45. See De Rijk 1962–7 II(2), 480.10–16; Averroes 1562–74b, f.84; Albert the Great 1890–9a, *tract.* IV, *cap.* 2, pp. 540–3.
46. De Rijk 1962–7, II(2), 501.21–6; Averroes 1562–74a, f.4–5; Albert the Great 1890–9a, *tract.* I, *cap.* 11–15, pp. 474–85.
47. Albert the Great 1890–9a, *tract.* IV, *cap.* 6, p. 550.

necessary, because in the preceding chapter, he insists that the predicate of an assertoric premiss is such that it can fail to belong to the subject (30ᵃ27–8). An inference of the form

A necessarily applies to all B
B applies to all C
A necessarily applies to all C

then means that because every B has A as its necessary property, this property is transferred to every C. Even if Cs cease to be B, they still are A because A is a necessary property which they cannot lose. When the corresponding valid modes in mixed necessary and contingent syllogisms are such that the conclusion is possible in the sense of possibility proper (*Pr. An.* 35ᵇ23–36), this can perhaps be understood so that in contingent universal and particular premisses the predicate may actually belong only to some of those beings to which the subject term refers.

Medieval solutions of the difficulties in mixed syllogisms

Albert the Great takes the first way out of the difficulty. He says that the assertoric premiss in valid syllogisms must be *de inesse simpliciter* and not *de inesse ut nunc*. The former type of predication is substantial, and as such it is necessary *secundum rem*.[48] When he tries to explain how the necessity of one premiss determines the second premiss to be *de inesse simpliciter* and not only *de inesse ut nunc*, he seeks arguments from the categorical structure of the real world. If, e.g., in the first figure the first premiss is necessary, then, in order to save the structure of the figure the predicate term of the second premiss must be either a proprium of the subject term or a term which is superior to the subject in the same category, as for example colour to white things.[49] The difficulties of this approach can be seen in the fact that Albert defines *de inesse simpliciter* differently while discussing mixed contingent and assertoric syllogisms.[50]

Averroes' solution is based on the statistical interpretation of modality. The terms of the necessary premiss are necessary (*semper ens*). In a mixed apodictic and assertoric syllogism of the first figure the predicate term of the second premiss must be necessary, too, because a term *de inesse* is not necessarily *semper ens*, and such a term does not follow from a necessary term. The subject of the second premiss is *de inesse*. Such a premiss is *de inesse*

---

48. Albert the Great 1890–9a, *tract.* III, *cap.* 3, p. 523.
49. Albert the Great 1890–9a, *tract.* III, *cap.* 4, p. 525; *tract.* IV, *cap.* 4, p. 545.
50. Albert the Great 1890–9a, *tract.* IV, *cap.* 10, pp. 558–9; see also Mignucci 1969, pp. 907–9.

per se and *necessarium per accidens* if the predicate always belongs to the subject when it is actual, as for example 'Everybody who writes is a man.' If the necessary premiss is 'Every man is an animal' the conclusion 'Everybody who is writing is necessarily an animal' is *de inesse per se* and necessary *per accidens.*[51]

Duns Scotus' theory of modality

These examples illustrate the difficulties of an Aristotelian modal logic in which modal notions are understood as classifying what happens in the actual world at different moments of time. A less troublesome treatment of modal syllogistic was offered in the late thirteenth and early fourteenth centuries in accordance with the new understanding of modality in which the apparent difficulties of the statistical model were realised. We have seen signs of a new kind of modal theory in the ideas of divine possibilities and, perhaps, in the ideas of the *nominales.*[52] It seems that Duns Scotus had a dominant role in creating the principles of modal thought which are no longer bound by the limitations of the statistical interpretation of modality.

In the fourth chapter of his *Tractatus de primo principio* Scotus criticises Aristotelian cosmology, in which the contingency of causally determined events is saved by the statistical interpretation of modality. He does not accept the Aristotelian line of thought as a proof of contingency, because it implies that at any given moment of time everything happens by necessity. For an indeterministic theory it is necessary that something (something that is or takes place) could have been or could have happened otherwise at the same moment of time. The crucial sentence in Scotus' argument runs as follows: 'I do not call contingent that which is not necessary or not always, but that the opposite of which could have happened at the very same time it actually did.'[53] The notion of contingency is thus understood to involve a consideration of several alternative states of affairs with respect to the same time.

It is instructive to see how Scotus applies this new way of understanding modality in his discussion of the freedom of the will. For Scotus, the will is not free in the sense that it could at the same time will a thing and its opposite. But the will is free with respect to the act of willing at any given

51. Averroes 1562–74b, ff. 84 ff.
52. For the ideas of this twelfth-century group see Knuuttila 1981, pp. 195–8.
53. See also *Ord.* I, d. 2, pars 1, q. 1–2, n. 79–88. (All references to Duns Scotus' Commentaries on the Sentences are to John Duns Scotus 1950–.)

time.[54] He refers to earlier attempts to explain the freedom of the will by means of the statistical interpretation of possibility – i.e., by asserting that the will can successively intend opposite objects.[55] This kind of contingency is not a sufficient basis for the freedom of will, however. It says nothing about the question whether the will while willing something could have not willed it then. That is why a satisfactory account of the freedom of the will presupposes a different concept of possibility. Scotus calls it a logical potency (*potentia logica*) or logical possibility (*possibilitas logica*). It characterises what is not contradictory regardless of whether or not it ever is actual.[56] Its function for Scotus in this connection is to show that contradictory sentences can be possible with respect to the same time. When Scotus says that there are real potencies which correspond to logical possibilities,[57] he means that realisation in the actual world is no longer the criterion of real possibility. The distinction between logical and real possibilities takes account of the fact that not all logical possibilities are real alternatives of the actual world. In Scotus' opinion the general structure of nature puts certain limits on real possibilities. But the possibility of willing otherwise is a real alternative because it does not demand that the structure of the actual world should be different.[58] The sentence 'He who is willing something at instant A can be not willing it at instant A' is then analysed by Scotus in accordance with the traditional distinction *secundum compositionem* and *secundum divisionem:* on the first interpretation it is false and on the second interpretation it is true. But it is historically important that Scotus goes on to point out that on the latter interpretation it is true not because the mutually exclusive predicates refer to different moments of time. Instead, the sentence must be interpreted as a conjunction of two sentences, in one of which an act of willing is said to occur, and in the other an opposite act of willing is said to be possible.[59]

The starting-point of Duns Scotus' modal theory is the concept of logical possibility. Every sentence which does not contain a contradiction is logically possible.[60] Each possibility can be thought of as being ac-

54. *Lect.* I, d. 39, q. 1–5, n. 45, 47.
55. *Ibid.* n. 48.
56. *Ibid.* n. 49–50.
57. *Ibid.*
58. *Ibid.* n. 50–4; see also Balić 1931, pp. 193–99, Roberts 1973 pp. 1ff. For examples of different logical possibilities see Sharp 1930, pp. 362–3. For real possibilities and the structure of the world see *Ord.* I, d. 3, pars 1, q. 4, n. 235–7, d. 8, pars 2, q.u., n. 306.
59. *Lect.* I, d. 39, q. 1–5, n. 51–2.
60. *Ord.* I, d. 2, pars 2, q. 1–4, n. 262, *Ord.* I, d. 7, q. 1, n. 27, *Ord.* I, d. 20, q. u., n. 11–12, *Lect.* I, d. 5, pars 2, q.u., n. 118. The concept *possibile logicum* does not occur in the literature before Scotus; see Faust 1931–2, II, pp. 247–59. Deku 1956, p. 15.

tualised. This does not mean, however, that every possibility could be actualised in the world, because not all possibilities are compossible.[61]

In Duns Scotus' modal theory modal notions are no longer understood as classifying the states of the actual world at different times. The domain of possibility is accepted as an *a priori* area of conceptual consistency which is then divided into different classes of compossible states of affairs, of which the actual world is one. Thus it was not Leibniz who invented the idea of possible worlds; the idea is present in Duns Scotus' modal theory, and this new view of modal notions constitutes the general basis of fourteenth-century modal logic.

Buridan's theory of modal consequences

As an example of the new modal logic I present the main lines of the theory of modal consequences in John Buridan. He first discusses the modal statements *in sensu diviso*, claiming that the domain of the subject term of both necessary and possible sentences must be ampliated so that in addition to the actual objects it contains those that are possible.[62] First the relationships between modal statements and *de inesse* statements are regulated. In the following formulations '⊢' indicates validity and '⊬' invalidity, '□' means 'necessarily' and '◇' 'possibly', while '(x)' and '∃x' mean 'all' and 'some', respectively. The domain over which the variable 'x' ranges in modal sentences is that of possible objects; they may be actual or merely possible.

The rules for necessary and *de inesse* sentences are as follows:

(1) $\nvdash (x)(\Diamond Ax \supset \Box Bx) \supset (x)(Ax \supset Bx)$

(2) $\nvdash \exists x(\Diamond Ax \,\&\, \Box Bx) \supset \exists x(Ax \,\&\, Bx)$

(3) $\nvdash \exists x(\Diamond Ax \,\&\, \Box \sim Bx) \supset \exists x(Ax \,\&\, \sim Bx)$

(4) $\vdash (x)(\Diamond Ax \supset \Box \sim Bx) \supset (x)(Ax \supset \sim Bx)$

None of the converse consequences are accepted.[63] (1) and (2) are not valid because the domain of the relevant individuals may be empty. In medieval logic it is usually supposed that in such a case affirmative sentences are not true although negative sentences can be true even if the subject is an empty term.[64] Therefore (4) is valid even if the extension of A in the actual world is empty. By contrast, (3) is not valid because it is compatible with the

---

61. *Ord.* I, d. 43, q.u., n. 16; *Lect.* I, d. 39, q. 1–5, n. 72. The idea of compossibility in the model entails that possibilities are classified into equivalence classes on the basis of the relations of compossibility (*Ord.* I, d. 43, q.u., n. 14, 16). One of the classes into which logical possibilities are partitioned is the actual world (*Lect.* I, d. 39, q. 1–5, n. 62–3).

62. Buridan 1976, *lib.* II, *cap.* 4, pp. 58–60.

63. *Ibid. lib.* II, *cap.* 6, *concl.* 3, pp. 64.106–65.138.

64. See, e.g., Ockham 1974a, I, *cap.* 72, p. 219.124–6.

antecedent that every actual A should be B. The corresponding rules for
possible and *de inesse* sentences are:

(5) $\nvDash (x)(\Diamond Ax \supset \Diamond Bx) \supset (x)(Ax \supset Bx)$
(6) $\nvDash (x)(\Diamond Ax \supset \Diamond \sim Bx) \supset (x)(Ax \supset \sim Bx)$
(7) $\nvDash \exists x(\Diamond Ax \& \Diamond Bx) \supset \exists x(Ax \& Bx)$
(8) $\nvDash \exists x(\Diamond Ax \& \Diamond \sim Bx) \supset \exists x(Ax \& \sim Bx)$
(9) $\vdash (x)(Ax \supset Bx) \supset \exists x(\Diamond Ax \& \Diamond Bx)$
(10) $\vdash \exists x(Ax \& Bx) \supset \exists x(\Diamond Ax \& \Diamond Bx)$
(11) $\nvDash (x)(Ax \supset \sim Bx) \supset (x)(\Diamond Ax \supset \Diamond \sim Bx)$
(12) $\nvDash \exists x(Ax \& \sim Bx) \supset \exists x(\Diamond Ax \& \Diamond \sim Bx)$[65]

Of these, (11) and (12) are not accepted because the subject of a true
negative *de inesse* statement can be empty – it can even be impossible, and
then the subject of a possible predicate is not one which actually is or can be.

The conversion rules for modal sentences *in sensu diviso* are such that
from an affirmative statement *de possibili* a particular affirmative statement
de possibili follows by the conversion of terms. But a negative sentence does
not imply any sentence *de possibili*. Of necessary statements only the
universal negative statement is convertible. Every statement *de contingenti
ad utrumlibet* can be converted into one of an opposite quality, but no
conversion of terms yields a statement *de contingenti ad utrumlibet*.[66]

After the rules for divided modal statements Buridan discusses those for
modal statements *in sensu composito*. If the *dictum* of the proposition is taken
to be the subject and the modal term the predicate, then there is a
conversion of the terms, except that a universal affirmative is converted
only into a particular affirmative, i.e., 'Every proposition "B is A" is
possible' is converted into 'Some possible proposition is "B is A"'.[67] As far
as the terms of the *dictum* are concerned, they are converted in the same way
as statements *de inesse*. This is based, according to Buridan, on the two rules
of inference which are basic in the modal logic of statements *in sensu
composito*:

(13) $$\frac{p \supset q}{\Diamond p \supset \Diamond q}$$

and

(14) $$\frac{p \supset q}{\Box p \supset \Box q}$$[68]

65. Buridan 1976, *lib.* II, *cap.* 6, *concl.* 4, pp. 65.140–66.170.
66. *Ibid. cap.* 6, *concl.* 5–8, pp. 66.172–69.254.
67. *Ibid. cap.* 7, *concl.* 10, pp. 71.68–72.88.
68. *Ibid. cap.* 7, *concl.* 12, pp. 72.98–73.129.

The rules governing the relationships between modal statements *in sensu composito* and *in sensu diviso* are similar to those between *de inesse* and *in sensu diviso*. Thus the following statements are accepted:

(15) $\vdash \Diamond(x)(Ax \supset Bx) \supset \exists x(\Diamond Ax \;\&\; \Diamond Bx)$

(16) $\vdash \Diamond\exists x(Ax \;\&\; Bx) \supset \exists x(\Diamond Ax \;\&\; \Diamond Bx)$

(17) $\vdash (x)(\Diamond Ax \supset \Box \sim Bx) \supset \Box(x)(Ax \supset \sim Bx)^{69}$

These rules are then applied by Buridan to modal syllogistic. If the conjunction of premisses *in sensu composito* is the antecedent and the conclusion is the consequent, then by rules (13) and (14) it follows that in every valid assertoric mode a necessary conclusion follows if the premisses together are necessary, and the same holds of possible premisses. Because the compossibility of two possible premisses is not assured, however, only conclusions from necessary premisses are acceptable. This is based on the following rules:

(18) $\vdash (\Box p \;\&\; \Box q) \supset \Box(p \;\&\; q)$

(19) $\nvdash (\Diamond p \;\&\; \Diamond q) \supset \Diamond(p \;\&\; q)^{70}$

While speaking of modal syllogisms in which the premisses are *in sensu diviso*, Buridan separately discusses the modes in which the domain of subject terms of modal premisses is restricted to actual beings and the modes in which it is ampliated to include possible beings as well.[71]

I have discussed Buridan as an example of the new fourteenth-century approach to modal logic. Similar treatments can be found, e.g., in Ockham and the Pseudo-Scotus.[72]

The formulations introduced above show that something like quantification into modal contexts was usual in fourteenth-century modal logic. It is interesting that certain recent problems connected with this type of quantification were discussed in the fourteenth century.[73] This side of medieval philosophical logic is, *ut nunc*, largely unexplored; the same holds of fourteenth-century epistemic logic and other branches of modal logic as well.[74]

69. *Ibid. cap.* 7, *concl.* 17–18, pp. 76.214–78.256.
70. *Ibid. lib.* IV, *cap.* 1, *concl.* 1, p. 113.69–90. Buridan does not discuss mixed modes here.
71. *Ibid. cap.* 2, pp. 114–28.
72. Ockham 1974a, II, *cap.* 24–9, pp. 327–45; III–1, *cap.* 20–64, pp. 411–97; III–3, *cap.* 10–16, pp. 631–49; Pseudo-Scotus 1639, qq. 25–33, pp. 309–25; McDermott 1972, pp. 273–306.
73. For the problem of reaching the reference of a term in different states of affairs see Ockham 1974a, I, *cap.* 72, pp. 216.58–217.80; Loux 1974, pp. 38–42. In Chapter IV of his *Sophismata* Buridan discusses extensively the principles of substitutivity of identity and existential generalisation in cognitive contexts. See Moody 1975, pp. 353–70.
74. See, e.g., Pseudo-Scotus 1639, q. 36, pp. 328–30; Buridan 1976, *lib.* IV, *cap.* 1, *concl.* 3, p. 114.107–12; Ockham 1974a, III–1, *cap.* 30, pp. 435–9.

18
FUTURE CONTINGENTS

Three problems involving future contingents

There is more than one problem of future contingents. There is first the problem raised by Aristotle[1] – that of reconciling the principle of bivalence (the principle that for any sentence P either P is true or not-P is true) with the view that some claims about the future are contingent, are such that neither the claim nor its denial is necessarily true.[2] Medieval discussions of this problem often rely on our intuitions that the past and the present are 'fixed' in some way in which the future is not, and so these discussions often illuminate medieval views on tense and modality.

A second problem has to do with the possibility of foreknowledge. Can one hold both that some future event is contingent and that it is foreknown?

A third problem is specifically theological. Can complete knowledge of the future by an immutable, infallible, impassible God be reconciled with the contingency of some aspects of the future?

These are distinct problems. Theories which solve the problem of contingent truth may fail to account for foreknowledge, and theories which account for both future contingent truth and foreknowledge may yet fail to explain how contingent future events, e.g. sins, can be known by a knower who cannot be causally acted upon.

Yet all three problems are variations on a single theme. We are inclined to think that there is an objective difference between the past and the future. What has happened happened as a result of earlier events including perhaps actions of our own but now that it has happened it does not depend

---

1. Aristotle discusses the contingency of the future in at least two places: *De interpretatione*, Ch. 9, and *Metaphysics*, Book VI, Ch. 3. This chapter will focus on the medieval response to the first discussion. The discussion in *Metaphysics* VI was typically understood by medieval writers to be of 'causal' rather than 'logical' determinism.
2. It is useful to distinguish what I here call the principle of bivalence from another principle, namely that for any sentence P, 'P or not-P' is true. The two are equivalent within the usual logical frameworks but can be distinguished. It seems to me, for example, that Ockham's reconstruction of Aristotle's account in *De interpretatione*, Ch. 9, separates them. For a discussion of the logical points involved, see Van Fraassen 1971, Ch. 5.3.

on anything agents will do. An adult may regret his misspent youth but cannot prevent it. On the other hand what will happen is dependent on what is happening and is, we think, in part dependent on what we and other agents will do. We think that some of what we will do we could avoid. The problems of future contingents arise because there seem to be various principles which connect every statement about the future with a corresponding statement about the past in such a way that it is impossible for one of the statements to be true and the other false. If any such principle is accepted, our intuitions about the objective difference between past and future may have to be revised.

Future contingents in antiquity and the patristic period

The later Middle Ages inherited the various problems of future contingents from antiquity and from the Church Fathers. The earliest extant discussion, in Chapter 9 of Aristotle's *De interpretatione*, was available throughout the medieval period, and this work, together with Boethius' two commentaries on it, formed part of the core of medieval curricula. The special problems raised by prophecy and divine omniscience were known through a number of sources, notably Augustine's comments on Cicero's views in *De civitate Dei*, Book V, Ch. 9, and Boethius' remarkable discussion in *De consolatione philosophiae* Book V. Although apparently little utilised, neo-Platonic conceptions of fate were available in Calcidius' commentary on Plato's *Timaeus*.

Anselm on future contingents, foreknowledge, and freedom

We can obtain a good picture of the state of the problem at the beginning of the later Middle Ages by considering the position defended by Anselm of Canterbury. Anselm discusses future contingents at length in his *De concordia praescientiae et praedestinationis et gratiae Dei cum libero arbitrio*, Q.1, and provides short discussions of particular aspects of the matter in *Cur Deus homo* II, c. 17, and in *De casu diaboli* XXI. His discussion centres on the compatibility of contingency and divine foreknowledge.

Anselm holds that God exists in eternity, and so events which occur at different times are 'simultaneous' for him – the doctrine of God's eternality on which Boethius had founded his rejection of the concept of divine *fore*knowledge.[3] Attempts to clarify the notion of eternity and show its

---

3. 'Habet enim aeternitas suum simul, in quo sunt omnia quae simul sunt loco vel tempore, et quae sunt diversis in locis vel temporibus.' 'For eternity has its own "simultaneity" wherein exist all things that occur at the same time and place and that occur at different times and places.' Anselm 1946d, p. 254.13–14. Cf. Boethius, *De consolatione philosophiae*, Book V, Prose 6.

relevance to the problem constitute one strand of the later medieval development.

The key to Anselm's treatment is his distinction between 'antecedent' and 'subsequent' necessity. The nature of 'antecedent necessity' is not entirely clear. Sometimes, notably in *Cur Deus homo* II, 17, Anselm speaks as if necessity is the basic notion and as if some situation is antecedently necessary just in case some force compels or constrains it to obtain. At other times, particularly in the drafts which have been published as the *Incomplete Work* (or *Philosophical Fragments*) and in *De libero arbitrii*, it seems that the basic notion is power or ability, and so it seems that some situation is necessary just in case there is no power which can prevent or undo it. These notions are not trivially equivalent. For example, if there were nothing at all, that there be nothing at all would be necessary on the second conception but not on the first. It is clear that some notion of what can and cannot *be done* underlies Anselm's picture of antecedent necessity. To illustrate this type of necessity he uses an example from Boethius, claiming that it is antecedently necessary that the sun will rise tomorrow and moreover that the sun will rise tomorrow *because* it is necessary that it rise (*De concordia* I, 3). 'Subsequent necessity', on the other hand, is pretty clearly relative necessity. If A then (subsequently) necessarily B if and only if it is impossible that A obtain and B not obtain (where 'impossible' is the correlate of *antecedently* necessary). It is in this sense of subsequent necessity that what is past is necessarily past, what is present is necessarily so, and what will be necessarily will be;[4] and it is in this sense that what God foreknows necessarily will come to pass. As Anselm insists, this sort of necessity is innocuous. It is only if we can be persuaded that what will be necessarily will be in some stronger sense of 'necessarily' that our belief in contingency is endangered. The problem of future contingents arises only if the future is antecedently necessary.

Anselm holds that God and the angels choose freely, but he also holds that one can choose freely even where what one chooses is the only available option.[5] This feature of Anselm's account of free choice is of

4. 'Pariter autem verum est quia fuit et est et erit aliquid non ex necessitate, et quia necesse est fuisse omne quod fuit, et esse quod est, et futurum esse quod erit.' 'However, it is equally true that there was and is and will be something which is not by necessity, and that all that was necessarily has been and what is [necessarily] is and what will be [necessarily] is going to be.' Anselm 1946d. p. 249, 10–12.
5. I take this to be implied by Anselm's argument that the ability to sin is not essential for freedom of the will. 'Magister. Libertatem arbitrii non puto esse potentiam peccandi et non peccandi. Quippe si haec eius esset definitio: nec deus nec angeli qui peccare nequeunt liberum haberent arbitrium; quod nefas est dicere.' Anselm 1946a, p. 207.

considerable importance for his account of future contingents. Because free choice requires absence of constraint but does not always require more than one alternative, many of the problems about the relation between prophecy and free action which beset later writers do not arise.

The one context in Anselm's work within which some of those problems do arise is his consideration of the problem whether one can foreknow one's own sin. In *De casu diaboli*, c. 21, Anselm argues that one could not do so, and at one place in his argument he seems to suggest that one cannot simultaneously will not to commit a sin and believe that one will commit it.[6] This principle would in particular raise puzzles about Peter's threefold denial of Christ and Christ's prediction to Peter of this denial. Not surprisingly it plays a role in fourteenth- and fifteenth-century discussions.

The interpretation of Aristotle's view of truth

In the period after Anselm much of the discussion of future contingents centred around the interpretation of Aristotle's view of truth, the view that a sentence is true if things are as the sentence says they are. On one interpretation of this view a sentence *is* true only if the way things *now* are verifies it. If one holds that a sentence is false only if the way things now are verifies its negation then this interpretation might lead one to abandon the principle of bivalence.

Abelard on future contingents

The first towering figure in this discussion after Anselm is Peter Abelard. Both the problem of future contingent truths and the problem of foreknowledge arise naturally in his discussions of Aristotle's *De interpretatione*, Ch. 9, and the problem of foreknowledge arises in many of his theological works as well. Abelard understands *De interpretatione* Ch. 9 as a defence of the claim made in *De interpretatione* Ch. 6 that every sentence has a contradictory. He considers two arguments against this which he extracts from *De interpretatione*, and in the course of replying to them he develops an unusual account of his own.

The second argument is sketched in his gloss *Editio super Aristotelem De*

---

6. 'M. Est et aliud quod mihi satis videtur ostendere nullo modo eum suam ante putavisse futuram prevaricationem. Nempe aut coactum putavisset aut spontaneam. Sed nec ullatenus erat unde se aliquando cogi suspicaretur, nec quamdiu voluit in veritate perseverare, ullo modo putare potuit se sola voluntate illam deserturum. Supra namque iam monstratum est eum, quamdiu rectam voluntatem habuit, in hac ipsa voluntate voluisse perseverare. Quapropter volendo tenere perseveranter quod tenebat, nullo modo video unde potuisset vel suspicari nulla alia antecedente causa sola se illud deserturum voluntate.' Anselm 1946c, c. 21, p. 268.

interpretatione.[7] It begins with the premiss that some contingent sentence P is true and proceeds in this way. If P is true then 'P will be true' was true, and since this is a sentence about the past, ' "P will be true" was true' is determinately true, or determinate. But then what makes it true, namely *that P*, is determinate, and hence P is determinate. Abelard's discussion of this argument naturally focuses on the sense of 'determinate'. In both his *Dialectica* and the commentary on *De interpretatione* in his *Logica 'Ingredientibus'* Abelard explains 'determinate' in epistemological terms, claiming that it applies primarily to states of affairs and secondarily to sentences which report them. In the *Dialectica* he explains that a state of affairs is determinate if it can be known either from the fact of its occurrence (*ex existentia sui*) or from its very nature (*ex natura rei*).[8]

In the *Logica 'Ingredientibus'* Abelard claims that future contingent sentences are not determinate; though they are true or false, they are indeterminately true or false. But he points out that since (1) ' "Socrates will eat" is true' entails (2) "Socrates will eat", we must either deny that (1) is determinate and so admit that not all sentences 'about' the past or present are determinate, or assert that valid inference does not preserve determinateness.[9] His reason for adopting the first alternative seems to be that

---

7. 'Et amplius probo quod perit casus et utrumlibet; tua sententia est quod si est album nunc in re verum erat dicere primo quoniam album est, id est vera erat propositio determinate quae prius enuntiavit; et si quia vera fuit determinate propositio quae hoc enuntiavit, ideo quia postea ita evenit in re: quare semper verum fuit dicere determinate quoniam erit quodlibet eorum quae facta sunt, id est omnes illae propositiones fuerunt verae determinate quarum res evenerunt.' Abelard 1969a, p. 103.

8. 'Determinatos autem eos rerum eventus dicimus quicumque vel ex existentia sui cognosci possunt vel ex natura rei certi sunt. Ex existentia quidem sui cognosci potuerunt tam presentia quam preterita. Ipsa namque preterita, quia quandoque presentia fuerunt, [quare] ex presentia sui cognosci valuerunt. Futura vero necessaria sive etiam naturalia ex proprietate nature determinata sunt.' Abelard 1970a, p. 211.5ff.

9. 'De quibusdam tamen praesentibus sive praeteritis restat quaestio, utrum definita sint vel indefinita, cum indefinita per futura indeterminata sciri queant. Ita cum dicitur "Socrates comedet", haec propositio iam profecto praesentaliter est vera vel falsa et haec propositio quae dicit ' "Socrates comedet" vera est" de praesenti est et ideo iam determinate vera est vel determinate falsa ... Sed nec istae de praesenti "Socrates est nomen hominis comesturi in crastino" vel "Homo comesturus in crastino est Socrates" ... determinari possunt nisi per futurum. ... Non itaque omnes de praesenti vel praeterito propositiones verae vel falsae determinate esse videntur, quando videlicet veritatis earum vel falsitatis discretio ex futuro pendet. ... Sunt autem qui dicunt, quod "Socrates comedet" quae fortasse se praesentaliter habet, quippe determinatus est eventus proprietatis praesentaliter ei inhaerentis et ipsam iam determinate veritatem habet. Sed licet determinate vera dicatur propositio quantum ad praesentem et determinatam inhaerentiam veritatis quantum tamen ad eventum, quem loquitur indeterminatum, indeterminate vera est. ... Aliud etiam "determinatum" sonare videtur quam "certum" quia determinatus dicitur eventus, qui ex se cognoscibilis nobis, ut paritas et imparitas astrorum ex ipsa praesentia, quam habent, de se cognitionem dare potest; certa vero sunt, quae quoquomodo actualiter cognita sunt, ut si quid de futuro contingenti testimonio angeli ad discretionem ⟨venerit⟩, certum quidem esset mihi non

there are some present-tensed truths which we cannot know and which are therefore not determinate as defined. In the *Dialectica*, however, he opts for the second alternative.[10]

Abelard on foreknowledge

Abelard's views on foreknowledge are straightforward by comparison. He thinks that God knows all future contingent truths and that these can be revealed to us by God.[11] But most of his discussion centres on reconciling the contingency of parts of the future with the view that God's foreknowledge is infallible. In particular he aims to show that 'It is possible for something other than what God foreknows to happen' has two senses. Read as claiming that 'Something other than what God foreknows happens' could be true it is false, but determinism is not thereby supported. Read as claiming of some particular event that it will not happen and so is not foreknown although it could happen, it is true, but divine infallibility is not thereby threatened.

Peter Lombard

The most influential twelfth-century work on future contingents is recorded in Book I, d. 38–40, of the *Sentences* of Peter Lombard. Lombard begins Book I, d. 38, c. 1, by asking 'whether the knowledge or foreknowledge of God is the cause of things or conversely?' Unlike Augustine and Anselm who seem to favour the view that God knows the future because he in some sense makes it, Lombard denies any causal connection between divine knowledge as such and its objects. He does not explain how knowledge without causal connection might work, however. He thus sets the stage for one of the most persistent later medieval controversies.

In distinction 39 Lombard is concerned largely with whether God *can* know what he *does not* know. His problem is thus to reconcile the contingency of the future with divine infallibility and immutability. His solution to the problem of divine infallibility is very like Abelard's. He

ex se, sed ex auctoritate angeli, sed determinatum non esset, quia ex se ipso cognoscibilis non esset . . . Unde etsi talis consequentia recipiatur: "Si 'Socrates comedet' est vera, Socrates comedet" et certum sit antecedens, certum est consequens. Sed non fortasse, si determinatum sit antecedens, et consequens, quia praesens eventus ex se cognoscibilis est, sed non ita futurus contingens.' Abelard 1919–27, pp. 427ff.

10. Abelard 1970a, p. 212.

11. In Abelard 1970a, p. 212.15ff., Abelard supposes that God can reveal future contingents: 'Futura vero ex se cognosci non valent, sed si aliquam certitudinem per reponsum divinum vel per signa aliqua de futuris habere contingeret, certa quidem esse possent quocumque modo cognita, sed non determinata, nisi ex proprio eventu cognoscerentur.' Cf. Abelard 1919–27, pp. 426–9.

distinguishes two senses of 'Things cannot be other than as God foreknows them', a compounded sense in which it is false and a divided sense in which it is true. The truth of the latter guards divine infallibility and the falsity of the former preserves the contingency of the future.

But Lombard's discussion of the immutability of divine knowledge differs markedly from Abelard's. In his *Logica 'Ingredientibus'* Abelard allows that God's knowledge can change as the world changes but insists that such change is not real change in God.[12] Lombard's view is that although God's knowledge is immutable, God can know what he does not know because he creates freely and hence can create what he does not create (a position disputed by Abelard), and because some creatures can do what they will not do.[13]

By insisting on God's freedom Lombard focuses attention on a sense of 'possible' which is sharply distinguished from mutability. God can know what he does not know, but his knowledge cannot change. For Lombard, then, there are claims which can be true but which never are true.

Robert Grosseteste

The distinction between necessity and immutability is taken up by Robert Grosseteste and used as the basis of one of the most penetrating and influential medieval approaches to the question. Grosseteste begins his treatise *De libero arbitrio* by distinguishing what is simply necessary from what is merely immutable.[14] The simply necessary is what could not be otherwise no matter how the history of the world had gone. (His example is 'Two and three is five.') The immutable is what cannot be one way after

---

12. 'Similiter cum modo me sedente, modo non sedente dicitur scire vel intelligere me sedentem et non intelligere vel scire me sedentem, nulla est in ipso variatio, sed in me; quocumque modo me habeam ipsum latere non possum. Cum itaque omnino in se Deus invariabilis subsistat, secundum variationem creaturum vel varios effectus ipsius quasi distenditur'. Abelard 1919–27, p. 428.

13. Lombard writes: 'Ex hac auctoritate clare ostenditur, scientiam Dei omnino invariabilem esse, sicut ipsa essentia Dei omnino invariabilis est . . . Et tamen conceditur posse scire quod non scit et posse non scire quod scit, quia posset aliquid esse subiectum eius scientiae, quod non est, et posset non esse subiectum aliquid quod est, sine permutatione ipsius scientiae.' Peter Lombard 1916, vol. I, p. 246.

14. 'Dico igitur quod est necessarium duplex: uno modo quod non habet posse aliquo modo ad eius oppositum vel cum initio vel fine, cuiusmodi est hoc: "Duo et tria esse quinque". Istud enim posse non habuit neque ante tempus, neque in tempore ad non esse verum. Et tale est necessarium simpliciter. Et est aliud necessarium, quod neque secundum praeteritum, neque secundum praesens, neque secundum futurum habet posse ad eius oppositum, sine tamen initio fuit posse ad hoc et fuit posse ad eius oppositum et tale est "Antichristum fore futurum" et omnium eorum quae sunt de futuro, quod eorum veritas, cum est, non potest habere non-esse post esse, ut supra ostensum est. Et tamen posse ad hoc, ut ab aeterno et sine initio fuerint falsa.' Grosseteste 1912a, Ch. 6.

being another, and so the truth of sentences about the future is immutable. For if 'The Antichrist will come' ever was true then (until the Antichrist comes) it will be true.[15] Grosseteste thus distinguishes three modal strengths: the simply contingent, – as in 'Socrates is white', which can be true at one time and false at another – the immutable, and the simply necessary. Grosseteste uses this distinction to explain how God can know what he does not know. God's knowledge is immutable but not simply necessary. Even though it is immutably true that the Antichrist will come, it is not simply necessary. Were its (simply contingent) contradictory to be true, God would always have known it.

Both claims about the past and claims about the future are immutable, and there is no indication that the past any more than the future is simply or absolutely necessary.[16] Yet Grosseteste does want to claim that an un-realised possibility can be realised only in the future.[17] He thus must still explain how God can know what he never has known even though his knowledge is immutable. The solution is that for God the act of knowing A is the very same act as that by which he would know not-A were not-A true.

Grosseteste's distinction between simple necessity and immutability enables him to provide a sense in which the future is contingent, but it does not explain how the past is necessary in a way in which the future is not. There are true past-tensed sentences which are immutably true whose true future-tensed analogues are not immutably true: 'Adam existed' is immutably true but 'The Antichrist will exist' will become false when the Antichrist dies. But there are also immutable future-tensed sentences

15. One might object that sentences such as 'The Antichrist will come' *will* cease to be true after being true; once the Antichrist comes it is false to say that he will come. Grosseteste is not unaware of this. Indeed, he writes: 'Sicut enim veritas huius "Deus scit A" vel "Antichristus fuit futurus" vel "Isias praedixit hoc verum" non potest desinere, sic veritas vel futuritio huius "Antichristus est futurus vel erit" non potest desinere *nisi per exhibitionem esse Antichristi*' (emphasis added). Grosseteste 1912a, Ch. 6, p. 170.23–8.

16. 'Unde illud simpliciter est necessarium, ad cuius aliquo modo non-esse nullo modo est posse. Est alio modo necessarium, scilicet quod cum est, non est posse ad ipsum habere non-esse post esse, quod habet. Sic vera de praeterito patenter sunt necessaria. Et hoc necessarium sequitur ad necessarium prius dictum. Unde necessarium simpliciter dividitur in necessarium supra dictum et in necessarium quod cum non-posse ad habere non esse post esse habet posse ad sine initio numquam esse vel fuisse vel fore. Talis est veritas dictorum de futuro, quia eorum veritas, cum est, non potest habere non-esse post esse, ut supra ostensum est, et tamen posse ad hoc, ut sine initio et ab aeterno fuerint vera; et posse ad hoc ut ab aeterno et sine initio fuerint falsa est posse ad falsitatem non initiabilem et ad veritatem non initiabilem in his. Sed cum habet veritatem et falsitatem, non est posse ad oppositum eius quod habeat post id, quod habet.' Grosseteste 1912a, p. 169.

17. 'Et tamen verum est, quod possibilitas sine actu solum est respectu futuri.' Grosseteste 1912a, p. 183.22–4.

whose past-tensed analogues are mutable. Thus Grosseteste's solution dissolves the problem by abandoning any deep difference between the modal status of the past and of the future. It is with this difference that much of the succeeding century is concerned.

Thomas Aquinas

Thomas Aquinas discusses the problem of future contingents in each of his comprehensive works, focusing on whether and how God can have foreknowledge of contingents. His position sometimes is that God can have such foreknowledge and that he has it through his knowledge of his own creative power: 'The knowledge of God is related to all created things just as the knowledge of a craftsman is related to his product.'[18] This raises a problem, however. A craftsman knows what he will make because his is the only free choice involved, but God is not always the only free agent involved in a *contingent* future. Either God's creative activity is a sufficient condition for my choosing to sin, in which case he can foreknow it but it is not clear that my choice is both free and efficacious, or God's creative activity is a necessary but not a sufficient condition, in which case it is not easy to see how knowledge of it alone constitutes foreknowledge. Aquinas seems to take the first horn of this dilemma. Like Anselm he denies that being able not to choose A is a necessary condition for choosing A freely, and so he can hold that a particular outcome is freely chosen by me even if God's activity guarantees its coming to pass.[19]

There is however another strand in Aquinas' thought – the view that God is able to know the future because all things, past, present, and future, are eternally present to him. This suggests a picture of the whole of time laid out before God, as does Aquinas' famous image of God as a man high up on a mountain watching others move along a road below.[20]

As interesting and as puzzling as Aquinas' account of God's mode of knowing the future is his discussion of the problems raised by the fact that it *was* true to say that God knew what is yet future, and that the past is in some

---

18. 'Dicendum quod scientia Dei est causa rerum. Sic enim scientia Dei se habet ad omnes res creatas, sicut scientia artificis se habet ad artificialia.' *ST*, I, Q. 14, art. 8.
19. At *ST*, I, Q. 62, art. 8, Aquinas argues that the good angels have free will though they cannot sin. Cf. *De veritate*, Q. 6.
20. The image of the road appears in *ST*, I, Q. 14, art. 13 *ad* 3. Following out this strain of Aquinas' thought one might conclude that he thinks that the past and the future in some sense *are*. But he denies this in *De veritate* Q. 1, art. 5, *ad* 6 and 7: 'Ad sextum et septimum dicendum quod id quod est futurum, in quantum est futurum non est, et similiter praeteritum, in quantum huiusmodi. Unde eadem est ratio de veritate praeteriti et futuri, sicut et de veritate non entis, ex qua non potest concludi aeternitas alicuius veritatis, nisi primae, ut dictum est' (Aquinas 1953a).

sense necessary.[21] The sentence 'If God knew that some contingent thing was going to be, then it will be' is true, and its antecedent is if true necessarily true because it is about the past. Hence if the antecedent is true the consequent is necessarily true. Aquinas agrees that the conditional is true, and that if the antecedent of a true conditional is necessary so is the consequent, and that a true sentence about the past is necessarily true. But he apparently doubts that the antecedent of this conditional really is about the past. Aquinas, following Boethius, argues that since God sees everything in an eternal present and since 'all that is, when it is, is necessarily', the antecedent and so the consequent of the conditional under discussion are necessary but with the relative (and harmless) necessity which attaches to present truths.[22]

John Duns Scotus

When considered against the background of Aquinas's position, Scotus' discussions of God's knowledge signal the clash of two fundamentally different ways of conceiving the nature of time. The first, which seems to have been Boethius' and may have been Aquinas', conceives the difference between past and future as perspectival rather than ontological. Human beings have relations to past events which differ from those we have to future events, but these differences are grounded in us rather than in the world outside us. The second view, the one for which Scotus argues and the one which seems to be taken more or less for granted in the first quarter of the fourteenth century, sees the difference between past and future as an objective difference, one that exists for God as well as for us.

Having rejected the possibility that God knows the contingent future by inspection, Scotus seeks another account. The one he adopts grounds God's infallible foreknowledge in the determinations of the divine will. As Scotus develops the account both in his *Lectura* and later in the *Ordinatio*, the truth-value of contingent claims about the future is not first apprehended by

21. 'Ad primum ergo dicendum quod, licet praeterita non fuisse sit impossibile per accidens, si consideretur id quod est praeteritum, idest cursus Socratis; tamen si consideretur praeteritum sub ratione praeteriti, ipsum non fuisse est impossibile non solum per se, sed absolute, contradictionem implicans.' *ST*, I, Q. 25, art. 4.

22. 'Et ideo aliter dicendum est quod quando in antecedente ponitur aliquid pertinens ad actum animae, consequens est accipiendum non secundum quod in se est, sed secundum quod est in anima. Aliud enim est esse rei in se ipsa, et esse rei in anima ut puta si dicam "si anima intelligit aliquid, illud est immateriale", intelligendum est quod illud est immateriale secundum quod est in intellectu, non secundum quod est in se ipso. Et similiter si dicam: "Si Deus scivit aliquid, illud erit", consequens intelligendum est prout subest divinae scientiae, scilicet prout est in sua praesentialitate. Et sic necessarium est, sicut et antecedens. Quia omne quod est, dum est, necesse est esse, ut dicitur in I Perih.' *ST*, I, Q. 14, art. 13, *ad* 2.

God.[23] Rather the divine intellect first considers such *unasserted complexa* as *that the Antichrist will come*. The divine will then makes these *complexa* true or false by asserting or denying them, and by inspecting the divine will the divine intellect then sees how things will turn out.[24]

As an account designed to reconcile foreknowledge with contingency this seems to leave too little to the created agent. If the divine will *chooses* to make *that Peter will deny Christ* true, then unless this choice is itself dependent on Peter's choice it does not seem that it is *Peter* who makes the sentence true.

But whether or not Scotus' own account of divine foreknowledge is successful, the theory of necessity and possibility with which he buttresses it is of great importance for the subsequent history of the problem. Unlike Aquinas, Scotus holds that if any effect is to be contingent the activity of the first cause on which that effect depends must be contingent. But all of God's activity is a single eternal act which is God himself. Hence if there is to be contingency God must be able to will the contrary of whatever he wills. Scotus insists that this is so and moreover that this is a power of created free agents as well.[25] Of course Scotus does not mean that an agent can at the same time will that a state of affairs and its contrary obtain. Rather he is proposing replacing the doctrine of the necessity of the present with a new criterion: a claim is possible if there is no '*repugnantia terminorum*', no semantical inconsistency, in supposing it to obtain.[26]

Scotus uses his abandonment of the necessity of the present to explain

---

23. According to Balić 1965, Scotus lectured on the *Sentences* at least three times, first in Cambridge and then, in a complex sequence, at Oxford and Paris. The *Lectura* is a transcription of the notes Scotus used for his Oxford lectures. The *Ordinatio* or *Opus Oxoniense* contains, in Balić's words (p. 20), 'the text that Scotus himself either wrote or dictated from his various lectures and writings and ordered in such a way as to present the material in the form of a Summa of his entire doctrine'. The material with which this section is chiefly concerned is found in distinctions 39 and 40 of Book I of the *Lectura* and the *Ordinatio*. The most detailed discussion of the problem of the truth of contingent claims about the future to be found in the Scotist corpus is presented in Scotus 1891, QQ. 7 and 8. This work is usually considered authentic, but there are features of the discussion – notably the apparent denial of a simultaneous capacity for opposites in Q. 8, 8 – that lead me to distrust it.

24. 'Unde quando intellectus divinus apprehendit "hoc esse faciendum" ante voluntatis actum, apprehendit ut neutram, sicut cum apprehendo "astra esse paria"; sed quando per actum voluntatis producitur in esse, tunc est apprehensum ab intellectu divino ut obiectum verum secundum alteram partem contradictionis. Oportet igitur assignare causam contingentiae in rebus ex parte voluntatis divinae.' Scotus 1960b, d. 39, q. 1–5, n. 44; p. 493.5–11.

25. Scotus 1960b, d. 39, q. 1–5, n. 53–4; p. 496.15–497.30.

26. 'Sed adhuc illam libertatem voluntatis consequitur alia potentia, quae est logica (cui etiam correspondet potentia realis). Potentia logica non est aliqua nisi quando extrema sic sunt possibilia quod non sibi invicem repugnant sed uniri possunt.' Scotus 1960b, d. 39, q. 1–5, n. 49; p. 494.20–5.

how it is that we can accept conditionals such as 'If God foresees X, X will happen' and accept that God from eternity foresees X without committing ourselves to the necessity of 'X will happen'. God's knowledge is a single act which never 'passes into the past' and so is as contingent as any present act. God knows what will happen, but he can know otherwise than he knows.[27]

Although Scotus claims a simultaneous capacity for opposites and with it the contingency of the present he clings tenaciously to the necessity of the past, but it is his own concept of possibility as semantic consistency which grounds fourteenth-century attempts to show the past contingent.

Peter Aureoli

At the beginning of the fourteenth century a series of conflicts about the nature of necessity and the development by Ockham and others of a theory of what it is for a claim to be about a time threw the problem of future contingents into sharp focus. The story begins with Peter Aureoli's attempt to defend the conflation of immutability and necessity.[28] Aureoli's view centres around a principle linking possibility and mutability: 'If a thing is A and can be not-A, then it can change from being A to being not-A.' From this principle it follows that if a thing is A and cannot change to being not-A, then it is necessarily A. In other words, what is immutably in a certain state is necessarily in that state. Given this identification, Aureoli sets out to show that if a sentence about the future is true it is immutably and hence necessarily true. If a contingent proposition about the future such as 'The Antichrist will come' is now true, then it cannot become false before the Antichrist does in fact come. For when could it *be* false? Neither now when

27. 'Ad primum argumentum, quando arguitur quod illud quod transit in praeteritum, est necessarium, concedatur. Et quando arguitur quod "istum praedestinari" transiit in praeteritum, dicendum quod hoc falsum est; si enim voluntas nostra semper haberet eandem volitionem in eodem instanti immobili non esset sua volitio praeterita sed semper in actu. Et sic est de volitione divina, quae semper eadem est; unde, sicut dictum est, eadem volitione qua vult aliquem praedestinare, potest velle eundem damnari pro eodem instanti aeternitatis.' Scotus 1960b, d. 40 q. 1, n. 5; pp. 512.27–513.7.

28. Aureoli discusses the relation between immutability and necessity at two places in his *Commentarium in primum librum Sententiarum*. The first is D. 8, Pars II, art. 1, where he argues: '... definitio necessitatis et immutabilitatis est eadem illa namque sunt unum et idem quae communicant in definitiva ratione nam definitio indicat quid est esse rei, sed definitio necessarii est quod est impossibile aliter se habere. Incommutabilis autem quod est impossibile mutari; mutari autem est aliter nunc se habere quam prius. Ergo "immutabile" et "necessarium" sunt idem.' Aureoli 1596–1605, D. 8. pars II, art. 1; p. 274. Aureoli advances other arguments here and in D. 39, art. 1; p. 893; but all of them seem to presuppose that *'aliter impossibile se habere'* and *'aliter impossibile nunc se habere quam prius'* are equivalent. It is precisely this which Aureoli's opponents are not likely to grant.

it is true nor later; for if it were false at some time later than now, that could only be because the Antichrist will not come after all; but in that case 'The Antichrist will come' is now false, contrary to our hypothesis.[29]

To save the contingency of the future Aureoli proposes abandoning the view that contingent sentences about the future are now true or false – apparently the first serious medieval attempt to argue that bivalence is not a fundamental logical principle. Aureoli did not work out the consequences of his view for logic, but he did ascribe the view to Aristotle; Ockham and Gregory of Rimini among others accepted the ascription.

William Ockham

Aureoli's view was never popular, but it had some influence in the fifteenth century, and it or another very like it was defended both in Oxford and at the papal court, according to Bradwardine.[30] The position which rapidly became the *opinio communis* of the early fourteenth century was rather that worked out and defended by Ockham. It is not entirely novel; indeed, it contains clear echoes of views expressed by Grosseteste and by Peter Lombard and of a view attacked by Aquinas, but Ockham's development of it is especially vigorous and sophisticated – one of his finest philosophical achievements.

29. 'Primum ergo assumptum patet ex multis, scilicet quod si haec propositio vera est "Antichristus erit" immutabiliter et inevitabiliter est vera. Si enim mutari potest, ne fit vera, aut mutabitur in illo instanti quo vera est, aut in instanti praecedenti, aut in instanti subsequenti usque ad instans quo res fiet aut in instanti quo res non fiet. Sed manifestum est quod non potest mutari in illo instanti quo est vera quia pro eodem instanti esset vera et non vera quod impossible est; nec in instanti praecedenti: tum quia, si in instanti dato, est vera et in omni praecedenti fuit vera, quia si hodie verum est quod Sortes erit cras, et heri verum fuit quod Sortes esset cras at ita si tunc poterat mutari in falsitatem, mutaretur in illo eodem tunc quo esset falsa et per consequens simul esset vera et non vera ... Nec potest dici quod mutari possit in aliquo instanti subsequenti in tempore signabili inter instans propositionis et instans quo res fiet quia si in aliquo instanti ut pote cras, falsa sit haec propositio "Sortes erit", impossibile est quod fuit heri vera et hodie falsa, hoc erit propter aliquam mutationem factam in re. Nulla autem mutatio facta est quia nondum res est ... nec potest dici quod in illo instanti in quo res fiet vel non fiet mutabitur illa veritas tum quia veritas illa transit in praeteritum ... quod autem transit in praeteritum immutabile est ... ergo cum non inveniatur instans in quo possit mutari propositio de futuro a veritate in falsitatem, necessario immutabiliter vera, si aliquo modo ponatur vera.' Aureoli 1596–1605, D. 38; pp. 883–4.
30. 'Opinio sexta fingit quod aliquid est futurum ad utrumlibet, vel non futurum in sensu composito, non autem in sensu diviso, quam sic astruere moliuntur. Nulla propositio simplex de futuro in materia contingente aequaliter est vera vel falsa, Philosopho I Peri Hermenias ultimo attestante, quare nec aliquid est futurum ad utrumlibet vel non futurum divisim. Hanc autem opinionem audivi in Curia Romana a quodam famoso Philosopho Tolosano in quadam disputatione solemne de contingentia futurorum, secundum eam totaliter publice respondente quam et Oxoniae similiter audiebam.' Bradwardine 1618, Book III, Ch. 17, p. 692A–B. In Baudry 1950 Peter of Candia and Pierre de Nugent are listed as supporters of Aureoli's view, and, as Baudry shows, it is Aureoli's position which was defended at Louvain in the fifteenth century by Petrus de Rivo.

Unlike Aureoli, Ockham is committed to bivalence and, more clearly than most of the major figures in the thirteenth century, to the view that the past is absolutely necessary. In fact, where A is a real quality he agrees with Aureoli that if something is immutably A it is necessarily A. Moreover unlike Scotus, Ockham accepts the doctrine of the necessity of the present.[31] But Ockham does not think that 'true' and 'false' signify real qualities inhering in the propositions of which those terms are predicated.[32] Thus while 'The Antichrist will come' is true, its being true is not a fact different from the fact that the Antichrist will come. So while '"The Antichrist will come" is true' is present-tensed and seems to be about the present, it is, Ockham thinks, really about the future; and so it is just as contingent as 'The Antichrist will come.' He distinguishes past- and present-tensed sentences which are merely verbally (*vocaliter*) about the past or present from those which are really (*secundum rem*) about the past or present. The latter are if true necessarily true; the former may be true and yet contingently true. A true sentence verbally about the past or present and yet really about the future will be contingently true if it is equivalent to or depends on a sentence which is uncontroversially about the future and is contingent.

For the Ockhamist programme to work, every present- or past-tensed sentence which is entailed by a future-tensed contingent sentence must be only verbally about the past or present. To make the programme credible Ockham must show us how to treat a variety of such past- and present-tensed sentences. This is relatively easily done for claims about the truth or

---

31. Indeed Ockham argues against Scotus that the necessity of the past entails the necessity of the present. 'Omnis propositio mere de praesenti, si sit vera, habet aliquam de praeterito necessariam; sed haec "voluntas vult hoc in *a* instanti" est vera per positum et est mere de praesenti; igitur haec erit semper postea necessaria "voluntas voluit hoc in *a* instanti"; igitur post *a* instans ista non potest esse vera "voluntas non voluit hoc in *a* instanti". Confirmatur: si post *a* haec semper fuit necessaria "voluntas voluit hoc pro *a* instanti", igitur post *a* sua opposita semper fuit impossibilis; et ultra: igitur post *a* semper fuit et erit verum dicere quod haec propositio non potuit esse vera in *a* "voluntas non vult hoc oppositum," quia tunc sua opposita fuit vera, haec scilicet "voluntas voluit hoc pro *a* instanti". Responsio igitur consistit in hoc, quia si voluntas vult hoc in *a*, post *a* erit semper haec necessaria "voluntas voluit hoc in *a*", et tunc si sua potentia non manifesta posset reduci ad actum in *a* instanti, vel contradictoria erunt simul vera post *a* instans, vel post *a* illa propositio quae est necessaria de praeterito, quia habuit aliquam mere de praesenti veram, erit falsa, quia sua opposita erit vera.' Ockham 1978, *De praedestinatione*, Q. III; *QT* II, p. 534.36–52. It seems that Ockham's argument requires a principle equivalent to 'If it was the case that possibly P, then possibly it was the case that P.' But that is what is in dispute.

32. 'Sed si veritas propositionis sit aliqua parva res distincta a propositione sive sit absoluta sive respectiva ille res essent subiective inherentes propositioni successive et per consequens illa propositio que aliquando est vera aliquando falsa realiter in se susciperet contraria quod est manifeste contra Philosophi determinationem. Praeterea si sic sequerentur quaedam absurda.' Ockham 1491, Quodlibet V, Q. 24.

falsity of contingent sentences and for attributions of predestination and reprobation, but how is the account to be extended to sentences such as 'God knew that the Antichrist will come' and 'Christ prophesied that Peter would deny him'? Ockham considers such cases in *Quodlibet* IV, Q. 4; Oxford theologians quickly took up the task of refining and extending his account.

Both in *Quodlibet* IV, Q. 4, and in his *De praedestinatione*[33] Ockham argues that sentences of the form 'X knew (or knows) that P' where P is a future contingent sentence depend on P, because 'X knew (or knows) that P' entails 'It is true that P' and this in turn entails 'P'. Hence if 'P' is contingent, so is the knowledge-claim. This seems plausible where X is a fallible creature but less plausible where X is God. God is infallible and omniscient, and if God knows that P only if he is in what we might metaphorically call a certain belief-state, (believing that P) then P is true just in case God is in that state. But whether God is in such a state is not a contingent matter; hence P is not contingent either.

Ockham solves this problem by denying that for God to know something is for God to be in a certain state.[34] Ockham is here echoing Grosseteste's doctrine that knowing A and knowing not-A is just the same in God. But however it is with God, with us there seems to be a (formal) difference between knowing A and knowing not-A. In one case we are in one mental state and in the other case in another. Again, if Christ reveals that Peter will deny him three times, the world seems really different from the way it would be if such a revelation were not made.

Ockham actually has two very different accounts of prophecy. In his *De praedestinatione*[35], he treats prophecies as disguised conditionals, usually as conditionals asserting what God would do under certain conditions. On Ockham's usual account a conditional sentence is true just in case the

33. 'Et sic non est necessaria, nec debet concedi quod Deus habeat scientiam necessariam de futuris contingentibus sed potius contingentem, quia sicut hoc futurum contingens contingenter erit, ita Deus scit ipsum contingenter fore, quia potest non scire ipsum fore, si ipsum scit.' Ockham 1978, Q. II, art. 4; p. 530.267–71.

34. 'Dico quod illud quod est in Deo vel potest esse in eo formaliter necessario est Deus; sed scire *a* non est sic in Deo sed tantum per praedicationem, quia est quidam conceptus vel nomen quod [aliquando] praedicatur de Deo et aliquando non.' Ockham 1978, Q. II, art. 4, p. 531.302–5.

35. 'Et concedo quod non fuit revelatum tamquam falsum, sed tamquam verum contingens et non tamquam verum necessarium, et per consequens tale potuit et potest esse falsum. Et tamen Prophetae non dixerunt falsum, quia omnes prophetiae de quibuscumque futuris contingentibus fuerunt condicionales, quamvis non semper exprimebatur conditio. Sed aliquando fuit expressa, sicut patet de David et throno suo; aliquando subintellecta, sicut patet de Ninive destructione a Iona prophetata: "Adhuc post quadraginta dies et Ninive subvertetur", nisi scilicet poeniterent; et quia poenituerunt, ideo non fuit destructa.' Ockham 1978, Q. I, *ad* 8, p. 513.173–82.

corresponding inference holds;[36] there is then no need to treat prophetic conditionals as contingent at all. But when Christ asserts 'Peter, before the cock crows you will thrice deny me', he seems to be making a categorical and not a conditional assertion. Indeed it is not easy to see what could be the suppressed antecedent in such a case.

In *Quodlibet* IV, Q. 4, Ockham proposes a different account of prophecy, one on which prophecies do turn out to be categorical. Here he argues that after God has revealed a future contingency it is necessary that the physical or mental things he used to reveal it have existed, but what is revealed is not necessary; for while 'God says that P; therefore P' is a valid inference 'God utters "P"; therefore God reveals that P' is not. If Peter had not denied Christ three times, Christ's utterance 'Peter, you will deny me three times' would not have been a revelation that Peter would deny him three times.[37]

Robert Holkot

Robert Holkot, one of Ockham's followers, devotes the last part of Book II, Q. II of his *Sentences*-commentary to a discussion of whether God is able to reveal a future contingent. Holkot begins by distinguishing two senses of 'reveal'. To reveal is to cause a new assent in the mind of some creature (1) to a true complex, or (2) to a complex whether true or not.[38] Holkot claims that in the first sense of 'reveal' 'God revealed that there will be a day of judgement' is contingent while in the second sense it is a sentence about the past involving no future-tensed sentence and hence necessary.[39] But it

---

36. '... condicionalis aequivalet uni consequentiae, ita quod tunc condicionalis est vera quando antecedens infert consequens et non aliter.' Ockham 1974a, Pars II, c. 31; p. 347.1–4.

37. 'Et si dices quod hec aliquando fuit vera "Deus creat hoc" demonstrata propositione de futuro, ergo semper postea haec erit necessaria: "Deus creavit hoc." Respondeo et dico "Deus creavit hoc" si per ly hoc demonstratur ista propositio de futuro vel ista qualitas quae est propositio post instans creationis ista de praeterito erit necessaria quia sua de praesenti non dependet a futuro. Sed si demonstratur per ly hoc revelatum vel notitia evidens tunc iste de praeterito est contingens quia ista de praesenti dependet ex futuro. Nam ista propositio "Deus creat revelatum vel notitiam evidentem" importat quod hoc revelatum erit quia falsum nec evidenter sciri nec revelari potest. Sed ista "Deus creat hanc propositionem vel qualitatem" non importat quod ista propositio sit vera vel falsa.' Ockham 1491, Quodl. IV, Q. 4.

38. 'Tertia distinctio est de isto termino "revelare" quia isto possumus uti dupliciter. Primo modo pro causatione novi assensus in intellectu alterius creaturae alicui complexo vero ... Secundo modo accipitur "revelare" pro causare assensum alicui complexo in intellectu alterius de novo.' Holkot 1518, Lib. II, Q. II, art. 8 AA.

39. 'Primo modo accipiendo hoc nomen "revelare" haec est contingens: "Deus revelavit Sorti dies iudicii fore" et postquam hoc revelavit Sorti haec est contingens: "Iste assensus fuit revelatio" – demonstrato assensu qui in rei veritate fuit revelatio quia sic iste terminus "revelatio" est unus terminus connotativus ... Si autem iste terminus "revelatio" exponatur secundo modo pro eo quod est simpliciter causare assensum alicui complexo, sic est necessaria haec: "Deus revelavit Sorti quod dies iudicii erit" et non dependet ab aliquo futuro quia sic potest Deus revelare falsum

seems that if God asserted that there would be a day of judgement and it is still contingent whether there will be one, then either God can be deceived or he can lie. Holkot denies that God can lie, for to lie is to speak a falsehood with an improper intention to deceive, and God can have no improper intentions. He also denies that God can be deceived; but he admits that God can utter a falsehood and can fail to fulfill a promise. God has deceived evil men; Holkot claims that God never will deceive good men, but not that he cannot do so.[40]

Thomas Bradwardine and the reaction to Ockhamism

The Achilles' heel of the Ockhamist theory appears to have been its inability to give a plausible, orthodox treatment of prophecy, but that was not the only feature likely to provoke a conservative theologian.[41] The strong reaction to the Ockhamist position began with Thomas Bradwardine.

Bradwardine's views on future contingents are intimately connected with his views about time and modality. Drawing to some extent on the *De libero arbitrio* of Grosseteste (which he quotes extensively in *De causa Dei*, e.g., III, c. 50) and to some extent on Anselm, Bradwardine insists that God is immutable and hence that the divine power is not affected by the passage of time.[42] Whenever it is correct to say that God was or will be able to do something it is correct to say that God *is* able to do it. Thus if God was able to bring it about that Adam never would exist, he is able to bring it about that Adam never did exist. His insistence on the immutability of the

si velit decipere et fallere creaturas et nullum inconveniens sequitur ex hoc quia nullum inconveniens est quod ille qui est veritas causet in aliquo falsitatem.' Holkot 1518, Lib. II, Q. II, art. 8 AA (but CC follows immediately).

40. Holkot takes up this complex of questions in Holkot 1518, Lib. II, Q. II, art. 9 and in his quodlibetal question 'Utrum generalis resurrectio necessaria sit futura' (MS Cambridge Pembroke Coll. Cod. 236f, 186vb–187ra). W. J. Courtenay and Paul Streveler have edited this question and two others of Holkot's on future contingents and kindly allowed me to examine their as yet unpublished edition.

41. We have a collection of epigrams from early in the fourteenth century – the *Notabilia* of Richard of Campsall (in Synan 1962) – which seem almost designed to startle theological conservatives. Several very similar epigrams appear in Holkot 1518, Lib. II, Q. II, art. 7, and in Peter of Ailly 1490, Q. XI, f. q2^{vb}. Campsall's *Notabilia* suggest the impact of the Ockhamist approach. Campsall has the skeleton of a very different theory of future contingents in his (presumably earlier) *Questiones super librum Priorum analeticorum* (in Campsall 1968).

42. Divine immutability is a major theme of *De causa Dei*; see, e.g., Lib. I, c. 23–5. That time does not affect the divine power follows from Bradwardine's view that the past, the present, and the future all depend on God's power: 'Si Deus esse desineret, nihil esset praeteritum, nec futurum, verum nec falsum, possibile vel impossibile, necessarium vel contingens, nec etiam posset esse.' Bradwardine 1618, Lib. I, c. 14, p. 209.

divine power provides Bradwardine with the core of his solution to the problem of future contingents: the future and the past are contingent in exactly the same sense – both depend upon the free will of God.

But to suggest that he sacrifices the necessity of the past to safeguard the contingency of the future would be to mistake Bradwardine's project. Both past and future are contingent on God's will, but given God's antecedent will, which is, Bradwardine claims, naturally prior to what God foresees, the whole history of the world is determined.[43] He distinguishes first between antecedent and consequent necessity (consciously echoing Anselm) and distinguishes antecedent necessity into two sorts: one 'wholly absolute' and another 'in some way relative'. This second sort in turn is divided into necessity relative to secondary causes and necessity relative to the first cause. Everything that happens is necessary relative to the first cause, the divine will.[44] Bradwardine is consciously reviving the view that God predestines everything. His forceful presentation of this view is central to its popularity in the fifteenth and sixteenth centuries.

Given his views about God's determination of the world, Bradwardine could have claimed that God knows the world perfectly in knowing his own intentions; but in fact his doctrine is more complex. In *De causa Dei* I, c. 24, he argues that God knows everything at once, reviving the image of a circle with God at the centre and the instants of time on the circumference. But in his use of the image God sees something first as future, then as present, and finally as past, much as an all-seeing eye located at the centre of a revolving circle would see a point first in one quarter and then in another. What God 'sees' changes with time (though God does not), and so God can know temporally indexical truths; God 'sees' by means of his causal power.[45]

---

43. 'Secundum hanc ergo distinctionem videtur mihi dicendum quod non omnia quae evenient, evenient de necessitate penitus absoluta sicut duodecimo huius probat, nec etiam respectiva, respectu scilicet aliquorum aut omnium inferiorum sive secundarum causarum sicut 5, 8 & 9 huius ostendunt, sed omnia quae evenient, evenient de necessitate respectiva, respectu scilicet superiorum sive primarum causarum, quae sunt voluntas et potentia summi Dei.' Bradwardine 1618, Lib. III, c. 27, p. 704 C & D.

44. 'Possunt autem haec omnia in unam syllogisticam rationem breviter sic reduci: Omnia quae evenient de necessitate naturaliter praecedente, de aliqua necessitate evenient. Omnia quae evenient, evenient de necessitate naturaliter praecedente quia voluntas divina quae omnibus suis volutis est necessitas naturaliter antecedens, ergo omnia quae evenient de ista necessitate evenient.' Bradwardine 1618, Lib. III, c. 27, p. 705B.

45. 'Aliter autem fortassis clarius et brevius dici potest, quod omnes sunt in Deo non realiter, sed causaliter, sicut secundum Philosophum 4 *Phys.* 23 res dicitur esse in sua causa'. Bradwardine 1618, Lib. III, c. 14, p. 690B–C.

The fourteenth-century controversy

Bradwardine's work is seminal in a conceptual revolution which was taking place in the fourteenth century. During the preceding millenium the concepts of possibility and necessity derived their content largely from theories about the powers of things. The Condemnation of 1277 had clearly established that God's power extended beyond the actual course of nature, but even this had not produced a fundamental change. One still looked to God's causal power for insight into possibility, and so intuitions about causality and power (for example the intuition that an effect could not precede its efficient cause) were still crucial to modal theories. Duns Scotus' insistence on a simultaneous power for opposites and his argument that this was possible simply because there was no *repugnantia terminorum* in the supposition that a being who in fact willed one contrary willed the other signalled a new focus. Bradwardine accepted Scotus' claim that only where there was a *repugnantia terminorum* in one contradictory was the other necessary and used it to argue that the past was no more necessary absolutely speaking than the future. In doing so he attacked a premiss on which the whole Ockhamist theory of future contingents had been constructed and so set the stage for a struggle which exercised the universities in the middle of the fourteenth century.

The nature and some of the details of this struggle have become clearer within the last decade.[46] It seems to have begun as a dispute centred at Oxford in the 1330s between Bradwardine and a number of representatives of the new Ockhamist *opinio communis*, notably Adam Wodeham and Robert Holkot. The issues involved include problems about foreknowledge, especially prophecy, but centre mainly on problems of predestination and the relative roles of merit and grace in salvation. At some point around 1340 the focus of the debate shifts to Paris, where, it seems, Thomas Buckingham champions the one side and Bradwardine (represented by writings earlier than the final version of the *De causa Dei*) the other. In 1342 Gregory of Rimini devotes a major part of his *Sentences* commentary to the questions involved in this debate. Gregory is a major figure in the controversy and seems to have been the architect of a position which reflects

---

46. The foundation for this recent activity was laid in part in Trapp 1956. Much recent work has been done by W. J. Courtenay; see, e.g., Courtenay 1972–3 and 1978. Bartholomew de la Torre has been working on a study of Thomas Buckingham's views on future contingents, and I have benefited from conversation with him.

Ockham's account of future contingent truth but accepts Bradwardine's criticisms of the view that the past is necessary.[47]

Peter of Ailly

The results of the debate may be seen in the work of the late fourteenth-century figure Peter of Ailly. His *Quaestiones super libros Sententiarum* were read at Paris probably in 1378 and so give us a picture of the situation after the initial controversy had somewhat subsided. Much of the difficulty of the problem of future contingent truth is generated by the tension between the supposed necessity of the past and the supposed contingency of the future. Hence it is rather startling to find d'Ailly arguing that the contingency of the future 'is only to be held on faith',[48] and maintaining that the necessity of the past is only *probabile*, not *evidens*.[49] His major arguments against the necessity of the past rest on his inability to find a relevant difference between past and future which would justify us in claiming that one was contingent and the other not. If God could once prevent the world ever having been but can no longer, it must be either because the divine power has changed or because something outside of God constrains his will, both of which are absurd.

Peter of Ailly's discussion of revelation[50] is heavily dependent on Adam Wodeham and Gregory of Rimini and is a good summing up of the state of the discussion near the end of the fourteenth century. He operates from within the framework of the Ockhamist approach and considers a number of ways of reconciling revelation with the approach. The first is the one proposed by Ockham in his *De praedestinatione* – namely that all revelations are disguised conditionals. This is rejected as too much limiting God's power to reveal. A second is a proposal made by Gregory of Rimini and

---

47. No philosophical consensus was produced in this controversy, and the position worked out by Gregory of Rimini and his followers by no means dominated later discussion. For example John Buridan, Albert of Saxony, and Marsilius of Inghen all adhered to the *Opinio communis* of the early fourteenth century. (See, e.g., Buridan 1588 and Marsilius of Inghen 1501.) And as Baudry (1950) has shown, several thirteenth- and fourteenth-century viewpoints were being debated at Louvain in the late fifteenth century.

48. 'Tertia est quod non est nobis evidens nec naturaliter demonstrabile quod aliquid futurum potest non fore. Patet quia in naturali lumine ita faciliter vel non magis difficiliter sustineretur quod praeteritum potest non fuisse sicut quod futurum potest non fore.' Peter of Ailly 1490, Q. XI, f. q4^vb C.

49. 'Quarto sequitur quod probabile est quod nullus de facto sic obligatur de peccato suo penitere quod teneatur velle peccatum suum non fuisse. Patet ex dictis suppositio quod impossibile sit non fuisse est probabile quamvis non evidens.' Peter of Ailly 1490, Principium, f. a4^r.

50. Peter of Ailly 1490, Q. 12, art. 3.

designed to save the possibility of infallible revelation. Gregory suggests that while the physical or mental sign by which God reveals something is part of the past, and hence it is necessary that it have existed in whatever sense of 'necessary' past things are necessary, yet the significance of the sign is no more part of the past than is the truth of a proposition. Hence just as Peter could make a true sentence about the future never to have been true, so Peter could make Christ's utterance 'Peter, you will deny me three times' never to have meant that Peter would deny Christ three times.[51] Ailly rejects this proposal as well, arguing that a sign's having a certain sense can have real effects over and above the effects the existence of the physical object which is the sign would have. Hence either Gregory is appealing to God's absolute power to change the past (in which case he need not stop with meanings) or his proposal fails. Peter finally settles for the view that Wodeham, Holkot, and Ockham all seem finally to have accepted: there can be no revelation of a future contingent to a creature which precludes the possibility of the creature having been deceived. This of course does not mean that there can be no *certain* revelation. We can know that God *will not* deceive us; what we cannot know (because it is false) is that God *cannot* deceive us.

Knowledge without causal connection: scientia media

Perhaps the least well-developed aspect of thirteenth- and fourteenth-century theories about contingent truth and foreknowledge is their account of *how* a contingent truth about the future can be known. The stumbling-block is the role causality ordinarily plays in knowledge. Ordinarily we know things because they (indirectly) causally affect us.

---

51. See Gregory of Rimini 1955, Lib. I, D. 42–4, Q. 3, art. 1, f. 168[ra]A: 'Unde si teneatur quod res praeterita potest per divinam potentiam non fuisse diceretur possibile esse ut Deus numquam illud dictum vel illum assensum creaverit et per consequens non dixit "*a* fore" et ille alius etiam non credidit. Si hoc vero non teneatur sicut aliqui antiqui doctores dixerunt quod possibile est illud dictum non fuisse significativum, aut non illius significati quid est "*a* fore" et similiter assensum alterius non fuisse assensum seu iudicium de *a* fore. Sicut etiam dicendum esset quod iudicium quo iudico Petrum sedentem sedere, si conservaretur in me a Deo postquam Petrus surrexit non esset iudicium quo iudicaret Petrum sedere. Vel adhuc aliter dici potest. Nam ut dicendum est ad hoc quod aliquis dicat aliquid proprie loquendo requiritur intentio significandi illud per suum dictum. Cum ergo Deus quid voluit possit non voluisse alias nullus praedestinatus posset non fuisse praedestinatus cuius oppositum communiter tenetur secundum sensum divisum. Possibile est Deum numquam voluisse significare per suum dictum "*a* fore" et per consequens numquam dixisse "*a* fore". Si vero nulla praedictarum viarum placet inveniatur alia melior. Et si invenire quis non possit potius iudico confitendum esse ignorantia quam praecipitandum se in tam horrendam auribus fidelium . . . qualis est si dicatur Deum posse mentiri aut dicere falsum aut decipere cum omnis scriptura catholica canonis et sanctorum clamet oppositum.' Note that Gregory does not endorse any of the views he suggests.

Occasionally we know things because we bring them about. But future contingents do not exist and so cannot have effects, and attempts to ground knowledge of them in their causes seem always to threaten their contingency. What is needed is a *via media*, a way of having knowledge without causal connection. Many writers, Ockham and Gregory of Rimini among them, were content to say that God knows the future intuitively and that it is a mystery how he knows it. It is not until the late sixteenth century that we find a well-developed and promising proposal.

The architect of the proposal seems to have been the Spanish Jesuit Luis de Molina,[52] and the proposal is that besides God's knowledge of all necessary truths and his knowledge of his own intentions, God has a *scientia media* – a knowledge of all true subjunctive conditionals regarding contingent matters. Molina couples this doctrine with the view that of any pair of conditionals 'If it were to be that A, it would be that B' and 'If it were to be that A, it would be that not-B' (where A is a complete specification of a context) exactly one is true. This is sometimes called the Principle of the Conditional Excluded Middle. The principle is far from obvious and, indeed, Dominican theologians contemporary with Molina argued against it. Their debate is important, and not only for the history of the problem of foreknowledge, for it is a lively issue today in the theory of counter-factual conditionals.[53]

The major argument against the Principle of the Conditional Excluded Middle is just that it seems false. There are cases in which it seems that if someone were in situation X he might do Y and might not. Indeed, one might take this as a partial account of what it is to be free in situation X. The arguments in favour of the principle are more subtle. The best of them, developed by Molina's contemporary Francisco Suárez,[54] exploits a putative connection between subjunctive and indicative conditionals. Many

52. The authoritative statement of Molina's views is in Molina 1876. Other works of Molina dealing with the question and an account of his life and work may be found in Stegmüller 1935. Perhaps the most central passage in Molina's work is this from Molina 1876, p. 317: 'Tertiam denique mediam scientiam, qua ex altissima et inscrutabili comprehensione cuius liberi arbitrii in sua essentia intuitus est, quid pro sua innata libertate, si in hoc, vel illo, vel etiam infinitis rerum ordinibus collocaretur, acturum esset, cum tamen posset, si vellet, facere re seipsa oppositum.'

53. The sixteenth- and seventeenth-century debate about the *scientia media* (and so about the Principle of the Conditional Excluded Middle) ranged Molina and his supporters against such opponents as Diego Alvarez and Domingo Bañez. On Bellarmine's work in support of Molina see Tromp 1933. For an enlightening discussion of the sixteenth-century debate in the light of twentieth-century issues, see R. Adams 1977.

54. 'Si Deus (verbi gratia) postquam voluit Petrum creare, et in tali opportunitate constituere aut permittere, vidit illum peccaturum, iam de illo conditionalis est vera: "Si Petrus creatur in tali occasione, peccabit"; ergo etiam si intelligeretur illa oratio proferri prius ratione, quam Deus

have supposed that one can test a conditional of the form 'If X were to happen Y would happen' by bringing it about that X does happen. If Y ensues, the original conditional was true; if Y does not, it was false, but in that case 'If X were to happen Y would *not* happen' is verified. Thus it seems that in a situation in which a subjunctive conditional has a true antecedent the Principle of the Conditional Excluded Middle holds. But how can it make a difference to the truth of the *conditional* whether one *in fact* brings about the antecedent or not? Suárez and Molina think it cannot make a difference.

Molina's position is that not only is the Principle of the Conditional Excluded Middle true but God knows which of each pair of conditionals is true and he knows this even though such conditionals are themselves contingent. If the doctrine of the *scientia media* is to help, it must not merely explain God's knowledge of one kind of contingent truth in terms of another more mysterious, but Molina himself appears to do just this. When pressed as to how God knows which of a pair of subjunctive conditionals (whose subject terms may even denote only non-existents) is true, Molina replies that we should not look for an explanation on the side of the known but on the side of the knower. It is because God's intellect is so keen that he has an especially acute comprehension of things and hence knows what they would do under any possible circumstance.[55]

This is not much of an advance beyond Ockham and Gregory of Rimini, and the view is mercilessly attacked by Molina's opponents, particularly by Domingo Bañez, as incoherent.[56] The theory of the *scientia media* is put on a surer footing by Suárez,[57] who argues that what a particular free agent would do in given circumstances is grounded in a *sui generis* property of that agent. On Suárez' view this is a contingent

vellet Petrum creare, etiam illa propositio esset vera determinate. Probatur consequentia, quia iam habuisset ex tunc conformitatem cum re significata; hanc enim non fecit, sed ostendit potius et manifestavit effectus subsecutus, postquam Deus voluit Petrum creare etc.; ergo eadem ratione omnis conditionalis similis intellecta vel cogitata in illo signo, antequam Deus aliquid decreverit aut voluerit de illo antecedente sub conditione sumpto, est determinate vera, aut determinate falsa, quia statim ac Deus ponere vult inesse illud antecedens, absolute determinatum est quid ex illo sequendum sit vel non sit; ergo illud ipsum antea sub conditione prolatum erat determinate verum, aut determinate falsum, iuxta exigentium obiecta.' Suárez, 'De scientia quam Deus habet de futuris contingentibus', Lib. II, c. 5, n. 13; in Suárez 1856–77, vol. 11, p. 359.

55. 'Neque enim ad intuendum in re libera in quam partem se inflectet satis est illius comprehensio, neque quaecumque major comprehensio quam sit res comprehensa, sed necessaria est altissima atque eminentissima comprehensio, qualis in solo Deo comparatione creaturarum reperitur.' Molina 1876, Q. 14, art. 13, disp. 52; p. 319.

56. See Bañez' *Apologia en Defensa de la Doctrina Antigua y Catholica* (in Heredia 1968), Pars Prima, c. 16; p. 185.

57. See his *De gratia*, prol. 2, c. 7; in Suárez 1856–77, vol. 7.

property, and so there remains some question about how God could know that a non-existent agent (for example a man before his birth) 'possesses' it. But on Suárez' view it is also a timeless property and so there is no special problem of *fore*knowledge. By knowing how he starts the world and how things would evolve were they to begin in that way God knows the world's entire history. This suggestion on the one hand echoes theories of complete individual divine ideas, and on the other hand suggests the theory of complete concepts which was to be proposed by Leibniz. But it differs from both these in that it does not claim that the property which grounds the conditional is an essential property of the individual who has it. On the contrary, since the conditional is contingently true the property which grounds it must be contingent. But how can even God know the contingent properties of non-existents? We seem to have come full circle.

VI

METAPHYSICS AND EPISTEMOLOGY

19
ESSENCE AND EXISTENCE

First philosophy, divine science, and the science of 'being as being'

The recovery of Aristotle's *Metaphysics* by medieval Western thinkers prepared the way for them to concentrate on the science of 'being as being' in the high Middle Ages. This work was enhanced by the translation into Latin of Avicenna's *Metaphysics* in the twelfth century and of Averroes' Commentary on Aristotle's *Metaphysics* in the early thirteenth century. But as medieval Latin thinkers began to examine Aristotle's text more closely, they encountered a problem of interpretation relating to the very nature of metaphysics.

In *Metaphysics* IV, c. 1 (1003^{a}21–32), Aristotle speaks of a science which studies being as being and contrasts it with more particular sciences which restrict themselves to investigating the attributes of a portion of being. But in *Metaphysics* VI, c. 1 (1026^{a}23–32), after referring to his investigation of 'beings as beings' and presumably, therefore, to his science of being as being, Aristotle distinguishes three theoretical sciences – physics, mathematics, and first philosophy or 'divine science' – and then seems to justify the viability of the last-mentioned one only insofar as it concerns itself with separate and immobile entities. One might wonder whether this first philosophy or divine science can be identified with Aristotle's general science of being as being, a difficulty which he himself recognises. He concludes the discussion by asserting that if there were no separate and immobile entity, then physics would be the first science. But if there is some immobile substance, then the science that considers it will 'be first and will be universal insofar as it is first. And it will pertain to this same science to study being as being' (1026^{a}30–1). Aristotelian scholars continue to debate his justification for this move and the degree to which he did or did not in fact succeed in bringing together his science of being as being and his first philosophy;[1] and this same problem exercised the philosophical skills

---

1. For reviews of recent discussions of this see Düring 1966, pp. 594–9; König 1970, pp. 226ff.; Owens 1978, pp. xiii–xxvii, 35–67.

of many of his followers during the high Middle Ages, although they tended to formulate it in terms of their efforts to identify the precise 'subject' of metaphysics.[2]

Avicenna and Averroes on the subject of metaphysics

The divergent positions of Avicenna and Averroes on this issue were well-known to thirteenth- and fourteenth-century Latin scholastics.[3] In his *Metaphysics* Avicenna examines in some detail the possibility that metaphysics might have as its subject God, but he rejects it. For him its subject can only be being as being. Since he is convinced that no science can demonstrate the existence of its own subject and since he also maintains that God's existence can be demonstrated in metaphysics and only in metaphysics, he seems to have no other choice.[4] But since God's existence will be established in metaphysics, for Avicenna the philosophical science that studies the divine is a part of the science of being as being.[5] And it would seem to follow that God, too, will be included under the notion of being as being.[6]

Averroes flatly rejected Avicenna's position on this question. While he agrees that no science can demonstrate the existence of its subject, he insists that it is in physics rather than in metaphysics that one demonstrates the existence of God, the first mover.[7] Hence while he does not reject 'being as

2. See Zimmermann 1965; Doig 1965, pp. 41–96; Doig 1972, pp. 172–213.
3. See for instance, Siger of Brabant 1948, *Introd.*, q. 1, pp. 3–4; and especially Duns Scotus, *Quaestiones super libros Metaphysicorum*, I. 1 (1891–5, v. 7, p. 11): 'Utrum subiectum Metaphysicae sit ens inquantum ens, sicut posuit Avicenna? vel Deus, et Intelligentiae, sicut posuit commentator Averroes?' In referring to Avicenna and Averroes in what follows I will be taking account of only the medieval Latin translations of their works.
4. In his *Opera* (1508, repr. Minerva, 1961), see I. 1–2. See f. 70ʳᵃᵇ: God is not the subject of metaphysics. Note in particular: 'Postquam autem inquiritur in hac scientia an sit, tunc non potest esse subiectum huius scientiae. Nulla enim scientiarum debet stabilire esse suum subiectum' (70ʳᵇ). Here too he rejects the suggestion that the causes might be its subject (ff. 70ʳᵇ–71ᵛᵃ). On being as being as the subject of metaphysics see f. 70ᵛᵃᵇ. For the above in the recently published critical edition (*Avicenna Latinus. Liber de philosophia prima*) see pp. 4–8, 10–13. On this in Avicenna see Zimmermann 1965, pp. 108–16; Doig 1965, pp. 73–82; Brown 1965, pp. 117–19; Gilson 1927, pp. 91–9; Goichon 1937, pp. 3–5.
5. See f. 71ʳᵃ; pp. 14–15 (crit. ed.). Here Avicenna divides metaphysics into different parts including one which investigates the ultimate causes insofar as they are causes of every caused being insofar as it is being ('omnis esse causati inquantum est esse'); others which study the first cause from which flows every caused being insofar as it is caused being ('et aliae inquirunt causam primam ex qua fluit omne esse causatum inquantum est esse causatum, non inquantum est esse mobile vel quantitativum'); others which inquire after the dispositions which 'happen' to being; and finally others which study the principles of the particular sciences.
6. Unfortunately, Avicenna does not make this point as clearly as one might wish. For discussion see Zimmermann 1965, pp. 112–14.
7. See Averroes 1562–74d, I, com. 83, ff. 47ʳᵇ–48ᵛᵃ: 'Sed notandum est quod istud genus entium, esse scilicet separatum a materia, non declaratur nisi in hac scientia naturali. Et qui dicit quod prima

being' as a description of the subject of metaphysics, he maintains that what is signified thereby is really substance.[8] And it is his view that it pertains to metaphysics to study substance in terms of its prime instance, that is, that separate substance which is the first form and the end or final cause of all other substance.[9] But such a study presupposes the demonstration in physics that such a substance, there established as the first mover, does in fact exist.[10] Averroes would apparently safeguard the general character of metaphysics by reasoning that in studying the substance that is the first form and ultimate end one also studies all other substance and thereby all other being as well.[11]

Thirteenth- and fourteenth-century thinkers tended to side with Avicenna against Averroes in their discussions of this issue. But although most were in agreement that being as being rather than divine being is the subject of metaphysics, the precise relationship between being as being and divine being continued to divide them.

Siger of Brabant and John Duns Scotus on metaphysics and God

First of all, one might reason that insofar as God is a being, he will be included under that notion of being which serves as the subject of meta-

---

Philosophia nititur declarare entia separabilia esse peccat. Haec enim entia sunt subiecta primae Philosophiae, et declaratum est in posterioribus Analyticis [76ᵇ1–23] quod impossibile est aliquam scientiam declarare suum subiectum esse.' See also II, com. 22, ff. 56ᵛᵇ–57ʳᵃ (where he interprets Avicenna as saying that no science can demonstrate the causes of its subject and counters that if this is true as regards demonstration *simpliciter* and demonstration *propter quid*, it is not true as regards demonstration *quia*. Thus Aristotle's demonstration of the first mover is proper to and peculiar to physics, and is a demonstration *quia* or, as he also refers to it, *per signum*); Averroes 1562–74f, XII, com. 5, f. 293ʳᵃ.

8. Averroes 1562–74c, I, com. 83, f. 47ᵛᵃᵇ: 'Omne enim de quo loquitur in hoc libro principaliter est propter illud principium; et iste est primus locus in quo naturalis inspicit alium modum essendi ab illo de quo considerat, et apud illum cessat, et dimisit considerationem de eo usque ad scientiam nobiliorem, quae considerat de ente secundum quod est ens.' See also 1562–74f, IV, com. 1, f. 64ʳᵃᵇ (on Aristotle's effort to define the subject of this science, and on 'being as being'); com. 2, ff. 65ʳᵇ–66ʳᵇ (on the meaning of being and its manifold predication by way of reference or attribution to substance).

9. Averroes 1562–74f, IV, com. 2, f. 66ʳᵃ (the philosopher, i.e., the metaphysician, must study the principles and causes of substance); XII, com. 5, f. 293ʳᵇ ('Et dicemus nos quidem quod Philosophus inquirit quae sunt principia substantiae secundum quod substantiae et declarat quod substantia abstracta est principium substantiae naturalis: sed hoc ponendo accepit pro constanti hoc quod declaratum est in naturalibus de principiis substantiae generabilis et corruptibilis, . . . et quod declaratum est in Octavo, scilicet, quod movens aeternam substantiam est abstractum a materia . . .); f. 293ᵛᵃ ('quod principium primae substantiae abstractae etiam est substantia et forma et finis et quod movet utroque modo . . .').

10. Averroes 1562–74f, XII, com. 5, f. 293ᵛᵃ.

11. His commentary on the final lines of Aristotle's *Metaphysics* VI, c. 1, is not very enlightening on this point. But see Doig 1965, pp. 53–60; also Zimmermann 1965, pp. 116–17; Gilson 1927, pp. 93ff.; Gilson 1948b, pp. 66–7; Gilson 1952a, pp. 77–8.

physics. Siger of Brabant in the 1270s and Duns Scotus around the turn of the fourteenth century may be regarded as representative of this position. Siger concludes that since the subject of metaphysics must be universal, God is not its subject.[12] He attempts to mediate between Avicenna and Averroes on the proof of God's existence by suggesting that the middle term whereby one establishes a conclusion in a given science need not be proper to that science. Thus the middle term employed by Aristotle to prove God's existence in *Metaphysics* XII is in fact taken from the *Physics*.[13] The implication seems to be that for Siger one may establish God's existence either in physics or in metaphysics, granted that the middle term for doing so is physical. And in other contexts he offers more properly metaphysical argumentation to show that this first mover is also the efficient cause of all caused beings, and that it is unique.[14]

Since Siger evidently regards as metaphysical the last-mentioned kind of effort to arrive at more precise knowledge of the divine, it seems that he does include God within the notion of being that serves as the subject of metaphysics. This inference is reinforced by his refusal (along with Avicenna) to admit that there are causes and principles for being as such. Granted that it pertains to metaphysics to investigate general causes and principles, these can be causes only of all caused being, not of being as being.[15] If God were not included under the being that serves as the subject of metaphysics, Siger could assign to metaphysics the study of the principles and causes of being as such.[16]

Duns Scotus touches on this problem more than once. By 'the subject of a science' he usually means that adequate object of study which implicitly contains the conclusions that may be drawn in a given science and which has sufficient unity to account for the unity of that science itself.[17] As he

12. Siger of Brabant 1948, *Intr.*, q. 1, p. 4.
13. *Ibid.* Also see Zimmermann 1965, pp. 181–2.
14. For discussion of these and appropriate references see Van Steenberghen 1977, pp. 296–300.
15. Siger of Brabant 1948, *Intr.*, q. 2, p. 5: 'Tamen entis, secundum quod ens, non est principium quia tunc omne ens haberet principium.' Also see his Commentary on Book IV, p. 185.60–80; also on Book VI, q. 1, p. 364.4–365.8.
16. Zimmermann 1965, pp. 185–6.
17. *Ordinatio, Prol.,* pars 3, qq. 1–3, nn. 142–4 (Duns Scotus 1950–, v. 1, pp. 96–7); *Lectura in I Sent.,* Prol., pars 2, qq. 1–3, n. 66 (Duns Scotus 1950–, v. 16, p. 26); and especially, his *Reportatio Parisiensis examinata* (*Reportatio* I-A according to the classification of the Scotus commission, for which see Duns Scotus 1950–, v. 1, 125*–6*), Prol., q. 1, a. 2 (MS *Vienna bibl. nat.* 1453, f. 1, pp. 1–2 of the transcription prepared by the late Victor Doucet). In light of recent findings by the Scotus Commission, one should no longer cite as Scotus' own work the version of Book One of the *Reportatio Parisiensis* contained in the Wadding and Vivès editions. On this see Duns Scotus 1950–, v. 7, pp. 4*–6*.

explains in the *Prologue* to his *Reportatio Parisiensis examinata*, the conclusions in any science are known only by reason of their principles. And these
principles, if they are immediate, are themselves known from their terms.
But the terms are known by reason of the subject of that science. Therefore,
'that is the first object (subject) of a science which contains virtually and
potentially knowledge of all the truths of that science'.[18]

It is clear that when Scotus so defines the subject or object of a science he
will not admit that God is the subject of metaphysics.[19] Hence in his
frequent contrasts between the positions of Avicenna and Averroes, he
usually defends Avicenna. The subject of metaphysics can only be being as
being. God cannot be the subject of metaphysics since the subject of any
science must be universal, not particular. Moreover, Scotus contends that it
is in metaphysics rather than in physics that one most effectively establishes
the existence of God, and so has another reason for not admitting God as
the subject of metaphysics.[20] On the other hand, since God is one of the
things investigated by metaphysics, it follows that for Scotus God, too, is in
some way included within that general notion of being that serves as its

18. '... dico quod illud est per se primum obiectum alicuius scientiae quod continet virtualiter et
potentialiter notitiam omnium veritatum illius scientiae ... quia conclusiones cognoscuntur ex
principiis, ut patet ex dictis; et principia tandem, si sint immediata, cognoscuntur ex terminis,
sicut dictum est. Terminus etiam praedicatus principii cognoscitur ex ratione subiecti, quia
principia communiter sunt per se primo modo. ... In isto ergo ordine tandem oportet devenire ad
aliquod subiectum simplex, quod est subiectum principii, vel principium principiorum, ex cuius
cognitione cognoscuntur omnia pertinentia ad scientiam." (MS *Vienna* 1453, f. 1, p. 2 of the
Doucet transcription).
19. Zimmermann 1965, pp. 267–9.
20. *Ordinatio, Prol.*, pars 3, q. 2, ad 2, nn. 189, 193–4 (Duns Scotus 1950–, v. 1, pp. 127, 129–31);
Lectura, Pról. pars 2, q. 2, ad arg., n. 97 (Duns Scotus 1950–, v. 16, pp. 34–5); *Report. Paris.
examinata, Prol.*, q. 3 (f. 8, p. 27 of Doucet transcription): 'De primo est controversia inter
Avicennam et Averroem. Posuit enim Avicenna quod Deus non est subiectum in metaphysica,
sed aliquid aliud ut ens, quia nulla scientia probat suum subiectum esse; metaphysicus probat
Deum esse et substantias separatas esse; ergo etc. Averroes reprehendit Avicennam in commento
ultimo I Physicorum: supposita maiori Avicennae, quod nulla scientia probat suum subiectum
esse, quae est communis utrique, capit quod Deus est subiectum in metaphysica et quod Deum esse
non probatur in metaphysica, sed in physica. ... Sed Avicenna bene dicit et Averroes valde male.
Et accipio propositionem utriusque communem, scilicet quod nulla scientia probat suum obiectum esse, quae vera est propter primitatem subiecti ad scientiam, quia si esset posterius, posset
ipsum probari esse in illa scientia in qua habet rationem posterioris et non obiecti adaequati. Sed
maiorem primitatem habet subiectum respectu scientiae posterioris quam prioris. Ergo, si scientia
prima non potest probare suum subiectum esse, quia est subiectum primum, ergo multo magis
nec scientia posterior ... Dico ergo ad quaestionem ... quod Deus non est subiectum in metaphysica.' In this same context Scotus again defends the superiority of the metaphysical demonstration of God. As is well known, Scotus spared no efforts in his concern to work out a
metaphysical demonstration of God's existence, one which has been described as 'what is, no
doubt, the most perfectly-elaborated proof of God's existence in the Middle Ages' (Maurer 1976,
p. 177). For full discussion of this argumentation and for appropriate references see Alluntis 1965,
pp. 133–70.

subject.[21] This can be seen from the fact that he denies that there are principles or causes of being as being, the subject of metaphysics, since this would mean that every being, God included, has a principle or cause.[22]

Thomas Aquinas on metaphysics and God

The position of Thomas Aquinas on this issue is almost unique. He agrees with Avicenna, Siger, and Duns Scotus in maintaining that the subject of metaphysics is being as being or being in general (*ens commune*),[23] but he denies that God is included under this notion of being in general.[24] In his view it belongs to a science to seek after knowledge of the principles or causes of its subject. And since Thomas regards God as the cause of *ens commune* (meaning thereby the cause of all that falls under *ens commune*), he proposes knowledge of God as the goal at which metaphysical investigation aims.[25] This would seem to imply that argumentation for the existence of God is a part of metaphysics. But there are some passages in his Commentary on Aristotle's *Metaphysics* which suggest that it is in physics that one establishes the existence of an immobile, separate entity, and that this conclusion is a necessary condition for beginning metaphysics.[26] Hence contemporary interpreters remain divided over two issues. According to Thomas, does it pertain to physics, or to metaphysics, or perhaps to both to establish the existence of God?[27] And does the very possibility of

---

21. Zimmermann 1965, pp. 271–3. 'Deus autem etsi non est primum subiectum in metaphysica, est tamen consideratum in illa scientia nobilissimo modo quo potest considerari in aliqua scientia naturaliter acquisita' (*Ord., Prol.*, pars 3, q. 2, n. 193, Duns Scotus 1950–, v. 1, p. 130).

22. '... quia entis in quantum ens, quod ponitur subiectum metaphysicae, nulla sunt principia, quia tunc essent cuiuslibet entis' (*op. cit.*, q. 1, n. 191 [p. 128]).

23. Aquinas 1955, Q. 5, a. 1, *ad* 6, p. 171; Q. 5, a. 4, p. 194: 'Et ideo pertractantur in illa doctrina, in qua ponuntur ea quae sunt communia omnibus entibus, quae habet subiectum ens in quantum est ens'; *In III Sent.*, d. 27, q. 2, a. 4. sol. 2; Aquinas 1971b, Prooemium, p. 2. On Aquinas' understanding of the subject of a science see Zimmermann 1965, pp. 160–5.

24. Aquinas 1950b, v. 2, no. 660, p. 245: '... omnia existentia continentur sub ipso esse communi, non autem Deus, sed magis esse commune continetur sub eius virtute'. *ST*, Ia IIae, q. 66, a. 5, *ad* 4: '... quia ens commune est proprius effectus causae altissimae, scilicet Dei'.

25. Aquinas 1955, Q. 5, a. 4 (p. 192.21–5; p. 195.6–24); Aquinas 1971b, Prooemium, p. 2: 'Unde oportet quod ad eamdem scientiam pertineat considerare substantias separatas, et ens commune, quod est genus, cuius sunt praedictae substantiae communes et universales causae ... Nam cognitio causarum alicuius generis, est finis ad quem consideratio scientiae pertingit'; cf. *SCG* III, c. 25. See Zimmermann 1965, pp. 174–5, especially on the different relationships of God and of other separate substances to *ens commune*.

26. See especially Aquinas 1971b, IV.i, no. 593; VI.i, nn. 1169–70; XI.vii, n. 2267, also III.vi, no. 398. On these see Wippel 1978, pp. 447–52.

27. On this see Owens 1953, pp. 109–21. For differing assessments as to whether in Thomas' eyes Aristotle's argumentation in the *Physics* leads merely to a sphere soul or to God, see Paulus 1933, pp. 259–94, 394–424; Owens 1966, pp. 119–50; Pegis 1973, pp. 67–117.

metaphysics presuppose that one has already demonstrated the existence of God or at least of some spiritual entity in physics?[28]

As regards the second of these disputed points, it seems that when Thomas is clearly writing in his own name rather than merely as the expositor of Aristotle, he does not maintain that one must base one's discovery of being as being, the subject of metaphysics, upon a conclusion already established in physics. But he does recommend that one study physics (as well as logic, mathematics, and ethics) before taking up metaphysics.[29] And as regards the first disputed point, it is fairly evident that Thomas does allow for strictly metaphysical argumentation for the existence of God, as one would expect from his discussions of the subject of metaphysics.[30] But when he is commenting on the *Physics*, he at least appears to regard purely physical argumentation as also sufficient for reaching this same conclusion.[31]

William Ockham on the subject of metaphysics

Quite different from any of these positions regarding the subject of metaphysics is the one taken by William Ockham,[32] who distinguished be-

28. For the view that for Aquinas the possibility of metaphysics does rest on such a conclusion from physics see, for instance, Smith 1954, pp. 78–94; Smith 1958, p. 382; O'Brien 1960, p. 160; Doig 1972, p. 243, n. 1; p. 303, n. 1; Weisheipl 1976, pp. 194–6. For a different interpretation see Klubertanz 1954a, pp. 13, 17; 1954b, pp. 196–8; Renard 1956.

29. See Wippel 1978, pp. 452–68. For texts in Thomas on the proper learning order see Aquinas 1964b, VI.vii, nn. 1209–11; Aquinas 1954d, Prooemium, p. 2; Aquinas 1955, Q. 5, a. 1, *ad* 9 (p. 172:3–11). For fuller discussion of this see Wippel 1973; Owens 1966, pp. 131–2. On the difficulty in determining when in his commentaries on Aristotle Thomas is simply interpreting Aristotle, when he is also accepting such an interpretation as his own position, and when he is going beyond the text to express his personal views, see Doig 1972, pp. ix–xiv, and the references given there; Wippel 1978, pp. 452ff. It seems evident enough that both in his Commentary on the *De Trinitate* and in the Prooemium to his Commentary on the *Metaphysics* Thomas is writing in his own name. If, as appears to be the case, it is difficult to reconcile certain statements taken from his Commentary proper (see n. 26 above) with those made when he is writing in his own name, preference should be given to the latter in any attempt to determine Thomas' own mind.

30. See, for instance, the argumentation presented in his *De ente et essentia*, c. 4, granted that in certain later writings Gilson has denied that this was really intended by Thomas to be a demonstration of God's existence. See Gilson 1950, pp. 257–60; Gilson 1961a, pp. 26–8. For another interpretation of this chapter together with references to others see Wippel 1979, pp. 279–95. Of Thomas' well known 'Five Ways' in *ST* I, 2, 3, the first argument, based on motion (along with its parallel version in *SCG*) has been interpreted by many as being physical rather than metaphysical. But for a different reading see Owens 1953, pp. 109–21.

31. See the conclusion of his Commentary on *Physics* VIII: 'Et sic terminat Philosophus considerationem communem de rebus naturalibus, in primo principio totius naturae, qui est super omnia Deus benedictus in saecula. Amen' (VIII.xxiii, n. 1172). One might argue, however, that this concluding remark is really not germane to Thomas' opinion about the physical or metaphysical nature of Aristotle's reasoning here; see above, n. 27.

32. On this see Guelluy 1947, pp. 277–93; Maurer 1958, pp. 98–112; Zimmermann 1965, pp. 330–38.

tween the object and the subject of a science. The object of a science is simply any proposition that is demonstrated within that science, but the subject of a science is the subject of such a proposition.[33] Since a given science, such as metaphysics, includes many propositions with different subjects, it will have many different subjects.[34] One of the many subjects of metaphysics is, of course, being, and it even enjoys a certain primacy; for the metaphysician is especially concerned with arriving at conclusions about being. From another vantage point God, also one of the subjects of metaphysics, may be regarded as primary by reason of his pre-eminent perfection.[35] But in Ockham's view there is no single unifying subject for metaphysics as envisaged by Avicenna, Siger, Thomas, or Scotus.[36]

Essence and existence in Boethius

Philosophers of the high Middle Ages felt a need to account for the metaphysical structure not only of corporeal beings but also of immaterial entities such as angels and separated souls. It was necessary to explain the caused, contingent, and composite character of such entities while distinguishing it from the absolutely uncaused, necessary, and simple nature of God. As a consequence, controversy arose concerning the relationship between essence and existence in creatures.[37] Although Boethius himself should not be regarded as a proponent of real distinction and composition of essence and existence in such entities, he had provided considerable impetus for those later discussions through a series of axioms at the beginning of his *De Hebdomadibus*. There he had written that 'being (*esse*) and that which exists are different'. He had also maintained that although in a simple entity 'its being and that which it is are one and the same', in any composite 'its being and that which it is are not one and the same'.[38] Such

---

33. William Ockham 1957b, Prologue, p. 9; see also Ockham 1967, Prologue, q. 9, p. 266.17–22.

34. Ockham 1957b, Prol., pp. 8–9; Ockham 1967, Prol., q. 9, pp. 247–9.

35. Ockham 1957b, Prol., p. 10; Ockham 1967, Prol., q. 9, pp. 255.12–257.2, 258.14–259.13.

36. See, for instance Ockham 1967, Prol., q. 9, p. 255.13–15: 'Ad tertium dico quod metaphysicae et similiter mathematicae non est unum subiectum, loquendo de virtute sermonis, sed quot sunt subiecta conclusionum tot sunt subiecta scientiarum.' See the immediately following context for his defence of some order between these various subjects. For some reservations as to whether this approach can really safeguard the unity of a science such as physics or metaphysics see Maurer 1958, pp. 109–10.

37. A complete history of this controversy concerning the relationship between essence and existence remains to be written. For helpful introductions see Grabmann 1924, pp. 131–90; Roland-Gosselin 1948, pp. 142–205; Gilson 1955, pp. 420–7; Paulus 1938, pp. 260–91.

38. Often referred to as the *De Hebdomadibus* by medieval authors, this work appears in the Rand edition under the title: 'Quomodo substantiae in eo quod sint bonae sint cum non sint substantialia bona' (p. 38). See Axioms II: 'Diversum est esse et id quod est ...'; VII: 'Omne simplex esse suum et id quod est unum habet'; VIII: 'Omni composito aliud est esse, aliud ipsum est'

Boethian texts were frequently cited by thirteenth-century participants in the controversy over the relationship between essence and existence.[39]

Essence and existence in Avicenna and Averroes

Avicenna was thought by many scholastics to have defended an extreme form of distinction between essence and existence. For instance, according to Aquinas, Siger of Brabant, and James of Viterbo, he had not only distinguished between them but had regarded existence as a kind of accident that is superadded to essence.[40] Averroes had already taxed Avicenna with having made this mistake both with respect to being and with respect to 'unity' or 'oneness', and it was an easy step for Latin critics to take up the Averroistic critique and sometimes also to apply it to thirteenth-century defenses of real distinction between essence and existence.[41] They would argue that if an entity enjoys real being only by reason of something that is superadded to its essence, then why not posit something else by reason of which that superadded thing (existence) itself enjoys reality, and so on *ad infinitum*?[42]

(pp. 40, 42). For different interpretations of these and the other axioms in Boethius himself see Bruder 1928, pp. 72ff. (who does see real distinction between essence and existence implied there); Brosch 1931, pp. 1–121; Roland-Gosselin 1948, pp. 142–5; Fabro 1950, pp. 98–105, 25–33; Fabro 1960, pp. 204–13; Fabro 1961, pp. 267–79; (in each of the above Fabro also considers Thomas' commentary on the Boethian text); Schrimpf 1966, pp. 5–26 (pp. 121ff. for a brief survey of other treatments of Thomas' commentary and for that commentary itself); Hadot 1970, pp. 143–56; McInerny 1974, pp. 227–45.

39. In his Commentary on the *De Hebdomadibus*, Thomas interprets Axiom II as cited above as implying only logical or intentional distinction. But he interprets Axiom VIII in the sense of real distinction between essence and existence (*esse*). See *In De Hebdomadibus*, L. II, n. 22: 'Quae quidem diversitas non est hic referenda ad res, de quibus adhuc non loquitur, sed ad ipsas rationes seu intentiones' (p. 396); n. 32: '. . . sicut esse et quod est differunt in simplicibus secundum intentiones, ita in compositis differunt realiter' (p. 398). For other passages in which Aquinas uses the Boethian terminology to express his own theory of composition of essence and *esse* in creatures see: *In I Sent.*, d. 8, q. 5, a. 1; *De ente*, c. 4; *ST* I, q. 50, a. 2, *ad* 3: Aquinas 1956, Quodl. 2, q. 2, a. 1 (p. 24); Quodl. 3, q. 8, a. 1 (p. 61). For Giles of Rome's citation of the Boethian axioms in support of his theory of real distinction of essence and existence see Giles of Rome 1503, q. 9, f. 18^{va-b}. There Giles also contests Henry of Ghent's 'theological' interpretation of the same, for which see Henry's Quodlibet 1, q. 9; Henry of Ghent 1518, ff. 7^v–8^r.

40. For Aquinas see Aquinas 1971b, IV.ii, nn. 556, 558; for Siger see Siger of Brabant 1948, *Intr.*, q. 7, pp. 16, 18, 20; for James see James of Viterbo 1968, Quodlibet 1, q. 4, p. 46.102–7. On the Avicennian position see Roland-Gosselin 1948, pp. 150–6; Goichon 1937. But for some recent attempts to defend the Arabic Avicenna against this interpretation see Rahman 1958, pp. 1–16; Rahman 1963, pp. 483–6; Morewedge 1972, pp. 425–35. But see also Verbeke 1977, pp. 34*–6*, 76*–9*.

41. For Averroes see Averroes 1562–74f, IV, com. 3, f. 67^{rab}. On this see Forest 1956, pp. 142ff.

42. See, e.g., Siger of Brabant 1948, *Intr.* q. 7, *sed contra*, p. 14 (the last two arguments, with which Siger apparently agrees); Godfrey of Fontaines 1904–37, Quodlibet 3, q. 1 (v. 2, p. 303) (short version), 163–4 (long version). Godfrey explicitly attributes this argument to Averroes.

Aquinas' theory of real composition and distinction of essence and existence

Among thirteenth- and fourteenth-century scholastics, a variety of positions developed with respect to this issue. On the one side there is Aquinas' well-known theory of real composition and distinction of essence and existence (*esse*) in all creatures.[43] He appears to defend this position already in his youthful *De ente et essentia*.[44] There in Ch. 4 he introduces this doctrine within the general context of his refutation of universal hylemorphism. According to that position, which Aquinas traces back to Avicebron, all beings other than God, including purely spiritual ones, are composed of matter and form. While Aquinas denies matter to purely spiritual entities, he proposes to establish their composite character by postulating another kind of composition for them, that of essence and *esse*. And he explicitly makes the point that because the quiddity or essence of a separate entity receives its existence from God, essence and existence are related to each other as potency and act.[45]

Frequently enough in writings dating from his more mature period Aquinas returns to and deepens his understanding of essence–*esse* composition in beings other than God.[46] It is clear that for Aquinas existence

---

43. For some studies by those who do find this position in Aquinas see De Finance 1960, pp. 94–111; Fabro 1950, pp. 212–44; Gilson 1952a, pp. 171–8; Gilson 1955, pp. 420–7; Grabmann 1924, pp. 131–90; Owens 1965, pp. 19–22, Sweeney 1963, pp. 97–131. But for some who deny that Thomas ever defended this position see Chossat 1939, col. 1180; Chossat 1932, pp. 129.465–177.513; Cunningham 1962, pp. 279–312; Cunningham 1964, pp. 283–306; Cunningham 1970, pp. 9–28. As will be clear from what follows, I agree with the former rather than the latter.

44. For references to some recent disputes over the interpretation of *De ente*, see Wippel 1979, p. 279, n. 1. For a fuller discussion of the interpretation of *De ente*, c. 4, presented here, see Wippel 1979, pp. 279–95.

45. *De ente* (1948b) p. 35.10–25. Central to his reasoning is the assumption that whatever is not included in one's understanding of an essence or quiddity can only come to it from without and unite in composition with it (p. 34.7–10). But even more important is his claim that there can be at most one being in which essence and existence are identical. Only after making that claim does he introduce argumentation for God's existence (pp. 34.15–35.9).

46. See *SCG* II, 52, 2nd arg., (*ca.* 1261 or thereafter); *Qu. disp. de spiritualibus creaturis* (1267–8), Aquinas 1953c, pp. 370b–371a. In contrast with the *De ente*, in each of these he accepts God's existence as given (for which he has already argued in *SCG* I, q. 13). In the latter text he then reasons that there can only be one being which is its *esse*, and hence that in every other being, since it is not its *esse*, it must have an *esse* that is received in something (essence) whereby it is limited. He then applies his metaphysics of participation: '... et sic in quolibet creato aliud est natura rei quae participat esse, et aliud ipsum esse participatum', and then correlates the participated *esse* and the participating nature in any such being as act and potency. For another text where he reasons from the factual existence of God as the only being in which essence and *esse* are identical to their distinction in others see his *Tractatus de substantiis separatis* (1271–3), Aquinas 1963, p. 79. For the increasing importance in Thomas' mature writings of arguments based on the participated character of beings other than God see Fabro 1950, pp. 222–44. Central to this reasoning is Thomas' conviction that: 'Quandocumque autem aliquid praedicatur de altero per participationem, oportet ibi aliquid esse praeter id quod participatur.' See Aquinas 1956, Quodl. 2, q. 2,

(*esse*) is not to be regarded as a thing (*res*) or as another kind of essence, or as a predicamental accident that would be superadded to essence; existence has no quidditative content in addition to that of the essence which it actualises.[47] Interpreters of Aquinas sometimes express this by saying that existence is a principle of being rather than a being in itself, that by reason of which an entity actually exists. Essence is another ontological principle of being, that by reason of which an entity is what it is and enjoys quidditative content. But neither essence nor existence can exist independently from the other.[48]

In his *De potentia* Aquinas describes *esse* as the 'actuality of all acts and the perfection of all perfections'.[49] It is not, then, a principle that simply accounts for a given being's existing. It is taken to account for this, to be sure, but it is also the ultimate intrinsic ontological principle of perfection in any existing entity.[50] And if existence actualises a distinct essence principle in every finite being, essence receives and limits existence.[51]

This same doctrine plays a central role in Aquinas' metaphysics of participation and in his solution to the classical problem of 'the one and the many'.[52] A finite being may be said to participate in being because of its

a. 1 (p. 24b). There he immediately concludes from this that in every creature: '... est aliud ipsa creatura quae habet esse, et ipsum esse eius', and cites Boethius' *De Hebdomadibus*.

47. See his critique of Avicenna in Aquinas 1971b, IV. ii, n. 558 (p. 155b). See also Aquinas 1956, Quodl. 12, q. 5, a. 1: '... dico quod esse substantiale rei non est accidens, sed actualitas cuiuslibet formae existentis, sive sine materia sive cum materia'. But he will admit that one can refer to existence (*esse*) as an 'accident' if one simply means thereby that it is not a part of the essence: '... accidens dicitur large omne quod non est pars essentiae' (p. 227a). For the same see Quodl. 2, q. 2, a. 1, and *ad* 2 (p. 24b).

48. See Gilson 1952a, pp. 172–6; De Raeymaeker 1954, pp. 106–7. See *ST*, I, q. 50, a. 2, *ad* 3: 'ipsum autem esse est quo substantia est, sicut cursus est quo currens currit' (where Thomas is again commenting on the Boethian couplet *esse* and *quod est*).

49. Aquinas 1953b, q. 7 a. 2, *ad* 9 (p. 192b): '... hoc quod dico esse est inter omnia perfectissimum ... Unde patet quod hoc quod dico esse est actualitas omnium actuum, et propter hoc est perfectio omnium perfectionum.' For parallels see *ST*, I, q. 3, a. 4; I, q. 4, a. 1, *ad* 3.

50. See Gilson 1952, pp. 172–86; De Finance 1960, pp. 111–19.

51. Aquinas 1954c, c. 18 (p. 18b): Nullus enim actus invenitur finiri nisi per potentiam, quae est vis receptiva.' As in the present context, Thomas frequently appeals to this notion in order to establish divine infinity. See, for instance, *De spiritualibus creaturis*, q. 1, art 1; *ST*, I, q. 7, a. 1c; *In I Sent.*, d. 8, q. 2, a. 1. In the following text he appeals to it to establish essence–*esse* composition in creatures: 'Praeterea, omnis creatura habet esse finitum. Sed esse non receptum in aliquo, non est finitum, immo absolutum. Ergo omnis creatura habet esse receptum in aliquo; et ita oportet quod habeat duo ad minus, scilicet esse, et id quod esse recipit' *In I Sent.*, d. 8, q. 5, a. 1. Though this appears in the *sed contra*, it reflects Thomas' own thinking.

52. Recognition of the major role played by Thomas' doctrine of participation in his overall metaphysics is one of the major achievements of twentieth-century Thomistic scholarship. Here greatest credit must be given to the groundbreaking studies in Fabro 1950 (1st ed., 1939), 1960, 1961; and in Geiger 1953 (1st ed., 1942). See also Little 1949 (to be used with caution); De Finance 1960, pp. 120–49; Clarke 1952a, 1952b.

essence–existence composition. As Aquinas frequently phrases it, no such being is identical with *esse*; it simply has or participates in *esse*.[53] In every such entity essence receives and limits *esse* and therefore accounts for its presence therein to this degree rather than any other. In such beings, therefore, the nature or essence that participates in *esse* must be distinct from the *esse* in which it participates.[54] In other words, real composition and distinction of essence and existence in any particular being is necessary if one is to account for its limitation, according to Aquinas.[55] He also maintains that any participated being is efficiently caused by God, pure and unparticipated *esse*.[56]

Giles of Rome on the real distinction

Shortly after the death of Aquinas in 1274, Giles of Rome emerged as a leading advocate of real distinction between essence and existence in creatures. By 1276 he appears to have been already identified as a defender of this position, and soon afterwards he devoted a systematic treatise to it, his *Theoremata de esse et essentia*.[57] Shortly after his return from his 'exile' from the theology faculty at Paris in 1285, he defended it again at great

---

53. See, for instance, Aquinas 1956, Quodl, 2. q. 2, a. 1 (p. 24a): '... ens ... de qualibet autem creatura praedicatur per participationem: nulla enim creatura est suum esse, sed est habens esse.' See *SCG* I, 22; II, 52; Aquinas 1953b, q. 3, a. 5: 'Unde oportet quod ab uno illo ente omnia alia sint, quaecumque non sunt suum esse, sed habent esse per modum participationis' (p. 49b).

54. See Aquinas 1956, Quodl, 2, a. 1; Aquinas 1953c, a. 1 (p. 371a): 'et sic in quolibet creato aliud est natura rei quae participat esse, et aliud ipsum esse participatum'.

55. Here Fabro and Nicolas appear to be correct in their criticisms of Geiger for having assigned priority to 'participation by similitude' in his account of Aquinas, and for having denied that Thomas appeals to composition of essence and existence in order to account for limitation and multiplicity of finite beings. See Fabro 1950, pp. 20–2; Fabro 1961, pp. 63–73; Nicolas 1948, pp. 561–4.

56. See for instance, *ST*, I, q. 61, a. 1: 'Omne autem quod est per participationem, causatur ab eo quod est per essentiam.' For many texts and fuller discussion of this see Fabro 1961, *passim*.

57. It seems clear that Giles was Henry of Ghent's target in his attack against the real distinction in his Quodlibet 1, q. 9 of 1276. Giles may even have participated personally in this Quodlibetal debate. See Hocedez 1928, pp. 100–1, 104; Paulus 1938, pp. 280–2. For early formulations of this doctrine by Giles see Giles of Rome 1521, d. 8, p. 2, pr. 1, q. 2, f. 52ᵛ; pr. 2, q. 1, ff. 53ᵛᵇ–54ʳᵇ. On this see Nash 1950, pp. 66–8; Nash 1950–1, pp. 15–18; Suárez 1948, pp. 94, 96; Pattin 1953, p. 84*, Trapé 1964, pp. 330–7. For the same in his *Theoremata de corpore Christi* see Giles of Rome 1481, ff. 119ʳᵇ–120ʳᵃ. Note in particular: 'Ex his clare patet quod esse accidit cuilibet creaturae et dicit aliquid receptum in natura cuiuslibet creati (et dicit additum cuiuslibet entis creati: omitted in the Venice 1502. ed., cited by Pattin 1953, p. 87*) et facit realem differentiam in rebus creatis' (f. 119ᵛᵇ). On this doctrine in this work see Pattin 1953, pp. 85*–7*; Suárez 1948, pp. 96–7; Trapé 1969, pp. 452–3. Both of these works appear to date *ca.* 1275–6, and before Henry's Quodlibet 1 of Advent, 1276. See Paulus 1938, p.281; Trapé 1969, p. 455; Pattin 1953, pp. 82*, 85*. For other studies of Giles' general position see Trapé 1966, pp. 49–86; 1967, pp. 170–93; 1968, pp. 351–68.

length against the criticisms of Henry of Ghent.[58] Giles insists that one must appeal to the real distinction in order to account for the contingent character of creatures.[59] He also draws a close parallel between matter–form composition and that of essence and existence: existence actualises essence even as form actualises matter. If substantial change points to matter–form composition of material beings, the fact of creation requires essence–existence composition of all creatures.[60]

A major difficulty in interpreting Giles' doctrine arises from his reference to the distinction between essence and existence as between thing (*res*) and thing (*res*).[61] His intent in using such language continues to be debated by scholars today, but his terminology is at least unfortunate.[62] For in addition to suggesting that a distinctive quidditative content might be assigned to *esse*, it leaves him open to charges similar to those raised by Averroes against Avicenna.[63] Although the Thomism or non-Thomism of

58. For the controversy between Giles and Henry see in addition to Hocedez 1928, and Paulus 1938, pp. 280–2; Hocedez 1927, pp. 358–84; 1929, pp. 365–86; 1930, pp. (82)–(84); Paulus 1940–42; pp. 323–58.

59. Giles' *Theoremata de esse et essentia* probably dates from 1278–1280. See Suárez 1948, p. 80; Pattin 1953, p. 91*; Paulus 1940–2, p. 328 (between 1278 and 1286); Hocedez 1930, p. (12), who also places it between 1278 and 1286; Siematkowska 1960, pp. 4–5, 31, 48 (before 1276). For the present point see Giles of Rome 1930, th. 19, p. 129; Giles of Rome 1503, q. 9: '... sic creatio facit scire quod essentia esset (*read:* est) aliud ab esse quia ex hoc est creatio inquantum essentia acquirit esse' (f. 21^{ra-b}). These *Quaestiones* date from 1285–7 (see Pattin 1953, p. 90*, n. 37). Qq. 9 and 11 are placed in 1286 by Paulus and before Henry's reply in Quodlibet 10, q. 7 (Christmas, 1286). See Paulus 1940–2, pp. 328, 334.

60. Giles of Rome 1930, th. 5, pp. 19–20; Giles of Rome 1503, q. 9, ff. 20vb–21ra: 'Dicemus ergo sicut generatio facit scire materiam aliud esse a forma, sic creatio facit nos scire essentiam esse aliud ab esse.' For some differences between matter – form and essence – existence composition see Giles of Rome 1930, th. 6, pp. 26–30.

61. In the *Theoremata* see Giles of Rome 1930, th. 16, p. 101; th. 19, p. 127: '... quod esse et essentia sunt duae res'; th. 19, p. 134: '... sicut materia et quantitas sunt duae res, sic essentia et esse sunt duae res realiter differentes'; Giles of Rome 1503, q. 9 (f. 20vb): 'Res ergo ipsa quae est esse est in genere substantiae'; q. 11 (f. 24vb): '... et per consequens intelligitur quod esse sit alia res ab essentia'.

62. For some who are highly critical of Giles and charge that he has in effect 'reified' or turned into things principles of being, that is to say, essence and existence, see Hocedez 1930, pp. (62)–(65), (117); Paulus 1938, pp. 283–4. For even sharper criticism see Nash 1950, pp. 57–91; 1957, pp. 103–15; 1967, pp. 484–5; Carlo 1966, pp. 14–19, 31, 66ff., 83. For much more sympathetic treatments see Suárez 1948, pp. 66–9, 251–4, 262–8, 270–1; Pattin 1953, pp. 90*, 102*–6*; Trapé 1969, pp. 445ff., 467–8.

63. See, for example, Henry of Ghent, Quodlibet 1, q. 9, f. 7^r; as well as some of Godfrey's arguments against the theory of real distinction as presented below. See Giles of Rome 1503, q. 9 (f. 20vb), for his refusal to reduce *esse* to the status of an accident. *Esse* rather belongs to the genus of substance, but only by way of reduction: 'Bene igitur dictum est quod res ipsa quae est esse [est] in genere substantiae, sicut res ipsa quae est punctus est in genere quantitatis.' See also Giles of Rome 1930, th. 22, pp. 155–9. While admitting that essence and existence are separable from one another, he denies that either can ever exist in separation from the other. See, th. 12 (pp. 67–70); th. 5 (pp. 21–2, 29); th. 7 (p. 37). On this see Pattin 1953, pp. 104*–5*; Suárez 1948, pp. 252–4, 270. See

Giles' position continues to be discussed, it is certain that his terminology is not that of Aquinas.[64] And it was Giles' terminology, not Thomas', that was to become standard in subsequent discussions of this issue in the late thirteenth and early fourteenth centuries.

Siger's rejection of real composition and real distinction

In reviewing some major positions on this problem in the early 1270s, Siger of Brabant presents Aquinas as defending an intermediary position.[65] He then cites from Thomas' Commentary on *Metaphysics IV*, but acknowledges that while the conclusion is correct, he does not understand Thomas' way of formulating it.[66] Siger eventually concludes by rejecting any kind of real composition or distinction of essence and existence in creatures.[67] Like Thomas, Siger was concerned with safeguarding the nonsimple or composite character of purely spiritual creatures such as intelligences, even though he, too, rejects matter–form composition of such entities.[68] Rather

also Giles of Rome 1481, ff. 119vb–120ra, and especially: '... videtur enim absurdum quod essentia et esse dicantur duae essentiae'.

64. See the studies cited above in n. 62.

65. Siger of Brabant 1948, *Intr.* q. 7 (p. 16.21–4; and p. 16.14–17). On the dating see Van Steenberghen 1977, p. 218. Siger here presents Thomas' position as intermediary between that defended by Avicenna (and apparently by Albert the Great) on the one hand, and that of Aristotle, as interpreted by Averroes. See p. 16.17–20. For confirmation of this see Vennebusch 1966, p. 168, and in the *Questiones metaphysice tres* of Siger there edited by him, pp. 179.133–180.154. On Albert and Avicenna as defending the view that *esse* is a disposition superadded to essence see Siger of Brabant 1948, pp. 14–15; Vennebusch 1966, p. 179. In the latter context Siger explicitly refers to Albert's exposition on the *Liber de causis* and even comments: 'et hoc eum dicentem viva voce audivi' (p. 179.110–11); for which see Albert 1890–9c, I, 1, 8; p. 377. In brief as he reports Albert's reasoning, because caused beings receive their *esse* from the first principle and not of themselves, and have their essence or that which they are of themselves, their essence and *esse* are not the same. On this see Maurer 1946, pp. 75–6. On the difficulty of determining Albert's definitive position on the essence–*esse* relationship see Roland-Gosselin 1948, pp. 172–84; Geyer 1963, p. 9.

66. See Siger of Brabant 1948, *Intr.* q. 7 (p. 16.21–32); Siger of Brabant 1966, p. 180.139–54. For Thomas' text see n. 47 above. According to Siger Thomas seems to be saying that though *esse* is added to a thing's essence, it is neither that essence (*res*) itself, not a part of the essence (such as matter and form), nor an accident. This appears to lead to the untenable conclusion that *esse* is some kind of fourth nature in reality, Siger reasons. For more on Siger's discussion of Thomas' text see Van Steenberghen 1977, pp. 284–9; Maurer 1946, pp. 76–7.

67. As Siger puts it, essence (*res*) and existence (*ens*) signify the same thing or essence and even the same intelligible content (*intentionem*), but in different ways: 'unum ... ut est per modum actus ut hoc quod dico ens, aliud per modum habitus ut res'. Siger of Brabant 1948, *Intr.* q. 7; p. 17.60–1. See Siger of Brabant 1966, pp. 180–1.

68. Siger of brabant 1948, *Intr.* q. 7; p. 13.50–4 (for an argument for the real distinction based on the fact that certain things apart from God are not composed of matter and form); p. 20.24–5 ('Ista et ultima ratio movit fratrem Thomam'). For the same argument see Siger of Brabant 1966, p. 177 (arg. 7).

than conclude to their essence–existence composition, however, he proposes two alternatives, the first of which he does not present as definitive. According to this first solution, one might maintain that all such entities fall short of the divine simplicity in that they recede from the actuality of the first being and approach potentiality.[69] In his second solution Siger appeals to a substance–accident composition of created separate entities.[70] In his only recently discovered and edited Commentary on the *Liber de causis*, which seems to be his final word on this topic, Siger's thinking shifts so much that there he at least approaches Thomas' theory of real composition of essence and *esse* in creatures.[71]

During the decades following Siger's work many others rejected any kind of real composition and real distinction of essence and existence. While some of these defended nothing more than a distinction of reason (a purely mental distinction), others proposed intermediate positions.[72]

Already in 1286 and continuing thereafter throughout his career as a Master in the theology faculty at Paris, Godfrey of Fontaines was unwavering in his refusal to admit anything more than a distinction of reason between essence and existence.[73] In his discussion of the theory that defends their real distinction, Godfrey assumes that according to that position existence (*esse*) is a thing (*res*) that is added to essence from

69. Siger of Brabant 1966, q. 7; p. 21. He expresses some doubt as to whether beings other than God must be composite, and as to whether Aristotle would admit this (p. 182), and stresses the point that insofar as they are not God, they are not pure act and approach potentiality. But, as he comments in the first passage: 'Hoc tamen non concludit quod habeant diversas essentias' (p. 21.33). Note that only this solution appears in the short version of the same (p. 21.60–3). This statement again indicates his failure to understand Thomas' position, since it implies that for him essence and *esse* are distinct essences!

70. Siger of Brabant 1948, p. 22.50–2; Siger of Brabant 1966, p. 182.229–31. On this see Van Steenberghen 1977, pp. 289–91.

71. See Siger 1972b, q. 53, pp. 183–4, and especially p. 184.35–8. On this see Van Steenberghen 1977, p. 292; Marlasca 1972, p. 21, n. 20.

72. By 'mental distinction' I here have in mind the scholastics' *distinctio secundum rationem*, which is to say, the kind of distinction that is imposed by the mind or intellect without implying any distinct realities in the thing. As developed by Siger with application to the present issue, it does not even seem to imply distinct concepts (*intentiones*), but only distinct ways of signifying one and the same thing (*modi significandi*).

73. For Godfrey's differentiation of the three basic positions known in his time see Quodlibet 2, q. 2 (*Les Philosophes Belges* 1904 (*PB*) 2, p. 60). Here he refers to the theory of real distinction as maintaining that *esse* is a distinctive *res* which is the actuality of essence. In other words, he uses Giles' language. Also see Quodlibet 4, q. 2 (*PB* 2.235) for another brief description of these same three opinions, namely, real distinction, intentional distinction (Henry of Ghent), and real identity with only mental distinction and distinction in terms of their *modi intelligendi et significandi*: 'omnino sint idem secundum rem et differunt solum secundum rationem et modum intelligendi et significandi ...' For fuller discussion of Godfrey's knowledge of and reaction to the theory of real distinction see Wippel 1964. For the dates of Godfrey's Quodlibets see Glorieux 1925, pp. 149–68.

without.[74] Godfrey is evidently heavily indebted to the terminology of Giles of Rome for his understanding of the theory of the real distinction. He follows Averroes' lead in reducing that position to an absurdity.[75]

Against the contention that one must appeal to essence–existence composition in order to account for the contingent character of creatures, Godfrey appeals to the notion of creation *ex nihilo*.[76] And against the claim that one must admit such composition in purely spiritual creatures in order to distinguish them from God, Godfrey develops more fully the first of the solutions proposed by Siger, while rejecting the second, the solution favored by Siger.[77] A less perfect essence may be regarded as potential in comparison with one that is more perfect, and as actual viewed in itself or in comparison with something else that is even less perfect. Godfrey offers as his source for this unusual doctrine of 'composition' of act and potency in separate intelligences Proclus' *Elementatio theologica* (prop. 2): 'That which participates in the One is both one and not one.'[78] And Godfrey would safeguard the participated character of any creature not by appealing to an intrinsic composition of a participating principle (essence) and

---

74. See Quodlibet 3, q. 1 (*PB* 2.158): 'esse existentiae est aliquid differens realiter ab essentia sive etiam ab esse essentiae'; and in the shorter version of the same (*PB* 2.301): 'dicunt quidam quod esse et essentia sunt diversae res ...'. Frequently enough in Giles, Godfrey, Henry, and others, the expressions '*esse existentiae*' (existential being) and '*esse essentiae*' (essential being) appear. For all practical purposes Godfrey takes them as synonyms and easily shifts from '*essentia*' to '*esse essentiae*', and from '*existentia*' or '*esse*' to '*esse existentiae*'.

75. Quodlibet 3, q. 1 (*PB* 2.163–4, for the long version; *PB* 2.303 for the shorter version (see arg. 3)). In the shorter version, Godfrey concludes this argument with the observation: 'Relinquitur ergo quod unumquodque sit ens per se et non per aliquam *rem* additam ...' (italics added). In both the longer and shorter versions Godfrey explicitly attributes this reasoning to Averroes.

76. Quodlibet 3, q. 1. See *PB* 2.160 for Godfrey's recognition of the importance of this argument for defenders (Giles) of the real distinction. For his reply see pp. 166–9, 171–3. In sum, Godfrey rejects the close parallel drawn by Giles between matter–form composition as entailed by generation of material entities and alleged essence – existence composition as implied by creation of any creature.

77. See Quodlibet 3, q. 1, *PB* 2.159; and p. 306 (shorter version). Also Quodlibet 3, q. 4 where, in the course of rejecting matter – form composition in angels, he again finds the appeal to substance – accident composition therein insufficient to account for the composite or nonsimple character of their essences. It is not by holding that such essences are composed of distinct *res* (essence and existence or matter and form) or by holding that the essence unites with something else (an accident) that one meets this difficulty. See *PB* 2.186; 309 (shorter version).

78. See Quodlibet 7, q. 7, where Godfrey is attempting to show that there is sufficient potentiality in angelic entities to allow for their being included in a logical genus, though not in a natural one (*PB* 3.354–5). For the point that all such entities are potential insofar as they are not identical with God, pure actuality, see pp. 355, 357–9. See in particular, p. 360: '... ita etiam in natura angeli, recedendo ab actualitate primi et accedendo ad potentialitatem simpliciter habet quodammodo compositionem, non rei, sed rationis ex potentia et actu'. For Proclus see Proclus 1951, p. 265: 'Omne quod participat uno est unum et non unum' (cited by Godfrey, p. 359). Both Godfrey and Siger (in his first reply) liken the different degrees of being to the different kinds of number. See Godfrey pp. 359–60; Siger of Brabant 1948, *Intr.* q. 7, pp. 21–2.

that in which it participates (*esse*) as both Thomas and Giles had proposed, but by noting that prior to its actual creation any such being is to be regarded as having potential being insofar as God has the capacity to bring it into being.[79]

Against Giles' reasoning based upon the possibility of conceiving an essence as not existing, Godfrey counters that an essence cannot be understood as actual unless its existence is also viewed as actual, that is, as actually existing. If one considers the essence as only potential, then its existence likewise can be understood only as potential. This follows for Godfrey, of course, because of his defense of the real identity of essence and existence. As he sees it, whatever is true of essence is true of existence, and vice versa.[80] According to Godfrey, then, essence and existence are related as that which is signified abstractly is related to the same signified concretely. Just as there is no real distinction between that which is signified by the abstract term 'light' and the concrete expression 'to give light', so too, there is no real distinction between that which is signified by the abstract term 'essence' and the concrete term 'existence' (*esse*). There is, he concedes, diversity in the way in which these terms signify. Essence and existence are neither really nor even 'intentionally' distinct (as Henry would have it), but only rationally (*secundum rationem*).[81]

William Ockham against the real distinction

William Ockham addresses himself to this same issue in some detail both in his *Summa logicae* and in his Quodlibet 2.[82] In each of these discussions he reacts critically to the theory according to which essence and existence are really distinct, and presents that theory according to the terminology introduced by Giles of Rome. In one of his arguments against this position he reasons that if existence is really distinct from essence, then it must either be a substance or an accident. Since it cannot be an accident (which for Ockham would amount to reducing it to a quality or a quantity), it can

---

79. For Godfrey's presentation of this argument for the real distinction see Q. 3, q. 1 (*PB* 2.158–9; 302 (shorter version)). For his refutation see pp. 169–71; 305 (shorter version).

80. For Godfrey's presentation of this argument, see Quodlibet 3, q. 1 (*PB* 2.158 and 302 (shorter version)). For this in Giles, see Giles of Rome 1503, q. 11; f. 24^(va–b); see also q. 9; f. 20^(va); also Giles of Rome 1930, th. 12; pp. 67–70. For Godfrey's reply, see pp. 171; 305 (shorter version). Also cf. Quodlibet 13, q. 3 (*PB* 5.208–9).

81. See Quodlibet 3, q. 1 (*PB* 2.164–5; 303–4 for the shorter version). Cf. Quodlibet 13, q. 3 (*PB* 5.207–8).

82. See Ockham 1974a Pars III-2, c. 27, pp. 553–5; Ockham 1491, Quodl. 2, q. 7. On this see Boehner 1958, pp. 388–97; Menges 1952, pp. 102–3; Leff 1975, pp. 165–6.

only be a substance. But this alternative will not do since every substance is either matter, or form, or a composite of the two, or a separate entity.[83] Again, if essence and existence are distinct things (*res*), they will unite either to constitute something that enjoys essential (*per se*) unity, or else only accidental unity. The first suggestion is unacceptable because then, one of these – existence, presumably – would be actuality and the other potentiality, and to admit this would be to identify one with form and the other with matter. But to hold that they unite to form an accidental aggregate is no more satisfactory. For this would again result in reducing one of them – existence, presumably – to the status of an accident.[84]

In another line of attack Ockham reasons that if essence and existence are distinct things (*res*), it would not be contradictory for God to preserve the essence (*entitas*) of a thing in being without its existence, or its existence without its essence.[85] In a somewhat similar vein, Ockham insists that one has no more right to conclude from the previous nonexistence of a given essence to a real distinction between that essence and its existence than to conclude to a real distinction between that essence and itself. For if there was ever a time when that essence did not enjoy existence, it was not then an essence either, but only nothingness.[86]

Ockham concludes, therefore, that 'essence' and 'existence' signify one and the same thing. Nonetheless, the Latin term '*esse*' can be taken either as a noun or as a verb. When used in the first way ('being'), it signifies the same thing as essence and even in the same grammatical and logical mode. When taken in the second way ('to be'), '*esse*' signifies as a verb that which 'essence' signifies as a noun.[87]

83. Ockham 1974a, p. 553.6–12. Note his final comment in this argument: '... nullum istorum potest dici "esse", si "esse" sit alia *res* ab entitate rei' (ital. mine). Cf. Siger's criticism of Thomas' argumentation in n. 69 above. See also Peter John Olivi 1922–6, qu. 8 (v. 1, pp. 147ff.).

84. Ockham 1974a, p. 553.13–18. This argument seems to move too quickly, in that it assumes that to correlate essence and existence as potentiality and actuality is to identify them with matter and form. But Giles of Rome had insisted that the essence–existence composition differs from that of matter and form in certain ways, granted that both are potency–act compositions. See above, n. 60. But for a similar refutation of Giles' position, see Godfrey of Fontaines, Quodlibet 3, q. 1 (PB 2.167–9; 304 (shorter version)).

85. Ockham 1974a, p. 553.19–21. See Olivi 1922–6, p. 149.

86. Ockham 1974a, p. 554.32–43; Ockham 1491, Quodl. 2, q. 7. Cf. Godfrey, Quodlibet 3, q. 1 (PB 2.171).

87. Ockham 1974a, p. 554.23–32; Ockham 1491, Quodl 2, q. 7. There see in particular: 'Tamen esse quandoque est nomen, et sic tunc significat omnimode grammaticaliter et logicaliter idem cum essentia. Aliquando vero est verbum: tunc idem significat verbaliter quod essentia significat nominaliter.'

Henry of Ghent's intermediate position

Quite different from any of the positions considered above is that developed by Henry of Ghent. From the time of his first Quodlibet of 1276 he had been unyielding in his opposition to Giles of Rome's defense of the real distinction between essence and existence. But he was not content to conclude that there is only a distinction of reason between them.[88] One of his major concerns is to account for the possibility of there being meaningful knowledge of nonexistent possibles, on the one hand, though not of merely imaginary entities such as chimeras, on the other.[89] In his solution to this issue he is heavily indebted to Avicenna's doctrine of the threefold way in which a nature or essence may be viewed: (1) absolutely or simply in itself; (2) as realised in singular things; (3) as present in the intellect. Avicenna had admitted that a nature can in fact exist only in the second or in the third way, even though it may be considered in the first way.[90] Henry appears to go somewhat farther in that he assigns a special kind of being, essential being (*esse essentiae*), to an essence when it is considered in this first way.[91]

Possible essences, prior to their realisation in individual existents, enjoy essential being from all eternity insofar as they are objects of God's knowledge. This essential being provides them with sufficient ontological consistency in themselves for them to be objects of knowledge prior to their realisation as individual existents in time. Because any such essential being is lacking to merely imaginary entities, true science concerning them is impossible. Creation of individual existents – that is to say, creation as it is normally understood – requires the added intervention of the divine will. God, now acting as an efficient cause, communicates actual existence (*esse existentiae*) to certain essences in time.[92]

88. See Henry of Ghent 1518a, Quodl. 1, q. 9; v. 1, ff. 6ᵛ–8ʳ. On the dates of Henry's Quodlibets see Glorieux 1925, pp. 87–93 and 177–99; Gómez Caffarena 1957, pp. 116–33. On this particular text in Henry see Hocedez 1928, pp. 92–117; Paulus 1940–2, pp. 324–7; Gómez Caffarena 1958, pp. 72–3.
89. See, e.g., Henry of Ghent 1518a, Quodl. 3, q. 9, f. 61ᵛ; Paulus 1938, p. 124. For a contemporary who recognises this concern on Henry's part see Godfrey, Quodlibet 2, q. 2 (*PB* 2.53–9). On this see Wippel 1974b, pp. 294–8.
90. For Henry see esp. Henry of Ghent 1518a, Quodl. 3, q. 9, (ff. 60ᵛ–61ʳ), where he cites Avicenna's *Metaphysica* I, c. 6 and V, c. 1. On this in Avicenna see Paulus 1938, pp. 69–74; Gómez Caffarena 1958, pp. 26–7; Hoeres 1965, pp. 122–3.
91. See Henry of Ghent 1518a, Quodl. 3, q. 1 (f. 61ʳ): 'Triplicem quidem habet intellectum verum sicut et tres modos habet in esse. Unum enim habet esse naturae extra in rebus; alterum vero habet esse rationis; tertium vero habet esse essentiae.'
92. Ibid., Quodl. 1, q. 9 (f. 7ʳ); Quodl. 3, q. 9 (ff. 61ʳ–62ᵛ); Quodl. 9, q. 2, v. 2, (f. 345ʳ–345ᵛ).

Henry also tries to determine more precisely the relationship between essence (*esse essentiae*) and existence (*esse existentiae*) in actually existing creatures. While existence does not add any new and distinct thing (*res*) to essence, it does add to it a new and distinct 'intention', a relation of actual dependence upon God as its efficient cause.[93] Hence Henry introduces a new kind of distinction, his 'intentional distinction', which falls between the real distinction and the mere distinction of reason. In order to illustrate this he observes that there is only a distinction of reason between a definition and that which is defined, for instance, between man and rational animal. Substance and accident, on the other hand, are really distinct from each other. But the distinction between a genus and its differentia – for instance, between animal and rational – must be more than a mere distinction of reason but less than real. Hence, contends Henry, these are intentionally distinct, and so, too, are essence and existence in any actually existing creature.[94] Given this, Henry is reluctant to say of any creature that its essence is its existence; this he would reserve for God alone.[95]

Although Henry's views on essential being and his defence of an intentional distinction between essence and existence were well known in his own time and immediately thereafter, they do not seem to have gained wide acceptance. Giles of Rome and Godfrey of Fontaines, to mention but two, rejected his intentional distinction as unintelligible. And both Godfrey and Duns Scotus submitted Henry's notion of essential being to sharp criticism.[96]

James of Viterbo's intermediate position

Shortly after Henry's retirement from active teaching at the University of Paris in 1292, James of Viterbo reviewed the three major positions on the essence–existence question which had been developed by then: Giles'

---

93. Ibid., Quodl. 1, q. 9 (f. 7ʳ–7ᵛ); Quodl. 10, q. 7 (ff. 417ʳ–418ʳ). Note in particular: 'Ut secundum hoc esse existentiae non addat super essentiam nisi respectum ad efficientem' (f. 417ʳ). See also Quodl. 11, q. 3 (f. 441ʳ–441ᵛ).

94. Ibid., Quodl. 10, q. 7 (ff. 417ᵛ–418ʳ). For discussion of Henry's intentional distinction and its application to essence and existence see Paulus 1938, pp. 220–36, 284–91; Hoeres 1965, pp. 129–50; Gómez Caffarena 1958, pp. 65–92.

95. Ibid., Quodl. 1, q. 9 (f. 7ʳ–7ᵛ); Quodl. 11, q. 3 (f. 441ʳ–441ᵛ). For another succinct presentation of Henry's overall theory see Henry of Ghent 1520, a. 28, q. 4 (vol. 1, ff. 167ᵛ–168ᵛ).

96. For Giles see Giles of Rome 1503, q. 9 (f. 19ᵛᵃ), and Paulus 1940–2 for Giles' running controversy with Henry. For Godfrey's explicit rejection of the intentional distinction see Godfrey of Fontaines 1973, p. 368: '... quia non est aliud differre ratione et intentione'. For Godfrey's general critique of Henry's position see Wippel, 1974b, *passim*. For Scotus see *Ord.* I, d. 36, q. 1, nn. 13–17; Scotus 1950–, VI, pp. 276–7. On this see Hoeres 1965, pp. 161–3; Paulus 1938, pp. 131ff.

theory of real distinction, Henry's intentional distinction, and the view that defends only a distinction of reason between them (probably known to James as defended by Godfrey).[97] Although James tries to find something good in each of these, he ends by differing with them all. While Giles' position strikes him as reasonable, he has difficulty with the way in which it is expressed, and especially with Giles' description of *esse* as a superadded actuality which is neither matter, nor form, nor the composite, nor an accident. With Henry he agrees that a creature is related to God as both its exemplar and its efficient cause, but doubts that the term 'existence' itself expresses this relationship, at least when taken in its primary meaning. Although James' own position seems closer to that which identifies essence and existence, he finds that solution unacceptable unless it be qualified as he himself proposes.[98]

According to James, existence (*esse*) and essence are related to one another as the concrete and the abstract. But a concrete term signifies something more than does its corresponding abstract term. While both signify a given form, the concrete term also signifies the subject in which that form is realised, although not with equal immediacy. First and foremost (*primo et principaliter*) it signifies the form, and the subject only in a secondary way. Essence and existence as realised in creatures are one and the same as regards their primary meaning: that is to say, 'essence' and 'existence' signify the same. But that which is signified by 'existence' in its secondary meaning really differs from that which is signified by 'essence'. For while the term 'existence' signifies essence first and foremost, in a secondary way it also signifies that which must be conjoined with essence when it is realised in a concrete existing subject.[99]

Duns Scotus' intermediate position

Duns Scotus also rejects any kind of real distinction or real composition of essence and existence.[100] Like his predecessors, Scotus is concerned with the

---

97. See James of Viterbo 1968, Quodl. 1, q. 4; pp. 45–7. For confirmation that James has Giles in mind as the representative of the theory of real distinction see his reference to 'pulcris theorematibus' (p. 54.383). James' Quodlibet 1 appears to date from 1293. For discussion as to whether it could be placed in the 1292–3 academic year or only that of 1293–4 see Wippel 1974a; Ypma 1975, p. 274, n. 147.
98. James of Viterbo 1968, pp. 54–6.
99. Ibid., pp. 47.120–49.214. For further discussion see pp. 50–6. One might wonder whether James' position really differs from that of Godfrey, since he, too distinguishes between existence and essence as between the concrete and the abstract (see n. 81 above). James goes farther, however, in stating that essence and existence are really distinct when existence is considered in this secondary way. This Godfrey will not do. See PB 5.208.
100. *Op. Oxon.* 4, d. 11, q. 3, n. 46 (Scotus 1891–5, vol. 17, p. 429a); d. 13, q. 1, n. 38 (Scotus 1891–5, vol. 17, p. 692b); *Op. Oxon.* 2, d. 16, q. 1, n. 10 (Scotus 1891–5, vol. 13, p. 28a).

need to distinguish every creature, including simple intelligences or angels, from God. But he does not do so by postulating composition of essence and existence in created spiritual entities. In reasoning that reminds one in part of Godfrey of Fontaines and in part of Siger of Brabant, he argues that if such an essence is not composed of distinct things, it is still in some way both composite and capable of entering into composition with something else (*componibilis*). It is composite insofar as it possesses only a given degree of being and at the same time lacks any greater degree. But he then observes that this composition of something positive and of privation is not intrinsic to the thing's essence, a criticism that Godfrey had already directed at Siger's preferred solution to this difficulty – substance–accident composition of such intelligences, which composition Scotus also defends.[101]

Although it is clear enough that Scotus rejects real distinction between essence and existence in creatures, it is more difficult to determine precisely how he does distinguish between them. Real distinction will not do because for him this can be realised only between things which are separable in fact, and, according to Scotus, essence and existence are not separable.[102] A number of modern commentators have stated that Scotus here applies the intermediate kind of distinction that is so often associated with his name, the 'formal distinction'.[103] But this interpretation has been challenged by others. With somewhat greater reason it has also been suggested that Scotus appeals to another intermediate kind of distinction, a modal distinction, which obtains here between a given essence and its intrinsic mode, existence.[104] In the absence of more positive indications by

101. *Ord.* 1, d. 8, pars 1, q. 2, n. 32 (Scotus 1950–, vol. 4, pp. 165–6). Note in particular: 'Componitur ergo non ex re et re positiva, sed ex re positiva et privatione ... Nec tamen ista compositio "ex positivo et privativo" est in essentia rei, quia privatio non est de essentia alicuius positivi.' See also *Lectura* 1, d. 8, pars 1, q. 2, nn. 31, 37 (Scotus 1950–, vol. 17, pp. 10, 12). For Godfrey see above, n. 77. For discussion of Scotus' theory of 'composition' see Gilson 1968, pp. 189–98. On substance–accident composition in angels, see *Ord.*, loc. cit., n. 34 (pp. 166–7), also *Lectura*, loc. cit., n. 30 (pp. 9–10). Gilson connects the diversity between Thomas and Scotus on the essence–existence question with their different understandings of being. Cf. Wolter 1946, pp. 66–71. On Scotus' doctrine of univocity see especially Barth 1939. pp. 181–206, 277–98, 373–92; Barth 1953, pp. 89–94; Wolter 1946, pp. 31–57. The literature on analogy in Thomas is vast. For an excellent study and for much of this literature see Montagnes 1963. As these authorities rightly indicate, Scotus' primary target in his critique of analogy was the unusual theory developed by Henry of Ghent.
102. For the point that for Scotus (and Ockham) real distinction implies separability see Wolter 1965b, p. 46 and n. 3. On the nonseparability of essence and existence for Scotus see *Op. Oxon.* 2, d. 1, q. 2, n. 7 (Scotus 1891–5, vol. 11, p. 63).
103. For references to some of these see O'Brien 1964, pp. 62–4. To these Wolter adds Day 1947, p. 63; Weinberg 1964, p. 218. See Wolter 1965b, p. 54, n. 26, and pp. 45–60 for a helpful discussion of Scotus' formal distinction.
104. See O'Brien 1964, pp. 65–77; also see Hoeres 1965, pp. 171–9; Gilson 1952a, pp. 202, n. 2, 235, 549, n. 2.

Scotus himself, however, this interpretation is also open to question.[105] Another way of attempting to convey his thought is the suggestion that for him the distinction between essence and existence simply expresses the aspect of an existing thing which is grasped by abstractive cognition on the one hand (its essence), and by intuitive cognition on the other (its existence).[106] In any event, for him this distinction is something more than a mere distinction of reason, and something less than a real distinction.

Potentiality and actuality, matter and form

Many of the thinkers discussed in the preceding sections, who did not accept matter–form composition of purely spiritual entities, were concerned with showing that even in these beings potentiality and composition are in some way realised.[107] According to those who defended real distinction of essence and existence, there is a real composition of potentiality (essence) and actuality (existence) in every actually existing creature. And insofar as the potency or essence principle receives and limits the existence or act principle, it came to be referred to by some participants in the discussion as 'subjective' potency. For those who rejected real composition and distinction of essence and existence, only what some of them termed 'objective' potency would be realised in created spiritual beings, meaning thereby that any such being was a potential object or terminus of God's creative activity. According to them essence is not a 'subjective' potency, since it does not receive a really distinct existence as its actuality.[108] As we have seen many would account for the act-potency

---

105. On the modal distinction see Wolter 1946, pp. 24–7. For more on this and for discussion of its applicability to essence and existence see Wolter 1965, pp. 54–60. (In brief, while the formal distinction obtains between two formalities, the modal distinction is rather that between a given formality and its intrinsic mode, as between wisdom and infinite in God, or between being and finite in a creature. Also see Alluntis-Wolter 1975, pp. 505–7, 508–9, 518–19.)

106. See Wolter 1965, pp. 58–60.

107. Because the *De rerum principio*, now attributed to Vital du Four, was formerly thought to be by Duns Scotus, and because it defends universal hylemorphism, this view was mistakenly ascribed to Scotus in the past. For James of Viterbo's appeal to substance–accident composition in order to assure the presence of act-potency even in simple creatures see James of Viterbo 1968, Quodl. 1, q. 4 (pp. 57–61). James adjusts this to his own views on essence and existence.

108. For the distinction between 'subjective' and 'objective' potency see Henry of Ghent 1518, Quodl. 1, q. 9 (f. 6ᵛ), where he distinguishes between two ways of understanding participation. The first (which he here rejects) would view essence as a subject and the existence in which it participates as received in it after the manner of a form. Here and in his subsequent discussion of this in Quodl. 10, q. 7 (f. 418ʳ–418ᵛ), Henry is refuting Giles of Rome's understanding of essence as potency vis à vis existence taken as actuality. According to Henry, the essence of a creature may be described as a potential object ('objectively potential') insofar as it is an object or terminus of the divine creative action which produces it from nothing. And existence may be viewed as the same essence insofar as it is regarded as an actual object and terminus of God's creative activity. He dubs as a *phantastica imaginatio* Giles' position according to which essence would be a subject

'composition' of creatures in other ways, whether by appealing to the union of being and nonbeing (absence or privation of greater being) therein or by having recourse to substance–accident composition even in spiritual entities insofar as they are capable of intellection and volition.

Universal hylemorphism

Reference has been made in passing to another tradition according to which there is matter–form composition in all beings other than God, including human souls and created separate intelligences or angels. Aquinas and other thirteenth-century thinkers traced this doctrine back to the *Fons vitae* of Avicebron, but certain defenders of this position attempted to show that it owed its origin to Augustine.[109] Perhaps best known among those who espoused this view in the thirteenth century was Bonaventure, but even before him Roger Bacon had developed it while teaching in the Arts Faculty at Paris in the 1240s.[110] It continued to be defended by other Franciscan thinkers later in the century such as John Peckham, William of La Mare, and Richard of Middleton, and early in the fourteenth century by Gonsalvus of Spain.[111]

This doctrine easily enabled its defenders to hold that all beings apart from God are composed and that they include potentiality – viz., matter. It also implies that in man two instances of matter are present, one which is intrinsic to his soul and with which the form of his soul is inseparably

which receives existence. Also see ff. 419ᵛ–420ʳ. See Giles of Rome 1503, q. 12 (f. 29ʳᵃ⁻ᵛᵇ). Giles concedes the distinction between the potential (possible) taken subjectively and objectively (*terminative*), but insists that the latter presupposes the former. For Henry's reaction see Quodl. 11, q. 3 (f. 443ᵛ). For Godfrey of Fontaines' use of this distinction in refuting argumentation (apparently Giles') for the real distinction based on participation see Quodlibet 3, q. 1 (*PB* 2.169–71). See Wippel 1964, pp. 404–5. For Scotus' use of this see *Lectura* 1, d. 8, pars 1, q. 2, nn. 31, 38; *Ord.*, 1, d. 8, pars 1, q. 2, n. 33.

109. For Thomas' attribution of this to Avicebron see his *De ente*, c. 4 (Aquinas 1948b, p. 30); *In II Sent.*, d. 3, q. 1, a. 1; *Treatise on Separate Substances*, c. 5 (Aquinas 1963, p. 56). On this doctrine in Avicebron see Forest 1956 (2nd edn.), pp. 109–10. Henry of Ghent also attributes it to Avicebron. See Henry of Ghent 1518, Quodl. 4, q. 16 (f. 130ᵛ). But Thomas of York and then Gonsalvus of Spain ascribe it to Augustine. See Zavalloni 1951, pp. 442–3 (on Thomas of York); and Gonsalvus' *Quaestiones disputatae . . .*, q. 11 (Gonsalvus 1935, p. 221). For modern scholars who stress Avicebron's influence upon medieval discussions of this see Crowley 1950, pp. 82, 90; Van Steenberghen 1966, pp. 46–7, 150, 245–6, 249. Zavalloni rather tends to stress the Augustinian influence (p. 422).

110. For a general discussion see Kleineidam 1930; Lottin 1932, pp. 21–4. For this in Bonaventure see Gilson 1953 (3rd edn.), pp. 198–201 (in angels), 255–6 (in the human soul); Forest 1956, pp. 116–19; Quinn 1973, pp. 139–50; Macken 1976. On Bacon see Crowley 1950, pp. 81–91.

111. For Peckham see his *Tractatus de anima*, John Peckham 1948, pp. 47–8, 61–3 (for discussion of his text). See William of La Mare 1927, pp. 49–52, 118–21. On this in Richard see Hocedez 1925, pp. 190–9; Sharp 1930, pp. 262–3. See Gonsalvus 1935, q. 11, pp. 204, 213–21.

united, a spiritual matter, and another which is extrinsic to the soul, the corporeal matter of the body.[112] But Bonaventure and other proponents of universal hylemorphism also attempt to determine whether the matter of spiritual and of corporeal entities is essentially the same in kind, or different. He acknowledges the difficulty of this question and attributes the diverse answers proposed by others to the different ways in which matter may be viewed. Thus one might simply consider it as it is in itself and as if it were devoid of all forms, or one might view it in relationship to the different kinds of forms that may actualise it. Ultimately, however, he sides with the view that matter is essentially the same and even one in number in all created substances.[113] Some decades later Gonsalvus of Spain is still troubled by this problem but also concludes that it is preferable to hold that matter as found in spirits and in corporeal entities is the same in kind.[114]

Critics of universal hylemorphism

Earlier in the thirteenth century universal hylemorphism had been criticised by William of Auvergne.[115] It was later rejected by Albert the Great, and then by Aquinas and other thinkers discussed above.[116] Central to Thomas's refutation in his *De ente*, for instance, is his contention that the presence of matter within an intelligence is incompatible with the latter's capacity to perform intellectual operations.[117] Godfrey of Fontaines maintains that if the soul or a separate intelligence were composed of matter and form, it would then be corruptible.[118]

Whether one wishes to credit Augustine or Avicebron with having inspired the medieval doctrine of universal hylemorphism, it is surely not

---

112. See Bonaventure 1882–1902a, II, d. 17, a 1, q. 2 (vol. 2, pp. 413–15); Quinn 1973, pp. 139–42. For Bonaventure's defense of matter–form composition in angels see II, d. 3, pars 1, a. 1, q. 1 (vol. 2, pp. 89–91).

113. *Ibid.*, II, d. 3, pars 1, a. 1, q. 2 (vol. 2, pp. 94–8). On the numerical sameness of matter in all substances see *loc. cit.*, q. 3 (pp. 100–1). On this see Quinn 1973, p. 148.

114. *Quaestiones disputatae*, q. 11 (pp. 204, 219–21).

115. For William see his *De universo* I.2, cc. 2–12. On this see Roland-Gosselin 1948, pp. 71–4; Forest 1956, pp. 121–3.

116. For Albert see in particular *In II Sent.*, d. 3., a. 4. On Albert's position see Forest 1956, pp. 123–6; Kleineidam 1930, pp. 51–7. On this in Siger see Van Steenberghen 1977, pp. 282–92. See Henry of Ghent 1518, Quodl 4, q. 16 (ff. 130ᵛ–131ʳ); Paulus 1938, p. 216. See Giles of Rome 1930, th. 19 (pp. 128–9), Quodl. 1, q. 8 (pp. 17–19). For James of Viterbo see Quodl. 3, q. 18, and for the same by implication see Quodl. 1, q. 4. For Ockham's rejection of matter–form composition in angels see his *Ord.* 1, d. 8, q. 1; *OT*, III, p. 176.1–2. Also see n. 110 above.

117. Aquinas 1948b, pp. 31–2. For more on Thomas' critique of universal hylemorphism see Collins 1947, Ch. 2, pp. 50–74.

118. See Quodl. 3, q. 3 (*PB* 2.183–4, 308 (shorter version)). For his detailed refutation of Gonsalvus of Spain's theory insofar as it applies to the human soul see Quodl. 15, q. 10 (*PB* 14.50–56).

an Aristotelian view. In his *Metaphysics* Aristotle had described matter as 'that which in itself is neither a something nor a quantity nor any of those other things by which being is determined'.[119] This description led many scholastics such as Albert, Thomas, Siger of Brabant, Giles of Rome, and Godfrey, to conclude that prime matter is pure potentiality, that is, that it is completely devoid of any actuality in and of itself and apart from its corresponding substantial form.[120] To assign any degree of actuality to matter in itself would, they feared, make of it something substantial in itself rather than a mere constituent or principle of an existing substance. And if matter were a substance in itself, then any superadded form or actuality acquired through change could only be accidental, not substantial.[121]

Not all of the schoolmen understood the nature of prime matter in that way. Many assigned some degree of actuality to matter in and of itself, and some even contended that it could be sustained in existence by God through his absolute power apart from any substantial form. Versions of this were defended especially by Franciscans such as John Peckham, Richard of Middleton, and, somewhat later, Duns Scotus and Ockham; but the secular Master, Henry of Ghent, also championed this position.[122] In sum, it numbered among its supporters not only defenders of universal hylemorphism but others who had rejected that position, such as Henry, Duns Scotus, and Ockham.

119. See *Metaphysics* VII, iii (1029ª20−21).
120. On this in Albert see Weisheipl 1965a, pp. 151−2. As Weisheipl indicates, Albert does allow for an 'incipient actuality' or *inchoatio formae* in prime matter, something which Thomas rejects. For Thomas on the purely potential character of matter see Weisheipl 1965, pp. 152ff.; Forest 1956, pp. 210−16. Also see *ST*, I, q. 115, a. 1, *ad* 2; *SCG* II, 43. For Siger see Van Steenberghen 1977, pp. 327−8. For Giles see especially Giles of Rome 1503, qu. 8, f. 98ᵛᵇ; also 1930, th. 10 (p. 58). For Godfrey see Quodl. 1, q. 4 (*PB* 2.7−9); Quodl. 2, q. 4 (*PB* 2.83); Quodl. 10, q. 9 (*PB* 4.336−41).
121. For this see, for instance, Aquinas 1971b, VIII.1, n. 1689; Godfrey, Quodl. 2, q. 4 (*PB* 2.83); Quodl. 10, q. 9 (*PB* 4.337−9).
122. See Sharp 1930, pp. 178−82 (on Peckham), 220−1 (Richard of Middleton); Zavalloni 1951, pp. 303−9. On Scotus and especially on Ockham see Wolter 1965a, pp. 131−46. Interestingly, precisely because matter is not merely in objective potency but also in subjective potency (to its form) Scotus concludes that it must enjoy some degree of actuality (see Wolter 1965a, p. 132; and *Ord.* 2, d. 12, qq. 1, 2 (Scotus 1891−5, vol. 12, pp. 558, 577)). For this in Henry see Henry of Ghent 1518, 1, q. 10 (ff. 8ʳ−9ᵛ). On this see Macken 1976a, pp. 107−13. For an excellent introduction to the related question which was heatedly debated during the closing decades of the thirteenth century − viz., unicity vs. plurality of substantial form in any given material substance, and especially in man, see Zavalloni 1951; for further texts see Roos 1977.

20

UNIVERSALS IN THE EARLY
FOURTEENTH CENTURY

Two sorts of questions for moderate realism

The vigorous early-fourteenth-century debate about universals was based on a rejection of Platonism, the theory that universal natures really exist independently of the particulars whose natures they are and independently of every mind. Fourteenth-century 'moderate' realists agreed that natures must be somehow common to particulars in reality, but Aristotle had convinced them that no one in his right mind could hold that the nature of a thing exists separated from it as Platonic forms were supposed to do.[1] They insisted instead that the natures really exist in the things whose natures they are, as metaphysical constituents of them. But this contention had its own problems. Since there can be more than one particular in a given genus or species, natures cannot be the only metaphysical constituents of particulars; there must also be individuating principles that serve to distinguish one particular from another.

But what are these individuating principles? William of Champeaux's position that accidental properties individuate[2] was denied by virtually everyone on the Aristotelian ground that substance is naturally prior to accidents but particular substances are not naturally prior to what individuates them. Thomas Aquinas held that prime matter, the ultimate property-bearer in composite substances, combines with quantitative dimensions to individuate.[3] But Duns Scotus found this tantamount to conceding that accidents individuate after all.[4] Besides, he argued, neither matter, quantitative dimensions, nor their combination was distinct and determinate in itself. Taking it as axiomatic that only what is distinct and determinate in itself *can* individuate, Scotus concluded that neither matter by itself, existence, nor any combination of accidents can do the job

---

1. William Ockham 1967, *Ordinatio* I, d. 2, q. 4; *OT* II, p. 117. Cf. Walter Burley 1507, *Super artem veterem Porphyrii et Aristotelis*, ff. 5va–6ra.
2. Peter Abelard 1919–27, *Glossae secundum magistrum Petrum Abaelardum super Porphyrium*, p. 13.
3. Aquinas, *De ente et essentia*, c. 2; *ST*, I, q. 75, a. 7, c.
4. *Ordinatio* II, d. 3, q. 4, n. 111; Duns Scotus 1950–, VII, p. 446.

(*Ordinatio* II, d. 3, qq. 5, 3, and 4, respectively). Since the numerical unity that belongs to particulars is more perfect than the specific unity of natures, and since what is merely potential cannot increase the perfection of what is actual, Scotus concluded that the individuating principles must be something positive and have an actuality of their own and not fall themselves under any of the ten categories.[5]

What is the relationship between the nature and the so-called individuating principles? There must be some distinction between them, or else the nature will not be in any way the same in many particulars. But what sort of distinction? Further, do the individuating principles individuate the nature, or can one nature numerically the same, be a member of many different collections of metaphysical constituents?

I will examine two of the various answers given to the second sort of questions by moderate realists of the early fourteenth century – viz., those of Duns Scotus and Walter Burley. Their positions were criticised, as we shall see, by the father of late fourteenth-century nominalism, William Ockham, and his older contemporary, Henry of Harclay, whose views occupy a middle ground.

Duns Scotus' theory of universals

Scotus' theory of universals develops his conviction that the nature must be somehow common in reality, even though it cannot exist apart from any and every particular. He defends the first part of his thesis with 'almost infinitely many arguments':[6] For example, he holds that 'the unity that is required to found a relation of similarity is real. And it is not numerical, since no one single thing is similar or equal to itself.'[7] Conversely, real opposition between numerically distinct things requires real extremes of opposition.[8] Again, if Socrates is to be more similar to Plato than to a line, it must be that some real thing is common to the former two that is not common to Socrates and a line.[9] Similarly, even 'if no intellect existed, fire

---

5. *Ordinatio* II, d. 3, q. 6, nn. 169–70; Duns Scotus 1950–, VII, pp. 474–5.
6. Henry of Harclay, 'Utrum universale significet aliquam rem extra animam, aliam a singulari vel supposito' in Gál 1971, sec. 4, p. 186.
7. *Ordinatio* II, d. 2, p. 1, q. 1, n. 18; Duns Scotus 1950–, VII, p. 398: 'Secundum Philosophum V *Metaphysicae* cap. de "Ad aliquid", idem, simile et aequale fundantur super "unum", ita quod licet similitudo habeat pro fundamento rem de genere qualitatis talis, tamen relatio non est realis nisi habeat fundamentum reale et rationem proximam fundandi realem; igitur unitas quae requiritur in fundamento relationis similitudinis, est realis: non est autem unitas numeralis, quia nihil unum et idem est simile vel aequale sibi ipsi.'
8. *Ibid.*, n. 19; Duns Scotus 1950–, VII, pp. 398–9.
9. *Ibid.*, n. 23; Duns Scotus 1950–, VII, pp. 400–1.

would still produce fire and destroy water. And there would be some real unity of form between the producer and the product, because of which unity the production would be univocal ...'[10]

Yet, Scotus argues that if the nature is essentially something that can really exist in and be common to numerically distinct real things, it cannot of itself be numerically one. For whatever pertains to a thing of itself, pertains to it in whatever it is in. 'Therefore, if the nature of stone were of itself *this*, the nature of stone, whatever it is in, would be this stone.'[11] Likewise, 'if one of a pair of opposites pertains to a thing of itself, the other of the pair of opposites is incompatible with that thing of itself. Therefore, if the nature is of itself numerically one, numerical multiplicity is incompatible with it.'[12] But Scotus contends that human nature is numerically one in Scorates and numerically many in numerically many distinct particulars, and concludes that there must be some individuating principles, or thisnesses, that are numerically one and particular of themselves and that contract the nature, which is common of itself, rendering the nature numerically one and particular as well. Since the nature is numerically one and particular only through the individual difference, it is said to be one denominatively as Socrates is said to be white denominatively by virtue of the inherence of whiteness.[13]

Just as the nature is not numerically one and particular of itself, so the nature is not of itself completely universal.[14] For as completely universal, the nature is in fact truly predicable of each and every particular in the species. But nothing that is essentially predicable of many could be numerically one and particular at all. Nor is the nature completely universal insofar as it exists in reality, since actually being truly predicable of many is incompatible with being numerically one and particular.[15] Rather, the nature is completely universal only insofar as it exists in the intellect as an object of thought.

---

10. *Ibid.*, n. 28; Duns Scotus 1950–, VII, pp. 401–2: 'Nullo exsistente intellectu ignis generaret ignem et corrumperet aquam, et aliqua unitas realis esset "generantis ad genitum" secundum formam, propter quam esset generatio univoca. Intellectus enim considerans non facit generationem esse univocam, sed cognoscit eam esse univocam.'

11. *Ibid.*, n. 3; Duns Scotus 1950, VII, p. 392: 'Quidquid inest alicui ex ratione sua per se, inest ei in quocumque; igitur si natura lapidis de se essent "haec", in quocumque esset natura lapidis, natura illa esset "hic lapis".'

12. *Ibid.*, n. 4; Duns Scotus 1950–, VII, p. 393: 'Praeterea, illi cui de se convenit unum oppositum, ei de se repugnat aliud oppositum; igitur si natura de se sit una numero, repugnat ei multitudo numeralis.'

13. *Ordinatio* II, d. 3, p. 1, q. 6, nn. 172–5; Duns Scotus 1950–, VII, pp. 476–8.

14. *Ordinatio* II, d. 3, p. 1, q. 1, nn. 33–4; Duns Scotus 1950–, VII, pp. 403–5.

15. *Ibid.*, n. 37; Duns Scotus 1950–, VII, pp. 406–7, n. 38; pp. 407–8.

So far, then, Scotus' view could be summarised in the following five theses: (T1) the nature is common of itself and is also common in reality; (T2) the principle of individuation or contracting difference is numerically one and particular of itself and cannot be common to numerically distinct particulars; (T3) both the nature and the contracting difference exist in reality as constituents of a particular and they can exist in reality only as such; (T4) as a result of combination with the contracting difference, the nature is numerically one denominatively and is numerically many in numerically distinct particulars; and (T5) the nature is completely universal only insofar as it exists in the intellect.

The most striking feature of Scotus' theory of universals, however, is his contention that the common nature and individuating principles are neither really distinct – in the sense of being distinct real things – nor distinct only in reason – in the sense of being thought of by means of distinct concepts. Rather Scotus holds that

(T6) The nature and contracting difference are formally distinct, or not formally the same.[16]

But Scotus' works contain at least two importantly different accounts of this alternative sort of non-identity or distinction, which he employs so often in his philosophy and theology.

(1.1) The first and earlier version stipulates that within what is really one and the same thing (*res*) there often is a plurality of entities or property-bearers whose non-identity or distinction in no way depends upon the activity of any intellect, created or divine. Scotus had two motives for making this stipulation. (1.1.1) The first is epistemological. Scotus thought, as Ockham was later to think, that if in reality, prior to every act of intellect, x and y are in every way the same, the intellect could not make x and y distinct. But, contrary to Ockham, he did not see how distinct concepts could genuinely signify a real thing without there being some non-identity or distinction in the thing corresponding to the distinction in conceived objects. Since it sometimes happens that, prior to every act of intellect, what is really one and the same thing is simultaneously apt to fall under or be signified by distinct concepts – e.g., a species falls under concepts of genus and differentia simultaneously – Scotus concluded that prior to every act of intellect there must be some sort of non-identity or

16. *Ordinatio* II, d. 3, p. 1, q. 6, nn. 187–8; Duns Scotus 1950–, VII, pp. 483–4.

distinction among entities within the real thing.[17] (1.1.2) Scotus' other motive is logical or metaphysical. He realized that often in philosophy and theology there is reason to deny that *x* and *y* are really distinct things (*res*) and yet apparent cause to affirm that *x* is *F* and *y* is not *F*. But according to the principle of the Indiscernibility of Identicals, which clearly applies to everything that exists in reality, nothing that is in every way the same can be both *F* and not *F* at once. Distinguishing non-identical or distinct property-bearers within what is really one and the same thing might seem to open the way for a solution to such problems.

Scotus labels the non-identical entities within what is really one and the same thing (*res*) 'realities' (*realitates*), 'formalities' (*formalitates*), 'aspects' (*rationes*), 'formal aspects' (*rationes formales*), 'intentions' (*intentiones*), or 'real aspects' (*rationes reales*). Likewise, because he claims that such entities are not formally the same, or are formally distinct, formally different, or formally diverse, the relation between them is best known as formal non-identity or distinction.

Scotus restricts the relations of formal identity and distinction to entities that are or are in what is really one and the same thing and understands that

(A) *x* and *y* are formally distinct or not formally the same, if and only if (a) *x* and *y* are or are in what is really one and the same thing (*res*); and (b) if *x* and *y* are capable of definition (in the strict Aristotelian sense, in terms of genus and differentia), the definition of *x* does not include *y* and the definition of *y* does not include *x*; and (c) if *x* and *y* are not capable of definition, then if they were capable of definition, the definition of *x* would not include *y* and the definition of *y* would not include *x*.[18]

Thus, Scotus' first account of formal non-identity or distinction presupposes an ontology that begins with formalities or realities that can have a double mode of existence: they can exist in reality as constituents of real things or they can have a non-real mode of existence in the intellect as objects of thought or concepts. Some properties belong to formalities of themselves – viz., their essential properties; others belong to them only insofar as they have one mode of existence or the other. Accordingly, Scotus says that man is of itself rational, mortal, and animal; and that man of itself is neither universal nor particular, but indifferent to each. Man is

17. *Quaestiones subtilissimae super libros Metaphysicorum Aristotelis* VII, q. 19, n. 5; Duns Scotus 1639c, p. 727.
18. *Lectura* I, d. 2, p. 2, q. 1–4, n. 275; Duns Scotus 1950–, XVI, p. 216. *Ordinatio* I, d. 2, p. 2, q. 1–4, n. 403; Duns Scotus 1950–, II, pp. 356–7.

completely universal only insofar as it exists in the intellect, and numerically one and particular only insofar as it exists in reality.

Some of Scotus' Parisian opponents charged that his application of formal identity and distinction to God compromised divine simplicity. Perhaps it was for this reason that Scotus took a different position in the *Reportata Parisiensia* I, d. 33, q. 2–3 and d. 34, q. 1.[19] In these works he still argues for the existence of some distinction in reality (*ex natura rei*) and prior to every act of intellect, but alternative to the real distinction between one thing and another. Yet he now denies that this involves distinguishing a plurality of property-bearers within what is really one and the same thing. Scotus elaborates this idea by contrasting absolute distinction (*distinctio simpliciter*) with distinction *secundum quid*. Distinct real things such as Socrates and Brownie the donkey are absolutely distinct. But a distinction between x and y may be *secundum quid* for one of two reasons: it may be that the being of x and y is somehow diminished (as it is when x and y have only a non-real mode of existence as objects of thought, or when x and y exist only virtually in their causes, or when x and y are elements in a mixture); or it may be that although x and y are both fully real and actual, they are not absolutely non-identical, but only non-identical *secundum quid*.[20] According to Scotus, x and y are non-identical *secundum quid* if and only if they lack either formal identity or adequate identity. Criterion (A) remains the criterion of the former, but it is no longer taken to signal the existence of any pluarlity of property-bearers within a single thing. Scotus says that x and y lack adequate identity when one of them exceeds the other according to predication or according to perfection. For example, animal is not adequately identical with man, because the former is predicated of more things than the latter is, while the latter is more perfect than the former is (presumably because the genus is in potentiality with respect to the specific difference, but the species is not).[21] And Scotus insists that the Indiscernibility of Identicals does not necessarily hold where x and y are

---

19. Cf. Gelber 1974, pp. 80ff. For some reactions to her interpretation and to the interpretation in Henry 1965, and Henry 1972, pp. 88–95, see Adams 1976.
20. *Reportatio Parisiensis* I, d. 33, q. 2; MS Civitas Vaticana bibl. apost., cod. Borgh. lat. 325, ff. 82[vb]–83[ra]; *Quaestiones miscellaneae de formalitatibus*, q. 1, n. 12; Duns Scotus 1639b, p. 444. Note that the Scotus commission has now identified the *Reportata Parisiensia* printed in Volume XI of Duns Scotus 1639a as the *Additiones magnae* written by Scotus' pupil William of Alnwick (cf. Modrić 1978, p. 83). While Alnwick had the intention of representing Scotus' teaching at Paris, he also drew heavily on Scotus' Oxford lectures and has heavily edited the text in places. I refer, therefore, to a manuscript of *Reportatio* I A, which the Scotus commission regards as the *Reportatio examinata* which was revised by Scotus himself.
21. *Reportatio* I A, d. 33, q. 2; MS Vat. Borgh. 325, f. 83[ra].

really but not formally the same nor do the Transitivity and Symmetry of Identity hold where x and y are really but not adequately the same.[22]

Ockham's attack on Scotus' formal distinction

Ockham attacked Scotus' theory on two independent grounds: first that the notion of formal non-identity or distinction presupposed by (T6) leads to ontological paradox or contradiction; and second, that in any case the conjunction of (T1)–(T4) and (T6) is contradictory.

Ockham charges that no creatures can be formally distinct without being really distinct.

> ... I argue this way: (i) Wherever there is any distinction or non-identity [between beings], there some contradictories can be truly asserted of those [beings]. (ii) But it is impossible that contradictories should be truly asserted of any [beings] unless they or those for which they supposit are (a) distinct real things or (b) distinct concepts or beings of reason or (c) a thing and a concept. But if (iii) they all exist in reality, (iv) they are not distinct concepts. (v) Nor are they a thing and a concept. Therefore, (vi) they will be distinct things.[23]

Premiss (i) is trivially true, and (iii) is maintained by Scotus. The crucial premiss (ii) combines an assertion of the Indiscernibility of Identicals, with the assumption that (a)–(c) constitutes an exhaustive list of the alternatives under which non-identity or distinction might obtain. But Scotus would insist on adding a fourth alternative: (d) x is formally distinct from y; or (e) x and y are distinct *secundum quid*.

The list of (a)–(c) reflects Ockham's ontology, according to which real things and beings of reason or concepts are the only beings there are, and there are no real beings that are not real things. But Scotus' first account of formal distinction is premissed on a wider ontology that allows for distinct formalities within one and the same real thing. He can, therefore, say that propositions of the forms 'x is F' and 'y is not F' are sometimes true about such mind-independent formalities.

Ockham's complaint is that the ontology that lies behind (d) leaves us with no resources for proving a real distinction among really existent

---

22. *Ibid.*, MS Vat. Borgh. 325, f. 83rb.

23. Ockham 1970, *Ordinatio* I, d. 2, q. 1; *OT* II, p. 14: "Contra istam opinionem arguo per unum argumentum quod est aequaliter contra distinctionem vel non-identitatem formalem ubicumque ponatur. Et arguo sic: ubicumque est aliqua distinctio vel non-identitas, ibi possunt aliqua contradictoria de illis verificari; sed impossibile est contradictoria verificari de quibuscumque nisi illa vel illa pro quibus supponunt sint distinctae res vel distinctae rationes sive entia rationis vel res et ratio; sed si omnia illa sint ex natura rei, non sunt distinctae rationes nec res et ratio; igitur erunt distinctae res.' Cf. *ibid.*, d. 2, q. 6; *OT* II, p. 173.

beings. He reasons that since all contradictories are equally contradictory, if some propositions of the forms 'x is F' and 'y is not F' can be true about really existent property-bearers that are only formally distinct, then any pair of contradictories can. For example, if 'Human nature is formally human nature and Socrateity is not formally human nature' entails only 'Human nature and Socrateity are formally distinct', what reason is there to suppose that 'A man is rational and a donkey is not rational' entails 'A man and a donkey are really distinct' rather than 'A man and a donkey are formally distinct'? Ockham rejects the suggestion that a proposition of the form 'x is F and y is not F' entails 'x and y are really distinct' while a proposition of the form 'x is formally F and y is not formally F' entails 'x and y are formally distinct'. For since 'formally F' and 'not formally F' are just as contradictory as 'F' and 'not F', there is no more reason why the latter should entail a real distinction than the former.[24]

Scotus' account of distinction *secundum quid* abandons the ontology that assumes a plurality of property-bearers within one and the same thing, but continues to insist that propositions of the forms 'x is F' and 'y is not F' might be simultaneously true even though x and y are distinct only *secundum quid*, i.e., where x and y are really the same but lack formal or adequate identity. But, Ockham observes, when Scotus says that x and y lack formal identity if and only if neither falls (or would fall) under the definition of the other, he is talking about *real*, not nominal, definitions. And while Ockham allows – contrary to Scotus's epistemological argument – that what is in every way the same in reality may simultaneously fall under distinct concepts with distinct nominal definitions, he insists that it is impossible that any x and y should be in every way the same in reality and have distinct real definitions; for there would be only one reality there to be defined.[25] Hence, it is impossible for any x and y to be really the same and lack formal identity.

Again, for x and y to lack adequate identity is for x and y to be really the same and yet for one to exceed the other in predication or perfection. For example, human nature and the contracting difference Socrateity would lack adequate identity; for while they are really the same, man is predicable of more than Socrateity is. This is tantamount to saying that x and y lack adequate identity where x and y are really the same, but for some F, x is F and y is not F. Where Scotus abandons the ontology according to which x

and *y* are distinct formalities within the same real thing, he is left asserting contradictories about what is in reality one and the same thing. And Ockham will again object that to relinquish the Indiscernibility of Identicals as a criterion of real distinction is to lose every way of proving distinction among real things.

It would be obviously circular to reply that Scotus never endorses contradictories about what is *in every way the same* in reality, but only about those that lack formal or adequate identity. For the lack of formal or adequate identity itself partially consists in the assertion of contradictories about what is really one and the same thing, and so it cannot be invoked to explain how those very predications are possible.

Ockham's claim that Scotus' theses are mutually inconsistent

Granting the formal distinction for the sake of argument, Ockham tries with varying success to show that Scotus' theory of universals is contradictory.

First, Ockham maintains that (T1) is incompatible with (T3) because together they entail the absurdity that something common is a constituent of a particular. Following Aristotle, Ockham insists that necessarily every particular is homogeneously particular in the sense of having no constituents that are not particular.[26] Scotus could reply, however, that he does not claim that any particulars have constituents that are not particular. For while (T1) asserts that the nature is common of itself and in reality, (T4) says that it is numerically one and particular denominatively, by virtue of its combination with the individuating principles.

Ockham would object, however, that the conjunction of (T1) and (T4) entails the absurdity 'that there are as many species as there are individuals'. For by (T1) this commonness or unity less than numerical unity pertains to the nature itself and so will accompany it wherever it exists. But by (T4) human nature existing in reality in Socrates is numerically distinct from human nature existing in reality in Plato. Hence 'there are two common entities in Socrates and Plato, and consequently two species'.[27] Scotus

---

26. *Ordinatio* I, d. 2, q. 5; Ockham 1970, *OT* II, pp. 158–9.
27. *Ordinatio* I, d. 2, q. 6; Ockham 1970, *OT* II, p. 181: 'Confirmatur, quia ad multiplicationem subiecti proximi sequitur multiplicatio passionis; sed secundum istum ista unitas minor est passio naturae; igitur sicut natura realiter multiplicatur, ita passio – cum sit realis – realiter multiplicabitur. Et per consequens sicut realiter sunt duae naturae in Sorte et Platone, ita erunt realiter duae unitates minores; sed ista unitas minor vel est communitas vel inseparabilis a communitate, et per consequens inseparabilis a communi; igitur sunt duo communia in Sorte et Platone, et per consequens duae species. Et per consequens Sortes esset sub uno communi et Plato sub alio, et ita tot essent communia – etiam generalissima – quot sunt individua, quae videntur absurda.'

would have to grant the first of Ockham's conclusions, but not the second. For he holds (T5) that the nature is incompletely universal in reality and completely universal only insofar as it exists in the intellect as an abstract general concept predicable of many. And the nature counts as a species only insofar as it is completely universal.

Ockham sees Scotus' theory of universals as running counter to a fundamental axiom of identity:

(B) Nothing is individuated through anything extrinsic to it; rather, being identical with itself and being distinct from everything else are properties that a thing has in and of itself.

A thing can be white because a really distinct quality of whiteness inheres in it or thought of because a really distinct intellect attends to it, but being the same as itself or distinct from others are properties that a thing has of itself or by virtue of something intrinsic to it.[28] It follows from (T4) and (T6), however, that the nature is individuated and numerically multiplied by combining with individuating principles formally distinct from it, so that neither is an essential constituent of the other. Scotus would doubtless have agreed that the nature cannot be individuated by anything really distinct from it, but would have rejected (B) and replaced it with his own axiom:

(C) Only what is distinct and determinate of itself can individuate something formally distinct from it.[29]

Nothing in this argument of Ockham's would compel Scotus to do otherwise.

Ockham's fourth argument – that (T1) is inconsistent with the conjunction of (T3) and (T4) – goes to the heart of Scotus' theory of universals in challenging the intelligibility of his contention that the nature is common or incompletely universal in reality. As noted above, Scotus argues that the nature is not 'this' of itself on the basis of the principle that

(D) 'If one of a pair of opposites pertains to something of itself, the other of the pair of opposites is incompatible with that thing of itself...'

Ockham insists that Scotus should equally grant the following:

(E) '... Whenever one of a pair of opposites really pertains to something in such a way that that thing is truly and really denominated from it, whether they pertain to it of itself or through something else – this fact remaining un-

28. *Ordinatio* I, d. 2, q. 6; Ockham 1970, *OT* II, pp. 184–5.
29. *Quaestiones in Metaphysicam Aristotelis* VII, q. 13; Duns Scotus 1639a, VII, pp. 417–18.

changed – the other of the opposites will not really pertain to it, but will be absolutely denied of it . . .'[30]

But, by (T3), the nature does not exist otherwise than together with some contracting difference or other; and, by (T4), the nature is numerically one and particular as a result of its combination with a contracting difference. Thus, by (E), no nature can simultaneously be common, as (T1) asserts it to be.

Ockham notes the objection that 'the two unities are not really opposed'.[31] But this seems inconsistent with Scotus' own claims. For he says that 'Multiplicity that cannot stand together with the greater unity, because it is opposed to it, can without contradiction stand together with the lesser unity.'[32] And he has appealed to this fact to justify regarding 'commonness' and 'numerical unity' or 'particularity' as opposites and proceeding to infer (by (D)) that if the nature is common of itself, it cannot be numerically one and particular of itself. Ockham argues analogously on the basis of (E) that if the nature is truly numerically one and particular – whether of itself or only denominatively – it cannot also be common, and vice versa.[33] Alternatively, a defender of Scotus might say that while (D) holds good – i.e., that if x of itself is F, not-F is incompatible with x of itself – it is not the case that if x is F – no matter whether of itself, *per se*, or denominatively – not-F is incompatible with x. For a man is white denominatively, and a white is white *per se*. But '. . . blackness goes together with man and does not go together with what is white, and yet a man is white, and a is a man and white'.[34] Likewise, being Plato's may be compatible with the nature, even though being Plato's is not compatible with being Socrates'; and numerical multiplicity may be compatible with the nature of itself, even though numerical multiplicity is not compatible with the particular.

30. *Ordinatio* I, d. 2, q. 6; Ockham 1970, *OT* II, p. 177: 'Primo sic: quandocumque convenit alicui realiter unum oppositorum, ita quod vere et realiter denominatur ab illo, sive conveniat sibi ex se sive per aliud, – hoc stante et non mutato –, reliquum oppositorum sibi non conveniet realiter, immo simpliciter ab eo negabitur. Sed per te omnis res extra animam est realiter singularis et una numero, quamvis aliqua de se sit singularis et aliqua tantum per aliquid additum; igitur nulla res extra animam est realiter communis nec una unitate opposita unitati singularitatis, igitur realiter non est aliqua unitas nisi unitas singularitatis.'

31. *Ordinatio* I, d. 2, q. 6; Ockham 1970, *OT* II, p. 177: 'Si dicatur quod istae duae unitates non sunt oppositae realiter, et eodem modo singularitas et communitas non opponuntur realiter.'

32. *Ordinatio* II, d. 3, p. 1, q. 1, n. 9; Duns Scotus 1950–, VII, p. 395: 'quia cum unitate minore sine contradictione potest stare multitudo opposita maiori unitati, quae multitudo non potest stare cum unitate maiore, quia sibi repugnat . . .'

33. *Ordinatio* I, d. 2, q. 6; Ockham 1970, *OT* II, p. 178.

34. *Ibid.*, p. 178: 'Si dicatur quod ista forma arguendi non valet, quia cum homine stat nigredo et cum albo non stat nigredo, et tamen homo est albus, et a est homo, et est album.'

Ockham thinks that this response is likewise mistaken. For 'to be compatible' can be taken actually or potentially. If Socrates is white, blackness is not actually compatible with Socrates, because 'Socrates is white and Socrates is black' is a contradiction. But blackness is potentially compatible with Socrates, because even if Socrates is in fact white, it is logically possible that whiteness not inhere in him and that blackness inhere in him instead. Likewise, if humanity in Socrates is Socrates' denominatively, it is not actually, but at most potentially compatible with Plato's contracting difference. And if humanity in Socrates is numerically one and particular, it is not actually, but at most potentially compatible with numerical multiplicity.

Scotus might reply, however, that this is exactly what he was claiming when he said that the nature in reality is common and _incompletely_ universal. Just as Socrates is not black while he is white, so humanity is not Plato's while it is Socrates' or numerically many while it is numerically one. Nevertheless, just as it is possible that Socrates should exist without whiteness inhering in him and have blackness inhering in him instead; so it is possible that the humanity in Socrates should not be combined with Socrates' contracting difference and possible that it should be combined with Plato's contracting difference instead; and possible that humanity should not be numerically one but should be numerically many instead.

Ockham also thinks Scotus' theory is unsatisfactory in virtue of his assertion of (T2) and (T6). For if humanity in Socrates is formally but not really distinct from Socrateity, it follows that it is not logically possible for the former to exist in a thing without the latter existing in the same thing, as it _is_ logically possible for Socrates to exist without whiteness inhering in him and to have blackness inhering in him instead. Consequently, it is not even logically possible for humanity in Socrates to exist without being determinately Socrates' and so not even logically possible that it should be determinately Plato's instead. Again, it is not even logically possible that it should actually exist in numerically many.[35] Thus, (T1) is inconsistent with the conjunction of (T2), (T3), (T4), and (T6); and Scotus' theory of universals is thereby shown to be unacceptable.

Walter Burley's moderate realism

Another version of moderate realism current in Ockham's time and apparently endorsed by his rival Walter Burley,[36] in effect concurs in

35. _Ibid._, p. 179.
36. Burley 1507, f. 4rb-va.

Scotus' theses (T1)–(T3) but rejects the troublesome (T4)–(T6). Invoking Aristotle, Burley maintains, with Ockham, that the Indiscernibility of Identicals is our chief criterion of distinction among real things. He then observes that 'every universal exists in many' but 'no particular exists in many';[37] that 'the universal is defined, but no particular is defined';[38] that universals but not particulars are the subject of demonstrative science;[39] and that 'the universal – e.g., genus – is divided by contrary differentiae, but no particular is divided by such differentiae'.[40] His conclusion is that

(T7) Universals are really distinct from particulars.

Analogous arguments would show that different universals – e.g., genus and differentia – are really distinct from one another. Again, like Scotus, Burley thinks that similarity and difference must have a real foundation in something common, but he holds that the common thing is really distinct from the particulars in which it exists.[41]

Further, while the particular is a composite of such universals and some individuating principles, the latter do not individuate or particularise the former. Rather

(T8) The whole universal (*secundum se totum*) exists in each of its particulars and is not numerically multiplied by its existence in numerically distinct particulars.[42]

Henry of Harclay and William Ockham both found many reasons for rejecting this position.[43]

---

37. *Ibid.*, f. 4va: 'Omne universale est in multis. Nullum singulare est in multis, ut patet ex libro *Periermenias*. Ergo aliquid vere affirmatur de universale quod negatur a quolibet suo singulari.'
38. *Ibid.*, f. 4va: 'Secundo sic: Universale diffinitur. Sed nullum singulare diffinitur, ut patet ex septimo *Metaphysicae*. Ergo etc.'
39. *Ibid.*, f. 4ra–b.
40. *Ibid.*, f. 4va: 'Item universale ut genus dividitur per differentias contrarias, ut animal per rationale et irrationale. Sed nullum singulare dividitur per huiusmodi differentias. Ergo etc.'
41. *Ibid.*, f. 4vb.
42. *Ibid.*, f. 4rb.
43. See Harclay in Gál 1971. In this question, it is Scotus' arguments that are presented in behalf of an affirmative answer, but the counter-arguments really attack the position Burley held. For this reason, Gál speculates that the question may be a record of an actual debate in which the students supplied the objections and Harclay is speaking only at the end when he gives and defends his own opinion (Gál 1971, pp. 184–5). See also Ockham 1970, *Ordinatio* I, d. 2, q. 4, who presents the position as one mistakenly attributed to Scotus. Gál shows that Ockham is drawing on Harclay's question; but Ockham never quotes Burley, and there is no positive evidence – other than the similarity of views under consideration and the spatio-temporal proximity of the two philosophers – that Ockham had Burley in mind. Burley's treatise does not quote from Harclay or Ockham either. But many of Harclay's and Ockham's arguments are directed against a position like Burley's, and many of the latter's remarks constitute replies to their objections.

Two attacks by Ockham on Burley's position

Ockham argues that the conjunction of (T3) and (T7) entails the absurd conclusion that the universal can exist without the particular or individuating principles, and vice versa. First, it was widely agreed that if *x* is naturally prior to and really distinct from *y*, then it is logically possible for *x* to exist without *y*. By (T7) the universal and particular or individuating principles are really distinct; and by (T3) the universal is a part of the particulars in which it exists. And the part is naturally prior to the whole. Consequently, the universal can exist without the particular or its individuating principles.[44] The latter conclusion is scarcely surprising by itself, since everyone would agree that human nature can exist without Socrates or his individuating principles; for human nature continues to exist in Plato after Socrates' death. But Ockham mistakenly reasons that when some real thing really distinct from other things can exist without each of them taken one by one, and can so exist by its nature, and does not essentially depend on any of them, it can exist without each of them taken in conjunction. And he concludes that universal human nature could exist without any and every particular human being.[45]

Conversely, Ockham observes that '... according to them [supporters of Burley's sort of moderate realism], the individual adds something to the nature, and this something combines with the universal real thing to make what is one *per se*', and he concludes that 'therefore, it does not seem contradictory that what is added should be preserved by God in the absence of any universal nature – which seems absurd'.[46] To be sure, moderate realists did not envisage either of these consequences; but it is far from clear why they should have found them impossible rather than merely unusual.

Harclay and Ockham vs. Burley

Harclay and Ockham agree that the conjunction of (T3) and (T8) entails the falsehood that numerically one thing exists wholly in numerically distinct particulars at the same time. (T8) does not, however, explicitly say that the universal *is numerically one*, but only that it is *not numerically many* in

---

44. *Ordinatio* I, d. 2, q. 4; Ockham 1970, *OT* II, p. 115.
45. *Ibid.*, 115.
46. *Ibid.*, 115: 'Confirmatur ista ratio, quia individuum aliquid addit supra naturam, secundum istos, et hoc aliquid faciens per se unum cum illa re universali, quia si non, tunc esset aliquid quod nec esset substantia nec accidens; igitur non videtur includere contradictionem quod illud additum conservetur a Deo sine omni natura universali adveniente, quod videtur absurdum.'

numerically distinct particulars. Harclay simply assumes[47] that Burley's position has this further consequence, but Ockham offers two arguments to prove it. In the first of these arguments Ockham claims that it follows from (T3) that the universal is a part of the particulars in which it exists. Now if each of a pair of really distinct things is equally simple and either is numerically one, the other will be numerically one as well; likewise if the more complex of a pair is numerically one. But a part is at least as simple as the whole of which it is a part. It follows that since the particular is numerically one, the universal that is a part of it will be numerically one. The second argument claims that the position under attack implies not only that universals and particulars are really distinct, but that universals are really distinct from one another. Thus, the genus substance, the genus animal, and the species man would be three really distinct things. Ockham plausibly supposes that 'every thing that combines with another thing really distinct from it to make a number [of things] is either numerically one or numerically many'.[48] But the view under attack would deny that the universal is numerically many.[49] Consequently, it follows, given (T3), that "humanity, which is numerically one and undivided in itself, exists in Socrates and Plato" simultaneously. When Harclay condemns this as impossible[50] and Ockham rejects it as false[51] they are only echoing Boethius' objection that genus or species cannot be numerically one in numerically distinct particulars.[52]

Responding to a similar objection, Burley maintains that 'numerically the same' or 'numerical unity' can be understood two ways: Commonly, it signifies 'what can combine with another to make or has constituted a number [of things], in such a way that it is true to say of it and the other that they are two'. But taken strictly, numerical unity is contrasted with specific and generic unity. Burley then, in effect, concedes to Ockham's second argument the conclusion that a universal is numerically one in the first

47. Harclay, in Gál 1971, sec. 41–2, p. 197.
48. *Ordinatio* I, d. 2, q. 4; Ockham 1970, *OT* II, p. 113: 'Tota ratio praecedens confirmatur sic: omnis res faciens numerum cum alia re realiter distincta est una res numero vel plures res numero; sed talis res universalis, si ponatur, vere facit numerum cum re singulari; igitur ipsa est una res numero vel plures res numero; sed non est plures res numero, quia tunc esset plura singularia, quia secundum istos et secundum veritatem omnis res una numero est singularis; igitur plures res numero sunt plura singularia; sed nulla res universalis est plura singularia secundum istos, quia secundum istos distinguitur realiter ab omnibus singularibus, igitur est una numero.' Cf. *ibid.*, pp. 112, 114.
49. *Ordinatio* I, d. 2, q. 4; Ockham 1970, *OT* II, pp. 113–14.
50. Harclay, in Gál 1971, sec. 41, p. 197.
51. *Ordinatio* I, d. 2, q. 4; Ockham 1970, *OT* II, pp. 108–12.
52. Boethius 1860h, *Commentaria in Porphyrium* Lib. I; *PL* 64, col. 83B.

sense, and further, that the species man and the species donkey are two really distinct things. But he denies that any universal is numerically one in the strict sense, the only sense in which, he contends, existing simultaneously in numerically distinct subjects is problematic.[53] Harclay and Ockham argue, on the contrary, that this conclusion has unacceptable consequences, even if 'numerically one' and 'numerically the same' are understood in this broader sense.

They argue first from creation and annihilation: for 'creation is absolutely out of nothing in such a way that nothing essential and intrinsic to the thing absolutely precedes it in real existence';[54] and 'when something is annihilated, nothing intrinsic to the real thing will remain in real existence – either in it or in anything else'.[55] Thus, if numerically the same universal pertained to the essence of numerically distinct particulars of a given species, no individual of that species could be created at a time when some individual of that species already existed, or be annihilated unless all members of that species were simultaneously destroyed[56] – which is absurd. Burley replies that 'the annihilation of something is the destruction of all its parts. But the species is not part of an individual.' For it follows from Aristotle's teachings that an individual or particular that is numerically one in the strict sense can have as parts only those things that are numerically one in the strict sense.[57] 'Therefore, it is not necessary that when the individual is annihilated, the species is annihilated.'[58]

Ockham accepts the thesis that particulars have only particulars as parts, and he has used it as a weapon against moderate realists. But he insisted that the position under attack implies the opposite: for by (T3) the universal

53. Burley 1507, f. 5ra–b; see esp. f. 5ra: 'Dicendum est ad primam rationem, quando dicitur quod idem numero esset in caelo et in terra et in inferno, dicendum est quod "idem numero" accipitur dupliciter – scilicet communiter et stricte. "Idem numero" acceptum communiter est illud quod cum alio potest facere numerum seu constituit numerum, ita quod de illo et de alio est verum dicere quod ista sunt duo. Et isto modo concedo quod natura hominis est una numero, quia illa et natura specifica asini sunt duae naturae. Sed "unum numero" stricte acceptum est solum illud quod distinguitur contra unum specie et unum genere, quomodo loquitur Philosophus de uno numero quinto et septimo *Metaphysicae*. Et eadem est divisio de "eodem numero". Nam idem numero uno modo est illud quod cum alio ponit in numerum et alio modo est illud quod distinguitur contra idem specie et idem genere, ut patet ex primo *Topicorum*.'
54. *Ordinatio* I, d. 2, q. 4; Ockham 1970, *OT* II, p. 115: '... sed creatio est simpliciter de nihilo, ita quod nihil essentiale et intrinsecum rei simpliciter praecedat in esse reali ...'
55. *Ibid.*, p. 116; 'Sed in adnihilatione nihil intrinsecum rei remanet nec in se nec in alio quocumque in esse reali ...'
56. *Ibid.*, pp. 115–16; for annihilation only in Harclay in Gál 1971, sec. 43, p. 197.
57. Burley 1507, f. 5ra; cf. f. 5va.
58. *Ibid.*, f. 5ra: 'Et si dicatur annihilatio alicuius est destructio quantum ad omnes partes eius. Sed species non est pars individui. Ideo non oportet quod annihilato individuo annihiletur species.'

exists in particulars as a constituent of them; and by (T7) it is really distinct from the particular and its individuating principles, as parts are really distinct from their wholes. Given these claims, Burley's denial would seem to amount to little more than the stipulation that only particular constituents of a particular count as its 'parts'. In any case, Ockham's creation and annihilation arguments depend, not on whether universals are parts of particulars, but on whether they are essential constituents of them; and surely Burley would not deny that human nature is essential to Socrates.

Even if it were granted that universals cannot be parts of particulars and that the annihilation of a particular involves only the destruction of its parts, an analogous difficulty would arise at the level of genera and species. And since genus and species are both universals, Burley cannot raise the previous objection to saying that the genus is part of its species. But if numerically the same genus exists in, as an essential part of, all its species, it would follow that 'God could not destroy the species of man without destroying every species of the genus of substance – which is absurd.'[59] To this line of argument Burley replies that 'annihilation is the destruction of all those things that are proper to the thing, not of all those things that are common to it and to others. Therefore, the species can be annihilated without the annihilation of the genus, because the genus is not a part proper to the species but a part common to it and to others.'[60]

Considering a similar move,[61] Ockham rightly insists that it does not accord with traditional definitions. For Socrates is not said to be created if his matter exists before he does. Yet the matter is not 'proper to' Socrates since it can exist as a part of something else, such as Socrates' corpse.[62] Surely genus is at least as essential to species and the species at least as essential to Socrates as Socrates' matter is to him.

Ockham and Harclay also argue that Burley's position will lead to contradictories, when it comes to accounting for the relation between

59. *Ibid.*, f. 5ʳᵃ: 'Contra: quicquid est de specie est et de individuo secundum istam opinionem est genus. Sed genus est pars speciei. Ergo sequitur quod non potest annihilare speciem hominis nisi destruat hoc genus animal, et etiam genus generalissimum substantiae. Sed destructo genere destruuntur omnes illius generis. Ergo Deus non posset destruere speciem hominis nisi destrueret omnem speciem de genere substantiae – quod est inconveniens.'
60. *Ibid.*, f. 5ᵛᵃ: 'Et quando arguitur in contrarium, quando dicitur quod ad minus sequitur istud inconveniens: quod Deus non posset annihilare speciem hominis nisi annihilaret totum genus substantiae, dicendum quod illud non sequitur, quia annihilatio est destructio rei quantum ad omnia quae sunt ei propria, non quantum ad omnia quae sunt communia sibi et aliis. Et ideo species potest annihilari absque annihilatione generis, quia genus non est pars propria speciei, sed communis sibi et aliis.'
61. *Ordinatio* I, d. 2, q. 4; Ockham 1970, *OT* II, p. 116.
62. *Ibid.*, p. 111.

substances and accidents. For it follows from the view as discussed so far that

(T9) A particular substance exists only if the real things that are its genera and species in the category of substance really exist in that particular.

But Aristotle says that substances are susceptible of contraries, and Ockham infers that the position would endorse the analogous theses for contraries as well:

(T10) Particular contraries do not really exist unless the universal contrary real things exist;

and

(T11) A particular accident inheres in a particular substance only by virtue of the universal accident's inhering in the universal substance.

Ockham then observes that frequently one of a pair of contraries inheres in one member of a given species and the other in another member of the same species at the same time. For example, Socrates may be white all over while an Ethiopian is black all over;[63] Christ is happy in heaven while Judas is damned and miserable in hell.[64] It follows from the conjunction of (T8), (T9), (T10), and (T11) that in such cases contraries simultaneously inhere in one and the same real thing – which is impossible.[65]

Burley's reply to a similar objection is, in effect, to deny that (T11) is true in general. Instead, the universal is the first subject of some accidents, such as spatial location and being in motion or at rest. But other accidents pertain primarily to the particular and pertain to the universal *per accidens*, insofar as it is a constituent of the particular to which they pertain *per se*. Thus Burley insists that where we are speaking about universals that are numerically one in the broad sense only, 'it is not absurd that numerically the same thing is in heaven and in hell and that it is simultaneously in motion and at rest'.[66] Universals exist in many subjects and hence in many places at once. Experiencing joy and sorrow pertain primarily to particulars, however, and so simultaneously pertain to the universal *man* only *per accidens*, insofar as it is a constituent of Christ and Judas respectively.[67]

63. *Ibid.*, pp. 121–2.
64. *Ibid.*, p. 121. Cf. Harclay in Gál 1971, sec. 43, p. 198.
65. *Ordinatio* I, d. 2, q. 4; Ockham 1970, *OT* II, pp. 120–2.
66. Burley 1507, f. 5ra: 'Dico igitur quod accipiendo idem numero communiter pro omni eo quod constituit cum alio numerum, sic non est inconveniens quod idem numero sit simul in caelo et in inferno et quod simul moveatur et quiescat.'
67. *Ibid.*, f. 5^{ra-b}.

One may wonder how the latter reply is supposed to avoid a violation of the Indiscernibility of Identicals, however. For if happiness pertains to the composite of the universal *man* with Christ's individuating principles, and misery to the composite of the universal *man* with Judas' individuation principles, it still follows that happiness and misery pertain to the universal *man* simultaneously. Burley's idea may be that just as apparent contradictions can be avoided by relativising the predications of contraries to different times – e.g., the table is white all over at one time and black all over at another – or to different parts of the particular – e.g., the table has a white top and black legs – so general ascriptions of the second sort of accidents to universal substances must be relativised to the particulars in which it has them – e.g., the universal *man* is happy in Christ and miserable in Judas. Ockham, for one, could not consistently object to this move, since he insists that no contradiction is involved even in the same *particular's* existing simultaneously in discontinuous places and in being simultaneously hot at one place and not hot at the other.[68]

Thus, whereas Ockham seems eventually to succeed in convicting Scotus' theory of contradiction, he is able to find Burley's theory guilty only of the odd or unexpected.

Henry of Harclay's position

While Scotus held, in (T2), that the individuating principles of things are logically incapable of existing in, as constituents of, numerically distinct things simultaneously, Harclay insists that

(T12) Everything that exists in reality is essentially singular – i.e., logically incapable of existing in, as a constituent of, numerically many simultaneously.[69]

Further, distinguishing singularity from universality and particularity, Harclay maintains that

(T13) Extra-mental (singular) things are neither universal nor particular of themselves or essentially.[70]

His thought is that essentially singular things such as Socrates are capable of acting on the intellect to produce two sorts of concepts of themselves: a distinct concept, by which the intellect conceives of that thing in such a way as to be able to distinguish it from others of the same kind; and a

---

68. Ockham 1494–6, *Reportatio* IV, q. 4, N; q. 5 J; cf. *Quaestiones in libros Physicorum*, q. 32.
69. Harclay in Gál 1971, sec. 67, p. 211.
70. *Ibid.*, p. 211.

confused (or generalised) concept by which the intellect cannot so distinguish it.[71]

(T14) The universal is a thing confusedly conceived, and a particular is the same thing distinctly conceived.[72]

Hence it follows that a universal and its particular are the same real thing, but distinct in reason. And Harclay says that 'what is superior to Socrates, such as "man" and "animal", signifies no real thing other than the thing that is Socrates, but insofar as he is confusedly conceived; that is, insofar as he moves the intellect to conceive of him in a confused way. And so I say that "Socrates is a man" is a case of the superior being predicated of the inferior, which is nothing other than that Socrates is Socrates, i.e., Socrates absolutely is Socrates, but insofar as he is confusedly thought of; and "Socrates is an animal" or "Socrates is a man" are the same.'[73] But Socrates is particular insofar as he is distinctly conceived. As for the claim that something essentially common or universal must exist in reality to be the object of definition or of the demonstrative sciences, Harclay replies that their objects are essentially singular extra-mental things considered not absolutely, but insofar as they are confusedly conceived.[74] Further, Harclay simply rejects the contention by Scotus and Burley that real similarity or agreement between things must be founded on the real unity of a constituent common to them both. On the contrary, 'if they agree, then they are not one in any third real thing'.[75]

Burley's attack on Harclay

Burley devotes considerable space to refuting this position, and Ockham declares Harclay's view to be 'absolutely false and unintelligible'.[76]

71. *Ibid.*, sec. 79, p. 216.
72. *Ibid.*, sec. 95, p. 222.
73. *Ibid.*, sec. 79, p. 216; 'Modo ego dico quod superius ad Sortem, puta "homo" et "animal", non significat rem aliam nisi rem quae est Sortes, ut tamen concipitur confuse, id est movet intellectum ad concipiendum ipsum modo confuso. Et sic dico quod hic "Sortes est homo" est praedicatio superioris de inferiori; quod non est aliud nisi quod Sortes est Sortes, id est Sortes absolute est Sortes, ut tamen confuse intellectus; et hoc est idem "Sortes est animal" vel "Sortes est homo" ...'
74. *Ibid.*, sec. 100, p. 224.
75. *Ibid.*, sec. 78, p. 215: '... quia concedo quod est unitas et convenientia realis inter mensuram et mensuratum inter comparabilia; pro secundo argumento: inter similia. Sed propter hoc non habent aliquam unam rem communem eis, distinctam ab omnibus. Nec convenientia aliqua realis, quantumcumque magna, hoc arguit, immo oppositum. Si enim sunt convenientia, ergo non sunt unum in aliquo reali tertio.'
76. *Ordinatio* I, d. 2, q. 7: Ockham 1970, *OT* II, p. 241.

First, Burley mounts a double-pronged attack on the claim that what is defined is a singular thing confusedly conceived. On the one hand, Burley appeals to the Aristotelian claim that the definition is a means of arriving at a distinct and perfect cognition of the object defined. Thus, if definition were of singular things, it would be no more of one singular thing of a given kind than another. Therefore no one would be able to know the definition *mortal rational animal* without having distinct and perfect knowledge of each and every individual human being – which is absurd.[77] To this Harclay could reply that, on the contrary, knowledge of the definition gives one at most confused knowledge of the singulars defined. For singular things are the objects of definition only insofar as they are confusedly conceived; and the confused concept caused by Socrates is indistinguishable from that caused by Plato.

More fundamentally, Burley charges that the definition is interchangeable with what is defined, while the definition is not interchangeable with any singular thing – e.g., *mortal rational animal* is not interchangeable with Socrates confusedly conceived.[78] Harclay considers the similar objection that, as superior to Socrates, animal will be predicated of more than Socrates. But if animal is Socrates confusedly conceived, and Plato is an animal, it will follow that Plato is Socrates confusedly conceived – which is absurd.[79] Harclay replies that that argument involves a fallacy of accident,[80] taking a position that Ockham rejects as 'neither true nor logical'.[81]

Again, Burley reasons, if universals were singulars confusedly conceived, then the most generic genus of substance would be a singular

77. Burley 1507, f. 4rb.
78. *Ibid.*, f. 4ra.
79. Harclay in Gál 1971, sec. 81, p. 217.
80. *Ibid.*, sec. 85, pp. 218–19.
81. *Ordinatio* I, d. 2, q. 7; Ockham 1970, *OT* II, pp. 242–3: 'Sed istud non est vere nec logice dictum, quia quando dicitur sic "animal est Sortes confuse conceptus" aut "animal" supponit simpliciter, aut personaliter. Si personaliter, "animal" non tantum est Sortes confuse conceptus, sed animal est Sortes distincte conceptus, quia tunc est una indefinita habens unam singularem veram, scilicet istam "hoc animal est Sortes distincte conceptus", demonstrando Sortem. Si autem "animal" supponat simpliciter, aut supponit pro aliqua vera re, aut pro ente tantum in anima, aut pro aggregato. Si pro re, igitur aliqua vera res est communis, et per consequens vera res praedicatur vere de alia re. Et ita, sicut haec est vera simpliciter "Sortes est animal" vel "asinus est animal", ita erit haec vera "asinus est Sortes conceptus", quia per te illud commune pro quo supponit "animal" in ista "animal est Sortes confuse conceptus" est Sortes conceptus, et nullo modo distinguitur a Sorte concepto; igitur de quocumque praedicatur unum et reliquum. Si utrumque supponat personaliter, igitur sicut haec est vera "asinus est animal", secundum quod "animal" supponit personaliter, ita haec erit vera "asinus est Sortes conceptus", secundum quod praedicatum supponit personaliter.'

substance confusedly conceived. But there is no more reason why it should
be one singular substance than another; hence, if it is one of them confusedly conceived, it is all of them confusedly conceived, and there would
be as many most generic genera of substance as there are individual
substances – which is absurd.[82]

Burley, following Scotus, assumes that where concepts have a genuine
application to reality, there is a distinction in things corresponding to the
distinction among concepts; but where Scotus allows that a formal distinction will do, Burley insists that there must be a real distinction. Thus he
reasons that 'the identity between universal and individual in extramental
things is not greater than that between universal and individual in concepts'. But Harclay admits that the distinct and confused concepts, the
inferior and superior concepts are different concepts. Therefore, the things
corresponding to them must be distinct.[83] Again, Burley remarks,
'everyone agrees that the universal is abstracted from singulars and from
material conditions by the intellect, but what is abstracted from such
material conditions really exists under them; otherwise abstraction would
deceive us. Therefore, the universal is really distinct from the singular from
which it is abstracted.'[84] But Harclay would reply with Ockham by
rejecting as one of the most fundamental errors in philosophy the notion
that distinctions in concepts must be mirrored by distinctions in reality.

Ockham's attack on Harclay

Unlike Burley, Ockham concedes Harclay's (T12), but argues that (T12)
entails not only (T13), but also the denial of (T14). For to say that a thing is
universal is to say that it is logically possible that it should be simultaneously
predicated of many, whereas to say that it is singular is to say that this is
logically impossible. Thus, it is a contradiction to say that one and the same
real thing is simultaneously singular and universal. As for Harclay's claim

82. Burley 1507, f. 4^{va-b}.
83. *Ibid.*, f. 4rb: 'Item non est maior identitas inter universale et individuum in rebus extra quam inter
universale et individuum in conceptum, quia ita essentialiter et in quid praedicatur universale de
individuo in conceptibus sicut in rebus extra. Sed in conceptibus conceptus universalis et
conceptus individualis sive conceptus superior et conceptus inferior non sunt idem. Ergo nec in
rebus erunt universale et individuum sive superius et inferius eadem.'
84. *Ibid.*, f. 4rb: 'Item in hoc conveniunt omnes quod universale abstrahitur a singularibus per
intellectum et a conditionibus materialibus. Nam Commentator primo *De anima* dicit quod
intellectus facit universalitatem in rebus. Et ex hoc sic arguitur: Illud quod per intellectum
abstrahitur a conditionibus et accidentibus materialibus realiter est sub illis; aliter enim ab-
strahentium esset mendacium – quod est contra Philosophum secundo *Physicorum*. Universale
ergo abstractum ab accidentibus realiter existens sub eisdem est aliqua res a singulari, et sic in rebus
universale et singulare sive individuum non sunt eadem res.'

that what is essentially singular is made universal through the consideration of the intellect, Ockham replies that the intellect is extrinsic to the thing. And nothing extrinsic to a thing can bring it about that the thing has a property that is incompatible with one of its essential properties.[85] Consequently, no matter how the intellect conceives of essentially singular things such as Socrates and Brownie the donkey, it will not be able to bring it about that either is universal, any more than it could bring it about that Socrates is a donkey or that Brownie is a human being.[86]

Harclay might grant that whereas 'Socrates is singular' and 'Socrates is universal' are contradictory, 'Socrates of himself is singular', 'Socrates distinctly conceived is particular', and 'Socrates confusedly conceived is universal' are not; for the modifiers 'of himself', 'distinctly conceived', and 'confusedly conceived' function to remove the contradiction just as much as 'on top' and 'on the bottom' do in 'The table is white on top and black on the bottom'.

Ockham replies that such modifiers could remove the contradictions only if they served to alter the supposition of the subject term, so that the resultant statements asserted the contradictory properties about different property-bearers. But Ockham believes that this can happen only (a) when the modifiers mention some part of the whole denominated by the subject, in which case they diminish the supposition from the whole to the part – e.g., in 'An Ethiopian is white with respect to his teeth', or (b) when the added determination is incompatible with the existence of the thing to which it is added, in which case it distracts the supposition to something else – e.g., adding 'dead' to 'man' distracts the supposition from the man to his corpse.[87] The above-mentioned modifers – 'of himself', 'distinctly conceived', and 'confusedly conceived' – neither mention part of Socrates nor signify anything incompatible with his existence, however, and so cannot alter the supposition of the subject term in Harclay's propositions. Thus, 'Socrates of himself is singular; therefore Socrates is singular', 'Socrates distinctly conceived is particular; therefore Socrates is particular', 'Socrates confusedly conceived is universal; therefore Socrates is universal' are all formal inferences. And if the last conclusion is incompatible with each of the first two conclusions, the last premiss is incompatible with each of the first two premisses as well.[88]

85. *Ordinatio* I, d. 2, q. 7; Ockham 1970, *OT* II, p. 241; cf. pp. 243, 249.
86. *Ibid.*, pp. 248–9; 251.
87. *Ibid.*, pp. 244–5.
88. *Ibid.*, pp. 244, 248.

Harclay might insist that he was not trying to argue that while 'universal' and 'singular' are genuinely incompatible predicates, they are not really asserted about the same thing. Rather he meant to contend that although the predications 'Socrates is singular', 'Socrates distinctly conceived is particular', and 'Socrates confusedly conceived is universal' are made about one and the same real thing – viz., Socrates – the predicates involved are not genuinely incompatible. In effect, Harclay has distinguished the one-place predicate '__ is singular' from the two-place predicates '__ is universal relative to __' and '__ is particular relative to __'. The first blank in those two-place predicates is to be filled by a proper name of an essential real singular thing, such as Socrates, the second blank by an expression designating a concept whose existence in the mind is caused by the real thing picked out by the expression filling the first blank. Thus 'Socrates is universal relative to a confused concept caused by Socrates' and 'Socrates is particular relative to a distinct concept caused by Socrates' are no more mutually contradictory than are 'Plato is older relative to Aristotle' and 'Plato is younger relative to Socrates'. Moreover, without further argument (which Ockham does not supply) there is no reason to think that 'Socrates is singular' and 'Socrates is universal relative to a confused concept caused by Socrates' are mutually contradictory either.

Ockham's own view

Throughout his career, Ockham insisted as Harclay did that

(T12) Everything that exists in reality is essentially singular – i.e., logically incapable of existing in, as a constituent of, numerically many simultaneously,

and concurred with Harclay against Scotus that one and the same singular thing can both cause and genuinely fall under both confused and distinct concepts, even though this distinction in concepts is in no way reflected by a distinction between nature and individuating principles in the singular thing. Unlike Harclay, however, Ockham maintained that universals are nothing other than names – naturally significant general concepts primarily, and secondarily the conventional signs corresponding to them. Ockham's nominalism is thus less misleadingly classified as a form of conceptualism.[89]

89. As noted in Boehner 1946.

Replies to opposing views

Replying to arguments in favour of moderate realism, Ockham says that Aristotle used the phrase 'primary object of definition' in several ways: When he says that the primary object of definition is interchangeable with the definition, he is referring to the fact that the terms 'man' and 'rational animal' are interchangeable,[90] contrary to Burley's contention.[91] On the other hand, when Aristotle says that definition is primarily of the thing whose parts it signifies, he takes the primary object of definition to be something other than a name. Ockham agrees with Burley that no particular man can be the primary object of the definition 'rational animal', in the sense that its parts are signified by 'rational animal' prior to those of anything else.[92] And he concludes that since only particulars can be real, nothing is the primary object of definition in this sense. Yet, each particular man is primarily defined by 'rational animal' in the sense that there is nothing whose parts are signified prior to the parts of it.[93] Thus Ockham insists with Harclay that knowledge of the definition cannot give one distinct and perfect knowledge, but only confused knowledge of the particulars thus primarily defined;[94] so that one can know, contrary to Burley, that every man is risible without having a distinct cognition of every peasant in India.[95] Similarly, in one sense the object of knowledge is mental, spoken, or written propositions and not any substance, universal or particular. Substances are known only in the sense that such propositions contain terms that supposit for them. And since only particular substances can really exist, only particular substances are known in this way.[96] Finally, Ockham joins Harclay in denying that real similarity between things requires the existence of something common to and existing in both.[97]

If Ockham was constant in his insistence that universals are in the first instance general concepts, he seems to have held two different views about the ontological status of concepts.[98] Early in his career,[99] Ockham main-

90. *Ordinatio* I, d. 2, q. 4; Ockham 1970, *OT* II, pp. 127–9.
91. Burley 1507, f. 4ra.
92. *Ordinatio* I, d. 2, q. 4; Ockham 1970, *OT* II, p. 132.
93. *Ibid.*, pp. 127–9.
94. *Ibid.*, p. 131.
95. Burley 1507, f. 4rb.
96. *Ordinatio* I, d. 2, q. 4; Ockham 1970, *OT* II, pp. 136–7.
97. *Ordinatio* I, d. 2, q. 6; Ockham 1970, *OT* II, pp. 211–12.
98. For a fuller discussion of these issues see Adams 1977.
99. *Ordinatio* I, d. 2, q. 8; Ockham 1970, *OT* II, pp. 273–4. *Expositio in librum Perihermenias Aristotelis*, Prooemium §§7, 9; Ockham 1978, *OP* II, pp. 359–60, 364–5.

tained that whatever is thought of must have some sort of existence. Yet, we sometimes think of objects that do not or cannot really exist: e.g., impossibles such as chimeras, abstract objects such as universals, and un-actualised possibles. He concludes that as objects of thought they must have some *non-real mode of existence*, which Ockham labels 'objective'[100] or 'cognized'[101] existence. Having analysed thoughts of such objects into a really existent mental act and an objectively existent object, Ockham seems to extend his conclusion to thoughts about real things as well.[102] He seems to have held further that what directs a really existent mental act towards one objectively existent entity rather than another is that the former bears an appropriate relation of comparative similarity or causality to the latter.[103]

Walter Chatton's objections and Ockham's replies

Ockham gave up the objective-existence theory, partly because of his own developing reservations and partly because of criticisms raised by his contemporary and fellow-Franciscan, Walter Chatton. Three objections challenged the application of the theory to our thoughts of particulars. (5.2.1) First, Chatton[104] charged that the objective-existence theory compromises direct realism in epistemology, because it identifies the immediate object of thought or awareness with the objectively existent entity and not with the mind–independent real particular. Although Ockham accepts this criticism and directs it against a similar theory held by Peter Aureoli,[105] he seems to have been mistaken in doing so. For his early theory claims that one and the same particular can simultaneously have both real and objective existence, and hence that the immediate object of awareness in intuitive cognitions is identical with the real particular.

Ockham himself criticises Aureoli's similar theory on the ground that it leads to ontological paradox: '"The trees appear to move; therefore some motion has objective existence" no more follows than that "The trees

---

100. *Ordinatio* I, d. 2, q. 8; Ockham 1970, *OT* II, pp. 272–4, 283.
101. *Expositio in librum Perihermenias Aristotelis*, Prooemium §7: Ockham 1978, *OP* II, p. 360.
102. The evidence here is indirect but seems to be implied in Ockham's discussion of divine ideas in Ockham 1979b, *Ordinatio* I, d. 35, q. 5 K and G, and in his suggestion that the objects of intuitive cognitions are the terms of propositions (Ockham 1494–6, *Reportatio* II, q. 15E; see Boehner 1943).
103. Ockham 1494–6, *Reportatio* II, q. 15 EE.
104. Chatton, *Lectura* I, d. 3, q. 2; quoted in Gál 1967, p. 203, n. 26; raised by Ockham against Aureoli in Ockham 1979b, *Ordinatio* I, d. 27, q. 3 H, and against his own objective-existence theory in Ockham 1491, Quodl. IV, q. 19.
105. Peter Aureoli 1952–6, p. 156; cf. I, d. 3, sec. 14, a. 1; II, pp. 696–700.

appear to move in reality; therefore a real motion appears" follows.'[106] It is as if Ockham assumes that Aureoli were operating with a system whose universe of discourse includes everything that exists either in reality or in a non-real mode. Within this system, statements of the form 'x is F' do not in general entail statements of the form 'x has objective existence' or statements of the form 'x has real existence', but only the disjunction of such statements. Further, this system is not one in which the predications are relativised to modes of existence, but one in which predicates attach absolutely. It will follow that things really have all of the properties that they appear really to have – which is absurd. This difficulty could be easily circumvented by relativising the predications to one mode of existence or another. Thus, 'Real motion appears' would become 'In the mode of objective existence, there is some motion and it really exists' which no more entails 'Motion really exists' than 'It is possible that motion really exists' does.

Since God is essentially omniscient and necessarily existent, He necessarily conceives of everything – actuals, possibles, and impossibles – from eternity. On the objective-existence theory, it will follow that all actuals, possibles, and impossibles necessarily have objective existence from eternity. And while this existence is not independent of the divine intellect, it is independent of the divine will, since God could no more destroy such objectively existent entities than He could alter His own nature.[107] But such a limitation on God's power is unacceptable.

Chatton objected to the application of the objective-existence theory even to our thoughts of universals, on the ground that it 'does with more what could be done with fewer'. While Ockham's early expositions of his theory make objective existence mind-dependent, they do not rule out the possibility that two people might simultaneously have the same objectively existent entity before their minds. Chatton judges this impossible on the apparently mistaken ground that if the objective existence of an entity does not logically presuppose the real existence of any act in particular, then it cannot logically presuppose the real existence of some act or other either.[108] But if objectively existent entity a logically presupposes the real existence of my act of intellect and objectively existent entity b logically

---

106. Ockham 1979b, *Ordinatio* I, d. 27, q. 3 K.

107. Raised by Chatton against Aureoli in *Lecturae Chaton Anglici in Sententias*, Prologi Quaestio Secunda; edited by O'Callaghan in O'Donnell 1955, p. 241; cited by Ockham against his own objective-existence theory in Ockham 1491, Quodl. IV, q. 19.

108. Chatton quoted in Gál 1967, p. 202.

presupposes the real existence of your act of intellect, then since my mental act can continue to exist when yours ceases and vice versa, it follows that *a* can continue to exist when *b* does not and vice versa. Hence, there are two objectively existent entities, just as there are two acts of intellect.[109]

Such multiplication of objectively existent entities would be futile, however, only if there were no theoretical role for them to play. But on the objective-existence theory, they are necessary, because they prevent our thoughts of chimeras, abstract objects, and impossibles from being thoughts of nothing. And in general, it is the fact that a really existent mental act is directed to an objectively existent entity and to one rather than another that explains why the thought has an object and has one object rather than another.

Chatton argues that such objectively existent entities cannot possibly fill the latter theoretical role, while the real things assumed by the theory can do so without them. He reasons that if one real thing can exist without any other really distinct (created thing), it can *a fortiori* exist without any and every objectively existent entity. But it is contradictory to suppose that an act of thought exists without being a thought *of* something. Chatton concludes that the direction of a thought towards an objectively existent entity and towards one rather than another cannot be what makes the thought have an object or have one object rather than another.[110] Further, Chatton rejects Ockham's contention that whatever is thought of must have some sort of existence. In order for us to think of a chimera or a golden mountain, it is not necessary that any existent entity *be* a chimera or a golden mountain; it is enough if some real thing has the property of being-of-a-chimera or being-of-a-golden-mountain.[111] And even on the objective-existence theory, Ockham has, in effect, allowed that really existent mental acts have such properties; for he claims that what directs a really existent mental act towards one objectively existent entity rather than another is appropriate relations of comparative similarity and causality. Ockham accepts Chatton's conclusion[112] and, abandoning the distinction between objective and real existence, identifies concepts with really existent acts of intellect and universals with really existent abstract general concepts.

Ockham's nominalism contrasts with modern nominalisms in identify-

109. *Ibid.*, p. 202.
110. *Ibid.*, p. 202.
111. *Ibid.*, p. 207.
112. Ockham 1491, Quodl. IV, q. 19.

ing universals primarily with naturally significant names (or concepts) and not with conventional names. But he does not devote much attention to explaining what this relation of natural signification is. His basic thought seems to be that a general concept C naturally signifies x if and only if there does not exist a y such that C resembles y more than C resembles x. Thus, the general concept *man* naturally signifies Socrates and Plato and not a gorilla, because there is nothing it resembles more than it resembles Socrates or more than it resembles Plato, but it resembles each of them more than it resembles a gorilla.[113] Many objections may be raised against this formulation, however. Indeed, it seems doubtful whether (on the objective-existence theory) the objectively existent universal *man* will be more similar in the relevant respects to the fully determinate particulars it is supposed to signify than to the objectively existent universal Australoid man or Negroid man respectively; or (on the mental-act theory) whether there is anything about an unextended mental quality by virtue of which it could resemble Socrates and Plato more than a particular gorilla.[114]

Conclusion

Although both the moderate realist and nominalist positions were developed with more variety and subtlety in the early fourteenth than they had been in the twelfth century debate over universals, the fundamental disagreements over identity, distinction, and similarity remained the same. Nominalists tried to show that any version of moderate realism was bound to be contradictory, while realists usually had more resources for preserving consistency than nominalists reckoned with. Ockham is no more successful in convicting Burley's position of contradiction than is Abelard in his attack on the first realist theory of William of Champeaux. Surprisingly, it is against his most distinguished opponent, Duns Scotus, that Ockham's onslaughts really do succeed. Even if Henry of Harclay's theory were consistent, however, his attempt to combine a nominalist ontology of singulars and concepts with a realist vocabulary is, as Ockham observed, obscurantist. In this respect, at least, Ockham's more straightforward nominalism enjoys a definite advantage.

113. *Expositio in librum Perihermenias Aristotelis*, Prooemium §6; Ockham 1978, *OP* II, 354–5.
114. For a fuller discussion of these topics, see Adams 1978.

21

FAITH, IDEAS, ILLUMINATION, AND EXPERIENCE

Medieval Platonism

In the later Middle Ages philosophical questions on the ordinary sources of human knowledge attracted continuous though uneven attention. The fundamental problem for the discussions involved taking account of two commonly recognised extremes.

On the one hand, Augustine had in summary fashion heralded a unified philosophy. For him the best in all preceding Greek thought had been assimilated into the Platonism current in his epoch, a type now conveniently designated by the nineteenth-century term 'Neoplatonism'. Within its own competence the perfected philosophy, as Augustine saw it, paralleled revealed biblical truth. His view set the framework for Christian intellectual tradition among the Latins for the eight ensuing centuries.

Medieval Aristotelianism

On the other hand, Boethius, from whose translations and commentaries medieval students learned their logic and received their general introduction to philosophy, had handed down an acquaintance with certain facets of Aristotle that resisted absorption into the Neoplatonic stream. By the mid twelfth century Aristotle had attained the status of the Philosopher *par excellence*.[1] His thought, as enhanced by Islamic writers translated during the latter half of that century, deepened medieval inquiry into subjects significant for problems of cognition. During the thirteenth century Aristotle's major works became available in direct translation and were read with the commentaries of Averroes. They rapidly imposed their philosophical techniques upon the intellectual training in the newly established universities and guided it for the rest of the medieval period.

---

1. 'Nam et antonomastice, id est excellenter, Philosophus appellatur.' John of Salisbury 1929, II, 16; p. 90.18–19.

Augustine and the ideal of Christian philosophy

Augustine's mature thinking had been entirely dominated by the Christian faith. Scriptural passages prompted him to reason:

Hence, because there is the one Word of God, through which all things were made, which is the unchangeable truth, all things in it are originally and unchangeably simultaneous ... In it, however, these things have not been, nor are they to be, but they only are; and all things are life, ... that life which was 'the light of men', the light certainly of rational minds, through which men differ from beasts and are, therefore, men. ... nor has it been placed far away from any of us, for in it we live and move and have our being.[2]

All things were within God, and in God men lived and thought. Philosophy, Augustine further reasoned, had come into harmony with those revealed tenets of faith:

... after many generations and many conflicts there is strained out at last, I should say, one system of really true philosophy. For that philosophy is not of this world – such a philosophy our sacred mysteries most justly detest – but of the other, intelligible, world.[3]

Philosophy and faith

Obviously this attitude ascribed to the Judeo-Christian revelation, as rationally developed through sacred theology, the primacy in one's overall world outlook. But it gladly recognised the autonomous even though not dominant role of philosophy. Philosophy by itself had come to know the intelligible world that had been revealed in the gospel as the eternal Word of God, but without recognising it as such. For Augustine the Word was in fact Christ, the second person of the Trinity. In that Word all things, including the human mind, really existed and were truly known.

---

2. *De Trin.*, IV, 1, 3 (tr. McKenna, pp. 132–3). 'Quia igitur unum Verbum Dei est, per quod facta sunt omnia, quod est incommutabilis veritas, ibi principaliter atque incommutabiliter sunt omnia simul; ... Ibi autem nec fuerunt, nec futura sunt, sed tantummodo sunt; et omnia vita sunt, ... sed *vita erat lux hominum*: lux utique rationalium mentium, per quas homines a pecoribus differunt, et ideo sunt homines ... nec longe posita ab unoquoque nostrum: in illa enim vivimus, et movemur, et sumus.' *PL*, 42, cols. 888–9. Cf. Augustine 1961, 40, 1; p. 49.2–5: 'docetur enim non verbis meis, sed ipsis rebus deo intus pandente manifestis'.
3. *Contra acad.*, III, 19, 42 (tr. O'Meara, p. 149). '... multis quidem saeculis multisque contentionibus, sed tamen eliquata est, ut opinor, una uerissimae philosophiae disciplina. Non enim est ista huius mundi philosophia, quam sacra nostra meritissime detestantur, sed alterius intellegibilis ...' Augustine 1950, p. 79.15–19. Cf. 'Lumen autem mentium esse dixerunt ad discenda omnia eundem ipsum Deum, a quo facta sunt omnia.' *De civ. Dei*, VIII, 7; Augustine 1899–1900, p. 366.21–2.

Religious faith, accordingly, was one distinct source of human knowledge. Through theology it was to maintain its dominating and judging role during later medieval times. From that viewpoint medieval thinking remained within the pattern set by Augustine, no matter how details varied in different writers.

Intellection and illumination

Philosophical knowledge, however, had to flow from other sources. For Augustine, sharing the Platonic tradition, these were intellection and sense experience.[4] Intellection was the interior vision of things in their true reality, reality that was vitally and luminously present within the mind in Neoplatonic fashion (see Plotinus, *En.*, V, 9, 6.1–10) as an intelligible object that was identified with each particular intelligible and yet was one intelligible. Augustine's use of this intelligible world to explain human thought is generally called today, as it was occasionally in the Middle Ages, the doctrine of 'divine illumination'.[5] That doctrine obviated any need to explain how external things could get into the mind in order to be known. They were already there, since they really existed in the mind's interior light, God himself; indeed, they had a higher type of being in the divine Word than in the external world.

Ideas and concepts

With things spread before the mind in that interior and living light, and with the mind's own vital response, explanation through metaphors of vision and birth seemed sufficient for Augustine. The things known were actually in front of the mind's eye. The mind saw them, thereby giving birth to human knowledge.[6] In this setting, ideas (which he called *ideae, rationes, formae,* or *species*)[7] were what the mind objectively confronted, not subjective mental features. Understandably, in this setting the 'idea' of a

---

4. '... duos esse mundos, unum intellegibilem, in quo ipsa veritas habitaret, istum autem sensibilem, quem manifestum est nos visu tactuque sentire'. Augustine 1950, III, 17, 37; p. 76.8–10. Cf. Augustine 1899–1900, VIII, 7; p. 366.18–21.
5. E.g. Roger Bacon 1897–1900, II, 5; I, p. 39.9. Bonaventure 1882–1902a, *III Sent.*, 23, 2, 2, Resp.; III, p. 491b (for faith). Henry of Ghent 1520 *Summa quaest. ord.*, I, 2; ff. 3ᵛ–4ᵛ ('illustratio divina', used repeatedly). Cf. Augustine 1894, *De Gen. ad lit.*, XII, 31: 'ipsum lumen, quo inlustratur anima, ... nam illud iam ipse Deus est', p. 425.22–4. 'Jam superior illa lux, qua mens humana illuminatur, Deus est', *In Joan. ev.*, XV, 4, 19; *PL*, 35, col. 1517. Augustine 1961, 40, 1; p. 48.25–6: '... interiore luce veritatis, qua ipse, qui dicitur homo interior, inlustratur....'
6. '... omnis res quamcumque cognoscimus, congenerat in nobis notitiam sui. Ab utroque enim notitia paritur, a cognoscente et cognito.' *De Trin.*, IX, 12, 18; *PL*, 42, col. 970.
7. 'Quas rationes, ut dictum est, sive ideas, sive formas, sive species, sive rationes licet vocare, et multis conceditur appellare quod libet ...' *De div. quaest.* LXXXIII, 42, 2; *PL*, 40, col. 31.

sensible object had much more reality than its external embodiment; in more exact phraseology, the same thing had greater reality in its idea than in its sensible existence. Yet in accord with the birth metaphor, Augustine could designate the mind's own representation of an idea as a 'word' that was conceived.[8] This use of 'word' was modelled on the way the term in theology helped to signify the difference between the divine persons. The mental word was an 'image' or 'likeness' of the thing, what medieval as well as modern writers call a 'concept'. Its presence was acknowledged by Augustine, but it remained peripheral in his account of cognition.

The role of the senses

Universal knowledge of a thing through its presence in the soul's interior light remained a persistent Augustinian heritage in medieval thought about cognition. But factual (quantitative and qualitative) acquaintance with corporeal things was not given in illumination only. For such cognition, the human mind had to be 'admonished'[9] by the senses. Yet even here the experiencing was by the mind, though through the senses.[10] The senses could not affect the soul, for nothing corporeal could act upon something incorporeal.[11] Such an account of experience of course avoids the difficulties of explaining transition from sense to intellect, since from the start the entire cognitive activity was in the mind.

The Aristotelian viewpoint transmitted by Boethius

Although there is no mention of illumination in Boethius' logical works, they exercised an influence that managed by and large to function within the Augustinian framework even while handing down in clear outline the basis of an Aristotelian theory of knowledge. Human cognition attained

---

8. '... visu mentis aspicimus: atque inde conceptam rerum veracem notitiam, tanquam verbum, apud nos habemus, et dicendo intus gignimus'. *De Trin.*, IX, 7, 12; *PL*, 42, col. 967.

9. Cf. 'aut admonitione a sensibus, ... cum intellegimus esse corpus', Augustine 1895, *Epist.*, XIII, 4; p. 31.21–2. '... nec idonea est ipsa mens noster, in ipsis rationibus, quibus facta sunt, ea uidere apud deum, ut per hoc sciamus, quot et quanta qualiaque sint, etiamsi non ea uidemus per corporis sensus', Augustine 1894, V, 16; p. 159.24–7. '... ad intelligibilia sua videnda a sensu admonetur potius quam aliquid accipit', Augustine 1895, VI, 2; p. 12.23–4. '... verbis fortasse ut consulamus admoniti', Augustine 1961, 11, 38; p. 47.9–10. '... admonetur, cum de istis partibus interrogatur,' *ibid.*, 12, 40; p. 49.10–11.

10. 'Mens itaque humana prius haec quae facta sunt, per sensus corporis experitur.' Augustine 1894, IV, 32; pp. 129.27–130.2. '... anima cum sentit in corpore, non ab illo aliquid pati, sed in ejus passionibus attentius agere, et has actiones ... non eam latere; et hoc totum est quod sentire dicitur'. *De musica*, VI, 10; *PL*, 32, col. 1169.

11. 'Nullo modo igitur anima fabricatori corpori est subjecta materies.' *De musica*, VI, 5, 8; *PL*, 32, cols. 1167–8.

one and the same corporeal thing in sensation (as singular) and in thought (as universal). But only singulars existed. Universals, which from this viewpoint were held to coincide with Platonic Ideas, did not exist at all. They were only thought about. The meaning was plain, though Boethius explicitly made the reservation that this Aristotelian view did not find particular favour with him.[12] In spite of his own Neoplatonic leanings, he transmitted a doctrine that gave ideas no real existence, and in the case of secondary substances far less substantiality than singulars. This was the opposite of the Neoplatonic gradation in which the ideas had greater reality than sensible things. Boethius, with Porphyry before him, had said enough to leave the question controversial, with the Neoplatonic position as the establishment and the Aristotelian viewpoint as the troublemaker.

The Neoplatonic – Aristotelian controversy of the early Middle Ages

The eleventh and twelfth centuries, lacking Aristotle's *Metaphysics* and *De anima*, were unable to resolve the controversy. At one extreme there arose a nominalism that is known today only through the rebuttals by its entrenched opponents. It accorded universal substances no reality other than the air emitted by the voice speaking about them.[13] On the other hand Anselm upheld the Augustinian tradition in a mildly expressed form, with God as the light of minds, and sense-experience as a requisite for the image from which the mind gave birth to the human concept (*verbum*).[14] With Abelard and others there was further concentration on the concept, with universals assessed as mental expressions (*sermones, conceptus*) abstracted from singulars.[15] The influential theologians of the school of Chartres,

---

12. '... singularitati et uniuersalitati, unum quidem subiectum est, sed alio modo uniuersale est, cûm cogitatur, alio singulare, cum sentitur in rebus in quibus esse suum habit. ... sed Plato genera et species ceteraque non modo intellegi uniuersalia, uerum etiam esse atque praeter corpora subsistere putat, Aristoteles uero intellegi quidem incorporalia et uniuersalia, sed subsistere in sensibilibus putat; ... studiosius Aristotelis sententiam executi sumus, non quod eam maxime probaremus, sed quod hic liber ad Praedicamenta conscriptus est, quorum Aristoteles est auctor'. Boethius 1896, *In Isag. Porph., editio secunda*, II, 11; p. 167.4–20.
13. '... dialecticae haeretici, qui non nisi flatum vocis putant universales esse substantias'. Anselm 1946e, *De incarn. verbi*, 2; p. 9.21–2. Cf. *ibid*., prior recensio, 4; Anselm 1946, I, p. 285.4–5. 'Alius ergo consistit in uocibus; licet hec opinio cum Rocelino suo fere omnino iam euanuerit.' John of Salisbury 1929, II, 17; p. 92.1–2.
14. 'Quanta namque est lux illa, de qua micat omne verum quod rationali menti lucet!' *Proslog*., 14; Anselm 1946, I, p. 112.5–6. 'Vere, domine, haec est lux inaccessibilis, in qua habitas. ... et tamen quidquid video, per illam video.' *Ibid*., 16; p. 112.20–2. '... non nascitur verbum cogitatae rei ex ipsa re ... sed ex rei aliqua similitudine vel imagine ...' *Monol*., 62; Anselm 1946, I, p. 72.15–16.
15. 'Eadem namque res ab universali nomine et particulari continetur et hoc loco hoc verbum "subsistit" de rebus ad sermonem transfertur per adiunctionem horum nominum: genus et species, quae sermonibus data sunt.' Peter Abelard 1919–27, p. 525.33–6. Cf. John of Salisbury 1929, II, 17; pp. 92.2–93.2.

though immersed in the Neoplatonism of Augustine and Dionysius the pseudo-Areopagite (fifth century A.D.?), tended in their commentaries on Boethius to describe universals as somehow abstracted from singulars by the activity of the intellect.[16] John of Salisbury, himself inclined towards considering universals as human concepts, recorded with facile humour the protracted efforts at reconciling the long-dead Plato and Aristotle, who had not been able to agree when alive.[17]

William of Auxerre and the material intellect

In the first quarter of the thirteenth century William of Auxerre was in full accord with the Aristotelian doctrines as transmitted by Boethius.[18] Yet he could neither accept sense experience as the sole source of philosophical knowledge, nor believe that Aristotle had done so.[19] Illumination, William reasoned, was necessary for religious faith, as well as for the first principles of the natural law and of the intellectual disciplines. Accordingly, he retained the doctrine of the existence of all things in the soul's interior light, as outlined in Augustine's *De magistro*, in connection with the notion of study in general.[20] In parallel fashion he accepted Aristotle's assertion (*De an.*, III 8, 431^{b}21) that the soul is in a way all things. In both cases, William claimed, the manner of expression was metaphorical. As for Augustine, we existed in God from eternity only potentially, insofar as we exist and live in virtue of the divine causality. And the meaning of the Aristotelian dictum is that the thing known is potentially in

16. '... substantiarum indiuiduarum uniuersalia quedam sunt, que ab ipsis indiuiduis humana ratio quodammodo abstrahit ... Id est: res uniuersales intellectus ex quibuslibet particularibus sumit.' Gilbert of Poitiers 1966, *Contra Eut.*, III, 31; p. 278.96–2. 'Sed intellectus uniuersalium rerum sumptus est ex particularibus.' Thierry of Chartres 1971, *Contra Eut.*, III, 17; p. 239.5–6. '... inductio est ex multis similibus particulatim inductis ad universalia progressio'. Clarembald of Arras 1965, *In Boeth. de Trin.*, II, 41; p. 123.25–6.

17. '... ut componerent inter Aristotilem et Platonem, sed eos tarde uenisse arbitror et laborasse in uanum ut reconciliarent mortuos qui, quamdiu in uita licuit, dissenserunt'. John of Salisbury 1929, II, 17; p. 94.23–6.

18. 'Dicimus ergo quod sensibile et intelligibile tantummodo differunt ratione ... genera et species non sunt ideae rerum, sicut dicebat Plato, sed sunt idem quod et ipsae res, sicut bene dicit Boethius.' William of Auxerre 1500, *Summa aurea*, I, q. add., a. 2; f. 33^{v}1.

19. 'Quod objicitur quod omnis scientia inchoatur a sensu. Dicimus quod hoc est falsum secundum Augustinum, nec Aristoteles dicit illud.' William of Auxerre 1500, III, 7, c. 1, q. 4; f. 154^{v}2.

20. '... sicut dicit Augustinus, fides est illuminatio mentis, quia illuminatur a prima luce sive a vera luce ad videndum bona spiritualia.' William of Auxerre 1500, III, 3, c. 2, q. 3; f. 135^{r}1. '... in intellectu angeli et animae impressa est notitia boni et ibi relucet prima veritas. In luce primae veritatis vident animae et angeli principia juris naturalis, sicut dicit beatus Augustinus in libro *Soliloquiorum*, et etiam principia facultatum.' *Ibid.*, II, 5, c. 1, q. 3; f. 47^{v}1. '... sicut dicit Augustinus in libro *De magistro*; et quidam philosophus ait, quod nihil aliud est studium quam supernae et internae illustrationis expectatio.' *Ibid.*, II, 12, q. 2; f. 66^{r}2.

the knower.[21] But in accord with the Aristotelian setting of William's position, the material intellect had to receive its *species* from the *species* of corporeal things, that is, from their sensible representations.[22]

The expression 'material intellect' goes back to about A.D. 200, when Alexander of Aphrodisias (*De an.*, 81.24–5) used it to designate the Aristotelian potential (or passible) intellect (*pathētikos nous* – Aristotle, *De an.*, III 5, 430^a24; Latin, *intellectus possibilis*) and justified the phrasing on the ground that what receives anything can be said to function as matter for it. The expression had been transmitted through the Islamic writers. The material intellect received the forms abstracted from sensible things, forms that were by William's time called by the Augustinian term '*species*' (see n. 7 above). The existence of things in the Augustinian intelligible world was being aligned with their potential existence in the soul's material intellect, and in each case 'existence' was regarded as metaphorical. In this way Augustine and the Boethian Aristotle were finally reconciled. Yet thinkers still felt a theoretical need for the doctrine of divine illumination, an illumination that was by then understood as the divine causation of existence and life.

William of Auvergne and the active intellect

William of Auxerre's interpretation of the material intellect leads naturally to the Aristotelian doctrine of the intellect that was causal and substantially actual (*De an.*, III 5, 430^a10–23). It had been illustrated by the simile of light, and had the function of actualising the potentialities of the material or potential intellect. To the medievals it became known as the active (or agent) intellect. William of Auvergne, the outstanding theologian of the second quarter of the thirteenth century, claimed that Aristotle was forced to invent it in trying – unsuccessfully – to accommodate the Platonic Ideal world within his own theory of knowledge. It was rejected outright by William. It would destroy moral responsibility as well as one's own

---

21. 'Secundum autem quod res dicuntur esse in Deo per cognitionem fuerunt res in Deo ab aeterno, et secundum hunc modum dicuntur unum esse in Deo, propter unam ideam qua omnia representantur. Secundum quem tropum dicit Aristoteles quod anima quodammodo est omnia.' *Ibid.*, II, 5, c. 1, q. 1; f. 47^r2. Cf. 'non aliter in eo sumus nisi quod id operatur unde vivimus et sumus. Secundum hunc modum non fuimus in Deo ab aeterno, scilicet per causam, nisi potentialiter.' *Ibid.* 'Amor enim et notitia sunt in anima cognoscente tanquam cognitum in cognoscente, propter assimilationem cognoscentis ad cognitum, sicut dicit Aristoteles quod anima quodammodo est omnia.' *Ibid.*, II, 10, c. 1, q. 6; f. 59^v1. But in Augustine: 'haec in anima existere,' Augustine, *De Trin.*, IX, 4, 5; *PL*, 42, col. 963.

22. '... intellectus enim materialis recipit species specierum rerum corporalium'. William of Auxerre 1500, IV, tr. ult., de suffragiis, q. 4; f. 305^v2.

initiative in study and invention. The material intellect is the essence of the soul and leaves no need for any other intellect. It knows singulars as well as universals and makes judgements about them, and it enjoys freedom in individual actions.[23] Yet it does not become a changing subject for material forms, even though the sensible things have the role of occasions on which it is aroused. The material intellect was equipped by nature to do its own work of thinking and of thereby producing the *species* in which it knows sensible things, the *species* being only similitudes by which the things themselves are known.[24] The notion of a *species* produced by thinking itself instead of being impressed on the intellect by a distinct agent was a significant insight that would have its history. For the production of those *species* the material intellect needed no further illumination from on high, nor action upon itself by the sensible things that merely occasion its knowledge. But besides being joined by sense experience to the corporeal world, man in his highest aspect is joined to the divine order, with illumination from above in order to know the first principles in the moral and intellectual orders.[25]

Albert the Great and the reception of forms

Albert the Great, whose writings date from at least 1245 onwards, bene-fited from closer interpretation of Aristotle's *De anima*. Sense experience, according to Albert, was the origin of all universal knowledge. But to abstract the universal from the image of the sensible particular an active

23. 'Causa autem, quae coegit ipsum hanc intelligentiam ponere, fuit positio Platonis de formis, sive de mundo specierum.' William of Auvergne 1674, *De universo*, II–II, 14; I, p. 821b (A). '... figmentum igitur est tantum, et vanissima positio intellectus agentis'. *Ibid., De an.,* VII, 4; Suppl. p. 209b. 'Quod si dixerit illam fieri ab intelligentia agente, quod est illuminatrix ... neque studium, neque inventio aliquid erit.' *Ibid.,* V, 7; p. 122a. '... alioquin ut praedixi nihil est in libera potestate ejusdem ex operationibus'. *Ibid.,* VII, 4; p. 208a. '... res ipsas sibi exhibet, et praesentat, et earum species ipse sibi in semetipso format'. *Ibid.,* II–III, 4; p. 1018b(EF). 'Quapropter ipsa anima non erit nisi intellectus materialis solus. ... Manifestum igitur est ipsi quod essentia sua non est nisi intellectus materialis; et propter hoc intellectus agens, sive formalis, nec ipsa essentia eius est, nec de ipsa.' *Ibid.,* VII, 3; p. 206b. '... destruxi errorem eorum qui dixerunt intellectivam virtutem esse apprehensivam universalium tantum'. *Ibid.,* VII, 1; p. 203a.

24. 'Quemadmodum audivisti in praecedentibus de intellectu, qui cum nihil patitur a formis ma-terialibus, et sensibilibus, per occasionem tamen alienae passionis, scilicet quae fit in aliquo ex organis sensuum, exeunt ab ipso novi cogitatus ...' *Ibid.,* II–II, 76; p. 929b (C). '... quia non ipsae imaginantur aut intelligantur, sed magis res, quarum sigillationes et similitudines sunt'. William of Auvergne 1674, *De retrib. sanct.*; I, 318a (H).

25. '... ponendum est animam humanam velut in horizonte duorum mundorum naturaliter esse constitutam et ordinatam'. *Ibid.,* VII, 6; p. 211b. '... creator ipse est liber naturalis et proprius intellectus humani. Ab illo igitur fiunt impressiones de quibus agitur, et inscriptiones signorum antedictorum in virtute nostra intellectiva, et ipse est lumen ...' *Ibid.* Cf. 'lucem veritatis per ipsum lumen eius, quod est verus fides ac salutaris'. William of Auvergne 1976, *De Trin.,* 26; p. 150.39–40.

intellect was indeed required, for a material thing could not bring about a form in the soul.[26] Since the soul itself performed the act of intellection, the active intellect as an intrinsic faculty of the soul had to act within the potential (material) intellect. It could not be something extrinsic. It possessed no intelligibles of its own; it had to abstract them from singulars.[27] Correspondingly the potential intellect was a *tabula rasa* for all intelligible objects. The *species* it received were in it not as in a subject but rather as light from the active intellect.[28] Accordingly no third thing was constituted by the cognitional union of knower and thing known, as would have been the case in a material reception of form.[29] The light of the agent intellect, however, was not self-sufficient; it had to be supplemented by the uncreated intelligible light.[30] Moreover, knowledge of God and self was naturally present in the soul, apart from sensible images.[31]

Albert's insistence on the reception of forms for the cognition of sensible things, and his understanding of it as different in kind from the reception of forms into a subject, are profoundly Aristotelian. But his interpretation of this reception in terms of light, as well as his emphasis on the dependence of the active intellect's light upon a higher light and his exemption of knowledge of God and self from its activity, show lingering traces of the Augustinian illumination. Albert recognises that cognition gives a new

26. '... unumquodque phantasma est particulare determinatum: et ideo necesse est ponere agens universale esse in intellectu.' Albert the Great 1890–9, *Summae de creat.*, II, 55, 1, *ad* 2m; XXXV, p. 456a. '... ita forma non habet a materia quod efficiatur in anima, sed ab actu intelligentiae agentis'. *De intellectu et intellig.*, II, tr. un., 1; 1890–9, IX, p. 504b.

27. 'Similiter dicimus intellectum agentem humanum esse conjunctum animae humanae, et esse simplicem, et non habere intelligibilia, sed agere ipsa in intellectu possibili ex phantasmatibus, sicut expresse dicit Averroes in commento libri de *Anima*.' *Summae de creat.*, II, 55, 3, Solut.; 1890–99, XXXV, p. 466b. '... intellectus vero agens non est extrinsecus animae intellectivae, sed est de constitutione ipsius'. *Ibid.*, 2, *ad* 1m; p. 460a.

28. '... se habet ad omnia intelligibilia sicut tabula rasa'. *De intellectu et intellig.*, II, tr. un., 4; 1890–9, IX, p. 508b. '... hoc modo movet lux agentis species intelligibiles ad possibilem, et sunt in ipso non sicut in subiecto, sed potius sunt in ipso sicut lumen agentis intentionatum intentione rei ...' *De unit. int.*, III, 2, *ad* 27m; 1890–9, XVII, 1, p. 29.38–41.

29. 'Et ideo cum fiat unum tertium a componentibus, quando aliquid componitur ex materia et forma, non fit sic unum; quando componitur intentio universalis cum intellectu possibili, sed fit unum actu, quia idem est actus intelligibilis qui est actus possibilis intellectus.' *De unit. int.*, III, 1; 1890–9, XVII, 1, p. 23.15–20. Cf. Averroes 1953, *Comm. magn. in De an.*, III, 5; p. 404.506–7.

30. 'Lux intellectus agentis non sufficit per se, nisi per applicationem lucis intellectus increati.' *I Sent.*, B, 5, Solut; 1890–9, XXV, p. 60a.

31. 'Unde cum non possit sine phantasmate secundum conditionem hujus vitae intelligere nisi ea quae sunt per essentiam in ipso, ut Deum et se, ...' *De coel. hierarch.*, II, 2, dub. 1, Solut.; 1890–9, XIV, 27a. '... quorum utriusque notitia insita est animae naturaliter, ut dicit Augustinus'. *I Sent.*, 3, G, 20, *ad* 2m; 1890–9, XXV, p. 120a. Yet Albert can maintain the sensible origin of all our knowledge: '... omnis nostra scientia oritur ex sensibilibus'. *De an.*, III, 2, 19; 1890–9, VII, 1, p. 206.70.

and spiritual existence to the thing known. He mentions Avicenna's pervasive doctrine that one and the same essence has material or natural being in the singular thing, spiritual being in the mind, and simple being in itself.[32] Yet he does not develop this insight into a full-fledged explanation of cognition in terms of being rather than of illumination.

Roger Bacon's Aristotelian explanation of Augustine

In the view of Roger Bacon, the soul's active intellect thought by means of innate exemplar ideas or *species* without being served by sense cognition, while the potential intellect, directed towards lower things, depended upon what was given it by the senses.[33] Bacon, however, maintained the doctrine of the overall illumination described by Augustine. From that viewpoint he could deny that the active intellect was part of the soul, since an agent had to be substantially other than the patient.[34] He opposed the doctrine that the same form can be the ground of both the being and the knowledge of the thing,[35] seeming content with the stand that the illumination itself allowed both intellects to *see* their objects. But he explicitly ranked the individual higher than the universal.[36]

In Bacon the notions of active and potential intellect are found accommodated to the Augustinian higher and lower reason, on the one hand, and on the other hand to the framework of the Augustinian illumination. The aim is still to explain Augustine by means of Aristotle. The Augustinian strain in Bacon appears also in his view that philosophy is not only in

32. 'Et ideo una et eadem est essentia in se et in anima et in singulari: sed in anima secundum esse spirituale, in singulari secundum esse materiale et naturale, in se autem in esse simplici.' *De praedicabilibus*, II, 6; 1890–9, I, 35a. Cf. '... prout est essentia quaedam absoluta in seipsa, et sic vocatur *essentia*, et est unum quid in se existens, nec habet esse nisi talis essentiae'. *De intellectu et intellig.*, I, 2, 2; 1890–9, IX, 493a. See Avicenna: 'Et est sicut esse proprium rei.' Avicenna 1508, *Metaph.*, I, 6; f. 72ᵛI. 'Essentiae vero rerum aut sunt in ipsis rebus: aut sunt in intellectu.' *Ibid.*, *Logica*, I; f. 2ᵛ2.

33. '... et hec vocatur intellectus agens, et hec non intelligit rem per administrationem sensuum, set per exempla sibi innata, confusa tamen; ... Alter est intellectus possibilis ... et hic intelligit per administrationem sensuum, de quo dicitur "nichil est in intellectu quin prius fuerit in sensu."' Roger Bacon 1905–40, *Quaest. XI. Metaph.*, VII, p. 110.4–13. '... quedam est principium cognoscendi tantum, ut ydea vel species alicujus rei; ... tertia est principium operandi et cognoscendi, et hec est exemplar.' *Ibid.*, p. 111.22–7. Cf. Roger Bacon 1897–1900, *Op. maj.*, II, 5; I, pp. 38–9.

34. '... agens semper est aliud a materia et extra eam secundum substantiam ... et sic nullo modo sequitur quod intellectus agens sit pars animae'. *Op. maj.*, II, 5; 1897–1900, I, pp. 40–1. 'Augustinus ... vult in pluribus locis quod non cognoscimus aliquam veritatem nisi in veritate increata et in regulis aeternis.' *Ibid.*, p. 41.

35. '... licet sit aliquo modo principium cognoscendi ipsam rem, non oportet quod sit principium essendi tamquam vera forma realis'. *Quaest. super Lib. de causis*, 11; 1905–40, XII, p. 63.9–11.

36. 'Item, cum probatum est quod individuum est prius secundum naturam, melius est sine comparacione quam universale.' *Comm. nat.*, I, 2, 2, 7; 1905–40, II, p. 95.29–31.

harmony with sacred theology, but necessary for it and engaged in on its account.[37]

Bonaventure's Aristotelian Augustinianism

Bonaventure likewise maintained that philosophy was necessary for the pursuit of theology, yet care had to be taken to avoid deception by it. Without faith philosophy had in fact held as impossible some things that are true; accordingly philosophy was not self-sufficient. As with Augustine and Anselm, understanding requires faith.[38]

On its own level according to Bonaventure, human reason travels the route of sense experience, with the soul impressing upon itself the *species* abstracted from material things.[39] Yet, as with Albert, knowledge of God and soul were exempt from that dependence. Knowledge of God did require a *species*, but impressed in a way different from abstraction.[40] In every case, however, the human intellect required a concept that emanated from itself.[41] Both the impressed *species* and the engendered concept were likenesses of the thing known. Things had existence in the divine exemplar ideas, in the created intellect, and in the world. In the divine exemplar they had being only as likenesses. In the world they exist in their own entity, a way of existence that was 'truer' and better for them.[42] But in their

---

37. 'Omnia quae tracto sunt propter theologiam.' *Comm. nat.*, I, 2, 2, 7; 1905–40, II, p. 95.9–10. '... manifestum est quod philosophia necessaria est legi divinae et fidelibus in ea gloriantibus'. *Op. maj.*, II, 7; 1897–1900, I, p. 43.

38. 'Sed quia ista scripta adducunt philosophorum verba, necesse est, quod homo sciat vel supponat ipsa.' Bonaventure 1882–1902, *In Hex.*, XIX, 10; V, pp. 421–2. 'Philosophi autem habent pro impossibili quae sunt summe vera.' *Ibid.*, III, 4; p. 343b. '... magistri cavere debent, ne nimis commendent vel appretientur dicta philosophorum. ... ad aquas philosophorum, in quibus est aeterna deceptio'. *Ibid.*, XIX, 12; V, p. 422a. '*Nisi credideritis, non intelligetis.* Hunc ordinem ignoraverunt philosophi.' *Sermo IV* ('Christus Unus Omnium Magister'), no. 15; 1882–1902, V, p. 571.

39. 'Ratio ... prout iudicio proprio relicta est, et sic procedit inspiciendo ad naturas et causas inferiores; acquirit enim scientiam per viam sensus et experientiae.' Bonaventure 1882–1902a, *II Sent.*, 30, 1, 1, Concl.; II p. 716a. 'Ideo anima non cognoscit rem, nisi speciem eius et formam sibi imprimat; et hoc non potest esse, nisi illa abstrahatur a materia.' *Ibid.*, 17, 1, 2, *ad* 4m; p. 415b.

40. 'Necessario enim oportet ponere, quod anima novit Deum et se ipsam et quae sunt in se ipsa, sine adminiculo *sensuum exteriorum*.' *II Sent.*, 39, 1, 2; 1882–1902a, II, p. 904b. 'Deus est praesens ipsi animae et omni intellectui per veritatem; ... dum cognoscitur ab intellectu, intellectus informatur quadam notitia, quae est velut similitudo quaedam non abstracta, sed impressa.' *I Sent.*, 3, 1, art. un., *ad* 5m; 1882–1902a, I, p. 70a.

41. 'Mens autem concipit intelligendo, et intelligendo aliud concipit simile alii, intelligendo se concipit simile sibi, quia intelligentia assimilatur intellecto.' *I Sent.*, 27, 2, art. un., q. 1, Resp.; 1882–1902a, V, p. 482b. Cf. '... verbum est quod emanat a mente per modum conceptionis'. *Ibid.*, arg. 4; p. 481a.

42. '... *triplex* est existentia rerum scilicet in *exemplari* aeterno, et in *intellectu* creato, et in ipso *mundo*. In *exemplari* aeterno et in *intellectu* creato sunt res secundum similitudinem; in ipso *mundo*

existence in the divine light they were able to illuminate the human mind
in the way described by Augustine in *De magistro*. That illumination was
required for every truth.[43] Though rejecting an explanation of cognition
solely in terms of causal influx, Bonaventure tended to align it with the
divine concurrence in human actions.[44] The illumination of faith is different in kind from the illumination of philosophy, and can accordingly
allow simultaneous belief and knowledge about the same thing.[45]

In Bonaventure, then, the doctrine of illumination continued in its full
Augustinian range and power. But Bonaventure had integrated it into an
Aristotelian framework of active and potential intellect and paralleled it
with the causality through which being is imparted by the first cause. Yet it
remained basically an account of cognition in terms of light rather than of
existence. The existence of things in their cognitional likeness was existence only from a particular viewpoint, and was not made to carry the
burden of explaining cognition considered as such.

secundum entitatem proprium. ... verius est unaquaeque res in proprio genere quam in
Deo ... *similitudo* rei verius et nobilius esse habet in Deo, quam *ipsa res* in mundo ratione eius quod
est; quia est ipse Deus'. *I Sent.*, 26, 2, 2, Resp.; 1882–1902a, V, 625b. '... eadem principia, quae
sunt principia essendi, sunt principia cognoscendi; sed tamen principia essendi conferunt esse per
se ipsa, sed cognitionem non conferunt per se, sed per suas similitudines'. *Ibid.*, p. 626b. Cf. '... in
Deo solum dicitur esse *secundum quid* ... sed in proprio genere *simpliciter*'. *Ibid.*, arg. 1 contra;
p. 625a. 'Item, verius est res, ubi est secundum propriam entitatem, quam ubi solum secundum
similitudinem.' *Ibid.*, arg. 3 contra; p. 625ab.

43. '... et constat secundum Augustinum et alios sanctos, quod "Christus habens cathedram in caelo
docet interius"; nec aliquo modo aliqua veritas sciri potest nisi per illam veritatem.' *In Hex.*, I, 13;
1882–1902, V, p. 331b. 'Lux ergo intellectus creati sibi non sufficit ad certam comprehensionem
rei cuiuscumque absque luce Verbi aeterni.' *Sermo IV*, 10; 1882–1902, V, pp. 569–70.

44. '... in opere vero, quod est a creatura per modum *imaginis*, cooperatur Deus per modum *rationis
moventis*; et tale est opus certitudinalis cognitionis, quod quidem non est a ratione inferiori sine
superiori'. *De scientia Christi*, IV, Resp.; 1882–1902, V, p. 24a. Cf. '... sed Deus sic est causa
essendi, quod nihil potest ab aliqua causa effici, quin ipse se ipso et sua aeterna virtute moveat
operantem: ergo nihil potest intelligi, quin ipse sua aeterna veritate immediate illustret intel-
ligentem'. *Ibid.*, arg. 24; p. 19b. 'Item omne ens in potentia reducitur ad actum per aliquid existens
in illo genere ... restat igitur, quod quidquid anima intelligens apprehendit, per aliquid quod est
supra animam apprehendat. Sed supra animam non est nisi Deus.' *Ibid.*, arg. 32; p. 20b. '*Alio modo*,
ut intelligatur, quod ad cognitionem certitudinalem necessario concurrit ratio aeterna quantum
ad suam *influentiam*, ita quod cognoscens in cognoscendo non ipsam rationem aeternam attingit,
sed influentiam eius solum. – Et hic quidem modus est insufficiens secundum verba beati
Augustini.' *Ibid.*, Resp.; p. 23a.

45. '... sic nihil impedit, unum et idem secundum alium et alium cognoscendi modum esse *infra* et
supra; et ita *scitum* et *creditum*.' *III Sent.*, 24, 3, 1, *ad* 4m; 1882–1902a, III, p. 524a. Cf. *ibid.*, *ad* 3m.
See also: 'unde aliquis credens, Deum esse unum, creatorem omnium, si ex rationibus necessariis
incipiat idem nosse, non propter hoc desinit fidem habere; vel si etiam *prius* nosset, fides
superveniens talem cognitionem non expelleret, sicut per experientiam patet'. *Ibid.*, Resp.;
p. 523a. 'Tertium lumen, quod illuminat ad *veritates intelligibiles* perscrutandas, est lumen
cognitionis philosophicae.' *De reduct. art.*, no. 4; 1882–1902, V, p. 320b. 'Quartum autem lumen,
quod illuminat ad *veritatem salutarem*, est lumen *sacrae Scripturae*.' *Ibid.*, no. 5; p. 321b.

Aquinas and the rejection of illumination

In Thomas Aquinas, on the other hand, cognition meant the existence of a thing in the knower.[46] In both sensation and intellection there was thorough identity of thing and cognitive agent, even though they were different in real existence.[47] This meant, in a recognisably Avicennian framework (see n. 32 above), that one and the same thing could have existence in reality and existence in cognition. Just in itself, however, the thing's nature had no being whatever. New in this regard was Aquinas' insight that a thing becomes known intellectually through two different but always concomitant acts of the human mind. It is apprehended in respect of its nature through an incomplex concept expressed by a single word (e.g., 'Socrates', 'man') and, simultaneously, in respect of its being through a synthesising act of apprehension expressed in a proposition (e.g., 'Socrates exists', 'Socrates is a man', 'Socrates is himself').[48] If the nature common to both ways of existing and known through the incomplex concept had any being at all of its own, it could not remain the same thing substantially under the different existential actualisations. Yet the common nature was what was predicated of all the singulars. With no being of its own, it could not be apprehended immediately; it had to be inferred. In that setting, obviously, absolute primacy was accorded to existence. When existing in the human mind, the nature was universal, even though the concept expressing it was something individual that was associated with a plurality of singulars.[49] Like other medieval writers, however, Aquinas

---

46. '... cognitio non dicit effluxum a cognoscente in cognitum, sicut est in actibus naturalibus, sed magis dicit existentiam cogniti in cognoscente'. Thomas Aquinas 1882–, *De ver.*, II, 5, *ad* 15m; XXII, p. 64b. '... secundum hoc cognitio perficitur quod cognitum est in cognoscente non quidem materialiter sed formaliter'. Aquinas 1954d, *In Lib. de causis*, 18; p. 101.14–16.

47. 'Secundum autem quod intelligit res alias, intellectum in actu fit unum cum intellectu in actu, inquantum forma intellecti fit forma intellectus, inquantum est intellectus in actu, non quod sit ipsamet essentia intellectus ... quia essentia intellectus manet una sub duabus formis, secundum quod intelligit res duas successive.' Aquinas 1874–89, *IV Sent.*, 49, 2, 1, *ad* 10m; XI, 486a.

48. 'Cum in re duo sunt, quidditas rei et esse ejus, his duobus respondet duplex operatio intellectus.' *I Sent.*, 38, 1, 3, Resp.; 1874–89, VII, p. 468b. Cf. 'Sed intellectus noster, cujus cognitio a rebus oritur, quae esse compositum habent, non apprehendit illud esse nisi componendo et dividendo.' *Ibid.*, *ad* 2m; p. 469a.

49. '... sed uerum est dicere quod homo, non in quantum est homo, habet quod sit in hoc singulari uel in illo aut in anima. Ergo patet quod natura hominis absolute considerata abstrahit a quolibet esse, ita tamen quod non fiat precisio alicuius eorum. Et hec natura sic considerata est que predicatur de indiuiduis omnibus.' *De ente et essentia*, III; 1882–, XLIII, p. 374.65–72. 'Et quamuis hec natura intellecta habeat rationem uniuersalis secundum quod comparatur ad res extra animam, quia est una similitudo omnium, tamen secundum quod habet esse in hoc intellectu uel in illo est quedam species intellecta particularis.' *Ibid.*, p. 375.102–7.

allowed the nature itself to be called a universal in a derived way, since it grounded the genuine universal that existed in the mind.[50]

On this view, existence in cognition was neither metaphorical nor dependent upon a particular viewpoint. Rather, both cognitional and real being were authentic ways of existing. Existence was undertood in various senses, all genuine, but in the order of primary and secondary instances. Primary was the thing's existence in God, secondary its existence in itself; dependent on both was its existence in human cognition.[51] But the thing confronted human intellection in the existence it had in itself, and not in the existence it had in the divine light. In consequence the primary existence in God did not ground a basic account of cognition in terms of illumination.[52] Though Aquinas like all his contemporaries made use of the traditional terminology of light, he developed his explanation of cognition in thoroughgoing terms of being. Philosophically God was reached only through reasoning based on the existence of sensible things in themselves and not on the basis of any Anselmian argument.[53] In this framework the sharp contrast between the *species* received by the intellect and the further *species* engendered by it became explicit.[54] The *species* was indeed *im*pressed by a really existent thing, yet the thing's nature had to be *ex*pressed in an incomplex concept that did not attain the being of the thing.

For Aquinas theology was the highest science. Its needs were served by the other sciences. It acknowledged the independent principles and methods of those sciences, yet had the role of judging through its own principles the validity of their findings. One could not have simultaneous faith and

---

50. '*Uno modo* potest dici universale ipsa natura communis, prout subjacet intentioni universalitatis. *Alio modo* secundum se.' Aquinas 1959, *In II De an.*, lect. 12, no. 378; p. 132b.

51. 'Unde in Deo est per esse increatum, in se autem per esse creatum, in quo est minus de veritate essendi quam in esse increato.' *I Sent.*, 36, 1, 3, *ad* 2m; 1874–89, VII, 434ab. 'Unde uniuscuiusque naturae causatae *prima* consideratio est secundum quod est in intellectu divino; *secunda* vero consideratio est ipsius naturae absolute; *tertia* secundum quod habet esse in rebus ipsis, vel in mente angelica; *quarta* secundum esse quod habet in intellectu nostro. . . . In his ergo illud quod est prius, semper est ratio posterioris.' Aquinas 1956, *Quodl.*, VIII, 1, 1, Resp.; pp. 158–9.

52. 'Quia tamen praeter lumen intellectuale in nobis, exiguntur species intelligibiles a rebus acceptae, ad scientiam de rebus materialibus habendam; ideo non solum per participationem rationum aeternarum de rebus materialibus notitiam habemus.' *ST*, I, q. 84, a. 5, Resp.; 1882–, V, p. 322b.

53. 'Nec potest argui quod sit in re, nisi daretur quod sit in re aliquid quo maius cogitari non potest: quod non est datum a ponentibus Deum non esse.' *ST*, I, q. 2, a. 1, *ad* 2m; 1882–, IV, p. 28b.

54. 'Unde necesse est quod species intelligibilis, quae est principium operationis intellectualis, differat a verbo cordis, quod est per operationem intellectus formatum; quamvis ipsum verbum possit dici forma vel species intelligibilis, sicut per intellectum constituta, prout forma artis quam intellectus adinvenit, dicitur quaedam species intelligibilis.' *Quodl.*, V, 5, 2, Resp.; 1956, p. 103b.

knowledge about the same thing, since faith involved assent without evidence of truth, while knowledge required that evidence.[55] The nature of the acts of faith and of knowledge themselves was the only reason offered by Aquinas for the conclusion. There was no further doctrine of illumination to make possible simultaneous presence of the two acts.

Henry of Ghent and the survival of illumination

In the final quarter of the century Henry of Ghent faced the traditional sceptical attacks – as transmitted through Cicero and Augustine – on the reliability of sense experience. He addressed himself to the Augustinian question whether any pure (*sincera*) truth, in the sense of truth unmixed with error, could be had from the senses. His answer was that it could be had by looking at the eternal exemplar ideas, attainable by men in the present state at the will of God. Divine illumination was accordingly required.[56] But the one *species* received in sensation sufficed to provide an object in the imagination from which the universal could be abstracted.[57] The intelligible *species* so abstracted was but the means of knowing, and not the object of the cognition.[58] In the object the essence of the thing enjoyed a being of its own (*esse essentiae*) that was distinguished intentionally from

55. '... theologia debet omnibus aliis scientiis imperare et uti his quae in eis traduntur'. *I Sent.*, *Prol.*, 1, 1, Solut.; 1874–89, VII, p. 5b. 'Et ideo non pertinet ad eam probare principia aliarum scientiarum, sed solum iudicare de eis.' *ST* I, q. 1, a. 6, *ad* 2m; 1882–, IV, p. 18a. 'Illa autem videri dicuntur quae per seipsa movent intellectum nostrum vel sensum ad sui cognitionem. Unde manifestum est quod nec fides nec opinio potest esse de visis aut secundum sensum aut secundum intellectum.' *ST*, IIaIIae, q. 1, a. 4, Resp.; 1882–, VIII, pp. 13–14. Cf. 'Sed sacra doctrina procedit ex articulis fidei, qui non sunt per se nota.' *ST*, I, q. 1, a. 2, arg. 1; 1882–, IV, p. 8a.

56. '... bene a sensibus sincera veritas expetenda est, et hoc quantum ex puris naturalibus judicio rationis in lumine puro naturali potest conspici: vel simpliciter judicio intellectus in claritate lucis aeternae.' Henry of Ghent, 1520 *Summa*, I, 1, *ad* 2m; f. 2ᵛ, F. 'Sincera igitur veritas ut dictum est non nisi ad exemplar aeternum conspici potest.' *Ibid.*, I, 2; f. 6ʳ, H. 'Ex puris igitur naturalibus exclusa omni divina illustratione nullo modo contingit hominem scire liquidam veritatem. ... Nunc autem ita est quod homo ex puris naturalibus attingere non potest ad regulas lucis aeternae, ut in eis videat rerum sinceram veritatem.... Sed illas Deus offert quibus vult: et quibus vult substrahit.' *Ibid.*, I, 2; f. 7ᵛ, LM.

57. '... ex parte autem intellectus nostri est ab ipso intelligibili universali, quod seipso est praesens intellectui in phantasmate actione intellectus agentis, propter quod seipso inclinat intellectum non mediante specie, quam solum ponimus in sensu.' Henry of Ghent 1518, *Quodl.*, XI, 5, Resp.; f. 451ʳ, S.

58. 'Abstractio tamen non fit neque a specie impressa: quia intellectus speciei materialis impressionem non recipit, quia vere esset alterabilis et transmutabilis sicut sensus ... Neque fit abstractio ab actu imaginandi eadem ratione, sed solum ab objecto imaginato, ut illud quod est sicut cognitum in imaginativa cognoscente uno modo, sit ut cognitum in intellecto cognoscente alio modo.' *Quodl.*, IV, 21, Resp.; 1518, f. 137ʳ, I.

the being of its actual existence (*esse actualis existentiae*).[59] This notion of essential being allowed ontological reasoning to God's existence.[60]

Though Henry utilized the distinction made by Aristotle (*De an.*, III, 6, 430^a26-^b31) between simple and complex intellection, and could readily say that the thing known is in the knower and is one with the knower, he did not show any tendency to explain cognition through existence as Aquinas had done.[61] His effort was a continuation of the doctrine of illumination as a requisite for explaining the truth of human knowledge in the present state. Illumination was likewise strongly defended by Franciscan theologians such as Matthew of Aquasparta (d. 1302) and Vital du Four (d. 1327).

Duns Scotus and the common nature

With John Duns Scotus the human intellect and its object, under the divine causality ordinarily required for the functioning of creatures, suffice for the attainment of truth. Consequently no special illumination was required.[62] But the intellect's basic object had to be sufficiently common to ground the universal, since the intellect could not be held to produce the universal from the singular alone without disastrous results. The widely accepted tenet that only singulars exist, while what is common springs just from the intellect, would make everything distinct from everything else in exactly the same utterly alienating way. It would provide no more ground for abstracting something common from Socrates and Plato than from Socrates and a line; it would make the universal a pure fiction. Prior to any work of the human intellect the specific nature of the sensible thing had to have its own type of unity and commonness outside the mind. In the thing

59. 'Et est hic distinguendum de esse secundum quod distinguit Avicenna in quinto in fine Metaphysicae suae, quod quoddam est esse rei quod habet essentialiter de se: quod appellatur esse essentiae. Quoddam vero quod recipit ab alio: quod appellatur esse actualis existentiae.' *Quodl.*, I, 9; 1518, f. 7^r, Y.
60. 'Ideo ex talibus conceptibus propositionum universalium contingit secundum Avicennam et Augustinum intelligere et scire Deum esse, non ex via testificationis sensibilium. . . . iste modus ortum sumit a cognitione essentiae creaturae.' *Summa*, XXII, 5; 1520, f. 134^v, DE.
61. 'Cognitione igitur intellectiva de re creata potest haberi duplex cognitio. Una qua praecise scitur sive cognoscitur simplici intelligentia id quod res est. Alia qua scitur et cognoscitur intelligentia componente et dividente veritas ipsius rei.' *Summa*, I, 2; 1520, f. 4^v, C.
62. 'Et ex isto apparet qualiter non est necessaria specialis illustratio ad videndum in regulis aeternis, quia Augustinus non ponit in eis videri nisi "vera" quae sunt necessaria ex vi terminorum. Et in talibus est maxima naturalitas – tam causae remotae quam proximae – respectu effectus, puta tam intellectus divini ad obiecta moventia, quam illorum obiectorum ad veritatem complexionis de eis. . . . quia termini apprehensi et compositi, sunt nati naturaliter causare evidentiam conformitatis compositionis ad terminos.' Scotus 1950–, *Ord.*, I, 3, 1, 4, no. 269; III, p. 164.13–165.2.

itself the nature had to be formally distinct from the individuating entity (*haecceitas*). The common nature, understood in this way, was in fact the first object of the human intellect.[63] Having its own distinct entity, it was not identified with the singular in the manner required for predication. But as grasped by the intellect it was actualised into the universal that was predicated with the requisite identity.[64] Socrates is not the common nature, humanity, but he is a man. This way of regarding the specific nature as common in reality to the singulars was a remarkable innovation with Duns Scotus. It did not involve a plurality of forms, for the common nature pervades the forms themselves as well as the matter and the composite; nor did it make possible the real existence of a non-individuated nature. It meant, rather, that if, *per impossibile*, the individuating entities could be removed, there would be nothing to separate the real humanity of Plato from that of other men.[65]

For Scotus the nature could be known either as existent by intuitive cognition, or without regard for existence by abstractive cognition.[66] Having its own proper entity it permitted valid reasoning to the existence of God in a version of the Anselmian argument, and it furnished a concept of being that was with requisite qualifications univocal to God and crea-

63. '... ita omnia essent aeque distincta; et tunc sequitur quod non plus posset intellectus a Socrate et Platone abstrahere aliquid commune, quam a Socrate et linea, et esset quodlibet universale purum figmentum intellectus'. *Ord.*, II, 3, 1, 1, no. 23; 1950–, VII, pp. 400.20–401.2. '... et secundum prioritatem naturalem est "quod quid est" per se obiectum intellectus, et per se, ut sic, consideratur a metaphysico et exprimitur per definitionem'. *Ibid.*, no. 32; p. 403.8–10. Cf. 'Primum actualiter cognitum confuse, est species specialissima, cuius singulare efficacius et fortius primo movet sensum.' *Ord.*, I, 3, 1–2, no. 73; 1950–, III, 50.8–9.

64. 'Est ergo in re "commune," quod non est de se hoc, et per consequens ei de se non repugnat non-hoc. Sed tale commune non est universale in actu, quia deficit ei illa indifferentia secundum quam completive universale est universale, secundum quam scilicet ipsum idem aliqua identitate est praedicabile de quolibet individuo, ita quod quodlibet sit ipsum.' *Ord.*, II, 3, 1, 1, no. 38; 1950– VII, pp. 407.20–408.3. Cf. 'Aliter dicitur, quod intellectus agens non causat universale, sed intellectus possibilis considerans illam quidditatem illimitatam, causat in eo universale.' Scotus 1891–5, *Metaph.*, I, 6, no. 7; VII, p. 74ab.

65. 'Et sicut compositum non includit suam entitatem (qua formaliter est "hoc") in quantum natura, ita nec materia "in quantum natura" includit suam entitatem (qua est "haec materia"), nec forma "in quantum natura" includit suam.' *Ord.*, II, 3, 1, 5–6, no. 187; 1950–, VII, p. 483.14–17. 'Respondeo, si loquamur realiter, humanitas quae est in Socrate, non est humanitas quae est in Platone, et est realis differentia ex differentiis individualibus unitive contentis, inseparabilibus hinc inde. Si autem circumscribamus differentiam hinc inde, sic ut nec natura intelligitur una maxima unitate in se, sed tantum illa unitate minori, quae est communis; sic nec est divisa ab humanitate Platonis divisione numerali, nec aliqua, quia non specifica,...' *Metaph.*, VII, 13, no. 21; 1891–5, VII, p. 421b.

66. 'Primam voco "abstractivam", quae est ipsius quidditatis, secundum quod abstrahitur ab existentia actuali et non-existentia. Secundam, scilicet quae est quidditatis rei secundum eius existentiam actualem (vel quae est rei praesentis secundum talem existentiam), voco intellectionem intuitivam.' *Ord.*, II, 3, 2, 2, no. 321; 1950–, VII, p. 553.6–11.

tures.[67] As an object present in its common status before the mind's intuitive or abstractive gaze, the nature continued to allow intellection to be described in visual terms in keeping with the doctrine of illumination, a version of which Scotus regarded as the 'common opinion'[68] of his day on divine causality. The Scotistic common nature diverges radically from that of Aquinas (*De ente et essentia*, c. II; pp. 20.2–23.7), for whom the nature taken just in itself had no being at all and though when abstracted precisively (i.e., in such a way as to be signified by an abstract term such as 'humanity') was not predicable of the singulars, nevertheless when abstracted non-precisively (i.e., in such a way as to be signified by a concrete term such as 'man') was exactly what was predicated, along with existence.

William Ockham and intuitive cognition

In the first part of the fourteenth century Durandus of Saint-Pourçain (d. 1334) developed the view that the acts of sensation and intellection are produced basically by the causes that created and engendered the knower, rather than by the object.[69] William Ockham followed this lead to the extreme in concluding that by way of miracle there could be intuitive cognition of something that did not exist. With special divine intervention all that was absolutely required to produce the intuitive cognition was the act on the part of the intellect. Accordingly the difference between abstractive cognition (not naturally requiring the real existence of its object) and intuitive cognition did not arise from the object but from the nature of the acts themselves.[70] Intelligible *species* in this setting were obviously

67. 'Per illud potest colorari illa ratio Anselmi ...' *Ord.*, I, 2, 1, 12, no. 137; 1950–, II, p. 208.16. 'Sed ponendo illam positionem quam posui ... de univocatione entis, potest aliquo modo salvari aliquod esse primum obiectum intellectus nostri.' *Ibid.*, I, 3, 1, 3, no. 129; III, pp. 80.21–81.2. '... dico quod primum obiectum intellectus nostri est ens, ... nam omne per se intelligibile aut includit essentialiter rationem entis, vel continetur virtualiter vel essentialiter in includente essentialiter rationem entis: omnia enim genera et species et individua, et omnes partes essentiales generum, et ens increatum includunt ens quiditative'. *Ibid.*, I, 3, 1, 3, no. 137; p. 85.12–18.

68. 'Si dicas quod lux increata cum intellectu et obiecto causat istam veritatem sinceram, haec est *opinio communis*, quae ponit lucem aeternam sicut "causam remotam" causare omnem certam veritatem.' *Ord.*, I, 3, 1, 4, no. 260; 1950–, III, p. 159.7–10.

69. '... quod sentire et intelligere non dicunt aliquid reale additum super sensum et intellectum, faciens cum eis realem compositionem; et ulterius, quod tales actus sunt in nobis per se a dante sensum et intellectum, quod est creans et generans, ab obiecto autem sicut a causa sine qua non'. *Quaest. de nat. cog.*; in Koch 1930, p. 18.24–30. Cf. '... et ideo ad hoc, quod reducatur in actum, non indiget agente dante novam formam'. *Ibid.*, p. 23.6–8.

70. 'Ideo dico quod notitia intuitiva et abstractiva se ipsis differunt et non penes obiecta nec penes causas quascumque, quamvis naturaliter notitia intuitiva non possit esse sine existentia rei ... Notitia autem abstractiva potest esse naturaliter ipsa re nota simpliciter destructa. ... Ex istis sequitur quod notitia intuitiva, tam sensitiva quam intellectiva, potest esse de re non existente.' William Ockham 1967, *Sent.* I, Prol., 1; *OT*, I, p. 38.5–16.

superfluous, as was likewise an agent intellect.[71] Further, intuitive cognition, both sensible and intellectual, was only of singulars. A universal, remaining something singular in the mind, was a sign for a plurality of individuals. It was a concept only, and formed no part of any substance.[72] As something singular the concept was a real being, whether in the first intention it signified things or in the second intention it signified concepts.[73] What is predicated universally is consequently a term referring indeterminately to a singular.[74] Since there is nothing common in either things or concepts, only the word is univocal.[75] Unlike his predecessors, Ockham does not regard theology as a single scientific *habitus*, though he was in accord with them in acknowledging its supremacy.[76]

From Ockham to Descartes

Ockham's nominalistic way of philosophising became widespread during the fourteenth and fifteenth centuries. Though divine illumination dropped out of the discussions, the deep Neoplatonic heritage continued through Meister Eckhart (1260–1327) and Nicholas of Cusa (1401–64). Followers of Aquinas and of Scotus engaged in continuous controversies, in the course of which the doctrine of essential being (*esse essentiae*) in the object of the incomplex concept came to be accepted by the Thomistic

---

71. '... talis species non est necessaria.' Ockham 1970, *Sent.*, I, 2, 8; *OT*, II, p. 269.7. 'Dico quod species neutro modo dicta est ponenda in intellectu, quia numquam ponenda est pluralitas sine necessitate. Sed sicut alias ostendetur, quidquid potest salvari per talem speciem, potest salvari sine ea aeque faciliter. Ergo talis species non est ponenda.' Ockham 1495–6, *Sent.*, I, 27, 2, K; III. 'Intellectus agens nullo modo distinguitur ab intellectu possibili, sed idem intellectus habet diversas denominationes.' *Sent.*, I, 3, 6; 1495–6, II, p. 520.11–13.

72. 'Conceptus et quodlibet universale est aliqua qualitas existens subiective in mente, quae ex natura sua ita est signum rei extra sicut vox est signum rei ad placitum instituentis.' *Sent.*, I, 2, 8; 1970, *OT*, II, p. 289.13–15. 'Hoc tamen teneo, quod nullum universale, nisi forte sit universale per voluntariam institutionem, est aliquid existens quocumque modo extra animam ... et quod nullum universale est de essentia seu quidditate cuiuscumque substantiae.' *Ibid.*, pp. 291.17–292.1.

73. '... tam intentiones primae quam secundae sunt vere entia realia, et sunt vere qualitates subiective existentes in anima'. Ockham 1491, *Quodl.*, IV, 19; f. 58ᵛ1.

74. 'Stat confuse tantum, hoc est semper in universali affirmativa praedicatum supponit confuse tantum.' Ockham 1974a *Summa logicae*, I, 73; *OP*, I, 204.4–6.

75. '... nihil a parte rei est univocum quibuscumque individuis, et tamen est aliquid praedicabile in quid de individuis'. *Sent.*, I, 2, 7; 1970, *OT*, II, p. 256.9–10. '"Univocum" proprie accipitur pro voce univoca.' *Ibid.*, 9; p. 306.18–19.

76. 'Ex istis sequitur quod diversarum partium theologiae sunt diversa subiecta, et quod theologiae non est unum subiectum.' *Sent.*, Prol., 9; 1967, *OT*, I, p. 269.17–18. 'Ideo aliter dico ad quaestionem quod theologia non est una notitia vel scientia, sed habet vel continet plures notitias realiter distinctas quarum aliquae sunt practicae simpliciter et aliquae speculativae.' *Ibid.*, 12; p. 337.17–20. '... dico quod aliae artes dicuntur eius ancillae, et quod de aliis habet iudicare propter maiorem veritatem in cognitis et propter firmiorem adhaesionem'. *Ibid.*, 7; p. 200.9–11. Cf. *ibid.*, p. 185.6–7.

participants. Against that background the 'objective concept'[77] in the meaning of what was known through the formal concept became established in Suárez (1548–1617) and Vasquez (1551–1604). This set the stage for the notion of 'idea' found in Descartes, with its long legacy of problems regarding its relation to its object.

Conclusion

For all representative thinkers in the later Middle Ages religious faith, meaning acceptance of truths on the authority of divine revelation,[78] was a source of knowledge necessary for man in his present state. They differed widely and radically on the roles played by divine illumination and sense experience in the formation of human ideas, with the doctrine of divine illumination becoming attenuated and finally disappearing for centuries till the seeing of 'all things in God' was revitalised by Malebranche. The notion of 'idea' gradually metamorphosed from the Neoplatonic forms through intelligible *species* into the 'formal' and 'objective' concepts familiar to students of Descartes. 'Innate' (*innata, inserta, insita, indita*) was used on occasion to designate knowledge possessed naturally or developed spontaneously by the mind.

In the medieval treatment of cognition, Aristotelian influence became dominant without the balance of a corresponding access to Plato.[79] The discussion of cognition, moreover, was carried on apart from any inkling that epistemology might be looked on as a distinct science, and its development was rendered still more uneven through its location in the context of various theological discussions. Its history is instructive, however, for understanding developments in early modern philosophy.

---

77. 'Conceptus objectivus dicitur res illa, vel ratio, quae proprie et immediate per conceptum formalem cognoscitur seu repraesentatur; . . . ut objectum et materia circa quam versatur formalis conceptio.' Suárez 1856–77, *Disp. metaph.*, II, 1, 1; XXV, p. 65a.
78. E.g. 'Non enim fides, de qua loquimur, assentit alicui, nisi quia est a Deo revelatum.' Aquinas, *ST*, IIaIIae, q. 1, a. 1, Resp.; 1882–, VIII, p. 7b.
79. E.g. 'Quae fuerunt rationes, vel probationes, Platonis non pervenit ad me. Ponam igitur rationes, quas vel habuisse videtur, vel habere potuisset.' William of Auvergne 1674, *De universo*, I–II, 14; I, p. 821b.

22
INTUITIVE AND ABSTRACTIVE COGNITION

Scotus and Ockham as the focal points of the discussion

The fourteenth century is especially rich in controversies about knowledge, but our understanding of them, while improving, is still limited. The relevant texts are not widely available, and as a result the analysis that has been produced is isolated and sketchy. Consequently, while we can frame tempting hypotheses about developments in the period and their influence on subsequent thought, it is still the familiar landmarks that best serve to present the themes of the time and the orientations of recent commentary.

Especially notable among those landmarks are the theories of intuitive cognition in Duns Scotus and William Ockham. Nearly all the medieval discussions of intuition that follow them are an attack on or defence of one or the other. Consequently, a presentation of the notion of intuition that focuses around Scotus and Ockham will provide a useful picture of the terrain on which subsequent battles have been fought.

The problem of the cognition of individuals

Around 1250 – the position of William of Auvergne suggests things may not have been so neat in the immediately preceding period[1] – writers of both Aristotelian and Augustinian persuasions could maintain as a matter of course that the province of the human intellect is the immaterial, so that with respect to the physical world our cognitive experience of existent individuals comes through sensation while the intellect contributes only the universal. Orthodox belief, of course, required that God's knowledge extend, as his providence does, to individuals. But, as is clear from disputes about what angels could know of material things, it had been traditional to locate the problem about an intellectual cognitive grasp of contingent and material individuals in the peculiarity of divine knowing.[2]

1. See Moody 1975, pp. 55 (notes), 59ff., 75 and 79.
2. Berube 1964 – a refreshingly non-polemical account of the controversy down to Ockham – lists among early proponents of 'non-intellection' of individuals Alexander of Hales, Robert Grosseteste, John of la Rochelle, Albert the Great, Bonaventure, and John Peckham.

Medieval philosophers were generally not inclined to scepticism, but the contrast with divine knowing provided an alternative base from which to project the limitations of human ways of knowing. It was to be expected, consequently, that the accommodation typical of the mid thirteenth century would eventually direct attention to the adequacy of its picture of human cognitive capabilities. And within a few years, for example with Thomas Aquinas, the emphasis was on making it clear that there is knowledge of material singulars at the level of intellect while preserving a special dependency on sensory experience.[3] Such a moderate liberalisation of the accepted opinion might have been expected to escape the full brunt of the anti-Aristotelian reaction that was productive of and stimulated by the Condemnation of 1277. But one feature of that reaction was an unprecedented sensitivity to any qualification on the immediacy of the intellectual awareness of individuals.[4] In 1282, the doctrine of the direct intellectual cognition of material singulars was officially adopted by Franciscan theologian-philosophers.[5] The emotionally charged atmosphere managed to obscure even some of the careful statements it occasioned.

The Augustinian background

The remote background of the issue is of more than ordinary interest, for the dispute offers a good example of modern-seeming developments carried by tradition-oriented attitudes. The tradition, of course, is Augustinian.[6] Augustine's world is exclusively individual. The phenomenon that interests him is necessity rather than generality and he locates its source in the mind of God.[7] What results is a familiar tripartite division of

3. The influential Augustianian Henry of Ghent also adopted 'indirect intellection', noting that it is not Aristotelian. Siger of Brabant, for that very reason, at first launched an Averroist attack against the theory, but seems eventually to have come around to it (Berube 1964, pp. 78–81).
4. Roger Bacon must be credited at least with an early emphasis on the cognition of singulars, but his polemical style makes it difficult to place his position accurately. Bacon's 'suspicious novelties' (Wolter 1967, p. 240) were a scandal to Franciscan authorities, and his direct influence on later theories of *cognitio singularis* is not as clear as is that of Matthew of Aquasparta and Peter John Olivi.
5. The philosophically undistinguished *Correctorium fratris Thomae* by William de la Mare achieved notoriety for being adopted officially by the order in 1282 (Lynch 1972, pp. 28–9). John Quidort is one of the better known authors of the Dominican rebuttals under the title *Correctorium corruptorii* (Berube 1964, pp. 89–91.)
6. Robert Grosseteste is an early example of the effort to accommodate Aristotle within an Augustinian scheme (cf. McEvoy 1977). For the later period, see note 61 below.
7. 'Plato is known as the first to have named ideas ... In fact, ideas are the primary forms or the permanent and immutable reasons [*rationes*] of real things ... It is denied that the soul can look upon [*intueri*] them unless it be rational, in that part whereby it excels, that is, in its mind and

knowledge, where only the soul's knowledge of itself is direct and unproblematic. Its knowledge of the physical world consists in organising the flux of sensory experience in the light of intelligible forms. Because those forms play an essential role in human knowing and yet can be located only in God's mind, problems arise regarding their accessibility and our objectivity, problems that Augustine tried to solve with his doctrine of divine illumination.

The influence of Aristotle

The interest medieval philosophers showed in the doctrine of illumination[8] is testimony equally to Augustine's authority and to the concern, as old as philosophy itself, with problems about knowledge that is necessary, abstract or universal. By the early thirteenth century there had been so much discussion of illumination that when an emphasis was placed on texts of Aristotle[9] in which the intellect is said to contribute the universal, the idea was accepted easily. But the problems involved in such an account of knowledge give rise to discussions in which claims about how we know things are not easily distinguished from claims about what we know.[10] For example, must one choose between the Aristotelian doctrine that the essential mode of intellectual cognition is universality and a straightforward application to the case of material singulars of the idea that the objects of knowledge must be real?

Cognition of individuals and Aristotelian demonstrative science

One might expect the emerging concern with the problem of an intellectual cognition of singulars to have generated explicit dissatisfaction with

reason, as it were in its face or interior and intellectual eye ... What religious man, infused with the true religion, even though not yet able to contemplate these objects, would nevertheless dare to deny and even refuse to confess that all things that are ... were created by God as their source ... ? Now where would we think these reasons are, if not in the mind of the Creator?' *Eighty-three Different Questions* q. 46, 1–2 (transl. in Bourke 1964, pp. 62–3).

8. Besides explicit philosophical discussion of the doctrine of illumination, there was also a special appeal to illumination in the mystical traditions of the Middle Ages and renaissance, and the doctrine is also thought to have inspired certain 'light theories' in medieval science (Weinberg 1964, pp. 163–4).

9. E.g., *Posterior Analytics* I, 18 (81^{b}6, 87^{b}35–40), *Physics* I, 5 (189^{a}7), *De anima* III, 4 & 8 (429^{b}10–11, 432^{a}3–14).

10. At least as early as Matthew of Aquasparta, there had developed the helpful distinction between the fact of our cognition of singulars and the manner of our knowing them (Lynch 1972, pp. 31–2). It is Vital du Four, however, who distinguished further between our knowledge of 'the singular' as existent and in its individuality (*ibid.*, p. 39), and showed some sensitivity to the difference between what the intellect 'knows' and what the human person does (see note 77 below).

the Aristotelian concept of a science, which we know to have been firmly entrenched on other grounds. But even Ockham, a staunch proponent of the importance of our knowledge of singulars, subscribed to the Aristotelian scientific ideal of demonstration from necessary premises, and he required that science be 'of terms' because it is 'of the universal'.[11] But even if sciences are only of the universal and necessary, knowledge is not. Some account is needed not only of how we might arrive at suitably scientific premises but also of the knowledge we obviously have of contingent facts about individuals and their existence.[12] And while it was the issue of individuality that raised the emotional temperature of the controversies, it was the problem of the knowledge of existents that determined the course of the major theories of intuition.

Duns Scotus and haecceitas

Neither the theory itself nor the term 'intuitive' which was used to mark it appeared without precedent; there were important and interesting transitional figures.[13] It was with Scotus, however, that a distinction between the knowledge of individuality and the knowledge of existent individuals was systematically developed, and the contrast between intuitive and abstract cognition was applied to the whole range of human knowing. His Franciscan heritage is evident in his advocacy of a positive principle of

---

11. *Expositio physicorum*, Prol. (in Boehner 1957, p. 11); and see *Ordinatio*, I, d.2, q. 4 (Ockham 1970, *OT.*, II, p. 34). Robert Holkot criticises Ockham for being insufficiently thorough regarding the reduction of terms to individuals: Moody 1975, pp. 345 and 352. But that issue is not usually taken as part of the dispute about *cognitio singularis*.

12. See Scotus, *Ordinatio*, I, prol., pt. 4, qq. 1 and 2; Scotus 1950–, pp. 142ff. (esp. p. 145), and *Opus Oxon.*, II, d. 3, q. 11, n. 11; and Bettoni 1961, pp. 123–5. A direct connection between intuitive cognition and the formation of scientific concepts is proposed by Scott 1969, p. 48.

13. The verb *'intueri'* has its non-technical uses (see note 7 above) but appears, perhaps for the first time, in Matthew of Aquasparta in connection with *cognitio singularis* (Lynch 1972, p. 124). The adverbial form, which became standard in Scotus and Ockham, was used by Matthew and by Vital du Four in a special triad: *intuitive, arguitive,* and *speculative* (*ibid.*, pp. 124–5). Vital says that we have knowledge *intuitive* of our own acts of the soul and allows for an extraordinary intuitive knowledge of the soul itself (*ibid.*, p. 144) – the latter providing an unusual use of 'intuitive' to mark the end rather than the beginning of a complex cognitive process. He objects that the theory of indirect intellection is not adequate but refrains from calling our intellectual cognition of material singulars 'intuitive': only the senses 'experience' material singulars so that the intellect knows them 'in the senses' (*ibid.*, pp. 40, 52, 92; Lynch thinks this amounts to intuitive cognition: p. 34, n. 25). This 'cognising in the senses' is reminiscent of Augustine's theory of vital attention, as is the account of another Augustinian, John Peckham (*ibid.*, pp. 98ff.). Vital's account is an elaborate and important description (see also note 10 above), but Lynch may be unduly enthusiastic in claiming that Vital had a theory to rival the developed accounts of Scotus and Ockham. (For the link between experience and intuition, see Berube 1964, pp. 127–8.)

individuation – the *haecceitas*,[14] as it came to be called – and in his use of the principle that the individual as 'primary being' must be intelligible if 'being' is.[15] Moreover, Scotus held that the human intellect, while less powerful than that of an angel, is not less capable of grasping the individual in its singularity.[16]

What set Scotus off from the more radical proponents of *cognitio singularis* was his contention that we lack an intuition of individuality since in its. present condition (*pro statu isto*) the human intellect does not realise its inherent capabilities.[17] For him, an intuition of individuality would involve a simple and formal understanding of merely numerically different individuals of the same kind. Beyond knowing that this table is an individual,[18] intuition as a grasp of *haecceitas* would as easily distinguish it from an otherwise similar one put in its place as if an altogether different kind of object had been substituted.[19] As Scotus saw it, such formal understanding as human beings do have of things derives from a process of abstraction of the sort Aristotle proposed.[20]

While the *haecceitas* of any actual thing will figure in a metaphysical description of the causality an object exercises in our experience of it, that alone does not imply that our experience involves a cognitive grasp of its individuality. Scotus did use the argument, characteristic of medieval proponents of intuition, that the intellect as a superior power is capable of whatever sensation is capable of.[21] But he denied to sensation the capacity for cognising the *haecceitas*,[22] so that argument supports no claim about our understanding of individuality, but only the more moderate conclusion that the intellect can cognise the individual as the senses can.

---

14. '[The term] designates the unique formal principle of individuation that makes the nature, which all individuals of the same species have in common, to be just this or that individual and no other.' Alluntis and Wolter 1975, p. 511.

15. *In Metaph.*, VII. q. 15, n. 4; and see Gilson 1952b, pp. 543–55. Walter Burley agrees with Scotus and Ockham on this point: Baudry 1943, p. 164.

16. *Quodl.*, q. 6 art. 3 (Alluntis and Wolter 1975, 6.19).

17. *Opus Oxon.*, II, d. 3, q. 6, n. 16; *Quodl.*, q. 13, a. 2 (Alluntis and Wolter 1975, 13.27–32). See also Bettoni 1961, p. 122, and Berube 1964, pp. 196 and 284ff. Peter Aureoli held the same position (II *Sent.*, 11, 4, 2), as did William of Auvergne (Moody 1975, p. 55, n. 38).

18. To know the universal in the singular is to 'know' the individual: *Opus Oxon.*, IV, d. 42, q. 4, n. 6; cf. also Aquinas, *ST*, I, q. 84, a. 7.

19. The *De anima* (22), whose authenticity is disputed, argues that a grasp of *haecceitas* would imply that we could recognise an individual substance even if all its accidents were removed. See Copleston 1963, II, p. 493.

20. But see Bettoni 1961, p. 100.

21. *Opus Oxon.*, IV, d. 45, q. 3, n. 11; *Quodl.*, q. 6, a. 1 (Alluntis and Wolter 1975, 6.19). The same argument appears in Ockham (*Ordinatio* I, d. 3, q. 6; Ockham 1967, *OT* I, p. 492) and in Burley (see Baudry 1943, p. 164). For the contrasting position of Aquinas, see below.

22. *Rep. Par.*, II, d. 3, q. 3, n. 15; d. 12, q. 8, n. 10; *In Metaph.*, VII, q. 13, n. 26 (all cited in Gilson 1952b, p. 546, n. 1).

Scotus' distinction between abstractive and intuitive cognition

Once the issue of a grasp of individuality is set aside – something that many of Scotus' disciples found hard to do – the orientation of the distinction Scotus drew between abstractive and intuitive cognition can be clearly seen in the analogy he frequently made with sensation. In the distinction of *visio* and *imaginatio* at the level of sensory awareness, perception of things is differentiated from a form of representation that can take place in their absence.[23] Accordingly Scotus posited pre-judgmental[24] acts at the intellectual level which are intuitive or abstractive depending on whether or not they are indifferent to the existence or non-existence of the objects they signify.[25]

Scotus sometimes described intuitive cognition within an Augustinian setting as an initial, confused awareness of what will come to be refracted into multiple, distinct (cognitive) elements.[26] The emphasis, however, is still on our experience of something real.[27] He extended that emphasis under the label 'imperfect intuition' to cover both the memory of experience and even a vision of the future – the latter to accommodate prophetic visions and, in particular, the foreknowledge of Christ in his human intelligence.[28] While such extensions put a strain on the definition of intuitive cognition as cognition of what is present and existent, one can understand their place in Scotus' scheme if, undistracted by the more familiar epistemological concern with certainty, one realises that for Scotus the fundamental distinction between intuitive and abstractive cognition is the difference between knowing what is actual and knowing what is merely possible or necessary.[29]

The same perspective helps to explain what might otherwise seem

---

23. *Quodl.*, q. 13, a. 2; q. 6, a. 1 (Alluntis and Wolter 1975, 13.28–9; 6.19).
24. *Quodl.*, q. 6, a. 1 (Alluntis and Wolter 1975, 6.17). See Bettoni 1961, p. 123, and Alluntis and Wolter 1975, p. 499.
25. As 'present and existing': *Opus Oxon.*, III, d. 14, q. 3, n. 14; and see II, d. 3, q. 6, n. 16. He says he means to contrast intuitive cognition with abstractive '... eo modo quo dicimur intueri rem, sicut est in se'. *Ibid.*, II, d. 3, q. 9, n. 6.
26. Bettoni 1961, p. 123; Berube 1964, pp. 172ff.; Alluntis and Wolter 1975, p. 500.
27. Scotus occasionally uses the term '*experimur*' (e.g., at *Opus Oxon.*, IV, d. 43, q. 2, nn. 9–10).
28. *Opus Oxon.*, IV, d. 10, q. 5, n. 4. The case of memory, of course, is not extraordinary. See *Opus Oxon.*, III, d. 14, q. 3, nn. 4–7; and *ibid.*, II, d. 9, q. 2, n. 19 and *Rep. Par.*, II, d. 3, q. 2, n. 11, where Scotus suggests one might postulate a special habit as an alternative to imperfect intuition. For Ockham on 'imperfect intuition', see *In Sent.*, II, q. 15 and the discussion in Baudry 1958, pp. 177–8.
29. *Quodl.*, q. 6, a. 1; q. 7, a. 2; q. 13, a. 2 (Alluntis and Wolter 1975, 6.18; 7.24–5; 3.33). In Scotus' scheme, experience serves the purpose of picking out (in a passive way) from the cognitive possibilities open to the human intellect what the Divine Will does (in a creative way) by determining one set of compossibles to actual existence. (For Scotus' theory of creative will and possibility, see Gilson 1955, pp. 460–1 and notes pp. 765–6 and the references given there.)

strange: Scotus found it obvious that we have abstractive cognition but thought an argument had to be given to show that there is an independent intuitive cognition.[30] Since what is possible can be non-actual, although what is actual cannot be impossible, it is to be expected that any case in which our thinking involves no claims about existence provides an example of the non-intuitive (abstractive); while every judgment of existence involves, so to speak, an admixture of what is possible. The difficulty is the same as that in trying to determine what it is that differentiates a drawing of an existent horse from one that is meant simply to illustrate the concept, as in a dictionary or biology text. It is also a difficulty that motivates in part Ockham's adjustments to the definition of intuitive and abstractive cognition.[31]

Ockham on concepts and individuals as objects of cognition

Although Ockham acknowledged a debt to Scotus' theory of intuition, it is characteristic of him to have taken up the whole issue of singular cognition in association with the question of what concepts signify. Convinced as he was that concepts, the mental correlates of terms, function as the basic components of our thought and that they are somehow caused by existent things, Ockham maintained that knowledge is either of concepts or of individuals outside the mind (*extra animam*) and that the latter is prior.[32] Ockham's penchant for parsimony put a heavy burden on this simple scheme, but one can imagine him insisting that whatever adjustments might have to be made to his account of the cognitive process, there is at least no need to expand one's ontology to admit non-individuals.

Ockham on evident cognition

Against this familiar background, Ockham proposed to demonstrate the need for a distinction among ways in which concepts can occur in the cognitive process.[33] There are cases, he says, where the same proposition can be known to be true in certain circumstances and not known to be true in others: for example, 'The wall is white' when I am looking at the white wall and when I am not. This knowledge-in-experience is one of three

30. *Quodl.*, q. 6, a. 1; cf., q. 7, a. 2 (Alluntis and Wolter 1975, 6.18–19; 7.22).
31. Peter Aureoli thinks one should define intuitive cognition only in terms of *purporting* to be about existents; see note 71 below.
32. See the extended discussion at *Ordinatio*, d. 3, qq. 5–8 (Ockham 1970, *OT* II, pp. 442–542); also *Quodl.*, I, q. 13 (translated in Boehner 1957, pp. 27–32). Walter Burley, who more often opposes Ockham, agrees about the intellectual cognition of material singulars: Baudry 1934, p. 164 and note 4.
33. *Ordinatio* I, Prol., q. 1 (Ockham 1967, *OT* I, pp. 22–3): translated in Boehner 1957, p. 20.

types of knowledge Ockham brings under the heading of what is 'cognised evidently'.[34] The others are conclusions seen to follow demonstratively from necessary premisses (that is, science in the strict sense), and *per se notae* propositions recognised as true without either an appeal to experience or any inference from other propositions.

Ockham defines evident cognition as '. . . cognition of some true complex [or proposition], the nature of which is to be adequately caused, immediately or mediately, by non-complex cognition of the terms . . .'[35] The truth of the cognised proposition is an obvious requirement if Ockham meant to introduce more than psychological certainty. But to put knowledge-in-experience in the class of knowledge that derives from apprehensions (i.e., terms) will strike a modern reader as an unusual handling of 'matters of fact'. At least part of Ockham's motivation here, however, was to insulate all evident cognition from the action of the will (a free agent) in favour of the unimpeded action of the intellect (a natural agent).[36]

Ockham on intuitive cognition

Intuitive cognition is precisely that incomplex apprehension in virtue of which contingent propositions are evidently cognised; abstractive cognition is non-intuitive.[37] Ockham argued his case in an extended account,

---

34. *Ordinatio*, I, Prol., q. 1 (Ockham 1967, *OT* I, pp. 5–7).
35. '. . . so that when a non-complex cognition of some terms, whether they are terms of that proposition or of another or of different propositions, adequately causes or is of a nature to cause, either mediately or immediately, cognition of a complex in any intellect having such a cognition, then that complex is cognised evidently'.
    '. . . notitia evidens est cognitio alicuius veri complexi ex notitia terminorum incomplexa immediate vel mediate nata sufficienter causari. Ita scilicet quod quando notitia incomplexa aliquorum terminorum sive sint termini illius propositionis sive alterius sive diversarum propositionum in quocumque intellectu habente talem notitiam sufficienter causat vel est nata causare mediate vel immediate notitiam complexi tunc illud complexum evidenter cognoscitur.' *Ordinatio*, Prol., q. 1 (Ockham 1967, *OT* I, pp. 5–6).
36. 'Praeterea, quicumque scit evidenter aliquod complexum, non potest dissentire illi complexo solo imperio voluntatis, sed oportet quod persuadeatur per rationem fortius moventem intellectum suum ad dissentiendum, vel oportet quod obliviscatur alicuius evidenter noti.' *Ordinatio*, Prol., q. 7 (Ockham 1967, *OT* I, p. 192).
37. 'Et universaliter omnis notitia incomplexa termini vel terminorum seu rei vel rerum virtute cuius potest evidenter cognosci aliqua veritas contingens, maxime de praesenti, est notitia intuitiva. . . . Et omnis notitia complexa terminorum vel rerum significatarum ultimate reducitur ad notitiam incomplexam terminorum. Igitur isti termini, vel res, una alia notitia possunt cognosci quam sit illa virtute cuius non possunt cognosci tales veritates contingentes, et illa erit intuitiva. Et ista est notitia a qua incipit notitia experimentalis, quia universaliter ille qui potest accipere experimentum de aliqua veritate contingente, et mediante illa de veritate necessaria, habet aliquam notitiam incomplexam de aliquo termino vel re quam non habet ille qui non potest sic experiri.' *Ordinatio* I, Prol., q. 1 (Ockham 1967, *OT* I, pp. 31–3).

the crucial premiss of which is that the proximate cause of assent to a proposition is the apprehension of its terms.[38] That premiss is supported by a less peculiar but no less carefully supported claim that assent to a proposition presupposes apprehension of the proposition, which in turn presupposes apprehension of the terms. Finally, if evident assent to the same contingent proposition is possible in one case and not in the other, the apprehension of terms in virtue of which the assent is made must be different in the two instances.

The argument supposes that the representative content of the differing apprehensions is in fact the same, and so Ockham's theory provides no more support than Scotus' for proponents of the intellectual grasp of singularity. Intuitive cognition pertains to an individual, Ockham says, because it is 'caused by this one rather than that'.[39] The character of intuitive cognition, therefore, is not captured by any logical or grammatical classification (e.g., the use of indexicals or proper names). Intuitive and abstractive cognition differ 'in themselves', but not by any mark other then having or lacking the capacity to cause evident assent with respect to contingent fact.

The structure of the argument in Ockham's explicit and detailed account of intuitive cognition in the Prologue to his commentary on the *Sentences* exhibits intuitive cognitions as a presupposition of our knowing contingent facts to be true. Ockham begins with a full-fledged case of knowledge and makes no special effort to hedge it against the possibilities of doubt. It is, moreover, knowledge expressible in the form of a proposition: 'The wall is white', 'I am sad'.[40] Ockham then proceeds to isolate the components of the proposition in terms of logical form, marking the steps and elements of a cognitive process in keeping with that structure. That one can truly say 'The wall is white' cannot, for Ockham, be explained directly as a matching of a proposition with some extra-mental

---

38. *Ordinatio* I, Prol., q. 1 (Ockham 1967, *OT* I, pp. 16–22). The extended argument is analysed in Boler 1976. The premiss that the proximate causes of assent must be intellective was attacked by Adam Wodeham on the grounds that it depends on a theory of plural substantial forms: *Quaestiones in librum Sententiarum* I, Prol., q. 1 (§20 '. . . quod visio sensitiva immediate accipitur in intellectu'.) The text was brought to my attention by Fr. Gedeon Gál, whose help in surveying the literature of the fourteenth century was invaluable to me.

39. *Quodl.*, I, q. 13; translated in Boehner 1957, p. 30 (see also pp. 28–9).

40. Scotus (*Opus Oxon.*, IV, d. 45, q. 3, n. 17) and Ockham (Ockham 1967, *OT* I, pp. 39ff.) hold that the intellect has intuitive cognition of mental acts. Walter Chatton argues that intuitive cognition is not needed to account for that knowledge: O'Callaghan 1955, article 5, pp. 255–61. The question of the soul's knowledge of itself is more complex and received various answers.

state of affairs. He has argued at length (in another context) that there is no extra-mental composition onto which predication is mapped.[41] But his definition of intuitive cognition very carefully reflects only the argument which produced it.[42]

Ockham on intuitive cognition of non-existent objects

On the other hand, Ockham was not fully in control of the implications of his having defined intuitive cognition in terms of true propositions, and he seems unaware of the troubles that arise because of his having set intuitive cognition in a causal sequence as well. The form of his definition is no accident, however, as is clear from the effort he takes to distinguish it from Scotus'.[43] For Scotus, it is impossible for there to be intuitive cognition of an object that is not present and existent. For Ockham, the necessary connection is between intuitive cognition and the true assent made in virtue of it.[44] That the two definitions are not equivalent is shown in Ockham's favourite if unfortunate device for displaying necessary connection. On Scotus' account, God cannot cause an intuitive cognition of a non-existent object; but on Ockham's definition, although the case would be extraordinary, God could cause an intuitive cognition so long as the ensuing judgement is true: namely, 'That object does not exist.'[45]

The most likely objection Ockham could think of is that his definition will seem faulty for implying that God could never deceive us. In reply, he simply denied the consequence. God can cause in us a 'creditative act' that, for example, something exists when it does not; but Ockham's definition requires only that the deception not be accomplished by means of an intuitive cognition.[46] The argument succeeds in what it is intended to accomplish. And Ockham's handling of the issue should dissolve any inclination to charge him with scepticism: one is hard pressed to imagine a

41. *Summa logicae* II, Chs. 2–20.
42. The definition is given in note 37 above.
43. Ockham considers a number of ways his position differs from that of Scotus: *Ordinatio* I, Prol., q. 1 (Ockham 1967, *OT* I, pp. 33–9). The requirement of an existent object is treated at pp. 38–9; a more detailed account is in *Quodlibeta* V, q. 5 and VI, q. 6 (tr. in McKeon 1929–30, II, pp. 368–75).
44. In an early text, Ockham does at one point characterise intuitive cognition in terms of the existence of its object (*Rep.*, II, q. 15: in Boehner 1943b, p. 248). For his later, more careful definition, see note 37 above.
45. Walter Chatton thinks Ockham's account is incoherent on this point (O'Callaghan 1955, articles 3–6: pp. 246–69). Of course, he uses, as Scotus does, the analogy of *visio* and *imaginatio* to distinguish intuitive and abstractive cognition (cf., *ibid.*, p. 248); see below.
46. *Quodl.*, V, q. 5 (McKeon 1929–30, II, p. 371).

sceptic who could leave the argument where Ockham leaves it.[47] But the issue is also something of a distraction, for the troubles in Ockham's account of intuition are not linked with the possibility of extraordinary exercise of God's absolute power.[48]

Present objects and unconditioned beginnings

The positions adopted by Scotus and Ockham, according to one interesting suggestion,[49] can be viewed as diverging along classical lines for intuition theories according to whether the emphasis is on the presence of the object or on an unconditioned beginning: 'a cognition not determined by previous cognitions'. Considering the way in which Scotus draws an analogy to vision, he is to be classed with those who adopt theories of the former sort. That such theories are probably more common, perhaps because they are less technical and more natural, may account for the continuing influence Scotus' theory had even after the publication of Ockham's criticisms. Ockham's weakening of the link between intuitive cognition and its object, along with other indications in the way he argued for intuitive cognition, favors his being classed with proponents of the unconditioned-beginnings sort of intuition theories. Since the question of where intuitions 'come from' is incidental for such theories, however, Ockham's concern for the causal origins of intuitive cognitions will appear from that perspective to be misplaced. But even if the causal link to objects were entirely dissolved, there would remain problems with Ockham's having defined intuitive cognition in terms of assent to *true* propositions. It is hard to see how he could have met the difficulties without adopting a rather sophisticated coherence theory of truth.[50]

Intuition and deception

One can, of course, argue that, despite the form Ockham's presentation takes in the Prologue, he was really engaged in a more straight-forwardly epistemological project where intuitive cognitions are introspectively re-

47. Sebastian Day (1947) brought to the boil a minor controversy about Ockham and scepticism which is not worth recounting (see Baudry 1958, p. 177 and Adams 1970, pp. 389–93). Day's book provides a useful collection of texts, but his interpretations of Scotus and Ockham must be read with caution; his account of Aquinas is altogether unreliable.
48. See Adams 1970, pp. 393ff., and Scott 1969, pp. 43–8.
49. The point is made by Robert Wengert in an unpublished manuscript concerning Hervaeus Natalis, who in *Quodl.* IV takes intuition as an unconditioned beginning.
50. Scott (1971, pp. 28ff.) is willing to claim that Nicholas of Autrecourt is only developing Ockham's position in maintaining that one must adopt the principle that what we are certain about is true.

coverable elements available for appeal in justifying knowledge claims about contingent facts.[51] Such a point of view puts into even starker relief the oddity of defining intuitive cognition in terms of true propositions and makes it impossible not to see a flaw in Ockham's having nowhere told us how to distinguish intuitive cognitions from deceptive creditative acts.

Mental language

Either approach to interpreting Ockham's theory will eventually uncover more radical anomalies. The basic structure and components of 'mental language', Ockham tells us, are determined by finding out what elements of a natural language are necessary for its statement-making functions.[52] If only for the appeal to the notorious 'razor', which Ockham himself points out is relevant only outside observational contexts,[53] the determination of intuitive cognitions – or on the theory that they should be introspectible, the correlation of intuitive cognitions with concepts (which are the basic components of mental language) – will be a complex and indirect procedure. It has even been persuasively argued that, when combined with Ockham's account of the derivation of scientific knowledge of fact, there results the paradox that we can have knowledge only if we do not know that we have it.[54]

Intuition, scepticism, and the absolute power of God

From a modern point of view, the project Ockham described, with its concern for first cognitions within a quasi-causal sequence from existent things through intuitive cognition to assent is so unmistakably pregnant with epistemological problems that it tends to foreshorten our perspective on philosophical developments between his time and that of Descartes.[55] An emphasis on scepticism, however, may distort our understanding of the actual development of fourteenth-century epistemology.

The sceptical proclivities of certain so-called 'Ockhamists' have been well advertised if not always well analysed.[56] The distinction characteristic

---

51. Adams 1970 gives a good account of this.
52. *Summa logicae* I, Ch. 3.
53. *Reportatio* II, q. 150 (quoted in Boehner 1957, p. xx, n. 2). Since the world results from a free act of creation, it contains more than only necessary things.
54. Scott 1969, pp. 43 and 46.
55. Intuitive cognition was still important for Suárez (Copleston 1963, III, p. 375), but the exact influence on Descartes' thought is not definitively established.
56. See Moody 1975, pp. 127–60. That such figures as Nicholas of Autrecourt and John of Mirecourt were called 'Ockhamists' tells us more about their social attitudes – or the attitudes of those who so labelled them – than about their philosophical positions.

of them is one between absolute certainty and ordinary certainty.[57] The former consists of what can be 'reduced'[58] to the principle of non-contradiction plus the knowledge of one's own existence and mental states which Augustine had established in arguments against the Academics.[59] As evidence that ordinary perceptual claims cannot meet this higher standard of certainty, these writers customarily alluded to God's ability to cause in us deceptive creditative acts about the existence of things.

The keystone of the argument, of course, is the doctrine of the absolute power of God, and deception with regard to intuitive or pseudo-intuitive cognition is introduced only to illustrate the range of that power. Ockham's theories were not likely to have been more than a mere occasion for this argument and his account of intuitive cognition served only the form in which it came to be expressed.[60] Like the accusation of scepticism, the adoption of scepticism usually stems from mixed motives, and the most powerful in this instance may have been social and political. The history of scepticism in the Middle Ages, the use of sceptical arguments and the efforts to avoid and counter them, is a complex story that deserves to be told. But its intersection with the history of the notion of intuition, while dramatic, may not be as important for either of them as has been supposed.

In general, throughout the thirteenth and fourteenth centuries, discussion of the knowledge of material singulars was oriented to the topics that gave rise to the original dispute: the domains of and relationship between sense and intellect, the limits of human knowing (in contrast with angelic and divine knowledge), and the knowledge of existence and singularity. With the appearance of explicit theories of intuition, attention was inevitably focused on the beginnings of the cognitive process. It is not easy to determine, however, for the individual studies which develop, whether their intentions were to inquire into the justification of knowledge claims or to provide a description of our ways of knowing. Moreover, the most prominent appeals to the possibilities of scepticism do not seem to function

57. Labelled 'special' and 'natural' by John of Mirecourt (Copleston 1963, III, p. 128). Peter of Ailly contrasts 'natural light' with 'reason' as concerned with the two types of certainty (Leff 1967c, p. 61). Buridan had proposed that science needed only practical or natural certainty (*In Metaphysicen Aristotelis quaestiones*, II, q. 1: tr. in Hyman and Walsh 1967, pp. 704–5). And Nicholas of Autrecourt consequently charges Buridan with scepticism! (Copleston 1963, III, pp. 137–8). Nicholas, however, denies that there are degrees of certainty; he allows a distinct type of certainty for matters of faith. however (*ibid.*).

58. Scott (1971, pp. 21–2, esp. n. 17) argues that Nicholas, at least, does not mean by this that we can only be certain of truths whose denial is a contradiction; he was, instead, talking of the relation of evidence to conclusion. For the more familiar interpretation see Weinberg 1964, p. 268.

59. See note 61 below.

60. See the discussion of Ockhamism in Moody 1975, pp. 127–60.

either as a base or as a foil for the development of explicit discussions of the perceptual process.[61]

From the perspective of the early modern era, it is striking that the intersection of theories of intuition and the principle of God's omnipotence could produce appeals to the possibility of deception but seem to have occasioned no developed accounts of the justification of perceptual claims.[62] Of course, in the absence of some reason to think that God is interfering with some or all of our perceptions, the mere possibility of deception is insufficient to render perceptual claims doubtful. As it happens, however, the target of the better known 'sceptics' of the post-Ockham period seems not to have been perception at all but rather the ideal of Aristotelian demonstration which was thought to provide an avenue to certainty that would rival or even undermine the faith.[63] In this connection, an appeal to God's omnipotence is a simple (if excessive) means for showing contingent claims to be contingent. And if the theory of intuitive cognition is supposed to provide the essential link (causal or otherwise) between the actual world and our perceptual claims, from which further transformations can produce scientific premises, the possibility of divine intervention is a legitimate consideration. For here, unlike the case for perceptual claims, the necessity of the demonstration is at stake, and the otherwise plausible rider: 'if God is not deceiving us', defeats its purpose.[64]

Intuition and intelligible species

The mixture of descriptive and justificatory purposes is a problem in the history of another theme which, during the period, was as prominent as

61. The model for this practice is again Augustine: see, for example, his *Contra academicos* and *De libero arbitrio*, Book II. The importance of Augustine for the epistemological developments of the later Middle Ages is easily overlooked: '... it is worthy of note that Gregory [of Rimini] should have been able to confirm by so many quotations from Augustine some theses one would otherwise feel tempted to explain by the spreading influence of Ockham.' (Gilson 1955, p. 502.)

62. The problem of scepticism is not ignored however. Scotus tried to counter what he took to be sceptical consequences in Henry of Ghent's theory of illumination (Gilson 1952b, p. 558); Ockham and Chatton are concerned with the sceptical elements in Peter Aureoli's idiosyncratic development of an *esse apparens* (see note 71 below); and Nicholas of Autrecourt works at articulating a rule for the inference from what appears to us to what is the case (discussed in both Scott 1971 and Weinberg 1948).

63. This was the primary reason at least of Peter John Olivi, Gregory of Rimini and Peter of Ailly. The picture developed in such classics as Michalski 1969 needs to be modified: cf. Copleston 1963, III, p. 148, and Gilson 1955, p. 759, n. 36.

64. For a discussion of some of these issues, see Scott 1971. Buridan's suggestion that science – and he may mean even Aristotelian science – does not need *that* sort of certainty could be either disingenuous or especially sophisticated: *In Metaph. Arist. quaest.*, II, q. 1 (Hyman and Walsh 1967, pp. 704–5). Scott takes the former alternative: 1971, p. 34.

and often linked with intuitive cognition: the role of the 'intelligible species'. Its history is too contorted to be straightened out in the present context, but it is a source of such confusion both in medieval writers and in the interpretation of them that the epistemological issues deserve a brief mention.

There is little enough in Aristotle's texts[65] to insure that a single meaning would be attached to the label. One is well advised to treat 'intelligible species' as equivocal in different theories and to be especially cautious when one writer presents the theory of another. There were two general types: causal and image theories.

Because of the analogy with *visio/imaginatio*, it is tempting to think Scotus' hesitations about an intelligible species in intuitive cognition derive from problems about images; but his theory is causal.[66] And so is Aquinas', for whom the intelligible species is like 'the form by which an agent acts'.[67] That Ockham was sensitive to the general lines of Scotus' account is clear from his conclusion that a mental habit will adequately serve the required purposes.[68] The change reflects the greater autonomy or independence in its activity which Ockham attributes to the human intellect.[69] But it should be kept separate from his criticism of the species as an image.

Ockham's complaint against images, echoed by opponents of an intelligible species in the period following him, was that the introduction of a medium or 'third thing' between concept and object is an opening to scepticism.[70] That critics of the species did not carry the day in the post-Ockham period was due not to a return to the causal theory – or a taste for

---

65. Primarily *De anima* III (e.g., 429^{a}27–8, 431^{b}2). For different 'species' in Aquinas, see Lonergan 1967, pp. 163–8.
66. See Alluntis and Wolter 1975, pp. 515–17 and the references there.
67. *ST*, I, q. 55, art. 1 and q. 85, art. 2; see also Lonergan 1967, pp. 82 and 155.
68. *In Sent.*, II, q. 15 R.
69. The rejection of intelligible species by Henry of Ghent and John Peckham is clearly connected to the Augustinian rejection of anything that suggests the passivity of the intellect with respect to material objects (see Lynch 1972, pp. 67–8 and 98ff.).
70. *In Sent.*, I, d. 27, q. 3. Even Peter Aureoli's strange-sounding claim that intuitive cognition is, like any concept, an *esse apparens* (cf. Gilson 1955, pp. 479–80; *In Sent.*, I, proem., sec. 2, a. 3; and see 14a.1: Peter Aureoli 1952–6, I, pp. 197ff., and II, pp. 696ff.) is motivated in part by the need to eliminate any 'medium' in knowledge: a thought of the object, for Aureoli, simply is the object in its intentional existence. However, when Aureoli says that an intuitive cognition can exist without the object, the sense is altogether different from that given the analogous claim in Ockham's theory. For a discussion of Ockham's criticism of the sceptical import of Aureoli's *esse apparens*, see Adams 1977, pp. 154–63. Walter Chatton's criticism of Aureoli can be found in O'Callaghan 1955, pp. 241–6.

scepticism – but to the resilience of image theories.[71] There were pre-cedents in the older tradition for adopting a triadic scheme in which thinking of an object is taking something as a sign of the object.[72] It is substantive concerns, of course, and not the history of labels that determine the philosophical value of various accounts; and students of the fourteenth century have to be especially sensitive to the difference.

Thomas Aquinas on the intellect and the cognitive process

These sketchy remarks on the intelligible species suggest the possibility of a more radical hypothesis that even 'intellect' may label significantly dif-ferent functions with the result that epistemological issues – at the very least their formulation – may be relative to the model of intellect in which they are embedded. It is a theme that allows us to return to the broader context introduced at the beginning of this section.

Compared to his Franciscan successors – and to Augustine – Aquinas offered a most unusual picture of radical incompleteness in the intellect's operation within the context of human knowing. It is a direct analogue to his account of the soul as incompletely human; and it seems to create a similar sort of scandal.[73] As the human being, for Aquinas, is a body and has a soul – so that the co-principle of soul is not body but matter[74] – so the human cognitive process, for him, is basically a sensory one that is or-ganised and structured by the intellect.[75] The intellect of an angel (an incorporeal being), he says, is not simply a more powerful version of our own; it corresponds in fact to the whole human cognitive apparatus including both sensation and understanding.[76] Consequently, Aquinas

---

71. Most adherents to a species theory in the thirteenth and fourteenth centuries treated the species as an image: a particularly clear case is Giles of Rome (see Lynch 1972, p. 87 and n. 68). See also John of Reading's defense of Scotus in *Super Sententias*, I, d. 3, q. 3, presented in Gál 1969. Fr. Gál's introductory remarks give a brief account of the dispute about the intelligible species from Aquinas to Reading.

72. A triadic definition of the sign relation was used by Augustine (for example in *De magistro*). For a discussion of Abelard's critical and complex account of ideas and images, see Tweedale 1976, pp. 169ff. and 210ff.

73. 'If [the] general theorem [that knowledge is by immateriality] is taken out of its historical context and made the premise of merely dialectical deductions, endless difficulties arise' (Lonergan 1967, p. 150). For Lonergan's account of individuation, see p. 153; for knowledge of individuals, see pp. 168–77 (which covers Aquinas' early and late theories), 179–80, and 184.

74. Anscombe and Geach 1961, p. 98.

75. That is, our experience is bodily: *De veritate*, q. 10 a. 5, and q. 8, a. 11. Contrast the experience of angels: *ST*, I, q. 54, a. 5; q. 57, a. 2; q. 75, a. 1.

76. *ST*, I, q. 57, a. 2. It is the human knower rather than the intellect which cognises the singular: *De veritate*, q. 2, a. 6, *ad* 3; *De anima* III, lect. 8, §§712–16.

uses the principle that a higher power can do what a lower power can to infer from the fact that sensation is a cognition of material singulars the conclusion that angels can cognise them intellectually.[77] But he denies that a similar conclusion can be drawn for the human intellect.[78]

It is sensory presentation, the 'matter' of our experience, that carries the presence of things for us within Aquinas' scheme.[79] That in itself was not unusual. But where the focal point of knowledge of singulars for Ockham was the application of concept to individual and for Scotus was the unity and reality of the individual thing represented by a complex of characterisations, the important polarity for Aquinas was not thought and thing but thought and data.[80] Our knowledge of a thing is a construct of sensory data organised by the intellect. The knowledge of angels is not; and were they to operate by abstraction from sensory experience, their more powerful intellects could not transform this 'artificial' process.[81]

The limited condition of physical objects, Aquinas thinks, is a match for our 'composite' or bodily mode of knowing.[82] They are individuals because the kind of things they are is differentiated only for being exemplified in this 'stuff' rather than that. And when he says that 'matter is not intelligible', it is not a self-defeating claim that we cannot think of matter, but that, as distinct from some structure which accounts for what something is, matter adds no property or specification. And consequently, if angels have a more complete, direct, and simple intellectual grasp of material singulars than we do, it does not result from their penetrating to something 'in' things which we fail to see but is due to their using a principle of intelligibility of a higher sort than the forms of material singulars themselves.[83]

The world of singular things then, according to Aquinas, is only potentially intelligible as it is sometimes only potentially sensible. It can be made actually sensible, however, by a non-cognitive process: a coloured body in the dark becomes actually visible if a light is lit;[84] and sensation follows unmediatedly when a well-disposed sense apparatus is in the presence of an

---

77. *De veritate*, q. 8, a. 11, *sed contra* §4.
78. *ST*, I, q. 86, a. 1, *ad* 4.
79. *Cognitio singularis* has precedence simply because sensation does: *ST*, I, q. 85, a. 3.
80. Cf. *ST*, I, q. 84, aa. 7–8; q. 86, a. 1; *De veritate*, q. 13, a. 3, *ad* 2 and 3.
81. *ST*, I, q. 57, a. 1, *ad* 3.
82. The forms of physical things do not even exhaust the potentialities of the matter which they inform: *ST*, I, q. 55, a. 2; q. 84, a. 3, *ad* 1. This limitation plays an important role in moral contexts: *ST*, IaIIae, q. 94, a. 4; IIaIIae, q. 120, aa. 1–2.
83. *ST*, I, q. 55, aa. 2–3; q. 56, a. 2; q. 57, a. 1, *ad* 3; q. 85, a. 5.
84. *SCG*, II, Ch. 59, §14.

actually sensible object. In contrast, the step from potential to actual intelligibility involves a cognitive operation.[85] We do not intellectually 'see' physical objects, according to Aquinas; our intellectual grasp of them is accomplished by structuring a sensory manifold, and the intellect's contribution to that construction is in providing the 'form'. This is a complex and perhaps unusual model for cognitive operations, but Aquinas' claims for the directness of sensation and the indirectness of intellection – that material singulars are actually sensible but not actually intelligible – take their significance from it.

Given the autonomy[86] that Scotus and Ockham accorded the intellect, they had to allow it a cognition of singulars in order to account for the knowledge we quite obviously have of existent individuals. The question about a cognitive grasp of singularity is independent and involves different philosophical issues precisely because our knowledge of singularity is already problematic at the level of ordinary claims about what and how we know. Even when that distinction is made, however, the approaches taken by Scotus and Ockham are likely to seem more familiar to a modern reader than does Aquinas' version of an 'incomplete' intellect because an autonomous intellect fits more readily our customary rhetoric of 'the mind'.[87] A similar fit obtains, significantly enough, if we focus the comparison and contrast on the writings of Augustine. And it was no small matter during the medieval period that the rhetoric in classics of Christian spirituality – the journey of the soul to God, the search within, and so on – was more easily accommodated in the model of an autonomous intellect, as were problems about the status and activities of the separated soul.

Conclusion

In sum, from the fact that Scotus and Ockham, in their differing ways, meant to be talking about the same thing as Aquinas was talking about – namely, our knowledge of reality – it does not follow that they must have meant the same thing even by a pivotal concept such as the intellect. And whether Aquinas' scheme was a deviant one for the medieval period or the norm for thirteenth-century theories, the pattern of change in models of intellect from Aquinas through Scotus to Ockham and of relative con-

---

85. *ST*, I, q. 84, a. 4, *ad* 2; *De veritate*, X, 6.
86. The autonomy of the intellect is a natural outcome of the Augustinian emphasis on the activity rather than passivity of the intellect: Gilson 1952b, p. 524 n. 2. See also Belmond 1928, pp. 463–87.
87. At least one more step is needed to transform the medieval idiom of '*extra animam*' into 'outside the mind'; see Matthews 1977.

stancy after that is actually clearer than the pattern of epistemological development.

Commentators on the later Middle Ages who are otherwise quite at odds in their approaches have long felt that something happened with Ockham which set the character of theories of knowledge until the time of Descartes. The growing interest in the epistemology of that period is sure to overthrow any too simple account of its development and will alter, perhaps radically, the now familiar picture of its sceptical tendencies. But the old hypothesis may prove to be right after all when directed not at the justification of knowledge but at its description.

23

INTENTIONS AND IMPOSITIONS

Sources of the concept of intention

The concept of intention played a key role in the discussions of epistemological, logical, and semantic questions in later medieval philosophy.[1] The significantly different use of 'intention' in other fields such as ethics or natural philosophy is not at issue here.[2]

'Intention' in the relevant sense is associated with two concepts that occur already in the writings of Al-farabi and Avicenna, where they are associated with the words "*ma'qul*" and "*ma'na*", both of which were translated into Latin as '*intentio*'.[3] In his commentary on the first chapter of Aristotle's *De interpretatione* Al-farabi understands by "*ma'qul*" – his translation of the Greek word '*noēma*'[4] – a concept or a thought that has to be examined by the logician in two respects: in its relation to things outside the soul and in its relation to words.[5] "*Ma'qul*" means nearly the same as "*ma'na*", which appears already in Al-farabi's *De intellectu et intellecto*[6] and was later used by Avicenna to signify the reality of the known considered as known. Thus *ma'qul*, *ma'na*, or *intentio* is that which is immediately before the mind, whether the object of the intention is outside the mind (in which case the intention is a *first* intention) or itself an intention (in which case the intention is a *second* intention). The distinction between first and second intentions was prefigured in Al-farabi's theory of abstraction.[7]

Second intentions associated with first or primarily known intentions

---

1. I have taken into consideration only such texts as have already been edited or partly edited and discussed by scholars of medieval philosophy. Too few texts have been studied, especially of the thirteenth and fourteenth centuries, to give more than a rather episodic history of the concept of *intentiones*.
2. For this use of '*intentio*' see Engelhardt 1976 with bibliography; and also articles on '*intentio*' in dictionaries of individual philosophers such as Schütz 1895, Baudry 1958, and Garcia 1910.
3. For the root of the concept of *intentio* in Arabic philosophy see Gyekye 1971.
4. Aristotle, *De interpretatione*, 16ᵃ3–18.
5. Al-farabi, *De interpretatione*, quoted by Gyekye 1971, p. 35, n. 16.
6. Al-farabi, *De intellectu et intellecto* in Gilson 1929–30, pp. 118, 119, 144.
7. See Madkour 1934, p. 140.

are designated by Avicenna as the subject of logic.[8] This association of logic with intentions considered as epistemological entities marks the starting point of the development of an 'intentionalistic' logic or logic considered as a *scientia rationalis*, parallel to and sometimes connected with the development of terminist logic, according to which logic was primarily concerned not with concepts but with language, a *scientia sermocinalis*.[9] According to Avicenna an intention is what the inner sense finds in things over and above the phantasms found by the exterior senses.[10] Thus an intention is nearly the same as a concept as well as the foundation of the concept's content – one reason why the ontological status of intentions was ambivalent from the beginning.[11]

Roger Bacon on intentions

Roger Bacon considered intentions as 'determinations' of the things acting upon the highest inner senses and leading to the cognitive operations of the mind. Ontological problems aside, however, Bacon's threefold distinction among modes of abstraction seems important for the epistemological and logical application of the notion of intentions. The first mode is the abstraction of a thing from a thing. This belongs to the domain of mathematics, where mathematical entities (*res mathematicae*) are abstracted from real things (*sensibilia*). Second is the abstraction of an intention from a thing. This belongs to the domain of physics, where such intentions as *man* and *horse* are abstracted from singulars. Finally, there is the abstraction of an intention from an intention. This belongs to the domain of logic, which deals with such second intentions as *species* in their association with first intentions. The second intention *species* may, for instance, be founded on the first intention *man*. The same is true of *genus* and other universal concepts with which logic deals.[12] (*Genus*, like *species*, is a second intention; third and higher intentions seem not to have been recognised.)

---

8. Avicenna 1508, *Metaphysica*, I, ii; f. 70ra: 'Subiectum vero logicae, sicut scisti, sunt intentiones intellectae secundo quae apponuntur intentionibus primo intellectis.'

9. For a characterisation of terminist logic see Kneale 1971, pp. 198–297, Boehner 1965, p. 228 and Kretzmann 1967, pp. 370ff.

10. Avicenna 1508, *De anima*, I, v; f. 5ra: 'Intentio autem est id quod apprehendit anima de sensibili quamvis non prius apprehendit illud sensus exterior.' ... 'Differentia autem inter apprehendere formas et apprehendere intentionem hec est quod forma est illa quam apprehendit sensus interior et sensus exterior simul.' (= Avicenna Latinus 1972, p. 86).

11. Avicenna 1508, says that an intention has a lesser being than its object has; *Metaphysica*, IX, iii; f. 103vb: 'Omnis enim intentio est propter id quod intenditur et est minoris esse quam id quod intenditur.' On further complications in the ontological status of intentions, see Vescovini 1965, pp. 64ff. and 80ff.

12. The basic text is Bacon's *Quaestiones super IV Metaphysicae*, IV, i (Bacon 1905–40, XI, pp. 89–90).

Thomas Aquinas on intentions and operations of the mind

Thomas Aquinas provided a much more detailed and systematic treatment of intentions than Bacon had done.[13] In epistemological contexts he uses the expression '*intentio intellecta*' and defines such an 'understood intention' as a likeness of the thing known, a likeness conceived within the intellect. The intention is not the thing itself in its physical reality nor is it the substance of the intellect itself; the intention is rather a sort of accident of the intellect, a likeness of the thing signified by extramental words. It is to be identified with the inner word (*verbum interius*, or *mentis*), which is the significate of the outer word. The being of the understood intention consists in its being known.[14]

Thomas distinguishes between what is primarily known – i.e., the extramental reality to which the intellect is first directed as its objects – which is the object of first intentions; and the secondarily known – i.e., the intellect itself in various modes of cognition, the domain of second intentions.[15] Second intentions (or *secunda intellecta*, as Thomas sometimes calls them) are indeed the subject of logic, as Avicenna had said; but logic is concerned with second intentions considered not as epistemological or psychological entities but only as representations of the objects from which they derive. Logic considers the concept or intention not in itself, but only in the relation of likeness it has to the object conceived of. What is represented in the intellect by a first intention is the intelligible nature (or essence) of the thing known apprehended absolutely – i.e., before it has been confined to either of the two possible modes of existence: in reality or in the soul. Since intentions are related both to the thing known and to the knower, two ways of studying their nature are possible: epistemology is concerned with the correspondence of the understood nature to the nature existing in reality, while logic studies the accidents that follow upon the existence of this nature in the soul. Logic is concerned with what happens to the absolute nature as a result of its being in the intellect. It is not the

---

13. The following remarks concerning Aquinas derive from Schmidt 1966, pp. 94ff.
14. Aquinas, *SCG*, IV, xi: 'Dico autem intentionem intellectam id quod intellectus in seipso concipit de re intellecta. Quae quidem in nobis neque est ipsa res, quae intelligitur; neque est ipsa substantia intellectus; sed est quaedam similitudo concepta in intellectu de re intellecta, quam voces exteriores significant; unde et ipsa intentio verbum interius nominatur, quod est exteriori verbo significatum.'
15. Aquinas, *De potentia* VII, ix: 'Prima enim intellecta sunt res extra animam, in quae primo intellectus intelligenda fertur. Secunda autem intellecta dicuntur intentiones consequentes modum intelligendi: hoc enim secundo intellectus intelligit in quantum reflectitur supra seipsum, intelligens se intelligere et modum quo intelligit.'

nature itself represented in the *intentio intellecta* that is the subject of the science of logic, but rather the accidents which that nature acquires from the manner (or mode) in which it exists in the intellect.[16]

According to Thomas' general division of the three operations of the mind (*operationes animae*, or *mentales*), the first operation, the abstractive apprehension of quiddities, gives rise to the intention of universality; the second operation, the composition of judgement, gives rise to the intention of attribution or predication; and the third operation, the discursive process from one thing to another, gives rise to the intention of consequence (*consequentia*).[17] Although they exist in the intellect, all these intentions are founded on natures that exist in the things themselves, and they are attributed by the intellect to those natures. For example, the intention *genus* does not exist in a donkey, but it is the nature of animal, which does exist in the donkey, to which that intention is attributed.[18]

Henry of Ghent on intentions and words

Henry of Ghent, referring to Thomas' doctrine of the '*intentio intellecta*',[19] took intentions to have being only within the actual consideration of the intellect. Thus the intellect is able to form two intentions of one and the same thing, although this duality must not be purely fictive. Just as leaves as well as fruits are drawn from one root, so different intentions may be drawn from one thing. An intention is the result of the relation or relations between the knower and the thing known. An extramentally existing thing is composed of intentions only virtually (not actually, as it is composed of parts). The universal '*in potentia*' becomes an intention '*in actu*' as soon as the thing is known in some way by the intellect.[20]

In his *Summa quaestionum ordinarium* Henry draws distinctions among three semantic levels:[21] (1) words signifying pure realities, (2) words signifying first intentions, (3) words signifying pure (second) intentions.

16. See Schmidt 1966, pp. 124ff., for further evidence.
17. See Schmidt 1966, p. 127.
18. Aquinas, *In I Sent.*, XXXIII, i, 1, *ad* 3: 'In omnibus autem intentionibus hoc communiter verum est, quod intentiones ipsae non sunt in rebus, sed in anima tantum: sed habent aliquid in re respondens, scilicet naturam, cui intellectus huiusmodi intentiones attribuit; sicut intentio generis non est in asino, sed natura animalis, cui per intellectum haec intentio attribuitur.'
19. See Brown 1971, p. 253.
20. Cf. Henry of Ghent 1518, *Quodl.* V, xii, c; 171 X–Y: 'Unde et intentio non dicitur esse aliquid in re ut est extra, sed solum ut cadit in intellectus actuali consideratione considerantis unum in re ut duo intentione, quod vere non fictive duo est intentione, quia in natura illius rei ut in fundamento et quasi in radice est utraque intentio educenda de ea opere intellectus tamquam res rationis et intellectus, quemadmodum in ligno velut in radice sunt folia et fructus ut diversa educenda opere naturae tamquam res naturae.'
21. The following passages are based upon Henry of Ghent 1520, LIII, v. H–K; f. 64ᵛ.

Words of level (1), such as 'this man' or 'Peter', signify singulars. The being of these singulars in no way depends on their being considered by the intellect. Words of level (2), such as 'man' or 'animal', are ambivalent in their signification. On the one hand they signify a universal considered as the product of abstraction from singulars; on the other hand they signify the reality itself considered as actually formed by that universal nature. Since the 'real sciences' (as distinct from the rational or sermocinal sciences) are concerned with things only in their universal natures, it is words of the second level rather than of the first that are used in the propositions of the 'real sciences'. Words of level (3) signify the relations between things that have already been taken into consideration by the intellect. But among words of the third level a further distinction is to be drawn between words of *logical* intentions, which are founded on things, and words of *grammatical* intentions, which have to do with *words* associated with things. Thus such words for words as 'name', 'substantive', and 'verb' are words of grammatical intentions. Third-level words of logical intentions, such as 'genus', 'species', and 'differentia', are used in logic, the science that studies reality insofar as it is expressible in words. Words for words are used in grammar, where words for things are considered only in their status as words. Logic thus has a stronger connection with reality than does grammar, which is truly a *scientia sermocinalis*.[22]

The Pseudo-Kilwardby on intentions and words

Another three-part division of word-levels appears in a commentary on the *'Priscianus maior'* which until recently has been wrongly ascribed to Robert Kilwardby.[23] We are to distinguish among words for things, words for intentions, and words for words. The imposition of words on things takes place in metaphysics, the imposition of words on intentions takes place in logic, and the imposition of words on words takes place in grammar.[24] The principles of grammar are the *'modi significandi'*; the

---

22. Cf. Henry of Ghent 1520, LIII, v. I; f. 64ᵛ: 'Consideratio primarum intentionum, quae est rerum secundum se, pertinet ad scientias reales. Consideratio vero secundarum intentionum, quae vel est circa res ut sunt expressibiles vocibus, et hoc quo ad intentiones logicales, vel est circa ipsas voces, et hoc quo ad intentiones grammaticales, pertinet ad scientias sermocinales; et tamen logica minus sermocinalis et magis realis est quam grammatica et quasi media inter scientias reales et grammaticam.'

23. For the text with an introduction including a discussion of the authorship see Pinborg *et al.* 1975.

24. *Commentary on 'Priscianus Maior'*, 2.1.11, in Pinborg *et al.* 1975, p. 77: 'Primorum nominum impositio pertinet ad metaphysicum, cuius est res generaliter et per se considerare. Secundorum nominum impositio pertinet ad logicum, cuius est per se intentiones considerare; est enim logica de secundis intentionibus adiunctis primis, ut dicit Avicenna. Tertiorum nominum impositio pertinet ad grammaticum, cuius est considerare nomina partium orationis secundum eorum proprias rationes.'

principles of logic are the common intentions that are founded on things. Since the principles of the two sciences have different causes, logic is not to be subordinated to grammar.[25]

Robert Kilwardby on intentions and words

In the undoubtedly authentic *De ortu scientiarum* Robert Kilwardby identifies first intentions with the things themselves.[26] Words of first intention, such as 'substance' or 'quantity', signify the things themselves. Second intentions are the '*rationes*' of the things, such as *universal* or *particular*. The relation between logic and grammar is not reflected within this context, however, as it is in the divisions considered above.

The connection between intentions and impositions

During the thirteenth and fourteenth centuries two distinctions that had been parallel distinctions in separate domains became increasingly interconnected: the distinction between first and second intentions (which has been discussed above) and the distinction between first and second impositions.[27] The latter distinction can be traced back to Porphyry[28] and Boethius[29] and is based on the observation that whereas some signs have been imposed in order to signify non-signs, others are signs of signs. Accordingly, words of first imposition are (conventional) signs of extralinguistic entities, and words of second imposition are (conventional) signs of linguistic entities. In terms of this distinction Aristotle's *Categories* was seen as a discussion of words of first imposition, while the subject matter of *De interpretatione* involved words of second imposition, such as

25. *Commentary on 'Priscianus Maior'* 1.3.4, in Pinborg *et al.* 1975, pp. 25–6: 'Sed principia grammaticae non habent ordinem ad principia logicae, quia principia grammaticae sunt modi significandi vel consignificandi, generales vel speciales dictionum. Principia per quae procedit logica et quae considerat sunt communes intentiones fundatae in rebus, sicut sunt universale, particulare, genus, species, causa, causatum et sic de aliis. Modi autem significandi res aut consignificandi et communes rerum intentiones non habent ordinem sed potius disparationem, cum a diversis causentur. Et ideo clarum est quod non subalternabit grammatica logicam.'

26. Robert Kilwardby 1976, 459, p. 157.24–32: 'Res enim ipsae sunt primae intentiones, et nomina eas significantia, cuiusmodi sunt substantia, quantitas et huiusmodi, sunt nomina primarum intentionum; sed rationes rerum, cuiusmodi sunt universale, particulare, antecedens, consequens et huiusmodi, sunt secundae intentiones, et nomina eas significantia nomina secundarum intentionum. Et dicuntur illae primae et istae secundae, quia primo comprehenduntur res et deinde ex consideratione et collatione rerum ad invicem colliguntur rationes earum.'

27. In the following passages I depend on Kretzmann 1967, pp. 369–71. For the history of the doctrine of first and second imposition see Dal Pra 1954.

28. Cf. Porphyry 1887, pp. 57–8.

29. Boethius 1860g, *PL* 64, c. 159 B–C: 'Ergo prima positio nominis secundum significationem vocabuli facta est, secunda vero secundum figuram: et est prima positio, ut nomina rebus imponerentur, secunda vero ut aliis nominibus ipsa nomina designarentur.'

'name', 'verb', 'proposition', and the like. The distinction between impositions is obviously a close parallel to the distinction between first and second intentions, since first intentions are (natural) signs of extramental entities and second intentions are (natural) signs of first intentions and so can be considered as signs of signs.

The two distinctions became complicated and confused for two main reasons. First, there were, of course, vocal or written terms imposed on first and second intentions – terms such as 'humanity' and 'genus'. Such terms were all of first imposition, since the intentions they were imposed upon were not conventional signs, but they could also be further described as names of first intention – 'humanity' – or of second intention – 'genus'. The second complicating factor was that the first and second intentions themselves were considered to be the terms in mental propositions. Thus whereas in the spoken or written proposition 'Animal is a genus' the subject and predicate terms are both of first imposition, in the mental proposition that animal is a genus the subject term is a first intention and the predicate term is a second intention. The relationship between the two distinctions was systematically elaborated by William Ockham.[30]

John Duns Scotus on intentions and knowledge

Scotus' theory of intentions[31] is characterised by a twofold understanding of the intention in an epistemological context: the intention as a formal structure in the thing itself and the intention as a concept.[32] Scotus defines the second intention as a rational relation (*relatio rationis*) of which one relatum is an act of judging on the part of the intellect.[33] Correspondingly, a first intention is to be understood as a rational relation of which one relatum is a *simple* act on the part of the intellect. First intentions are

30. See below.
31. The theory has been carefully examined in Swiezawski 1934. In the following passages concerning Scotus I draw on this article, but I do not present Swiezawski's conclusions, since they are true only of the Scotists, not of Scotus himself.
32. *Reportata Parisiensia*, II, d. 13, q. 1, n. 4; Scotus 1891–5, XXIII, p. 440: '... nomen intentio aequivocum uno modo dicitur actus voluntatis; secundo ratio formalis in re, sicut intentio rei, a qua accipitur genus, differt ab intentione, a qua accipitur differentia; tertio modo dicitur conceptus; quarto ratio tendendi in obiectum, sicut similitudo dicitur ratio tendendi in illud cuius est; et isto modo dicitur lumen intentio, vel species lucis.' For present purposes the definitions given in 'secundo' and 'tertio' are essential.
33. Scotus, *Ordinatio*, I, d. 23, q. unica, 10; Scotus 1950–, V, p. 352.12–18: '... omnis intentio secunda est relatio rationis, non quaecumque, sed pertinens ad extremum actus intellectus componentis et dividentis vel saltem conferentis unum ad alterum (hoc patet, quia intentio secunda – secundum omnes – causatur per actum intellectus negotiantis circa rem primae intentionis, qui non potest causare circa obiectum nisi tantum relationem vel relationes rationis).' Cf. also *Lectura*, I, d. 23, q. unica, 12; Scotus 1950–, XVII, p. 306.10–13*.

directed towards the absolute forms that determine the objects of simple intellectual acts. A second intention is produced by a complex act that compares two objects previously apprehended by simple acts and formed into first intentions.[34] Every object in its being known can be a first intention. Even a second intention considered simply as being known can become a first intention. Likewise, second intentions can be based on other second intentions. The second intention *genus* considered as a formal structure in the thing that is animal – i.e., the universal structure by which animal is a genus of the species *man* – can be comprehended by a simple act and as such can be a first intention. Put in relation to another first intention it can constitute a further second intention. Every intention exists to the degree to which it is effectively and concretely thought. In comparison with extramental reality, an intention has diminished being, an '*esse diminutum*' or '*esse cognitum*'.[35] The logician has to study intentions as such, while the metaphysician is concerned with them insofar as they are things. The proper subject of logic is the second intention founded on the first, the prime example of such a combination being the syllogism.[36]

The role of intentions in speculative grammar

In the period between Aquinas and Scotus, the second half of the thirteenth century, intentions were very eagerly discussed by an unusual group of philosophers working in linguistic theory, the Modistae.[37] The Modistae differ from the terminist logicians in that they all give a special ontological interpretation of the *modi significandi*, one that determines the ontological interpretation of logic. The key concept of terminist logic, supposition, is seldom used by the Modistae, and then only in a rudimentary way. Their interests tend more to metalogical questions, to the character of logical laws and logical concepts, than to the development of logic itself. The logic of the Modistae is even further from Aristotelian logic than is terminist logic, although it, too, finds its source in Aristotle's logical writings. And although its non-Aristotelian developments are quite different from those of terminism, it is also influenced by some theories of terminist logic. The

---

34. See Swiezawski 1934, pp. 221ff.
35. See Swiezawski 1934, p. 236.
36. See Swiezawski 1934, pp. 238ff.
37. To these belong, among others, Thomas of Erfurt, Peter of Auvergne, and Simon of Faversham as well as Duns Scotus (as a commentator on Aristotle's logical works), and Radulphus Brito. For the history of the '*modi significandi*' see Pinborg 1967a; 1972, pp. 102ff.; Bursill-Hall 1971, pp. 42ff. For manuscripts and editions of philosophers mentioned above see Pinborg 1975, pp. 41ff.

Modistae chiefly taught at Paris, while the Oxford tradition remained more closely associated with terminism.

According to the Modistae, logic is to be divided on the basis of the three operations of the mind: apprehension, judgement, and ratiocination. Each of these operations represents an act from which special logical concepts or second intentions result. These are the main subject of logic. To the first operation, the simple apprehension of quiddities, belong simple intentions – i.e., such non-complex terms as are treated in Porphyry's *Isagoge* and Aristotle's *Categories*: 'genus', 'species', 'differentia', and so on. Intentions referring to propositions belong to the second operation, predication and judgement. They are treated in Aristotle's *De interpretatione* and in the first book of the *Posterior Analytics*. Intentions referring to a set of propositions belong to the third operation, ratiocination – e.g., the intention *syllogism* – and these are treated in the *Prior Analytics*, the second book of the *Posterior Analytics*, the *Topics*, and the *Sophistici elenchi*.[38]

All the intentional entities, first intentions as well as second intentions, are drawn from the properties of the objects signified. A proper *modus essendi* corresponds to each first intention, a common *modus essendi* to each second intention.

Intentions and speculative grammar in Radulphus Brito

In the writings of Radulphus Brito[39] the modistic analyses are refined and extended. Partly in connection with grammatical analysis Brito develops the following theory of intentions, based on the triad of thing, concrete intention, and abstract intention. Whenever a thing is known, a cognition arises in respect of an abstract intention. The act of cognition and that intention are identical.[40] The intentions originate from the fact that the object and the active intellect act together on the potential intellect, the active intellect's role being to abstract from all the particular and material conditions of the object.[41] The resulting abstract intention is signified by such abstract words as 'humanity' or 'animality'; it is the essence or pure form of the object or of the feature conceived. This abstract intention has

38. See, e.g. Boethius of Dacia 1976, pp. 3ff.; Radulphus Brito, Prooemium to his *Quaestiones super Porphyrium* (forthcoming).
39. The important texts are to be found in Brito's commentary on Porphyry, in his *Quaestiones* on Aristotle's *De anima*, in his commentary on the Sentences and in various *Sophismata*, especially in the sophisma '*Aliquis homo est species*'. For a survey of Brito's life and works, manuscripts and editions, see Pinborg 1975a, pp. 71–97, Fauser 1973, pp. 3–36, and the forthcoming edition of Brito's *Quaestiones super Porphyrium*.
40. Brito, *De anima* III, q. 25; in Fauser 1973, pp. 296–7.
41. Brito, *De anima* III, q. 16; in Fauser 1973, p. 236.

being only in the intellect and is a psychological entity.[42] What is known is not the intention, however, but rather the thing as it stands under that abstract intention.[43] The complex aggregate consisting of the thing and the abstract intention is called the concrete intention. The abstract intention is the same as the cognition, and the concrete intention is the same as the thing known. In its material part – i.e., the thing – the concrete intention exists extramentally; in its formal part – i.e., the intention *per se* – it exists in the intellect. Thus the two intentions, abstract and concrete, are formally identical but materially distinct. In an analogy with real accidents, it might be said that there is a relation of denomination between the intention and the thing. Just as real accidents denominate their subjects, so intentions denominate their objects. For example, the whiteness inherent in a man is the reason why the man can be correctly called white; that same whiteness is also the reason why the intellect can form the intention *whiteness* and associate it with that man in a concrete intention. Objects thus cause intentions and are in turn denominated by them; but this must not be taken to mean that the intention thus formed is a part of the object.[44] Only a concrete intention is predicable of an object, not qua concept (its formal aspect) but only qua thing (its material aspect). The abstract intention represents the formal aspect under which the predication is accomplished. The real man is predicated under the aspect of his *humanity*.[45]

Whenever the cognition of an object occurs under the aspect of a proper *modus essendi* of the thing, an absolute and primary cognition arises, a first intention. Whenever the cognition occurs under the aspect of a *modus essendi* which the thing has in common with other things, a relative, secondary cognition arises. The common *modi essendi*, from which the second intentions are drawn, do not belong to the essence of the object but are rather the foundation of an external relation.[46] The foundation of the cognition of a second intention – e.g., as expressed in the proposition 'Man is a species' – is the same man as constitutes the foundation of the cognition of a first intention, as expressed in the proposition 'Man is an animal'. The

42. Brito, *In Porphyrium*, q. 11; in Pinborg 1974, p. 52, n. 18: 'intentio in abstracto est de consideratione naturalis'.
43. Brito, *De anima*, III, q. 7; in Fauser 1973, p. 176: 'Illud quod intelligitur, de se est quiditas rei secundum se, cui accidit et esse signatum et esse abstractum. Tamen intelligitur sub esse quod habet in anima, ita quod illud esse quod habet in anima, non est illud quod intelligitur, sed illud, sub quo res intelligitur.'
44. Brito, *In Porphyrium*, q. 8; in Pinborg 1974, pp. 51–2.
45. Brito, *In Porphyrium*, q. 13 and q. 8; in Pinborg 1974, p. 53.
46. Brito, *In Porphyrium*, q. 5 and q. 7; in Pinborg 1974, pp. 52–3.

modus essendi is different in each case, but in both cases the real man is the subject.[47]

The predicates of second intention are the logician's concern. He has to work out the accidental relations of those predicates and to establish the logical rules that are accidental in relation to the quidditative cognition of the things. The second intentions belong to the category of quality. They are *passiones animae* caused by the real *modi essendi*. The logician does not consider them in this respect, however, but rather in their accidental relations when they are considered as the likenesses of the things.[48]

In the domain of the first mental operation, the apprehension of quiddities, the connection between the corresponding second intentions, such as the universals *genus* or *species*, and the thing itself is guaranteed in the sense mentioned above. On the level of the second and third mental operations, judgement and ratiocination, however, it becomes difficult to preserve the connection between second intentions and the things. Within these latter operations it is not really the things that are the immediate objects, but rather certain constructs of the intellect – complex objects, as Brito calls them – and the relations of these objects to other '*complexa*' existing only on a mental level. Thus it seems that not all second intentions share the same degree of reality.[49]

According to a revised version of Brito's theory,[50] even the intentions of the higher mental operations are materially connected with the thing, because the relation between the terms (concepts) in a proposition or in a syllogism corresponds to a *modus essendi* of the thing in virtue of the fact that all logical operations have to be interpreted and verified of the things. This interpretation and verification is not the task of the logician, however. He need not concern himself with the specific nature of the objects. Instead, the logician considers them as genus, as species, and so on. In this way he is able to draw conclusions, but not in his role as logician to verify them.[51] The bond between logic and the real sciences is not broken in principle, however. According to Brito and the Modistae, logic is the speculative

---

47. Brito, *In Porphyrium*, q. 8; in Pinborg 1974, p. 53, n. 19.
48. See Pinborg 1974, p. 54, and Pinborg 1969, p. 174, where Pinborg gives an extract from the text of Brito's sophisma '*Aliquis homo est species*'.
49. In this sense Brito discusses the intentions which belong to the higher operations in the sophisma mentioned above. See Pinborg 1972, pp. 91–2. For another extract from the text see ibid. 197–9 and in Pinborg 1975, p. 58, n. 69.
50. Given in Brito's sophisma '*Omnis homo est homo/omnis homo de necessitate est animal*'. Cf. Pinborg 1975b, p. 58, and Pinborg 1969, pp. 170–4.
51. See Pinborg 1972, pp. 80ff., and Pinborg 1975a, pp. 58–9.

science of 'the conceptual order that parallels the synthetic structure internal to the things'.[52]

By his treatment of second intentions as the subject of logic Brito secured the foundations of a logic that was developed by various thinkers, especially by the Thomists and the Scotists. Treatises on this sort of logic continued to be written in the sixteenth century.[53] Reflections on the intentions found their natural place in the commentaries on Aristotle and on the Sentences (especially in the context of the question concerning the theology of the Trinity, whether 'person' is a word of first or of second intention: I, d. 23) as well as in special treatises *De intentionibus*.

Reactions to Brito

In the writings of Hervaeus Natalis[54] and Peter Aureoli the theory of intentions developed by Brito was more or less modified. But it was also attacked rather forcefully both by nominalists (especially Ockham) and by realists (especially Walter Burley).

Peter Aureoli on intentions

According to Peter Aureoli[55] an intention is not to be identified with the act of cognition. What is being predicated (both in first and in second order predications) is neither acts of cognition nor extramental things, but rather the objective concept of the thing. ('Objective' here is taken in the medieval sense in which it indicates the conceptual content that appears to the intellect but is strictly speaking not a component [*subiective*] part of the intellect in the way actually formed concepts considered as psychological entities are component parts of the intellect.) Thus second intentions are not founded on the primary cognition of the thing but rather on the objective content of the first order concept that is formed.[56] The cognition establishes not only a relation of denomination between intention and thing but also a special 'intentional being' (*esse intentionale*). It is in its

52. Moody 1935, p. 303.
53. For the history of this development see Hickmann 1971.
54. See Pinborg 1974, pp. 54–5, who gives some information about Hervaeus' theory in his treatise 'De secundis intentionibus' (MS Basel UB B III, 22, especially f. 143), and Domanski 1966.
55. For the discussion of Aureoli I depend on Pinborg 1974, pp. 56–9. The basic text is Peter Aureoli, *In Sententias*, I, d. 23, art. 2 (MS Vat. Borgh. lat. 329, ff. 260ʳ–264ʳ). A short survey of Aureoli's arguments is provided by the list of '*Capitula*' in Aureoli 1952–6, pp. 59–61.
56. Aureoli, *In Sententias*, I, d. 23, art. 2 (f. 260ʳᵃ): 'Actus autem intellectus quo universalitas apprehenditur non inest tamquam subiecto actui quo intelligitur animal. Quamvis enim inter eos sit ordo praesuppositionis, non tamen inhaerentiae habitudo. Ergo prima et secunda intentio per prius et formalius se tenent ex parte obiectivorum conceptuum quam ex parte actus intellectus.'

intentional being that the thing appears to the intellect, but the appearance takes on different forms according to the intellect's settling on one or another objective concept. For example, the concepts *man* and *animal*, which are both predicable of Socrates, are distinct intentional entities of this kind, not to be found in Socrates himself.[57] Aureoli himself gives the following concise account of his theory of intentions:

An intention is the objective concept formed by the intellect containing in itself indistinguishably the passive conception and the thing conceived. 'Intention' is the same as 'concept', and 'first intention' the same as 'concept of the first order', which the intellect forms of the things without reflecting on its own concepts. Second intentions are concepts of the second order, which the intellect constructs by reflection on the first concepts: *universality*, *predicability*, and the like concerning the simple mental operation of apprehension; *affirmation* or *negation* concerning the second mental operation of judgement; and *the connection of the extremes of a syllogism* concerning the third mental operation, the discursive and ratiocinative act.[58]

Walter Chatton and William Ockham on intentions and impositions

Aureoli's separation of the content of the concept from the act of cognition and his association of intentions with a special *esse obiective* brought onto-logical problems to the fore again. These problems were clearly discerned by Walter Chatton, a contemporary of Aureoli and Ockham. Chatton's criticism was directed against the *esse obiectivum* of the concept, which he saw as an unnecessary mediator between object and cognition. Ockham accepted Chatton's view after having propagated the so-called *fictum*-theory for some time.[59] For Ockham, however, this question was a secondary problem for his theory of concepts or intentions.[60] According to Ockham the primary problem is whether the intentions are not simply to be identified with the mental terms of propositions and arguments.

During an earlier period, in his commentary on the Sentences, Ockham had defined the first intention as the really existing thing itself, the second intention as something in the soul that bears a relation to the things and can be predicated by means of words which in a proposition have simple rather than personal supposition.[61] In his later *Summa logicae* Ockham provided

57. See for the text Pinborg 1974, pp. 56–7.
58. See for the text Pinborg 1974, pp. 58–9.
59. For the controversy between Ockham and Chatton see Gál 1967c, pp. 191–212.
60. See Knudsen 1975, pp. 10–14.
61. Ockham 1495–6, *In Sententias*, I, d. 23 D: '... intentio prima vocatur res realiter existens. Intentio autem secunda vocatur aliquid in anima rebus applicabile praedicabile de nominibus rerum, quando non habent suppositionem personalem, sed simplicem'.

definitions of intentions that are suited to the *intellectio*-theory propagated by Chatton, according to which a concept is the act of cognition itself.[62]

According to Ockham there are no *intentiones ex parte rei* corresponding to the intentions properly so-called, as in Brito's theory. There is no need for entities intermediate between intentions and objects. An intention is something in the soul which is a natural sign signifying something for which it can stand, or which can be a part of a mental proposition.[63] A first intention is a natural sign of something that is not itself a sign. A second intention is a natural sign that signifies other natural signs or first intentions. The first intention or concept *man* naturally signifies all men and each individual man; the second intention *species* is a natural sign of the natural sign *man* and of other species-intentions. The signs of spoken language correspond in a special way to the intentions considered as natural language signs: they are arbitrarily (*ad placitum*) connected with certain significates – i.e., they have been imposed by men on certain objects in the relation of signification, the intellectual side of which involves the intentions.

Ockham makes use of the traditional distinction between words of first and of second imposition in the following way. Spoken names (nouns or adjectives) are either of first or of second imposition, and within this general distinction of names the distinction between first and second intentions is a sub-distinction. Names of second imposition are names of names – i.e., they are conventional signs that signify conventional signs as such. For instance, the spoken word 'name' signifies every name such as 'man' or 'animal'. In this connection Ockham distinguishes between names of second imposition in the strict sense – those that have no corresponding elements in mental language, e.g., the name 'conjugation' – and names of second imposition in the broad sense – those that do have such corresponding elements, e.g., 'verb' and 'name'.[64] Names of first imposition are all those that are not names of second imposition either in the strict sense or in the broad sense; but syncategorematic words such as 'not' or 'only' do not belong to names of first imposition in the strict sense; indeed, they are not names at all.

Ockham introduced the distinction between names of first and second

---

62. In the following discussion I depend on Boehner 1958, pp. 201–32; the basic text is *Summa logicae* I, Chapter 12; Ockham 1974a, pp. 41–4. An English translation of *Summa logicae* I is in Loux 1974; for our text see pp. 73–4.
63. Ockham 1974a, I, c. 12; p. 43.41–4.
64. Ockham 1974a, I, c. 11; pp. 38.4–39.31.

intention (a distinction applied here of course to spoken signs and not to intentions themselves or mental signs) within the class of names of first imposition in the strict sense.[65] Names of second intention in the strict sense are imposed precisely in order to signify intentions of the soul, which are natural signs. Names of second intention in the broad sense are imposed on conventional signs in their capacity as signs. In this broad sense names of second intention can be names either of first or of second imposition.

Names of first intention are imposed in order to signify things or objects that are neither signs nor derived from signs – e.g., 'Plato', 'whiteness'. Some names, however, signify both things and signs; these are the so-called transcendentals: *'unum'*, *'verum'*, *'bonum'*, etc. The transcendentals are nevertheless considered names of first intention.

Names of second imposition belong to the domain of grammar, names of first imposition and second intention belong to the domain of logic, names of first imposition and first intention belong to the domain of the real sciences, and names imposed on the transcendentals belong to the domain of metaphysics.[66]

A controversy arose between Ockham and Chatton concerning the distinction between first and second intentions and their respective supposition in a proposition.[67] For Ockham a first intention is what has personal supposition in a proposition, suppositing for really existing singulars. Words of first imposition and first intention signify singulars directly, and so in their case what is supposited and what is signified coincide. A second intention is a concept that is predicated of a subject that has simple supposition. Thus in the proposition 'Man is a species', 'species' is a second intention and supposits for the same as the word 'man' supposits for in simple supposition – viz., the concept *man*. Words of first imposition and second intention signify concepts as concepts.[68] A first intention extensionally intends singulars; a second intention intends concepts of singulars insofar as those concepts are used for themselves rather than for the singulars – i.e., insofar as they have simple rather than personal supposition. Logic deals with second intentions.

For Chatton a first intention is a natural sign of singulars in their quiddity (or essence). A word of first intention – e.g., 'man' – supposits for

---

65. Ockham 1974a, I, c. 11; pp. 39.36–40.55.
66. Ockham 1974a, I, c. 11; pp. 40.56–41.78.
67. For Ockham's theory of supposition see Boehner 1958, pp. 232–67; the main text is Ockham 1974a, I, cc. 63–7; pp. 193–238.
68. Ockham 1495–6, I, d. 22, C; see also Knudsen 1975, pp. 7–8.

the thing signified in its quiddity. What is supposited and what is signified coincide only *de facto*, not *per se*. A word of second intention stands in a proposition of logic for a concept suppositing simply, but not only for the concept as concept, also for the concept in its function as a sign of many things. The word 'species' signifies the concept *man* not insofar as it is a concept but insofar as it is predicable of many. A second intention is a connotative concept that signifies a concept as a sign of singulars.[69] According to Chatton a concept is signified by a word of second intention not only in its extensionality but also in its intensionality – i.e., in its character as a sign, which derives its applicability to many singulars from the inner structure of the things. Logic deals with the relation between the sign (second intention) and its significate (first intention), which is not a *real* relation. Thus logic is not a 'real science' – i.e., science of reality.[70]

Walter Burley on intentions and the nature of logic

Ockham criticised the logic of intentions introduced by the Modistae particularly because he rejected any sort of reification of the relations between extramental things and concepts or intentions. Realists such as Walter Burley also opposed the Modistic theory, however.[71] According to Burley a word can exercise its function of signification without a special form mediating the act of signification. Just as a corporeal sign, which is a natural thing, can be introduced (or imposed) to signify something – e.g., the hanging barrel-hoop to signify the presence of wine in a tavern – so a natural vocal sound can be introduced to signify something without a new artificial form being added to the sound.[72] Second intentions inhere in the

69. Chatton, *In Sententias*, I, d. 23, art. 2, in Knudsen 1975, p. 24: 'Dico, quod difficile est assignare bonam differentiam. Dico tamen, quod intentio prima est illa, quae significat rem esse talem, qualis est in essendo, secunda, quae significat rem esse signum alterius rei, cuiusmodi sunt praedicari de pluribus vel praedicari de uno solo. Nam conceptum hominis praedicari de pluribus est ipsum esse signum plurium, non quidem significans conceptum esse talem naturam, sed esse signum. Est igitur intentio secunda conceptus relativus significans conceptum illum esse signum plurium vel unius.'

70. *Ibid.* in Knudsen 1975a, pp. 25–6: 'Sed contra ... tunc logica esset scientia realis, quia relatio signi ad significatum est realis, de qua tractat logica ... dico, quod supponit, quod relatio signi ad significatum esset realis, et non est sic.'

71. For this passage see Pinborg 1975a, p. 60.

72. Walter Burley, *In Perihermenias*, cap. '*de nomine*' (for the text and the manuscripts see Pinborg 1975a, p. 60, n. 83): '... quamvis nomen sit nomen per institutionem imponentis tamen non est res artificialis, quia per hoc quod instituitur ad significandum nulla forma accidentalis sibi inhaerens acquiritur. Res enim praesupposita omni impositione imponitur ad significandum. Unde signum, quod est res naturalis, puta circulus, potest institui ad significandum vinum in taberna, ita vox naturalis potest institui ad significandum absque hoc quod aliqua forma nova sibi acquiratur.'

things; they are parts of extramental reality. Whereas Ockham located the intentions strictly within the mind, Burley locates them strictly outside the mind, each man in his different way opposing the Modistae. Since according to Burley the intentions are features of reality, logic, which deals with the intentions, is indeed a 'real science'.[73] This extraordinary interpretation of the nature of the intentions and of the nature of logic was carried on by the so-called Averroists of Bologna.[74]

73. Walter Burley 1478, f. 14ᵛ): '... liber praedicamentorum est de rebus secundum quod eis insunt intentiones secundae, scilicet intentio generis generalissimi et generis subalterni, intentio speciei et sic de aliis'.
74. See Pinborg 1975a.

24
DEMONSTRATIVE SCIENCE

Scientia demonstrativa in the Middle Ages

From the thirteenth century down to the Renaissance, philosophers attempted to forge plausible accounts of Aristotelian 'demonstrative science' and its basis, the 'knowledge-producing syllogism' (*syllogismus faciens scire*). The term '*scientia demonstrativa*' is ambiguous, referring both to the knowledge a demonstrative syllogism effects in someone who understands it and to a system of syllogisms comprising propositions which satisfy the requirements for demonstration stipulated in Aristotle's *Posterior Analytics*. In expounding Aristotle's theory, medieval authors typically interpret and criticise it in the light of their own conceptions and doctrines; for example, their treatments of the requirements that premises of demonstrative syllogisms be true, necessary, and certain invoke various views of truth, necessity, and certainty.[1] So while it is true that almost all the major figures of medieval philosophy in some sense endorse what is traditionally called 'the Aristotelian ideal of demonstrative science', this appearance of unanimity can be misleading. The generalisation that this ideal dominated medieval thinking regarding scientific knowledge obscures or ignores the variety in philosophical accounts of its foundation and scope.[2]

Much of our current understanding of medieval epistemology is based on doctrines concerning acquaintance with and knowledge of particular entities or states of affairs, and the subsequent formation of general concepts. Because discussions of more elaborate cognitive activities, those involving relatively complex judgements and inferences, have until recently received less attention, the full significance of theories of demonstrative science in late medieval epistemology remains to be determined. Similarly, the relationship of those highly abstract theories to the actual

---

1. For reports of the medieval Latin commentaries on the *Posterior Analytics*, see Lohr 1967–74. Discussions relevant to demonstrative science are also regularly found in comments on Book VI, Chapter 6 of the *Nicomachean Ethics* and on Book I, Dist. 39 of the *Sentences*.
2. Barnes summarises a frequently held view: '... the *Analytics* imposed on the learned world a narrow, blinkered logic, and a stultifying theory of science' (Barnes 1975, ix).

practice of natural philosophy and other medieval 'sciences' remains to be established. These topics are closely connected, since the question whether it is possible to attain *scientia demonstrativa* of the natural world was itself at issue. Mathematics – particularly geometry – was often thought to come closest to satisfying Aristotle's requirements for demonstrative science.[3] But the status of natural sciences with respect to the demonstrative ideal was suspect insofar as their premisses fell short of the truth, necessity, or certainty of geometrical axioms. Thus the import of a philosopher's allegiance to the ideal of demonstrative science varies according to his position on at least three topics: (1) the interpretation of the requirements for a demonstrative syllogism; (2) the relationship between demonstrative science and other sorts of knowledge; and (3) the possibility of attaining a demonstrative science of nature.

The theory of demonstrative science in the Posterior Analytics

The basic tenets of the theory of demonstrative science Aristotle presents in the *Posterior Analytics* are simple to identify but difficult to understand and assess. According to Aristotle, full-fledged scientific knowledge of something requires understanding its necessitating causes; this knowledge is produced or best manifested by a demonstrative syllogism.[4] A demonstrative syllogism yields knowledge of a 'reasoned fact' by showing not just that something is so, but why it always must be so; the medievals marked this distinction by the phrases '*demonstratio quia*' (demonstration of the fact) and '*demonstratio propter quid*' (demonstration of the reason why).[5] Such explanatory demonstrations must be syllogisms in *Barbara* whose premisses are true, necessary, certain, immediate, and appropriate to the phenom-

---

3. Many, though certainly not all, of Aristotle's examples are mathematical, and in particular, geometrical; for a discussion of ancient geometrical method and its subsequent history, see Hintikka and Remes 1974.

4. 'Hence that of which there is understanding simpliciter cannot be otherwise ... [It is what we] know through demonstration. By demonstration I mean a scientific deduction; and by scientific I mean one in virtue of which, by having it, we understand something' (*Post. An.* 71[b]16–19; see also 73[a]21–5). (All quotations from the *Posterior Analytics* follow the translation in Barnes 1975.) In part because Aristotle provides no examples which clearly meet all his requirements for demonstrative syllogisms, commentators often emphasise the potential utility of demonstrative syllogisms for displaying or teaching scientific explanations, rather than their efficacy for the discovery of scientific knowledge. See, for example, Barnes *et al.* 1975, pp. 77–87. An example which appears to meet the requirements for demonstration is this: 'Having incisors belongs necessarily to every carnivore. Being carnivorous belongs necessarily to every dog. Therefore: having incisors belongs necessarily to every dog.' See Barnes *et al.* 1975, p. 66.

5. *Post. An.* I, Ch. 13.

enon to be explained.[6] As a proximate cause of what is explained, the middle must be simultaneous with its effect.[7] If a syllogism which meets these requirements is to manifest the nature or necessity of its 'reasoned fact' to a particular person, he must realise that it satisfies all these requirements and thereby explains the fact.[8] While the logical structure of demonstrative or 'scientific' syllogisms is simple, the additional requirements severely limit the number of full-fledged 'scientific' syllogisms. Perhaps Aristotle was content to posit demonstrative syllogisms as an ideal for scientific explanation which could be only approximated in the practice of most sciences.

The early reception of the Posterior Analytics

From John of Salisbury's *Metalogicon*, we know that the *Posterior Analytics* was translated by 1159,[9] but the first full Latin commentary now known was composed by Robert Grosseteste only towards the end of the first quarter of the thirteenth century.[10] The slow reception of the *Posterior Analytics* by twelfth- and even thirteenth-century philosophers is not surprising in view of the difficulty of the text and the differences between its doctrine and the Augustinian assumptions about truth and knowledge which pervaded early medieval thought.

The Augustinian background

While the details of Augustine's theory of knowledge fluctuate somewhat, several fundamental tenets are fixed. God is identified with Truth or Supreme Truth, and the forms or eternal exemplars of things are identified

---

6. '... it is necessary for demonstrative understanding in particular to depend on things which are true and primitive and immediate and more familiar than and prior to and explanatory of the conclusion (for in this way the principles will also be appropriate to what is being proved)' (*Post. An.* 71^{b}20–3). 'Demonstration is deduction from what is necessary' (73^{a}24–5).

7. 'For the middle term must be coeval – something that came about for what came about, something that will be for what will be, ... something that is for what is; but it is not possible for anything to be coeval with "it has come about" and "it will be"' (*Post. An.* 95^{a}38–42).

8. 'Similarly, (there is) both knowledge and opinion of the same thing. For the one is of animal in such a way that it cannot be an animal, and the other in such a way that it can be – e.g. if the one is of just what is man, and the other of man but not of just what is man' (*Post. An.* 89^{a}33–8).

9. The summary occurs in Book IV, Chs. 6–8. It is interesting to note that John emphasises the connection between demonstrative science and pedagogy; one of the merits of having demonstrative knowledge of a subject, he says in Ch. 7, is that it enables one to teach the subject well. Although there were several subsequent translations, the first translation, by James of Venice, remained the standard one. These texts are contained in Minio-Paluello 1968; for a discussion of the quality of James' text, see Dod 1971.

10. For a discussion of the dating of this work, see Dod 1971, pp. 46ff.

with ideas in the divine mind.[11] Insofar as human knowledge involves access to these exemplars, it requires divine aid of some sort.[12] Augustine's most frequent metaphor for knowledge is vision which provides a clear and direct acquaintance with its object; hence the divine aid requisite for knowledge came to be known as divine illumination.[13] Since full understanding or comprehension involves direct acquaintance with eternal exemplars, the highest epistemic state is reached only in a vision of Truth itself.[14]

But this ideal does not exclude the possibility of our having knowledge of temporal objects or of truths given in propositions.[15] Augustine relates his epistemic ideal to his account of mundane knowledge by explaining that in its proper sense the term '*scientia*' refers to knowledge of temporal things, while in its improper or extended sense it refers to knowledge of eternal things, which is more properly called wisdom.[16] Because he believes that wisdom supersedes knowledge, he accords primarily instru-

---

11. 'And Truth is our God who liberates us . . .'; 'Haec est libertas nostra, cum isti subdimur veritati; et ipse est deus noster qui nos liberat . . .' (*De libero arbitrio*, Book II, sec. 37). 'But he does not, therefore, know all his creatures, both spiritual and corporeal, because they are, but they are because he knows them. . . . He created, therefore, because he knew . . . this knowledge, therefore, is quite unlike our knowledge.'
    'Universas autem creaturas suas, et spirituales et corporales, non quia sunt ideo novit; sed ideo sunt quia novit. . . . Quia ergo scivit, creavit . . . longe est ergo huic scientiae scientia nostra dissimilis' (*De Trinitate* Book XV, sec. 13).
12. 'Concerning universals of which we have knowledge, we do not listen to anyone speaking and making sounds outside ourselves. We listen to the truth within us which presides over our minds . . . our real teacher is Christ.'
    'De universis autem, quae intelligimus, non loquentem, qui personat foris, sed intus ipsi menti praesidentem consulimus veritatem . . . Ille autem, qui consultitur, docet . . . est Christus . . .' (*De magistro*, sec. 38).
13. 'But when we have to do . . . with the intelligence and with reason we speak of things which we look upon directly in the inner light of truth which illumines the inner man and is inwardly enjoyed.'
    'Cum vero de his agitur . . . intellectu atque ratione, ea quidem loquimur, quae praesentia contuemur in illa interiore luce veritatis, qua ipse, qui dicitur homo interior, inlustratur et fruitur . . .' (*De magistro*, sec. 40).
14. 'In the preceding book . . . we were occupied in distinguishing the function of the rational mind with respect to temporal things . . . from the more excellent function of this same mind when it is employed in the contemplation of eternal things.'
    'In libro superiore . . . egimus discernere rationalis mentis officium in temporalibus rebus . . . ab excellentiore eiusdem mentis officio, quod contemplandis aeternis rebus impenditur . . .' (*De Trinitate* Book XIII, sec. 1).
15. 'A human mind, therefore, knows all these things which it has acquired through itself, through the senses of its body, and through the reports of others.'
    'Haec igitur omnia, et quae per se ipsum, et quae per sensus sui corporis, et quae testimoniis aliorum percepta scit animus humanus' (*De Trinitate* Book XV, sec. 12, 22).
16. 'If this is the correct distinction between wisdom and knowledge, that intellectual cognition of eternal things should pertain to wisdom, but rational cognition of temporal things to knowledge, then it is not hard to judge which is to be ranked above and which below.'

mental value to knowledge of the natural world, which is a source of signs of the attributes of its creator.[17] And so it is not surprising that Augustine's writings fail to provide extensive analyses of such topics as cognition, induction, and judgement.

Augustine's view of truth and knowledge left several tasks for subsequent Christian thinkers. They had to show how any additional or alternative account of knowledge relates to the putative fact of divine illumination, and then provide a fuller treatment of our acquisition of knowledge of the natural world and of the truth of our judgements about its states of affairs. Augustine's characterisation of God as Truth led to a conception of truths as relationships between something in the world and the relevant divine idea. On the one hand, things in the world are true if they are genuine tokens of the types which God conceives; on the other hand, our thoughts are true when they correspond to what God thinks.[18] The relationship of states of affairs in the natural world to concepts, and the nature of the truth of concepts, judgements, or propositions required considerable clarification.

'Si ergo haec est sapientiae et scientiae recta distinctio, ut ad sapientiam pertineat aeternarum rerum cognitio intellectualis; ad scientiam vero, temporalium rerum cognitio rationalis: quid cui praeponendum sive postponendum sit, non est difficile judicare' (*Ibid.*, Book XII, sec. 15, 25).
'But now we speak of knowledge, later of wisdom ... And we do not take these terms so strictly that one cannot speak either of wisdom in human affairs or knowledge in divine ones. When speaking in broader fashion, one can talk in both cases of wisdom or of knowledge.'
'Sed nunc de scientia loquimur, post de sapientia ... Nec ista duo sic accipiamus, quasi non licet dicere, vel istam sapientiam quae in rebus humanis est, vel illam scientiam quae in divinis. Loquendi enim latiore consuetudine, utraque sapientia, utraque scientia dici potest' (*Ibid.*, Book XIII, sec. 19, 24).

17. 'For without knowledge we cannot even possess the very virtues by which we live rightly ... and arrive at that eternal life which is truly blessed.'
'Sine scientia quippe nec virtutes ipsae, quibus recte vivitur ... ut ad illam quae vere beata est, perveniatur aeternam' (*Ibid.*, Book XII, sec. 14, 21).
'... whoever ... does not inquire further to learn the source of truths ... can be seen to be in no way wise.'
'... quisquis ... non potius quaerere, unde sint vera ... videri potest, esse autem sapiens nullo modo' (*De doctrina christiana* Book II, sec. 38, 57).

18. Augustine characterises the foundation of thought as an inner, prelinguistic word: '... a true word is produced when we say what we know ... the word is most similar to the thing known, and is that word of no language from which its image is also produced.'
'... gignitur verbum verum, quando quod scimus loquimur ... est verbum simillimum rei notae, de qua gignitur et imago eius ... quod est verbum linguae nullius' (*De Trinitate* Book XV, sec. 12, 22).
The 'inner word' resembles either a temporal state of affairs, in the case of sensible truths, or an eternal exemplar, in the case of intelligible truths. See also Book XV, sec. 14, 24. Later Augustine describes the inner word as 'knowledge of knowledge, vision of vision' 'scientia de scientia, et visio de visione' (*Ibid.*, Book XV, sec. 21, 40).

Anselm's Augustinianism

Anselm of Canterbury followed Augustine in identifying God as Truth, but he constructed a more explicit account of the relationship between Truth and particular truths, one that rests on his general definition of truth as 'rightness perceptible by the mind alone'.[19] The standard of rightness for particular things remains God's idea of the essence of things of that type, while the standard of rightness in judgements is their correspondence to what God knows or wills to be the case.[20] In the first sense, someone is a 'true friend' or a 'true artist' when his nature corresponds to the divine idea of a friend or an artist. Anselm explains the truth of propositions or judgements in terms of the second sense of rightness. Here he relies on a view of truth as the correspondence between a proposition and what is the case, but he depicts this correspondence as a species of rightness by reasoning that if a proposition is true, it is doing what it ought to do, i.e. affirming what is the case or denying what is not the case.[21]

Augustinianism in Grosseteste's interpretation of the Posterior Analytics

The first known commentator on the entire *Posterior Analytics* in the Latin West, Robert Grosseteste, in effect endorsed Anselm's Augustinian treatment of the nature of truth. He agrees that the truth of things is their adequate conformity to their 'reasons' in God's mind, while the truth of propositions is a function of the adequate conformity between what they

19. 'Possumus igitur, nisi fallor, definire quia veritas est rectitudo mente sola perceptibilis' (Anselm 1946b, p. 191.19–20).
20. 'If there is no rectitude in those things which ought to have rectitude, except when they are as they ought to be, and this alone amounts to their being right, it is clear that there is one sole rectitude for all these things.'
 'Si rectitudo non est in rebus illis quae debent rectitudinem, nisi cum sunt secundum quod debent, et hoc solum est illis rectas esse: manifestum est earum omnium unam solam esse rectitudinem' (*Ibid.*, p. 199.7–9).
 'Thus there is truth in the being of all things that exist, because they are what they are in the highest truth.'
 'Est igitur veritas in omnium quae sunt essentia, quia hoc sunt quod in summa veritate sunt' (*Ibid.*, p. 185.18–19).
21. 'Thus it is the same for it to be right and to be true, that is, to signify to be the case what is the case . . . It is similar, when an utterance signifies not to be the case what is not so.'
 'Idem igitur est illi et rectam et veram esse, id est significare esse quod est . . . Similiter est, cum enuntiatio significat non esse quod non est' (*Ibid.*, p. 178.22–3 and 27). 'Proposition' is used in its medieval sense here, in which it refers primarily to a spoken sentence. For discussions of the medieval senses of this term, see Kretzmann 1970 and Nuchelmans 1973.

assert and what is the case.[22] He also follows Anselm's account of the unity of truth in asserting that the truths of things and of propositions are simply manifestations of the same exemplar, Truth. But Grosseteste adds a metaphysical explanation of the participation of instances of truth in their exemplar. He maintains the view that things are created and conserved through emanations of divine light; according to this theory, the forms of things which give them their truth are not entirely distinct from the divine emanation, or Truth itself.[23] Drawing an epistemic moral from his metaphysics, Grosseteste infers that whether one understands something as a particular or as a participant in its divine idea, he understands it by means of indirect or direct divine illumination. Since divine light gives things the forms through which they are intelligible, it always plays a role in knowledge, regardless of the knower's awareness of it.[24]

Grosseteste's Augustinian assumptions about truth and knowledge influence his interpretation of the *Posterior Analytics*. Although he generally agrees with what he takes to be Aristotle's account of demonstrative science, he places it within the framework of his metaphysical and epistemological theory of divine illumination. His theocentric theory of truth provides a cosmic context for understanding the requirement that demonstrative premises be true. The commitment to divine illumination also affects his treatment of the requirement that the premises of scientific syllogisms which are indemonstrable first principles or definitions must be more certain than their conclusion. Aristotle indicates that experience and

---

22. '... the truth of each thing is its conformity to its reason in the eternal word ...'
    '... veritas cuiuscunque est eius conformitas rationi suae in aeterno Verbo ...' (Grosseteste 1912c, p. 137.1–2).
    '... the truth [of a declarative sentence] will be an adequate conformity between interior speech and a thing ...'
    '... erit veritas [orationis enuntiativae] adaequatio sermonis interioris et rei ...' (*Ibid.*, p. 134.23–4).
23. 'And the species and perfection of all bodies is light ... the lower bodies participate in the form of the higher bodies ...'
    'Et species et perfectio corporum omnium est lux ... corpora inferiora participant formam superiorum corporum ...' (Grosseteste 1912b, p. 56.36 and p. 57.9–10).
24. '... no truth is perceived except in the light of the highest truth ... many of the impure of heart see the highest truth [in conjunction with true things] and many of them do not realise that they see it in any way ... But the pure of heart and the perfectly purified mentally perceive the light itself ... Therefore, there is no one who knows any truth, who does not also know the highest truth in some way, either knowingly or ignorantly.'
    '... nulla conspicitur veritas nisi in luce summae veritatis ... immundi multi summam veritatem vident [in conjunctione ... rebus veris] et multi eorum nec percipiunt se videre eam aliquo modo ... Mundicores vero et perfecte purgati ipsam lucem in se conspiciunt ... Nemo est igitur, qui verum aliquid novit, qui non aut scienter aut ignoranter etiam ipsam summam veritatem aliquo modo novit' (Grosseteste 1912c, p. 138.3–21).

induction lead to an intuitive grasp of such premisses, but he hardly considers the question of providing criteria to determine the correctness of our apprehension of indemonstrable premisses.[25] So to a reader who raises this question, Aristotle's account of indemonstrable premisses appears implicitly conditional: If one has understood a first principle or definition correctly, one grasps something which is in some sense more certain than its consequences. But Grosseteste's assumptions allow him to make an explicit case for the possibility of certainty in demonstrative science. He characterises a person's intuitive apprehension of an indemonstrable premiss as a direct or indirect irradiation of his mind by divine light, and insists that no certainty is possible without such illumination.[26]

Grosseteste is optimistic about the possibility of attaining a demonstrative science of nature. He realises that the stipulation that demonstrative syllogisms identify the necessitating causes of phenomena creates a presumption against the applicability of scientific demonstration to nature, on the grounds that what is necessary is always the case, while many natural phenomena occur frequently rather than always. Even the lunar eclipse – Aristotle's favorite example – appears to be only an intermittent phenomenon. But Grosseteste emphasises that one can have scientific knowledge of such frequently occurring events, since whenever their necessitating causes obtain, the effect occurs.[27] In his summary of the virtues of Aristotle's theory of demonstrative science, he says that it enables us

---

25. *Post. An.* Book II, Ch. 19; Serene 1979, pp. 99–101.
26. 'Pure intellects receive direct irradiation from the divine light; generally human intellects are not directly irradiated by the light of the divine ideas, but by the created light of their minds.'
 'Et apud intellectum purum et separatum a phantasmatibus possibile est contemplari lucem primam quae est causa prima ... et intellectus humanus ... multotiens recipit irradiationem a luce creata quae est intelligentia' (Grosseteste 1514, I, 7, f. 8va).
 In any case, we know first principles by a spiritual light: '... that by which something is an immediately accepted first principle has the same nature as intellectual capacity, because this nature is a spiritual light directly visible to the mind's eye, as was said above.'
 '... eadem natura quae est virtus intellectiva est id secundum quod aliquid est principium et sine medio acceptum. Quia ut superius dictum est lux spiritualis per se visibilis a mentis aspectu est haec natura' (*Ibid.*, II, 6, f. 40rb).
27. 'For the eclipse *simpliciter* always exists in its causal reasons, although no particular eclipse always exists in its causal reasons ... whenever the moon falls into the earth's shadow it is eclipsed.'
 'Eclipsis enim simpliciter semper est in rationibus suis causalibus nulla tamen eclipsis particularis semper est in ratione sua causali ... quotienscumque luna cadit in umbram terrae eclipsatur' (*Ibid.*, I, 8, f. 9ra). A recent interpretation of this passage suggests that according to Grosseteste: 'The eclipse demonstration is just one step away from being verified at any time, *est proximo habens veritatem in omni hora*, in this sense: it specifies the exact conditions under which an eclipse will occur at any time, and the moment such conditions are verified, the demonstration itself is true' (Wallace 1972, pp. 32–3). But the more plausible reading of '*probatio*' for '*proximo*' yields the simpler point that the demonstration is always true, provided that its premisses are qualified by the key term 'whenever'.

to judge easily when an explanation produces scientific knowledge.[28] Lacking the concept of a divine guarantee, Aristotle had not made such a strong claim for his theory.

Aquinas on the truth, necessity, and certainty of scientific premisses

Thomas Aquinas is better known for treating theology as a demonstrative science than for contributing to the theory of science. But his consideration of demonstrative science is interesting just because he seems so sympathetic to the details and spirit of Aristotle's enterprise, as is clear from his exposition of the requirements that demonstrative premisses be true, necessary, and certain.

Augustinian accounts of truth are relevant primarily to the hereafter, though they are not denied; the end of man is a vision of God which will include acquaintance with the eternal exemplars, but even now the speculative intellect can work toward its end, to attain truths which are expressed in judgements.[29] Truth, 'the conformity of the understanding with reality, such that the understanding says that what is the case is so, and that what is not is not', is a correspondence between a judgement and the reality which is its object.[30] Although it is not easy to say exactly what Aquinas means by 'reality' or 'thing' (*res*) in the definition of truth, it is clear that he does not think the relevant extra-mental *relatum* for human knowledge of the natural world is a divine idea. In his treatment of the requirement that demonstrative premisses be necessary, Aquinas assumes that no proposition which is ever false can be absolutely necessary.[31] When he discusses the demonstrability of frequently occurring phenomena, he follows Grosseteste's justification for considering the lunar eclipse demonstrable: whenever the causes of an eclipse occur, the effect occurs.[32] But he refuses

28. 'And by this science which has been exhibited it is easy to recognise whether a proposed syllogism is demonstrative.'
   'Et hac scientia habita facile est cognoscere de syllogismo proposito an sit demonstrativus' (Grosseteste 1514, II, 5, f. 39[rb]). For discussions of Grosseteste's view of the utility of demonstrative science, see Crombie 1953.
29. '... and therefore the intellect does not recognise truth except in composing and dividing through its judgement.'
   '... et ideo intellectus non cognoscit veritatem, nisi componendo vel dividendo per suum judicium' (*Comm. De Trin.* V, 1). See also *In Periherm.* I, lect. 3, n. 9; *ST*, I, 16, 1–2; *Quaest. disp. de ver.* I, 3. For a discussion of the nature of judgement, see Maritain 1959, pp. 84–100.
30. 'Cum enim veritas intellectus sit adaequatio intellectus et rei, secundum quod intellectus dicit esse quod est vel non esse quod non est ...' (*SCG*, I, 59, n. 2).
31. *In Periherm.* I, lect. 15, n. 2; see also *Comm. Post. an.* I, lect., 42. For interpretations of Thomas' conception of modality, see Jalbert 1961 and Knuuttila 1975.
32. 'But there cannot be demonstration of particulars, as we have shown, but only of universals. Hence it is clear that such [frequently occurring] things are always so, insofar as there is a

to extend the mantle of genuine demonstrability to frequent phenomena whose causes can obtain without bringing about their usual effect. Syllogisms which explain what we now call statistical phenomena, such as the generation of trees from some but not all seeds under the same general conditions, differ in kind from demonstrative syllogisms because they have only qualified necessity, do not yield demonstrative knowledge of what is true absolutely, and are less certain than fully demonstrative syllogisms.[33] In his characterisation of the certainty of demonstrative premisses, Aquinas recapitulates Aristotle's views, holding that we naturally grasp first principles and definitions through experience without needing a special learning process.[34]

Aquinas on knowledge and opinion

When Aquinas speaks of science or demonstrative knowledge in the strict sense, he follows the firm version of Aristotle's distinction between knowledge and opinion. The objects of knowledge include only what can be demonstrated by syllogisms meeting all the proper criteria; anything else is an object of opinion.[35] Thus one has only opinion with respect to truths which have not been demonstrated, including all contingent truths, and even with respect to the conclusions of demonstrative syllogisms in the

demonstration of them. As is the case with the lunar eclipse, so it is with all other similar things . . . For some things are not always so with respect to time, but are always so in relation to a cause.'
'De particularibus autem non potest esse demonstratio, ut ostensum est, sed solum de universalibus. Unde patet huiusmodi, secundum quod de eis est demonstratio, sunt semper. Et sicut est de defectu lunae, ita est de omnibus aliis similibus . . . Quaedam enim non sunt semper secundum tempus, sunt autem semper per comparationem ad causam' (*Comm. Post. an.* I, lect. 16, n. 8).

33. 'Yet such demonstrations do not make one know that what is concluded is true *simpliciter*, but only in a qualified sense, namely, that it is true in most cases . . . Hence sciences of this kind fall short of sciences which concern absolutely necessary things with respect to the certitude of the demonstration.'
'Huiusmodi tamen demonstrationes non faciunt simpliciter scire verum esse quod concluditur, sed secundum quid, scilicet quod sit verum ut in pluribus . . . Unde huiusmodi scientiae deficiunt a scientiis, quae sunt de necessariis absolute, quantum ad certitudinem demonstrationis' (*Comm. Post. an.* II, lect. 12, n. 5).

34. 'Hence every aspect of the speculative sciences is reduced to some first principle, which someone should not necessarily have to learn or find out . . . but should recognise naturally.'
'Unde omnis consideratio scientiarum speculativarum reducitur in aliqua prima, quae quidam homo non habet necesse addiscere aut invenire . . . sed eorum notitiam naturaliter habet' (*Comm. De Trin.* VI, 4). Thomas agrees with Aristotle that one cannot err in the apprehension of a first principle; see *In Metaph.* IV, lect. 6.

35. For the view that all propositions not seen as necessarily connected to first principles yield only opinion, see *Quaest. disp. de ver.* II, 1; *Comm. De Trin.* VI, 1; *Comm. Post. an.* I, lect. 44; and *ST*, II, II, 116. In particular, Aquinas stresses that we have only opinion and neither understanding nor knowledge with respect to contingents: 'Sic enim se habet [opinio] circa contingentia, sicut intellectus et scientia circa necessaria.' See Byrne 1968, p. 184.

absence of an apprehension of their premisses. Demonstrated truths, then, are a small subset of truths. And since Aquinas' definition of certitude parallels his definition of truth, it follows that one can be certain of many more truths than one knows by demonstration.[36] When Aquinas considers the work of the natural and moral sciences, however, he relaxes the distinction between knowledge and opinion, using the terms '*scientia*' and '*demonstratio*' broadly to refer to these areas of inquiry and their arguments. His concession that the sciences which deal with singulars and so fall short of the necessity found in geometry can nevertheless produce some certitude is as important as his caveat that they cannot produce absolute knowledge or certitude.[37] Aquinas does not expect investigators to construct a strictly demonstrative science of the physical world, but he is sanguine about the development of sciences in the broad sense, although they can only approximate the ideal of producing scientific knowledge through fully demonstrative syllogisms.[38]

Aquinas on the importance of final causation

This is a natural attitude for Aquinas to take, since it squares with his special interest in the explanatory power of final causes, whose metaphysical priority he thought Aristotle had overlooked.[39] Aquinas extends the

---

36. 'This, indeed, is certitude of cognition: when the cognition does not deviate at all from what was found in the thing, but rather considers the thing in this way: just as it is.'
   'Cognitionis quidem certitudo est, quando cognitio non declinat in aliquo ab eo quod in re invenitur, sed hoc modo existimat de re sicut est' (*Quaest. disp. de ver.* VI, 3). Byrne 1968 notes: '... certainty as a characteristic of human science differs from opinion or probable knowledge not in kind but only in degree' (p. 269).

37. 'And so also to the extent to which any science has more to do with singulars, such as ... medicine, alchemy, and ethics, they can have less certitude because of the great number of singulars that must be considered in such sciences – if any of them is omitted, error will follow – and because of the variability of singulars.'
   'Et ideo etiam quanto aliqua scientia magis appropinquat ad singularia, sicut ... medicina, alchimia et moralis, minus possunt habere de certitudine propter multitudinem eorum, quae consideranda sunt in talibus scientiis, quorum quodlibet si omittatur, sequetur error, et propter eorum variabilitatem' (*Comm. De Trin.* VI, 1). See also *In I Eth.*, lect. 3, n. 36 and *In Metaph.* XI. lect. 7, n. 2249.

38. 'But the necessary ... is one way in natural things which are true for the most part and fail to be true in a few cases; and it is another way in disciplines such as mathematics which are always true.'
   'Necessarium autem ... aliter est in naturalibus, quae sunt vera ut frequenter, et deficiunt in minori parte; et aliter in disciplinis, idest in mathematicis, quae sunt semper vera' (*Comm. Post. an.* I, lect. 42, n. 3).

39. '... but the end is prior to the efficient cause insofar as it is bringing something about in a substance and its complement [i.e. its accidents or the new substance it is becoming] since the action of the efficient cause is completed only on account of the end.'
   '... sed finis est prior efficiente ... inquantum est efficiens in substantia et complemento, cum actio efficientis non compleatur nisi per finem' (*De principiis naturae* IV, 25).

notion of final causality in various ways, including applying it to the problem of providing a necessary causal explanation for statistical phenomena by describing the effect as a final cause. If, for example, the flourishing of a tree is the final cause of its seed, then one can argue that whenever the final cause occurs, its correlative efficient cause must have occurred; thus if there is a flourishing tree, there was a seed.[40] As Aquinas' successors hastened to point out, however, such arguments cannot yield plausible scientific explanations.[41] Even if such explanations 'on the supposition that the effect has occurred' were plausible, they still would not satisfy all the requirements for genuine demonstration. But his attempt shows that while in principle Aquinas remains a strict adherent to 'the Aristotelian ideal of demonstrative science', in practice he welcomes various sorts of scientific explanations which do not satisfy its requirements.[42]

Duns Scotus' modifications of the concept of demonstrative science

In the writings of Duns Scotus the concept of demonstrative science undergoes a substantial change which may have had roots in the Condemnation of 1277. Among the propositions condemned by bishop Tempier we find the assertion that: 'One should not hold anything unless it is self-evident or can be manifested from self-evident principles.'[43] The view that the canons of demonstrative science cannot provide the sole

40. '... we will adduce as proof that if it happens that an ultimate end occurs, that through which the end was attained must precede.'
'... argumentabimur quod si fieri contingit finem ultimum, oportet praecedere ea per quae pervenitur ad finem' (*Comm. Post. an.* II, lect. 9, n. 11). Aquinas was not the only philosopher interested in enhancing the status of explanations from final causes. According to Longeway 1977, pp. 320–55, Simon of Faversham held that a *demonstratio potissima* comprises a major premiss which identifies an essential cause of a subject *s* of type *T*, a minor which identifies the final cause *f* of *T* things, and a conclusion which shows that *f* necessarily inheres in any token of type *T*. The fact that the property *f* ascribed in the minor and in the conclusion is extensionally the same property apparently does not detract, in Simon's eyes, from the interest of establishing its inherence as a reasoned fact.
41. For example, Scotus writes, 'For the end is not the cause of the efficient cause.'
'Nam illud quod est finis non est causa eius quod est efficiens' (Scotus 1966, pp. 28–9).
Ockham writes, 'But to say that a thing outside the mind is mutable according to one consideration of mine and that it is immutable according to another is simply false and asinine.'
'Sed quod illa res quae est extra propter unam considerationem meam sit mutabilis et propter aliam considerationem meam sit immutabilis, est simpliciter falsum et asinine dictum' (Ockham 1957b, p. 14). In Ockham 1974a, III, II, 17, he explains that a definition taken from a final cause cannot serve as a middle term because it is a nominal, not a real definition.
42. For Boethius of Dacia's different interpretation of the relationship between demonstration and the objects of natural science, see Pinborg 1975a.
43. 'Quod nichil est credendum, nisi per se notum, vel ex per se notis possit declari' (Denifle and Chatelain 1889–97, I, p. 545). For a discussion of the condemnation, including detailed treatment of both primary and secondary sources, see Wippel 1977. See esp. Hissette 1977.

criteria for knowledge found redoubtable advocates in Scotus and later in Ockham. Although Scotus agrees that demonstrative syllogisms yield knowledge of reasoned facts, other aspects of his thinking undermine the traditional status of demonstration. These include renewed attention to God's relation to knowledge and a revived interest in the Augustinian paradigm of knowledge as vision.

Scotus on truth

For Scotus, truth is a 'likeness through imitation, as a copy is to a pattern'.[44] Arguing against Henry of Ghent, he proposes three interpretations of this correspondence relation in support of the view that there is genuine knowledge of truths apart from special instances of divine illumination.[45] Truth can be understood as the correspondence between terms in an indubitable proposition such as: 'The whole is equal to the sum of its parts.' Or it can be taken as the relationship between a particular idea and the particular individual or state of affairs which is its object. In a third sense, truth can be the correspondence between a general idea and the essence of objects of that genus. Scotus' criterion for successful apprehension of truths suggests that he espouses at least the first two interpretations of the correspondence relation. He uses the evidentness of cognition as a criterion for truth and certainty, even though it is not part of his definition of truth. 'Evident cognition' is a technical term which designates both the possible objects and the quality of the cognition; its possible objects are the existence of particular individuals or states of affairs a person is perceiving and propositions whose truth is known from their terms alone.[46] Because evident cognitions are clear and indubitable, they serve as an epistemic ideal and a criterion for truth.

44. '... similitudo per imitationem sicut est ideati ad ideam' (*Quaest. quodl.* Q. 13, n. 12). For a discussion of this point, see Vier 1951, pp. 31–8.
45. 'From all this, it is clear why a special illumination is not necessary in order to see in the eternal rules, for Augustine assumes that we see in them only such "truths" as are necessary by the force of their terms.'
   'Et ex isto apparet qualiter non est necessaria specialis illustratio ad videndum in regulis aeternis, quia Augustinus non ponit in eis videri nisi "vera" quae sunt necessaria ex vi terminorum' (Scotus 1954, dist. 3, 1, Q. 4; p. 164.13–15).
46. Scotus' ideal of certain and evident cognition echoes the Augustinian paradigm of knowledge as direct vision of its objects: 'Perfect knowledge is certain and evident cognition. ... Furthermore, vision of the extremes of a contingent truth and of their union necessarily causes evident certitude concerning such evident truth.'
   '... in scientia illud perfectionis est, quod sit cognitio certa et evidens ... Visio autem extremorum veritatis contingentis et unionis eorum necessario causat evidentem certitudinem de tali veritate evidente' (Scotus 1950–, I, 4, Q. 1–2; p. 144.10–11 and p. 145.10–12). The same ideal of certain and evident cognition is satisfied in grasping a self-evident proposition, i.e., one which

Scotus on evidentness and necessity

Although Scotus' view of truth does not decisively distinguish his theory of science from that of earlier authors, his interest in evidentness does. Like Aristotle and Aquinas, he believes that first principles can be evident on the basis of experience,[47] but he insists that the apprehension of the correct premisses of a scientific syllogism does not suffice for scientific knowledge. We also need evident cognition of the phenomenon being explained by the demonstration.[48] To follow the difficulties this apparently innocuous point creates in Scotus' treatment of demonstrative science, it is helpful to attend to his innovative view of necessity. The most significant divergence from the Aristotelian theory of science in Scotus is his denial of necessity in the natural world. He agrees with the traditional requirement that demonstrations of reasoned facts have some sort of necessity, but for theological reasons denies that there are any unconditionally necessary truths about the natural world. In the first place, the laws of nature cannot be absolutely

derives its evident truth from knowledge of its terms and contains within itself the sole source of its certitude: '... illa propositio est per se nota ... quae ex terminis cognitis habet veritatem evidentem et quae non habet certitudinem nisi ex aliquo in se' (Scotus 1960a, I, dist. 2, Q. 2; p. 117.17–18). Scotus insists that if a proposition can be demonstrated to anyone, it is not self-evident: '... illa non est per se nota ex notitia terminorum quae potest esse conclusio demonstrationis' (*Ibid.*, p. 115.5–8).

47. The senses merely serve as an occasion for grasping the evidence of such a relationship: 'I reply that with respect to knowledge [of principles], the intellect has the senses not as a cause but as an occasion, because it can have knowledge of simples [i.e., terms] only from the senses.'
'Respondeo quantum ad istam notitiam [principiorum], quod intellectus non habet sensus pro causa, sed tantum pro occasione, quia intellectus non potest habere notitiam simplicium nisi acceptam a sensibus' (Scotus 1954, dist. 3, 1, Q. 4; p. 140.18–20). Scotus' example of a self-evident truth here is this: '... Every whole is greater than its part – the intellect by its own power and by the force of those terms should assent without doubt to this complex.' '... omne totum est maius sua partee, intellectus virtute sui et istorum terminorum assentiet indubitanter isti complexioni' (*Ibid.*, p. 141.4–6).

48. '... unless we first have a simple idea of something in itself, nothing about it is demonstrated scientifically.'
'... quod quia nihil scientifice concluditur de aliquo, nisi in se simpliciter praeconcepto' (Scotus 1966, IV, p. 111). In the *Quaest. quodl.*, Q. 7, 2, Scotus says that the objects of scientific knowledge are concepts and definitions which do not always require intuitive cognition of their extra-mental referents. Here he is defending the view that the scientific status of theology is not contingent on the theologian's intuitive cognition of God; it requires only that he have evident cognition of the concept of God. But the best understanding of natural phenomena requires evident cognition of an actual effect together with demonstrative knowledge of its causes: 'When you say that cognition through a cause is more perfect, I say that simple cognition of the effect, which it causes itself, must be included here. Cognition of a complex is caused by cognition of the cause and the effect together; and it is true that [a cognition caused] by the first cause and the second together is more perfect than that [caused] by the second alone.'
'Cum dicis: cognitio per causam est perfectior, dico quod ibi includitur cognitio effectus simplex causata ab ipso. Cognitio complexi causatur simul a cognitionibus causae et causati; et verum est quod a causa prima et secunda simul est aliquid perfectius quam a secunda sola' (*loc. cit.*).

necessary because the creator chose them by a free act of his will.[49] Secondly, God could at any moment will to abrogate the laws he originally ordained. Since demonstrative premisses were to be necessary in and of themselves, this theologically based scepticism appears to undermine the possibility of a demonstrative science of nature as Aristotle conceived it.

Scotus on the purpose of demonstrative science

But rather than rejecting demonstrative science, Scotus reinterprets its purpose; its new object is to discover not what is necessary in nature but what is possible or compossible.[50] Thus science primarily concerns not phenomena as they actually stand, but propositions about what can occur; its truths are now *de dicto*, not *de re* assertions. In this new view, science deals primarily with relations among ideas, but these ideas are grounded in reality by the assumption that indemonstrable premisses are found in experience and by the requirement that scientific knowledge of natural phenomena include evident cognition of the effect explained.

Unfortunately, this new philosophy of science creates some confusion about the explanatory power of demonstrations in natural science. If evidentness is the criterion for truth, and scientific knowledge requires evident cognition of an effect, what additional insight does a demonstration contribute? It seems that an evidently cognised particular fact must always be more evident than its premisses. Aristotelian science was designed to explain a particular phenomenon by showing it to be a token of a type whose essential nature always necessitates that exact kind of phenomenon under the specified conditions. Scotist science is designed to elicit answers to two different questions: what laws of nature make this type of phenomenon possible? What particular causes brought about this particular instance of its occurrence? There is some reason to believe that Scotus himself did not always fully appreciate the distinction between these two questions, as the following examples suggest.

---

49. 'Proof: Whatever God causes immediately he causes contingently ... therefore, [he causes] everything [in this way], because the contingent does not naturally precede the necessary, nor does the necessary depend on the contingent.'
   'Probatur, quid quod immediate causat, contingenter causat ... igitur et quidlibet, quia contingens non praecedit naturaliter necessarium, nec necessarium dependet a contingente' (Scotus 1966, IV, p. 91).
50. While this conclusion appears more clearly in Ockham, Scotus recognises in the *Quaest. quodl.*, Q. 7, 2, that there are necessary truths about the possibilities of contingent things; see Scotus 1895, p. 292.

Scotus on the regularity of nature

Scotus believes that nature functions in a regular manner, deeming it evident that: 'Whatever occurs in many instances by means of a cause that is not free is the natural effect of that cause.'[51] Experience enables us to identify 'unfree' causes, i.e. causes which do not directly express an agent's will, and to associate these causes with their frequent effects.[52] It is natural to expect that having introduced this principle Scotus will apply it to the problem of explaining statistical phenomena; but he encounters some difficulty in doing so when he takes up the traditional example of the lunar eclipse. The problem is that he assumes the *explanandum* is a particular eclipse which is now being observed; since what is intermittent is not a given instance of an eclipse but the occurrence of that type of celestial event, there is nothing intermittent left to explain by means of the principle of the regularity of nature.[53]

The second case Scotus considers involves the proposition that a certain herb or particular sprig of an herb is hot to the taste.[54] The standard interpretation of Scotus' treatment of the example runs as follows. On the basis of the principle of the regularity of nature, together with our inductive evidence that sprigs of, say, coriander are hot, we can conclude with the lowest grade of scientific certainty that the next sprig tasted will be hot, or at least that it is apt to be hot. According to this interpretation, Scotus is pointing out that even the principle of the regularity of nature cannot fully

---

51. 'Quidquid evenit ut in pluribus ab aliqua causa non libera, est effectus naturalis illius causae' (Scotus 1954, dist. 3, 1, Q. 4, p. 142.1–2).

52. 'A natural cause brings about its effect to the best of its power whenever it is not impeded.' 'Causa naturalis agit ad effectum suum secundum ultimum potentie suae quando non est impedita' (*Ibid.*, dist. 3, 1, QQ. 1–2, p. 52.1–3). It is interesting that Leonardo Da Vinci makes a similar point: 'A principle being given, it is necessary that its consequences flow from it, if it has not been hindered . . .' (*Frammenti letterari e filosofici*, ed. Salmi 1925, quoted in Blake, Ducasse, and Madden 1966, p. 18).

53. 'And if someone will have discovered by way of division that the earth is such a body interposed between sun and moon, our conclusion will no longer be known merely by experience as was the case before we discovered this principle. It will now be known most certainly by a demonstration of the reasoned fact, for it is known through its cause.' 'Et si inventum fuerit per divisionem quod terra tale est corpus, interpositum inter solem et lunam, scietur certissime demonstratione propter quid (quia per causam) et non tantum per experientiam, sicut sciebatur ista conclusio ante inventionem principii' (Scotus 1954, dist. 3, 1, Q. 4, p. 143.12–16).

54. Vier 1951 (p. 147) and Wolter 1962 (p. 111) suppose Scotus is discussing a generalisation about a type of herb; but a literal translation of the relevant passage suggests that he is interested in a particular instance, e.g., a particular sprig of coriander: 'suppose that this herb of such a species is hot', 'puta quod haec herba talis speciei est calida' (Scotus 1954, p. 143.20–144.1).

overcome the fallibility of induction, since the next sprig may not be hot.[55] But another reading of the example yields a different interpretation which parallels the treatment of the lunar eclipse. If the assumption of the example is that Scotus has tasted a particular sprig of coriander, and so has an evident cognition of its hotness, reference to the principle of the regularity of nature can add nothing to the evidentness of his cognition that it is hot.[56]

The failure of these examples to provide a clear illustration of the utility of the principle of the regularity of nature which Scotus introduced with some emphasis suggests that he may not have fully understood that his theory entails a radical revision of Aristotelian science. Addressing the challenge he raises of explaining a particular event in its particularity would involve abandoning the demonstrative format as it was traditionally conceived. Although the laws of nature have no absolute necessity, Scotus holds that what occurs at a given moment is uniquely determined by a concatenation of causes, including what God wills then.[57] In principle a particular event, for example that this seed germinated at this moment, could be explained if one could specify in sufficient detail the set of relevant conditions. But if, *per impossibile*, we could give such an explanation, it would involve so many additional causes, conditions, and principles that it would hardly resemble the traditionally simple demonstrative syllogism. It is no wonder that Scotus seems uncertain about what demonstrative

55. Vier 1951 supports this interpretation in maintaining that: 'The only infallible knowledge the inductive process conveys is that the herb is *capable* of producing warmth. It is for this reason that the knowledge resulting from the application of the inductive process is termed by Scotus the lowest degree of scientific knowledge' (p. 147). This reading supposes that the principle of the regularity of nature, together with appropriate experiences of coriander, tells us only that a particular sprig of coriander has 'an aptitude for warmth'; but it cannot tell us with certainty that a particular sprig will be hot. In this view, the fallibility and uncertainty of the supposition that an untasted sprig of coriander will be hot is removed to some extent by adverting to the regularity of nature. Vier's point requires reading 'licet tunc *certitudo* et *infallibilitas* removeantur per istam propositionem' rather than 'licet tunc *incertitudo* et *fallibilitas* ...'. The manuscripts provide no decisive witness for either reading; a number of them omit at least part of this vexed point; see Scotus 1954, p. 144n.
56. On this interpretation, the text reads: 'although the certitude and infallibility [of a present evident cognition] may be put aside through that proposition [that coriander is only usually hot] ...'. Thus the evidentness of a particular present experience of a sprig's hotness may be ignored in favour of a less evident and certain explanation of the cause of the general phenomenon that coriander is hot. This reading squares with Scotus' comment that, 'individuals are only imperfectly understood in a universal reason, since they are not understood according to the full positive entity in them, as I have shown in the question concerning individuation'.
'Individua in ratione universalis imperfecte intelliguntur, quia non secundum quidlibet entitatis positivae in eis, sicut in quaestione de individuatione ostendi' (Scotus 1966, IV, p. 107).
57. He writes in Scotus 1966, III: '... for whatever can be produced has some cause [to which it is] essentially ordered'.
'... nam omne effectibile habet aliquam causam essentialiter ordinatam' (p. 61).

syllogisms can contribute to the understanding of particular events in their particularity.[58]

Ockham on propositions as the objects of science

William Ockham endorsed many of the tenets of Aristotle's theory of demonstrative science while using the notions of evidentness and divine power to erode its epistemic importance. He holds that: 'A demonstrative syllogism is one in which primary cognition of a conclusion can be obtained from propositions that are necessary and evidently known.'[59] But he maintains that the resulting sciences are collections of true propositions, and not necessarily a mirror of the inner constitution of nature.[60] The premisses and objects of demonstrative science must be propositions rather than natural phenomena because God is the only necessary being.[61] These necessary premisses may be derived from matters of fact by a two-step process; first we learn contingent truths about what is the case by experience, then we transform them into correlative necessary truths about what must be possible.[62] Even though Ockham insists that properly speaking demonstrative science concerns ideas and propositions, 'mental contents which are common', he confidently assumes that it reflects the causes of these ideas in the physical world.[63] His confidence stems from the

---

58. Thus Scotus' view should not be assimilated to Humean scepticism about induction. He is not worried about induction *per se*, but about how to reconcile his belief in the explanatory power of demonstration with his commitment to using the evidence of cognition as a criterion for truth and certainty.

59. 'Syllogismus demonstrativus est ille, in quo ex propositionibus necessariis evidenter notis potest adquiri prima notitia conclusionis' (Ockham 1974a, III, I, 1; p. 359.14–16).

60. 'For the object of science is the whole known proposition.'
'Nam obiectum scientiae est tota propositio nota' (Ockham 1957, p. 9).

61. 'In one way something is called necessary ... because it can begin or cease being through no power; and thus God alone is ... necessary. ... In another sense, a proposition which cannot be false is called necessary. ... And in this sense demonstration is of necessities ... that is, of propositions which cannot be false, but always true.'
'Uno modo dicitur aliquid necessarium ... quia per nullam potentiam potest incipere vel desinere esse; et sic solus Deus est ... necessarius. ... Aliter dicitur necessarium ... propositio quae non potest esse falsa. ... Et isto modo demonstratio est necessariorum ... hoc est propositionum, quae non possunt esse falsae sed tantum verae' (Ockham 1974a, III, II, 5; p. 512.27–32).

62. '... propositions in a demonstration are necessary which are negative or hypothetical or which concern the possible ...'
'... propositiones ... in demonstratione sunt necessariae quae ... sunt negativae vel hypotheticae vel de possibili ...' (*Ibid.*, p. 513.65–514.2).

63. 'But, properly speaking, natural science is about mental intentions common to such [corruptible and mutable] things and suppositing precisely for such things in many propositions ... Nevertheless, metaphorically and improperly speaking, natural science is said to be about corruptible and mutable things, because it is about those terms which supposit for such things'.
'Sed, proprie loquendo, scientia naturalis est de intentionibus animae communibus talibus rebus [rebus corruptibilibus et mobilibus] et supponentibus praecise pro talibus rebus in multis pro-

belief that intuitive, evident cognition of particulars, which provides the basis for knowledge, is by definition true.[64]

Ockham's devaluation of demonstrative science

But his conception of evidentness dramatically devalues demonstrative science. If the conclusions of demonstrative syllogisms are known only indirectly rather than directly and evidently, they must be dubitable in some sense.[65] Hence, he contends, scientific knowledge is not epistemically decisive; a demonstrative syllogism is in principle no more certain than a dialectical one which rests on probable premisses – those which are considered true by everyone, or by most people, or by the wisest – since such a syllogism may 'produce firm faith without any doubt'.[66] Further challenging the claims of demonstration to epistemic priority, Ockham argues that cognition acquired by demonstration and that acquired from experience do not differ in kind.[67] But even while denying demonstrative science its traditional pre-eminence, Ockham presents nominalist interpretations of traditional features of the demonstrative syllogism, such as the necessity of the premisses and their priority with respect to the conclusions derived.[68] He raises and discusses various questions (stimulated by Scotus' work) concerning the relationship between experience and demonstration e.g.: 'Can there be demonstration *propter quid* of a currently observed pheno-

positionibus ... Tamen, metaphorice et improprie loquendo, dicitur scientia naturalis esse de corruptibilibus et de mobilibus, quia est de illis terminis qui pro talibus supponunt' (Ockham 1957, p. 11).

64. For exposition and criticism of this tenet, see Adams 1970, Scott 1971, and Boler 1976.

65. '... every conclusion of a [full-fledged] demonstration is dubitable, thus ... it is not self-evident', '... omnis conclusio demonstrationis [potissimae] est dubitabilis, ita ... non est per se nota'. (Ockham 1974a, III, II, 9; p. 521.7–8). For a discussion of this point, see Webering 1953, p. 76; for a related point in Scotus, see n. 46 above.

66. 'A topical [or dialectical] syllogism is not deficient in matter or in form but often even produces firm belief without any doubt.' '... syllogismus topicus nec peccat in materia nec in forma ... sed etiam frequenter facit firmam fidem, sine omni dubitatione' (Ockham 1974a, III, I, 1; p. 360.35–6 and 40–1).

67. 'And if it should be asked whether cognition of some conclusion acquired through experience and that acquired through demonstration are of the same species; and similarly whether cognition acquired through diverse premisses is of the same species, it can probably be said that if such a cognition should be precisely cognition of the conclusion and nothing else, it is not inappropriate to posit that such a cognition is of the exact same species.' 'Et si quaeratur an notitia accepta per experientiam alicuius conclusionis et notitia eiusdem accepta per demonstrationem sint eiusdem speciei; et similiter, notitia accepta per diversas praemissas sit eiusdem speciei, potest probabiliter dici quod si talis notitia praecise sit notitia conclusionis et nihil aliud, non est inconveniens ponere quod talis notitia sit eiusdem speciei specialissimae.' (*Ibid.*, III, II, 11; p. 524.13–18).

68. See esp. Ockham 1974a, III, II, chapters 3, 5, 11, and 15.

menon?'[69] 'Can current experience serve in lieu of a definition, principle, or term?'[70]

Nicholas of Autrecourt

Some philosophers who extended the nominalist programme thought that Ockham had not gone far enough in applying his razor to demonstrative science.[71] For example, Nicholas of Autrecourt thought that Ockham had not interpreted the concept of evidentness strictly enough, since only immediate experience and the law of non-contradiction are truly evident and certain.[72] The vast majority of true propositions are only probable because theoretically they could be falsified by God's exercise of his absolute power.[73] Since non-mathematical demonstrative premises fall into this class, it is impossible for them to produce absolutely certain knowledge of natural phenomena.

John Buridan

In response to Autrecourt's strict interpretation of evidentness, John Buridan took up the defence of natural science. His strategy was to concede that its principles and conclusions are not absolutely evident in Autrecourt's sense, but nevertheless to insist that they are sound if they have been confirmed in many instances and have not been falsified.[74] It has been suggested that Buridan's methodological stricture that a single exception in nature falsifies an explanatory principle enables him to maintain – without entering into complex metaphysical controversies – that natural phenomena as well as propositions are the immediate objects of science.[75]

---

69. *Ibid.*, III, II, 23.
70. *Ibid.*, III, II, 29.
71. For a detailed exposition and discussion of these doctrines in Ockham, see Adams 1977.
72. '... I am evidently certain concerning the objects of the five senses and concerning my actions. ... Every certitude had by us is reduced to this principle [that contradictories cannot be simultaneously true].' '... sum certus evidenter de obiectis quinque sensuum et de actibus meis. ... Omnis certitudo a nobis habita resolvitur in istud principium [contradictoria non possunt simul vera]' (Nicholas of Autrecourt 1908, p. 6.15–6; p. 7.5–6, and p. 6.33).
73. Nicholas rejects the strategy of defending the evidentness of scientific inferences by adding the proviso that God is not engaging in miraculous intervention, on the grounds that we cannot be certain if or when the proviso is satisfied (*Ibid.*, pp. 2–3 and p. 13.26–30).
74. 'It is therefore concluded ... that certain people argue very badly wanting to undermine the natural sciences, ... because ... in possible cases they can be falsified supernaturally, because strict evidentness is not required in such sciences ...'
'Ideo conclusum est ... quod aliqui valde male dicunt, volentes interimere scientias naturales ... eo quod ... possunt falsificari per casus supernaturaliter possibiles, quia non requiritur ad tales scientias evidentia simpliciter ...' (Buridan 1588 (actually 1518), Book II, Q. 1, f. 9rb).
75. Moody 1970, p. 605.

Buridan does make the traditional assumption that scientists can pursue their investigation without giving an account of the metaphysical constituents of what they study;[76] and he evidently believes, correctly, that scientific explanations which lack the absolute certitude or necessity of demonstration can be well enough established to be interesting and enlightening. But these assumptions need not rest on an innovative falsificationist methodology; indeed, it would be misleading to consider Buridan a strict falsificationist. He admits, for example, that miracles do not negate scientific truths, which deal only with the common course of nature.[77] He adds a more significant qualification in response to the observation that even in the common course of nature, expected effects are often impeded by other natural phenomena: explanations in natural science implicitly assume the proviso that no impediments occur.[78] Thus at least some sorts of exceptions will not falsify explanatory principles. In the light of these qualifications, it is not surprising that Buridan considers demonstrative science only a small subset of science. Only propositions or phenomena which happen all or almost all the time can be objects of demonstrative, as opposed to natural, science; most natural phenomena are only objects of natural science. Thus for Buridan the phenomenon of the lunar eclipse cannot be an object of demonstrative science, nor can the dispositional property of the heavens to have eclipses from time to time.[79]

76. '... for no science besides metaphysics has to consider the quiddity of a thing *simpliciter*. ... the natural scientist does not have to know *simpliciter* what a man is or what an ass is; he should describe such things by some change or by some operations.'
  '... nulla enim scientia praeter metaphysicam habet considerare de quiditate rei simpliciter ... physicus non habet scire simpliciter quid est homo vel quid est asinus: licet possit talia describere per aliquos motus vel per aliquas operationes' (Buridan 1588, Book I, Q. 1, f. 3vb).
77. '... there is firmness of truth [e.g. that "fire is hot"] on the supposition of the common course of nature ... even though God could thus make it cold, and so that [principle] "every fire is hot" is falsified'.
  '... est firmitas veritatis [quod "ignis est calidus"] ex suppositione communis cursus naturae ... non obstante quod deus posset sic facere ignem frigidum et sic falsificatur ista "omnis ignis est calidus"' (*Ibid.*, Book I, Q. 1, f. 8vb).
78. 'Although we naturally should assent to principles of this sort ["every fire is hot"] nevertheless this [proviso] must be understood, "if an impediment does not occur".'
  'Unde quamvis naturaliter assentiamus huiusmodi principiis ["omnis ignis est calidus"] hoc tamen est intelligendum "si non occurrat impedimentum"' (*Ibid.*, Book II, Q. 2, f. 9vb).
79. '... only in the first way is science about propositions and not about all things, but only about true and necessary things or at least those which are true in most cases ... In a second way, science is very much about all things of the world, but not as though (it was only) about demonstrable conclusions.'
  '... primo modo solum est scientia de propositionibus et non de omnibus: sed solum de veris et necessariis vel saltem de illis que (sic) ut in pluribus sunt vere ... Secundo modo est bene scientia de omnibus rebus mundi ... sed non tanquam de conclusionis demonstrabilibus' (*Ibid.*, Book VI, Q. 3, f. 34^{ra-b}).

Buridan seems willing in practice to relegate demonstrative science to a peripheral status, and he devotes himself to defending the reliability of natural science in a number of commonsensical anti-sceptical arguments.[80]

Conclusion

The revival of explicitly realist interpretations of demonstrative science and the elaboration of its methodology by Aristotelians of the Renaissance lie beyond the scope of this survey.[81] But it is clear that even in the medieval portion of its history, the so-called 'Aristotelian ideal of demonstrative science', like most long-lived ideals, underwent numerous transformations, many of them theologically motivated. What accounts for the persistent interest and influence of this theory of demonstrative science? On the basis of our survey, it is tempting to begin a response to this question by speculating that the malleability of the notion of demonstrative science in the hands of diverse philosophers is part of the answer.

80. *Ibid.*, Book I, Q. 1, f. 8[vb]. See also Scott 1965.
81. For a view of the extensive Renaissance discussion of methodological issues, see Gilbert 1960. Traditional versions of the theory of demonstrative science survived well past the fourteenth century; indeed, in many texts even Galileo seems to espouse such a strict version of the theory that interpreters have been hard-pressed to identify the novelties one might expect. For recent discussions, see Butts and Pitt 1978.

VII
NATURAL PHILOSOPHY

25
THE INTERPRETATION OF
ARISTOTLE'S PHYSICS AND THE
SCIENCE OF MOTION

Natural philosophy, first philosophy, and moral philosophy

When the 'new' Aristotelian books of philosophy were incorporated into the curriculum of the medieval Faculty of Arts by 1252, they were simply added as 'the three philosophies' to an existing curriculum of the seven liberal arts, a course requiring up to eight years before one became a Regent Master. The 'new logic' (*logica nova*), namely the two *Analytics*, *Topics*, and *Elenchi*, had merely expanded the old study of logic, which had even assimilated the *logica modernorum* without substantially changing the curriculum. But the addition of the hitherto proscribed (1210–*ca.* 1237) *libri naturales* and *Metaphysics*, together with the *Nicomachean Ethics* translated in full (1245–7) by Robert Grosseteste, expanded the curriculum substantially to include three new 'sciences': natural philosophy, first philosophy (or metaphysics), and moral philosophy. Thus during the second half of the thirteenth century was inaugurated what might be called the Faculty of Arts and Sciences.

The assimilation of the new learning

It was a period that saw an unprecedented assimilation of 'the new learning' not only in the Faculty of Arts, but more especially in the Faculty of Theology. However, the most notable assimilation and syntheses of the new learning both in philosophy and in theology were accomplished by theologians who had already passed through the university system and embarked on their own re-thinking of Christian truths 'new and old'. This was particularly true of such leading scholars as Robert Grosseteste, Albert the Great, Thomas Aquinas, Roger Bacon, and later Thomas Bradwardine. In most cases their writings (philosophical and theological) are extra-curricular in the sense that they were not delivered in the lecture halls or intended for the classroom. On the other hand, by far the most numerous writings of most thirteenth-century Masters do stem from the classroom, either as lectures by Masters in Arts or Bachelors in Theology commenting on the *Sentences*, or Masters disputing questions or commenting on Scripture. In this latter group, some of the more outstanding scholars were Siger of Brabant, Bonaventure, Henry of Ghent, John Duns Scotus, and in the early fourteenth century, William Ockham.

While the tendency of mid-thirteenth-century Masters was to effect a harmony of faith and reason, using the once-proscribed Aristotle as an aid to reason and faith, the tendency of early fourteenth-century Masters was to separate the demands of 'demonstration' from the simplicity of the Christian faith, seeing Aristotle as a pagan and his followers as hostile to the faith. This was particularly true among the Franciscans and the Austin Friars. (It may well be that this change in the intellectual climate is in part a consequence of the Condemnation of 1270 at Paris and the Condemnations of 1277 at Paris and Oxford.) During the second half of the thirteenth century all three of the new sciences were avidly studied and commented upon. Indeed, commentaries on the entire Aristotelian Corpus (as it was then conceived of) abound during this period, as they do not in the fourteenth century.

The special status of natural philosophy

But obviously all the Aristotelian books together with the seven liberal arts could not be covered in the eight years one spent in the Faculty of Arts. The books of logic were naturally given special emphasis, since they were the indispensable tool (*organon*) of all scientific knowledge. Inevitably logic remained one of the main pillars of medieval education and of scholastic thought, even in the later Middle Ages. Among the 'real' sciences, however, natural philosophy was acknowledged as fundamentally important by all the scholastics, whatever their views of the status of moral philosophy or metaphysics. All acknowledged that the *libri naturales*, the Aristotelian and pseudo-Aristotelian books of natural science, provided the foundation of ethics, metaphysics and – to a certain extent – theology, in the sense in which Anselm had described it as 'faith seeking understanding'. While interest in moral philosophy and metaphysics declined in the later Middle Ages, as is evident from both university requirements and extant commentaries, interest in natural science never flagged, although different emphases developed with succeeding generations and different centres of learning. Amid all vicissitudes, two Aristotelian books of natural philosophy stand out as of primary importance: the *Physics* and the *De anima*. Around them centred many of the problems that methodologically would have arisen in the context of other books, had they been treated. The eight books of Aristotle's *Physics* became the focal point of all basic problems of natural science, while the three books of Aristotle's *De anima* became the focal point of all basic problems of human psychology, especially that of the separated soul. Few bothered to deal with *De caelo*, *De generatione et corruptione*, *Meteora* or with the details of *De animalibus*, while the so-called *parva naturalia* were covered in class in a matter of a few weeks.

Aristotelian natural philosophy extended from very general considerations in the *Physics* to particular subjects discussed in the other books dealing with the heavens, metals, minerals, flora, fauna, environment and human behaviour. The most remarkable example of the medieval version of this kind of Aristotelian science is found in the writings of Albert the Great. There was also a non-Aristotelian medieval approach to natural science, one that sought explanations of natural species and phenomena in perspective and the mathematics of light rays; perhaps the most remarkable examples of this 'Pythagorean' approach – the term is Albert's – are found in the writings of Robert Grosseteste and later in Roger Bacon. The Aristotelian approach remained clearly dominant, however. Even while Walter Burley was concerned with a wide range of problems for the 'realist' dialectician in natural philosophy, and John Buridan was concerned with new problems of 'impetus' and the *via moderna* in its widest application, the *Physics* of Aristotle remained the cornerstone of medieval natural philosophy. William Ockham wrote no commentaries on moral philosophy or metaphysics, but he composed both an *Expositio* and *Quaestiones* on Aristotle's *Physics*, and made it the focal point of his logical analysis of motion and quantity. The influential *De proportionibus velocitatum in motibus* of Thomas Bradwardine centred on the problem of ratios in Aristotle's *Physics* VII, 4–5, while his *De continuo* (against Grosseteste, Walter Chatton, and Henry of Harclay) developed the basic principle in Aristotle's *Physics* VI, 1–2. In the later Middle Ages, *pro forma* requirements of the curriculum notwithstanding, logic and natural philosophy were the two pillars of philosophical education. Aristotle's *Physics* clearly ranked as the base of the second pillar, with the whole of psychology (including 'philosophy of mind') considered as an integral part of one single science, variously called *scientia naturalis*, *philosophia naturalis*, *scientia de naturalibus* or the like.

The medieval understanding of the structure of Aristotle's Physics

Medieval schoolmen took the eight Books of Aristotle's *Physics* as they received them from the Greek (divided into chapters) and from the Arabic (divided into texts), without raising questions about authenticity, possible autonomy of books, recensions, or possible posthumous compilation. They were, however, very much concerned with the arrangement and content of its Books. As to their arrangement, all the scholastics saw the first two Books as dealing with the general subject of natural philosophy, *ens mobile*, which had 'motion' (Bks III–VIII) as its proper attribute (*propria passio*).

Interpretations of Physics I

Thomas Aquinas saw more clearly than Albert that Book I discussed the possibility of all change (natural or unnatural) in the face of the pre-Socratic dilemma concerning *genesis* (*fieri*): 'no thing can come from nothing' and 'what is does not come to be'. Aristotle's resolution of this dilemma in terms of potentiality and actuality was not uniformly appreciated by all scholastics. Many, clinging to imagination, conceived 'first matter' as a substratum having some minimal actuality of its own, even prior to first actuality, or 'form'. Aquinas, however, and many others insisted that unless this 'first matter' were pure potentiality (*pura potentia*), having no actuality whatever of its own (not even *esse*), the dilemma faced by Aristotle could not be resolved. It would still be impossible for the ultimate substance and reality of anything truly to change (*fieri, mutari*). For this reason, the whole of Aquinas' natural philosophy is based on the absolute unicity of substantial form in every material composite. For him, the one and only *esse* a substance has comes entirely from the actualising form (*forma dat esse*); whatever is posterior to the first, immediate actualising form must consequently be accidental to the composite. The many opponents of this position conceded not only a minimal *esse* and actuality to 'first matter', but insisted that a plurality of substantial forms, hierarchically arranged, was necessary to safeguard certain truths of the Christian faith. This 'Christian' position was the one defended by Robert Kilwardby, Dominican Archbishop of Canterbury, when he condemned the unicity doctrine at Oxford on 18 March 1277, a condemnation that was reiterated by his successor, the Franciscan John Peckham, seven years later.

Interpretations of Physics II

While Book I discussed the possibility of any change taking place in the world, Book II was seen to limit 'the subject of this science' to *nature*, which was identified as 'a principle of motion and rest in those things to which it belongs *per se* and not accidentally' (192^b21-3). Thus the natural philosopher is not properly concerned with those things that come about in the world by human ingenuity (art) or by pure chance. But, as is evident from Book I, the word 'nature' can be used in two senses: in the active sense of 'form' as a formal principle (*ut principium formale seu activum*) or in the passive sense of 'matter' as a material principle (*ut principium materiale seu passivum*). Therefore the natural philosopher must study both the active principle (form) and the passive principle (matter) of all natural things. But since no passive principle can be actualised without some extrinsic, efficient cause acting for a definite purpose, the natural philosopher must also study the efficient and final causes of all natural things. In this regard he differs from the mathematician who applies his mathematical principles to the same natural phenomena, since the mathematician 'abstracts from sensible matter and from motion as such'[1] and is concerned only with the measurable aspects of those phenomena. For Albert, Thomas, and even Grosseteste, those measurable aspects constitute the objects of special sciences really distinct from natural science. Thomas called them *scientiae mediae*,[2] – e.g., astronomy and optics – intermediate between natural philosophy and pure mathematical sciences, but formally mathematical, not natural. Thus, for Thomas, the astronomer and the naturalist may demonstrate the same conclusion, e.g., the sphericity of the earth, but they do so through formally different principles of demonstration.[3] This vast area of intermediate science developed rapidly in succeeding centuries; its concern was the measurable aspects of natural phenomena and what could be demonstrated about them, disregarding the 'natural causes' that brought them about, whether they be strictly material, formal, efficient or final.

Medieval attitudes towards the role of chance in Aristotelian natural philosophy

Surprisingly, not all the scholastics appreciated the important role 'chance' (*tuchē*, *casus*) played in Aristotelian natural philosophy. While 'nature' necessarily and *per se* tends toward one predetermined end as to a final cause, by definition there can be no *per se* cause of a 'chance event'. Precisely because a 'chance event' is indeterminable, it cannot have a *per se* cause or be a *per se* cause (196^b22–3). Thus, for Aristotle 'chance is a *per accidens* cause, happening in a minority of cases and in the sphere of those

---

1. Boethius 1860, i, 2; *PL* 64; col. 1250; cf. Aquinas, *In Boeth. De trin.*, q. 5, a. 3 (*per totum*); *In V Metaph.*, lect. 16, n. 989. See analysis in Laso 1952, pp. 1–29.
2. *In Boeth. De trin.*, q. 5, a. 3 *ad* 6; also *In II Phys.*, lect. 3, n. 8; *ST*, IIaIIae, q. 9, a. 2 *ad* 3. See Pseudo-Albertus 1977, c. 3, p. 14.11–2.
3. Aquinas, *ST*, IIaIIae, q. 1, a. 1.

actions that are done for the sake of something involving purpose'
(197ᵃ5−6). Aristotle's world was not fatalistic or mechanistic. Nevertheless,
many Christians in the Middle Ages sought to explain apparently chance
events on earth by astrology (*astronomia iudicialis*) or some other form of
divination. That is, they sought to explain future events by Fate, the stars,
or some created superpower, short of divine providence itself.[4] The problem with this fatalism is that it denies man's free will, which is of course
important for Christianity. Medieval scholastics were nevertheless imbued
with the idea of the influences of celestial bodies and intelligences on
terrestrial phenomena. Many of the scholastics, notably Albert the Great
and Roger Bacon, were highly credulous about these influences on the
atmosphere, bodily humours and human emotions. But even apart from
the influences of celestial bodies, man's free will (*ad utrumlibet*), and nature's
predetermination to an end actually attained in most cases (*ut in pluribus*),
medieval natural philosophy recognised a whole range of events that do
genuinely happen by chance (*ut in paucioribus*), which are outside the range
of true 'scientific' knowledge. Regarding those chance events we can have
only 'probability' or 'likelihood', not certainty.

Interpretations of Physics III−VIII

Physics III−VIII was seen as a systematic examination of all the basic aspects
of motion in general: its essential nature (Book III), its natural conditions of
place and time (Book IV), types of true motion (Book V), continuity and
quantitative divisibility (Book VI), and efficient causes of various motions
ordered *per se* ultimately to a First Unmoved Mover, itself devoid of
motion, matter, quantity, and limitation of power (Books VII−VIII).

The study of Aristotelian natural philosophy

The entire ensemble of the eight Books presented only the basic theory of
natural philosophy, presupposed by subsequent investigation, but needing
to be filled out with increasingly detailed studies of celestial and terrestrial
motions down to the most specific differences of metals, minerals, flora,
fauna, and mankind in its complex nature, races, and sexuality. Although
medieval students had numerous summaries and manuals of Aristotelian
natural philosophy and studied some of the actual texts in class together
with various commentaries, notably that of Averroes, there was not
enough time assigned in the university calendar to study the whole of

---

4. The principal source of medieval astrology was not Stoic determinism but Muslim fatalism,
particularly that of Albumbazar (Abū Ma'shar).

Aristotle's natural science. The most that could be hoped for was a general idea of some of the main principles and a serious study of at least the *Physics* and the *De anima*, a study that always presupposed logic, grammar, and some of the mathematical sciences.

Aristotle's account of motion

Aristotle clearly stated that since 'nature' is 'a principle of motion and change' and is the subject of natural philosophy, it is obviously necessary 'that we understand the meaning of "motion"; for if it were unknown, the meaning of "nature" too would be unknown' (200^b12-14). The facts that some things really move and that moving is objectively different from not moving Aristotle took as primary data of sense (185^a12-14), within which he included *genesis* (*fieri*). For him there is an obvious difference between the state of a body before it moves (potency) and its state after it has begun to move (actuality). The reality of movement itself must somehow be a kind of actualisation of that potentiality, precisely as it is potential, toward completed actuality, just as the process of 'building' is the actualisation of the 'buildable' only as long as the building is 'being built' (cf. 201^b9-15).

Albert the Great's exposition of Aristotle on motion

In this exposition the scholastics, notably Albert the Great,[5] recognised three kinds of 'definition' of motion: (i) 'the actualising of what exists potentially, insofar as it exists potentially' (201^a10-11), which they called *formal*; (ii) 'the actualising of the movable *qua* movable' (201^a28-9), which they called *material*, because it is better known to us and demonstrable from the prior definition; (iii) the simultaneous actuality of the mover as cause and of the moved as that in which the change takes place, which Albert called a *total definition*, because it includes the efficient (and implicitly the final) cause whereby motion takes place. Hence, for Albert, the category of *agere* (acting) belongs to the agent as coming from him (*a quo*), while the category of *pati* (undergoing) belongs to the recipient as existing in him (*in quo*).

Medieval misunderstandings of Albert's exposition

Some misunderstanding arose among later scholastics concerning Albert's exposition of Aristotle's doctrine.[6] The background was Avicenna's insistence, based on his conception of all nature as predominantly passive,

5. *Physica* III, tr. 1, cc. 1–8; Albert the Great 1890–9, III, pp. 177–202.
6. This misunderstanding has persisted in some modern historians. See, e.g., Maier 1944; 1949, pp. 9–25; 1958, pp. 61–76; Dijksterhuis 1961, pp. 174–6; Pedersen 1953.

that all motion, of whatever kind, belongs to the category of *passio* as a *fluxus formae*, caused by intelligences. But Averroes, in a famous text (*Phys.* III, comm. 4; V, comm. 9), insisted that motion cannot belong to any one category; it must be a *forma* reducible to one of the three terms or ends of motion: quantity, quality, or place. The alternative conceptions of motion as *fluxus formae* (a succession of form) or *forma fluens* (a successive form) are nowhere presented in Avicenna, Averroes, or Albert; further, Albert in no way aligns himself with either Avicenna or Averroes, nor does he present Averroes simply as a defender of any *forma-fluens* theory; finally, no fourteenth-century misreading of Albert could have prepared the way for Ockham's denial of motion as a reality distinct from form.[7]

Albert and Thomas on 'motion' as an analogical term

Albert's main objection to Avicenna is that he places motion in a single category of *passio*, essentially different from the term of motion, as though it were a univocal concept. His main objection to Averroes is that he fails to distinguish sufficiently between motion as a *via* (or process) and the term (or end) of motion. For Albert, motion is essentially a *fluxus alicuius entis* (a succession of a certain being) existing in the moved, but belonging to the agent as its cause. He even defines motion as a *continuus exitus formae* (a continuous flow of a form), which belongs to the same category as its term, differing from it not as a distinct category (as Avicenna had held), but as a process differs from its term. The main point for Albert (and for Thomas) is that 'motion' is an analogical term, more easily applied by us to locomotion, but also true of growth and of the intension and remission of qualities. The analogical term becomes even more diverse when applied to 'substantial change' (*mutatio substantialis*), and most tenuous when applied to 'creation' (*creatio*), where there is no pre-existent matter.

Albert and Thomas on sources of motion

Unlike Averroes, neither Albert nor Thomas ever spoke of the substantial form of an inanimate body as a conjoined mover (*motor coniunctus*); this term was reserved exclusively for the substantial form of higher living things which by definition 'move themselves'. Although Albert himself denied the view, he explained that Aristotle and most of the Peripatetics thought the heavens to be 'animated' with a *motor coniunctus* that moved with the celestial body under the influence of a separated intelligence.[8] On

---

7. Anneliese Maier to the contrary notwithstanding.
8. Albert, *Liber de causis*, II, tr. 1, c. 2; II, tr. 2, c. 1, etc.

the other hand, for Averroes the Aristotelian principle 'everything that is moved is moved by another' required the constant presence of a conjoined mover to account for natural as well as violent motions. Thus, although Averroes recognised the difference between living and non-living things, he created a separation between the 'form' as mover of the medium and 'matter' as moved by the form through the medium (i.e., *per accidens*), which meant that there could be no motion whatever in a void.[9] For Albert and Thomas, however, the 'form' of any inanimate body is simply a formal, active principle from which natural motion spontaneously and immediately flows toward an end unless impeded.[10] Such a 'form' is in no way the efficient cause of its natural motion. But a 'living form', an *anima*, is not only a formal principle of certain elemental natural motions, but also a vital principle of other natural motions such as growth that cannot be classified as 'self-motion'. In most animals, the 'form' is not only the active principle of elemental motions, spontaneous growth and digestion, but it is also the real efficient cause of some of its own motions, such as walking, swimming, crawling, or flying.[11] Only in this last case can the *anima* or *forma* be called a conjoined mover in any proper sense of the term, for it is truly an efficient cause of some of its movements.

The basic problem, however, is that each of these bodies must 'be moved' in some way in the first place, and therefore 'moved by another'. It is obvious that every terrestrial body must be generated in the first place in order to have the nature it has, whereby it acts naturally. Celestial bodies 'are moved' perpetually without coming to any final term, or rest; moreover their 'souls' (if such there be, according to Aristotle) are themselves 'moved' by reason of the bodies they animate, i.e., *per accidens*. But the whole point of Aristotle's Books VII and VIII is that all such motions have no 'explanation' unless there is some First Mover, itself entirely unmoved *per se* and *per accidens*, immaterial (separated from matter), having infinite power to move the entire universe as a whole by means of the first heaven for all eternity. Albert and Thomas thought that even if the universe moved and existed from all eternity, the First Uncaused Mover would still, as First Being, have 'to create' (*producere*, or *movere*) the entire universe *ex nihilo* – even on Aristotle's own principles.[12]

9. See Weisheipl 1974b and Moody 1951.
10. Weisheipl 1955, pp. 1–32.
11. Albert the Great 1951a, *Liber de principiis motus processivi*, pp. 47–75; cf. *Liber de causis* II, tr. 3, c. 11, and c. 17; Albert the Great 1890–9c, pp. 560–1a, 568–9a.
12. Albert the Great 1890–9c, II, tr. 1, c. 17; tr. 2, c. 17; Aquinas, *In II Sent.*, dist. 1, q. 1, a. 2; *De potentia*, q. 3, a. 5.

Ockham and the 'common view' of motion

William Ockham, lecturing on the *Sentences* at Oxford around 1317–18, was not troubled about any controversy over motion as *forma fluens* or *fluxus formae*.[13] Rather, he was concerned with 'a common view' of motion, defended by Walter Burley and others, that motion is (i) a *forma diminuta* distinct from the body in motion,[14] and (ii) increased and decreased by a succession of distinct forms, more or less intense, of indivisible duration,[15] a view Burley claimed to have taken from Godfrey of Fontaines, if not from Aristotle.

Theories of motion and Ockham's razor

The problem of motion for Ockham was only one of many that seemed to multiply entities not at all required by sound philosophy or the Christian faith. For him, the problem of what has real existence in itself reduces to the basic question of distinguishing a *res absoluta* as distinct from what is only relative or connotative – i.e., from what is not a thing but only a way of knowing things or of talking about them. But for Ockham there are only two kinds of *res absolutae*, substances and qualities: 'Besides absolute things, namely substance and qualities, there is nothing imaginable either in act or in potency.'[16] An 'absolute thing' (*res absoluta*), for Ockham, is an objectively existing reality (a *res permanens*), distinct in place and subject from every other permanent thing, capable of existing, at least by God's absolute power, with nothing prior or posterior to it. On this basis, only individual substances (either matter or form) and individual qualities (such as colour, heat, shape, and weight) are *res absolutae* (the latter because of their occurrence in the Eucharist). All the other Aristotelian 'categories' are therefore simply ways of understanding things or talking about them.

Motion not a distinct reality

Concerning the first point on motion, the Aristotelian text to which Ockham constantly appeals is: 'There is no such thing as motion over and above things' (200^{b}34). Aristotle merely meant that there is no special

---

13. Ockham was under the impression that Averroes defended the view of motion as *fluxus formae* (Ockham 1494–6, *Sent.* II, q. 9, obj. 7 H), and he seems to have misunderstood the presumed point of the distinction as presented by A. Maier (*ibid.*, *ad* 7 S); cf. Ockham 1944, pp. 49–52.
14. *Super octo libros Physicorum*, III, text. 4; Burley 1501, f. 60vb and f. 62va.
15. *De intensione et remissione formarum*, Burley 1496, ff. 2^r–15^v. This view is summarised and rejected by Gregory of Rimini, *Sent.* I, dist. 17, q. 4, a. 2; Gregory of Rimini 1522, ff. 104vb–107va. Cf. Godfrey of Fontaines 1914, Quodl. VII, q. 7; discussed in Duhem 1906–13, III, pp. 327–8.
16. *Summa logicae* I, c. 49; Ockham 1974a, *OP* I, p. 154.23–4.

category of 'motion' over and above the ten discussed in the *Categories*, but for Ockham this meant that motion is not a distinct reality over and above the body in motion. In fact, 'to move' means simply to be in one place after another 'without interruption'. Consequently, 'motion' is not something over and above the body in motion, but is the body itself acquiring part after part successively, i.e., without interruption. Since being 'without interruption' signifies an absence, a negation, an *ens rationis*, it cannot be something real and positive added to the body in reality. Therefore, motion, as such, cannot be a reality over and above the body in motion, but only a way of speaking about individual bodies.[17]

One of Ockham's major concerns was about 'the fiction of abstract nouns', since many philosophers erroneously imagine that distinct nouns correspond to distinct realities outside the mind.[18] Abstract nouns, such as 'motion,' 'change,' 'action,' or 'passion', which are derived from verbs, are used in human speech, according to Ockham, only 'for the sake of brevity of speech or ornamentation of language'.[19] Thus the noun 'locomotion' briefly expresses the cumbersome phrase: 'a body that is in one place and later in another place in such a way that at no time does it rest in any place'. But this should not be taken to mean that locomotion (or any other motion) is a reality over and above the body in a place.[20] Hence, according to Ockham the term 'motion' has a double signification: one positive, signifying the body (*res absoluta*) itself, the other negative (an *ens rationis*), connoting uninterrupted succession of part after part. Since negation is an *ens rationis*, it cannot be a reality over and above the body in motion.

Motion and the absence of forms yet to come

Concerning the second point on motion noted above, the essence of motion consists in the acquisition of part after part, not in the loss of previous parts or degrees, as Burley proposed. In the obvious case of natural augmentation (invariably exemplified by rarefaction in the fourteenth century) the preceding part remains, but a new extension is added, quantity itself not being distinct from the quantified body according to Ockham. In condensation a body naturally decreases its dimensions while retaining all of its previous parts. According to the doctrine of the Eucharist, God can so decrease the extension of matter by his absolute power as to make a body

17. Ockham 1495–6, *Sent.* II, q. 9 (*per totum*); Cf. Ockham 1944, pp. 32–69.
18. Ockham 1944, p. 46; Ockham 1930, I, q. 1; pp. 52–66.
19. Ockham 1944, p. 37.
20. *Ibid.*, p. 45.

exist without any extension whatever. That is to say, by his absolute power God can make all the parts of the material universe to exist *simul*, as at a point, in such a way that the distinct parts would be without any extension in space, although not without existing in some place. Therefore, Ockham argued, 'quantity' or extension in space cannot be a *res absoluta* distinct from substance or qualities.

According to Ockham, although it is true that in local motion, in decrease (in condensation), and in remission (in qualities), the preceding 'form' is lost or left behind, this is by no means essential to the concept of motion:

For in the motion of augmentation and alteration [i.e., intension of qualities] it is obvious that prior parts remain with those to be acquired, since increase is achieved by the addition of one part to another . . . , likewise in local motion, although in fact one place or location is continuously lost just as another is continuously acquired, nevertheless by God's power all the lost parts could remain simultaneously, since God could make a body move locally in such a way that when it acquired a new place, it retained the previous one, and so on, because God can make the same body exist [simultaneously] in different places.[21]

The point is that although motion sometimes involves a 'loss' of some kind, it is essentially the absence of forms yet-to-come that is connoted by the fact of motion. Thus 'motion' signifies principally the existing *res permanens*, the individual substance or quality, and connotes the non-existence of forms yet to come: 'And through such negations and affirmations "succession" is explained in motion'.[22] For Ockham the 'negation' implied in motion is not the non-existence of a previous form, but of a future form; all successive motion is essentially the acquisition of additional parts or designations. Just as in augmentation and increase of qualities the previous form of quantity or quality is not lost, but remains with the additional form, so it *can* be in local motion.

From this it follows that intension and remission of forms presented Ockham with no real problems. Intension, for him, simply meant more by

---

21. 'Nam in motu augmentationis et alterationis manifestum est quod partes priores manent cum posterioribus, quia augmentatio fit per additionem unius partis ad partem . . ., similiter in motu locali, licet de facto unus locus vel ubi continue deperdatur sicut aliud continue acquiritur, tamen de potentia dei possunt omnia acquisita simul manere, quia deus potest facere quod corpus moveatur localiter, et quod semper quando acquirit novum locum retineat primum locum et secundum, et sic deinceps, quia deus potest facere ut idem corpus sit in diversis locis.' Ockham 1495–6, *Sent.* II, q. 9 H. The same conception of motion is found in Peter John Olivi 1922–6, *Quaestiones in secundum librum Sententiarum*, q. 27; I, p. 470.
22. Ockham 1495–6, *Sent.* II, q. 9 H.

addition; remission simply meant less by subtraction.[23] Ockham never clearly distinguished between the extension and the intension of any quality, much less between mass and velocity.

Bradwardine and the commensurability of motions

In 1328 Thomas Bradwardine, Fellow of Merton College and theology student at Oxford, published an influential treatise entitled *De proportione velocitatum in motibus*, which dealt directly with the commensurability of motions, discussed by Aristotle in *Physics* VII, 4–5. Since all successive motions are proportionate to one another in velocity (with direction intended), natural philosophy, which studies motion, must not ignore the proportions of motions and velocities. But Bradwardine recognised that this essential and extremely difficult part of natural philosophy requires a sound knowledge of mathematics, 'for, as Boethius says, whoever dismisses mathematical studies has destroyed the whole of philosophical knowledge'.[24]

For Aristotle not all motions are comparable, neither according to term nor according to velocity, but only those which are of the same species. Hence alteration cannot be compared with local motion, and even rectilinear motion cannot be compared with rotational motion since a straight line and a circle are specifically different (248^a18–$^b7$; 248^b10–12). But even within a given species of motion, there are limits beyond which motions cannot be compared, as when a moving body is divided in such a way that its power is less than the resistance offered by the body to be moved, and conversely, when the body to be moved is doubled beyond the capacity of the moving power.

Moving power and velocity

The two notions essential to this doctrine are that of 'moving power' (*potentia motiva*) over resistance and that of velocity (*velocitas in motibus*) in the direction of motion. While motion itself, for Aristotle, is not 'speed' or 'velocity', all natural motions (unlike rest) have a velocity, in each case involving both a time and kind of 'distance', which accelerates toward its natural end. Hence the basic motion in the whole terrestrial world is accelerated motion toward a goal, even if the motion be irregular as in the case of growth and alteration. For this reason Aristotle had no difficulty in

---

23. See *Sent.* I, dist. 17, q. 4; Ockham 1977a, *OT* III, pp. 479–519.
24. Thomas Bradwardine 1955, p. 65. Cf. Boethius 1847, *De arithmetica* I, c. 1; *PL* 63, col. 1081.

explaining 'gravitational motion' or 'the acceleration of freely falling bodies'; it was the natural kind of motion for a heavy body to have.

Velocity considered in respect of its cause or of its effect

To appreciate the significance of Bradwardine's treatise, two essential distinctions must be noted. Although Bradwardine discussed them only in passing and took them for granted, they are fundamental to all subsequent discussions of motion at Oxford and elsewhere. The first is between velocity considered *penes causam* (in respect of its cause) and velocity considered *penes effectum* (in respect of its effect). The first had to do with what Gaetano di Thiene called the *a priori* conditions of the proportion of force over resistance productive of different speeds in a given direction,[25] a consideration that later came to be called 'dynamics'. The important point is that 'velocity considered in respect of its cause' was a variable ratio (*proportio*) of force to resistance that was the *cause* (an efficient cause, so to speak) of variable velocities. The second consideration had to do with what Gaetano called the *a posteriori* conditions of speeds effected, regardless of direction. This consideration of motion later came to be called 'kinematics'. Regarding this distinction, it should be noted first that these questions were asked not only about local motion, as with Bradwardine, but also about augmentation and alteration, as with John Dumbleton, William Heytesbury, and others. Second, Bradwardine was concerned not only with the variable proportion of moving power and resistance (dynamics), but also with the variable proportion of distance to time, that is, with velocity in the original direction of motion.

Total velocity and instantaneous velocity

The second basic distinction is between the whole motion (*velocitas totalis*) from beginning to end and motion at any given instant (*velocitas instantanea*).[26] No Aristotelian maintained that true motion could take place in an instant, i.e., without time. '*Velocitas instantanea*' was the expression used to designate the 'intensity' or 'degree' (*gradus*) of a motion at any particular instant. It was measured by the *velocitas totalis* a body would have if it were moving at a constant speed at the rate it had at that instant, for example, 50 km. per hour. This distinction corresponded to the older distinction between the 'quantity of motion' (the time it takes) and the 'quality of motion' (its intensity).

25. Gaetano di Thiene 1494, f. 37ra; see Duhem 1906–13, III, pp. 302–9; Clagett 1959, pp. 207–9.
26. See esp. Maier 1951, pp. 111–31; 1958, pp. 147–86; Clagett 1959, pp. 199–219.

The initial problem for Bradwardine and the Mertonians (the philosophers associated with him at Oxford)[27] was to give some definite meaning
to the expression 'instantaneous velocity' when talking of a uniformly
accelerated body moving from zero to maximum degree compared to the
more intelligible expression *velocitas totalis*. Their solution, known in the
history of science as 'the Mertonian mean speed theorem', was to say that
the 'total velocity' of a body moving with constant speed 'corresponds' to
the speed at the *middle instant* of the time taken by a body moving with
uniform acceleration from zero to maximum degree.[28] Obviously, no
general rule can be established for nonuniformly accelerated or decelerated
motions, such as growing and decaying, but a rough mid-point can be
established, although it is only widely analogous to *velocitas instantanea*. It is
also clear that in questions of pure kinematics such as the Mertonians were
interested in, there was concern only over the spatial-temporal conditions
of speed, not over the direction of motion.

Bradwardine's laws

The aim of Bradwardine's treatise was to determine a universal rule that
would govern proportions between moving power and resistance, on the
one hand, and between distance and time on the other. For him there had
to be a proportion of velocities between motions of the same kind. The
difficulty Bradwardine found with the traditional Aristotelian formula was
twofold: (i) 'it is insufficient, because it does not determine the proportion
of the velocity of motion *except* in cases where either the mover is the same
or equal, or when the mobile body is the same or equal'.[29] (ii) 'It produces a
fallacy of the consequent', because it would then follow that 'any mobile
body could be moved by any mover', whereas for motion to occur, 'the
proportion of the mover to the moved must *always* be one of greater
inequality'.[30] Bradwardine devised a universal formula in which both
forces and resistances could vary and yet maintain a proportion of greater
inequality and always produce a proportionate velocity in moving bodies.
The formula he suggested was a function for any given ratio of greater
inequality. In this way any exponential variation of a given ratio of greater
inequality would always produce a definite, proportional variation of
speeds in moving bodies. Although Bradwardine's laws primarily concern

27. See Sylla's contribution to this volume.
28. Texts and comment in Clagett 1959, pp. 255–329; Grant 1974, pp. 237–43.
29. Bradwardine 1955, pp. 96–9.
30. *Ibid.*, pp. 98–105.

kinematic representation, i.e., speed (*penes effectum*), they are firmly grounded in a dynamical cause of motion (*penes causam*).[31]

The influence of Bradwardine's work

Bradwardine's treatise became immediately popular both in England and on the Continent. But undergraduates were introduced to Bradwardine's doctrine of 'geometrical proportionality' more often through shorter and simpler summaries, often called *Proportiones breves* or *De proportionibus*.[32]

The new conception of motion at least suggested by Bradwardine can be seen in the author of an anonymous *Tractatus de motu locali difformi*, possibly Richard Swineshead, despite its expression in terms of the traditional Aristotelian causes:

The material cause of motion is whatever is acquired through motion; the formal cause is a certain transmutation conjoined with time; the efficient cause is a proportion of greater inequality of the moving power over resistance; and the final cause is the goal intended.[33]

One significant point is that 'velocity' or 'speed' was conceived of as an *intensive quality*, a 'form', that could be intensified and remitted as any other 'form'. In the later Middle Ages *velocitas*, whether considered with a vector quantity or not, was always discussed under the general heading of the 'intension and remission of forms'. But after Bradwardine every attempt was made to reduce the kinematics of all intensive qualities to some kind of measurement that would be amenable to Bradwardine's formula. While this attempt was doomed to failure, the attempt to mathematise all motions, including celestial motions (as Bradwardine himself attempted in Chapter 4 of his treatise) was destined for considerable success.

---

31. On Bradwardine's mathematics see Molland 1967; 1968a; 1968b; and Mahoney 1978.
32. Besides Albert of Saxony's well-known treatise produced at Paris, two in particular were in common use among undergraduates. One has been edited and translated in Clagett 1959, pp. 481–94; the other exists in many MSS and begins, 'Omnis proporcio aut est communiter dicta, proprie dicta, vel magis proprie dicta . . .'
33. 'Unde causa materialis motus seu materia motus est ipsum acquisitum per motum; causa formalis est ipsa transmutatio quedam coniuncta cum tempore; causa efficiens est proportio maioris inequalitatis potentie motive super potentiam resistivam; causa finalis est terminus intentus per motum.' Anon., *Tractatus de motu locali difformi*, MS Cambridge, Gonville & Caius 499/268, f. 212ᵃ. This treatise occurs between two other short treatises ascribed to Swineshead and with the *Calculationes*.

26
THE EFFECT OF THE CONDEMNATION
OF 1277

Potentia Dei absoluta

The Condemnation of 219 articles in theology and natural philosophy by the bishop of Paris in 1277 points to a significant development in the history of medieval philosophy generally, but especially natural philosophy.[1] Whatever may have induced bishop Stephen Tempier and his advisers to promulgate the condemnation, the most significant outcome was an emphasis on the reality and importance of God's absolute power (*potentia Dei absoluta*) to do whatever He pleases short of bringing about a logical contradiction. Although the doctrine of God's absolute power was hardly new in the thirteenth century, the introduction into the Latin West of Greco-Arabic physics and natural philosophy, with their independent, and often deterministic, philosophical and scientific explanatory principles, conferred on that doctrine a new and more significant status. After 1277, appeals to God's absolute power were frequently introduced into discussions of Aristotelian physics and cosmology.

The range of the Condemnation

The wide range of topics covered by the Condemnation indicates its potential impact on natural philosophy. Among the themes at which several articles were directed are God's knowability, nature, will, and power; the causation and eternality of the world; the nature and function of intelligences; the nature and operation of the heavens and the generation of terrestrial things; the necessity and contingency of events; the principles of material objects; man and the active intellect. Whether implicitly or explicitly, many of the articles asserted God's infinite and absolute creative

---

1. The Latin text appears in *CUP* I, pp. 543–55, and, reorganised by subject matter, in Mandonnet 1908, pp. 175–91. For an edition of the text with a discussion of its possible sources see Hissette 1977. For a translation of all the articles see Fortin and O'Neill 1963 (reprinted in Hyman and Walsh 1967, pp. 540–9). A selection of the articles relevant to medieval science appears in Grant 1974, pp. 45–50.

and causative power against those who thought to circumscribe it by the principles of natural philosophy. Nowhere is the spirit of the Condemnation better revealed than in Article 147, which condemned the opinion 'That the absolutely impossible cannot be done by God or another agent', if '"impossible" is understood according to nature'.[2]

The effect of the Condemnation

The Condemnation was in effect at Paris throughout the fourteenth century. The seriousness with which it was taken is shown by numerous direct and indirect references to its articles by such eminent scholastics as Richard of Middleton, John Duns Scotus, William Ockham, Walter Burley, Peter Aureoli, John of Ripa, John Buridan, and Nicole Oresme. As the most characteristic feature of the Condemnation, God's absolute power was invoked in a variety of hypothetical physical situations. The novel supernatural alternatives considered in the aftermath of the Condemnation conditioned scholastics to contemplate physical possibilities outside the ken of Aristotelian natural philosophy, and frequently in direct conflict with it; indeed, a concern with such possibilities became a characteristic of late medieval scholastic thought.

The Condemnation and the concept of a vacuum

No area of physical thought was more affected by the Condemnation and its emphasis on God's absolute power than the concept of a vacuum. Here two articles played a paramount role, the thirty-fourth, which condemned the claim that the First Cause, or God, could not produce more than one world[3] and the forty-ninth, which condemned the claim that God could not move the world with a rectilinear motion because a vacuum would be left behind.[4] In exploring the consequences of these possibilities, concepts contrary to Aristotelian physics and cosmology were found plausible rather than impossible. Not only could God create other worlds, but each would be a closed system like ours with its own proper centre and circumference. With the simultaneous existence of a plurality of centres and circumferences rendered hypothetically intelligible, Aristotle's argument for the necessary existence of a single centre and circumference,

2. 'Quod impossibile simpliciter non potest fieri a Deo, vel ab agente alio. – Error, si de impossibili secundum naturam intelligatur.' *CUP* I, p. 552.
3. 'Quod prima causa non posset plures mundos facere.' *CUP* I, p. 545.
4. 'Quod Deus non possit movere celum motu recto. Et ratio est, quia tunc relinqueret vacuum.' *CUP* I, p. 546.

on which he had founded his belief in a unique world, was plainly subverted.

Articles 34 and 49 also made it appear plausible to suppose that an infinite empty space existed beyond our world. For if God did make other worlds, empty space would intervene between them; and if God moved the world rectilinearly not only would an empty space be left behind but also the world would move into and out of other empty spaces that lay beyond. To John of Ripa, for example, the mere possibility that God could move the world suggested the actual existence of an extra-cosmic empty space; for otherwise there could be no places or spaces capable of receiving the world or any part of it, and so God would be unable to move the world, which would restrict His power (and violate the intent of article 49).[5]

Although no articles of the Condemnation concerned vacua within the cosmos itself, it seemed obvious that if God could create or allow a vacuum beyond the world, He surely could do the same within the world; and so God was frequently imagined to annihilate all or part of the matter within the material plenum of our world. Potential problems that would arise from such divine action were often discussed. Thus it was asked: Was the empty interval a proper space? Would the concave surface surrounding that space be a proper place? Would a stone placed in such a void be capable of rectilinear motion? Could distances be measured within such emptiness? Would vision and hearing be possible there? Analysis of these and similar 'thought experiments' in the late Middle Ages were often made in terms of Aristotelian principles even though the conditions imagined were 'contrary to fact' and impossible within Aristotelian natural philosophy.

Conclusion

As a consequence of the Condemnation of 1277, God's absolute power became a convenient vehicle for the introduction of subtle, imaginative questions which generated novel replies. Although the speculative responses did not replace, or cause the overthrow of, the Aristotelian world view, they did challenge some of its fundamental principles and assumptions. For some four centuries many were made aware that things might be quite otherwise than had been dreamt of in Aristotle's philosophy.

5. Combes and Ruello 1967, pp. 232.66–8 and 234.6–9.

27

THE OXFORD CALCULATORS

The identity and the writings of the Calculators or 'Mertonians'

In the second quarter of the fourteenth century a collection of works was produced at Oxford whose joint impact on European natural philosophy lasted well into the sixteenth century. The works at the core of this collection are Thomas Bradwardine's *De proportionibus velocitatum* (1328), William Heytesbury's *Regulae solvendi sophismata* (1335), and Richard Swineshead's *Liber calculationum* (usually dated *ca.* 1350, but probably earlier). Other treatises were linked with these three through common interests and approaches in logic, in mathematics, and in physics or natural philosophy. Among the most closely linked works were Richard Kilvington's *Sophismata*, Walter Burley's *De primo et ultimo instanti* and *Tractatus primus et secundus de formis accidentalibus* (the *Tractatus secundus* is known better as *De intensione et remissione formarum*), Richard Billingham's *Conclusiones*, Heytesbury's *Sophismata* and the *Probationes Conclusionum* of his *Regulae*, Roger Swineshead's *De motibus naturalibus*, John Bode's treatise on the sophisma '*A est unum calidum*' and others, the anonymous *Sex inconvenientia*, and John Dumbleton's *Summa logicae et philosophiae naturalis*, not to mention many treatises on the usual subjects of fourteenth-century logic – supposition, consequences, *obligationes*, *insolubilia*, etc. – or commentaries on Aristotle's physical works and other set books of the medieval curriculum.

Since many of the most famous authors of these works, including Bradwardine, Heytesbury, Richard Swineshead, Burley, Dumbleton, and possibly also Bode, had been fellows of Merton College, Oxford, some recent historians of science call this group of authors the Merton School, although there is little contemporary evidence that they were called Mertonians.[1] Contemporary and slightly later Continental philosophers

---

1. See, e.g., Gunther 1923, which has a chapter on the 'Merton School of Astronomy'. Also Maier 1952, p. 265; Clagett 1959, pp. 199–329; Molland 1968a; Weisheipl 1968, 1969; Sylla 1971; Bottin 1973, p. 127. The appropriateness of the term is questioned by Weisheipl 1959, pp. 439–40. One instance of a fourteenth-century identification with Merton is Thomas Bradwardine's addressing

tended to call the members of the group simply '*Anglici*' or '*Britannici*', doubtless associating them with the larger group of British logicians whose contribution to logic was considered noteworthy.[2] By the late fifteenth and early sixteenth centuries the members of the narrower group were being called Calculators, with Richard Swineshead known as 'the Calculator'.[3] In what follows, I will treat these authors insofar as the label 'Oxford Calculators' fits them.[4]

The Calculators considered as natural philosophers

The fifteenth- and sixteenth-century Continental authors who quoted the arguments of the Oxford Calculators did so most often in the context of natural philosophy.[5] Consequently, it was twentieth-century historians of science such as Pierre Duhem, Anneliese Maier, and Marshall Clagett, looking for the scientific background of Leonardo da Vinci and Galileo, who rekindled an interest in the work of the Calculators.[6] Seen from this perspective, the Oxford Calculators have been credited with distinguishing between kinematics and dynamics, with developing a concept of instantaneous velocity, and with the proof of the so-called mean speed theorem for uniformly accelerated motion.[7] Bradwardine's *De propor-*

his *De causa Dei contra Pelagios* 'ad suos Mertonenses', but such a term of address is, of course, no evidence of the conscious association of a particular school of thought with Merton.

2. For example, in many of the manuscripts of the relevant works the author is identified as '*anglicus*'. Richard de Bury in his *Philobiblon*, in referring to the University of Paris, says; 'Involvunt sententias sermonibus imperitis, et omnis logicae proprietates privantur; nisi quod Anglicanas subtilitates, quibus palam detrahunt, vigiliis furtivis addiscunt', p. 89 in Thomas 1888, quoted by Gilbert 1976, p. 232. Gaetano di Thiene, in his *De reactione* (1491), says, 'Sed haec oppositio est britannica. Et melius est tenere opinionem realium.' Thus he seems to associate the British with nominalism.

3. Swineshead is called the Calculator by, e.g., Angelo of Fossambruno in the early fifteenth century, as well as by Marliani, Scaliger, Leibniz, and others later. Cf. Clagett 1959, pp. 649, 659; Duhem 1906–13, III, pp. 497–8.

4. This label seems preferable to 'Merton School' because not all scholars whose work seems to be associated with that of the group can be shown to have been members of Merton College, though the core certainly was there. I am here retaining 'Oxford Calculators' rather than 'English Calculators', which would have much more early support, not in order to exclude the possibility of Calculators at Cambridge, but rather because I want to exclude members of the English nation at Paris who were never at Oxford.

5. I am thinking of such authors as Blaise of Parma, Messinus, Angelo of Fossambruno, Jacopo of Forli, Paul of Venice, Gaetano di Thiene, Giovanni Marliani, John Dullaert, Luiz Coronel, Juan Celaya, Alvarus Thomas, Domingo de Soto, Hieronymus Picus, *et al.* See Clagett 1941; also 1959, pp. 645–59; Wallace 1969, 1971; Lewis 1975, 1976.

6. See Pierre Duhem 1906–13, Anneliese Maier 1952 *et seq.*, and Marshall Clagett 1950, 1969. Others who have studied the Calculators from the perspective of natural philosophy or mathematics are Michalski 1922 etc.; Molland 1967 etc.; Murdoch 1957 etc.; Sylla 1970 etc.; Thorndike 1934; Weisheipl 1956 etc.; and Wilson 1956.

7. Clagett 1959, p. 205. Cf. Murdoch 1974a, p. 55n.

tionibus (*On the Ratios of Velocities in Motions*), Roger Swineshead's *De motibus* (*On Natural Motions*), and Dumbleton's *Summa* (*Compendium of Logic and Natural Philosophy*) certainly are primarily works of natural philosophy. To the modern ear, the name 'Calculators' tends to link the bearers of the name with mathematics and with science. But if later scholars have noticed and valued the work of the Oxford Calculators for its physical and mathematical content, nevertheless, within the fourteenth-century Oxford academic context, the work of the Calculators probably arose not in the guise of recognised mathematics or natural philosophy, but within the standard practice of logical disputations. The specific characteristics of the work of the Oxford Calculators are much easier to understand if the work is seen in this disputational context.

The disputational context for the work of the Calculators

The three pedagogical techniques most commonly used in medieval universities were the lecture, the question, and the disputation.[8] The student was, first of all, required to hear certain textbooks read, both in cursory lectures, most often given by bachelors of arts, and in ordinary lectures given by masters of arts, the latter lectures including the raising and answering of pertinent questions about the text. The main subjects covered in the Faculty of Arts at Oxford were the seven liberal arts and the three philosophies: natural, moral, and metaphysical. The fourteenth-century Oxford undergraduate heard lectures on grammar, logic, and natural philosophy or the quadrivium (arithmetic, geometry, astronomy, and music). The bachelor of arts heard lectures mainly on philosophical topics and lectured cursorily on logic and natural philosophy. Ideally, the master of arts was expected to be able to teach all ten disciplines.[9]

8. I have based the following survey of the Oxford curriculum mainly on Gibson 1931 and Weisheipl 1964a. Lectures and disputations are clearly distinct – in the former a single lecturer reads and expounds the text, and in the latter several people debate with one another. Questions are closely related to both lectures and disputations. They may be integral parts of lectures, merely mimicking the form of disputation, they may be subjects of independent disputations, or, thirdly, they may arise from lectures, become the subjects of disputations, and then receive definitive answers in later lectures (Wallerand 1913, p. 20).

9. Logic dominated the undergraduate curriculum, as is clear from the statutes of 1268 (Gibson 1931, p. 26) and 1409 (Gibson 1931, p. 200). The 1268 statutes, but not those of 1409, also require attendance at lectures on the *Physics*, *De anima*, and *De generatione et corruptione*. Bachelors studied mainly the three philosophies, as is shown by the requirements for inception in the statutes prior to 1350 (Gibson 1931, pp. 32–3) and in 1431 (Gibson 1931, pp. 234–5). Both sets of statutes require attendance at lectures on the *libri naturales*. *Inter alia* the 1431 statutes specify three terms to be spent on the *Physics* or the *De caelo*, the *De anima*, or other books of natural philosophy.

It seems clear that in 1431 there was greater effort to cover all the seven liberal arts and three philosophies than there had been earlier. The statutes for determiners and inceptors before 1350

But besides hearing lectures with or without questions, the student was required to assist at disputations. After two years of hearing lectures, the undergraduate might first serve as 'opponent' and then as 'respondent' in disputations *de sophismatibus* (1268) or *in parviso* (before 1350, 1409). When he had done this for a year, he might be admitted to respond *de quaestione*. And when he had responded *de quaestione* for at least part of a year, he might be given permission to 'determine' in the school of his or some other master during Lent.[10] At this point he became a bachelor of arts.

do not, for instance, mention any books of music or metaphysics. In 1268 natural philosophy was required for determination, but nothing from the quadrivium, it apparently being possible to postpone hearing the books of the quadrivium until the bachelor years. (See Gibson 1931, p. 33. 14–20, quoted above.) In 1409, on the other hand, at least the most elementary parts of the quadrivium were required for determination, but nothing was required of natural philosophy until inception. According to a statute of 1340, the bachelor was supposed to lecture on a book of natural philosophy, such as *De caelo, De anima, Meteora, De generatione et corruptione*, or the *Parva naturalia*; so he would have had to have heard at least one of those books earlier (see Gibson 1931, p. 32).

(It would appear that at least in certain decades of the fourteenth and fifteenth centuries the *Physics* could be omitted altogether, replaced by *De caelo*. Cf. Gibson 1931, p. 32.8–13; p. 200; pp. 234.32–235.3.)

As far as the masters are concerned, it seems that at some periods they could choose the subjects of their own lectures. (Cf. Weisheipl 1964a, pp. 149, 160.) But in later periods a certain organisation was imposed to insure that there were ordinary lectures on all the books required *pro forma* (Gibson 1931, pp. 235–6, for 1431).

In this more regulated situation a master might well be expected to change the subject of his lectures from term to term. Similarly, a late statute for responses of bachelors, citing ancient custom, supposes that they might respond in disputations concerning each of the ten disciplines in turn (Gibson 1931, p. 247 for 1432). This statute is perhaps evidence that the ordinary solemn disputations of the masters were linked to the disciplines or ordinary lectures. This is argued further in the next two notes.

10. The statutes of 1268 oblige candidates for the determination 'publice de sophismatibus per annum integre ... respondisse' and in the summer before the Lent term of their degree 'de questione respondisse' (Gibson 1931, p. 26). In the 1409 statutes they must have responded 'de questione' before the Hilary term of their degree, and they must previously have been 'arciste generales, parvisum interim frequentantes, et se ibidem disputando, arguendo, et respondendo doctrinaliter exercentes' (Gibson 1931, p. 200). Disputations 'in parviso' (in a place out of doors) as contrasted with 'in scolis' are mentioned also in statutes of *ca.* 1350 and 1607 (Gibson 1931, p. 358).

A comparison of the 1268 and the 1409 statutes leads to the conclusion that the disputations *in parviso* were either identical with the disputations *de sophismatibus* or else took their place. Weisheipl (1964a, p. 154) says that disputations *de sophismatibus* were disputations on logic whereas disputations *de quaestione* were on natural philosophy. I am inclined to believe that the responses *de quaestione* are to be identified not by their subject matter as much as by their location; in particular, I think that the responses *de quaestione* at issue may be the ones that occurred in the schools. It seems likely that the regent masters giving ordinary morning lectures on required books also held ordinary disputations on questions or problems arising from them, and that both undergraduates and bachelors acted as the respondents in these disputations held in the schools, usually in the afternoon. (Cf. Gibson 1931, pp. 192 and 194 for 1407 or before.) The advanced undergraduate would respond *de quaestione* at the same ordinary or solemn disputations of the masters at which bachelors were supposed to oppose or respond (Gibson 1931, pp. 235–6, 247).

As a bachelor of arts the student would continue to oppose and respond in disputations. At the end of three years he could be licensed to incept as master of arts, participating in two disputations as part of inception, and, after that, disputing on every 'disputable day' for the next forty days and giving ordinary lectures with accompanying ordinary disputations as a 'necessary regent' for the next two years.[11]

The master might give a formal reply during a subsequent morning lecture (Gibson 1931, p. 56, for before 1350).

Undergraduates who were admitted to determine were supposed to dispute only in logic except on Fridays and special days (Gibson 1931, pp. 27, 201–2). From the emphasis on logic in determinations we may infer that in the disputation *in parviso* the emphasis was similarly on logic, as indeed one statute indicates (Gibson 1931, p. 27). This would fit with the fact that in hearing lectures undergraduates concentrated on logic and with the fact that even if the disputations *in parviso* were not, as has been assumed, identical with the disputations *de sophismatibus* required in 1268, they nevertheless held the same place in the curriculum.

11. The main sources concerning disputations of bachelors of arts are from 1340 and 1431. The statutes for 1340 state (Gibson 1931, p. 32): '*Quociens tenentur arciste arguere et respondere in disputacionibus bachilariorum.* Item ordinatum est quod arguat quilibet incepturus quater ad minus puplice in disputacionibus magistrorum, et quod semel disputet vel respondeat quilibet in disputacione generali bachilariorum facultatis predicte, et hoc pertinencia argumenta adducendo tantummodo ad questionem vel problema quam vel quod eum contigerit disputare. (*Quociens arciste tenentur respondere magistris antequam incipiant.*) Item, ordinatum est quod quilibet incepturus, ante licenciam suam in artibus, respondeat bis ad minus magistris regentibus in disputacionibus solempnibus, que non fuerint de quolibet, et hoc de questionibus vel semel de questione et de problemate alias.'

There are at least two sorts of disputations mentioned here. First, there are the solemn disputations of the masters, which are probably the disputations of single masters in their schools with responding sophistae and bachelors, as argued in the previous note. At these ordinary or solemn disputations the bachelor was, in 1340, expected to act as opponent at least four times and as respondent at least twice, either both times *de quaestione* or once *de quaestione* and once *de problemate*.

The second sort of disputation mentioned is that *apud Augustinienses*, or the general disputation of the bachelors. It is supposed that questions or problems will be disputed there and these are supposed to be announced at least three days in advance (Gibson 1931, p. 287). Apparently the role of respondent was more popular than that of opponent. If there was disagreement over roles, the senior bachelor was to be respondent (Gibson 1931, pp. 286–7, for before 1477). In 1346 it was ordained that each bachelor, when called upon, should take part in these general disputations of the bachelors twice a year, once as opponent and once as respondent (Gibson 1931, p. 147).

The disputations connected with inception in arts were 'vesperies' and investiture; there were formal differences between the disputations associated with the two occasions. See Gibson 1931, pp. 36–9; Weisheipl 1964a, pp. 164–5; Little and Pelster 1934, pp. 44–52. These disputations seem to have concerned mainly the quadrivium or one of the philosophies. Such disputations can be found in MS London, Lambeth Palace 221, ff. 262–309, and in MS Oxford Magd. College 38, ff. 16ᵛ–48ᵛ. See Gibson 1930 and 1931, pp. 643–7. The inceptor took the role of opponent while those who had most recently incepted responded. (Gibson 1931, p. 38, for before 1350.)

For the disputations for forty days after inception there is a statute for before 1350 (Gibson 1931, p. 39).

In theology faculties there were, besides the disputations so far described, quodlibetal disputations. Most recent commentators believe that there were also quodlibets in the arts faculty (e.g. Glorieux 1925–35, II, p. 19; Gibson 1931, p. xcv; p. 32.26; pp. 404, 406; Weisheipl 1964a, pp. 182–5). I think this has yet to be shown. Weisheipl 1964a, p. 182, reports that the editors of Rashdall 1936 similarly doubt the existence of arts quodlibets at Paris before a late date; I, p. 460, n. 2. It should, of course, not be forgotten that in the extant quodlibets of Oxford theologians arts

As I interpret the statutes, the ordinary disputations of the masters which, along with the ordinary lectures, formed the backbone of university instruction were linked to the lectures and open to participation by men from all levels of the university. The disputation was held in a school by a master of arts who, at the end or on a subsequent day as part of his lecture, 'determined' or gave a final answer concerning the subject of the dispute. Beyond these ordinary disputations held by masters in their schools there were other sorts of disputations, typically designed for students at a particular level.

Disputations on sophismata

Although the extant university statutes and other evidence for fourteenth-century Oxford are frustratingly full of gaps, it appears (from information given in more detail in the notes) that at Oxford there were disputations *de sophismatibus*, which were understood mainly as aids to learning logic, which were held (or called) *in parviso*, and which were primarily intended for advanced undergraduates, who were called *sophistae* because of their participation in these disputations.[12] Masters or perhaps bachelors of arts attended and supervised these disputations, but the real work of the disputation was done by the undergraduate respondent. If the master made a determination of the sophisma at all, the point of the exercise remained the activity of the undergraduate. It appears likely that the most typical works of the Oxford Calculators, especially Heytesbury's *Regulae* and *Sophismata*, were connected with these undergraduate disputations *in parviso*.

Sophismata at Paris and at Oxford

Quite a few sophismata determined by named masters of arts survive from the University of Paris.[13] This fits the evidence that at Paris sophismata were disputed *in scolis*. Many of these sophismata, even in their written

questions are treated as well as more obviously theological ones. But surely theological quodlibets were not an arena in which sophismata were determined. A consideration of all these various types of disputation leads to the conclusion that disputation of sophismata at Oxford took place mainly *in parviso* or also in ordinary disputations of the masters linked to the ordinary lectures on logic, but not usually elsewhere. In the present state of our knowledge it seems most likely that the works of the Oxford Calculators are to be linked with disputations *in parviso*.

12. Cf. Weisheipl 1964a, pp. 177–81. One cannot claim an absolute identity between disputations *de sophismatibus* and disputations *in parviso*. There were certainly disputations *de sophismatibus* not *in parviso* – for instance in the 'determinations' of new bachelors in Lent and probably also in disputations connected with the ordinary lectures on logic. Later there may have been disputations *in parviso* not on logic. I am arguing that in the period of the Oxford Calculators most disputations *in parviso* would have been *de sophismatibus* and vice versa.

13. See Grabmann 1940a.

form, show clear evidence of the live debate in which they originated, and some are not really sophismata but merely disputed questions.[14] The sophismata of the Oxford Calculators, on the other hand, do not contain so much evidence of live debate and are almost always real sophismata and not disputed questions.[15] I assume that the works of the Oxford Calculators were composed by men who were masters of arts and not students, but I doubt that the sophismata of Kilvington and Heytesbury were publicly determined by them in live debate, although Kilvington's sophismata are usually determined by him in their literary format. Rather than being records of live debate, the works of Kilvington, Heytesbury, and Richard Swineshead seem to have originated as written works intended primarily to provide ammunition for future undergraduate disputes with little emphasis on a particular magisterial determination. In its literary format, Heytesbury's *Regulae solvendi sophismata* may be seen as developing a set of theories which are then extended and applied by means of sophismata.[16] In its historical genesis, however, the order was most likely the other way around, as the title of the work would indicate: posing and solving sophismata was the live activity in the service of which the rules were compiled. Perhaps with the help of such works, the undergraduate disputations in fourteenth-century Oxford were carried on with a level of energy and expertise high enough to merit outside attention.[17]

The alleged distinction between 'physical' and 'logical' sophismata

This, then, is the disputational context in which the core works of the Oxford Calculators should be viewed.[18] But, if so, why, we might ask, are

14. See note 10 above. Also Grabmann 1940a and Pinborg 1975b.
15. Pinborg 1979, pp. 28–9.
16. Cf. Wallerand 1913, pp. (29)–(32). Wallerand distinguishes between the use of sophismata as exercises applying a theory and their use to extend theory. Murdoch 1974, pp. 63–70; Murdoch 1975e, pp. 304–7.
17. It is striking that the *forma* for determination in 1409 is introduced by a statement that Oxford has received many honours for the determinations of its bachelors and that the logical subtlety for which Oxford is world-famous receives its greatest increase from exercise in determinations (Gibson 1931, p. 199): 'Quia per sollennes determinaciones bachillariorum in facultate arcium nostra mater Oxonie universitas, et precipue ipsa arcium facultas, multipliciter honoratur, ac mira sciencie logicalis subtilitas, qua prefata mater nostra supra cetera mundi studia dinoscitur actenus claruisse, per fructuosum exercicium in eisdem potissimum suscipit incrementum, utile et expediens visum est magistris ut certa forma provideretur, sub qua bachillarii sufficientes et ydonei, exclusis indignis, ad determinacionis actum forent admittendi, modumque et condiciones exprimere, quos in suo introitu, processu et exitu debeant observare ...' For the fame of Oxford logic at Paris, see Gilbert 1976; Coleman 1975; Murdoch 1978b.
18. Cf. Duhem 1906–13, III, pp. 441–51; Pedersen 1953, p. 141: 'The result ... was a new kind of literature, the so-called *sophismata*, viz. tracts containing huge collections of calculations in the most various fields with Suiseth's own book as the most famous example.'

physical as well as logical subjects involved in these rules and sophismata? What are we to make of the so-called 'physical sophismata'?[19] For all the physics used in these works, it appears that they were not intended to be part of the student's education in natural philosophy, though they might use philosophical knowledge already gained. As will be clear from the more detailed description of the works to follow, in Kilvington's or Heytesbury's work one cannot separate 'physical sophismata' from logical or grammatical sophismata; physical concepts are used in traditional logical sophismata where they might not have been expected.[20] And wherever natural philosophy or calculations are used, they are used for the sake of the disputation, either to set up the puzzling results typical of sophismata or else to unravel such results once they have been set up. Just as one could derive and explain counterintuitive results using the techniques of syncategoremata and supposition theory, so one could do so using *calculationes*.[21]

This at least would be the rationale for introducing calculations. We are not forced to conclude that there is no natural philosophy or mathematics in the works of the Oxford Calculators. It may have been the case that because the general disputations of the *sophistae in parviso* were somewhat separated from the ordinary lectures there was a greater chance there to introduce material from non-logical disciplines than would have been the case in an ordinary disputation covering questions arising from the reading of a particular book of logic. Perhaps *sophistae* attracted by the more advanced topics of natural philosophy and mathematics were tempted to smuggle these topics into disputations *in parviso* originally meant as logical exercises. But even if this is the correct explanation of the appearance of natural philosophy and mathematics in sophismata, the work would nevertheless have been done in the context and under the influence of logical disputations.

19. For discussions of physical sophismata, see Duhem 1906–13, III, pp. 441–54; Michalski 1926, pp. 59–61; Maier 1952, pp. 264–70; Weisheipl 1964a, p. 178, n. 96; Bottin 1973, p. 126; Murdoch 1975a, p. 306.
20. Wilson 1956, pp. 21–5. Physical subject matter could seem to fall under *scientiae sermocinales* when the emphasis was put upon an analysis of the semantics of the propositions comprising science. John Murdoch has drawn attention to the 'second intentional' or 'metalinguistic' approach of fourteenth-century natural philosophy in a recent series of important articles which give examples of how this occurred in detail and explores various ways in which it may have come about. See Murdoch 1974a, pp. 60–2, 68–70, 73–4, 100, 105, 111–12; Murdoch 1975a, pp. 287–8, 303–7; Murdoch 1979 and his other recent articles, some still in press at the time of this writing.
21. Alvarus Thomas 1509 provides some vivid descriptions of how calculations might be involved in disputations. See Duhem 1906–13, III, pp. 537, 541–3.

Richard Kilvington's Sophismata

Kilvington's *Sophismata* exemplifies as perfectly as one might desire how close disputations *de sophismatibus* might come to questions of mathematics and natural philosophy without ever leaving the confines of logic and semantics proper and without bringing in calculations to any extent.[22] It seems likely that this work was composed before Bradwardine's *De proportionibus* in 1328.[23] Although not bringing in mathematics or natural philosophy directly, Kilvington's work was so close to it, so ready for it, that it was only a very small step for Heytesbury to bring in mathematics and physics explicitly in his sophismata. Whether this happened primarily because of a felt need within the sophismata tradition or because of the impressiveness of Bradwardine's achievement (after Kilvington's?) is not clear, but both factors must have had an important influence.

Kilvington's sophismata are individually short and topically unified in comparison with Heytesbury's, but they are organised and connected in a way that allows a sustained examination of certain problem areas. The first eleven sophismata all involve combinations of beginning, ceasing, and comparisons of degrees of whiteness. In the twelfth sophisma the problems of traversing a space are introduced and these are treated, sometimes in combination with problems of beginning and ceasing, of motive power,

22. I have based my study of Kilvington on the forthcoming edition of his *Sophismata* prepared by Norman and Barbara Kretzmann. I would like to thank them for generously providing me with the typescript of their edition. Wilson 1956, pp. 163–8, gives a list of the sophisma sentences with some indications of parts of the arguments. In Wilson's numbering, Sophisma 30 should be omitted and the subsequent numbers decreased by one. In general I here follow Kretzmann's terminology, according to which the typical sophisma has the following parts: (1) the 'sophisma sentence' which is frequently called the sophism in recent literature; (2) the 'hypothesis' or hypothetical case in light of which the sophisma sentence is to be interpreted; (3) the proof of the sophisma sentence; (4) the disproof of the sophisma sentence; (5) the solution of the sophisma; (6) the reply to arguments for the opposing side. All these parts together are called the 'sophisma', retaining the medieval term to guard against the too easy assumption that medieval sophismata are all considered sophisms or sophistical in the modern sense. While in many cases the sophisma sentences are strange or bizarre, often they are not – for instance '*A* begins to be true' (Kilvington, Sophisma 16) or 'Socrates does not move faster than Plato' (Kilvington, Sophisma 32). What does characterise the sophismata of the Oxford Calculators more universally is that there are plausible proofs and disproofs of the same sophisma sentence, a plausible proof of something that appears obviously false, or a plausible disproof of something that seems obviously true.

23. The *Sophismata* shows no familiarity with Bradwardine's work – for instance it does not draw a distinction between total (or average) and instantaneous velocity where such a distinction would have been most useful. Kilvington was a bachelor of theology by 1335. If we assume that seven years of study of theology were required for that degree, Kilvington's 'necessary regency' in the arts would have occurred *ca.* 1326–8 or before. The *Sophismata* was cited by Adam Wodeham in 1330–1. See Courtenay 1978, pp. 86–9. Courtenay suggests that Kilvington became a bachelor of theology between 1332 and 1335. It should be noted, however, that Kilvington's *Questions on the Physics* are said to take up Bradwardine's dynamics (Maier 1964, p. 253). For a more detailed consideration of the historical questions surrounding Kilvington's work, see the Introduction to the forthcoming edition of his *Sophismata* by Norman and Barbara Kretzmann.

or of comparisons of velocities, in Sophismata 12–19, 27–35, and 42–4. The intermediate sophismata deal with generation and corruption (20, 39–41), whitening involving non-uniformity of whiteness (21–3, 26), division of a body (24–5), and strength (36–8). The last four sophismata are somewhat separate and deal with problems associated with the verb 'to know'.

What is remarkable about these sophismata is that all but the last four (and Sophisma 17 which treats an issue subsidiary to 16) deal with problems of motion (or change) and yet physical issues concerning motion are very rarely raised. Thus the first sophisma sentence is 'Socrates is whiter than Plato begins to be white', for the interpretation of which it is supposed that Socrates is white in the highest degree and that Plato now is not white and begins to be white.[24] In the whole discussion of the sophisma it is tacitly assumed that the whiteness Plato takes on increases continuously from zero degree as an extrinsic limit, but nothing is said (a) about how whiteness is measured or determined when it may be non-uniformly distributed within a body, or (b) about what theory of the intension and remission of forms is assumed – among the many theories hotly debated in the fourteenth century.[25]

To put the matter in modern terms, the problem at issue in the first sophisma arises from the fact that the set of degrees that Plato takes on has no least member and no intrinsic bound on the smaller side, but rather contains degrees lower than any given degree. If it is admitted that Socrates is whiter than Plato begins to be white, then it would seem to follow that he is infinitely whiter proportionally, since there is no intrinsic lower bound to Plato's whitenesses: given any ratio between Socrates' whiteness and some degree of whiteness Plato takes on, there is a greater ratio between Socrates' whiteness and a smaller whiteness that Plato takes on. But Plato begins to have not zero whiteness but some whiteness, and so it seems to follow that if Socrates is infinitely whiter than Plato then Socrates must be infinitely white, which is false.[26]

24. This sophisma has been discussed several times in the recent literature. See Bottin 1973 (Latin text of the initial sophismata); Kretzmann 1977 (English translation of the first sophisma); Knuuttila and Lehtinen 1979.
25. For these theories see Sylla 1973.
26. As Kilvington recognises in his reply to the sophisma, this is a good argument except for the last sentence. 'Socrates is infinitely whiter than Plato begins to be white' is a true proposition if 'infinitely' is taken in the syncategorematic sense. Then the sense of the proposition is simply that given any ratio between Socrates' whiteness and some degree of whiteness Plato takes on, there is a greater ratio between Socrates' whiteness and a degree of whiteness that Plato takes on earlier. This does not entitle one to conclude that there is an infinite ratio between Socrates' whiteness and some given degree of whiteness taken on by Plato, and so it does not entitle one to conclude that Socrates is infinitely white.

Kilvington responds that the sophisma sentence is true, and concedes that Socrates is infinitely whiter than Plato begins to be white; but he denies that Socrates is infinitely white on the grounds that there is no given first and most remiss degree of whiteness that Plato will have.[27]

In reply to the second sophisma – 'Socrates is infinitely whiter than Plato begins to be white' – Kilvington again accepts the sophisma sentence, but denies that it implies that Plato begins to be infinitely less white than Socrates is now, again on the grounds that there is no first degree of whiteness with which Plato begins to be white.[28] The ostensible basis for the distinction between the two accepted and rejected propositions is word order. Expressions standing first in a proposition, before any syncategorematic word, refer to determinate supposita, such as given degrees of whiteness in Socrates or Plato. But expressions occurring later in the proposition or after some syncategorematic word may refer indeterminately to a whole set of supposita, such as all the degrees of whiteness Plato takes on.[29] Thus Kilvington has solved these sophismata not by using physical theory or mathematics, but rather by using the standard techniques of terminist logic.

A second example of the logical orientation of Kilvington's sophismata can be found in the sophismata about traversing a distance. The main issue raised concerning traversing a distance A is whether one should say that Socrates traverses it (a) at any time he is in the process of traversing A, or (b) only when he has completely traversed A. Against the first interpretation is the consequence that Socrates traverses A infinitely many times, since infinitely many times he will be in the process of traversing A; but Socrates traverses A only once. Against the second interpretation is the consideration that when Socrates has traversed A completely, then he is no longer traversing it; so it hardly makes sense to say that he traverses A only when he has traversed A completely.

In Sophisma 13 – 'Socrates will traverse distance A' – Kilvington concludes only by distinguishing the two senses of 'Socrates will traverse distance A' – either it is equivalent to 'Socrates will be in the process of traversing distance A', in which case the sophisma sentence is true, and it is true that Socrates will traverse A infinitely many times, or it is equivalent to 'Distance A will have been traversed by Socrates', in which case the

27. Bottin 1973, pp. 139–40; Kretzmann 1977, p. 15.
28. Bottin 1973, pp. 140–1.
29. For this standard use of supposition theory see the discussions of supposition and syncategoremata elsewhere in this volume.

sophisma sentence will not be true before the last instant of the time period during which Socrates will move over distance A.[30]

The replies to Sophisma 12 – 'Socrates has traversed distance A' – are much more complicated. The main question is whether or not the instant at which Socrates first reaches the end of distance A (call it instant C) is the first instant at which he has traversed distance A. Kilvington's preferred answer is that at C it is not true that Socrates has traversed A, because in that case he would have ceased moving over A, which is false (he has not ceased moving over A because at C he is still touching the end of A).[31] From the fact that distance A has been traversed by Socrates it does not follow that Socrates has traversed distance A, but only that he begins to have traversed A (in the sense that at C he has not traversed A but immediately after C he will have traversed A).[32] An alternative reply, which Kilvington finds less satisfactory, interprets 'Socrates has traversed A' as equivalent to 'Socrates was in the process of traversing A'.[33]

Thus in his preferred reply Kilvington interprets 'Socrates has traversed A' as equivalent to 'A was previously traversed by Socrates'. A third alternative which Kilvington mentions but does not develop would be to interpret 'Socrates has traversed A' as equivalent to 'A has been traversed by Socrates', which would leave open the possibility that A has just now been traversed and was not previously traversed by Socrates.[34] Given

---

30. 'Socrates pertransibit A spatium. . . . Ad sophisma dicitur distinguendo de isto termino "pertransibit". Uno modo sic exponitur: "Socrates pertransibit A spatium" id est, "Socrates erit in pertranseundo A spatium." Et sic est sophisma verum. Et ulterius conceditur conclusio ultima, quod infinities isto modo pertransibit Socrates A spatium, quia infinities erit Socrates in pertranseundo A spatium. Alio modo potest sophisma exponi sic: "Socrates pertransibit A spatium" – id est, "A spatium erit pertransitum a Socrate." Et ita loquendo ante C non pertransibit Socrates A spatium' (ed. Kretzmann, forthcoming).

31. 'Socrates pertransivit A spatium . . . Ad sophisma dicitur quod est falsum, quia si Socrates pertransivit A spatium et nullam aliam partem B spatii Socrates pertransivit, ut suppono – sit B quoddam totum spatium cuius medietas est A spatium – igitur Socrates desinebat moveri super A spatium, quod est falsum' (ed. Kretzmann, forthcoming).

32. 'Ad probationem dicitur quod non valet illa consequentia: "A spatium est pertransitum a Socrate; igitur Socrates pertransivit A spatium." Sed bene sequitur "A spatium est pertransitum a Socrate; igitur Socrates pertransivit A spatium vel incipit pertransivisse A spatium"' (ed. Kretzmann, forthcoming).

33. 'Aliter tamen dicunt quidam concedendo quod Socrates pertransivit A spatium. Et ulterius, quando arguitur "Socrates pertransivit A spatium; igitur Socrates prius pertransivit A spatium", concedunt conclusionem. Et ulterius concedunt quod Socrates incepit pertransire A spatium quando Socrates incepit moveri super A spatium, et quod per totum tempus quo Socrates movebatur super A spatium fuit haec propositio vera: "Socrates pertransivit A spatium"' (ed. Kretzmann, forthcoming).

34. 'Alio modo exponitur iste terminus "pertransivit" per verbum passivum sic: "Socrates pertransivit A spatium" – id est, "A spatium est pertransitum a Socrate." Et sic exponendo istum terminum "pertransivit" non sequitur "Socrates pertransivit A spatium; igitur Socrates prius

Kilvington's preferred reply, Socrates will not begin to traverse A any sooner than he will begin to *have* traversed A previously (neither will be true until immediately after instant C). On the third alternative reply Socrates will traverse A when he will not have traversed it previously – at instant C 'A has been traversed by Socrates' will be true, but 'A was previously traversed by Socrates' will not be true. Nevertheless, even on this alternative interpretation both propositions will begin to be true at C; the first will be true at C and at no time before (one of the two standard expositions of 'begins'), and the second will not be true at C but at any time thereafter (the other standard exposition of 'begins'). All of this is said in reply to Sophisma 14.[35]

Having explored in Sophismata 12–14 the results of assuming that Socrates traverses a distance either (a) when he is in the process of traversing it or (b) when he has completely traversed it, Kilvington, in Sophisma 15, considers the results of assuming (c) that a distance is traversed when more than half of it is traversed. These results need not detain us here, but the overall circumstances are worth noting. The issues Kilvington considers in Sophismata 12–15 are very close to the Oxford Calculators' later common concern with the proper measures of local motion with respect to effect.[36]

There is little mathematical or calculatory about Kilvington's procedure except in Sophisma 15 where he argues that if something is traversed when more than half of it is traversed, it follows that if distance B is traversed, then C, equal to three-halves B, will be traversed. But if C is traversed, then

pertransivit A spatium," quia non sequitur "A spatium est pertransitum a Socrate; igitur A spatium est prius pertransitum a Socrate"' (ed. Kretzmann, forthcoming).

35. 'Socrates incipiet pertransire A spatium, et Socrates incipiet pertransivisse A spatium, et non prius incipiet pertransire A spatium quam incipiet pertransivisse A spatium. Et hoc probatur per expositionem istorum terminorum "pertransire" et "pertransivisse". Nam non prius incipiet Socrates esse in pertranseundo A spatium quam incipiet fuisse in pertranseundo A spatium, quia sine tempore medio postquam Socrates incipiet moveri super A spatium erit in pertranseundo A spatium, et sine medio postquam Socrates incipiet moveri erit verum quod Socrates fuit in pertranseundo A spatium. Ideo in hoc sensu et secundum hanc expositionem concedendum est sophisma. Sed alio modo exponendo eosdem terminos sophisma est falsum. Quia prius incipiet A spatium esse pertransitum quam debet fuisse pertransitum, quia prius erit verum A spatium esse pertransitum quam A spatium fuisse pertransitum. Quod patet quia in primo instanti in quo motor deveniet ad B terminum A spatii erit haec propositio vera: "A est pertransitum." Et tunc non erit haec propositio vera: "A fuit pertransitum", posito quod A non erit pertransitum nisi semel ante C instans. Unde licet concedenda sit haec propositio "Prius incipiet A spatium esse pertransitum quam debet fuisse pertransitum", haec tamen propositio est neganda: "Prius incipiet A spatium esse pertransitum quam incipiet fuisse pertransitum", quia in C incipiet A spatium esse pertransitum, exponendo li "incipit" per positionem de praesenti et remotionem de praeterito, et in C incipiet A spatium fuisse pertransitum, alio tamen modo exponendo li "incipit" – scilicet, per remotionem de praesenti et positionem de futuro' (ed. Kretzmann, forthcoming).

36. Cf. Clagett 1959, pp. 208–9.

D, equal to 2B, will be traversed since C is more than half D, etc.[37] But with or without this small foray into calculations on Kilvington's part it is obvious how, beginning from Kilvington's logico-semantical approach, one could be drawn by progressive stages into calculations.

Bradwardine's De proportionibus

Although this work of Bradwardine's does not represent the Oxford calculatory tradition at its most typical, it was highly influential in that tradition.[38] Bradwardine devoted the first main section of his treatise to an exposition of a mathematical theory of ratios. This theory was based on Book V of Euclid's *Elements*, but it took advantage of a theoretical tradition in mathematics that treated ratios as *sui generis* and entirely different from fractions in order to develop a system of operations on ratios different from the normal system of operations on fractions.[39]

In the second and third chapters of the work, Bradwardine used this system of ratios to defend a new theory of how forces, resistances, and velocities are to be correlated in local motions.[40] Bradwardine's new theory became the dominant one in the succeeding period, being rejected primarily by those philosophers who rejected his distinction between ratios and fractions.[41]

In the fourth chapter Bradwardine argued that velocities of rotation should be measured by the speed of the fastest moved point.[42] This attempt to establish a measure for rotations soon blossomed in the work of Heytesbury and others into attempts to find measures of all sorts of local

---

37. 'A spatium incipit esse pertransitum. Posito quod A spatium dicatur pertransitum quando maior pars eius fuerit pertransita, et sit A spatium non pertransitum quando maior pars eius fuerit non pertransita. Et ponatur quod aliquid incipiat moveri super A spatium. Tunc probatur sophisma sic. A spatium non est pertransitum et erit pertransitum, et nullum tempus erit antequam A spatium erit pertransitum; igitur A spatium incipit esse pertransitum. Consequentia patet et maior similiter. Et minorem probo, quia si aliquod tempus erit antequam A spatium erit pertransitum, sit igitur, gratia exempli, quod hora erit antequam A spatium erit pertransitum. Sed probo quod non, quia lapsa medietate illius horae, verum erit quod A est pertransitum. Quod probo, quia lapsa medietate illius horae, verum erit quod aliqua pars A est pertransita. Sit igitur quod B pars tunc sit pertransita. Tunc sic. B est pertransitum, et B est plus quam medietas C; igitur per casum C tunc erit pertransitum – posito quod C sit unum compositum ex B et alia parte A aequali medietati B. Et per consimile argumentum D erit tunc pertransitum – posito quod D sit duplum ad B. Et sic arguendo, sequitur quod lapsa medietate illius horae praedictae, totum A erit pertransitum' (ed. Kretzmann, forthcoming).
38. The full text of the work is in Crosby 1955. See also Murdoch 1969, pp. 225–33.
39. See Molland 1968a and 1978, pp. 150–60. I have written a paper which tries to trace these traditions for the Festschrift for I. B. Cohen (forthcoming).
40. See Weisheipl's contribution to this volume.
41. See Clagett 1959, p. 443.
42. Crosby 1955, pp. 128–33, and Clagett 1959, pp. 215–16, 220–2.

motions, augmentations, and alterations.[43] Thus if Bradwardine's contemporaries were tempted by sophismata like Kilvington's to want to introduce mathematical physics into their sophismata, Bradwardine provided them with excellent starting materials.

Burley's De primo et ultimo instanti and De intensione et remissione formarum

Although Burley's works were used by Italian philosophers of the fifteenth and sixteenth centuries as if they belonged to the same universe of discourse as the works of Heytesbury and Swineshead, it can be seen that, from a fourteenth-century point of view, they represent stages leading into the calculatory tradition rather than full-fledged parts of it. Burley, like Kilvington, very rarely calculates. Nevertheless, for at least two reasons, Burley's work became very important to the calculatory tradition.

First of all, Burley's question (delivered at Toulouse) *De primo et ultimo instanti* (*On the First and Last Instant*) took the existing logical tradition of discussing the syncategorematic words 'begins' and 'ceases', a tradition which had already incorporated some Aristotelian physics in the thirteenth-century works of Peter of Spain and William of Sherwood,[44] and connected it even more inextricably with physics. Henceforth, if one wanted to know, for instance, whether in a given case of beginning there would be a last instant of non-existence or a first instant of existence, it was clear that one ought to look at the underlying physics of the situation to find an answer. Whereas the earlier tradition had distinguished between permanent entities for which there would be a first and no last instant of existence and successive entities (like motion) for which there would be only a last instant of non-existence in beginning and only a first instant of non-existence in ceasing, Burley broke down the category of permanent entities into many sub-categories, e.g. permanent things having an indivisible degree of perfection (for which there would be a first and last instant of existence) versus permanent things existing within a range or latitude of degrees (for which there would be a first and no last instant of existence).[45]

Secondly, Burley's treatises on the intension and remission of forms were important to the calculatory tradition because they offered a well-

---

43. Cf. Clagett 1959, Ch. 4–6; Wilson 1960, Ch. 4.
44. Cf. Wilson 1960, Ch. 2; Kretzmann 1976; Murdoch 1979; and Murdoch forthcoming a. A preliminary edition of the Burley question has been published (Shapiro 1965).
45. Shapiro 1965, pp. 164–6.

developed theory of alteration in terms of the succession of forms, opposed to the more commonly accepted addition theory of alteration.[46] These treatises also gave clear expositions of a third theory, the admixture theory, which was sometimes combined with the addition theory. The competition among these three theories left open a wide range of possible assumptions concerning qualities which could be exploited by the Calculators. On Burley's theory a body that was hot would at each point have some degree of heat and no degrees of cold. On the admixture theory the sum of hot and cold at any given point of a body always equalled some maximum degree (usually taken as eight) with a hot body having more hot than cold and a cold body more cold than hot. The Calculators, who usually hold the addition theory, vacillated inconsistently between assuming that there was one quality of a given type at one place and assuming that both qualities could be present at a given place. This vacillation gave them far more opportunities for calculation than would otherwise have been the case.

Kilvington and logic, Bradwardine and mathematics, Burley and natural philosophy

Thus, very generally speaking, while Kilvington contributed to the origins of the calculatory movement from the logical side and Bradwardine from the mathematical side, Burley's contribution came mainly from natural philosophy and from bringing natural philosophy into juxtaposition with what had once been simply logical problems. Of course William Ockham and the Ockhamists also contributed very importantly to the habit of bringing physical considerations into logic – for instance considerations of what sorts of entities actually exist in the outside world.[47]

Heytesbury's Regulae

I take the work of Heytesbury and Swineshead as representing the peak of the Oxford calculatory tradition. In the prohemium to his *Regulae solvendi sophismata* (*Rules for Solving Sophismata*) Heytesbury says that it is meant for the young men engaged in the first year of the study of logic and that it will deal not with sophismata presenting enormous difficulties, but with those which come up in common and everyday exercises and which any re-

---

46. The *Second Treatise* was published at Venice in 1496. See Shapiro 1959; Maier 1968, pp. 315–52; Sylla 1973, pp. 233–8.
47. See Murdoch forthcoming b.

sponder ought to come to know how to unravel.[48] In saying this, although modern historians have doubted it,[49] Heytesbury clearly does intend to write for beginners and not for the older and more advanced *sophistae*; but in his reference to responders, there is an indication that the book is not for the most junior students who would simply listen to lectures on logic, but rather for those who had advanced to the stage of responding in disputations *de sophismatibus* or *in parviso*.

In the prohemium Heytesbury goes on to say that he has organised the subject matter to make it possible to find a given subject more quickly.[50] Although the *Regulae* consists mainly of fully resolved sophismata, these are meant as examples which, along with the explicitly stated rules, will make it easy for a respondent to solve any sophisma put to him. Almost every section of the work contains the remark that many other sophismata can be produced concerning the same subject-matter, all of which can be solved using the rules stated.[51]

The major sections of the *Regulae* are on (1) self-reference (*insolubilia*); (2) 'to know' and 'to doubt'; (3) relative terms; (4) 'begins' and 'ceases'; (5) maxima and minima; and (6) the three categories of motion, – viz., local motion, augmentation, and alteration.[52] One might suppose that the earlier sections concern logic while the later sections pertain to natural philosophy, but in fact problems associated with traversing spaces and alteration are introduced into earlier sections as well as later ones. Each section provides a separate vocabulary and rules, or what might be called an 'analytical language', to use John Murdoch's terminology, which will

48. William Heytesbury 1494, f. 4[va]: 'Regulas solvendi sophismata non ea quidem quae apparenti contradictione undique vallavit iuventorum subtilitas aut quae latere solent quempiam logicorum, sed quae adeo existunt communia ut communis quotidianaque exercitatio ea doceat atque responsalem quemlibet oportet noscere evolvere: vestrae sollicitudini iuvenes studio logicalium agentes annum primum prout facultatis meae administraret sterilitas: traderem brevi summa: si non verbosus tumor sophistarum veterum provectorumque indignatio altiora quaerentium huic operi obviarent. Nescio, enim, nec video inter tot et tantas inventiones novas opinionesque tam varias sicut iam de die in diem pullulant et frondescunt qualiter declinarent murmura dum quae certa sunt omnibus ulterius attentarem. Verum quoniam est iste labor facilis ipsumque utilitatem quamdam spero posse amplecti praetensam hanc causam non causabor ut causam sed opusculum istud ut praemissis studentibus offerre proposui moderata brevitate veluti quodam introductionis modo aggredi temptabo. Et in sex capitula dividens summulam ne dispendiosae et incompositae narrationis ob prolixitatem lectorum fastidiat oculos. Viso primum quid in singulis inferius agetur capitulis ut inveniat quisque promptius quod voluerit.'

49. Weisheipl 1968, pp. 196–7.

50. See text in note 48.

51. Heytesbury 1494, ff. 16[rb], 21[rb], 21[va], 26[va], 27[ra], 41[vb], 42[va], 44[ra], 44[rb].

52. For the later sections, see Wilson 1956. Paul Spade has translated the section on insolubilia (Spade 1979b).

be useful in solving certain sophismata – often with two or more of the 'analytical languages' applied seriatim to the same sophisma.[53]

In its structure and purpose Heytesbury's *Regulae* is very nearly the prototype of the late fifteenth- and early sixteenth-century printed *Libelli Sophistarum ad usum Oxoniensium* and *Cantabrigiensem*.[54] These later printed books, also designed for the use of *sophistae* or advanced undergraduates, generally contain a collection of short works on basic logic along with treatises on *obligationes* and *insolubilia*, a short work on fallacies, a vocabulary of the basic terms of natural philosophy, and a treatise on proportions or ratios like Bradwardine's. The booklet for Cambridge *sophistae* has a section devoted specifically to sophismata which deals with many of the sophismata found in Heytesbury's collection, but treated more briefly.[55] Within its treatise on insolubilia there is a long section on maxima and minima.[56] The preface to the *Libellus ... Oxoniensium* (*Booklet for the Use of Sophistae at Oxford*) indicates that it will help the student impress others with his solutions of sophismata.[57]

One final indication that all of Heytesbury's *Regulae* has an essentially logical rather than natural philosophical intent is that in several places it is remarked that the cases treated are impossible in nature, although they are given consideration as imaginable. Thus, for instance, Heytesbury considers acceleration to infinity as imaginable and so available for consideration, but he thought it physically impossible.[58] In dealing with a case of diminution to zero quantity, Heytesbury says, 'assume for the sake of argument that numerically the same magnitude can be diminished part by

---

53. Murdoch 1974a, pp. 58–60; Murdoch 1975a, pp. 282–7. Among these conceptual languages are the languages of intension and remission of forms, proportions, beginning and ceasing, first and last instants, maxima and minima, continuity and infinity, and supposition theory. Such an 'analytical language' would have, not only a set of technical terms, but also a set of standard moves used to analyse any problem.

54. See Ashworth 1979. For fifteenth-century manuscripts of similar works see De Rijk 1975.

55. It is the seventh tract in the book and appears also in MS Cambridge, Gonville and Caius 182/215, pp. 73–91. See De Rijk 1975, pp. 302–3. I have used the edition of London, Wynandus de Worde, 1524.

56. This is the sixteenth tract in the book. The main treatise on insolubilia is that of Roger Swineshead, but other material has been added.

57. London, Richard Pynson, 1499–1500, f. Ai verso: '... quoniam tam inter se congruentes sunt logica et sophistria ut qui logicam laudat sophistriam bonum logice seminarium laudet necesse sit. Haec enim tractat subtilissima sophismata quae si quis bene doctique intellexerit videbitur apud omnes mirabiles sapientiae et disciplinae.'

58. Heytesbury 1494b, 43vb: 'Sed contra illud forte arguitur posito quod A et B motus sic intendantur saltem difformiter A continue in duplo velocius B quousque uterque illorum habuerit omnem gradum velocitatis imaginabilem, videlicet usque ad gradum velocitatis infinitum secundum imaginationem ...' Cf. Heytesbury 1494c, f. 161vb.

part until it has no quantity. Although, indeed, this is not possible literally speaking, nevertheless since the case is not self-contradictory it can satisfactorily be admitted for the sake of disputation.'[59] Gaetano di Thiene comments that 'calculators should not flee from a case'.[60] Thus the point is not to discuss what really happens physically, but rather to dispute imaginary cases in the usual fourteenth-century manner.[61] Here it is clear that it is not God's absolute power that leads to the introduction of imaginary cases, but rather the disputational rules under which a Calculator is supposed to operate. Heytesbury in one case gives alternate responses to a single argument and comments: 'The first response is more fitting for the *sophista* and the second pertains more to the facts (*ad rem*).'[62]

Heytesbury's Sophismata

Heytesbury's *Sophismata* provides an excellent example of the use of physical theory and calculations in sophismata. At the same time, I believe, this treatise shows that the whole investigation was still considered a part of logic and not partly logic, partly physics. Of Heytesbury's thirty-two sophismata, Constantin Michalski and others have characterised the last two as physical and the others as logical because of their sophisma sentences (and on the basis of the colophon of a Parisian manuscript).[63] Many of Heytesbury's first thirty sophismata are familiar from the sophisma-literature of the thirteenth century.[64] By contrast, the last two sophismata are (31) 'It is necessary that something be condensed if something should be rarefied' and (32) 'It is impossible that something be heated unless some-

---

59. Heytesbury 1494b, f. 48ᵛᵃ: 'Posito gratia argumenti quod eadem magnitudo numero poterit diminui per partem ante partem usque ad non quantum. Quamvis enim hoc non sit possibile de virtute sermonis tamen ex quo casus non claudit contradictionem satis poterit admitti gratia disputationis.'

60. *Ibid.*: 'Cum quantitas sit aeterna mere est impossibile quod illa magnitudo condensetur usque ad non quantum. Sed dicit ille magister bene scis hoc, sed quia non implicat contradictionem et est satis imaginabile, ideo calculatores non debent fugere casum quia est fuga baranorum.' The significance of the last four words is not clear to me.

61. Cf. Wilson 1956, pp. 24–5; Murdoch 1974a, pp. 64–70; Murdoch 1975a, pp. 281, 292; Murdoch and Sylla 1978, pp. 246–7.

62. Heytesbury 1494b, f. 21ᵛᵃ: 'Prima responsio plus convenit sophistae et secunda ad rem magis pertinet.'

63. Michalski 1926, pp. 59–60. The MS is Paris BN lat. 16134. Weisheipl 1964a, pp. 178–80.

64. Heytesbury, *Sophismata*. Cf. Wilson 1956, pp. 153–63 for a list of the sophisma sentences and a sketch of the argumentation. The first ten sophisma sentences are: (1) 'Omnis homo est omnis homo'; (2) 'Omne coloratum est'; (3) 'Omnis homo est totum in quantitate'; (4) 'Omnis homo est unus solus homo'; (5) 'Omnis homo qui est albus currit'; (6) 'Anima Antichristi necessario erit'; (7) 'Omnis propositio vel eius contradictoria est vera'; (8) 'Isti ferunt lapidem'; (9) 'Neutrum oculum habendo tu potes videre'; (10) 'Quilibet homo morietur quando unus solus homo morietur.'

thing be cooled.'[65] But a prominent feature of the last two sophismata is that they are modal propositions involving 'necessary' and 'impossible'; despite their presentation of physical considerations, they might well be disputed in connection with logical problems of modality. Conversely, the earlier sophismata might well be proved or disproved on the basis of physical considerations. Thus the fifth sophisma – 'Every man who is white is running' – is used to consider the way in which the distribution of a quality in a body affects what is said about the whole body: how white does a man have to be to be called white? This might raise the whole issue of the proper measures of qualities.

Thus one must distinguish between the 'sophisma sentence' and the 'sophisma', the whole development consisting of the sophisma sentence, hypothesis, proof, disproof, and resolution. The appearance of physics in sophisma sentences and the appearance of physics in the full sophismata are sufficiently independent of each other to argue against assuming that there were 'physical sophismata', which were considered parts of natural philosophy.

Looking only at Heytesbury's first ten sophismata, it is clear that physical and calculatory elements are present throughout and are not reserved for the last two sophismata. And yet, again, these elements are applied not to natural cases, but rather only to imaginary cases.[66] Again Gaetano comments: 'For although these cases now posited are not possible *de facto*, nevertheless they are imaginable without contradiction, and so they should be admitted by the logician'.[67]

If we turn to the last two so-called physical sophismata, we find indeed that mainly physical arguments are used there, but that logical arguments are also used, and that the physical cases proposed are not naturally possible, but only imaginable. In discussing whether it is true that, in the words of the last sophisma 'It is impossible for something to be heated unless something should be cooled', Heytesbury must first of all, for the sake of disputation, agree to use words loosely, because he believes that, strictly speaking, nothing is heated or cooled, since whenever something is acted on by a heating or cooling agent it undergoes a substantial as well as an accidental change and hence does not remain the same thing. Water is

65. (31) 'Necesse est aliquid condensari si aliquid rarefiat'; (32) 'Impossibile est aliquid calefieri nisi aliquid frigefiat.'
66. Cf. Heytesbury 1494c, 133ra, and esp. 161vb and 162va. Cf. Wilson 1956, p. 25, n. 65.
67. Heytesbury 1494c, f. 89ra: 'Nam licet casus nunc positi de facto non sint possibiles, sunt tamen imaginabiles absque contradictione, quare a logico admittendi.'

never heated because as soon as a heating agent is applied it begins to convert the water to air.[68]

Even beyond this, however, much of Heytesbury's argumentation is based on cases that are naturally impossible. Supposing that bodies often simultaneously contain degrees of hot and cold, Heytesbury concedes that if, *per impossibile*, there were a body with no hot or cold, then it could simultaneously be heated and cooled.[69] Indeed, he thought that any body in which the sum of the degrees or latitudes of hot and cold was less than the maximum degree or latitude could be simultaneously heated and cooled until the sum of its degrees reached the maximum degree, at which time any further heating would require a reduction of the cold present and vice versa.[70] But since it would never occur naturally that a body was qualified with degrees totalling less than the maximum degree, Heytesbury's interest in the last two sophismata is no more truly physical than in the earlier ones; he is interested in performing thought experiments, but he is unconcerned with even their theoretical realisability.

Swineshead's Liber calculationum

If Swineshead's *Liber calculationum* (Book of Calculations) is considered in the light of Heytesbury's works, it becomes clear that, for all its exclusive concern with physical topics, the *Liber calculationum*, too, is a work concerning not real but imaginable cases and designed to be used in disputations. The treatises of the *Liber calculationum* consider (1) intension and remission: (2) non-uniformly qualified bodies; (3) the intensity of an element having two unequally intense qualities: (4) the intensity of mixed bodies; (5) rarity and density; (6) augmentation; (7) reaction; (8) powers of things; (9) difficulty of action; (10) maxima and minima; (11) the place of an element; (12) light sources; (13) the action of light sources; (14) local motion; (15) non-resisting media; (16) the induction of the maximum degree.[71]

The typical treatise first lists the various positions usually taken concern-

---

68. *Ibid.*, ff. 164va, 165vb.
69. *Ibid.*, f. 170va: '... dato per impossibile quod esset aliquod corpus alterabile quod nullam caliditatem nec frigiditatem haberet et esset sibi approximatum aliquod aliud corpus quod esset uniforme per totum aequaliter omnino habens de caliditate sicut de frigiditate, conceditur tunc quod illud agens ageret in illud alterabile simul caliditatem et frigiditatem quousque totum esset assimilatum illi agenti'.
70. *Ibid.*, f. 170vb: 'verumtamen quamvis aliqui duo gradus caliditatis et frigiditatis possunt simul intendi, non tamen sic possunt omnes gradus, quia nulli duo gradus ultra gradum medium sue latitudinis possunt intendi. Unde si sint duo gradus caliditatis et frigiditatis medii coextensi simul, et unus illorum incipit intendi, alius remitti, ideo etc.'
71. Richard Swineshead 1520. See Murdoch and Sylla 1976 and 1978, pp. 236–7.

ing the subject matter of the section, next recites various conclusions or sophismata that might be raised against each given position, and finally shows how the sophismata apparently opposed to the preferred position might either be accepted as unobjectionable or resolved. Sometimes more than one position is considered sustainable.[72] Several sections end with the statement that many other sophismata might be raised and solved using the preceding material.[73]

This, at least, is the pattern of the earlier treatises of the book. Some of the later treatises consist only of sets of conclusions following from a given position, and these conclusions are generally very prominently of a calculatory nature – as in the fourteenth treatise, which gives rules for local motion following from Bradwardine's law concerning the relations of forces, resistances, and velocities. Nevertheless, from the juxtaposition of these treatises, the purpose of the calculations seems clear: they are used to derive surprising or counter-intuitive results and to determine whether or not these must be accepted.

Bradwardine and Heytesbury were often content to inspect mathematical relationships in order to give a general classification of the results to be expected. Thus Bradwardine asserts that if one starts with a force less than twice a resistance, then by doubling that force one will produce a velocity more than double the original velocity.[74] He does not indicate how to determine exactly the ratio by which the velocity will increase. Heytesbury likewise is content to say that given any uniformly accelerated motion not starting from zero velocity, the ratio of the distance traversed in the second half of the time to the distance traversed in the first half of the time will be as the mean velocity of the second half of the motion to the mean velocity of the first half of the motion. He even seems to suggest that to calculate the actual numerical values would be more bothersome than helpful.[75]

But both Bradwardine and Heytesbury made enough progress toward deriving mathematical results that their successors were stimulated to go further, and Swineshead's *Liber calculationum* is the result of many such further steps toward actual calculation.

Still, it should be pointed out that even in the *Liber calculationum* most of the mathematics involved is not very numerical and does not give rise to

---

72. See Murdoch and Sylla 1976, pp. 190–1.
73. Swineshead 1520, ff. 9[ra], 9[rb], 15[rb], 16[va], 22[rb].
74. Crosby 1955, pp. 112–13. Conclusion 6.
75. Heytesbury 1494b, f. 41[rb]. The printed version actually says less difficulty ('sed huiusmodi calculatio minorem sollicitudinem ageret quam profectum'), but compare Gaetano's comment on the passage. Cf. Swineshead 1520, f. 52[ra].

many computations or calculations in the usual modern senses of those terms. Instead, one has to do with verbal reasoning in which many variables and their relations are kept in mind and equivalences derived with very little use of numbers.[76] It is in this broad sense of 'calculation' that Heytesbury can say concerning insolubilia; 'Many very prolix and useless cases arise in this matter in which it is necessary to calculate diligently and to run from one proposition to another until it appears which of them is insoluble.'[77] In this broad sense, too, any of the familiar fourteenth-century arguments *in terminis*, in which the letters A, B, C, etc., were used to represent, for example, velocities, or degrees of quality, or propositions, or distances, or instants, may have been considered calculations.[78]

If Swineshead's book covers only physical topics, it is nevertheless no more genuine physics than are Heytesbury's works. Having treated many different distributions of hot and cold, Swineshead remarks, 'All of these must be conceded imaginarily, and they are to be denied *de facto*; for in all these cases it is posited that unequal colds are extended with equal heat.'[79] In another place Swineshead supposes that there are in half a body infinite heats of infinite intensity and infinite colds of infinite intensity, something obviously not possible in nature.[80]

The Oxford disputations in the light of the Calculators' writings

If, then, the core works of the Calculators were meant to be used as aids in preparing for disputations, does this prove anything about the disputations themselves? Unfortunately, there need not have been a simple connection between, say, the contents of Heytesbury's *Regulae* and some particular series or type of disputations.[81] Nevertheless, putting the works of the Calculators together with the Oxford statutes discussed earlier, the series of disputations described in the statutes providing the best match with Heytesbury's and Swineshead's work seems to be the disputations *in*

76. Cf. Murdoch 1974a, p. 67 and n. 39.
77. Heytesbury 1494b, f. 7rb: 'Multi etiam fiunt casus in hac parte prolixi nimis et inutiles in quibus oportet diligenter calculare et discurrere ab una propositione ad aliam quousque appareat quae illarum sit insolubilis.'
78. Maier 1952, pp. 257–88, esp. 258–60.
79. Swineshead 1520, f. 15ra: 'Omnes istae concedendae sunt imaginarie et negentur de facto. Nam in omnibus casibus istis ponitur cum aequali caliditate inaequales frigiditates extendi.' Compare ff. 8va, 13vb, 15^{va-b}, 16ra, 16va.
80. *Ibid.*, f. 8ra.
81. It would be useful to look for more direct records of such disputations. Some of the works already known but not carefully examined with this issue in mind may prove to be of help. Perhaps one should not expect undergraduate disputations to be recorded, but more evidence would be desirable.

parviso. Calculatory techniques could be introduced into disputations on natural philosophy, but then the results of those disputations were much more recognisably physical than are the core works of the Oxford Calculators. The result would be something like Roger Swineshead's *De motibus* or Dumbleton's *Summa*, but not Swineshead's *Liber calculationum*. When the techniques of the Calculators were brought into the areas of the three philosophies, their application was perhaps questionable because so many of the cases they considered were thought to be possible only in imagination.

Conclusion

Although there is excellent precedent in fourteenth-century theories of scientific method for considering logical analysis as a method of scientific discovery,[82] nevertheless the Calculators carried their analyses and calculations a bit too far for it to be plausible that their main goal was discoveries in natural philosophy. If some later natural philosophers found the calculations subtle and 'beautiful speculations',[83] it is not surprising that others considered them unduly complicated and irrelevant. When later humanists complained that the English disputational subtleties made too much of what should have been schoolboy exercises, they may have been right, at least concerning the context in which the subtleties developed.[84] The historian inclined to admire the work of the Oxford Calculators may wish to assert that it was indeed the work of masters and not of schoolboys. While this is no doubt true, it nevertheless seems to be the case that the work was to be used in disputations *de sophismatibus* or *in parviso*, which were meant primarily for advanced undergraduates. Even while thinking of the work as that of masters, we ought also to wonder at the level of logical sophistication that advanced undergraduates in fourteenth-century Oxford must have attained.

82. See Sylla 1979, esp. pp. 176–7.
83. There is a marginal note in Swineshead's *Liber calculationum* to this effect (f. 64rb): 'Nota pulchram speculationem.'
84. Cf. Garin 1969a; Guerlac 1979.

28
INFINITY AND CONTINUITY

The prevalence of issues involving infinity and continuity

Natural philosophy in the fourteenth century is, when compared to that of the preceding century, more extensive, less repetitious, and more varied in the problems it treats, the solutions it sets forth, and the approaches and methods it employs in reaching those solutions. However, if one examines in some depth not merely the expositions and questions dealing with the relevant works of Aristotle but also the numerous non-commentatorial works constituting this literature, one cannot but be impressed by the unusual amount of time and effort spent in dealing with problems involving in one manner or another the infinite and the continuous.

Often these problems concern infinity or continuity from the outset; but equally often the problems are extended or developed by the fourteenth-century scholar to take into account some aspect of the infinite or the continuous in a manner that was not apparent in the problem as initially stated. A discussion of the way in which one should measure a quantity that varies in intensity throughout its subject might, for example, be carried so far as to accommodate 'infinite values'. Alternatively, a discussion of angelic motion might involve one in a rather full investigation of the composition of all continuous quantities. Indeed, the prevalence of issues involving the infinite or the continuous in later medieval natural philosophy is such that an exhaustive history of these two notions in the later Middle Ages would constitute a very large part of the history of natural philosophy during this period.

The Aristotelian background

Aristotle had himself devoted considerable attention to the infinite and the continuous: the major portion of Book III and all of Book VI of the *Physics*, as well as three substantial chapters in the first book of *De caelo*, deal expressly with these notions. And many other, less extensive discussions, especially in the later books of the *Physics*, also take up aspects of these notions. Aristotle's evident concern in this regard was not lost on his later medieval expositors. When one considers that the *Physics* was the most commented upon of Aristotle's natural philosophical works through the first half of the fourteenth century and, further, that it received more attention at Oxford – where preoccupation with problems involving infinity and continuity was proportionally greater than on the Continent – it seems obvious that Aristotle provided a considerable part of the background and impetus for the later medieval concern with these two notions. Just how Aristotle served in this regard will be made clearer when we turn to the specific issues of the infinite and the continuous that were treated by medieval scholars and cite the Aristotelian source for the problem at hand.

Aristotle stimulated and influenced the medieval preoccupation with infinity and continuity not only because of his explicit discussions of those notions but also because of the central importance of continuous, infinitely divisible quantities and processes throughout Aristotelian natural philosophy.[1] Indeed, even if the processes are not themselves continuous – like locomotion or qualitative change – they are considered as taking place within an absolutely continuous time, so that the concept of the continuous is always relevant if only in respect of analysing just how some discontinuous change – some substance passing into or out of existence, for example – could be precisely described against the background of continuous time.

The medieval development of the Aristotelian material

For all the importance of the Aristotelian background to medieval discussions of infinity and continuity, there are few areas in later medieval natural philosophy in which one can more clearly observe the medievals going beyond their inherited Aristotelian material. This development of what could be gleaned from Aristotle with respect to the infinite and the continuous is apparent even in the very kinds of medieval writings that provide the sources for the history of these two notions. For we find an immense amount of relevant material not only in commentaries on Aristotelian works and in one or another *Summa* of natural philosophy, but also a surprising number of special treatises and *quaestiones* dealing exclusively with some aspect of the infinite or continuous.[2]

---

1. For an account of the importance of continuity for Aristotle, see W. Wieland 1970, pp. 278–316.
2. This will be evident from some of the works to be cited in what follows, but there are many other separate works on infinity and continuity, especially in the fourteenth century.

The influence of theological considerations

Writings produced in the Faculties of Theology were as important as those produced in the Faculties of Arts; thus theological considerations were influential, especially in furthering the analysis of the infinite. For example, the extensive thirteenth- and fourteenth-century debates over the possible eternality of the world provided a stimulating setting in which to puzzle over the difficulties involved in the notion of an infinite past time. And discussions of God's infinity or of the possibility of His knowing an infinite had similar effects.[3]

Fourteenth-century commentaries on the *Sentences* often contained extensive deliberations concerned with the infinite and the continuous in less obviously appropriate contexts, such as discussions of whether the will acts instantaneously or continuously over time, of how one might best 'measure' its meritorious and demeritorious acts, or of how one might compare the perfections of various creatures with one another and with God.[4]

The most influential theological element was the newly precise concept of God's omnipotence. Writers began to base their analyses of the infinite and the continuous upon what could obtain in respect of the absolute power of God. But since God's absolute power extended to everything that did not include a contradiction, to invoke this power in examining infinity or continuity was to transfer one's analysis from the realm of the physically possible (within the confines of Aristotelian natural philosophy) to the broader realm of the logically possible.

Although this appeal to divine omnipotence arose within a theological context, it appears as well in works that are clearly devoted to natural philosophy.[5] Yet whether such an appeal occurred within the one context or the other, it had the effect of extending the discussion at hand so that in principle it would take into account all logical possibilities. Invoking the absolute power of God thus supplied one with a warrant to reason *secundum imaginationem*, a manner of reasoning which, when applied to the infinite and the continuous (or to almost any other area of late medieval philosophy), permitted the exercise of a number of new methods and tools of

---

3. On God's infinity, see Sweeney & Ermatinger 1958 for a single instance of the kinds of things at issue. For the problem of God's knowledge of the infinite – a problem that derives from Augustine, *De civ. Dei*, XII, 18 – see William of Alnwick 1937, pp. 488–551.

4. References to such less obviously appropriate contexts can be found in Murdoch 1975a, pp. 289–303.

5. For example, John Buridan 1509, *Quaestiones Physicorum*, III, QQ. 14, 19.

analysis in resolving (in some cases first creating and then resolving) problems.

Actual and potential infinity

Of all the points made by Aristotle in his treatment of the infinite in Book III of the *Physics*, undoubtedly the one most often repeated by the medieval philosopher was his denying the possibility of an 'actual infinite' of any sort and admitting only the 'potential infinite' that was associated with the infinite divisibility of continuous magnitudes. As Aristotle put it, any permissible infinite is not that beyond which there is nothing (for that would be a completed infinite *in actu*), but rather that beyond which there is always something (the infinite *in potentia*).[6]

Almost all the scholastics followed Aristotle's distinction of permissible from non-permissible infinites, formulating a variety of alternative ways of expressing this distinction. The most popular of these alternative expressions was the claim that the rejected actual infinite was a quantity so great that it could not be greater (*tantum quod non maius*), while the permissible potential infinite was a quantity that was not so great but that it could be greater (*non tantum quin maius*).[7] The scholastics themselves often pointed out that the latter was really only an indefinite finite, as was made explicit in any number of 'expositions' of propositions involving this type of infinite.[8]

The logic of the infinite

The exposition of propositions involving infinity is at the heart of what might be called the medieval logic of the infinite. The fundamental distinction in this logic, or analysis, is between the 'categorematic' and 'syncategorematic' uses of the term 'infinite' (or 'infinitely', or 'infinitely many'). Taken categorematically, the term functioned collectively, very

---

6. *Physics*, III, 6, 207ª1, 7–8. The medieval Latin is: 'Non enim cuius nihil est extra, sed cuius semper aliquid est extra, hoc infinitum est. . . . Infinitum quidem igitur hoc est, cuius secundum quantitatem accipientibus, semper est aliquid accipere extra.'

7. The same distinction for multitudes was expressed, respectively, as 'tot quod non plura' and 'non tot quin plura'. Another frequently used manner of expressing the distinction between Aristotle's two infinites was to speak of an *infinitum in facto esse* (= actual) vs. an *infinitum in fieri* (= potential). On these distinctions, see Maier 1964, pp. 41–4.

8. Hence in his *Tractatus de continuo*, Thomas Bradwardine characterises the potential infinite as 'infinitum privative secundum quid est quantum finitum, et finitum maius isto, et finitum maius isto maiori, et sic sine fine ultimo terminante; et hoc est quantum, et non tantum quin maius' (MSS Torun R, 4°, 2, p. 153; Erfurt, Amplon. Q° 385, 17ʳ; Paris BN n.a.1. 625, 71ᵛ). Note that because of this 'always finite' character of the Aristotelian (and hence also of the scholastic) infinite, Georg Cantor was later to term it an *Uneigentlich-unendliche* (Cantor 1932, pp. 165, 180).

much like an ordinary numerical adjective or modifier; but taken syncategorematically it was held to function as a distributive sign. Thus, '*homines infiniti currunt*' means that an actually infinite number or collection of men are running, the key to the proper exposition of this proposition being that the term '*infiniti*' follows the subject term '*homines*' and hence functions categorematically. On the other hand, if the term '*infiniti*' precedes the subject term it modifies, then it occurs in its syncategorematic sense, so that the proper exposition of '*infiniti homines currunt*' is that some men are running but not so many that no more are running. But this is to say only that a potentially infinite number of men are running.[9] In this latter syncategorematic sense, 'infinitely many' ('*infiniti*') was taken as a distributive sign, that is, as 'distributing' (or 'multiplying') the common subject term relative to the predicate.[10] For example, Peter of Spain explains the syncategorematic use of 'infinitely many' by claiming that in that use it functions as equivalent to the phrase 'more than any [number] you choose' (*quolibet plura*).[11]

The re-examination of the possibility of actual infinity

In Book III of the *Physics* and Book I of *De caelo* Aristotle had argued against the existence of actual, completed infinites largely on the basis of the inconsistency of an actual infinite with the doctrines of natural place and the contrary opposition and transformation of the elements; con-

9. See Maier 1964, p. 44. Using the same doctrine of the position of 'infinite' relative to what it modifies, Albert of Saxony distinguishes 'in infinitum continuum est divisibile' from 'continuum est divisibile in infinitum' (*Quaestiones Physicorum*, III, Q.9; Albert of Saxony 1518a, f. 37ᵛ). The former takes '*infinitum*' syncategorematically and is a true statement about the potentially infinite divisibility of continua, while the latter takes '*infinitum*' categorematically and is a false statement about the divisibility of continua, since it would imply an actually infinite, completed division. John Buridan, however, at times does not agree that it makes a difference if 'infinite' precedes or follows what it qualifies: 'non refert dicere infinita magnitudo et magnitudo infinita, sicut non refert dicere homo albus et albus homo' (*Quaestiones Phys*. III, 18; (Buridan 1509, f. 61ᵛ).

10. Thus in '*infiniti homines currunt*,' '*infiniti*' distributes '*homines*' relative to '*currunt*.'

11. Peter of Spain 1972, p. 231: 'Solet autem poni quod "*infinitum*" quandoque sumitur pro termino communi, et tunc hec propositio "*infinita sunt finita*" equipollet huic: "*aliqua infinita sunt finita*"; quandoque autem sumitur pro signo distributivo, et tunc ista "*infinita sunt finita*" equipollet huic quoad distributionem, scilicet "*quolibet plura sunt finita*". Et probatur sic: uno plura sunt finita, doubus plura sunt finita, tribus plura sunt finita, et sic de aliis; ergo quolibet plura sunt finita. Et tunc dicitur facere interscalarem distributionem, sive interruptam vel discontinuam, quia hec dictio "*plura*" in prima propositione supponit pro duobus et deinceps, et in secunda pro tribus et deinceps, et sic semper gradatim sive scalariter ascendendo. Et ideo hec oratio: "*quolibet plura*" facit interscalarem distributionem, quia pro aliis supponit hoc quod dico "*quolibet*" et pro aliis hoc quod dico "*plura*", secundum numerum ascendendo, ut dictum est.' For other analyses of the categorematic and syncategorematic uses of '*infiniti*' see William of Sherwood 1941, pp. 54–5; 1968, pp. 41–3; Peter of Spain 1945, pp. 118–22 (which contains the probably spurious *Tractatus exponibilium*); Albert of Saxony 1502, Sophisma 53; Thomas Bradwardine, *Tractatus de continuo*, MSS Torun R. 4°. 2, pp. 153–6; Erfurt Amplon. Q° 385, 17ʳ–18ʳ.

sequently, the arguments elucidating this inconsistency were for the most part physical in character. But it was not physical possibilities that were in question when the medievals went beyond Aristotle and asked whether God in his absolute power could create an actually infinite stone or could complete the infinite division of a continuous magnitude.[12] If the absolute power of God could not accomplish such 'tasks', it was certainly not mere *de facto* principles of natural philosophy that ruled them out. Some stronger inconsistency would have to be involved were such a restriction validly to be placed upon God's omnipotence, and the one which seems to have been most compelling to the medievals is the paradox occasioned by the implied existence of unequal infinites.

The paradox of unequal infinites used against actual infinity

The structure of the paradox was uncommonly simple and straightforward: if one allows the existence of actual infinites, then it appears that some infinites will clearly be greater than other infinites which are equally clearly parts of the former; but it is axiomatic that all actual infinites are equal; therefore in this instance a part is not less than, but equal to, its whole – which is absurd.

The discussion of this paradox was not something the medieval philosopher could cull from Aristotle, and although the paradox was treated in other ancient sources,[13] they were either not available in the Latin Middle Ages or were never cited; the same must be said for Islamic discussions of the paradox.[14] On the basis of presently available evidence, then, philosophers and theologians in the Latin West appear to have realised the importance of the paradox on their own. Discussions of it can be found in any number of thirteenth- and fourteenth-century texts, but it was probably Bonaventure's inclusion of it in his examination of the possibility of an

12. These examples are quite common, but see, e.g., John Buridan 1509, III, Q. 19; f. 64^{r-v}: 'Hec est impossibilis: in qualibet medietate proportionali huius diei Deus creat unum lapidem pedalem et etiam ista: in qualibet medietate proportionali huius diei creabit unum lapidem pedalem. ... Omnes partes linee B Deus potest separare ab invicem et separatim conservare. ... In qualibet medietate proportionali huius diei potest Deus facere unum lapidem pedalem conservando ipsum semper post.' (Note the presence of 'potest' in the last two propositions and its absence in the first.)
13. See, for example, Plutarch, *De comm. not. adv. Stoicos*, 1079a; John Philoponus, *De aeternitate mundi contra Proclum*, I, 3, and *apud Simplicium*, *Phys.*, VIII, 1, ed. Diels, p. 1179; Alexander of Aphrodisias, *Quaest. naturales*, III, p. 12; Proclus, *Comm. in Euclidem*, def. 17; Proclus, *Elem. theol.*, prop. 1; Lucretius, I, 615–26. Only Lucretius and Proclus' *Elements of Theology* were available to the Latin West, but neither was cited relative to the paradox in question.
14. Al-Shahrastānī, *Kitāb Nihāyatu 'l-Iqdām fī 'Ilmi'l-Kalām*, ed. A. Guillaume, Ch. 1; Averroes, *Tahafut al-Tahafut*, tr. Van den Bergh, pp. 9–10, 14, 162–3; Maimonides, *Guide for the Perplexed*, tr. Friedländer, p. 138. Maimonides was translated into Latin, but was not cited in this context. The translation of Averroes' *Tahafut* occurred too late (1328) to enter effectively into the debate in the Latin West.

eternal world that gave it the status of an essential ingredient in almost all subsequent discussions of that possibility.[15] The use to which Bonaventure put the paradox represents one of three basic attitudes exhibited by the medievals towards unequal infinites, the one a part of the other – i.e., regarding them as strictly impossible, and maintaining, therefore, that one had to reject as equally impossible the situation that appeared to generate such infinites in the first place (in Bonaventure's case, the possibility of an eternal world).[16]

Resolutions of the paradox of unequal infinites

However, not all the medievals used the paradox in this way; some attempted to resolve it. One group simply concluded that the fact that the same infinites could be shown to be both equal and unequal meant that one could not apply 'equal to', 'greater than', and 'less than' to actual infinites at all.[17] But a second group of those who attempted a resolution of the

15. Bonaventure, 1882–1902a, *Comm. Sent.*, II, dist. 1, pars. 1, art. 1, Q. 2 (the first of his arguments against an eternal world): 'Prima est: Impossibile est infinito addi. Haec est manifesta per se, quia omne illud quod recipit additionem fit maius, infinito autem nihil maius. Sed si mundus est sine principio, duravit in infinitum; ergo durationi eius non potest addi. Sed constat, hoc esse falsum, quia revolutio additur revolutioni omni die; ergo, etc. Si dicas quod infinitum est quantum ad praeterita, tamen quantum ad praesens quod nunc est est finitum actu, et ideo ex ea parte qua finitum est actu est reperire maius; contra, ostenditur quod in praeterito est reperire maius. Haec est veritas infallibilis: quod, si mundus est aeternus, revolutiones solis in orbe suo sunt infinitae; rursus, pro una revolutione solis necesse est fuisse duodecim ipsius lunae; ergo plus revoluta est luna quam sol; et sol infinities, ergo infinitorum ex ea parte qua infinita sunt est reperire excessum. Hoc autem est impossibile; ergo etc'.
16. The impossibility of unequal infinites became one of the most popular, and most telling, ways of disposing of the eternity of the world, especially among Franciscans who, steadfastly refusing to consider the possibility of an eternal world as a *problema neutrum* as had Thomas Aquinas (e.g., *ST*, I, Q. 46, art. 1–2), did their utmost to establish its impossibility. However, it was not only a Franciscan trait (which, admittedly, becomes less universal among *fratres minores* in the fourteenth century) to wield the paradox of unequal infinites against the eternity of the world; one finds a highly developed version of the paradox put to the same task, for example, in Thomas Bradwardine's *De causa Dei*, Lib. I, cap. 1, coroll., pars 40; Bradwardine 1618, pp. 121–6; Cf. Murdoch 1962, pp. 18–20. Mention should also be made of the fact that, like Lucretius (I, 615–26), Walter Chatton used the paradox to refute the possibility of the infinite divisibility of continuous magnitudes (see his *Comm. Sent.*, Lib. II, dist. 2, Q. 3: MS Paris BN 15887, 94ᵛ). Chatton (who does not mention Lucretius in this connection) was a 'finitist', holding the extremely strange view that a continuum was composed of a finite number of non-extended indivisibles. On Chatton and continua, see Murdoch and Synan 1966.
17. For example, Nicole Oresme, *Quest. phys.*, III, Q. 12 (MS Sevilla Colomb. 7–6–30, 37ᵛ–39ᵛ), where the major conclusion is: 'Nullum infinitum alteri comparatum per ymaginationem est ipso minus vel equale vel maius, sed omne omni est incomparabile.' Albert of Saxony's treatment of the issue parallels that of Oresme; see Albert of Saxony 1518b, I, Q. 10. Although one cannot maintain that they knew either Oresme or Albert, both Galileo and Newton come to a similar conclusion about the inapplicability of 'equal to', 'less than,' and 'greater than' to infinites. (See Galileo, *Discorsi* (ed. naz.), p. 79; Newton, *Letter to Richard Bentley*, 1693, in I. B. Cohen (ed.), *Newton's Papers and Letters on Natural Philosophy* (Cambridge, Mass., 1958), pp. 293–9.)

paradox asked instead whether different 'axioms' of equality and part-whole might not be applicable to infinite magnitudes and multitudes. One might consider, we are told, an infinite line AB beginning at some arbitrary point A and extended *ad infinitum* toward B; now if one specifies a determinate point C on the line at some finite distance from A, then our paradox arises with respect to the whole infinite line AB and its equally infinite part CB. Yet one can resolve the paradox by noting that, while AB is indeed equal to CB relative to the terminus B, they are unequal relative to the termini A and C.[18] Infinites can have, as it were, 'finite ends', and can hence simultaneously suffer equality and inequality depending upon 'direction'.[19]

Henry of Harclay

A more fruitful attempt to uncover a way to tailor part–whole and equality relations for infinites began, it seems, with Henry of Harclay, Chancellor of Oxford in 1312. A proponent of the existence of actual infinites and the composition of continua out of indivisibles, Harclay believed that there can be, and are, unequal infinites and realised that the crucial issue one must resolve if one is to hold such a belief is to explain just what kind of part–whole axiom governs such infinites. In anticipation of his adversaries, he asserts that the traditional Euclidean axiom 'every whole is greater than its part' is naturally applicable only to finite quantities. Nevertheless, one must realise that it is subordinate to a more general axiom which does apply to infinites and in terms of which the inequality of infinites must be understood: 'that which (e.g., an infinite set) contains another thing (e.g., an infinite proper subset) and something else beyond (*ultra*) it, or in addition to (*praeter*) it, is a whole with respect to that other thing'.[20]

William of Alnwick and Gregory of Rimini

Harclay's first critic, the Franciscan William of Alnwick, claims that there is a significant difference between the terms 'beyond' and 'in addition to' which Harclay employed in a seemingly innocuous disjunction in his

18. The argument is that of an unnamed opponent in Peter John Olivi 1922–6, I, pp. 38–9.
19. The 'finite end' of infinites is frequently considered in attempting to resolve the paradox. So it is, for example, in Gerard of Odo's *Comm. Sent.*, Lib. II, dist. 2, Q. 2 (MS Valencia Cated. 200, 17^r–17^v); and in Michael of Massa's *Comm. Sent.*, additiones libri secundi (MS Vat. lat. 1087, 151^r–154^v).
20. Henry of Harclay, *Questio de infinito et continuo* (MSS Tortosa Cated. 88, 83^v; Firenze Naz. II.II.281, 95^r): 'Illud quod continet aliud et aliquid ultra illud vel praeter illud est totum respectu illius.'

generalised axiom: 'beyond' entails having more absolutely, while 'in addition to' entails having more only when it is a question of *finite* things of a certain quantity. Among *infinite* things, Alnwick maintains, 'in addition to' entails diversity but not a greater plurality.[21]

Although in drawing this latter distinction Alnwick may have begun to move in the direction of what we today consider set-subset relations on the one hand and cardinality relations on the other, he had still not faced the question of precisely what it is that is involved in the inequality which can, or cannot, be inferred on the basis of the distinction he had drawn between mere diversity and greater plurality. A reasonably satisfactory treatment of that question is provided in the lectures on the *Sentences* given at Paris in 1342 by Gregory of Rimini.[22] If one is to apply 'part' and 'whole', 'greater than', and 'less than' to infinites, one must realise, Gregory claims, that there are two senses for each term. In one way, everything is 'a whole which includes something that is something and something else in addition to (*praeter*) that something'. But in a second, more restricted sense that is 'a whole which includes something in the first way and also includes as many things as that included does not include'. An infinite multitude can, Gregory continues, very well function as a whole with respect to another infinite multitude in the first sense, but not in the second sense. It seems clear, then, that what Gregory intends is, in our terms, distinctions between whole and part in the sense of set and subset (his first sense) and between whole and part in the sense of unequal cardinality of the sets involved (his second sense).[23] By such means Gregory, who believed in the

---

21. William of Alnwick, *Determinatio* 2 (MS Vat. Pal. lat. 1805, 10ᵛ): 'Dicendum quod refert dicere "habere aliquid in se et aliquid *ultra* illud", et dicere "habere in se aliquid *praeter* illud". Quod enim habet in se aliquid et aliquid aliud *ultra* illud est maius illo, quia habere in se *ultra* aliquam quantitatem, est habere plus. Sed habere aliquid et *praeter* illud habere aliud, non includit habere plus nisi in rebus finitis; sed includit diversitatem sed non maiorem pluralitatem in infinitis. Tempus igitur habens in se infinitos menses februarios et ianuarios non habet in se aliquod tempus *ultra* hos menses aut illos; habet tamen in se aliquid *praeter* istos menses aut *praeter* illos.'

22. Although one can find similar attempts to resolve the paradox between Alnwick and Rimini (e.g., in Ockham 1495–6, *Comm. Sent.*, Lib. II, Q. 8; and Ockham 1491, *Quodl.* II, Q. 6), they are not as successful as that of Rimini.

23. Gregory of Rimini 1522, *Comm. Sent.*, Lib. I, dist. 42–44, Q. 4; f. 173ᵛ: 'Primo modo omne quod includit aliquid quod est aliquid et aliud praeter illud aliquid et quodlibet illius dicitur totum ad illud; et omne sic inclusum dicitur pars includentis. Secundo modo dicitur totum illud quod includit aliquid primo modo et includit tanta tot quot non includit inclusum; et econverso tale inclusum non includens tot tanta quot includens dicitur pars eius. ... Secundo distinguo hos terminos maius et minus ... uno modo sumuntur proprie et sic multitudo ... dicitur maior quae pluries continet unum vel plures unitates; illa vero minor quae paucies seu pauciores. Alio modo sumitur improprie, et sic omnis multitudo quae includit unitates omnes alterius multitudinis et quasdam alias unitates ab illis dicitur maior illa, esto quod non includat plures unitates quam illa. Et hoc modo esse maiorem multitudinem alia non est aliud quam includere illam et esse totum respectu illius primo modo.'

existence of actual infinites,[24] removed what was perhaps the most telling objection to such a belief.

Infinity in continua

Late medieval discussions of the infinite as involved in the divisibility of continuous magnitudes were perhaps richer and more varied in the new considerations they brought to the fore than were discussions of actual infinity. It was all but universally agreed that continua in some way or other contained, at least potentially, an infinite number of indivisibles.[25] They contained them 'in some way or other' because it was realised that the very existence of indivisibles was itself exceedingly problematic. Indeed, although Aristotle had devoted considerable attention to issues involving the presence of indivisibles within continua, he had not spent much effort in examining their existence as such. The medievals, however, did so, led by William Ockham.

Ockham on indivisibles

Put succinctly, Ockham's position was that indivisibles do not exist at all. A point, for example, is not a *thing* in any proper sense. Points are, of course, traditionally regarded as the termini of lines. But in Ockham's view we do not need separately existing points to account for the termination of lines; all we need are finite lines of this or that length. Indeed, he is willing to say that the term 'point' is equivalent to the expression (*complexum*) 'a line of such and such a length' or something of that sort.[26] But if we can use such an equivalence to rid ourselves of points, it follows that we do not need separately existing points to account for the termination of lines; the lines

---

24. See Maier 1964, pp. 82–4.

25. The fact that continua *contained* indivisibles is not to say, of course, that they were *composed* of indivisibles. (The latter was a quite different issue and will be treated briefly below.) These 'contained' indivisibles would be points (for one-dimensional geometrical magnitudes), lines (for two-dimensional magnitudes), or surfaces (for three-dimensional magnitudes), instants for time, and degrees for intensible and remissible qualities or forms.

26. William Ockham 1930, pp. 36–8 (MSS Basel F.II.24, 23ʳ; Rome, Angelica 1017, 66ʳ): 'Et si queratur quid est punctus, aut est res divisibilis aut indivisibilis, dicendum est quod, si sic dicendo "punctus est aliquid" vel "punctus est res" vel huiusmodi li "punctus" supponat pro aliquo ita quod habeat precise vim nominis et non includat equivalenter unum complexum ex nomine et verbo vel aliquid consimile quod secundum proprietatem vocis potest reddere suppositum verbo, debet concedi quod punctus est aliquid et quod punctus est res; et hoc quia debet concedi quod punctus est linea et punctus est quantitas, quia tunc hoc nomen "punctus" equivalet toti isti: "linea tante vel tante longitudinis" sive "linea non ulterius protensa vel extensa" vel alicui toti composito ex adiectivo et substantivo vel alicui toti composito ex nomine et verbo mediante coniunctione vel adverbio vel hoc pronomine "qui", secundum quod placet dare diversas diffinitiones exprimentes quid nominis illius nominis "punctus". Et ideo sicut hoc predicatum "res divisibilis" predicatur de tali substantivo et per consequens de composito ex adiectivo et substantivo, ita predicatur de puncto.'

are terminated *per se ipsas*.[27] Of course, the term 'point' occurs everywhere in the propositions of natural philosophy, and there is nothing wrong with using the term 'point' in these propositions; we should merely realise that in so doing we are but employing the term in place of more complex expressions or propositions in which the term 'point' does not appear and which thus reveal that we need not be committed to the existence of any such *thing* as a point.[28]

Ockham's attempted removal of such fictive elements as points and instants parallels his removal of such connotative terms as 'motion' or 'time' from natural philosophy. For just as one must realise that there is no separately existing *thing* called motion above and beyond the moving body itself and the places it successively occupies or the forms it successively possesses, so one must realise that there are no separately existing *things* called points above and beyond terminated lines.[29] Further, just as one accounts for the fact that there is no thing directly corresponding to the term 'motion' by reducing all propositions in which this term occurs to another proposition or other propositions in which only terms standing for moving bodies and other real things occur, so one can provide for the fact that there is no thing corresponding to the term 'point' by reducing all propositions in which this term occurs to other propositions or expressions in which only terms standing for lines of one sort or another occur.[30] The technique of propositional analysis employed by Ockham in such cases preserved a particularist ontology that allowed the existence of only individual permanent things.[31]

Ockham's influence

Although the sparseness of Ockham's ontology for such conceptions as motion was opposed by some of his successors,[32] his denial of the reality of

---

27. Ockham 1930, p. 32: 'Linea sufficienter est continua et finita per naturam propriam sine omni alia re addita sibi.' Note that since lines are themselves indivisible in two dimensions and surfaces are indivisible in one, Ockham must perform the same 'reduction' of lines to surfaces and surfaces to bodies as he does for points to lines. Then, with three-dimensional bodies, he will have reached the level of individual *res permanentes*, of really existing things. Of course, parallel reductions must be carried out for instants relative to time intervals.
28. Ockham 1930, p. 44.
29. Although lines themselves are no more *things* than are points (see note 27), once we have performed the same reduction operations for lines and then for surfaces, we are at the level of real things.
30. On Ockham's analysis of the term 'motion' see Shapiro 1957.
31. On such 'propositional analysis' in general in fourteenth-century philosophy, see Murdoch forthcoming a and b.
32. Ockham's influence is most evident from the fact that after him the question about the 'reality' of

such entities as points and instants was more warmly received. At Paris, John Buridan and Albert of Saxony left no doubt of this in following and developing Ockham's denial of the reality of indivisibles, while closer to home the Mertonians Thomas Bradwardine and William Heytesbury assert an equally firm Ockhamist position in this matter.[33] Thus, at the end of his *Tractatus de continuo*, Bradwardine draws things together concerning the indivisibles he has been dealing with throughout his treatise in the explicit claim that 'there are no surfaces, lines, or points at all', adding the equally Ockhamist corollary that 'a continuum is neither continued nor rendered finite by such (indivisibles), but by its very self'.[34] And Heytesbury in his *Regulae solvendi sophismata* allows himself the rare onto-logical remark that there are no such things in nature as instants, or even time or motion, even though he alludes to such things in the *Regulae* at every turn in his examples and arguments.[35]

The rise of indivisibilism

In Book VI of the *Physics*, Aristotle had set forth several arguments against the possibility that continua are composed of indivisibles. Almost all medieval philosophers accepted Aristotle's arguments, but a minority opposition arose at the beginning of the fourteenth century. Indivisi-bilists or atomists such as Henry of Harclay, Walter Chatton, Gerard of Odo, and Nicholas Bonet – to mention only those most frequently cited and criticised – began to maintain that continua were indeed composed of

motion was most often raised in the Ockhamist form of whether motion was some entity above and beyond permanent things, but his conclusion that there were only such permanent things involved in motion or change was far from universally accepted. To cite only the most notable instance of such disagreement, John Buridan accepted Ockham's conclusions with respect to the motions of alteration and augmentation or diminution, but disagreed with him concerning local motion (see Murdoch and Sylla 1978, pp. 217–18).

33. For the relevant references to Buridan and Albert, see Zoubov 1961 (which contains an edition of Buridan's *De puncto*). Note that Buridan's and Albert's treatments of points occur in works of natural philosophy, while Ockham's is most fully developed in a theological work because of Ockham's conviction that an analysis of quantity was required in order to give an appropriate account of the Eucharist. In this instance theology appears to have provided an important starting-point for philosophy.

34. Thomas Bradwardine, *Tractatus de continuo* (MS Torun R. 4°, 2, p. 192): 'Superficiem, lineam sive punctum omnino non esse. Unde manifeste: Continuum non continuari nec finitari per talia, sed seipso.'

35. Heytesbury 1494b, f. 26ʳ: 'Quid autem instans sit in rerum natura et qualiter continue sit aliud instans et aliud, longe est alterius perscrutationis; et multa figmenta falsa admittit modus loquendi hominis de instanti, tempore, et motu propter breviloquium et mentis conceptum facilius exprimendum, quia in rerum natura non est aliquid quod est instans ut instans nec tempus ut tempus aut motus ut motus, sicut nihil est Sortes prout ipse est homo albus, nec aliquid est Plato prout ipse est disputaturus cras aut prout ipse debet hodie respondere.'

indivisibles.[36] In most instances the component indivisibles were taken to be extensionless, whether an infinite or only a finite number of them was thought to compose this or that continuum. Unfortunately, almost all this indivisibilist literature is devoted to arguing against the Aristotelian position and to establishing that continua *can* be composed in this or that fashion of indivisibles; very little is said that helps to explain precisely why this current of indivisibilism arose in the first third of the fourteenth century or what function it was held to serve. There seems to be no sign of a resurgence of ancient physical atomism among these late medieval indivisibilists, nor anything resembling a consciously atomistic interpretation of mathematics. Yet perhaps two motives can be gleaned from the texts themselves. The first is that indivisibilism may have resulted from attempts to account for the motion of angels. In Book VI of the *Physics* (Ch. 10; 240^{b}8–241^{a}26) Aristotle had proved that the motion of an indivisible implies the composition of spatial and temporal continua out of indivisibles and so had rejected the possibility of the motion of an indivisible. But angels are indivisibles that move.[37] An even more specific motive is found

36. On this fourteenth-century development of indivisibilism, see Murdoch & Synan 1966; Murdoch 1974b. Chatton seems to be alone in holding that continua are composed of finite numbers of indivisibles. Further, although almost all medieval indivisibilists held their indivisibles to be extensionless, Nicholas Bonet was an exception in that, like Democritus, he opted for indivisibles having magnitude. On Bonet, Chatton, and Odo, see Zoubov 1959. Thomas Bradwardine includes both Harclay and Chatton in the classification he gives in his *Tractatus de continuo* of the various kinds of indivisibilism: 'Pro intellectu huius conclusionis est sciendum, quod circa compositionem continui sunt 5 opiniones famose inter veteres philosophos et modernos. Ponunt enim quidam, ut Aristoteles et Averroys et plurimi modernorum, continuum non componi ex athomis, sed ex partibus divisibilibus sine fine. Alii autem dicunt ipsum componi ex indivisibilibus dupliciter variantes, quoniam Democritus ponit continuum componi ex corporibus indivisibilibus. Alii autem ex punctis, et hii dupliciter, quia Pythagoras, pater huius secte, et Plato et Waltherus modernus, ponunt ipsum componi ex finitis indivisibilibus. Alii autem ex infinitis, et sunt bipartiti, quia quidam eorum, ut Henricus modernus, dicit ipsum componi ex infinitis indivisibilibus inmediate coniunctis; alii autem, ut Lyncul⟨niensis⟩, ex infinitis ad invicem mediatis . . .' (MSS Torun, R. 4° 2, p. 165; Erfurt, Amplon. Q° 385, ff. 25^v–26^r). There were, in addition to the four mentioned above, many other supporters of indivisibilism in the fourteenth century, some of whom are little known or anonymous. Still, at least two further proponents should be mentioned: Nicholas Autrecourt (see the relevant text in Nicholas of Autrecourt 1939, pp. 206–17, and the analysis in Weinberg 1948, Ch. 9) and John Wyclif (see the text in Wyclif 1899, Ch. 9), who had several indivisibilist followers at Oxford in the later fourteenth century. Indeed, Wyclif's condemnation at the Council of Constance in 1414 included (guilt by association!) what seems to have been the only medieval condemnation of indivisibilism (Hermann von der Hardt (ed.), *Corpus actorum et decretorum magni Constantiensis concilii*, vol. 4, p. 406).

37. Thus in his *Comm. Sent.* Walter Chatton introduces his discussion of the composition of continua as follows: 'Et quia non potest sciri de motu angeli utrum sit continuus vel discretus nisi sciatur utrum motus et alia continua componantur ex indivisibilibus, ideo quero propter motum angeli: Utrum quantum componatur ex indivisibilibus . . .' (MSS BN 15887, 93^r; Firenze Naz. conv. sopp. C.5.357, 187^r). Gerard of Odo's discussion of continua occurs in the context of a discussion of God's ubiquity (Dist. 37 of Book I of his *Comm. Sent.*). Four questions are relevant to this context,

in the earliest of the indivisibilists, Henry of Harclay; for it was his view that the composition of continua out of indivisibles was required by the possible inequality of infinites.[38] Nevertheless, these 'motives' do not seem to tell the whole story; except for the two or three sentences in which they are expressed, they receive no attention in the texts themselves. Indeed, it appears equally attractive to suppose that these fourteenth-century indivisibilists were drawn to their views largely because their analysis of Aristotle's arguments against indivisibilism uncovered loopholes in them.

Harclay's attempted refutation of Aristotle's 'touching' argument

Whatever may have been the occasion for the development of this indivisibilism, the first task each of its proponents had to face was the refutation of the standard arguments against such a position, those of Aristotle being the first in line. Foremost among Aristotle's arguments was the one that proved that no continuum could be composed of indivisibles not merely because indivisibles cannot be continuous, but because there is no way in which they can even be in contact with one another. This is so, Aristotle argued, because indivisibles can have no extremities or parts, which they must have if they are to be in contact with one another; for if one whole indivisible were somehow to be in contact with another indivisible as a whole, the two could not constitute a continuum of a size greater than a single indivisible (*Physics* VI, 1; 231^{a}21–^{b}6). Thus, the fourteenth-century indivisibilists reasoned, if continua are to be composed of indivisibles, there must be some way in which they can touch or be 'connected to' one another. Harclay's solution is that they do touch whole to whole but 'in respect of distinct locations' (*secundum distinctos situs*), since in that way, he thinks, they could account for the increase in size (*faciunt maius*) required for the continuum which they composed, something they could not do if they were in contact as wholes 'in one and the same location' (*in eodem situ*).[39]

one of which is 'utrum motus angeli habeat partem aliquam simpliciter primam'. He then discusses the composition of continua as the central difficulty to be resolved 'pro solutione istarum [quatuor] questionum' (MSS Napoli, Bib. naz. VII.B.25, 234^v–235^r; Valencia Cated. 139, 120^v). It is noteworthy that Duns Scotus' influential (non-indivisibilist) treatment of the composition of continua (see note 44 below) also occurs in the context of a discussion of angelic motion.

38. Harclay, *Questio de infinito et continuo* (MS Tortosa Cated. 88, 86^v–87^r): 'Contra hoc [viz., the inequality of infinites] sunt omnia argumenta que probant continuum non posse componi ex indivisibilibus; probant enim etiam quod in uno continuo non sint plura puncta quam in alio.'

39. Harclay, *Questio de infinito et continuo* (MSS Tortosa Cated. 88, 89^r; Firenze Naz. II.II.281, 98^r–98^v): 'Dico quod indivisibile tangit indivisibile secundum totum, sed potest hoc esse dupliciter: vel totum tangit totum *in eodem situ*, et tunc est superpositio sicut dicit Commentator, et non faciunt

Bradwardine against Harclay

Harclay's attempted refutation of Aristotle's 'touching' argument against indivisibilism did not go unchallenged. Thomas Bradwardine, for example, overturned Harclay's contentions more impressively than did Harclay's other critics. Appealing to geometry, Bradwardine grants Harclay the Euclidean notion of superposition as a way of interpreting or accounting for his notion of indivisibles touching 'in respect of distinct locations' or being immediately next to one another.[40] But he proceeds to show that all occurrences of superposition in geometry are systematically disassociated from continuity; that is, no superposed geometrical magnitude can form a continuum or be continuous with the magnitude on which it is superposed.[41] And so even the most favorable interpretation of Harclay's immediate indivisibles will not allow them to serve as components of continua.[42]

infinita indivisibilia plus quam unum.... Eodem modo dico ego superficies vel corpora, in quibus sunt huiusmodi puncta, si essent applicata *secundum eundem situm*, non facerent aliquid maius. Et ideo dico quod non propter indivisibilitatem quod unum indivisibile sic additum indivisibili non facit maius extensive, sed quia additur ei *secundum eundem situm* et ⟨non⟩ *secundum distinctum situm*. Si tamen indivisibile applicetur immediate ad indivisibile *secundum distinctum situm*, potest magis facere secundum situm.' Gerard of Odo has a similar notion of touching indivisibles; see Murdoch 1964, pp. 431–5.

40. Euclid appeals to superposition in proving the congruence of figures in several basic theorems (I, 4, 8; III, 24). The technique is to apply or superpose one of the figures upon the other. Although Bradwardine uses the notion of superposition in a sense that is faithful to Euclid, the term '*superpositio*' also had other meanings (deriving basically from Averroes) in the medieval tradition (see, for example, the use of the term in the preceding note). On all of this, as well as the history of superposition in medieval mathematics, see Murdoch 1964.

41. Bradwardine, *Tractatus de continuo*, Conclusiones 9–13 (MSS Torun R. 4°, 2, pp. 158–60; Erfurt Amplon. Q° 385, 19ʳ–21ʳ): '9 – Lineam rectam secundum totum vel partem magnam recte alteri superponi et habere aliquod punctum intrinsecum commune cum ista non contingit. 10 – Linee recte unam partem magnam alii recte imponi et aliam partem magnam superponi eidem vel ad latus distare ab illa impossibile comprobatur. 11 – Unius recte duo puncta in alia continuari et per partem eius magnam superponi eidem vel ad latus distare ab illa non posse. 12 – Linee recte unam partem magnam recte alteri superponi et [ad!] aliam ad latus distare ab ista est impossibile manifestum. 13 – Unius recte duo puncta alteri superponi vel unum imponi, aliud vero superponi, et magnam eius partem ad latus distare ab ista non posse contingere.'

42. Bradwardine intended his arguments to be valid not only against Harclay, but against any brand of immediate indivisibilism. In addition, he gives many effective arguments against any view maintaining that continua are composed of a finite number of indivisibles (and hence against another English indivisibilist, Chatton). He also believed that he had overturned the position maintaining that continua are composed of an infinite number of indivisibles between any two of which there is always another (something Bradwardine himself refers to – see note 36 above – as composition *ex infinitis* [*indivisibilibus*] *ad invicem mediatis*), but he was not successful in this regard. Incidentally, Bradwardine's ascription of this last brand of indivisibilism to Grosseteste ('*ut Lyncul⟨niensis⟩*') is not accurate. Grosseteste held that an infinity (indeed, differing infinities) of indivisibles were *contained in* differing continua, but he did not hold them to be *composed of* indivisibles (see Robert Grosseteste 1963, pp. 91–5).

Mathematical arguments against indivisibilism

Some medieval arguments against indivisibilism were not Aristotelian, and the most interesting and formidable of them were essentially mathematical. Such arguments can be found in the *Metaphysics* of Algazel[43] but also, and more importantly, in John Duns Scotus.[44] These arguments as well as all the variants which they generated in later philosophers, might be characterised basically as attempts to reveal the absolute incompatibility of indivisibilism and geometry. For example, parallel lines drawn from each indivisible in one side of a square to each indivisible in the opposite side will destroy the incommensurability of the diagonal with the side, since these parallels will meet the diagonal in as many, and only as many, indivisibles as they meet the sides. Similarly, the construction of all the radii of two concentric circles will entail the absurdity that they have equal circumferences if both circumferences are composed of indivisibles.[45]

These arguments, too, had to be answered by the medieval indivisibilist, but in attempting to answer them he was often forced to introduce inappropriate material notions into the mathematics of the arguments or even to reveal himself quite incompetent to deal with the mathematics at all.[46]

Euclidean considerations against indivisibilism

These arguments against the indivisibilist composition of geometrical continua were not the only mathematical factors in the medieval analysis of continuity. A few scholars were also aware of the assumptions made about continuity (and about infinity too) within Euclidean geometry itself. Thomas Bradwardine, for instance, had in effect rested his whole case against indivisibilism in his *Tractatus de continuo* on a series of geometrical propositions he had established at the beginning of his treatise. Yet at the end of his refutation he astutely asked just which 'axioms' concerning the composition of continua were assumed in the first place by the very

---

43. Algazel 1933, pp. 10–13.
44. Duns Scotus, *Opus Oxoniense*, Lib. II, dist. 2, quest. 9.
45. Examples of these arguments can be found in Murdoch 1962, pp. 24–30; also Murdoch and Synan 1966, pp. 254–6.
46. Thus, an indivisibilist might account for the intersection of lines in terms appropriate only to the crossing or overlapping of something having physical magnitude like sticks, since one could then explain how the parallel 'lines' cutting the diagonal of a square consumed more of the diagonal (which they intersected 'obliquely') than they did when they cut the sides (which they intersected at right angles). See, e.g., Murdoch and Synan 1966, pp. 259–62, where Chatton also shows his lack of understanding of incommensurability when he tries to relate it to odd vs. even numbers.

geometry he was using; by basing his refutation so completely on geometry, had he perhaps begged the whole question? No, he replies, for one *can* allow the composition of geometrical magnitudes out of indivisibles of a certain sort and still prove all the standard theorems of geometry.[47]

Campanus of Novara on curvilinear angles

A quite different and less unusual awareness of the continuity assumptions in geometry can be found in the medieval comments on Euclid. The first proposition of Book X of the *Elements* states that, given any magnitude A greater than some magnitude B, we can, in continuing to subtract parts from A, at some point reach a magnitude less than B.[48] The effect of this proposition was to exclude infinitely large, infinitely small, and minimal magnitudes. The thirteenth-century mathematician Campanus of Novara revealed himself to be quite aware of this effect, when, in preparing his version of the *Elements*, he commented that certain magnitudes, namely certain angles formed by straight lines and the circumference of a circle, appeared to contradict this proposition. For if we consider (Figure 1) the rectilinear angle ABC greater than the curvilinear angle DBC, it is evident that in decreasing or subtracting parts from ABC, we shall never reach an angle less than DBC. 'Therefore it is clear', Campanus adds, 'that any

47. *Bradwardine, *Tractatus de continuo*, (MS Torun, R. 4° 2, p. 188): 'Posset autem circa predicta fieri una falsigraphia: Avroys in commento suo super Physicorum (III, c. 31), ubi dicit, quod naturalis demonstrat continuum esse divisibile in infinitum et geometer hoc non probat, sed supponit tamquam demonstratum in scientia naturali, potest igitur impugnare demonstrationes geometricas prius factas dicendo: Geometriam ubique supponere continuum ex indivisibilibus non componi et illud demonstrari non posse. Sed illud non valet, quia suppositum falsum. Non enim ponitur inter demonstrationes geometricas continuum non componi ex indivisibilibus nec dyalecticer indiget⟨ur⟩ ubique, quoniam ⟨non⟩ in 5to Elementorum Euclidis. Et similiter, nec geometer in aliqua demonstratione supponit continuum non componi ex infinitis indivisibilibus mediatis, quia, dato eius opposito, quelibet demonstratio non minus procedit, ut patet inductive scienti conclusiones geometricas demonstrare.' Bradwardine also claims that maintaining that continua were composed of indivisibles immediately next to one another would cause difficulties in proving the fourth and eighth propositions of Book I of Euclid, since these propositions appeal to superposition in their proof and superposition is the geometrical notion used by Bradwardine to interpret the immediacy of indivisibles (see Murdoch 1964, p. 440). What Bradwardine was doing in this place and in the passage quoted above amounts to probing the logic of assumptions made in mathematics and (in modern terms) to asking just which axioms were independent of the system of geometry as he knew it and which were not.

48. This is a simplification of X, 1. Euclid speaks not of subtracting parts in general from the greater magnitude, but of subtracting more than half (or, in a corollary, just half) the difference between the greater and lesser magnitudes. On the difficulties caused by this restriction in Euclid (as well as by the fact that most medieval Latin versions of the *Elements* lacked another form [V, def. 4] of the continuity assumption asserted by X, 1), see Murdoch 1963, pp. 240–51. These difficulties are not, however, germane to the point being made here.

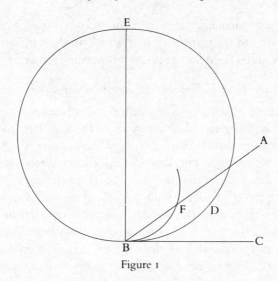

Figure 1

rectilinear angle is greater than an infinite number of angles of contingence' (that is, curvilinear angles like DBC). Campanus had correctly identified what in fact was an infinitesimal magnitude which does not obey the continuity principle set down by Euclid's X, 1, and he appropriately specifies that the fact that such curvilinear angles are not of the same genus as rectilinear angles is the reason why the former do not obey this principle.[49] What is more, in his comment on the proposition in Euclid in which such curvilinear angles are mentioned, Campanus notes that they violate yet another continuity principle. For the right angle EBC (Figure 1) is greater than the angle of the semicircle EBD, while the acute angle EBA is less than EBD. Yet one can decrease the right angle EBC by rotating the tangent BC about B toward BA and in so doing reach an acute angle less than the angle of the semicircle EBD. But this means one has violated the continuity principle that claims that if one moves from a magnitude (EBC) greater than some second magnitude (EBD) to a third magnitude (EBA)

---

49. Euclid, *Elementorum geometricorum libri XV cum expositione ... Campani in omnes* (ed. Basel, 1558), p. 244: 'Attendere autem oportet, quod huic propositioni videtur decimaquinta tertii contradicere, proponens angulum contingentiae minorem fore quolibet angulo a duabus lineis rectis contento. Posito enim angulo quolibet rectilineo, si ab ipso maius dimidio dematur, itemque de residuo maius dimidio, necesse videtur hoc toties posse fieri, quousque angulus rectilineus, minor angulo contingentiae relinquatur, cuius oppositum 15 tertii syllogisat. Sed hi non sunt univoce anguli, non enim eiusdem sunt generis simpliciter curvum et rectum. ... Planum ergo est etiam, quemlibet angulum rectilineum, infinitis angulis contingentiae esse maiorem.' (In modern terms, because it does not obey the continuity principle in X, 1, an angle of contingence is a non-Archimedean magnitude.)

less than the second magnitude, then one moves through a magnitude
equal to this second magnitude.[50] In a word, angles of contingence and
angles of semicircles need not obey this continuity principle.

Peter Ceffons and the measure of species

The relevance of this particular portion of medieval mathematics to
medieval philosophy derived not only from the fact that any number of
fourteenth-century philosophers and theologians were aware of the peculiar properties of these curvilinear angles (and often aware of what
Campanus had said about them),[51] but also from the discovery that such
angles could be put to use in providing a scale of measure that would prove
effective when applied to the different perfections of radically distinct
species. The paradigm of this application of curvilinear angles was undoubtedly the one produced by Peter Ceffons. Lecturing on the *Sentences* at
Paris in 1348–9, Ceffons spent what seems to be an inordinate amount of
time explaining how his 'calculus of angles' could measure the 'distances'
between species. There is, to begin with, an infinite distance between
individuals of distinct species, between (say) a man and a donkey, a distance
that can be represented by the infinite excess of a rectilinear angle representing man over an angle of contingence representing the donkey. For,
like distinct species, these angles are *finite* things allowing of mutually
infinite excess. Moreover, these angles of contingence can themselves be
increased or decreased (by drawing smaller or larger circles to the relevant
point of tangency) and they are still infinitely exceeded by rectilinear
angles (thus angle ABC (Figure 1) infinitely exceeds angle FBC as well as
angle DBC). This phenomenon corresponds to an allowable increase or
decrease of individuals *within* a given species while preserving the infinite
distance between individuals of distinct species.[52] Ceffons' fancies in this
regard appear to have drawn fire from at least one of his Parisian successors,
John of Ripa, who did not hold with the value of such '*exempla mathe-
matica*'.[53]

50. Euclid, *op. cit.*, p. 67, *additio ad prop.* III, 15 (= III, 16 of the Greek): 'Ex hoc notandum, quod non
    valet ista argumentatio: Hoc transit a minori ad maius, et per omnia media: ergo per aequale. Nec
    ista: Contingit reperire maius hoc, et minus eodem: ergo contingit reperire aequale'. Campanus
    goes on to specify that angles of contingence and angles of semicircles provide instances of
    magnitudes which, relative to rectilinear angles, violate these 'continuity principles'.
51. Thomas Bradwardine, *Geometria speculativa* (ed. Paris, 1503), Tract. 2, Ch. 3, concl. 6.
52. Something more of Ceffons' machinations with curvilinear angles and the perfections of species
    can be found in Murdoch 1978a, pp. 61–3 and Murdoch 1969, pp. 242–6, the latter of which
    contains other material (pp. 238–41) relating to the 'measure' of species. Ceffons' *Comm. Sent.* is
    unedited. The basic article on him is Trapp 1957.
53. See the text in Murdoch 1969, n. 107.

Harclay, Alnwick, and terminist logic in the analysis of continua

Mathematics was not the only discipline to which the late medieval scholar turned in analysing continua; logic provided an even more fruitful source in this regard, especially when it was a question of analysing the limits one ascribed to continuous magnitudes and processes.

An instance of this application of logic can be found in one of Henry of Harclay's positive arguments in support of his indivisibilism. Although men cannot perceive or know all the points of a finite line, Harclay argued, God surely can. But if God does perceive *all* the points of a line, then either he perceives that there is some line segment between the first point of the line and *every* other point of the line, or he does not. If he does, then, since points can obviously be assigned in any such segment, there are points in the original line which he did not perceive, contrary to the hypothesis. If he does not, then some point must be immediate to the first point of the line, which proves that at least one continuum is composed of points in contact – which, as we have seen, is Harclay's position.[54] In criticising this argument of Harclay's, William of Alnwick insists that we must distinguish two different propositions: (1) 'between the first point of a line and every other point known by God of the same line, there is a mean point'; (2) 'there is a mean point between the first point and every other point perceived by God of the same line'. Alnwick claims that the first proposition is true while the second is false, because, in the first proposition, the term 'mean point' has a type of 'merely confused supposition' (or indeterminate reference) (as a result of the fact that 'every' precedes it in the proposition), while 'mean point' in the second proposition has 'determinate supposition'. On the principles of terminist logic employed by Alnwick here, in the second proposition we can 'descend' from the term 'mean point' to the specification of either 'this (particular) mean point' or 'that (particular) mean point' or 'that other (particular) mean point', etc. But this means that the second proposition is false, because there is no one particular mean point that falls between the initial point of the line and *all* other points in the line. On the other hand, the fact that in the first

---

54. Since in what follows I discuss William of Alnwick's refutation of Harclay's argument, I present Alnwick's version of the argument here: it is in essence, if not in language, the same as Harclay's original. 'Deus actualiter videt sive cognoscit primum punctum inchoativum linee et quodlibet aliud punctum possibile signari in eadem linea. Aut igitur Deus videt quod inter hoc punctum inchoativum linee et quodlibet aliud punctum in eadem linea potest linea intercipi aut non. Si non, igitur videt punctum puncto immediatum, quod est propositum. Si sic, cum in linea media possint assignari puncta, illa puncta media non essent visa a Deo, quod falsum est.' (MS *Vat. pal. lat.* 1805, f. 11ʳ).

proposition the term 'mean point' has merely confused supposition means that one *cannot* descend to such a disjunction of singular propositions – which represents what as a matter of fact is the case, namely, that there is no one mean point between the initial point of the line and all others. Hence the first proposition is true.[55]

Alnwick's criticism of Harclay is but a single instance of the application of the doctrine of supposition to the analysis of continua, in particular to the analysis of the order and denseness of elements within a continuum. If we look to Ockham, for example, we find him employing the same technique in dealing with continua and the infinite.[56]

55. I have given a resumé of William of Alnwick's reply to Harclay's argument (which he cites, naming Harclay as its author): Alnwick, *Determinatio 2* (MS *Vat. pal. lat.* 1805, 14^{r-v}): 'Dico autem breviter quod ista est vera: "inter primum punctum linee et omnem alium punctum eiusdem linee cognitum a Deo est linea media". Quelibet enim singularis est vera et eius contradictoria est falsa. Et hoc ideo est, quia "linea media" in predicato sequens mediate signum universale stat confuse tantum. Hec tamen est falsa: "est linea media inter primum punctum et omnem alium punctum eiusdem linee visum a Deo", quia nulla est linea media inter primum punctum et omnem alium punctum visum a Deo. Non enim contingit dare aliquam talem lineam mediam, sic enim mediaret inter primum punctum et seipsam; nec illa linea esset visa a Deo. Et ideo, cum infertur: si sic, igitur cum in linea possent puncta signari, et cetera, ibi "linea" stat particulariter; et ideo arguitur a superiori ad inferius affirmative et sic facit fallaciam consequentis. Similiter arguitur a termino stante confuse tantum ad eundem terminum stantem determinate sive particulariter, et commutatur quale quid in hoc aliquid, et fit fallacia figure dictionis.' (In summarising Alnwick's reply, I have spoken of 'mean points' in place of the 'mean line' in which such points can be designated, but the structure of the argument is precisely the same.) Cf. William of Alnwick 1937, pp. 501–3.

56. Ockham, *Exp. phys.*, III, ad text. 60 (206^{b}16), MS Mert. 293, 71^v: 'Est autem istis adiciendum quod quamvis hec sit vera: "omni magnitudine est minor magnitudo", hec tamen est impossibilis: "aliqua magnitudo est minor omni magnitudine". Ista enim est vera: "omni magnitudine est minor magnitudo", quia est una universalis cuius quelibet singularis est vera. Hec tamen est falsa: "aliqua magnitudo est minor omni magnitudine", quia est una particularis cuius quelibet singularis est falsa. Et est simile sicut de istis duobus: hec est vera: "omnis homo est animal", et hec falsa: "aliquod animal est omnis homo". Et ratio diversitatis est quia in ista: "omni magnitudine est minor magnitudo" ly "minor magnitudo" supponit confuse tantum propter signum universale precedens a parte subiecti, et ideo ad veritatem sufficit quod ista magnitudine sit una magnitudo minor et illa magnitudine sit una alia magnitudo minor et sic de aliis. Sed in ista: "aliqua magnitudo est minor omni magnitudine" ly "magnitudo" supponit determinate, et ideo oportet quod aliqua una magnitudo numero esset minor omni magnitudine, et per consequens esset minor seipsa.' (Note that Ockham dispenses with the unnecessary 'aliqua' in the first proposition; it was included in other treatments.) Ockham, *Exp. phys.*, VI, ad text. 52 (236^{b}3), MS Mert. 293, 133^v: 'Tertio sciendum est pro sophisticis quod ista propositio de virtute sermonis est concedenda: "ante omne mutari est mutatum esse", quia quelibet singularis est vera, scilicet ista: "ante hoc mutari est mutatum esse" et "ante illud mutari" et sic de singulis. Sed ista falsa est: "aliquod mutatum esse est ante omne mutari", quia est una indiffinita cuius quelibet singularis est falsa. Nec sequitur: "ante ⟨omne⟩ mutari est mutatum esse, igitur aliquod mutatum esse est ante omne mutari", quia in prima "mutatum esse" stat confuse tantum propter hoc quod sequitur signum universale affirmativum mediate; in consequente autem stat determinate, quia precedit signum, et ideo est fallacia figure dictionis et etiam fallacia consequentis.'

Contradictory opposites and the instant of change in Aristotle

Logic also provided the conceptual toolkit for another problem concerning continua, one which received so much attention by late scholastics that whole treatises were devoted to it. In this case, however, the problem underwent a development within natural philosophy proper before it was submitted to logical analysis. Two passages in Aristotle's *Physics* furnished the raw material. In the fifth chapter of Book VI of the *Physics* ($235^b32-236^a27$), Aristotle had raised the question whether there is a first instant, a 'primary when', at the *beginning* of a continuous change or motion and, secondly, whether there is such a primary element for the *completion* of such a change, an instant when one can first truly say 'this change is now over'. Aristotle's reply was that one should *deny* that there is a first instant of a continuous change, but *affirm* that there is an instant at the end of it – that is, a 'primary when' signifying that the change has been concluded. The second Aristotelian ingredient also came from the *Physics*: Book VIII, Chapter 8 (263^b9-26). There Aristotle had dealt with the 'contradictory change' involved in (say) changing from being not-white to being white.[57] Here his decision was that the relevant first instant should be assigned to the later segment of the time interval in question; that is, there would be a first instant at which the changing subject is white. Unlike his reply in Chapter 5 of Book VI maintaining that there is no first element to a continuous change, this passage maintains that there is such a first element.

De primo et ultimo instanti

These Aristotelian problems were expanded and systematised in the fourteenth century in questions and treatises usually entitled *De primo et ultimo instanti*, the most popular of them by far being Walter Burley's.[58] In sum, these treatises stipulated that since one must, with Aristotle, deny a first instant at the beginning of a continuous change, one could, indeed one must, designate a *last instant before* the beginning of the change, a last instant of the period of the change's not yet occurring. Similarly, if one turns to the ending of such a change, since one must, again with Aristotle, affirm a first instant of the change's no longer occurring, one must also deny a last

---

57. Aristotle's example is of a change from being white to being not-white, but since the scholastics reversed the example, I have done so here.
58. The text of Burley's treatise is printed in Shapiro 1965, but it is not a critical edition.

instant of the change itself. One can thus say that any continuous change or motion is limited at its beginning by a last instant of its not-being and at its end by a first instant of its not-being. But the restriction to not-being means that the change or motion is *extrinsically* limited at both its ends, since if it were intrinsically limited, that would entail the existence of first or last instants belonging to the change itself, which is categorically denied.

The rules were different, however, when one turned from continuous changes, *res successivae*, to *res permanentes*, a case of which is provided by the example of something changing from not-white to white.[59] Here, following Aristotle's decision, there was a first instant of being white, and thus a (non-continuous) change that was *intrinsically* limited at its beginning. On the other hand, when that being white came to an end, it would do so without there being a last instant of its existence; there would merely be another first instant of the existence of whatever the subject changed into (or even a first instant of the non-existence of the subject itself). Thus a *res permanens* like being white was intrinsically limited at its beginning but extrinsically limited at its end.

Incipit/desinit

Such an interpretation of Aristotle's views about the ascription of limits to both successive and permanent things was, however, only one cornerstone of the medieval literature dealing with the topic. And of all this literature, unquestionably the most important was that which transferred the whole problem to the context of logic. There was already existent in that context a new and altogether suitable home for this problem of limits: namely, the logical tradition of treating as problematic propositions in which the verbs 'begins' ('*incipit*') or 'ceases' ('*desinit*') occurred.[60]

The new context made a difference. For in the literature of first and last instants (*de primo et ultimo instanti*) one spoke directly about the things to which limits were ascribed and about the instants or limits themselves; but once the problem of limits was placed within the logical context of discussions of '*incipit*' and '*desinit*' the elements of analysis became the terms '*incipit*' and '*desinit*' and the propositions embodying those terms. Instead of

---

59. Being white was considered a *res permanens* because it had all of its 'parts' at once, and not, like a *res successiva* (any continuous motion, for example), one after the other.

60. This earlier tradition is sketched in Kretzmann 1976. Note, however, that the earliest of the literature constituting that tradition did not contain treatments of the problem of limits presently in question. The introduction of that problem had occurred by the time of the discussions of '*incipit*' and '*desinit*' by William of Sherwood and Peter of Spain (for which see Kretzmann, *op. cit.*).

asking, for example, whether Socrates' being white was limited at its beginning by a first instant of his being white, one carried out an analysis of the proposition 'Socrates begins to be white' (*'Sortes incipit esse albus'*). Accordingly, the considerations regarding first and last instants which differentiated intrinsic from extrinsic limits were represented by different kinds of logical 'expositions' that could be given of propositions involving the terms *'incipit'* and *'desinit.'* [61] The difference between the treatment of these problems of limits in the literature of first and last instants and their treatment in the literature of *'incipit'* and *'desinit'* might be described as a difference between an object-language treatment and a metalinguistic treatment of the same problems. This sort of difference can be seen in the thirteenth century in the sections on *'incipit'* and *'desinit'* in the works of William of Sherwood and Peter of Spain, and in the fourteenth century in Thomas Bradwardine's treatise on the subject.[62] But something additional happens when we follow this *incipit/desinit* literature further into the fourteenth century, especially in the works of Richard Kilvington,[63] William Heytesbury,[64] and, at the close of the century, Paul of Venice.[65] The keynote of this later literature was the construction of limit-decision problems as sophismata, the motive behind this new turn apparently being the formulation of problems complicated and ingenious enough to allow, perhaps even compel, the hearer or reader of them to develop real expertise in the application of the techniques and rules relevant to the resolution of limit-problems, especially as cast in their *incipit/desinit* form.

De maximo et minimo

In the literature of first and last instants or of *'incipit'* and *'desinit'*, the fundamental continuum in question was that of time. For it is against the 'background' of an absolutely continuous time that the changes whose limits were at stake occur, whether they are continuous or instantaneous. But fourteenth-century scholastics also struggled with the problem of ascribing limits in cases in which the continuum of time was not relevant. Such cases occur when one attempts to set limits to powers or capacities,

---

61. See, for instance, the expositions provided in the *Tractatus syncategorematum* ascribed to Peter of Spain. The whole section of this work dealing with *'incipit'* and *'desinit'* is conveniently available in translation in Kretzmann 1976, pp. 122–8.

62. For Sherwood and Peter of Spain, see Kretzmann 1976. For Thomas Bradwardine's *Tractatus de incipit* (unedited), see Murdoch 1979, pp. 125–6.

63. Richard Kilvington, *Sophismata*, currently being edited and translated by Norman and Barbara Kretzmann.

64. William Heytesbury 1494b, cap. 4: 'De incipit et desinit'; ff. 23^v–27^r.

65. Paul of Venice 1499, Prima pars, tractatus 18; ff. 65^v–70^v.

maxima that a power (of lifting, for example) can accomplish vs. minima it cannot. Although the treatment of this kind of limit-problems was more thoroughly physical than that of setting limits to the existence of things and events in time, it too had its decidedly logical elements. But this story cannot be told here.[66]

Richard Swineshead's Liber calculationum

Instead, for the final example let us return from continua to the infinite. We shall at the same time be turning from logic to something more distinctively mathematical even though the treatment of the problems is carried out in the format of sophismata. The work in question is Richard Swineshead's *Liber calculationum*. The context is the measurement of the overall intensity of a given quality (heat, for example) in a given subject when varying intensities of that quality are distributed in certain specifiable ways over the subject.[67] One two-part example of the distribution of these varying intensities brings Swineshead face to face with the infinite. Imagine, as a first hypothesis, that a given subject is (say) hot in degree 1 over its first half, in degree 2 over its next quarter, in degree 3 over its next eighth, in degree 4 over its next sixteenth, and so on *in infinitum*. As a

---

66. The problem had its origins in Aristotle's contention (*De caelo*, I, Ch. 11, 281^{a}1–27) that a capacity should be defined in terms of the maximum it can accomplish, a contention to which he added the correlative information that, if some capacity can accomplish so much, it certainly can accomplish less, while if it cannot accomplish so much, it surely cannot accomplish more. Aristotle did not raise the question of a possible boundary between what a capacity can and cannot accomplish, but Averroes moved in the direction of formulating such a question when he commented that a capacity should be defined in terms of the maximum it can do, while its correlative incapacity should be defined in terms of the minimum it cannot do. These notions of maxima and minima became standard when, in later medieval analyses, the problem was transformed into one of ascribing limits. Should a capacity such as Socrates' ability to lift things be limited by a maximum weight he can lift or by a minimum weight he cannot lift? What criteria can be used to decide such a question one way or another? Although some solutions to this problem were reasonably physical (such as that of Richard Swineshead in Tract. 10 of his *Liber calculationum*), others', and especially Heytesbury's (in Ch. 5 of his *Regulae*), bring logical considerations to bear. Thus, Heytesbury's approach to the problem amounts to asserting that the kind of *terms* occurring in the very formulation of the question will enable one to decide whether a *maximum quod sic* or a *minimum quod non* is appropriate. Thus, the prime consideration is what kind of quantifier modifies the common noun (for example, 'weight', 'lifting power', etc.) by means of which one determines a maximum or minimum, and how many things (*supposita*) the quantified noun stands for. Heytesbury even appeals to the verifiability of propositions in order to express a number of the conditions that must obtain in order that a capacity have a range susceptible to maxima and minima. On the whole problem, Heytesbury and Swineshead included, see Wilson 1956, Ch. 3.

67. On the context in question, see Murdoch & Sylla 1976, pp. 190–3. The example in question is drawn from Tractatus II (*De difformibus*), of Swineshead 1520, ff. 6^v–7^r.

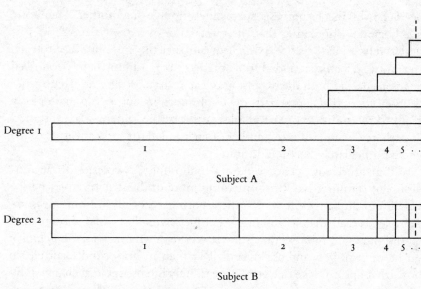

Subject A

Subject B

Figure 2

whole, the subject is hot in degree 2.[68] That is, it is *finitely* hot as a whole even though the heat throughout it increases *infinitely*. Secondly, Swineshead takes the very same subject having varying intensities of a quality distributed *in infinitum* over its decreasing proportional parts in the manner just described and submits this subject to rarefaction in a specified fashion. Rarefy the second proportional part (that is, its third quarter) by any amount howsoever small, rarefy the fourth proportional part (that is, its fifteenth sixteenth) by an amount half as much (or, as Swineshead says, rarefy the fourth proportional part half as slowly as the second), and so on, taking only every 2^{nth} proportional part and rarefying each twice as slowly as the preceding one. Given this hypothesis, how hot is the whole? Answer: infinitely hot. For in selecting only the 2^{nth} proportional parts of the subject, Swineshead had chosen parts whose intensities were, as he has

68. If we allow ourselves a geometric representation (Figure 2) which is not present in Swineshead, we can see more clearly how he went about establishing his conclusion. Take subject A with increasing intensities (beginning from an intensity of degree 1 over its first half) 'stacked up' over its succeeding proportional parts; A clearly has 'just as much quality' as does subject B. For all we have to do is redistribute the 'top layer' of B over the succeeding proportional parts of A as uniformly intense in degree 1 to obtain A with the increasing intensities *ad infinitum*. But B as a whole is clearly hot (or of whatever quality) in degree 2; therefore, so is A with increasing intensities *in infinitum*. In modern terms, what we have is the convergent series $\frac{1}{2} + \frac{2}{4} + \frac{3}{8} + \frac{4}{16} + \ldots + \frac{n}{2^n} = 2$, but it is anachronistic to speak of infinite series in Swineshead. See the text of this segment of Swineshead's example in Clagett 1968, pp. 58–61.

specified in his first hypothesis, successively double one another. Therefore, in deliberately stipulating that the rarefaction over these parts should be successively 'twice as slow' (which means that the amount *added* to each part is always half that added to its predecessor), it immediately followed that, considering both the extension of each part added by rarefaction and the intensity in that added part, the resulting contribution (no matter how small) to the measure of the whole would be the same in each instance. Since there were an infinite number of such added parts, the measure of the whole immediately becomes infinite.[69]

Within fourteenth-century natural philosophy, Swineshead's accomplishment is impressive. But something more of the structure of what he was doing can be seen if we compare both parts of his 'infinite measure' example. Recall that in his first example Swineshead had shown that, astonishing as it might seem, a subject whose quality increases *in infinitum* can be only finitely intense overall. But then in his second example he shows that one can take this very same finitely intense subject, change it by a finite amount as small as one wishes, and it immediately becomes infinitely intense. The switch from infinite to finite and then back to infinite again was more than incidental; it was a feature of Swineshead's indulgence in the (by then very fashionable) tradition of creating and solving sophismata. In fact, he even refers to the problem he was dealing with as a *sophisma*; the fact that it involved mathematics instead of logic made no difference.

69. Swineshead 1520, f. 7^r: 'Sit A tale cuius prima pars proportionalis sit aliqualiter intensa, et secunda in duplo intensior et tripla in triplo intensior, et sic in infinitum [this much gives the initial "convergent series" mentioned in n. 68 above]. Tunc A est solum finite intensum, ut predicitur. Ponatur igitur quod secunda pars proportionalis A aliqualiter velociter rarefiet acquirendo quantitatem, et quarta pars proportionalis in duplo intensior secunda parte proportionali in duplo tardius acquirat de quantitate, et pars in quadruplo intensior illa secunda in quadruplo tardius acquiret quantitatem quam illa secunda, et sic in infinitum; et nunc incipiat huiusmodi rarefactio in illis partibus, stantibus omnibus aliis partibus non rarefactis nec condensatis. Et sequitur quod A solum finite velociter rarefiet seu maiorabitur et secunda in duplo tardius et sic in infinitum. Et quod A subito in infinitum intendatur patet, quia ante quodcumque instans habebit A infinitas partes quarum quelibet tantum faciet ad intensionem totius, sicut est hoc certum datum, demonstrando illud quod faciet quantitas acquisita secunde parti proportionali; nam sicut aliqua pars acquisita alicui parti proportionali erit minor quam quantitas acquisita secunde parti proportionali, ita eadem pars erit intensior quam secunda pars proportionalis et quam quantitas sibi acquisita, ut ponit casus, addendo quod quelibet pars proportionalis in principio et continue sit uniformis. Sed hoc est generaliter verum: quod si proportionaliter sicut una quantitas seu pars alicuius est alia parte minor, ita eadem sit alia parte maiori intensior, equaliter facient omnes huiusmodi partes ad totius intensionem; ergo omnes iste quantitates acquisite infinite facient equaliter ad totius denominationem, id est, ante quodcumque instans, et per consequens cum erunt huiusmodi partes infinite, sequitur quod in infinitum facient ante quodcumque instans datum.' We would, anachronistically, interpret Swineshead at this point by saying that the series he had constructed, was divergent, for its general term is $2^n/2^{2^n} - 2^n/2^{n-1}K$, where K represents the rarefaction undergone by the first rarefied part.

Logic and mathematics

The absence of a recognised difference between logic and mathematics is symptomatic of what transpired methodologically throughout fourteenth-century natural philosophy of the infinite and the continuous, especially in its more creative phases. Mathematical considerations on the one hand and logical considerations on the other consistently provided concepts, doctrines, and techniques for the analysis at hand. In some instances, the mathematics was drawn from, or at least rooted in, what had been inherited from the Greeks. But in other cases, the medievals were forced to go well beyond their mathematical heritage, perhaps even go against it, since a 'mathematics of the infinite' was certainly not a Greek predilection. A fair share of the mathematical considerations that were employed in the medieval treatment of infinity and continuity was, then, 'home grown'.

Moreover, almost all the logic that was employed was similarly a medieval creation. This is surely the case with respect to the doctrine of supposition, but it is perhaps less obviously true regarding the propositional analysis of problems of the infinite and the continuous. Of course, the invocation of logic and logical considerations was far more frequent in fourteenth-century philosophy and theology than an appeal to anything mathematical. Yet judgements of this sort are probably guilty of separating logical and mathematical techniques in a way in which they were not separated in the minds of the fourteenth-century thinkers who applied these techniques. Not only were the techniques often mixed in their application of them, but it is frequently difficult to determine, as we have seen, whether in a given instance it might be the mathematics that was more determinative of the problem or the sophisma-mould deriving from logic into which the mathematics was poured. In any event, the application of both mathematical and logical notions was a hallmark of the analytical bent of the fourteenth century, throughout its philosophy and its theology.

VIII

PHILOSOPHY OF
MIND AND ACTION

29

THE POTENTIAL AND THE AGENT INTELLECT

The Aristotelian origins of the doctrine

The conception of potential and agent intellect came to Western medieval philosophy with the assimilation of Aristotle's theory of soul in his *De anima*. In this text, intellective cognition was understood as the reception of abstract concepts; therefore Aristotle conceived an intellective power capable of receiving which, in order to accomplish this function, had a purely potential nature. In several passages of the *De anima*, this power is called *nous pathētikos* (Lat. *intellectus possibilis*). The process of cognition starts, however, with the data of sensitive cognition, which are particular and not universal. Therefore the reception of abstract concepts must be preceded by the abstraction of the universal content from sensible images. In order to explain this action, Aristotle conceived of an active power which his Greek commentators named *nous poietikos* (Lat. *intellectus agens*). Neither the exact functions of the two powers nor the relation between them was very clear in the *De anima*. In some portions of the text, the intellect was described as a part of the soul, which was defined by Aristotle as a substantial form of the body, but other sections considered the intellect as having a nature different from the soul-form of the body. This difference was especially stressed in the case of the active power, which was at various points described as being separate from the body and surviving death, or as inseparably joined to the body. These and other inconsistencies in Aristotle's text opened the way to different interpretations beginning with such Greek commentators as Themistius and Alexander of Aphrodisias, and carrying on through medieval Arabic 'Aristotelian' theories of the soul.

Avicenna and Averroes

Western medieval philosophers became acquainted with Aristotle's theory along with its earlier interpretations, the most important and influential among them being Averroes' and Avicenna's. Averroes and Avicenna had accepted some fundamental theses common to different currents of

'Aristotelianism': there exist both a potential and an agent intellect, each of which differs in nature (i.e. potentiality/act) and in function (i.e. passivity/activity). Avicenna endowed man with a potential intellect which was the highest part of the soul, spiritual substance accidentally joined to the body as its form. The agent intellect, however, was according to Avicenna a separate, spiritual substance, the one and only intelligence for all men – 'a treasury of concepts' – whose function was to transmit intelligible forms – concepts – into the individual human mind (possible intellect). According to Averroes' conception, on the other hand, both intellects were separate substances, common to all humanity and connected to each man by his individual sensitive cognition. When the sensitive data came into contact with the potential intellect, they were illuminated by the agent intellect, their universal content was separated from their individual conditions, and the abstract concepts thus produced were then received in the potential intellect. The whole process of intellective cognition proceeded, therefore, inside the separate psychic substances and was only communicated to individual men.

The Christian Platonist tradition and the new Aristotelianism

The new texts presenting various interpretations of Aristotle's theory of the potential and agent intellect came to the West in the twelfth and early thirteenth centuries. At the time this process began, Western philosophy conceived of the soul and the process of intellective cognition in a Christian perspective against the philosophical background of a Platonist tradition with Boethius and Augustine as its main sources. The human soul was treated as a spiritual substance, having innate knowledge, illuminated by God, composed of a *ratio superior* directed toward the spiritual world and a *ratio inferior* tending toward lower beings, not dependent on the body, and accomplishing its cognitive function all by itself. The encounter of the new Aristotelian conception with the old Christian tradition produced a conflict which was never resolved in the Middle Ages and which provided an important stimulus for the evolution and development of a new theory of the soul, incorporating the conception of the potential and agent intellect. Because of the strong position of this old Christian tradition, the first attempts to assimilate the Aristotelian theory of the potential and agent intellect favored those interpretations which stressed 'Platonic' residues in Aristotle's conception, especially the transcendent nature of the intellect.

Dominicus Gundissalinus

The first Western assimilation of the theory of the intellect occurred in Spain, in Toledo, where Avicenna's translator, Dominicus Gundissalinus, wrote his *De anima* between 1142 and 1152. According to Gundissalinus, the human soul is a spiritual substance, mover of the body and its perfection or form. His conception of the intellect is basically Avicennian: the human soul contains the potential intellect only, and the agent intellect is a spiritual substance distinct from man. The function of both intellects is Avicennian too: the potential intellect gives its attention to phantasmata and this attention prepares it to receive enlightenment from the agent intellect. Thus, the agent intellect illuminates phantasmata and creates abstract concepts in the potential intellect.[1]

John Blund

No sequel to this Spanish twelfth-century reception of the Avicennian or Aristotelian theory of the intellect is known until the beginning of the thirteenth century when John Blund, student and professor at the Faculty of Arts in Paris commented on Aristotle's *De anima* before 1210.[2] The main sources of his commentary were Augustine, Boethius, and Avicenna, and these philosophers lay behind his conception of the soul as a spiritual substance, simple, like a disembodied intelligence, but linked somehow with the body, directed by its higher part toward contemplation of spiritual beings and by its lower part toward sensible things. This lower activity proceeds by way of abstraction, vaguely conceived in an Avicennian sense. John Blund's sparse remarks on the intellect and its cognition are very imprecise. He accepts the potential intellect as receiver of abstract concepts and the active intellect as a distinct substance, a *dator formarum* or angelic intelligence, which is necessary for the impression of universal concepts in the possible intellect because sensible data initiating the process of intellective cognition are 'too far' from the intellect.[3]

William of Auvergne, Philip the Chancellor, and John of La Rochelle

The prohibition of 1210 against teaching Aristotle's texts dealing with natural philosophy stopped the process of assimilation of the Aristotelian

---

1. Gilson 1929–30, pp. 82–3, 95, 87.
2. Edited by D. A. Callus and R. M. Hunt, 1970. See also Callus 1955, p. 432.
3. MS Vat. lat. 833, f. 99va, 99vb, 100ra, 100rb, 100vb.

theory of the intellect in the Paris Arts Faculty for thirty years. However, the process continued slowly in the Paris Faculty of Theology, where no Aristotle texts of any kind had been taught and consequently no prohibition was enforced. William of Auvergne, Philip the Chancellor, and John of La Rochelle were the main links in this process. It started in 1230 with the *De anima* of William of Auvergne. William was aware of the Avicennian conception of the intellect and rejected it in order to maintain the traditional Christian theory of man. The process continued with Philip the Chancellor (d. 1236), who incorporated Aristotelian concepts of the potential and agent intellect in the traditional Christian theory of soul, and it came to its full development with John of La Rochelle (d. 1245), who also attempted to incorporate the new conception of the soul and the role of the possible and active intellect into the tradition. In his *Summa de anima* he created a new conception of the soul as a spiritual substance, composed of *quo est* and *quod est*, which was at the same time a perfection of the body. He also accepted the Avicennian agent intellect, identified, however, with an angelic intelligence who illuminates human souls giving them knowledge of supra-sensible beings. Nevertheless, he regarded not only the potential but also the active intellect as internal to the human soul; the latter has the nature of an actuality and is identical with divine light in the soul, while the former is described in Aristotelian fashion as a *tabula non scripta*. The function of both intellects in the soul is basically Aristotelian: the agent intellect purifies sensible images of their individual characteristics and produces universals for reception in the potential intellect.[4]

The elements of the early assimilation

Thus was the first step accomplished in the Christian interpretation of Aristotle: each man was endowed with an individual active intellect. The agent intellect, which in the *De anima* was treated sometimes as separate from the soul and sometimes as belonging to it, and which in Avicenna's conception was considered a single distinct substance, was now divided into two different beings: the first was part of the human soul, and the second identical to an angelic intelligence and thus separate.

Roger Bacon

After thirty years of prohibition, Aristotle texts again appeared in the Paris Faculty of Arts in 1240, and the first philosopher to comment upon

---

4. John of la Rochelle 1881, pp. 118–21, 161–3, 290–5.

Aristotle's works on *philosophia naturalis* was Roger Bacon, master there between 1240 and 1247. His opinion on the soul and the potential and agent intellect evolved between his *Quaestiones* and *Quaestiones alterae* on Aristotle's *Physics* and *Metaphysics*: in the first phase he considered the agent intellect as part of the human soul, in the second as a separate Avicennian substance.

Bacon began by accepting the general Avicennian conception of the soul as a spiritual substance which can be conceived in union with the body, but he rejected his concept of the separate agent intellect. In this way he took the second step on the road first taken by John of La Rochelle. Considered in its union with the body, the soul contains the potential and agent intellect, the former being a lower, the latter a higher part of the soul. The potential intellect is connected with sensitive powers, it is directed toward spiritual beings, and its object is the material thing. The agent intellect does not use sensitive powers, it is directed toward spiritual beings and knows them by its own essence. Conforming to Platonic and Augustinian tradition, Bacon also accepts some kind of 'confused innate knowledge', *exempla* in the soul. However, he weakens the meaning of this expression and understands innate knowledge only as a disposition which inclines the human intellect to cognition of truth, in other words, there is innate knowledge only of the first principles of understanding.[5]

Roger Bacon's conception of the cognition and function of both intellects is dependent on his interpretation of their objects. Individual beings have a common nature, but this nature can be known by the intellect only through universals, which are unclear, indictinct images. The agent intellect illuminates phantasmata, dematerialised to some extent by sensitive powers, liberates them definitively from material conditions and impresses them upon the potential intellect as concepts, intentions, or universals. The process of intellective cognition is, however, not limited to this abstraction, because the agent intellect performs some kind of illumination through its 'innate knowledge' also, but this illumination has a merely regulative role: the illumination by *exempla* is not a necessary condition of the cognition but only of the veracity of knowledge.[6]

In the second phase of the evolution of his position, Roger Bacon separates the agent intellect from the intellective soul which becomes identical with the sole potential intellect. Thus the potential intellect is now

5. Roger Bacon 1909–40, VII, pp. 15–16, 110, 111–12; VIII, pp. 2–3, 15–16; XI, p. 9.
6. Bacon 1909–40, VII, p. 31; VIII, pp. 4, 97.

considered from a twofold point of view – as spiritual substance, or as a form of the body. Considered as substance, it has its innate confused knowledge and is able to know spiritual substances. The potential intellect as a form of the body is not able to know spiritual substances, although it was created with innate knowledge, it has lost it as a result of separation from God and become a *tabula rasa* with no knowledge at all. The agent intellect, a distinct spiritual substance, gives its confused knowledge to the potential intellect by means of impressed intelligible species. Having thus obtained its confused knowledge, the potential intellect is enabled to proceed to further cognition.[7] The concept of the cognition and function of the potential intellect is, however, not elaborated in this second phase of Bacon's developing position. The conception of the intellect explained in *Opus maius* and *Communia naturalium* between 1265 and 1268 belongs to another period of his scientific activity, and represents a type common in Augustinian theory.

Other theories in the first half of the thirteenth century

An anonymous *Commentary on the Ethics* written in Paris before 1250 presents an opinion similar to the first phase of Bacon's evolution, but it seems to eliminate any kind of collaboration between the potential and active intellect.[8] Peter of Spain's *Scientia de anima*, written probably around 1250 in Salerno or Portugal, conceives of the soul as containing the potential and agent intellect, but accepts a second agent intellect distinct from the soul in accordance with Avicenna's model.

The Augustinian – Aristotelian synthesis

The new Aristotelian material became well known by the second half of the thirteenth century. Elements taken from Aristotle and Avicenna, as assimilated by theologians in Paris, were welded with the Platonic and Augustinian Christian tradition into the synthesis of Bonaventure. A deep analysis of the texts of Aristotle and his commentators undertaken with the aim of modernising Christian thought gave rise to the works of Albert the Great and Thomas Aquinas. Scholarly interest in original Aristotelian ideas, clarified by his commentators, gave rise to the work of Siger of Brabant.[9] The work of Albert, Thomas, and Siger will be the subject

7. Bacon 1909–40, X, p. 11; XII, pp. 73, 74; XIII, pp. 7, 8, 10, 11.
8. Lottin 1957, Vol. 1, pp. 512–15.
9. Kuksewicz 1968, pp. 63–6.

of the next chapter: meanwhile something should here be said about Bonaventure.

Bonaventure

Bonaventure did not approve of the infiltration of Aristotle into Christian tradition, and his theory of the potential and agent intellect explained in II *Sententiarum* and *Breviloquium* between 1250 and 1257 is only a minor part of his Augustinian conception of the soul, almost free of Avicenna's influence and including some elements of Aristotle. There is no separate agent intellect, because the sole illuminative function belongs to God, who illuminates souls giving them the possibility of true knowledge and regulating their intellective activity. (See the contribution to this volume by J. Owens.) The human soul possess its 'higher' and 'lower face'. By means of the former it achieves the cognition of itself and supra-sensible beings, and in this field of activity there is no need for Aristotelian concepts of the potential and agent intellect. However, when describing the cognition of material objects, Bonaventure introduces Aristotelian terminology. The 'lower face' of the soul, which is connected with the material world, operates through the potential and agent intellect which are understood not as different faculties or parts but as two kinds of activity of the same substance – the soul. The conception of the potential and the agent intellect is, however, far from Aristotelian. The potential intellect does not have the nature of pure potentiality, because, according to Bonaventure, it not only receives but also produces knowledge: it proceeds to abstraction based upon particular images produced by the senses, consequently, it is active. Even the process of abstraction is not conceived of in the Aristotelian sense: it is merely an act of attaching the human mind to a particular image of a given object and not a process of purification from individual characteristics. Therefore, there is no need to accept the active intellect as the agent of abstraction; but Bonaventure endows the soul with this traditional Aristotelian faculty and gives it the function of illuminating the possible intellect as a necessary condition for the operation of this intellect.

30

SENSE, INTELLECT, AND IMAGINATION IN ALBERT, THOMAS, AND SIGER

Albert the Great

Albert the Great reveals the influence of Avicenna and Averroes in his psychology, though he certainly does not agree with them on all points.[1] Although he maintains that sense as such is a material and passive power, Albert admits that after it has been actualised by the sensible form, it can make judgements. However, it appears to do so only through the common sense. Albert rejects the argument that just as there is in the soul an agent intellect which abstracts and thus actualises intelligible species so there must be an active sense which abstracts and thus actualises the sensible. He replies that it is something in the nature of the intellect which renders the potentially intelligible actually intelligible, but it is something in external reality, not anything in the powers of the soul, which renders material things actually sensible. However, what is in the sense is certainly not the form united in existence with matter as found in the external thing, but rather an intention (*intentio*) or species of the material thing which enables us to have sense knowledge of that thing. Since sense apprehends the sensible object through such an intention, the first grade of abstraction is

---

1. On Albert's life, see Meersseman 1931; Weisheipl 1980, pp. 13–51. The most ambitious study of his psychology is Schneider 1903–6. Other general monographs on the subject are Reilly 1934, Pegis 1934, and Michaud-Quantin 1966. The impact of Albert's own psychological doctrines on later medieval and Renaissance philosophy has received attention from Park 1980, pp. 501–35 and Mahoney 1980a, pp. 537–63. For Albert's relationship to Averroes and Averroism see Nardi 1960, pp. 108–50; Van Steenberghen 1966, pp. 289–306. Nardi argues that for Albert philosophy has to do with interpreting Aristotle and the Aristotelian tradition, setting aside miracles and theological principles so that we do not confuse philosophy and theology. He cites Albert, *De generatione et corruptione*, I, tr. 1, c. 22, ad t. c. 14: 'dico quod nihil ad me de Dei miraculis cum ego de naturalibus disseram'. Nardi finds Albert frankly Averroist on the possibility of the human intellect's union with a separate intellect. While admitting the influence of Averroes on Albert's interpretation of Aristotle, Van Steenberghen argues that Albert's Aristotelianism is orthodox or Christian, since Albert does not hesitate to denounce Aristotle's errors and those of other pagan philosophers. He also notes that Albert himself insists that Aristotle was a human being, not a god, and he could therefore err just as we can (Albert, *Physica*, VIII, tr. 1, c. 14). For further discussion on the thorny question of whether Albert's philosophical commentaries contain his own philosophical position, see Kennedy 1959–60, pp. 121–3 and Kaiser 1962, pp. 53–62.

found in sensation, namely, separation from the matter of the external thing. However, in so far as sensation is of actually existing sensible things, which are individuated by matter, there must remain in sense apprehension a reference to matter as present and to the individuating conditions of matter. The other three grades of abstraction and apprehension occur in the internal senses and the intellect.[2]

The internal senses provided Albert with a topic of discussion in several of his works, and scholars have sometimes seen inconsistencies in these accounts. It has been argued, however, that two principles unite these discussions, namely, the principle of the grades of abstraction and the theory of animal spirit and its role in the brain.[3] In his *De homine*, Albert classifies the common sense, along with the external senses, as a power of the sensible soul which apprehends what occurs externally (*apprehensiva deforis*), while elsewhere he follows Avicenna and lists it as one of the internal senses (*virtutes interiores*). The common sense enables us to be aware of the operations of our external sense, such as seeing and hearing, and also to make comparisons between the objects sensed by the different external senses.[4] With imagination we advance to the second grade of abstraction, for imagination retains the images of sensible things when the latter are no longer present, though it does not abstract from reference to conditions of matter, that is, uniquely individuating characteristics. It is also imagination which enables us to form an image before our interior eyes (*prae oculis interioribus facere imaginem*) and to prepare images for the use of phantasy and intellect, which represent the third and fourth grade of abstraction respectively. Only on the level of the intellect is there apprehension of

---

2. Albert, *De anima*, II, tr. 3, c. 1, 3, 4 and 6, pp. 96a–98a, 100b–102b; *De homine*, q. 34, a. 1, pp. 294a–296a; a. 3, p. 303a. Steneck 1980, pp. 263–90, carefully examines the physical basis of the grades of abstraction in the sense organs and the brain. For a detailed analysis of the four grades of abstraction according to Albert, see Dähnert 1934, pp. 27–90. Albert considers the sensible species which is generated in the sense organ to be a *similitudo* caused by the sensible object, an *imago* of that object. By bringing about an *intentio* in the sense organ, the sensible object provides us with knowledge of itself. See *De homine*, q. 45, a. 2, p. 414ab.

3. See Steneck 1974, pp. 193–211. Steneck argues (p. 209) that these two principles set up a graded hierarchy among the internal senses. The principle of greater abstraction of the form from the object is connected to the doctrine of spirit in that the higher internal sense is located in a more subtle spirit in the brain. Albert shows far greater interest than Aquinas in establishing the relationship between the internal senses and the brain. See also Noble 1905, pp. 91–101; Steneck 1980, pp. 275–8; and Dewan 1980, pp. 291–320. Both Schneider 1903–5, pp. 154–7, and Wolfson 1935, pp. 116–20 and 1973, pp. 197–301, have discerned discrepancies in Albert's various accounts of the internal senses. But see Klubertanz 1952, pp. 134–44.

4. Albert, *De homine*, q. 19, p. 164; q. 37, p. 323; *De anima*, II, tr. 4, c. 7, p. 157a. Cf. Steneck 1974, p. 198; Schneider 1903–6, pp. 157–8. See also Ryan 1951, pp. 56–73.

essences which have been separated from all material conditions so as to be common to many and thus universal.[5]

Despite his interest in Avicenna and Averroes, Albert insists that both the potential and the agent intellect are parts of the human soul and are therefore multiplied according to the number of individual human beings.[6] While Albert had denied the need of an agent sense, since the sensed objects themselves serve as agents, he argues that an intellect acting in a universal manner (*intellectus agens universaliter*) is required in each human soul. Phantasms provide only knowledge of individuals, and they therefore cannot move the potential intellect to the universal knowledge proper to it.[7] Consequently, the agent intellect must abstract both from all material characteristics which individuate forms and also from the particular itself.[8] There are two tasks which the agent intellect must perform, namely, to abstract intelligible forms from phantasms and to illuminate the potential intellect directly. This means that when the universal intelligible species are received by the potential intellect, which then achieves intellectual knowledge, they are received in the light of the agent intellect.[9]

Although Albert rejects the view that the agent intellect is a transcendent being, he does not exclude God as a causal factor in human cognition.[10]

---

5. Albert, *De anima*, II, tr. 3, c. 4, pp. 101b–102a; tr. 4, c. 7, p. 157ab; *De homine*, q. 37, a. 4, pp. 328a–329b; q. 38, a. 1, p. 331a. On phantasy and estimation, see Schneider 1903–6, pp. 161–5; Dähnert 1934, pp. 66–9; Michaud-Quantin 1966, pp. 63–76. Presumably phantasy is the sense power which enables us to imagine things which in no way exist outside the mind, as when we invent (*fingimus*) chimeras, goat-stags and other monsters simply by imagining them. See *De anima*, III, tr. 1, c. 4, p. 169b; *De homine*, q. 38, a. 1, p. 332a. Albert shows keen interest in explaining sleep and dreams in terms of the internal senses and the 'spirit' in the brain. See *De homine*, q. 38, a. 5, p. 335b; q. 43, a. 1, pp. 366a and 368a; q. 44, a. 1, p. 404ab, a. 3, p. 406b; a. 4, p. 407a; q. 45, a. 1, p. 412a and a. 3, p. 417a.

6. Albert, *De homine*, q. 55, a. 4, part 1, p. 470a; a. 6, p. 476a; *De anima*, III, tr. 2, c. 19, pp. 203b–205b. In his early *De homine*, q. 55, a. 3, p. 466, Albert believed that Averroes held that the agent intellect was not a separate substance. Albert later realised that Averroes in fact taught that it was. For an explanation of why Albert may perhaps have been misled and also an account of how Albert transposed key concepts of Averroes' psychology into his own, see Miller 1954, pp. 57–71.

7. *De homine*, q. 55, a. 1, pp. 455b–456a. See also *De natura et origine animae*, tr. 1, c. 6, pp. 15b–16b for reference to the *intellectus universaliter agens* within the human soul. When Albert refers to God by this same term he sometimes adds that God is such *simpliciter*, since he alone illuminates all else which exists and is not himself illuminated by anything else before him. See *De causis et processu universitatis*, I, tr. 2, c. 1, p. 388a.

8. Albert, *De intellectu et intelligibili*, I, tr. 2, c. 1, pp. 490b–491a; *Summa Theol.*, II, q. 14, p. 193a. On abstraction or separation from the 'appendicies' of matter, see *De anima*, II, tr. 3, c. 4, pp. 101b–102a; III, tr. 2, c. 13, pp. 195b–196a; *De homine*, q. 57, a. 2, p. 491a; q. 61, a. 1, pp. 519b–20b.

9. Albert, *De anima*, III, tr. 2, c. 19, p. 205b; III, tr. 3, c. 11, p. 221ab; *De natura et origine animae*, I, c. 7, p. 16a; *De intellectu et intelligibili*, II, c. 3, pp. 506a–508a; I *Sent.*, d. 3, a. 29, p. 130ab.

10. Albert, I *Sent.*, d. 2, a. 5, pp. 59–60; *Summa Theol.*, I, tr. 3, q. 15, a. 3, pp. 110b–111a. Albert rejects making God an agent intellect in the Avicennian sense. See *De homine*, q. 55, *ad* 18 and 20, p. 468b.

The agent intellect in the human soul and its abstractive action are not sufficient to account for our knowledge of natural objects – the light of the uncreated intellect must also be operative. However, illumination from God seems to be required in a very special way in the case of 'divine' things, that is, beings such as God and the angels which are wholly separate from matter. These beings, which are studied by metaphysics, are known through the intellect's direct union with the divine light and in complete independence of phantasms and abstraction.[11] Albert shows particular interest in earlier discussions of such philosophers as Alexander, Themistius, Avicenna, and Averroes regarding the union of the human intellect with a separate intellect.[12] He explains in some detail how the potential intellect is first joined to the light of the agent intellect operating universally within the soul itself, then to the lights of the different intelligences, and finally to the light of the divine intellect itself, which is the goal of the human intellect's strivings.[13]

Thomas Aquinas

Albert's student, Thomas Aquinas, was also much interested in Avicenna, Averroes, and the Greek commentators, though he makes a somewhat more cautious use of them.[14] Thomas maintains that sense is primarily a passive power, one which is naturally suited to be modified or changed by an external sensible object. In sensation there is both a material modification of the sense organ and also a 'spiritual' or intentional modification brought about by the production of a species (*species*) or intention

For discussion regarding Albert's doctrine of divine illumination, see Schneider 1903–6, pp. 342–8; Michaud-Quantin 1955, pp. 73–5; Nardi 1960, pp. 111–17; Johnston 1960, pp. 210–11; Kennedy 1962–3, pp. 23–37.

11. Albert, *Summa Theol.*, II, tr. 4, q. 14, a. 2, part 4, *ad* 1, p. 196a.

12. Albert, *De anima*, III, tr. 3, c. 6–11, pp. 214b–223b. See also II, tr. 2, c. 5, pp. 183b–184a.

13. Albert, *De intellectu et intelligibili*, II, c. 9–12, pp. 516a–521b. See also *De anima*, III, tr. 3, c. 11, pp. 221b–222b. On this striking doctrine, see Schneider 1903–6; Nardi 1960, pp. 147–50; Kennedy 1962–3, pp. 28–37. The resemblance of Albert's doctrine to Averroes here is brought out by Kennedy 1959–60, pp. 131–7 and Nardi 1958, pp. 127–37. Albert himself indicates how close he is to Averroes on the topic of conjunction: 'Nos autem in paucis dissentimus ab Averroe, qui inducit istam quaestionem in commento super librum de anima.' *De anima*, III, tr. 3, c. 11, p. 221a, lin. 9–11.

14. On the life and works of Aquinas, see Walz 1962; Chenu 1964; and Weisheipl 1974. For this philosophical sources, see Callus 1957, pp. 93–174, and for his use of Themistius' paraphrases on the *De anima*, see Verbeke 1957, pp. ix–lxii. Information on the relation of his thought to Avicenna and Averroes is provided by Goichon 1951, pp. 114–30; Vansteenkiste 1953, pp. 457–507; idem 1957, pp. 585–623; idem 1960, pp. 336–401; de Contenson 1958, pp. 3–31; idem 1959, pp. 31–4, 53, 63–4, 68, 82–3 and 93–4; Gardet 1974, pp. 419–48; idem 1976, pp. 139–49; Anawati 1974, pp. 449–65; Gómez Nogales 1976, pp. 161–77.

(*intentio*), that is, a likeness (*similitudo*) of the sensible object. Besides this passive aspect of sensation, there is also an active side: the individual sense power is able to distinguish or judge among its own proper sensible objects.[15] However, like Albert, Thomas rejects the need for an agent sense to render the material object fit to be sensed, arguing that sensible things outside the soul are already in act, that is, actually sensible. On the other hand, since things outside the soul are not already actually intelligible, an active element as well as a passive element is needed in the intellect.[16]

In his analysis of the internal senses in the *Summa theologiae*, Thomas refers to Avicenna's list of five internal senses, but his own discussion reveals the influence of Averroes and also some original developments. Thomas takes the internal senses to be four in number, namely, the common sense, the imagination, the estimative or cogitative power, and memory, all of which are located in the brain. Although he does allow that the individual senses can make a judgement regarding their own proper sensibles, for example, sight can discern white from green, he insists that a separate sense power is needed to make a judgement of discernment in regard to the objects of all five senses. This separate power, which is called the common sense, also enables the animal or the man to be aware of the activity of his external senses.[17] The imagination or phantasy serves as the storehouse of forms (*thesaurus formarum*), that is, phantasms, of sensible things when the latter are no longer present to the external senses.[18] When

---

15. Aquinas, *Summa theol.*, I, q. 12, a. 2; q. 78, a. 3–4; q. 84, a. 3; q. 85, a. 1, *ad* 3; I–II, q. 22, a. 2, *ad* 3; *In II Sent.*, d. 19, q. 1, a. 3, *ad* 1; *In de anima*, II, lect. 24; *Quodl.* VIII, q. 2, a. 1; *De malo*, q. 16, a. 8, *ad* 10. For discussion regarding the intentionality of sensation, see Boyer 1925, pp. 97–116; Picard 1926; Rohmer 1951, pp. 5–39; Van Riet 1953, pp. 374–408. On the judgements made by the senses and by the common sense, see Garceau 1968, pp. 242–8 and Owens 1970, pp. 138–47. For Thomas all knowledge involves the assimilation of the knower to the known, but this assimilation is brought about only by means of a likeness (*similitudo*) of the thing known existing in the knower. See *Summa theol.*, I, q. 85, a. 2; *S.C.G.*, II, c. 65 and 77; *De ver.*, q. 2, a. 3, *ad* 3; q. 8, a. 5; q. 10, a. 4 and 8. The likeness (*similitudo*) serves as the principle of knowing a thing not by reason of its existing in a knowing power but by reason of the relationship it has to the thing known, that is, as it is representative of the thing (*repraesentativa rei*). See *De ver.*, q. 2, a. 5, *ad* 7. For studies on Aquinas' doctrine of *intentio*, see Gómez Izquierdo 1924, pp. 169–88; Simonin 1930a, pp. 445–63; Rabeau 1938, pp. 13–22; Hayen 1954; Regis 1959.
16. Aquinas, *Summa theol.*, I, q. 79, a. 3, *ad* 1; *Q.D. de anima*, a. 4, *ad* 5; *Quodl.* VIII, q. 2, a. 1; *De ver.*, q. 26, a. 3, *ad* 4. See the appropriate remarks of Van Riet 1953, pp. 400–7. Thomas' target appears to be William of Auvergne, who argued in his *De anima*, c. 7, part 3, p. 207 that just as no agent sense is required between the sensibles and the senses, so no agent intellect is required between the intelligibles and the material intellect.
17. Aquinas, *Summa theol.*, I, q. 78, a. 4, c. and *ad* 2; q. 87, a. 3, *ad* 3; *Q.D. de anima*, a. 13; *In de anima*, II, lect. 13. For discussion see Garceau 1968, pp. 242–8.
18. Aquinas, *Summa theol.*, I, q. 12, a. 9, *ad* 2; q. 78, a. 4; q. 84, a. 6, *ad* 2; *Quodl.* VIII, q. 2, a. 1; *De ver.*,

imagination operates in conjunction with the human intellect, it enables human beings to form new combinations of the stored phantasms, as for example the image of a golden mountain. It is the task of the common sense to judge between the images found in imagination and external reality. However, since the normal functioning of common sense is suspended in sleep, we frequently are led to take our dreams for true likenesses of the external world. On the other hand, the role of the estimative power is to enable animals to perceive intentions not known directly to the external senses, such as danger, and to form an instinctive judgement, such as that they should flee. However, since man makes some rational comparisons among these intentions and acts by a free judgement, this sense in man is given the special name of the cogitative power.[19] Thomas sometimes identifies the corruptible 'passive intellect' (*intellectus passivus*) with this cogitative power, at other times with the imagination, and on occasion with the complex of the cogitative power, the imagination, and memory, all of which prepare the phantasm for the intellect.[20] Indeed, Thomas explains the variation in understanding among human beings in terms of the difference in development of these three internal senses.[21]

For Thomas both the potential intellect and the agent intellect are powers of the human soul, and they are therefore multiplied according to the number of human beings.[22] Thomas denies, in opposition to Avicenna

q. 8, a. 5. Thomas rejects Avicenna's distinction of two imaginative powers, arguing that since creative imagination appears only in man a distinct power is not required. For two strikingly different approaches to Thomas' doctrine on imagination, see Brennan 1941 pp. 149–61 and Kenny 1969, pp. 273–96. Thomas' terminology regarding sensible species and phantasms needs to be carefully understood. He reserves the word 'phantasm' for the species found in the imagination, the cogitative power and memory. See *Summa theol.*, I, q. 89, a. 5; *S.C.G.*, II, c. 73. It is not used of the sensible species as found in the external senses or the common sense. In *Summa theol.*, I, q. 85, a. 1, *ad* 3, phantasms are called likenesses just after it is said that colours can impress (*imprimere*) their likeness (*similitudo*) on sight. It would be a misreading, however, to take Aquinas to mean that the species produced in the power of sight are phantasms.

19. Aquinas, *Summa theol.*, I, q. 78, a. 4; q. 83, a. 1; *Q.D. de anima*, a. 13. On Thomas's originality regarding the cogitative power in comparison with Averroes, see Klubertanz 1952, pp. 276–82. The central role of the cogitative power is also brought out by Peghaire 1942–3 and Naus 1959, pp. 123–6 and 192–8. Thomas allows for the possibility that some people will retain some use of their common sense during sleep and so be able to judge that what they are seeing are dreams. However, he adds that they will be deceived in taking some similitudes for the real thing. See *Summa theol.*, I, q. 84, a. 8, *ad* 2; *De ver.*, q. 12, a. 3, *ad* 2; q. 28, a. 3, *ad* 6. See n. 5 above.
20. For the relevant texts, see Klubertanz 1952, pp. 161, 183–90, 194–6 and 244–5. Hamlyn 1961, p. 48 confuses matters somewhat by referring to the potential intellect as the 'passive intellect'. The distinction between them goes back to Themistius and Averroes.
21. Aquinas, *Summa theol.*, I, q. 76, a. 5; q. 85, a. 7; *In de anima*, II, lect. 19.
22. Aquinas, *De unitate intellectus*, c. 1 and 4; *Summa theol.*, I, q. 76, a. 2; q. 79, a. 1 and 4; *De spiritualibus creaturis*, a. 10, *ad* 4; *Q.D. de anima*, a. 3 and 5; *S.C.G.*, II, c. 59, 73, 75–8; *Comp. theol.*, I, c. 85–9.

and Averroes, that Aristotle ever taught that either intellect was a separate substance.[23] Moreover, he rejects those accounts of intellectual cognition which involve representations that are innate to the soul or that are sent into the soul from a higher being, and he likewise denies that the human intellect knows material things in the exemplars of the divine mind.[24] The potential intellect stands wholly in potency to the intelligible, but the natures of the sensible things in the world about us are not of themselves intelligible. It is the task of the agent intellect to render intelligible the phantasm or image of the external thing. This it does by abstracting the nature or form from matter and the individuating conditions of the particular individual which is represented in the phantasm.[25] Since a phantasm in the senses and in imagination is material and individual, it is incapable of producing a universal likeness of a nature or essence. The agent intellect must therefore abstract the bare essence or quiddity of the sensible thing from all the accidental material conditions presented in the phantasm.[26] The resulting universal likeness, which is called the intelligible species, actualises the potential intellect, and the latter forms in turn its own likeness of the abstracted nature, namely, the 'concept' or mental word.[27] Although Thomas is clear that the intelligible species and the concept, just like the phantasm, are not themselves the objects of cognition but serve rather as the means by which one knows, later critics would argue

23. Aquinas, *Summa theol.*, I, q. 76, a. 2; q. 79, a. 4–5; *De unitate intellectus*, c. 1; *De spiritualibus creaturis*, a. 9–10; *S.C.G.*, II, c. 74 and 78. However, in the early *In II Sent.*, d. 17, q. 2, a. 1, Thomas appears to accept that Aristotle held the agent intellect to be a separate substance, namely, the lowest of the intelligences. This passage is analysed by Gilson 1926–7, pp. 111–13. See n. 33 below.
24. Aquinas, *Summa theol.*, I, q. 84, a. 3–5; *De ver.*, q. 10, a. 6; *Q.D. de anima*, a. 15.
25. Aquinas, *Summa theol.*, I, q. 54, a. 4; q. 79, a. 3–4; q. 84, a. 2 and 6; q. 85, a. 1; q. 86, a. 1; *Q.D. de anima*, a. 4. The phantasm is the *similitudo rei particularis* (*Summa theol.*, I, q. 84, a. 7, *ad* 2). In *Summa theol.*, I, q. 85, a. 1, *ad* 4, Thomas emphasises that the agent intellect illuminates the phantasms in order that they will be rendered fit to have intelligible species abstracted from them. For discussion regarding the nature of this illumination and the interpretations offered in the Thomist tradition, see Garin 1931, pp. 395–485. On the agent intellect as a *lumen naturale*, see n. 34 below.
26. Aquinas, *Summa theol.*, I, q. 85, a. 1; *S.C.G.*, II, c. 77; *De spiritualibus creaturis*, a. 10, *ad* 4 and 17; *De ver.*, q. 10, a. 6, *ad* 2 and 7; *In de anima*, III, lect. 8 and 10. On the various meanings of abstraction in Aquinas, see Blanche 1934, pp. 237–51. Santeler 1939, pp. 4–66 presents a detailed examination of Thomas' doctrine on the agent intellect as found in his various works.
27. Aquinas, *Summa theol.*, I, q. 85, a. 2, *ad* 3; I–II, q. 93, a. 1, *ad* 2; *De ver.*, q. 4, a. 2; q. 10, a. 6; *S.C.G.*, I, c. 53 and IV, c. 11; *De pot. Dei*, q. 8, a. 1; q. 9, a. 5; *Comp. theol.*, I, c. 38–9; *Quodl.* V, q. 5, a. 2. On the doctrine of the mental word in Thomas' thought, see Garin 1931, pp. 621–828; Paissac 1951, pp. 101–236; Peifer 1952, pp. 132–79; Chenevert 1961, pp. 192–223 and 370–92; Lonergan 1967, pp. 1–10, 124–33 and 191–6. The presentation of Thomas' theory of knowledge and doctrine of the mental word by Colish 1968, pp. 161–83 is not wholly accurate. See Bloomfield 1970, pp. 119–22; Mahoney 1973b, pp. 258–62.

that it was dangerous to postulate such intermediaries in the process of cognition since they appeared to veil reality from the mind.[28]

A related doctrine of Thomas also became the object of later criticism, namely, his insistence that the intellect as such knows universals directly and individuals only indirectly. Since the intellect abstracts from the individual as presented in the phantasm, it has to reflect on that phantasm if it is to know the individual.[29] Thomas himself points out that the nature of a material thing can in fact be known completely only when it is known as existing in an individual. And since we grasp the individual only through the phantasms of sense and imagination, we must turn back to the phantasm. Indeed, Thomas insists that in this life we cannot actually understand anything unless we turn in some way to phantasms. This can be seen in the fact that when we want to understand something, we form phantasms to help us do so, just as we offer others concrete examples in order to help them to understand. One consequence of Thomas' position is that humans can understand purely immaterial things such as God and the angels only by comparison to things of which they do have phantasms.[30] Another

28. Aquinas, *Summa theol.*, I, q. 85, a. 2; q. 87, a. 3; *S.C.G.*, II, c. 75; *De spiritualibus creaturis*, a. 9, *ad* 6; *De ver.*, q. 10, a. 8, *ad* 2; *In de anima*, III, lect. 8. The intelligible species can of course become the object of knowledge but only secondarily, that is, by a reflection of the intellect back on itself and its acts of thinking. Historians who have written about Thomas' theory of knowledge have tended to emphasise that the intelligible species and the concept are merely the means in or by which we know and are not the object of knowledge itself. See for example Gómez Izquierdo 1924, pp. 169–88; Garin 1931, pp. 692–828; Peifer 1952, pp. 165–79; Regis 1959, pp. 210–21 and 248–52; Carlo 1966, pp. 47–66; Owens 1974, pp. 189–205. However, some of Thomas' own contemporaries opposed intelligible species precisely because they would be the object of knowledge and block the intellect's grasp of extramental reality. See Henry of Ghent, *Quodlibeta*, III, q. 1; IV, q. 7; V, q. 14; Peter John Olivi, *Quaestiones in secundum librum sententiarum*, q. 58 and q. 74. Olivi's remark that anything between the gaze of the intellect and the external object, such as an intelligible species, would 'veil' (*velaret*) the object may seem familiar to the contemporary reader. Similar language is found in Russell 1910–11, p. 119 and Bennett 1965, pp. 2–3.
29. Aquinas, *Summa theol.*, I, q. 86, a. 1; *De ver.*, q. 2, a. 6; q. 10, a. 5; *S.C.G.*, I, c. 65; *Q.D. de anima*, a. 20, *ad* 1; *In de anima*, III, lect. 8; *Quodl.* VII, q. 1, a. 3. In these texts Thomas himself connects abstraction and the need to reflect back on phantasms with his view that individuation is through matter. Not surprisingly, there has been disagreement as to what Aquinas meant by the reflection back on the phantasm. Among the more helpful studies are Allers 1941, pp. 95–163; Isaac 1948, pp. 338–40; Klubertanz 1952b, pp. 135–66; Lonergan 1967, pp. 25–33 and 159–71; Kenny 1969, pp. 288–94. Thomas' doctrine that the intellect only knows the universal directly and can know sensible individuals only indirectly by a reflection on the phantasm (*Summa theol.*, I, q. 86, a. 1) was already the subject of attack by thirteenth-century Franciscans such as William of la Mare and Matthew of Aquasparta. See Simonin 1930b, pp. 289–303.
30. Aquinas, *Summa theol.*, I, q. 12, a. 2, 11 and 12; q. 32, a. 1; q. 84, a. 7–8; q. 88, a. 1–2; q. 117, a. 1; *De ver.*, q. 10, a. 2, *ad* 7, and a. 11; *S.C.G.*, II, c. 73; III, c. 51–2; IV, c. 1. Actual sensing and thinking are necessary conditions for self-consciousness. See *Summa theol.*, I, q. 14, a. 2, *ad* 3; q. 87, a. 1 and 3; *In III Sent.*, d. 23, q. 1, a. 2, *ad* 3; *De ver.*, q. 10, a. 8; *Q.D. de an.*, a. 16, *ad* 8. For a helpful analysis of how the soul knows itself see Gardeil 1934, pp. 219–36.

consequence is that in order to explain how the disembodied soul after death can know anything Thomas is forced to postulate that God sends into the soul likenesses (*similitudines*) or species which are not phantasms but which can provide the soul with knowledge of individuals.[31]

One of the most striking aspects of Thomas' psychology of knowledge is the rejection of such key Augustinian doctrines as the active theory of sensation and the need for divine illumination to achieve necessary and certain knowledge.[32] Thomas also opposes some of the theses put forth by those who pursued the path of Avicennised Augustinianism, to borrow Gilson's useful term.[33] For example, it is clear that for Thomas God in fact has no special role to play in man's achieving knowledge of the natural order, even that knowledge which is necessary and certain. The 'natural light' of the human intellect does not entail for Thomas either God as an agent intellect or divine illumination.[34] Unlike Albert, Thomas sees no need to postulate any divine illumination to account for man's natural knowledge, and unlike Bonaventure, he believes that the human intellect's own abstractive abilities are sufficient to account for its necessary and

31. For an appreciation of the nuances of his thought on this thorny topic, see Aquinas, *Summa theol.*, I, q. 89, a. 1–8; *Q.D. de an.*, a. 15 and 17–21; *De ver.*, q. 19, a. 1–2, *S.C.G.*, II, c. 80–1; *Quodl.* III, q. 9, a. 1. For general discussion see Pegis 1974, pp. 131–58.
32. Aquinas rejects Augustine's active theory of sensation in *Summa theol.*, I, q. 75, a. 4; q. 84, a. 6. For a contrast of Augustine and Thomas on the nature of sensation, see Hessen 1960, pp. 251–4 and 258–60. Moreover, Aquinas rejects the need for any divine illumination and also the possibility that God himself is the first object of human cognition. See *Expositio super De trinitate*, q. 1, a. 1 and 3; *Summa theol.*, I, q. 12, a. 11, *ad* 3; q. 84, a. 5; q. 88, a. 3, *ad* 1–2; I–II, q. 109, a. 1; *De ver.*, q. 10, a. 11; *Quodl.* X, q. 4, a. 1; *De spiritualibus creaturis*, a. 10, *ad* 8. For comment, see Grabmann 1931, pp. 57–63; idem 1948, pp. 66–86.
33. For references to God as agent intellect, see *Summa theol.*, I, q. 79, a. 4; *In II Sent.*, d. 17, q. 2, a. 1; d. 28, q. 1, a. 5; *S.C.G.*, II, c. 85; *Q.D. de anima*, a. 5; *De spiritualibus creaturis*, a. 10, especially obj. 1; *De unitate intellectus*, c. 5. For clear rejection of any direct and special role for God or an intelligence in man's natural knowledge and for an emphasis on the relative autonomy of the agent and possible intellects in man, see *Summa theol.*, I, q. 79, a. 4; q. 84, a. 4, *ad* 1 and 3; I–II, q. 93, a. 2; *Q.D. de anima*, a. 4, *ad* 7; a. 5, c. and *ad* 6; *De spiritualibus creaturis*, a. 10, c. and *ad* 8–9; *S.C.G.*, II, c. 76–8. For discussion see Grabmann 1931, pp. 53–68. By 'Avicennised Augustinianism', Gilson meant a psychological theory which attributes to God the functions of Avicenna's agent intellect. That is to say, the intelligible is received into the human soul from the God who illuminates. Gilson listed as adherents of this theory William of Auvergne, Roger Bacon, and John Peckham. See Gilson 1926–7, pp. 5–127; idem 1929, pp. 5–107. For a careful and helpful re-examination of the appropriateness of Gilson's term, see Bertola 1967, pp. 318–34, and 1971, pp. 278–320.
34. Sometimes Thomas speaks simply of the *lumen naturale* of the intellect, of the soul, or of reason (*Summa theol.*, I, q. 12, a. 12, *ad* 3 and a. 13; q. 88, a. 3, *ad* 1; I–II, q. 68, a. 2; q. 109, a. 1, *ad* 2; II–II, q. 8, a. 1; *In III Sent.*, d. 39, q. 3, a. 1, *ad* 3), whereas at other times he speaks of the *lumen naturale* of the agent intellect (*In II Sent.*, d. 28, q. 1, a. 5; *In IV Sent.*, d. 49, q. 2, a. 4). Thomas occasionally connects the concept of the *lumen naturale* with our ability to know self-evident first principles. See for example *Summa theol.*, I–II, q. 63, a. 3; *S.C.G.*, III, c. 154. The classic paper on Thomas' doctrine on the *lumen naturale* is by Guillet 1927, pp. 79–88.

certain knowledge.[35] Finally, Thomas is highly critical of any suggestion that during this life the human intellect can achieve an intuitive cognition of separated substances, whether they be intelligences, angels, or God.[36] In this opposition, he is making one of his sharpest breaks with Albert and also setting himself against Avicenna and Averroes. His opposition would be duly noted by the Latin Averroist tradition.

Siger of Brabant

Siger of Brabant is without doubt the most celebrated representative of so-called Latin Averroism.[37] A member of the Arts Faculty at the University of Paris in the 1260s and 1270s, he played a key role in controversies with other members of that faculty, with theologians such as Thomas, and with Church authorities such as Etienne Tempier. While it would be an exaggeration to say that he eventually became a loyal follower of Thomas, there is certainly evidence that his views on the soul and intellect underwent a dramatic evolution and that his final position was close to that of Thomas on some key points. That evolution, long a topic of modern scholarly debate, has been definitively established with the discovery and publication of his questions on the *Liber de causis*.[38]

The major works of Siger which are dedicated to philosophical psychology and which are also generally accepted as genuine are the *Quaestiones in librum tertium de anima*, the *Tractatus de anima intellectiva*, and the *De intellectu*.[39] In the first of these works, which was probably com-

---

35. Aquinas, *Summa theol.*, I, q. 84, a. 1; *De spiritualibus creaturis*, a. 10, *ad* 8; *Expositio super De trinitate*, q. 5, a. 2, c. and *ad* 4. Thomas relates the possibility of knowledge with certitude to our grasping first principles or resolving things back into such principles. See *Summa theol.*, I, q. 85, a. 6; I–II, q. 90, a. 2, *ad* 3; q. 112, a. 5; S.C.G., III, c. 47; IV, c. 54; *De ver.*, q. 1, a. 4, *ad* 5; q. 10, a. 6, c. and *ad* 6; q. 11, a. 1, *ad* 13. For comparison of Thomas with Bonaventure and the Augustinian approach, see Grabmann 1931, pp. 68–71; idem 1948, pp. 45–51; Quinn 1973, pp. 443–663; idem 1974, pp. 105–40. On Aquinas' theory of judgement and assent, see Wilpert 1931, pp. 56–75; Keeler 1934, pp. 83–111; Tyrrell 1948; Hoenen 1952; Garceau 1968; Owens 1970, pp. 138–58.
36. Aquinas, *Summa theol.*, I, q. 12, a. 1–2, 4–5 and 11; q. 88, a. 1–2; S.C.G., III, c. 42–8 and 51–3; *De ver.*, q. 10, a. 11; *Expositio super De trinitate*, q. 1, a. 2; q. 6, a. 3. Man's ultimate beatitude for Thomas was a direct vision of God in the hereafter which involved no intelligible species or concept and which was given as a free gift by God. See *Summa theol.*, I, q. 12, a. 2–5, 9 and 11; I–II, q. 3, a. 8.
37. For a brief sketch of Siger's life, see Glorieux 1941. There is a detailed account of his life and career in Van Steenberghen 1977, pp. 9–176. For earlier reviews of Siger scholarship, see Van Steenberghen 1956, pp. 130–47; Maurer 1956, pp. 49–56; Zimmermann 1967–8, pp. 206–17.
38. Various scholars have affirmed that evolution on the basis of the questions on the *De causis*. See Dondaine and Bataillon 1966, pp. 206–10; Marlasca 1971, pp. 3–27 and 1974, pp. 431–9; Fioravanti 1972, pp. 407–64; Mahoney 1974a, pp. 531–53; Van Steenberghen 1977, pp. 338–403.
39. In 1923, Martin Grabmann discovered *Quaestiones in libros tres de anima* in Clm 9559, a manuscript of the Staatsbibliothek at Munich. The find was announced in Grabmann 1924. The work

posed during the academic year 1269–70,[40] Siger begins by accepting Averroes' doctrine that there is one intellect for all men. It comes from without and unites with the vegetative and sensitive parts within the human being to form a composite soul (*anima composita*).[41] However, the intellect cannot be united in its substance to human bodies, since it would then be inseparable from the body. The intellect exists in the body by operating in it, namely, by moving the body and also by thinking in the body.[42] The latter occurs as the intellect works with the actually operative imaginations of particular human beings. Indeed, Siger argues both that the single intellect is numbered or diversified among humans through the different intentions present in their imaginations and also that men have different shares in the universal intelligibles of the one intellect according to the number of imagined intentions they possess.[43]

Our senses know a sensible object by means of a sensible species or a likeness (*similitudo*) which that particular sensible object causes in the sense organ.[44] The senses and imagination apprehend things only under

contained a psychology resembling Thomas'. Van Steenberghen accepted Grabmann's attribution of the work to Siger and edited and published the Munich questions along with similar questions from Codex 275 belonging to Merton College, Oxford. See Van Steenberghen 1931, pp. 21–156. However, Grabmann's ascription of the Munich questions to Siger was subsequently attacked by Nardi 1936, pp. 26–35 and 1937, pp. 160–4. Van Steenberghen replied in a brief monograph, 1938, pp. 24–45, but Nardi 1939, pp. 453–71 and 1940, pp. 149–56 continued his attack. He was supported by Gilson 1939, pp. 316–23. Van Steenberghen's case was seriously weakened by Sajo 1958, pp. 21–58, who proved that two of the other works in the Munich manuscript were by Boethius of Dacia. Van Steenberghen 1971, pp. 131–3 and 1978, pp. 66–8 now accepts the ascription of these works to Boethius and even considers him the possible author of the questions on the *De anima*.

40. Bazán 1972b, pp. 70*–74* has argued for this dating on the grounds that Siger's work must have been written after Thomas' disputed question on the *De anima*, whose final redaction he dates as 1269.

41. Siger of Brabant, *In tertium de anima*, q. 1, pp. 2–3, lin. 42–68; q. 2, p. 5, lin. 32–41. Nardi 1960, pp. 160–1 argued that Siger's conception of a composite soul reflected the influence of Albert the Great's *De natura et origine animae*, but this thesis has been severely criticized by Van Steenberghen 1977, pp. 341–2 and Bazán 1975, pp. 32–4. See also Vennebusch 1966, p. 59, n. 50. Siger's use of the term *anima composita* for the union of the intellect with the vegetative and sensitive parts must be distinguished from his use of the terms 'intellective soul' (*anima intellectiva*), 'rational soul' (*anima rationalis*) and 'our intellect' (*noster intellectus*) for the unitary and separate intellect. For discussion, see Da Palma 1955a, pp. 30–3.

42. *Ibid.*, q. 7, pp. 22–4; q. 8, p. 25. Siger uses (p. 24, lin. 54) the celebrated sailor-ship analogy (*De anima*, II, c. 1, 413ᵃ7–9) for his own purposes. For a summary of the various ways in which it was adopted by different ancient and medieval philosophers, see Mansion 1953, pp. 457–65.

43. *Ibid.*, q. 9, p. 28, lines 74–96. Siger points out that this is what Averroes meant when he spoke of the speculative intellect. Bazán 1975, pp. 27–30, considers Siger's conception of the speculative intellect to be a weakness in his theory and not to do justice to its importance in Averroes' thought.

44. *Ibid.*, q. 18, pp. 67–8. Siger's example is that of sight, which will have a likeness of this particular coloured thing.

their material conditions, that is, as particulars. Sense and imagination differ, however, in that a sense can receive the sensible form only when the sensible object is actually present, while imagination can also receive that form in the absence of the sensible object. While Siger admits that the estimative power (*existimativa*) receives something beside sensible forms, for example the enmity which the sheep apprehends in a wolf, he argues that it can apprehend such an insensible form only when it simultaneously apprehends a sensible form such as colour or size.[45] On the other hand, Siger claims that we are aware of the reception of immaterial and universal intelligible forms or essences within us which cannot be explained by any sensible species. That is to say, we experience in ourselves two immaterial activities and the two powers of the intellect causing those activities in us, namely, the abstracting by the agent intellect of the universal intelligibles which previously were intentions of our imagination (*intentiones imaginatae*) and the reception by the material or possible intellect (*intellectus possibilis*) of those universal intelligibles.[46] Siger seems very doubtful, however, that the intellect itself can know individuals as individual, even by a reflection on the phantasm, since he takes it as axiomatic that the intellect of itself knows only that which is universal.[47]

Aquinas against the Averroists

Thomas' *Tractatus de unitate intellectus contra Averroistas*, completed early in 1270, was probably not directed specifically against Siger's *In tertium librum de anima* but rather against the oral teaching of Siger and his circle in the Arts Faculty.[48] The critique which it presents eventually undermined

---

45. *Ibid.*, q. 4, p. 14, lin. 12–15 and p. 16, lin. 67–82. The imagination receives the sensible form (*sensitiva forma*) only by means of a sensible image (*imago*). Siger is of course following Averroes when he claims that Aristotle called the imagination the 'passive intellect' (*intellectus passivus*).

46. *Ibid.*, q. 4, pp. 12–13, lin. 70–5 and p. 14, lin. 23–9; q. 13, p. 45, lin. 50–5; q. 14, p. 47, lin. 28–32. The three principles of intellectual knowledge are therefore the possible intellect, the agent intellect, and the phantasms or intentions of the imagination which are rendered intelligible by abstraction. See q. 12, p. 37, lin. 63–9 and p. 40, lin. 21–4; q. 14, p. 47, lin. 30–2, 38–50 and 64–82, and p. 50, lin. 1–11. Siger does not consider the agent and the possible intellects to be two individual substances. On the contrary, they are powers of the same single substance, namely, 'our intellect', the unitary intellect of all human beings. See q. 15, p. 58, lin. 42–8.

47. *Ibid.*, q. 18, pp. 65–7. Da Palma 1958, p. 71 sees Aquinas as Siger's target.

48. Van Steenberghen 1942, p. 558 and 1966, p. 435 states that it would be difficult to determine with certitude whether Thomas had Siger's *In tertium de anima* specifically in view when he wrote the *De unitate intellectus*. He admits (1942, p. 557) that Thomas' final paragraphs are directed to some writing or lesson of Siger. More recently Van Steenberghen 1977, pp. 59 and 347 has suggested that Thomas seems to have made use of course notes reflecting the oral teaching of Siger and his party. Wéber 1970, pp. 29–33 and 41–5 has attempted to reconstruct Siger's teaching from apparent references to it in Thomas's opusculum. Bazán 1974, pp. 57–66 has justifiably ques-

Siger's confidence in the Averroist psychology.[49] The two major errors of Averroes regarding Aristotle which Thomas singles out for attack are the denial that the possible or potential intellect is the substantial form of the human body and the doctrine that it is one for all men and therefore not multiplied according to the number of existing human beings.[50] He marshals passages from Aristotle himself as well as from Alexander, Theophrastus, Themistius, Avicenna, and Algazel to prove that not just Latin philosophers but also Greeks and Muslims take Aristotle to maintain that the potential intellect is part of the individual human soul, which is itself the form of the body.[51] It is particularly noteworthy that in two different passages Thomas quotes at length from William of Moerbeke's translation of Themistius' paraphrases of the *De anima* to prove that Themistius had held that while there may be a single agent intellect illuminating all other intellects, there is in each human soul an agent intellect which, having been illuminated by that transcendent intellect, illuminates in turn the individual potential intellect that is also found in the soul.[52] These citations embolden Thomas to denounce Averroes as 'the depraver of Peripatetic philosophy' for having falsely presented Themistius as a proponent of the unity of the intellect.

Thomas attacks the Averroists not for having said that the agent intellect is one for all men, but for having held to the unity of the potential intellect.[53] Like Siger, Thomas appeals to our own psychological experience. The difference is that Thomas emphasises that it reveals to us that in thinking it is *this* individual man who thinks and not some separate intellect whose cognition we merely share. Pursuing this theme of the

tioned how Wéber can distinguish Siger's teaching from that of his colleagues, and he has gone on to challenge the specific doctrines which Wéber attributes to Siger. Moreover, Bazán has effectively discredited Wéber's fundamental thesis, namely, that Thomas dramatically changed his own doctrine on the relation between the human soul and its intellect after studying Siger's position. See the replies by Wéber 1974, pp. 15–16 and 435 and 1976, pp. 294 and 309. Van Steenberghen 1977, pp. 357–9 and 412–15 has entered the fray to attack anew Wéber's 1970 book and his scholarship.

49. Much of Thomas' critique can actually be found in his earlier works, where it is directed simply against Averroes. See Nardi 1947, pp. 56–67. More recent studies on the topic include Verbeke 1960, pp. 220–49; Mazzarella 1974, pp. 246–83; Mahoney 1974a, pp. 535–8; Nédoncelle 1974, pp. 284–92.

50. Aquinas, *De unitate intellectus* (1957), c. 1, par. 1, pp. 1–2.

51. *Ibid.*, c. 1, par. 3–43, pp. 3–29; c. 2, par. 51–9, pp. 33–8; c. 5, par. 119–21, pp. 76–8.

52. *Ibid.*, c. 2, par. 51–4, pp. 33–5; c. 5, par. 120–1, pp. 77–8. For discussion of the impact of Moerbeke's translation on Thomas and other late-thirteenth and early-fourteenth-century philosophers, see Verbeke 1957, pp. xxxix–lxii; Mahoney 1973a, pp. 422–67.

53. *Ibid.*, c. 4, par. 86, pp. 54–5; c. 5, par. 120, p. 77. Thomas well knew that some of his contemporaries taught that there is only one agent intellect, namely, God himself. See n. 33 above. On the Franciscans' discussions regarding the agent intellect and whether it is to be identified with God, see Bowman 1972–3, pp. 251–79.

individuation of cognition in the individual, he analyses the Averroist theory of the interrelationship of the phantasm, the intelligible species, and the potential and agent intellects. Thomas takes Averroes to postulate two subjects for the intelligible species, namely, the separate potential intellect and the phantasm in the individual human being. Pointing out that when the intelligible species is in the phantasm it is there only potentially, that is, before abstraction by the agent intellect has rendered it actually intelligible, he argues that the potential or possible intellect cannot therefore be joined to the phantasms of individual men through the intelligible species. The obvious consequence is that Averroes has no way to account for the individual person actually thinking.[54] Thomas himself explains the individuation of universal cognition by means of his own doctrine of intelligible species.[55] While the intelligible object (*intellectum*) is certainly one and the same for all men, namely, the universal nature or essence abstracted from phantasms, it must be distinguished from the intelligible species (*species intelligibilis*). It is the different intelligible species found in the intellects of individual men which allow universal intellectual cognition of the same intelligible object to be individuated in these different individuals. That is to say, while each of them will know the same intelligible object, they will do so by means of different intelligible species in their individual intellects. The consequence will be that we can truly say of each of them that it is *this* individual human being who is thinking.

Siger's treatise *De intellectu*

Siger's initial reply to Thomas' *De unitate intellectus* was his now lost *De intellectu*, probably written in 1270 before Tempier's condemnation.[56] It

54. *Ibid.*, c. 3, par. 62–6, pp. 39–42. See also c. 4, par. 91, p. 58. Thomas considers it absurd to believe that the separate substances could receive anything from the phantasms of humans. See c. 4, par. 95, p. 61.

55. *Ibid.*, c. 5, par. 106–13, pp. 68–73. Both Wéber and Bazán have rightly emphasised that Thomas' doctrine on intelligible species represents a radical departure from Aristotle. Wéber 1970 explains that Thomas introduced intelligible species in his account of intellectual cognition in order to break with Aristotle's pure and simple identity between the intellect and the intelligible (*De anima*, III, 4, 430^{a}2–4), presumably a fundamental principle leading to Averroes' doctrine of the unity of the intellect (pp. 221, 226–9, 237–8 and 291). Bazán 1974, pp. 98–9 rightly praises Wéber for underscoring the importance of the intelligible species in Thomas' critique of and reply to Averroes.

56. Bazán 1972b, p. 75*; Van Steenberghen 1966, p. 447 and 1977, p. 63. The proposal of Kuksewicz 1968, p. 44, 72–3 and 76 that the *De intellectu* was written after Siger's *De anima intellectiva* in 1272 or 1273 and was thus sent to Thomas after he had left Paris is implausible. Such an ordering of the two works would make the evolution of Siger's thought erratic in the light of his final position in the questions on the *De causis*. Nardi 1945, pp. 20–1 was the first to establish that the *De intellectu* and the *De anima intellectiva* were distinct works and that the former, not the latter, was Siger's initial reply to Thomas' *De unitate intellectus*. Mandonnet 1911a, p. 110 claimed that Thomas' opusculum was a reply to Siger's *De anima intellectiva*. Doncoeur 1910, p. 501 rejected

has been reconstructed by Bruno Nardi from citations to be found in the writings of Agostino Nifo.[57] Siger reveals himself to be on the defensive in regard to Thomas and to have made some readjustments in his own Averroist psychology in order to save the unity of the intellect and yet be able to evade some of Thomas' arguments. To Thomas' objection that the intellect must be united to man as his form if he is to be put in the species of the rational, Siger replies that the intellect, that is, the potential intellect, is united to man according to its operation and also according to existence. Consequently, it is the form of the human body, providing man with his specific difference.[58] The potential intellect is united to our cogitative power from our birth as a natural form which gives us existence (*dans esse*) and puts us in the human species. However, the intellect is united to our phantasms in a different way when it serves as a principle of knowing.[59] The agent intellect is a distinct separate substance, for it is God, who appears to play here a dual role for Siger. He illuminates and abstracts the phantasms in men which the potential intellect then knows, and he also can be the object of an intuitive knowledge providing the potential intellect and the human being joined to it with complete beatitude.[60]

Siger's *Tractatus de anima intellectiva*

These modifications, which were meant to shore up the Averroist psychology against Thomas' attack, did not long satisfy Siger.[61] About three

Mandonnet's thesis, which had been published in the first edition of his book, and proposed that either Thomas was attacking another work or he was attacking other Averroists. Chossat 1914, pp. 25–52 showed that Siger drew arguments against the unity of the intellect from Thomas himself, and he therefore argued that Siger no longer holds the doctrine himself in the *De anima intellectiva*. Van Steenberghen 1938, pp. 64–75 and 1942, pp. 551–8 has summarised in admirably clear fashion the results of these earlier investigations.

57. Nardi 1945, pp. 11–90. For a summary of the major doctrines of Siger's *De intellectu* and his *De felicitate*, see pp. 46–7.
58. Agostino Nifo, *De intellectu*, I, tr. 2, c. 8–9, cited by Nardi 1945, pp. 14–15. See Aquinas, *De unitate intellectus*, c. 3, par. 80, p. 50.
59. Agostino Nifo, *In libros de anima*, III, comm. 5, cited by Nardi 1945, pp. 15–17. See also his *De intellectu*, I, tr. 3, c. 18, cited by Nardi 1945, pp. 17–19. By the potential intellect Siger means the lowest of the separate substances, that is, an intellect that is one for all men.
60. Nifo, *De intellectu*, I, tr. 4, c. 10; II, tr. 2, c. 17; *De beatitudine animae*, II, comm. 21, cited by Nardi 1945, pp. 21 and 25–7. Nifo himself incorporated Siger's suggestion that God is the agent intellect into his own more complicated interpretation of Averroes. For details see Mahoney 1970, pp. 387–409.
61. Bazán 1972, p. 77*; Van Steenberghen 1977, pp. 99, 218 and 220–1. Siger's caution regarding the conflict of faith and reason no doubt reflects some concern on his part resulting from the Condemnation of 1270. For the text of the latter, see Mandonnet 1911a, p. 111, n. 1; Denifle and Chatelain 1889, pp. 486–7. For thorough discussion of the condemnations of 1270 and 1277 see Wippel 1977, pp. 169–201; Van Steenberghen 1977, pp. 74–80 and 149–59; Hissette 1977.

or four years later, that is, in 1273 or more likely in 1274, he completed his *Tractatus de anima intellectiva*. The focus of attention is now Aristotle himself, and the commentator used most frequently to determine his mind is Themistius, the very authority whom Thomas had used to discredit Averroes' reliability.[62] Averroes himself, the 'Commentator', is mentioned by name only twice.[63]

Siger again accepts that for Aristotle the intellect, which operates in an immaterial fashion, comes from without and unites with the vegetative and sensitive parts, which have only bodily activities and are educed from matter. The result of this union is a composite form (*forma composita*).[64] Siger attacks both Albert and Thomas, 'distinguished men in philosophy', for maintaining that the substance of the intellective soul is so united to the body that it gives existence to it, while its power, the intellect, is wholly separate from matter since it needs no bodily organ to operate. They have thereby contradicted Aristotle. Nonetheless, while Siger emphasises that the thinking of the intellective soul, which is a form subsisting apart from matter, is somehow separate from matter, he also admits that that thinking must somehow be united to matter if we are truly to say *this* man is thinking. Siger points out that the intellect by its nature requires both the phantasm and the imagination if it is to carry out its proper activity, but he is quick to add that it depends on the phantasm provided by the body only as an object (*obiectum*) of cognition and not as an underlying subject (*subiectum*) required for its own existence. Thinking can be truly attributed to the individual human being insofar as he operates by one of his 'parts', namely, the single intellect. That is to say, when the intellect thinks, by its very nature it operates within the human body.[65] Since that which is

---

62. For reference to Themistius by name, see Siger of Brabant, *De anima intellectiva*, c. 3, p. 83, lin. 43, p. 85, lin. 88 and p. 88, lin. 42. In his edition, Bazán has identified many other pasages in which Siger is relying on Themistius. For further discussion, see Bruckmüller 1908, pp. 13, 16–18, 50, 55–6, 93; Nardi 1947, pp. 75–8; Verbeke 1957, pp. xlvii–xlviii; Mahoney 1966, pp. 163–4 and 170–2; idem 1973a, pp. 438–41; idem 1974a, pp. 540 and 544, n. 25. Although Van Steenberghen 1942, p. 653 and 1977, pp. 100, 207 and 400–1 does indicate that Themistius' paraphrases on the *De anima* helped to undercut Siger's allegiance to Averroes, he does not bring out how much Themistius influenced the psychology which Siger himself develops in the *De anima intellectiva*. On the other hand, Kuksewicz 1968, pp. 32–44 never mentions Themistius at all when analysing Siger's *De anima intellectiva*.

63. Siger of Brabant, *De anima intellectiva*, Prol., p. 70, lin. 9 and c. 6, p. 97, lin. 54. See Bruckmüller 1908, p. 13.

64. *Ibid.*, c. 8, pp. 109–10.

65. *Ibid.*, c. 3, pp. 80–7. Siger's implausible claim (p. 86, lin. 11–12) that the intellect is not man's 'mover' when it functions within him in the process of thinking probably represents an attempt to circumvent Thomas' attack on Averroes for making the intellect a mover and the human being something moved. See Aquinas, *De unitate intellectus*, c. 3, par. 57–63 and 79, pp. 42–6 and

an intrinsic agent (*operans intrinsecum*) in regard to matter can be called its 'form', at least in an extended sense of the word, the intellect proves to be the form or perfection of the human body. Though it subsists in itself, the intellect is like a true form both because that which operates intrinsic to a body is not spatially separate (*non loco separatum*) from that body, and also because the operation of such an intrinsic agent denominates the whole composite.[66]

Despite all these tortured distinctions, Siger admits in the seventh chapter of the *De anima intellectiva* that there are philosophical arguments and authorities for the view that the intellective soul is multiplied according to the number of human bodies: he cites Algazel, Avicenna, and Themistius, authorities used by Thomas in his *De unitate intellectus*.[67] He also adopts two of Thomas' arguments for the multiplicity of intellects, namely, that on the supposition of the unity of the intellect all men would have the same knowledge and there would be no need for the agent intellect, since the intellect would always be filled with all intelligibles. Siger recounts that because of the difficulty of these and other arguments he has long been in doubt as to what natural reason should hold regarding the problem and what Aristotle in fact thought about it. He concludes that in such a state of doubt he must adhere to faith, which surpasses all human reason.[68]

50, and also c. 4, par. 87–8, pp. 56–7. It is ironic that while Thomas insists that the soul is united to the body as its form and not as a sailor to his ship (*ibid.*, c. 1, par. 10, pp. 8–9; see also c. 1, par. 5, p. 5; and c. 3, par. 69, p. 44), Siger deliberately cites (*De anima intellectiva*, c. 3, p. 79, lin. 38–42 and p. 85, lin. 85–9) Themistius as an authority to argue that for Aristotle the intellect is related in its operations in regard to the body precisely as a sailor to a ship. He does so when presenting his theory of the *operans intrinsecum* as the form or perfection of that in which it operates. Chossat 1914, pp. 573–4 characterises Siger's theory as a miserable subterfuge. For a more sympathetic judgement, see MacClintock 1954–5, pp. 187–94 who shows the influence of Siger's doctrine on John of Jandun. For the relevant text see Jandun, *Super libros de anima*, III, q. 5, f. 58ᵛᵇ, who mentions Siger by name as the source of the *operans intrinsecum* theory (f. 60ʳᵃ).

66. 'Ad ultimum dicendum quod anima intellectiva perfectio corporis est, secundum quod intrinsecum operans ad corpus perfectio et forma corporis habet dici. Convenit enim cum forma in hoc quod intrinsecum corpori non loco separatum, et quia etiam operatio sic intrinseci operantis totum denominat.' Siger of Brabant, *De anima intellectiva*, c. 3, p. 87, lin. 33–7. For a full discussion, see Ermatinger 1963, especially pp. 28–40.

67. *Ibid.*, c. 7, p. 107, lin. 42–7. See Aquinas, *De unitate intellectus*, c. 5, par. 119–20, pp. 76–7. The strong influence of Thomas' doctrine of individuation on Siger here was first delineated by Bruckmüller 1908, pp. 140–53. See n. 76 below.

68. *Ibid.*, c. 7, p. 108, lin. 76–87. See Aquinas, *De unitate intellectus*, c. 4, par. 90–1 and 95, pp. 57–8; *Q. D. de anima*, a. 1; *De spiritualibus creaturis*, a. 9. See n. 74 below. Since Siger admits his uncertainty as to Aristotle's position on the intellective soul, it seems out of the question to consider him to be a convinced 'Averroist' in this work. Furthermore, since he gives Themistius precedence over Averroes as an interpreter of Aristotle and takes Themistius to maintain the multiplicity of both agent and possible intellects in human beings, it would be erratic for him to present Aristotle as a proponent of the unity of the intellect. Siger also raises the problem of the relation between faith

Several points remain to be made regarding the psychology assumed by Siger in the *De anima intellectiva*. First of all, it must be emphasised that Siger breaks with Averroes and his own *In librum tertium de anima* in that he denies that it is through the phantasms or intentions of the imagination that the separate intellect is united to man and made his form and holds instead that the intellective soul is directly united with the human body itself.[69] Secondly, although he agrees with Thomas that the intellective soul knows by receiving intelligible species of material things, he holds against Thomas that according to Aristotle it receives those species into its very substance and not merely in its power.[70] Thirdly, since the intellective soul is described only as understanding or receiving forms, which is the proper task of the possible or potential intellect, and is never said to be the source of abstraction, it appears that the intellective soul is identical with the possible intellect, whereas the agent intellect is some other, unspecified separate substance.[71] And finally, we are told nothing in the work about how the intellect can know individuals or whether man, when united to the possible intellect, can have an intuitive knowledge of God and the other separate substances.

Siger's questions on the Liber de causis

Siger's questions on the *Liber de causis* were composed sometime after the *De anima intellectiva*, but presumedly before his flight from Paris in 1276.[72] Siger now rejects the notion of a composite soul, arguing that the substantial form of each individual thing must be simple and provide the basis of all

and reason in *De anima intellectiva*, c. 7, p. 83, lin. 44 to p. 84, lin. 48, where he ends by quoting almost to the word Albert the Great, *In de gen. et corr.*, I, tr. 1, c. 22, ad t. c. 14, cited in n. 1 above. Siger did not maintain the so-called 'double truth theory', but neither did any of his contemporaries. For discussion see Van Steenberghen 1974, pp. 555–70; idem 1976, pp. 351–60; and Pine 1973, pp. 31–7.

69. *Ibid.*, c. 3, p. 85, lin. 76–89. See the discussion in Bruckmüller 1908, pp. 22–3, 30 and 114–15. See also Van Steenberghen 1942, pp. 676–7; 1966, pp. 450–1; and 1977, pp. 369–70.
70. *Ibid.*, c. 3, p. 83, lin. 22–38. Siger will not surrender this view in his questions on the *De causis*.
71. *Ibid.*, c. 3, p. 83, lin. 23–5 and c. 4, p. 90, lin. 36–42. While it is true that Siger mentions the agent intellect in two passages of the treatise, in neither case does he state that the agent intellect is part of the intellective soul. See c. 5, p. 93, lin. 62–5 and c. 7, p. 108, lin. 79–82. It is therefore difficult to accept the confident assertion of Van Steenberghen 1977, p. 376, n. 82 to the contrary. For further discussion, see Mahoney 1966, pp. 177–8 and Kuksewicz 1968, pp. 37–8. It should be noted that in the Lisbon *Quaestiones naturales* Siger maintains that the agent intellect and the possible intellect belong to different separate substances. It should also be recalled that in his earlier *De intellectu* Siger had taken the possible or potential intellect and the agent intellect to be two separate substances. Consequently, we would perhaps do best to consider Siger as non-committal in the *De anima intellectiva*.
72. Dondaine and Bataillon 1966, pp. 206–7 and 210–11; Marlasca 1972, pp. 25–9. On Siger's flight, see Dondaine 1947, pp. 186–92.

that is predicated of that individual, rationality included.[73] Averroes'
doctrine of the unity of the intellect is denounced as heretical and also as
irrational, and whether or not Aristotle agreed with Averroes on this
question, he too was human and could err.[74] Although Siger adopts some
of Thomas' arguments to show that the intellective soul is truly the form
and actuality of the human body, he still rejects Thomas' conception of the
soul as united by its essence to matter as its form while separated from it by
its power, the intellect. However, he carefully distinguishes the soul from
ordinary material forms by characterising it is subsistent in itself even
though it perfects matter and is thereby individuated.[75] Siger has here
abandoned the standard Averroist dichotomy of forms wholly separate
from matter and forms wholly material. That is to say, he is claiming that
between the ordinary material forms, which are completely bound to
matter and multiplied in the same species, and the wholly separate forms,
of which there can be only one in each species, there is a middle kind of
form, namely, the intellective soul or human intellect. Unlike the forms
which are totally separated from matter and cannot be multiplied, human
intellects are multiplied since they do communicate with matter and have
relationships to individual human bodies as their respective forms. On
the other hand, unlike ordinary material forms they maintain an individual
and subsistent existence in themselves which they even maintain in a
disembodied state after death.[76]

The intellective soul does not depend on the body as on an underlying
subject (*subiectum*) for its existence or its act of intellectual cognition, but it

73. Siger of Brabant, *Super librum de causis*, q. 4, pp. 47–9.
74. *Ibid.*, q. 27, p. 111, lin. 114–15; p. 112, lin. 147–52; and p. 115, lin. 248–52. While Siger might still
    concede that there can be some debate as to what Aristotle himself taught regarding the unity or
    multiplicity of the intellect, he now has no doubts that natural reason and philosophy can prove
    its multiplicity. This is surely a dramatic change from the lingering doubt which he had expressed
    in the *De anima intellectiva*. See n. 68 above and also Zimmermann 1973, pp. 426–7. Siger now
    appears to demarcate more clearly natural reason and philosophy from the text and teachings
    of Aristotle. Siger doubtless borrowed his remark (p. 115) that Aristotle was not a god but
    rather a human being who could err from Albert, *Physica*, VIII, tr. 1, c. 14, cited in n. 1 above.
    On possible personal contacts between Siger and Albert, see Vennebusch 1966, pp. 168–9 and
    Van Steenberghen 1977, pp. 395–7.
75. Siger of Brabant, *Super librum de causis*, q. 26, pp. 104–7.
76. *Ibid.*, q. 9bis, p. 59, lin. 19–31; q. 18, p. 81, lin. 29–36; q. 27, pp. 108–17; q. 53, p. 182, lin. 165–70.
    Siger's account of the individuation of the soul through its relationship to matter closely
    resembles the position of Thomas. See q. 27, pp. 112–16; q. 32, p. 126; q. 33, p. 127; q. 53,
    pp. 183–4. Moreover, Siger's explanation of how the disembodied human soul remains in-
    dividuated despite the loss of its body (q. 27, pp. 114–15, lin. 205–37) is much like that of Thomas
    in *De spiritualibus creaturis*, a. 9, *ad* 3 and 4; *De unitate intellectus*, c. 5, par. 104, p. 67, and other
    works.

does depend on the body to provide it with an object (*obiectum*), namely, the phantasm.[77] However, while the phantasm or sensible species is a principle of knowledge, it brings with it all the individuating characteristics of a particular sensible thing. Only by abstracting the intelligible species from the phantasm will the intellect have a principle of universal cognition. That is to say, just as Plato and Socrates have their own individual sensible species by which they see the same individual sensible nature, for example, this colour, so by their own distinct intelligible species, which are likenesses (*similitudines*) of one same thing, they know the same intelligible object (*intellectum*) or universal nature.[78] The intellective soul extends itself in a universal fashion to all material forms, both abstracting and receiving those forms: the agent intellect abstracts from the phantasm the universal intelligible species which is then received by the potential or possible intellect.[79] It is thus the agent intellect and the phantasm as rendered intelligible which together reduce the possible intellect from potency to act.[80]

While Siger does still maintain some doctrines of his own in these questions, it is obvious that he has moved very close to Thomas on the nature of the soul and intellect. This rapprochement may be one of the reasons why Dante placed them together in the fourth heaven of the *Divine Comedy*.[81]

Despite Siger's abandonment of Averroes as the true interpreter of Aristotle and the heavy blow of Tempier's condemnation of 1277, Averroism did not disappear from the University of Paris.[82] John of Jandun (d. 1328), who taught there in the Arts Faculty in the early fourteenth century, followed Averroes as the best guide to Aristotle, and he

77. *Ibid.*, q. 26, p. 182, lin. 156–61; q. 26, p. 105, lin. 88–91. This distinction was already used by Siger in the *De anima intellectiva*, c. 3, p. 85, lin. 70–1.
78. *Ibid.*, q. 28, pp. 116–17. Siger has made his own the critical distinction which Thomas used against Averroes. See Marlasca 1971, pp. 20–1 and 25–7. However, it would be a mistake to believe that Siger capitulated to Thomas on all major philosophical topics. On the remaining differences between them see Zimmermann 1967–8, pp. 212–21 and 1973, pp. 438–45.
79. *Ibid.*, q. 52, p. 181, lin. 134–6. See also q. 37, p. 146. I do not believe, as does Marlasca 1971, p. 14, either that the intellective soul is identical with the potential intellect or that the nature of the agent intellect is left somewhat unclear.
80. *Ibid.*, q. 41, pp. 151–2 and q. 52, p. 178, lin. 30–7.
81. See *Paradiso*, X, lin. 133–8, where Thomas indicates Siger to Dante. For discussion of this passage and of Dante's own philosophical views, see Nardi 1944, pp. 207–45; idem 1947, pp. 81–9; Gilson 1949, pp. 257–81; Zimmermann 1967–8, pp. 206 and 214; Van Steenberghen 1977, pp. 165–76; idem 1978, pp. 64–8.
82. On Averroism in the late thirteenth and early fourteenth centuries, see De Wulf 1937, pp. 125 and 128; Gauthier 1947–8, especially pp. 187–9 and 331–6; Kuksewicz 1968, pp. 97–9 and 118–20.

also defended him against both Albert and Thomas.[83] Jandun's writings would have influence on fourteenth- and fifteenth-century philosophy in Italy, especially at Bologna, and they would continue to be read and cited during the Renaissance.[84] Toward the end of the fifteenth century, both Jandun's questions on the *De anima* and also Siger's *De intellectu* were closely studied at the University of Padua.[85] This represented no clear victory for Averroism, however, since there was also close interest in Albert and Thomas. Indeed, Albert's psychological ideas had such great impact on philosophers like Nicoletto Vernia (d. 1499) and Agostino Nifo (*ca.* 1470–1538) that their thought can to some extent be described as Albertistic.[86] This interest in Siger, Thomas, and Albert testifies to the continuing vitality of thirteenth-century philosophical discussions during the Renaissance and beyond.[87]

83. On Jandun's life and works, see Valois 1906, pp. 528–602; MacClintock 1956, pp. 4–7 and 103–30; Terrero 1960, pp. 331–43; Schmugge 1966, pp. 1–26 and 121–32.
84. On Jandun and Bolognese Averroism, see Maier 1944, pp. 150 and 157; eadem 1949, pp. 251–78; eadem 1964, pp. 1–40; eadem 1967, pp. 335–66; Kristeller 1952, pp. 59–65; Ermatinger 1954, pp. 35–6; Kuksewicz 1968, pp. 315–52; Vanni-Rovighi 1971, pp. 161–83. His role in Renaissance Aristotelianism remains to be studied more carefully.
85. Nardi 1945 is the classic study of Siger's *De intellectu* and its diffusion in Italy. Jandun's psychological doctrines and interpretations of Aristotle, Alexander, and Averroes played a central role in philosophical discussions at Padua. See Mahoney 1968, pp. 281 and 294–5; idem 1976b, pp. 153–5; idem 1976c, pp. 291–2 and 298–300; Poppi 1970b, passim.
86. On Thomas' influence at Padua, see Kristeller 1974, pp. 46, 49–53 and 62; Mahoney 1974b, pp. 277–85; idem 1976a, pp. 195–211. The Albertistic tendencies of Vernia and Nifo have been underlined by Mahoney 1980, pp. 546–55.
87. This essay was completed during the tenure of a fellowship from the John Simon Guggenheim Foundation. I am indebted to Professors George W. Roberts and John F. Wippel for criticisms of earlier drafts.

31

CRITICISMS OF ARISTOTELIAN PSYCHOLOGY AND THE AUGUSTINIAN – ARISTOTELIAN SYNTHESIS

Thirteenth-century criticism of Aquinas' Aristotelianism

Strong reaction among traditional theologians in Paris and Oxford against the massive introduction of new Aristotelian ideas was still growing at the time Albert, Thomas, and Siger taught and wrote. It culminated in the formal act of condemnation by Bishop Tempier in 1277. For a while the Averroistic trend was halted, and the main target of criticism was Thomas Aquinas. A conception of the soul too closely connected to the body, too near to matter was an offense against the entire Christian tradition, which derived so much from Platonism and Augustine. The criticism also attacked the concept of the potential and agent intellect. It rejected the potential nature of the intellect which received and did not produce cognition, it rejected the effect of sensible species on the intellect, and the independence attributed to human cognition, unassisted by divine illumination.

Reactions to the criticism

Even Thomas' pupils and defenders stepped back in the face of this overwhelming pressure. Giles of Rome, although he basically agreed with Thomas' conception of the potential and agent intellect, described the agent intellect also as a quasi-Avicennian storehouse of pre-empirical knowledge and rules of understanding, conceived of as complete potential knowledge.[1] Godfrey of Fontaines defended Thomas in his *Quodlibeta*, written between 1285 and 1297, and gave his conception of the soul an even firmer Aristotelian character, but he denied the possibility that phantasmata can be turned into intelligible species by the agent intellect, and indeed eliminated intelligible species altogether as an element of intellective cognition.

---

1. Giles of Rome 1476, *In Aristotelis De anima commentum*, f. 69[rb–va]. Cf. Kuksewicz 1973.

Early attempts at an Augustinian–Aristotelian synthesis: Roger Marston

Most theologians of that time preferred the old Augustinian tradition systematised by Bonaventure, and tried to create doctrines which would absorb some generally admitted Aristotelian ideas, but include them as subordinate parts of a basically Platonic and Augustinian conception of a spiritual and active soul. Roger Marston, for instance, the author of *Quaestiones disputatae* dated between 1280 and 1294, accepted not only the potential and agent intellect in the human soul, but also a second agent intellect, separate from men and identified with God who illuminates human souls.

Matthew of Aquasparta

Less simple, and more interesting and original, was the conception of Matthew of Aquasparta, author of the *Quaestiones de cognitione* written before 1280.[2] Matthew accepts the agent and potential intellects as cognitive faculties of the soul, assisted by divine illumination. This Augustinian correction of the Aristotelian conception was based on the Augustinian idea of the soul and the Avicennian interpretation of the object of cognition. The perfect spiritual nature of the soul makes it impossible for it to be affected by sensible objects. Furthermore, the object of human intellective cognition is not the quiddity or essence of material objects as it was in Thomas' theory, but simply *quiditas* which exists in particular objects and is neutral between particularity and universality. The role of both intellects founded on these principles could not be conceived of in terms of the abstraction of universals from their individuation. It is not possible for sensible species to act on the potential intellect, nor is the action by the agent intellect on these species necessary; since the quiddity is not particularised it does not need to be freed. The agent intellect, therefore, assisted by divine illumination, creates intelligible species by itself and impresses them on the potential intellect. The role of sensible species is therefore only that of a necessary condition of intellection.

The conception of neutral quiddity, Avicenna's contribution to the development of Aristotelianism, became an important element of other solutions. (See J. Wippel's contribution to this volume.) The deep gulf between spiritual intellect and material sensory data was admitted too, but Matthew of Aquasparta's limitation of the role of these sensory data to a

---

2. Matthew of Aquasparta 1903, *Quaestiones disputatae selectae* vol. 1, *Quaestiones de fide et cognitione*, pp. 226–7, 231, 154, 428.

mere necessary condition did not convince other philosophers. Henry of Ghent and Duns Scotus looked for a better foundation of the content of human knowledge and its link with objects to be known.

Henry of Ghent

Henry of Ghent, who in his *Quodlibet* of 1270 represented a conception of the potential and agent intellect quite close to the theory of Aquinas, influenced by the generally critical mood after 1277 and by the turbulent disputes concerning the concept of the intellect, changed his conception some years later and elaborated one of the most interesting theories of the late thirteenth century.[3]

The potential and agent intellect are, according to Henry, faculties of the soul (which is a spiritual substance and form of the body), and they are characterised in medieval Aristotelian language: the potential intellect receives the concept, the agent intellect illuminates sense images and activates the process of abstraction. However, Henry rejects some specific theses which were basic to medieval Aristotelianism as represented by Thomas Aquinas. First, he denies that an accident could be impressed on a spiritual subject, and this rule applies to the potential intellect. Second, he does not accept a transmutation performed by the agent intellect upon phantasmata transforming them from particular to universal, nor does he allow an impression by sensory faculties on the potential intellect. Third, the representation of universals by intelligible species is not possible because only a universal being can give a universal representation of itself; universal concepts cannot be impressed by individual objects of the material world, nor can they be impressed by spiritual beings, because such concepts would not represent material objects.[4]

These principles completely changed the Aristotelian conception of the role of both intellects. The agent intellect acts upon particular phantasmata and upon the potential intellect. By the latter operation, it prepares the potential intellect for intellection; by the former, it proceeds to abstraction. However, this abstraction has little similarity to the Aristotelian or Thomistic concept of abstraction. The active intellect does not transform sensible species into universal concepts: its action upon particular phantasmata contained in the imagination relieves them only of their rich, particular character of clear images and transforms them into shapes, indistinct

3. Bettoni 1954, p. 18.
4. Henry of Ghent 1502, *Summa quarumdam ordinarium theologiae*, f. 14ᵛ; idem, 1613, *Quodlibeta aurea*, ff. 78ᵛ, 206ᵛ, 262ᵛ.

images called 'universal phantasmata'. These phantasmata, in no way identical with quiddity, can initiate the act of understanding, which arises as produced by and impressed in the potential intellect.[5]

The role of the potential and agent intellect does not end there. The resulting knowledge is not a cognition of essence, nor can it be called 'science'. Scientific knowledge is 'necessary', and cannot, therefore, be caused by changeable material objects and their nebulous images – the universal phantasmata – in the intellect. Full perfect knowledge must concern the nature of the given object, and that is possible only when this object is conceived under the most general categories. The second stage of cognition begins in the following way. The moment the potential intellect is stimulated by the universal phantasma, not only the act of understanding but also the most general notion of 'being' appear in it, and then, with the illumination of the initial knowledge by the agent intellect, the potential intellect starts the process of cognition whose result is full knowledge of the essence of the given object. This last process is assisted by divine illumination directed toward the concept and giving it full validity.[6]

More drastic criticisms of Aristotelianism

A positive synthesis of the Aristotelian and Augustinian traditions was not the only aim of the late-thirteenth-century philosophers. More drastic criticisms of the Aristotelian notions of the potential and agent intellect were also made at that time. Peter John Olivi, who founded his conception on the basic Platonic and Augustinian opposition between the spiritual soul and the material world, rejected the potential and agent intellect along with the process of abstraction, phantasmata, and species.

Duns Scotus

The turbulent disputes about Aristotelian, Platonic, and Augustinian concepts of the intellect were the occasion of a new and final synthesis by Duns Scotus, who in his lectures in Paris and Oxford in 1297–1302 tried once more to provide an unshakable theory of human cognition aimed at satisfying growing doubts.

Duns Scotus' conception of the intellect and its activity, was based upon the Avicennian concept of the nature of a thing. The nature of each being, *natura communis*, is neither individual nor universal and this nature is contained in each individual being in its pure state, without any individuation. The human soul is conceived of in a twofold way: *pro statu naturae*

---

5. Henry of Ghent 1613, p. 200[r]; 1502, p. 129[v]–131[r].
6. Henry of Ghent 1502, ff. 14[v], 130[r]–131[v], 153[r].

(according to its nature) it is a spiritual substance, and *pro statu isto* (in its earthly life) it is connected to the body. The proper objects of cognition are real individual beings and their natures. However, in this life, the human soul joined to the material body cannot achieve this kind of cognition. Therefore, the soul *pro statu isto* perceives the common nature of each object in a twofold way: through the senses as it exists in individual beings and through the intellect as a universal. The soul and its cognition *pro statu isto* fit well with the Aristotelian conception, and the potential and agent intellect seemed to Scotus adequate for explaining the process of intellective cognition, starting with the senses and ending with universals.[7]

The active intellect is characterised, in line with medieval Aristotelian tradition, as an active power which produces a real effect in the potential intellect. The potential intellect, however, loses its Aristotelian character: it becomes actuality and not potentiality; since it is treated as spiritual in nature, and so knowable in itself, it must be *in actu*. Nevertheless, Scotus saves its description as *tabula rasa* in the sense that it is able to know all beings and is, therefore, indeterminate. The potential intellect is thus an active potency which acts through its own power and needs only a determination of the content of its act.[8]

The function of both intellects depends mainly on the conception of their object. Since the quiddity (neutral nature) existing in particular things is not particularised, there is no need to free it from individual conditions, and no abstraction effected by the active intellect is necessary. The presence of the nature in the phantasma joined to the illumination of the potential intellect by the agent effects the intelligible species. The agent intellect is therefore the real cause of the species, but the phantasma collaborates in this act, determining its content. Therefore, there are two causes of species, which are named *causae partiales*, where the active intellect is the principal cause. However, the intelligible species is not identical with the act of cognition. This act is produced jointly by the intelligible species and the potential intellect, where the potential intellect – an active power – is the cause of the act and the species is the cause of this act being about what it is.[9]

Thus a new Augustinian conception was created at the turn of the fourteenth century founded partly on Aristotelian principles. But these principles have profoundly changed their original meaning. The role of the agent intellect has become limited to action on the potential intellect and to

7. John Duns Scotus 1639, *Reportata Parisiensia*, I. 3, q. 3, n6. *Opus Oxoniense*, I. 1, d. 3, q. 6, n8.
8. Idem, *Reportata Parisiensia* I. 1, d. 3, q. 4, n4. *Opus Oxoniense*, I. 2, d. 3, q. 8, n11.
9. Idem, *Opus Oxoniense*, I. 1, d. 3, I. 6, n15, n8.

the production of intelligible species; the potential intellect became an active power of the act of understanding, whose potentiality was limited to the indeterminacy of the content of its act. And the intellect as a whole became the sole cause of the act of cognition. The separation of the material from the spiritual was once more deep and unbridged.[10]

Criticism and stagnation in the fourteenth and fifteenth centuries

Fourteenth-century philosophy presents a great variety of solutions to the problem we have been dealing with. In that period, human cognition interested philosophers and theologians much more than the nature of the soul and its faculties. Thus the analyses of William Ockham treat kinds of knowledge, intuition, abstraction, and experience much more than the faculties of the soul. Peter Auriol, Durand de Saint-Pourçain and Henry of Harclay tend to simplify the process of intellective cognition, eliminating steps in the process. Durand acknowledges only the possible intellect, and eliminates the active intellect and intelligible species. John of Mirecourt rejects the process of abstraction; Nicolas of Autrecourt eliminates the cognitive faculties of the soul.

However, the Aristotelian tradition is by no means non-existent in the fourteenth century. Aristotle's *De anima* was included in the programme of the Faculty of Arts, and commented on by all masters, who were thus obliged to explain the conception of the possible and active intellects. However, the main interest of these commentaries was centred not on the nature of the possible and agent intellects, but on their function and the process of abstraction. Problems concerning the necessity of the active intellect, the production of intelligible species, the relation of the species to the act of intellection and the possibility of simultaneous intellection of several objects became the topics of chief interest.

After the intellectual revolution of Ockham, Auriol, Durand, John of Mirecourt, and Nicolas of Autrecourt which overturned the traditional conception of abstraction, the second half of the fourteenth century re-turned to medieval Aristotelianism and its concepts, with an admixture, in varying degrees, of neoplatonic ideas. By the end of the century, different solutions coming from different schools blended together. Various solutions discussed earlier were repeated and revived, but there were hardly any new ideas of lasting importance.

---

10. For Ockham's theory of the intellect's role in knowledge, see J. Boler's contribution to this volume.

32

FREE WILL AND FREE CHOICE

Aristotelian and Christian backgrounds for the medieval discussion

Medieval teaching on free choice was inspired on the one hand by Christian thinking and on the other by the moral philosophy of Aristotle as expounded in the *Nicomachean Ethics*. According to Christian thinkers man is given by God the possibility of choosing between good and evil, so that his conscious decisions affect his ultimate fate, although salvation is impossible without the intervention of divine grace. For Aristotle the consequences of free choice are limited to life on this earth; but in other respects there are similarities between his view and the Christian teaching. For both, man can choose between good and evil as a consequence of his capacity for rational judgement, which makes him significantly more independent of his environment than other beings. According to Aristotle man has a will or desire (*boulēsis*) for what is good for him: when this is combined with a judgement about what, in concrete circumstances, is conducive to his good there results a choice (*prohairesis*). The criteria by which such choices are made may differ from individual to individual and are by no means uniform for all men.[1]

Medieval thinkers derived their Christian view of free will principally from the Book of Genesis and from the Epistles of St Paul, but they were also acquainted with Augustine and John of Damascus. The former, in speaking of free choice, emphasised on the one hand the freedom and spontaneity of human aspirations, and on the other the moral and theoretical problems associated with the liberation of human beings from the fetters of doubt, suffering, and sin.[2]

In addition to the problems concerning human freedom of choice, medieval Christian thought was concerned with the degree of freedom

---

1. Aristotle, *Ethics*, 1112^{a}13–18.
2. Genesis 3.1–8; 2 Cor. 3.17; Rom. 20–3; Augustine, *De gratia et libero arbitrio, PL* 44, I, 1, col. 881; II, 2, col. 882; x, 22, col. 894; Augustine, *De libero arbitrio, PL* 32, I, 12, 26, col. 1235; II, 1, 1, col. 1240; II, 1, 3, col. 1241; III, 3, 7; Augustine, *Retractationes, PL* 32, I, 9, 4, col. 596. John of Dramascus, *De fide orthodoxa, PG* 94, 928 B–C, 941 C, 944 B–C, 945 A–C.

accorded to angels, and with the independence and freedom which belonged to God in virtue of his omnipotence, limited to some degree as this was through the laws established by him. This last problem was linked on the one hand with the question of predestination, and on the other with the miraculous intervention of the Creator in a natural world governed by laws of his own making.[3]

Liberum arbitrium

In presenting in English the thought of medieval philosophers on freedom of choice, we meet with a linguistic difficulty. The cluster of problems concerning human freedom and action which are discussed by modern and contemporary English-speaking philosophers under the title 'freedom of the will' were discussed in the Middle Ages under the heading '*liberum arbitrium*'. But the Latin expression cannot simply be translated by the English one, because it does not contain the Latin word for will (*voluntas*), and it was a matter of debate, among those who believed in the existence of *liberum arbitrium*, whether it was the will, or some other faculty, which was the bearer of the freedom involved in *liberum arbitrium*, and indeed whether the will is free at all. The will itself was defined as the rational appetite, or the desire for the good apprehended by reason, and not in terms of a capacity for choosing between alternatives; hence its relation to *liberum arbitrium* was something which required investigation. 'Freedom of choice' is probably a less misleading translation of '*liberum arbitrium*'; but here too there is the difficulty that the Latin expression does not contain the technical word for choice (*electio*). In what follows, therefore, we shall use 'freedom of decision' or else leave '*liberum arbitrium*' untranslated.

Independence of spirit and determinism of matter

It was a matter of general agreement from the beginning of the Middle Ages that freedom and the capacity of independent action were a prerogative of beings who possessed intellectual understanding. In accordance with this belief freedom was attributed in an absolute degree to God, in a lesser degree to angels, and in a still lesser degree to human beings. From the beginning of the thirteenth century, under the influence of Aristotle, we find the notion of freedom associated with that of immateriality: the less a being is conditioned by matter and material forces, the freer and less

3. Gilson 1932, II, pp. 100–18.

determined is its activity.[4] Thus, Philip the Chancellor writes:

Aristotle says that the potential intellect can understand pairs of contraries, because it is separate, or separable, with respect to matter, from either of them. Similarly, the practical intellect is capable of operating in opposite directions, because it is free in general from the bonds of matter.[5]

The contrast between the independence of spirit and the determinism of matter became a characteristic feature of Franciscan thought. Merely corporeal beings are enslaved by the necessity of nature and compelled by its laws; irrational animals act by instinct and have no power to judge their own actions and approve or disapprove them. Driven on by natural forces, they have no freedom of decision because they lack the power of abstraction which is necessary in order to compare actions with standards of right and wrong.[6]

Various aspects of human freedom

Among corporeal beings, then, only human beings enjoy freedom: but human freedom has more than one aspect. Freedom from evil is not the same thing as freedom from coercion. Only in the eternal happiness of heaven can a man hope to be free from all evil and the many kinds of misery on earth; the way to heaven is by freedom from the moral evil which is sin. Freedom from sin is something different from the freedom from coercion without which neither sin nor right action would be possible in the first place. These contrasts were frequently drawn early in the Middle Ages.

Thus Bernard of Clairvaux distinguishes between freedom from necessity, freedom from sin, and freedom from misery. Every rational creature, whether good or bad, enjoys freedom from necessity; freedom from sin may be called the freedom of grace (*libertas gratiae*) since only grace can confer it; freedom from misery may be called the freedom of glory (*libertas gloriae*) since it is the prerogative of the glorious saints and angels in heaven.[7] Many medieval thinkers adopt this hierarchy of freedoms, with the freedom of the blessed in heaven at its apex.[8] Thus William of Auxerre

---

4. Cf. Lottin 1957, pp. 12–13; Gilson 1932, pp. 104–8.
5. Lottin 1957, p. 73.
6. Thus John of La Rochelle (Lottin 1957, p. 133); Alexander of Hales, *Summa* II, 403; Odo Regaldus (Lottin 1957, pp. 160–1).
7. Bernard of Clairvaux, *De gratia et libero arbitrio tractatus*, PL 182, col. 1006.
8. Thus John of La Rochelle (Lottin 1957, p. 132); Philip the Chancellor (*ibid.*, pp. 80–1) and Odo Regaldus (*ibid.*, p. 162).

rejects the definition of *liberum arbitrium* as the freedom to do what you want, on the grounds that such a definition would make the damned more free than the blessed, whose wills are fixed on God.[9] Other thinkers used similar arguments.

Freedom to sin

If freedom is, as this view suggests, essentially freedom from evil, does this mean that sinful action is not really free? This conclusion was drawn by Anselm of Canterbury, who defined *liberum arbitrium* as the power to maintain a righteous will.[10] By contrast, Anselm of Laon defined freedom of decision as 'the power of acting well or badly'. According to him angels and Christ possessed the power to do evil, but it would be absurd to think of Christ making use of that power; it was used only by the angels who proved unfaithful to God. Albert the Great agreed with Anselm of Laon that when a human being wills evil he acts freely; but he did not agree that God and the saints have the power to do wrong. Their inability to will evil does not take away their freedom, however; it is the result not of coercion but of the irrevocable fixing of their wills on goodness.[11]

Superior and inferior reason

Just as it became common to deny that God and the saints could do wrong, similarly there is a suggestion in some authors that even in this life reason, which is the highest part of man, is incapable of sinning. Thus the author of the *Summa Porretana* (between 1195 and 1210) offers a definition of *liberum arbitrium* as the power of consenting to the reason or to the will. The will may be a rational will or a sensual will; if the latter is consented to, an evil choice results; if the former, the free decision is made for the better part. According to this definition, then, if a choice is in accordance with reason, the rightness of the choice is guaranteed. Reason can be said to be responsible for sin only in the sense in which the king can be said to be responsible for the crimes committed in Paris in virtue of not repressing them. But the author adds that this all applies only to the superior part of the reason, or *synderesis*. Inferior reason possesses the ability to sin.[12]

Like the author of the *Summa Porretana*, Roland of Cremona (a Domi-

---

9. William of Auxerre 1500, *Summa aurea in quattuor libros Sententiarum a subtilissimo doctore magistro Guillelmo Altissiodorensi edita*, f. 64ra.
10. Anselm, *Dialogus de libero arbitrio*, PL 158, col. 494. On Anselm of Laon, cf. Bliemetzrieder 1919, pp. 27–8.
11. Albert the Great 1899, *Summa de homine*, pp. 585–6, 589–90.
12. Lottin 1957, p. 49.

nican writing *ca.* 1230) made use of the distinction between superior and inferior reason; but though only inferior reason can sin, in his view, both superior and inferior reasons are free. Just as there are two reasons, there are two types of *liberum arbitrium*. Superior reason is the reason which is the bearer of *sapientia* (philosophical wisdom and learning), inferior reason is the locus of *prudentia* (practical wisdom or prudence). Inferior reason can turn itself in the direction either of good or of evil: it has freedom in respect of the lower goods that are the subject matter of prudence. Superior reason or intellect has freedom with respect to the higher goods: it cannot choose evil, but it can will one good rather than another. Human beings, therefore, make two kinds of free decisions; the really free ones are those which are made by superior reason, which govern its own actions and the actions of inferior reason as well.[13]

Theoretical and practical reason

Instead of, or as well as, the distinction between superior and inferior reason, other authors in their treatment of freedom of decision made use of a distinction between practical and theoretical reason. Thus, William of Auxerre observed that reason makes judgements of two kinds. In a judgement of theoretical reason we simply judge what ought to be done and what ought not to be done; the other kind of judgement involves not only deliberation but also a consequent imperative to do one thing rather than another. It is this imperative judgement of practical reason which is the act of the power of choice and which constitutes *liberum arbitrium*.[14]

Reason, will, and liberum arbitrium

For William of Auxerre, therefore, free decision is essentially an act of the reason; Philip the Chancellor, by contrast, maintained that freedom was principally a matter of the will. But his position was not as distant from William's as might appear, because he regarded reason and will as being in substance the same faculty, given two different names because of two different activities. Yet a third view appears in an anonymous treatise of the first part of the thirteenth century: *liberum arbitrium* is to be identified neither with reason nor with will, but is a third power distinct from both. Whatever will and reason may tell us to do, it is still in our power to do it if

13. Lottin 1957, pp. 106–7.
14. Lottin 1957, p. 67.

we choose or not do it if we choose not. It is this power which is freedom of decision, and which is the most powerful element in the soul.[15]

The relationship between reason, will, and freedom of decision was a major topic of debate throughout the thirteenth century. Eventually it came to be characteristic of Dominican writers to link freedom very closely with reason, and of Franciscan writers to locate *liberum arbitrium* rather in the will. But in the earlier part of the thirteenth century there was considerable variety of opinion among Dominican masters.

Thus Hugh of St Cher, writing *ca.* 1230–5, adopted a position resembling that of Philip the Chancellor. Reason and will are a single faculty which can perform different actions: telling the difference between good and bad is called an act of the reason, choosing to enact one of a number of proposed courses of action is called an act of the will. *Liberum arbitrium*, considered as an act, is a combination of the reason's act of judgement and the will's act of choice; if we consider them as powers or faculties, however, *liberum arbitrium*, reason, and will are one and the same.[16]

We find, however, a clear distinction between the will and *liberum arbitrium* in the writings of the early Oxford Dominican, Richard Fishacre. Richard distinguished between two types of volition, complete and incomplete. Incomplete volition is the spontaneous motion of the will which precedes rational reflection. *Liberum arbitrium* consists precisely in the power of rational reflection upon spontaneous volition: it is thus essentially an intellectual power, a manifestation of the power of self-reflection peculiar to intellectual beings. Complete volition leads to the carrying out of action after this reflection upon its moral value. *Liberum arbitrium* thus operates to turn incomplete volition into complete volition and is itself neither one nor the other.[17]

Albert the Great regarded *liberum arbitrium* as a power distinct from reason and will which arbitrates (hence its name) between the dictates of reason and the aims of will in cases where there is a conflict between the two. Reason judges a proposed action as good or bad, and will endorses or rejects an object of desire; free decision chooses either the object approved by the reason or the object pursued by the will.[18]

Three stages may be distinguished in the evolution of Albert's thought. In his *Summa de homine* he emphasised the role of free decision as mediator

15. Lottin 1957, pp. 88–9.
16. Lottin 1957, pp. 100–1.
17. Lottin 1957, pp. 110–11.
18. Albert the Great 1899, *Summa de homine*, p. 575.

or arbitrator between the two distinct faculties of reason and will. In the commentary on the *Sentences* the function of *liberum arbitrium* is to link the desires of will with the judgements of reason, and the notion of arbitration is not stressed. Finally, in the commentary on Aristotle's *Ethics* free decision, while remaining distinct from both reason and will, is described as involving the activity of both faculties. In being a judgement, free decision involves the activity of reason; in being free, it involves the activity of the will.

Thomas Aquinas likewise adopted different approaches to the relationship between reason, will, and freedom at different periods of his life, from the early commentary on the *Sentences* through the *De veritate* and the commentary on the *Ethics* to the *Summa theologiae* in the last years of his life. Having said in the commentary on the *Sentences* that choice is an act of the will influenced by preceding rational deliberation, he explained in the *De veritate* that *liberum arbitrium* is not a faculty distinct from the will, but the will itself considered as the power of choosing, choice being just one of the several kinds of act it can perform. It is the power by which we judge freely. Judgement itself is an act of reason, but what gives freedom to judgement is the will. In the commentary on the *Ethics* he describes the function of the will as aiming at the ultimate goal, while choice selects the means conducive to this goal. Finally, in the *Summa theologiae* he drew a comparison between cognitive and volitional capacities. Understanding self-evident truths and drawing conclusions from them are two different actions, but both are acts of the same faculty, the intellect; similarly, aiming at an ultimate goal and freely choosing means to that goal are two different actions, but both are acts of the same faculty, the will. Hence *liberum arbitrium* is not a faculty distinct from the will. But for Thomas it is not the will but the intellect which has the major role in the moral activity of human beings. For the intellect is the final or teleological cause of the will's action: it is the intellect which presents to the will its ultimate aims. This last opinion gained wide popularity through its acceptance by the Thomist school, and also had an influence on the outlook of many thinkers from other schools such as Buridan and his followers.[19]

The Franciscan masters of the thirteenth century were much more unified in their approach than the Dominicans. However, three different positions can be identified. John of la Rochelle followed Philip the

---

19. Thomas Aquinas, *In II Sententiarum*, dist. 24, quaest. 1, art. 2; *De veritate*, quaest. 24, art. 6; Thomas Aquinas 1969, *Sententia libri Ethicorum.*, pp. 133–4; *ST*, I, q. 82, 1, 2; cf. Siewerth 1954.

Chancellor in identifying reason with will and regarding *liberum arbitrium* as being itself identical with this single faculty of rational appetition. Alexander of Hales thought that freedom of decision was a power distinct from reason and will which was supreme in the soul and could command both the other faculties. *Liberum arbitrium*, reason, and will, he maintained, formed a trinity in the appetitive part of the soul comparable to the divine Trinity of Father, Son, and Holy Ghost. Bonaventure, on the other hand, thought that *liberum arbitrium* was not a faculty at all, but a *habitus* or disposition. Neither reason nor will alone suffices to exercise control over human action: freedom of decision is a disposition created by the co-operation of the two faculties.[20] Bonaventure's view that freedom of decision is not a faculty but a *habitus* was followed at Oxford by the Franciscan Richard Rufus of Cornwall and by the Dominican Robert Kilwardby.[21]

Radical voluntarism

In the second half of the thirteenth century the writers of the Franciscan school began to espouse a radical form of voluntarism. Thomas Aquinas had taught that the will acts according to the directives it receives from the reason. Walter of Bruges attacked this doctrine. He distinguished between the natural will, a passive appetite which tends towards good, and the real will which has the power to judge and decide, an active power which can freely accept or reject what is presented to it by reason. The will is independent of the intellect in the sense that whatever object the intellect presents to it may be freely chosen or rejected. The judgement of practical reason is also free, but not to the same degree as the will, which has absolute power over its own actions.[22] William de la Mare, likewise, thought that the will was both a passive and an active power: passive in that it must receive its object from the intellect, active in that it moves itself and activates all other parts of the soul.[23] Similarly Matthew of Aquasparta: the will while needing enlightenment by the intellect itself activates the intellect, giving it commands and stimulating it to action. The will is superior to the intellect because its virtue, charity, is superior to the intellect's virtue,

---

20. John of la Rochelle (Lottin 1959, pp. 129–34); Alexander of Hales, *De libero arbitrio*, MS Todi Bibl. Commun. 121, ff. 45ᵛᵃ–46ᵛᵃ; Odo Regaldus (Lottin 1959, pp. 152 ff.); Bonaventure, *In II Sententiarum*, 25, 1, 2 and 6.
21. Lottin 1959, pp. 190–2.
22. Lottin 1959, p. 243; similar views were held by Gerard of Abbeville, *ibid.*, pp. 249–50.
23. Lottin 1959, pp. 272–3.

faith; and its object, goodness, is superior to the intellect's object, truth.[24]

One who was influenced by the voluntarism of the Franciscan school was the bishop of Paris, Stephen Tempier, who in 1277 condemned a number of propositions concerning freedom of choice. He declared unorthodox the view that the will is a merely passive power and that human action can be necessitated by external forces. He also condemned the view taught by Thomas in the *De veritate* that the will must follow the dictates of reason.[25]

Tempier's condemnation of determinism led the majority of thinkers at the end of the thirteenth and beginning of the fourteenth centuries to maintain that the will, and not the reason, was the seat of freedom and autonomy. This, at least, is the impression we get from the writing of Peter de Falco, who maintained that the will was the root of human freedom. Reason is necessary to enable us to conceive the possibilities of choice open to us, and to deliberate about them; but it is the will which produces free human action since it depends on the will whether a man accepts or rejects what the reason proposes.[26]

Attempts to re-establish the supremacy of reason

The Augustinian Giles of Rome attempted to reconcile Aquinas' doctrine of the superiority of reason to will with the Franciscan thesis that the will was self-determining. According to Giles, when reason presents the will with absolute good the will cannot help but desire it; but the will is free to control its own actions where a choice between relative degrees of goodness is concerned: it can attend to the good or evil aspects of the object presented by reason.[27]

In Paris the Dominican John Quidort defended against the Franciscan thinkers the doctrine of Thomas in the *De veritate* that the will cannot but desire what reason presents to it as the better. Similarly, Godfrey of Fontaines maintained that the Franciscan theory of the self-determination of the will was unintelligible.

In Oxford as in Paris Aquinas found defenders. Thomas Sutton and Nicholas Trivet took his side in the debate about the superiority of the intellect over the will. Sutton maintained that the will is passive with

24. Mathew of Aquasparta 1903, 8, *ad* 4, *ad* 22; 9, *ad* 4, *ad* 10. For a similar position see Henry of Ghent 1613, *Quodl.* 1, qq. 14–16.
25. *CUP*, 543–58, propositiones 151, 152, 157, 158, 160, 163–6. See Hissette 1977, pp. 230–63.
26. Lottin 1959, pp. 283–5; see also Richard Middleton (Lottin 1959) and Roger Marston 1932, *Quaestiones disputatae*, pp. 438–9, 441–2, 447–50.
27. Giles of Rome 1646, pp. 177–9.

respect to the object of its desire, but free in its choice of means to achieve its object. But even in this choice of means it is dependent on the judgements of reason. Trivet, likewise, maintains that both will and reason are free, though each in a different way. The dependence of will on reason does not conflict with its freedom, which is freedom of choice of means in the endeavour to achieve the aim presented by reason. Unlike Jean Quidort, these Oxford masters do not defend Thomas outright: they make smaller or larger concessions to Tempier's condemnations.[28]

Voluntarism in Scotus and Ockham

But again, in Oxford as in Paris, it was the Franciscan supporters of voluntarism who were dominant at the end of the thirteenth century. The most important of these was John Duns Scotus. Scotus saw the problem in terms of a contrast between an order or system of nature and an order or system of liberty. A single human act with a single object cannot belong to both of these orders at the same time: it cannot be both the result of natural necessity and of the freedom of the will. In God, indeed, willing and necessity can coincide: God necessarily loves (his own) infinite goodness, but it is not thus with created wills. God's love and God's will are identical with God's essence, but a human being's love and will are not identical with his essence. A human will need not aspire to a goal presented to it by the human intellect; it can act or not act, and it can act in any way it pleases. It is the will which controls the exercise of other human abilities: thus it is superior to the intellect since it controls it too. In line with the Franciscan tradition Scotus argues that the will is superior to the intellect because charity is superior to knowledge and goodness is superior to truth.[29]

William Ockham's theory of the will is similar to Scotus'. Ockham has a twofold concept of freedom: as independence of constraint, and as spontaneity of action. Will is a free and active force, which can desire or not desire whatever is presented to it or dictated to it by reason. The will is free to choose its own goal as well as being free in the choice of means to a goal. Nature is determined by the laws which govern it; in virtue of possessing free will man belongs not to the order of nature but the order of liberty.[30]

28. John of Paris, *Quaestiones*, MS Basel Bibl. Univ. B. III, 13, f. 31^{ra-rb}, 100va–101ra; Sutton (Lottin 1959, pp. 365–71, 349–54); Trivet (Lottin 1959, pp. 378–82).
29. *Quaestiones quodlibetales* XIV–XXI; John Duns Scotus 1895, pp. 180–1, 184, 188–9, 199, 241; *Quaestiones in quartum librum Sententiarum (Opus Oxoniense)*; John Duns Scotus 1891–5, XXI, pp. 97, 123, 151, 155; Cf. Gilson 1952b, pp. 586–7, 597.
30. William Ockham 1483, *In IV Sententiarum*, d. 16, q. 1; Ockham 1481, *Quodlibeta septem*, f. b 3vb, b 4^a; Ockham 1491, *Expositio super Physicam Aristotelis*, f. 117^a.

Buridan on two types of human freedom

One of the fullest and most interesting medieval accounts of human freedom was that of John Buridan, presented between 1342 and 1354. Buridan distinguished between two types of freedom possessed by human beings: freedom of choice (*libertas oppositionis*) and freedom to aspire to a goal (*libertas finalis ordinationis*). Freedom of choice is not absolute, because a man must necessarily aim at what is good; but he is free in choosing different paths to its attainment. In the act of choice both the intellect and the will are involved, and each of the two faculties is both active and passive. The intellect derives the content of its knowledge from the external world, and to that extent is passive; but in informing the will what to seek and what to avoid it is active. Similarly, the will is passive in taking information from the intellect, but active in making a free choice among various possible courses. When it first learns of a good or of an evil, the will spontaneously, but necessarily, feels pleasure or displeasure; but this reaction is not its specific activity, which is the acceptance or rejection of the object in question. In this act it is free and independent of the dictates of the intellect.

Besides this freedom of choice human beings possess another freedom: the freedom to aspire to a goal selected by the intellect. It is this *libertas finalis ordinationis* which is the more perfect freedom. So Buridan, though he might be called a voluntarist, emphasises the role of the cognitive faculty in fixing the goals of action. Since it is the intellect which selects the objects of human aspiration, the intellect is superior to the will.[31]

Buridan's followers, especially in central Europe (e.g. in Prague, Vienna, and Cracow) concentrated on the topic of freedom of choice, and ignored Buridan's second type of freedom. In doing so they made Buridan appear a more thoroughgoing voluntarist than he really was.

Divine power and freedom

In the fourteenth century, alongside the debates on human freedom there was much discussion of the omnipotence and freedom of God. Duns Scotus emphasised that God was independent of the laws of nature and could suspend these laws which he had himself established. His omnipotence was twofold: absolute omnipotence (*potentia absoluta*) and omnipotence within the limits of the laws which he has himself established (*potentia*

---

31. John Buridan 1513, *Quaestiones super decem libros Ethicorum* III, quaest, 1–6; X, quaest. 1–3. Cf. Monahan 1954, pp. 72–8; Walsh 1964, pp. 50–61; 1966, 1–13; Korolec 1974a, 1974b.

ordinata). If we consider the first kind of freedom we can say that God has the power to order men to hate him, thus suspending the law of love which he has given. The only limits of this omnipotence are laws of logic such as the principle of non-contradiction. Ockham defended a similar view, saying that in respect of his absolute will (*voluntas beneplaciti*, corresponding to *potentia absoluta*) he can do whatever he wants, whereas in respect of his manifested will (*voluntas signi*) he wills only in accordance with the commands he has given.[32]

The divine will and the human will

The relationship between the human will and the divine will is most fully discussed in Thomas Bradwardine's treatise *De causa Dei*, written before 1325 against the Pelagian heresy. Bradwardine emphasises the absolute dependence of man's will on God's: human beings can free themselves from the influence of psychological forces and from the influence of the stars, but they cannot become independent of God. But in spite of the absolute divine influence on human behaviour, it is man and not God who is the cause of sin. The action itself is caused by God, but its sinfulness is caused by man himself.[33]

Robert Holkot, by contrast, is prepared to admit a sense in which God is the author of sin. Using Ockham's distinction between *voluntas beneplaciti* and *voluntas signi*, he says that God is the author of sin in so far as he can do what he desires, but cannot be the author of sin because of the will which manifests itself in the commandments.[34] The same problem was also discussed by Thomas Buckingham (1333 or 1338) who maintained that every human action was performed in direct dependence on God. By his prescriptive will (*voluntas approbationis*) God desires actions which are morally good; by his absolute will he permits sin and the corruption of human action. What counts as good action and what counts as evil action depends only on the decision of God.[35]

Conclusion

The most striking feature of the medieval discussions of the problem of the freedom of choice is the number of scholars who supported a moderate

---

32. Gilson 1952, p. 366; Ockham 1483, *In IV Sententiarum*, d. 16, q. 1.
33. Leff 1957, pp. 57–64, 91–7; Michalski 1937, 320–2, 326, 344–5, 350–1.
34. Michalski 1937, 303–97, 345–6.
35. *Ibid.* 307–10, 347–8. A similar set of distinctions was drawn up in Paris by John of Mirecourt; see *ibid.* 275–9, 326–31, 346–7, 352–8.

voluntarism, in contrast to the rationalism of Thomas Aquinas and his followers. It was voluntarism which had far the greater influence on the European mind in the second half of the thirteenth century and in the two succeeding centuries.

33
THOMAS AQUINAS ON
HUMAN ACTION

Philosophical and theological motivations for Aquinas' work

At least two distinct purposes may be discerned in Aquinas' various writings on human action. One is to complete and correct Aristotle's treatment of it in the *Nicomachean Ethics*, to which he of course pays close and respectful attention. A second springs from his primary commitment to theology. Reflecting on what is said in the Scriptures and the writings of the Fathers about such topics as the fall of Adam, sin, conversion, and the operation of grace, theologians produced a body of doctrine about various aspects of human acts. To Aquinas' mind, this teaching settles certain questions authoritatively: as when it declares that voluntary human acts are commanded by their agents freely, and not by necessity. In addition it introduces certain concepts into the theory of action, for example, those of enjoyment and consent. Aquinas undertakes to incorporate these contributions of theology, where sound, into a revised Aristotelian theory.

Aristotelian causal theories

Aristotelian theories of action are causal, and causal in a distinctive way. To do something, to perform an act, is to cause something. And causing something is always to be investigated in terms of a pair of fundamental concepts, *dynamis* and *energeia*, which appear in Thomas' Latin as *potentia* (potency) and *actus* (act). The power or capacity of an object to cause something – whether a change of state, or a persistence in a state – largely determines what that object is. Brute animals are distinguished by their possession of powers of sensation and bodily movement. Human beings are differentiated from brute animals by their further possession of intellectual powers, making it possible for them to cause changes or persistences in the state of things in rationally pursuing ends they have rationally set themselves. So to cause a change or persistence is to perform a human act.

Fundamental distinctions regarding actions

Two distinctions pervade Aquinas' treatise on the nature of human acts (*de conditione humanorum actuum*), his final and most elaborate discussion of human action, which occupies *Summa theologiae* IaIIae, 6–17. The first, drawn in *Summa theologiae* IaIIae, 1, 1, is that between those doings of human beings that are human properly speaking and those that are not. A human act, properly speaking, is an act in which the human agent exercises the distinctively human capacities of reason and will. Accordingly, acts in which those capacities are not exercised, like absent-minded twitches of hand or foot, or strokings of the beard, although acts of a human being (*actus hominis*) are not human acts (*actus humani*). The second is Aquinas' equally sharp distinction between the complete human acts in which the human capacities of will and intellect are exercised, and the exercises of those powers which go to make up complete human acts. A complete human act is a unity in which, by virtue of certain intellectual acts, some possible act is commanded, and by virtue of certain acts of will, the commanded act is performed.[1] Neither an intellectual act, such as thinking that it would be good to have a higher salary, nor an act of will, such as willing to do what needs to be done to get more money, are by themselves considered complete human acts by Aquinas. Yet both may be components in a given person's complete act of working overtime.

Aristotle on voluntariness and choice

According to Aristotle, an act is voluntary if its moving principle is in the agent himself, he being aware of the circumstances of his act and of the objects with which it is concerned (*Nic. Eth.* 1110^{b}32–3; 1111^{a}22–3). Hence brute animals, acting from bodily appetites such as hunger, act voluntarily (1111^{b}8). Human action is distinguished from that of brutes as exemplifying not only voluntariness, but also choice. Choice involves not only will for an end, but also deliberation about how to attain it (1139^{a}31–2). Both call for intellect; for deliberation is an intellectual operation, and will presupposes an intellectual grasp of what is willed. However, since he held that human beings by nature will to live a good life, and that their characters reveal what they take a good life to be, Aristotle was reluctant to acknowledge that a man acting out of character or on impulse genuinely chooses at all (1139^{a}31–4).

Aquinas' modifications of Aristotle

Aquinas rejected this. He retained the structure of Aristotle's analysis of chosen acts; but he insisted that if human acts as such involve choice, then

---

1. '... imperium et actus imperatus sunt unus actus hominis, sicut quoddam totum est unum, sed est secundum partes multa' (*ST*, IaIIae, 17, 4c.). '... nihil prohibet, in his quae sunt multa partibus et unum toto, unum est prius alio; sicut anima quodammodo est prius corpore' (ibid. *ad* 3).

choice cannot be subject to restrictions according to which acts that are out of character cannot be chosen. Aristotle's restricted concept of choice follows from his restricted concept of will. Aquinas therefore proposed a new and less restricted concept of willing an end, which in turn made it possible for him to introduce, as the fundamental explanatory concept in the theory of action, the derivative concept of intention.

Will as rational appetite

In Aquinas' theory, voluntary human acts are identical with human acts involving choice. All such acts are exercises of the same power, the power of will, in defining which Aquinas simply appropriates Aristotle's definition of the power of choice: '"Will"', he writes, "means rational appetite" (IaIIae, 6, 2; cf. *Nic. Eth.* 1139^{b}4). As rational, will is moved to activity by the activity of the related power of intellect; as appetitive, its activities are for the attainment of ends. The power of will, as rational appetite, is directed to the rationally appetible, that is, to the character of good (*ratio boni*), which is intellectually grasped as being common to all things (*bonum in communi*) (IaIIae, 8, 1 and 2; 10, 1 and 2). A particular act in which the power of will is exercised can be directed to an object only inasmuch as it is taken to be good (*sub ratione boni*) (IaIIae, 8, 1c.).

Exercises of an appetitive power, which by its nature has to do with the attainment of an end, necessarily involve two kinds of subordinate acts: acts directed to the end to be attained, and acts directed to the means by which the end is to be attained.

Simple acts of the will

The power of will, according to Aquinas, is exercised in no fewer than three kinds of acts directed towards ends. One, however, is fundamental; and, with unfortunate ambiguity, Aquinas calls it by the same name as the power of will itself, namely, '*voluntas*'. Fortunately, when using this ambiguous word would mislead, he usually has recourse to the less ambiguous phrases '*actus voluntatis*' (act of will), sometimes preceded by the epithet '*simplex*' (simple), and '*motus voluntatis*' (motion of the will) (e.g., IaIIae 8, 2 and 3; 10, 2 and 3). A simple act of will is a 'motion' of an agent inasmuch as he is intellectual (an interior motion, therefore, and not an exterior bodily one) towards the attainment of a particular thing taken to be good as an end.

It is of the first importance to follow Aquinas' example (in IaIIae, 8, 2c.) and to distinguish between what he says about the power of will and what he says of the acts in which that power is exercised. Only of the power of will is the object said to be the character of good (*ratio boni*) (Ia IIae, 8, 2c.). And the sense of saying that is clear: namely, that nothing can be an object of an act of that power except as having that character. Acts of will, accordingly, have as their objects particular ends *sub ratione boni*. By contrast, the traditional interpretation is obscure, according to which Aquinas holds that the first act of will in a complete human act has good *in communi* for its object.[2] What would it be to will something incompatible with good *in communi*? Aquinas insists that the simple acts of the power of will have only ends as their objects, while at the same time arguing that the power of will has as objects means as well as ends 'because the character of good, which is the object of the power of will, is found not only in the end, but also in those things which are for the end' (IaIIae, 8, 2c.). Hence, to foist on him the doctrine that there is a simple act of will having the character of good as its object, with the implication that there are simple acts of will extending to means as well as to ends, would gratuitously make him contradict himself.

Any intellectual act in which something is affirmed to be an attainable good can give rise to a simple act of will directed to attaining it. Aquinas insists that an end willed need not be good as a matter of fact (*in rei veritate*), finding for his departure Aristotelian credentials of a sort in *Physics* II, 195^{a}26 (IaIIae, 8, 1c.). From this, taken together with the theological doctrine that the only good attainable by man that is complete and lacks nothing, namely, the beatific vision, cannot be intellectually grasped by natural means, he further concludes that in this life the will is not moved to any end necessarily (IaIIae, 10, 2). No end any human being can think of by his natural powers can move his will necessarily, because, since no such end is completely good, it is open to him to incline instead to some good he recognises that end to lack (IaIIae 10, 2c.).

Enjoyment and intention

Besides what he called simple acts of will, Aquinas recognises two other kinds of acts of will directed towards ends: enjoyment (*fruitio*) and intention (*intentio*). By the former, he enriches the Aristotelian theory from theological sources, above all from the writings of Augustine, whence are

---

2. By the 'traditional' interpretation, I mean the interpretation that was to be found in most manuals of Thomist philosophy until very recently. The source of many of these treatments appears to be the article 'Acte' in *Dictionnaire de Théologie Catholique*, by A. Gardeil. Compare the scheme presented by Thomas Gilby in *Thomas Aquinas* 1964–76, vol. 17, p. 211.

drawn the proof texts in all four articles of the question *de fruitione* (IaIIae, 11). By the latter, he further develops his revision of Aristotle.

Enjoyment

The Aristotelian characterisation of the will as rational appetite says both less than can be said about why human beings persist in ends despite accumulating evidence of their unsatisfactoriness, and less than theologians have taught about the rewards of persisting in ends that are satisfactory. Augustine had distinguished enjoyment from passive pleasure by maintaining that it is through the will that we enjoy.[3] And he had defined enjoying as 'cleaving with love to something for its own sake'.[4] Since anything simply willed as an end is willed for its own sake, although it may be willed for the sake of some further end as well, it is natural to ask whether every simple act of will is accompanied by an act of enjoyment. Aquinas' answer is implicit. 'Anyone', he declares, 'has love or delight from what he ultimately looks for (*de ultimo exspectato*), which is [his] end' (IaIIae, 11, 1c.). This implies that every simple act of will must have an act of enjoyment as its counterpart.

Why did Aquinas not simply add 'involving cleaving with love' to his account of a simple act of will as an interior motion to something as an end *sub ratione boni*? Two reasons can be found in his text. First, although either one simply wills something as an end or one does not, one enjoys an end more the better it seems, and only the beatific vision completely (IaIIae, 11, 3c.); moreover, one enjoys an end perfectly only when it is possessed, and imperfectly when it is merely intended (IaIIae, 11, 4c.). Enjoyment, in short, has degrees, but simple willing has not. Secondly, with the actual possession of the beatific vision, 'the delighted will comes to rest' (IaIIae, 11, 3c.); but that is when enjoyment is at its height.

Intention

The fundamental theme of an Aristotelian theory of action is that willing an end generates action by way of the agent's deliberation about means (literally, 'those things that are for the end'). Following Nemesius, Aquinas held that means are possible acts by which the end can be attained (IaIIae, 14, 4c.). Unless an appropriate act of deliberation ensues, simple acts of will remain barren. But once an appropriate act of deliberation has disclosed means by which an end willed can be attained, the simple act of willing that

---

3. Augustine, *De trinitate* X, 10 (*PL* 42, col. 981); quoted in *ST*, IaIIae, 11, 3 obj. 3.
4. Augustine, *De doctrina christiana*, I, 4 (*PL* 34, col. 30); quoted in *ST*, IaIIae, 11, 1c.

end generates a further act directed towards it: namely, an act of willing it through the means. Aquinas offers a simple but effective illustration. When we simply will to be healthy, our act is a simple act of will, and no more; but when we will to be healthy as an end to which some possible act is ordered, we perform a further act, an intention (IaIIae, 12, 1 ad 4; cf. 4c.). The deliberation by which an intention is generated can be more or less complete. Aquinas remarks that 'there can be an intention of an end even though the means have not yet been determined' (IaIIae, 12, 4 ad 3). As soon as it is judged that there is a possible act by which an end can be attained, the end may be willed through that possible act. Intentions, in short, may be more or less determinate.

Choice

For reasons which will become plain, Aquinas' treatment of choice largely recapitulates his treatment of intention. He adopted not only Aristotle's view that willing an end gives rise to choice by way of deliberation, but also his conception of acts of deliberation as consisting of analytical questioning (*quaerere et resolvere*), terminating in a judgement, in which the end willed as the effect of the contemplated action is resolved into its simple causes – the means by which it may be attained (IaIIae, 14, 1 and 5; cf. *Nic. Eth.* 1112^{b}12–31).

Complete acts and component acts

A further complication can no longer be put aside. Deliberation is itself often a complete human act; for example, doing a sum in my head, as part of the act of balancing my monthly accounts. Hence many human acts must be complex, in the sense of having other complete human acts as components. Familiar examples given today are repetitious acts, such as driving home a nail by repeated blows with a hammer.[5] But what may be called organised acts, consisting in a number of different complete human acts, the performance of which in a certain temporal order (some or all may be simultaneous) is designed to bring about a certain result, are more common and more important. Making a cake and tying a complicated knot are homely examples.

Deliberation as a component of any complete act

The fact that the act of deliberation which, according to any Aristotelian theory, is a component of any complete human act, may itself be a

---

5. Cf. Goldman 1970, pp. 35–7.

complete human act, raises the spectre that deliberation is a process that must go on *in infinitum*. This would necessarily be the case if *every* act of deliberation were a complete human act. However, Aquinas argues that some are not. It is true that any question may be made an occasion for a complete human act of deliberation. But since human action does occur, there must be simple human acts in which the act of deliberation is not itself a complete human act. This will be so when the agent's end is resolved into means unproblematically, because the resolution is a matter either of the agent's scientific knowledge (*disciplina*) or technical skill (*ars*), or has to do with a trifle in which nothing that might come to mind would seem possibly to be in error (IaIIae, 14, 4 and 6). Thus in making a cake according to a recipe I know by heart, my technical skill enables me to judge how much of a given ingredient it is good to add as soon as the question comes up, without any process of calculation.

Choosing the means

Aquinas points out that the judgement or verdict in which a 'practical syllogism' of deliberation terminates (IaIIae, 13, 1 ad 2) is not apodictic.[6] An agent resolving the attainment of an end into its simple causes will produce a premiss to the effect that it will be attained on a certain condition: say 'If M is adopted, E will be attained.' Quite obviously, from such a premiss, taken together with the judgement, 'E is good to attain', which led to E's attainment being willed, it does not follow that 'M is the suitable means to adopt.' For the conditional premiss does not exclude others: for example, 'If N is adopted instead of M, E will be attained' (IaIIae, 13, 6 ad 2).

As soon as his deliberation has resulted in a judgement that it would be well to adopt some determinate means for the sake of the end willed, it is open to the agent to exercise his will and choose that means – or not to, either abandoning the end willed, or choosing to deliberate further. If he chooses the means indicated by his deliberation, however, is his choice not identical with his intention?

Aquinas leaves no doubt that in certain circumstances it is. In the body of IaIIae, 12, 4 he lays it down that 'to tend towards an end and to tend towards that which is for the end is one and the same motion of the will in subject (*subiecto*)'; and he goes on to say that that same motion of the will, which is one in subject, differs according as we think about it either

6. Anscombe 1965, pp. 152–3.

primarily in terms of the means (choice), or primarily in terms of the end (intention) (IaIIae, 12, 4 ad 3). The reason why Aquinas' treatment of choice largely recapitulates his treatment of intention is now plain: when its object is determinate, an intention is the same act as the corresponding choice.

Just as an agent does not merely tend to his ends, but cleaves to them with love, so having in deliberation arrived at a judgement as to what means to his ends are good, he does not simply tend to those means, but approves and loves them (IaIIae, 15, 3). This Aquinas calls consent (*consensus*), identifying it with what the translators of John Damascene referred to as '*sententia*'. However, unlike enjoyment, which is full only when the end of all human action has been attained, consent is logically prior to choice, and may precede it in time. For consent, unlike choice, is accorded to suitable means to one's ends as soon as they are judged to be such. In most simple human acts, only one means to his end ever comes into the agent's mind, and he consents to it and chooses it together; but, as Aquinas remarks, it may happen that deliberation discloses several suitable means, one of which is judged most suitable, and in such cases, the agent approves and loves all the means judged suitable, while going on to choose the one judged most suitable (IaIIae, 15, 3 ad 3).

Commanded acts and acts of command

Aquinas has now developed his revision of Aristotle's theory of action sufficiently to elucidate his own conception of a complete human act as a unity, among the components of which are a commanded act and an act of command (IaIIae, 17, 4c.). Commanded acts are commanded by the will, but only as a subordinate power (IaIIae, 1, 1 ad 2): ultimately they are commanded by the intellect (IaIIae, 17, 1c.). This follows from his definition of commanding as 'ordering (*ordinare*) somebody to something that is to be done, with a certain intimating motion (*intimativa motione*)' (IaIIae, 17, 2c.). He explains that intimating is primarily expressed by indicative sentences containing gerundives, of the form '*Hoc est tibi faciendum*' (This is to be done by you), and only secondarily by imperatives (IaIIae, 17, 1c.). In a complete human act, a commanded act will be that component which the agent judges is to be made to happen, and which *does* happen as a result of an act of will which he performs in view of that judgement. Taking Aquinas' theory as so far developed, it is natural to identify the act of command (*imperium*) with the judgement that terminates deliberation; and to identify the mediating act of will, as a result of which the commanded act happens, with the act of choice. Aquinas, as we shall see, adds a further act of will (namely, *usus*), and provides it with an appropriate generating intellectual act; but that, I shall argue, is muddled.

Commanded acts, elicited acts, and executive powers

Yet it is essential to Aquinas' theory, as nobody seriously disputes, that in no complete human act can the component commanded act be identical with any of the acts of intellect and will that give rise to it. For every one of those latter acts – judging an end good, willing to attain it, enjoying it, deliberating about what would be the suitable means of attaining it, consenting to such means as there are, and choosing the most suitable – is an immediate exercise of the power of intellect or of will, which excludes any exercise of any subordinate power (IaIIae, 1, 1 ad 2; 6, 4c.). Each of them is *elicited*, not commanded.

What acts, then, *are* commanded? The most obvious complete human acts are bodily, for example, raising one's arm.[7] When an act is a bodily act, the commanded act will be a motion of one's bodily members, for example, one's arm's going up. The occurrence of such a commanded act is always an exercise of what Aquinas calls the agent's executive power with regard to his body, an exercise that is immediately caused by some act of will (IaIIae, 16, 2c.; 17, 9c.). Each human being finds out by experience the range of his executive power with regard to his body (IaIIae, 17, 9 ad 2 and 3). Aquinas expressly declares that both acts of intellect and acts of will can also be commanded, and even, up to a point, acts of sensitive appetite (IaIIae, 17, 5–7).

Why he does so appears most clearly from what he says about commanded acts of intellect. It follows from the nature of elicited acts, as we have seen, that no elicited act of intellect can be commanded: one cannot command dissent from what immediately strikes one as true. But not all acts of intellect are elicited. When human beings ask themselves whether a certain answer to a question is true or false, it often happens that no judgement is immediately elicited. Should their intellectual powers fail them in this way, it is open to them to deliberate whether their ends will be served better by assenting to a given answer, or by dissenting from it. And so, in the absence of an elicited act of assent or dissent, assent and dissent themselves may be commanded (IaIIae, 17, 6).

---

7. Wittgenstein, *Philosophical Investigations* I §621, has made this example the standard one.

The article (IaIIae, 17, 5) in which Aquinas treats of commanded acts of will is perilously succinct. It will be misunderstood if it is forgotten that, when a certain possible act is commanded in an act of intellect and then chosen in an act of will, what is commanded is the possible act that is chosen, and not the act of choosing or willing it. The crucial premiss in Aquinas' demonstration that acts of will are commanded is that a man 'can judge that it is good that [he] will a certain thing' (IaIIae, 17, 5c.). He has not forgotten that what is judged in deliberation is that a certain means is most suitable: his point is that sometimes the means judged most suitable for attaining an end may itself be an act of will. And so the act of choice that ensues, if one does, will be an act of willing that act of will. Although Aquinas gives no examples, they are not far to seek. Resolving to act in a certain way in the future, one of the means by which moral virtues are acquired, is one kind of act of will that can be commanded.

The carrying out or execution of a commanded act, as Aquinas describes it, is a matter of the operation of certain human interior principles, namely, the powers of the soul such as intellect, will, and sensible appetite, their trained dispositions (*habitus*), and the organs or bodily members, each conceived as the seat of powers such as to see, to feel, to move in such and such a way, and the like (IaIIae, 16, 1c.). These principles are also referred to as executive powers (IaIIae, 17, 8c.). They are set in operation by acts of will (IaIIae, 16, 1). Aquinas therefore holds that, in a complete human act, the actual execution of the commanded act is related to a certain elicited act of will – necessarily the last one – as effect to cause. And the causal relation will not be that of an agent to his complete human acts, or to those of their component acts that are elicited, but that of any event that is an effect to any event that is its cause.

The last act of will in a complete act

It remains to determine what is the last act of will in a complete human act: the act of will which causes the operation of the executive powers that constitutes the commanded act. There is an obvious reason for identifying it with the act of choice, and so for identifying the intellectual act of command with the act of judgement that terminates deliberation: namely, that Aquinas himself lays it down that, 'inasmuch as [the power of will] is in the person willing as having a certain proportion or order to that which is willed', the last act of will with respect to the means is choice (IaIIae, 16, 4c.).

Usus

Aquinas' argument for interpolating a further act of will between choice and the commanded act begins with the premiss that, besides the relation which the power of will can have to the willed inasmuch as it is in the person willing as having a certain proportion or order to the willed, there is a second relation which it can have inasmuch as the willed is in the person willing as an end which he really possesses (IaIIae, 16, 4c.). The means, as well as the end, is then declared to be included in this second relation. And finally, it is argued that, since choice is the last act of will in the first relation: '*Usus* belongs to the second relation of the will to the thing willed by which it tends to its bringing about. From which it is manifest that *usus* follows choice, provided that the word "*usus*" is adopted inasmuch as the will uses the executive power, by moving it' (IaIIae, 16, 4c.). This seems to be one of those sheer blunders into which even the greatest philosophers fall. For if the second relation of the will to the willed in fact obtains – namely, the relation it has when the willed is something really possessed – then the executive power by which the willed has been brought about must already have been exercised. Hence if *usus* is an act which belongs to the second relation of the will to the willed, it cannot be directed to the operation of an executive power which *ex hypothesi* has already operated. 'Using' the executive powers can only be an act belonging to the *first* relation of the will to the willed. And Aquinas himself concedes that the last act of will in that first relation is choice. *Usus*, understood as the 'using' of the executive powers, should therefore be identified with choice. And *imperium*, as the act of judgement which gives rise to *usus*, need not be identified with an elicited intellectual act alleged to follow choice (cf. IaIIae, 17, 3 ad 1): it should simply be identified with the judgement with which deliberation terminates.

Shorn of excrescences that contradict his own principles, Aquinas' analysis of the structure of a simple complete human act can be set out in the schematic table below (see Figure 1).

Standard philosophical objections

Aquinas' analysis of human action is rightly held by his admirers to be a major contribution to philosophy. To his immediate successors, the most controversial point in Aquinas' theory of action was the priority it affirms of intellect over will. Freedom of will, according to it, is wholly a matter of the non-necessity of any judgement a man can arrive at by his natural

FIGURE 1

Aquinas' Analysis of a Human Act,
Corrected according to the Present Interpretation

A SIMPLE COMPLETE HUMAN ACT
(e.g. Socrates' raising of his arm)
consists of

I. Acts of intellect   II. Acts of will

A. *with regard to the end*

1. Judging that an attainable end is good (e.g. Socrates' judging that it would be good to attract Plato's attention and that he can).

2. Willing to attain that end (e.g. Socrates' willing to attract Plato's attention).
3. Enjoying that end.
4. Intending that end through suitable means (cf. 7.).

B. *with regard to the means*

5. Deliberating how to attain that end, that is:
(a) asking what within one's power would most suitably cause the attainment of the end willed, and
(b) judging that a certain act (= the commanded act) in one's power would be most suitable (e.g. Socrates' judging that the most suitable means would be his arm's going up.). [Aquinas should have identified this judgement with *imperium*, or command.]

6. Consenting to all the means judged suitable.
7. Choosing the means judged most suitable (e.g. Socrates' choosing that his arm go up.) [This is identical with intending, given that one's intention is fully determinate.]

Elicited acts

III. Act of the executive power caused
by the last elicited act of will

Executed act

8. The commanded act takes place, the relevant executive powers having been set in operation by the act of choice (e.g. Socrates' arm's going up.).

powers as to the goodness of an end or the suitability of a means. Even when will seems to fly in the face of intellect, there is always a (foolish, perhaps vicious) judgement which directs it. Duns Scotus was to develop the doctrine that the source of the will's freedom is internal to it, and not external, as Aquinas holds.[8] To many twentieth-century philosophers, the feature of Aquinas' theory that is most objectionable is his retention of

8. See Bonansea 1965, esp. pp. 97–113.

Aristotle's conception of causation as the exercise of a power or capacity, which allows him to think of human beings themselves, and not only of events occurring within them, as genuine causes of their actions – 'agent causes'.

Familiar uninformed objections

Little has been said of the vulgar objections, or rather slogans, by which the philosophical work of Aquinas and other scholastics is now and then ignorantly dismissed. The commonest, probably, is that Aquinas' theory of action is a 'faculty-psychology' in which human beings are resolved into a collection of faculties or powers, each of which is then treated as a quasi-agent. For convenience, Aquinas often speaks of what a power such as the intellect does or can do. But such statements, if they are indispensable to his theory of action, can readily, if sometimes cumbrously, be reformulated as statements of about what human beings, as possessing that power, do or can do. He himself annihilates the objection that acts of will cannot be commanded because 'the will cannot understand a command' (IaIIae, 17, 5 obj. 2) by pointing out that 'a *man* enjoins an act of will on *himself* inasmuch as *he* understands and wills' (IaIIae, 17, 5 ad 2).

As for the scarcely less common objection that the elicited acts which according to Aquinas are components of even the simplest complete human acts are too numerous to be credible, and correspond to nothing in our experience of our own acts, the reply – made also by action theorists today – must be that the components of simple human acts are ascertained, not by introspecting what happens when we perform them, but by examining various cases in which an act is begun but not completed. We recognise cases in which we or others will to attain an end, and then do not bother to consider means at all; cases in which we or others think about suitable means but fail to settle on any as most suitable; cases in which we or others settle upon some means as most suitable, and then do not choose to adopt it; and finally (as when we or others suffer some unanticipated impairment of our executive powers) cases in which we choose to bring about some act which we think possible, and find that it is beyond our power. It is by reflection on such cases, and not by introspection, that Aquinas constructs his theory (e.g., IaIIae, 12, 2 ad 4; 12, ad 3; 15, 3 ad 3; 16, 4 ad 3; 17, 5 ad 2).

IX

ETHICS

34
THE RECEPTION AND INTERPRETATION OF ARISTOTLE'S *ETHICS*

The first translations

During the Middle Ages[1] the *Nicomachean Ethics* received less attention than Aristotle's writings on natural philosophy and metaphysics, and still less than his logical writings. Although the *Ethics* was never condemned in any form, it was apparently not until the second half of the fourteenth century that it was adopted as a regular textbook in the Arts faculties;[2] and it was only in the fifteenth century, as the number of commentaries shows, that it began to be studied really intensively.

We are not so well informed about this period as we are about the beginnings of philosophical ethics in the Middle Ages. According to the latest historical research,[3] the first translation of the *Nicomachean Ethics* appeared in the twelfth century; but it covered only the second and third books (*ethica vetus*). A second translation, of which only the first book (*ethica nova*) and a few fragments remain, came at the start of the thirteenth century.

The new conception of philosophical ethics

The texts thus made available to Latin readers make two claims for philosophy: (a) happiness and human perfection are a legitimate object of philosophical concern; (b) virtue, or good human character, can be rationally discussed without recourse to theology.

These philosophical claims were not easy to accept. The problem does not lie in the conception of a natural virtue. Such an idea was already present in twelfth-century theology,[4] and so the reception of the Aristotelian concept of virtue was not a revolutionary step. The difficulty lay rather in the assertion that the goal of human life, no less than virtue, was a topic for philosophy. Earlier thinkers had allowed that even pagan

---

1. The best and most informative survey is in Gauthier 1970, pp. 111–46.
2. Heidingsfelder 1921, pp. 55ff.
3. Gauthier 1974, pp. XVI–CLI.
4. Wieland (forthcoming), Ch. 6, 1.

philosophers might deal with the path to the goal, but not with the goal itself, because that was something reserved exclusively for Christian theology.[5] The consequence of their view was plain: in so far as ethics is merely the theory of virtue it is subordinate to theology because the end determines the means to the end. Whether philosophical ethics could hold its own in medieval Christendom against theology would depend on the treatment of happiness.

Determining a role for philosophical ethics

In commentaries written before the whole *Nicomachean Ethics* was translated (*ca.* 1246–7) it is on the whole the theological view which prevails.[6] What is probably the oldest commentary on the *ethica vetus* (Avranches, MS Bibl. munc. 232), sees the epitome of happiness in God; so too do the Paris Commentary on the *ethica nova*[7] and *vetus* (MSS Bibl. nat. lat. 3804 A and 3572) and the commentaries on the *ethica nova* and *vetus* wrongly ascribed to John Peckham,[8] which are the most important of these early texts.

This identification of happiness and God conflicts with the Aristotelian text, which, in criticising Plato's idea of the Good, rejects the notion of a self-subsistent entity constituting happiness. Moreover, happiness for Aristotle is a human achievement rather than a divine gift. So the commentators were at pains to make distinctions to square the traditional Christian view with the new philosophical view.

The basic question is whether there is happiness in this life in addition to the true bliss of everlasting life. According to the commentary on the *ethica nova* and *vetus* perhaps written by Robert Kilwardby, the answer is yes.[9] If so, philosophical ethics has its own field marked out, at least in principle, and is thus guaranteed a certain independence from theology.

Theological misinterpretations

The first commentators on Aristotle's *Ethics* misunderstood important passages of their text in a theological sense. This is strikingly shown by their treatment of prudence.[10] Latin writers at the time of the early commentaries knew only the short passage at the end of the first book where

5. Peter Abelard 1970b, *Dialogus*, p. 137.
6. Wieland (forthcoming), Ch. 5, 3.
7. Gauthier 1975, pp. 71–141.
8. MSS Oxford, Bodl. misc. lat. 71; Florence, Bibl. naz. conv. soppr. G. 4.853. See Spettmann 1923, pp. 221–2.
9. MS Cambridge, Peterhouse 206. See Wieland (forthcoming), Ch. 5, 3e.
10. Gauthier 1963, pp. 129–74.

Aristotle introduces his fundamental distinction between moral and intellectual virtues, mentioning wisdom, insight, and prudence only briefly and without further explication. Thus the Pseudo-Peckham's commentary defines intellectual virtue as knowledge and love of the highest good for its own sake, and sees in prudence the highest of these virtues because prudence originates in intelligent creatures in whom the purest image of the creator appears. This position makes the intellectual virtues into Christian virtues and interprets them as Christian contemplation, which differs from merely theoretical speculation by involving the love of the object of contemplation.

This misinterpretation of the intellectual virtues is easily explained by the fact that these Latin writers knew only the first three books of the *Nicomachean Ethics*. Their lack of the tenth book, in which Aristotle further develops the concept of happiness in its theoretical aspects, was especially important. Even after the translation of the whole of the *Nicomachean Ethics* it was difficult for the Latins to reproduce faithfully the Aristotelian distinction between *theoria* and *praxis*.[11] This is shown, for example, in the work of Roger Bacon, who subordinates metaphysics to ethics and ethics to theology because – like the commentators on the *ethica nova* and *vetus* – he does not see *theoria* as an independent value in Aristotle's sense.

The contribution of Robert Grosseteste

The Latin translation of the *Nicomachean Ethics* which became the standard one throughout the Middle Ages was made about 1246–7 by Robert Grosseteste,[12] who simultaneously published a collection of Greek commentaries in Latin translation.[13] These commentaries were of varied provenance: Eustratius' commentaries on Books I and VI; an anonymous third-century commentary on Books II–V; one by Michael of Ephesus on Books V, IX, and X; an anonymous twelfth-century one on Book VI; and one by Aspasius on Book VIII.

Now the Latins possessed the resources for a better understanding of the *Nicomachean Ethics*, but this did not lead to any substantial improvement of the position of ethics in the context of the philosophical disciplines. In its statute of 1245,[14] the Paris Faculty of Arts devotes the same amount of time

11. Wieland 1974, pp. 147–73.
12. Gauthier 1974, p. CCI.
13. Mercken 1973.
14. *Chartularium Universitatis Parisiensis* (= *CUP*) I, n. 246.

to the *Nicomachean Ethics* as to the *Liber de sex principiis* or Aristotle's *De sensu et sensato* or *De somno et vigilia*.

Albert the Great's commentaries

The first complete Latin commentary on the *Nicomachean Ethics* was compiled by Albert the Great, who made use of a great deal of the material prepared by Grosseteste. While the earlier commentaries originated in the Faculty of Arts, Albert commented on the Aristotelian text as a theologian during his time in Cologne during the years 1248–52. He adopted the same method as his predecessors from the Faculty of Arts: first came the exposition of the text (*expositio litterae*), which followed Aristotle's train of thought step by step, then *quaestiones*, in which the difficulties arising from the text were treated individually.

Some years later (*ca.* 1263–67),[15] Albert wrote a second commentary in the form of a paraphrase of the *Nicomachean Ethics*, as part of his massive project to comment on all the works of Aristotle. Later medieval commentators quoted Albert's two commentaries more than any others, and he thus became the greatest Latin authority in the field of philosophical ethics.[16] One reason for this status is that he gives a clear and distinct exposition of the philosophical point of view. On the question of happiness he stresses human agency: 'Our actions constitute the cause of the happiness of which the Philosopher is speaking here.'[17] On the question of the virtues Albert firmly rejects any reference to theological categories: 'Here we are discussing not theological but natural virtues.'[18] He regards human beings as the immediate and direct cause of happiness in this life, while believing, as a Christian, that God is the first and all-embracing cause here too. He is convinced of the fundamental harmony of the Aristotelian and the Christian positions; and he reads and interprets the *Nicomachean Ethics* in the light of that conviction. When his work is considered as a whole, he is seen to have departed remarkably little from Aristotle.

There is, however, a significant difference between Aristotle and Albert concerning the relation of *theoria* and *praxis*. The Aristotelian conception of ethics as a practical science can easily be misunderstood if ethics is regarded either as strictly theoretical or as immediately practical. The

15. Gauthier 1970, p. 123; n. 123; Dunbabin 1963, pp. 232–50.
16. Grabmann 1936a, pp. 324–412; Gauthier 1947–8, pp. 269ff.
17. Albert *Super Ethica* I, 10, 55: 'operationes nostrae sunt causa felicitatis, de qua hic loquitur Philosophus'.
18. Albert *In Eth.* I, tr. 7, c. 5: 'iam non de theologicis, sed de physicis (scl. virtutibus) disputamus'.

commentators on the *ethica nova* and *vetus*, who as theologians had a low opinion of mere speculation, tended to interpret ethics as an immediately applicable guide to virtuous living;[19] but this is to mistake the philosophical (scientific) character of the discipline. Albert gives a simple-sounding answer to the question: what is the goal of ethics?[20] In its theoretical aspect – as *ethica docens* – ethics is for the sake of knowledge; in its practical aspect – as *ethica utens* – its purpose is 'to make us good'. Albert can thus see ethics as a unified whole; but he fails to distinguish between the rationality of moral action and the philosophical rationality of ethics.

Thomas Aquinas on ethics

Thomas Aquinas is the first to see the point clearly. 'Moral science is indeed for the sake of action, but this action is not an act of science but rather of virtue.'[21] Accordingly philosophical ethics is bound to stand at a distance from the concrete individual action; it is therefore not the immediate cause of moral behaviour. For the rationality of moral action is guaranteed not by science, but by prudence, the virtue which recognises, judges, and prescribes what is actually to be done. Prudence mediates between the general rules and concrete individual actions. This is possible because it is both the perfection of reason and immediately linked to desire.[22] Thus according to Thomas prudence is no less a moral than an intellectual virtue.[23] Prudence does indeed depend on the moral virtues, but the dependence is mutual, not one-sided. The moral virtues cannot exist without prudence, and prudence cannot exist without the moral virtues.

As is well known, it is in the second part of the *Summa theologiae* that Thomas develops his moral theory. The doctrine is unambiguously theological but philosophy is not discarded; on the contrary, in the field of ethics philosophical thought is quite clearly determinative. Thomas had already become acquainted with the *Nicomachean Ethics* during his studies in Cologne (1248–52); he heard his teacher Albert lecture learnedly on the text, and it was he who edited the text of Albert's lectures. No doubt this fostered his obvious natural interest in questions of ethics.

19. Wieland (forthcoming) Ch. 4, 5b.
20. Albert *Super Ethica*, Prologus, 5: 'Dupliciter potest considerari scientia ista: secundum quod est docens, et sic finis est scire; vel secundum quod est utens, et sic finis est, ut boni fiamus.'
21. Aquinas 1948c, *In librum Boethii De trinitate* 5, 1 *ad* 3: 'Scientia vero moralis, quamvis sit propter operationem, tamen illa operatio non est actus scientiae, sed magis virtutis.'
22. Kluxen 1964, pp. 30–40.
23. Aquinas ST, IIaIIae, 47, 4: 'prudentia non solum habet rationem virtutis quam habent aliae virtutes intellectuales, sed etiam habet rationem virtutis quam habent virtutes morales, quibus etiam connumeratur'.

In 1271−2 he himself wrote a commentary on the *Nicomachean Ethics*. He based it on a revised but still imperfect text of Grosseteste's translation. (These is no evidence for a revision of the translation by William of Moerbeke, comissioned by Thomas himself.)[24] Thomas never, or hardly ever, makes explicit use of Albert's Cologne lectures, but many passages show that the influence of his teacher is still strong. The number of mistakes Thomas makes in quoting or paraphrasing Albert show that he was not consulting Albert's lectures as he wrote.[25] Methodologically, Thomas' commentary belongs with the earlier commentaries of the Faculty of Arts; the style of textual explication (*expositio litterae*) is substantially the same, but the usual *quaestiones* are missing. The commentary is based not on actual lectures, but is the result of Thomas' private study of the *Ethics*; it seems to have served as a preparation for the substantive moral theory of his *Summa theologiae*.

Thomas' theological interest is shown in the fact that he draws the boundaries of philosophical ethics more sharply than his predecessors and his teacher. Thus, for example, he thinks that Aristotle had consciously restricted himself to imperfect happiness, because perfect happiness is incompatible with 'mortal human life'.[26] This restriction of the competence of philosophers does not imply a low estimation of philosophy or the ethics. On the contrary, it seems that Thomas was the first of the Latin masters to develop a clear awareness of the distinctiveness of a practical science, because of his correspondingly clear grasp of the Aristotelian concept of *theoria*. From this point of view one can say that medieval philosophical ethics came to be an independent discipline only when metaphysics was firmly established as the basic theoretical science.

The commentaries of the radical Aristotelians of the thirteenth century

As we have seen, the first commentaries on the *Nicomachean Ethics* after a complete translation became available were written by theologians anxious to avoid any flat contradiction between Aristotelian philosophy and Christian doctrine. But at Paris ethical questions continued to be treated in the Arts Faculty also, and there sometimes without consideration of the Christian tradition. The amount of literary evidence before 1277 is indeed not very great − it includes the *Quaestiones morales* and fragments of the

24. Gauthier 1970, pp. 125−31.
25. Gauthier 1969, pp. 254*−57*.
26. Aquinas 1969, *Sententia libri Ethicorum* X 13: 'in hac vita non ponit perfectam felicitatem, sed talem qualis potest competere humanae et mortali vitae'.

Liber de felicitate of Siger of Brabant[27] and the *De summo bono* of Boethius of Dacia – but it is enough to show, on the question of happiness if on no others, a strikingly self-confident philosophy which sets itself on a par with theology or even above it.

The philosophical life is not just one way of life amongst others, but is the absolute standard of human living. 'Whoever does not lead this life does not lead the right life.'[28] Thus, the happiness of political life, which had been given an independent significance by Aristotle, is eliminated, or made merely relative. This doctrine involves an exaggerated evaluation of the theoretical life – something as far removed from Aristotle as was the interpretation of happiness as Christian contemplation in the commentaries on the *ethica nova*.

The self-affirmation of the philosophers led to a strong theological reaction. The question of the *ordo vivendi* is one of the topics of Bonaventure's conflict with contemporary Aristotelians.[29]

On 7 March 1277 Stephen Tempier, the bishop of Paris, condemned 219 theses.[30] These included propositions which corresponded to the manifestoes of contemporary Aristotelians: 'No station in life is to be preferred to the study of philosophy';[31] 'Philosophers alone are the wise ones of the world.'[32] Some propositions are concerned with happiness, for example: 'God cannot infuse happiness directly';[33] 'Happiness is to be had in this life and not in another'.[34] Other propositions concern the nature of virtue: 'The only good which can be achieved by men consists in the intellectual virtues";[35] 'No virtues are possible other than those which are acquired or innate';[36] continence and humility are not to be classified as virtues.[37]

Wherever these theses may have come from, the commentaries of the thirteenth century so far known can hardly be the immediate source. For both the commentators on the *ethica nova* and *vetus* and the theologians Albert and Thomas adhere so closely to Christian doctrine that they cannot

---

27. These fragments survive in Agostino Nifo. See Nardi 1945, pp. 24–9 and 36–8.
28. Boethius of Dacia 1936, *De summo bono*, p. 377: 'haec est vita philosophi, quam quicumque non habuerit non habet rectam vitam'.
29. Bonaventure, *Coll. in Hexaemeron*, VIII, 16.
30. *CUP* I, n. 473.
31. *CUP* I, n. 473, Sent. 40: 'quod non est excellentior status quam vacare philosophiae'.
32. Sent. 154: 'quod sapientes mundi sunt philosophi tantum'.
33. Sent. 22: 'quod felicitas non potest a Deo immitti immediate'.
34. Sent. 176: 'quod felicitas habetur in ista vita et non in alia'.
35. Sent. 144: 'quod omne bonum, quod homini possibile est, consistit in virtutibus intellectualibus'.
36. Sent. 177: 'quod non sunt possibiles aliae virtutes, nisi acquisitae vel innatae'.
37. Sent. 168 and 171.

be the authors of these obviously anti-Christian propositions. The other surviving commentaries[38] must probably be dated after 1277; they are in any case far from unambiguous on these topics.

In the Paris MS Bibl. nat. lat. 14698, there is an incomplete commentary on the *Nicomachean Ethics*; it includes *quaestiones* on Books I–V. Its author was perhaps James of Douai, a master in the Paris Faculty of Arts who appears in a list of the Faculty in 1275. The commentary may have been written shortly after 1277; that would explain the commentator's reticence on the question of happiness. He conspicuously avoids positions which conflict with Christian doctrine, as for example the thesis: 'God cannot infuse happiness directly.' On this point as on others he follows the doctrine developed by Albert the Great.[39] Nonetheless, the commentator, following Aristotle but in conflict with Christian doctrine, sees poverty as a hindrance for a virtuous life; moreover, he regards philosophical errors as basically useful because they promote rational discussion. The author of the commentary, like Boethius of Dacia, also believes that philosophers spontaneously live a life of virtue, because the pleasure of philosophical contemplation far outweighs sensual pleasures;[40] but here he misinterprets Aristotle, who does not derive the moral virtues from the theoretical life.[41]

The commentary ascribed to Peter of Auvergne (Leipzig MS Univ. lat. 1386) comes from the same time and the same milieu; there is an unmistakable affinity between the two texts. Only the *quaestiones* on the first two books have survived. As in his other commentaries, Peter interprets the Aristotelian doctrine here in such a way as to avoid any contradiction between philosophy and theology. In doing so he frequently follows the teaching of Thomas Aquinas, even if he does not always understand it correctly.[42]

The Erlangen commentary (MS Univ. 213) is rather different. It does not hesitate to make clear the contradiction between philosophy and theology and to take up the philosophical side of the argument.[43] This is shown above all in the treatment of happiness. Here questions are discussed which have hardly anything to do with Aristotle, for example the problem whether and how God gives happiness. For Aristotle this is not a topic for ethics; but in this commentary the question is given serious philosophical

38. Grabmann 1931, pp. 30–60; Gauthier 1947–8, pp. 197–336; Hissette 1976, pp. 79–83.
39. Gauthier 1947–8, pp. 269ff.
40. F. 130^{ra–b}; Gauthier 1947–8, pp. 226ff.
41. X, 8; 1178^{b}5ff.
42. Gauthier 1964, pp. 233–60.
43. Grabmann 1931, p. 54.

discussion, despite its being of theological origin. In the opinion of the commentator, God cannot infuse happiness directly, because as the absolutely unmoved principle he has a single and eternal effect – namely, the first Intelligence – from which other effects proceed in a hierarchy of emanations producing multiplicity and variety in the world. Happiness, as something newly brought about in individual cases, belongs to the world of multiplicity and is derivable from God only by means of this series of intermediate steps. This neoplatonic thought, stemming from the *Liber de causis* and Avicenna, abolishes God's freedom, and the commentator is aware that such a view contradicts the faith. Still, like most of these commentators, he proceeds on the methodological principle that every practitioner of a scientific discipline must stay within the boundaries set by his principles.[44] Accordingly, theology cannot assume the function of a regulative, much less a constitutive, principle in philosophy. In spite of this clear distinction between philosophy and theology, the author often alludes to Thomas Aquinas, and indeed not just to his *Ethics* commentary, but also to the *Summa theologiae*.

Related to the Erlangen commentary is that of Giles of Orleans (Paris MS Bibl. nat. lat. 16089), another master in the Faculty of Arts at Paris. Both commentaries are probably to be dated after 1286. Giles is an exponent of the philosophical viewpoint and does not take Christian doctrine into consideration. He comes to the same conclusions as the Erlangen commentator. (The anonymous *Ethics* commentary from Erfurt (MS Amplon. F. 13) is a member of this same group.)

The Vatican commentary (MSS Vat. lat. 832 and Vat. lat. 2172), possibly by Radulphus Brito, follows substantially the same lines of thought as the commentaries so far discussed.[45] One argument of this commentator deserves special mention because it rejects Aquinas' theological answer to the question whether earthly happiness is possible. Thomas distinguishes perfect happiness, which consists in the immediate contemplation of the nature of God, from the imperfect happiness of this life represented by the Aristotelian conception. It is obvious that this distinction is made from a theological point of view. Against this the commentator defends the philosophical standpoint: the happiness of this life deserves to be called perfect for it corresponds perfectly to what is possible for human nature

---

44. The paradigmatic formulation of this principle is by Boethius of Dacia, e.g., *De aeternitate mundi*, p. 347: 'Nullus artifex potest aliquid causare, concedere vel negare nisi ex principiis sui scientiae.'
45. Gauthier 1947–53, pp. 75–85.

under the conditions of this life, even though theologically, earthly happiness can rightly be called imperfect.[46]

In the *Ethics* commentaries of the late thirteenth century, the *quaestio*-form becomes predominant. This shows that the original Aristotelian problems, while not actually abandoned, were increasingly overshadowed by topical issues of the time. The *reception* of Aristotle is now complete, and internal scholastic discussion more and more takes its place.

The commentaries of the fourteenth and fifteenth centuries

We are far less well-informed about the development of philosophical ethics and the corresponding commentaries in the fourteenth and fifteenth centuries than in the preceding period. Nonetheless, ethics seems to have aroused increasing interest. Thus in 1335 the study of the *Nicomachean Ethics* became a requirement for the Dominicans of Provence.[47] In 1366 the Faculty of Arts in Paris made it an absolute requirement for the M.A. degree that every candidate must have attended lectures on the *Ethics*.[48] Towards the end of the century (1392) a *lector Ethicorum*[49] is mentioned in Paris. But the two most significant and influential thinkers of the time, John Duns Scotus and William Ockham, did not compose commentaries on the *Nicomachean Ethics*.

All the same, the number of theologians commenting on the *Ethics* increased. These include[50] the Augustinian Henry of Friemar, whose commentary comes from the first decade of the fourteenth century; the Carmelite Guy Terrena who wrote about 1313; the Franciscans Gerard of Odo (commentary before 1329) and Peter Coruheda; the Dominicans Conrad of Ascoli and Guy of Rimini, who discuss Thomas' commentary rather than the *Nicomachean Ethics* itself. (Richard Kilvington's *Quaestiones* is an independent elementary treatment of individual problems of ethics rather than a real commentary.) Despite this theological interest in philosophical ethics, there remain conflicts in the fourteenth century though they are no longer reflected in the form of binding condemnations. Thus the Augustinian Ugolino of Orvieto, like Bonaventure in the thirteenth century, regarded ethics as superfluous and largely misleading.[51]

---

46. MS Vat. lat. 832, f. 9rb (2172, f. 12va): 'sed dico, quod in hac vita aliquis homo potest esse felix felicitate humana, perfecta etiam, secundum quod est possibile in hac vita'. Gauthier 1947–8, p. 279.
47. Gauthier 1970, p. 135.
48. *CUP* III, n. 1319.
49. *Auctuarium Chartularii Universitatis Parisiensis* I, 667.
50. Gauthier 1970, pp. 134–6; cf. Gerard of Odo 1482.
51. *Sent.* Prologus, qu. 4, art. 1.

Walter Burley's commentary

More influential than the theological commentaries mentioned is the commentary on the *Nicomachean Ethics* composed between 1333 and 1345 by Walter Burley[52] who according to his own statements had already written a more extensive but now lost commentary on the first six books. Burley very often quotes the comments (*notulae*) made by Robert Grosseteste on his Latin translation. He also often cites Eustratius, Averroes, and Albert the Great; despite clear dependence on Aquinas he mentions his name remarkably rarely.

Albert of Saxony's commentary and Ockham's influence

The *Ethics* commentary of Albert of Saxony[53] is evidence of Burley's influence, sometimes following him word for word. It is remarkable that Albert, a follower of Ockham, should in ethics follow the lead of a declared opponent of Ockham. This suggests the question whether *any* influence of Ockham's thought is discernible in the *Ethics* commentaries. Such an influence would be expected in the case of John Buridan, whose commentary was more popular than any other among the adherents of nominalism.[54] Ockham believed that human action is good if it follows God's commands: for which there is no other ground than the will of God, itself limited only by the principle of non-contradiction. If this is taken as the foundation of a nominalist ethics, the result would be completely incompatible with the ethics of Aristotle. On the other hand, Ockham regarded what we would call meta-ethics as one of the most secure sciences because it contains many self-evident principles, as, for example, that the will must agree with right reason.[55]

John Buridan's commentary

There is no trace in Buridan's commentary of a voluntaristic conception which stresses the absolute freedom and omnipotence of God and restricts morality to obligations in the face of merely arbitrary commands. In his opinion Ockham's view of God's *potentia absoluta* is no part of philosophy.[56] One might perhaps think that Buridan's ethics operates on the plane of the order prescribed by God, the order of the *potentia ordinata*; but

52. Walter Burley 1481, 1500, 1521.
53. Heidingsfelder 1921.
54. John Buridan 1513; see also Walsh 1966, p. 4.
55. William Ockham 1491, II, 14.
56. John Buridan 1513, X, qu. 5, f. 213[rb].

in this commentary there is no room for a concept of the type of obligation which would follow from such an ordering. And this conception of earthly good as being similar to and part of the supreme good[57] cannot be interpreted as the result of a voluntary decision of God. Altogether Buridan's commentary on the *Nicomachean Ethics*, at least so far as concerns *praxis*, seems to be anything but nominalistic, even though on other issues it takes a thoroughly Ockhamist stand – e.g., the rejection of realist doctrines of universals and of the Scotist *distinctio formalis*.

The question of the nominalist character of this commentary needs further examination, but one thing is clear: for Buridan philosophical ethics is a practical science. It is practical in a sense stronger than that upheld by Aristotle and Thomas Aquinas, who regarded ethics as a science which does not immediately determine human action. For them, that is rather the task of prudence, which is clearly distinguished from science. In contrast to this Buridan clearly emphasises the immediate practical character of ethics as productive of goodness; he goes so far as to identify prudence with knowledge of ethics.[58] Because of the immediately practical task of ethics Buridan believed that a special moral logic was required, a logic operative in poetry and rhetoric and appealing not to abstract reason but to human beings determined by their passions.[59] This may explain, too, why Buridan quotes Seneca so strikingly often; perhaps his *Epistolae ad Lucilium* gave support to this interpretation of the task of philosophical ethics.

Scholastic commentaries after Buridan

The influence of Buridan extended well beyond Paris. Prague, especially, where the *Quaestiones* were presented in shortened form,[60] became a new centre of Buridanism. There ethics apparently took its place amongst the regular lectures right from the beginning; it was accorded as much time in the curriculum as physics.[61]

One commentary which may derive from Buridan's is that of Henry Totting of Oyta.[62] Apart from this there is a series of mostly anonymous

57. John Buridan 1513, I, qu. 5, f. 6ra: '... quodlibet aliquid sibi adipiscitur boni proprii; per quod bonum, inquantum est quaedam participata similitudo primi boni, ipsum refertur ad primum et finale bonum'.
58. John Buridan 1513, VI, qu. 17, f. 131va: 'videtur mihi, quod habitus acquisitus ex doctrina librorum legum, decretorum et universaliter librorum moralium pertinet ad prudentiam'. Korolec 1975, pp. 56ff.
59. John Buridan 1513, Prooemium, f. 2rb.
60. Korolec 1974a, p. 198.
61. Heidingsfelder 1921, p. 56.
62. Lang 1937, p. 133.

editions and abridgements of the Buridan commentary dating from the fourteenth and fifteenth centuries.[63] Textbooks in the form of abridgements are characteristic of the treatment of ethics at the universities of central Europe, including Cracow, where Buridan's influence extended beyond the middle of the fifteenth century.[64] Probably the most significant Cracow commentary is that of Paul of Worczyn. The Cracow commentaries are noticeable for restricting themselves to the first four or five books of the *Nicomachean Ethics* thus omitting consideration of the intellectual virtues and the theoretical life.

One indication of the ever-increasing interest in ethics is the translation of the *Nicomachean Ethics* into French done by Nicole Oresme in 1370 at the command of King Charles V. Oresme used the Latin text of Robert Grosseteste and added short comments mainly derivative from the commentary of Thomas Aquinas.[65]

In the fifteenth century it seems to be mainly the universities of central Europe where ethics is treated in a comprehensive way. Many commentaries come from masters of the University of Vienna,[66] such as Thomas Eberdorfer of Haselbach, Urban of Melk, Thomas of Wuldersdorf, Andreas of Schärding, who also expounds Buridan's commentary, and Andreas Wall of Walzheim, who refers to the Viennese custom of using only the first five books of the *Nicomachean Ethics* as the basis of a disputation, which explains why many of these commentaries cover only five books, as in Cracow.

The commentary of John Versor of Paris was reprinted several times; it deals only with the first six books.[67] Another commentary on the *Ethics* was written by Paul of Venice; he does not claim originality, but follows the received commentators.

Alongside these works composed by philosophers, the fifteenth century also offered theological commentaries on the *Nicomachean Ethics*. It is especially interesting that we now find commentaries which clearly appeal to Duns Scotus as their authority. Nicholas of Orbelles wrote a three-part commentary on the whole philosophy of Aristotle, the third part of which, concerning practical philosophy, is essentially a commentary on the *Nicomachean Ethics*.[68] The Scotist Peter Tartaretus wrote *quaestiones* on the

63. Korolec 1974a, pp. 198–202.
64. Korolec 1974a, pp. 202–8.
65. Gauthier 1970, p. 138.
66. Gauthier 1970, pp. 139ff.
67. First edition Cologne 1491; Cologne 1495 (reprint, Frankfurt 1966).
68. Basel 1494, 2 vols; cf. Gauthier 1970, p. 142, n. 169.

first six books of the *Ethics* which were reprinted several times.[69] The Franciscan Peter of Castrovol is one of the first to base his commentary on Aretino's new translation of the *Nicomachean Ethics*; in his comments he remains true to the scholastic method.

In the course of the fourteenth and fifteenth centuries philosophical and theological schools gained in strength and significance, and disputes broke out between the *via antiqua* and the *via moderna*, but ethics remained comparatively free from controversy. The reason for this is still unclear.

Humanist translations, editions, and interpretations

The fourteenth century in Italy saw the development of *studia humanitatis*, governed not by the theoretical interests of scholasticism, but by primarily educational considerations. Grammar, rhetoric, poetics, history, and ethics are the topics of humanistic study.[70] Thus ethics is given a dominant place amongst the disciplines and treated as primarily practical, not theoretical. Despite the change, Aristotle remains among the preferred authors – alongside Cicero and Seneca. He is no longer read as a witness to the truth, however, but as an ancient author who writes in a particular historical context.

This explains the fact that the main contribution of the humanists to the study of Aristotle consists of new translations. In 1416–17 Leonardo Bruni, called Aretino, completed his translation of the *Nicomachean Ethics*; it is hardly more than a revision of the Grosseteste translation.[71] Aretino's project gave rise to a controversy in which defenders of the old translation espoused the ideal of philosophical truth against elegance of style;[72] but the controversy did not prevent the translation from being a great success. Another widely-read translation was that of John Argyropoulos (1457). Towards the end of the fifteenth century the first editions of the Greek text appeared.

On the basis of the new translations there soon emerged new interpretations. While Aretino's *Isagogicon moralis philosophiae* gave only a short introduction to the *Ethics*, Niccolo of Foligno wrote a commentary on the basis of Aretino's translation. Donato Acciaiuoli used the Argyropoulos version for his *Expositio super librum Ethicorum Aristotelis*. The commentaries of Ermelao Barbaro and of Agostino Nifo are well known. The last

---

69. First edition 1497; further editions Venice 1503, 1513, 1571, 1621.
70. Cf. Kristeller 1961b, pp. 289–335.
71. Gauthier 1970, pp. 147ff.
72. Grabmann 1926, pp. 440–8.

of this line of humanist introductions and commentaries on the *Nicomachean Ethics* is that of Faber Stapulensis.

Philip Melanchthon

Martin Luther's attack on scholasticism and its philosopher Aristotle was much sharper than that of the humanists. It is due to the work of Philip Melanchton that the study of Aristotle and above all of the *Ethics* was revived for two further centuries in the schools and universities of Germany. He was guided less by his humanist interests than by the need to delimit the new faith in the face of fanaticism, and the realisation that the gospel contains no teaching about political life.

Melanchthon wrote on the *Nicomachean Ethics* on several occasions. In 1529 he published a commentary on the first and second books, in 1532 he extended it to Books III and V. In 1538 he composed the *Philosophiae moralis epitome* and in 1550 the *Ethicae doctrinae elementa*, written completely in the spirit of Aristotelian ethics. Unlike Aristotle, however, he made a sharp separation between the political – social and the individual aspects of human action.

According to Melanchthon, ethics is 'that part of divine law which prescribes external actions'.[73] Thus it is confined to the habits and customs of civil life. Consequently, the Aristotelian distinction between ethics and politics becomes meaningless: ethics is in reality politics.[74] Accordingly it primarily concerns the lawyers and the theologians who deal with political institutions. Ethics does not deal with the inner relation of man to God, which eludes reason and philosophy. Consistently with this interpretation of ethics, Melanchthon commented only on Books I–III and V of the *Nicomachean Ethics*, that is, on the texts which treat of civil happiness, the basic principles of the ethical virtues, and justice. It was no accident that politics was studied in the Protestant universities to a greater extent than elsewhere.[75]

Even independently of Melanchthon's efforts the study of the *Ethics* was very much on the increase in the middle of the sixteenth century. New Latin and vernacular translations appeared and the number of commen-

---

73. *Philosophiae moralis epitome* 1850, p. 21: 'Philosophia moralis est pars illa legis divinae, quae de externis actionibus praecipit.'
74. *In primum librum Ethicorum Aristotelis enarratio*, cap. I, 1850, p. 285: 'Aristoteles hoc loco admonet hanc ipsam ethicen vere esse eam politicam seu practicam, quae principaliter privatos mores et publica officia regit.'
75. Maier 1966, pp. 59–116.

taries further increased. The influence of Aristotelian ethics in the schools and universities of the sixteenth and seventeenth centuries may well have been greater than it had ever been in the Middle Ages; but philosophical ethics itself underwent its new development outside the universities, in an atmosphere of indifference or even open hostility to Aristotle.

35

HAPPINESS: THE PERFECTION
OF MAN

The Aristotelian concept of happiness and the Christian tradition

The medieval discussion of happiness both before and after the reception of Aristotle is governed by two basic thoughts: there is no happiness in this world because 'all men, so long as they are mortal, are also necessarily wretched';[1] true happiness is to be found only in the enjoyment of the contemplation of God (*frui Deo*) in the world to come. Thus the concept of happiness involves an element that transcends human capacities. But the Aristotelian and Christian conceptions also understand happiness as the perfection of human nature, the actualisation of the possibilities inherent in man. This rules out all definitions of happiness in terms of something like worldly wealth, which is external to human nature, or like the satisfaction of sensual desire, which is not specific to human nature. For Aristotle as for others the essence of happiness is to be found in perfection. It is in that spirit, for instance, that Anselm regards the contemplation of God as the perfection of human rationality, because without this form of happiness man would be rational to no purpose.[2]

The difference between the Christian and the philosophical conception is particularly clear in the *Dialogus inter philosophum, Iudaeum, et Christianum* of Peter Abelard. While the philosophers speak only of ethics, aiming primarily for the way to the highest good, and accordingly deal mainly with the virtues, Christians take the goal itself as their starting point. The best the philosophers can offer as the highest human perfection is a state in which sin and suffering are *de facto* absent, not one in which they are necessarily eliminated. But what is wanted is 'a life quite free of sin', where 'not only is there no sin, but there can be no sin'.[3] Such a life cannot

1. Augustine, *De civitate Dei*, IX, 15: 'omnes homines, quamdiu mortales sunt, etiam miseri sint necesse est'.
2. Anselm, *Cur Deus homo*, II, 1.
3. Abelard 1970b, p. 103: 'ut eam ... meliorem esse vitam intelligas, quam et ab istis malis omnino constat esse immunem et in tantum a peccato prorsus remotam, ut non solum ibi non peccetur, sed nec peccari possit'.

be grasped by merely philosophical means. The adequate description of happiness as the contemplation of God can be given only by a Christian who realises that there can be no happiness in this life.

Given such a background, there were bound to be difficulties in assimilating the Aristotelian concept of happiness. Moreover, the Boethian concept of happiness, which was generally accepted, is not compatible with Aristotle's; for Boethius, too, regards the perfecting of man in this life as impossible. The multiplicity and fragility of earthly things admits of no perfect condition; there is happiness only in another world, in which the multiplicity is made one and the fragility is exchanged for permanence.[4]

Compared with this Christian Platonist interpretation of happiness, the Aristotelian conception makes a far more modest claim. It is not measured in terms of an absolute ideal of perfection, but restricts itself to the humanly possible. Happiness is accordingly a human good: the highest of human goals to be sure, and one which is sought for its own sake, but one that man can attain by his own actions.

Medieval thinkers had no difficulty in accepting the Aristotelian analysis of human action and its results; like Aristotle they assume that the ultimate goal of action is happiness. The problem is whether human action suffices to attain this ultimate goal; whether the highest human perfection is to be understood as a gift of God or as an achievement of man. Aristotle's position is clear: happiness is an achievement of man in which an absolute supreme Good plays no part, because such a Good 'is not a good humanly realisable or attainable; but that is the kind of good we are looking for'.[5] According to the Christian view, God alone is the source of true perfection; human achievement cannot be compared on the same scale.

A further difficulty is presented by the distinction Aristotle makes between kinds of happiness. On the one hand there is social or political happiness, which consists in the exercise of the moral virtues and characterises the good life of the free citizen. Contrasted with this there is the theoretical life, which consists in pure contemplation of ultimate grounds and causes. This way of life is superior to social happiness because it is more stable, pleasant, and self-sufficient; it presupposes leisure and stands out as the higher form of happiness. Aristotle does not reduce the two forms of happiness to each other: a philosopher leading a theoretical life has no

4. Boethius, *Consolatio*, III, pr. 9 and 10.
5. I, 6; 1096^b34.

obligation to lead a political one, even though he 'is a man and lives in a community'.[6]

How would Aristotle's distinction be justified in a medieval context? Aristotle himself recognises, simply as a practical matter, that there is a plurality of forms of life; he does not need to justify this plurality. However, as soon as one regards God as the one final goal, it is not easy to see why there should be various forms of human perfection.

The Aristotelian conception of happiness and the relation of man to God

The first commentators on the *Nicomachean Ethics*[7] found Aristotle's conception of happiness particularly difficult: not only were they influenced by the theological doctrine that God is the quintessence of happiness, but until about 1250 they had access to only the first three books of the *Ethics*, and so remained unaware of the doctrine of the theoretical life, which Aristotle develops in the tenth book. Hence a number of important questions arose: (a) What is the relation between the absolute perfection of the one God in whom true happiness consists and the imperfections of the many individual men whose happiness it is? (b) How is man to be united to God and thus made happy? (c) What sort of happiness is Aristotle talking about in the *Nicomachean Ethics*? (I will consider each of these questions in turn.)

God and human happiness

Theologians had long distinguished between uncreated happiness, which is identical with God, and created happiness, which is the individual perfection of man.[8] The first philosophers who attempted to deal with the *Ethics* made use of this distinction. A collection of *quaestiones* stemming from the Paris Faculty of Arts, for example, asks whether there is one single happiness in which all (or many) participate, and gives the answer: 'Happiness is a single common good, which is caused in order that many may share in it as one.'[9] How is this proposition to be understood? God cannot be this 'one single common good', because it is created (caused); equally it cannot be

---

6. X, 8; 1178^{b}5–8.
7. Wieland (forthcoming), chap. 5, 3.
8. William of Auxerre 1500, *Summa aurea*, III, tr. 20, f. 195ra: 'Tamen dicimus quod, cum dicitur: Deus diligitur quia bonus, haec dictio "bonus" praeter divinam essentiam, quam signat, connotat aliquid creatum, scilicet suavitatem vel dilectionem vel beatitudinem creatam, quae est finis quo quiescitur in Deo; Deus autem est finis in quo quiescitur.'
9. MS Ripoll 109 (Archivo de la Corona de Aragon), f. 136rb: 'felicitas est enim unum commune bonum causatum, ut a pluribus participetur una'.

the individual actuality of happiness, because there are as many actualities as there are persons who are happy as happy subjects.

The anonymous commentary of Naples gives an explanation: happiness is numerically one but at the same time general (*communis*), 'because everything tends towards it'.[10] This thought has nothing to do with Aristotelian ethics, which regards happiness not as a numerical but as a specific unity: men are happy through virtuous activity and not through participation in an hypostasised form of happiness. The commentator apparently sees the problem in a neoplatonic context: something is required to mediate between the absolute One and the multiplicity of men, and this is created happiness.

The Pseudo-Peckham's commentary tries to solve the problem without the neoplatonic metaphysics. Two aspects of created happiness can be distinguished: in relation to individual subjects happiness is manifold, in relation to the cause there is just one happiness.[11] Given such an answer, it is not clear whether the category of created happiness is necessary at all.

Human happiness as the union of man with God

While the concept of created happiness as a hypostasis mediating between God and man is completely foreign to Aristotle, there is nothing *prima facie* unaristotelian about the general conviction of the early commentators that contemplation is the activity in which individual happiness consists: 'the means by which happiness (= God) is united with us'.[12] Because Aristotle himself regards *theoria* as the highest form of human perfection, the medieval authors seem to be in general agreement with him here; but the appearance is deceptive.

The concept of contemplation cannot be properly understood in terms of knowledge alone; for 'mere knowledge' (*simplex notitia*) has no essential emotional component, while contemplation is incomplete without loving (*notitia amantis*).[13] Thus it is to practical reason that the Paris commentary ascribes the activity in which contemplation essentially consists: affective

---

10. MS Naples, Bibl. naz. VIII G 8, f. 9rb: 'necque dico, quod sit communis [scl. felicitas] sicut universale, sed est unum et idem numero sicut commune, quia omnia tendunt ad ipsum'.
11. MS Oxford, Bodl. misc. lat. 71, f. 18va: 'similiter et de beatitudine causata: ipsa enim considerata in sua causa una est; ipsa vero considerata in recipientibus multae est'.
12. Cf. the anonymous Commentary on the *ethica nova*, Gauthier (ed.) 1975, p. 115: 'virtus secundum quam attenditur vita contemplativa est medium quo nobis unitur felicitas'.
13. Robert Kilwardby 1935, *De natura theologiae*, p. 31: 'est scientia notitiae simplicis tantum, quae radicatur in consensu aspectus nudi ad ratiocinationem aliquam vel visionem; et est scientia notitiae amantis, quae radicatur in consensu affectus per amorem rectum'.

knowledge.[14] Knowledge finds its perfection and specific form in love. Aristotle indeed recognises pleasure as part of the happiness associated with contemplation; but this is an accompaniment of theoretical activity, not joy in the object of contemplation, not an element of the essential nature of happiness.

Early medieval views of the Aristotelian notion of happiness

What of the social happiness which Aristotle describes in the first book? How can this concept be reconciled with traditional Christian categories? There is nothing to suggest that Aristotle is speaking of anything other than created happiness;[15] from a Christian viewpoint that much goes without saying. What is far more suprising is the suggestion in the *quaestiones* from the Paris Faculty of Arts and in the Pseudo-Peckham's commentary that Aristotle is dealing with happiness after death. According to these texts, the boundary between the philosophical and theological kinds of happiness is marked not by death, but by the kind of entity that is to be considered happy. According to philosophy, it is the soul alone that can be happy after death; according to theology it is the soul in union with the body.[16]

This shows two things: first, the *Nicomachean Ethics* was not initially interpreted as hostile to the Christian tradition; second, even philosophical commentators regard theological categories as the decisive guides to interpretation. On the point of happiness after death it did not take long to reach clarity. An early commentary, probably by Robert Kilwardby, explains that in the *Ethics* Aristotle is talking only about the happiness which belongs to the realm of politics; the question of happiness after death and of the true happiness of contemplation lies beyond that realm.[17] The author of this commentary was not in a position to know that for Aristotle too it is theoretical life which constitutes real happiness, for he composed his commentary just before Robert Grosseteste's translation of the whole *Nicomachean Ethics*.

---

14. Gauthier (ed.) 1975, p. 102.
15. MS Ripoll 109, f. 136ra.
16. Ibid.: 'Anima enim maxime vivit in se post mortem, cum sit a corpore separata, et ideo innuit hic [= *Nic. Eth.* 1100ᵃ10] Aristoteles felicitatem esse post mortem.' MS Oxford, Bodl. misc. lat. 71, f. 21vb.
17. MS Cambridge, Peterhouse 206, f. 293va: 'unde forte intendit non nisi de illa felicitate quae dicitur vita secundum ius doctrinae civilis, nec debuit forte doctrina civilis de alia felicitate perscrutari. Utrum enim post mortem felicitatur animal vel totus homo, forte non pertinet ad ipsam, nec hoc determinat Aristoteles.'

The relation between philosophical and theological
concepts of happiness in Thomas Aquinas

The reception and adaptation of the Aristotelian concept of happiness was completed by Thomas Aquinas.[18] Thomas does not merely reproduce the Aristotelian concept; he is a theologian, guided by theological interests, and he fully accepts the Christian tradition. For him it is clear 'that the happiness of the life to come lies beyond any inquiry of the reason' and that 'perfect human happiness is reserved for the life to come'.[19] Since happiness means the complete satisfaction of human aspirations, and since human aspirations are infinite because of human spirituality, only an infinite object, namely God, can perfectly satisfy man.[20] Human beings cannot achieve this by themselves, because insofar as they are potential, they cannot actualise their own potentialities.

If God is taken to be the object of the desire for happiness in this way, something important follows: since God does not belong to the sphere of human action, to the extent to which happiness is identified with him it cannot become an object of practical knowledge. Thus, if a theologian takes God, the ultimate goal, as his starting point, his treatment of happiness must be theoretical. But the essence of human happiness does not consist in the object which makes men happy but in the activity or relationship of human beings vis-à-vis this object. To describe this distinction between the object and the activity of happiness, Thomas uses the traditional concepts of uncreated and created happiness.[21] He appeals to Aristotle, who defines happiness as strictly an activity (*operatio*), since activity is the final and complete realisation of every active being.

What is the precise activity in which happiness consists? Here Thomas' answer goes against the tradition. His analysis of the essence of happiness shows that ultimately it can consist only in a cognitive mental activity. It is knowledge which constitutes happiness and the possession of God, knowledge accompanied in the will by the pleasure which arises from this possession.[22] But the cognitive activity which constitutes happiness is not an exercise of practical reason concerned with human emotions and actions; this would be the case only if man were his own ultimate goal.[23]

---

18. Kluxen 1978, pp. 77–91.
19. Aquinas 1964b, I, 9, p. 32: 'felicitas alterius vitae omnem investigationem rationis excedit'; I, 16, p. 60: 'reservatur homini perfecta beatitudo post hanc vitam'.
20. *ST*, IaIIae, 2, 8.
21. *ST*, IaIIae, 3, 2.
22. *ST*, IaIIae, 3, 4.
23. *ST*, IaIIae, 3, 5 *ad* 3.

Since the ultimate goal of infinite human aspiration is God, happiness must consist in an activity of theoretical reason.

Thus far Thomas agrees with Aristotle; he differs from him only in that he takes the concept of perfection in the very strict sense familiar from theology. According to this, human happiness is nothing less than the vision of God's essence – an activity of theoretical reason – without interruption, without end, and unaccompanied by other activities. In other words, perfect human happiness is a single, continuous, eternal activity. Obviously such an activity is not possible in this life.[24]

Given such a strict concept of happiness, one can look on the present life in various ways. It can be regarded as a condition of misery and unhappiness, impossibly far removed from true happiness; or one can emphasise those elements of the present life which bear a certain relationship to perfect happiness. Thomas chooses the second alternative. As a theologian he judges the happiness of this life to be imperfect; but it is *happiness* in no merely equivocal sense. The theological distinction between perfect and imperfect happiness goes back to William of Auxerre,[25] but it was Thomas who was the first to make it fruitful by treating the concept of happiness in the *Nicomachean Ethics* as a paradigm of imperfect happiness.

In accordance with the strict sense of perfection, happiness is realised in a single eternal activity; what is possible in this life, by contrast, is a double happiness (*duplex felicitas*), the happiness of the theoretical life and the happiness of social life. In the state of perfect happiness there is no room for such a distinction because the union of man with God, brought about by contemplation, automatically brings about the perfection of the whole man. It is different with imperfect happiness; the social and the theoretical forms of life do not coincide. The perfection of theoretical reason as such does not mean *eo ipso* the perfection of the whole man; the ordering of human action and emotions is the task of practical reason. In general in the area of imperfect happiness the perfection of the lower faculties is a necessary condition for the perfection of the higher faculties.[26] If the philosopher is a good man, it is not simply because he is a philosopher. This is a genuinely Aristotelian idea, but, as we shall see, it is interpreted differently by some of his most enthusiastic followers.

Unquestionably, Thomas himself understands certain doctrines of the

---

24. *ST*, IaIIae, 3, 2 *ad* 4.
25. William of Auxerre 1500, *Summa aurea* III, tr. 20, f. 222[rb]: 'distinguenda est beatitudo perfecta et beatitudo imperfecta; beatitudinem perfectam habebunt sancti in futuro, in praesenti vero habent beatitudinem imperfectam'.
26. *ST*, IaIIae, 3, 3 *ad* 3.

Nicomachean Ethics in a manner unintended by Aristotle. This is especially true of the doctrine of the two types of happiness. Thomas agrees with Aristotle that the active and contemplative lives cannot be made to coincide and that theorising is to be regarded more highly than the activity of the moral life. But, unlike Aristotle, Thomas regards the life of political action as directed towards theoretical happiness. For him the duality of happiness is thus only relative.[27] The main reason for this difference is that because of the unity of human nature Thomas can allow only a single goal for human life.[28]

There can be no doubt that the Thomistic conception of happiness is basically intellectualist. This intellectualism is the result of his analysis of the nature of happiness. From the point of view of *praxis*, in the conditions of the present life, Thomas values the will more highly than reason, because the will can reach God directly while reason remains subjected to the senses.[29] Happiness in its perfect, intellectual form is realised only in the other life.

The theoretical life as the paradigm of human happiness: Boethius of Dacia and Siger of Brabant

Some philosophers who were acquainted with the whole *Nicomachean Ethics* and therefore familiar with the Aristotelian concept of *theoria* were unwilling to adapt these philosophical doctrines to a theological context. One such philosopher was Boethius of Dacia, who in his work *De summo bono* dealt with happiness, outside the context of theology. For him, the highest good of man consists in the perfect actualisation of the highest human capacity, reason. Reason involves both a theoretical and a practical faculty, the theoretical capacity orientated to knowing truth and the practical one to doing good. The highest good of man, human happiness, consists in the exercise of both capacities and in the pleasure derived from each. All action should be directed to this goal. A man who acts for the sake of this goal acts correctly and naturally because this is the goal to which he is orientated by nature. Moral failure occurs when a man sets up as his goal something other than his highest capacity – for instance, if all his action is directed to sensuality. For Boethius this amounts to a disorder which clashes with nature.

---

27. Aquinas 1964b, X, 11, p. 587.
28. Aquinas 1964b, I, 9, p. 31: 'necesse est enim unum esse ultimum finem hominis inquantum est homo propter unitatem humanae naturae'.
29. *ST*, I, 82, 3; IaIIae, 27, 2 *ad* 2.

The distinction between theoretical and practical reason is to a certain extent reminiscent of the Aristotelian distinction according to which social happiness consists in the complete exercise of the moral virtues and contemplative happiness in the exercise of wisdom. Aristotle is talking of two goals which are independent of each other; he emphasises that *theoria* is neither the cause of nor a precondition for a good social life. Thomas Aquinas too takes this view, although he regards active happiness as belonging to practical *reason*. Does Boethius of Dacia also maintain the doctrine of the double happiness? Does he think a good life is possible without theoretical reason operating as its standard? Boethius is aware that almost all men follow their disordered desires rather than their natural appetite for knowledge. This shows that almost everyone leads an unnatural and blameworthy life, but it does not answer our question. Matters become clearer when he says that philosophers alone follow the innate appetite for knowledge and lead a life which corresponds to the natural ordering; they alone achieve the best condition which is possible for man.[30]

In fact according to Boethius, philosophy is not just one form of life amongst others; it is not even simply the highest life, it is the one test of human life in general: 'whoever does not lead this (life), does not lead the right life'.[31] Boethius does not recognise social happiness as an independent form of human perfection; only the philosopher can really live the life of *praxis*, because his theoretical activity gives him an intuition of virtue and vice, which enables him to reach correct decisions. Again, it is the philosopher who prefers the greater intellectual pleasures to sensual enjoyment; in his purely intellectual activity there is no room for wrongdoing. Boethius is quite consistent in drawing the conclusion: 'it is easier for a philosopher to be virtuous than for anyone else'.[32] Thus Boethius abolishes the difference between 'man' and 'philosopher', which was so important in Aristotelian ethics: the philosopher is the epitome of man; all others simply 'do not lead the right life'.

Is there any limit to philosophical happiness? For Boethius, philosophical knowledge reaches its term with knowledge of the principle of all things, namely, 'uncreated Being'.[33] This end is not its limit but its perfection. Boethius, however, retains the Aristotelian assumption that philosophical

---

30. Boethius of Dacia 1936, *De summo bono*, pp. 373ff.
31. Ibid., p. 377: 'Haec est vita philosophi, quam quicumque non habuerit non habet rectam vitam'.
32. Ibid., p. 375: 'Ideo philosophus est facilius virtuosus quam alius'.
33. Ibid., p. 375: 'numquam enim satiatur appetitus sciendi, donec sciatur ens increatum'.

knowledge of the divine starts with created beings and remains bound up with them. The philosopher can demonstrate the necessity of a first cause, and he can also recognise the dependence of the world and of man on this cause. But Boethius does not speak of a knowledge of the essence of 'uncreated being', and this may be looked on as a limitation of philosophical happiness. By contrast, the perfect happiness of theology, as explained by Thomas, consists in the knowledge of the essence of God.

According to the testimony of Agostino Nifo (1472–1538), Siger of Brabant (a contemporary of Boethius of Dacia and of Thomas Aquinas) in his lost *Liber de felicitate* rejected this difference between philosophical and theological conceptions of happiness.[34] According to him, human happiness consists in the immediate contemplation of the nature of God: 'we shall finally be made blessed [happy] by the essence of God itself and not by any intermediary'.[35] This is of course not a usual state or one often encountered even in the philosophical life; it is the maximum which is finally possible for the philosopher, for one who 'is very skilled in philosophy'.[36] It is obvious that such a notion, even more than that of Boethius, neglects the practical aspect of happiness.

Such an interpretation of the nature of happiness places philosophy on a par with theology. This explains the reaction of the theologians which took shape in the Paris condemnation of 1277. The 219 condemned theses include some concerning happiness and the self-aggrandisement of philosophy. 'There is no better calling than to dedicate oneself to philosophy.'[37] This proposition fits well with Boethius' views. The thesis that 'we can understand God in his essence in this mortal life'[38] is propounded in Boethius' *Liber de felicitate*. 'A man whose understanding and appetite is properly ordered ... is sufficiently disposed for eternal bliss'.[39] Such a proposition appears to abolish the necessity for divine grace and turns the 'perfect' happiness of the theologians into an object of human activity.

The condemnation of 1277 does not seem to have intimidated the philosophers. The Vatican commentary on the *Ethics* (MSS Vat. lat. 832 and 2172), probably written around the end of the thirteenth century, took a

34. Nardi 1945, pp. 24–9 and 34–8.
35. Ibid., p. 27: 'nos quandoque beabimur per essentiam Dei, ut ille, et per nihil medians'.
36. Siger of Brabant 1948, III, 1, p. 84: 'homo multum expertus in philosophia a causatis a primo posset pervenire ad intellectum essentiae Primi'.
37. CUP I, n. 473, sent. 40: 'quod non est excellentior status quam vacare philosophiae'.
38. Sent. 36: 'quod Deum in hac vita mortali possumus intelligere per essentiam'. Cf. note 35.
39. Sent. 157: 'quod homo ordinatus quantum ad intellectum et affectum ... est sufficienter dispositus ad felicitatem aeternam'.

position similar to that of the *Liber de felicitate*: Talking of the happiness of the present life, the anonymous author says 'happiness consists in the knowledge of the divine essence'.[40] The author draws the conclusion that if happiness consists in the knowledge of the nature of God and such knowledge is possible in this life, then the will must restrict itself to loving what is presented to it by knowledge. This contradicts the thought of Aquinas, who gives the will priority over reason in this life: as long as the essence of God is not yet seen, the will can get closer to the final goal than reason can.

These thirteenth-century philosophers never entirely lost sight of the practical aspect of the *Nicomachean Ethics*. For Aristotle happiness is something possible for most or many men. Happiness as the highest good of man is, for him, something possible even without the philosophical life; such practical happiness is a 'second-best' life,[41] but nonetheless in its way a highest good. Most philosophers of the thirteenth century make this second-best life a mere appendix of the philosophical life – an elitist position that sacrifices the proper claims of the practical life on the altar of *theoria*.

John Buridan and the concept of the contemplative life

Not all theologians accepted the philosophers' decision that *theoria* is the epitome of happiness. Bonaventure opposed the thesis of Aquinas that the reason and not the will is the real bearer of happiness.[42] Duns Scotus saw happiness basically as an act of the will and valued the will more highly than the reason. Scotus rejected the claim of the philosophers to recognise the final goal and to reach it by their own powers. Philosophy can recognise the goal only 'in general', in a way which is not sufficient to guide conduct. The science which directs human action to its eternal goal is theology, which through revelation grasps this goal 'in detail'.[43]

John Buridan's commentary on the *Ethics* gives us some idea of the philosophical response to these criticisms in the fourteenth century. His description of ethics as an immediately practical science, and his identification of ethics with prudence can be seen as a reaction against the one-sided theoretical conception of the philosophers at the end of the thirteenth century. The topic of freedom plays an important part in his commen-

---

40. MS Vat. lat. 892, f. 10va (2172, f. 14rb); 'quando dicitur: felicitas consistit in cognitione divinae essentiae, verum est'; Gauthier 1947–8, p. 290, n. 1.
41. X, 8; 1178 ^{a}9.
42. *Coll. in Hexaemeron*, II, 22–9.
43. Honnefelder 1975, pp. 239 and 274.

tary;[44] a notable example of this is his assertion that it is the free man who is the specific object of ethics.[45] His commentary treats extensively of the problem of the relation of reason to will and the relation of both to happiness.[46]

In the same context, Buridan mentions a question that had often been asked since John of Paris: whether happiness consists in the direct contemplation of God or in some consequence thereof – e.g., in reflexive knowledge of it. Buridan took the side of those who identify happiness with contemplation.[47] Others, he was aware, drawing a distinction between the *potentia absoluta* and the *potentia ordinata* of God, had argued that in his absolute power God could turn the joy and love arising from the contemplation of God into sorrow and hate, or, conversely, he could detach the love from the act of knowledge. But Buridan's own mind is made up: 'I am certain that I do not want such a happiness'.[48]

In other respects Buridan separates philosophical topics quite clearly from theological ones: his aim is 'to proceed throughout the book purely philosophically'.[49] But this does not exclude the consideration of theological positions. He distinguishes between the true happiness of the life to come (*in patria*), about which he will not speak, and the happiness of this life, with which the philosophers deal.[50] The happiness of this life is achieved by human exertion; God comes into consideration only as general cause, being the origin of all good things. Here Buridan is repeating the reading of Albert the Great.[51]

A man can be called happy in the present life, but not in the strict sense (*secundum imaginationem mathematicam*) that he has reached the highest point of all his possibilities. That was true only of Christ. The average happy man must enjoy certain basic elements of happiness: physical health or at least the lack of serious physical defect, the moral virtues, prudence and wisdom, wealth and good fortune. These individual elements admit of degrees, so that human happiness does not entail a condition of absolute perfection.[52]

This description of happiness corresponds to the well-known definition

44. Korolec 1974b, pp. 190–252.
45. John Buridan 1513, I, qu. 3, f. 4[va].
46. Ibid., X, qu. 1–3.
47. Ibid., X, qu. 5, f. 213[ra]; cf. Gauthier 1947–8, p. 197, n. 2.
48. Ibid., X, qu. 4, f. 209[rb]: 'constat mihi, quod ego non vellem talem felicitatem'.
49. Ibid., I, qu. 18, vol. 18[ra]: '... redeuntes ad nostram intentionem, quae est in hoc toto libro nihil nisi pure philosophice tractare'.
50. Ibid., I, qu. 10, f. 10[rb].
51. Ibid., I, qu. 17, f. 17[ra]; Albert, *Super Ethica* I, 10, 55.
52. Ibid., X, qu. 4, f. 211[va–b].

of Boethius, according to which happiness is a perfect condition consisting in the union of all goods.[53] Buridan mentions a second definition of happiness, as the most excellent activity of the noblest capacity upon the noblest object. This definition he ascribes to Aristotle. The two definitions do not contradict each other, says Buridan. If one starts synthetically (*via compositionis*) from the individual elements, one arrives at 'the unification of all goods'; if one asks analytically (*via resolutionis*) about the relation of the elements to one another, one arrives at the most excellent element to which all the others are subordinated.[54]

Neither of the two methods makes quite clear how Buridan understands the Aristotelian distinction between active and contemplative happiness. He describes active happiness as the exercise of prudence and contemplative happiness as the activity of theoretical reason.[55] How does this distinction fit the definitions just mentioned? In the 'Boethian' definition prudence and wisdom (contemplation) are both equally elements of happiness; the 'Aristotelian' definition admits only *one* act and *one* object of happiness, namely the act of contemplating the divine nature (*actus speculationis circa divinam essentiam*).[56] We may raise the questions whether Buridan regards active happiness as an independent item in a philosophical ethics or thinks of it as merely preparatory to true human happiness.

An answer becomes clear when we inquire how Buridan regards the status of people who do not achieve *theoria*. He mentions workmen (*mechanici*) who look after others and thus without themselves achieving happiness bring others closer to it.[57] Thus on his view there is only *one* happiness to which the activity of all men has to be orientated; active happiness can only be regarded as preparatory to contemplative happiness.

This interpretation is confirmed by two further remarks of Buridan. 'The true metaphysician', he says, 'is a good and perfect man without qualification', while the prudent man, who is also a good man, does not achieve the same completion and perfection as the metaphysician. Pru-

---

53. Ibid., X, qu. 4, f. 210ra; Boethius, *Consolatio* III, pr. 2: 'liquet igitur esse beatitudinem statum bonorum omnium congregatione perfectum'.
54. Ibid., X, qu. 4, f. 210ra: 'via resolutionis optimum in homine diceretur illa dispositio vel ille actus aut quocumque nomine nominetur, quae vel qui in praedicta congregatione resoluta in suas partes esset optimum et finalissimum aliorum ... et certum est, quod istum modum loquendi tenuit Aristoteles'.
55. Ibid., X, qu. 4, f. 209vb.
56. Ibid., X, qu. 4, f. 210ra.
57. Ibid., I, qu. 5, f. 6ra: 'sciendum etiam non omnes illos homines esse frustratos suo fine, qui ipsum formaliter non adipiscuntur ... sicut sunt mechanici, qui procurant aliis vitae necessaria, quibus habitis alii possunt tendere iam ad maiora et propinquiora fini'.

dence is the rule and the measure of the moral quality of a man in the area of politics or of *praxis*, but it is not an absolute rule and standard except as preparatory for perfect happiness.[58] Conversely, it is true that prudence receives its rule from wisdom: 'It is wisdom which enables prudence to prescribe.'[59] This means that politics and ethics are subordinated to metaphysics.

Buridan ends his commentary with the question whether human happiness consists of an act of reason or of the will.[60] His answer is in full accord with the philosophical tradition of the thirteenth century: happiness is an act of knowledge by which man is united to God directly, while desire and love reach their object only through the mediation of knowledge. According to Buridan this is true not only of the perfect happiness of the life to come, but in this life too, even when this knowledge is founded not on self-evident principles, but on faith. 'A simple woman' may have a greater love for God based on greater faith and accordingly a greater knowledge than a scholar who may have evidence and proofs at his disposal.[61]

After Buridan

From the second half of the fourteenth century commentators frequently restrict their consideration to the first five books of the *Nicomachean Ethics*. This suggests that interest in theoretical happiness had begun to recede. But it is uncertain whether this is related to a particular conception of ethics as primarily practical or whether it is simply the result of teaching schedules in the universities. Melanchthon, for example, gives the impression of being unwilling to take the Aristotelian conception of theoretical happiness into account. Given his theological background, he naturally judges sceptically any philosophical claim to provide a true ultimate goal for man. But his attitude is perhaps also a sign that people are beginning to doubt fundamentally the possibility of human perfection by *theoria*.

---

58. Ibid., V, qu. 22, f. 139vb: 'verus metaphysicus est simpliciter bonus homo et perfectus; prudens autem non metaphysicus est simpliciter, idest absoluto sermone loquendo, bonus homo, sed non perfecte et consummate ... [f. 140ra] prudentia est regula et mensura totius bonitatis humanae politicae, non totius bonitatis humanae simpliciter nisi praeparative sicut ministra'.
59. Ibid., I, qu. 6, f. 7ra: 'prudentia praecipit gratia sapientiae'.
60. Ibid., X, qu. 5, f. 211vb.
61. Ibid., X, qu. 5, f. 214^{ra-b}.

36
CONSCIENCE

Origins of the medieval discussion: Peter Lombard

Medieval treatises on conscience were divided into two parts, one headed
'*synderesis*' and the other '*conscientia*'. '*Synderesis*' is just a corrupted trans-
literation of '*suneidēsis*' the Greek word for 'conscience', so the medieval
distinction between *synderesis* and *conscientia* requires explanation. In the
first instance, the explanation is historical. Conscience was not directly
treated either by Plato or by Aristotle; the way in which it became a
standard topic of later medieval philosophy was curious, almost an
accident. Like many other topics regularly discussed by medieval philosophers, it came to their attention through a passage in Peter Lombard's
Sentences and most of the medieval treatises on conscience are to be found
in commentaries on that work.

Yet Peter Lombard does not actually discuss conscience at all: his
question is how the will can be bad (2.39). As usual, he reports several
answers, though, exceptionally, without pronouncing judgement upon
them at the end. He notes, first, that some people distinguish two senses of
'*voluntas*', in one of which it is a power, in the other the exercise of that
power (1.3). This distinction was probably inspired by a parallel Aristotelian distinction, between two senses of 'know', the first dispositional, but
the second involving actually thinking about what one knows, as is sometimes necessary when using one's knowledge.[1] Similarly, we each have a
host of desires, but it is only at certain times that any one of them makes
itself felt or that we pay attention to it, so that it is then actualised in the
sense of being called to mind.

The problem which Peter sets out requires this interpretation, for, he
continues, the will is part of man's natural endowment, and he rejects the
solution that *qua* potentiality it is always good but *qua* actualisation sometimes bad, on the ground that there is nothing wrong with calling to mind
what one knows, so why should there be anything wrong with calling to

---

1. *De anima* III, 4; 429ᵃ29 ff.

mind what one wants? He admits, though, that there may be some occasions when it is bad to call to mind what we know: 'for now and again a person remembers something bad in order to do it, and seeks to understand the truth in order to attack it'.[2]

Yet these are exceptional, rather than typical cases, whereas evil desires are commonplace, and this leads him on to the famous passage in Romans 7 where St Paul describes his own internal conflicts: 'For I do not do what I want, but do what I do not want' (7.15). Are there, then, asks Peter, two wills in man? Those who say 'Yes' fall into two camps. The first group holds that the will by which a man wants to do good in such a conflict is the will with which he is naturally endowed; it is the spark of conscience which, as Jerome said, was not extinguished even in Cain, whereas the other will is a result of the fall of Adam and Eve. The second group takes the opposite view: the will by which a man wants to do what is bad is embraced by free choice and is in the ascendant unless and until God's grace gives greater strength to the will that wants to do what is good. Finally, there are those who maintain that there is only one will in man, by which he 'naturally wants what is good and through a defect in it wants and takes pleasure in what is evil; so that, to the extent that he wants what is good he is naturally good, but to the extent that he wants what is bad he is evil'.[3]

Origins of the medieval discussion: Jerome

Peter concludes that the question whether there are two wills in man is a deep one, leaving it to his successors to decide among the three solutions. Thus the topic by which he was exercised here is the classical one of weakness of will, which had been discussed in some detail by Plato, Aristotle, and Augustine, as well as by St Paul. Conscience is no more than mentioned, and then only with a reference to Jerome. But his commentators followed up that reference, which is to an allegorical interpretation of Ezekiel's vision. Ezekiel saw four living creatures coming out of a fiery cloud; each of them had the form of a man, but with four faces: the front face was human, the right face that of a lion, the left that of an ox and the back face that of an eagle (Ezekiel 1.4−14). Jerome interpreted the four faces as representing the structure of the human soul, correlating the first three with Plato's tripartite division in the *Republic* (IV, 436B−441B). The eagle, however, he identified with conscience:

---

2. 'Memorat enim interdum quis malum ut faciat; et quaerit intelligere verum ut sciat impugnare' (2.1).

3. '... quo naturaliter vult homo bonum et ex vitio vult malum eoque delectatur; et in quantum vult bonum, naturaliter bonus est; in quantum malum vult, malus est' (3.4).

Most people interpret the man, the lion and the ox as the rational, emotional and appetitive parts of the soul ... And they posit a fourth part which is above and beyond these three, and which the Greeks call *synteresis:* that spark of conscience which was not even extinguished in the breast of Cain after he was turned out of paradise, and by which we discern that we sin, when we are overcome by pleasures or frenzy and meanwhile are misled by an imitation of reason. They reckon that this is, strictly speaking, the eagle, which is not mixed up with the other three, but corrects them when they go wrong ... However, we also see that this conscience is cast down among some people, who have neither shame nor insight regarding their offences, and loses its place ...[4]

Peter's citation of Jerome was thus very apposite, since Plato invoked the tripartite division of the soul precisely to explain weakness of will. But Jerome's remarks gave his medieval readers many headaches, although they took no interest in them as exegesis: the text of Ezekiel and its meaning play no further part in the discussion.

Jerome proposes, in this passage, a quadripartite soul. By the middle ages, Aristotle's interpretation of the 'parts' of the soul as basic psychological potentialities was generally accepted. On this reading, Jerome is saying that conscience is a fourth potentiality, irreducible to any of the other three. But he then goes on to ask whether a person can cease to have a conscience and, *prima facie*, his answer is inconsistent. First, he seems to say 'No', because he tells us that even Cain did not cease to have a conscience, a rather surprising remark in view of the story of Cain and Abel, for at no point in the story does Cain show the slightest sign of being sorry for having murdered his brother. When the Lord asks him: 'Where is Abel your brother?' he tries to disown any responsibility: 'I do not know, Am I my brother's keeper?' (Genesis 4.9). Subsequently, after being sentenced to a nomadic life, he merely complains: 'My punishment is greater than I can bear' (Genesis 4.13). However, Jerome then goes on to say that very wicked people *do* cease to have any conscience, quoting other passages of Scripture in support (Proverbs 18.3, Jeremiah 3.3).

Medieval philosophers thought that they could resolve this apparent inconsistency. Jerome introduces the example of Cain in apposition to the word *'synteresis'*, 'that spark of conscience which was not extinguished

---

4. 'Plerique ... rationale animae, et irascitivum, et concupiscitivum ... ad hominem et leonem ac vitulum referunt. ... Quartamque ponunt quae super haec et extra haec tria est, quam Graeci vocant συντήρησιν, quae scintilla conscientiae in Cain quoque pectore, postquam ejectus est de paradiso, non extinguitur, et qua victi voluptatibus vel furore, ipsaque interdum rationis decepti similitudine, nos peccare sentimus. Quam proprie aquilae deputant, non se miscentem tribus, sed tria errantia corrigentem ... Et tamen hanc quoque conscientiam ... cernimus praecipitari apud quosdam et suum locum amittere, qui ne pudorem quidem et verecundiam habent in delictis ...' (Lottin 1948, pp. 103–4).

even in the breast of Cain ... and by which we discern that we sin'. At the end of the passage, however, he uses the Latin '*conscientia*' when he says 'this conscience is cast down among some people ... and loses its place'. Few western medieval philosophers knew any Greek, so this suggested a distinction to them between *synderesis* and *conscientia*, *synderesis* being the 'spark of *conscientia*'. Cain at least regretted the consequences of his action; though he did not regret the action as such, this residue of regret witnessed to a spark of conscience remaining within him.

To medieval philosophers, this would have seemed an honest attempt to make sense of a puzzling passage in Jerome, although, as exegesis, it will hardly convince a modern reader. For when Jerome says that *this* conscience *loses its place* in some people, he must be referring to its place in the quadripartite soul. Moreover, he would have known that '*conscientia*' was the exact Latin equivalent of '*syneidesis*': the latter is a nominalisation from the compound verb '*sun-oida*', meaning originally 'I know in common with', so that '*con-scio*' is exactly parallel to it.[5] Disagreement with the medieval interpretation of Jerome does not necessarily force us, though, to write off any distinction between *synderesis* and *conscientia* as an unfortunate mistake. There could be independent reasons for drawing a distinction *within* what we simply call 'conscience' – never mind the labels for it – and the right question to ask is whether the medieval distinction, in spite of its muddled origin, turned out to be productive. Do the two terms mark a distinction which is essential for understanding and speaking clearly about the notion of conscience? If so, then the original motivation for its introduction need not trouble us further.

Philip the Chancellor

The first treatise on conscience, which set the pattern for subsequent ones, was written by Philip the Chancellor about 1235. Philip poses four questions; he distinguishes between *synderesis* and *conscientia* in the third, whether *synderesis* can lead us to do wrong. He begins with four arguments to the effect that it can, of which the first runs as follows: '*Conscientia* is sometimes mistaken, sometimes right. But in whatever power there is any mistake over what is to be done, in that power there is sin.'[6] Now (citing Jerome), *synderesis* is the same as *conscientia*, so *synderesis* can lead us to do wrong. In his subsequent discussion, however, Philip denies that they are the same,

---

5. See Davies 1962, p. 672.
6. '... conscientia aliquando est erronea, aliquando recta. Sed in qua vi est error in operandis, in ea vi est peccatum' (Lottin 1948, p. 150.3–5).

holding that *conscientia* comes from a conjunction of *synderesis* with free choice, and illustrating his position with an example:

... suppose that it is written in *synderesis* that everyone who makes himself out to be the Son of God and is not, should die the death; and that this man (indicating Christ) makes himself out to be the Son of God, and yet is not (so it is thought); therefore he should die the death. What was contributed by *synderesis* was unchangeable and dictated only good, but this conjoined with what was contributed by reason dictated sin. So, therefore, *synderesis* plus the reason for a free choice makes *conscientia* right or mistaken, and *conscientia* sticks more to the side of reason; *synderesis* itself, however, which is the spark of *conscientia*, ... is not mistaken.[7]

In his fourth question, whether a person can lose *synderesis*, Philip discusses a closely related example, that of heretics whose *conscientia* urged them to die for their faith. *Prima facie*, *synderesis* did not murmur in them in answer to sin, but Philip replies:

... the effect of *synderesis*, considered as such, is paralysed in them because of the lack of faith, which is the basis of everything good. But the exercise of *conscientia* thrives in them, the evidence of which is that the man is ready to undergo martyrdom, because he supposes that what he believes is the faith. It is not, however, *synderesis* which does this, but what belongs to free choice or reason. Moreover, *synderesis* is not extinguished in such a person because, although he may be mistaken about the particular matter, evil in general still displeases him.[8]

This contrast between the general and the particular occurs again in an addendum to the second question, devoted to the sense in which *synderesis* is said to murmur back in answer to sin:

... *synderesis* affects free choice by telling it to do good and restraining it from evil, and moves us to the general good which is found in this or that good. Hence it is not in itself directed to particular good deeds, but to the general [good] which is present in them.[9]

---

7. '... si in synderesi sit scriptum quod omnis qui se fecerit filium Dei et non sit, morte moriatur; sed iste se faciat filium Dei, demonstrato Christo, et non est; ita opinantur: morte ergo moriatur. Quod erat syndereseos erat immutabile et non dictabat nisi bonum; sed illum coniunctum cum eo quod erat rationis dictabat peccatum. Sic ergo synderesis cum ratione liberi arbitrii facit conscientiam rectam vel erroneam; et conscientia magis se tenet ex parte rationis; ipsa tamen synderesis non est erronea, que est scintilla conscientie ...' (Lottin 1948, pp. 151–2. 61–9).
8. '... in hiis debilitatur effectus syndereseos per se sumpte propter privationem fidei que est fundamentum omnium bonorum; sed in hiis conscientie actus viget, ratione cuius paratus est ipse subire martyrium; supponit enim hanc quam credit esse fidem. Hoc autem non facit synderesis, sed ea que sunt liberi arbitrii aut rationis. Tamen non est in tali extincta synderesis; quia licet erret in particulari, tamen in generali displicet ei malum ...' (Lottin 1948, pp. 154–5. 53–9).
9. '... synderesis movet liberum arbitrium dictando bonum et cohibendo a malo, et movet in bonum commune quod invenitur in isto bono aut in illo. Non ergo est in bonum particulare secundum se, sed in commune inventum in eo' (Lottin 1948, p. 148.128–31).

Philip's argument is thus that we need to distinguish between *general* and *particular* propositions which are of the form: '*A* ought to φ', where the proper name of any person may be substituted for '*A*' and any verb-phrase containing a verb of action for 'φ' (I shall henceforth call these 'deontic propositions'). His reason is that a person, in spite of holding a correct general principle, can always misapply it to particular circumstances and so mistakenly believe himself obliged to a certain action. If both are subsumed under a single, undifferentiated notion of conscience, then, faced with examples of the type Philip cites, we cannot answer the question: 'Is the man's conscience mistaken?' If, however, we distinguish between *synderesis* and *conscientia*, then we can say that his *synderesis* is not mistaken but his *conscientia* is. Yet we now need a more precise characterisation of the difference between a general and a particular deontic proposition, which, apart from his examples, Philip does not give us.

Philip's *motivation* for distinguishing between *synderesis* and *conscientia* is that, although he allows that *conscientia* can be mistaken, he holds that *synderesis* cannot. This should not be confused with his *ground* for distinguishing between them, namely, that general deontic propositions can be misapplied to particular circumstances. He gives us a good reason for distinguishing between two senses of 'conscience', but we are not compelled, in accepting it, to agree that in one of these senses conscience cannot be mistaken. This remains as a further question, which was controversial even at the time, for he was taking issue with William of Auxerre.[10] The distinction could be made out just as well by an example in which the general proposition was false, yet misapplied to yield a true particular proposition. But then we should have to regard *synderesis* as consisting in the set of our deontic *beliefs*, i.e. those which could be reported in the form: '*A* believes that he ought to φ', whereas the etymology of 'conscience', as well as many of the things which we ordinarily say about it, suggest that it is a form of *knowledge*.

Philip also holds that *conscientia* involves free choice, whereas *synderesis* is non-deliberative. The same motivation is at work here: only where choice comes into play is wrong-doing possible. But we can easily concoct examples which, like Philip's, support a distinction between two senses of 'conscience' but which afford no ground to posit choice as a factor in assent to the minor premiss. Suppose that a man believes that he ought to give alms to the poor, but mistakenly believes of a certain very rich widow that

10. See Lottin 1948, p. 150.

she is destitute, and concludes that he ought to give alms to this widow. He may simply have been misinformed about her and have made a purely factual mistake totally unconnected with his desires. It seems, then, that Philip is again asking his distinction between general and particular deontic propositions to do too much work and that he has been misled by his choice of examples.

In his first and second questions, Philip is trying to determine how *synderesis* fits into the structure of the soul. The first asks whether it is a potentiality or a disposition, the second how it is related to reason. He finds a clue to these problems in the impulse to sin, of which he sees conscience as the counterpart:

Since the soul is not abandoned by its creator so that it has no help in doing what is good, just as it contains an impulse to sin inclining free choice towards sin or evil, so, therefore, there will be some aid which, to the extent that it works of itself, always directs it to what is good and makes it shun what is bad, in the same way as the impulse to sin works in the contrary direction. But what else can this be except *synderesis*?[11]

This counterpart theory of conscience seems to derive from the Rabbinic doctrine of the two impulses in man, according to which every man is born with an evil inclination, manifested primarily in bodily and especially in sexual desires. At the age of puberty it begins to be opposed by an impulse to good, the struggle between the two impulses continuing for the rest of a man's life.[12] St Paul was writing within this tradition in his description of chronic conflicts of desires, in which the evil impulse appears as the 'law of sin', and in Augustine (*Confessions*, VIII) it is neatly meshed into the Platonic and Aristotelian analyses of weakness of will. But it was also modified in Christian hands, the impulse to sin now being seen, not as part of God's design for men, but as a consequence of the Fall. Thus Philip is able to say that it is 'outside the substance of the soul'[13] and to conclude from this that the same applies to *synderesis*, i.e. that neither is a basic psychological potentiality.

If *synderesis* is the counterpart of the impulse to sin, then it should be

11. 'Cum non sit destituta anima a creatore suo ut non habeat adiutorium in bonum, sicut habet fomitem peccati inclinantem liberum arbitrium in peccatum aut in malum, erit ergo aliquod adiutorium semper dirigens, quantum est de se, in bonum et retrahens a malo, quemadmodum fomes peccati opposito modo se habet. Sed quid aliud erit a synderesi?' (Lottin 1948, p. 141.66–71).
12. Davies 1955, pp. 21–5.
13. Lottin 1948, p. 141.

related to rational desire as the latter is related to bodily appetites. So Philip concludes that it is an innate tendency of rational desires, what remains of

... the original righteousness of man's powers, which Adam had in the state of innocence, which remained as a little light leading him to God, lest his reason should be totally turned or bent to temporal things. ... For it is established that Adam was naturally righteous by virtue of his judgement, will, and emotions ... And each of these looks to the highest good, to which it primarily relates. It will not, accordingly, be a potentiality separated from these powers to the extent that they are pliable, but will exist in them inflexibly, the same as each one of them.[14]

By 'pliable', he means that they can be directed towards good or bad, whereas *synderesis* is inflexible, being always directed towards good. His conclusion, then, is that *synderesis* is innate and not acquired: that it is not a grace to compensate for the impulse to sin (a view which Peter Lombard reports, *Sentences* 2.39.3.3), but what remains of the full control of bodily appetites which man possessed in the state of innocence: and that, *pace* Jerome, it is not a potentiality distinct from reason.

Is it, then, a potentiality or a disposition? His final answer is that it is neither, but a dispositional potentiality, a term which was his own invention but which may have been suggested by William of Auxerre:[15]

Synderesis, although the morphology of its name makes it sound more like a disposition than a potentiality, is nevertheless the name of a dispositional potentiality: I do not say of an acquired disposition, but of an innate one. And thus, *qua* disposition it can be applied to what occurs as a disposition, *qua* potentiality to what occurs as a potentiality. From this it follows that it has a certain difference from ... the impulse [to sin] and sensuality. ... *qua* potentiality, it is disparate from ... sensuality ... So, if anyone asks whether it is a potentiality or a disposition, the right answer lies in taking something in between: a dispositional potentiality.[16]

14. '... rectitudinis prime virium, quam habebat Adam in statu innocentie, que remansit tamquam modicum lumen in Deum ductivum, ne non esset ex toto ratio ad temporalia inclinata vel incurvata.... Constat enim quod Adam habuit rectitudinem a principio iudicii et voluntatis et irascentie naturalem... Et horum omnium est inspectrix relatione ad summum bonum ad quod principaliter se habet. Et secundum hoc non erit seiuncta potentia ab illis viribus in quantum flexibiles sunt, sed in illis existens inflexibilis, eadem cum unaquaque illarum' (Lottin 1948, p. 147.78–90).
15. See Lottin 1948, p. 139 n.
16. '... synderesis, licet secundum formam nominis magis sonare videatur habitum quam potentiam, tamen est nomen habitualis potentie, non dico de habitu acquisito, sed innato. Et ita ratione habitus potest apponi ei quod per modum habitus se habet, ratione potentie ei quod per modum potentie se habet. Unde habet quamdam disparationem ... a fomite et sensualitate ...: secundum rationem potentie, disparationem habet ... a sensualitate; ... Si ergo quaeratur utrum sit potentia aut habitus, respondendum est accipiendo medium: potentia habitualis' (Lottin 1948, pp. 141–2.79–90).

The point of the reference to the etymology of *synderesis* is, of course, that it is a compound of *oida* and that knowledge is a disposition. With this solution, Philip appears to be trying to have the best of both worlds; yet rather than worrying too much about his new category of dispositional potentialities, we might construe his main contention as being that *synderesis* is akin to a potentiality in being innate, but akin to a disposition in embodying a tendency, namely, to what is good.

Bonaventure

The history of the treatise on conscience until the end of the thirteenth century has been ably documented in Lottin 1948. Here I must be highly selective, and so have chosen Bonaventure and Aquinas as able representatives of views which differ almost as much as the constraints of the medieval philosophical tradition allowed, while yet exhibiting a progression from and continuity with Philip's treatment of conscience. Of the three, Bonaventure is the odd man out. To begin with, he virtually reverses the *synderesis/conscientia* distinction and deals with *conscientia* first; though that could be misleading, because he also draws the distinction in a somewhat different way from Philip. His first question on *conscientia* is whether it belongs to the thinking or to the desiring part of the soul (*pars intellectus, affectus*), his first question on *synderesis* whether it is to be classified with apprehension or with desire (*cognitio, affectus*). These questions relate to the Aristotelian distinction between theoretical and practical: apprehension, which may be perceptory or intellectual, aims at truth, the world as it is; desire, which may be instinctual/emotional (the 'passions' of the soul) or rational (will), aims at the good, the world as one would like it to be and, thus, at changing it.

Nor does Bonaventure make any use of Philip's distinction between general and particular deontic propositions, though he reports Philip's view, without committing himself to it.[17] Instead, he takes his cue from John of Damascus' remark that conscience is the law of our thought[18] and avers that 'a law is what we recognise by means of *conscientia*'.[19] But this does not distinguish *conscientia* from *synderesis*, since both are related to natural law. The latter, however, can be understood both as a set of injunctions and as a psychological disposition. As a set of injunctions, it is the object both of *conscientia* and of *synderesis*, the first telling us them and

17. Bonaventure 1882–1902a, II, dist. 39, 2. 1.
18. John Damascene 1955, 95.
19. 'lex enim est illud quod per conscientiam novimus' (1.1, *corpus*).

the second inclining us to observe them; moreover, *conscientia* is a disposition of practical reason, *synderesis* a potentiality of desire, because it tends towards what is good.[20] In other words, the set of injunctions has first to be *known* to us (the job of *conscientia*) but, once we know them, we shall in some sense *want* to follow them (the job of *synderesis*).

Bonaventure develops this line of thought in his discussion of the question whether *conscientia* pertains to thought or to desire, after distinguishing three senses of *conscientia:* its object (that of which we are conscious, the natural law), the potentiality of being conscious (ability to become conscious of the natural law) and the disposition in virtue of which we are conscious (knowing the natural law but not continuously exercising our knowledge). Etymological influence is marked here: conscience is not clearly distinguished from consciousness (a very recent development) and it is taken for granted that conscience is a form of knowledge rather than of belief. Bonaventure then comments upon the third sense, which he holds to be the most usual one:

If, then, it be asked of what potentiality it is a disposition, it should be said that it is a disposition of a cognitive potentiality, but not in the same way in which theoretical knowledge [is a disposition of a cognitive faculty], because theoretical knowledge perfects our understanding insofar as it is theoretical, whereas *conscientia* is a disposition perfecting our understanding insofar as it is practical, or insofar as it directs us towards deeds. And thus understanding has in a way a motivating character, not because it produces motion, but because it directs and inclines us towards motion. Such a disposition is, accordingly, not called just 'knowledge' (*scientia*) but 'conscience' (*conscientia*), in order to signify that this disposition does not perfect the potentiality for theoretical knowledge itself, but as [that potentiality] is joined in some way to desire and deed. Because of this, we do not say that conscience dictates principles like 'every whole is greater than any of its parts', but rightly say that it tells us 'God is to be honoured' and similar principles, which are like rules for what is to be done.[21]

20. 2.1, *ad finem*.
21. 'Si ergo quaeratur, cuius potentiae sit habitus; dicendum, quod est habitus potentiae *cognitivae*, aliter tamen, quam sit ipsa speculativa scientia: quia scientia speculativa est perfectio intellectus nostri, in quantum est *speculativus*; conscientia vero est habitus perficiens intellectum nostrum, in quantum est *practicus*, sive in quantum dirigit in opere. Et sic intellectus habet quodam modo rationem *motivi*, non quia efficiat motum, sed quia dictat et inclinat ad motum. – Et propterea talis habitus non simpliciter nominatur *scientia*, sed *conscientia*, ut in hoc significetur, quod habitus iste non perficit ipsam potentiam speculativam *in se*, sed prout est quodam modo *iuncta affectioni et operationi*. Propter quod nos non dicimus, quod dictamen conscientiae sit ad hoc principium: omne totum est maius sua parte, et ad consimilia; sed bene dicimus, quod conscientia dictat, Deum esse honorandum, et consimilia principia, quae sunt sicut regulae agendorum' (1.1, *corpus*).

It is, then, concerned with the knowledge of *ends* and, in the last sentence, the comparison with a stock example of a first principle of theoretical reasoning already hints at Bonaventure's account of how we come to know these ends.

He pursues this in discussing his second question, whether *conscientia* is an innate or an acquired disposition:

> ... since it is necessary to apprehension that two things should be present concurrently, namely, what can be apprehended and light by means of which we judge the former, as we see in the case of sight . . . , apprehensory dispositions are partly innate because of a light imparted to the soul, but also partly acquired because of the forms... For everyone agrees that there is a light imparted to the apprehensory potentiality, which is called 'natural judgement', but we acquire forms and likenesses of things by means of the senses . . . For no one would apprehend *whole* or *part*, or *father* and *mother*, unless he received its form through one of the external senses; . . . However, the light of natural judgement directs the soul itself in judging both of what can be apprehended and of what can be done . . . Since *conscientia* thus names a disposition which directs our judgement with respect to what can be done, it follows that in one way it names an innate disposition with regard to the basic dictates of nature, but an acquired disposition with regard to what is added by education . . . For I have a natural light which is enough to apprehend that one's parents are to be honoured and that one's neighbours are not to be harmed, but I do not have the form of *father* or form of *neighbour* naturally impressed upon me.[22]

Transposing this account into modern terminology, Bonaventure's contention is that we have to learn a language before we can have any deontic knowledge, but that, having once done so, we see immediately that certain deontic propositions are true *a priori*. But Bonaventure does not maintain that this applies to *all* deontic propositions:

22. 'Cum enim ad cognitionem duo concurrant necessario, videlicet praesentia cognoscibilis et lumen, quo mediante de illo iudicamus, sicut videmus in visu . . . ; habitus cognitivi sunt quodam modo nobis *innati* ratione *luminis animae inditi*, sunt etiam quodam modo *acquisiti* ratione *speciei* . . . Omnes enim in hoc concordant, quod potentiae cognitivae sit *lumen inditum*, quod vocatur naturale iudicatorium; *species* autem et similitudines rerum acquiruntur in nobis mediante sensu . . . Nemo enim unquam cognosceret *totum*, aut *partem*, aut *patrem*, aut *matrem*, nisi sensu aliquo exteriori speciem eius acciperet . . . Illud autem *lumen* sive naturale iudicatorium dirigit ipsam animam in iudicando tam de cognoscibilibus quam de operabilibus . . . – Quoniam igitur *conscientia* nominat habitum directivum nostri iudicii respectu operabilium, hinc est, quod quodam modo habitum nominat *innatum*, et quodam modo nominat *acquisitum*. Habitum, inquam, *innatum* nominat respectu eorum quae sunt de primo dictamine naturae; habitum vero *acquisitum* respectu eorum quae sunt institutionis superadditae. . . . Naturale enim habeo *lumen*, quod sufficit ad cognoscendum, quod parentes sunt honorandi, et quod proximi non sunt laedendi; non tamen habeo naturaliter mihi impressam *speciem* patris, vel speciem proximi' (1.2, *corpus*).

... the following point is especially to be noted. Just as certain things which can be apprehended are exceedingly plain, e.g. axioms and first principles, but some things less plain, e.g. particular conclusions; so, too, some things which can be done are maximally plain, e.g. 'Do not do to others what you do not want to be done to you', that one ought to submit to God, and so on. Apprehension of first principles is said to be innate in us in virtue of that light, because that light is enough to apprehend them by, once the forms have been assimilated, without any further persuasion, on account of their own clarity ... Moreover, apprehension of the particular conclusions of the various branches of knowledge is acquired in that the light which is innate to us is not enough to apprehend them, but demands some persuasion and a new aptitude. This is also to be understood as applying to deeds ....[23]

As an example, the Jews, arguing from the basic deontic premiss that God is to be obeyed, conclude that circumcision and the dietary prescriptions of the Mosaic law are still obligatory. But there is a suppressed non-deontic premiss of the argument, that God commands certain dietary practices and the circumcision of male children, which, in Bonaventure's view, is no longer true.[24]

Conscientia nevertheless includes derived deontic propositions as well as basic ones; it is infallible only with respect to the latter, and so can be mistaken. Bonaventure therefore asks whether we are bound to do everything which it tells us to be necessary to salvation. He replies that we are, provided that it does not tell us to do something which is against the law of God; in that case, such a

... *conscientia* does not bind us to act or not to act, but binds us to get rid of it ... since whether a man does what it says or the opposite, he sins mortally. For if he does what his *conscientia* tells him, and that is against the law of God, and to act against the law of God is mortal sin, then without any doubt he sins mortally. But if he does the opposite of what his *conscientia* tells him, ... he still sins mortally, not in virtue of the deed which he does but because he does it in an evil way. For he does it in despite of God, so long as he believes, his *conscientia* telling him so, that

---

23. 'hoc attendendum est praecipue; quia, sicut inter cognoscibilia quaedam sunt *valde evidentia*, sicut dignitates et prima principia; quaedam sunt *minus evidentia*, sicut conclusiones particulares; sic et in operabilibus quaedam sunt *maxime evidentia*, utpote illud: "quod tibi non vis fieri, alii ne feceris", et quod Deo obtemperandum est, et consimilia. Quemadmodum igitur cognitio primorum principiorum ratione illius luminis dicitur esse nobis innata, quia lumen illud sufficit ad illa cognoscenda, post receptionem specierum, sine aliqua persuasione superaddita, propter sui evidentiam ... *Rursus*, quemadmodum cognitio particularium conclusionum scientiarum acquisita est, pro eo quod nobis lumen innatum non plene sufficit ad illa cognoscenda, sed indiget aliqua persuasione et habilitatione nova: sic etiam intelligendum est ex parte operabilium ...' (1.2, *corpus*).

24. 2.3 *ad* 4.

this displeases God ... God does not merely take notice of *what* a man does, but with what intention he does it.[25]

The poor man is thus caught in a double bind, for the moment he recognises his conscience to be mistaken, he will, *ipso facto*, have changed it. This would be reasonable only if no one could have a mistaken conscience in good faith but, *ex hypothesi*, the situation can arise only where a derived deontic proposition is involved, and Bonaventure allows that man's reasoning is fallible.

His account of *synderesis* leads him to reject the counterpart theory of conscience espoused by Philip. *Synderesis*, he argues, is an innate tendency to want to do what is honourable rather than useful, a natural bias of desire corresponding to the natural light of *conscientia* by which basic deontic propositions are known (2.1). It cannot, therefore, be extinguished by sin; the worst that can happen is that its exercise is temporarily prevented, e.g. 'sometimes in sins of the flesh a man is so engrossed ... that a sense of guilt has no place, because men of the flesh are so far carried away by the impulse to pleasure that reason has then no place [in them]'.[26] This is at once reminiscent of the impulse to sin, which also features explicitly in an argument he considers to the effect that *synderesis* can be extinguished, on the ground that the impulse to sin can be extinguished (as in the Virgin Mary). His reply is that they are not comparable, because the impulse to sin is not constitutive of human nature, whereas *synderesis* (and *conscientia*) are.[27] He is equally adamant that the impulse to sin is no guide to *conscientia*; replying to the argument that, since the law of the flesh is opposed to the law of the mind and the former is related to desire, so must be the latter, he says that the law of the flesh presupposes that imagination and apprehension represent bodily things to us in a disordered way and, hence, corruption of the perceptory potentiality, which pertains to apprehension, not desire.[28] But this very point also casts doubt upon his hypothesis that

25. 'conscientia non ligat ad faciendum, vel non faciendum, sed ligat ad se deponendum, ... quia, sive homo faciat quod dicit, sive eius oppositum, mortaliter peccat. – Si enim faciat quod conscientia dictat, et illud est contra legem Dei, et facere contra legem Dei sit mortale peccatum; absque dubio mortaliter peccat. Si vero facit oppositum eius quod conscientia dictat, ... adhuc peccat mortaliter, non ratione *operis*, quod facit, sed quia *malo modo facit*. Facit enim in contemptum Dei, dum credit, dictante sibi conscientia, hoc Deo displicere ... ... non tantum attendit Deus, *quid* homo faciat, sed *quo animo* faciat' (1.3, *corpus*)
26. 'aliquando enim in peccatis carnalibus ita absorbetur homo ... ut remorsus locum non habeat, quia carnales homines tanto impetu delectationis feruntur, ut ratio tunc non habeat locum' (2.2, *corpus*).
27. 2.2 *ad* 4.
28. 1.1 *ad* 3.

desire is naturally biased to what is honourable, for, of the ways in which the exercise of *synderesis* can be hampered, the first two (the darkness of blindness and the wantonness of pleasure) are failures of apprehension, while the third (obstinacy) involves the conviction that one is right.

Thomas Aquinas

Aquinas consolidated Philip's way of distinguishing between *synderesis* and *conscientia* with Bonaventure's distinction between basic and derived deontic propositions. He made a significant modification to Bonaventure's treatment of mistaken conscience, but his most original contribution was an account of the meaning of deontic propositions. He discussed conscience on three occasions; here I shall concentrate upon the *Disputed Questions on Truth*, 16–17, which date from 1257–58. Although he wrote on the topic again ten years later, he did so much more briefly and made no significant modifications to his previous exposition. He begins, like Philip, with *synderesis*.

Synderesis, according to Aquinas, is a natural disposition of the human mind by which we apprehend the basic principles of behaviour, parallel to that by which we apprehend the basic principles of theoretical disciplines, and in both cases these principles are apprehended without inquiry. Just as there is a natural disposition of the human mind by which it apprehends the principles of theoretical disciplines, which we call the understanding of principles, so too it has a natural disposition concerned with the basic principles of behaviour, which are the general principles of natural law.

The disposition in question, he concludes, is a disposition of the potentiality of reason, but *synderesis* can be used either to mean this disposition, which is comparable to that by which theoretical principles are apprehended, or to mean the potentiality of reason as endowed with this disposition.[29]

Conscientia, by contrast, Aquinas holds to be an actualisation, the application of deontic first principles known by *synderesis*. He distinguishes two kinds of application: the case in which a person asks himself the question, before acting, 'What ought I to do?' from that in which, afterwards, he asks himself 'Did I do the right thing?'[30]

29. Cf. 2.2.
30. '*uno modo* secundum quod consideratur an actus sit vel fuerit: *alio modo* secundum quod consideratur an actus sit rectus vel non ... Et *haec duplex* via in operativis distinguitur secundum duplicem viam quae est in speculativis; scilicet viam quae est inveniendi et iudicandi. Illa enim via qua per scientiam inspicimus quid agendum est, quasi consiliantes, est similis inventioni, per quam ex principiis investigamus conclusiones. Illa autem via per quam ea quae iam facta sunt,

Since Aquinas holds that basic deontic propositions are known to us without inquiry, we should expect him to say that *synderesis* cannot do wrong. He does indeed say that, but for a different reason – viz., that the whole edifice of knowledge, whether theoretical or practical, rests upon first principles, so that, if we could be wrong about them, nothing would be certain.[31] He is here assuming an Aristotelian view of the 'edifice of knowledge' as a deductive system, which few would agree with today; mathematics is probably the only discipline for which such a characterisation is plausible. However, his reason for thinking that deontic first principles are known to us without inquiry is that they are necessarily true.[32] It has been very widely assumed throughout the history of philosophy that necessary propositions are self-evident, but this is to confuse epistemology with logic. To classify propositions as necessary or contingent is to draw a *logical* distinction, with the implication that a different method will be appropriate in each case to determining whether they are true or false. Kant made the first breach in the traditional epistemological assumption by distinguishing *a priori* propositions into analytic and synthetic and showing that synthetic *a priori* propositions, far from being self-evident, had to be justified by transcendental arguments: arguments to the effect that our experience could not be what it is were they false. But even he thought that philosophy need not concern itself with analytic *a priori* propositions because they were self-evident. The development of logic in the last hundred years has taught us otherwise; even with regard to tautologies and their negations, only a little complexity need be present for people's intuitions about their truth or falsity to become very fallible.

Aquinas does allow, of course, that *conscientia* can be mistaken, and illustrates two ways in which this can happen: first, through invalid reasoning; second, by combining a deontic first principle with a false premiss, when valid reasoning will not be enough to guarantee a true conclusion. His example of the latter is those who killed the apostles, thinking that thereby they did God a service.[33] He thinks, nevertheless, that *conscientia* is infallible when the derived deontic proposition 'falls directly' under the first principle, but his examples, 'God is not to be loved by me' and 'Something bad ought to be done' appear to be negated transformations of

examinamus et discutimus an recta sint, est sicut via iudicii, per quam conclusiones in principia resolvuntur' (17.1, *corpus*).
31. 16.2.
32. 16.1 *ad* 9.
33. 17.2; cf. 16.2 *ad* 1, 2.

deontic first principles and, again, people can and do make mistakes in this type of reasoning, especially when multiple quantification is involved. He also says nothing about the *misapplication* of deontic propositions to particular circumstances, as distinct from the *derivation* of deontic propositions by inference.

Despite these criticisms, Bonaventure's replacement of Philip's distinction between general and particular deontic propositions with one between necessary and contingent deontic propositions, and Aquinas' development of the latter, was an extremely important advance, because it provides the basis for a justification of change in ethics.

Aquinas' most important and original contributions to the medieval debate about conscience are made in his answer to the question whether conscience binds us. He says immediately that it does, but goes on to explain:

> 'binding', used of spiritual things, is a metaphor taken from bodily ones, which implies the imposition of necessity. . . . There are two kinds of necessity which can be imposed by another agent. The first is a necessity of force, through which everything absolutely necessarily has to do what is determined by the action of the agent; the other should not strictly be called force but, rather, inducement. This is a conditional necessity, that is, deriving from a goal; e.g. there may be a necessity imposed upon someone that, if he does not do such-and-such, he will not obtain his reward.
> . . . The second kind of necessity can be imposed upon the will, e.g. it may be necessary to choose such-and-such, if a certain good is to result, or if a certain evil is to be avoided . . .[34]

This reply distinguishes psychological from physical necessity, but can also be taken as an exposition of the meaning of 'ought' in deontic propositions. It is now recognised that there is a close, though not exact, analogy between 'obligatory' and 'necessary' on the one hand, and 'permissible' and 'possible' on the other. Thus interpreted, Aquinas' first contention is that deontic propositions are to be expounded as implicit conditionals. He is aligning the meaning of 'ought' in the deontic propositions with which ethics is concerned with its meaning in a much wider range of contexts, those in which it introduces a necessary *means* to a *goal*.

---

34. 'ligatio metaphorice a corporalibus ad spiritualia sumpta, necessitatis impositionem importat . . . Est autem *duplex* necessitas quae ab alio agente imponi potest. *Una* quidem *coactionis*, per quam omnis absolute necesse habet facere hoc ad quod determinatur ex actione agentis; alias coactio non proprie diceretur: sed magis *inductio*. *Alia* vero est necessitas *conditionata*, scilicet ex finis suppositione; sicut imponitur alicui necessitas ut si non fecerit hoc, non consequatur suum praemium . . . *Secunda* necessitas voluntati imponi potest; ut scilicet necessarium sit hoc eligere, si hoc bonum debeat consequi, vel si hoc malum debeat vitare' (17.3, *corpus*).

What, then, is the presupposed goal in ethical contexts? To Aquinas, this presents no difficulty: it is obedience to God's commands. Aquinas is most explicit about this in his answer to the question whether a mistaken conscience binds:

It does not seem possible for someone to escape sin if his *conscientia*, however much mistaken, tells him that something is an injunction of God which is indifferent or bad *per se* and, such *conscientia* remaining, he arranges to do the contrary. For so far as in him lies, by this itself he has the wish that the law of God be not observed; hence he sins mortally.[35]

Aquinas is talking only about *conscientia* and not about *synderesis*: on his view, a man *cannot* be mistaken about basic deontic propositions. So the sense in which the man envisaged has a mistaken conscience is either that he has drawn a false deontic conclusion from his stock of basic deontic propositions or that he has misapplied a deontic proposition to particular circumstances. Nevertheless, the man in question thinks that God enjoins upon him a certain type of action or a particular action. But his desire to obey the law of God will be a concomitant of his belief that God ought to be obeyed, and this, being a basic deontic proposition, will belong to *synderesis* and not to *conscientia*. So it is not because he acts against his *conscientia* that he does wrong but because, in acting against his *conscientia*, he is also acting against his *synderesis*, which is infallible.

Aquinas argues that the way in which *conscientia* binds us is a special case of the way in which we are bound by the commands of a ruler, namely, by the threat of sanctions for disobedience or promise of a reward for obedience: 'e.g. there may be a necessity imposed upon someone that, if he does not do such-and-such, he will not obtain his reward'. God being the ruler *par excellence*, his rewards and sanctions are then the ultimate ones.[36]

We have already seen that Aquinas holds that a mistaken *conscientia* is, in general, binding, but not how he deals with the case in which a man believes that be is obliged to do something but the action in question is evil. His view about this case is slightly more lenient than Bonaventure's, but only slightly. If the mistake is not itself sinful, e.g. when it arises from some factual mistake, then the man who follows his mistaken *conscientia* is excused; but if the mistake is one of law, then he is not excused, any more than a plea of ignorance of the law excuses in the courts, because the

---

35. 'Non videtur autem possibile quod aliquis peccatum evadat, si conscientia, quantumcumque errans, dictet aliquod esse praeceptum Dei quod sit indifferens sive per se malum; si contrarium, tali conscientia manente, agere disponat. Quantum enim in se est, ex hoc ipso habet voluntatem legem Dei non observandi; unde mortaliter peccat' (17.4, *corpus*).

36. 4 *ad* 5.

mistake has arisen from ignorance of something he ought to have known. Aquinas realises that in this situation whatever a man does will be wrong, but this is not an impossible state of affairs.

As a parallel example, he cites a man who is bound to give alms to someone, but is going to do so with an intention of vainglory: if that is his intention, then he is obliged not to give the alms, but *ex hypothesi* he is obliged to give them. The dilemma can be resolved quite simply by giving up the bad intention.[37]

Yet Aquinas does allow that a mistaken *conscientia* excuses except where we can say that the person ought to have known better, and he does justify his position that a man who is mistaken about a matter of law, i.e. about a deontic proposition, can never be mistaken in good faith. Basic deontic propositions are not in question for Aquinas here, because *synderesis*, according to him, cannot be mistaken. Hence the objects of a mistaken *conscientia* must always be false *derived* deontic propositions or else misapplications of deontic propositions. But the former, on his own admission, can arise only from fallacious reasoning or from the use of false non-deontic premises. Moreover, the latter would not count as ignorance of fact in the sense in which he is contrasting it with ignorance of law; ignorance of fact in this legal sense is concerned with mistaken descriptions of circumstances to which a law is *applied*. Deriving conclusions from premises often *is* difficult to do correctly, whether in theoretical or practical matters, so what right has Aquinas to impute evil to everyone who believes false *derived* deontic propositions?

Unwittingly, perhaps, Aquinas laid the foundations of an argument which could lead to a much more lenient position than he himself envisaged. For if there are relatively few basic deontic propositions, then the scope for a mistaken *conscientia* which is in good faith will be correspondingly wide. It then becomes important for us to identify the basic deontic propositions, and it is one of the most remarkable features of the medieval treatment of conscience, in view of the central role of the *synderesis/conscientia* distinction, that no serious attempt to do this was ever made. If we abandon the attempt, and say, unlike Aquinas, that *synderesis* is fallible no less than *conscientia*, then a man with a mistaken *conscientia* may not, after all, be caught in a double bind: he may be justified in acting against it. This is the opposite of what people commonly say today, so the study of medieval philosophy can help them, at least, to think more deeply about issues upon which, perhaps, they conclude too hastily.

37. 4 *ad* 3.

37
NATURAL MORALITY AND NATURAL LAW

Sources of the medieval concept of natural law

The chief sources on which the scholastics drew for their knowledge of natural law were Cicero, the *Digest*, St Paul, the Fathers and, later, Aristotle.

St Paul observed in his Epistle to the Romans, 2.12–16, that even without knowledge of the Old Testament Law pagans have its substance written on their hearts. Conscience and reason lead men to do by nature what the Law commands.[1] Natural law thus accords with the Decalogue. Lactantius recorded Cicero's definition of law: true law is right reason in agreement with nature, being found among all men, summoning them to duty and prohibiting wrongdoing. True law may not be abolished by Senate or People; it is not different in Rome or in Athens, now or in the future. Its originator and promulgator is God; disobedience to it constitutes a denial of the nature of man.[2]

The *Digest* in its first chapter distinguished three types of law: *ius civile* or the law of the state, *ius gentium* or the law of nations, and *ius naturale* or the law of nature. The jurists cited defined the natural law variously. Ulpian described it as the common instinct of animals; the union of male and female, the procreation of offspring and their education have been taught to animals by nature. But Gaius defined the natural law as those human laws practised by all nations and dictated to all men by natural reason, and Paulus said that the natural law consists of what is equitable and good. The *Digest* does not establish natural law as a law able to override the laws of the courts, but it affirms that good laws are those that are grounded on nature, reason, equity and justice. Among the Christian Fathers, Isidore knew the definitions of the Roman lawyers, and in the fifth book of his *Etymologies* he too described the natural law as the law that is common to all nations and that is set up by a natural instinct, not by any positive constitution. It

---

1. 'Gentes quae legem non habent naturaliter quae legis sunt faciunt.'
2. Lactantius *Divinarum institutionum* lib. VI, c. 8 (*PL*. 6, 660–1); Cicero *De republica*, III, xxii, 33. Cf. Cicero *De legibus*, I, xii, 33.

enjoins the union of male and female, the procreation and education of children, the common possession of all things, universal liberty and the acquisition of things taken in the sky, on earth, and in the sea. It also includes the restitution of goods held in trust and the repulsion of violence by force.[3] Following the revival of the study of the Roman law from the end of the eleventh century, the definitions given in the *Digest* became more widely available. Ulpian's declaration that natural law is the common instinct which nature has taught all animals found the most favour with the civilians of the twelfth and thirteenth centuries.

Natural law in twelfth-century philosophy

Before the wide diffusion of the new Aristotle, and among the philosophers of the twelfth century, notably Peter Abelard and William of Conches, there was a particular insistence on the equivalence of nature and reason. Nature is a force implanted in things (*vis insita in rebus*); it operates according to the reason of God. Plato's *Timaeus* and Calcidius' commentary on it were central texts in the discussion of *natura* which was sometimes personified (e.g. by Alan of Lille in *De planctu naturae*) as a goddess who presided over the universe and taught the natural law. Peter Abelard in his *Dialogus inter philosophum, iudaeum et christianum* distinguished *ius naturale*, which is the reason within men which stipulates what is necessary for all men, and *ius positivum* which is instituted by men.[4] The natural law is the primitive law followed according to human reason before the giving of the Mosaic Law, which consists chiefly of a writing down of the content of the natural law.[5] The gentile philosophers, however, not knowing this revelation, pursued the *summum bonum* through the practice of virtue according to reason, and their lives are as exemplary as those of the Prophets.[6] The moral precepts of the Gospel constitute a reformation of the natural law followed by the philosophers.[7]

The Aristotelian contribution

With the broadening of knowledge of the Aristotelian *corpus*, beginning in the late twelfth century, the scholastics were not only able to give natural

---

3. *Etymologiarum*, lib. V, c. 4.
4. *Dialogus inter philosophum, iudaeum et christianum*, in PL. 178, 1656. On this see Gagner 1960, pp. 210–24.
5. *Dialogus*, in PL. 178, 619–23.
6. *Theologia Christiana*, II.
7. 'Si enim diligenter moralia Evangelii praecepta consideremus, nihil ea aliud quam reformationem legis naturalis inveniemus, quam secutos esse philosophos constat', *Theologia Christiana*, II (PL. 178, 1179D).

morality and natural law a metaphysical foundation but were also able to read Aristotle's own statement about natural justice. In his *Rhetoric* I, XIII, 2 (1373b) Aristotle distinguished between laws which are particular to individual states and general laws which are in accordance with nature and which reflect a universal idea of natural justice. Similarly in the *Nicomachean Ethics* V, vii (1134b–1135a) Aristotle affirmed the existence of natural justice and, in writing about political justice which regulates relations among citizens, he distinguished between natural rules which have the same validity everywhere and do not depend upon enactment, and conventional or legal rules, which, for example, lay down the cost of a ransom or the detailed requirements of sacrifice. These latter rules differ from state to state.

Gratian and the decretists

In the introductory distinctions of the *Concordia discordantium canonum*, Gratian followed Isidore in defining natural law as the law common to all nations by virtue of being found everywhere because of natural instinct and not because of any positive constitution. It came into existence with the very creation of man as a rational being; it does not vary in time, but remains unchangeable.[8] But Gratian said more than Cicero or the Roman lawyers: 'Natural law prevails in antiquity and in dignity over all laws'. 'Whatever has been recognised by custom, or laid down in writing, if it contradicts natural law, must be considered null and void.'[9] He cites Isidore, *Etymologies* V, 2: 'All laws are either divine or human. Divine laws are based on nature, human laws on custom. The reason why the latter differ from one another is that different nations prefer different laws.'[10] Gratian equated the natural law with the basic moral precept contained in the divine law regarding neighbourly love: 'Mankind is ruled by two things: Natural law and custom. Natural law is that which is contained in the Law and the Gospel where everyone is commanded to do to another as he would be done by and forbidden to do to another what he does not wish to have done to himself.'[11]

---

8. D.V.1.

9. 'Naturale ius inter omnia primatum obtinet et tempore et dignitate,' D.V.1. 'Quecumque enim vel moribus recepta sunt, vel scriptis comprehensa, si naturali iuri fuerint adversa, vana et irrita sunt habenda', D.VIII.11.

10. 'Omnes leges aut divinae sunt, aut humanae. Divinae natura, humanae moribus constant, ideoque hae discrepant, quoniam aliae aliis gentibus placent', D.I.

11. 'Humanum genus duobus regitur, naturali videlicet iure et moribus. Ius naturae est, quod in lege et evangelio continetur, quo quisque iubetur alii facere, quod sibi vult fieri, et prohibetur alii inferre, quod sibi nolit fieri', D.I.

The Decretists who explained Gratian's text tended to follow him in defining natural law as that which is contained in the Scriptures and which teaches man to do to others what he would have others do to himself. They pushed into the background Isidore's natural law common to all nations. But like the philosophers they readily invoked the concept of natural justice with references to the *Timaeus* or to Stoic morality. Thus Rufinus of Assisi (d. *ca.* 1190) drew upon Cicero to describe man's capacity to distinguish between good and evil as a natural power.[12] The Decretists were aware of the different senses of the natural law. They began to list the various definitions more or less systematically: natural law is the teaching of Scripture, or it is what is left undetermined by divine command or prohibition; it is the human capacity to distinguish right from wrong; it is natural equity; it is also the natural instinct of all animals and as well a general law of all creation.

Early Franciscan masters

The task of trying to classify and analyse these descriptions was taken up by the scholastics of the thirteenth century, and particularly by the early Franciscan masters. The treatise on law by John of La Rochelle (contained in the third part of the *Summa* attributed to Alexander of Hales) distinguished three modes of natural law: *nativum*, *humanum*, and *divinum*. The first is the natural law which has regard to all animate creatures; the second is that which refers to the order of rational creatures and is the *ius gentium*; the third is the law regulating human actions in respect of divine grace, e.g. the Mosaic Law. Each of these modes derives from the eternal law of God.[13] Discussion also developed regarding the permanence or impermanence of the precepts of the natural law. Problems were raised by the doctrine of the Fall and by Old Testament examples of such irregular actions as cases of polygamy among the Prophets and the Mosaic bill of divorce. The question whether God could dispense from the natural law or whether man could adjust it was treated by the *Summa fratris Alexandri* in the light of the distinction between immutable precepts (e.g. the law of charity) and variable demonstrations of these precepts (e.g. communal property, human equality and liberty). The demonstrations can be adjusted to suit changing needs.[14] The natural law regulates human reason

---

12. 'Vis quaedam humanae creaturae a natura insita ad faciendum bonum cavendumque contrarium,' *Summa Magistri Rufini*, ed. von Schulte, p. 4.
13. *Alexandri de Hales ... Summa theologica.* Liber III, pars II, Inq. II, q. IV, c. 1.
14. *Alexandri de Hales ... Summa theologica.* Lib. III, pars II, Inq. II, q. III.

through the medium of conscience which is formed by the natural law, and human will through *synderesis*, the spark of conscience (*scintilla conscientiae*). The law lays down that good should be done and evil avoided; man makes a judgement of reason in the light of this principle before committing an action and this forms conscience; having made his judgement, *synderesis* prompts the will to do what is good.[15]

Albert the Great

Albert the Great reacted against the practice of the lawyers who enumerated the different senses of the natural law, and he rejected Ulpian's definition of the natural law as that which nature has taught all animals. Natural law exists only for man and is nothing other than the law of reason.[16] Thus, the procreative instinct of the animals is not part of natural law or of natural justice because it lacks the rationality required for human marriage. However, human reason has in the past justifiably permitted dispensations from the law of monogamy.[17] In his commentary on Aristotle's *Ethics*, V, where he treats of Aristotle's distinction between natural and legal justice, Albert also rejects the cosmic notion of justice associated with the *Timaeus*. Natural justice, which Albert assimilates to the moral nature of man, proceeds from human reason.[18] He interprets Cicero's definition of the natural law as an innate force (*innata vis*) to mean the light of the agent intellect.[19]

Thomas Aquinas

The foundation of Aquinas' classic formulation of the doctrine of natural law is the teleological principle that all beings by their nature have within themselves inclinations which direct them to the end which is proper to them. Good has the nature of an end and evil is its contrary.[20] There is a difference between animals which are driven by instinct (*aestimatio naturalis*) and men who also have the capacity of knowing their end and the relationship of the means to the end. However, human actions arise both from a natural inclination in the appetitive faculty and from a natural

15. Op. cit., Lib. III, pars II, Inq. II, q. II, c. 3.
16. *De bono* (*ca.* 1242), Tractatus V, De iustitia, q. 1, a. 1–2(12). *Ethica* (after 1260), lib. V, tract. III, cap. III. Cf. *Super Ethica commentum et quaestiones*, lib. V, lectio XI, 421 (written 1250–2).
17. *De sacramentis*, Tractatus IX, De matrimonio, Q. 3. Cf. *Commentary on the Sentences* (1244–9), lib. IV, dist. 33 A, a.1–3.
18. *Super Ethica*, lib. V, lectio XI, 419. *De bono*, Tract. V, q. 1, a. 2.
19. *De bono*, Tract. V, q. 1. a. 1 (12).
20. 'Bonum est faciendum et prosequendum et malum vitandum', Aquinas *ST*, IaIIae, q. 94, a. 2.

concept in the cognitive faculty. In his commentary on Aristotle's *Ethics* (lib. V, lectio XII; written 1271–2), Aquinas distinguished between man's animal nature, which is obliged by natural instinct to mate and to rear offspring, and his rational nature which is obliged by the *ius gentium* to keep agreements, to grant immunity to envoys, and so on. Aquinas did not reject Ulpian's definition of the natural law. Indeed, his reason for admitting that polygamy was allowed by the natural law was that not all the animals restrict themselves to having one mate. The Old Testament examples of polygamy and of divorce are thus not dispensations or breaches of the natural law specially allowed by God.[21]

In his *Summa theologiae* (IaIIae, q. 94, a. 2) Aquinas provided a ranking of the precepts of the natural law which corresponds to an order of natural inclinations. First, man shares with all substances the inclination to self-preservation, and the natural law enjoins those things that preserve human life. Secondly, man shares with all animals a more particular inclination towards the union of male and female and the education of offspring. Thirdly, man by virtue of his rational nature has an inclination to do good and to know the truth about God and to live in society. Human, moral obligation is therefore imposed by reason and the rational is natural, because it has a basis in human nature, which is rational. 'In human affairs a thing is said to be just by virtue of its being right according to the rule of reason. The first rule of reason is the law of nature.'[22] Man's natural desire includes the desire to know God. In the *Summa theologiae* (IaIIae, q. 4) Aquinas went beyond Aristotle's ethics of human conduct in this life. The human will and the human intellect cannot be fully satisfied unless they achieve their supernatural end, which is the vision of God.[23] Aquinas distinguished two ends for man: the natural end, which consists in an imperfect knowledge of God through his creatures and in the practice of the natural virtues, and the supernatural end, which transcends the power of nature, consists of life eternal, and requires the infusion of the theological or supernatural virtues into the soul.

In *ST*, IaIIae, q. 91, art. 1–2, Aquinas gave a detailed formulation of the place of natural law in the eternal and divine order. Since the universe is governed by divine providence and by divine reason, and since this is

---

21. In *SCG*, III, c. 122, Aquinas condemns fornication as contrary to the divine law which supports the natural law.
22. 'In rebus autem humanis dicitur esse aliquid iustum ex eo quod est rectum secundum regulam rationis. Rationis autem prima regula est lex naturae', *ST*, IaIIae, q. 95, a. 2.
23. Cf. Aquinas *SCG*, III, 39.

outside the limits of time, there is also an eternal law to which all creatures are subject. The end or final cause of all natures is to be what they are, and all things derive from the eternal law certain inclinations to those actions and aims that are proper to them. Rational creatures participate in the eternal law intellectually and rationally and this participation is the natural law.[24]

The first and fundamental precept of natural law is 'good is to be done and pursued and evil avoided' and this precept is self-evident since all creatures act on account of their end, which is the good for them.[25] In his commentary on the *Sentences* Aquinas identifies what is 'written in everyone's practical intellect' with the Law given to Moses, which re-iterates what is known to human reason. He also distinguishes between primary and secondary precepts of the natural law in the light of a distinction between primary and secondary ends of nature.[26] The primary ends of nature include the use of food, bodily health, procreation and the upbringing of children. Anything which prevents the achievement of those ends is forbidden by the primary precepts of the natural law. Here Aquinas treats a primary precept of the natural law as one which embraces all animal behaviour, as in Ulpian's definition, although man has in addition a certain inclination to know the truth about God. The secondary precepts regulate specifically human and rational behaviour; they relate to whatever makes the achievement of human ends more possible or im-possible. The primary precepts are self-evident; secondary precepts are deduced by the process of reasoning and may, as in the case of monogamy, be modified in rare circumstances.

Aquinas' distinction between the primary and secondary precepts of the natural law is presented afresh in *ST*, IaIIae, q. 94, a. 4. The primary and secondary precepts are, respectively, common principles that are self-evident to the theoretical or speculative reason and conclusions deduced by the practical reason from the common principles and relating to the sphere of contingent happenings. The practical reason is not immune from making erroneous judgements and it does not everywhere and at all times draw the same conclusions regarding particular situations. The further the practical reason goes into detail regarding moral judgements and human events, the more it is likely to fall into error and to provide divergent

---

24. 'Lex naturalis nihil aliud est quam participatio legis aeternae in rationali creatura', *ST*, IaIIae, q. 91 a. 2.
25. *ST*, IaIIae, q. 94, a. 2.
26. *In IV Sent.* d. 33. Cf. *In IV Sent.* d. 26, q. 1. a. 1, *ad* 1.

decisions. However, the primary or common principles are equally well known to all men and are wholly immutable; they have a kind of necessity (*aliqua necessitas*). The secondary or particular principles that follow closely by way of conclusion from these first principles are the same among most people, although in a few societies passion or entrenched social custom may obscure their appreciation, as happened, according to Caesar, among the Germans who turned robbery into a virtue. Aquinas says little about the content of the two kinds of precept, and what he does say is provided by way of illustration. For example, it is a common principle that man should do good according to reason, and this leads to the conclusion that what is borrowed should be returned. But this conclusion is not invariable because it might be unreasonable in certain circumstances to return borrowed goods, e.g. if their owner wished to use them to harm the state.

Natural law in Thomas' expositions stands between eternal law on the one hand and positive law – both divine and human – on the other. It is linked with both. It is neither an ultimate nor a detailed source of law or morality. In a long discussion of the divine law in *SCG*, III, 114ff. Thomas presents the divine law not as the Old Testament Law and the Gospel but as a development of the requirements of nature and as a help to the natural law, commanding explicitly what is intrinsically and objectively right. Divine law is the reason of God in relation to the governance of human beings.[27] Its end is the love of God and of one's neighbour. The things that are prescribed by the divine law are right not only because they have been established by law but also because they are in accordance with nature and are naturally right (*SCG*, III, 129). The divine law prescribes that man observe the order of reason in those things that are given over to his use; it confirms the rational distinction between good and evil.

Human positive law is also, like all law, an act of reason.[28] Its purpose is to benefit human life by deriving conclusions from the natural law that suit particular needs and by adding to the precepts of the natural law, just as the written law is said to supply what was wanting in the natural law. Through human positive law private property and slavery have been instituted to meet the convenience of man (*ST*, IaIIae, q. 94, a. 5 and q. 95). In his Commentary on the *Ethics*, V (lectio XII) Aquinas uses the terms '*conclusio*' in respect of principles derived from natural justice (e.g. thieves

---

27. 'Lex ... est quaedam ratio divinae providentiae gubernantis rationali creaturae proposita', *SCG*, III, 115; 'lex divina est quaedam ratio divinae providentiae ad homines gubernandos', ibid., 128.
28. '[Lex] nihil est aliud quam quaedam rationis ordinatio ad bonum commune ab eo qui curam habet communitatis promulgata', *ST*, IaIIae, q. 90, a. 4.

should be punished) and '*determinatio*' in respect of positive laws also derived therefrom (e.g. such or such a penalty should be inflicted). Law is commanded by the ruler's will, but command (*imperare*) is an act of reason that springs from the will (*ST*, IaIIae, q. 90, 1 ad 3). If the will of the legislator is not regulated by reason, and if human law is at variance with natural law, it is not law but a corruption of it (*ST*, IaIIae, q. 95, a. 2).

Duns Scotus

By contrast with Aquinas' emphasis on reason, Franciscan thinkers tended to base moral values on the free will of God, limited only by the bounds of logical possibility.

For Duns Scotus law and morality are primarily the product of the divine will. The divine will is the first rule or rectitude.[29] It is the cause of good, and so by the fact that God wills something it is good.[30] But Scotus also states that God cannot will anything that is not good (e.g. hatred of himself) and that an act is naturally good (*naturaliter bonus*) when it is in conformity with right reason (*recta ratio*). The Ten Commandments are divine precepts that condemn what is wrong also by the law of nature.[31] Scotus distinguished between immutable moral laws that are self-evident and moral laws that are merely in accordance with the primary principles but are not absolutely necessary. The first group belongs to the natural law in the strictest sense and is contained in the first two commandments which are concerned with the very notion of good and of God. The second, which are provided by the commandments of the second Table from Sabbath observance onwards, may be dispensed with by God since they regulate the conduct of human beings in particular ways that admit of exception and variation. Thus, the Old Testament incidents relating to Abraham's duty to slay Isaac, the polygamy of the Patriarchs, the spoliation of the goods of the Egyptians and the fornication of Hosea illustrate the fact that the secondary precepts are not necessary but arise from the will of

---

29. 'Voluntas divina quae est prima regula omnium agibilium et omnium actionum, et actio divinae voluntatis, ex quo est prima regula, est prima rectitudo', *Reportata Parisiensia*, lib. IV, dist. XLVI, qu. IV, n. VIII.

30. 'Voluntas divina est causa boni et ideo eo ipso quod vult aliquod, ipsum est bonum', *Reportata Parisiensia*, lib. I, dist. XLVIII, qu. unica.

31. 'Omnia peccata, quae sunt circa decem praecepta, formaliter non tantum sunt mala quia prohibita, sed quia mala, ideo prohibita, quia ex lege naturae oppositum cujuslibet fuit malum, et per naturalem rationem potest homo videre, quod quodlibet praeceptum ex illis est tenendum', *Reportata Parisiensia*, lib. II, dist. XXII, qu. unica. n. 3. On *recta ratio* see *Opus Oxoniense*, II, XL. qu. unica, n. 3.

God.[32] Aquinas had not allowed that the secondary precepts could be dispensed with; cases of apparent dispensation were cases in which the circumstances were so altered that the precept no longer applied. But Scotus saw that the precepts relating, for example, to the inviolability of private property and the wrongness of stealing admitted of legitimate exceptions and are not self-evident. They depend on the divine will and although they are reasonable, they are neither necessary nor strictly of the natural law. For God is free to command anything except that which contradicts itself.

William Ockham

Ockham considerably developed the implications of the 'voluntarist ethics' of the Franciscans. Perhaps he meant to exaggerate when he supported his view that God could have sanctioned anything that falls short of logical contradiction by saying that he could have commanded even hatred of himself.[33] But he emphasised that God is not under any obligation to do anything; whatever he wills is by this fact just.[34] All obligation has its foundation in divine command and in man's dependence on God. 'Evil is nothing else than to do something when one is under an obligation to do the opposite.'[35] Yet Ockham did not abandon natural morality or the natural law. In his Commentary on the *Sentences* where this radical 'voluntarism' finds its expression, Ockham also wrote, like Scotus, that 'every right will is in conformity with right reason'[36] and that 'there is no such thing as moral virtue or virtuous action unless it is in conformity with right reason, for right reason is included in the definition of virtue in the second book of the *Ethics*'.[37] And in his political tract entitled *Dialogus de imperio ac pontificia potestate* Ockham spoke of the *ius naturale* and distinguished it into three modes. The first consists of absolutely immutable norms conforming to the natural reason, e.g. the prohibition of lying and adultery. The

---

32. *Opus Oxoniense*, III, 37, qu. unica. Cf. *Reportata Parisiensia*, IV, d. XVII, qu. unica, scholium primum.
33. *In Sent.* II, qu. 19P.
34. 'Obligatio non cadit in deum quia ille ad nihil faciendum obligatur', *In Sent.* II, qu. 5H. 'Deus ad nullum actum causandum obligatur, ideo quemlibet actum absolutum potest sine omni malo culpe causare et eius oppositum', *In Sent.* II, qu. 19P. 'Deus autem ad nullum actum potest obligari; et ideo eo ipso, quod Deus vult, hoc est iustum fieri', *In Sent.* IV, qu. 9E.
35. 'Malum nihil aliud est quam facere aliquid ad cuius oppositum faciendum aliquis obligatur', *In Sent.* II, qu. 5H.
36. 'Omnis voluntas recta est conformis rationi recte', *In Sent.* I, dist. 41K.
37. 'Nulla virtus moralis nec actus ... est virtuosus nisi conformis recte rationi quia recta ratio ponitur in diffinitione virtutis secundo ethicorum', *In Sent.* III, qu. 12NN. Cf. Aristotle, *Nic. Eth.*, 1107a. See also Ockham, *In Sent.* III, qu. 12CCC.

second consists of *ius naturale* that may be legitimately modified by positive law, e.g. the common ownership of property and universal liberty; this is what man should uphold through natural equity if there were no customs or institutions. The third consists of norms that may be deduced by evident reason and by supposition from the *ius gentium* or from human behaviour, e.g. that violence, being against the law of nature, may be lawfully repelled by force.[38]

The fourteenth and fifteenth centuries

Whether the nominalist movement of the fourteenth century resulted in a growing preference by thinkers to move natural law closer to divine law and to divine will is a question that has produced varying answers. Thomas Bradwardine found no place for the natural law and forged no such link between God's will and man's reason. On the other hand Gabriel Biel did not break radically with Aquinas and accepted natural-law teaching. Some scholars have seen Luther's emphasis on the corruption of human nature as the climax of the retreat by many thinkers at the end of the Middle Ages from the 'classical' scholastic theory that natural law is different from the law that comes from revelation; others have doubted the extent of such an abandonment of natural-law principles. The general picture as regards the fourteenth and fifteenth centuries is less clear than one might wish it to be.

The sixteenth century

However, in the sixteenth century there was a revival of discussion of the natural law and a marked renewal of interest in Aquinas' teaching. Substantial treatments of natural law doctrine were provided by Robert Bellarmine, Gabriel Vásquez, Dominic de Soto, Richard Hooker and Francisco Suárez. Richard Hooker restated Aquinas' arguments regarding the divisions of law in the first book of *The Laws of Ecclesiastical Polity* (1594). Francisco Suárez in his *De legibus ac Deo legislatore* (1612) likewise returned to Thomas but provided as well (in Book II) a notable review and critique of subsequent scholastic thinking from Ockham down to Vásquez in his own time.

Francisco Suárez

At the very beginning of his treatise Suárez seeks to establish that natural law is truly law. He comments upon Aquinas' definition of law as a certain

---

38. *Dialogus de imperio ac pontificia potestate*, III, tr. 2, p. 3, c. 6.

rule and measure in accordance with which one is induced to act or is restrained from acting.[39] This he criticises as too broad and general. It appears to suit all creatures, not only those that are human and rational, and it appears to embrace other actions than moral ones; it also includes counsels which are clearly distinct from precepts. The expression 'natural law' may broadly and metaphorically refer to the inclinations of all natural things, as it seems to do in Plato's *Timaeus* and also here in Aquinas' *Summa*, or it may just refer to all animate creatures as in the Roman law. But, strictly speaking, things that lack reason are not susceptible to law and are not capable of obedience; law is strictly a rule, not a working out or an effect of a rule.[40] Suárez accordingly attempts a tighter definition of the natural law as 'a certain measure of moral acts in the sense that such acts are characterised by moral rectitude through their conformity to law, and by perversity, if they are out of harmony with law'.[41] The natural law is 'that form of law which dwells within the human mind in order that right may be distinguished from wrong'.[42]

In Book II, c. V, of *De legibus* Suárez concentrates his criticism upon Vásquez and disagrees that natural law is right reason or the faculty of rational judgement. While rational nature is the foundation of the natural law and provides the measure or standard of objective right and wrong, law is a more specific concept than that of a standard or measure. Conscience too is a broader term than that of law and, moreover, conscience, unlike natural law, can err (II, V, 15). Law has to be commanded; it requires a lawgiver, and law and command are not provided by rational nature. If natural law is rational nature, it merely indicates what should or should not be done and is thus *lex indicativa* or *demonstrativa*. Suárez traces this view back to Gregory of Rimini and to Gabriel Biel, who, he says (II, VI, 3), appear to hold that natural law does not come from a lawgiving God and does not depend on God's will. Since it consists of the dictates of right reason and manifests the evil that resides intrinsically in evil acts (e.g. lying), it would have the character of law (or at least of indicative law) even if God did not exist. Suárez himself believed that only a preceptive law (*lex praeceptiva*) which commands and prohibits is truly a law because law

---

39. Suárez 1971–7, I, I, 1. Cf. Aquinas *ST*, IaIIae, qu. 90, a. 1: 'Lex est quaedam regula et mensura secundum quam inducitur aliquis ad agendum vel ab agendo retrahitur.'
40. Suárez 1971–7, loc. cit. Cf. I, III, 5.
41. 'Mensura quaedam actuum moralium, ita ut per conformitatem ad illam rectitudinem moralem recti, et si ab illa discordent obliqui sint', Suárez 1971–77, I, I, 5.
42. 'Lex ergo naturalis propria quae ad moralem doctrinam et theologiam pertinet est illa quae humanae menti insidet ad discernendum honestum a turpi', Suárez 1971–77, I, III, 9.

cannot exist apart from a legislator or *praecipiens* whose will it imposes. On the other hand, Suárez does not wish to subscribe to the extreme view, which he finds in Ockham,[43] and according to which natural law is simply and entirely what is commanded or prohibited by God as the author and ruler of nature. In saying that no act is evil except in so far as it is forbidden by God and that God can abolish or change the whole natural law, Ockham and those who agree with him (Suárez cites John Gerson and Peter of Ailly in *De legibus*, II, VI, 4) assimilate the natural law into the eternal law which issues the divine commands and prohibitions. The role of the natural reason is to reveal God's will to man.

Suárez thus provides an admirable appreciation of the divisions of opinion towards the end of the medieval period. He proceeds in *De legibus* (II, VI, 5ff.), to expand fully a *via media* that is based on Aquinas and comprises three principal theses. The first is that natural law is genuinely preceptive or prescriptive law. It is more than a knowledge of self-evident principles because contravention of it is an offence against God's will and mandate. Secondly, natural law is more than precept and prohibition. God's will prescribes acts that are good or evil for rational nature. Human reason demonstrates this natural law to mankind and shows as well that acts contrary to natural law are also contrary to divine law. Thirdly, natural law is truly divine law and God is its legislator. Suárez sees (*De legibus*, II, VI, 14ff.) that the matter turns upon the admissibility of the hypothesis that intrinsic goodness has to be sought and intrinsic evil has to be avoided even if God were not to exist. He considers an argument put by Bartholomew Medina and urges that, even if a preceptive divine law is put aside, an evil action is still not only morally wrong but also a sin apart from its relation to God because it transgresses the law of nature.

The remainder of Suárez' treatment of the natural law is not without importance both in itself and in view of the light it sheds on the divergence of teachings up to his own time. In *De legibus*, II, VII Suárez discussed the scope of the contents of the natural law. He roundly affirmed that the natural law embraces all moral precepts which are characterised by the goodness necessary to right conduct. Natural law includes as well as self-evident principles – both general (e.g. do good and avoid evil) and specific (e.g. worship God; observe justice) – deductions from self-evident precepts which may not be equally clear to all men (e.g. the prohibitions of adultery, usury, and lying). Far from hesitating over the necessity or

43. Ockham, *In Sent. II*, qu. 19 *ad* 3, 4.

properly natural-law character of these deductions, Suárez holds that the truth of a principle becomes clearer in the conclusion; natural reason works more through the specific conclusions that can be applied to individual acts and virtues than through universal principles.

Suárez also provided a defence of the immutable character of the natural law by distinguishing between intrinsic and extrinsic change and between positive and negative precepts (*De legibus*, II, XIII). Intrinsically the precepts of the natural law cannot vary, but since they cannot cover all the particular circumstances which may arise (e.g. killing in self-defence, breaking a secret to safeguard a third party), the precepts may be adapted extrinsically to fit altering circumstances. Moreover, many things (e.g. common ownership of goods) fall under the natural law which are not commanded by it. Common ownership would naturally occur, as would nakedness unless man introduced a different arrangement; it was permitted to man and private ownership was not prohibited (*De legibus*, II, XIV). So the institution of private property is not a sign that man can alter the natural law, for private property falls negatively under the natural law in the sense that it is not prohibited by it. Natural law positively prescribes not that all should own all but that all should be able to use what is necessary for each; consequently, natural law prohibits such undue taking of property as prevents reasonable use. Just as man cannot alter the natural law, neither can God. Against Ockham Suárez argued that the precepts of the natural law cannot be altered by God because they pertain to intrinsic goodness or wrongness (e.g. God cannot command man to hate him). Against Scotus, Suárez maintained that God cannot alter or dispense with any of the Ten Commandments and he argued, like Aquinas, that the alleged instances of dispensations in the Old Testament (e.g. the spoliation of the goods of the Egyptians by the Hebrews) are apparent examples only since dominion over these goods belonged rightfully to the Hebrews by divine judgement (*De legibus*, II, XV).

Finally, and especially because Suárez is considered an authority on international law, it may be noted that he firmly distinguished the *ius gentium* and the natural law. Although, like the natural law, the *ius gentium* is common to all men, Suárez sees a distinction between, on the one hand, the conclusions which are drawn from the primary moral principles of the natural law and which are themselves natural law, and, on the other hand, the common unwritten customs of the nations and the detailed regulations that govern relations between nations. These are part of positive, human law (*De legibus*, II, XVII–XIX).

The seventeenth century

Later in the seventeenth century Pufendorf came to denounce the schoolmen's doctrine of the natural law. Hugo Grotius in his *De iure belli ac pacis* (1625) paved the way to the future by writing about natural and about international law not as a theologian but as a lawyer. But it is clear that he followed the later scholastics when he made his famous pronouncement that natural law would retain its validity even if God did not exist. He built his theory of laws independently of theological assumptions but his definition of the natural law is not revolutionary: 'The law of nature is a dictate of right reason which points out that an act, according as it is or is not in conformity with rational nature, has in it a quality of moral baseness or moral necessity; and that, in consequence, such an act is either forbidden or enjoined by the author of nature, God.'[44] With this Suárez, and many before him, would not have disagreed.

44. 'Ius naturale est dictatum rectae rationis indicans, actui alicui, ex ejus convenientia aut disconvenientia cum ipsa natura rationali inesse moralem turpitudinem aut necessitatem moralem, ac consequenter ab auctore naturae Deo talem actum aut vetari aut praecipi', *De iure belli ac pacis*, I, I, 10, 1.

X
POLITICS

38

THE RECEPTION AND INTERPRETATION OF ARISTOTLE'S *POLITICS*

The scope of this study

This study makes no pretensions to being a comprehensive survey of medieval commentaries on the *Politics*; it is confined to a few of the known commentaries on Moerbeke's translation, all dated to the late thirteenth and the fourteenth centuries. Within this narrow range, it aims to discuss, firstly, how close the earliest commentaries, those of Albert the Great and of Thomas Aquinas with the *Continuation* by Peter of Auvergne, came to explaining Aristotle's meaning accurately and, secondly, what motives later commentators had in writing, what arguments they considered valid, and how far, if at all, their own views can be inferred from what they wrote. To make some useful comparison between the texts, I shall, after a few introductory remarks on each commentary, concentrate on what each scholar made of Aristotle's arguments for the proposition that the multitude of freemen in a state should participate in its political life (*Politics* III, 1281b and 1282a). Because they recognised its importance, all the commentators expanded, illustrated, or interpreted this passage in a way which brings out their individual characters and sometimes their political ideas.

William of Moerbeke's translation

The exact date at which Moerbeke finished his translation of the *Politics* is still uncertain, but it was probably around 1260. Moerbeke tried to render Aristotle's meaning without the slightest interpretation of his own – an aim which he believed could be best fulfilled by translating word for word, preserving the Greek word order, some Greek double negatives, and even an occasional Greek term – e.g., *'epikeia'* – for which there was no exact Latin equivalent. The last chapter of Book II is full of mistakes, and there are some errors in Books VI and VII;[1] but, in general, it is a very accurate rendering. Unfortunately, accuracy is more than counterbalanced by unintelligibility. So the first function of the earliest Latin commentators,

1. Newman 1887, vol. 2, p. xiv, note 1.

Albert, Thomas, and Peter of Auvergne, was to engage in the task which
Moerbeke had declined, to explain what Aristotle was saying, using
methods of exposition and philosophical terms familiar to late-thirteenth-
century scholars and students. Though not without their mistakes, the
commentaries are in general far more correct than incorrect.[2]

Albert the Great's commentary

Albert's commentary has been tentatively dated to around 1265,[3] which
would make it the earliest written in the Latin West. It ends with his often-
quoted diatribe against the anti-Aristotelian party in the schools, whom he
compares with the slayers of Socrates; their criticisms he ascribes to laziness
and a desire to paralyse others into their own inertia.[4] But despite the
violence of its ending, and the vast storehouse of knowledge revealed in his
citations from other authorities, this commentary was not among his most
important or influential works. He adopts the normal method of literal
exposition, dividing each book into chapters (not the ones conventionally
adopted by later authors), stating the theme, breaking each chapter into
sections, stating the main arguments, then sub-dividing till he comes to
each individual phrase. But here, instead of paraphrasing loosely, as was his
normal habit, he keeps very close to the wording of the Moerbeke translation, changing only what is strictly necessary in order to make the phrase
intelligible. To this, he adds comments on the grammatical constructions,
additional information on persons or places mentioned, the occasional
contemporary example of a phenomenon discussed by Aristotle or quotations from other authorities (classical, biblical, patristic or Arabic)
making the same point as Aristotle. But there is comparatively little
interpretation of the text, and no chance to find out what he himself thinks
of it.

Given this method, what Albert makes of the passage on the participation of free men is in general predictable: by stating the main lines of
argument first, he makes Aristotle's aporetic style somewhat more trenchant, and certainly easier to understand; when he gets down to the
individual sentences, he renders them succinctly, usually accurately, and
without judgement on the merit of the line being pursued. He gives the
kind of assistance which might be expected of a good crib. But there is one
point at which his comment can only confuse the reader: where Aristotle

2. Martin 1951, p. 36.
3. Aquinas 1971a, p. A8.
4. Albert the Great 1890–9d, pp. 803–4.

states that there is an element of truth in the view that the multitude ought to be supreme (1281a), the Moerbeke translation renders this *oportet dominos esse liberos et multitudinem civium*. Albert, in explaining the *multitudinem civium*, goes back to the definition given at 1278a: a citizen in the strictest sense is he who shares in the offices and honours of the state.[5] This definition looks odd in conjunction with Albert's very next phrase, which states that these men have no special standing. His misunderstanding robs the passage of its radical import. Again, when Aristotle says that it is dangerous to exclude the multitude totally from office and concludes that they should have some deliberative and judicial functions, Albert explains these words as applying only to citizens understood in an elitist sense,[6] although he has just correctly explained Aristotle's opposition to their holding office on ground of their folly. Despite Albert's very great reputation, no later commentators followed him in this reading.[7]

The commentary of Thomas Aquinas and Peter of Auvergne

The second, and far more influential, commentary which sought to make Moerbeke intelligible was that of Thomas Aquinas, continued by his disciple Peter of Auvergne. Thomas' part, perhaps to be dated to his second Paris regency, 1269–72,[8] covers Books I–III 6, and there are some, by no means indisputable, signs that he knew Albert's work.[9] Peter's part, which starts at the beginning of Book III,[10] probably dates from 1274–90.[11] He certainly had access to Albert's commentary. Both include the same amount of literal exposition, but are more willing to paraphrase. The general level of accuracy in rendering individual phrases of the text is high, though there are some errors – mostly of detail, and commoner in Books V and VI, replete as they are with historical allusions unfamiliar to the thirteenth century. More impressively, the summing up of arguments at the beginning of each section is remarkably accurate – it is certainly Aristotle's point of view which is being given.

Thomas' part has recently been edited, with a full introduction; no more need be said of it here. But Peter's has been less intensively studied; and

---

5. *Ibid.*, p. 259
6. *Ibid.*, p. 260.
7. It is possible, however, that it is to be found in some of the fifteenth-, sixteenth- and seventeenth-century commentaries, strongly influenced by Albert, discussed in Czartoryski 1960, pp. 3–44.
8. Weisheipl 1974a, p. 381.
9. Aquinas 1971a, p. A10.
10. Grech 1967.
11. *Ibid.*, p. 55.

because his influence on later commentators was very powerful, it justifies a more extended examination of his method than will be accorded to others in this study. Unlike Albert, Peter is prepared to interpret his text when he gets down to the detail of the argument and even to make additions to it. The best known of these[12] was made at III 1284b, where Aristotle says that kingship is one of the true forms of government; Peter, however, says that it is the best constitution. It may be that this reflects his own opinion, though there can be no certainty on the point, and the fact that he was a loyal subject of the French king will not prove it. It certainly does reflect his belief that all Aristotle's writings form a unity; he has simply inserted here the statement Aristotle makes in Book VIII of the *Nicomachean Ethics* (1108b). Another, much less controversial, addition comes at the end of 1283b; there he concludes from what Aristotle says that the question whether the legislator who desires to make the justest laws ought to legislate with a view to the good of the higher classes or of the many is answered in favour of the many.[13] This is indeed what the text implies. But Peter, by stating the implication, gives it greater significance in the course of the argument than it has in Aristotle's text; and the impact of this addition on later commentators was enormous. Walter Burley even argues that this is the most important question in the whole of Book III,[14] an impression he could never have got from the original text alone; and since it was an idea particularly congenial to medieval thinkers, no doubt they were glad to find it in Aristotle. A third addition comes at V 1301b, where Aristotle says that those who excel in virtue have the best right to rebel, but are of all men least inclined to do so; Peter adds to his explanation of this remark that, if the virtuous have a just cause and also the power to rebel, they ought to do so, and they sin if they do not.[15]

Aristotle asks whether the principle that the multitude collectively are better judges than the few good men applies to all multitudes, then says it is not clear. 'Or rather, by heaven, in some cases it is impossible of application; for the argument would equally hold about brutes; and wherein, it will be asked, do some men differ from brutes?' (1281b). Peter fits this into a neat shape; multitudes can be of two kinds: either *bestialis*, without reason, individually or corporately, and therefore having no claim to a political

---

12. Daly 1968, p. 43; Thomas Aquinas 1951, p. 169, section 474.
13. Thomas Aquinas 1951, p. 164, section 461.
14. Oxford Balliol MS 95, f. 183ᵛ, 'haec quaestio est principalis huius libri'.
15. Thomas Aquinas 1951, p. 247, section 714 – a remark hard to reconcile with the authoritarianism attributed to Peter in Martin 1951, p. 39.

role; or one in which each man has some inclination to virtue (called by later commentators *multitudo bene ordinata*), where corporately the whole has more prudence than a small group of good men, and therefore a role in political life is merited. The effect of Peter's tidying operation is undoubtedly to give greater prominence to the *multitudo bestialis* than it has in Aristotle's argument, and to make quite explicit the fact that it is denied a political role.[16] But whether there is any substantial innovation here, which can be ascribed to an anti-democratic bias,[17] is far more doubtful. Peter defines this multitude entirely in moral and rational terms, not social ones. Aristotle cites with apparent approval Solon's system, in which the people elected and called to account the magistrates. Peter specifies this as the role of the *multitudo bene ordinata*, thus introducing a new and potent element into medieval political thinking.

Peter also seeks to explain why Aristotle is so hesitant in concluding that the people, if not degraded, are probably better judges corporately than a few good men (1282a). He cannot ascribe this, as a modern critic might, to a slightly irritating stylistic habit; for him everything the Philosopher says has significance. So the *'forte'* ('perhaps') with which Aristotle introduces his conclusion is ascribed to the fact that this conclusion does not apply to all constitutions, and in particular not to monarchies, where the people have no right to elect or punish but must simply obey their moral superior.[18]

When Aristotle raises again the claim of the multitude to rule (1283b) on the grounds that it is stronger than a few men, Peter uses this opportunity to sum up the whole argument. He states that a multitude which is made up of some wise and prudent men and others who, though not wise in themselves, can be persuaded to accept reason, ought to rule, in the sense of electing and punishing rulers, because such a multitude has the two requirements for rule, both knowledge of how it should be done, and (in virtue of its numbers) the power to repel enemies.[19] By putting together two pieces of argument which are separated in the text, and thus stressing that power is a necessary part of the popular claim to be involved in the state, Peter has in effect strengthened Aristotle's case for popular participation.

These three additions to the passage all seem to be inspired simply by a

16. Thomas Aquinas 1951, pp. 151–2, section 427–31.
17. Grignashi 1966, p. 83.
18. Thomas Aquinas 1951, p. 152m, section 435.
19. *Ibid.*, pp. 161–2, section 549.

desire to bring out the inner logic of the argument, for its own sake and not for the sake of putting a different political complexion on Aristotle's words. A disciplined approach is imposed upon a notoriously undisciplined text, sometimes successfully, in that underlying implications are made plain, sometimes forcedly, in that a phrase in an aporetic argument is burdened with rather more weight than most modern critics would think it could stand. But there is no serious distortion of Aristotle's argument.

The effect of the Thomas – Peter commentary

With the appearance of the Thomas–Peter commentary, the job of rendering the Moerbeke translation intelligible was done, and it did not have to be done again. Many, if not most, other medieval commentators simply plagiarised it wholesale. But the other commentators considered in this study managed to contribute something distinctive of their own. The first three, Guy of Rimini, Walter Burley and Nicole Oresme, used the literal form, though in very different ways; the other three commentaries used the question form.

Guy of Rimini's commentary

Guy of Rimini's commentary[20] written in the early years of the fourteenth century, is presented in a simpler style than either Albert's or that of Thomas–Peter; it is generally free from scholastic distinctions, uses familiar thirteenth-century words, and has some rhetorical flourishes, along with a few light-hearted digressions. Unlike Thomas–Peter, Guy regularly points out the differences between what Aristotle is saying and what orthodox Christians believe – he is, for example, the only commentator to say that the doctrine of natural slavery looks harsh to Christian eyes[21] – and, like Albert, he uses contemporary examples to explain what Aristotle means, Lombard tyrants, Italian overseas trade and the organisation of chanceries being just a few of his illustrations. All this suggests that he is aiming his work at a fairly unscholarly readership, an impression which is proved by an incidental remark he makes while discussing Aristotle's criticisms of Plato.[22] One of the manuscripts in which Guy's commentary survives (Venice Marciana 2492), is a beautiful and rather extravagant

---

20. For some discussion of this, see Aquinas 1971a, p. A14.
21. MS. Venice Marciana 2492. f. 87ᵛ. 'Sed ut hoc videtur crudele dictum et contra naturalem amorem qui debet esse inter homines et contra doctrinam et pietatem Christianae religionis, quae praecepit quod unusquisque proximum diligat sicut seipsum ...'
22. 'Hoc opus facimus propter eos qui non multum vel nihil de profundis cognoscunt.' f. 124ʳ.

production, far removed from the usual cramped, messy volumes which circulated in the university world, and in itself suggestive that Guy's work was regarded as of more than academic importance. But his work was used by scholars, too: it forms the basis for an eccentric commentary on Books I and II of the *Politics* by the canonist John of Legnano,[23] and extracts from it were used in the form of scholia in manuscripts of the Moerbeke text.[24]

In his discussion on popular rights in political life Guy simply follows Peter, including all three additions to the text.

Walter Burley's commentary

Walter Burley's commentary, written about 1338–9[25] and based on Thomas–Peter, is a brief paraphrase. Each book of the *Politics* is introduced by a list of the questions Aristotle discusses there; each has an index of headings at the end; and there are occasional diagrams to clarify the argument. The mere imposition of such a format on the *Politics* gives it a novel character; and the assumption that it is a series of questions with solutions leads Burley to greater clarity than Aristotle in providing the answers. A condensed summary of this sort must surely have been a handbook for students; that they were mainly English students is made plain by the examples.[26]

Burley's reliance on Peter is immediately evident in his discussion of popular rights in political life. According to Aristotle, he says, 'a bestial multitude should in no wise rule (*principari*), but a multitude of men who have virtue, even if imperfectly, and an inclination to virtuous actions, ought to rule, for the reason given above [that is, that corporately they may have more virtue than a few virtuous men]. However, it does not seem that this multitude ought to rule with supreme authority (*principari summo principatu*) because of its lack of prudence, which leads to poor judgement, and its injustice.'[27] Burley follows Aristotle in arguing that when the

---

23. Contained in MS Venice Marciana 2653, ff. 117^r–130^r. I am grateful to Dr Maurice Keen for telling me of the existence of this commentary.
24. See for example MSS Phillips 891, contained in British Library Photocopy R.P. 60, which contains Guy's introduction, then the Moerbeke translation, with marginal notes taken mainly, though not exclusively, from his commentary.
25. Martin 1964, p. 225.
26. The dedications, first to Richard de Bury and then to the Pope, do not seem to me to give more than a partial indication of whom he was writing for.
27. MS Balliol 95, f. 182^r: 'Solvit quaestionem, intendens quod multitudo bestialis nullo modo debet principari; sed multitudo hominum qui habent virtutem quamvis imperfecte et inclinationem ad actus virtuosos debet principari propter rationem superius dictum. Talis tamen multitudo non videtur quod debet principari sumo principatu propter imprudentiam ad non recte iudicandum et iniustitiam.'

magistrates, counsellors, judges and leaders of the assembly (*contionatores*) are incorporated into the multitude, that multitude is sovereign in the state.[28] Then, following a line of thought very likely incited by Peter's exclusion of monarchy from the constitutions described by Aristotle in this passage, Burley produces an original, though enigmatic, comment: 'It is to be understood that in true constitutions, other than monarchies, a multitude rules, and this means many men; and in addition, in a kingdom, a multitude made up of the king and the nobles and the wise men of the kingdom in some way rules.' [29] He then cites the English parliament, called to expedite important business, as an example. It is difficult to know what to make of this. It may be that Burley read this whole passage in the *Politics* as an argument for power-sharing and broadly-based government rather than for the participation of the man in the street; but it is also possible that he believed parliament to be in some way representative of the people, offering them participation, though very indirectly, in the *ordo principatus* which is the life of the state. But Burley's terse style leaves his real meaning a mystery.

Nicole Oresme's commentary

Both Guy of Rimini and Walter Burley had as their main aim in commenting the desire to render the *Politics* easily understood, though by rather different groups of people. Nicole Oresme, writing around 1371,[30] only partially shared this aim, because, for the most part, he had made the task redundant by translating the text into straightforward French. Consequently he has time to expand on Aristotle and to relate the text to the world as he knows it. He is the only one of the commentators whose own political views emerge without equivocations. When he misinterprets Aristotle, it is not because medieval political preconceptions blur his understanding, but because it suits his book to do so. One of his more startling uses or abuses of the text comes when Aristotle talks of the supremacy of law; Oresme applies this passage to the church in his own day, arguing that it would be well if the papacy could see itself as bound by

---

28. *Ibid.*, f. 182ʳ: 'Magis videtur conveniens quod multitudo principatur quam unus vel pauci virtuosi, et hoc loquendo de multitudine quae comprehendit in se consiliarios, iudices, contionatores et alios prudentes.'
29. *Ibid.*, f. 182ʳ: 'Intelligendum quod in rectis principatibus aliis a regno principatur multitudo, et haec est plures; et adhuc in regno multitudo constituta ex rege et proceribus et sapientibus regni quodammodo principatur.'
30. Menut 1970, p. 19.

law, instead of priding itself on its *plenitudo potestatis*.[31] In the same way, Aristotle's teaching on the proper distribution of offices is applied to ecclesiastical benefices;[32] and his comment that the priesthood ought not to be given to husbandmen or mechanics is turned into a criticism of the friars.[33]

On popular participation in political life, Oresme begins in the conventional way by explaining the text; but at the end of the first section, he adds a gloss of his own: '[Aristotle] means, it seems to me, firstly, that it is better for a few men to have the sovereign authority, though not all lordship; then, that another multitude, if it is not bestial, should have rights or authority to counsel or judge, as is said; and thirdly, that everyone should have a voice in the election or correction of the princes and their deeds.'[34] The distinction between the multitude which counsels and the whole people which elects is unique to him. In his next excursus he declares that what Aristotle says on elections may be sensible for aristocracies, but does not relate to monarchies; he echoes Peter in interpreting Aristotle's 'perhaps' as limiting the application of the remark. But he goes far beyond Peter in aruging that election is in itself undesirable for three reasons: even where the multitude is well-ordered at the time when the power to elect is given to it, it may degenerate over the years; even if it does not degenerate, the process of election can cause discord; and even a rational multitude can be seduced into false decisions.[35] In the past open election of kings may have been a good thing, now hereditary succession is expedient.[36]

Aristotle argues that the master of the house is a better judge of it than the builder. Oresme notes that in a book entitled *Defensor Pacis* this argument is invoked to demonstrate that human law should be made, promulgated, corrected, or changed by the authority and consent of the whole community or of its weightier part.[37] Thus, he says that Aristotle

---

31. *Ibid.*, pp. 159–60.
32. *Ibid.*, p. 139.
33. *Ibid.*, p. 307.
34. *Ibid.*, p. 135: 'Il veult dire, ce me semble, premierement que ce est mieux que un peu de gens vertueux aient non pas toute la seigneurie, mes la souveraine dominacion. Item, que l'autre multitude, se elle ne est bestial, ait dominacion ou auctorité quant a conseillier et a jugier comme dit est. Item, que tous ensemble aient voies en election et en la correction des princes et de leur fais.'
35. *Ibid.*, p. 136.
36. *Ibid.*, p. 109.
37. *Ibid.*, p. 137: 'En un livre intitulé *Defensor Pacis* ceste raison est alleguee a monstrer que lays humaines positives doivent estre faictes, promulguees, corrigees ou muees de l'auctorité et consentement de toute la communité ou de la plus vaillant partie.'

would have regarded the Romans as having behaved bestially in handing over to their emperor the right to legislate.[38] In a later context, he goes on to remark that he sees no difference between arbitrary rule without the law and rule according to laws made only by the governors, without the consent of the multitude, and not in accord with public good.[39] Oresme has twisted Aristotle on popular participation into a statement on the legislative supremacy of the people. The only question is, whom does he have in mind when he talks of the consent of the multitude?

Oresme's multitude is clearly aristocratic. In Book VI, when discussing sovereignty, he says that the body which is sovereign in polities and aristocracies is the multitude, 'not the populace, but the multitude or universal congregation of all princes or office-holders and of the principal citizens'. This he compares with the assembly of the Masters in the University of Paris. In monarchies, he says, the king and his council are only a small part of the political multitude who ought to consider and ordian where the public good lies; by implication, all office-holders and the principal citizens have rights here too. He goes on to argue for the rights of a similar multitude in the government of the Church, in other words for the conciliarist principle.[40] Oresme's multitude is clearly an aristocratic one of properly qualified men, to whom rights of counselling and judging can entirely safely be given. In a work undertaken at the request of the king of France, and dedicated to him, written in a language easily understood by those men who stood most to gain by using his arguments, Oresme is demanding a radical programme of reform, both in church and in state.

Peter of Auvergne's Questions on the Politics

The use of the question form (in place of the literal commentary) allows the master who employs it a greater freedom to select topics for discussion and to offer his own conclusions. But, as in the case of the literal commentaries, plagiarism was the rule; and again, the key commentary was by Peter of Auvergne. Peter's *Quaestiones*[41] cover the first seven books of the *Politics*, a hundred and twenty-six questions in all, with notably wider coverage on Books I and III than the others. In arguing, he employs a tight syllogistic

---

38. *Ibid.*, p. 138.
39. *Ibid.*, p. 178.
40. *Ibid.*, p. 274: 'La multitude non pas la populaire mes la multitude et congregation universele de tous les princeys ou offices et des principalz citoiens.'
41. I have used MS Paris Nat. Lat. 16089, ff. 274^r–319^r. I have not been able to compare it with MS Bologna Bibl. Univ. 1625, which is a shortened form of the *Quaestiones*, but with a little new material.

form, applies learning culled from other Aristotelian works to the elucidation of the *Politics*, and relentlessly drags out the implications of Aristotle's tentative statements. He also echoes a number of the themes which occur in the political writings of Thomas Aquinas, whose disciple he was.

On popular participation, Peter first asks whether it is better for the whole multitude or for a few virtuous men to rule. In favour of the few virtuous, he argues that it must be good for the state to be ruled by those who further the purpose for which it was instituted, the life of virtue. Also since that state which most closely approximates the best is better, and since aristocracy approximates to kingship, which is the best, aristocracy must be better than rule by the multitude. In favour of rule by the multitude, Peter says that they are corporately more prudent than the few good men and that they aim at the common good. To rule, however, it is necessary to have not only both prudence and virtue *per se*, but also power *per accidens*, on Peter's view; and this leads to his solution: multitudes are divided into the bestial and the mixed, in which there are some wise men and all the rest can be persuaded to reason. Bestial multitudes are deprived of all right to rule, but mixed ones ought to do so, in the sense that they should elect and punish princes. Such a multitude has all three requisites for rule, whereas the few virtuous men have only two, lacking the power which comes from numbers.[42]

Peter then asks if the multitude should rule with supreme authority.[43] He argues against this, on the ground that it has prudence and virtue only in respect of the wise men among it, who are like the heart to the whole animal, and this is not enough for the task of holding office. And secondly, the multitude can rule only if it is unanimous, which means it can rule only if it is like one man; therefore rule by one man is better. One man of prudence and virtue elected to office by the multitude, would obtain the necessary power from the fact of his election, and would thus combine all that was needful.

Then comes the problem of whether the multitude should have the right to elect the princes and call them to account. In the course of his discussion,

---

42. MS Paris Nat. Lat. 16089, f. 295ʳ: 'Haec est multitudo bestialis et nata subesse principatu despotico. Alia autem est multitudo bene persuadibilis, mixta ex sapientibus et ex vulgaribus bene persuadibilibus ... Dicendum quod multitudinem vilem et bestialem non expedit ad istam [electionem] attingere; multitudinem tamen mixtam et ordinatam iustum est attingere ad istam ... quia electio principis duo requirit, scilicet consilium de principe bono investigando et potentiam ad cogendum electum.'

43. *Ibid.*, f. 295ᵛ: 'Utrum oportet multitudinem principari principatu maximo in civitate bene ordinata.'

Peter points out that he is talking only of cities which are wholly independent, since, if there is a superior authority, it will be up to it to elect
and correct the prince (a point which recalls the argument of Aquinas in *De
regno*, Ch. 6). Peter easily shows that the multitude ought to elect, in
virtue of its corporate prudence and its power. Because men love what they
themselves have made, they will more easily obey a prince whom they
have elected. Equally, the multitude ought to punish a prince who fails in
his duty: punishment ought always to be inflicted by those whose action
will breed the least resentment in the punished – which is the multitude
(presumably because its great numbers make it an impersonal force).[44]

The Milan commentator

Whatever may have been his own political preferences, Peter in writing
the *Quaestiones* was aspiring to the detachment which is so marked a
characteristic of his master's work. Such detachment, however, did not
attract others. An interesting commentary, dating from the late thirteenth
or the early fourteenth centuries, and clearly closely related to Peter's
Quaestiones, is to be found in the MS Milan Ambrosiana A 100 Inf.
(ff. 1^r–54^r). The author asks only ninety questions; but they are almost
identical with those asked by Peter, and many of the arguments are the
same. Because this anonymous author and Peter are usually so similar, their
differences on popular participation in political life are all the more
interesting.

In discussing how the multitude ought to participate, the Milan commentator points out that it must be a very varied body; just as the animal
needs many parts to be effective, so the multitude must be made up of
many different kinds of men. Some of them will be naturally good, others
can be persuaded to goodness, and on others no form of persuasion will be
effective.[45] He excludes the last category from political rights, calling them
multitudo bestialis et servilis et non persuadibilis aliquo modo ad virtutes; uniquely
among the commentators, he offers an example of such a group, a crowd of
mechanics, presumably because they are corrupted by their work.[46] But
all others are comprehended within the multitude which deserves political

---

44. *Ibid.*, f. 296^r: 'Ergo maxime expedit eligere quod in se habet consilium et potestatem; sed haec est
multitudo; quia per sapientes partes sui habet prudentiam, per se autem potentiam; et iterum
homines diligunt sua opera ut filios . . . et multitudo principi quem eligit magis obediet. Item ad
correctionem dum princeps peccaverit, exigatur discretio penam inveniendi et potentiam eam
infligandi. Haec autem conveniunt in multitudine.'
45. Taken from the *Ethics*, Book X, 1179b–1180a.
46. MS Milan Ambrosiana A 100 Inf. f. 28^r.

rights. As a consequence, the commentator departs in form from Peter, allowing such a multitude the right to wield supreme authority (*principari summo principatu*), but only in the sense that the few prudent men will actually hold office, while all the rest participate in some way, either in counselling or electing.[47] The Milan commentator even tells us how the elections should be organised, and in so doing, he passes from the abstract sphere of Peter to concrete political facts. Elections are out of place, he observes, in principalities where hereditary succession is normal; but where elections do take place, they should not be democratic in the full sense. Representatives should be chosen from the principal families and crafts (*artes*) to choose the prince; then they should present their candidate to the whole people to be accepted; but the people have the right to reject him if one of their number makes out a case against him. The process is defended by citing the maxim of Roman law that what affects everyone ought to be decided by everyone (*quod omnes tangit ab omnibus debet pertractari*).[48]

The blend of a representative system with popular right to acclaim or veto is compatible with Aristotle's intentions in this passage, but it is far too concrete a notion to emerge just from the reading of the text. Our author is using the text to urge a particular policy in circumstances which our ignorance of his identity and background hide from us. The passage stands out in the Milan commentary as extraordinary; elsewhere the author exhibits the same attitude towards the text as Peter does, one of detachment and philosophical, rather than political, reflection.

John Buridan's Questions on the Politics

If the discussion of popular participation is a particularly good one for bringing out the individual character of the Milan commentary, it is not suitable for the *Quaestiones* of John Buridan,[49] the teacher of Nicole Oresme. When Buridan turned to the *Politics* at some unknown date in the middle of the fourteenth century, he used it to provide an extremely loose

---

47. *Ibid.*, f. 28ʳ: 'Ad hoc dicendum est quod expedit multitudinem principari in maximo principatu intelligendo quaestionem illo secundo modo, sicut dicebatur, ita quod aliqui virtuosi principentur in tali multitudine simpliciter et dirigant alios in finem determinatum talis principatus, et alii habeant aliquod principatum sicut consilium vel principentur aliquo modo exsequendo vel in eligendo alios qui debent simpliciter principari.'

48. *Ibid.*, f. 28ʳ: 'Ulterius est intelligendum quod non oportet sic multitudinem eligere principem quod quilibet existens in civitate habeat vocem in eligendo principem; sed sic quod unus de una tota progenie et in istis artibus quae principaliores [sunt] habeat vocem in eligendo, et non omnis ... isti sic deputati a tota multitudine ducunt illum quem elegerunt praesentare multitudini, videndum utrum placeat multitudini, et si non placet, potest electio impediri.'

49. John Buridan 1640.

framework for discussing his own views on moral and legal questions, showing a particular interest in the proper processes for law courts and judgements, which he introduced into the text with very little justification from Aristotle. It is these parts which would best exemplify his commentary. Yet, for our purposes it is worth looking at what he says on the topic here selected for discussion.[50]

Buridan asks whether it is permissible for the multitude to elect a prince and afterwards to punish him if he errs. The arguments put against the multitude's doing so are that prudence is necessary for election, but multitudes often lack it; that rules of expediency do not apply to serious matters, of which this is one; that the right to elect or punish rulers confers on the multitude a form of sovereignty which vile persons ought not to enjoy over their superiors; and finally that election encourages division. The only point made in favour of the multitude at this point is that Aristotle believes in it. Buridan then offers six *notabilia*, five of which clearly derive from Peter's *Quaestiones*. They are that a true prince needs three qualities, virtue, prudence, and power; that multitudes can be divided into bestial (*constituta ex hominibus vilibus*) and well-ordered (*constituta ex potentibus viris, virtuosis et sapientibus*); the bestial can be divided into the totally sensual, who cannot participate in reason, and the *persuadibiles*, who can be brought to it; the body which is to elect a prince needs to have both prudence and power, since it may need to force a good man to accept office; and a prince elected by the multitude will be loved by it. The sixth point, his own, is that a good prince is an interpreter of the law; if he is ignorant of the laws, he is not good; and if he knowingly despises them, he ought to be punished or deposed. This leads him to his own conclusions: that the bestial multitude which, in his argument, though not Peter's, includes the *persuadibiles*, should not elect or punish; but the well-ordered both can and should, since it has prudence, love of the community and strength of numbers; such an election will serve peace and concord, and these will be preserved by allowing the multitude to punish the prince if he strays from rule according to the law. All the arguments originally put against the conclusion apply only to bestial multitudes.[51]

It is striking how Buridan is content to copy almost verbatim from Peter, a man who ought to have been reckoned among his philosophical opponents. What is less clear is whether Buridan has added a new dimen-

50. See Grignashi 1960, p. 138.
51. John Buridan 1640, pp. 140–2.

sion to the argument in his description of the make-up of the two multitudes. He is certainly more exclusive than Peter in including the *persuadibiles* among the bestial, though he makes nothing of this in his conclusion. But it has been claimed that by describing the bestial multitude as made up of vile men, and the well-ordered of the powerful, Buridan was aiming to limit political rights to the nobility and *haute bourgeoisie*.[52] This is possible; but Buridan's words are susceptible of another interpretation. And the word '*viles*' he applies to the bestial multitude may be a moral rather than a social adjective; even if it is social, it is as likely in a medieval context to mean servile as common, and thus preserve a genuinely Aristotelian distinction.

Conclusion

In conclusion, it is worth emphasising what has been the chief finding of this study: though the medieval commentaries on the *Politics* have a common source, they still differ in their approach, partly as a result of the needs of the readership for which they were written, partly because they follow different academic conventions, and partly because some show a genuine originality of mind.

52. Grignashi 1960, p. 138.

39

RIGHTS, NATURAL RIGHTS,
AND THE PHILOSOPHY OF LAW

Rights derived from above: John of Salisbury

In the period from John of Salisbury to Richard Hooker and Francisco
Suárez the concept of a right and the theory of natural rights emerged from
a religious view of society with which the subsequent politics of rights has
more or less willingly dispensed. At the outset sacral kingship and, more
convincingly, the authority of the Church, especially the papacy, claimed
divine warrant and support. At the same time those who wished to resist
their superiors could usually allege violation of mutual obligation, or
failure to conform to the requirements of rulership, and Christian impulses
to condemn, flee, or find a radical alternative to ordinary worldly life were
always active.

John of Salisbury's *Policraticus*, although a highly personal work, shows
important aspects of the original view. John regards rights (*iura*) as the vital
means which an ideal court (an Areopagus) would give each class or
profession in a community as required to perform its proper functions
(*Policr.* I.3) – functions in an organic social whole, which has as its soul the
priesthood and whose princely head of government is an earthly image of
the divine majesty.[1] John draws his organic model for society from classical
sources but adapts it to medieval Christian needs by making the sacerdotal
soul a distinct class, of which the prince is in some sense a minister.[2] In the
same way, he takes over the Roman jurists' impersonal definition of
fairness or equity as a rational equilibration of disparate things with respect
to the same laws (*iura*), bestowing on each what is his own, but identifies
such *aequitas* with the justice of God, to which rulers are emphatically
subordinate.[3] Rights, in his view, are bestowed on their possessors from
above, that is, from God or from the exigencies of the organic social whole.
They are not in theory arbitrarily determinable by government, however,

1. John of Salisbury 1909, IV.1, VI.25.
2. *Ibid.*, IV.3; V, prol., 1–2, 6; III.1.
3. *Ibid.*, IV.2–7.

and in John's case corporatist principles are compatible with vigorous individuality. The potential for a theory of natural rights is clearly present.

Virtue as the determiner of rights: Thomas Aquinas

With some exceptions (for example, Roger Bacon's *Opus maius*) the philosophically significant political thought of the thirteenth and fourteenth centuries was part of a struggle within Christian society to accommodate, control, or exploit the naturalistic resources of Aristotle's *Politics*. According to Thomas Aquinas, an individual man is a part of the community in all that he is and has; hence his proper good is subordinate to the more perfect common good.[4] Determination and achievement of both public and private good take place, however, through the virtues of charity, prudence, and justice. In his complex analysis of these virtues (*ST*, IaIIae) as well as in his treatment of law (*ST*, IaIIae, qq. 90–108), Thomas provides both inspiration and criticism for the attempt to base politics on a theory of persons and their rights. A right in the sense of an action in some sense owed to another person, is the object of the moral virtue justice,[5] while the discernment of rules of action by which right or just relationships among persons and things may be achieved is the work of another cardinal virtue, the intellectual virtue of prudence.[6] An individual's concern for the good of the community is supported by the theological virtue of charity (discord, strife, and sedition are vices[7] opposed to peace, which is an effect of charity) and is also a matter of rational prudence,[8] but the community in question is primarily a unity of right (or law) and common utility, not simply an existing power structure. Hence, the tyrant is seditious, not those who resist him, for it is he who violates this unity.[9] With respect to the principles of justice we are subject to God, not mediately, through a human superior, but immediately, for God instructs each man by divine and natural law.[10] Again, both the justification of private property rights and their limitations turn on considerations of rational communal utility more basic than positive titles. Appropriation can indeed be justified, but only with respect to care and responsibility for material things, not their use.[11]

---

4. *ST*, IaIIae, q. 96, a. 4; q. 90, a. 2.
5. *ST*, IIaIIae, q. 57, a. 1; q. 58, a. 1.
6. *ST*, IIaIIae, q. 47, a. 6.
7. *ST*, IIaIIae, qq. 37, 41–2.
8. *ST*, IIaIIae, q. 47, a. 10.
9. *ST*, IIaIIae, q. 42, aa. 2–3.
10. *ST*, IIaIIae, q. 104, a. 5, *ad* 2.
11. *ST*, IIaIIae, q. 66, a. 2.

Accordingly, theft from necessity does not violate the commandment against stealing (although open robbery with a threat to life does).[12]

Thomas' account of the objective order of justice yields a rather short list of universal human rights. Because all men are equals in nature, all have rights at a fundamental natural level, such as the right to contract marriage or vow virginity.[13] Because human law concerns only outward acts, the mind, as Seneca says, is free;[14] this freedom must be respected even when it is a matter of accepting or not accepting Christianity.[15] The right to active participation in political affairs is not universal. It is appropriate for a morally responsible people, but a corrupt people is more suitably ruled by others.[16] Thomas thought the former situation more desirable than the latter, holding that the best political regime (as exemplified in the Old Testament) is one 'well mixed' from royal, aristocratic, and democratic elements.[17] Even on an occasion (*De regno* I) when he extolled the merits of pure kingship and deplored tyrannicide, he tied this to an emphasis on virtuous subjects as the goal of good kings and the chief fear of tyrants. In every case, then, the powers and virtues of persons are central in Thomas' political thought, but of persons seen in relation to other persons, including God, not in isolation.

Powers and rights: Fourteenth-century papalism and its radical opponents

Both the term '*plenitudo potestatis*' and the papal *Rechtsidee* associated with it have a long history in the earlier Middle Ages.[18] The most philosophically systematic expositions of this view, however, were those presented in the early fourteenth century in the face of new theoretical, institutional, and ethical challenges by such writers as Giles of Rome, James of Viterbo, and Augustinus Triumphus.

Augustinus Triumphus

Augustinus' work, for example, is a *Summa de ecclesiastica potestate*, a consideration of the pope's power, first in itself,[19] then in relation to the acts of temporal and spiritual dominion or lordship (*dominium*) for which it

---

12. *ST*, IIaIIae, q. 66, aa. 7–8.
13. *ST*, IIaIIae, q. 104, a. 5.
14. *ST*, IIaIIae, q. 104, a. 5.
15. *ST*, IIaIIae, q. 10, a. 8.
16. *ST*, IaIIae, q. 97, a. 1; a. 3, *ad* 3. IIaIIae, q. 47, a. 12; q. 50, aa. 1–2.
17. *ST*, IaIIae, q. 95, a. 4; q. 105, a. 1.
18. Ullmann 1966a, 1966b, 1970.
19. qq. 1–34.

is ordained,[20] and finally in relation to the graded perfections of institutional status accruing to men from such power.[21] Just as God cannot deny Himself to be lord of all, so His vicar cannot exempt anyone from papal jurisdiction, cannot deny that he has universal *dominium*. To do so would be to fall into Manichaeism.[22] Accordingly, all other rights are derived from God to men through the pope, and it pertains principally to him to maintain others in these derived rights.[23] No one else could judge the pope, but a heretical pope (a possibility often discussed in earlier canonistic literature) judged, and deposed, himself.[24] Augustinus also incorporated into his treatise on papal power ideals of natural law involving no particular reference to the Church. His enumeration, under the heading of theft, of various forms of injustice perpetrated by secular lords against their subjects is an example of this.[25]

Marsilius of Padua

Early-fourteenth-century opponents of papal claims to comprehensive secular power included such distinguished Aristotelian successors of Aquinas as John of Paris and Dante, both of whom based the autonomy of secular governments on the rational and moral competence of human nature, but by far the most radical, if not the most Aristotelian, antihierocratic theoretician was Marsilius of Padua.[26] For Marsilius, more than for any earlier thinker, the natural process of earthly politics had a self-sufficiency which not only needed no completion or rectification from higher sources but could be represented as mortally endangered by such interference.[27] The normal human desire for a peaceful life must itself be allowed to generate the means necessary for its realisation. That is, the people as a whole must consent to the power of their rulers and, above all, popular consultation and consent must determine the laws by which government is to operate.[28] The government and laws thus established will in turn establish and control such other offices or parts of the state (including the priesthood) as are necessary for the healthy existence of the com-

---

20. qq. 35–75.
21. qq. 76–112.
22. q. 61, aa. 2–3.
23. q. 1, aa. 3, 7–8; qq. 44–6; q. 75, a. 1.
24. q. 5, a. 1; q. 22, a. 1, *ad* 2; q. 1, a. 2.
25. q. 54, a. 4; cf. q. 26.
26. Gewirth's comparative method makes his penetrating study of Marsilius (Gewirth 1951) an exceptionally valuable account of major aspects of political philosophy in the period.
27. *Defensor pacis*, Dictio I, cc. 4, 9.
28. *Def. pac.* I.9, sections 5–9; I.12.3.

munity.[29] Should the government signally or persistently fail in its mission of implementing the popular will, the people may correct or replace it.[30]

If Marsilius so directly asserted the natural right of the people as a whole to control its own political situation, his contribution to the theory of individual rights was both less direct and less affirmative. While his definition of the right of ownership, for example, as a power of legal control over a thing[31] may mark a stage in the doctrine of 'subjective right' central to much modern jurisprudence and political theory,[32] Marsilius did not regard such rights either as based on natural law or as the building-blocks of politics. His interest in them was negative: he held a *lack* of them to be the hallmark of a genuinely Christian ministry.[33]

William Ockham

Like Marsilius, William Ockham became involved in politics as an opponent of the contemporary papacy, but although he eventually developed detailed ideas on both papal and secular government, the initial basis for his opposition was religious, not political. Ockham and most other Franciscans of the time held that Christ and the apostles had abdicated all ownership of material things and that a life imitating this poverty was the most perfect *status* available to a Christian. An important part of the Franciscan position expounded in the *Opus nonaginta dierum*, a detailed attack on John XXII's constitutions on the poverty questions, was the idea of a natural right to use material things possessed by the human race in common. Property rights in positive law were seen as excluding the exercise of this natural right by persons other than the owner or those he authorised. The 'licenses of using' granted the Franciscans could then be viewed, not as conferring a new positive-legal right, but simply as cancelling the exclusion created by the owner's legal right, with the result that the friars were placed in a state of nature with respect to the things they used.[34] For the sake of clarity in the extremely intricate discussions of rights which the poverty controversy by this time required, Ockham in the second

29. *Ibid.*, I.7, 15.
30. *Ibid.*, I.18.
31. *Ibid.*, II.12.10.
32. Subjective right may be defined as an individual's legally recognised power or freedom with respect to some good. However, the definition, historical antecedents, and juristic and philosophical significance of the idea are all debated (see especially Bucher 1965 and Kasper 1967).
33. *Def. pac.* II.14.6–16.
34. William Ockham 1963–74, *Opus nonaginta dierum*, cc. 61–2, 65, 87–92; Miethke 1969, pp. 458–502.

chapter of the *Opus nonaginta dierum* defined a series of key terms, including right of use (*ius utendi*) and ownership (*dominium*). In these definitions a legal right is said to be a judicially enforceable 'licit power' to use something, and this has been taken to be an important appearance of the concept of subjective right.[35] Certainly, later Ockhamists made telling use of the notion that a ruler's power (or lordship, *dominium*) over his people was *not* to be identified with any such right of ownership.[36] It may be doubted, however, whether Ockham himself intended to do anything more in these definitions than spell out the concrete meaning of having a (legal) right in such a way as to draw clearly the issues between his own party of rebel friars and John XXII.

Another feature of Ockham's early polemic with at least indirect implications for later discussion of rights is his assertion of what might be called the right to a reasonable explanation in religion. The theory, accepted by Ockham and his group, that a heretical pope was *ipso facto* deprived of all spiritual power and was therefore no longer really pope, required for practical effectiveness a general awareness of the pope's defection from the faith. But since the pope was normally in charge of examinations of faith, the legitimacy of even discussing his own orthodoxy was questionable, and it was difficult to work out the obligations towards one another of Christians holding different views on the subject. In the labyrinth of the first part of Ockham's *Dialogus*, the thesis that an *erring* inferior is not obligated to give up his opinions at the bare rebuke of an *orthodox* ecclesiastical superior has important bearing on such issues. Ockham argues that a reasonable explanation of the error must be given the mistaken party before he is obligated to change his position. This line of argument, like Ockham's whole anti-papal project, has sometimes been seen as an attack on the foundations of medieval Christianity, sometimes as a sign of vitality in a system too often perceived as monolithic.

Doing without rights: Wyclif

Augustine had said that 'everything belongs to the just',[37] and such an idea of a better kind of relationship to things and persons than the legal relations of ownership and lordship actually obtaining in the world was richly developed in the course of the Middle Ages. In his *De civili dominio* Wyclif used this idea as the basis for a political philosophy. A soul infected by

35. Villey 1964; McGrade 1980.
36. Skinner 1978, II, pp. 117–22; 176–7, 320.
37. *Epist.* 93, c. 12.

mortal sin lacks the justice required for possessing or using things well, he argued, while a just person through God's grace dominates the whole sensible world with a lordship that cannot be taken from him.[38] Wyclif is scornful of those who base lordship on conquest or the fictions of blind sinners rather than the creation and re-creation of God, or who hold that it requires coercive power rather than virtue.[39] True *dominium* is an effect of charity, through which all the just possess the world in common and are reciprocally one another's lords and servants.[40] This is not to say that charity justifies a redistribution of material goods among the godly. On the contrary, the ideal is to follow Christ – the *primum metrum et mensura* of the genus Christian as fire is the first measure of hot things – in a life of evangelical poverty free from the temptations to sin which are inherent in owning property or exercising coercive power.[41] It is a diabolical error to suppose that any legal right is unconditional or that a person can do what he pleases with his own possessions. All are merely custodians of what is God's.[42]

In denying absolute standing to conventional principles of justice, Wyclif contributes much to the negative, revolutionary side of thought regarding natural rights; but he equally denies the legitimacy of natural rights themselves, if these are construed in secular fashion as items of moral property held without continuing reference to God. It is controversial whether Wyclif's work is the culmination of an earlier tradition (as he suggests with his quotations from such figures as Augustine, Grosseteste, and Bernard) or a serious distortion of it. In any case, his work represents a final stage of some distinctively medieval lines of thought as well as an example for later reformers who were not always appreciative of its traditional premises.

Later developments

In the Italian Renaissance, in the midst of despotism and foreign invasions, a variety of issues concerning man's nature, powers, dignity, present condition, and prospects were discussed by humanists and others with searching eloquence. Scholars give a more positive weight to medieval contributions to this discussion now than previously, but very disparate

38. John Wyclif 1885–1904, *De civ. dom.*, Book I, cc. 7, 9, 15.
39. *Ibid.*, I.11, 20–1.
40. *Ibid.*, I.11, 14.
41. *Ibid.*, III.4–6, 10.
42. *Ibid.*, I.19–21, II.15.

assessments are still defensible. Machiavelli, for example, so modern in his analysis of human affairs, can also be regarded as an Augustine or John of Salisbury *manqué*. Much political thought in Italy and elsewhere was connected in one way or another with the Great Schism in the papacy. Ideas about the authority of church councils elaborated in response to the temporary disintegration of papal monarchy were developed further in unsuccessful attempts to constitutionalise, first, ecclesiastical and then secular government. Detection of Marsilian and Ockhamist influences on conciliarism and kindred developments depends heavily on the view taken of these thinkers and of the later movements.[43] Marsilius clearly asserted the regular superiority of general council to pope, which Ockham denied, but Ockham discussed constitutional questions in both spiritual and temporal government in a way that emphasised the power of a community (the congregation of believers or the community of mortals) to take decisive action if ill served by its rulers. Marsilius, whose attack on the whole conception of a spiritually governed society has been considered as radical as Marx's attack on capitalism, was undoubtedly more often read than cited. Ockham, on the other hand, continued to be a dominant influence in academic theology and philosophy. A convincing history of political Ockhamism remains to be written, but it would include chapters on such important thinkers as Peter of Ailly and John Gerson in the fifteenth century, James Almain and John Major in the sixteenth, and very likely a chapter on Locke.

Locke's conception of government as the delegate of a community of reasonable but imperfect individuals, set up to protect the natural rights of its principals rather than to confer rights on them, and restrained in its religious power, draws from (while, of course, modifying), not only Ockhamism, but also the Thomistic tradition, to which Locke was exposed through Hooker as well as in his own wider reading. The more corporatist modern natural-rights tradition culminating in Rousseau has medieval antecedents in the general tendency to think of human association in terms of organic analogies or principles of ideal justice and in doctrines of consent, such as those of Marsilius of Padua and Nicholas of Cusa, calling for a genuine synthesis or concord of desires as a basis for legitimate social action. The idea of rights against the state or civil society has roots in medieval forms of scepticism about secular political and economic institutions, varying from hierocratic insistence on the corrigibility of all

43. For the influence of the canonists, see Tierney 1954, 1955a, 1955b, 1966, 1975.

secular rulers in the light of ecclesiastically administered divine law to Franciscan and Wyclifite renunciation of legal rights in favor of evangelical poverty and charity.

Philosophy of law

Much later medieval philosophy of law can be understood only in relation to factors usually excluded from modern legal discussions: cosmic religious values and moral leadership. There is other important material, easier to absorb, in which law appears as a rational response to the problems of communal existence; and modern legal positivism also has a medieval background. Some of the relations among positions held may be clearer in a thematic than in a chronological survey.

Law as the expression of higher values: Augustinus Triumphus and Richard Hooker

The idea that human society has its value in relation to something beyond the individuals composing it has two main expressions in our period, one in the hierocratic conception of the papacy as an institution mediating the relation of man to God and regulating on God's behalf all relations of man to man, the other in the conception of law itself as an expression of the divine order. Augustinus Triumphus will serve as an example of the first tradition, Richard Hooker of the second.

Augustinus begins his argument that papal authorisation is required for the validity of imperial civil law with an exegesis of Augustine's reference to an eternal law, a highest divine reason, by which it is just that all things should be done 'most orderedly'. Every just law depends doubly on divine law, he argues: first, effectively and derivatively, simply in being just, since what is just and what is unjust is discerned only through divine law; second, materially and subjectively, because the first imperial laws were materially composed from divine speeches (for example, the Roman law of the twelve tables from Solomon's laws). Imperial law, therefore, depends on the pope's authority by the same right by which it depends on divine law, of which the pope is vicar and minister, especially since, according to Dionysius, the law of divinity is such that its influence does not pass to lower things except by intermediates (*media*). But the intermediate between God and the Christian people is the pope (*Summa de ecclesiastica potestate*, q. 44, a. 1).[44] Since Christ by his passion has merited judicial

---

44. Cf. q. 1, aa. 1, 3–9.

power over every creature, his vicar's authority extends to pagans as well as Christians.[45] The pope can correct, depose, or institute (without the request or consent of others) the rulers of any realm (q. 46, aa. 1–3). Anyone suffering unjustly may appeal to him from the sentence of any man whatsoever, whether king or emperor.[46]

Augustinus argues at one point that a papal precept binds more than the law of nature, since it binds not only potentially but also actually, not only universally but also particularly. Moreover, its 'impression' in Christ's commission of the Church to Peter (Matt. 16.18) is more unfailing than the impression of the law of nature (which is only habitual and can in its actual exercise fall into evil or be reformed to good) (q. 63, a. 1; cf. q. 60, a. 1). This greater concrete effectiveness of papal authority is not, of course, a license to violate natural law. Augustinus is intent on claiming all ultimate legal or governmental authority for the papacy – the whole worldly machine is a single governmental unit and needs a single ruler[47] – but in exercising this authority the pope only mediates a higher justice and must act accordingly. He is not to be obeyed if he commands anything contrary to natural or divine law, for example (q. 22, a. 1). Similarly, it behooves him to set an example of obedience to imperial laws, and he cannot justly deprive pagans of political authority (q. 23, a. 3), free slaves (q. 22, a. 5), or arbitrarily take one person's property and give it to another (q. 54, a. 4, *ad* 1). For Augustinus Triumphus the hierarchical structure of ecclesiastical offices, however unworthy the men who held them, reflected or represented the perfection of Christ and the Apostles.[48] Similarly, Richard Hooker defended the laws of English ecclesiastical polity rather than the faulty men who administered them.[49] He held these laws to be superior to the crown, so that a royal grant contrary to law could be null,[50] and he held them to be warranted by the systematic survey of 'laws and their several kinds in general' with which he began his work. But Hooker's defence was itself necessary because of an appeal to higher law, divine law, made by the Anglican establishment's Puritan opponents. They held that Scripture provided a rule for every action of life[51] and, especially, that it contained a

45. q. 23, a. 1.
46. q. 45, a. 3.
47. q. 22, a. 3; q. 49, a. 2; q. 60, a. 4.
48. q. 1, a. 2; qq. 76–112. On the distinction between office and person in medieval political thought generally, see Kantorowicz 1957.
49. Hooker 1977–81, *Of the Laws of Ecclesiastical Polity*, Book II, c. 1, sect. 1; I.16.1; VII.18 and 24.2–16.
50. *Ibid.*, VIII.2.13.
51. *Ibid.*, II.

complete form of church government,[52] including a penitential judicial system replacing episcopal courts with consistories of local laymen.[53] Hooker must thus be read as working out a substantially medieval problem the problem of how, not whether, a Christian society should conform to the divine order. Much of Hooker's *Laws* is a defense of human reason as a factor in both the acceptance and the application of Scripture, as well as in deciding matters not addressed by Scripture.[54] In this rational aspect Hooker's concept of law reflects his vision of reality as wonderfully ordered and intelligible, yet he clearly declines to present Anglican law as a unique and necessary consequence of cosmic reason. Accordingly, he is much concerned with the authority of human law over a range of 'probable' determinations in religious practices and with the autonomy of a national human community and its comprehensive power over individual members.[55] In this dynamic or voluntarist aspect, too, his concept of human law also reflects his view of the nature of things. Departing from tradition, Hooker does not include imposition by a superior as a necessary element in his definition of law.[56] The immediate result is that he can speak of God Himself as voluntarily adopting a law for His own actions, but in addition he can present the English church as free to make laws for itself in matters of religion.

It is sometimes thought that Hooker gave legal omnipotence to a positivist public reason.[57] On the contrary, he regarded natural and divine law as limiting the range of human legislation,[58] his interpretation of the English royal supremacy was strikingly constitutionalist,[59] and his whole work expresses a sense that history is a process of communal development and activity, guided by government but not simply a product of rulers' decisions. Hooker's contention that a political community's laws should reflect and promote its religion – that church and commonwealth are one if every citizen is a Christian (*Laws* VIII.1.2; 6.6.11) – is a late expression of medieval belief in the wholeness of the aims of human association.

52. *Ibid.*, III.
53. Hooker's treatment of the spiritual-legal topic of lay-elders in *Laws* VI is largely lost. On the significance of the treatment of penance which remains, see McGrade (1978).
54. Hooker 1977–81, II.7–8, III.8.
55. *Ibid.*, Preface, 6; III.1, 9–11; V.8, 10.
56. *Ibid.*, I.2.1, I.3.1; but cf. I.10.7–8, VIII.6.13.
57. See Munz 1952, McGrade 1963, Cargill Thompson 1972.
58. Hooker 1977–81, I.8.5–8, 10.1; VIII.6.5.
59. *Ibid.*, VIII.2. 3, 7, 12–13, 17; 6.8, 13; 8.9. Munz 1952, pp. 107ff.

Moral leadership, revolution, and reform: John of Salisbury and John Wyclif

Political philosophers who regard law or government as an expression of higher values – and nearly every medieval thinker did so in one way or another – have special problems in providing against human failings. While a distinction between office and person or laws and men is easy enough to draw in theory, it is difficult to set up procedural safeguards 'over' institutions that are themselves endowed with supreme spiritual or moral power. A natural twofold response to this situation consists of first, seeking to engender the highest possible ethical qualities in rulers (the aim of numerous 'mirrors' for princes) and, if that fails, countenancing revolution or extra-legal reform.

While John of Salisbury regarded a true king as an image of deity he viewed tyrants as the greatest of political horrors. The sole or greatest difference between a legitimate ruler and a tyrant is rule in accordance with law (*Policr.* IV.1, VII.17). Law itself John describes in the highest terms as a gift of God, interpreter or form of equity, norm of justice, image of the divine will, safeguard of safety, union and consolidation of peoples, rule of offices, exclusion and extermination of vices, and punishment of all violence and injury (*Policr.* IV.2, VII.17). To encourage proper regard for law by those in power he uses both theological and philosophical tactics. Against 'whitewashers' citing Roman law maxims that the prince is *legibus solutus* and what pleases him has the force of law, John deploys a sustained exegesis of Deuteronomy enforcing the subordination of rulers to justice as a religious principle,[60] and he attempts to make such subordination more plausible psychologically through a sustained philosophical criticism of the current courtly ethos.[61] This provides the framework as well as the subtitle (*On the Follies of Courtiers and Footsteps of Philosophers*) of his work. The brutalising effect of the successful exercise of power, the cultivation of bizarre means to foretell the future and exciting ways to waste the present, and the courtier's self-avoiding narcissism are reviewed with a rare combination of astuteness, stylistic elegance, and fervour.

Instead of the court life so described, John proposes, not heroic sanctity, but a philosophically moderated *civilitas*, and existence including the delights of literature and the truth of self-knowledge as well as love of justice, country, and liberty.[62] John's aim is to alter a form of life. Literature, in the

---

60. John of Salisbury 1909, IV.7.
61. *Ibid.*, I–III, VII–VIII.
62. *Ibid.*, VIII.5, 8–9; III.2; VII.25.

broadest sense, serves the function of a constitutional check, providing both standards of criticism for courtly life and a viable alternative to it. And if this form of philosophy fails as a check, it supports the most radical ethical action, tyrannicide. Like most of the *Policraticus*, the treatment of tyrannicide combines Biblical and classical inspiration.[63] Tyranny is outrageous as a violation of both divine law and republican liberty. It creates a climate of violence and deceit and at the same time legitimates these as tactics against itself. John presents both aspects of the situation effectively in recounting Judith's assassination of Holofernes and in epigrams adapted from Cicero on friendship (it is licit to flatter whom it is licit to kill). John's commendation of tyrannicide is not standard medieval doctrine, but it deserves attention as the response of a widely admired writer to a widely recognised problem.

Whereas John of Salisbury sought to augment virtue in order to bring about royal government in accordance with law, Wyclif urged the king to override merely human law in order to bring about the rule of virtue. For both, obedience to divine law is central. Wyclif, however, uses this idea as a basis, not for subjecting government to moderation by human law, but for virtually dispensing with human law in favour of the law of charity. Charity suffices for governing the soul, therefore it suffices for the government of whatever is accessory to the soul, such as bodily goods and the goods of fortune;[64] and this applies not only to religious matters but also to the commonwealth, for Christ's law teaches completely how every sin should be destroyed and avoided, but it is impossible for a commonwealth to deteriorate except by occasion of sin.[65] The sharp contrast in Wyclif's thought between spiritual and material goods[66] and his insistence that such human law as may be necessary should be directed by a vision of the higher goods had striking implications for the reform of social attitudes and practices. Christ came for the gradual abolition of private civil property.[67] It would be better even from the standpoint of earthly polity – and Wyclif assures us Aristotle would agree – if all things were held in common.[68] Accordingly, social distinctions based on inequalities of wealth and power are fallacious. Servile status, for example, is nothing to be ashamed of

63. *Ibid.*, III.15; IV.1, 12; VII.20; VIII.17–21.
64. John Wyclif 1885–1904, I.17, III.2–3.
65. *Ibid.*, I.44.
66. *Ibid.*, I.12–13.
67. *Ibid.*, II.16, III.4.
68. *Ibid.*, I.14, III.12.

(hereditary servitude is of doubtful legitimacy), while wealth and political power are more to be feared than sought.[69]

For Wyclif, leadership in a good society would necessarily be moral leadership and would have to come from the Christian ministry. The ideal picture of England's priests guiding their flocks by the light of charity is like that of the best (aristocratic or natural) Biblical polity, in which judges ruled by the law of the Lord. Given the sinfulness of the present human condition, firm coercion by kings using civil punishments will also be necessary, but this must be directed theologically.[70] Unfortunately, the condition of the Christian ministry at the time struck Wyclif as the heart of the problem.[71] Accordingly, he proceeded to a typically medieval political paradox, a call for coercively enforced reform to purify an essentially spiritual governing authority.[72] On one level, the expropriation of excessive or misused ecclesiastical property Wyclif advocated can be understood as a simple redistribution of wealth. He held that the poor were defrauded of their share of the Church's goods under present arrangements and that if clerics were remiss in administering such goods layman might properly step in.[73] But this is not, of course, the primary level on which he sought to operate. He sought to make the ideal of a Christian transformation of human life effective in a world where, as he saw it, human life had largely transformed Christianity instead.

Law as a product of human reason: Thomas Aquinas and William Ockham

Aquinas' famous definition of law as an ordinance of reason for the common good, made by one having the care of the community, and promulgated (*ST*, IaIIae, q. 90, a. 4), has both traditional and positivistic elements, but its essence is practical reason. The definition is intended to apply to law in general, including[74] an eternal law (the divine reason conceived as providentially governing all creation), natural law (the rational creature's participation in eternal law), and divine law (supernaturally revealed certifications of natural law and determinations of it with a view to man's ultimate end of eternal blessedness), as well as human law (which to be legitimate must be derived from natural law and not contrary to divine law). By situating human law in the context of these

69. *Ibid.*, I.22, 32–4.
70. *Ibid.*, I.26–7, II.2; cf. III.13, I.10.
71. *Ibid.*, I.44, III.2–3.
72. *Ibid.*, I.37, II.5.
73. *Ibid.*, I.42, III.14.
74. *ST*, IaIIae, q. 91; q. 99, a. 4; q. 100, a. 1.

other laws, Thomas follows medieval Christian precedent. By including
authoritative enactment and promulgation in the concept of law, he
accords some weight to power. Yet even when rules for human action
seem most clearly to be given from above, for Thomas it is a matter of
instruction rather than command, and the instruction is in first principles
constituted by and self-evident to practical reason, and in reason's elaboration of those principles.[75] Conversely, the primary function of legal
penalties is to supplement the family *disciplina* by which the young,
especially, may be educated to perform good acts voluntarily; only in
extreme cases is law a matter of repressing the wicked in order to leave the
good in peace.[76] Similarly, in so far as tyrannical law is contrary to reason,
it is not law but a perversion of law, and to that extent it is not binding in
conscience.[77]

In reason's direction of human life, it moves from determinate ends,
fixed by our various natural inclinations, to rules for action that will be
effective in achieving these ends in particular, indefinitely varied circumstances.[78] Thomas' own work, then, is partly concerned with making
evident the necessity of the more general practical rational principles. He
does this, for example, in his treatment of the Decalogue (traditionally
taken as a divine prescription of natural law), which he expounds in a
remarkably systematic fashion, so that the self-evidence of these precepts is
not a matter of isolated intuitions but of seeing the point of certain forms of
action as constituents or preconditions of human well-being.[79] The more
specific one attempts to make the indispensable principles of reason, however, the more difficult it is to formulate rules which actually realise the
principles in all cases.[80] Accordingly, Thomas also discusses various sorts of
contingency in human affairs and the functions of law and government in
meeting them.

While all legitimate human law is in some way derived from natural
law, some is essentially only a restatement of it. The most properly human
part of our legislation, however, is derived from natural law by way of
'determinations' fitting it to specific circumstances, rather as an artist
embodies a form in a particular matter.[81] The implication seems to be that

75. *ST*, IaIIae, q. 90, a. 1, *ad* 2; q. 94, a. 1. On natural law as practical reason in Aquinas, Grisez 1969.
76. *ST*, IaIIae, q. 95, a. 1.
77. *ST*, IaIIae, q. 92, a. 1, *ad* 4; q. 96, a. 4.
78. *ST*, IaIIae, q. 51, a. 1; q. 91, a. 2; IIaIIae, q. 47, a. 15; q. 120, a. 1.
79. *ST*, IaIIae, q. 99, aa. 1–2; q. 100; IIaIIae, q. 122.
80. *ST*, IaIIae, q. 94, a. 4.
81. *ST*, IaIIae, q. 95, a. 2.

there is a permissible range of choice for human lawmakers here, within which there may be better or worse laws but where even the less adequate rules are ethically acceptable in themselves and become obligatory through legitimate enactment. Human law is rightly subject to change, either because of change in the circumstances to which the law is addressed or because of the progressive character of human reason, which may discover better legislative solutions to continuing problems. Contemplated new legislation must, however, be a considerable improvement if change is to be justified.[82]

While practical reason is in principle universally valid as is any other kind of reason, non-rational factors of various kinds may impede its operation in particular men or societies.[83] Although human law is essentially concerned with making its subjects good, it properly does not command all virtuous acts or forbid all evil deeds but issues only such commands and prohibitions as most people are capable of observing without intolerable strain and resultant greater evils (Thomas quotes Augustine for the legality of prostitution).[84] This and other imperfections of human law are made good by divine law. Besides allowing everyone to have certain knowledge of the most necessary principles of natural law, divine law prescribes all the acts of all the virtues (including inner acts and acts bearing on personal excellence rather than the common good) and punishes all vicious acts;[85] and divine law calls men to membership in a higher community, with God, the *principalitas* of which is love inspired by the Holy Spirit.[86]

Human law and government have positive ethical value, and Christians are subject to secular government, even though its authority is founded on nature, not grace.[87] On the other hand, Christians should not be politically subject to non-believers, for even though their authority may be in principle legitimate, it would in most concrete circumstances pose dangers to the Christians' faith.[88] Heresy, as distinct from simple non-belief, is not merely a vice but a legally punishable crime, for it is a violation of commitments that a person has explicitly professed.[89]

82. *ST*, IaIIae, q. 97, aa. 1–2.
83. *ST*, IaIIae, q. 94, a. 6.
84. *ST*, IaIIae, q. 96, a. 2; IIaIIae, q. 10, a. 11.
85. *ST*, IaIIae, q. 91, a. 4; q. 100, a. 2.
86. *ST*, IaIIae, q. 108, a. 1.
87. *ST*, IIaIIae, q. 104, a. 6.
88. *ST*, IIaIIae, q. 10, a. 10.
89. *ST*, IIaIIae, q. 10, aa. 8, 12.

Notwithstanding Suárez' opinion that the issues involved are more verbal than real (*Tractatus de legibus ac Deo legislatore*, I.5.1), Ockham's 'voluntarist' view of law is sometimes sharply contrasted with Thomas' definition of law as reason. Ockham's conception of coercion of wrongdoers as the principal purpose of secular government[90] and his concern with questions of power throughout his political writings may seem to indicate a legal positivism consonant with the theological and philosophical positivism sometimes found in his academic writings. The sceptical or positivist interpretation of these earlier writings is questionable, however. Certainly, Ockham made commitment to *recta ratio* essential to a good will in ethics.[91] Rationality, as against arbitrary power, is also a dominant theme in such major political works as the third part of the *Dialogus* and the *Octo quaestiones de potestate papae*,[92] but it is a rationality which gives unusually full attention to contingent, often irrational circumstances. For example, Ockham holds that monarchy is normally the best regime, for the world as well as for a single realm, since one ruler can discharge the functions for which governments are instituted more effectively than many. In spite of his role as an imperial apologist, however, his endorsement of monarchy is qualified: it is expedient to vary regimes or dominions according to the variety, quality, and needs of the times. Sometimes it may be expedient to have one secular or ecclesiastical ruler over all mortals, sometimes many secular or ecclesiastical rulers governing together; at other times it may be useful for many independent rulers to preside over the different parts of the world.[93]

Ockham allows that the subjects of any government may in some cases (but not without cause) depose their rulers and set up new regimes,[94] and he explicitly rejects the common axiom of papalist and Marsilian political theory,[95] that avoidance of strife requires a unity of jurisdiction between spiritual and secular governments (*Octo quaestiones* III. 3). The apparent anarchy of these Ockhamist positions[96] is offset by certain principles Ockham sought to establish concerning what is ordinarily desirable in

---

90. William Ockham 1974b, *Octo quaestiones*, Q. III. c. 8.
91. William Ockham 1495–6, III, qq. 12, 13.
92. The less nuanced and less widely circulated *Breviloquium* and *De imperatorum et pontificum potestate* are now more accessible.
93. Part III of the *Dialogus*, Tract II, Book 1, cc. 1, 5–6; *Octo quaestiones* III.11.
94. III *Dialogus* I.1.16, 2.28: II.1.7, 29, 31. *Octo Quaestiones* II.2, 9–10; VIII. 6. *Breviloquium* IV.12–13, VI.2.
95. Gewirth 1951, pp. 14–20, 30, 115–25.
96. Lagarde 1956–70, V, 258–9 and *passim*.

politics. Rejecting the Aristotelian monarchic ideal of a legally absolute outstandingly virtuous ruler as unsuitable to the present day, he argued that government should ordinarily operate under legal restraints.[97] Again, while he found no absolute line between secular and spiritual affairs and hence held that lay and ecclesiastical authorities might in extraordinary circumstances act in one another's jurisdictions,[98] acceptance of a considerable distance between secular and spiritual government as normally desirable was one of his main aims in writing.[99] Finally, Ockham's strong emphasis on personal liberty, though unaccompanied by endorsements of popular participation in politics, favours a situation in which rulers must show cause for restricting their subjects' freedom and in which subjects have scope for opposition should occasion require it.[100]

Law as command

Every political theory has something to say about effectiveness as a feature of law, but when the sheer survival of a government or of endurable political life is the paramount concern, it becomes natural to think of coercive enforceability as law's essence.[101] In our period, Marsilius of Padua is the pre-eminent representative of this viewpoint. It may mislead to say that whatever a ruler effectively wills has the force of law for Marsilius, but the needed qualifications of this positivistic formulation all rest on deeper considerations of effectiveness or political viability. Marsilius does not admit the legitimacy of just any ruler; though indifferent to the type of regime as between one, few, or many rulers, he insists that whatever the government is, it should be subordinate to the popular will.[102] But this is because governments lacking popular control are ineffective, in his view, not merely in achieving or preserving the common good but even in preserving themselves.[103] Again, he holds that governmental action should be determined by law, rather than law being a product of government, but this is because only in the universal formulations of law can the healthy will of the people find effective expression in contrast with the partial or diseased wills of individuals.[104] Finally, he holds

97. III *Dialogus* I.2.6.
98. III *Dialogus* I.1.16–17; *Octo quaestiones* III.12; *De imperatorum et pontificum potestate*, c. 12.
99. McGrade 1974, pp. 84–5.
100. *Octo quaestiones* I.6, III.6; III *Dialogus* I.1.5–8; *Breviloquium* II.3–4.
101. Gewirth 1951, pp. 131–6; but see Lewis 1963 and Rubenstein 1965.
102. *Defensor pacis* I.8.4, 9.9, 17.2.
103. *Ibid.*, I.12.6–7.
104. *Ibid.*, I.11–12.

that what the people would will if impediments to the operation of their desire were removed would not be capricious or irrational, but this is not because the people have insight into, or commitment to, abstract principles of rectitude but rather because determining the contents of proposed legislation in an objectively adequate way is less important in his theory than the wholesomeness of the popular desire which gives such recommendations legal force.[105] Within very broad limits, then, whatever the people as a whole approve as a legal command *will* have legitimacy, in the sense of effectively promoting the peace and tranquillity that the people as a whole necessarily desire.

If Marsilian legal positivism grew from an urgently felt need for governmental unity, a higher positivism can be found as part of the hierocratic tradition. The ruling idea here is that of an omnicompetent authority whose status is warranted religiously, 'from above'. The popes were acutely conscious of their legislative power in the area of canon law and typically claimed superiority to every other positive law as well. In collaboration or competition with the papal model, fortified by the tradition of theocratic kingship, and often instructed by Roman law, secular monarchs could sometimes vindicate claims to a similar supra-legal authority. It has been beyond the scope of this survey to determine what, if anything, can make political authority sacred, or whether true religion best supports positivism or an illuminated legal rationalism. Much of later medieval political philosophy seems understandable without such determinations, and in the current philosophical climate it is naturally tempting to take up that portion and leave the rest. The temptation is yet stronger if one feels unhappy with the combination of *ius divinum* and Marsilian positivism (in versions of the latter worked out by Bodin and Hobbes) used to sustain absolutism in the seventeenth and eighteenth centuries. Separating the purely reasonable parts of medieval political thought from the spiritual concerns that originally animated them is surely bad history, however; and in the present disspirited condition of Western political theory it is arguably bad philosophy as well.

105. *Ibid.*, I.13.1–4.

40

THE STATE OF NATURE AND THE ORIGIN OF THE STATE

Lordship and ownership

Before the arrival in the west of Aristotle's *Politics*, the origin of organised society was usually discussed in terms of the institution of lordship and ownership (*dominium*). *Dominium* was seen to arise from an act of force, an act of God, human agreement or an amalgam of these, just as in fact the assumption of power often proved to be a combination of events such as usurpation, the test of utility and merit, 'divine right', hereditary claims and election or confirmation by the community or its clerical part.

The view that lordship arose from the forceful assumption of power and the subjection of other men had been handed down by Patristic writers. It was illustrated by the story of the Fall and of the appearance with Cain and Nimrod of sinful ambition and dominion, and it reflected too the Stoic assumption (cf. Seneca, *Epistola*, XIV.2 (90)) that men had enjoyed equality, freedom, and self-sufficiency in an original state of innocence which had been lost through the appearance of human wickedness. The history of the ancient Roman empire attracted much interest since it had obviously gained authority from conquest. Government, then, was the consequence of sin and it arose from the lust for power and domination. But in so far as coercive authority restrained further abuse of free will, it was a necessary and legitimate remedy of sin. After the loss of innocence many men were no longer fit to enjoy freedom and equality or to practice common ownership.

The divine origin of rulership

The ultimately divine origin of rulership was generally accepted. Even on the assumption that government is rooted in sin, it acquires a moral and sacred function as a remedy of sin. St Paul had written: 'There is no power but of God. For the powers that be are ordained of God' (Romans 13.1). For this reason Hugh of Fleury, writing after 1102, dismissed as foolish the assertion that royal authority sprang from greed, crime, and pride or through the agitation of the devil.[1] Following the example of the writings of Denis the pseudo-Areopagite many scholastics, including William of Auvergne[2] and Giles of Rome,[3] explained the existence of ranks and offices on earth as an aspect of the hierarchic order of the universe and, in particular, as an extension to earth of the celestial model in which God is king and under him stand nine orders of angels in descending order. Although men, like angels, are equal by nature, they are divided into a hierarchy of unequal orders for the maintenance of harmony and for the effective exercise of different functions. To bring multiplicity to unity, the lowest must be subjected to the highest through intermediaries, as much in the temporal as in the spiritual sphere.

There were many demonstrations of the claims of the priesthood to mediate God's will in the establishment of rulership. Giles of Rome[4] and James of Viterbo[5] supported the theory that temporal power is caused by and is subject to spiritual power even in temporal as distinct from spiritual matters, just as in the universe inferior, corporeal bodies are moved by spirits and intelligences. Nature is perfected by grace, and the means to an end is judged in relation to the final end. Some writers, particularly imperialist writers, argued that the ruler's authority is derived immediately from God and not mediately through the Church. One of the most interesting supporters of such 'divine right' theory was Dante who, like many others in his time, distinguished a twofold end for man corresponding to his double nature, part corruptible and temporal and part incorruptible and spiritual. The means to each of these ends differ and man needs a double direction. The emperor guides man to temporal felicity in accordance with philosophic teachings regarding the practice of the moral and intellectual virtues and the pope leads the human race to eternal felicity in accordance with revealed truth. But although both ends are divinely ordained, and although one is inferior to the other, they are distinct.[6] At the root of many disagreements, as John of Paris saw,[7] lay the problem of evaluating what was meant by the principle that temporal ends are ordained to spiritual ends.

---

1. *De regia potestate et sacerdotali dignitate*, I, 1.
2. *De universo*, II, 2.
3. Giles of Rome 1929, *De ecclesiastica potestate*, II, 13.
4. *Ibid.*, I, 4, 5.
5. James of Viterbo 1926, *De regimine christiano*, II, 6, 7.
6. Dante 1963, *De monarchia*, III, 16.
7. John of Paris 1968, *De regia potestate et papali*, 5; 13; 17.

Agreement as the basis for government

Roman law provided material for the conception that government sprang from the voluntary agreement of the people or the corporate community. By the *lex regia* the people of Rome had 'conferred upon the prince all their power and authority'.[8] That the relationship between ruler and ruled rested on a sort of compact or *pactum* was evident to many writers, among them Manegold of Lautenbach.[9] Marsilius of Padua provided a systematic statement of the role of the community as the corporate *Legislator* from whom the power of the ruler is derived.[10] By the fifteenth century the idea that secular lordship had originated in a free grant of authority by the ruled had come to be applied by conciliarist thinkers to spiritual authority. In his *De concordantia catholica* Nicholas of Cusa argued that since men are by nature free, the regulation of freedom requires agreement; rulers should be constituted through election.[11] Suárez rejected the view that political authority was possessed by 'divine right'; the decision to create a political jurisdiction must be made by the community.[12]

Only from the thirteenth century onwards did the origin of the political community itself receive sustained examination as a natural necessity. The 'organic metaphor' or analogy of the state with a living organism had already been deployed to indicate the interdependence of all the members of a community under the purposeful direction of its higher parts, and the metaphor continued to find favour in later centuries.[13] So too did Cicero's conception of the virtuousness of public life.[14] But the decisive development was the discovery of Aristotle's teaching that man, unless he was a beast or a god, could not exist without the state. He is a political animal by nature. A state or body of citizens is required to meet man's natural needs – physical, moral and rational. Although the state was 'made for the sake of living, it exists for the sake of living well'.[15] Writers as different as Aquinas,[16] Giles of Rome[17] and Marsilius of Padua[18] found in the *Politics*

---

8. '... cum lege regia ... populus ei et in eum omne suum imperium et potestatem conferat', *Digest*, I, 4, 1.
9. *Liber ad Gebehardum.*
10. *Defensor pacis*, I, 15.
11. Nicholas of Cusa 1964–8, *De concordantia catholica*, II, 14; II, 19; II, 34; III, 4.
12. Suárez 1971–7, *De legibus ac Deo legislatore*, III, ii, 3–4.
13. Cf. John of Salisbury 1909, *Policraticus*, V, 1; Marsilius, *Defensor pacis*, I, 2; Nicholas of Cusa, *De concordantia catholica*, III, 41. Also Aristotle, *Politics*, I, 55; VI, 4, 2.
14. *De republica*, I, 1–7. Cf. Lactantius, *Divinae institutiones*, VI, 10 (man as a social animal).
15. *Politics*, I, i, 8 and 12.
16. *Sententia libri Politicorum*, I, 1.
17. *De regimine principum*, III, 1.
18. *Defensor pacis*, I, 3 and 4.

the source of their account of the origin of the state. The state is the consummation of the development of the family, of villages, and of townships. It reflects the natural increase of population. It is a natural, not a conventional, institution. But it is the product of natural human reasoning and issues from rational agreement.

The naturalness or unnaturalness of the state

In his *De regimine principum*, Aquinas followed Aristotle to the extent that he argued that man cannot live alone. If he could live alone, he would be king over himself under God, but by nature he is both a social and a political animal. Men would not pursue their common end, which is their common good, without the direction of a ruler. Aquinas invoked the analogy of a ship blown about by diverse winds and of its helmsman who selects the course to be taken and steers it to port. But the ultimate end for Aquinas is not virtue or living well; it is the vision of God, and to attain the ultimate end a government of priests has been instituted which is distinct from the government of kings. To kings belongs the duty to order the good life in a way that is congruous with the achievement of eternal felicity.[19]

Discussion of the origin of rulership and of the state was closely bound to an assessment of the state of nature. If men are naturally innocent, equal, and free, if property is naturally held in common, if natural law is unchanging and perpetual, the state through its maintenance of private property, unequal liberties, and serfdom, is a contradiction of nature or at best it is based on conventions that qualify nature. Many thought that serfdom, private property, and coercive power do not belong to the state of nature. The appearance of sin having altered all, arguments had to be advanced and distinctions had to be found to justify these institutions.

From the canonist Rufinus in the twelfth century[20] to Suárez in the early seventeenth,[21] there were thinkers who met the problem by distinguishing what is commanded by the natural law and what is indicated or demonstrated by it without being commanded. Thus, according to Rufinus, liberty is one of the demonstrations of the natural law. Natural law neither commands nor forbids it but shows it to be good. It was expedient before the Fall but now it is no longer expedient and the civil

19. *De regimine principum*, I, 1, 14; *Sententia libri Ethicorum*, I, 1; *Sententia libri Politicorum*, I, 1.
20. *Summa decretorum*, D. 1, *Dictum Gratiani ad c.* 1.
21. Suárez 1971–7, II, 5.

laws rightly deprive most men of freedom. This is necessary because crime must be punished and virtue inculcated through discipline. Even slavery is a means to virtue; thus, slavery is a part of the natural law although it is not found in the state of nature. Other institutions also arose subsequent to the state of nature and modify the natural law, but they do not conflict with it. Customs have wisely developed regarding the union of male and female that limit this to certain persons after marriage; otherwise ephemeral and precipitous unions would occur.[22]

The recovery of Aristotle's natural philosophy led people to take note of the naturalness of the political community itself; the actual state was itself a natural state. Aquinas consequently distinguished two types of lordship.[23] Lordship in the sense of rule in the interest of the ruler was, as the Stoics and the Fathers and the medieval lawyers had maintained, absent from the state of nature or innocence. But lordship in the sense of the direction of free men for the sake of their common good is, as Aristotle showed, natural, for man is by nature a political animal and the common good of a society requires an organising and directing authority. Moreover, men are by nature unequal in respect of knowledge and the capacity for justice, and it would be unsuitable for the superior members of society not to be able to use their superiority for the benefit of others. Thus subjection is natural, and although slavery is not found in the state of nature, it is not against nature, for it is an addition made to nature by human reason for the benefit of man following the introduction of sin.

The naturalness or unnaturalness of private property

Aquinas also bowed to Aristotle in respect of private property.[24] He recognised the strength of traditional teaching that by natural law all things belong to all men in common. But he refused to see private property as a contradiction of nature. He appealed to the distinction between possession and use. Natural law does not prohibit the acquisition or division of possessions; it arises by human and reasonable agreement under positive law as an addition to the natural law. The tranquillity and order of society are better assured if men are encouraged to acquire property through their own effort and to maintain it themselves. But the common use of things prevails over private possession and in cases of necessity goods should be

22. On the handling by the canonists of Plato's teaching regarding the community of wives see Kuttner 1976.
23. *ST*, I, q. 92, a. 1 *ad* 2. Also IIaIIae, q. 57, a. 3.
24. *ST*, I, 2, q. 94, a. 5. Also IIaIIae, q. 32, a. 7 *ad* 3; IIaIIae, q. 66. Cf. *Politics*, I, 3.

transferred to those in need. Aquinas forthrightly condoned the reasonableness of a poor man's taking what he needs from a well-endowed person, because by natural law inferior things exist for the common use of men and human law cannot abrogate natural law. The ruler, for the sake of the common utility, may tax or confiscate private property.[25]

Aquinas' doctrines that lordship and private ownership belonged to the state of nature rapidly gained a wide influence. John of Paris, for example, held that 'true lordship' over things belonged to those who acquired them by their own labour. Men may dispose of their property at their pleasure as long as no injury is done to another. But the prince is the judge of rights; he must punish usurpations of property when found and redistribute it when the common 'necessity or utility' requires it.[26] Ockham taught likewise.[27] But the controversies over the question of apostolic poverty brought these discussions into sharper focus. Many scholastics in the fourteenth century applied a moral or religious test to ownership and held that the right enjoyed by an individual possessor was dependent on his relationship to God. The Spiritual Franciscans argued that by nature property is held in common and therefore those who seek perfection should renounce personal possession. When applied to the Church or to the wealthy or to those outside the church such doctrines were of far more than academic interest. The question, too, of the ruler's powers over the property of his subjects was crucial to the discussion of lordship.

Giles of Rome, basing himself upon Augustine's *De civitate Dei*, II.22 ('true justice does not exist except in that commonwealth whose founder and ruler is Christ'), argued that valid titles to property could not be enjoyed by infidels and excommunicates and could only be held under the general lordship of the Church.[28] John of Paris rejected this, except in cases of supreme necessity.[29] So did Ockham who taught that the Church's mission was purely spiritual and was not concerned with social utility.[30] But Richard FitzRalph argued that since lordship is found in the state of nature and since by nature men are just and hold all things in common, original lordship is exercised by all just men in common. Ownership which makes a thing the property of one man is not original lordship and it may exclude the just man from the use or the right to use that thing. Ownership

25. *De regimine iudaeorum.*
26. *De potestate regia et papali*, 7.
27. *Opus nonaginta dierum*, II, 88; *Breviloquium de principatu tyrannico*, III, 14.
28. *De ecclesiastica potestate*, II, 7 and 12.
29. *De potestate regia et papali*, 7.
30. *De imperatorum et pontificum potestate*, 9–10.

is acquired lordship which is also called civil or political or positive lordship. Original or pure lordship, on the other hand, is the right of the just man alone.[31] Wyclif, who borrowed many of his premisses from FitzRalph, also wrote in support of the view that the man who is in grace is lord of all the world, and if there is a multitude of such men they should have to hold all in common. Misuse of goods, even by the ecclesiastical community, creates a ground for their expropriation.[32] But Wyclif and FitzRalph did not urge an immediate or unconditional transfer of property from the unjust to the just. Viewed spiritually, men who are in grace do have a full right to all property, but the presence of sin constrains all to accept the fact of private ownership.

In the sixteenth century some Thomist thinkers vigorously reaffirmed the equal capacity of all men, including unjust men and non-Christians, to establish, under natural law, their own political societies with true rulers and legitimate ownership. The Spanish conquests in the Americas and the seizure of Indian possessions were attacked on these grounds by, among others, Vitoria in the 1530s in his lectures on *The Recently Discovered Indies*.

Rulers as delegates of the people

In the scholastic period populist principles – 'people-sovereignty' or the 'ascending' theme of government – challenged 'ruler-sovereignty' and hierocratic theory – the 'descending' theme of government – even in the ecclesiastical sphere. The Roman law teaching that rulership is derived from the people by the *lex regia* (*Digest*, I, I, 4) and Aristotle's view that man is by nature a political animal, capable of being a citizen as distinct from being a subject (*subditus*), underlay much of the development of political philosophy.

Absolute rulership

Roman law did not uncontrovertibly point to the conclusion that the people retained any control over the authority it had created. In Roman law the prince is freed from the laws (*legibus solutus*); his will has the force of law. The revival of Roman law from the end of the eleventh century encouraged a growing appreciation that a legislative authority – e.g. a king or emperor – is the sole, immediate, active source of law, and that only the prince can make positive, written law. Hence the bold claims of, for

---

31. Richard Fitzralph 1890, *De pauperie salvatoris*, I, 2; IV, 1.
32. *De civili dominio*, I, 14 and 37.

example, Aeneas Sylvius: the emperor is absolute, he is lord of the laws and he must be obeyed, however unjust he is.[33] From the thirteenth century at least the conception emerged more clearly that there is in the state a sovereign power, caesar or pope, which alone can provide law (*legem ponere; lex posit(iv)a*) and against which there can be no appeal.

The sovereignty of the people and other restraints on rulership

However, the civilians and others who knew about Roman law also debated another theory, namely that the people had merely conceded authority to the emperor (through a *concessio*) and is entitled to resume it. The *Corpus iuris civilis* had also laid down that 'it is a thing greater than empire that a prince submit his government to the laws'.[34] Many were far from agreeing that the emperor might issue law arbitrarily. For one thing, law must conform to justice. As John of Salisbury wrote, 'the prince is said to be loosed from the bonds of law, not because unjust deeds are permitted him, but because he ought to be one who cultivates equity from the love of justice rather than from fear of punishment'.[35] And Bracton, while affirming that the king has no peer in his kingdom and that no writ runs against the king, held that the king is under the law; what pleases the prince has the force of law (*Digest*, I, 4, 1), but the prince should will only what is right and just and agreed after taking counsel with his great men.[36] Moreover, the prince should respect the customs of the people. Bartolus took this further: if the people can by tacit consent create usages and customs, they can also by explicit consent create the written law as well; the state was itself sovereign (*civitas sibi princeps*).[37] Later in the sixteenth century Jacques Almain argued forthrightly that no community can wholly alienate its authority to a ruler any more than an individual can renounce his right to self-preservation; although monarchy is the best form of government, it is limited by being a rule over free men.[38] At the very beginning of the revival of Roman law, Irnerius had defined law as an ordinance of the people promulgated after consultation with wise men, especially the Senate.[39] Richard Hooker reflected many thinkers in the centuries that

---

33. *De ortu et auctoritate imperii romani*, 16; 20; 21.
34. 'Maius imperio est legibus submittere principatum', *Cod.* I, 14, 4.
35. 'Princeps tamen legis nexibus dicitur absolutus, non quia ei iniqua liceant, sed quia is esse debet, qui non timore poenae sed amore iustitiae aequitatem colat ...' *Policraticus*, IV, 2.
36. Henry of Bracton 1968, *De legibus et consuetudinibus*, I, 8, 5; III, 9, 3.
37. Woolf 1913.
38. Almain 1706, *De dominio naturali civili et ecclesiastico*. Cf. Almain 1525, *De auctoritate ecclesiae*, I.
39. *Summa codicis*, I, 14, 3.

intervene when he wrote that, while wise men may devise laws, their coercive character may only be given by the whole community or its representatives or by the prince if he has received this authority from the community. 'Laws they are not therefore which public approbation hath not made so.'[40]

Limited monarchy

In the thirteenth century the case for a middle road between ruler-sovereignty and people-sovereignty was developed and the theory of limited monarchy or of the mixed constitution emerged. The question was not basically whether rule by one man was better than rule by many. Under the influence of Aristotle's *Politics*, I, 1, a distinction came to be drawn between political government according to law and despotic or arbitrary government. The value put upon each and the position of the line between the two varied from thinker to thinker. Aristotle in his *Politics* had himself indicated a relativist view of the value of different constitutions. Aquinas in his Commentary on the *Politics*[41] and Ptolemy of Lucca in his *De regimine principum*, II, 8–9 and III, 11, regarded political government (*regimen politicum*) as government in which the ruler – whether one or many – was limited by the laws of the state and governed according to established laws. *Regimen regale* was government in which the ruler has absolute power (*plenaria potestas*) and is not bound by the laws of which he is the living source. The form of government to be preferred depended largely on the qualities of the people to be governed.

Giles of Rome expressed a clear preference for *regimen regale* over *regimen politicum* in his *De regimine principum*, II, 1, 14 and II, 2, 29: the king should rule according to his own will and according to the laws he has himself made, not according to the laws made by the citizens. But he is obliged by the natural law to maintain justice and to seek the common good, not to pursue his private interest (I, 1, 12; I, 3, 3). The case for rule by one man received a universal extension in Dante's *De monarchia*. In this treatise Dante sought to maximise the liberty of the human race by placing the affairs common to all men under the rule of one supreme, universal monarch. Ockham called a monarchy in which one man rules without legal limit for the benefit of the common good a pure, regal monarchy; this is 'the best, when it is at its best'.[42] Regal monarchy, in Ockham's terms, is

---

40. *Of the Laws of Ecclesiastical Polity*, I, 10, 4–8; VIII, 2, 9–11.
41. *Sententia libri Politicorum*, I, 1.
42. *Dialogus*, pars III, tr. I, lib. II, c. 6.

government over free men that does not use men or their goods despotically for its own advantage. But this is nowhere to be found: 'in these days
there is perhaps in the whole world no instance of regal monarchy'.[43] The
best in practice is kingship according to law in which the ruler is bound by
certain laws or customs introduced by men. Sir John Fortescue reconciled
regal and political lordship in a combined *dominium politicum et regale*. By
this Fortescue meant that the king should rule by such laws as he makes
himself (*dominium regale*), but such laws should receive the assent of his
people (*dominium politicum*).[44]

Aquinas had earlier expressed an influential preference for mixed, constitutional rule. In *De regimine principum*, I, 2 and 3, and also in I, 6, Aquinas
held that a monarchy devoted to the common good was the best form of
government because it tended to the unity of the state. But to prevent the
monarch becoming a tyrant his power must be limited (*temperatur*). In the
Summa theologiae Aquinas describes as the best government that of one man
of virtue when other men of virtue govern under him and when the rulers
are elected from all and by all (*politia bene commixta*).[45] The mixed constitution includes the elements of monarchy, aristocracy, and democracy
(*regimen commixtum*) and in it laws are made by the nobles with the
participation of the people (*majores natu simul cum plebibus*).[46]

In the *Summa theologiae* Aquinas outlined a case for giving everyone a
share in the ruler's authority: the ruler should be elected by all and from all.
John of Paris argued that the climatic, linguistic and political differences
between communities constituted a reason why separate communities
should choose their own rulers and not, *pace* Dante, be subject to one
supreme monarch.[47] Marsilius used a utilitarian argument in favour of
popular participation in government: the involvement of all the citizens
would make government more efficient.[48] Nicholas of Cusa went further:
since by nature all men are free and equal in respect of authority, valid rule
and legal coercion can only arise from the voluntary consent of men. All
power, spiritual as well as corporeal, is latent in the people in potency, and
if it is to be actualised so as to regulate and coerce men, the people must
freely subject themselves. The elective principle is the origin of every

---

43. 'Forte his diebus non est in universo orbe talis principatus scilicet primus regalis', *Dialogus*, ibid.
44. *De natura legis naturae*, I, 16 and 24–5; *De laudibus legum angliae*, 9.
45. *ST*, IaIIae, q. 105, a. 1.
46. *ST*, IaIIae, q. 95, a. 4.
47. *De potestate regia et papali*, 3.
48. *Defensor pacis*, I, 12.

ordered superiority.[49] Suárez thought likewise: the authority to make law resides in the community for men are by nature equal and no man naturally has jurisdiction over other men. The community creates government in such a form as it wishes.[50]

The ruler as private and public person

It was very hard in some concrete situations to disentangle the private, proprietary rights and actions of kings from their public capacities and the property of the state entrusted to them. But Roman law distinguished public and private law and John of Salisbury echoes it when he describes the king as 'the minister of the public utility': 'the power of all the subjects is gathered together in him that he may be strong enough to seek out and perform what is useful for the welfare of each and all ... The prince is, as some define him, a public power and a certain image of the divine majesty on earth.'[51] Aquinas spoke of the prince as 'the bearer of the person of the community'.[52] Gerson, in *Vivat rex*, reminded the king of France that a king is not a private person but a public power ordained for the welfare of the whole community. The development of elective and representative institutions and of ideas of consent and the common good, and the development, moreover, of the notion of the community itself or of the *communitas regni*, was intertwined with reflection on the links that bind together the ruler and the ruled. Marsilius of Padua brought out in a decisive manner the implications for political philosophy of the idea of popular sovereignty and of representative government. Following Aristotle's *Politics*, III, 11, Marsilius argued that in every 'perfect community' the authority to make law and to institute the governing head (*pars principans*) must belong ultimately to the people or all the citizens (*populus seu civium universitas*) or their weightier part (*valentior pars*).[53] Law made by the citizen body as a whole will secure the common benefit, and will be better observed, than law made by one man or by a few. The people must be the *legislator*. The *pars principans* is not necessarily elected; it might consist of one individual or a small council and inheritance may enter into it, but the authority granted to it is delegated to it immediately by the

49. *De concordantia catholica*, II; III, 4.
50. *De legibus ac Deo legislatore*, III, 2, 3.
51. 'In eum omnium subditorum potestas confertur, ut in utilitate singulorum et omnium exquirenda et facienda sibi ipse sufficiat ... Est ergo, ut eum plerique diffiniunt, princeps potestas publica et in terris quaedam divinae maiestatis imago', *Policraticus*, IV, 1.
52. 'Princeps qui curam populi habet et eius personam gerit', *ST*, IIaIIae, q. 57, a. 2.
53. *Defensor pacis*, I, 12.

Legislator. Thus the *pars principans* is the executive part (*secundaria quasi instrumentalis seu executiva pars*) of the community and is bound by the law. The doctrine of popular sovereignty and of elective, representative government was also applied to the ecclesiastical community.[54] Marsilius applied the principle that coercive authority is located in the whole community to the Christian community of believers who, in a Christian republic, are identical with the community of citizens. They should therefore be governed by a general council organised by the 'faithful, human legislator which lacks a superior'.[55] Other conciliarist writers argued towards similar conclusions.

The limits set upon a ruler's authority varied according to the nature and source of his authority. Likewise the arguments that were elaborated to cope with abuse of authority and with tyranny also varied. There were writers, particularly earlier in the Middle Ages, who argued that since royal authority was sacred and of divine institution, it could not lawfully be resisted even when it acted unjustly. 'All power is from God . . . he who resists the power resists the ordinance of God' (Romans, 13. 1 and 2). Even Nero, as Augustine remarked,[56] owed his power to divine providence which decided that man's condition deserved such a master. Gregory the Great provided support for a theory of 'divine right' when he put the bad ruler beyond criticism by men and made him accountable to God alone.[57] Imperialist writers in the eleventh century tended to agree.

The legitimacy of resisting authority

But this was not the whole story, for the patristic inheritance overwhelmingly proclaimed that the purpose of society and of rulership was the attainment of justice. By this standard the tyrant enjoyed no rightful power. There were several ways along which theories allowing control of the ruler might develop and admit of resistance to him and ultimately justify assassination. One of these starts from the distinction between a king and a tyrant. Isidore of Seville had drawn a sharp contrast between them.[58] John of Salisbury, too, in his *Policraticus*[59] describes tyranny as the contradiction of kingship which consists in the government of the people in the interest of public utility and equity and which upholds the law out of

54. *Ibid.*, I, 15–17.
55. *Ibid.*, II, 16–17; II, 20–1.
56. *De civitate Dei*, V, 19.
57. *Regula pastoralis*, III, 4; *Moralia in Iob*, XXII, 24; XXV, 16.
58. Isidore of Seville 1911, *Etymologiae*, IX, 3; *Sententiae*, III, 48.
59. *Policraticus*, III, 15; IV; VIII, 17–21.

the love of justice. A tyrant who oppresses the people by the sword and who voids the law has no rights against the people and deserves to die by the sword. But every ruler is the image and vicar of God, and killing a tyrant is an act that signifies divine vengeance. The tyrant's assassin does not really act in the name of the outraged community.

Aquinas also based his argument in favour of resistance to tyranny upon the tyrant's lack of divine sanction. In his Commentary on the *Sentences*, II, d. 44, 2, 2, he stated that authority (*praelatio*) derives from God or it is defective. However, Aquinas is also careful to indicate the limitations to be put upon a theory of resistance. Authority may be defective either through the manner of its acquisition or through the use to which it is put. Resistance to defective authority is not allowable if the ruler is simply unsuitable, nor is it allowable if the ruler obtains power illegally but subsequently gains acceptance by his subjects. But it is allowable if the ruler uses his authority to command acts of sin or to command what is beyond his rights. Aquinas, through his support of the idea of a mixed constitution, hoped that the ruler's authority might be limited (*temperare*) in its use in such a way that the opportunity for tyranny would be removed.[60] But he clearly affirmed that resistance to a tyrant is not sedition, because it is the tyrant who is seditious.[61] It may be better to obey the tyrant if a worse evil is likely to ensue from his deposition, but he cannot be obeyed in acts of sin. Aquinas also applied Aristotle's test of good government which is good if it serves the common good. The obedience due to a ruler by virtue of his divinely ordained authority extends only as far as the order of justice requires.[62]

Another form of resistance theory rested on the idea of contract. The argument used by Manegold of Lautenbach in his *Liber ad Gebehardum* was one that reappeared frequently in later centuries: the king is hired or contracted by the people to do a job. The elective principle was an aspect of the making of a king and oaths were taken at royal coronations. If the king chooses to act the tyrant, he can no longer claim fidelity because he has broken faith and the compact. Hence the people should be free of his lordship. Manegold also used the argument that the tyrant lacks the essential qualities of a king who is meant to excel all men in wisdom, justice and piety. Loss of honour by corruption justifies loss of the royal title. Aquinas is one of many who appealed to the notion of contract. In *De*

---

60. *De regimine principum*, I, 6.
61. *ST*, IIaIIae, q. 42, a. 2.
62. *ST*, IIaIIae, q. 104, a. 6; also q. 42, 2. Cf. Giles of Rome, *De regimine principum*, I, 1, 12; I, 3, 3; III, 2, 34.

regimine principum, I, 6, he held that public authority – though not private individuals – may remove a tyrant who breaks the contract with the people, just as it may establish the king. Giles of Rome, too, although he favoured absolute and hereditary monarchy, nonetheless maintained in *De renuntiatione papae*, XVI, 1, that the ruler must be established by the consent of men and by that same consent he may be deposed. Contract theory was, however, two-edged. Richard Hooker shrewdly observed that the community may require the consent of the ruler before withdrawing from his dominion.[63]

A further ground for the removal or correction of a ruler lay in the notion that the community possesses sovereignty. Marsilius' doctrine of popular sovereignty allows the community, or the representatives whom it appoints, to correct or depose the ruler because Marsilius transfers the function of making law from the ruler to the community. The ruler (*pars principans*) is simply the executive part of the community which is the *legislator*; hence the *pars principans* is accountable at law.[64] Jacques Almain hardened the argument when he wrote that the people cannot abdicate; under natural law any person who menaces the community may be resisted.[65]

Among the later scholastics the assumption that authority is a concession by the community was paramount. Molina treated tyranny as the exercise of more authority than is granted to the ruler by the community which determines the extent of the ruler's authority.[66] Soto argued that since authority is conferred by the community it may be withdrawn by it in the event of manifest tyranny. Soto, although he had a high view of the authority of the king, represents the view that a legitimately appointed ruler who becomes tyrannical may be assassinated, after a public judgement, by a duly appointed agent; a tyrant usurper may be killed by anyone.[67] The scholastics in general expressed firm support for the possibility of resistance based on the principles of justice and of contract. Such principles gained ground in a number of different countries. The Wars of Religion and the divisions following the Reformation were not a prelude to the rise of resistance theory. To a certain extent they may have been a sequel.

63. *Of the Laws of Ecclesiastical Polity*, VIII, 2, 10.
64. *Defensor pacis*, I, 18.
65. *De dominio naturali civili et ecclesiastico*.
66. Luis de Molina 1659, *De iustitia et iure*, I, 2, 23.
67. Domingo de Soto 1567, *De iustitia et iure*, V, 1, 3. Cf. Mariana, *De rege*, I, 6.

41
THE JUST WAR

The medieval development of theories of war

In the preface to his *Tree of Battles*, written in 1387 and dedicated to Charles VI of France, Honoré Bouvet laments that 'all holy Christendom is so burdened by wars and hatreds, robberies and dissensions, that it is hard to name but one little region, be it duchy or county, that enjoys good peace'. War was the normal condition of society in medieval Europe; and pessimistic doctors argued, on theological or astrological grounds, that 'in this age it is necessary for there to be wars, and the slaughters and infinite sufferings of war'.[1] Some men were dazzled by the pomp and circumstance of glorious war; most doubtless agreed that 'warres & bataylles shold be acursed thyng, & not due'.[2]

About that cursed thing arose a prodigious literature – legal and theological, philosophical and practical, historical, strategical, and ecclesiastical. The centrepiece of the medieval discussions, to which they owe their abiding philosophical interest, is the theory of just war.

That theory is now most familiar from Aquinas' brief essay *De bello* (*ST*, IIaIIae, q. 40); but in this instance Aquinas was no innovator: he stands in a long line of theorists, the *fons et origo* of whose ruminations is to be found in the writings of Augustine.[3] The scattered observations of Augustine and his successors were collected and ordered by the canon lawyers of the twelfth century, whose work is best represented by Gratian's *Decretum*. The commentators on the *Decretum*, of whom Rufinus was the first, developed a theory of war; and the theory was elaborated in the thirteenth

---

1. Baldus, *Consilia* V, cons. 439; see esp. John of Legnano, *De bello*, Ch. 6; Bouvet, *Tree of Battles*, III. 2.
2. Christine de Pisan, *Fayttes of Armes* I.2.
3. The main Augustinian texts, in chronological order, are: *Contra Faustum* XXII.74–8; *Ep.* 138; *De civ. Dei* XV. 4; XIX. 7, 12–15; *Ep.* 189; *Serm.* 302; *QQ. in Hept.* IV.44; VI.10; *Ep.* 229. The influence of Augustine was all-pervasive; he is cited frequently in this chapter only because he was constantly quoted by the medieval theorists. By contrast, Aristotle's influence was negligible (but see below, nn. 30, 58); for his views see *Politics* 1256^{b}23–6, 1333^{b}38–1334^{a}2.

century by Decretalists such as Raymond of Pennaforte and by theologians such as Alexander of Hales and Thomas Aquinas. The theory was vigorous in the fourteenth century – John of Legnano and Baldus de Ubaldis may serve as representative figures – and in the sixteenth it was discussed by men of the stature of Vitoria and Suárez. The final flowering of the tradition may properly be seen in Hugo Grotius' *De jure belli et pacis*, a masterpiece standardly taken to mark the beginning of modern political theory.[4]

Early Christian thinkers inclined to pacifism;[5] for the New Testament seemed firmly opposed to any form of military enterprise: 'All soldiering is instituted either to repel injury or to inflict punishment – injury is repelled either from one's own person or from one's associates – and both things are prohibited by the law of the gospels.'[6] Augustine checked that pacifist inclination: on his view, Christ's 'precepts of patience' do not outlaw war; for 'those precepts are addressed rather to the preparation of the heart, which is internal, than to the deed, which takes place publicly.'[7] The evil of war lies in the mind: the soldier who strikes down his enemy from benevolence and pity acts in accordance with Christ's teaching.[8]

Augustine's scriptural exegesis may raise a sceptical eyebrow or an

---

4. My sketch of the just war theory is based primarily on the following sources: Augustine (texts listed above, n. 3; and see. e.g., De la Brière 1930); Gratian, *Decretum* Causa XXIII (see, e.g., Hubrecht 1955); Rufinus, *Summa decretorum* ad Causa XXIII; Raymond of Pennaforte, *Summa de casibus* II.v.17–18; Alexander of Hales, *Summa theologica* III, §§466–70; Aquinas, *ST*, IIaIIae, q. 40; John of Legnano, *Tractatus de bello*; Baldus de Ubaldis, *Consilia* V, cons. 439; Francisco de Vitoria, *De Indis sive de iure belli Hispanorum in barbaros*, relectio posterior; Francisco Suárez, *De triplice uirtute theologica*, tract. III. disp. XIII, 'De bello'. For the earlier part of the period there is an exhaustive study, citing numerous supplementary texts, in Russell 1975; for the later Middle Ages see Keen 1965 and Tooke 1965. Grotius 1853 is a mine of historical information.
5. On early Church attitudes to war see, e.g., Bainton 1946; Russell 1975, Ch. 2.
6. Gratian, C XXIII, q. 1, introd.: 'Omnis militia vel ob iniuriam propulsandam vel propter vindictam inferendam est instituta – iniuria autem vel a propria persona vel a socio repellitur – quod utrumque evangelica lege prohibetur.'
7. *Ep.* 138.2: 'Ista praecepta magis ad praeparationem cordis, quae intus est, pertinent quam ad opus, quod in aperto fit' (quoted by Gratian, C XXIII, q. 1, canon 2; cf. Aquinas, *ST*, IIaIIae, q. 40, art. 1, *ad* 2); cf. Augustine, *Ep.* 189.14 (quoted below, n. 8); *Contra Faustum* XXII. 76.
8. *Contra Faustum* XXII.74: 'quid enim culpatur in bello? . . . nocendi cupiditas, ulciscendi crudelitas, inpacatus atque implacabilis animus, feritas rebellandi, libido dominandi, et si qua similia, haec sunt quae in bellis iure culpantur' (quoted by Gratian, C XXIII, q. 1, canon 4; Aquinas, *ST*, IIaIIae, q. 40, art. 1, resp.; Alexander, *Summa*, III, §466); cf. Augustine, *Ep.* 189.14: 'Sunt ergo ista praecepta patientiae semper in cordis praeparatione retinenda, ipsaque benevolentia ne reddatur malum pro malo semper in voluntate complenda est. Agenda sunt autem multa cum invitis benigna quadam asperitate plectendis . . . Ac per hoc si terrena ista res publica praecepta Christiana custodiat, et ipsa bella sine benevolentia non gerentur, ut ad pietatis iustitiaeque pacatam societatem victis facilius consulatur . . . Misericorditer enim si fieri posset etiam bella gererentur a bonis, ut licentiosis cupiditatibus domitis haec vitia perderentur quae iusto imperio vel extirpari vel premi debuerunt.'

outraged hackle;[9] but it was gratefully accepted and piously parroted by the medieval political theorists: by returning a negative answer to the question 'Is soldiering always a sin?', Augustine made room for a morality of warfare and a theory of just war.

Conditions of a just war

The theory states that *X* wars justly upon *Y* if and only if certain conditions are satisfied. The conditions were arranged under formal headings; but there was no uniformity, either of enumeration or of nomenclature, to the arrangement. The most elaborate system is that of Alexander of Hales: 'In order to determine if a war is just or unjust you must mark the authority (*auctoritas*), the state of mind (*affectus*), the intention (*intentio*), the condition (*conditio*), the desert (*meritum*), and the cause (*causa*). The state of mind and the authority must be considered in the person of him who declares war; the condition and the intention in the person of him who wages war; the desert in the person of him who is warred upon; the cause in the person of him for whom the war is waged.'[10] Raymond[11] and Baldus[12] list five conditions: where Alexander writes *conditio* they write *persona*, and his *meritum* they express by *res*; his *affectus* becomes *animus*; and they omit *intentio*.[13] John of Legnano also has a list of five items: he has nothing answering to *affectus*, *intentio*, or *conditio*, and he makes up his numbers by somewhat obscure references to 'the enemy' and 'the law which allows the war'.[14] Rufinus specifies four conditions: the declarer of the war must have authority; the soldiery must fight with the right spirit and be men of the

---

9. E.g., on Matt. 26.52 ('all they that take the sword shall perish with the sword'), he comments: 'Ille utitur gladio qui nulla superiori ac legitima potestate vel iubente vel concedente in sanguinem alicuius armatur' (*Contra Faustum*, XXII.70, quoted by Gratian, C XXIII, q. 4, canon 36; Aquinas, *ST*, IIaIIae, q. 40, art. 1, *ad* 1). For the scriptural texts against war, and the standard way of dealing with them, see, e.g., John of Legnano, *De bello*, Ch. 10; Suárez, *De bello*, I.1–5; cf. Grotius 1853, I.ii.5–10.

10. Alexander, *Summa*, III, §466: 'Notandum autem ad hoc ut discernas quod bellum iustum sit vel iniustum, auctoritatem affectum intentionem conditionem meritum et causam. Affectus et auctoritas debent considerari in persona indicentis bellum; conditio et intentio in persona peragentis bellum; meritum in persona sustinentis bellum; causa in persona pro qua agitur bellum.'

11. Raymond, *Summa*, II.v.17: 'Ut autem plane liqueat de bello, nota quod quinque exiguntur ad hoc ut bellum sit iustum, scilicet persona res causa animus et auctoritas.'

12. Baldus, *Consilia* V, cons. 439: 'Ad bellum iustum requiruntur quinque: sunt persona res causa animus et auctoritas.'

13. Unless *animus* embraces both *affectus* and *intentio* (see below, n. 19).

14. John of Legnano, *De bello* Ch. 76: 'Nam licita dicuntur [sc. bella] ratione indicentis, illius contra quem, rei, et causae, et iuris permittentis.'

right type; the enemy must deserve – or be justly deemed to deserve – his fate. Thus Rufinus ignores *affectus* and *causa*.[15] Aquinas holds that 'for any war to be just, three things are required. First, authority . . . Secondly, a just cause. . . . Thirdly, it is required that the intention of the warriors be correct . . .'[16] Aquinas omits *conditio*; his *causa* is Alexander's *meritum*; his *intentio* perhaps embraces *intentio*, *affectus*, and *causa*. Finally, Suárez says that 'for war to occur honourably, several conditions must be observed, which can be reduced to three heads: first, it must be declared by a legitimate authority; secondly, there must be a just cause and title; thirdly, the proper mean and proportion must be preserved in its inception, prosecution, and victory'.[17] *Causa* again answers to *meritum*; and Suárez' third condition is, as it were, the external correlate to *affectus* and *intentio*.

Conditio

Of the two conditions Alexander lays on the soldiery, the first, *conditio*, demands that they be secular, not clerical.[18] The question of what part the clergy might play in warfare looms large in the medieval discussions; but its interest is purely antiquarian and theological.

Intentio and affectus

The second condition on the soldiery, and the first on the declarer of the war, are psychological: just *intentio* demands that the soldiers do not fight from cupidity or a desire for booty (Alexander has no objection to their fighting for pay); and a just *affectus* excludes cruelty. Both conditions derive

15. Rufinus, *Summa* ad C XXIII, q. 2: 'Iustum bellum dicitur propter indicentem, propter belligerentem, et propter eum qui bello pulsatur. Propter indicentem: ut ille qui vi bellum indicit vel permittit huius rei indulgendae ordinariam habeat potestatem; propter belligerentem: ut ille qui bellum gerit et bono zelo hoc faciat et talis persona sit quam bellare non dedeceat; propter eum qui bello fatigatur: ut scilicet mereatur bello lacerari vel si non meretur iustis tamen praesumptionibus mereri putetur.'
16. Aquinas, *ST*, IIaIIae, q. 40, art. 1, resp.: 'respondeo dicendum quod ad hoc quod aliquod bellum sit iustum tria requiruntur. Primo quidem, auctoritas . . . Secundo, requiritur causa iusta. . . . Tertio, requiritur ut sit intentio bellantium recta.'
17. Suárez, *De bello*, I.7: 'Ut bellum honeste fiat, nonnullae conditiones sunt observandae, quae ad tria capita revocantur: primum, ut sit a legitima potestate; secundum, ut causa iusta et titulus; tertium, ut servetur debitus modus et aequalitas in illius initio prosecutione et victoria.'
18. Alexander, *Summa*, III, §466: 'ut non sit persona clericalis'; cf., e.g., Raymond, *Summa*, II.v.17: 'ut sit saecularis, cui licitum est fundere sanguinem, non autem ecclesiastica, cui est prohibitum'. The more nuanced view in Gratian (C XXIII, q. 8; cf. Rufinus, *Summa*, ad C XXIII, q. 8) is expressly rejected by Alexander, *Summa*, III, §470. Those authors who do not make *conditio* a requirement on justice still discuss the question: e.g., Aquinas, *ST*, IIaIIae, q. 40, art. 2; q. 64, art. 4; q. 188, art. 3; John of Legnano, *De bello*, Ch. 82–7; Suárez, *De bello*, III.

from Augustine's emphasis on the mental aspects of warfare;[19] and it is tempting to dismiss them. For, as Grotius says, 'these things ... may argue a sin, but they do not make the war itself properly unjust':[20] cruelty and greed, whether in the prince or in the private, are evil; for they will lead to breaches of the laws of war and to violations of agreements governing its conduct. But if a war is fought unjustly, it does not follow that it is unjustly waged; and the theory of just war is a theory of warring, not of fighting.[21]

That is largely right. But two reservations should be made. First, if a war cannot be fought justly (if, say, innocent non-combatants are bound to be killed), then perhaps it cannot be justly waged: a just war requires at least the possibility of effectively upright intentions. Secondly, although the cruelties and hatreds of a prince may be strictly irrelevant to the justice of his war, his intentions, in a broader sense, are not; for his war aims will affect the justice of his venture. But that issue perhaps falls under Alexander's heading of *causa*.

Auctoritas

Anyone who declares war must have 'just authority' to do so.[22] 'War begins', according to Grotius, 'where the lawcourts end';[23] and Aquinas explains the condition of authority thus: 'first, the authority of a prince, at

19. On *intentio* Alexander, *Summa*, III, §466, quotes a text he ascribes to Augustine: 'Apud veros Dei cultores etiam illa bella pacata sunt quae non cupiditate aut crudelitate sed pacis studio geruntur, ut mali coerceantur et boni subleventur' (Gratian, C XXIII, q. 1, canon 6, and Aquinas, *ST*, IIaIIae, q. 40, art. 1, resp., also quote the passage; but it is not found in our texts of Augustine); on *affectus* Alexander quotes Augustine *Contra Faustum*, XXII.74 (above, n. 7) and *Ep*. 189.4 (in Gratian, C XXIII, q. 1, canon 3). Cf. Raymond, *Summa*, II.v.17: 'animus, ut non fiat propter odium vel ultionem vel cupiditatem ...'; Baldus, *Consilia* V, cons. 439: 'ut non fiat propter odium vel insatiabilem crudelitatem, sed propter caritatem iustitiam et oboedentiam, et ut sine perturbatione in securitate vivatur'. Raymond and Baldus seem to be thinking primarily of *affectus*.
20. Grotius 1853, II.xxii.17: 'Sed haec, ubi causa iustifica non deest, peccatum quidem arguunt, ipsum tamen bellum proprie iniustum non faciunt.'
21. On the distinction between *ius ad bellum* and *ius in bello* see Walzer 1977, Ch. 2–3.
22. Augustine, *Contra Faustum*, XXII.75: 'Interest enim quibus causis quibusque auctoribus homines gerenda bella suscipiant; ordo tamen ille naturalis mortalium paci accommodatus hoc poscit ut suscipiendi belli auctoritas atque consilium penes principem sit ...' (quoted by Gratian, C XXIII, q. 1, canon 2; Alexander, *Summa*, III §466; Aquinas, *ST*, IIaIIae, q. 40, art. 1, resp.). On the controversies over the condition of authority, and its practical importance, see Keen 1965, pp. 72–81.
23. Grotius 1853, II.i.2: 'Ubi iudicia deficiunt, incipit bellum.' The view that war is legal action carried on by other means underlies the whole just war theory; it derives from Rome – see e.g. Cicero, *Off*. I.xi.34: 'Cum sint duo genera decertandi, unum per disceptationem, alterum per vim, cumque illud proprium sit hominis, hoc beluarum, confugiendum est ad posterius si uti non licet superiore.' Cf., e.g., John of Legnano, *De bello*, Ch. 76: 'Cum ergo ab eo qui obnoxius est iustitia haberi non potest, tunc licet bellum indicere'; Christine de Pisan, *Fayttes of Armes*, I.2: 'Warre & bataill whiche is made by iuste quarell is non other thing but right execucion of iustyce, for to gyve the right there as it apperteyneth.'

whose command the war is to be waged; for it does not belong to a private person to start a war, since he can prosecute his rights in the court of a superior'.[24] John of Legnano writes: 'the prince alone is competent to declare war on his own authority, since he has no superior to whom he may have recourse for obtaining justice'.[25] In short, *X* may war upon *Y* only if *X* is a sovereign state; for otherwise *X* has legal means by which it may and must settle its claim against *Y*.

In medieval theory, all Christendom was one realm, of which the Emperor was sovereign;[26] and a few theorists drew the consequence, that wars were just only if declared on ᵔimperial authority.[27] But the sovereignty of the Emperor was a polite fiction; and that doctrine would render most medieval wars unjust.[28] More liberal theorists allowed authority to the various princes within the Empire: 'it apperteyneth to none to empryse warre or bataylle for ony maner cause but yf it be to prynces souerayn lyke as emperours kynges dukes & other lordes terryens which ben merely princypall heedes of Iuredictions temporall'.[29] (Vitoria derived authority not from sovereignty, but from the Aristotelian principle that 'a

---

24. Aquinas, *ST*, IIaIIae, q. 40, art. 1, resp.: 'primo quidem, auctoritas principis, cuius mandato bellum est gerendum. Non enim pertinet ad personam privatam bellum movere quia potest ius suum in iudicio superioris prosequi.'

25. John of Legnano, *De bello*, Ch. 14: 'Soli ergo principi competit sua auctoritate, cum non habeat superiorem ad quem recurret pro iustitia consequenda'; cf. Suárez, *De bello*, II.2: 'Princeps et res publica imperfecta, et quicumque superiorem habet in temporalibus, non potest iuste bellum indicere sine sui superioris auctoritate. Ratio est: huiusmodi princeps potest petere ius a superiore suo; ergo non habet ius indicendi bellum, quia quoad hoc se habet ut privata persona.'

26. See, e.g., John of Legnano, *De bello*, Ch. 13: 'Omnes gentes fere quae oboediunt sacrae matri ecclesiae sunt de populo Romano' (and therefore subject to the emperor). Cf. the remarkable comment on the Hundred Years War by Jacob Meyer, *Commentaria sive annales rerum Flandicarum* (quoted by Keen 1965, p. 75 n. 5): 'Bellum Anglicum exordium habuit quod omnium longissimum atque atrocissimum fuit; quodque per intervalla centesimum excessit annum. Seditio potius domestica quam bellum dicendum. Christiana respublica unum regnum unaque domus est; quaecumque in ea geruntur bella cum magno dedecore geruntur; nec, si verum fateamur, bella sunt sed turpissimae seditiones.'

27. See, e.g. Odofredus, *Lectura Codicis* in Cod. 11.47: 'Nullus poterit movere guerram et arma portare sine licentia imperatoris' (quoted by Russell 1975, p. 46 n. 31). Many theorists also grant *auctoritas* to the Pope or the Church; e.g. Raymond, *Summa*, II.v.17: 'auctoritas: ut si auctoritate ecclesiae, praesertim cum pugnatur pro fide vel auctoritate principis'; Aquinas, *ST*, IIaIIae, q. 188, art. 3, *ad* 4: war may be waged 'solum auctoritate principum vel ecclesiae' (see also his *Comm. in Sent.* III, dist. 30, art. 3, *ad* 8, quoted below, n. 60); Baldus, *Consilia* V, cons. 439: 'Dominus Papa potest dare licentias probo religioso ut utatur armis, non tamen ita quod effundat sanguinem sed pro statu fidei et ecclesiae et pro salute patriae.' Alanus Anglicus (cited by Russell 1975, p. 140, n. 41) appears to assign *auctoritas* to the Pope alone. The question raises complex historical issues.

28. See John of Legnano, *De bello*, Ch. 13: 'Hodie quia sunt populi non recognoscentes superiorem de facto, non requiritur superioris auctoritas cum non recognoscent. Immo tota die bella indicuntur a populo contra populum nullo alio requisito.'

29. Christine de Pisan, *Fayttes of Armes*, I.3.

republic must be self-sufficient';[30] he also allowed that a republic might go to war if, through the impotence or indolence of its sovereign, it could not obtain legal redress.)[31] The problem here is partly historical (for in medieval Europe it was hard to determine with whom sovereignty lay); but it was partly theoretical (for the concept of sovereignty required more careful articulation).

The condition of authority was derived ultimately from Cicero; and according to the Roman theory, on which Augustine drew, 'no war is held to be just unless it is declared, unless it is announced, unless it concerns wrongs for which redress has been demanded'.[32] The requirement that war must be formally declared found its way, *via* Isidore, into Gratian's *Decretum*;[33] but it was generally ignored by the medieval theorists,[34] and indeed it appears to be a requirement of decency rather than of justice – to make war without giving notice is unsporting; but it does not follow that the war itself is unjust.[35]

Meritum

Next comes *meritum* or, in Aquinas' terminology, *causa*; and 'whether a war is just or unjust is judged principally from the cause of warring'.[36] Aquinas comments: 'secondly, a just cause is required, viz. that those who are to be warred upon should deserve to be warred upon because of some fault. Hence Augustine says: "Just wars are customarily determined as

30. Vitoria, *De Indis*, q. 2, §8; for the Aristotelian principle ('respublica debet esse sibi sufficiens') see *Politics* 1280^{b}33–5.
31. Vitoria, *De Indis*, q. 2, §9; cf. Suárez, *De bello*, II.1–2. Note that in Suárez' view (*ibid.* II.1) *auctoritas* is required only for aggressive wars: 'nam potestas se defendendi ab iniusto invasore penes omnes datur.' (Raymond, *Summa*, II.v.18, strangely states that *auctoritas* is not needed in wars fought *pro rebus repetendis* or *pro defensione patriae*, i.e., not in just wars.)
32. Cicero, *Rep.* III.xxiii.35 (a fragment preserved by Isidore, *Etym.* XVIII.i.3): 'nullum bellum iustum habetur nisi denuntiatum, nisi indictum, nisi de rebus repetitis' (see below, n. 51); cf. *Rep.* II.xvii; *Off.* I.xi.36; for *de rebus repetitis* and the formal demand for redress see, e.g., Livy vii.9; x. 45 (cf. Philippson 1911, pp. 327–40).
33. Isidore, *Etym.*, XVIII.i.2: 'iustum bellum est quod ex praedicto geritur de rebus repetitis aut propulsandorum hostium causa' (quoted by Gratian, C XXIII, q. 2, canon 1).
34. But see, e.g., More, *Utopia*, p. 200 (the Utopians wage war only 'repetitis ac non redditis rebus'). When Gratian quotes Isidore (above, n. 34) he writes '*edicto*' for '*praedicto*', '*repetendis*' for '*repetitis*', and '*hominum*' for '*hostium*': the second alteration at least may be significant.
35. Grotius 1853, III.iii.5, asserts that 'ut iustum ... bellum sit, ... oportet ... ut ... publice decretum sit'; and he cites the passages from Cicero and Isidore quoted above in nn. 32 and 33. But at *ibid.* 6–8 he allows that the requirement of public declaration is not absolute, commenting thus: 'verum etiam ubi ius naturae non praecipit talem interpellationem fieri, honeste tamen et laudabiliter interponitur.'
36. Alanus Anglicus (quoted by Russell 1975, p. 128, n. 2): 'quod bellum sit iustum vel iniustum ex causa bellandi praecipue iudicatur.'

those which avenge injuries, if a nation or state which is to be warred upon has neglected to punish crimes committed by its people or to restore what has been unjustly taken away." '[37] In general, X may war on Y only if Y has condoned some injury.[38]

To whom must the injury have been done? Evidently, X has a case against Y if the people of Y have injured the people of X. Gratian adds that 'injury to associates (*socii*) is to be repelled by arms';[39] for, as Ambrose says, 'he who does not defend his associate against injury when he can, is as much to blame as he who inflicts the injury'.[40] Aquinas concurs;[41] and Suárez specifies that injury 'against allies or friends' is a cause for war.[42] More generally, 'the prynce may iustly yf it please hym to ayde & helpe euery prynce baron or other hys alye or frende or ony contre or londe yf he be requyred in caas that the quarell be iuste'.[43] Thus if Y injures Z and Z calls on X, relying on a treaty or a bond of friendship or merely on hope, then X has just cause to war on Y.

Suppose that Y injures its own nationals: may X war upon Y to avenge injuries done to members of Y? Are such 'humanitarian' wars sanctioned by the medieval theory? The letter of the theory appears to countenance them; and More's Utopians will go to war when, 'pitying a people oppressed by tyranny, they may, for humanitarian reasons, free them from the tyrant's yoke and bondage'.[44] But the spirit of the theory is against such

37. Aquinas, *ST*, IIaIIae, q. 40, art. 1, resp.: 'Secundo requiritur causa iusta, ut scilicet illi qui impugnantur propter aliquam culpam impugnationem mereantur. Unde Augustinus dicit [*QQ. in Hept.*, IV.10]: iusta autem bella ea definiri solent quae ulciscuntur iniurias, si qua gens vel civitas quae bello petenda est vel vindicare neglexerit quod a suis improbe factum est vel reddere quod per iniurias ablatum est.' (I have given Augustine's text: Aquinas quotes it in slightly different form; it is badly garbled by Gratian, C XXIII, q. 2, canon 2. The text continues: 'sed etiam hoc genus belli sine dubitatione iustum est, quod deus imperat' – cf. *Contra Faustum*, XXII.74, 75.)

38. Rufinus' view, that the enemy need only be thought to deserve attack (above, n. 15), is unusual; for discussion see Vitoria, *De Indis* §20.

39. Gratian, C XXIII, q. 3, p. canon 10: 'Ecce quod nonnumquam est obviandum perversis, et iniuria sociorum armis est propulsanda, ut et malis adempta facultas delinquendi prosit et bonis optata facultas libere consulendi ecclesiae ministretur.'

40. Ambrose, *Off.*, I.xxxvi: 'qui enim non repellit a socio iniuriam si potest, tam est in vitio quam ille qui facit' (quoted by Gratian, C XXIII, q. 3, canon 7).

41. Aquinas, *ST*, IIaIIae, q. 188, art. 3, *ad* 1: 'aliquis potest non resistere malo dupliciter … Alio modo, tolerando patienter iniurias aliorum. Et hoc ad imperfectionem pertinet, vel etiam ad vitium, si aliquis potest convenienter iniurianti resistere' (he quotes Ambrose, *Off.*, I.xxvii, cited by Gratian, C XXIII, q. 3, canon 5).

42. Suárez, *De bello* IV.3, says explicitly that *iniuria contra foederatos sive amicos* provides just cause for war. See also More, *Utopia*, p. 200, quoted below, n. 44.

43. Christine de Pisan, *Fayttes of Armes*, I.4.

44. More, *Utopia*, p. 200: 'non temere capessunt nisi quo aut suos fines tueantur aut amicorum terris infusos hostes propulsent aut populum quempiam tyrannide pressum miserati (quod humanitatis gratia faciunt) suis viribus tyranni iugo et servitute liberent.' Cf. Grotius 1853, II.xx.40:

interventions; and Suárez is right when he says that 'what some assert, that sovereign kings have power to punish injuries over the whole world, is altogether false, and confounds all order and distinction of jurisdictions'.[45]

A war can redress wrongs only if wrongs have been done. Vitoria affirms that 'there is one and only one just cause for waging war, viz. an injury received'; and he adds, correctly, that 'this is the opinion of all the doctors'.[46] Francis Bacon rejected that view: 'neither is the opinion of some of the schoolmen to be received, that a war cannot justly be made, but upon a precedent injury or provocation. For there is no question, but a just fear of an imminent danger, though no blow be given, is a lawful cause of war'.[47] If Y threatens to attack X, may not X indulge in 'anticipatory defence' and attack Y? (Thus Israel attacked Egypt in 1967.) If Y threatens to occupy Z to the detriment of X, may not X indulge in 'anticipatory breach of neutrality' and attack Z? (Thus was Iceland invaded in 1940.) The schoolmen might have replied that if Y puts X in 'imminent danger', then Y has thereby injured X, so that 'anticipatory' wars can be justified by Vitoria's cause of 'injury received'.[48] But there is a better reply: 'imminent danger' does not warrant war; the appropriate (and prudent) response to a threat is mobilisation and military vigilance, for that both guards against the danger and preserves the possibility of peace.[49]

What injuries give cause for war? An *iniuria* is the violation of a right; and the general answer to the question is given by Grotius: 'the sources of war are as many as those of legal actions'.[50] Augustine's reference to the

'Sciendum quoque est reges et qui par regibus ius obtinent ius habere poenas poscendi non tantum ob iniurias in se aut subditos suos commissas, sed et ob eas quae ipsos non peculiariter tangunt sed in quibusvis personis ius naturae aut gentium immaniter violant' (Grotius cites Augustine, *De civ. Dei*, V. 1, in support of his view; but he wrenches a sentence out of context). On humanitarian wars see Walzer 1977, Ch. 6.

45. Suárez, *De bello*, IV. 3: 'Quod quidam aiunt, supremos reges habere potestatem ad vindicandas iniurias totius orbis, est omnino falsum et confundit omnem ordinem et distinctionem iurisdictionum.'

46. Vitoria, *De Indis*, q. 3, §13: 'Unica est et sola causa iusta inferendi bellum iniuria accepta', citing Augustine and Aquinas, he remarks that that 'est determinatio omnium doctorum;' cf., e.g., Suárez, *De bello*, IV. 1: 'Causa haec iusta et sufficiens est gravis iniuria quae alia ratione vindicari aut reparari nequit;' Grotius 1853, II. i. 1: 'Causa iusta belli suscipiendi nulla esse alia potest nisi iniuria' (citing Augustine and Livy, i. 32).

47. Bacon, *Of Empire*, quoted by Walzer 1977, p. 77.

48. Cf. Grotius 1853, II. i. 1: 'dantur autem actiones aut ob iniuriam non factam aut ob factam' – *iniuria non facta* is nevertheless *iniuria*.

49. For considerations *pro* and *contra* anticipatory wars see Walzer 1977, pp. 74–85; Brownlie 1963, pp. 257–61.

50. Grotius 1853, II. i. 2: 'ac plane quot actionum forensium sunt fontes, totidem sunt belli; nam ubi iudicia deficiunt, incipit bellum' (see above, n. 23). Claims not actionable at law cannot be prosecuted in war: 'sicut in foro exigi non potest, ita nec armis deposci' (*ibid.*, II. xxii. 16).

'customary determination' of justice in war suggests the Roman formula, which was adopted by Isidore and frequently repeated: 'a war is just if it is waged ... for the restitution of goods or for defending one's country'.[51]

Defence is an elastic notion; but here it should be narrowly construed: if *Y* invades the territory of *X*, then *Y* injures *X* and *X* has just cause for war. Under twentieth-century international law (as defined by the Kellogg–Briand Pact and the United Nations Charter), self-defence is the only legitimate excuse for war.[52] That excuse, or right, was universally recognised by the medieval theorists, who grounded it on the domestic analogy: as a private person may violently defend himself against an assailant, so a state may repel an invader by force of arms.[53] The right of self-defence carries a proviso and implies certain restrictions. The proviso is that the invader be acting unjustly: there is no right to defence against legitimate attack. The restrictions are that the defence should be immediate (*incontinenti* and not *ex intervallo*) and that it should observe the rule of proportionality (*moderamen inculpatae tutelae*): self-defence cannot justify war unless it is a response to a present danger; and it cannot justify more than the minimal force needed to repel the attack.[54].

---

51. Isidore, *Etym.* XVIII.i.2 (quoted above, n. 33). Isidore cites Cicero, *Rep.*, III.xxiii.35 (see above, n. 32): 'illa iniusta bella sunt quae sine causa suscepta; nam extra ⟨quam iniurias?⟩ ulciscendi aut propulsandorum hostium causa bellum geri iustum nullum potest.' Cf., e.g., Raymond, *Summa*, II.v.17: 'res, ut sit pro rebus repetendis et pro defensione patriae'; Baldus, *Consilia* V, cons. 439: 'ut fiat pro rebus repetendis et pro defensione patriae'; John of Legnano, *De bello* Ch. 76: 'septimum [sc. genus bellorum] dicitur necessarium et licitum, quod faciunt fideles iuris auctoritate se defendendo contra ipsos invadentes; nam vim vi repellere licet'; More, *Utopia*, p. 200: 'Auxilium gratificantur amicis non semper quidem quo se defendant sed interdum quoque illatas retalient atque ulciscentur iniurias.' Christine de Pisan, *Fayttes of Armes*, I.4, distinguishes three just causes: 'The first ... is for to susteyne right & iustice. The second for to withstonde the euyl that wold defowle grieve & oppresse the londe the contree & the people and the thirde for to recoure londes seignoryes or other thynges by other taken & vsurped by iniuste cause.' Her discussion seems to imply that the first cause in fact embraces the other two.
52. See Brownlie 1963, pp. 74–92: 'apart from self-defence [and police action taken under the U. N. Charter] war, and indeed any use of armed force, is prohibited for all purposes, and is placed outside the legal competence of states' (p. 91).
53. On the right of self-defence see, e.g., Aquinas, *ST*, IIaIIae, q. 64, art. 7; for self-defence as a ground for war see also *ibid.* q. 40, art. 1, resp.: 'gladio bellico ad eos [i.e. principes] pertinet rempublicam tueri ab exterioribus hostibus'; *ibid.* q. 188, art. 3, resp.: 'propter defensionem divini cultus et publicae salutis.' Cf. Ambrose, *Off.*, I.xxvii: 'fortitudo quae ... in bello tuetur a barbaris patriam ... plena iustitia est' (quoted by Gratian, C XXIII, q. 3, canon 5; Aquinas, *ST*, IIaIIae, q. 188, art. 3, *ad* 1 [see above, n. 41]); Augustine, *Ep.* 87: 'non quod hos persequantur, sed quia se defendant' (quoted by Gratian, C XXIII, q. 3, canon 3).
54. On the limits of self-defence see esp. John of Legnano, *De bello*, ch. 111–120: cf. e.g. Vitoria, *De Indis* q. 2, §3; and the Decretalist Johannes Teutonicus, quoted in Russell 1975, p. 132 n. 11.

The medieval theory did not regard self-defence as a necessary condition for just warring: aggressive war, in their eyes, might be just;[55] for clearly Y may do injury – and do injury to X – without invading X's territory. Suárez remarks that 'various kinds of injuries may be causes of just war, but they reduce to three heads: first, if a prince appropriates someone else's goods and will not restore them; secondly, if he denies the common rights of nations without reasonable cause (e.g. the right to passage,[56] common trade, etc); thirdly, severe harm to reputation or honour'.[57] It would not be profitable to attempt a subtler classification of actionable injuries; but it is worth observing that 'self-help' in the redressing of wrongs has always been the most common reason for going to war. Nor is it an implausible reason: the modern law, which implicitly prohibits war *de rebus repetendis*, is not a principle of justice.

Causa

Alexander's final condition on justice in war is not easy to interpret: 'there must be a just cause, which is the support of the good, the coercion of the bad, peace for all'.[58] The text Alexander proceeds to cite is used by Aquinas to explicate his claim that 'the intention of the warriors must be correct, viz., they should intend to promote good or to avoid evil'.[59] Those passages have been taken to support a doctrine of 'ameliorative' warfare: X

---

55. So, explicitly, Suárez, *De bello* I.5: 'bellum etiam aggressivum non est per se malum, sed potest esse honestum et necessarium.'

56. Augustine invoked this right to justify the Israelites' attack on the Amorites (Num. 21.21–5), QQ. *in Hept.*, IV.44: 'notandum est sane quemadmodum iusta bella gerebantur. Innoxius enim transitus negabatur, qui iure humanae societatis aequissimo patere debebat' (quoted by Gratian, C XXIII, q. 2, canon 3); the text was frequently repeated – see esp. Bouvet, *Tree of Battles* IV.61. On the comparable Corfu Channel case of 1946 see Brownlie 1963, pp. 283–9.

57. Suárez, *De bello* IV.3: 'Varia esse iniuriarum genera pro iusti belli causa, quae ad tria capita revocantur: unum, si princeps res alterius occupet ac nolit restituere; alterum, si neget communia iura gentium sine rationabili causa, ut transitum viarum, commune commercium, etc.; tertium, gravis laesio in fama vel honore.' Suárez does not mention self-defence, since he is dealing only with aggressive wars.

58. Alexander, *Summa*, III, §466: 'in persona illius pro quo pugnatur attendenda est causa iusta, quae est sublevatio bonorum, coertio malorum, pax omnium;' cf. Raymond, *Summa*, II.v.17: 'causa, si propter necessitatem pugnetur ut per pugnam pax acquiratur;' Baldus, *Consilia* V, cons. 439: 'ut propter necessitatem pugnetur ut propter pugnam pax acquiratur'. The slogan that 'war is for the sake of peace' is associated with Augustine (*Ep.* 189.5: 'non enim pax quaeritur ut bellum excitetur, sed bellum geritur ut pax acquiratur' – cited by Gratian, C XXIII, q. 1, canon 2; Aquinas, *ST*, IIaIIae, q. 40, art. 1, *ad* 3; cf. Augustine, *Ep.* 229; *De civ. Dei*, XIX. 12); it derives from Aristotle, *Nic. Eth.* 1177^{b}5, to which Baldus alludes, and ultimately from Plato (*Laws* 628E, 803D; see also Cicero, *Off.* I.xi.35; cf. Defourny 1977).

59. Aquinas, *ST*, IIaIIae, q. 40, art. 1, resp.: 'ut sit intentio bellantium recta – qua scilicet intenditur vel ut bonum promoveatur vel ut malum vitetur.' The Augustinian text is cited above, n. 19.

wars justly upon *Y* if the overall consequences of war are better, or less bad, than the overall consequences of abstaining from war. In such cases, justice is determined not by the antecedent misdeeds of *Y* (there may be none) but by the anticipated results of going to war.[60] But neither Alexander nor Aquinas is concerned with ameliorative war; both texts impose a condition on just wars additional and not alternative to the condition of *meritum* or just cause. Alexander seems to mean, in part, that *X* may go to war only if good men have been injured by bad men – a pernicious principle. Aquinas may mean, in part, that *X* may go to war only if redressing the injuries by force of arms will not do more harm than leaving the injuries unredressed. Trivial injuries will not warrant war; as Vitoria notes, 'one must beware lest greater evils follow from the war itself than are avoided by the war'.[61]

Alexander's reference to peace may be intended to advert to the war aims of the belligerents, although it determines them only in the vaguest terms. In fact, the legal analogy implicitly specifies the goals of legitimate warfare, as Vitoria saw most clearly: if *X* wars justly on *Y*, then *X* may claim, first, compensation for those injuries which were the *casus belli*; secondly, compensation for any losses incurred in the course of the war; and thirdly, punitive damages against the malefactors of *Y* who precipitated the war.[62] The Utopians, it is true, 'seek only this in war – that they may obtain that which, had they had it before, they would not have gone to war'.[63] But the Utopians were foolish, and they sought less than justice allows.

Those rights effectively determine the legitimate war aims of *X*: a prince who aims at the annihilation of his enemies, or a belligerent who demands their unconditional surrender, is not engaged in a just war. At this point, Augustine's psychological requirement, that the belligerent not be moved by hatred, and the legal condition, that the action be proportionate to the offence, conspire to set a further limit on the scope of legitimate warfare.

---

60. A third text, contrasting *iustitia* and *bonum*, does seem to allow ameliorative wars; see Aquinas, *Comm. in Sent.* III, dist. 30, art. 4, ad 8: 'ecclesia hoc modo movet bella adversus iniquos, vel ut iustitiam faciat vel ut maius malum evitet aut maius bonum inducat.' But this view is idiosyncratic.
61. Vitoria, *De Indis*, §37: 'Oportet cavere ne ex ipso bello sequantur maiora mala quam vitentur per ipsum bellum;' cf. Grotius 1853, II.xxiv, title: 'monita de non temere etiam ex iustis causis suscipiendo bello' (*ibid.* 1: 'contra enim evenit ut plerumque magis pium rectumque sit de iure suo cedere'). This condition will doubtless rule out wars to avenge libel, of the sort envisaged by Suárez (above, n. 57).
62. Vitoria, *De Indis*, q. 4, §§15–19; cf., e.g., Suárez, *De bello*, IV.5.
63. More, *Utopia*, p. 202: 'Hoc unum illi in bello spectant, uti id obtineant quod si fuissent ante consequuti bellum non fuerant illaturi.'

Issues associated with the theory of the just war

Such, in outline, is the theory of just war: *X* justly wars upon *Y* if and only if each of the conditions described above is satisfied. Some theorists explicitly add that the war must be 'necessary'; that is to say, that there are no means short of war by which *X* can achieve its aims.[64] But the requirement of 'necessity' was implicit in every statement of the theory.

About the theory clustered a variety of related considerations: the issue of conscientious objection was debated; the duty to obey military orders was discussed; rules of war, dealing with the rights of non-combatants, the legitimacy of technologically sophisticated weaponry, the use of deception and espionage, the propriety of fighting on holidays, were elaborated and analysed; trials of war criminals were held and argued over; the matter of the spoils of war was at once a theoretical and a practical issue; the crusades posed problems of their own. Those questions were raised and answered in the context of the theory of just war.[65]

The significance of the theory

But how significant was the theory? Did it prevent a single bloody battle? Did it curb a single ambitious prince? Cynics will observe, with Lactantius, 'how far expediency departs from justice: we are taught that by the Romans – for they solemnly declared wars and legally inflicted injuries and eternally desired and appropriated other men's goods, and thereby gained for themselves possession of the whole world'.[66] Theory is impotent: 'this present werke by somm enuyous myght be reproched sayeng that it is but ydlenes & losse of tyme'.[67]

In general, cynics underestimate the effect of theory on action; but their dismissive suggestions can be refuted only by detailed historical research. One episode in that history is the notorious assault on Constantinople by the soldiers of the Fourth Crusade. Contemporary chroniclers record the debates which preceded their attack; and it is plain that, whatever else was in

---

64. E. g. Raymond and Baldus, quoted above, n. 58; Nicholas I, *Responsa ad consulta Bulgarorum* 46: 'si nulla urgeat necessitas, non solum quadragesimali tempore sed etiam omni tempore a proeliis abstinendum' (quoted by Gratian, C XXIII, q. 8, canon 15); Suárez, *De bello* IV. 1 (quoted above, n. 46); cf. Livy, ix.1: 'iustum bellum quibus necessarium, et pia arma quibus nulla nisi in armis relinquitur spes.'

65. On these questions see Russell 1975; Keen 1965; on the special problems of the Crusades see Riley-Smith 1977.

66. Lactantius, *Inst.*, VI.xi.4: 'Quantum autem ab iustitia recedat utilitas populus ipse Romanus docet, qui per fetiales bella indicendo et legitime iniurias faciendo semperque aliena cupiendo et rapiendo possessionem sibi totius orbis comparavit.'

67. Christine de Pisan, *Fayttes of Armes* I.2.

their minds, the Crusaders were concerned with, and moved to action by, the very considerations of justice which the theorists were debating. Even in the heat of a campaign, the just war theory could affect the course of events.[68] But the cynic may remain unimpressed; for, having decided to take Constantinople, the Crusaders ravaged the city with unbridled ferocity.

68. On this episode see Schmandt 1975.

XI

THE DEFEAT, NEGLECT AND REVIVAL OF SCHOLASTICISM

42
THE ECLIPSE OF MEDIEVAL LOGIC

A revised dating of the eclipse

The view that the insights and developments of medieval logic were eclipsed during the fifteenth century by a humanist, rhetorically-oriented logic has long been popular, but it needs considerable revision and modification. In what follows I shall first give a brief account of what happened to the writing, teaching, and publication of logical works in the medieval style, by which I mean those which discuss such topics as consequences, insolubles, exponibles, and supposition. I shall then examine in more detail what was actually said about certain medieval doctrines in the late fifteenth and sixteenth centuries in order to indicate both where logicians of the period had something new to contribute, and where there were departures from medieval doctrines which cannot be attributed to new logical insight.[1] My conclusion will be that medieval logic as a living tradition did largely disappear, but that the eclipse dates from about 1530 (in so far as a specific date can ever sensibly be offered) rather than the mid fifteenth century.

Fifteenth-century logicians

After the death of Paul of Venice in 1429, the fifteenth century did not give rise to much important logical writing. There were various logicians in Italy who deserve mention for their contributions to logic in the medieval style, including Domenico Bianchelli (Menghus Blanchellus Faventinus), who wrote a long commentary on Paul of Venice's *Logica parva*; Paul of Pergula, who wrote on Ralph Strode's *Consequentiae* as well as producing his own *Logica*; and Gaetano di Thiene, who wrote on Strode, William Heytesbury, and Richard Ferrybridge. The latter thinkers all formed part of the logic curriculum at Padua where both Paul of Pergula and Gaetano

---

1. For further details about the period as a whole, and for some of the doctrines mentioned below, see Ashworth 1974a, and Risse 1964. For a bibliography of primary sources, see Risse 1965. For a bibliography of secondary sources, see Ashworth 1978.

taught. Outside Italy we find a few lesser figures such as John Heynlyn (Johannes de Lapide), author of commentaries on Aristotle's logical works and a treatise on exponibles, who between 1446 and 1478 studied and taught at Heidelberg, Leipzig, Louvain, Basle, Paris, and Tübingen. Perhaps the most successful commentator was the Thomist John Versor (d. *ca.* 1480) whose commentary on Peter of Spain was first printed in 1473 and was reprinted in Cologne as late as 1622. There were many other commentators on Aristotelian and scholastic logical writings, but their work seems to have had little effect on subsequent developments.

The end of medieval logic outside France

In most European countries work on logic in the strictly medieval style came to an end during the sixteenth century, though, as will be noted below, medieval doctrines survived in textbooks. In Italy medieval texts continued to be printed and read, but there was no important logician who genuinely belongs to the medieval tradition. In Poland the tradition produced its last original thinker with John of Glogow (*ca.* 1445–1507) who taught at Cracow and wrote a commentary on Peter of Spain. There were some good synthesisers in Germany in the early years of the sixteenth century, notably Jodocus Trutvetter (Isenachensis) (d. 1519) who taught at both Erfurt and Wittenberg, and Johann von Eck (1486–1543), a noted humanist and theologian as well as a good logician. England presents a particularly dreary picture. The 1483 *Logici* published in Oxford shows some signs of having been organised by one man, though it is largely composed of earlier writings. But the popular *Libellus sophistarum ad usum Cantabrigiensium*, published four times between 1497 and 1524, and the *Libellus sophistarum ad usum Oxoniensium*, published seven times between 1499 and 1530, were both unadorned reprints of early-fifteenth-century manuscript collections, the actual writing having been done during the fourteenth century.[2] It is no wonder that humanism triumphed so easily in the English universities.

2. Pollard and Redgrave 1976 give the title '*Logici*' to a work which is in fact untitled. It contains much of Paul of Venice's *Logica parva* (without acknowledgement) together with treatises relating to the separate parts of Aristotle's Organon. It has only two treatises – Swineshead's *Insolubilia* and Bradwardine's *Proportiones* – in common with the *Libelli sophistarum*. Despite the judgement of Pollard and Redgrave that the two *Libelli* have 'essentially the same text', the Cambridge text contains six treatises which are not in the Oxford text, and the Oxford text contains five treatises which are not in the Cambridge text. Nor are the ten treatises they have (more or less) in common fully identical. James McConica has pointed out to me that at least one of the surviving copies bears ownership marks which indicate use throughout the sixteenth century. For further discussion and complete references, see Ashworth 1979. It should be noted

The resurgence of medieval logic in France and Spain

In France, however, we find a renaissance of medieval work which lasted from about 1490 to about 1520 and which strongly influenced the Spanish universities, where medieval logic flourished into the 1530s. A possible starting point for this logical renaissance is the royal decree of 1474 which forbade the study of nominalism at the University of Paris. So far from crushing nominalism, the decree, which was rescinded in 1481, aroused fresh interest in the writings of William Ockham, John Buridan, Albert of Saxony, Marsilius of Inghen, Peter of Ailly and John Dorp, and this led in turn to a great increase in new writings on standard medieval topics. The authors involved are far too numerous to list here; I will mention just a few of the more outstanding names. The most distinguished of the earlier writers were the Scotist Peter Tartaret and the nominalist Thomas Bricot (d. 1516), both of whom completed their logical work before 1500. In the sixteenth century the leading figure was the Scotsman John Major (1469–1550), who attracted a brilliant and diverse group of men to the college of Montaigu where he taught from 1505 to 1517. (He was in Paris again from 1525 to 1531, but the earlier period is the important one.) The group included several Scotsmen, several Frenchmen, and a large number of Spaniards, among whom were Gaspar Lax and Domingo Soto. Apart from Pierre Crockaert (Peter of Brussels) (d. 1514), who became a leading Thomist, and Soto, also a Thomist, though eclectic, they tended to be nominalist in orientation. Other Spaniards working in Paris during this period included Jerónimo Pardo (d. 1505), Juan Dolz and Fernando de Enzinas. Most of the Spaniards returned to Spain, and under their leadership the teaching of logic at Alcalá and Salamanca reached great heights.

A study of the publication of logic texts in France and Spain provides evidence of the richness of the logical work done in these countries in the first decades of the sixteenth century, as well as revealing the sudden decline which occurred after 1530. Leaving aside the publication of such medieval authors as Buridan and Ailly, and leaving aside compendia of various sorts including commentaries on the *parva logicalia*, I know of the following texts. There are twenty separate treatises on terms, by well-known men such as John Major as well as by such lesser figures as Gilbert Crab and Gerard Columel. The only treatises on terms published after 1530 are by

that all my claims about the number of times logic texts were printed are subject to revision. On the one hand, we know there were sixteenth-century editions of which no copies seem to have survived; on the other hand, copies of hitherto unknown editions are frequently discovered.

Ferdinando de Enzinas (which first appeared in 1533) and Hermosilla (1553). There are nine treatises on exponibles; apart from Soto's treatise (1529) the last is by George Lokert (*ca.* 1522). There are ten treatises on insolubles; again, apart from Soto's (1529), the latest is by Celaya (*ca.* 1518), and the same is true of the eight treatises I know of on obligations. Of the five treatises on consequences, the latest is by Lax (1532). Various works by Enzinas and Lax were reprinted in the 1530s, but only Soto was reprinted after 1540. A much revised edition of his *Introductiones dialecticae* or *Summulae*, a collection of virtually independent treatises, appeared in 1547 and was reprinted several times.

The decline after 1530

The impression one gets of a sudden decline in medieval logic after 1530 is considerably strengthened by an investigation of the publication of medieval authors and of commentaries on Peter of Spain between 1530 and 1600. Authors who contributed most to the development of late medieval logic – such men as Buridan, Strode, Heytesbury, Peter of Ailly, Albert of Saxony, and Marsilius of Inghen – drop out of the picture altogether. Walter Burley's *Super artem veterem expositio* was published once during this period (Venice 1541) as was Ockham's *Summa logicae* (Venice 1591). John Duns Scotus' *In universam Aristotelis logicam quaestiones* was published twice (Venice 1586 and 1600). The only popular work was the *Logica parva* of Paul of Venice, which was published at least eight times in Venice between 1535 and 1580. Of the late fifteenth-century commentaries on Peter of Spain, two appeared in print: Versor's once in Naples (1577) and at least five times in Venice between 1550 and 1593, Tartaret's three times in Venice, in 1571, 1591 and 1592. The only new commentaries on Peter of Spain were those of Agostino Sbarroya (treatises 1 and 4, Seville 1533); Pedro Sánchez Ciruelo (Salamanca, 1537); Alphonso de Veracruz (Mexico, 1554, 1562, Salamanca 1561, 1562, 1569, 1572, 1573, 1593); and Thomas de Mercado (Salamanca 1571). In addition we find Peter of Spain's *Tractatus de locis dialecticis cum Versorii Parisiensis annotationibus* included in the works of Chrysostom Javellus (Lyon 1580). Somewhat later the *Gymnasium Speculativum* edited by F. Aúgustinus Gothutius (Paris 1605) included tracts 1, 2, 4, 5, 8, and 9 of Peter of Spain, together with such works as Josse Clichtove (1472–1543) on terms, Tartaret on the *Posterior Analytics*, and Thomas of Erfurt's *Grammatica speculativa*, which was attributed to Duns Scotus.

The survival of medieval logic in sixteenth-century textbooks

Despite the enormous changes signalled by the record of publication in the sixteenth century, medieval doctrines were to some extent retained in the textbooks which were written during that period, particularly in Spain. Two important Spanish authors, who appeared on the Jesuit *ratio studiorum* of 1595, were Francisco de Toledo whose *Introductio in dialecticam Aristotelis* (Rome 1561) was reprinted more than twenty times, and Pedro de Fonseca whose *Institutionum dialecticarum libri octo* (Lisbon 1564) was printed at least fifty-three times up to 1625. Both works included discussions of such medieval elements as consequences and supposition, as well as the newly emphasised traditional subject matter of categorical propositions, syllogisms, and fallacies. Similar authors are to be found in Italy, including the Dominican Chrysostom Javellus (d. *ca.* 1538), and Ludovico Carbo, who taught at Perugia in the second half of the century and published his *Introductiones in logicam* in 1597. They both discussed consequences, supposition, and insolubles in their textbooks. Even in England echoes of medieval doctrines are to be found in the works of John Seton (d. 1567) and John Sanderson (d. 1602), though the level of discussion is much lower than that prevailing on the continent then.

Non-scholastic sixteenth-century logic

Most sixteenth-century logical writings bear no trace of specifically medieval doctrines and developments, however. They fall roughly into four overlapping categories: humanist logic, Ramist logic, Aristotelian textbooks, and commentaries on the Greek Aristotle. The figure most directly responsible for the spread of humanist logic in the sixteenth century was Rudolph Agricola (1444–85), whose *De inventione dialectica* circulated in manuscript for many years before it was printed in 1515. Agricola influenced Philip Melanchthon, who wrote a large number of simplified textbooks, including at least three logic texts for use in German schools; he also influenced Johann Sturm, Johannes Caesarius, and Bartholomaeus Latomus, all of whom taught Agricola's work at Paris after it was printed there in 1529. Peter Ramus (Pierre de la Ramée) developed this tradition further. Francis Titelman's *Compendium dialecticae* (1535) is a good example of the straightforward Aristotelian textbooks. Among the commentators on Aristotle the three Italians, Agostino Nifo, J. F. Burana, and Jacopo Zabarella are perhaps most noteworthy.

Late developments: the properties of terms

Against the background of this survey of authors and their works, I want now to examine the fate of the medieval doctrines themselves during the sixteenth century. About supposition and the distinctively medieval treatment of terms there is little to say. In the first decades of the sixteenth century these doctrines were discussed in great detail; in the later textbooks they were merely summarised. Appellation as a property of terms either ceased to be mentioned, or was mentioned only with scorn, as for instance by Augustin Huens (1521–78),[3] but otherwise there was no obvious novelty in the nature of the theories presented. The one original development found in the works of Parisian logicians and later satirised by Vives concerned the use of 'a' and 'b' as special signs of supposition, to be used especially in the analysis of such propositions as 'Of every man some donkey is running' and 'Every man has a head', which posed special problems for the theory of supposition.[4] A simple example of how the signs were used is 'Every man is b animal' which, unlike 'Every man is animal', signifies, by virtue of the special sign 'b', that every man is identical to one and the same animal.

Exponibilia

The discussion of exponibles exhibits more significant advances.[5] In the first part of the century we find treatises which in their detail, organisation, and clarity mark a great improvement over the rather muddled discussions found in Paul of Venice. If we turn to the accounts presented by such later authors as Francisco de Toledo and Pedro de Fonseca, however, we find three great changes. First, among the exponibles only exclusive, exceptive, and reduplicative propositions are discussed; propositions employing such exponible terms as '*incipit*' and '*desinit*' are ignored. Second, the analyses offered of these propositions are much simpler than those that had been developed by medieval logicians. For instance, the reduplicative 'Every A inasmuch as it is B is C' is no longer analysed as 'Every A is B, and every A is C, and every B is C, and if something is B it is C' but simply rewritten as 'Every A because it is B is C.' Third, there is none of the characteristic concern of the scholastic logicians with especially difficult cases for the suggested analysis, or with such issues as the relationship between spoken or written exponibles and the corresponding mental propositions.

3. Ashworth 1974a, p. 97.
4. See Ashworth 1978a; Guerlac 1979.
5. See Ashworth 1973.

Consequences

The changes in the discussion of consequences follow a similar pattern. At the beginning of the century we find not just detailed analyses of propositions and arguments but also a discussion of wider issues such as the definition of a valid inference. We also find some relatively original work, particularly that concerned with the distinction between 'illative' conditionals, in which it is impossible for the antecedent to be true when the consequent is false, and 'promissory' conditionals, in which truth demands only that the antecedent not be true when the consequent is false. In the later textbooks, however, there is no discussion of wider issues, there is nothing original, and there are clear classical influences. For instance, the textbooks contain the five Stoic indemonstrables, two of which (*modus ponendo ponens* and *modus tollendo tollens*) were found in medieval works, but three of which (two concerning strong disjunction and one concerning negated conjunction) were not. The standard list of consequences narrows to consist mainly of those concerned with truth and modality, and they are presented without analysis or comment.

Obligationes and insolubilia

The treatises of the period have not yet been studied in sufficient depth to say much about the theories of obligationes presented in them. In the latter part of the century only Cardillo de Villalpandeo discussed obligationes in his *Summa Summularum* (1557). The companion treatises on insolubilia are better known, however, and here we can definitely say that at least one original theory is to be found in the early period. Thomas Bricot took Roger Swineshead's solution, which was adopted by Major and Soto among others, and revised it in such a way as to avoid the consequences that two contradictories can be false and that there can be valid inferences with a true antecedent and a false consequent.[6] His view was that an affirmative proposition is true if and only if it meets both of two conditions, namely that it signifies things to be as they are and does not falsify itself, whereas a negative proposition is true if and only if it meets one of two conditions, namely that it signifies things not to be as they are not, or that its contradictory falsifies itself. Thus 'This is false' said of itself is false, but 'This is not false', said of the first proposition, is true. Other popular solutions were drawn from Ailly, Ockham, and Paul of Venice's *Logica parva*. By the second part of the century most writers on logic had ceased to refer to

6. See Ashworth 1977b.

insolubles at all, and significant chapters are to be found only in Cardillo de Villalpandeo and in M. Doniensis Ormazius' *De instrumento instrumentorum sive de dialectica* (1569). What is most noteworthy is the sudden appearance of classical influences. The term '*insolubilia*' is replaced by '*inexplicabiles*', and the references are to Cicero and Aulus Gellius rather than to medieval authors. Solutions were rarely offered by these authors, but Doniensis Ormazius did argue that insolubles were not genuine propositions, but *orationes imperfectae*.

The semantics of propositions

Semantic theory underwent some developments at Paris in the first three decades of the sixteenth century which were not echoed at all in later writings. The developments are of two sorts. In the first place we find lengthy discussions of *complexe significabilia*, in which the views of Juan Dolz and Fernando de Enzinas are particularly significant.[7] They argued that indicative sentences signified *aliqualiter* – in some way – rather than *aliquid* – some thing. They explained this by arguing that propositions are analogous to syncategorematic rather than to categorematic words in their manner of signifying, performing a function other than that of naming. To the question, 'What does this sentence signify?' one could reply only by a paraphrase. In particular, questions about the *dictum* of a sentence were answered by replacing the *dictum* with a that-phrase. For instance, ' "Man is an animal" signifies man being an animal (*hominem esse animal*)' was rewritten as ' "Man is an animal" signifies that man is an animal (*quod homo est animal*)', thus removing the temptation to think that the *dictum* 'man being an animal' functions as a name. However, they recognised that there were some contexts in which the question. 'What is this sentence about?' could be answered by naming or pointing to an object. On such occasions a sentence was said to signify categorematically.

The semantics of terms

In the second place we find an interesting series of attempts to provide a unified theory of the reference of general terms by arguing that the word 'horse' refers to actual objects both in intentional contexts, such as 'I promise you a horse', and in modal contexts, such as 'For riding is required a horse', and by arguing that the word 'chimera' could be taken to refer to actual objects in order to save the truth of such propositions as 'A chimera is

7. See Ashworth forthcoming.

imagined.'[8] The solution to the second problem proposed by Celaya and Enzinas involved the claim that the sentence is a disguised conditional, being more properly written as 'If an act of riding takes place, a horse is ridden', so that the truth of the antecedent always involves successful reference to a particular horse. The solution to the third problem proposed by the same authors involved the postulation of imaginary objects to serve as referents, but the universe was not thereby populated with extra entities, for they explained that an imaginary chimera was just an actual object which could be imagined to be a chimera. In the last analysis, however, Enzinas and others were forced to admit that there were a few sentences such as '"Chimera" signifies a donkey' of whose general terms a purely extensionalist account could not be given if one wished to prevent the sentence containing them from being construed as true. The sentence in question, said Enzinas, can be true only if the word 'chimera' picks out those donkeys which can be imagined to be chimeras by means of the concept *chimera*, which in fact it does not.

Conclusion

Why did these interesting and varied treatments of medieval logical themes cease so abruptly after 1530?[9] Humanism alone cannot be the answer, since it apparently triumphed only by default. Italian universities continued to teach medieval logic long after the attacks on it by such men as Lorenzo Valla; and Agricola's logic did not capture Paris until the production of texts in the medieval style had already ceased.[10] Humanism certainly had a part to play in the process, however. Soto, for instance, came to believe as a result of humanist influences that doctrines which were difficult and not clearly expressed by Aristotle should be omitted from logic, and that too much time was devoted to summulist doctrines in the teaching of logic. Accordingly, the later editions of his *Introductiones dia-*

---

8. See Ashworth 1974b, 1976a, 1977a.
9. Schmitt 1975, p. 512, notes that certain branches of medieval physics also declined. He writes: '. . . several fourteenth-century traditions – including nominalism, the logical traditions of *sophismata* and *insolubilia*, and the Merton and Paris schools of philosophy of motion – continued on into the first few decades of the sixteenth century and after that quickly lost ground to other approaches and sets of problems. The printing-history of the medieval texts in question as well as new commentaries being written on Aristotle indicate this. Why this happened is not clear. Humanism had a strong impact, as did the reintroduction of the writings of the Greek commentators on Aristotle, but neither of these facts explains why the *calculatores* and writers on *sophismata* lost out, while the commentaries of Averroes did not. In brief, certain medieval aspects of the tradition expired in the early sixteenth century, while other equally medieval aspects continued to play an important role.'
10. For a discussion of Valla, Agricola, and their influence, see Jardine 1977.

lecticae were very much altered and simplified. Another instructive example is Agostino Nifo's *Dialectica ludicra* (1520). Here we have an introductory text written by a leading Aristotelian who had a good knowledge of medieval doctrines, yet he distorts them completely by describing only those parts of the scholastic theory of terms and supposition theory which are directly applicable to standard categorical propositions.[11] No one who became acquainted with medieval logic through Nifo would understand the function of the non-Aristotelian parts at all. A very plausible account of the indirect effect of humanism on logic teaching is provided by Terrence Heath, whose study of the teaching of grammar at three German universities at the end of the fifteenth century and beginning of the sixteenth century shows that the change to non-medieval logic was preceded by the change to humanistic grammar.[12] The significance of this sequence of changes is brought out in Heath's claim that medieval grammar prepared the student for medieval logic, whereas humanist grammar did not. One may also speculate that social changes were influential in creating a need for men with a new style of education. The rise of modern physics has been cited as a possible cause, but this suggestion cannot be accepted, given that modern physics can hardly be said to have risen before the end of the sixteenth century.[13] The judgement of a contemporary logician might be that medieval logic came to an end because no further progress was possible without the concept of a formal system and without the development of a logic of relations. This view is borne out by the desperate, complicated attempts to analyse such propositions as 'Every man has a head' that are to be found in the writings of the Parisian logicians. They certainly pushed medieval logic to its limits, but whether they gave up in despair because they realised that that was what they had done is another matter. For the moment our question must remain without a fully satisfactory answer.

11. See Ashworth 1976b.
12. Heath 1971.
13. Kneale 1962, p. 307. It should be noted that the Kneales speak as if interest in formal logic declined only during the *seventeenth* century, so that their reference to modern physics is not implausible in its context.

43
HUMANISM AND THE TEACHING OF LOGIC

The humanists' reassessment of the study of language

The traditional account of the impact of humanism on the logic curriculum blames the supposed 'barbarousness' of the mediaeval logicians' use of language for the humanists' hostility to the logic of the traditional curriculum. In their standard history of logic the Kneales wrote:

> The first blow to the prestige of logic came from the humanists, or classical scholars, of the Renaissance, i.e. in the fifteenth century. Their objection to scholasticism, and to medieval logic in particular, was not that it was false in any details, but rather that it was barbarous in style and unattractive in content by contrast with the rediscovered literature of antiquity. Who but a dullard would devote his life to the *proprietates terminorum* when he might read the newly found poem of Lucretius *De Rerum Natura* or learn Greek and study Plato?[1]

According to this account, a commitment to eloquence as the basis for all learning led humanists to turn from logic, the study of the technical manipulation of a formal language, to rhetoric:

> The writing of elegant Latin was now the chief accomplishment to be learnt, and for this Cicero and Quintilian were the authorities. From them the men of the Renaissance acquired the Roman attitude to scholarship, with the result that genuine logic was neglected for rhetoric and books which purported to be on logic quoted Cicero as often as Aristotle.[2]

In actual fact, the shift of interest amongst humanist students of language derived from different motives. And what is masked by the so-called 'rhetoricisation' of logic by humanist teachers is a more far-reaching reassessment of the study of language as part of a general arts education. The humanist most closely associated with such a reassessment, and whose influence is to be found in most subsequent humanist work on dialectic, is Lorenzo Valla (1407–57).

1. Kneale 1962, p. 300.
2. *Ibid.*

Lorenzo Valla and the revival of dialectic

Valla was a grammarian whose view of language was coloured by his commitment to *consuetudo* (the established linguistic usage of the great Roman authors of antiquity) as the standard for eloquent Latin. The study of grammar in the curriculum ought, he maintained, to be based on Latin usage in the period of its fullest currency as a living language, and ought to be regulatively descriptive, rather than prescriptive.[3] In his most influential work, the *Elegantiae linguae Latinae libri sex* (written around 1444), Valla showed how the precise use of Latin can be decided by careful reference to classical quotations in which the appropriate lexical item figures; usage legislates for future employment of the Latin language.

Valla's emphasis on *consuetudo* as the ultimate arbiter in the study of language led him to a drastic reassessment of the study of dialectic in the curriculum, which he put forward in his *Dialecticae disputationes* (written in 1439).[4] The major part of actual argumentation and controversy, Valla maintained, is concerned not with *certainty* (that area of ratiocination appropriately systematised in formal syllogistic as traditionally taught), but with persuasion and probability.[5] Here the central issue is not whether the conclusion of the argument has been validly inferred from the premisses; it might be, instead, how tellingly the position taken up by an orator is supported by evidence and testimony *prior* to the formation of a valid chain of arguments; or it might be how convincingly the speaker discriminates by choice of supporting material and citation of authorities between two

3. An eloquent statement of this point of view is to be found in an early work by Juan Luis Vives, an enthusiastic follower of Valla. In his *Adversus pseudodialecticos* (1782–90), I.42, he writes (1519): '"Homo est albus" is a Latin sentence not because grammar makes it so (any more than rhetorical figures impart splendor and refinement to speaking because rhetoric decrees it), but rather because the Roman people, who spoke true Latin, judged that sentence to be Latin. Therefore the grammarian does not decree that this is Latin, but he teaches that it is; and it is because certain figures of speech seemed beautiful and fine to speakers that rhetoric diligently observed and handed them on.' The translation is from Guerlac 1979, p. 57. Valla's *Elegantiae* in its entirety is an example of this approach to Latin usage.

4. On Valla see in particular Di Napoli 1971, Camporeale 1972, and Adorno 1954. On the various versions of the *Dialecticae disputationes* and their dates of completion, see also Zippel 1957. Zippel gives the first printed edition of the *Dialecticae disputationes* as 1509, but Risse 1965 lists two editions for 1499. See also Jardine 1977.

5. A succinct statement of this position on dialectic is given by another disciple of Valla's, Rudolph Agricola. In his *De inventione dialectica* he writes (*ca.* 1480): 'Exigua enim portio eorum [humanorum studiorum] quae discimus, certa et immota est, adeoque si Academiae credimus, hoc solum scimus, quod nihil scimus. Certe pleraque, pro cuiusque ingenio, ut accommodatissime ad probandum quisque excogitare potuerit, alio atque alio trahuntur' (Agricola 1539, p. 2).

widely held views. And it may be that coercive strategies such as *sorites*[6] or *dilemma*,[7] whose inferential status is dubious, play as great a part as reliable syllogistic inference in driving an opponent in debate to a desired conclusion.[8]

Although such considerations had traditionally found their way into the curriculum of the schools under the heading of rhetoric or sophistic, Valla argued that they rightly belonged in *dialectic*, not simply as subsidiary instruction, but as the very core of the study. He adduced the oratorical texts of Cicero and Quintilian (in particular the *Institutio oratoria* of the latter, which had recently been recovered in its entirety through the efforts of humanist scholars)[9] to support this view. Concerned as these authors were with ratiocination in the context of the law-courts, they tackled the practical problems of instruction in proving one's case where certain proof was unlikely to be available and putting a convincing case was a serious option.[10]

The effect and influence of Valla's revisions in dialectic

This was the thinking which prompted Valla's revisions in dialectic. Their *effect*, in terms of traditional teaching, was to shift the focus of the curriculum away from syllogistic and its associated analysis of terms which facilitates the formal employment of terms in syllogisms. Instead, the theory of the Topics became the centre of the course. As developed by the Roman orators and systematised in Boethius' *De topicis differentiis*,[11] the theory of the Topics provided a system of classification for oratorical material according to its appropriateness for a range of strategies used in

6. *Sorites* is the 'heap' or *acervus* argument, which proceeds by small, unobjectionable steps to a controversial conclusion. It takes its name from the case in which an interlocutor accepts a mound of sand as a 'heap', and is then asked to decide at which point it ceases to be a heap if the grains are withdrawn one by one. See Jardine 1977, pp. 161–2.

7. *Dilemma* or *antestrephon* is another technically undecidable form, of which the most celebrated example is probably the one attributed to Bion in Aulus Gellius' *Noctes Atticae*. The man who argues for celibacy urges, 'You are sure to marry a woman who is beautiful or ugly; if she is beautiful you will share her; if she is ugly she will be a trial to you.' The uxorious man retaliates: 'If I marry a beautiful woman she will not be a trial to me; if an ugly one I alone shall possess her' (*Noctes Atticae* V.xi.1–14).

8. See Hamblin 1970 for a modern attempt to derive a formal logic of question and answer from strategies such as these.

9. Quintilian's *Institutio oratoria* had been available only in mutilated form until Poggio discovered a complete manuscript at Saint Gall in 1416. See Reynolds and Wilson 1974, p. 121. See also Sabbadini 1905. On Valla's work on the newly recovered text see Winterbottom 1967, esp. pp. 356ff. On Valla's textual activities see Gaeta 1955.

10. See Michel 1960.

11. On Boethius and the theory of the Topics in antiquity see Stump 1978.

debating, of which the syllogism was only one. Even a single example will help to show the potentially greater flexibility of this focus on the Topics. The extrinsic Topic *from the greater*,[12] under which are classified propositions of the form '*a* is greater than *b*', provides the orator with arguments of the form '*a* is greater than *b*; *b* is greater than *c*; therefore *a* is greater than *c*', which although entirely reliable is nevertheless unavailable to those confined to syllogistic argument.

During the fifty years after Valla completed his *Dialecticae disputationes* there is evidence of its being given serious consideration by Aristotelian logicians.[13] But it was not until the early decades of the sixteenth century that Valla's humanist dialectic came into its own as a serious competitor with traditional Aristotelian logic within the traditional teaching establishments of Europe. Its appearance in university records correlates closely with the introduction into those universities of programmes in classical reading and the study of Greek and Roman eloquence which in the early decades of the sixteenth century transformed the arts courses of the northern European universities. Having been a technical introduction to the linguistic tools needed for solving problems in philosophy and theology, the arts course became a general introduction to Latin and Greek language and literature for students destined for professional careers.[14] The textbook which we find displacing Peter of Spain and Paul of Venice as the introduction to dialectic within these programmes is the *De inventione dialectica* of Rudolph Agricola (1444–85),[15] which plainly advocates Valla's approach to dialectic.

Rudolph Agricola's De inventione dialectica

In 1523 Zasius wrote to Amerbach that at his university of Freiburg, 'Peter of Spain has disappeared, all of logic has disappeared, except that which some profess from Melanchthon's little works, some from the books of Rudolph Agricola.'[16] In 1531 a visitation at the University of Tübingen reported that Agricola was being studied by the '*moderni*' in place of the set

---

12. See Boethius, *De topicis differentiis*, *PL* 64, 1190D, for his discussion of 'greater than' and 'less than'.
13. On the importance of Valla's dialectic see Vasoli 1968a, Jardine 1977, Kristeller 1972, p. 145, and 1964, pp. 33–5. Agostino Nifo's *Dialectica ludicra* (1520) invokes Valla's dialectic as a matter of course (as it appears), as representing an opposed, 'grammatical' approach to dialectic. He quotes him verbatim without acknowledgement throughout this work and its companion volume, *Epitomata rethorica ludicra*, published in the same year. See Jardine forthcoming.
14. On the changing function of the arts course in education see Stelling-Michaud 1967, pp. 71–142. On the changed role of Oxford and Cambridge in this period see Stone 1975.
15. On Agricola see Vasoli 1968a, pp. 147–82; Howell 1961; Gilbert 1960; and Ong 1958a.
16. *Amerbach Korrespondenz* II, Ep. 923, pp. 429–31, cited in Guerlac 1979, p. 24.

text, Peter of Spain's *Tractatus*.[17] By the 1530s revisions to existing statutes for the northern universities replace the traditional scholastic manual for the arts course with Agricola's *De inventione dialectica* or a humanist dialectic manual derivative from it. Henry VIII's 1535 injunctions for Oxford and Cambridge stipulate that students in arts should learn their dialectic from 'the purest authors', including Rudolph Agricola and Philip Melanchthon, rather than from scholastic texts.[18] Of the five college lecturers out of a total of nine appointed to the task of dialectic instruction in the 1560 statutes for Trinity College, Cambridge, one was to lecture on Agricola – the only 'modern' text specified.[19]

Between 1515 and 1590 Agricola's *De inventione dialectica* went through at least 35 editions, not including epitomes of the work designed explicitly for the classroom. Latomus' epitome alone went through 13 editions between 1530 and 1575.[20] It was followed by a spate of textbooks closer in format to traditional texts (and therefore more readily incorporated into existing teaching programmes), with Agricolan emphasis on the theory of the Topics, the priority of discovery (*inventio*), understood as the selection and organisation of material, over confirmation (*iudicium*), understood as the deployment of such material syllogistically or persuasively, and ratiocinative strategies other than the syllogism. Most prominent amongst these were the textbooks of Philip Melanchthon, Johannes Caesarius, and Peter Ramus.

Melanchthon and Caesarius

Melanchthon (1497–1560)[21] produced a number of teaching texts in dialectic, co-ordinated with his programme for the humanist education of reformed Christians. Between 1520 and the turn of the century these went through a staggering ninety-one editions.[22] His *Erotemata dialectices* (1547)[23] preserves the key characteristics of Agricola's and Valla's dialectical approach. It provides an attenuated treatment of syllogistic, which is not allowed an important place in the text as a whole. Treatment of the predicables and categories is minimised (doing little more than familiarise

17. Teufel 1977, p. 80. See also Heath 1971.
18. *Statuta academiae Cantabrigiensis* (Cambridge, 1785), pp. 137–8.
19. Mullinger 1884, appendix to vol. II. See also Jardine 1974 and 1976.
20. All these figures are taken from Risse 1965. See also Ong 1958b.
21. For biographical details see Vasoli 1968a, pp. 278–309.
22. Risse 1965, passim.
23. On the chronology of Melanchthon's various texts on dialectic see Vasoli 1968a. The first was the *Compendiosa dialectices ratio* (1520).

the student with the terminology), demonstration gets cursory treatment, and there is a bare reference to the *parva logicalia*, the treatises presenting the innovations of terminist logic, with the statement that all the problems the *parva logicalia* are supposed to tackle are the province of the grammarian and do not arise at all if the precepts of grammar are carefully applied.[24] The same pattern is followed by Caesarius (1467–1550) in his *Dialectica* (1532),[25] which matched Melanchthon's in popularity, and confirmed the position of Agricolan dialectic at the heart of the curriculum.[26] Both Caesarius' *Dialectica* and one of Melanchthon's manuals were in use at the University of Wittenberg in the 1530s.[27]

Peter Ramus

But the 'best-seller' amongst dialectic texts was undoubtedly that of the infamous Peter Ramus,[28] whose calibre as a traditional logician in the medieval mould has been queried by historians of logic ever since W. J. Ong's work on the popularity and influence of his *Dialectica* brought him to their attention.[29] Ramus (1515–72) was trained at the Collège de Navarre of the University of Paris during the late 1520s,[30] a crucial period for the teaching of dialectic in the University. The introduction of Agricola's *De inventione dialectica* into the dialectic course at Paris is generally dated from 1529, when Sturm came to the city. Latomus was also teaching in Paris in 1533.[31] Two editions of Agricola's work appeared from the Paris presses in 1529.[32] Juan Luis Vives (1493–1540),[33] who had

24. *Erotemata dialectices* (Wittenberg 1555), p. 418: 'Addita est Aristotelis Dialecticae doctrina, uerius Grammatica quam Dialectica, quam nominarunt parua logicalia, in qua dum praecepta immodice cumularunt, et labyrinthos inextricabiles, sine aliqua utilitate finxerunt ...'
25. For biographical details see Vasoli 1968a, p. 260. For the widespread influence of both Melanchthon's and Caesarius' dialectic texts see Risse 1964, pp. 25–31 and 79–121.
26. Both Caesarius and Melanchthon acknowledge their debt to Agricola. See Caesarius, *Dialectica* (1568), f. 8ʳ. See Vasoli 1968a, passim, for additional evidence of Agricola's direct influence on later dialecticians.
27. See Caesarius 1559, preface (dated 1532): '... intellexeram Dialecticam meam uel qualemcunque ipsius Philippi [Melanchthonis] cura et subornatione publice nunc praelegi atque doceri in Academia Vuittenbergensi'.
28. See Vasoli 1968a, pp. 333–589 passim; Ong 1958a and 1958b.
29. See most recently Ashworth 1974.
30. See Ong 1958a.
31. The evidence for Sturm's having actually introduced Agricola to Paris is rather vague. Lefranc 1893 attributes this statement to Schmidt 1855, pp. 120–1. It may, therefore, reflect the prejudice of a biographer of Sturm. There is, however, no doubt that Sturm's and Latomus' arrival in Paris ensured widespread dissemination of Agricolan dialectic at Paris, whether or not it had preceded them there.
32. Ong 1958a, p. 96.
33. On Vives see Guerlac 1979; Vasoli 1968a, pp. 214–46.

studied scholastic logic intensively under Gaspar Lax at the Collège de Montaigu, between 1509 and 1512, had produced his *Adversus pseudodialecticos* in 1519.[34] This highly polemical little work outspokenly attacked the entire tradition of scholastic logic, rejecting it in favour of a humanistic study of usage and everyday ratiocination as pioneered by Valla and Agricola.[35] In this atmosphere Ramus set about a ruthless reduction and schematisation of Agricolan dialectic to produce an all-purpose, accessible, and undemanding introduction to the tools necessary for 'clear thinking'. If Valla and Agricola had pioneered the reform of dialectic instruction, Ramus pioneered popular education: his manuals were designed for the humblest members of the intellectual community.

Ramus was probably the last of the dialectical innovators to have been trained both in the scholastic tradition and in the 'Ciceronian' tradition of the new humanist arts schools. Much of the 'ignorance' and 'uncouthness' of which Ramist dialectic is accused stemmed from the fact that his texts fell into the hands of students who had received no systematic introduction to traditional Aristotelian logic. There is some evidence that scholastic manuals lingered on in the universities in the latter half of the sixteenth century because teachers found it necessary to provide some genuine formal logic to support the humanist programme.[36]

Ramus was involved in a programme of reform of the entire arts programme at Paris and produced textbooks which achieved great vogue in each subject of the curriculum (and also in such new subjects as vernacular grammar). He contended that the oratorical focus of a vocational arts course (no longer a technical training for clerics and teachers, but a higher education for a literate laity) called for simplification in the teaching of dialectic. Most specifically (and this emphasis is already to be found in the writings of Vives and Melanchthon),[37] the arts training was now directed towards ethics, civics, and politics (the active sciences of the professional man), in which areas opinion and persuasive discourse had traditionally

34. See Guerlac 1979.
35. 'Aristotle did not define even the smallest rule in his entire dialectic so that it would not conform to the same meaning of Greek speech that scholars and children and women and all the common people used. For a dialectician does not fashion and transmit a new meaning of language, but teaches rules taken from that old and familiar meaning.' *Opera*, p. 53, translated Guerlac 1979, p. 79.
36. See McConica 1979. McConica records the persistence of scholastic manuals alongside humanist manuals, and suggests that an eclectic pedagogy allowed both to be used.
37. Melanchthon argues energetically in his *Erotemata dialectices* that there is room for the study of dialectic as part of an education directed at the spiritual and moral welfare of the Christian individual. All his examples of logical argument are taken from ethical and scriptural questions.

held sway. For such studies a systematic logic of plausibility or probability (what may be argued as reasonable with the majority of reasonable men) is not merely an indulgence, but a necessity.

Like his predecessors in humanist logic, Ramus took as his fundamental distinction in logic the division into *inventio* and *iudicium*. Cicero, Quintilian, and Boethius provided the precedent for his move, which by now was the hallmark of a humanist dialectical approach. Ramus used grammatical well-formedness as the unique test of the appropriateness of a proposition for dialectical use (any well-formed, affirmative proposition is 'true' for his purposes), thus stressing the contingent nature of the study as he envisages it. He taught only an abbreviated list of Topics as the means of classifying dialectical material; these Topics (as in Boethius) serve as a checklist for the strategies of argument appropriate to the material stored under any one head. He curtailed discussion of the syllogism and entirely ignored the *logica moderna*. And he introduced *method* as the rallying point for his aggressively simplified programme of instruction, using 'method' to designate all the accumulated strategies for organising units of discourse in blocks larger than single syllogisms.

Ramus appears to have imagined that a dichotomous key, arranging the major propositions relating to any of the arts in descending order of generality, would provide a *grid* enabling teacher or student to display everything relevant to that art (including complex argumentation) in a way that would guarantee clarity and completeness.[38] In practice, in the Ramist handbooks which multiplied in the later sixteenth century, this Ramist method became a crude and restrictive device for running over the subject matter of a syllabus, or a clumsy mnemonic device for rote recall in extemporaneous speaking. It is probably fair to say that the protracted discussions of Ramist method as the solution for all the intellectual ills of the later sixteenth century represent the lowest ebb of the pioneering reforms of the humanists. But it should be remembered that this pedagogic aberration does not represent the entire achievement of humanist thinking on dialectic.

The function of the humanist textbooks

A good deal of the manoeuvring which takes place within humanist texts on dialectic is a direct consequence of their function – to provide elementary instruction in the art of discourse for students enrolled in an arts course

---

38. On Ramist method see Ong 1958a, Gilbert 1960, and Jardine 1974.

with an increasingly humanistic bias. In all of them philosophical questions are subordinated to pragmatic concerns. Check-lists to simplify standard procedures for selecting material pertinent to a theme and arguing consistently to a desired conclusion figure prominently. Latomus' successful epitome of Agricola's *De inventione dialectica* (a much more discursive work) is a striking example of the way in which the dialectic *manual* of the 1530s and thereafter is expected to be a pocket blueprint for successful performance in set disputations. The object of the text is unashamedly to enable the student to make the appropriate debating moves; the only criterion for preferring one strategy to another is its effectiveness in polemic. From the point of view of the historian of logic, it no longer makes very good sense when considering these manuals to isolate treatment of a traditional section like the categories in order to assess the humanist dialectician's intellectual contribution to it: he makes of it only as much as will carry his student to the next heading in his survey course. In this respect a recent historian of logic is correct in saying that the humanist dialecticians 'perverted the purpose of scholastic logic, which was also to teach, but to teach a developed formal logic rather than the art of thinking clearly'.[39]

Summary and conclusion

We may summarise the changes in dialectic teaching brought about by the impact of humanistic studies on the arts course as follows. In the early decades of the sixteenth century, across northern Europe, we find the introductory arts course being adapted to meet the requirements of an influx of students from the professional classes.[40] Within this arts course, with its humanist predilection for Greek and Latin eloquence, and legal and ethical instruction, there was an acknowledged need for some rigorous underpinning of instruction in 'clear thinking'. But the meticulous introduction to formal logic and semantic theory provided by the scholastic programme came to look increasingly unsuitable for this purpose.

One should, however, add that where the introductory arts course continued to be the preliminary stage in a programme directed toward the

---

39. Ashworth 1974a, p. 9.
40. It is becoming increasingly clear that despite a certain inertia in the statutes, humanist texts began to be studied in arts courses throughout northern Europe in the early decades of the sixteenth century, as study of book inventories of students, commonplace books, and teachers' lecture notes proves. See Curtis 1959 for the persisting discrepancy between statute requirements and the books students actually studied and owned. See also Jardine 1974, 1975, 1976, 1977, and forthcoming; also Kearney 1970.

study of philosophy and theology, scholastic logic continued to be taught with its traditional rigour. This was the case at the universities of southern Europe such as Padua, with its thriving philosophy faculty, and Bologna, with its sophisticated medical school.[41] Humanist studies in the Italian universities became assimilated into what had always been a thriving *grammar* course.[42] Aristotelian logicians teaching in the Italian universities show themselves aware of the alternative programme in practical dialectic,[43] and sometimes wrote elementary manuals suitable for a humanist course, while concentrating most of their attention on the enduring scholastic tradition.[44] One might even suggest that contact with the humanists' emphasis on the Topics led some of these logicians to introduce fruitful and original treatments of Topics into their formal and philosophical treatises.[45]

What was needed in the way of dialectic for the humanist arts course was a simple introduction to the analysis and use of ordinary language (elegant Latin) for formal debating and clear thinking. Such an analysis was provided in the 'alternative' dialectics deriving from the work of Valla and Agricola. These were committed to 'plausibility' as the measure of successful argumentation. Their authors impressively argued the case for giving serious consideration to non-syllogistic forms of argument, and strategies which support or convince rather than prove, as an intrinsic part of the 'art of discourse'.

In practice, the pedagogues working from the innovatory treatises of Valla and Agricola tended to discard those earlier authors' intellectual justifications for their refocused textbooks. But they stuck faithfully to the selection of subjects for treatment to which those authors had given emphasis. Thus Caesarius and Melanchthon both give space to non-syllogistic *sorites* in their textbooks, although they give no indication *why*

41. On the school of Padua see Randall 1940, reprinted in Randall 1961. For a full bibliography see Schmitt 1971.
42. See Rashdall 1936, I, 92, for an account of this fundamental difference between the structures of the arts courses north and south of the Alps.
43. Nifo, Zimara, and Zabarella all allude to the humanist programme, and sometimes appear to incorporate some of the devices (particularly for presentation) from those courses in their more traditional treatises. For an account of the close contact between humanism and the enduring Aristotelianism at Padua see Poppi 1970 and Vasoli 1968b.
44. See Nifo's *Dialectica ludicra*, which in many ways deviates from traditional Aristotelianism in its selection of topics and presentation. See also the *Tabulae logicae* by Zabarella, printed at the end of his *Opera logica*.
45. This may well be the case with Nifo, whose commentary on Aristotle's *Topics*, widely used in the sixteenth century, incorporates many non-Aristotelian attitudes towards the use and flexibility of the teaching of the Topics. See Ashworth 1976b.

this topic is of peculiar interest to them.[46] They also tend to be extremely sketchy on just those traditional areas of logic in which the historian of logic is particularly interested. This may well be because there already existed a body of standard textbooks of quality in these areas, to which the student could be referred. There has not yet been an adequate study of the intellectual contribution of the humanist dialecticians on the issues with which they are particularly concerned, such as extended argumentation over units larger than the syllogism, or coercive forms of argument.[47] Until such a study is made, we shall not be in a position to decide whether the humanist intervention in the history of logic represents a decisive impoverishment or a possible enrichment of the tradition.

46. *Sorites* is allowed a heading to itself, although no attempt is made at more than a description of the argument form.
47. The work of Vasoli, Howell, and Gilbert is in the end too descriptive to make much headway.

44

CHANGES IN THE APPROACH TO LANGUAGE

The humanists' attitude towards scholastic philosophy

There is a certain irony in the fact that it was the humanists with their enthusiasm for the literature of the ancient world who were in large part responsible for the demise of scholastic grammar. For inasmuch as humanism was a literary and educational, not a philosophical movement, the attitude of most humanists towards scholastic philosophy was one of indifference; they seldom manifested outright hostility, and such opposition as they professed was not, for the most part, philosophical.[1]

Humanists outside the university

The early humanists were, in fact, either independent men of letters or, more typically, members of the legal profession holding high office in church or state.[2] Petrarch (1304–74) is the best-known representative of the first category. Famous nowadays for having written some of the most magnificent sonnets in the Italian language, he was known to his contemporaries primarily as a promoter of classical studies and the author of a number of highly regarded original works in Latin as well as a voluminous correspondence, likewise in Latin. An outstanding example of the second type of humanist is Petrarch's younger friend Coluccio Salutati (1331–1406), who was trained as a notary at Bologna University and for the last twenty-six years of his life held the office of chancellor in Florence.

---

1. On the relation between humanism and scholasticism, see Kristeller 1944–5; 1956, pp. 553–83; Garin 1965, pp. 1–4. The word 'humanist', a fifteenth-century creation, was originally applied to teachers of classical literature, later to anybody, whether teacher or not, who cultivated the so-called *studia humanitatis*; see Campana 1946, esp. p. 66; Avesani 1970. The abstract noun 'humanism', on the other hand, is of very recent date. Note that while humanism was not a philosophical movement, many humanists had profound philosophical commitments, witness the platonism of Marsilio Ficino; see Garin 1965, pp. 78–135; Kristeller 1961a, pp. 48–69.
2. On early humanism, see Weiss 1947. A classic account of Italian and German humanism is Geiger 1882. Voigt 1893 is also still valuable. On the concept of the Renaissance a great deal has been written, see especially Ferguson 1948; Chabod 1958, pp. 149–200; Garin 1969b, pp. 1–20.

The humanists' involvement in education

Then, from the early fifteenth century onwards, many humanists became involved in education and left their stamp on generations of students, at first drawn predominantly from northern Italy, but in course of time from as far afield as England and Hungary. The two foremost educators, Guarino Veronese (1374–1406) at the d'Este court in Ferrara, and Vittorino da Feltre (1373–1446) at Mantua, developed a comprehensive course of studies for the young men in their charge, embracing a wide variety of physical as well as intellectual pursuits.[3] The literary curriculum was largely based on the principles laid down by Quintilian and comprised a thorough initiation into both Latin and Greek, together with the intensive study of classical authors, including the then much-esteemed works on moral philosophy by Cicero, Plato, and Aristotle. One might perhaps characterise the ideal products of the new educational programme as all-round individuals capable of turning their talents to any form of public service. It was this conception of the liberally educated man which distinguished the humanistic schools from the scholastically dominated universities of the time.

The humanists' attitude towards the study of grammar

As regards the more narrowly linguistic aspects of the movement, the foremost aim of the humanists was to model their Latin style on that of the ancients whom they so admired: one of the primary targets of their disapproval was the level of contemporary Latinity. At first this ideal was achieved without the aid of special textbooks. Petrarch spent his life saturating himself in the works of Cicero and other Latin authors, which did not fail to affect his own Latin prose style in a profound way, but he expressed no dissatisfaction with the grammatical literature in general use at that time. Indeed, he included two medieval dictionaries in his list of favourite books, namely the anonymous *Papias* (mid-eleventh century) and the *Catholicon* of John of Genoa (late thirteenth century).[4]

Early humanist grammars

Even when the humanists turned their attention to the composition of new textbooks, they did so without any explicit criticism of the medieval

---

3. On Guarino Veronese, see Sabbadini 1891; also 1896, esp. pp. 26–38; on Vittorino da Feltre, see Woodward 1921.
4. On Petrarch's favourite books, see Ullman 1955, pp. 117–37.

grammarians. The earliest humanist grammar of Latin was the *Regulae grammaticales* of Guarino Veronese, composed before 1418.[5] The two salient characteristics of this remarkable work are its exteme brevity and its omission of the logical and metaphysical underpinnings characteristic of the grammatical products of the late Middle Ages. Of genuine originality there is little, if any: Guarino drew his material from the Latin grammars of his immediate predecessors, not directly from the Roman grammarians of antiquity. It is noteworthy too that he made no attempt to support his rules by means of quotations from the classical authors; indeed many of his examples are concocted ones of the kind familiar from earlier grammatical works.[6]

In spite of the unoriginality of Guarino's grammar it was a considerable success, but copyists in transcribing it often put back some of the medieval features which Guarino had been at such pains to remove.[7] At least in that negative respect Guarino was clearly in advance of his age.

The Latin grammars written in the wake of Guarino's *Regulae* are characterised by a gradual accentuation of humanistic features and a progressive rejection of medieval traits, but the development is by no means linear. Thus the grammar of Gasparo Veronese, composed in Rome some time during the pontificate of Nicholas V (1447–55), shows if anything more medieval features than Guarino's.[8]

Fully developed humanist grammars

The work which most profoundly influenced all humanists in the area of Latin prose style was the voluminous *Elegantiarum linguae Latinae libri sex* by Lorenzo Valla (1407–57), which circulated beginning in the early 1440s. The revolutionary feature of Valla's manual was the extensive, though not exclusive, use of direct quotations from the authors of antiquity to back up the stylistic precepts. Valla was not concerned with syntax or

---

5. On Guarino's Latin grammatical works, see Sabbadini 1896, pp. 38–47; 1902; 1906; 1919, pp. 79–80; 1922, pp. 3–15; Percival 1972; 1975; 1976a.
6. The following are typical of the examples to be found in Guarino's grammar: 'Me taedet vitiorum', 'Ego emo equum decem ducatorum', 'Mulier trunca manum', 'Animal homo currit.' The quotations from the classics are almost all stock examples carried over from earlier grammars, such as 'Urbem quam statuo vestra est' (Vergil, *Aen.*, i. 573), quoted by Priscian and also by the author of the *Graecismus* (Wrobel 1887, p. 5.40).
7. For instance, some manuscripts of the *Regulae* contain the modistic definitions of the parts of speech – e.g., 'Nomen est pars orationis declinabilis, significans per modum habitus et quietis et determinatae apprehensionis' (MS Naples, Biblioteca Governativa dei Gerolamini, *A 60*, f. 1ʳ). See Roos 1961, p. 10, lines 19–21.
8. On the grammar of Gasparo Veronese, see Sabbadini 1896, pp. 45–6.

composition, however; the bulk of the *Elegantiae* is devoted to the proper meaning and choice of single words and the avoidance of barbarisms, i.e., non-classical words. What is truly novel in Valla's work is a pervasive critical attitude, which extends also to the grammatical authorities of antiquity: Valla indeed went so far as to criticise Priscian on occasion, for which he appears to have been censured by his contemporaries.[9]

After Valla's death, the next major contribution to Latin grammatical writing was the *Rudimenta grammatices* by Niccolò Perotti (1429–80), which was completed in Viterbo in 1468. This neatly organised manual, which soon appeared in many printed editions and was widely used in Italy and northern Europe until well into the sixteenth century, was the first humanistic grammar of Latin to include elementary morphology (the noun and verb paradigms, for instance) in addition to more advanced topics, and the last third of it is devoted to epistolary style. It could, therefore, be used as the basis of a complete course of studies in Latin, and it may be that it owed its popularity to this fact as well as to its perspicuous organisation.[10]

An even more comprehensive grammar was shortly afterwards produced by the Salamanca humanist Antonio de Nebrija (*ca.* 1441–1522). The first printed edition of his *Introductiones Latinae* appeared in 1481; the work assumed final shape in 1495 and was reprinted many times, in Spain and elsewhere.[11] Like Perotti's grammar it is lucid and well-organised, and it also treats topics such as orthography, prosody, and metrics, ending with a short dictionary, based predominantly on Valla's *Elegantiae* and the monumental *Orthographia* of Giovanni Tortelli (*ca.* 1400–66), a work which had appeared in the early 1450s. Nebrija was self-consciously innovative, and all the editions from 1495 on are provided with a copious commentary in which he meticulously explains and justifies his intentions. His most drastic innovation was perhaps his addition of the gerund and the supine to the eight canonical parts of speech, which he justified on the grounds that there had been no consensus among the grammarians of antiquity as to the number of the parts of speech.[12]

---

9. On Valla's *Elegantiae*, see Barozzi and Sabbadini 1891, pp. 161–73; Casacci 1926; Stevens 1975.
10. A thorough analysis of Perotti's *Rudimenta* is an urgent desideratum. See, however, Mercati 1925, pp. 59–61, 131–2; Baebler 1885, pp. 135–9.
11. Nebrija is chiefly known for his grammar of Castilian, which appeared in 1492. On Nebrija's life and works, see González-Llubera 1926, pp. xvii–xl. His Latin grammar has so far not received the attention it deserves.
12. After arguing that the gerund is a separate part of speech, he says: 'Neque id mirum videri debet, cum multi plures, multi pauciores quam octo partes orationis posuerint' (Nebrija 1481, sig. c6ᵛ).

The influence of the rediscovered classics

It is important to realise that Nebrija's sort of statement could not have been made by grammarians who lived before those spectacular discoveries of previously unknown, or little known, Latin authors which we associate with such men as Poggio Bracciolini (1380–1459).[13] It was, in fact, the discovery of the works of Probus, Diomedes, Charisius, and other Roman grammarians which made books such as Tortelli's *Orthographia* possible.[14] In this general category the most important find was undoubtedly the fragments of Varro's *De lingua Latina* (first century B.C.), on which the humanist Giulio Pomponio Leto (1428–98) lectured in Rome and which he subsequently edited for publication (1471).[15] The discovery of Varro was especially important for grammarians because his much earlier approach to grammatical questions differed in many important respects from that of the two canonical authors Donatus (*ca.* 350 A.D.) and Priscian (*ca.* 500 A.D.). Thus, the humanists' critical attitude to traditional theory was reinforced, if not brought on, by this exposure to more ancient, hitherto unfamiliar doctrine.

Another factor which contributed to the widening of linguistic horizons was the initiation of Greek studies in Italy, first by Chrysoloras in Florence in the final decade of the fourteenth century, then by other Greek émigrés, notably Theodore Gaza and Constantine Lascaris, and as time went on by an ever-increasing number of Italians, among them Guarino Veronese, who was perhaps the first westerner to study Greek in Constantinople (1403–8).[16] Chrysoloras, Guarino's teacher, wrote a grammatical textbook, the *Erotemata*, in the traditional catechetical style, which Guarino abridged. This epitome was subsequently translated into Latin, and the resulting bilingual version was the first Greek grammar widely disseminated in the West.[17] The amount of Greek which the general run of

---

13. On the discoveries of manuscripts made by the humanists, see Sabbadini 1905; 1914.

14. The epistle dedicatory in Tortelli's *Orthographia* makes this abundantly clear; see Garin 1958, pp. 495–7. On the *Orthographia*, see Rinaldi 1973.

15. On Pomponio Leto's grammatical works, see Ruysschaert 1954; 1961. The standard treatment of this humanist is Zabughin 1909–12.

16. On the Greek grammars of the Renaissance, see Pertusi 1962. The impact of Greek émigré scholars on the Italian Renaissance has at times been somewhat exaggerated in the popular imagination, especially in northern Europe. Garin comments as follows: 'The actual contribution made by Byzantium to humanism consisted mainly in new tools and in precious materials which enriched occidental civilisation. The East was able to provide useful formulas to a western system of thought which had already reached an autonomous maturity' (1965, p. 81). In this connection see also Geanakoplos 1966, esp. p. 112.

17. The curious methodology of Greek instruction in the West is described in Sabbadini 1922, pp. 19–22. On Chrysoloras' grammar, see Pertusi 1962; Sabbadini 1919, pp. 76–7, 128.

fifteenth-century humanists commanded should not be over-estimated. But learning a language in many ways so different from Latin posed a considerable intellectual challenge to the student of those days and may even have stimulated many teachers to scrutinise traditional grammatical doctrine.

A similar broadening of perspectives must have resulted from the beginnings of Hebrew studies. It should perhaps not surprise us that Nebrija, who taught Greek and Hebrew as well as Latin, was the first humanist grammarian to state explicitly that the rules of syntactic agreement observed in Latin are common to all languages, but it is noteworthy that he appealed to the authority of Aristotle (*De int.* 16ᵃ8) in so doing.[18]

The humanists' treatment of logical syntax

This raises the complex issue of logical syntax, an area which had but recently been developed by the scholastic grammarians with little help from their classical forebears. An elaborate and theoretically sophisticated framework for the analysis of sentences had taken shape by the fourteenth century. It is worthy of remark that while the humanist teachers reduced the grammatical baggage to the minimum in order to facilitate and hasten their students' initiation into classical literature, they nonetheless retained the essential features of the system of logical syntax they had inherited from the immediate past. Terms such as '*suppositum*' ('subject'), '*appositum*' ('object', or sometimes 'predicate'), '*agens*' ('initiator of the action'), '*patiens*' ('recipient of the action'), and above all '*antecedens*' ('antecedent of a pronoun'), which had constituted the stock-in-trade of the Latin grammarians of the fourteenth century, survived well into the sixteenth century, and some of them, such as 'agent' and 'antecedent', have remained in use to this day.

This retention of medieval syntactic concepts is especially evident in the grammatical textbooks written by the humanists of northern Europe. Thus the *Syntax* of Anthonius Haneron (*ca.* 1400–90), presumably written in the 1430s and perhaps the earliest grammatical work of the humanistic variety composed north of the Alps, includes a careful discussion of sentential

---

18. Nebrija's three universal rules are the agreement of adjective with substantive, of relative with antecedent, and of subject nominative with verb. He comments as follows: 'Ponit tria praecepta quae non sermonis latini propria, verum etiam omnibus linguis communia, publica, et quodam modo naturalia sunt, si quidem naturale est, ut inquit Aristoteles, quod apud omnes gentes idem est' (*Introductiones Latinae cum commento*, 1495, sig. c8ᵛ).

analysis.[19] It is also significant that in the version of Perotti's grammar edited by Bernard Perger of the University of Vienna with the impressive title *Grammatica Nova* (the first printed editions date from the early 1480s), Perger adds an extra set of syntactic rules after Perotti's.[20]

The humanists' attitude towards modistic grammar

Regarding the modistic literature, the humanists' attitude was, not surprisingly, one of indifference, if not outright disdain. Their explicit references to the *modi significandi* are rather few, but consistently hostile. A passage from Valla's encomium on Thomas Aquinas perhaps typifies the ambivalence the humanists felt towards certain manifestations of scholasticism. Valla first reproves the theologians for their superstitious reverence for the *modi significandi* – it is, he says, almost as if they regarded them as a newly discovered sphere or planetary epicycle – then declares that it really makes no difference to him whether one knows about the modes or not, and finally hastens to add that it is perhaps preferable to remain ignorant of them altogether since they are obstacles in the way of better things.[21]

An organised attack on modistic grammar was launched by the Westphalian humanist Alexander Hegius (*ca.* 1433–98), who taught for many years at the school of the Brethren of the Common Life in Deventer. His pungent *Invectiva in modos significandi*, composed around 1480, contains all the expected humanistic charges, such as the contention that the *modistae* were corrupters of Latinity, that the church fathers had written excellent Latin without knowing anything about the *modi significandi*, and so forth. But Hegius offers at least one argument of a more substantive nature, namely the contention that words which have the same *modus significandi* do not necessarily behave the same syntactically. He points out, for instance, that while the genitive of '*Johannes*' can be used in the expression '*liber Johannis*' ('John's book'), the genitive of the personal pronoun '*ego*' ('I'), cannot be used in that way: '*liber mei*' is not permissible. From this the reader is to conclude that knowing the *modi significandi* does not entail knowing Latin syntax.[22]

---

19. On Anthonius Haneron, see Ijsewijn 1975, pp. 217–19; Ijsewijn–Jacobs 1976, pp. 29–33.
20. On Bernard Perger and the impact of the new humanistic textbooks in German-speaking universities, see Heath 1971.
21. See Ijsewijn 1971, pp. 301–2; Vahlen 1886, p. 394.
22. For the full text of Hegius' invective, see Ijsewijn 1971. On Hegius, see Lindeboom 1913, pp. 70–81; Hyma, 1951, pp. 151–9; 1965, pp. 125–8. In philosophical penetration Hegius' arguments against modistic grammar cannot compare with those of the nominalists a hundred and fifty years earlier; see Pinborg 1967a, pp. 172–85.

The humanists' attitude towards the verse grammars

As for the verse grammars (in particular the *Doctrinale* of Alexandre de Villedieu and the *Graecismus* of Evrard de Bethune), which had been a staple of the curriculum from the thirteenth century onwards, the attitude of the humanists towards them seems initially to have been favourable, or at least tolerant. The *Doctrinale* was still being used in Guarino's school.[23] A wholesale reaction against the verse grammars did not take place until the second half of the fifteenth century. There is, for instance, a sharply worded invective aimed at the *Doctrinale* in one of the grammatical textbooks written by the Roman humanist Giovanni Sulpizio Verulano (*ca.* 1470).[24] Significantly, however, his criticisms were motivated primarily by pedagogical considerations: he censured the work for its density and obscurity, not its factual unreliability.

In northern Europe, the attack on the verse grammars generated more acrimony, and they were all but completely banished from the classroom by the middle of the sixteenth century.[25] Nevertheless, the custom of casting grammatical rules in verse for mnemonic purposes was by no means abandoned by the humanist grammarians: parts of Guarino's and Nebrija's grammars were written in verse, and in general this practice persisted until well into the nineteenth century.

Universal grammar

The belief that all languages share certain basic grammatical categories was another medieval legacy, a notion which had been clearly stated by Gundissalinus in his *De divisione philosophiae* (late twelfth century)[26] and was presupposed by all the writers of modistic treatises. The early humanists do not mention the idea, but it would be rash to assume that they took exception to it. As we have seen, Nebrija grants universal status to the Latin rules of concord. After suffering what appears to have been a complete eclipse, philosophical grammar came back into fashion in the seventeenth century,[27] and some of its new votaries acknowledged that they were not starting from scratch. Both Campanella, in a treatise published in Paris in 1638, and John Wilkins, author of *An Essay Towards a Real Character and a*

---

23. See Sabbadini 1896, pp. 36, 42, 56–7; Woodward 1921, p. 165.
24. For the complete text, see Percival 1976b, pp. 87–8; cf. pp. 82–3.
25. See Reichling 1893, pp. XCIII–CIII; Heath 1971.
26. See Baur 1903, pp. 45–6.
27. On seventeenth-century philosophical grammar, see Padley 1976, pp. 154–209. On the Port-Royal language textbooks, see Donzé 1967; Padley 1976, pp. 210–59.

Philosophical Language (1668) allude explicitly to medieval predecessors.[28]

Whether we should posit an unbroken tradition of philosophical grammar linking the *modistae* and the seventeenth-century universal grammarians has not yet been established. The famous Port-Royal *Grammaire générale et raisonée* (1660) emphasised the difference between substantives and adjectives in their modes of signifying (Part II, Chap. 2),[29] but the same point had been made by the nominalist Mario Nizzoli in his *De veris principiis et vera ratione philosophandi* a little over a hundred years earlier.[30] We know that the Port-Royal educators were familiar with such works as the elder Scaliger's *De causis linguae Latinae* (1540), a blistering attack on traditional grammatical terminology and concepts from an avowedly Aristotelian standpoint, but it is not clear to what extent, if any, they had first-hand acquaintance with medieval approaches to language. It is perhaps more likely that they were influenced by scholastic logic than by survivals of the medieval grammatical tradition.[31]

The influence of the humanists' approach to language

Even the more narrowly linguistic aspects of humanism could not fail to have a profound and lasting influence on philosophy as a whole. Already in the first half of the fifteenth century Valla had subjected some of the key terms used by the schoolmen, such as *quiditas* and *ens*, to destructive grammatical analysis. As Valla viewed the matter, a word such as *quiditas* is a morphological impossibility in Latin, and the notion of universality implied in the term *ens* can have no grammatical justification whatever.[32]

---

28. Campanella 1638, Pars prima, I. i., p. 3; Wilkins 1668, III. i., p. 297.
29. *Grammaire générale et raisonnée*, II. ii., p. 31 (in the first (1660) edition).
30. *De veris principiis* (Parma 1553), I. iii., sigs. C2ʳ–C3ʳ.
31. Thus the famous analysis of the sentence 'Dieu invisible a créé le monde visible' into the three judgements 'Dieu est invisible', 'Il a créé le monde', and 'Le monde est visible' (*Grammaire générale et raisonnée*, (1660) II. ix, pp. 68–9) can be traced back to the discussions centring on 'restrictions' and 'exponibles' by the medieval logicians, see Salmon 1969, pp. 180–3; Kretzmann 1975, pp. 189–95.
32. *Dialecticae disputationes*, I. ii and iv (*Opera*, sigs. 2S3ᵛ–5ʳ, 2S6ᵛ–7ʳ). Fresh light has recently been shed on this work by the discovery of two previously unpublished versions, one earlier and the other later than the version to be found in the *Opera*. See Zippel 1957 and subsequent studies, such as Vasoli 1968a and Camporeale 1972 (esp. pp. 149–71). The pedagogical implementation of the new humanistic approach to logic can be observed in the manuals of George of Trebizond (see Monfasani 1976, pp. 300–17) and Rudolph Agricola (see Faust 1922; Crescini 1965, pp. 49–67). The philological method was almost immediately applied to biblical criticism, witness the *Adnotationes in Novum Testamentum*, written by Lorenzo Valla in the last years of his life and published half a century later by Erasmus (Paris 1505). On the theological aspects of humanism see Fois 1969, Trinkaus 1970, Camporeale 1972, pp. 211–468; and Kristeller 1961a, pp. 79–80; 1974, p. 65. Procedures which had proved effective in the study of belles-lettres were inevitably turned to good account by theologians themselves. On the relation between biblical exegesis and present-day canons of textual criticism, see Pasquali 1952, pp. 8–12.

Another important service provided by the humanists was to make available hitherto unknown or imperfectly known philosophical texts, and concomitantly to bring about a re-evaluation of already familiar texts. In this area, one may point to the many translations of Greek philosophical works which began to appear from the early fifteenth century onwards. The humanists published bilingual Greek–Latin editions of many such works and provided them with elaborate new commentaries, composed, naturally, in Latin.[33]

The greater accessibility of the rich Platonic corpus was a novel and especially potent factor. As is now widely recognised, a vigorous Aristotelian tradition, increasingly revitalised by the availability of new texts and fresh translations, maintained itself throughout the Renaissance and into the early modern period. At the same time, however, Platonism undoubtedly provided philosophers with valuable new concepts, which were utilised in a wide variety of contexts. For instance, the recovery of Plato's *Cratylus* stimulated and enriched speculation about the nature of language.[34]

33. The new humanistic translations of *De anima*, for example, had to compete with the familiar version by William of Moerbeke (late thirteenth century), which had provided the schoolmen with a stock of useful terms for a number of fundamental psychological concepts; see Garin 1951; Cranz 1976. It is clear from such cases that the medieval philosophical tradition, while undergoing a profound change, survived the humanistic revolution to a considerable extent.
34. See, for instance, Scaliger 1540, III. lxvii, sigs. p3ʳ–4ᵛ; Sanctius 1587, I. i, sigs. A5ʳ–6ᵛ.

45

SCHOLASTICISM

IN THE SEVENTEENTH CENTURY

Spain as the bastion of late scholasticism

After the attacks of humanists, Ramists, reformers, and plain haters of philosophy over much of two centuries, it is amazing that scholasticism survived at all. Not only did it survive, it experienced a notable revival throughout much of western Europe towards the end of the sixteenth century and beginning of the seventeenth. Humanists and reformers were by no means unanimous in opposing the medieval scholastics. More important, the Iberian peninsula was comparatively unaffected by the intellectual and religious ferment of most of the rest of Europe. The schools of Spain and Portugal had a more or less continuous tradition of scholastic philosophy, and the leading figures in the general revival of scholastic thought round the end of the sixteenth century tend to be Spaniards like Bañez, Vásquez, and Suárez. In northern Europe the scholastic revival looks more like a self-conscious and deliberate Aristotelian reaction to Ramists, humanists, and the like, but the northerners of whatever religious allegiance were happy enough to take guidance and inspiration from Spain.

New trends in late scholasticism

Although in obvious ways continuous with the main medieval tradition, late scholasticism, whether in its Iberian form or in its northern revival, shows certain very distinctive characteristics of its own which may be seen as marking a transition to some of the most prominent themes of early modern philosophy.

While these philosophers were nearly unanimous in rejecting medieval nominalism (indeed, in the north this was another of the things they were reacting against), Scotus, Ockham, and the later nominalistic tradition had a very powerful influence on them. What is particularly notable is their tendency to internalise order, to direct our attention away from an order given in the external world and towards an internal order, the structure of the mind and patterns in the way in which the mind acts. In what follows I shall try to trace the result of this internalising of order in logic, in metaphysics, and in the study of law and morals.

Late scholastic logic

It is hard to praise the late scholastics for their contributions to formal logic.[1] For reasons that are complex and a little obscure, progress and inventiveness in formal logic dried up early in the sixteenth century. With hindsight we can conjecture that the medieval logicians had gone about as far as they could go without the mathematical tools of a later age. We find no new contributions to formal logic in the treatises of the late sixteenth and early seventeenth centuries, and medieval achievements are misrepresented or not reported at all. Some of these treatises give little more formal logic than a rather garbled treatment of syllogistic. Few include any discussion of supposition theory at all, and those that do either give a very truncated survey, as Sanderson does,[2] or put together doctrines that would have horrified their medieval predecessors.

In fact, these authors were not much interested in formal logic as such. They were far more interested in the philosophy of logic and language than in formal logic. On these matters, while they made few if any original contributions, they carried on the medieval discussion at a high level of competence and were the means of transmitting some of the characteristic doctrines of medieval speculative grammar and the philosophical study of language to the early modern period. This is a matter of some interest because we can here trace the history of what Chomsky has called 'Cartesian linguistics' from the medieval logicians and grammarians to the Cartesians themselves.[3] Many of the logicians of the period also show some Ramist influence in their concern for methodological questions. They are sometimes accused of psychologising logic; but the genuine scholastics – as opposed to the out-and-out Ramists or the 'mixts' who tried to combine Aristotle and Ramus – were concerned about an ideal, inner order of thought, fit to represent the most general formal characteristics of being. In this their philosophy of logic was no more psychologistic than that of their medieval predecessors.

The logic of John of St Thomas

A well-known logic of the period and the only one that has attracted much attention in our time is that of John of St Thomas. His logical works were incorporated during his lifetime in his *Cursus philosophicus Thomisticus*, although in his first editions he used such titles as *Artis logicae pars prima, de*

---

1. Thomas 1964, pp. 297–311.
2. Sanderson 1640.
3. Chomsky 1966. See Trentman 1975; 1976; also Kretzmann 1975.

dialecticis institutionibus, quas summulas vocant and *pars secunda, de instrumentis logicalibus ex parte materiae.*[4] The 'first part' is a shorter text intended as an introduction to logic; the 'second part' is a more extensive work for more mature students of philosophy. It takes up such Aristotelian subjects as the predicables, the ten categories, and demonstration, including of course an account of necessary propositions and *per se* predication.

In his general logic John, unlike most of his contemporaries, includes a relatively extensive treatment of supposition theory. He very insistently claims to be a follower of Thomas Aquinas, and it is interesting to compare what he gives of supposition theory with that of an earlier *soi-disant* Thomist, Vincent Ferrer (1350–1419).[5]

John's divisions of supposition are the same as Ferrer's. He has not much to say about natural supposition, which obtains in necessary propositions and which Ferrer discussed at very considerable length, but he includes it in his account, and he also defines simple supposition in the characteristic anti-Ockhamist way as obtaining when a term stands for what it primarily and immediately signifies.[6] He had no objection whatever to assigning the property of supposition to predicates as well as subjects. In this he was no true follower of his master, Aquinas, if Ferrer was right.[7] Worse yet, he makes full use of what the medievals had called 'merely confused supposition', which Ferrer had argued does not occur – is, indeed, a merely confused notion. Furthermore, John uses the notion exactly as Ockham had done. So at least so far as supposition theory goes John of St Thomas turns out to be a strange Thomist.[8]

Noam Chomsky has identified three principal doctrines that characterise what he calls 'Cartesian linguistics'.[9] First, there is a creative aspect of human language that defies the possibility of mechanistic explanations and distinguishes our use of language from animal behaviour generally. Secondly, there are 'grammatical principles' that are universal to all human languages in the sense that they stand as constraints on possible grammars of natural languages. Thirdly, one can and must distinguish the deep structure of language, shared with other rational beings who speak different languages, from the surface structures of these tongues. All these

---

4. For bibliography see John of St Thomas 1955a.
5. Vincent Ferrer 1977.
6. A good account of these debates can be found in Pinborg 1972.
7. Vincent Ferrer 1977. Cf. Geach 1972; 1961, pp. 76–80. In fact, Aquinas was not consistent on this point; see Vincent Ferrer 1977, p. 97, n. 1.
8. Cf. Vincent Ferrer 1977, pp. 43 and 141f.
9. Chomsky 1966.

principles are clearly found in John of St Thomas' logic, but in this he was only following the long tradition of medieval scholastic study of language.[10] Indeed, John's insistence that *entia rationis* of second intention are the formal object of the study of logic is tantamount to the claim that logic has to do with structures universal to all rational minds. The logician must give an account of this internal order and relate it, on the one hand, to the conventional sounds and marks we produce and, on the other, to the things in the world we want to talk about. Nothing could be more 'Cartesian'.

Scholastic logics of the seventeenth century

We find the same thing wherever we look in scholastic logics of this period. Franco Burgersdijck's *Institutionum logicum libri duo* was widely used throughout northern Europe and in 1646 was translated into Dutch and went into 'school editions' in the author's homeland.[11] It presents little formal logic and shows no logical originality. There are signs of Ramist influence in its concern about questions of method, although its author records his proper scholastic-revival disapproval of Ramus. On 'Cartesian' principles, however, Burgersdijck is sound. Much the same can be said of two other popular logics of the time, the *Logica* of the Polish Jesuit, Martin Smiglecki, and the *Logicae libri quinque* of the Anglican, Richard Crakanthorpe.[12]

Much the same can be said of the earlier work of Seton, which was first printed 'with Peter Carter's annotations' in 1572.[13] As a formal logic it is tedious and uninspired; as philosophy of language it faithfully records the standard medieval doctrine. Likewise, Edward Brerewood in two logic texts does little formal logic and none to deserve special notice, but he does produce a quite interesting discussion of problems in the philosophy of language that has much in common with Thomas of Erfurt's *Grammatica speculativa*.[14] A rather more interesting English logic of this period is Robert Sanderson's *Logicae artis compendium*.[15] Unlike most of his contemporaries, Sanderson gives a brief survey of supposition theory; he also includes as an appendix an interesting survey of the history of logic, in which he praises the logic of his medieval predecessors but not their Latin

---

10. Cf. Trentman 1975.
11. See Risse 1964, pp. 515–16, and Guerault 1968.
12. Smiglecki 1634; Crakanthorpe 1622.
13. Seton 1631; cf. Trentman 1976, pp. 180–1 and 184–5.
14. Brerewood 1614 and 1628; cf. Trentman 1976, pp. 187–8.
15. Sanderson 1640.

style. His account of the task of the logician is quite interesting.[16] The logician, using his own appropriate tools, can clarify and make explicit the structures that may have been hidden in the idiomatic expressions of everyday speech. This is good medieval doctrine; it also points ahead to 'Cartesian' linguistics in its concern with the inner order of mind and mental acts.

Late scholastic metaphysics in general

The metaphysics of the late scholastics, like their logic, mixes old and new. We may note the influence of Ockham and his followers on philosophers who were by no means Ockhamists and indeed, regarded themselves as Thomists, as well as the emphasis on the activity of mind and the internal structure of mental activity. The metaphysics of Francisco Suárez was particularly prominent and influential.

Suárez on essence and existence

The Suarezian idea that has occasioned the most interest and controversy through the centuries is his understanding of the distinction between essence and existence. Suárez inherited the question and its background from his medieval predecessors. It was the old problem of understanding the idea of creation and relating the belief in creation to a philosophical analysis of created being. It is a tenet of orthodox Judaeo-Christian belief that God exists by his own nature; it is in the very nature of what it means to be God that God must exist. As it was put, in God essence and existence are identical. What it means to be a creature is that this is true of no created thing. For all created things essence must somehow be distinguished from existence. But how? Suárez distinguishes three possible positions that one might take in response to this question.[17] First, one can say that for finite beings existence and essence are really distinct. Suárez expresses this option in a way that requires its defender to hold that existence and essence are distinct things; existence is a kind of object (*rem quandam distinctam*). He says that this 'seems to be St Thomas' opinion',[18] but he is sure that it is the opinion of a wide variety of later Thomists including Cajetan. The second option holds that existence and essence are not really distinct; they are formally distinct, i.e., existence can be regarded as a mode of essence. Mention of the formal distinction suggests Scotus, and Suárez identifies

16. *Ibid.*, p. 75.
17. Suárez 1965, 31, 1; vol. II, pp. 224–8.
18. 'Haec existimatur esse opinio D. Thomae'; cf. pp. 225–31.

this position with him. The third opinion is that existence and essence are only mentally distinct (*tantum ratione*). According to Suárez, this opinion was held by Alexander of Hales, Peter Aureoli, Durandus, Gabriel Biel, and nominalists generally. Suárez asserts that the first two positions are false and the third true, but true only if the terms are understood in the proper sense. By 'existence' we must understand 'actual existence' and by 'essence' 'actually existing essence'.[19] Understood in this way the existence and essence of any created being can be regarded as mentally distinct or mentally distinguishable. For Suárez, then, the distinction has its origin in the mind; making such distinctions is one of the things that minds do. But the mind is not at complete liberty to do what it pleases here; while it is responsible for the distinction, something about the way things are with finite beings in the world is the occasion for it to make the distinction. The distinction itself is something that minds do, but their performing such an action is somehow grounded in things; this is what he means by his expression '*distinctio rationis cum fundamento in re*'.[20]

Suárez on individuals and universals

One of the major turning points in the history of western philosophy was Scotus' formulation of the idea of intuitive cognition. The old problem of individuation was, crudely, this: given the knowledge of universals, find the individuals. After Scotus there was a new problem: given the knowledge of individuals, find the universals. Suárez addressed the new problem, and although he was sharply critical of Scotus, his doctrines of individuality and universality show their influence throughout Suárez' discussion. All actually existing things, immediately existing things as distinct from what can exist only dependently in an individual object, are singular and individual.[21] Furthermore, they can be known in their individuality. Suárez agreed with Scotus that to say that a thing is individual is to talk about some thing (*aliquid reale*) in addition to the nature of the thing, which is common to many, but he saw no reason for positing a special individuator like the *haecceitas* to account for this individuality.[22] The composite of form and matter itself contains in its union its own principle of individuation.[23] As he puts it, 'the adequate principle of individuation is this matter

---

19. 31, 1, 13; vol. II, p. 228.
20. 31, 6, 23; vol. II, p. 250. Cf. 7, 1, 4–5; vol. I, p. 251.
21. 5, 1, 4; vol. I, pp. 146–7.
22. 5, 2, 8–9; vol. I, pp. 150–1.
23. 5, 3; vol. I, pp. 161–75.

and this form in union. The form alone is the sufficient and chief principle so that the composite, as an individual thing of a certain species, can be considered numerically one and the same thing'.[24] In many ways this argumentation in Suárez curiously foreshadows the twentieth-century debate about so-called bare particulars. Modern logical atomists have argued that in order to account for the individuality of two things that are identical in all their nonrelational properties one must posit individuators that in themselves have no properties (hence their bareness) but ground the individuality and thereby the distinctness of the things. But the idea of the bare particular, like that of the Scotist's *haecceitas*, has a strangeness about it that does not appeal to many philosophers.[25]

Suárez certainly did not regard himself as a nominalist. Nevertheless, it is interesting to notice how close his position on this issue is to Ockham's.[26] Again we see that at the heart of Suárez' doctrine there is a strong emphasis on the activity of the mind. He insists that the unity of the universal is not a real, extramental unity but a rational unity, a unity imposed by the mind. But it would be quite wrong to conclude that there is little more than Ockhamism in his doctrine. Suárez thought minds are no more at liberty to impose whatever they will on external reality than they are to distinguish existence and essence without some basis or grounding for the distinction. Universal words are not names that refer to independent entities in the world, but acts of minds have an ontological grounding in the structure of external reality; once more in Suárez we meet the concept *cum fundamento in re*.[27] In his discussion of universals Suárez often appeals to Aquinas, picking out for special attention Aquinas' insistence on the creativity of minds to the possible neglect of other elements in his thought. In the game whose rules had been drawn up by Scotus, Thomism can be made to look very much like Ockhamism.

Suarezian individuals, then, are composites of form and matter that contain in their unity their own principles of individuality. They can be known directly by the mind, and the mind accounts for what they share with each other by imposing on them its conceptual scheme, its acts of universalisation. But its doing so has a ground in reality although not in the existence of distinct, real things, i.e., extramental universals. Some have

24. '... adaequatum individuationis principium esse hanc materiam et hanc formam inter se unitas, inter quae praecipuum principium est forma, quae sola sufficit, ut hoc compositum, quatenus est individuum talis speciei, idem numero censeatur'. 5, 6, 15; vol. I, p. 186.
25. See, e.g., Bergmann 1964.
26. His position is worked out in Dist. 6; vol. I, pp. 201–50. See especially sections 5 and 6; pp. 222–8.
27. 'Universalitas est per intellectum cum fúndamento in re.' 6, 5, 1; vol. I, p. 222.

said that Suárez gives the mind too much to do, so that he runs the danger, if he does not indeed succumb to it, of letting the mind have such a creative function that its hold on external reality is weakened if not lost entirely. This is the burden of the complaint by some Thomists (whose best known modern representative is Gilson) that Suárez is a philosopher of essence not existence, that in contrast with Aquinas he is left with an 'essentialist' metaphysics.[28]

Suárez on creation

The distinction between essence and existence, it was noted, was the result of an attempt to provide a philosophical understanding of what is involved in the theological doctrine of creation. This doctrine requires that, while it is in God's nature necessarily to exist, created things exist contingently in dependence on God's creative action. Furthermore, in his act of creation God must not be thought to work with any kind of raw material and, therefore, to bring about a kind of change in individual things. Creating differs from making. Geach has expressed this difference succinctly in the following way.[29] When we mean to say that God (or anybody, A) makes something, what we say can be expressed in the form

M — ($\exists$x) (A brought it about that x is an F)

To say however that something is created is to say

C — (Not M) and (A brought it about that ($\exists$x) (x is an F))

Thomists maintain that their doctrine meets the principles expressed in this analysis completely. Suarezians would deny that Suárez' doctrine of existing essences causes him the theological embarrassment of having provided God with uncreated material to work with in creation or the philosophical embarrassment of a proliferation of odd entities. A Thomistic critic would maintain that if Suarezians insist that the actualised essence is just as contingent and dependent on God's creative act as the Thomist's created individual, they only push the difficulty back.[30]

What is at issue in this dispute can be usefully illuminated by making some more modern comparisons. Suárez certainly insists that no created being exists necessarily. We can think of essences abstracted from their existence, but in actuality essence and existence cannot exist separately. Indeed, for Suárez such a supposition makes no sense. Just as it is absurd to suppose that essence without existence would leave some existing thing as a

28. Gilson 1952, pp. 96–120.
29. Geach 1969, pp. 75–85.
30. Gilson 1952, p. 104.

remainder, so it is absurd to suppose that before God brought it about that there was this particular actually existing essence there was some part of it; in denying the real distinction Suárez supposed that he was denying that such part-whole talk makes sense. Nevertheless, one can *think* of essence in abstraction from its existence.

Suárez on possibility and reality

This brings us back to another important Suarezian distinction. Suárez maintains that we can talk about being in two different ways, distinguished, he claims, by the use of a noun (*esse*) and the use of a participle (*ens*). The use of the noun signifies what has a genuine essence whether it actually exists or not; the use of the participle indicates the act of existence, and by it we understand that the thing in question actually exists.[31] Moreover, corresponding to this distinction between two ways to talk about being, Suárez distinguishes two senses of the term 'real'. It can mean 'capable of existing in the real world', i.e., possibly producible by a cause; something real in this sense has 'objective potential being', which in turn means that we can think of its possibly existing. The second sense of 'real', which Suárez calls its 'proper' sense, is 'actually existing in the real world'.[32] All this talk of worlds and the real world, actual beings and possible beings reminds one of Leibniz, who was after all a great admirer of Suárez. It also reminds one of Leibniz' modern followers who use the language of set theory to talk about necessity, contingency, and possibility. It is no accident that some of these tools can easily be made to work with Suárez' ideas.

We can think of a possible world as an overall state of affairs, the way things can be or could have been. Obviously, things are and have been a certain way, but they could have been different. There will be individual beings that exist in the various possible worlds, some in all, others only in some possible worlds. Suárez would maintain that God exists in all possible worlds but Francisco Suárez, for instance, only in some. These beings have properties in the various worlds, and the properties they have in the various worlds may of course be described by propositions. In distinguishing his two senses of 'being', Suárez points out that a real essence signified by the noun *'esse'* is something that may not but could exist in the real world. By

31. Suárez 1965, 2, 4, 9; vol. I, p. 90.
32. 31, 2, 1; vol. II, p. 229. Also 31, 2, 10; vol. II, p. 232.

this he means to rule out two possibilities. First, a real essence must be something that can be coherently thought; 'the round square', 'the thing that both is F and is not F' cannot designate real essences. So the idea of possibility utilised in his concept of objective potential being must, first of all, mean what is in a broad sense logically possible; the round square exists in no possible world. Secondly, Suárez means to rule out pure flights of fancy. According to Suárez, fictional characters have no sort of being, not even possible being,[33] and things like the chimera are not possible beings. Because certain properties are essential to the nature of what we call goats, no goat can have a lion's head and a serpent's tail; therefore, no such things can be truly said to exist in any possible world.

Real essences exist in possible worlds, but obviously not all of them exist in the actual world. We can clearly think of objects that are describable in logically coherent ways, are not fictional characters, are of such a nature that they could exist in the actual world; but they do not. Do they yet have some kind of being or reality? Such things are real in the sense of 'having objective potential being', not in the sense of 'actually existing in the real world'. But this is too quick, Suárez' critic will say. Surely everything that exists in a possible world exists, is real, in that world; the so-called actual world, which we may designate W^+, is only one element in the set of worlds W. Why should we give such prominence to one member of the set? For any world, W, to say 'This individual x exists in W' is tantamount to saying 'X actually exists in W'; to say 'x exists in W^+', therefore, is to say 'x actually exists in W^+'. How does this give any preferred status to W^+, which we have chosen to call the 'actual world'? It looks as if

(A) This is the actual world

is logically equivalent to

(B) This world is this world.

Plantinga's response to this kind of objection is very much to the point in discussing Suárez. Plantinga argues that the objector's conclusion is based on a mistake. B is obviously tautologically true; but if A means 'W^+ is the actual world', it is contingently true.[34] This is exactly Suárez' point; God has chosen to make this world the actual world, and there's an end on't. Why he chose to create what he chose to create we shall never know and is none of our business. As a matter of contingent fact he created the actual world.

---

33. 31, 2, 2; vol. II, p. 229. Cf. Plantinga 1974, pp. 153–63.
34. Plantinga 1974, pp. 49–51.

The concept of natural law in late scholasticism

Both Suárez himself and also the other philosophers of the scholastic revival are probably better known for their contributions to theories of natural law than for their metaphysics. It has often been thought that their doctrines of natural law developed in a more and more secularistic direction, culminating in Grotius' famous comment that the natural law would still hold and oblige us even if God did not exist. But it is anachronistic to read this sort of secularisation into Grotius, and those who do so often show no awareness of the context of Grotius' remark or, indeed, of exactly what he wrote. He certainly thought God required things and forbade others because they were in and of themselves right or wrong, and he also thought it makes no sense to say that God can change the natural law; but he tells us that the speculation that, even if God did not exist, the natural law would hold cannot be considered without the most profane wickedness (*quod sine summo scelere dari nequit*)[35] – hardly the remark of a secular moralist. Later natural-law theorists may seriously have tried to secularise the theory; in the period under consideration here the changes in natural-law theory were different. In fact, they directly parallel the changes we have noted in the philosophy of language and in metaphysics. Again we see the influence of Scotus, Ockham, and the Ockhamist tradition on people who were at some pains to refute Ockhamism, and we see the shift of interest from order in external nature to an internal order in the minds of rational beings. And it can also be claimed that few if any of the raw materials of this philosophy of law and morals were original. Indeed, in the thought of Thomas Aquinas (and in that of his followers down to the present) there has always been a certain tension between the extent to which the precepts of natural law are seen to be read off the order of external nature and the extent to which minds are illuminated in an Augustinian fashion to know them. The complex and difficult doctrine of *synderesis* is adequate testimony to this tension. What happens in the period under consideration is that the illumination theme tends to assume ever greater prominence at the expense of confidence in finding the precepts of natural law in an external order.

Richard Hooker on natural law

Of course, not everyone moved so far so quickly, and within the period itself we can see this tension working itself out. A good place to start is with

---

35. Grotius 1853, Prolegomena.

Richard Hooker. Hooker is in many ways a typical product of the northern scholastic revival. He has often been regarded as a transitional figure,
and so he is; but in comparison with others I shall consider shortly, like
Suárez, Holdsworth, and Grotius, he is a man who is constantly looking
back over his shoulder. To put it in his own language, we can say that he
would prefer to inquire 'into the causes of goodness' (by which he means
Aristotelian *aitiai*), but 'this present age full of tongue and weak of brain'
forces us to settle for second best.[36] There is a theological as well as a
philosophical presupposition behind this. Hooker was explicitly reacting
against the doctrines of English Calvinists, who held a low view of the
possibilities for natural knowledge and whom C. S. Lewis aptly characterised as Barthians.[37] Luther was little better help; he thought our minds
had capacities sufficient only for recognising that we were sinners and
needed salvation. Melanchthon, who was an Aristotelian and in many
ways a kind of precursor to the later Aristotelian revival, was unable to
improve on this gloomy diagnosis by much. It is the theological problem
of the consequences of the Fall for human knowledge that sets the task for
later protestant defenders of natural law and provides the context of
Hooker's revival of natural law. What can the human mind know of law
and morals on its own without God's grace and revelation? He thinks we
should (in principle) be able to have something like an Aristotelian science
of morals, but it is uncertain how far he actually thought a demonstrative
science of morals a real possibility. He is content to argue that certain
general (mostly formal) principles of natural law are self-evidently known
to us. Otherwise we must go by 'signs and tokens to know good'.[38] As for
these signs and tokens, Hooker lays great stress on what he calls the
'universal consent of men',[39] that these Laws of Reason are generally
known – 'the world hath always been acquainted with them'.[40] In a later
age defenders of kinds of natural-law doctrine commonly appealed to the
supposed fact that all men agreed about certain obligations and prohibitions, while opponents thought the discovery of apparent exceptions
constituted a refutation of such claims. Hooker, however, certainly did not
appeal to any nose-count, nor can one imagine him with a tally-board
recording responses to questionnaires. Indeed, he hedges his appeal to

36. Hooker 1977, I, viii, 2.
37. Lewis 1954, p. 449.
38. Hooker 1977, I, viii, 3.
39. *Ibid.*
40. I, viii, 9.

universality with a number of crucial qualifications. Children, innocents, and madmen get no vote;[41] indeed, it is those 'having natural perfection of wit and ripeness of judgement' who are to be listened to.[42] It is those who comprehend the principles of natural law by the light of natural understanding, Melancthon's *lumen naturale* and Aquinas' *synderesis*.

Hooker, however, has no truck with voluntarism; 'They err therefore who think that of the will of God to do this or that there is no reason besides his will.'[43] We may not know the reason for the precepts of natural law, but we are to be assured that there is one; God in his unsearchable counsel knows the right and rational order of things, knows it to be good, and consequently wills accordingly.

Suárez and Vásquez on natural law

The problem I have introduced was at the heart of the controversy between Suárez and one of his countrymen, Vásquez, who like Hooker had a hankering for an independently knowable external order. Vásquez maintained that the natural law is identical with rational nature, by which he meant that good acts are those that conform to the ideal nature of human beings and bad acts are those that violate it. This nature is objectively knowable and constitutes the foundation of all law and morals.[44] Suárez objected that all this is false to the meaning of the term 'law'. Law in itself is a matter of will, and Suárez defines 'law' as 'an act of a just and right will by which a superior wills to oblige his inferiors to do this or that'.[45] Will, therefore, is essential to the meaning of 'law', which definition identifies Suárez' doctrine with the tradition of medieval voluntarism. But the divine will is not the sole basis of morality. Will is essential to law, but God's will attaches to what is intrinsically good and his prohibitions to what is intrinsically bad in the nature of things. Gregory of Rimini had held that the natural law is not prescriptive but demonstrative of the order of things; Ockham (as Suárez interprets him) had held that good is simply what God wills and God is free to attach his will to anything that can be consistently described. Suárez aims at avoiding both extremes. Will is essential to the concept of law, but God's will is not arbitrary; He wills what is in the nature of things good.

41. I, vii, 4.
42. I, viii, 9.
43. I, ii, 5.
44. Vásquez 1620, disp. 150, 3; cf. q. 94, ar. 2 and q. 94, ar. 5.
45. Suárez 1944, I, 5, 24, '... actum voluntatis iustae et rectae, quo superior vult inferiorem obligare ad hoc, vel illud faciendum.'

In support of this *via media* Suárez offers an important, influential argument. Aristotle contends in the *Ethics* (1107^a8-27) that some actions or passions do not admit of an extreme; they are described by names that in and of themselves imply badness. Aristotle's examples are spite, envy, shamelessness, adultery, theft, murder. If an action or passion is truly described in one of these ways, there can be no debate about when, where, how to perform the action or indulge the passion; it has already been condemned in the description. Suárez attributes the same doctrine to a wide variety of authors including the Ockhamist, Gabriel Biel.[46] In fact, Ockham himself gave a certain prominence to this Aristotelian argument.[47]

Richard Holdsworth on natural law

An author who gives this argument a central significance in his doctrine of natural law is Richard Holdsworth, a seventeenth-century English theologian. Holdsworth was very influential in his own time but has since been almost entirely forgotten.[48] Holdsworth was very much a product of the scholastic revival, and although he was not only an Anglican but associated with the Puritans, he readily acknowledged his debt to Suárez and other scholastics. He went to some pains to try to explicate and use the scholastic notion of *synderesis*, but he was unsatisfied either with an appeal to our supposed awareness of an external order or with any sort of intuitionist claim that we all really know in our hearts what is right and wrong. Rather he appeals to Aristotle's argument and adds that anyone who can understand a description expressed in terms of one of Aristotle's 'bad names' must (assuming him to be in his right mind) be embarrassed and insulted. Thus to call a person a perjurer, he claims, is to describe his actions in such a way that the description is as good as an insult. Anyone truly so described is properly insulted (or corrected, or brought to repentance). Here we see the basis of natural law sought in a kind of linguistic fact, the fact that certain concepts not only describe acts but imply a condemnation of anyone whose doings can be truthfully described by them. As Holdsworth puts it, this is in effect the voice of nature itself pronouncing judgement on one who does these things (*Natura ipsa clamat quod malum sit, Naturae Lex*

---

46. Suárez 1944, II, vi, 11.
47. William Ockham 1495–6, III, 12, d. 16; cf. McGrade 1964, p. 190, and Trentman 1978, pp. 29–39.
48. See, e.g., Curtis 1959, and Hill 1965. Holdsworth's lectures were edited and put out by his nephew after the restoration (Holdsworth 1661).

arguit.)[49] What this means, according to Holdsworth, is that natural law is founded in the nature of things, but not in any natural order we can readily observe around us; rather it is found in what he calls 'integral nature', an ideal order, which has only left us its traces.[50] These traces are to be found in language, in concepts that all rational beings share whatever their national languages. In this way natural law is an expression of the community of language users, which of course presupposes that all human beings as such share certain concepts. This sharing constitutes a community that in principle unites all human beings and provides them with a rather tenuous link with integral nature; here, in Holdsworth's terminology, we find the *vestigia* of ideal order.

Natural law and the order of nature

What has become of the external order of nature? Hooker, for all his qualifications, still felt confident enough to assert '. . . God being the author of Nature, her voice is but his instrument. By her from Him we receive whatsoever in such sort we learn.'[51] The new scholasticism as represented by such thinkers as Suárez and Holdsworth had far more in common with another contemporary, John Donne, whose well-known lines express his feeling about the effect of 'new philosophy':

> 'Tis all in pieces, all coherence gone;
> All just supply, and all Relation.[52]

In the response of the new scholastics to a picture of the world from which all coherence was gone we see the themes I have been stressing come together. As I have noted, Suárez, following the Ockhamist tradition, insisted that will is essential to the concept of law. Likewise Holdsworth rejects what he calls the traditional jurists' definition of natural law – that natural law is what Nature teaches all living beings. First, he insists that natural law is essentially about prescriptions for human beings; secondly, he is sceptical about Nature's directly teaching anything. We need our reasons, expressed in our linguistic competence and use, to reflect an ideal,

---

49. Holdsworth 1661, lect. xxviii, pp. 247–8. It might be noted that it would be both anachronistic and too crude to interpret this in terms of analyticity or, worse, some vague idea of what is 'true by definition'; it is the nature of the acts in question that requires necessary connections in our thought.
50. Holdsworth 1661, p. 246.
51. Hooker 1977, I, viii, 3.
52. 'The First Anniversarie' in John T. Shawcross (ed.), *The Complete Poetry of John Donne*, New York University Press, 1968, p. 278.

divinely ordered order to make sense of any kind of lawfulness.[53] Incidentally, it should be obvious that the natural-law doctrines of these authors do no violence to the principle of the autonomy of ethics understood as the rule that ethical conclusions cannot be derived from admittedly non-ethical premisses.[54] Indeed, they insist that the right ordering of rational wills is at the heart of the definition of law.

This account of the scholastic revival has in a way come full circle in that we find the doctrine of natural law rooted in an internal order to be found in what is innate in all minds. What is innate is an ordered conceptual scheme shared by all rational beings, and this idea is explicated in terms of the 'Cartesian' doctrines in the philosophy of language, inherited from the logicians and speculative grammarians of the Middle Ages.

Hugo Grotius on natural law

As a final example of the new scholastic doctrine of natural law, we can turn to Grotius. Much that he says in the Prolegomena to his *De jure belli et pacis* sounds very like the theories of Suárez and Holdsworth I have just discussed. The idea of natural law or natural right is based not on general ideas of order in nature but on an analysis of human nature. Human beings naturally desire to live in society. This is no news; everybody in the scholastic tradition would have agreed with Plato and Aristotle about this. Grotius accounts for it, however, by appealing to the fact that language-use is a differentia of human beings, and society is based on linguistic community. Furthermore, Grotius' arguments about the species-specific characteristics of language use are almost identical to Descartes'.[55] One can see that the raw materials for the new scholasticism were all very old. It was the proportion, the emphasis, that was new, but this produced a distinctively different-looking result, a result that looks much more like what we call early modern philosophy.

The survival of scholasticism in the universities

Obviously the transition from medieval to modern philosophy was neither so smooth nor so evident as this may suggest. First, at least some Aristotelian texts continued to hold a prominent place in the curriculum for a very long time. How seriously they were taken and how they were

53. Holdsworth 1661, pp. 239–40.
54. Cf. a similar point made about Aquinas in Donagan 1969.
55. Grotius 1660; cf. Descartes, René (1897 & 1913). *Discours de la méthode* in Charles Adam and Paul Tannery, *Oeuvres de Descartes*, vol. VI, Cerf, pp. 56–9.

read and studied we shall soon consider. Secondly, many of the formalities of medieval scholastic university training – the lecture, the disputation, other scholastic acts or exercises – continued to be observed, at least after a fashion, until quite recent times; indeed, their traces are obviously still with us. Thirdly, the works of medieval philosophers continued to be printed and came out in new editions. Fourthly, and most important, despite superficial continuities, the most influential and most read scholastic works in the seventeenth century and thereafter were not Aristotelian texts, nor the works of medieval scholastics, but the new textbooks. They were the main vehicle for transmitting scholasticism to the succeeding centuries. This may be a cause for lament, since what was criticised as medieval scholastic doctrine may often have been a demonstrably garbled account by a seventeenth-century textbook-writer.

Little need here be said about the continuation of Aristotelian texts in university curricula. The texts prescribed tended often to be Aristotle's scientific works rather than what we should call the philosophical works, although the *Nicomachean Ethics* turns up with some frequency in lists of prescribed books. Whether the logical works do or do not appear depended perhaps on the degree to which the institution prescribing the books had been influenced by Ramism. Aristotle's philosophical works were rarely allowed to speak for themselves, however. In most lists of prescribed books or directions for students drawn up in the seventeenth century Aristotelian works are accompanied by some of the new textbooks to 'explain' them. One suspects that while lip service was given to Aristotle for a long time, it was the explanations by textbook-writers that were read.

The continued reprinting of works by medieval scholastic authors poses a similar problem. Even leaving out of account reprints in Roman Catholic countries, where the influence of the commitments of religious orders was instrumental, the number of new editions and reprints throughout the seventeenth and into the eighteenth century is astounding. Who read these books? They generally do not appear in reading-lists for students. Of course, they were available in university libraries, and we know from catalogues of personal libraries that they were evidently bought by individual scholars. Yet they seem not to have influenced them very much. One example might help to make this point. Ockham's *Summa logicae* appeared in a new printing in Oxford in 1675,[56] but it is very hard to find any evidence that the book found perceptive readers who made much of its

---

56. Printed by O. Walker, Oxford.

contents. Formal logic was in a dreary state; Sanderson, perhaps the best of a bad lot, gives only a very superficial treatment of supposition theory.[57] Furthermore, there is little trace in the period of the medieval theory of consequences; the formal logic is once again syllogistic, not infrequently garbled. What then did people make of the medieval texts that kept coming out in new editions? Very little, it seems. They were too busy reading the new textbooks.

The shift from scholastic commentaries to modern treatises

Where medieval philosophers had commonly worked out their doctrine in the course of commentaries, either on the works of Aristotle or on the *Sentences* of Peter Lombard, the scholastics of the early seventeenth century took to writing systematic treatises on their own. Suárez' *Disputationes metaphysicae* was a prominent example of the new style, a work that aimed at a systematic treatment of the subject, full of references to other philosophers, to be sure, but organised according to its author's view of a methodical, systematic presentation of the subject rather than as a commentary on what others had written. The *Disputationes metaphysicae* hardly looks like a text for beginners, but the systematic style could easily be used both for general and purportedly exhaustive treatments of a subject and for introductions aimed at beginning students. One of the most popular writers of such textbooks in northern Europe was Franco Burgersdijck, who produced texts on every branch of philosophy which were very widely read in the seventeenth century. Another such person was Bartholomew Keckermann. It was authors like these who were most widely read and who represented scholasticism to most people in the seventeenth and eighteenth centuries. Unfortunately, not only were they not very original, they did not always understand or adequately transmit the doctrine they had inherited from the Middle Ages.

The best way to get an impression of what in fact was being read in the universities of the seventeenth and early eighteenth centuries is to examine a guide for students. An excellent one for our purposes is the *Directions for a Student in the Universitie* by Richard Holdsworth.[58] We know that the

---

57. Sanderson 1640.
58. Holdsworth, Richard (1648?), *Directions for a Student in the Universitie*, Emmanuel College (Cambridge) MS 48; reprinted in H. F. Fletcher, *The Intellectual Development of John Milton*, 1961, University of Illinois Press, vol. II, pp. 623–55. Cf. Bodleian MS Rawlinson D200; in a forthcoming paper I argue that its ascription of the work to John Merryweather is mistaken. Trentman, J. A. 'The Authorship of the Seventeenth-century Cambridge *Directions for a Student in the Universitie*', *Transactions of the Cambridge Bibliographical Society*.

Directions not only represents university education during its author's lifetime but also for at least fifty years after his death. When Josiah Barnes (1654–1712), Regius Professor of Greek in Cambridge University from 1695 until his death, wrote his own directions and advice to students,[59] in the middle of it he copied out the whole of Holdsworth's *Directions* as giving the essence of what he had to say. What Holdsworth prescribed was clearly still being followed or at least urged sixty years later.

It is interesting to note how similar in certain general principles and presuppositions the *Directions* is to the Jesuit *Ratio Studiorum* of 1599. Both show the influence of humanism in their emphasis on the study of ancient languages and, further, their emphasis on writing and speaking 'good' Latin, i.e., the Latin of Cicero and Quintilian. With this a wide range of Greek and Latin literature is prescribed. And, of course, both include much moral and religious counsel. For both, however, the study of philosophy is rooted firmly in scholastic Aristotelianism. Holdsworth supposes that the serious student will read all of Aristotle (in Greek, of course) and all of both of Aquinas' *Summae*, but what is much more interesting is how he thinks these things should be read and where his real emphasis lies. Concerning philosophical controversies (the successors of the medieval disputations), which are to be a primary concern of the third year of university study, Holdsworth writes, 'The reading of Aristotle, will not only conduce much to your study of Controversy, being read with a Comentator, but all so help you in Greeke, & indeed crown all your other learning, for he can hardly deserve the name of a Scholar, that is not in some measure acquainted with his works.'[60] The important phrase here is 'being read with a Comentator', and much more space is given in the *Directions* to the commentators than to Aristotle and medieval scholastics put together. It is useful here simply to note who some of these authors were. In logic Burgersdijck is most highly praised, but we are directed also to Brierwood, Eustachius, Smiglesius, the Complutenses and the Conimbricenses, Crakanthorpe, Keckermann, Molinaeus, and Sanderson.[61] In ethics Burgersdijck again, Golius,

---

59. Emmanuel College (Cambridge) ms 179.
60. Holdsworth 1648 (?), p. 33.
61. Brerewood (Brierwood) 1614 and 1628. Eustachius (a Sancto Paulo) (1609), *Summa philosophiae quadripartita*, Paris. Smiglesius: Smiglecki 1634. Complutenses: the Carmelite professors of the University of Alcalá (formerly Complutum) published a *Cursus Artium* there in 1624; the author of the Logic was Diego de Jesus. Conimbricenses: a similar group-venture produced by the Jesuit professors at the university of Coimbra in Portugal; they wrote a variety of commentaries and a *Cursus philosophicus*. Crakanthorpe 1622, Keckermann, Bartholomew (1613), *Systema Systematum*, Hanover. Molinaeus: du Moulin, Pierre (1603), *Elementa logica*, Antwerp, Sanderson 1640.

Eustachius, Morisanus;[62] in metaphysics Scheibler, Fonseca, Eustachius, Suárez, 'or the like'.[63] These were the authors that both students and teachers of philosophy read. And there is abundant evidence that the spirit and even many of the details of the *Ratio studiorum* and Holdsworth's *Directions* were widely characteristic of university training in western Europe into the eighteenth century. The pity is that scholasticism was not represented in the universities either by the best medieval philosophers or even very often by the more interesting late scholastics. Indeed, Holdsworth himself wrote more interesting things than many of the authors he recommends to students.[64] Instead scholasticism was transmitted to later generations by philosophical hacks like Burgersdijck and Keckermann or ill-tempered clerics like Crakanthorpe. It is little wonder that real scholastic insights were misunderstood and that Aristotelian scholasticism was often 'refuted' by *ignoratio elenchi*.

62. Burgersdijck, Franco (1623), *Idea Morali Philosophiae*, Leyden. Golius, Theophilus (1631), *Epitome doctrinae moralis*, Argentorati (i.e. Strasbourg). Eustachius 1609. Morisanus: Morisan, Bernard (1625), *Commentarii et disputationes in libros logicos, physicos, et ethicos Aristotelis*, Frankfort.
63. Scheibler, Christoph (1628), *Philosophia compendiosa*, Oxford. Fonseca, Petrus da (1577), *Commentariorum . . . in libros metaphysicorum Aristotelis*, Rome. Eustachius 1609. Suárez 1965.
64. Holdsworth was, however, very reluctant to see his writings published. The only thing to come out in his lifetime was his sermon 'The Valley of Vision', which was printed as a pamphlet after, he says, he was three times begged to allow its distribution. It appeared in more permanent form shortly after his death in Holdsworth, Richard (1651), *The Valley of Vision*, London.

46
NEOSCHOLASTICISM

Intellectual and religious reaction to the French Revolution

The upheaval of the French Revolution destroyed many academic and ecclesiastical organisations belonging to the old order, but a reaction was not slow in coming. As Sainte-Beuve noticed in 1854, the number of *Le Moniteur* for Easter Sunday 1802, which published news of the Peace of Amiens and of the Concordat between Napoleon and the Pope, also published a review of a recent book: *Le Génie du Christianisme*, by Chateaubriand (1768–1848). An appeal to tradition against the excesses that had followed from rationalism found romantic expression in Chateaubriand's book, but the concept of tradition was to receive a more philosophical cast from others – De Maistre (1763–1852), De Bonald (1754–1840), and Lamennais (1782–1854). All three had idiosyncratic views on the role of language, and the opposition they provoked influenced the form taken by the revival of scholasticism. Writing in 1809, De Maistre claimed that the content of language depends upon the life and customs of those who use it; it eludes arbitrary enactments; it was not invented by men, nor can its diversity be attributed to human means.[1] For De Bonald, the disagreements of philosophers oblige us to seek for moral science what physical sciences have already: a fixed point, a criterion of truth, something that will be public, readily accessible, and evident. He believed this to be 'the primordial and indispensable gift of language, bestowed upon the human race'. Reason and experience in individuals need the setting and tradition of society, and of the language it hands on, to reach truths that go beyond particular facts.[2] Lamennais is the best known of the three, and drew political conclusions of a very different sort, but he too gives a special place to society and to language. The eccentricities of individual reason are to be corrected by the beliefs that are held by the human race as a whole, for these traditions – 'common sense', as he calls

---

1. De Maistre 1844, §§XLVII–LVII.
2. De Bonald 1830, I, pp. 57f.

them – go back to the truths primordially bestowed by God, bestowed along with the gift of language.[3] His political conclusions were of a theocratic and 'democratic' character, threatened the relations established between Church and State after the Napoleonic wars, and were one cause of his condemnation by Rome in 1832 and 1834.[4]

The condemnation of Lamennais

In so far as the intervention by Rome had any philosophical motivation, it was the novelty of what Lamennais wrote that caused offence,[5] for there was little official interest at Rome in philosophical matters. The teaching of it to ecclesiastics at the Jesuit Collegio Romano was not based upon any one tradition or authority.[6] A good part of the course there then seems to have been devoted to mathematics and science;[7] indeed, a pupil at the Collegio Romano in 1830 wrote afterwards that the only tenet held by all was a contempt for Aristotle.[8]

The condemnation of Lamennais was taken by some at Rome as an encouragement to return to the scholastics, but a statement[9] from one teaching philosophy there shows that the matter was regarded with tempered enthusiasm. Lamennais and others, it said, had attacked the rationalism of Descartes; but such attacks are rarely mortal, and Cartesianism has much to offer. And if not Cartesianism, why not the scholastic philosophy on which Descartes built his own? The Church has endured through the ages, and does not need novelties in speculation.

The disciplining of Bautain

The opinions of Lamennais were not the only novelty of which the writer disapproved. He goes on to mention someone else whose opinions were to be opposed by the neoscholastic revival: Louis Bautain (1796–1867). Bautain had attacked the scholastic method in philosophy, and had made

---

3. Lamennais 1819, cc. xiii, xx.
4. *DS*, 2730f.; *DB* 1617f.; for contemporary comment by a journal we shall meet again, see *JHL* 1; the political consequences of Lamennais' opinions are reprobated in Boyer 1835. (*DS* is *Enchiridion symbolorum ... quod primum edidit Henricus Denzinger et quod funditus retractavit ... Adolfus Schönmetzer S. I. DS* gives extracts from ecclesiastical documents, with ample bibliographical information. First edited by Denzinger in the nineteenth century, it was repeatedly revised; the revision by Schönmetzer changed the numbering of the paragraphs found in the earlier standard edition by Bannwart (*DB*). *JHL* is *Journal historique et littéraire*.)
5. *DS* 2732.
6. Dmowski 1836, p. 511, in a passage about Lamennais.
7. *JHL* 1: 197, part of a general account of studies at Rome.
8. Cited by Pelzer 1911, p. 251.
9. Anonymous 1834.

both the validity of arguments in favour of religious belief and the acceptance of miracles depend upon faith. Denounced by his bishop, he went to
Rome in 1838 to present his case.[10] While recording the indifference at
Rome to philosophy as such, he also shows that it was felt there that too
severe a condemnation of his fideistic views would be invoked in favour of
yet another school of thought – theologians in Germany sympathetic to
Georg Hermes (1775–1831), who had been condemned in 1835.[11]
Hermes, trying to come to terms with Kant's philosophy, would have
theology begin with a sceptical doubt about everything – including religion – and then recover the tenets of Christianity by an adaptation of
Kantian techniques of argument. The disfavour shown by Rome towards
what was seen as rationalism mitigated its reaction to Bautain, when he had
to sign a formula in 1844.[12] Disapproval of Bautain, and of the other
philosophical innovations, did at least imply a preference for older ways of
thought, and the disapproval was eventually to strengthen the hands of
those who wished to revive them.

Victor Cousin

Meanwhile, however, interest in the older ways was being shown in purely
secular contexts. Victor Cousin (1792–1867) was the best known if not the
most skilful pioneer of the history of medieval philosophy,[13] and this
discipline was, eventually, to exercise the most important influence of all
on the neoscholastic revival.

Early nineteenth-century Thomism

Among the places that had preserved a teaching of scholastic philosophy
was, not surprisingly, Spain, and the Catalan Cardinal Boxadors had issued
a letter in 1757 demanding that St Thomas Aquinas be studied. One of
those who followed the lead which Boxadors had given was another
Catalan, the Jesuit B. Masdeu. When the Society was expelled from Spain
in 1767, Masdeu and others went to Italy. From 1799 to 1806 he taught at
Piacenza, in the Collegio Alberoni, and among the pupils he converted to
Thomism was V. Buzzetti (1777–1824), who was dissatisfied with the
teaching he had been receiving there – Condillac had lived at Parma, and

10. His Roman Journal, in Poupard 1964, is in my opinion a minor literary masterpiece.
11. *DS* 2738f.
12. *DS* 2756f.; Poupard 1964 and 1961 give a careful estimate of its force and setting.
13. In works such as Cousin 1836 and 1838.

his philosophy was popular in that part of Italy.[14] At all events, Buzzetti himself taught Thomism at Piacenza to some who were to carry it to Rome and (eventually) to favour there. Among these were Domenico and Serafino Sordi, who both became Jesuits, and played a part in the curious mixture of intrigue and politics that followed. During his novitiate in the Society, Serafino handed on the doctrine to Luigi Taparelli d'Azeglio (1793–1862) who in 1824 became the Rector of the newly-restored Collegio Romano. We have already seen what variety of philosophical teaching obtained there. Taparelli was grieved by this, and recruited a group of students to whom, under pledge of secrecy, he imparted the teaching he had himself received.[15] One thing at least is clear: all those involved in the affair touched up their memoirs in later years so as to read back as much Thomism into their old selves as possible. Why, we shall soon see; for the present, we can notice that one of the pupils so initiated was Gioacchino Pecci, the future Leo XIII (1878–1903). Among the Jesuits themselves, there was much opposition to the revival of scholasticism, and Taparelli and one of the Sordi brothers were removed, first to Naples, then to Sicily.[16] The revolution of 1848 changed the balance of opinion at Rome: the upheaval seemed a consequence of modern thought, and some new instrument was needed for the defence of the Church. At the insistence of the new Pope (Pius IX, 1846–1878), the Jesuits founded the periodical *Civiltà Cattolica*; its editorial board was dominated by those who favoured a return to scholasticism,[17] and from 1850 onwards the periodical was advocating it as part of a more general policy of militant ultramontanism.

The neoscholasticism of Joseph Kleutgen

The victory of ultramontanism still lay in the future. There existed a variety of philosophical opinions in Roman Catholic institutions, and some were to shape the development of neoscholasticism by the debates and disagreements they caused. In Germany, for instance, Hermes had

---

14. In giving this account, I have followed Pelzer 1911, Batllori 1944, and Jacquin 1943. On Boxadors, see also Tusquets 1923, and for an anthology of early neoscholastic writing in Italy, see Dezza 1942–4. For other works, not seen by me (especially Masnovo's investigations), see the exhaustive Rossi 1959, who himself minimises the influence of Masdeu, on grounds that Scholastic philosophy had never been wholly neglected in Piacenza.
15. I follow here the works cited in n. 14 above, and notice that the footnotes in Jacquin 1943 are valuable for their lengthy extracts from sources not easily available.
16. For Pelzer 1911, the reasons were philosophical; Jacquin 1943, c. 3, gives evidence that administrative difficulties also played a part.
17. Jacquin 1943, c. 5.

been followed by Günther (1783–1863) and Frohschammer (1821–93), who went to Hegel and Fichte respectively for categories in which traditional doctrines might be expressed. Their condemnations at Rome[18] are associated with polemical activities by one of the first Germans to join the cause of neoscholasticism, Joseph Kleutgen (1811–83). Kleutgen came to scholastic philosophy only as an afterthought. Strongly opposed to all forms of idealism, he wrote a defence of traditional theology against it; but Günther's attacks on the scholastic method as such led to his defending the older philosophy as well in a much-translated book.[19] Kleutgen had come to live in Rome in the 1840s as a teacher of rhetoric, and his profession shows in the crusading style of his book – a precedent that was to be widely followed. In one sense, he does what Lamennais had done: he appeals to tradition. But the tradition is one of approved philosophical speculation in the Church, and to this believers must return;[20] tradition in the sense that Lamennais and others had used – the socially transmitted and primaevally linguistic embodiment of knowledge – he rejects, just as he rejects the fideism of Bautain and the rationalism of the Germans. For Kleutgen, what matters most is a defence of objectivity in knowledge against idealism, and the first half of his book is entirely concerned with epistemology. His preoccupations made him see the scholastic revival in a way that many would see it after him: a rejection of idealism, a rational vindication of elements in religious belief, a call to return to a neglected but enduring heritage. These preoccupations made him, just as they were to make others, insensitive to values in what he was opposing: the creative function of the understanding, the relation of arguments about religion to the setting of religious belief, the role of language and of social instruction, the historical setting of philosophical speculation.

Cartesian scholasticism

Another (French) tradition tended to neglect those same issues. A readily accessible source, Renan's *Souvenirs*, shows us something of this tradition in Renan's own time as a student. At Tréguier, the clergy at the college he attended in the 1830s distrusted Chateaubriand, just as the Sulpician priests at the seminary at Issy distrusted Lamennais.[21] At Issy, the college for

---

18. 1857 and 1862; *DS* 2828f. and 2850f.
19. Kleutgen 1860; see also Lakner 1933.
20. 1860, Einleitung §1.
21. Renan 1975: III, i, p. 106; IV, i, p. 142; IV, ii, p. 155. Boyer, cited earlier as opposing Lamennais, was superior at Issy; Renan writes of his contact with Rome at IV, i, p. 142.

philosophy, various traditions of speculative thought were represented,[22] but the textbook was scholastic and in Latin. However, the scholasticism taught was not 'the barbarous and childish scholasticism of the thirteenth century, but what might be called cartesian scholasticism, that modified form of cartesianism which was widely adopted for ecclesiastical instruction and set down in three volumes known as the *Philosophie de Lyon*'.[23] It was this modified cartesianism that was to be the greatest obstacle to the neoscholastic revival, and yet was to have so great an effect on it. In the first place, it took for granted Descartes' starting-point in philosophy: by reflection and criticism, the individual was to scrutinise in himself what purported to be knowledge, and to discern the genuine from the spurious. The neoscholastics were to oppose the cartesians and others in the name of a revived medieval philosophy, but their starting-point was to be the same. A full return to the Middle Ages would have called it in question, but the neoscholastics did not do this; indeed, their rejection of theories that gave pride of place to language and to society confirmed them in their cartesianism.

That they were so confirmed, they showed by sharing the belief of contemporaries that medieval logic was unworthy of serious notice. For Renan, the vocabulary of medieval scholasticism was barbarous and childish; an ecclesiastical writer of the time on philosophy could deplore the Middle Ages, when 'the sacred sciences were held in the harsh bondage of dialectic';[24] and the Jesuit we saw opposing Taparelli could list 'Barbara Celarent' along with alchemy as among the absurdities that a revival of scholasticism would bring.[25] That neoscholastics thought much the same can be seen from the flood of textbooks that started in the 1860s: whatever else in them constitutes a revival, the section on logic does not. Indeed, the editor of one of the first (it was a translation of a seventeenth-century book) defends his printing of obsolete scientific opinions, but concedes that late medieval logic had become over-subtle,[26] and a similar remark about over-subtlety is about the only qualification to the praises of Aquinas in a Letter of Leo XIII.[27]

22. Renan 1975: IV, ii, p. 157.
23. '... non la scolastique du XIIIe siècle, barbare et enfantine, mais ce qu'on peut appeler la scolastique cartésienne, c'est-à-dire ce cartésianisme mitigé qui fut adopté en général pour l'enseignement ecclésiastique, au XVIIIe siècle, et fixé dans les trois volumes connus sous le nom de *Philosophie de Lyon*' (Renan 1975: IV, ii, p. 156).
24. Ferrari 1833, p. XVII.
25. Jacquin 1943, p. 295, n. 150.
26. Goudin 1864, p. xvii.
27. *DS* 3140.

Ontologism

There was a third school of thought which neoscholasticism opposed, and which left its mark thereby upon the revival. Its defenders were largely in Belgium, at the University of Louvain.[28] To understand it, we must realise that 'cartesian scholasticism' of the kind taught to Renan regarded itself as the heir to a tradition going back to Plato. Augustine had reformed Platonism according to Christian belief, and had spoken of God as the illuminating sun of knowledge, making all else to be understood.[29] In medieval times, the tradition had been represented by Bonaventure; the innate ideas of Descartes, and even more Malebranche's vision of all things in God, were in the same line of thought, making our understanding depend upon divine enlightenment.[30] At Louvain, G. C. Ubaghs and others combined this 'Augustinian' tradition with that emphasis upon language and upon the social transmission of knowledge that we saw held earlier in the century. Under the influence of the Italian philosopher Gioberti (1802–53), then exiled to Brussels for republicanism, they saw his 'ontologism' as a continuation of Augustine's view.[31] An intuition of God is the base of all further knowledge, and divine illumination gives knowledge its necessity.[32] In controversy with neoscholastics, Ubaghs used medieval sources then being made available to show the variety of opinion permitted in medieval times, and to suggest that a dangerous tendency to empiricism lay in Aristotelian elements in the opinions of Aquinas about knowledge.[33] It is this point, rather than the quasi-religious terminology of the debate, that was important for the development of neoscholasticism. Precisely because the ontologists appealed to the 'Augustinian' strain in traditional theories of knowledge, neoscholastics like Liberatore stressed whatever in Aquinas was distinct from it.[34] Conceptual thinking was explained by them in terms of an 'abstraction' that did not do justice to the 'illuminating' or active nature of such thinking.[35]

28. A good account of this Louvain school is in Henry 1924; apart from the primary sources to be quoted, the *JHL* and the *Revue Catholique* have an abundance of material from the 1840s to the 1860s.
29. A favourite text was *Soliloquia*, I 8; *PL* 32: 877.
30. For a statement of this belief, see Branchereau 1855, iii.
31. Labis, 1845.
32. Ubaghs 1860.
33. Ubaghs 1861; see also Fabre 1862 and Claessens 1860.
34. Liberatore 1855.
35. A comment on the debate from an English admirer of Branchereau is Meynell 1866. For Meynell's use of Branchereau, see letters of his in 1869 to Newman, who sought his criticism when writing the *Grammar of Assent*, Newman 1961–, XXIV: 306, 353.

The victory of neoscholasticism

If neoscholasticism was affected by its disagreement with all these other schools of thought, the disagreement itself was solved by political rather than by philosophical means. The advance of ultramontane opinions favoured the adoption of a uniform system of philosophy throughout the Church.[36] A further pragmatic and extraneous consideration was that Aquinas was used in theology, and that his technical terms there are unintelligible without some instruction in his philosophy.[37] In Goudin 1851, the editor's introduction contains personal reminiscence to this effect. In all this, the ambiguity latent in the revival from the start becomes palpable: neoscholasticism is rationally preferable; it must be, because the preference has been part of Catholic tradition. That the revival bore the marks of recent debates, and shared quite unmedieval presuppositions and preferences with its opponents, was beyond the grasp or concern of many who were promoting it. There was something especially paradoxical in reviving a philosophy conspicuous for its attention to language, while at the same time discounting the role of language.[38] But the battle with ontologism was canonically over by the late 1860s, although Rome was slower to move than the *Civiltà Cattolica*. By then, supposedly ontologist theses had been condemned as tending to pantheism and irrationalism,[39] but even the Vatican Council of 1870 did not commit itself to specific philosophical positions.[40] Matters changed when, in 1878, Leo XIII succeeded Pius IX. As a student in Rome, he had had scholasticism imparted to him in secret at the Collegio Romano; as Nuncio in Brussels in the 1840s, he had seen the beginning of the debates over ontologism; as Archbishop of Perugia from 1846, he had (with his ex-Jesuit brother) enforced its teaching there; as Pope, one of his first Encyclical letters was a call for the philosophy of Aquinas to be taught and honoured throughout the Roman Church. Aquinas has gathered together and increased the wisdom of all earlier teaching: 'he has refuted by himself the errors of preceding times, and has

---

36. Ramière 1861 uses this argument among others (pp. 10–12, 40–3); see also Ventura 1861, vol. i, pp. cxv, 618–19; on the preposterous Padre Ventura, and on much else, see the valuable Foucher 1955.
37. Ramière 1861, pp. 21–3.
38. See, e.g., Ramière 1861, p. 84.
39. DS 2841; ASS 3 : 204–24; further details in Henry 1924, p. 135f. (ASS is the *Acta Sanctae Sedis in compendium opportune redacta*, which was succeeded in 1909 by the *Acta Apostolicae Sedis* as the official journal for Roman documents and decrees.)
40. DS 3000f.

provided invincible weapons for the refutation of errors that were to be ever springing up in days to come.'[41]

Neoscholastic attention to medieval philosophy

It is fair to say that the circumstances of the victory of neoscholasticism brought out its most conspicuous defect: the lack of a sense of history. The need to place all human utterances in their cultural and temporal setting had not been felt in the Middle Ages as it was being felt in the nineteenth century; yet the patronage accorded to the revival was accorded by a Church which found it difficult to place its own doctrines in that way, and for which the elaborate vocabulary and distinctions of scholasticism seemed to offer a way out. A neglect of the role of history in theology both confirmed and was confirmed by an analogous neglect in philosophy. Neoscholasticism took its first step towards maturity only when it began a dispassionate examination of just what medieval philosophy had been, and an inventory of just what had survived of it. One scholar to be mentioned here links this study of history with an institute that played a special part in the neoscholastic revival: Maurice De Wulf (1867–1947), who from 1894 to 1939 held the Chair of The History of Medieval Philosophy at the Institut Supérieur de Philosophie at Louvain. Leo XIII, aware of the popularity that ontologism had enjoyed at that university, wanted a chair of Thomistic philosophy there. The first holder was D. Mercier (1851–1926), whose foresight and determination eventually secured the founding in 1890 of the Institute as a place for graduate studies.[42] Among this generation of historians, M. Grabmann (1875–1959) contributed more than anyone else to the discovery and editing of previously unknown texts.[43] Of the results achieved by these and by others, none was more important than the display of the sheer *variety* in medieval philosophy – a variety not only in opinions and interests, but in the *genres* of philosophical and theological writing then.[44] We can measure the advance made by the

41. The text of the letter – in the drafting of which Kleutgen is said to have played a part – is in *ASS* 12: 97–115; extracts are in *DS* 3135f., where omissions have given it an air of reasonableness. Reactions to it in England are given in Holmes 1975; for its eventual effect on philosophical teaching in a seminary there, see Milburn 1964, pp. 302–6.
42. An entertaining and well-documented account of the politics of the matter is in De Raeymaeker 1951; Tambuyser 1958, gives details of its complicated pre-history. Judicious estimates of Mercier's own philosophical work are in De Raeymaeker 1952, and in Van Riet 1946, p. 134f. De Wulf's example and influence were of the highest order; for an affectionate and perceptive account, see Van Steenberghen 1948.
43. Schmaus 1959 shows just how monumental his achievements were.
44. For examples of how work done here could affect estimates by neoscholastics of their own past, see Moreau 1951, in a volume dedicated to De Ghellinck.

history of medieval philosophy if we take a theme already mentioned – the balance in it between the 'Augustinian' and 'Aristotelian' traditions – and look back to the state of affairs at the turn of the century. At that time pressure from Leo XIII[45] obliged the editors of Bonaventure to claim his identity in thought with Aquinas; and at that time a history like Picavet's (1905), defending the interesting thesis that the clue to the scholastics lay in an understanding of Plotinus, exhibited the exaggerations of a pioneering book. Since those days, a debate in works by Gilson[46] and Van Steenberghen[47] has successively explored and appraised the diversity of elements in the thought of the thirteenth century; the synthesis in Van Steenberghen 1966 has the strength it has because of the long tradition on which it builds. The study of the history of medieval philosophy has changed the concept of what a scholastic revival might be.

Neoscholasticism in relation to the philosophy and science of its own time

But if historical work showed medieval philosophy to be varied and complex, and to have been occupied with its own particular range of philosophical problems, it thereby pointed to the need for neoscholasticism to consider the philosophical questions of its own day. The need was most readily met in epistemology, concerning which, as we have seen, the neoscholastics shared presuppositions of their contemporaries. If epistemological questions come again to be put where they are now out of fashion, the sheer quantity and variety of answers offered will prove useful.[48] Things were very different for any kind of philosophy of nature, for medieval questions here seemed bound up with so much that had been abandoned. The very obviousness of the difficulty has led to a multiplicity of answers. Some have been as much historical as philosophical. At the beginning of this century, Duhem had shown continuities between the 'new sciences' and what had gone before, and his example has been followed. A work like Maier 1949 can be seen as doing for Galileo what Gilson 1912 did for Descartes: showing, without compromising his place in a long history, just how much he was part of that history. Philosophical answers have not always been as successful. One has been to separate the findings of modern science from natural philosophy, and to make the latter

45. *ASS* 31:264–7.
46. 1936, 1955, 1961a.
47. 1930, 1955, 1966.
48. Van Riet 1946 is a lucid and wide-ranging account, which also throws light on other interests of neoscholasticism.

alone concerned with the ultimate principles of things. For Maritain, physical science of our day is concerned only that the final results of its calculations should coincide with measurements made, and, unlike philosophy, is not concerned with the inner ontological nature of reality.[49] The view goes back to the early neoscholastic Zigliara, for whom metaphysics decides on the essence of bodies, while physics touches only their 'threshold'.[50] For obvious reasons, it has remained popular with theologians. Other neoscholastics have taken a more serious view of modern science, and have submitted that medieval developments of Aristotle can do it justice in a way that mechanistic philosophy, with its reduction of all things to extension and motion, cannot. An adversary such as 'mechanistic science' is not only vague, but – modern science being what it is – can be little more than a straw man. However, this claim too goes back to the early days of the revival.[51] It is difficult to see how the conceptual distinctions of medieval Aristotelianism can be combined with experimental evidence expressed in terms of modern science. Thus, a scholastic adversary of Hoenen holds that chemistry shows him to be wrong in claiming that elements in a compound remain 'virtually, not formally'; they rather remain 'formally, but without a new form of the compound'.[52] How the matter could conceivably be settled, and what contribution by what discipline would effect the settlement, is not investigated by either party,

Metaphysics in neoscholasticism

We saw that Kleutgen had argued against Kant as against other idealists, and later neoscholastics such as Mercier devoted attention to him.[53] It was, however, in the work of J. Maréchal (1878–1944) that neoscholasticism tried most elaborately to come to terms with the challenge of the critical philosophy. In a series of 'Cahiers' from 1922, he examined theories of knowledge, and in particular the Kantian position.[54] His contention was that, by beginning where Kant did, and by analysing what was involved in

49. Maritain 1959, p. 60.
50. Zigliara 1876, vol. 2, p. 81.
51. Cornoldi 1893 is an English version of a work of 1864. The classic exposition of this claim, supported with a massive background of science and history, is Hoenen 1945, part of which is in English as Hoenen 1967.
52. Moran 1951, pp. 413–36, who gives references to Hoenen; the passages in Hoenen 1945 are nn. 308–10, referring to nn. 275, 291.
53. Van Riet 1946, p. 177.
54. Maréchal 1926.

that starting-point, we can regain the metaphysics that Kant had banished from the speculative intellect. Maréchal was influenced by Blondel (1861–1949), whose philosophical speculations were based on analyses of human action and of the implications of its needs.[55] This attempt to begin with a theory of understanding and to end with metaphysics has found much support among German neoscholastics, of whom the best known is probably the theologian, Karl Rahner – indeed, for Rahner, the 'transcendental method', as it is called, is the legitimate heir to what was neoscholasticism.[56] Bernard Lonergan writes in this general tradition: his work of 1957 will be admired for its aphorisms and phenomenological descriptions even when its remoter purposes fail to win assent, or comprehension. Earlier articles assembled in Lonergan 1968 should be consulted (despite their plethora of undiscriminated references to the text of Aquinas) for an elaborate account and appraisal of what Aquinas says about conceptual thinking and for comparisons with the views of other scholastics.

Some neoscholastic contributions worthy of note have dealt with the notion of *esse* ('existence', approximately) in Aquinas.[57] Gilson and Fabro, for instance, seek to vindicate for the speculations of Aquinas, and in particular for what he says about God, a distinctive role for *esse*, a role that, they claim, has been obscured by his successors. The philosophical part of their claim raises questions that have been answered in different senses by two writers on Aquinas outside the neoscholastic tradition. For Geach the account of *esse* in what Aquinas writes about God in his mature works is coherent, while for Kenny it is not.[58] I am not concerned with the merits of their disagreement, but I point out that they are agreed about the kind of argument to be used; that the arguments they do use – often with close reference to the text of Aquinas – are not of the sort found in Fabro or Gilson.[59] What causes the gap here – and, of course, not only here – between two types of attention to Aquinas? Are we faced with a consequence of the lack of interest in logic shown by neoscholastics? Certainly,

55. See, e.g., Blondel 1893.
56. Foreword to Muck 1968. Well-written examples of what this tradition is attempting, and of its contact with other schools, are the essays in Lotz 1955.
57. Gilson 1952a is a well-known example, while Fabro 1939, Geiger 1942, and Fabro 1960, combine the investigation with an account of those elements in the thought of Aquinas that are concerned with the relation of participation in creatures towards God.
58. Geach 1961; Kenny 1969.
59. Geach has expressed elsewhere (1972, pp. 263–5) dissent from arguments employed by Gilson.

the lack is worthy of note, and we should also note that the exceptions themselves are odd.

Logic in neoscholasticism

It is the rambling and at times ridiculous Sanseverino who shows an acquaintance with the then recent controversy of De Morgan with Hamilton, and who speaks with respect of Stoic logic, citing Diogenes Laertius and Sextus Empiricus.[60] And, by a strange turn of history, the chief logical influences of neoscholasticism in a broad sense came through two men who had broken with the Roman Church: Franz Brentano (1838–1917) and Anton Marty (1847–1914). Brentano was above all a student of Aristotle, but he had also studied medieval philosophy under Clemens, a friend of Kleutgen.[61] His philosophical influence in Poland was to have important results. Twardowski was impressed with 'scholastic' elements in Brentano's philosophy, such as an insistence on clear definitions and on logical rigour. He passed on these standards to his pupil Łukasiewicz, who had attended, but had not valued, lectures at the Institut Supérieur at Louvain.[62] This zeal for exactness of statement was found in Marty's writings by Leśniewski, another logician from Poland.[63] And indeed Marty sets a similar goal for philosophy, and gives logic and grammar a place in it that is thoroughly 'scholastic', but which no neoscholastic had given them.[64] The influence of Łukasiewicz on the study of ancient and medieval logic is notorious: it is worth recalling the deviousness of the route by which it all started.

Methodological obscurity

Nonetheless, I see this lack of interest in logic as only part of a more general weakness in neoscholasticism, which I would describe as a lack of *methodological* clarity, already noticed when considering neoscholastic approaches to natural science. The growth of the new sciences is more than a juxtaposition of new questions with old; it calls for an account of the old questions that will show them to be still worth asking.[65] We can go for

---

60. Sanseverino 1862, I, vol. 2, cap. 2, art. IX; cap. 3, art. IV.
61. Biographical and critical material is in McAlister 1976; Brentano 1968 gives an interesting appreciation of Aquinas (written in 1908), with remarks on neoscholasticism.
62. Sobociński 1956, pp. 3f.
63. Kotarbiński 1967.
64. See Marty 1908, dedicated to Brentano.
65. McMullin 1963, which contains an exchange between a neoscholastic and an analytic philosopher, shows an awareness of how real the difficulty is.

another example of the difficulty to a topic already met – the scholastic account of conceptual thinking. It has an elaborate terminology of 'active intellect', 'passive intellect', 'phantasm', 'illumination', 'abstraction', and the rest. That we have metaphors here need be no demerit in so fundamental a matter. But what check has been made upon the growth of the metaphor? How far does each term have an independent sense? What are we supposed to be *doing* in drawing the distinctions? Too often, qualifying words like 'metaphysical' or significantly untranslatable terms like *'entia quibus'* have been used to block questions that needed putting, here as in the metaphysical speculations on *'esse'*. Methodological obscurity can be said to go with a lack of attention to logic and language, for a greater attention might at least have brought out the varied functions of words, and the impossibility of getting a satisfactory semantics by simply making all words 'mean things', and then affixing deterrent labels to the things meant. Philosophy can err in the matter of self-examination by defect as well as by excess.

Neoscholasticism's loss of distinctiveness

These obscurities have lost the significance they once had, because neoscholasticism is no longer the distinctive body of thought it once was. One reason for this development lies in the Roman Church. From the turn of the century, it has been trying to face the relationship between doctrine and history, and neoscholasticism proved of little assistance in the modernist crisis of the early 1900s.[66] Further dissent, especially since 1945, found expression in the Second Vatican Council, where philosophical pluralism was acknowledged.[67] Another reason has been the absorption of neoscholastic activities into the general stream of philosophy. The extent of the absorption can be seen by an inspection of periodicals over the years,[68] or by surveying the unrivalled 'Chroniques' in the *Revue Philosophique de Louvain*. The Institut Supérieur itself has seen a shift of interest towards Husserl, whose *Nachlass* is deposited there.[69] And, as its 'Centre De Wulf-Mansion', research goes on into medieval logic among other things.[70] The entry of the neoscholastic revival into the general course of philosophy can

66. I have argued this in FitzPatrick 1973.
67. Baldanza 1970; McInerny 1966 illustrates the problems this has created.
68. On them, and on other activities among neoscholastics, ample information is to be found in De Raeymaeker 1947.
69. On which, see Van Breda 1971; on the division of the University in 1970, see *Revue Philosophique de Louvain* 69:164, and later 'Chroniques'.
70. See, e.g., the commemorative articles of 1977 in *Revue Philosophique de Louvain* 75.

be seen in this *History* itself. It would hardly have been written if the revival had not taken place, but it reflects many interests that would not have been stressed by those who, from a mixture of motives, worked a century and more ago for a revived scholasticism. That it can reflect those interests is a tribute to the rich diversity of what was being revived.

BIOGRAPHIES

BIOGRAPHICAL INFORMATION ON MEDIEVAL AUTHORS

These very concise presentations of biographical information are intended solely as a convenience for readers of this volume. They cannot replace the biographies in such standard reference works as *The New Catholic Encyclopedia*, *The Encyclopedia of Philosophy*, or *The Dictionary of Scientific Biography*. Only the more prominent medieval Latin authors who belong to the period specifically covered by this *History* are included here, and only so much of their careers and writings as is directly pertinent to the purposes of the *History* is presented. For most medieval authors very little biographical information of any kind is available. We have tried in general to provide at least the following information: the author's name (along with well-known or confusing variants); dates (or the death date, or the *floruit*); texts of the author's works (editions whenever possible, manuscripts when necessary); secondary literature (a selection chosen with a view to guiding the reader to other articles and books on the author and his work).

ADAM WODEHAM (Wodham, Wodam, Godam)
BIOGRAPHICAL DATA: b. *ca.* 1298; d. 1358.
TEXTS: *Quaestiones in libros Sententiarum* (1512). Editio media, ed. Henry of Oyta, published by John Major, Paris; Prologue to Ockham's *Summa logicae*, *q. v.*; *Tractatus de indivisibilibus*: MS Flor. Bibl. Naz. Conv. Soppr. A III 508 ff. 135ra–147rb; MS Flor. Bibl. Naz. Conv. Soppr. B VII ff. 133^r–143^r.
SECONDARY LITERATURE: Courtenay, William J. (1978). *Adam Wodeham: An Introduction to His Life and Writings*, E. J. Brill; Murdoch, John and Edward Synan (1966). 'On the Composition of Continua', *Franciscan Studies* 26:267–88.

AENEAS SYLVIUS (Pope Pius II)
BIOGRAPHICAL DATA: b. 1405; d. 1464.
TEXTS: *De ortu et auctoritate imperii romani* (1446); *De iurisdictione, auctoritate et preaeeminentia imperiali* (1566), ed. S. Schard, Basle.

ALAN OF LILLE (Alanus ab Insulis)
BIOGRAPHICAL DATA: d. 1203.
TEXTS: *De planctu naturae*, PL 210; *The Complaint of Nature* (1908), D.M. Moffat (tr.) (Yale Studies in English, XXXVI), H. Holt.
SECONDARY LITERATURE: D'Alverny, M. T. (1965). *Alain de Lille: Textes inédits*, J. Vrin.

ALBERT THE GREAT (Albertus Magnus, Albert of Cologne)
BIOGRAPHICAL DATA: b. *ca.* 1200; d. 1280. Joined Dominican order 1223 while studying at Padua. Lector of theology in Germany, 1220s to 1230s. Sent to Paris, 1240s. Master of Sacred Theology, 1245. Taught at Cologne, 1249, where Thomas Aquinas was one of his students. Paraphrased or commented on most of Aristotle's works, 1250s to 1260s.
TEXTS: *Opera omnia* (1651), ed. P. Jammy (21 vols.), Lyon; *Opera omnia* (1890–9), ed. A. Borgnet (38 vols.), Vivès; *Opera omnia* (1951–), ed. Bernard Geyer *et al.*, Aschendorff.

SECONDARY LITERATURE: Catania, Francis J. (1959). 'A Bibliography of St. Albert the Great', *The Modern Schoolman* 37:11–28; Houde, R. (1961). 'A Bibliography of Albert the Great: Some Addenda', *The Modern Schoolman* 39:61–4; Meersemann, G. G. (1931). *Introductio in Opera Omnia B. Alberti Magni*, Bruges, Beyaert; Pelster, Franz (1920). *Kritische Studien zum Leben und zu den Schriften Alberts des Grossen*, Stimmen der Zeit; Schooyans, M. (1961). 'Bibliographie philosophique de S. Albert le Grand (1931–1960)', *Revista da Universidade Católica de São Paolo* 21:36–88; Schwertner, T. M. (1932). *St Albert the Great*, Marquette University; Weisheipl, J. A., ed. (1980). *Albertus Magnus and the Sciences*, Pontifical Institute of Mediaeval Studies.

ALBERT OF SAXONY (Albertus Parvus, Albertutius, Albertus de Saxonia)

BIOGRAPHICAL DATA: d. 1390. Studied in Prague and Paris. Master of Arts at Paris, 1351. Taught in arts faculty at Paris, 1351–62. Helped to found University of Vienna, of which he became the first rector in 1365.

TEXTS: *Commentarius in Posteriora Aristotelis* (1497, 1522), Venice; *Expositio aurea et admodum utilis super artem veterem edita per venerabilem inceptorem fratrem Gullielmum de Ockham cum quaestionibus Alberti parvi de Saxonia* (1496), Bologna; *Perutilis Logica* (1518, 1522), Venice (Reprinted Olms 1974); *Quaestiones de caelo et mundo* (1520), Venice; *Quaestiones de generatione et corruptione* (1568), Paris; *Quaestiones totius libri Physicorum* (1518), Paris; *Sophismata* (1495, 1502), Paris (Reprinted Olms 1975).

SECONDARY LITERATURE: Boehner, Philotheus (1952). *Medieval Logic*, Manchester University Press; Clagett, Marshall (1959). *The Science of Mechanics in the Middle Ages*, University of Wisconsin Press; González, Atanasio (1958–9). 'The Theory of Assertoric Consequences in Albert of Saxony', *Franciscan Studies* 18:290–354 and 19:13–114; Heidingsfelder, Georg (1927). *Albert von Sachsen: Sein Lebensgang und sein Kommentar zur nikomachischen Ethik des Aristoteles* (*BGPM* XXII, 3–4), Aschendorff; Moody, E. A. (1970). 'Albert of Saxony', in *Dictionary of Scientific Biography*.

ALEXANDER OF HALES

BIOGRAPHICAL DATA: b. *ca.* 1185 in Gloucestershire; d. 1245. Studied and taught theology at Paris. His *Summa* is the earliest philosophical contribution by a Franciscan and one of the earliest medieval works to be based on full knowledge of the Aristotelian *corpus* and the Arabic commentators.

TEXTS: *Summa theologica* (1924–48), Collegium S. Bonaventurae; *Glossa in quatuor libros sententiarum* (1951–7), Collegium S. Bonaventurae.

SECONDARY LITERATURE: Gössmann, Elisabeth (1964). *Metaphysik und Heilsgeschichte: eine theologische Untersuchung der Summa Halensis*, Hueber.

ANDRÉ DE NEUFCHÂTEAU (Andreas de Novo Castro)

BIOGRAPHICAL DATA: fl. *ca.* 1360.

TEXTS: *In primum librum Sententiarum* (1514), Paris. Parts translated into French in Hubert Elie (1937), *Le Complexe significabile*, J. Vrin; pp. 83–138.

SECONDARY LITERATURE: Elie, Hubert (1937). 'André de Neufchâteau, dit "Le docteur très ingénieux", Étude bio-bibliographique', in his *Le Complexe significabile*, J. Vrin; pp. 225–52.

ANSELM OF CANTERBURY (Anselmus Beccensis)

BIOGRAPHICAL DATA: b. *ca.* 1033; d. 1109.

TEXTS: *Sancti Anselmi Opera Omnia* (1938–61), ed. F. S. Schmitt, Nelson (Reprinted Stuttgart, Frommann 1968); Schmitt, F. S. (1936). 'Ein neues unvollendetes Werk des hl.

Anselm von Canterbury' (*BGPM* XXXIII, 3), Aschendorff; Schmitt, F. S. and R. W. Southern (1969). *Memorials of St Anselm*, British Academy.
SECONDARY LITERATURE: Henry, D. P. (1964). *The De Grammatico of St Anselm* (Publications in Medieval Studies, 18), University of Notre Dame Press; Henry, D. P. (1967). *The Logic of Saint Anselm*, Clarendon Press; Henry, D. P. (1974). *Commentary on 'De Grammatico'* (Synthese Historical Library, 8), Reidel; Hopkins, Jasper (1972). *A Companion to the Study of St Anselm*, University of Minnesota Press; Hopkins, Jasper and H. Richardson (1974–6). *Anselm of Canterbury* (4 vols.), Edwin Mellen.

AUGUSTINUS TRIUMPHUS (Agostino Trionfo; of Ancona)

BIOGRAPHICAL DATA: b. *ca.* 1270/3; d. 1328. Augustinian Order of Hermits. Studied at Paris 1297–1300; lectured on *Sentences* there 1302–4 or 1304–6. Lector in the Augustinian School at Padua; returned to Paris as Master of Theology 1313–15. Chaplain to Charles, son of King Robert of Naples, in 1322.
TEXTS: *Summa de potestate ecclesiastica* (1582, 1583, 1584, 1585), Rome; *Tractatus brevis de duplici potestate prelatorum et laicorum* (1903), ed. R. Scholz (Kirchenrechtliche Abhandlungen, 6–8), Enke.
SECONDARY LITERATURE: McCready, William D. (1974). 'The Problem of the empire in Augustinus Triumphus and late medieval papal hierocratic theory', *Traditio* 30:325–49; McCready, William D. (1977). 'The papal sovereign in the ecclesiology of Augustinus Triumphus', *Medieval Studies* 39:117–205; Ministeri, B. (1953). *De Vita et Operibus Augustini de Ancona O.E.S.A.* (†1328); Wilks, Michael (1963). *The Problem of Sovereignty in the Later Middle Ages: The Papal Monarchy with Augustinus Triumphus and the Publicists* (Cambridge Studies in Medieval Life and Thought, New Series 9), Cambridge University Press.

BALDUS DE UBALDIS

BIOGRAPHICAL DATA: b. *ca.* 1320; d. 1400. Roman lawyer and canonist who taught at Bologna, Perugia, Pisa, Florence, Padua, and Pavia.
TEXTS: *Consilia* (1608–9), Venice; *L'opera di Baldo nel V centenario della morte del grande giureconsulto (1900–1)* ed. I. Tarducci (Annali dell' Università di Perugia, Facoltà di Giurisprudenza, 10–11), University of Perugia Press.
SECONDARY LITERATURE: Horn, Norbert (1968). *Aequitas in den Lehren des Balduis* Böhlau; Lange, Hermann (1973). *Die Consilien des Baldus de Ubaldis († 1400)*, Verlag der Akademie der Wissenschaften und der Literatur (Mainz).

BARTHOLOMEW KECKERMAN

BIOGRAPHICAL DATA: b. 1571; d. 1609. Student at Wittenberg, Leipzig, and Heidelberg. Taught at Heidelberg and Danzig. Wrote and published widely in astronomy, physics, and mathematics, in addition to theology and philosophy.
TEXTS: *Opera Omnia* (1614), Geneva.
SECONDARY LITERATURE: Rose, Paul Lawrence (1973). 'Keckerman, Bartholomew' in *Dictionary of Scientific Biography*.

BARTOLUS OF SASSOFERRATO

BIOGRAPHICAL DATA: d. 1357.
TEXTS: *Opera omnia* (1588), Basle.
SECONDARY LITERATURE: C. N. S. Woolf (1913). *Bartolus of Sassoferrato*, Cambridge University Press; Calasso, F. (1964). 'Bartolo da Sassoferrato' in *Dizionario biografico degli italiani*, Istituto della Enciclopedia italiana, Società Grafica Romana; vol. 6, pp. 640–9.

BOETHIUS OF DACIA (Boethius Dacus)
BIOGRAPHICAL DATA: fl. 1275. Master of arts in Paris *ca.* 1270. Involved in the condemnation of 1277.
TEXTS: *Opera omnia* (1969–), in *Corpus Philosophorum Danicorum Medii Aevi,* ed. Jan Pinborg, Gad; *Godfrey of Fontaine's Abridgement of Boethius of Dacia's Modi Significandi* (1980), ed. and tr. A. Charlene Senape McDermott, Benjamins.
SECONDARY LITERATURE: Fioravanti, G. (1969–70). 'Scientia, fides, theologia in Boezio di Dacia', *Atti della Accademia delle scienze di Torino (Classe di scienze morale),* pp. 525–632; Pinborg, Jan (1974). 'Zur Philosophie des Boethius de Dacia. Ein Ueberblick', *Studia Mediewistyczne* 15:165–85.

BONAVENTURE (John of Fidanza)
BIOGRAPHICAL DATA: b. *ca.* 1217; d. 1274. Studied in Paris beginning 1234/5. Master of arts in Paris around 1243. Joined Franciscans 1243/4. Master of theology 1254/5. Elected minister general of Franciscans 1257. Active against radical Aristotelians (the so-called Latin Averroists) in Paris from 1260s until his death.
TEXTS: *Opera Omnia* (1882–1902), ed. Collegium S. Bonaventurae.
SECONDARY LITERATURE: Bougerol, J. Guy (1964). *Introduction to the Works of Bonaventure,* St Anthony Guild Press; Brady, I. (1975). 'The *Opera Omnia* of Saint Bonaventure Revisited', *Proceedings of the Seventh Centenary Celebration of the Death of Saint Bonaventure,* The Franciscan Institute; Quinn, J. F. (1973). *The Historical Constitution of St Bonaventure's Philosophy,* The Pontifical Institute of Mediaeval Studies.

BONSEMBIANTE BEDUARIUS OF PADUA
BIOGRAPHICAL DATA: b. 1332; d. 1389.
TEXTS: *Quattuor principia;* MSS Codex Latinus Monacensis 26. 711; Codex Vaticanus Latinus 981.
SECONDARY LITERATURE: Elie, Hubert (1937). *Le complexe significabile,* J. Vrin.

CAMPANUS OF NOVARA
BIOGRAPHICAL DATA: b. *ca.* 1205; d. 1296. Primarily a mathematician; cited by Roger Bacon in 1267 as excellent in mathematics. Probably a master at Paris or Bologna. Closely associated with Pope Urban IV (1261–64).
TEXTS: *Euclidis Megarensis mathematici clarissimi Elementorum geometricorum libri XV cum expositione Theonis in priores XIII a Bartholomaeo Veneto Latinitate donata, Campani in omnes et Hypsicles Alexandrini in duos postremos* (1546), Basle; *Theorica planetarum* (1971), ed. and tr. F. S. Benjamin and G. J. Toomer in *Campanus of Novara and Medieval Planetary Theory* (University of Wisconsin Publications in Medieval Science, 16), University of Wisconsin Press.
SECONDARY LITERATURE: Murdoch, John E. (1968). 'The Medieval Euclid: Salient Aspects of the Translations of the *Elements* by Adelard of Bath and Campanus of Novara', *Revue de Synthese* 89:67–94; Toomer, G. J. (1971). 'Campanus of Novara' in *Dictionary of Scientific Biography.*

DANTE ALIGHIERI
BIOGRAPHICAL DATA: b. 1265; d. 1321.
TEXTS: *De monarchia* (1963), ed. E. Moore and P. Toynbee in *Le Opere di Dante Alighieri* (5th edn.), Oxford University Press; *Dante Alighieri: Monarchia* (1965), ed. P. G. Ricci, Mondadori.
SECONDARY LITERATURE: Gilson, Étienne (1939). *Dante et la philosophie,* J. Vrin.

DOMINGO BÁÑEZ

BIOGRAPHICAL DATA: b. 1528; d. 1604. Joined Dominicans 1547. Studied under Melchior Cano at Salamanca. Taught at Salamanca, Avila, Alcalá, Valladolid. Advisor and confessor of St Teresa.

TEXTS: *Scholastica commentaria in primam partem Summae theologiae D. Thomae Aquinatis* (1934), ed. L. Urbuno, F.E.D.A. (Valencia); *Commentarium in libros De generatione et corruptione* (1585), Salamanca; *Institutiones minores dialecticae* (1590), Salamanca.

DOMINGO DE SOTO

BIOGRAPHICAL DATA: b. 1494/95; d. 1560. Studied at Paris. Returned to Spain, 1519. Entered Dominican order, 1525. Taught at Salamanca. Attended council of Trent, 1545. Confessor to Charles V.

TEXTS: *De iustitia et iure* (1553/54, 1556/57), Salamanca.

SECONDARY LITERATURE: Muñoz-Delgado, V. (1964). *Logica formal y filosofia en Domingo de Soto* (Publicaciones del Monasterio de Poyo, 16), Estudios de Madrid.

EDWARD BREREWOOD (Brierwood)

BIOGRAPHICAL DATA: b. *ca.* 1565; d. 1613. Studied at Brasenose College, Oxford. Professor of Astronomy at Gresham College, London.

TEXTS: *Commentarii in Ethica Aristotelis* (1640), Oxford; *Elementa logica* (1614), London; *Enquiries touching the Diversities of Languages and Religions Through the Chief Parts of the World* (1614), London; *Tractatus quidam logici de praedicabilibus et praedicamentis* (1628), Oxford.

FRANCISCO SUÁREZ

BIOGRAPHICAL DATA: b. 1548; d. 1617. Entered Society of Jesus in 1564. Studied canon law at Salamanca. Taught at Avila, Segovia, Valladolid, Rome, Alcalá, Salamanca, and Coimbra. His theological writings include a commentary on Aquinas' *Summa theologiae*.

TEXTS: *De bello* [= *De triplici virtute theologica*, tr. III, disp. XIII] (1954), ed. L. P. Vincente, Madrid Instituto Francisco de Vitoria; *De legibus* (1971–), ed. L. Perena *et al.* (Corpus Hispanorum de Pace, 11), Madrid Consejo Superior de Investigaciones Cientificas, Instituto Francisco de Vitoria; *On Formal and Universal Unity* (1964), J. F. Ross (tr.), Marquette University Press; *On the Various Kinds of Distinctions* (1947), C. Vollert (tr.), Marquette University Press; *Opera omnia* (1856–78), Vivés; *Disputationes metaphysicae* (Reprinted from *Opera omnia*, Olms 1965); *Selections from Three Works* (1944), G. W. Williams and James Brown Scott (ed. and tr.) (Classics of International Law, 20), Clarendon Press.

SECONDARY LITERATURE: Grabmann, Martin (1926). 'Die *Disputationes Metaphysicae* der Franz Suarez in ihrer methodischen Eigenart und Fortwirkung' in his *Mittelalterliches Geistesleben*, vol. 1, Hueber; Mahieu, L. (1921). *François Suarez, sa philosophie et les rapports qu'elle a avec sa théologie*, Desclée; Mugica, Plácido (1948). *Bibliografia suareciana*, Universidad de Granada; Wilenius, Reijo (1963). *The Social and Political Theory of Francisco Suárez* (Acta Philosophica Fennica, 15), Societas Philosophica Fennica.

FRANCISCO DE VITORIA

BIOGRAPHICAL DATA: b. 1483/86; d. 1546. Spanish theologian and jurist. Studied and taught in Paris around 1506–23. Held chair of philosophy at Salamanca from 1526.

TEXTS: *Relecciones teológicas* (1960), ed. T. Urdánoz, Biblioteca de Autores Cristianos; *Francisci de Victoria De Indis et De iure belli relectiones* (1917), ed. E. Nys, Carnegie Institution of Washington.

SECONDARY LITERATURE: Hamilton, Bernice (1963). *Political Thought in sixteenth-century Spain: A study of the Political Ideas of Vitoria, De Soto, Suárez, and Molina*, Clarendon Press.

FRANCO BURGERSDIJCK (Burgersdicius)
BIOGRAPHICAL DATA: b. 1590; d. 1629. Studied at the University of Leiden. Studied theology and taught at Samur. Professor of logic and moral philosophy (later also natural philosophy) at Leiden.
TEXTS: *Idea philosophiae moralis* (1623), Leiden; *Institutionum logicarum libri duo* (1626), Leiden; *Institutionum logicarum synopsis sive rudimenta logica* (1626), Leiden.

GABRIEL VÁSQUEZ
BIOGRAPHICAL DATA: b. *ca.* 1551; d. 1604. Entered Society of Jesus in 1569. Student at Alcalá. Taught at Alcalá, Ocaña, Madrid, Rome.
TEXTS: *Commentaria ac disputationes in primam partem S. Thomae* (1620), Antwerp; (1631), Lyon.
SECONDARY LITERATURE: Gilson, Étienne (1930). *Études sur le rôle de la pensée médiévale dans la formation du système cartésien*, J. Vrin; Maurer, Armand (1962). *Medieval Philosophy*, Random House.

GAETANO DI THIENE
BIOGRAPHICAL DATA: b. 1387; d. 1465. Taught at Padua and held the chair of logic there between 1422 and 1430.
TEXTS: *Complementum expositionis Messini de tribus praedicamentis* (1494), Venice; *Declaratio super tractatu Hentisberi Regularum* (1494), Venice; *De intensione et remissione formarum* (1491), Venice; *Expositio in libros De coelo et mundo* (1484), Venice; *Recollectae super Consequentias Strodi*; MS Venice, San Marco, lat. VI. 160, ff. 109^r–118^r; *Recollectae super octo libros Physicorum Aristotelis* (1496), Venice; *Recollectae super Sophismatibus Hentisberi* (1494), Venice.
SECONDARY LITERATURE: Clagett, Marshall (1959). *The Science of Mechanics in the Middle Ages*, University of Wisconsin Press; Valsanzibio, P. S. da (1948). *Vita e Dottrina di Gaetano di Thiene*, Scuola tipografica Madonna di Castelmonte; Wilson, Curtis (1956). *William Heytesbury: Medieval Logic and the Rise of Mathematical Physics*, University of Wisconsin Press.

GARLANDUS COMPOTISTA
BIOGRAPHICAL DATA: fl. 11th century. Native of Lorraine. Studied at one of the Liégian schools. Went to England under the reign of Harald I (1036–40). *Magister scholarum* at Besançon in 1084.
TEXTS: *Garlandus Compotista, Dialectica* (1959), ed. L. M. De Rijk, Van Gorcum.
SECONDARY LITERATURE: Henry, D. P. (1975). 'The Singular Syllogisms of Garlandus Compotista', *Revue internationale de philosophie*. 113:243–70; Stump, Eleonore (1980). 'Dialectic in the Eleventh and Twelfth Centuries: Garlandus Compotista', *History and Philosophy of Logic* 1:1–18.

GEOFFREY OF HASPHALL (Aspall)
BIOGRAPHICAL DATA: fl. 1270. Master and regent of arts in Paris before 1265. Prominent at Oxford around 1270. Wrote several commentaries on Aristotle's works.
TEXTS: *Quaestiones in Metaphysicam*, MS Cambridge Gonville and Caius College 509.
SECONDARY LITERATURE: Callus, D. A. (1943). 'The Introduction of Aristotelian

Learning to Oxford', *Proceedings of the British Academy* 29:229–81; Macrae, E. (1968). 'Geoffrey of Aspall's Commentaries on Aristotle', *Medieval and Renaissance Studies* 6:94–134; Pinborg, Jan (1979). 'The English Contribution to Logic Before Ockham', *Synthese* 40:19–42.

GERARD OF ODO (Guiral Ot, Geraldus Odonis)
BIOGRAPHICAL DATA: fl. *ca.* 1325, in Paris. Elected Franciscan minister general in 1329. As a result of criticism by John the Canon, he became known for his unorthodox views on the existence of a void and the composition of continua.
TEXTS: *In quatuor libros sententiarum*, MS Paris, BN lat. 3068; *De suppositionibus* (1975). ed. S. Brown, *Franciscan Studies* 35:5–44; *Expositio in Aristotelis Ethicam* (1482), Brescia.
SECONDARY LITERATURE: Bartolomé, L. (1928). *Fray Gerardo de Odón, Ministro General de la Orden Franciscana (1329–42)*, Tipografia San Francisco; Langlois, C. (1927). 'Guiral Ot (Geraldus Odonis), Frère mineur', *Histoire littéraire de la France* 36:203–25; Teetaert A. (1932). 'Ot, Guiral,' *Dictionnaire de théologie Catholique*, vol. 11, 1658–63; Walsh, J. (1975). 'Some Relationships Between Gerald Odo's and John Buridan's Commentaries on Aristotle's Ethics', *Franciscan Studies* 25:237–75.

GILES OF ROME (Aegidius Romanus, Egidius Colonna)
BIOGRAPHICAL DATA: b. *ca.* 1243–7 in Rome; d. 1316. Joined Hermits of St Augustine at age fourteen. Sent to Paris to study in 1260. Completed study of liberal arts, 1266. Studied theology, probably under Thomas Aquinas, 1269–72. Involved in the condemnation of 1277 and returned to Italy. Resumed teaching as master of theology at Paris 1285–91 and was the Augustinians' first regent master in theology. Elected General of his order in 1292.
TEXTS: *De ecclesiastica potestate* (1929), ed. R. Scholz, H. Boehlaus Nachfolger (Reprinted Aalen, Scientia Verlag 1961); *De medio in demonstratione potissima* (1976), ed. Jan Pinborg, *Miscellanea Medievalia* 10:254–68; *De regimine principum* (1502), Venice; (1607), Rome; *De renuntiatione papae* (1698), ed. J. T. Rocaberti, Bibliotheca maxima pontificia, Rome; *Theoremata de esse et essentia*, ed. E. Hocedez, Louvain, Museum Lessianum (1930). Also in *Theorems on Existence and Essence* (1952), M. V. Murray (tr.), Marquette University Press.
SECONDARY LITERATURE: Bruni, G. (1936). *Le Opere di Egidio Romano*, Olschki; Huebener, W. (1968). *Studien zur Theorie der kognitiven Repräsentation in der mittelalterlichen Philosophie*, unpublished Habilitationsschrift, Freie Universität, Berlin; Mandonnet, P. (1910). 'La carrière scolaire de Giles de Rome', *Revue des sciences philosophiques et théologiques* 4:480–99; Nash, P. (1967). 'Giles of Rome', *New Catholic Encyclopedia*.

GODFREY OF FONTAINES
BIOGRAPHICAL DATA: b. *ca.* 1250; d. 1306–9. Studied arts at Paris in the early 1270s. Studied theology under Henry of Ghent and Gervais of Mt St Elias at the Sorbonne beginning at least as early as 1274. Master in the theology faculty from 1285 to 1298–9 and again *ca.* 1303–4.
TEXTS: *Disputed Questions* 1, 7, 8, 13, 15, in Neumann, B. (1958), *Der Mensch und die himmlische Seligkeit nach der Lehre Gottfrieds von Fontaines*, Limburg, Lahn-Verlag, pp. 152–66; *Disputed Questions* 4 and 5, in Lottin, O. (1954), *Psychologie et morale au XIIᵉ et XIIIᵉ siècles*, Abbaye du Mont César, vol. 4, pt. 3, pp. 581–8 and 591–7; *Disputed Questions* 9, 10, and 12, in Wippel, J. F. (1973), 'Godfrey of Fontaines: Disputed Questions 9, 10, and 12', *Franciscan Studies* 33:351–72; *Disputed Question* 11, in Lottin, O. (1949), *Psychologie et morale au XIIᵉ et XIIIᵉ siècles*, Abbaye du Mont César, vol. 3, pt. 2, pp. 497–502; *Disputed Question* 15, in Koch, J. (1930), *Durandi de S. Porciano O. P. Tractatus de habitibus Quaestio Quarta* (Opuscula et Textus, Series scolastica, 8), Münster, Aschendorff, pp. 60–6; *Disputed*

Question 19, in Lottin, O. (1954) 'Les vertus morales acquises son-telles de vraies vertues?', *Recherches de Théologie ancienne et médiévale* 21 : 114–22; *Les Quodlibets*, in *Les Philosophes Belges*, l'Institut Supérieur de Philosophie de Louvain.
SECONDARY LITERATURE: Arway, R. J. (1962). 'A Half Century of Research on Godfrey of Fontaines', *The New Scholasticism* 36 : 192–218; Neumann, B. (1958). *Der Mensch und die himmlische Seligkeit nach der Lehre Gottfrieds von Fontaines*, Lahn-Verlag; Tihon, P. (1966). *Foi et théologie selon Godefroid de Fontaines*, Desclée de Brouwer; Wippel, J. F. (1967). 'Godfrey of Fontaines', *New Catholic Encyclopedia* 6 : 577–8; (1980). *The Metaphysical Thought of Godfrey of Fontaines; A Study in Late Thirteenth-Century Philosophy*, Catholic University of America Press.

GRATIAN OF BOLOGNA (Franciscus Gratianus)
BIOGRAPHICAL DATA: fl. 1140. Entered Camaldulian monastery in early life and wrote his compilation of canon law in the monastery of San Felice in Bologna. Generally considered the founder of the science of canon law.
TEXTS: *Concordia discordantium canonum* (1879), ed. A. Friedberg (*Corpus Juris Canonici*, 1), Tauchnitz.

GREGORY OF RIMINI (Gregorius Ariminensis)
BIOGRAPHICAL DATA: b. *ca.* 1300 at Rimini; d. 1358. Studied in Italy, at Paris (B.A. *ca.* 1323), and in England. Taught at Paris, Bologna, Padua, Perugia. Returned to Paris 1341–51. Taught at Rimini 1351–6. Elected prior general of the Augustinians 1357.
TEXTS: *Super primum et secundum Sententiarum* (1522), Venice (Reprinted, The Franciscan Institute 1955); *Lectura super primum et secundum Sententiarum* (1979–), ed. D. Trapp *et al.* (Spätmittelalter und Reformation, Texte und Untersuchungen, 9), De Gruyter.
SECONDARY LITERATURE: Elie, Hubert (1937). *Le Complexe significabile*, J. Vrin; Gál, Gedeon (1967). 'Gregory of Rimini', in *New Catholic Encyclopedia* 6 : 797; Leff, Gordon (1961). *Gregory of Rimini: Tradition and Innovation in Fourteenth Century Thought*, Manchester University Press; Nuchelmans, Gabriel (1973). *Theories of the Proposition: Ancient and Medieval Conceptions of the Bearers of Truth and Falsity* (North-Holland Linguistic Series, 8), North-Holland; Trapp, Damasus (1958). 'Gregory of Rimini: Manuscripts, Editions, and Additions' *Augustiniana* 8 : 425–43; Trapp, Damasus (1962). 'New Approaches to Gregory of Rimini', *Augustinianum* 2 : 115–30.

GUARINO VERONESE (Guarino da Verona, Guarinus Veronensis)
BIOGRAPHICAL DATA: b. 1373; d. 1460. Studied in Padua under Giovani di Conversino, in Constantinople under Manuel Chrysoloras (1403–8). Taught in Florence (1410–14), Verona (1419–29), and Ferrara (1430–60).
TEXTS: *Epistolario di Guarino Veronese* (1915–19), ed. R. Sabbadini (Miscellanea di storia veneta, 3rd ser., vols. 8, 11, 14), (Reprinted Bottega d'Erasmo 1967); *Regulae grammaticales*. MSS Milan, Biblioteca Trivulziana, Cod. 631; Oxford, Bodleian Library, Lat. misc. e. 123; Venice, Biblioteca Marciana, Lat. XIII. 113 (= 4042).

GUY OF RIMINI (Guido Vernani de Arimino)
BIOGRAPHICAL DATA: d. after 1344. Twice lector in studium generale in Bologna between 1310 and 1324.
TEXTS: *De potestate summi pontificis* (1746), Bologna; *De reprobatione Monarchiae compositae a Dante Alighiero* (1746), Bologna; *Expositio super decretale: Unam Sanctam edita a domino Bonifacio papa octavo* (1934), ed. Martin Grabmann (*Sitzungsberichte der Akademie der Wissenschaften*, Munich; Philosophisch-historische Abteilung, 2 : 144–57).

SECONDARY LITERATURE: Grabmann, Martin (1934). 'Studien über den Einfluss der aristotelischen Philosophie auf die mittelalterlichen Theorien über das Verhältnis von Kirche und Staat', *Sitzungsberichte der Akademie der Wissenschaften*, Munich; Philosophisch-historische Abteilung, 2:76–100; Käppeli, T. (1937–8). 'Der Dantegegner Guido Vernani O. P. von Rimini', *Quellen und Forschungen aus italienischen Archiven und Bibliotheken* 28:107–46.

HENRY BRACTON
BIOGRAPHICAL DATA: d. 1268.
TEXTS: *Bracton on the laws and customs of England* (1968–). S. E. Thorne (tr.), Belknap Press of Harvard University Press; *De legibus et consuetudinibus Angliae*, (1915–42), ed. G. E. Woodbine, Yale University Press.
SECONDARY LITERATURE: Fesefeldt, W. (1962). *Englische Staatstheorie des 13. Jahrhunderts: Henry de Bracton und sein Werk*, Musterschmidt.

HENRY OF GHENT (Henricus Gandavensis, Henricus de Gandavo)
BIOGRAPHICAL DATA: b. *ca.* 1217; d. 1293. Taught at the University of Paris, 1276–92.
TEXTS: *La 'Lectura ordinaria super sacram scripturam' attribuée à Henri de Gand* (1972), ed. R. Macken, Editions Universitaires de Louvain; *Quodlibeta* (1518), Paris. (Reprinted Bibliothèque S. J. de Louvain 1961) *Les 'Quaestiones in librum De causis' attribuées à Henri de Gand*, (1974), ed. J. P. Zwaenepoel, Editions Universitaires de Louvain; *Summa quaestionum ordinariorum* (1520), Paris (Reprinted The Franciscan Institute 1943); *Henrici de Gandavo Opera omnia* (1979–), ed. Raymond Macken *et al.* E. J. Brill.
SECONDARY LITERATURE: Bettoni, E. (1954). *Il processo astrattivo nella concezione di Enrico di Gand*, Società editrice 'Vita e Pensiero'; Huet, F. (1838). *Recherches historiques et critiques sur la vie, les ouvrages et la doctrine de Henri de Gand*, Leroux; Maurer, Armand (1948). 'Henry of Ghent and the Unity of Man', *Mediaeval Studies* 10:1–20. Paulus, J. (1938). *Henri de Gand: Essai sur les tendances de sa metaphysique*, J. Vrin.

HENRY OF HARCLAY
BIOGRAPHICAL DATA: b. 1270; d. 1317. Master of arts by 1296. Ordained priest in 1297. Studied theology at Paris while Duns Scotus was there. Bachelor of theology by 1308. Master of theology in 1312. Elected Chancellor of Oxford in 1312.
TEXTS: Gál, Gedeon (1971). 'Henricus de Harclay: Quaestio de Significato Conceptus Universalis', *Franciscan Studies* 31:178–234; Maurer, Armand (1954). 'Henry of Harclay's Question on the Univocity of Being', *Mediaeval Studies* 16:1–18; Maurer, Armand (1957). 'Henry of Harclay's Questions on Immortality', *Mediaeval Studies* 19:79–107; Maurer, Armand (1961). 'Henry of Harclay's Questions on the Divine Ideas', *Mediaeval Studies* 23:163–93.
SECONDARY LITERATURE: Balić, C. (1959). 'Henricus de Harclay et Ioannes Duns Scotus', *Mélanges offerts à Etienne Gilson*, Pontifical Institute of Mediaeval Studies; Kraus, J. (1932). 'Die Universalienlehre des Oxforder Kanzlers Heinrich von Harclay und ihre Mittelstellung zwischen skotistischem Realismus und ockhamistischem Nominalismus', *Divus Thomas* (Freiburg) 10, 11; Pelster, F. (1924). 'Heinrich von Harclay, Kanzler von Oxford und seine Quästionen', *Miscellanea Francesco Ehrle* I (Studi e Testi, 37), pp. 307–56.

HERVAEUS NATALIS (Harvey Nedellec, Noel)
BIOGRAPHICAL DATA: b. *ca.* 1250/60; d. 1323.
TEXTS: *Quaestiones in quatuor libros sententiarum* (1505), Venice; (1647) Paris (Reprinted Gregg 1966); *Quaestiones disputatae* (1513), Venice; *Quodlibeta* (1486, 1513), Venice (Reprinted Gregg 1966); *Tractatus de secundis intentionibus* (1489), Paris; (1513), Venice.

SECONDARY LITERATURE: Allen, E. (1960). 'Hervaeus Natalis: An Early Thomist on the Notion of Being', *Mediaeval Studies* 22 : 1–14; Glorieux, P. (1933). *Répertoire des Maîtres en Théologie de Paris au XIIIe Siècle*, (n. 64) J. Vrin; Stella, P. (1959). 'La prima critica di Hervaeus Natalis O.P., alla Noetica di Enrico di Gand: il 'De intellectu et specie' del cosidetto 'De quattuor materiis', *Salesianum* 21 : 125–70; Vollert, C. O. (1947). *The Doctrine of Hervaeus Natalis on Primitive Justice and Original Sin* (Analecta Gregoriana, 42), Gregorian University.

HUGO GROTIUS (Huigh de Groot)

BIOGRAPHICAL DATA: b. 1583; d. 1645. Entered the University of Delft in 1594. Doctor of law at Orleans in 1598. Diplomat and lawyer. Studied with Arminius at Leiden. Involved in controversy with mainstream Calvinists; imprisoned but fled to France in 1621. Became Swedish Ambassador to France.

TEXTS: *De iure belli ac pacis* (1625), Paris. Reprinted with English translation by F. W. Kelsey *et. al.* (1925) (Classics of International Law, 3), Oxford, Clarendon Press.

SECONDARY LITERATURE: Dumbauld, Edward (1969). *The Life and Legal Writings of Hugo Grotius*, University of Oklahoma Press; Eysinga, Willem J. M. van (1945). *Huigh de Groot, een Schets*, H. D. Tjeenk Willink; Friedmann, Wolfgang (1967). 'Grotius, Hugo' in Paul Edwards (ed.), *The Encyclopedia of Philosophy*, vol. 3; Meulen, Jacob ter and P.J.J. Diermanse (1950). *Bibliographie des écrits imprimés de Hugo Grotius*, Martinus Nijhoff.

IRNERIUS OF BOLOGNA (Guarnerius)

BIOGRAPHICAL DATA: fl. 1118.

TEXTS: *Summa codicis* (1894), ed. H. Fitting, Guttentag; *Questiones de iuris subtilitatibus* (1894), ed. H. Fitting, Guttentag.

SECONDARY LITERATURE: Besta, E. (1896). *L'opera d'Irnerio: Contributo alla storia del diritto italiano* (2 vols.), Loescher; Fitting, H. (1888). *Die Anfänge der Rechtsschule zu Bologna*, Guttentag; Kantorowicz, H. and W. W. Buckland (1938). *Studies in the Glossators of the Roman Law*, Cambridge University Press.

JAMES ALMAIN (Jaques Almain)

BIOGRAPHICAL DATA: b. *ca.* 1480; d. 1515. Studied under John Major. Asked by the Sorbonne in 1512 to compose its official response to Louis XII's request for a rebuttal of papal claims to supremacy over church councils.

TEXTS: *Libellus de auctoritate ecclesiae; Quaestio resumptiva; De dominio naturali, civili, et ecclesiastico;* and *Expositio de suprema potestate ecclesiastica et laica, circa quaestionum decisiones Magistri Guillermi de Ockham super potestate summi pontificis,* in Jean Gerson's *Opera Omnia,* ed. L. E. DuPin (1706), Antwerp, Sumptibus Societatis, vol. 2; *Opuscula* (1518), Paris.

SECONDARY LITERATURE: LaBrosse, Olivier (1965). *Le pape et le concile,* Editions du Cerf; Oakley, Francis (1965). 'Almain and Major: conciliar theory on the eve of the Reformation', *The American Historical Review* 70 : 673–90; Skinner, Quentin (1978). *The Foundations of modern Political Thought,* 2, Cambridge University Press.

JAMES OF DOUAI

BIOGRAPHICAL DATA: fl. 1275. Master of arts in Paris.

TEXTS: Commentaries on the *Prior* and *Posterior Analytics* and *De anima; Quaestiones in Physicam.* MSS Paris Bibl. nat. lat. 14721 and 14698.

SECONDARY LITERATURE: Grabmann, Martin (1956). 'Jakob von Douai, ein Aristoteleskommentator zur Zeit des heiligen Thomas von Aquin und des Siger von Brabant', in his *Mittelalterliches Geistesleben* 3 : 158–79, Munich, Hueber.

JAMES OF VITERBO

BIOGRAPHICAL DATA: b. *ca.* 1255; d. 1308. Joined the order of Augustinian Hermits around 1270 in Viterbo. Studied theology at Paris from 1278/9–1282/3. Became master of theology at Paris *ca.* 1293 and succeeded Giles of Rome in the Augustinian chair, functioning as regent master until 1296/7. In charge of *studium generale* in Naples beginning 1300. Bishop of Benevento 1302. Archbishop of Naples 1303.

TEXTS: *De regimine christiano*, in H.-X. Arquillière (1926), *Le plus ancien traité de l'église: Jacques de Viterbe, De Regimine Christiano (1301–2)*, Gabriel Beauchesne; *Quodlibeta*, in *Jacobi de Viterbio O.E.S.A. Disputatio Prima de Quolibet* (1967), *Jacobi de Viterbio O.E.S.A. Disputatio Secunda de Quolibet* (1969), *Jacobi de Viterbio, O.E.S.A. Disputatio Tertia de Quolibet* (1973), *Jacobi de Viterbio Disputatio Quarta de Quolibet* (1975), ed. E. Ypma, Augustinus-Verlag.

SECONDARY LITERATURE: Gutiérrez, David (1939). *De B. Iacobi Viterbiensis O.E.S.A. Vita, Operibus, et Doctrina Theologica*, Analecta Augustiniana; Ypma, E. (1974). 'Recherches sur la carrière scolaire et la bibliothèque de Jacques de Viterbe † 1308', *Augustiniana* 24: 247–82; Ypma, E. (1975). 'Recherches sur la productivité littéraire de Jacques de Viterbe jusqu' à 1300', *Augustiniana* 25: 223–82.

JOHN AURIFABER

BIOGRAPHICAL DATA: fl. *ca.* 1330, Erfurt.

TEXTS: *Commentary on the Tractatus of Peter of Spain*, possible fragment in MS Krakow, BJ 742, ff. 130–44.
Sophism against the modi significandi, in Jan Pinborg (1967), *Die Entwicklung der Sprachtheorie im Mittelalter* (BGPM XLII, 2), Aschendorff; *Sophism on dimensions*, MS Leipzig, UB, 1444, ff. 149^v–152^v; *Tractatus de demonstratione*, MSS Harburg I, 2, 80, 10, ff. 123–127; München Clm. 331, ff. 45–7.

SECONDARY LITERATURE: Pinborg, Jan (1975). 'A Note on Some Theoretical Concepts of [Medieval] Logic and Grammar', *Revue Internationale de Philosophie* 113: 286–96.

JOHN BODE (John Body, Bodi)

BIOGRAPHICAL DATA: fl. mid-fourteenth century. Fellow of Merton College, Oxford, possibly in 1334, 1338. Benedictine monk; D. Th. mentioned in 1357, 1358.

TEXTS: *A est unum calidum*, MSS Paris B. N. lat. 16134, ff. 73^r–80^v; Venice, San Marco, lat. VI. 30, ff. 113^r–133^r; Venice, San Marco, lat. VI. 155. ff. 65^r–82^v; Vatican, lat. 4447, ff. 229ra–303vb.

SECONDARY LITERATURE: Busard, H. L. L. (1965). 'Unendliche Reihen in *A est unum calidum*', *Archive for History of Exact Sciences* 2: 387–97; Duhem, Pierre (1906–13). *Études sur Léonard de Vinci*, Hermann et Fils; Vol. 3, pp. 474–7; Duhem, Pierre (1913–59). *Le Système du Monde*, Hermann et Fils; Vol. 7, pp. 648–50; Maier, Anneliese (1952). *An der Grenze von Scholastik und Naturwissenschaft* (2nd ed.), Edizioni di Storia e Letteratura.

JOHN BURIDAN (Jean Buridan, Ioannes Buridanus)

BIOGRAPHICAL DATA: b. *ca.* 1295/1300; d. after 1358. Studied at Paris and obtained master of arts there around 1320. Rector of the university in 1328 and again in 1340. Lecturer in the faculty of arts at Paris. Taught Albert of Saxony, Marsilius of Inghen, Nicole Oresme.

TEXTS: *Consequentiae*, in *Iohannis Buridani Tractatus de consequentiis* (1976), ed. H. Hubien, Publications universitaires de Louvain; *De motibus animalium* (1967), ed. F. Scott and H. Shapiro, *Isis* 58: 533–52; *In Metaphysicam Aristotelis Quaestiones* (1518), Paris (Reprinted Minerva 1964); *Quaestio de punctis* (1961), ed. V. Zoubov, *Mediaeval and Renaissance Studies* 5: 63–95; *Quaestiones et decisiones physicales insignium virorum* (1489), Paris (Reprinted Minerva 1966); *Quaestiones super libris quattuor de caelo et mundo* (1942), ed. E. A. Moody, The Mediaeval Academy of America; *Quaestiones super decem libros Ethicorum* (1513), Paris

(Reprinted Minerva 1968); *Quaestiones super octo Physicorum libros* (1509), Paris (Reprinted Minerva 1963); *Sophismata*, in *Johannes Buridanus: Sophismata* (1977), ed. T. K. Scott, (Grammatica Speculativa, 1) Frommann-Holzboog. Also in *Sophisms on Meaning and Truth* (1966), T. K. Scott (tr.) (Century Philosophy Sourcebooks), Appleton-Century-Crofts; *Summulae de dialectica* (also called *Summulae dialecticae, Summulae logicae, Compendium logicae, Compendium totius logicae*), Tractatus IV (De suppositionibus) (1957) in Maria Elena Reina (ed.) 'Giovanni Buridano: Tractatus de suppositionibus,' *Rivista critica di storia della filosofia* 12:175–208 and 323–52. Also *Perutile compendium totius logicae Joannis Buridani cum praeclarissima solertissimi viri Joannis Dorp expositione* (1499), Venice (Reprinted Minerva 1965). SECONDARY LITERATURE: Faral, Edmond (1946). 'Jean Buridan: Notes sur les manuscrits, les éditions et le contenu de ses ouvrages', *Archives d'histoire doctrinale et littéraire du moyen âge* 21:1–53; Faral, Edmond (1949). 'Jean Buridan: Maître ès arts de l'Université de Paris', in *Histoire littéraire de la France*, Imprimerie nationale; vol. 38; Ghisalberti, A. (1975). *Giovanni Buridano dalla metafisica alla fisica* (Publicazioni della Università Catolica del Sacro Cuore), Vita e pensiero; Moody, E. A. (1975). 'Jean Buridan', in *Studies in Medieval Philosophy, Science, and Logic. Collected Papers 1933–1969* (Publications of the Center for Medieval and Renaissance Studies at UCLA, 7) University of California Press, pp. 441–53; Pinborg, Jan, ed. (1976). *The Logic of John Buridan* (Opuscula graecolatina, 9), Museum Tusculanum.

JOHN CAPREOLUS

BIOGRAPHICAL DATA: b. 1380; d. 1444.
TEXTS: *Defensiones theologiae divi Thomae Aquinatis* (1900–8), ed. C. Paban and T. Pègues (7 vols.), Cattier (Reprinted Minerva 1967).
SECONDARY LITERATURE: Degl'Innocenti, U. (1967). 'Capreolo, Giovanni' in *Enciclopedia Filosofica* 1, Sansoni; pp. 1202–3; Grabmann, Martin (1944). 'Joannes Capreolus, der "Princeps Thomistarum" und seine Stellung in der Geschichte der Thomistenschule', *Divus Thomas* (Freiburg) 22:85–109, 145–70.

JOHN DUMBLETON

BIOGRAPHICAL DATA: fl. mid-fourteenth century. Fellow of Merton College, Oxford from 1338 through 1347/8.
TEXTS: *Compendium sex conclusionum* (*Expositio capituli quarti Bradwardini De proportionibus*). MS Paris, B. N. Nouv. acq. lat. 625, ff. 70^v–71^v; *Summa logicae et philosophiae naturalis*. MSS Cambridge, Peterhouse 272, ff. 1–111; Cambridge, Gonville and Caius 499/268, ff. 1–162; Vatican, lat. 6750, ff. 1–202.
SECONDARY LITERATURE: Clagett, Marshall (1959). *The Science of Mechanics in the Middle Ages*, University of Wisconsin Press; Maier, Anneliese (1968). *Zwei Grundprobleme der scholastischen Naturphilosophie* (3rd ed.), Edizioni di Storia e Letteratura; Molland, A. G. (1973). 'John of Dumbleton', *Dictionary of Scientific Biography*; Sylla, Edith (1970). *The Oxford Calculators and the Mathematics of Motion 1320–1350*. Unpublished Ph.D. dissertation, Harvard University; Sylla, Edith (1973). 'Medieval Concepts of the Latitude of Forms: the Oxford Calculators', *Archives d'histoire doctrinale et littéraire du moyen-âge* 40:251–71; Weisheipl, James A. (1956). *Early 14th-Century Physics and the Merton 'School' with special reference to Dumbleton and Heytesbury*, unpublished D.Phil. thesis, Oxford University; Weisheipl, James A. (1959). 'The Place of John Dumbleton in the Merton School'. *Isis* 50:439–54; Weisheipl, James A. (1969). 'Repertorium Mertonense', *Mediaeval Studies* 31:174–224.

JOHN DUNS SCOTUS

BIOGRAPHICAL DATA: b. *ca.* 1265; d. 1308. Ordained in St. Andrews, Northhampton in 1291. Studied at Oxford between 1288 and 1301. Lectured on Sentences at Oxford during that time, again at Paris in 1302–3, and possibly also at Cambridge in 1303–4. Returned to Paris in 1304. Probably became master in 1305. Lectured as professor of theology at Franciscan study house in Cologne from 1307 until his death.

TEXTS: *Ioannis Duns Scoti Doctoris Subtilis et Mariani Opera Omnia* (1950–), ed. Carl Balić *et al.*, Typis Polyglottis Vaticanis; *Joannis Duns Scoti Doctoris Subtilis Ordinis Minorum Opera Omnia* (1639), ed. Luke Wadding, Lyon. Republished by Vivès, Paris (1891–5); *John Duns Scotus, A Treatise on God as First Principle* (1966). A. B. Wolter (ed. and tr.) (Forum Books), Franciscan Herald Press; *Johannes Duns Scotus, Abhandlung über das erste Prinzip* (1974), W. Kluxen (ed. and tr.) (Texte zur Forschung, 20), Wissenschaftliche Buchgesellschaft; *Johannis Duns Scoti Tractatus de Primo Principio* (1941), ed. M. Müller (Bücher Augustinischer und Franziskanischer Geistigkeit, Erste Reihe A 1), Herder; *The De Primo Principio of John Duns Scotus* (1949), E. Roche (ed. and tr.), The Franciscan Institute.

SECONDARY LITERATURE: Balić, Carl (1965). 'The Life and Works of John Duns Scotus', in John K. Ryan and Bernardine M. Bonansea (eds.) *John Duns Scotus 1265–1965*, Catholic University of America; Gieben, S. (1965). 'Bibliographia Scotistica recentior (1953–1965)', *Laurentianum* 6; Schaefer, Odulf (1955). *Bibliographia de vita, operibus et doctrina Ioannis Duns Scoti, Saec. XIX–XX*, Orbis–Catholicus–Herder; Schaefer, Odulf (1967). 'Resenha abreviada da bibliografia escotista mais recente (1954–1966)', *Revista Portuguesa de Filosofia* 23 : 338–63.

SIR JOHN FORTESCUE

BIOGRAPHICAL DATA: b. *ca.* 1394; d. *ca.* 1476.

TEXTS: *De laudibus legum angliae* (1942), ed. S. B. Chrimes, Cambridge University Press; *De natura legis naturae* (1869), in Lord Claremont (ed.) *Works*, London.

JOHN GERSON

BIOGRAPHICAL DATA: d. 1429. Chancellor of the University of Paris in 1395, succeeding Peter of Ailly, with whom he played an important part in the conciliar movement culminating in the Council of Constance.

TEXTS: *Oeuvres Complètes* (1960–5), ed. P. Glorieux, Desclée; *Opera omnia* (1706), ed. L. DuPin, Antwerp: Sumptibus Societatis, vol. 2.

SECONDARY LITERATURE: Combes, A. (1940). *Jean Gerson, commentateur dionysien*, J. Vrin; Figgis, J. N. (1907). *Studies of Political Thought from Gerson to Grotius*, Cambridge University Press; Morrall, John B. (1960). *Gerson and the Great Schism*, Manchester University Press; Pascoe, Louis B. (1973). *Jean Gerson: Principles of Church Reform* (Studies in Medieval and Reformation Thought, 7), E. J. Brill; Schafer, Carl (1953). *Die Staatslehre des Johannes Gerson*, Buchdruckerei Beyer und Hausknecht K.-G.

JOHN OF JANDUN

BIOGRAPHICAL DATA: b. *ca.* 1285/9; d. 1328. Master of arts in Paris in 1310. Fled to the Emperor Ludwig of Bavaria with Marsilius of Padua in 1326.

TEXTS: *Quaestiones in XII libros Metaphysicae et super libros Aristotelis De anima* (1553, 1583), Venice (Reprinted Minerva 1966); *Quaestiones super VIII libros Physicorum Aristotelis* (1551), Venice (Reprinted Minerva 1969).

SECONDARY LITERATURE: MacClintock, S. (1956). *Perversity and Error*, Indiana University Press; Schmugge, L. (1966). *Johannes von Jandun* (Pariser Historische Studien, 5), Hiersemann.

JOHN OF LEGNANO

BIOGRAPHICAL DATA: b. *ca.* 1320; d. 1382/83. A lawyer of Bologna. Wrote on theology, law, politics, astrology; very active in Italian politics.

TEXTS: *Tractatus de bello* (1917), ed. T. E. Holland, Oxford University Press.
SECONDARY LITERATURE: Ermini, G. (1933). *I trattati della guerra e della pace di Giovanni da Legnano*, Imola.

JOHN MAJOR (John Mair)

BIOGRAPHICAL DATA: b. 1467/69; d. 1550. Studied at Cambridge and then at Paris, where he received his master's degree in 1495. Taught at the University of Glasgow and at St Andrews between 1518 and 1526, after which he returned to Paris, 1526–31. An Ockhamist in theology and politics. Taught Pierre Crockaert, George Buchanan, John Calvin, and John Knox.
TEXTS: *De statu et potestate ecclesiae* and *De Potestate Papae in Temporalibus*, in Gerson's *Opera Omnia* (1706), ed. L. DuPin, Antwerp, Sumptibus Societatis, vol. 2; *Le traité 'De l'infini' de Jean Mair* (1938), ed. H. Elie, J. Vrin.
SECONDARY LITERATURE: Burns, J. H. (1954). 'New Light on John Major', *The Innes Review* 5:83–100; Oakley, Francis (1962). 'On the road from Constance to 1688: the political thought of John Major and George Buchanan', *The Journal of British Studies* 2:1–31; Oakley, Francis (1965). 'Almain and Major: conciliar theory on the eve of the Reformation', *The American Historical Review* 70:673–90; Renaudet, Augustin (1953). *Préréforme et humanisme à Paris pendant les premières guerres d'Italie (1494–1517)* (2nd edn), Librairie d'Argences; Skinner, Quentin (1978). *The Foundations of Modern Political Thought*, 2, Cambridge University Press.

JOHN OF MIRECOURT

BIOGRAPHICAL DATA: fl. 1345.
TEXTS: 'Questioni inedite di Giovanni di Mirecourt sulla conoscenza (Sent. I, q. 2–6)' (1958), A. Franzinelli (ed.), *Rivista critica di storia della filosofia* 13:319–40, 415–49; 'Questioni inedite tratte dal I libro del Commento alle Sentenze di Giovanni di Mirecourt (q. 13–16)' (1978), M. Parodi (ed.), *Medioevo* 3, 237–84.
SECONDARY LITERATURE: Birkenmaïer, A. (1922). *Ein Rechtfertigungsschreiben Johannes von Mirecourt* (*BGPM* XX, 5), Aschendorff; Parodi, M. (1978). 'Recenti studi su Giovanni di Mirecourt', *Rivista critica di storia della filosofia* 33:297–307; Stegmueller, F. (1933). 'Die zwei Apologien des Jean de Mirecourt', *Recherches de théologie ancienne et moderne* 5:40–78 and 192–204.

JOHN LE PAGE (Johannes Pagus)

BIOGRAPHICAL DATA: fl. 1230
TEXTS: *Rationes super Praedicamenta Aristotelis* (1934), excerpted in E. Franceschini, 'Giovanni Pago: Le sue "Rationes super Predicamenta Aristotelis" e la loro posizione nel movimento aristotelico del secolo XIII', *Sophia* 2:172–82; 329–50; 476–86.
SECONDARY LITERATURE: Gründel, J. (1958). 'Die Sentenzenglosse des Johannes Pagus (ca. 1243–45) in Padua Bibl. Ant. 139', *Münchener theologische Zeitschrift* 9:171–85; Pelster, F. (1930). 'Literaturgeschichtliches zur Pariser theologischen Schule aus den Jahren 1230 bis 1256', *Scholastik* 5:46–78; Braakhuis, H. A. G. (1979). *De 13de eeuwse tractaten over syncategorematische termen* (Deel I), Krips Repro Meppel.

JOHN OF PARIS (John Quidort, Johannes Dormiens, Surdus, Soardus)

BIOGRAPHICAL DATA: d. 1306. Dominican. Lectured on the Sentences at Paris, 1293–4. Master of theology at Paris, 1304. Involved in both political and theological controversy: supported Philip the Fair's call for a general council against Boniface VIII. Object of theological censure by an episcopal board under Giles of Rome and suspended from teaching in 1305.

TEXTS: *Correctorium corruptorii 'Circa'* (1941), ed. J. P. Muller (Studia Anselmiana, 12–13), Herder; *De regia potestate et papali*, in F. Bleienstein (1968), *Johannes Quidort von Paris über königliche und päpstliche Gewalt* (*De Regia Potestate et Papali*) (Frankfurter Studien zur Wissenschaft von der Politik), E. Klett. Translated in *On Royal and Papal Power* (1971), J. A. Watt (tr.), Rome Pontifical Institute of Mediaeval Studies; and *John of Paris on Royal and Papal Power* (1974), Arthur Monahan (tr.), Columbia University Press.

SECONDARY LITERATURE: Grabmann, Martin (1922). 'Studien zu Johannes Quidort von Paris O. Pr.', *Sitzungsberichte der bayerischen Akademie der Wissenschaften*, (Philosophisch-Historische Klasse), 3; Kaeppeli, Thomas (1975). *Scriptores Ordinis Praedicatorum medii aevi*, Istituto Storico Domenicano Roma; II, 517–24; Leclercq, Jean (1942). *Jean de Paris et l'ecclésiologie du XIIIᵉ siècle*, J. Vrin; Tierney, Brian (1955). *Foundations of the Conciliar Theory*, Cambridge University Press.

JOHN PECKHAM (John Peckam, John Pecham)

BIOGRAPHICAL DATA: b. *ca.* 1225; d. 1292. Archbishop of Canterbury, 1278–92.

TEXTS: *Perspectiva communis* (1970), ed. and tr. D. C. Lindberg in *John Pecham and the Science of Optics* (University of Wisconsin Publications in Medieval Science, 14), University of Wisconsin Press; *Quaestiones tractantes de anima* (1918), ed. H. Spettmann (*BGPM* XIX, 5–6), Münster, Aschendorff; *Quodlibet Romanum* (1938), ed. F. Delorme (Spicilegium Pontificii Athenaei Antoniani, 1), Pontificium Athenaeum Antonianum; *Summa de esse et essentia* (1928), ed. F. Delorme, *Studi francescani* 14:1–18; *Tractatus de anima* (1949), ed. G. Melani, (Biblioteca di studi francescani, 1), Edizioni Studi Francescani; *Tractatus de perspectiva* (1972), ed. D. C. Lindberg (Franciscan Institute Text Series, 16), The Franciscan Institute.

SECONDARY LITERATURE: Callebaut, A. (1925). 'Jean Peckham O. F. M. et l'augustinisme', *Archivum Franciscanum Historicum* 18:441–72; Douie, D. L. (1952). *Archbishop Pecham*, Clarendon Press; Spettmann, H. (1919). *Die Psychologie des Johannes Pecham* (*BGPM* XX, 6), Aschendorff.

JOHN OF READING

BIOGRAPHICAL DATA: b. *ca.* 1285; d. 1346. A Franciscan and one of the earliest & staunchest supporters of Duns Scotus. Lectured on the Sentences in Oxford before 1320. Became regent master in theology, 1320/21. Strongly opposed Ockham's nominalism.

TEXTS: *Super Sententias* I, 4.3, q. 3, in Gedeon Gál (1969), 'Quaestio Joannis de Reading de Necessitate Specierum Intelligibilium Defensio Doctrinae Scoti', *Franciscan Studies* 7:66–156.

SECONDARY LITERATURE: Longpré, P. (1924). 'Jean de Reading et le B. Jean Duns Scot', *La France Franciscaine* 7:99–109.

JOHN OF RIPA

BIOGRAPHICAL DATA: fl. *ca.* 1355, in Paris. His work influenced a number of later theologians, including Peter of Candia.

TEXTS: *Conclusiones* (1957), ed. A. Combes (Études de philosophie médiévale, 44), Vrin; *Determinationes* (1957), ed. A. Combes (Textes philosophiques du moyen âge, 4), Vrin; *Lectura super 'Primum Sententiarum'* (1961–70), ed. A. Combes and F. Ruello (Textes philosophiques du moyen âge, 8, 16), Vrin; *Quaestio de gradu supremo* (1964), ed. A. Combes and P. Vignaux (Textes philosophiques du moyen âge, 12), Vrin.

SECONDARY LITERATURE: Combes, André (1956). 'Présentation de Jean de Ripa', *Archives d'histoire doctrinale et littéraire du moyen âge* 22:145–242.

JOHN OF ST THOMAS (Jean Poinsot)

BIOGRAPHICAL DATA: b. 1589; d. 1644. Entered Dominican order 1612. Studied at Coimbra and Louvain. Taught at Piacenza, Madrid, and Alcalá. Advisor and confessor of Philip IV of Spain.

TEXTS: *Cursus Philosophicus Thomisticus* (1930–7), ed. B. Reiser, Marietti; *Cursus Theologicus* (1930–53), ed. Benedictines of Solesmes, Desclée; *Outlines of Formal Logic* (1955). Francis C. Wade (tr.), Marquette University Press; *The Material Logic of John of St Thomas* (1955). Y. R. Simon, J. J. Glanville, G. D. Hollenhorst (trs.), University of Chicago Press.

JOHN OF SALISBURY

BIOGRAPHICAL DATA: b. *ca.* 1120; d. 1180. Studied at Paris under Abelard and at Chartres under Gilbert de la Porrée. Recommended by St Bernard, he served for several years as secretary to Theobald, Archbishop of Canterbury. Close friend to Thomas Becket. Bishop of Chartres in 1176.

TEXTS: *Entheticus de Dogmate Philosophorum* (1843), ed. Christian Petersen, Meisser; *Historia Pontificalis* (1927), ed. R. Lane Poole, Clarendon Press; *Metalogicon* (1929), ed. C. C. J. Webb, Clarendon Press; *Policraticus* (1909), ed. C. C. J. Webb, Clarendon Press (Reprinted Minerva 1965.), Portions translated in *The Statesman's Book of John of Salisbury* (1927), John Dickinson (tr.), Knopf, and in *Frivolties of Courtiers and Footsteps of Philosophers* (1938), Joseph B. Pike (tr.), Oxford University Press.

SECONDARY LITERATURE: Eberenz, James H. (1969). *The Concept of Sovereignty in Four Medieval Philosophers: John of Salisbury, St Thomas Aquinas, Egidius Colonna and Marsilius of Padua*, University Microfilms; Liebeschütz, H. (1950). *Humanism in the Life and Writings of John of Salisbury*, Warburg Institute; Liebeschütz, H. (1968). 'Chartres and Bologna: Naturbegriff und Staatsidee bei Johannes von Salisbury', *Archiv für Kulturgeschichte* 50:3–32; Rouse, Richard H. and Mary A. (1967). 'John of Salisbury and the doctrine of tyrannicide', *Speculum* 42:693–709; Smalley, Beryl (1973). *The Becket Conflict and the Schools: A Study of Intellectuals in Politics*, Rowman and Littlefield; Türk, Egbert (1977). *Nugae curialium: Le règne d'Henri II Plantagenet (1145–1189) et l'éthique politique* (Publications du Centre de Recherche d'Histoire et Philologie de la IVe Section de l'École pratique des Hautes Études, 5: Hautes Médiévales et Modernes, 28), Droz; Webb, C. C. J. (1932). *John of Salisbury*, Methuen.

JOHN SETON

BIOGRAPHICAL DATA: b. *ca.* 1498; d. 1567. Student and Fellow of St John's College, Cambridge. Chaplain to Bishop Gardiner. Disputed with Cranmer, Ridley, and Latimer at Oxford. Imprisoned after accession of Elizabeth I. Fled to Rome.

TEXTS: *Dialectica: annotationibus Petri Carteri, ut clarissimis, ita brevissimis, explicata* (1572), London.

JOHN WYCLIF

BIOGRAPHICAL DATA: b. *ca.* 1330; d. 1384. Fellow of Merton College, Oxford, in 1356. Master of Balliol College in 1360; doctor of divinity in 1372. Involved in theological controversies; forty-five articles from his works were proscribed at the Council of Constance in 1415.

TEXTS: *Select English Works of John Wyclif* (1869–71), ed. Thomas Arnold, Clarendon Press; *The English Works of Wyclif Hitherto Unprinted* (1880), ed. F. D. Matthew, Clarendon Press; *Works* (1882–1924) (Wyclif Society), London, Tübner (Reprinted Johnson Reprint Corporation 1966).

SECONDARY LITERATURE: Daly, Lowrie John (1962). *The Political Theory of John Wyclif*, Chicago, Loyola University Press; Farr, William (1974). *John Wyclif as Legal Reformer*, E. J. Brill; Leff, Gordon (1967). *Heresy in the Later Middle Ages*, Manchester University Press; Robson, J. A. (1961). *Wyclif and the Oxford Schools* (Cambridge Studies in Medieval Life and Thought, Second Series, 8), Cambridge University Press; Tatnall, Edith Comfort (1965). *Church and State According to John Wyclyf*, London, University Microfilms.

JUAN DE MARIANA
BIOGRAPHICAL DATA: b. 1536; d. 1623/4.
TEXTS: *De rege et regis institutione* (1605), Mainz.
SECONDARY LITERATURE: Lewry, G. (1960). *Constitutionalism and Statecraft during the Golden Age of Spain. A Study of the Political Philosophy of Juan de Mariana, S.J.* (Travaux d'humanisme et renaissance, 36), Droz.

LAMBERT OF AUXERRE
BIOGRAPHICAL DATA: fl. 1250, in Paris. Dominican. See Alessio's 'Introduzione' in Lambert of Auxerre 1971.
TEXTS: *Logica*, or *Summa Lamberti* (*De propositionibus, De praedicabilibus, De praedicamentis, De postpraedicamentis, De sillogismo, De locis, De fallaciis, De suppositionibus et de significationibus*) edited in Lambert of Auxerre 1971, La Nuova Italia Editrice.

LORENZO VALLA (Laurentius Vallensis)
BIOGRAPHICAL DATA: b. 1407; d. 1457. Studied under Giovanni Aurispa and Ranuccio da Castiglion Fiorentino. Taught in Pavia, 1430–3, and in Milan, 1433–4. Entered the service of Alfonso of Aragon, King of Naples, in 1435. Worked for Nicholas V in the papal curia beginning in 1448.
TEXTS: *Opera* (1543), Basle (Reprinted Bottega d'Erasmo 1962); *Opuscula quaedam* (1503), Venice (Reprinted Bottega d'Erasmo 1962).
SECONDARY LITERATURE: Camporeale, Salvatore I. (1972). *Lorenzo Valla: umanesimo e teologia*, Istituto Nazionale di Studi sul Rinascimento; Fois, Mario (1969). *Il pensiero cristiano di Lorenzo Valla nel quadro storico-culturale del suo ambiente* (Analecta Gregoriana, 174), Libreria Editrice dell' Università Gregoriana; Garin, E. (1952). *Prosatori Latini del Quattrocento* (La letteratura italiana: storia e testi, 13), Ricciardi; Gerl, Hanna–Barbara (1974). *Rhetorik als Philosophie: Lorenzo Valla* (Humanistische Bibliothek, 13), Fink Verlag.

LUIS DE MOLINA
BIOGRAPHICAL DATA: b. 1535; d. 1600.
TEXTS: *De iustitia et iure* (1876), P. Lethielleux.
SECONDARY LITERATURE: Stegmüller, F. (1935). *Geschichte des Molinismus* (BGPM XXXII), Aschendorff.

MANEGOLD OF LAUTENBACH
BIOGRAPHICAL DATA: d. 1103.
TEXTS: *Liber ad Gebehardum* (1891) (Monumenta Germaniae historica, I), Impensis Bibliopolii Hahniani.

MARSILIUS OF INGHEN (Marsilius of Inghem, Marsilius de Novimagio)
BIOGRAPHICAL DATA: b. *ca.* 1330; d. 1396. Probably studied at Paris under John Buridan. Became master of arts at Paris in 1362. Served twice as rector of the University of Paris (1367 and 1371). Went to the University of Heidelberg in 1382, where he became the first rector (1386–92).

TEXTS: *Abbreviationes Libri Physicorum* (1521), Venice; *De Generatione* (1518), Venice; *Parva Logicalia* (forthcoming), ed. E. P. Bos; *Quaestiones super libros Priorum Analyticorum* (1516), Venice. (Reprinted Minerva 1968); *Quaestiones super quattuor libros Sententiarum* (1501), Strassburg. (Reprinted Minerva 1966).

SECONDARY LITERATURE: Clagett, Marshall (1959). *The Science of Mechanics in the Middle Ages*, University of Wisconsin Press; Maier, Anneliese (1964, 1967). *Ausgehendes Mittelalter* I and II, Edizioni Storia e Letteratura; Möhler, W. (1949). *Die Trinitätslehre des Marsilius von Inghen: ein Beitrag zur Geschichte der Theologie des Spätmittelalters*, Limburg; Nardi, B. (1967). 'Marsilio di Inghen', in *Enciclopedia filosofica* 4, Sansoni; Ritter, G. (1921). *Studien zur Spätscholastik: I. Marsilius von Inghen und die okkamistische Schule in Deutschland*, Sitzungsberichte der Heidelberger Akademie der Wissenschaften, 4. Abhandlung, Winter.

MARSILIUS OF PADUA (Menandrinus of Padua, Marsiglio dei Mainardini di Padova)

BIOGRAPHICAL DATA: b. 1275/80; d. 1342/3. Rector of the University of Paris in 1313, where he lectured on natural philosophy and engaged in medical research. Completed the *Defensor Pacis* in 1324. When his authorship of the work became known in 1326, he fled with John of Jandun to the court of Ludwig of Bavaria. Remained under Ludwig's protection until his death.

TEXTS: *Defensor minor* (1922), ed. C. K. Brampton, Cornish Brothers; *Defensor pacis* (1928), ed. C. S. Previté-Orton, Cambridge University Press. Also (1932–3), ed. R. Scholz, Hahnsche Buchhandlung. Translated A. Gewirth (1956), *Marsilius of Padua: The Defender of Peace* (The Records of Civilization, Sources and Studies, 46), Columbia University Press; *De translatione imperii* and *De iurisdictione imperatoris in causis matrimonialibus* (1960), in M. Goldast (ed.) *Monarchia Sancti Romani Imperii*, Akademische Druck und Verlagsanstalt; *Oeuvres mineures* (*Defensor Minor, De translatione imperii*) (1979), ed. Colette Jeudy and Jeannine Quillet, Editions du Centre National de la Recherche Scientifique.

SECONDARY LITERATURE: D'Entrèves, A. Passerin (1939). *The Medieval Contribution to Political Thought: Thomas Aquinas, Marsilius of Padua, Richard Hooker*, Oxford University Press; Eberenz, James H. (1969). *The Concept of Sovereignty in Four Medieval Philosophers: John of Salisbury, St. Thomas Aquinas, Egidius Colonna, and Marsilius of Padua*, University Microfilms; Quillet, J. (1970). *La Philosophie politique de Marsile de Padoue* (L'Église et l'état au Moyen Age, 14), J. Vrin; Stout, Harry S. (1974). 'Marsilius of Padua and the Henrician Reformation', *Church History* 43:308–18.

MARTIN OF DACIA (Martinus Dacus)

BIOGRAPHICAL DATA: d. 1304. Professor at the arts faculty at Paris in the 1270s. Master of theology at Paris around 1285. Chancellor of the Danish King Erik VI around 1288–1300. Afterwards returned to Paris.

TEXTS: *Opera* (1961), ed. H. Roos (Corpus Philosophorum Danicorum Medii Aevi, 2), Gad.

SECONDARY LITERATURE: Roos, H. (1952). 'Die Modi significandi des Martinus de Dacia', (*BGPM* XXXVII, 2), Aschendorff.

MARTIN SMIGLECKI (Smiglesius)

BIOGRAPHICAL DATA: b. 1564; d. 1618. Joined the Society of Jesus in 1581. Professor of Philosophy and Theology at Vilna. Governor of Colleges of Pubtusk, Posen, and Kalisch.

TEXTS: *Logica* (1618), Ingolstad; (1634, 1638) Oxford.

MATTHEW OF AQUASPARTA

BIOGRAPHICAL DATA: b. *ca.* 1237; d. 1302.

TEXTS: *Quaestiones De Anima VI* (1958), ed. A.-J. Gondras, *Archives d'histoire doctrinale et littéraire du moyen âge* 24:203–52; *Quaestiones disputatae De Anima XIII* (1961), ed. A.-J. Gondras, *Études de philosophie médiévale 50*; *Quaestiones disputatae de gratia, cum introductione critica* (1935), ed. V. Doucet, Collegium s. Bonaventurae; *Qu. disp. de anima separata, de anima beata, de ieiunio, et de legibus* (1959), Collegium s. Bonaventurae; *Qu. disp. de fide et de cognitione* (1957), Collegium s. Bonaventurae; *Qu. disp. de productione rerum et de providentia* (1956), ed. G. Gál, Collegium s. Bonaventurae.

SECONDARY LITERATURE: Beha, H. M. (1960–1). 'Matthew of Acquasparta's Theory of Cognition', *Franciscan Studies* 20:161–204; 21:1–79; Prezioso, F. (1950). 'L'attività del soggetto pensante nella gnoseologia di Matteo d'Acquasparta e di Ruggiero Marston', *Antonianum* 25:259–326.

MICHAEL OF MASSA

BIOGRAPHICAL DATA: fl. *ca.* 1325. Augustinian friar, still almost entirely unknown. The second book of his Commentary on the Sentences contains many lengthy *additiones* dealing with topics in natural philosophy.

TEXTS: *Commentary on the Sentences,* MS Vat. lat. 1087.

SECONDARY LITERATURE: Trapp, Damasus (1956). 'Augustinian Theology of the Fourteenth Century', *Augustiniana* 6:146–274, esp. 163–75; Trapp, Damasus (1965). 'Notes on some Manuscripts of the Augustinian Michael of Massa († 1337)', *Augustianum* 5: 58–133.

NICHOLAS OF AUTRECOURT (Nicolaus de Ultricuria, Autricuria)

BIOGRAPHICAL DATA: b. *ca.* 1300; d. after 1350.

TEXTS: *Exigit ordo executionis* (*Tractatus universalis magistri Nicholai de Ultricuria ad videndum an sermones Peripateticorum fuerint demonstrati*) (1939), ed. J. R. O'Donnell, *Mediaeval Studies* 1:179–280; *Letters* (1908), ed. J. Lappe, 'Nikolaus von Autrecourt' (*BGPM* VI, 2), Aschendorff. Translated E. A. Moody, in H. Shapiro, ed. (1964), *Medieval Philosophy*, Modern Library; *The Universal Treatise of Nicholas of Autrecourt* (1971), tr. L. A. Kennedy et al. (Medieval Texts in Translation, 20), Marquette University Press.

SECONDARY LITERATURE: Dal Pra, Mario (1951). *Nicola di Autrecourt*, Fratelli Bocca; Dal Pra, Mario (1952). 'La fondazione del empirismo e le sue aporie nel pensiero di Nicola di Autre-court', *Rivista critica di storia della filosofia* 5:389–402; Moody, E. A. (1947). 'Ockham, Buridan, and Nicholas of Autrecourt', *Franciscan Studies* 7:113–46; Scott, T. K. (1971). 'Nicholas of Autrecourt, Buridan, and Ockhamism', *Journal of the History of Philosophy* 9:15–41; Weinberg, Julius (1948). *Nicholas of Autrecourt*, Princeton University Press.

NICHOLAS BONET

BIOGRAPHICAL DATA: d. 1343. Taught in Paris. Known to have followed Gerard of Odo in many of his contentions concerning indivisibles and continua.

TEXTS: *Praedicamenta; Philosophia naturalis; Metaphysica; Theologia naturalis* (1505), Venice.

SECONDARY LITERATURE: Barcelone, Martin de (1925). 'Nicolas Bonet († 1343), Tourangeau, Doctor Proficuus O. M.', *Études franciscaines* 37:638–57; O'Briain; F. (1937). 'Nicolas Bonet' in *Dictionnaire d'histoire et géographie ecclésiastiques* 9:849–52.

NICHOLAS OF CUSA

BIOGRAPHICAL DATA: b. 1401; d. 1464.

TEXTS: *Opera omnia* (1932–), (Heidelberger Akademie), Meiner; *Nicholas of Cusa on Learned*

Ignorance: A Translation and Appraisal of De docta ignorantia (1981), tr. Jasper Hopkins, A. J. Banning; *Nicholas of Cusa's Debate with John Wenck: A Translation and Appraisal of De ignota litteratura and Apologia doctae ignorantiae*, tr. Jasper Hopkins, A. J. Banning.

SECONDARY LITERATURE: Danzer, R. (1964). 'Cusanus-Bibliographie 1961–64 und Nachträge', *Mitteilungen und Forschungsbeiträge der Cusanus-Gesellschaft* 3:223–37; Gandillac, M. de (1941). *La Philosophie de Nicolas de Cues*, Éditions Montaigne; Hopkins, Jasper (1978). *A Concise Introduction to the Philosophy of Nicholas of Cusa*, University of Minnesota Press; Kleinen, H. and R. Danzer (1961). 'Cusanus-Bibliographie 1920–61', *Mitteilungen und Forschungsbeiträge der Cusanus-Gesellschaft* 1:95–126; Schnarr, H. (1973). *Modi essendi. Interpretationen zu den Schriften De docta ignorantia, De coniecturis, und De venatione sapientiae von Nikolaus von Kues* (Buchreihe der Cusanus-Gesellschaft, 5), Aschendorff; Sigmund, P. E. (1963). *Nicholas of Cusa and Medieval Political Thought*, Harvard University Press; Traut, W. (1967). 'Cusanus-Bibliographie 1964–67 und Nachträge', *Mitteilungen und Forschungsbeiträge der Cusanus-Gesellschaft* 6:178–202; Watanabe, M. (1963). *The Political Ideas of Nicholas of Cusa* (Travaux d'Humanisme et Renaissance, 58), Droz; Zellinger, H. (1960). *Cusanus-Konkordanz*, Hueber.

NICHOLAS OF PARIS

BIOGRAPHICAL DATA: fl. 1250.

TEXTS: *Syncategoremata* (1979), ed. H. A. G. Braakhuis in his *De 13de eeuwse tractaten over syncategorematische termen*, Krips Repro Meppel; *Summe Metenses* (1967), in L. M. De Rijk 1962–7, II (2).

SECONDARY LITERATURE: Grabmann, Martin (1926). 'Die logische Schriften des Nikolaus von Paris und ihre Stellung in der aristotelischen Bewegung des XIII. Jahrhunderts', in his *Mittelalterliches Geistesleben*, Hueber.

NICOLE ORESME

BIOGRAPHICAL DATA: fl. at Paris 1345–60; d. 1382. Wrote *Quaestiones* on Aristotle's *Physics, De caelo, De generatione et corruptione, De anima, De sensu,* and *Meteorologica*; a group of works (in French as well as Latin) opposing astrology; and four important treatises in natural philosophy. Towards the end of his career he translated Aristotelian and other treatises into French, often with commentary.

TEXTS: *Ad pauca respicientes; De proportionibus proportionum* (1966), ed. and tr. Edward Grant in *Nicole Oresme: De proportionibus and Ad pauca respicientes* (University of Wisconsin Publications in Medieval Science, 9), University of Wisconsin Press; *Le livre du ciel et du monde* (1968), ed. and tr. A. D. Menut and A. J. Denomy in *Nicole Oresme: Le livre du ciel et du monde* (University of Wisconsin Publications in Medieval Science, 11), University of Wisconsin Press; *Quaestiones in libros De anima* (1980), ed. Peter Marshall, with introduction and commentary, unpublished Ph.D. dissertation, Cornell University; *Questiones super libros De celo* (1965), ed. Claudia Kren, unpublished Ph.D. dissertation, University of Wisconsin; *Tractatus de commensurabilitate vel incommensurabilitate motuum celi* (1971), ed. and tr. Edward Grant in *Nicole Oresme and the Kinematics of Circular Motion* (University of Wisconsin Publications in Medieval Science, 15), University of Wisconsin Press; *Tractatus de configurationibus qualitatum et motuum* (1968), ed. and tr. Marshall Clagett in *Nicole Oresme and the Medieval Geometry of Qualities and Motions* (University of Wisconsin Publications in Medieval Science, 12), University of Wisconsin Press.

SECONDARY LITERATURE: [See Introductions and Commentaries in volumes listed above.] Clagett, Marshall (1974). 'Nicole Oresme' in *Dictionary of Scientific Biography*.

PAUL OF PERGULA (Paulus Pergulensis)
BIOGRAPHICAL DATA: d. 1451/5. Studied under Paul of Venice in Padua. Master of arts *ca.* 1420. Doctor of theology by 1430. Taught in Venice from 1421 to his death.
TEXTS: *Paul of Pergula: Logica* and *Tractatus de sensu composito et diviso* (1961), ed. M. A. Brown (Text Series, 13), Franciscan Institute.
SECONDARY LITERATURE: Boh, Ivan (1965). 'Paul of Pergula on suppositions and consequences', *Franciscan Studies* 25:30–89.

PAUL OF VENICE (Paolo Nicoletti, Paulus Venetus)
BIOGRAPHICAL DATA: b. *ca.* 1369; d. 1429.
TEXTS: *Logica magna* (1499), Venice; *Paul of Venice: Logica Magna Part I, Fascicule 1* (1979). Norman Kretzmann (ed. and tr.), The British Academy and Oxford University Press; *Paul of Venice: Logica Magna Part II, Fascicule 6* (1978). Francesco del Punta and Marilyn M. Adams (ed. and tr.), The British Academy and Oxford University Press; *Paul of Venice: Logica Magna (Tractatus de Suppositionibus)* (1971). A. R. Perreiah (ed. and tr.), Franciscan Institute.
SECONDARY LITERATURE: Lohr, C. H. (1973). 'A Note on the Manuscripts of Paulus Venetus, Logica', *Manuscripta* 17:35–6; Perreiah, A. R. (1967). 'A Biographical Introduction to Paul of Venice', *Augustiniana* 17:450–61.

PETER ABELARD (Petrus Abaelardus, Abailardus, Abaielardus, Adbaielardus)
BIOGRAPHICAL DATA: b. 1079; d. 1142. Studied with a number of teachers, notably Roscelin and William of Champeaux. Disagreement with the latter led him to set up his own school at Melun in 1104 and later at Corbeil. Because of ill health, he stayed in Brittany 1106–8. Returned to Paris and began teaching first at Melun and then at Mont-Sainte-Geneviève. Studied theology under Anselm of Laon beginning in 1113. Returned again to teach in Paris in 1116. There followed the famous love affair with Heloise, their secret marriage, and the castration ordered by her uncle in 1118. Wrote the *Theologia summi boni* in 1118–20, which was condemned by the synod of Soissons in 1121. Abbot of St Gildas in Brittany 1125–32. Teaching again in Paris, 1136–40. St Bernard of Clairvaux succeeded in getting his theology condemned at the synod of Sens in 1140. Peter the Venerable of Cluny mediated the dispute and arranged for Abelard to spend his last days in quiet study.
TEXTS: *Dialectica* (1970), ed. L. M. de Rijk (Wijsgerige teksten en studies, 1) (2nd ed.), Van Gorcum; *Dialogus inter Philosophum, Iudaeum et Christianum* (1970), ed. R. Thomas, Friedrich Frommann; *Ethica* or *Scito te ipsum* (1971), in D. E. Luscombe (ed.) *Peter Abelard's Ethics* (Oxford Medieval Texts), Clarendon Press; *Logica 'Nostrorum Petitioni'* and *Logica 'Ingredientibus'*, in B. Geyer, ed. (1919–27), *Peter Abaelards Philosophische Schriften* (BGPM XXI, 1–4), Aschendorff; *Theologia 'Summi Boni'* (1939), ed. H. Ostlender (BGPM XXXV, 2–3), Aschendorff; *Petri Abaelardi Opera theologica I–II* (1969), ed. E. M. Buytaert (Corpus Christianorum, Continuatio Mediaevalis, 11–12), Brepols; *Pietro Abelardo Scritti filosofici: Editio super Porphyrium, Glossae in Categorias, Editio super Aristotelem De interpretatione, De divisionibus, Super Topica glossae* (1954), ed. Mario dal Pra, Fratelli Bocca; *Theologia 'Scholarium'* (or *Introductio ad theologiam*), in Victor Cousin (ed.) (1859), *Petri Abaelardi Opera*, II, Durand; *Twelfth Century Logic, Texts and Studies: Abaelardiana inedita* (1958). L. Minio-Paluello (ed.), Edizioni di storia e letteratura.
SECONDARY LITERATURE: Fumagalli, M. T. Beonio-Brocchieri (1970). *The Logic of Abelard* (Synthese Historical Library, 1), Reidel; Jolivet, Jean (1969). *Arts du Language et Théologie chez Abélard* (Études de Philosophie Médiévale, 57), J. Vrin; Luscombe, D. E. (1969). *The School of Peter Abelard: The Influence of Abelard's Thought in the Early Scholastic Period*, Cambridge University Press; Sikes, J. G. (1932). *Peter Abailard*, Cambridge

University Press; Tweedale, M. M. (1976). *Abailard on Universals*, North-Holland; Ulivi, L. U. (1976). *La psicologia di Abelardo e il 'Tractatus de intellectibus'*, Edizioni di Storia e Letteratura.

PETER OF AILLY (Pierre d'Ailly, Petrus de Aliaco)
BIOGRAPHICAL DATA: b. 1350. d. 1420/1. Entered Collège de Navarre at University of Paris as bursar (recipient of a scholarship) in 1364. Became bachelor of arts in 1367. Entered faculty of theology in 1368. Became doctor of theology in 1381. Named Cardinal 1411. Active in Council of Constance (1414–18).
TEXTS: *Conceptus et insolubilia* (1495), Paris. Translated in Peter of Ailly (1980). *Concepts and Insolubles*, tr. Paul Vincent Spade, Reidel; *Destructiones modorum significandi* (*ca.* 1490–5), Lyons; *Quaestiones super libros Sententiarum* (1474), Brussels; (1490) Strassburg (Reprinted Minerva 1968); *Tractatus de arte obligandi* (1489), Paris. (Of doubtful authenticity; perhaps by Marsilius of Inghen.); *Tractatus exponibilium* (1494), Paris.
SECONDARY LITERATURE: Bottin, Francesco (1976). *Le antinomie semantiche nella logica medioevale* (Publicazioni dell'istituto di storia della filosofia e del centro per ricerche di filosofia medioevale, nuova serie, 23), Editrice Antenore; Cardin, A. (1967). 'Ailly, Pierre de', in *Enciclopedia filosofica* 1, Sansoni; Elie, Hubert (1937). *Le Complexe significabile*, J. Vrin; Gandillac, Maurice Patronnier de (1933). 'De l'usage et de la valeur des arguments probables dans les questions du cardinal Pierre d'Aily sur le "Livre des Sentences"', *Archives d'histoire doctrinale et littéraire du moyen âge* 8:43–91; Glorieux, Palémon (1965). 'L'oeuvre littéraire de Pierre d'Ailly', *Mélanges de science religieuse* 22:61–78; Meller, Bernhard (1954). *Studien zur Erkenntnislehre des Peter von Ailly* (Freiburger theologischen Studien, 67), Herder; Oakley, Francis (1964). *The Political Thought of Pierre d'Ailly: The Voluntarist Tradition* (Yale Historical Publications, Miscellany 81), Yale University Press; Salembier, Louis (1931). *Le Cardinal Pierre d'Ailly*, Georges Frères; Tschackert, Paul (1877). *Peter von Ailly (Petrus de Alliaco): Zur Geschichte des grossen abendländischen Schisma und der Reformconcilien von Pisa und Constanz*, Friedrich Andreas Perthes.

PETER AUREOLI (Aureolus, Aureol, Oriole)
BIOGRAPHICAL DATA: b. *ca.* 1280; d. 1322.
TEXTS: *Compendiosa expositio evangelis Joannis* (1951), ed. Friedrich Stegmüller, *Franziskanische Studien* 33:207–19; *Compendium sensus litteralis sacrae scripturae* (1896), ed. P. Seebaeck, Collegium S. Bonaventurae; *Scriptum super primum Sententiarum* (1953), ed. E. M. Buytaert, Franciscan Institute.
SECONDARY LITERATURE: Dreiling, R. (1913). 'Der Konzeptualismus in der Universalienfrage des Franziskaner Erzbischofs Petrus Aureoli' (*BGPM* II, 6), Aschendorff; Teetaert, A. (1934). 'Pierre Auriol', in *Dictionnaire de Théologie Catholique*, vol. 12.

PETER OF AUVERGNE (Petrus de Alvernia, Peter of Alverny)
BIOGRAPHICAL DATA: d. 1303. Probably rector of the university of Paris around 1275. Master of theology by 1296. Became Bishop of Claremont in 1302.
TEXTS: Hocedez, E. (1932). 'Les *Quaestiones in metaphysicam* de Pierre d'Auvergne', *Archives de Philosophie* 9:515–70; 'Quaestiones in Metaphysicam Petri de Alvernia' (1955), ed. A. P. Monahan in J. R. O'Donnell (ed.) *Nine Mediaeval Thinkers* (Studies and Texts, 1), Pontifical Institute of Mediaeval Studies; *The Commentary of Peter of Auvergne on Aristotle's Politics* (1967). G. M. Grech (ed.), Desclée; 'A New Ms. of the Questions on the *Post. Anal.* Attributed to Petrus de Alvernia with the Transcription of some Questions Related to Problems of Meaning' (1973). Jan Pinborg (ed.) *CIMAGL* 10:48–62.

SECONDARY LITERATURE: Grech, G. M. (1964), 'Recent Bibliography on Peter of Auvergne', *Angelicum* 41 : 446–9; Hocedez, E. (1930). 'La théologie de Pierre d'Auvergne', *Gregorianum* 11 : 520–2; Hocedez, E. (1933). 'La vie et les oeuvres de Pierre d'Auvergne', *Gregorianum* 14 : 3–36; Monahan, A. P. (1954). 'The Subject of Metaphysics for Peter of Auvergne', *Mediaeval Studies* 16 : 118–30.

PETER CEFFONS

BIOGRAPHICAL DATA: fl. at Paris, *ca.* 1350. A Cistercian who lectured on the *Sentences* at Paris, 1348–49. His Commentary on the Sentences is an immense work showing the influence of fourteenth-century English philosophy and theology.

TEXTS: Commentary on the Sentences, MS Troyes 62.

SECONDARY LITERATURE: Murdoch, John E. (1978). 'Subtilitates Anglicanae in Fourteenth-Century Paris: John of Mirecourt and Peter Ceffons' in *Machaut's World: Science and Art in the Fourteenth Century, Annals of the New York Academy of Sciences* 314 : 51–86; Trapp, Damasus (1957). 'Peter Ceffons of Clairvaux', *Recherches de Théologie ancienne et médiévale* 24 : 101–54.

PETER HELIAS (Petrus Heliae)

BIOGRAPHICAL DATA: fl. *ca.* 1140, Paris.

TEXTS: *Summa super Priscianum, Books I–III* (1975), in Reilly, *Petrus Helias' summa super Priscianum I–III, an edition and study*, unpublished Ph.D. dissertation, University of Toronto; *Summa super Priscianum, Books XVII–XVIII* (1978), in J. H. Tolson (ed.), 'The Summa of Petrus Helias on Priscianus Minor', *CIMAGL* 27–28 : 1–210.

SECONDARY LITERATURE: Fredborg, K. M. (1973). 'The Dependence of Petrus Helias' *Summa super Priscianum* on William of Conches' *Glose super Priscianum*', *CIMAGL* 11 : 1–57; Fredborg, K. M. (1975). 'Petrus Helias on Rhetoric', *CIMAGL* 13 : 31–41; Hunt, R. W. (1949–50). 'Studies on Priscian in the Twelfth Century', *Mediaeval and Renaissance Studies* 1 : 194–231; 2 : 1–55. Rijk, L. M. de (1967), in De Rijk 1962–7, II(1), 227–34.

PETER JOHN OLIVI

BIOGRAPHICAL DATA: b. 1248; d. 1298.

TEXTS: *Quaestiones in secundum librum Sententiarum* (1922–6), ed. B. Jansen (3 vols.), Collegium S. Bonaventurae.

SECONDARY LITERATURE: Bettoni, E. (1959). *Le dottrine filosofiche di Pier di Giovanni Olivi*, Publicazione dell'Università del S. Cuore; Burr, David (1976). *The Persecution of Peter Olivi* (Transactions of the American Philosophical Society, n.s., 66, pt. 5), American Philosophical Society; Gieben, S. (1968). 'Bibliographia Oliviana 1885–1967', *Collectanea Franciscana* 38 : 167–95; Partee, C. (1960). 'Peter John Olivi: Historical and Doctrinal Study', *Franciscan Studies* 20 : 215–60.

PETER LOMBARD

BIOGRAPHICAL DATA: b. *ca.* 1095; d. 1160. Taught in the cathedral school of Paris from 1140.

TEXTS: *Libri IV Sententiarum* (1916), ed. A. Heysse, Collegium S. Bonaventurae; *Sententiae in IV libris distinctae* (1971–), Collegium S. Bonaventurae.

SECONDARY LITERATURE: Delhaye, P. (1961). *Pierre Lombard, sa vie, ses oeuvres, sa morale*, Institut d'études médiévales de Montréal.

PETER OF SPAIN (Petrus Hispanus Portugalensis, Petrus Juliani, Pope John XXI)

BIOGRAPHICAL DATA: Born in Portugal; d. 1277. Studied arts at the University of Paris, then medicine perhaps in Montpellier or Salerno. Professor of medicine at the University of Siena, 1245–9. Dean of Lisbon and Archdeacon of Braga in 1250. Became court physician of Pope Gregory X in 1272. Archbishop of Braga in 1273 and then Cardinal Archbishop of Tusculum. Elected Pope (John XXI) in 1276.

TEXTS: *Exposição sobre os livros de Beato Dionisio Areopagita* (1957), ed. M. Alonso, Instituto de alta cultura, Universidade de Lisboa; *Obras filosóficas* (1941–52), ed. M. Alonso (Consejo superior de investigaciones científicas. Madrid, Instituto filosófico Luis Vives); *Syncategoremata* (1502), Venice. Also translated in J. P. Mullally, tr. (1964), *Peter of Spain, Tractatus Syncategorematum and selected anonymous treatises* (Medieval Philosophical Texts in Translation, 13), Marquette University Press; *Tractatus called afterwards Summule logicales* (1972), ed. L. M. de Rijk (Wijsgerige teksten en studies, 22), Van Gorcum.

SECONDARY LITERATURE: Grabmann, Martin (1936). 'Handschriftliche Forschungen und Funde zu den philosophischen Schriften des Petrus Hispanus, des späteren Papstes Johannes XXI' (Sitzungsberichte der Bayerischen Akademie der Wissenschaften, Phil.-hist. Abt., 9), Hueber; Rijk, L. M. de (1970). 'On the life of Peter of Spain, the author of the *Tractatus* called afterwards *Summule logicales*', Vivarium 8:123–54; Rijk, L. M. de (1972). 'Introduction' in De Rijk (1972).

PETER OF TARANTASIA (Pope Innocentius V)
BIOGRAPHICAL DATA: b. *ca.* 1225; d. 1276.
TEXTS: *In quattuor libros Sententiarum commentaria* (1649–52), ed. T. Turco and G. B. De Marinis, Toulouse (Reprinted The Gregg Press 1964).
SECONDARY LITERATURE: Stella, P. (1967). 'Pietro di Tarantasia,' in *Enciclopedia filosofica* 4, Sansoni.

PHILIP THE CHANCELLOR
BIOGRAPHICAL DATA: d. 1236. Studied theology and probably Canon Law in Paris.
TEXTS: *Quaestiones de anima* (1937), in *Ex Summa Philippi cancellarii Quaestiones de anima*, ed. L. W. Keeler, Aschendorff.
SECONDARY LITERATURE: Lottin, O. (1927). 'Le Créateur du traité de la syndérèse', *Révue Néo-Scholastique de Philosophie* 29:197–220; Schneyer, J. B. (1963). *Die Sittenkritik in den Predigten Philipp des Kanzlers* (BGPM XXXIX, 4), Aschendorff.

PHILIPP MELANCHTHON
BIOGRAPHICAL DATA: b. 1497; d. 1560.
TEXTS: *Opera quae supersunt omnia* (1834–60), ed. C. G. Bretschneider (28 vols.), Schwetzke.
SECONDARY LITERATURE: Huschke, R. B. (1968). *Melanchthons Lehre vom Ordo politicus*, Gütersloh; Kisch, G. (1967). *Melanchthons Reechts- und Soziallehre*, De Gruyter.

PSEUDO-PETRUS
BIOGRAPHICAL DATA: The Pseudo-Petrus is the author or authors of material printed in the Cologne editions (1489 and 1496) of the logical works of Peter of Spain and either mistakenly attributed to Peter (*e.g.*, the *Tractatus exponibilium*) or presented in ways that make the attribution confusing or doubtful (*e.g.*, the *Tractatus syncategorematum*).

PTOLEMY OF LUCCA (Tolomeo)
BIOGRAPHICAL DATA: d. 1326/7.
TEXTS: *De regimine principum*, in R. M. Spiazzi, ed. (1954), *Divi Thomae Aquinatis Opuscula Philosophica*, Marietti.

RADULPHUS BRITO

BIOGRAPHICAL DATA: d. 1320. Professor in the arts faculty at the University of Paris around 1296–1306. Lectured on the Sentences at Paris, 1308–9. Master of theology around 1311–12. Provisor of the Sorbonne, 1315–20.

TEXTS: 'Der Kommentar des Radulphus Britonis zu Buch III *De Anima*' (1974). W. Fauser (ed.) (*BGPM*, neue Folge, 12), Aschendorff; 'Radulphus Brito's Commentary on Boethius' *De differentiis topicis* and the sophism "Omnis homo est omnis homo"' (1978), ed. N. J. Green-Pedersen, *CIMAGL* 26:1–121; 'Radulphus Brito on Universals' (1980). ed. Jan Pinborg, *CIMAGL* 35:56–142 *Radulphus Brito's Quaestiones super Priscianum minorem* (1980), ed. H. W. Enders and Jan Pinborg (Grammatica Speculativa, 3), Frommann-Holzboog; 'Radulphus Brito's Sophism on Second Intentions' (1975), Jan Pinborg (ed.), *Vivarium* 13:119–52.

SECONDARY LITERATURE: Glorieux, Palemon (1966). *Aux Origines de la Sorbonne*, J. Vrin; Pinborg, Jan (1974). 'Zum Begriff der *Secunda Intentio*: Radulphus Brito, Hervaeus Natalis, und Petrus Aureoli in Diskussion', *CIMAGL* 13:49–59; Pinborg, Jan (1975). 'Die Logik der *Modistae*', *Studia Mediewistyczne* 16:39–97.

RALPH STRODE

BIOGRAPHICAL DATA: Fellow of Merton College, 1359–60. Friend of Chaucer. May be identical with a London lawyer of the same name who died in 1387, survived by his wife Emma and his son Ralph. See Blackley 1967; Emden 1957–9, 3:1807–8; Workman 1926, 1:125–9, 242–3, 2:412–4.

TEXTS: *Logica* (*De arte logica, De principiis logicalibus, De suppositionibus, Consequentiae, Obligationes, De insolubilibus*). The *Consequentiae* and *Obligationes*, which were required texts at several universities, were printed in several renaissance editions; see Hain 1948, 15093–15100. MSS: Oxford, Bodleian, MS Canon. Misc. 219, ff. 13ra–52vb; individual treatises of the *Logica* are preserved in several other manuscripts. Alfonso Maierù is preparing a partial edition of the *Logica*. The *Consequentiae* have been edited and translated by W. K. Seaton in an unpublished Ph.D. dissertation, 1973, University of California at Berkeley.

RAYMOND LULL

BIOGRAPHICAL DATA: b. *ca.* 1232; d. 1315/6. Received informal education as courtier. At the age of 30, he experienced a religious conversion and joined the Franciscans. Considered it his mission to convert Muslims. Studied Arabic; vigorously attacked Latin Averroism at the University of Paris. Active in Mallorca, Montpellier, Paris, and Naples. Made three missionary journeys to North Africa: to Tunis in 1293, to Algeria in 1307, and again to Tunis in 1314–15. Some 280 works are attributed to him, of which 240 survive.

TEXTS: *Ars Generalis Ultima* (1645), Palma de Mallorca (Reprinted Minerva 1970); *Obres de Ramón Llull* (1901–3), ed. Roselló, Palma de Mallorca; *Obres de Ramón Lull* (1906–50), ed. M. Obrador *et al.*, Palma de Mallorca; *Opera Latina* (1959–), ed. Friedrich Stegmüller *et al.*, (Maiorcensis Schola Lullistica), Palma de Mallorca. (Vol. VII onwards published in Corpus Christianorum, Continuatio Medievalis, 32, Brepols.); *Opera Omnia* (1721–42), ed. I. Salzinger, Mainz (Reprinted Minerva 1965).

SECONDARY LITERATURE: Brummer, R. (1976). *Bibliographia Lulliana, Ramon-Lull-Schrifttum 1870–1973*, Gerstenberg; Colomer, E. (1961). *Nikolaus von Kues und Raimund Llull. Quellen und Studien zur Geschichte*, De Gruyter; Hillgarth, J. N. (1971). *Ramon Lull and Lullism in Fourteenth Century France* (Oxford-Warburg Studies), Clarendon Press; Platzeck, E. W. (1962–4). *Raimund Lull, sein Leben, seine Werke* (Biblioteca Franciscana, 5–6), Roma-Düsseldorf.

RAYMOND OF PENNAFORTE

BIOGRAPHICAL DATA: b. *ca.* 1180; d. 1275. Spanish canon lawyer. Studied in Bologna around 1210–20 before returning to teach law at Barcelona. Master General of the Dominicans. Thomas Aquinas wrote the *Summa contra gentiles* on his advice.

TEXTS: *Opera omnia* (1945–), ed. J. Rius et Serra, University of Barcelona.

SECONDARY LITERATURE: Balmé, F. and C. Paban, eds. (1900–). *Raymundiana; seu documenta quae pertinent ad S. Raymondi de Pennaforti vitam et scripta*, In domo generalitia.

RICARDUS SOPHISTA (Magister Abstractionum)

BIOGRAPHICAL DATA: '*Ricardus Sophista*' is the designation used for the author of the *Abstractiones* found in at least five MSS; the designation appears in MS Oxford, Bodleian, Digby 24, and MS Bruges, Bibliothéque de la Ville, 497. Manuscript evidence and internal evidence suggest that this author must have written in the first decades of the thirteenth century. Both Richard Fishacre and Richard Rufus of Cornwall have been recently suggested in attempts to identify *Ricardus Sophista*.

RICHARD BILLINGHAM (Belyngham, Bilegam)

BIOGRAPHICAL DATA: fl. mid-fourteenth century. Fellow of Merton College 1344–61. TEXTS: *Conclusiones*, MS Vatican lat. 3065 ff. 21rb–25va; *De sensu composito et diviso*, MS Paris, B. N. lat. 14715 ff. 79ra–82rb; *De significato proposicionis*, MS Worcester, Bibl. Cathed. F35 ff. 109vb–110va; *Sophisma*, MS Worcester, Bibl. Cathed. F 35 ff. 107–109vb; *Speculum puerorum* [see Maierù 1969, below].

SECONDARY LITERATURE: Knuuttila, Simo and Anja Inkeri Lehtinen (1979). 'Plato in infinitum remisse incipit esse albus', in E. Saarinen *et al.* (eds.), *Essays in Honour of Jaako Hintikka*, Reidel; Maierù, Alfonso (1969). 'Lo *Speculum puerorum sive Terminus est in quem* di Riccardo Billingham', *Studi Medievali*, 3^a serie, 10, *A Giuseppe Ermini*, vol. 3, pp. 297–397; Rijk, L. M. de (1976). 'Richard Billingham's Works on Logic', *Vivarium* 14:121–38; Weisheipl, James (1969). 'Repertorium Mertonense', *Mediaeval Studies* 31:174–224.

RICHARD BRINKLEY (Brenkell, Brinchil, Brinkel, Brinkil, etc.)

BIOGRAPHICAL DATA: fl. 3rd quarter of fourteenth century; O.F.M.

TEXTS: Several theological writings, including a *Lectura* on the Sentences and a *Distinctiones*, attributed to him; *Summa logicae* (*De termino in genere, De universalibus, De praedicamentis, De suppositionibus terminorum, De propositionibus in genere, De insolubilibus, De obligationibus*). MSS: Leipzig, Karl Marx Universität, MS 1360, ff. 1ra–105vb (an inferior copy); Prague, Statni Knihovan CSR, MS III.A. 11, ff. 31ra–104ra (formerly Univ. Library 396); London, British Library, MS Harley 3243, ff. 49ra–56rb (*De insolubilibus* only). *De insolubilibus* edited in Spade, Paul Vincent (1969), *An Anonymous Fourteenth-Century Treatise on Insolubles: Text and Study*, L.S.M. Thesis, Pontifical Institute of Mediaeval Studies.

SECONDARY LITERATURE: Gál, Gedeon, and Wood, Rega (forthcoming), 'Richard Brinkley and his *Summa logicae*', *Franciscan Studies*.

RICHARD OF CAMPSALL

BIOGRAPHICAL DATA: d. *ca.* 1350/60. Cleric of the archdiocese of York. Master of theology; fellow of Balliol and later of Merton Colleges at Oxford.

TEXTS: *Logica Campsale Anglici valde utilis et realis contra Ockham*, MS University of Bologna, 2635. Parts transcribed in 'The Universal and Supposition in a *Logica* attributed to Richard of Campsall' (1955), ed. Edward Synan in J. R. O'Donnell (ed.) *Nine Mediaeval Thinkers*, Rome, Pontifical Institute of Mediaeval Studies; *Notabilia quedam Magistri Richardi camassale pro materia de contingencia et presciencia dei*, in 'Sixteen Sayings by Richard of Campsall on

Contingency and Foreknowledge' (1962), Edward Synan (ed.) *Mediaeval Studies* 24:250–62; *The Works of Richard of Campsall*, vol. I: *Questiones super librum Priorum Analeticorum* (1968), ed. Edward Synan, Pontifical Institute of Mediaeval Studies.
SECONDARY LITERATURE: Synan, Edward (1952). 'Richard of Campsall, an English Theologian of the Fourteenth Century', *Mediaeval Studies* 14:1–8; Synan, Edward (1968). 'Introduction' to his edition of Campsall's *Questiones super librum Priorum Analeticorum*, Pontifical Institute of Mediaeval Studies.

RICHARD OF CORNWALL (Ricardus Rufus, Ricardus de Cornubia, Ricardus Rufus Cornubiensis)
BIOGRAPHICAL DATA: fl. mid-thirteenth century. Probably joined Franciscan order in Paris sometime before 1238. Lectured on the Sentences at Oxford, 1250–3. Lectured on the Sentences in Paris, 1253–5. Became regent master at Oxford around 1256, the fifth Franciscan master at Oxford.
SECONDARY LITERATURE: Callus, D. A. (1939). 'Two Early Oxford Masters on the Problem of Plurality of Forms, Adam of Buckfield, Richard Rufus of Cornwall', *Revue Néoscolastique de Philosophie* 42:439–45; Ebbesen, Sten and Jan Pinborg (1970). 'Studies in the Logical Writings Attributed to Boethius de Dacia', *CIMAGL* 3:1–54; Henquinet, F. M. (1936). 'Autour des écrits d'Alexandre de Halès et Richard Rufus', *Antonianum* 2:197–9 and 201–9; Pelster, F. (1929). 'Roger Bacons *Compendium studii theologiae* und der Sentenzkommentar des Richardus Rufus', *Scholastik* 4:410–6; Pelster, F. (1949). 'Der Oxforder Theolog Richardus Rufus O.F.M. über die Frage: *Utrum Christus in triduo mortis fuerit homo*', *Recherches de Théologie ancienne et médiévale* 16:259–80.

RICHARD CRAKANTHORPE
BIOGRAPHICAL DATA: b. 1567; d. 1624. Studied at Queen's College, Oxford, where he was also a Fellow. Chaplain to diplomats and bishops; involved in theological controversies.
TEXTS: *Introductio in Metaphysicam* (1619), Oxford; *Logicae libri quinque de Praedicabilibus, Praedicamentis*, etc. (1622), London.

RICHARD FISHACRE
BIOGRAPHICAL DATA: d. 1248.
SECONDARY LITERATURE: Callus, D. A. (1943). 'The Introduction of Aristotelian Learning to Oxford', *Proceedings of the British Academy* 29:229–81; Pelster, F. (1930). 'Das Leben und die Schriften des Oxforder Dominikanerlehrers Richard Fishacre', *Zeitschrift für Katholische Theologie* 54:518–53; Sharp, D. E. (1933). 'The Philosophy of Richard Fishacre', *The New Scholasticism* 7:281–97.

RICHARD FITZRALPH (Armacanus)
BIOGRAPHICAL DATA: b. *ca.* 1295; d. 1360. A native of Dundalk, Ireland; Fellow of Balliol College, Oxford; Vice-chancellor 1333; Archbishop of Armagh 1347.
TEXTS: *De pauperie salvatoris*, in R. Lane Poole, ed. (1890), *Wyclif's Latin Works*, VIII: *De dominio divino*, Trübner; pp. 257–476.
SECONDARY LITERATURE: Leff, Gordon (1964). *Richard FitzRalph, Commentator of the Sentences, A Study in Theological Orthodoxy*, Manchester University Press.

RICHARD HOLDSWORTH
BIOGRAPHICAL DATA: b. 1590; d. 1649. Studied at St John's College, Cambridge, where he was also a Fellow. Professor of Divinity, Gresham College, London. Master, Emmanuel College, Cambridge. Vice-Chancellor, Cambridge. Deprived of his appointments and imprisoned by parliament in 1643. Named Dean of Worcester by Charles I in 1647.

TEXTS: *Directions for a Student in the Universitie*, transcribed in H. F. Fletcher (1961), *The Intellectual Development of John Milton* (vol. 2), University of Illinois Press; *Praelectiones Theologicae, habitae in Collegio Greshamensi apud Londinenses* (1661), ed. Richard Pearson, London; *The Valley of Vision* (1651), London.

RICHARD HOOKER

BIOGRAPHICAL DATA: b. *ca.* 1554; d. 1600. Studied at the Latin School at Exeter and at Corpus Christi College, Oxford, where he was also a Fellow. Lecturer in logic and deputy professor of Hebrew at Oxford. Master of Temple Church in London, 1585–91. Rector of Bishopsbourne.

TEXTS: *Of the Laws of Ecclesiastical Polity*, in W. Speed Hill (ed.) (1977–), *The Folger Library Edition of the Works of Richard Hooker* (5 vols.), Cambridge, Mass., The Belknap Press of Harvard University Press.

SECONDARY LITERATURE: D'Entrèves, Alessandro Passerin (1939). *The Medieval Contribution to Political Thought: Thomas Aquinas, Marsilius of Padua, Richard Hooker*, Oxford University Press; Hill, W. Speed, ed. (1972). *Studies in Richard Hooker: Essays Preliminary to an Edition of His Works*, Case Western Reserve University Press; Munz, Peter (1952). *The Place of Hooker in the History of Thought*, Routledge and Kegan Paul.

RICHARD KILVINGTON (Kilmington, Chillington, Climenton, etc.)

BIOGRAPHICAL DATA: d. 1361. At Oxford, perhaps Oriel College, before 1330. Along with Thomas Bradwardine and others, a member of Richard de Bury's circle. Dean of St Paul's, London.

TEXTS: *Sophismata* (forthcoming), ed. N. and B. Kretzmann.

SECONDARY LITERATURE: Bottin, Francesco (1973). 'Analisi linguistica e fisica Aristotelica nei "Sophysmata" di Richard Kilmyngton', in C. Giacon (ed.) *Filosofia e Politica e altri saggi*, Editrice Antenore; Bottin, Francesco (1974). 'Un testo fondamentale nell' ambito della "Nuova Fisica" di Oxford: I Sophismata di Richard Kilmington', *Miscellanea Mediaevalia* 9:201–5; Kretzmann, Norman (1977). 'Socrates is Whiter than Plato begins to be White', *Noûs* 11:3–15.

RICHARD LAVENHAM

BIOGRAPHICAL DATA: d. 1399. Born at Lavenham in Suffolk. Became Carmelite friar at Ipswich. Received doctorate in theology from Oxford. Prior of Bristol convent of Carmelites. Confessor to Richard II.

TEXTS: At least sixty-three works attributed to him. Compiled a collection of heresies drawn from works of the Wyclifite John Purvey. Wrote commentaries on Aristotle's *Physics* and *Ethics*, treatises on astronomy, logic, natural philosophy, and other topics. See Klingsford 1949–50 and Emden 1957–9, 2:1109–10; Treatises on logic and natural philosophy in MS British Library Sloane 3899, ff. 1ʳ–90ᵛ; *Consequentiae, Exceptivae, Suppositiones, Tractatus exclusivarum, Tractatus qui differt et aliud nuncupatur* edited in Spade, Paul Vincent (1974a); 'Five Logical Tracts by Richard Lavenham' in J. Reginald O'Donnell (ed.), *Essays in Honour of Anton Charles Pegis*, Pontifical Institute of Mediaeval Studies; *De propositionibus modalibus* edited in Spade, Paul Vincent (1973a), 'The Treatises On Modal Propositions and On Hypothetical Propositions by Richard Lavenham', *Mediaeval Studies* 35:49–59; *De propositionibus hypotheticis* partially edited in Spade 1973a; edition completed in Spade, Paul Vincent (1975b), 'Notes on Some Manuscripts of Logical and Physical Works by Richard Lavenham', *Manuscripta* 19:139–46; *Obligationes* edited in Spade, Paul Vincent (1978b), 'Richard Lavenham's *Obligationes*: Edition and Comments', *Rivista Critica di Storia della Filosofia* 33:225–42, *Summulae logicales* partially edited in Spade,

Paul Vincent (forthcoming a), 'Notes on Richard Lavenham's So-called *Summulae logicales*, with a Partial Edition of the Text', *Franciscan Studies*. (Edition completed in Spade 1973a and Spade 1975b.)
SECONDARY LITERATURE: Spade, Paul Vincent (1980a), 'Richard Lavenham and the Cambridge Logic', *Historiographia Linguistica* 7:241–7.

RICHARD SWINESHEAD (Calculator, Suisseth, Suiset)
BIOGRAPHICAL DATA: fl. 1340–55. Fellow of Merton College, Oxford. Later commonly called 'The Calculator' because of his major work *Liber calculationum* (*ca.* 1350).
TEXTS: *De motu, De motu locali*, and *De caelo*, MS Cambridge, Gonville and Caius 499/268, ff. 212ra–213rb, 213rb–215rb, 204ra–211vb; *Liber Calculationum* (1477), Padua; (1520), Venice.
SECONDARY LITERATURE: Clagett, Marshall (1941). *Giovanni Marliani and Late Medieval Physics*, Columbia University Press; Clagett, Marshall (1950). 'Richard Swineshead and Late Medieval Physics', *Osiris* 9:131–61; Clagett, Marshall (1959). *The Science of Mechanics in the Middle Ages*, University of Wisconsin Press; Murdoch, John and Edith Sylla (1976). 'Swineshead, Richard', *Dictionary of Scientific Biography*, vol. 13; Sylla, Edith (1971). 'Medieval Quantifications of Qualities: the "Merton School"', *Archive for History of Exact Sciences* 8:9–39; Sylla, Edith (1973). 'Medieval Concepts of the Latitudes of Forms: the Oxford Calculators', *Archives d'histoire doctrinale et littéraire du moyen âge* 40:223–83; Weisheipl, J. A. (1964). 'Roger Swyneshed, O.S.B., Logician, Natural Philosopher, and Theologian', in *Oxford Studies Presented to Daniel Callus*, Oxford University Press; Weisheipl, J. A. (1969). 'Repertorium Mertonense', *Mediaeval Studies* 31:174–224.

ROBERT BACON
BIOGRAPHICAL DATA: d. 1248.
TEXTS: *Syncategoremata* (forthcoming), ed. H. A. G. Braakhuis.
SECONDARY LITERATURE: Callus, D. A. (1943). 'The Introduction of Aristotelian Learning to Oxford', *Proceedings of the British Academy* 29:229–81; Smalley, Beryl (1948). 'Robert Bacon and the Early Dominican School at Oxford', *Transactions of the Royal Historical Society* (Fourth Series) 30:1–19; Braakhuis, H. A. G. (1979). *De 13de eeuwse tractaten over syncategorematische termen* (Deel I), Krips Repro Meppel.

ROBERT FLAND
BIOGRAPHICAL DATA: Wrote between 1335 and 1370. Probably associated with the University of Oxford, perhaps with Merton College. See Spade 1978c.
TEXTS: *Consequentiae, Insolubilia, Obligationes*, in MS Bruges, Bibliothèque publique de la Ville, 497, ff. 41ra–46ra; *Consequentiae* edited in Spade, Paul Vincent (1976), 'Robert Fland's *Consequentiae*: An edition', *Mediaeval Studies* 38:54–84; *Insolubilia* edited in Spade, Paul Vincent (1978c), 'Robert Fland's *Insolubilia*: An Edition, with Comments on the Dating of Fland's Works', *Mediaeval Studies* 40:56–80; *Obligationes* edited in Spade, Paul Vincent (1980), 'Robert Fland's *Obligationes*: An Edition', *Mediaeval Studies* 42:41–60.

ROBERT GROSSETESTE (Lincolniensis)
BIOGRAPHICAL DATA: b. *ca.* 1168/75; d. 1253. Studied at Oxford, possibly also at Paris, 1209–14. First chancellor of Oxford and first teacher to Friars Minor (1224/32–35). Elected bishop of Lincoln, 1235. Translated many works from Greek, including Aristotle's *Nicomachean Ethics*, but more inclined to Augustinian Neo-Platonism than to Aristotelianism.
TEXTS: *Commentarius in Posteriorum analyticorum libros* (1981), ed. P. Rossi, Leo S. Olschki *Die philosophischen Werke des Robert Grosseteste* (1912), ed. L. Baur (*BGPM*, IX), Aschendorff; *Roberti Grossetesste Commentarius in VIII libros Physicorum Aristotelis* (1963), ed. R. C. Dales, University of Colorado Press.

SECONDARY LITERATURE: Callus, D. A., ed. (1955). *Robert Grosseteste, Scholar and Bishop*, Oxford University Press; Crombie, A. C. (1953). *Robert Grosseteste and the Origins of Experimental Science*, Oxford University Press; Thomson, S. H. (1940). *The Writings of Robert Grosseteste*, Cambridge University Press.

ROBERT HOLKOT (Holcot)
BIOGRAPHICAL DATA: b. *ca.* 1290; d. 1349. Oxford Dominican commentator, theologian, and philosopher. Studied and taught at Oxford ca. 1326–34. Became master in theology in 1332. His view that God is the cause but not the author of sin was condemned at Paris in 1347.
TEXTS: 'A Quodlibetal Question of Robert Holkot, O. P., on the Problem of the Objects of Knowledge and Belief' (1964), E. A. Moody (ed.), *Speculum* 39:53–74; *In quattuor libros Sententiarum quaestiones* (1518), Lyon (Reprinted Minerva 1967); *Quodlibeta* I, 6, in William J. Courtenay (1971), 'A revised text of Robert Holkot's quodlibetal dispute on whether God is able to know more than he knows', *Archiv für Geschichte der Philosophie* 53:1–21; 'Utrum theologia sit scientia: A quodlibetal question' (1958), J. T. Muckle (ed.), *Medieval Studies* 20:127–53.
SECONDARY LITERATURE: Schepers, H. (1970). 'Holkot contra dicta Crathorn I; Quellenkritik und biographische Auswertung der Bakkalareatsschriften zweier Oxforder Dominikaner des XIV. Jahrhunderts', *Philosophisches Jahrbuch der Görres-Gesellschaft* 77:320–54.

ROBERT KILWARDBY
BIOGRAPHICAL DATA: d. 1279.
TEXTS: *De natura theologiae* (1935), ed. Friedrich Stegmüller (Opuscula et Textus, Series Scholastica, 17), Aschendorff; *De ortu scientiarum* (1976), ed. A. G. Judy (Auctores Britannici Medii Aevi, 4), British Academy; 'The Commentary on "Priscianus Maior" Ascribed to Robert Kilwardby' (1975), Jan Pinborg *et al.*, *CIMAGL* 15:1–146.
SECONDARY LITERATURE: Sommer-Seckendorff, E. M. F. (1937). *Studies in the Life of Robert Kilwardby, O. P.* (Dissertationes Historicae, 7), Institutum Historicum FF. Praedicatorum Romae ad S. Sabinae.

ROBERT SANDERSON
BIOGRAPHICAL DATA: b. 1587; d. 1663. Student and Fellow at Lincoln College, Oxford. Regius Professor of Divinity, Oxford. Ousted by parliament in 1648; reinstated in 1660. Held various ecclesiastical appointments, including chaplain to Charles I and Bishop of Lincoln after the Restoration. Participated in the revision of the *Book of Common Prayer* in 1661.
TEXTS: *Logicae Artis Compendium* (1615, 1618), Oxford.

ROGER BACON
BIOGRAPHICAL DATA: b. *ca.* 1214; d. 1292/4. Studied at Oxford. Master of arts in Paris by 1237, where he lectured on Aristotle for at least ten years. Relinquished his position and turned to experimental science and astronomical tables. Joined the Franciscans around 1252–7. At the request of Pope Clement IV (1265–8), he outlined his reform of learning, the *Opus maius*, in 1267. The *Opus minus* and *Opus tertium* followed in 1268. Condemned for certain suspect doctrines (probably Joachite positions) by the Minister General of his order and Pope Nicholas III (1277–80). Imprisoned around 1254–7. Later allowed to return to England.

TEXTS: 'An Unedited Part of Roger Bacon's *Opus maius*: De signis' (1978). K. M. Fredborg, L. Nielsen, and Jan Pinborg (eds.), *Traditio* 34:75–136; *Compendium studii theologiae* (1911), ed. H. Rashdall, Aberdeen University Press (Reprinted Gregg 1966); *Moralis Philosophia* (1953), ed. F. Delorme and E. Massa, Antenore; *Opera hactenus inedita R. Baconis* (1905–40), ed. R. Steele, Oxford, Clarendon Press; *Opera inedita* (1859), ed. J. S. Brewer (Rerum Britannicarum Medii Aevi Scriptores), London (Reprinted Kraus 1966); *Opus Maius* (1897–1900), ed. J. H. Bridges, Oxford University Press (Reprinted Minerva 1964); *The Greek Grammar of Roger Bacon* (1902), ed. E. Nolan and S. A. Hirsch, Cambridge University Press.
SECONDARY LITERATURE: Alessio, F. (1959). 'Un secolo di studi su Ruggero Bacone', *Rivista critica di storia della filosofia* 14:81–102; Crowley, T. (1950). *Roger Bacon: The Problem of the Soul in His Philosophical Commentaries*, Louvain, Publications Universitaires; Easton, S. C. (1952). *Roger Bacon and His Search for a Universal Science*, Blackwell; Little, A. G., ed. (1914). *Roger Bacon Essays*, Oxford University Press (Reprinted New York, Russell and Russell 1972).

ROGER SWINESHEAD (Swyneshed, Sineshead, Schweinshaupt, Suicet, Suiseth, etc.)
BIOGRAPHICAL DATA: fl. before 1335; d. *ca.* 1365. Master of theology. Benedictine monk of Glastonbury.
TEXTS: *De motibus naturalibus*, MS Erfurt, Amplon. F. 135, ff. 25va–47rb; *Insolubilia*, in Paul Vincent Spade, ed. (1979a), 'Roger Swyneshed's *Insolubilia*: Edition and Comments', *Archives d'histoire doctrinale et littéraire du moyen âge* 46:177–220; *Obligationes*, in Paul Vincent Spade, ed. (1977), 'Roger Swyneshed's *Obligationes*: Edition and Comments', *Archives d'histoire doctrinale et littéraire du moyen âge* 44:243–85.
SECONDARY LITERATURE: Clagett, Marshall (1941). *Giovanni Marliani and Late Medieval Physics*, Columbia University Press; Sylla, Edith (1973). 'Medieval Concepts of the Latitude of Forms: the Oxford Calculators', *Archives d'histoire doctrinale et littéraire du moyen âge* 40:223–83; Weisheipl, James (1964). 'Roger Swyneshed, O. S. B., Logician, Natural Philosopher, and Theologian', in *Oxford Studies Presented to Daniel Callus*, Clarendon Press.

RUFINUS OF ASSISI
BIOGRAPHICAL DATA: d. *ca.* 1190. Bishop of Assisi, Archbishop of Sorrento. Canon lawyer and theologian. Taught at Bologna from *ca.* 1150. Wrote a popular, systematic commentary on Gratian.
TEXTS: *Die Summa Decretorum des Magister Rufinus* (1902), ed. H. Singer, Schöningh; *Die Summi magistri Rufini zum Dekretum Gratiani* (1892), ed. J. F. von Schulte, Roth.

SIGER OF BRABANT (Sigerus, Segerus, Sogerus, Sugerus)
BIOGRAPHICAL DATA: b. *ca.* 1240; d. 1284. Cited by the papal legate Simon of Brion in 1266 in connection with political disturbances in the arts faculty at the University of Paris, where he was a master of arts, and one of the leaders of the radical Aristotelian movement. Some of his beliefs condemned by St Bonaventure in his Lenten Conferences of 1267 and 1268 and in 1273, and by Stephen Tempier, Bishop of Paris in 1270. Thomas Aquinas' attack in 1270 on the doctrine of the unicity of the intellect caused Siger to modify his views somewhat, but his career continued to be stormy. Called to appear before the tribunal of the Inquisitor of France, Simon du Val, in 1276, but was already away from Paris. Appealed to the papal curia and ended his days in Italy, without being convicted of the charge of heresy.
TEXTS: *Les Quaestiones super librum de causis de Siger de Brabant* (1972), ed. A. Marlasca (Philosophes Médiévaux, 12). Publications universitaires de Louvain; *Quaestiones in tertium*

De Anima, De anima intellectiva, De aeternitate mundi (1972), ed. B. Bazán (Philosophes Médiévaux, 13), Publications universitaires de Louvain; *Questions sur la Métaphysique* (1948), ed. C. A. Graiff (Philosophes Médiévaux, 1), Publications universitaires de Louvain; 'Die Questiones metaphysice tres des Siger von Brabant' (1966), ed. J. Vennebusch, *Archiv für Geschichte der Philosophie* 48 : 163–89; *Siger de Brabant. Ecrits de logique, de morale et de physique* (1974), ed. B. Bazán (Philosophes Médiévaux, 14), Béatrice-Nauwelaerts.
SECONDARY LITERATURE: Steenberghen, F. Van (1977). *Maître Siger de Brabant* (Philosophes Médiévaux, 21), Béatrice-Nauwelaerts.

SIGER OF COURTRAI

BIOGRAPHICAL DATA: d. 1341. Studied in Paris around 1300. Appointed dean of the chapter of the Church of Our Lady at Courtrai in Flanders shortly after 1305; remained in office till shortly before 1330. Again in Paris in 1315. Belonged to the school of the *modistae*.
TEXTS: *Les oeuvres de Siger de Courtrai* (1913), ed. G. Wallerand (Les philosophes Belges, 8), Louvain, Publications Universitaires; *Summa modorum significandi, Sophismata* (1977), ed. Jan Pinborg (Amsterdam Studies in the Theory and History of Linguistic Science, 14), John Benjamins; *Zeger van Kortrijk, Commentator van Perihermeneias* (1964), ed. C. Verhaak, Paleis der Academiën.
SECONDARY LITERATURE: Bursill-Hall, G. L. (1971). *Speculative Grammars of the Middle Ages*, Mouton; Trentman, John (1976). 'Speculative Grammar and Transformational Grammar: A Comparison of Philosophical Presuppositions' in Herman Parret (ed.) *History of Linguistic Thought and Contemporary Linguistics*, De Gruyter.

SIMON OF FAVERSHAM (Symon Anglicus)

BIOGRAPHICAL DATA: b. *ca.* 1260; d. 1306/7 Master of Arts and Doctor of Theology at Oxford. Chancellor of Oxford, 1304. Archdeacon of Canterbury, 1305.
TEXTS: *Opera omnia. Vol. I, Opera logica, tomus prior: Quaestiones super libro Porphyrii, Quaestiones super libro Praedicamentorum, Quaestiones super libro Perihermeneias* (1957), ed. P. Mazzarella, Cedam; *Quaestiones in tres libros De anima* (1963) in J. Vennebusch, *Ein anonymer Aristoteles Kommentar des XIII. Jahrhunderts: Quaestiones in tres libros De anima*, Schöningh; *Quaestiones super tertium De anima* (1934) in D. Sharp, 'Simon of Faversham's Quaestiones super tertium De anima', *Archives d'histoire doctrinale et littéraire du moyen âge* 9 : 307–68; *Sophisma 'Universale est intentio'* (1969) in T. Yokoyama, 'Simon of Faversham's Sophisma 'Universale est intentio', *Mediaeval Studies* 31 : 1–14; *Quaestiones novae et veteres super librum Elenchorum* (forthcoming), ed. Del Punta *et al.*, Pontifical Institute of Mediaeval Studies.
SECONDARY LITERATURE: Grabmann, Martin (1933). *Die Aristoteleskommentare des Simon von Faversham: Handschriftliche Mitteilungen* (Sitzungsberichte der Bayerischen Akademie der Wissenschaften, Philosophisch-historische Abteilung, 3), Verlag der Bayerischen Akademie; Longeway, John (1977). *Simon of Faversham's Questions on the Posterior Analytics: A Thirteenth-Century View of Science*, unpublished Ph.D. dissertation, Cornell University; Pinborg, Jan (1971). 'Simon of Faversham's *Sophisma: Universale est intentio:* A Supplementary Note', *Mediaeval Studies* 33 : 360–5; Rijk, L. M. de (1968). 'On the Genuine Text of Peter of Spain's *Summule logicales.* II Simon of Faversham (d. 1306) as a Commentator of the Tracts I–V of the *Summule*', *Vivarium* 6 : 69–101; Vennebusch, J. (1965). 'Die Quaestiones in tres libros De anima des Simon von Faversham', *Archiv für Geschichte der Philosophie* 47 : 20–39; Wolf, F. J. (1966). *Die Intellektlehre des Simon von Faversham nach seinem De anima Kommentaren*, Inaugural dissertation, University of Bonn.

THOMAS AQUINAS (Thomas d'Aquino)

BIOGRAPHICAL DATA: b. *ca.* 1225; d. 1274. Studied with the Benedictines at Monte Cassino beginning in 1231 and then with secular masters at the University of Naples,

1239–44. Joined Dominicans at Naples in 1244. Studied in Paris, 1245–8. Studied and taught under Albert the Great at Cologne, 1248–52. Master of theology at Paris in 1256, where he taught until 1259. Spent next ten years in Italy, where he wrote the first part of his *Summa theologiae*. Ordered back to Paris in 1269, where he composed the second part of the *Summa* and most of his commentaries on Aristotle. During this time, he was active in the defense of the mendicant Orders against secular clerics and of his own orthodox use of Aristotle against the Augustinians and the Latin Averroists. Died on his way to the Council of Lyon, leaving unfinished the third part of his *Summa* and various commentaries on Aristotle.

TEXTS: *De regimine principum*, in R. M. Spiazzi, ed. (1954). *Divi Thomae Aquinatis Opuscula Philosophica*, Turin, Marietti. Translated in *On Kingship to the King of Cyprus* (1949), G. Phelan and I. T. Eschmann (trs.), Pontifical Institute of Mediaeval Studies; *In decem libros Ethicorum Aristotelis ad Nicomachum expositio* (1964), ed. R. M. Spiazzi (3rd edn.), Marietti; *In octo libros Politicorum Aristotelis expositio* (1966), ed. R. M. Spiazzi, Marietti; *Opera omnia* (1852–73), Parma, Tipis Petri Fiaccadori (Reprinted Musurgia 1948–50); *Opera omnia* (1871–80), ed. S. E. Fretté and Paul Maré Vivès; *Opera omnia* (1882–), ed. Leonine Commission, Vatican Polyglot Press; *S. Thomae Aquinatis opuscula omnia* (1927), ed. P. Mandonnet, Lethielleux.

SECONDARY LITERATURE: Eckert, W. P., ed. (1974). *Thomas von Aquino. Interpretation und Rezeption*, Grünewald; Gilson, Etienne (1956). *The Christian Philosophy of St Thomas Aquinas*, Random House; Kluxen, W., ed. (1975). *Thomas von Aquinas im philosophischen Gespräch*, Alber; Oeing-Hanhoff, L., ed. (1974). *Thomas von Aquin 1274–1974*, Kösel; Walz, A. (1962). *Saint Thomas D'Aquin* (Philosophes médiévaux, 5), Béatrice-Nauwelaerts; Weisheipl, J. A. (1974). *Friar Thomas d'Aquino: His Life, Thought and Works*, Blackwell.

THOMAS BRADWARDINE (Thomas Beer de Hertefeld)
BIOGRAPHICAL DATA: b. *ca.* 1295; d. 1349. Fellow of Balliol College in 1321 and of Merton College by 1323. Proctor of University of Oxford in 1325 and again in 1327. Master of arts before 1326. Left Merton College in 1335 to join household of Richard de Bury. Master of theology at Oxford and then Chancellor of Saint Paul's, London, 1337–49. Confessor to King Edward in 1346. Doctor of theology before 1348. Archbishop of Canterbury in 1349. Vigorous opponent of contemporary Pelagianism.

TEXTS: *Insolubilia*, in Marie-Louise Roure (1970), 'La problématique des propositions insolubles au XIIIe siècle et au début du XIVe, suivie de l'édition des traités de W. Shyreswood, W. Burleigh et Th. Bradwardine', *Archives d'histoire doctrinale et littéraire du moyen âge* 37:205–326; *Summa de causa Dei contra Pelagium et de virtute causarum ad suos Mertonenses libri tres* (1618), ed. H. Savile, London (Reprinted Minerva 1964); *Thomas Bradwardine His Tractatus de Proportionibus* (1955), ed. H. Lamar Crosby, Jr., University of Wisconsin Press.

SECONDARY LITERATURE: Clagett, Marshall (1959). *The Science of Mechanics in the Middle Ages*, University of Wisconsin Press; Leff, Gordon (1957). *Bradwardine and the Pelagians*, Cambridge University Press; Murdoch, John (1976). 'Bradwardine, Thomas', in *Dictionary of Scientific Biography*; Oberman, H. A. (1957). *Archbishop Thomas Bradwardine. A Fourteenth Century Augustinian*, Zemink and Zoon; Weisheipl, James A. (1968). 'Ockham and Some Mertonians', *Mediaeval Studies* 30:163–213; Weisheipl, James A. (1969). 'Repertorium Mertonense', *Mediaeval Studies* 31: 174–224.

THOMAS OF ERFURT
BIOGRAPHICAL DATA: fl. *ca.* 1300.
TEXTS: *Grammatica speculativa* (1972). G. L. Bursill-Hall (ed. and tr.) (The Classics of Linguistics, 1), Longmans.

SECONDARY LITERATURE: Bursill-Hall, G. L. (1971). *Speculative Grammars of the Middle Ages. The Doctrine of the partes orationis of the Modistae*, Mouton; Grabmann, Martin (1943). *Thomas von Erfurt und die Sprachlogik des Mittelalterlichen Aristotelismus* (Sitzungsberichte der Bayerischen Akademie der Wissenschaft, Heft 2), Hueber; Pinborg, Jan (1967). *Die Entwicklung der Sprachtheorie im Mittelalter* (*BGPM*, XLII, 2), Aschendorff.

UGOLINO OF ORVIETO (Hugolin)
BIOGRAPHICAL DATA: b. *ca.* 1300; d. 1373.
TEXTS: *Prologus* to *Commentaria in quattuor libros Sententiarum*, in A. Zumkeller (1941), *Hugolin von Orvieto und seine theologische Erkenntnislehre* (Cassiciacum, Eine Sammlung wissenschaftlicher Forschungen über den hl. Augustinus und den Augustinerorden, Band IX, 2. Reihe, 3. Band) Augustinus-Verlag; *Der Physikkommentar Hugolins von Orvieto OESA* (1972), ed. Willigis Eckermann, De Gruyter.
SECONDARY LITERATURE: Corvino, F. (1967). 'Ugolino di Orvieto', in *Enciclopedia filosofica* 6, Sansoni.

VITAL DU FOUR (Vitalis de Furno)
BIOGRAPHICAL DATA: b. *ca.* 1260; d. 1327.
TEXTS: *De rerum principio*, in *Johannis Duns Scoti Opera omnia* (1639), ed. L. Wadding, Vivés; *Quaestiones disputatae*, in F. M. Delorme, ed. (1927), 'Le Cardinal Vital du Four, Huit questions disputées sur le probleme de la connaissance', *Archives d'histoire doctrinal et littéraire du moyen âge* 2:151–337; *Quodlibeta Tria* (1947), ed. F. M. Delorme, Spicilegium Pontificii Athenaei Antoniani; *Speculum morale totius sacrae scripturae* (1513), Lyon.
SECONDARY LITERATURE: Lynch, John E. (1972). *The Theory of Knowledge of Vital du Four*, The Franciscan Institute; Pisvin, A. (1949). 'Die Intuition und ihre metaphysische Wert nach Vitalis de Furno und Gonsalvus Hispanus', *Wissenschaft und Weisheit* 12:147–73; Untervintl, L. von (1955). 'Die Intuitionslehre bei Vitalis de Furno', *Collectanea Franciscana* 25:53–113, 225–53.

WALTER BURLEY (Burleigh, Bayle, Borle, Bourle, Brulleus, Burghle, Burlaeus, Burle, Burlie)
BIOGRAPHICAL DATA: b. *ca.* 1275; d. 1344/5. Master of arts at Oxford and Fellow of Merton College by 1301. Remained Fellow of Merton until 1305. Ordained in 1309. Studied theology under Thomas Wilton at Paris beginning before 1310. Master of theology at Paris around 1320–2. Fellow of the Sorbonne by 1324. Appointed envoy to the papal court at Avignon by Edward III in 1327. Held quodlibetal disputation in Toulouse in 1327 and in Bologna in 1341. Clerk of the household of Richard de Bury, Bishop of Durham in 1333, and of the King's household in 1336. Held a number of benefices, including a canonry at York and one at Salisbury.
TEXTS: *An Introduction to the Treatise 'De obligationibus' With Critical Editions of the Treatises of William of Sherwood (?) and Walter Burley* (1963), ed. Romuald Green, unpublished doctoral dissertation, Institut Supérieur de Philosophie de Louvain; *De primo et ultimo instanti* (1965), ed. H. and C. Shapiro, *Archiv für Geschichte der Philosophie* 47:157–73; *De puritate artis logicae tractatus longior, with a revised edition of the Tractatus brevior* (1955), ed. Philotheus Boehner, Franciscan Institute; *De relativis* (1962), ed. H. Shapiro, *Franciscan Studies* 22:155–71; 'La problématique des propositions insolubles au XIIIᵉ siècle et au début du XIVᵉ, suivie de l'édition des traités de W. Shyreswood, W. Burleigh et Th. Bradwardine' (1970). M.-L. Roure (ed.), *Archives d'histoire doctrinale et littéraire du moyen âge* 37:205–326; 'The *De potentiis animae* of Walter Burley' (1974). J. M. Kitchel (ed.), *Mediaeval Studies* 33:85–113; 'Walter Burleigh's Middle Commentary on Aristotle's *Perihermeneias*' (1973). S. F. Brown (ed.), *Franciscan Studies* 33:42–134; 'Walter Burleigh's

Quaestiones in librum Perihermeneias' (1974). S. F. Brown (ed.), *Franciscan Studies* 34:200–95; 'Walter Burleigh's Treatise *De Suppositionibus* and Its Influence on William of Ockham' (1972). S. F. Brown, *Franciscan Studies* 32:15–64; 'Walter Burley's Treatise *De formis*' (1970). F. J. D. Scott (ed.), Bayerische Akademie der Wissenschaften (*Veröffentlichungen d. Kommiss. f. d. Hrsg. ungedr. Texte aus d. Mittelalt. Geisteswelt*, 4).

SECONDARY LITERATURE: Martin, C. (1964). 'Walter Burley', in *Oxford Studies Presented to Daniel Callus* (Oxford Historical Society, n.s., 16), Clarendon Press; Murdoch, John and Edith Sylla (1970). 'Burley, Walter', in *Dictionary of Scientific Biography*; Uña Juárez, A. (1978). *La filosofía del siglo XIV. Contexto cultural de Walter Burley*, Biblioteca 'La Ciudad de Dios', Real Monasterio de El Escorial; Weisheipl, James A. (1968). 'Ockham and Some Mertonians', *Mediaeval Studies* 30:163–213; Weisheipl, James A. (1969). 'Repertorium Mertonense', *Mediaeval Studies* 31:174–224.

WALTER CHATTON (Chaton, Catton, Caton, Cepton, Schaton)
BIOGRAPHICAL DATA: b. 1285; d. 1344. Entered the Franciscan order as a boy. Ordained subdeacon in 1307. Commented twice on the Sentences, once (the *Reportatio*) in 1322/3 at Oxford, and again later (*Lectura*) at some unknown place and date. May have used Ockham's Sentence commentary in producing his own. Adam Wodeham attended Chatton's lectures and showed his notes to Ockham. Returned to Oxford as fifty-third regent in 1330. Was in Assisi with Gerard of Odo, Minister General of the Franciscans, in 1332. At the papal court in Avignon in 1333, where, as one of the Pope's advisors, he was involved in various theological controversies and proceedings.

TEXTS: *Commento alle Sentenza Prologo–Questione Terza* (1973). Luciano Cova (ed.), Edizioni dell'Ateneo; *De paupertate evangelica*, in D. Douie, ed. (1931–2), 'Three Treatises on Evangelical Poverty', *Archivum Franciscanum Historicum* 14:341–69, 15:36–58, 210–40; 'Ein ockhamkritischer Text zu Signifikation und Supposition und zum Verhältnis von erster und zweiter Intention' [*In Sent.* I d. 22–23] (1975). Christian Knudsen (ed.), *CIMAGL* 14:1–26; 'Gauthier de Chatton et son Commentaire des Sentences' (1943). L. Baudry (ed.), *Archives d'histoire doctrinale et littéraire du moyen âge* 14:337–69; 'Gualteri de Chatton and Guillelmi de Ockham Controversia de Natura Conceptus Universalis' (1967). Gedeon Gál (ed.), *Franciscan Studies* 27: 191–212; 'La prima questione del Prologo del Commento alle Sentenze di Walter Catton' (1970). M. E. Reina (ed.), *Rivista critica di storia della filosofia* 25: 48–74, 290–314; 'La quarta questione del Prologo del Commento alle Sentenze di Walter Catton' (1975). Luciano Cova (ed.), *Rivista critica di storia della filosofia* 30: 303–16; 'The Second Question of the Prologue to Walter Chatton's Commentary on the Sentences' (1955). J. J. O'Callaghan (ed.), in R. O'Donnell (ed.) *Nine Mediaeval Thinkers*, Pontifical Institute of Mediaeval Studies; 'Two Questions on the Continuum: Walter Chatton (?), O. F. M. and Adam Wodeham, O. F. M.' (1966). E. Synan and J. Murdoch (eds.), *Franciscan Studies* 26:212–88; 'Walter Chatton on the Univocity of Being: A Reaction to Peter Aureoli and William Ockham' (1971). Noel A. Fitzpatrick (ed.), *Franciscan Studies* 31:88–177.

SECONDARY LITERATURE: Auer, J. (1953). 'Die "skotistische" Lehre von der Heilsgewissheit: Walter von Chatton der erste "Skotist"', *Wissenschaft und Weisheit* 16: 1–19; Brady, Ignatius (1967). 'Walter of Chatton', in *The New Catholic Encyclopedia*; Knudsen, Christian (1975). *Walter Chattons Kritik an Wilhelm von Ockhams Wissenschaftslehre*, unpublished doctoral dissertation, Rheinische Friedrich-Wilhelms universität, Bonn.

WILLIAM OF ALNWICK
BIOGRAPHICAL DATA: fl. *ca.* 1315. Lectured on the Sentences at Paris before 1314. He was associated with Duns Scotus in the opening years of the fourteenth century and may be the

author of the *additiones* to Books I and II of Scotus' Commentary on the Sentences. His unedited *Determinationes* is a collection of questions dealing largely with topics in natural philosophy.

TEXTS: *Quaestiones disputatae de esse intelligibili et de quolibet* (1937), ed. A. Ledoux, Collegium S. Bonaventurae.

SECONDARY LITERATURE: Ledoux, A. (1937). 'Introduction' in his edition of *Quaestiones disputatae*.

WILLIAM ARNAUD (Guillielmus Arnaldi)

BIOGRAPHICAL DATA: fl. mid-thirteenth century. Master of arts at Toulouse in 1235–44. Wrote one of the earliest commentaries on Peter of Spain's *Tractatus*.

TEXTS: 'On the genuine text of Peter of Spain's *Summulae logicales, IV:* The *Lectura Tractatuum* by Guilelmus Arnaldi, Master of arts at Toulouse (1235–1244)' (1969). L. M. de Rijk (ed.), *Vivarium* 7:120–62.

WILLIAM OF AUVERGNE (William of Paris, Guilelmus Alvernus, Guilelmus Arvernus)

BIOGRAPHICAL DATA: b. *ca.* 1180; d. 1249. Taught theology at Paris. Bishop of Paris from 1228–49.

TEXTS: *De universo* (1516), Paris. *Opera omnia* (1674), Paris (Reprinted Minerva 1963); 'Tractatus magistr. Guillelmi Alvernensis *De bono et malo*' (1946). J. R. O'Donnell (ed.), *Mediaeval Studies* 8:245–99; 'Tractatus secundus Guillelmi Alvernensis *De bono et malo*' (1954). J. R. O'Donnell (ed.), *Mediaeval Studies* 16:219–71.

SECONDARY LITERATURE: Baumgartner, Matthias (1893). 'Die Erkenntnislehre des Wilhelm von Auvergne' (*BGPM* II, 1), Aschendorff; Charland, T. M. (1936). *Artes praedicandi*, Vrin, Forest, A. (1952). 'Guillaume d'Auvergne, critique d'Aristote', in *Études médiévales offertes à M. la doyen A. Fliche*, Presses universitaires françaises; Masnovo, A. (1930–45). *Da Guglielmo d'Auvergne a S. Tommaso d'Aquino* (2 vols.), 'Vita e pensiero'. Moody, E. A. (1975). 'William of Auvergne and His Treatise *De anima*' in his *Studies in Medieval Philosophy, Science, and Logic*, University of California Press; Valois, Noël (1880). *Guillaume d'Auvergne, évêque de Paris (1228–1249), sa vie et ses ouvrages*, Alphonse Picard.

WILLIAM OF AUXERRE (Guilelmus Autissiodorensis)

BIOGRAPHICAL DATA: b. *ca.* 1140/50; d. 1231. Master of theology at Paris. Archdeacon of Beauvais.

TEXTS: *Summa aurea in quattuor libros Sententiarum* (1500), Paris (Reprinted Minerva 1964); (1518), Paris; (1591), Venice.

SECONDARY LITERATURE: Ottaviano, Carmelo (1931). *Guglielmo d'Auxerre, la vita, le opere, il pensiero*, "L'Universale" Tipografia Poliglotta; Principe, Walter H. (1963). *William of Auxerre's Theology of the Hypostatic Union*, Pontifical Institute of Mediaeval Studies.

WILLIAM OF CONCHES

BIOGRAPHICAL DATA: b. *ca.* 1080; d. *ca.* 1154.

TEXTS: *Dragmaticon* (1567), ed. G. Gratarolus under the title *Dialogus de substantiis physicis . . .*, Argentorati (= Strasbourg); *Glosae super Platonem* (1965), ed. E. Jeaneau, Vrin; *Philosophia mundi*, among the works of Bede, in *PL* 90, and of Honorius, in *PL* 172; *Philosophia mundi*, Book I (1974), ed. G. Maurach, E. J. Brill.

SECONDARY LITERATURE: Fredborg, K. M. (1973). 'The Dependence of Petrus Helias' *Summa super Priscianum* on William of Conches' *Glose super Priscianum*', *CIMAGL* 11:1–57; Rijk, L. M. de (1967), in De Rijk 1962–7, II (1), 221–8.

WILLIAM HEYTESBURY (Hentisberius, Hentisburius, Hesberi, Hesbri, Tisberius, Tisbery)

BIOGRAPHICAL DATA: b. before 1313; d. 1372/3. Fellow of Merton College by 1330. Foundation Fellow of Queen's College in 1340, but soon returned to Merton. Doctor of theology by 1348.

TEXTS: *Tractatus Gulielmi Hentisberi de sensu composito et diviso, Regulae ejusdem cum Sophismatibus* ... (1494), Venice; *William Heytesbury: On 'Insoluble' Sentences: Chapter One of His Rules for Solving Sophisms* (1979). ed. Paul Vincent Spade, Pontifical Institute of Mediaeval Studies.

SECONDARY LITERATURE: Clagett, Marshall (1959). *The Science of Mechanics in the Middle Ages*, University of Wisconsin Press; Maier, Anneliese (1952). *An der Grenze von Scholastik und Naturwissenschaft* (2nd ed.), Edizioni di Storia e Letteratura; Maierù, Alfonso (1966). 'Il "Tractatus de sensu composito et diviso" di Guglielmo Heytesbury', *Rivista critica di Storia della Filosofia* 21:243–63; Maierù, Alfonso (1969). 'Il problema della verità nelle opere di G. Heytesbury', *Studi Medievali* 7:40–74; Murdoch, John (1979). 'Propositional analysis in Fourteenth-Century Natural Philosophy', *Synthese* 40:126–38; Weisheipl, James A. (1968). 'Ockham and Some Mertonians', *Mediaeval Studies* 30:163–213; Weisheipl, James A. (1969). 'Repertorium Mertonense', *Mediaeval Studies* 31:174–224; Wilson, Curtis (1956). *William Heytesbury: Medieval Logic and the Rise of Mathematical Physics* (Publications in Medieval Science, 3), University of Wisconsin Press; Wilson, Curtis (1972). 'Heytesbury, William', in *Dictionary of Scientific Biography*.

WILLIAM DE LA MARE

BIOGRAPHICAL DATA: d. *ca.* 1290.

TEXTS: *Correctorium Corruptorii*, in P. Glorieux, ed. (1927), *Les premières polemiques thomistes* (Bibliothèque thomiste, 9), Kain.

SECONDARY LITERATURE: Pelzer, F. (1955). 'Einige ergänzende Angaben zum Leben und zur Schriften des Wilhelm de la Mare O. F. M.', *Franziskanische Studien* 37:75–80.

WILLIAM OCKHAM (Guillelmus de Ockham, Occam, Hockham)

BIOGRAPHICAL DATA: b. *ca.* 1285; d. 1347/9. Joined Franciscans, probably subdeacon in 1306. Student of theology at Oxford. Lectured on Sentences there, 1317–19. Completed all requirements as bachelor before going to London friary in 1320 to await his turn to incept as master. Never became regent master, partly because there were many waiting to occupy the Franciscan chair and partly because of the opposition of the chancellor of the university John Lutterell. Taught and wrote at the *studium generale* of the London Custody until 1324. Probably lived in the same house as Walter Chatton; their running debate is reflected in the writings of both men. Summoned to Avignon in 1324 to answer charges of heresy. While in Avignon he became involved in the controversy concerning Franciscan poverty. Fled Avignon with the Minister General of the order Michael of Cesena in 1328. After being excommunicated, took refuge in Munich under the protection of Ludwig of Bavaria. Carried on polemic against Pope John XXII and his successors, writing numerous political treatises.

TEXTS: *Breviloquium de potestate papae* (1944: reprinted 1952) in R. Scholz (ed.) *Wilhelm von Ockham als politischer Denker und sein Breviloquium* (Schriften des Reichsinstituts für ältere deutsche Geschichtskunde, 8), K. W. Hiersemann. Also L. Baudry, ed. (1937) (Études de philosophie médiévale, 24), J. Vrin; *De imperatorum et pontificum potestate* (1944) in R. Scholz (ed.) *Unbekannte Kirchenpolitische Streitschriften aus der Zeit Ludwigs des Bayern 1327–1354*, Loescher. Also C. K. Brampton, ed. (1927), Clarendon Press; *Opera philosophica et theologica* (1967–), ed. Gedeon Gál, Stephen Brown, *et al.*, Franciscan Institute; *Opera plurima*

(1494–6), Lyon. (Reprinted Gregg Press 1962); *Opera politica* (1956–), ed. J. G. Sikes, R. F. Bennett, and H. S. Offler, Manchester University Press; *The De Sacramento Altaris of William of Ockham* (1930). T. B. Birch (ed. and tr.), Lutheran Literary Board; *The Tractatus de praedestinatione et de praescientia dei et de futuris contingentibus of William Ockham* (1945), ed. Philotheus Boehner, Franciscan Institute. Also in *William Ockham: Predestination, God's Foreknowledge and Future Contingents* (1969). M. M. Adams and N. Kretzmann (trs.), Appleton-Century-Crofts/Hackett.

SECONDARY LITERATURE: Baudry, Léon (1949). *Guillaume d'Occam: Sa vie, ses oeuvres, ses idées sociales et politiques*, J. Vrin; Baudry, Léon (1958). *Lexique philosophique de Guillaume d'Occam: Étude des notions fondamentales*, P. Léthielleux; Boehner, Philotheus (1958). *Collected Articles on Ockham*, ed. E. M. Buytaert, Franciscan Institute; Ghisalberti, Alessandro (1972). *Guglielmo di Ockham*, Vita e Pensiero; Heynck, Valens (1950). 'Ockham-Literatur: 1919–1949', *Franziskanische Studien* 32:164–83; Junghans, Helmar (1968). *Ockham im Lichte der neueren Forschung*, Lutherisches Verlaghaus; Koelmel, W. (1962). *Wilhelm Ockham und seine Kirchenpolitischen Schriften*, Ludgerus Verlag; Leff, Gordon (1975). *William of Ockham: The Metamorphosis of Scholastic Discourse*, Manchester University Press/Rowman and Littlefield; McGrade, Arthur S. (1974). *The Political Thought of William of Ockham*, Cambridge University Press; Miethke, J. (1969). *Ockhams Weg zur Sozialphilosophie*, De Gruyter; Reilly, James P. (1968). 'Ockham Bibliography: 1950–1967', *Franciscan Studies* 28:197–214; Weisheipl, James A. (1968). 'Ockham and Some Mertonians', *Mediaeval Studies* 30:163–213.

WILLIAM OF SHERWOOD (Guilelmus de Shyreswood, Shyreswode, Schirewode, Syrewude)

BIOGRAPHICAL DATA: b. *ca.* 1200/1210; d. between 1266 and 1272. Studied and taught at Oxford; master at Oxford in 1252. Treasurer of Lincoln from 1254/8 onwards. Rector of Aylesbury.

TEXTS: *De obligationibus*, in Romuald Green, ed. (1963), *The Logical Treatises De obligationibus: An Introduction with Critical Texts of William of Sherwood (?) and Walter Burley*, unpublished doctoral dissertation, Louvain; *Introductiones in logicam* (1937), ed. Martin Grabmann, (*Sitzungsberichte Bayerischen Akademie der Wissenschaften, Phil.-hist. Abteilung*, Heft 10), Hueber. Also in *William of Sherwood's Introduction to Logic* (1966), Norman Kretzmann (tr.), University of Minnesota Press; *Syncategoremata* (1941), ed. J. R. O'Donnell, *Mediaeval Studies* 3:46–93. Also in *William of Sherwood's Treatise on Syncategorematic Words* (1968), Norman Kretzmann (tr.), University of Minnesota Press.

SECONDARY LITERATURE: Braakhuis, H. A. G. (1977). 'The views of William of Sherwood on some semantical topics and their relation to those of Roger Bacon', *Vivarium* 15:111–42; Kretzmann, Norman (1967). 'William of Sherwood', in *The Encyclopedia of Philosophy*; Malcolm, J. (1971). 'On Grabmann's text of William of Sherwood', *Vivarium* 9:108–18; Rijk, L. M. de (1976). 'Some thirteenth-century tracts on the game of obligation', *Vivarium* 14:26–49. Spade, Paul Vincent and Eleonore Stump (forthcoming), 'The Treatise on Obligations Attributed to William of Sherwood'; Stump, Eleonore (1980). 'William of Sherwood's Treatise on Obligations', *Historiographia Linguistica* 7:249–61.

BIBLIOGRAPHY

Note: Because of the length of time required for the preparation of this History, works published after 1976 could not always be taken into account; and many works published before the publication of this History are listed here as forthcoming.

For additional bibliographical information on individual philosophers see also the Biographies.

Abelard, Peter. *See* Peter Abelard

Ackrill, J. L. (1963). *Aristotle's Categories and De Interpretatione*. Translated, with notes. Clarendon Press

Adams, Marilyn McCord (1970). 'Intuitive Cognition, Certainty and Scepticism in William of Ockham', *Traditio* 26:389–98

(1973). 'Did Ockham Know of Material and Strict Implication? A Reconsideration', *Franciscan Studies* 33:5–37

(1976). 'Ockham on Identity and Distinction', *Franciscan Studies* 36:5–74

(1977). 'Ockham's Nominalism and Unreal Entities', *Philosophical Review* 86:144–76

(1978). 'Ockham's Theory of Natural Signification', *Monist* 62:444–59

Adams, Robert M. (1977). 'Middle Knowledge and the Problem of Evil', *American Philosophical Quarterly* 14:109–17

Adorno, F. (1954). 'Di alcune orazioni e prefazioni di Lorenzo Valla', *Rinascimento* 5:191–225

Agricola, Rudolph (1539). *De inventione dialectica*. Cologne

Alan of Lille (1855). *Regulae de sacra theologia*, PL 210

Albert the Great (1890–9). *Opera omnia* (38 vols., ed. Augustus Borgnet), Vivès

(1890–9a). *Liber I Priorum analyticorum* (vol. 1), Vivès

(1890–9b). *De anima libri tres* (vol. 5), Vivès

(1890–9c). *Liber de causis et processu universitatis* (vol. 10), Vivès

(1890–9d). *Politicorum Aristotelis commentarii* (vol. 8), Vivès

(1890–9e). *Super Ethica* (vol. 7), Vivès

(1899). *Summa de homine* (vol. 38), Vivès

(1951–). *Opera omnia* (50 vols., ed. Bernhard Geyer, *et al.*), Institutum Alberti Magni

(1951a). *Liber de principiis motus processivi* (vol. 12), Institutum Alberti Magni

Albert of Saxony (1495). *Sophismata*, Paris

(1496). *Quaestiones super artem veterem*, in *Expositio aurea et admodum utilis super artem veterem edita per venerabilem inceptorem fratrem Gullielmum de Ockham cum quaestionibus Alberti parvi de Saxonia*, Bologna

(1497a). *Commentarius in Posteriora Aristotelis*, Venice

(1497b). *Quaestiones super Analytica posteriora*, Venice

(1502). *Sophismata*, Paris

(1518). *Perutilis logica*, Venice

(1518a). *Quaestiones Physicorum*, Paris

(1518b). *Quaestiones in De caelo*, Paris

(1522). *Perutilis logica*, Venice

Albinus (1858). *Didascalicus* (in *Platonis dialogi* ... vol. 6, ed. C. F. Hermann), Teubner

Alcuin (1851). *Dialectica, PL* 101

(1941). *The Rhetoric of Alcuin and Charlemagne*, tr. W. S. Howell, Princeton University Press

Alexander of Aphrodisias (1883). *In Aristotelis Analyticorum priorum librum I commentarium*, ed. M. Wallies (Commentaria in Aristotelem Graeca, II. 1), Reimer

(1891). *In Aristotelis Topicorum libros octo commentaria*, ed. M. Wallies (Commentaria in Aristotelem Graeca, II, 2), Reimer

(1892). *De fato*, ed. I. Bruns (Commentaria in Aristotelem Graeca, Suppl. II, 2), Reimer

Alexander of Hales (1924–48). *Summa theologica* (4 vols. in 5), Collegium S. Bonaventurae

Alexander of St Elpidius (1969). *Tractatus de Ecclesiastica Potestate* in J. T. Rocaberti (ed.) *Bibliotheca Maxima Pontificia*, 2, Akademische Druck- und Verlagsanstalt

Algazel (1933). *Metaphysics. A Medieval Translation*, ed. J. T. Muckle, C.S.B., Pontifical Institute of Mediaeval Studies

Allan, D. J. (1950). 'Mediaeval Versions of Aristotle, *De Caelo*, and the Commentary of Simplicius', *Mediaeval and Renaissance Studies* 2 : 82–120

Allen, J. W. (1957). *A History of Political Thought in the Sixteenth Century*, revised ed., Methuen

Allers, Rudolf (1941). 'The Intellectual Cognition of Particulars', *The Thomist* 3 : 95–163

Allmand, C. T., ed. (1973). *Society at War, the Experience of England and France during the Hundred Years War*, Oliver and Boyd

ed. (1976). *War, Literature and Politics in the Late Middle Ages*, Liverpool University Press

Alluntis, F. (1965). 'Demonstrability and Demonstration of the Existence of God', in J. K. Ryan and B. M. Bonansea (eds.) *John Duns Scotus 1265–1965*, Catholic University of America

Alluntis, F., and Wolter, A. (1975). *John Duns Scotus. God and Creatures: The Quodlibetal Questions*, Princeton University Press

Almain, Jacques (1611). *Expositio de Suprema Potestate Ecclesiastica et Laica, circa Quaestionum Decisiones Magistri Guillermi de Ockham super Potestate Summi Pontificis* in M. Goldast (ed.) *Monarchia Sancti Romani Imperii*, 1 : 588–647, Conrad Biermann. (Reprinted 1960 Akademische Druck- und Verlagsanstalt) (Also in L. Du Pin (ed.) *Jean Gerson, Opera Omnia*, 2: cols. 1013–1120, Sumptibus Societatis Antwerp)

(1525). *Moralia ... et Libellus de Auctoritate Ecclesiae*, Claudius Chevallon. (*Libellus* also in L. Du Pin (ed.) *Jean Gerson, Opera Omnia*, 2: cols. 976–1021, Sumptibus Societatis Antwerp)

(1706). *Quaestio Resumptiva, De Dominio Naturali, Civili et Ecclesiastico* in L. Du Pin (ed.) *Jean Gerson, Opera Omnia*, 2: cols. 961–76, Sumptibus Societatis Antwerp

Altschul, Michael (1971). 'Kingship, government, and politics in the middle ages: some recent studies', *Medievalia et Humanistica*, N.S. 2 : 133–52

Alvarus Pelagius (1969). *De Planctu Ecclesiae* in J. T. Rocaberti (ed.) *Bibliotheca Maxima Pontificia*, vol. 3, Akademische Druck- und Verlagsanstalt

Alvarus Thomas (1509). *Liber de triplici motu*. Paris

Ammonius (1895). *In Aristotelis Categorias commentarius*, ed. A. Busse (Commentaria in Aristotelem Graeca IV.4), Reimer

(1897). *In Aristotelis De Interpretatione commentarius*, ed. A. Busse (Commentaria in Aristotelem Graeca IV.5), Reimer

Anawati, Georges C. (1974). *Études de philosophie musulmane* (Études musulmanes, No. 15), Vrin

André de Neufchâteau (1514). *In primum librum Sententiarum*, Paris

Andrés, Teodoro de (1969). *El nominalismo de Guillermo de Ockham como filosofia del lenguaje* (Biblioteca hispánica de filosofia), Editorial Gredos

Angelelli, I. 1970. 'The Techniques of Disputation in the History of Logic'. *Journal of Philosophy* 67:800–15

   (1972). 'Franciscus Sebastiani's *Logica* (1791)', *Journal of the History of Philosophy* 10:76–82

Anonymous (14th c.). *Tractatus de motu locali difformi*, Cambridge, Gonville & Caius MS 499/268, ff. 213rb–215rb

Anonymous (1611a) *Disputatio inter Militem et Clericum* in M. Goldast (ed.) *Monarchia Sancti Romani Imperii*, 1:13–18; Conrad Biermann (Reprinted 1960 Akademische Druck- und Verlagsanstalt)

Anonymous (1611b). *Somnium Viridarii de Iurisdictione Regia et Sacerdotali* in M. Goldast (ed.) *Monarchia Sancti Romani Imperii*, 1:58–229; Conrad Biermann (Reprinted 1960 Akademische Druck- und Verlagsanstalt)

Anonymous (1834). 'Lettre écrite de Rome à un professeur de philosophie', *Journal historique et littéraire* 1:541–51

Anonymous (1902). *Vita beati Joannis Psichaitae*, in Ven, P. van den 'La vie grecque de S. Jean le Psichaïte', *Le muséon. Études philologiques et religieuses*. N.S. 3:97–125

Anonymous (1929). *Anonymi logica et quadrivium cum scholiis antiquis*, ed. J. L. Heiberg (Det Kongelige Danske Videnskabernes Selskab. Historisk-filologiske Meddelelser XV.1)

Anonymous (1940a). *Quoniam ignoratis communibus* in Grabmann 1940, pp. 27–9 (excerpts)

Anonymous (1940b). *Sophismata logicalia* in Grabmann 1940, pp. 50–1 (excerpts)

Anonymous (1940c). *Sophismata Parisius determinata* in Grabmann 1940, pp. 33–41 (excerpts); supplemented in Braakhuis 1979, p. 81

Anonymous (1954). *Rhetorica ad Herennium*, tr. Harry Caplan (Loeb Classical Library), Harvard University Press

Anonymous (1962–7a). *Ars Emmerana* in De Rijk 1962–7, II (2), 143–74

Anonymous (1962–7b). *Ars Meliduna* in De Rijk 1962–7, II (1), 292–390 (excerpts)

Anonymous (1962–7c). *Dialectica Monacensis* in De Rijk 1962–7, II (2), 453–638

Anonymous (1962–7d). *Quaestiones Victorinae* in De Rijk 1962–7, II (2), 731–69

Anonymous (1962–7e). *Tractatus Anagnini* in De Rijk 1962–7, II (2), 215–332

Anonymous (1962–7f). *Tractatus de univocatione Monacensis* in De Rijk 1962–7, II (2), 33–51

Anonymous (1977). *Tractatus implicitarum* in Giusberti 1977

Anonymous (1979). *Sincategoreumata Monacensia* in Braakhuis 1979, I, pp. 95–104

Anonymous of York (1897). *Tractatus Eboracenses* in *Monumenta Germaniae Historica* (Libelli de Lite) 3:645–87. Impensis Bibliopolii Hahniani

   (1977). *Der Codex 415 des Corpus Christi College Cambridge*, ed. Karl Pellens and Ruth Nineham, Steiner

Anscombe, G. E. M. (1965). 'Thought and Action in Aristotle' in Renford Bambrough (ed.) *New Essays on Plato and Aristotle*, Routledge and Kegan Paul

Anscombe, G. E. M., and P. T. Geach (1961). *Three Philosophers: Aristotle, Aquinas, Frege*, Cornell University Press

Anselm of Canterbury (1936). *Ein neues unvollendetes Werk des hl. Anselm von Canterbury*, ed. F. S. Schmitt (*BGPM*, XXXIII.3), Aschendorff

(1946). *Opera omnia*, ed. F. S. Schmitt, Nelson

(1946a). *De libertate arbitrii* in F. S. Schmitt (ed.) *Opera omnia*, vol. 1, Nelson

(1946b). *De veritate* in F. S. Schmitt (ed.) *Opera omnia*, vol. 1, Nelson

(1946c). *De casu diaboli* in F. S. Schmitt (ed.) *Opera omnia*, vol. 1, Nelson

(1946d). *De concordia praescientiae et praedestinationis et gratiae Dei cum libero arbitrio* in F. S. Schmitt (ed.) *Opera omnia*, vol. 2, Nelson

(1946e). *De incarnatione verbi* in F. S. Schmitt (ed.) *Opera omnia*, vol. 2, Nelson

Apollonius Dyscolus (1878). *Scripta minora*, ed. R. Schneider (Grammatici Graeci II.1), Teubner

(1910a). *De syntaxi*, ed. G. Uhlig (Grammatici Graeci II.2), Teubner

(1910b). *Fragmenta*, ed. R. Schneider (Grammatici Graeci II.3), Teubner

Apuleius (1908). *De philosophia libri*, ed. P. Thomas (Apulei opera quae supersunt, vol. III), Teubner

Aquinas, Thomas, *see* Thomas Aquinas

Arbus, M.-R. (1957). 'Le droit romain dans l'oeuvre de saint Thomas', *Revue Thomiste* 57:325–49

[Aristoteles Latinus] (1939). *Codices: Pars prior*, ed. G. Lacombe *et al.*, La Libreria dello Stato

(1955). *Codices: Pars posterior*, ed. G. Lacombe *et al.*, Cambridge University Press

(1957). VII.2, *Physica: Translatio Vaticana*, ed. A. Mansion, Desclée de Brouwer

(1961a). *Codices: Supplementa altera*, ed. L. Minio-Paluello, Desclée de Brouwer

(1961b). I.1–5, *Categoriae vel Praedicamenta*, ed. L. Minio-Paluello, Desclée de Brouwer

(1961c). XXIX.1, *Politica: Translatio imperfecta*, ed. P. Michaud-Quantin, Desclée de Brouwer

(1962). III.1–4, *Analytica priora*, ed. L. Minio-Paluello, Desclée de Brouwer

(1965a). II.1–2, *De interpretatione vel Periermenias*, ed. L. Minio-Paluello and G. Verbeke, Desclée de Brouwer

(1965b). XI.1–2, *De mundo*, ed. W. L. Lorimer, rev. L. Minio-Paluello, Desclée de Brouwer

(1966a). I.6–7, *Categoriarum supplementa: Porphyrii Isagoge et Liber sex principiorum*, ed. L. Minio-Paluello, Desclée de Brouwer

(1966b). XVII.2, *De generatione animalium*, ed. H. J. Drossaart-Lulofs, Desclée de Brouwer

(1968a). IV.1–4, *Analytica posteriora*, ed. L. Minio-Paluello and B. G. Dod, Desclée de Brouwer

(1968b). XXXIII.1–2, *De arte poetica*, ed. L. Minio-Paluello, Desclée de Brouwer

(1969). V.1–3, *Topica*, ed. L. Minio-Paluello, Desclée de Brouwer

(1970). XXV.1–1a, *Metaphysica: Translatio Iacobi ('Vetustissima') et Translatio composita ('Vetus')*, ed. G. Vuillemin-Diem, Desclée de Brouwer

(1972–4). XXVI.1–3, *Ethica Nicomachea*, ed. R. A. Gauthier, Brill/Desclée de Brouwer

(1975). VI.1–3, *De sophisticis elenchis*, ed. B. G. Dod, Brill/Desclée de Brouwer

(1976). XXV.2, *Metaphysica: Translatio anonyma ('Media')*, ed. G. Vuillemin-Diem, Brill

Armstrong, A. H., ed. (1967). *The Cambridge History of Later Greek and Early Medieval Philosophy*, Cambridge University Press

Armstrong, R. A. (1966). *Primary and Secondary Precepts in Thomistic Natural Law Teaching*, Martinus Nijhoff

Arway, R. J. (1962). 'A Half Century of Research on Godfrey of Fontaines', *The New Scholasticism* 36:192–218

Ashworth, E. J. (1972). 'The Treatment of Semantic Paradoxes from 1400 to 1700',
  Notre Dame Journal of Formal Logic 13:34–52
  (1973). 'The Doctrine of Exponibilia in the Fifteenth and Sixteenth Centuries',
  Vivarium 11:137–67
  (1974a). *Language and Logic in the Post-medieval Period* (Synthese Historical Library, 12),
  Reidel
  (1974b). '"For Riding is Required a Horse": A Problem of Meaning and Reference
  in Late Fifteenth- and Early Sixteenth-Century Logic', *Vivarium* 12:94–123
  (1976a). '"I Promise You a Horse": A Second Problem of Meaning and Reference in
  Late Fifteenth- and Early Sixteenth-Century Logic', I, *Vivarium* 14:62–79, II, *Ibid.*,
  14:149–55
  (1976b). 'Agostino Nifo's Reinterpretation of Medieval Logic', *Rivista critica di storia
  della filosofia* 31:355–74
  (1977a). 'Chimeras and Imaginary Objects: A Study in the Post-medieval Theory of
  Signification', *Vivarium* 15:57–79
  (1977b). 'Thomas Bricot (d. 1516) and the Liar Paradox', *Journal of the History of
  Philosophy* 15:267–80
  (1978). *The Tradition of Medieval Logic and Speculative Grammar from Anselm to the End
  of the Seventeenth Century: A Bibliography from 1836 Onwards* (Subsidia Mediaevalia,
  9), Pontifical Institute of Mediaeval Studies
  (1978a). 'Multiple Quantification and the Use of Special Quantifiers in Early Sixteenth
  Century Logic', *Notre Dame Journal of Formal Logic* 19:599–613
  (1979). 'The "Libelli Sophistarum" and the Use of Medieval Logic Texts at Oxford and
  Cambridge in the Early Sixteenth Century', *Vivarium* 17:134–58
  (forthcoming). 'Theories of the Proposition: Some Early Sixteenth-Century
  Discussions', *Franciscan Studies*
Atti del XVII Convegno di Studi, Todi (1978). *Le scuole degli Ordini Mendicanti (secoli
  XIII–XIV)*, Accademia Tudertina
Aubert, Jean Marie (1955). *Le droit romain dans l'oeuvre de Saint Thomas*, Vrin
Augustine (1845a). *In Johannis evangelium tractatus*, PL 35
  (1845b). *De nuptiis et concupiscentia*, PL 44
  (1877). *De magistro*, PL 32
  (1894). *De Genesi ad litteram*, ed. J. Zycha (*CSEL*, 28), Tempsky
  (1895). *Epistulae*, ed. A. Goldbacher (*CSEL*, 44), Tempsky
  (1899–1900). *De civitate Dei*, ed. E. Hoffmann (*CSEL*, 40), Tempsky
  (1922). *Contra academicos*, ed. P. Knöll (*CSEL*, 63), Tempsky
  (1950). *Against the Academics*, tr. J. J. O'Meara (Ancient Christian Writers, 12),
  Newman
  (1955). *De civitate Dei*, ed. B. Domhart and A. Kalb (Corpus Christianorum. Series
  Latina, 47–8), Brepols
  (1956). *De libero arbitrio* (*CSEL*, 74), Hoelder-Pichler-Tempsky
  (1961). *De magistro*, ed. G. Weigel (*CSEL*, 77), Hoelder-Pichler-Tempsky
  (1963a). *De doctrina Christiana* (*CSEL*, 80), Hoelder-Pichler-Tempsky
  (1963b). *The Trinity*, tr. S. McKenna (The Fathers of the Church, 45), Catholic
  University of America
  (1968). *De Trinitate*, ed. W. J. Mountain (Corpus Christianorum. Series Latina, 50–
  50A), Brepols
  (1975). *De dialectica*, tr. wth introduction and notes by B. D. Jackson from the text
  newly edited by J. Pinborg (Synthese Historical Library, 16), Reidel
Augustinus Triumphus (1479). *Summa de ecclesiastica potestate*, Rome
  (1903). *Tractatus Brevis de Duplici Potestate Prelatorum et Laicorum* in R. Scholz (ed.) *Die*

Publizistik zur Zeit Philipps des Schönen und Bonifaz' VIII, Enke

Aureoli, Peter, *see* Peter Aureoli

Averroes (1562–74a). *Media expositio in libros Priorum resolutoriorum* (Aristotelis opera cum Averrois commentariis, I.1), Venice

(1562–74b). *Quaesita octo in libros Priorum analyticorum* (Aristotelis opera cum Averrois commentariis, I.2b and 3), Venice

(1562–74c). *Media expositio Topicorum Aristotelis* (Aristotelis opera cum Averrois commentariis, I.3), Venice

(1562–74d). *Commentary on the Physics* (Aristotelis opera cum Averrois commentariis, IV), Venice

(1562–74e). *In libros De coelo commentarii* (Aristotelis opera cum Averrois commentariis, V), Venice

(1562–74f). *Commentary on the Metaphysics* (Aristotelis opera cum Averrois commentariis, VIII), Venice

(1953). *Commentarium magnum in Aristotelis De anima*, ed. F. S. Crawford (Corpus commentariorum Averrois in Aristotelem), Mediaeval Academy of America

(1954). *Tahafut al-Tahafut*, tr. S. Van den Bergh, Luzac

(1974). *Averroes on Plato's Republic*, tr. with introduction and notes by R. Lerner, Cornell University Press

Avesani, A. (1970). 'La professione dell' "umanista" nel cinquecento', *Italia medioevale e umanistica* 13:205–32

Avicenna (1508). *Avicennae perhypatetici philosophi ac medicorum facile primi opera . . .*, Venice (Reprinted Minerva and Bibliothèque S. J. de Louvain 1961)

[Avicenna Latinus] (1968) *Liber De anima IV–V*, ed. S. Van Riet, Éditions Orientalistes/Brill

(1972). *Liber De anima I–III*, ed. S. Van Riet, E. Peeters/Brill

(1977). *Liber de philosophia prima*, ed. S. Van Riet, E. Peeters

Bacon, Roger, *see* Roger Bacon

Baebler, J. J. (1885). *Beiträge zu einer Geschichte der lateinischen Grammatik im Mittelalter*, Buchhandlung des Waisenhauses

Baeumker, Clemens (1895). *Avencebrolis (Ibn Gebirol) Fons vitae ex Arabico in Latinum translatus ab Johanne Hispano et Dominico Gundissalino (BGPM, I)*, Aschendorff

(1913). 'Die Stellung des Alfred von Sareshel und seiner Schrift "De Motu Cordis" in der Wissenschaft des beginnenden XIII. Jahrhunderts', *Sitzungsberichte der königliche Bayerische Akademie der Wissenschaften*, Philos.-philol. u. hist. Klasse 9:35–40

(1923). *Des Alfred von Sareshel (Alfredus Anglicanus) Schrift 'De Motu Cordis' (BGPM, XXIII)*, Aschendorff

Bainton, R. H. (1946). 'The Early Church and War', *Harvard Theological Review* 39:189–212

Baldanza, G. (1970). 'Il Problema della filosofia in "Optatam totius"', *Seminarium* n.s. 10:1–18

Baldus de Ubaldis (1608–9). *Consilia* (2 vols.), Venice

Balić, C. (1931). 'Une question inédite de J. Duns Scot sur la volonté', *Recherches de théologie ancienne et médiévale* 3:191–208

(1965). 'The Life and Works of John Duns Scotus', in J. K. Ryan and B. M. Bonansea (ed.), *John Duns Scotus 1265–1965*, Catholic University of America

Báñez, Dominic (1934). *Scholastica commentaria in primam partem Summae Theologiae S. Thomae Aquinatis*, ed. L. Urbano, Editorial F.E.D.A. (Reprinted Brown Reprint Library 1966)

Barcia Trelles, Camilo (1933). 'Francisco Suárez (1548–1617)', *Académie de droit international: recueil des cours* 43:385–553

Barnes, Jonathan (1972). *The Ontological Argument*, Macmillan and St Martin's Press
(1975). *Aristotle's Posterior Analytics*, tr. with notes by Jonathan Barnes, Clarendon Press

Barnes, Jonathan, Malcolm Schofield, and Richard Sorabji (1975–9). *Articles on Aristotle* (4 vols.), Duckworth

Barozzi, L. and R. Sabbadini (1891). *Studi sul Panormita e sul Valla* (R. Istituto di studi superiori pratici e di perfezionamento in Firenze), Le Monier

Barth, T. (1939). 'De fundamento univocationis apud Joannem Duns Scotum', *Antonianum* 14:181–206, 277–98, 373–92
(1953). 'De univocationis entis scotisticae intentione principali necnon valore critico', *Antonianum* 28:72–110
(1965). 'Being, Univocity, and Analogy According to Duns Scotus', in J. K. Ryan and B. M. Bonansea (ed.), *John Duns Scotus, 1265–1965*, Catholic University of America

Batllori, M. (1944). *Baltasar Masdeu y el neoscolasticismo italiano*, Balmesiana

Battaglia, F. (1965). *Metafisica religione e politica nel pensiero di Nicolò da Cusa*, Pàtron

Baudry, Léon (1934). 'Les rapports de Guillaume d'Occam et de Walter Burleigh', *Archives d'histoire doctrinale et littéraire du moyen âge* 9:155–73
(1943). 'Gauthier de Chatton et son commentaire des Sentences', *Archives d'histoire doctrinale et littéraire du moyen âge* 18:337–69
(1949). *Guillaume d'Occam: Sa vie, ses oeuvres, ses idées sociales et politiques*, vol. 1 (Études de Philosophie Médiévale, 39), Vrin
(1950). *La Querelle des futurs contingents (Louvain 1465–1475)* (Études de Philosophie Médiévale, 38), Vrin
(1958). *Lexique Philosophique de Guillaume d'Ockham*, Lethielleux

Baur, Ludwig (1903). *Dominicus Gundissalinus: De divisione philosophiae* (BGPM, IV.2–3), Aschendorff
(1912). *Die philosophische Werke des Robert Grosseteste, Bischofs von Lincoln* (BGPM, IX), Aschendorff
(1917). *Die Philosophie des Robert Grosseteste* (BGPM XVIII), Aschendorff

Bayley, C. C. (1949). 'Pivotal concepts in the political philosophy of William of Ockham', *Journal of the History of Ideas* 10:199–218

Bazán, Bernardo Carlos (1972). *Siger de Brabant: Quaestiones in tertium de anima, De anima intellectiva, De aeternitate mundi, Édition critique* (Philosophes médiévaux, Tome 13), Publications Universitaires and Béatrice-Nauwelaerts
(1973). 'La eternidad y la contingencia del intelecto en Sigerio de Brabante', *Philosophia* (Mendoza), No. 39:63–84
(1974). 'Le dialogue philosophique entre Siger de Brabant et Thomas d'Aquin. A Propos d'un ouvrage récent de E. H. Weber O.P.', *Revue philosophique de Louvain* 72:53–155
(1975). 'La unión entre el intelecto separado y los individuos, según Sigerio de Brabante', *Patristica et mediaevalia* (Buenos Aires), 1:5–35

Becker, A. (1933). *Die Aristotelische Theorie der Möglichkeitsschlüsse*, Junker und Dünnhaupt Verlag

Becker, O. (1952). *Untersuchungen über den Modalkalkül*, Westkulturverlag Anton Hain

Becker-Freyseng, A. (1938). *Die Vorgeschichte des philosophischen Terminus "contingens"* (Quellen und Studien zur Geschichte und Kultur des Mittelalters, Reihe D, Heft 7), Selbstverlag F. Bilabel

Beha, H. (1960–1). 'Matthew of Aquasparta's Theory of Cognition', *Franciscan Studies*

20:161–204; 21:1–79, 383–465

Bellarmine, Robert

(1870). *De Summo Pontifice* in Justin Fèvre (ed.) *Politiani Opera omnia*, 1:449–615 and 2:5–167 (Reprinted Minerva 1965)

(1870–4). *De Conciliis* in Justin Fèvre (ed.) *Politiani Opera omnia*, 2:187–407 (Reprinted Minerva 1965)

(1950). *The Power of the Pope in Temporal Affairs, against William Barclay*, tr. and ed. George Albert Moore, 2nd ed., Country Dollar Press

(1951). *Extracts on Politics and Government from the Supreme Pontiff*, tr. and ed. George Albert Moore, Country Dollar Press

Belmond, S. (1928). 'Le mechanisme de la connaissance après Pierre Olieu, dit Olivi', *La France Franciscaine* 12:291–401; 463–87

(1930). 'L'Intellect actif après Jean Duns Scot', *Revue de philosophie* 30:31–54

Beltran de Heredia, V. (1968). *Domingo Bañez y las controversias sobre la gracia: textos y documentos*, Consejo superior de Investigaciones Cientificas

Bendiek, J. (1952). 'Die Lehre von den Konsequenzen bei Pseudo-Scotus', *Franziskanische Studien* 34:205–34.

Berges, W. (1938). *Die Fürstenspiegel des hohen und späten Mittelalters*, K. W. Hiersemann

Bergh, B. (1978). *Paleography and Textual Criticism* (Scripta Minora Regiae Societatis Humaniorum litterarum Lundensis 1979–80:2), CWK Gleerup

Bergmann, Gustav (1964). *Logic and Reality*, University of Wisconsin Press

Bernard of Clairvaux (1963). *De Consideratione ad Eugenium Papam* in J. Leclercq and H. Rochais (eds.) *S. Bernardi Opera*, 3:381–493, Editiones Cistercienses

(1976). *Five Books on Consideration: Advice to a Pope*, ed. John D. Anderson and Elizabeth T. Kennan (Cistercian Fathers 13, Works of Bernard of Clairvaux 13), Cistercian Publications

Bernard Morisan (1625). *Commentarii et disputationes in libros logicos, physicos, et ethicos Aristotelis*, Frankfurt

Bertola, Ermenegildo (1967). 'E esistito un avicennismo latino nel medioevo?', *Sophia* 35:318–334

(1971). 'E esistito un avicennismo latino nel medieovo?', *Sophia* 39:278–320

Berube, C. (1964). *La connaissance de l'individuel au moyen âge*, Presse Universitaire de Montréal

Bettoni, Efrem (1954). *Il processo astrattivo nella concezione di Enrico di Gand*, Vita e Pensiero

(1961). *Duns Scotus*, tr. B. M. Bonansea, Catholic University of America

Bird, Otto (1959). 'The logical interest of the topics as seen in Abelard', *The Modern Schoolman*, 37:53–7

(1960). 'The Formalizing of Topics in Mediaeval Logic', *Notre Dame Journal of Formal Logic* 1:138–49

(1961). 'Topic and Consequence in Ockham's Logic', *Notre Dame Journal of Formal Logic*, 2:65–78

(1962a). 'The Tradition of the Logical Topics: Aristotle to Ockham', *Journal of the History of Ideas* 23:307–23

(1962b). 'What Peirce Means by Leading Principles', *Notre Dame Journal of Formal Logic* 3:175–8

Black, Anthony (1970). *Monarchy and Community: Political Ideas in the Later Conciliar Controversy 1430–1450*, Cambridge University Press

Blackley, F. D. (1967). 'Ralph Strode', *New Catholic Encyclopedia*, 12:71

Blake, Ralph, Curt Ducasse, and Edward Madden (1966). *Theories of Scientific Method:*

The Renaissance through the Nineteenth Century, University of Washington Press

Blanche, F.-A. (1934). 'La théorie de l'abstraction chez Saint Thomas d'Aquin' in *Mélanges Thomistes* (Bibliothèque Thomiste, vol. 3), Vrin

Blanché, Robert (1970). *La Logique et son Histoire: d'Aristote à Russell*, Armand Colin

Blemmydes, Nicephorus. *see* Nicephorus Blemmydes

Bliemetzrieder, F. (1919). *Anselmus von Laon systematische Sentenzen* (*BGPM*, XVIII, 2–3), Aschendorff

Bloch, M. (1973). *The Royal Touch: Sacred Monarchy and Scrofula in England and France*, tr. J. E. Anderson, Routledge and Kegan Paul

Blondel, Maurice (1893). *L'Action*, Alcan

Bloomfield, Morton W. (1970). Review of Marcia L. Colish, *The Mirror of Language: A Study in the Medieval Theory of Knowledge*, Yale University Press, 1968, in *Speculum* 45:119–22

Bocheński, I. M. (1938). 'De Consequentiis Scholasticorum Earumque Origine', *Angelicum* 15:92–109

  (1947a). *La Logique de Théophraste* (Collectanea Friburgensia, n.s. 32), Librairie de l'Université Fribourg en Suisse

  ed. (1947b). *Petri Hispani Summulae logicales*, Marietti

  (1951). *Ancient Formal Logic* (Studies in Logic and the Foundations of Mathematics), North-Holland

  (1956). *Formale Logik* (Orbis Academicus III, 2), Karl Alber

  (1961). *History of Formal Logic*, tr. and ed. Ivo Thomas, University of Notre Dame Press

Bodin, Jean (1641). *De Republica libri sex*, Frankfurt

  (1962). *The Six Bookes of a Commonweale*, Richard Knolles' trans. of 1606 edn. with introd. and notes by Kenneth Douglas McRae, Harvard University Press

  (1975). *Colloquium of the Seven about Secrets of the Sublime*, tr. Marion L. D. Kuntz, Princeton University Press

Boehner, Philotheus (1943a). 'Ockham's political ideas', *Review of Politics* 5:426–87

  (1943b). 'The Notitia Intuitiva of Non-Existents According to William Ockham', *Traditio* 1, 245–75

  (1946). 'The Realistic Conceptualism of William Ockham', *Traditio* 4:307–35

  (1951a). 'Bemerkungen zur Geschichte der De Morganschen Gesetze in der Scholastik', *Archiv für Philosophie* 4:113–46

  (1951b). 'Does Ockham Know of Material Implication?', *Franciscan Studies* 11:203–50

  (1952). *Medieval Logic: An Outline of Its Development from 1250–c. 1400*, Manchester University Press

  ed. (1955). *Walter Burleigh: De puritate artis logicae Tractatus longior with a revised edition of the Tractatus brevior* (Franciscan Institute Publications, Text Series, 9), The Franciscan Institute

  (1957). *Ockham: Philosophical Writings*, Nelson

  (1958). *Collected Articles on Ockham*, ed. E. M. Buytaert (Franciscan Institute Publications, Philosophy Series, 12), The Franciscan Institute

  (1965). 'History of Logic III – Scholastic Logic', *Encyclopedia Britannica* 14:226–31

Boethius (1847). *De arithmetica*, PL 63

  (1860a). *De differentiis topicis libri quattuor*, PL 64

  (1860b). *De syllogismo categorico*, PL 64

  (1860c). *De trinitate*, PL 64

  (1860d). *In Topica Ciceronis Commentariorum libri sex*, PL 64

  (1860e). *Introductio ad syllogismos categoricos*, PL 64

(1860f). *Liber de divisione, PL* 64

(1860g). *In Categorias Aristotelis libri quattuor, PL* 64

(1860h). *Commentaria in Porphyrium, PL* 64

(1860i). *De unitate Trinitatis cum Gilberti Porretae commentario, PL* 64

(1877). *Commentarii in librum Aristotelis ΠΕΡΙ ΕΡΜΗΝΕΙΑΣ pars prior versionem continuam et primam editionem continens*, ed. Carl Meiser, Teubner

(1880). *Commentarii in librum Aristotelis ΠΕΡΙ ΕΡΜΗΝΕΙΑΣ pars posterior secundam editionem et indices continens*, ed. Carl Meiser, Teubner

(1906). *In Isagogen Porphyrii Commenta*, ed. S. Brandt (Corpus Scriptorum Ecclesiasticorum Latinorum, 48), F. Tempsky

(1918). *De trinitate* in *Tractates, De consolatione philosophiae*, ed. H. F. Stewart and E. K. Rand (Loeb Classical Library), William Heinemann, Ltd

(1957). *Philosophiae consolatio*, ed. L. Bieler (Corpus Christianorum, Series Latina, 94), Brepols

(1969). *De hypotheticis syllogismis*, ed. L. Obertello, Paideia editrice

(1978). *Boethius's De topicis differentiis*, tr. Eleonore Stump, with introduction, commentary, and supplementary essays, Cornell University Press

Boethius of Dacia (1936). *De Summo Bono sive De Vita Philosophiae* in M. Grabmann, *Mittelalterliches Geistesleben*, 2:209–16, M. Hüber

(1969). *Quaestiones super Priscianum maiorem* ed. J. Pinborg and H. Roos (Corpus Philosophorum Danicorum Medii Aevi 4), Gad

(1976). *De aeternitate mundi*, ed. N. J. Green-Pedersen in *Boethii Daci Opera* (Corpus Philosophorum Danicorum Medii Aevi, 6), Gad

(1976). *Quaestiones super librum Topicorum*, ed. N. J. Green-Pedersen and J. Pinborg (Corpus Philosophorum Danicorum Medii Aevi VI, 1), Gad

Boggess, W. F. (1971). 'Hermannus Alemannus' Rhetorical Translations', *Viator* 2:227–50

Boh, Ivan (1962). 'A Study in Burleigh: Tractatus de Regulis Generalibus Consequentiarum', *Notre Dame Journal of Formal Logic* 2:83–101

(1963a). 'Burleigh: On Conditional Hypothetical Propositions', *Franciscan Studies* 23:4–67

(1963b). 'Walter Burleigh's Hypothetical Syllogistic', *Notre Dame Journal of Formal Logic* 4:241–69

(1964). 'An Examination of Some Proofs in Burleigh's Propositional Logic', *The New Scholasticism* 38:44–60

(1965). 'Paul of Pergula on Suppositions and Consequences', *Franciscan Studies* 25:30–89

(1966). 'Propositional Connectives, Supposition and Consequence in Paul of Pergula', *Notre Dame Journal of Formal Logic* 7:109–28

(1977). 'The "*Conditionatim*"-Clause: One of the Problems of Existential Import in the History of Logic', *Notre Dame Journal of Formal Logic* 18:459–66

Boler, J. F. (1963). 'Abailard and the Problem of Universals', *Journal of the History of Philosophy* 1:37–51

(1973). 'Ockham on Intuition', *Journal of the History of Philosophy* 11:95–106

(1976). 'Ockham on Evident Cognition', *Franciscan Studies* 36:85–98

Bonald, L. G. A. de (1830). *Recherches philosophiques sur les premiers objets des connaissances morales* (2 vols.), Vanryckegem-Hovaere

Bonansea, Bernadino M. (1965) 'Duns Scotus's Voluntarism' in J. K. Ryan and B. M. Bonansea (eds.) *John Duns Scotus 1265–1965*. Catholic University of America

Bonaventure (1882–1902). *Opera omnia* (10 vols.), Collegium S. Bonaventurae

(1882–1902a). *Commentarius in quattuor libros Sententiarum Petri Lombardi* (Opera omnia, I–IV), Collegium S. Bonaventurae

(1911). *Tria opuscula: Breviloquium, Itinerarium mentis in Deum, De reductione artium ad theologiam*, Collegium S. Bonaventurae

Borak, H. (1964). 'Principia doctrinae politicae apud S. Bonaventuram', *Laurentianum* 5:301–20, 487–523

Bos, E. P. (1976). 'John Buridan and Marsilius of Inghen on Consequences', in Jan Pinborg (ed.), *The Logic of John Buridan* (Opuscula Graecolatina, Supplementa Musei Tusculani, 9) Museum Tusculanum

Bosley, R. (1978). 'In Support of an Interpretation of On Int. 9', *Ajatus* 37:29–40

Bottin, Francesco (1973). 'Analisi linguistica e fisica Aristotelica nei "Sophismata" di Richard Kilmyngton' in Carlo Giacon (ed.) *Filosofia Politica e altri saggi* (Università di Padova, Pubblicazioni dell' Istituto di Storia della Filosofia e del Centro per Ricerche di Filosofia Medioevale, n.s. 14), Antenore

(1973a). 'L'Opinio de Insolubilibus di Richard Kilmington', *Rivista Critica di storia della filosofia* 28:568–90

(1974). 'Un testo fondamentale nell' ambito della "Nuova Fisica" di Oxford: I Sophismata di Richard Kilmington', *Miscellanea Mediaevalia* 9:201–5

(1976). *Le antinomie semantiche nella logica medievale* (Pubblicazioni dell' Istituto di Storia della Filosofia e del Centro per Ricerche di Filosofia Medioevale, n.s. 23), Antenore.

Bougerol, J. Guy (1964). *Introduction to the Works of Bonaventure*, St Anthony Guild Press

Bouillard, H. (1949). 'L' Intention fondamentale de Maurice Blondel et la théologie', *Recherches de Science Religieuse* 36:321–402

Bourgeois, R. (1936). 'La théorie de la connaissance intellectuelle chez Henri de Gand', *Revue de Philosophie* 36:238–59

Bourke, V. J. (1964). *The Essential Augustine*, The New American Library

Bowman, Leonard J. (1972–3). 'The Development of the Doctrine of the Agent Intellect in the Franciscan School of the Thirteenth Century', *The Modern Schoolman* 50:251–79

Boyer, Charles (1925). 'Réflexions sur la connaissance sensible selon Saint Thomas', *Archives de philosophie*, vol. 3, Cahier 2, Gabriel Beauchesne

Boyer, M. (1835). *Défense de l'ordre social contre le carbonarisme modern avec un jugement sur M. de La Mennais considéré comme écrivain et une dissertation sur le romantisme*, Le Clerc

Braakhuis, H. A. G. (1967). 'The Second Tract on *Insolubilia* Found in Paris, B.N. Lat. 16.617: An Edition of the Text with an Analysis of Its Contents', *Vivarium* 5:111–45

(1977). 'The Views of William of Sherwood on Some Semantical Topics and Their Relation to Those of Roger Bacon', *Vivarium* 15:111–42

(1978). *I. De Ontwikkeling van de theorie van de syncategoremata tot aan de 13de eeuw; II. De 13de eeuwse syncategoremata-tractaten; III. Enkele aspecten van de ontwikkeling van de theorie van de syncategoremata in de 13de eeuw*, Typescript; preliminary version

(1978a). Preliminary editions of Robert Bacon (?), *Sincategoreumata*, and Henry of Ghent, *Sincathegoreumata*, Typescript; preliminary version

(1979). *De 13de eeuwse Tractaten over syncategorematische Termen* (Deel I: Inleidende studie; Deel II: Uitgave van Nicolaas van Parijs' Sincategoreumata), Krips Repro Meppel

Brady, Ignatius (1950). 'Law in the *Summa Fratris Alexandri*', *Proceedings of the American Catholic Philosophical Association* 24:133–47

(1967). 'Bonaventure, St', *New Catholic Encyclopedia* 2:658–64

(1975). 'The *Opera Omnia* of Saint Bonaventure Revisited', *Proceedings of the Seventh Centenary Celebration of the Death of Saint Bonaventure*, pp. 47–59, The Franciscan Institute

Brampton, C. K. (1963). 'The Probable Order of Ockham's Non-Polemical Works', *Traditio* 19:469–83

B[ranchereau], L. (1855). *Praelectiones philosophiae in majori seminario Claromontensi primum habitae*, Leroux & Jouby

Breda, H. L. van (1971). 'The Actual State of the work on Husserl's Inedita: achievements and projects', *Analecta Husserliana* 2:149–59

Brennan, Robert E. (1941). 'The Thomistic Concept of Imagination', *The New Scholasticism* 15:149–61

Brentano, F. (1968). 'Thomas von Aquin' in *Die vier Phasen der Philosophie ... nebst Abhandlungen über Plotinus, Thomas von Aquin ...* (Philosophische Bibliothek, 195), Felix Meiner

Brerewood, Edward (1614). *Elementa Logicae*, London

(1614a). *Enquiries touching the Diversities of Languages and Religions through the chief parts of the World*, London

(1628). *Tractatus quidam logici de Praedicabilibus et Praedicamentis*, Oxford

(1640). *Commentarii in Ethica Aristotelis*, Oxford

Brosch, H. J. (1931). *Der Seinsbegriff bei Boethius, mit besonderer Berücksichtigung der Beziehung von Sosein und Dasein* (Philosophie und Grenzwissenschaften 4, pt. 1:1–120) Rauch

Brounts, A. (1970). 'Nouvelles précisions sur la pecia'. *Scriptorium* 24:343–59

Brown, J. V. (1971). 'Sensation in Henry of Ghent', *Archiv für Geschichte der Philosophie* 53:238–66

Brown, Mary A. (1966). 'The Role of the Tractatus de Obligationibus in Medieval Logic', *Franciscan Studies* 26:26–35

Brown, Stephen F. (1965). 'Avicenna and the Unity of the Concept of Being', *Franciscan Studies* 25:117–50

(1972). 'Walter Burleigh's Treatise *De suppositionibus* and Its Influence on William of Ockham', *Franciscan Studies* 32:15–64

(1973). 'Walter Burleigh's Middle Commentary on Aristotle's *Perihermeneias*', *Franciscan Studies* 33:42–134

(1974). 'Walter Burley's *Quaestiones in librum Perihermeneias*', *Franciscan Studies* 34:200–95

Browne, I. (1963). *International Law and the Use of Force by States*, Clarendon Press

Browne, M. (1932). 'Circa intellectum et eius illuminationem apud S. Albertum Magnum', *Angelicum* 9:187–202

Bruckmüller, Franz (1908). *Untersuchungen über Sigers (von Brabant) Anima intellectiva*, G. J. Manz (Inauguraldissertation, Ludwig-Maximilians-Universität, Munich)

Bruder, K. (1928). *Die philosophischen Elemente in den Opuscula sacra des Boethius*, Meinar

Bruni, G. (1936). *Le Opere di Egidio Romano*, Olschki

Brunner, F. (1963). *Platonisme et Aristotélisme*, Publications Universitaires de Louvain

Bucher, Eugen (1965). *Das subjektive Recht als Normsetzungsbefugnis*, J. C. B. Mohr

Bucher, T. (1948). *Theologischen Grundlegung der menschlichen Sozialanlage nach der Lehre des hl. Bonaventura*, Weger

Buchner, H. (1970). *Plotins Möglichkeitslehre* (Epimeleia, Beiträge zur Philosophie, 16), Anton Pustet

Buisson, L. (1958). *Potestas und Caritas: die päpstliche Gewalt in Spätmittelalter* (Forschungen zur kirchlichen Rechtsgeschichte und zum Kirchenrecht, 2), Böhlau

Burgersdijck, Franco (1623). *Idea Morali Philosophiae*, Leyden
  (1626a). *Institutionum logicarum synopsis sive rudimenta logica*, Leyden
  (1626b). *Institutionum logicarum libri duo*, Leyden
Buridan, John, *see* John Buridan
Burley, Walter, *see* Walter Burley
Burns, J. H. (1954). 'New light on John Major', *The Innes Review* 5:83–100
Bursill-Hall, G. L. (1971). *Speculative Grammars of the Middle Ages* (Approaches to
  Semantics, 11), Mouton
Busard, H. L. L. (1965). 'Unendliche Reihen in *A est unum calidum*', *Archive for History of
  Exact Sciences* 2:387–97
Butts, Robert and Joseph Pitt (1978). *New Perspectives on Galileo*, Reidel
Buytaert, E. M. (1964). 'The Tractatus Logicae Minor of Ockham', *Franciscan Studies* 24:
  34–100
  ed. (1974). *Peter Abelard* (Mediaevalia Lovaniensia series I/studia II), Louvain, Presses
  Universitaires
Byrne, Edmund F. (1968). *Probability and Opinion*, Mouton

Caesarius, Johannes (1559). *Dialectica*, Cologne
Cairns, H. (1949). *Legal Philosophy from Plato to Hegel*, Johns Hopkins University Press
Cajetan, Thomas (1938–9). *Commentaria in De anima Aristotelis*, ed. P. I. Coquelle
  (2 vols.), Angelicum
Callus, D. A. (1943). 'The Introduction of Aristotelian Learning at Oxford', *Proceedings
  of the British Academy* 29:229–81.
  ed. (1955a). *Robert Grosseteste, Scholar and Bishop*, Clarendon Press
  (1955b). 'The Treatise of John Blund On the Soul' in *Autour d'Aristote*, Publications
  Universitaires de Louvain
  (1957). 'Les sources de saint Thomas: État de la question' in *Aristote et saint Thomas
  d'Aquin* (Chaire Cardinal Mercier, 1955), Publications Universitaires de Louvain
  and Éditions Beatrice-Nauwelaerts
  (1960). 'San Tommaso d'Aquino e Sant'Alberto Magno', *Angelicum* 37:133–61
Callus, D.A., and R. W. Hunt, eds. (1970). *Johannes Blund, Tractatus de Anima*, British
  Academy
Camara, Helder (1978). 'What would Saint Thomas Aquinas, the Aristotle commen-
  tator, do if faced with Karl Marx?' *The Journal of Religion* 58 Supplement: S 174–82
Campana, A. (1946). 'The origin of the word 'humanist', *Journal of the Warburg and
  Courtauld Institutes* 9:60–73
Campanella, Tommaso (1638). *Philosophiae rationalis partes quinque*, Paris
Camporeale, S. I. (1972). *Lorenzo Valla, umanesimo e teologia*, Nella Sede dell 'Istituto
  Palazzo Strozzi
Canizzo, G. (1961). 'La dottrina del "Verbum mentis" in Pietro d'Auvergne', *Rivista di
  filosofia neoscolastica* 53:152–68
Cantor, Georg (1932). *Gesammelte Abhandlungen*, ed. E. Zermelo, Springer
Capelli, A. (1961). *Lexicon Abbreviaturarum* (6th ed.) Hoepli
Cargill Thompson, W. D. J. (1972). 'The philosopher of the "politic society": Richard
  Hooker as a political thinker' in W. Speed Hill (ed.) *Studies in Richard Hooker:
  Essays Preliminary to an Edition of his Works*, Case Western Reserve University
Carlo, William (1966a). 'Idea and Concept: A Key to Epistemology' in Frederick J.
  Adelmann (ed.) *The Quest for the Absolute* (Boston College Studies in Philosophy,
  No. 1), Boston College and Martinus Nijhoff
  (1966b). *The Ultimate Reducibility of Essence to Existence in Existential Metaphysics*,

Martinus Nijhoff
Carlyle, R. W. and A. J. (1903–36). *A History of Medieval Political Theory in the West* (6 vols.), Blackwood
Casacci, A. (1926). 'Gli "Elegantiarum libri" di Lorenzo Valla', *Atene e Roma* (ser. 2) 7:187–203
Casado, F. (1951–3). 'El pensamiento filosófico del beato Santiago de Viterbo', *La Ciudad de Dios* 163:437–54; 164:301–31; 165:103–44, 283–302, 489–500
Cassiodorus (1937). *Institutiones*, ed. R. A. B. Mynors, Clarendon Press
Cassirer, Ernst (1946). *The Myth of the State*, Yale University Press
Chabod, F. (1958). *Machiavelli and the Renaissance*, Bowes & Bowes
Charette, Léon (1972). 'Philosophie politique et méthode chez Saint Thomas d'Aquin', *Revue de l'Université d'Ottawa* 42:83–96
Chenevert, Jacques (1961). 'Le verbum dans le Commentaire sur les Sentences de Saint Thomas d'Aquin', *Sciences ecclésiastiques* 13:191–223 and 359–390
Chenu, M.-D. (1934). 'Contribution à l'histoire du traité de la foi. Commentaire historique de II^{a}II^{ae} q. 1, a. 2' in *Mélanges Thomistes, publiés par les Dominicains de la province de France à l'occasion du VIe centenaire de la canonisation de Saint Thomas d'Aquin (18 juillet 1323)*, Bibliothèque Thomiste III, Le Saulchoir, 1923, 2e édition, J. Vrin, 1934
  (1936). 'Grammaire et théologie aux XIIe et XIIIe siècles', *Archives d'histoire doctrinale et littéraire du moyen âge* 10:5–28
  (1954). *Introduction à l'étude de Saint Thomas d'Aquin*, J. Vrin
  (1964). *Toward Understanding Saint Thomas*, trans. A. M. Landry and D. Hughes, Henry Regnery
Chevrier, G. (1952). 'Remarques sur l'introduction et les vicissitudes de la distinction du *ius privatum* et du *ius publicum* dans les oeuvres des anciens juristes français', *Archives de philosophie du droit*, 1:5–77
Chodorow, Stanley (1972). *Christian Political Theory and Church Politics in the Mid-Twelfth Century: The Ecclesiology of Gratian's Decretum*, University of California Press
Chomsky, Noam (1966). *Cartesian Linguistics*, Harper and Row
Chossat, M. (1914). 'Saint Thomas d'Aquin et Siger de Brabant', *Revue de philosophie* 24:553–575, 25:25–52
  (1932). 'L'Averroisme de saint Thomas. Notes sur la distinction d'essence et d'existence à la fin du XIIIe siècle', *Archives de philosophie* 9:129(465)–177(513)
  (1939). 'Dieu', *Dictionnaire de théologie catholique* 4:1180
Chrimes, S. B. (1936). *English Constitutional Ideas in the Fifteenth Century*, Cambridge University Press
Christine de Pisan (1937). *The Boke of Fayttes of Armes and Chyvalrye* trans. William Caxton, ed. A. T. P. Byles (Early English Text Society 184), Oxford University
  (1973). *Fayttes of Armes*, excerpted in Allmand 1973
Chroust, A. H. (1947). 'The Corporate Idea and the Body Politic in the Middle Ages', *Review of Politics* 9:423–52
Chroust, A. H. and Corbett, J. A. (1949). 'The fifteenth century *Review of Politics* of Laurentius of Arezzo', *Mediaeval Studies* 11:62–76
Church, Alonzo (1960). 'Intention' in D. D. Runes (ed.) *Dictionary of Philosophy*, Philosophical Library
Claessens, P. (1860). *Raison et Révélation. Exposé sommaire de quelques notions et de principes généraux auxiliaires d'une philosophie catholique*, Lethielleux
Clagett, Marshall (1941). *Giovanni Marliani and Late Medieval Physics*, Columbia

University Press
(1950). 'Richard Swineshead and Late Medieval Physics', *Osiris* 9:131–61
(1959). *The Science of Mechanics in the Middle Ages*, University of Wisconsin Press
(1968). *Nicole Oresme and the Medieval Geometry of Qualities and Motions*, University of Wisconsin Press
Clarembald of Arras (1965). *Life and Works of Clarembald of Arras*, ed. Nikolaus Häring, Pontifical Institute of Mediaeval Studies
Clark, David W. (1971). 'Voluntarism and rationalism in the ethics of Ockham', *Franciscan Studies* 31:72–87
(1973). 'William of Ockham on right reason', *Speculum* 48:13–36
Clarke, W. N. (1952a). 'The Limitation of Act by Potency: Aristotelianism or Neoplatonism?', *The New Scholasticism* 26:167–94
(1952b). 'The Meaning of Participation in St Thomas', *Proceedings of the American Catholic Philosophical Association* 26:147–57
Classen, P. (1960). *Gerhoch von Reichersberg*, F. Steiner
Classen, S. (1960). 'Collectanea zum Studien- und Buchwesen des Mittelalters mit besonderer Berücksichtigung der Kölner Universität und der Mendikantenstudien', *Archiv für Geschichte der Philosophie* 42:159–206 & 247–71
Cobban, A. B. (1975). *The Medieval Universities: their Development and Organisation*, Methuen
Coing, Helmut (ed.) (1973). *Handbuch der Quellen und Literatur der neueren europäischen Privatrechtsgeschichte, I; Mittelalter (1100–1500). Die gelehrten Rechte und die Gesetzgebung*, C. H. Beck
Coleman, Janet (1975), 'Jean de Ripa, O. F. M. and the Oxford Calculators', *Mediaeval Studies* 37:130–89
Coleman, T. (1971). *Modistic Grammar*. Unpublished dissertation, University of Toronto
Colish, M. L. (1968). *The Mirror of Language: A Study in the Medieval Theory of Knowledge*, Yale University Press
Collins, J. (1947). *The Thomistic Philosophy of the Angels*, The Catholic University of America
Combes, A. (1940). *Jean Gerson, commentateur dionysien*, J. Vrin
Combes, A. and Ruello, F. (eds.) (1967). 'Jean de Ripa I Sent. Dist. XXXVII: De modo inexistendi divine essentie in omnibus creaturis', *Traditio* 23:191–267
Composta, D. (1954). 'Il diritto naturale in Graziano', *Studia Gratiana* 2:151–210
Contenson, P.-M. (1959a). 'S. Thomas et l'avicennisme latin', *Revue des sciences philosophiques et théologiques* 43:3–31
(1959b). 'Avicennisme latin et vision de Dieu au début du XIIIᵉ siècle', *Archives d'histoire doctrinale et littéraire du moyen âge* 34:29–97
Copleston, Frederick (1963). *A History of Philosophy*, vol. 3, Part II, Doubleday Image Books
Cornoldi, G. M. (1893). *The physical system of St Thomas*, tr. Edward Heneage Dering, London & Leamington Art & Book Co.
Costello, Frank B. (1974). *The Political Philosophy of Luis de Molina, S. J. (1535–1600)* (Bibliotheca Instituti Historici S. I.), Institutum Historicum S. I.
Cotta, S. (1955). *Il concetto di legge nella Summa theologiae di S. Tommaso d'Aquino* (Università di Torino. Memorie dell'Istituto Giuridico, serie 2, mem. 89), G. Giappichelli
Courtenay, William J. (1971). 'A revised text of Robert Holcot's quodlibetal dispute on whether God is able to know more than he knows', *Archiv für Geschichte der Philosophie* 53:1–21

(1972–3). 'John of Mirecourt and Gregory of Rimini on Whether God Can Undo the Past', *Recherches de Théologie Ancienne et Médiévale* 39:224–56; 40:147–74

(1978). *Adam Wodeham. An Introduction to His Life and Writings*, E. J. Brill

Cousin, Victor (1836). *Ouvrages inédites d'Abélard, pour servir à l'histoire de la philosophie scolastique en France*, Imprimerie Royale

(1838). *Historie générale de la Philosophie*, Didier

(1849). *Petri Abaelardi Opera* (2 vols.), A. Durand

Crakanthorpe, Richard (1619). *Introductio in metaphysicam*, Oxford

(1622). *Logicae Libri Quinque*, London

Cranz, F. E. (1940). *Aristotelianism in Medieval Political Theory: a study of the reception of the Politics*, Harvard University Graduate School: Summaries of theses, pp. 133–6

(1971). *A Bibliography of Aristotle Editions, 1501–1600* (Bibliotheca Bibliographica Aureliana, 37), Valentin Koerner

(1976). 'The Renaissance reading of the *De Anima*', *De Pétrarque à Descartes* 32:359–76

Crawford, F. S., ed. (1953). *Averrois Cordubensis Commentarium Magnum in Aristotelis De Anima* (Corpus Commentariorum Averrois in Aristotelem), Mediaeval Academy of America

Crescini, A. (1965). *Le origini del metodo analitico: il Cinquecento*, Del Bianco

Crombie, A. C. (1953). *Robert Grosseteste and the origins of experimental science: 1100–1700*, Clarendon Press

Crosby, H. Lamar, Jr. (1955). *Thomas of Bradwardine: His Tractatus de Proportionibus; Its Significance for the Development of Mathematical Physics*, (Publications in Medieval Science, 2), University of Wisconsin Press

Crowe, M. B. (1974). 'St Thomas and Ulpian's natural law' in A. Maurer *et al.* (eds.) *St Thomas Aquinas, 1274–1974*, 1, Pontifical Institute of Mediaeval Studies

(1977). *The Changing Profile of the Natural law*, Martinus Nijhoff

Crowley, T. (1950). *Roger Bacon. The problem of the Soul in his Philosophical Commentaries*, Duffy

(1952). 'Roger Bacon and Avicenna', *Philosophical Studies* (Maynooth) 2:82–8

Cunningham, F. (1962). 'Distinction According to St Thomas', *The New Scholasticism* 36:279–312

(1964). 'Textos de Santo Tomas sobre el *esse* y *esencia*', *Pensamiento* 20:283–306

(1970). 'The "Real Distinction" in John Quidort', *Journal of the History of Philosophy* 8:9–28

Curtis, Mark H. (1959). *Oxford and Cambridge in Transition 1558–1642*, Clarendon Press

Czartoryski, P. (1960). 'Gloses et commentaires inconnus sur la *Politique* d'Aristote d'après les mss. de la bibliothèque Jagellone de Cracovie', *Mediaevalia Philosophica Polonorum* 5:3–44

Dabin, P. (1950). *Le sacerdoce royal des fidèles dans la tradition ancienne et moderne*, L'Édition Universelle

Dähnert, Ulrich (1934). *Die Erkenntnislehre des Albertus Magnus gemessen an den Stufen der "Abstractio"* (Studien und Bibliographien zur Gegenwartsphilosophie, vol. 4), S. Hirzel

Dales, R. C., ed. (1963). *Roberti Grosseteste Commentarius in VIII Libros Physicorum Aristotelis*, University of Colorado Press

Dal Pra, Mario, ed. (1954a). *Pietro Abelardo Scritti Filosofici, Editio Super Porphyrium, Glossae in Categorias, Editio Super Aristotelem De Interpretatione, De Divisionibus, Super Topica Glossae*, Bocca

(1954b). 'Sulla dottrina della impositio prima et secunda', *Rivista critica di storia della filosofia* 9:390–9

D'Alverny, M.-T. (1952). 'Notes sur les traductions médiévales des oeuvres philosophiques d'Avicenne', *Archives d'histoire doctrinale et littéraire du moyen âge* 19:337–58

(1957). 'Les traductions d'Avicenne (Moyen âge et Renaissance)' in *Avicenne nella storia della cultura medioevale. Relazioni e discussione*, Accademia Nazionale dei Liucei

(1961–72). 'Avicenna Latinus', *Archives d'histoire doctrinale et littéraire du moyen âge* 28–39

Daly, Lowrie J. (1962). *The Political Theory of John Wyclif*, Loyola University Press

(1968). 'Medieval and Renaissance Commentaries on the *Politics* of Aristotle', *Duquesne Review* 13:41–55

(1973). 'Wyclif's political theory: a century of study', *Medievalia et Humanistica*, 4:177–87

Damascene, John. *See* John Damascene

D'Angelo, Francesco Saverio (1968). *La filosofia della politica in S. Tommaso d'Aquino*, Caltanissetta: A cura del Seminario vescovile

Dante Alighieri (1963). *Monarchia* in E. Moore and P. Toynbee (eds.) *Le Opere di Dante Alighieri*, 5th ed., Oxford University Press

Danto A. C. (1973). *Analytical Philosophy of Action*, Cambridge University Press

Da Palma Campania, G. (1955). *La dottrina sull'unità dell'intelletto in Sigieri di Brabante*, CEDAM

David, M. (1954). *La souveraineté et les limites juridiques du pouvoir monarchique du IXᵉ au XVᵉ siècle*, Librairie Dalloz

Davies, William David (1955). *Paul and Rabbinic Judaism*, S.P.C.K.

(1962). 'Conscience' in Buttrick *et al.* (eds.) *The Interpreter's Dictionary of the Bible* 1:671–6, Abingdon Press

Davis, C. T. (1957). *Dante and the Idea of Rome*, Clarendon Press

Davitt, T. E. (1951). *The Nature of Law*, Herder

Day, S. (1947). *Intuitive Cognition: A Key to the Significance of the Later Scholastics*, The Franciscan Institute

De Andrés, Teodoro, *see* Andrés, Teodoro de

De Benedictis, M. M. (1946). *The Social Thought of Saint Bonaventure*, Catholic University of America

De Bonald, L. G. A., *see* Bonald, L. G. A. de

Decker, B. (1967). *Die Gotteslehre des Jakob von Metz* (*BGPM* XLII, 1), Aschendorff

De Finance, J., *see* Finance, J. de

De Fourny, Maurice (1977). 'The Aim of the State: Peace', in J. Barnes, M. Schofield, R. Sorabji (eds.) *Articles on Aristotle: 2. Ethics and Politics*, Duckworth

Deku, H. (1956). 'Possibile logicum', *Philosophisches Jahrbuch der Görres-Gesellschaft*, 64:1–21

De la Brière, Y., *see* La Brière, Y. de

De Lagarde, G., *see* Lagarde, G. de

De Lapparent, P., *see* Lapparent, P. de

De La Vaissière, J., *see* La Vaissière, J. de

De Libera, A., *see* Libera, A. de

Delhaye, P. (1947). 'L'organisation scolaire au XIIᵉ siècle', *Traditio* 5:211–68

(1964). 'Notes sur l'histoire et le sens actuel de la vertu de justice', *Mélanges de sciences religieuses* 21:1–14

Del Prado, N. (1911). *De veritate fundamentali philosophiae Christianae*, Ex typis consociationis sancti Pauli, Friburgi Helvetiorum

De Maistre, J., *see* Maistre, J. de

Dempf, A. (1929). *Sacrum Imperium: Geschichts- und Staatsphilosophie des Mittelalters und der politischen Renaissance*, R. Oldenbourg
  (1931). *Die Ethik des Mittelalters*, R. Oldenbourg

Denifle, H., and A. Chatelain (1889–97). *Chartularium Universitatis Parisiensis* (4 vols.), Delalain

D'Entrèves, Alessandro Passerin (1932). *Riccardo Hooker: Contributo alla teoria e alla storia del diritto naturale*, Presso L'Istituto Giuridico della R. Università
  (1939). *The Medieval Contribution to Political Thought: Thomas Aquinas, Marsilius of Padua, Richard Hooker*, Oxford University Press
  (1951). *Natural Law. An introduction to legal philosophy*, Hutchinson's University Library
  (1952). *Dante as a Political Thinker*, Oxford University Press

De Pater, W., *see* Pater, W. de

De Raeymaeker, L., *see* Raeymaeker, L. de

De Rijk, L. M., see Rijk, L. M. de

Descartes, René (1897 and 1913). *Discours de la méthode* in Charles Adam et Paul Tannery (eds.), *Oeuvres de Descartes*, L. Cerf

Destrez, J. (1935). *La Pecia dans les manuscrits universitaires du XIIIᵉ et du XIVᵉ siècle*, Paris

De Vaux, R., *see* Vaux, R. de

Dewan, Lawrence (1980). 'St Albert, the Sensibles, and Spiritual Being' in James A. Weisheipl (ed.) *Albertus Magnus and the Sciences: Commemorative Essays 1980*, Pontifical Institute of Mediaeval Studies

De Wulf, Maurice, *see* Wulf, Maurice de

Dexippus (1888). *In Aristotelis Categorias commentarium*, ed. A. Busse (Commentaria in Aristotelem Graeca IV. 2), Teubner

Dezza, P., ed. (1942–4). *I neotomisti italiani del XIX secolo* (2 vols.), Fratelli Bocca.

Diem, G. (1967). 'Les Traductions gréco-latines de la Métaphysique au moyen âge: le problème de la *Metaphysica Vetus*', *Archiv für Geschichte der Philosophie* 49:7–71.

Dijksterhuis, E. J. (1961). *The Mechanization of the World Picture*, tr. C. Dikshoorne, Clarendon Press

Di Napoli, G. (1971). *Lorenzo Valla: filosofia e religione nell' umanesimo italiano*, Edizioni di storia e letteratura

Diogenes Laertius (1925). *Lives of Eminent Philosophers I–II*. With an English translation by R. D. Hicks (Loeb Classical Library), William Heinemann and Harvard University Press
  (1964). *Vitae philosophorum*, ed. H. S. Long (Oxford Classical Texts), Clarendon Press

Dirks, Heinrich (1928). *Des hl. Bonaventura Ideen über Staat und Recht*, Görres-Druckerei (Koblenzer Volkszeitung)

Dmowski, J. (1836). *Logica et metaphysica quae traduntur in Collegio Romano Societatis Iesu a R. P. Dmowski in exeunte anno 1836 et proximo 1837*, Collegio Romano

Dod, B. G. (1970). 'The Study of Aristotle's *Posterior Analytics* in the Twelfth and Thirteenth Centuries', Unpublished B. Litt. thesis, Oxford University

Döring, K. (1972). *Die Megariker. Kommentierte Sammlung der Testimonien* (Studien zur antiken Philosophie, 2), B. R. Grüner

Doig, J. (1965). 'Science première et science universelle dans le "Commentaire de la métaphysique" de saint Thomas d'Aquin', *Revue philosophique de Louvain* 63:41–96
  (1972). *Aquinas on Metaphysics. A historico-doctrinal study of the Commentary on the Metaphysics*, Martinus Nijhoff

Domański, J. (1966). 'Stephani de Reate de secundis intentionibus', *Mediaevalia*

Philosophica Polonorum 12:67–106

(1967). 'Claves intentionum', *Materialy* 7:3–22

Donagan, Alan (1969). 'The Scholastic Theory of Moral Law in the Modern World' in Anthony Kenny (ed.) *Aquinas: A Collection of Critical Essays*, Anchor Books

Doncoeur, P. (1910). 'Notes sur les averroistes latins: Boèce le Dace', *Revue des sciences philosophiques* 4:500–11

Dondaine, A. (1947). 'Le manuel de l'inquisiteur (1230–1330)', *Archivum Fratrum Praedicatorum* 17:85–194

(1956). *Les secrétaires de Saint Thomas*, Commissio Leonina

(1967). 'Un cas majeur d'utilisation d'un argument paléographique en critique textuelle', *Scriptorium* 21:261–76

Dondaine, A. and Bataillon, L. J. (1966). 'Le manuscrit Vindob. lat. 2330 et Siger de Brabant', *Archivum Fratrum Praedicatorum* 36:153–261

Donzé, R. (1967). *La grammaire générale et raisonnée de Port-Royal: contribution à l'histoire des idées grammaticales en France*, Francke

Dowdall, H. C. (1923). 'The word "state"', *Law Quarterly Review* 39:98–125

Duhem, Pierre (1906–13). *Études sur Léonard de Vinci* (3 vols.), Hermann

(1913–59). *Le système du monde: histoire des doctrines cosmologiques de Platon à Copernic* (10 vols.), Hermann

Duin, J. J. (1954). *La doctrine de la providence dans les écrits de Siger de Brabant*, Éditions de l'Institut Supérieur de Philosophie de Louvain

Dumbauld, Edward (1969). *The Life and Legal Writings of Hugo Grotius*, University of Oklahoma Press

Dumitriu, Anton (1977). *History of Logic*, (4 vols.), vol. II, Abacus Press

Dunbabin, Jean (1963). 'The Two Commentaries of Albertus Magnus on the Nicomachean Ethics', *Recherches de Théologie Ancienne et Médiévale* 30:232–50

(1972). 'Robert Grosseteste as Translator, Transmitter, and Commentator: the *Nicomachean Ethics*', *Traditio* 28:460–72

Duns Scotus, John, *see* John Duns Scotus

Durand of Saint-Pourçain (1506). *De Iurisdictione Ecclesiastica*, J. Petit

(1677). *De Origine et Usu Iurisdictionum* in *Maxima Bibliotheca Veterum Patrum* 26:127–35, Lyon

(1929). *Quaestio de natura cognitionis*, ed. J. Koch (*BGPM*, XXVI), Aschendorff

Düring, I. (1966). *Aristoteles. Darstellung und Interpretation seines Denkens*, Winter

Dürr, Karl (1942). 'Alte und neue Logik', *Jahrbuch der Schweizerischen Philosophischen Gesellschaft* 2:104–22

(1951). *The Propositional Logic of Boethius*, North-Holland

Duzy, Erminius Stanislaus (1944). *Philosophy of Social Change according to the Principles of Saint Thomas*, Catholic University of America

Dyckmans, W. (1937). *Das mittelalterliche Gemeinschaftsdenken unter dem Gesichtspunkt der Totalität: eine rechtsphilosophische Untersuchung* (Görresgesellschaft Veröffentlichungen der Sektion für Rechts- und Staatswissenschaften 73), Schöningh

Dziewicki, Michael, ed. (1893–9). *John Wyclif. Tractatus de Logica* (Wyclif's Latin Works) (3 vols.), Trübner, for the Wyclif Society

Ebbesen, S. (1972). 'Anonymi Bodleiani in Sophisticos Elenchos Aristotelis Commentarii fragmentum', *CIMAGL* 8:3–32

(1973a). 'Manlius Boethius on Aristotle's Analytica Posteriora', *CIMAGL* 9:68–73

(1973b). 'Paris 4720A. A 12th-Century Compendium of Aristotle's *Sophistici Elenchi*',

CIMAGL 10:1–20

(1976a). 'Anonymus Aurelianensis II, Aristotle, Alexander, Porphyry and Boethius. Ancient Scholasticism and 12th century Western Europe', *CIMAGL* 16:1–128

(1976b). 'The Summulae, Tractatus VII De Fallaciis' in J. Pinborg (ed.) *The Logic of John Buridan. Acts of the 3rd European Symposium on Medieval Logic and Semantics* (Opuscula graecolatina, 9), Museum Tusculanum

ed. (1977a). *Incertorum auctorum Quaestiones super Sophisticos Elenchos* (Corpus Philosophorum Danicorum Medii Aevi, 7), Gad

(1977b). 'Jacobus Veneticus on the Posterior Analytics and some early 13th-Century Oxford Masters on the Elenchi', *CIMAGL* 21:1–9

(1977c). 'Can Equivocation Be Eliminated?', *Studia Mediewistyczne* 18:103–24

(1979). 'The Dead Man is Alive', *Synthese* 40:43–70

(1979b). 'Anonymi Aurelianensis I Commentarium in Sophisticos Elenchos', *CIMAGL* 34

(1981a). 'Analyzing Syllogisms or Anonymus Aurelianensis III – the (presumably) Earliest Extant Latin Commentary on the Prior Analytics, and its Greek Model', *CIMAGL* 37:1–20

(1981b). *Commentators and Commentaries on Aristotle's Sophistici Elenchi*, 3 vols., Brill

Ebbesen, S. and J. Pinborg (1970). 'Studies in the Logical Writings Attributed to Boethius de Dacia', *CIMAGL* 3:1–54

Eberenz, James H. (1969). *The Concept of Sovereignty in Four Medieval Philosophers: John of Salisbury, St Thomas Aquinas, Egidius Colonna and Marsilius of Padua*, University Microfilms

Eckermann, Willigis (1972). *Der Physikkommentar Hugolins von Orvieto OESA*, De Gruyter

Ehrle, Franz (1925). 'Der Sentenzenkommentar Peters von Candia', *Franziskanische Studien* Beiheft 9

(1954). *Zur Enzyklika "Aeterni Patris", Text und Kommentar. Zum 75 jährigen Jubiläum der Enzyklika neu herausgegeben von Franz Pelster S. J.* (Sussidi Eruditi, 6), Edizioni di Storia e Letteratura

Elie, Hubert (1937). *Le complexe significabile*, J. Vrin

Emden, A. B. (1957–9). *A Biographical Register of the University of Oxford to a.d. 1500* (3 vols.), Clarendon Press

Enders, Heinz (1975). *Sprachlogische Traktate des Mittelalters und der Semantikbegriff* (Veröffentlichungen des Grabmann-Instituts, neue Folge, 20), Schöningh

Engelbert of Admont (1614). *De Ortu, Progressu et Fine Regnorum, et Praecipue Regni seu Imperii Romani* in M. Goldast (ed.) *Politica Imperialia*, pp. 754–73, John Bringer

Engelhardt, P. (1976). 'Intentio' in J. Ritter and K. Gründer (eds.) *Historisches Wörterbuch der Philosophie* 4:466–74, Wissenschaftliche Buchgessellschaft

Epictetus (1898). *Dissertationes*, ed. H. Schenkl, Teubner

Ermatinger, Charles J. (1954). 'Averroism in Early Fourteenth Century Bologna', *Mediaeval Studies* 16:35–56

(1963). *The Coalescent Soul in Post-Thomistic Debate*. Ph.D. Dissertation, Saint Louis University

(1969). 'John of Jandun in his Relations with Arts Masters and Theologians' in *Arts libéraux et philosophie au moyen âge*, Institut d'Études médiévales and J. Vrin

Eschmann, I. T. (1943). 'A Thomistic Glossary on the Principle of the Preeminence of a Common Good', *Mediaeval Studies* 5:123–65

(1944). 'Bonum commune melius est quam bonum unius', *Mediaeval Studies* 6:62–120

(1946). 'Studies on the notion of society in St Thomas Aquinas', *Mediaeval Studies*

8:1–42

(1947). 'Thomistic Social Philosophy and the Theory of Original Sin', *Mediaeval Studies* 9:19–55

(1958). 'St Thomas Aquinas on the two powers', *Mediaeval Studies* 20:177–205

Eustachius a Sancto Paulo (1609). *Summa philosophiae quadripartita*, Paris

Evans, G. R. (1977). 'Inopes verborum sunt Latini: Technical Language and Technical Terms in the Writings of St Anselm and some Commentaries of the Mid-Twelfth century', *Archives d'histoire doctrinale et littéraire du moyen âge* 54:115–34

(1978). *Anselm and Talking about God*, Clarendon Press

Eynde, D. Van den (1957). *L'oeuvre littéraire de Geroch de Reichersberg*, Pontificium Athenaeum Antonianum

(1962). 'Les écrits perdus d'Abélard', *Antonianum* 37:467–80

Eysinga, Willem J. M. Van (1945). *Huigh de Groot, een Schets*, H. D. Tjeenk Willink

Fabre [J.] (1862). *Défense de l'Ontologisme contre les attaques récentes de quelques écrivains qui se disent disciples de Saint Thomas*, Casterman

Fabro, Cornelio (1939). *La nozione metafisca di partecipazione secondo San Tommaso d'Aquino*, Vita e Pensiero

(1950). *La nozione metafisica di partecipazione secondo s. Tommaso d'Aquino* (2nd ed.), Società Editrice Internazionale

(1960). *Partecipazione e causalità secondo San Tommaso*, Società Editrice Internazionale

(1961). *Participation et causalité*, Publications Universitaires de Louvain

Faral, Edmond (1946). 'Jean Buridan: Notes sur les manuscrits, les éditions et le contenu de ses ouvrages', *Archives d'histoire doctrinale et littéraire du moyen âge* 21:1–53

(1949). 'Jean Buridan: Maître ès arts de l'Université de Paris' in *Histoire littéraire de la France* Vol. 38, pp. 462–605, Imprimerie nationale

Farr, William (1974). *John Wyclif as legal Reformer*, Brill

Farrel, W. (1930). *The Natural Moral Law according to St Thomas and Suárez*, St Dominic's Press

Fassò, G. (1964). *La legge della ragione*, Il Mulino

(1966–70). *Storia della filosofia del diritto* (3 vols.), Il Mulino

Faulkner, Robert K. (forthcoming). *Richard Hooker and the Politics of a Christian England*, University of California Press

Fauser, W. (1973) *Der Kommentar des Radulphus Brito zu Buch III De Anima* (*BGPM*, n. F., XII), Aschendorff

Faust, A. (1922). 'Die Dialektik Rudolf Agricolas: ein Beitrag zur Charakteristik des deutschen Humanismus', *Archiv für Geschichte der Philosophie* 34 (n. F. 27):118–35

(1931–2). *Der Möglichkeitsgedanke. Systemgeschichtliche Untersuchungen* I–II (Synthesis, 6–7), Winter

Ferguson, W. K. (1948). *The Renaissance in Historical Thought: Five Centuries of Interpretation*, Houghton Mifflin

Fernández-Santamaria, J. A. (1977). *The State, War and Peace: Spanish Political Thought in the Renaissance, 1516–1559*, Cambridge University Press

Ferrari, A. (1833). *Ethices Christianae institutiones ad usum clericorum deductae* (4 vols.), G. Vincenzi

Ferree, William (1942). *The Act of Social Justice: An Analysis of the Thomistic concept of Legal Justice ...*, Catholic University of America

Figgis, J. N. (1907). *Studies of Political Thought from Gerson to Grotius*, Cambridge University Press

(1914). *The Divine Right of Kings*, Cambridge University Press

Finance, J. de (1960). *Être et agir*, Librairie Éditrice de l'Université Grégorienne

Fink-Errera, G. (1960). 'De l'édition universitaire', *L'homme et son destin. Actes du Ier congrès international de philosophie médiévale*, pp. 221–8, Nauwelaerts
(1962). 'Une institution du monde médiéval: la pecia'. *Revue Philosophique de Louvain* 60 (III. série, 66): 184–243

Fioravanti, G. (1972). 'Sull' evoluzione del monopsichismo di Sigieri di Brabante', *Atti della Accademia delle Scienze di Torino* 106: 407–64

Fisher, Luke Francis (1948). *A Philosophy of Social Leadership according to Thomistic Principles*, Catholic University of America

Fitch, Frederic B. (1970). 'Comments and A Suggestion', in Robert L. Martin (ed.), *The Paradox of the Liar*, pp. 75–7, Yale University Press

FitzPatrick, P. J. (1973). 'Fact and Fiat: one theme in the modernist crisis', *Durham University Journal*, n. s. 34: 151–80

Fletcher, H. F. (1961). *The Intellectual Development of John Milton*, University of Illinois Press

Flückiger, F. (1955). *Geschichte des Naturrechts*, Evangelischer Verlag

Fobes, F. H., and Kurland, S., eds. (1956). *Averrois Cordubensis Commentarium medium in Aristotelis De Generatione et Corruptione Libros* (Corpus Commentariorum Averrois in Aristotelem), Mediaeval Academy of America

Fois, Mario (1969). *Il pensiero cristiano di Lorenzo Valla nel quadro storico-culturale del suo ambiente* (Analecta Gregoriana, 174), Libreria Editrice dell'Università Gregoriana

Folz, R. (1969). *The Concept of Empire in Western Europe from the Fifth to the Fourteenth Century*, tr. S. A. Ogilvie, Arnold

Fonseca, Pierre da. *See* Petrus da Fonseca

Forest, A. (1956). *La structure métaphysique du concret selon saint Thomas d'Aquin* (2nd ed.), J. Vrin

Fortescue, Sir John (1864). *De natura legis naturae*. Printed from a manuscript in the Lambeth Library for Lord Clermont
(1942). *De Laudibus Legum Anglie – The Praise of the Laws of England*, tr. and ed. S. B. Chrimes, Cambridge University Press

Fortin, E. L. and O'Neill, P. D. (tr.) (1963). 'The Condemnation of 1277', in R. Lerner and M. Mahdi (eds.) *Medieval Political Philosophy: A Source Book*, The Free Press of Glencoe

Foucher, L. (1955). *La philosophie catholique en France avant la renaissance thomiste, et en rapport avec elle (1800–1880)*, J. Vrin

Fraassen, Bas C. Van (1971). *Formal Semantics and Logic*, Macmillan

Franceschini, E. (1933). *Roberto Grossatesta, vescovo di Lincoln, e le sue traduzioni latine* (Atti del Reale Istituto Veneto di Scienze, Lettere ed Arti, 93, 2), C. Ferrari

Francis of Mayron (1940–2). 'L'oeuvre politique de François de Mayronnes', ed. P. de Lapparent, *Archives d'histoire doctrinale et littéraire du moyen âge* 15–17: 5–151

Franklin, J. H. (1973). *Jean Bodin and the Rise of Absolutist Theory*, Cambridge University Press

Fredborg, K. M. (1973). 'The Dependence of Petrus Helias' Summa super Priscianum on William of Conches' Glose super Priscianum', *CIMAGL* 11: 1–57
(1977). 'Tractatus glosarum Prisciani in MS Vat. lat. 1486', *CIMAGL* 21: 21–44

Fredborg, K. M., N. J. Green-Pedersen, L. Nielsen, and Jan Pinborg (1975). 'The Commentary on "Priscianus Maior" ascribed to Robert Kilwardby', *CIMAGL* 15: 1–143

Fredborg, K. M., L. Nielsen and J. Pinborg (1978). 'An Unedited Part of Roger Bacon's Opus Maius: De signis', *Traditio* 34: 75–136

Frede, Michael (1974a). *Die stoische Logik* (Abhandlungen der Akademie der

Wissenschaften in Göttingen, Phil.-hist. Klasse, Dritte Folge, 88), Vandenhoeck und Ruprecht

(1974b). 'Stoic vs. Aristotelian Syllogistic', *Archiv für Geschichte der Philosophie* 56:1–32

(1977). 'The Origins of Traditional Grammar' in Butts and Hintikka (ed.) *Historical and Philosophical Dimensions of Logic, Methodology and Philosophy of Science*, Reidel

(1978). 'Principles of Stoic Grammar' in J. N. Rist (ed.) *The Stoics*, University of California Press

Friedmann, Wolfgang (1967). 'Grotius, Hugo' in Paul Edwards (ed.) *The Encyclopedia of Philosophy* (vol. 3), Collier-Macmillan

Friedrich, C. J. (1958). *The Philosophy of Law in Historical Perspective*, University of Chicago Press

Fumagalli, M. T. B-B. (1970). *The Logic of Abelard*, Reidel

Gabriel, A. (1977). *The Economic and Material Frame of the Medieval University* (Texts and Studies in the History of Medieval Education 15), Notre Dame University Press

Gaeta, F. (1955). *Lorenzo Valla: filologia e storia nell' umanesimo italiano*, Istituto italiano per gli studi storici

Gaetano di Thiene (1491). *De reactione*, Venice

(1494). *Recollecte super De motu locali*, Venice

Gagnér, Sten (1960). *Studien zur Ideengeschiclite der Gesetzgebung* (Acta Universitatis Upsaliensis. Studia Iuridica Upsaliensia, I), Almqvist and Wiksell

Gál, Gedeon (1967a). 'Gregory of Rimini' in *New Catholic Encyclopedia* 6:797

(1967b). 'William of Ockham' in *New Catholic Encyclopedia* 14:932–5

(1967c). 'Gualteri de Chatton et Guillelmi de Ockham Controversia de Natura Conceptus Universalis', *Franciscan Studies* 27:191–212

(1969). 'Quaestio Ioannis de Reading de Necessitate Specierum Intelligibilium Defensio Doctrinae Scoti', *Franciscan Studies* 29:66–156

(1971). 'Henricus de Harclay: Quaestio de Significato Conceptus Universalis', *Franciscan Studies* 31:178–234

(1977). 'Adam of Wodeham's Question on the "Complexe Significabile" as the Immediate Object of Scientific Knowledge', *Franciscan Studies* 37:66–102

Gál, Gedeon, and Rega Wood (forthcoming). 'Richard Brinkley and His *Summa logicae*', *Franciscan Studies*

Galen (1874). *De placitis Hippocratis et Platonis libri novem*, ed. I. Mueller, Teubner

(1884–93). *Scripta minora.* ed. Marquardt, Mueller, Helmreich (3 vols.), Teubner

(1896). *Institutio logica*, ed. C. Kalbfleisch, Teubner

(1977). *Libellus de captionibus quae per dictionem fiunt*, ed. C. G. Gabler, in R. B. Edlow (ed.) *Galen on Language and Ambiguity* (Philosophia Antiqua, 31), Brill

Galindo Romeo, P. and L. Ortiz Muñoz (1946). *Antonio de Nebrija, Gramática castellana, texto establecido sobre la ed. "princeps" de 1492*, Edición de la Junta del Centenario

Gandillac, Maurice Patronnier de (1933). 'De l'usage et de la valeur des arguments probables dans les questions du cardinal Pierre d'Ailly sur le "Livre des Sentences"', *Archives d'histoire doctrinale et littéraire du moyen âge* 8:43–91

Garceau, Benoit (1968). *Judicium: Vocabulaire, sources, doctrine de Saint Thomas d'Aquin* (Université de Montréal, L'Institut d'Études Médiévales, No. 20), Institut d'Études Médiévales and Vrin

Garcia, F. M. (1910). *Lexicon scholasticum philosophico-theologicum*, Ad Claras Aquas

Gardeil, A. (1934). 'La perception expérimentale de l'âme par elle-même d'après Saint Thomas' in *Mélanges Thomistes* (Bibliothèque Thomiste, vol. 3), Vrin

Gardet, Louis (1974). 'Saint Thomas et ses predecesseurs arabes' in *St. Thomas Aquinas 1274–1974: Commemorative Studies*, vol. 1, Pontifical Institute of Mediaeval Studies (1976). 'La connaissance que Thomas d'Aquin put avoir du monde islamque' in G. Verbeke and D. Verhelst (eds.) *Aquinas and the Problems of His Time* (Mediaevalia Lovaniensia, Series I, Studia 5), Louvain, Publications Universitaires

Gardiner, Stephen (1930). *The Oration of True Obedience* in P. Janelle (ed.) *Obedience in Church and State*, Cambridge University Press

Garin, E. (1951). 'Le traduzioni umanistiche di Aristotele nel secolo XV', *Atti e memorie dell'Accademia Fiorentina di Scienze Morali, La Colombaria* 8:57–104

(1952). *Prosatori latini del quattrocento* (La letteratura italiana: storia e testi, 13), Ricciardi

(1958). *Il pensiero pedagogico dell' umanesimo*, Giuntine e Sansoni

(1965). *Italian Humanism: Philosophy and Civic Life in the Renaissance*, tr. P. Munz, Blackwell

(1969a). 'La cultura fiorentina nella secunda meta dell Trecento e i "barbari Britanni"', in his *L'età nuova. Richerche di storia della cultura dal XII al XVI secolo*, Morano

(1969b). *Science and Civic Life in the Italian Renaissance*, Doubleday

Garin, Pierre (1931). *La théorie de l'idée suivant l'école thomiste*, Desclée De Brouwer

Garlandus Compotista (1959). *Garlandus Compotista. Dialectica*, ed. L. M. de Rijk, Van Gorcum

Gauthier, R.-A. (1947–8). 'Trois commentaires "averroistes" sur l' Éthique à Nicomaque', *Archives d'histoire doctrinale et littéraire du moyen âge* 22/23:187–336

(1947–53). Review of Lottin 1942–60, II–III, *Bulletin thomiste* 8, no. 1:60–86

(1963). 'Arnoul de Provence et la doctrine de la *fronesis*, vertu mystique suprême', *Revue du Moyen Âge latin* 19:129–70

(1964). 'Les *Questiones supra Librum Ethicorum* de Pierre d'Auvergne', *Revue du Moyen Âge latin* 20:233–60

(1969). 'Praefatio' in Thomas Aquinas (1969), pt. 1

(1970). *Aristote. L'Ethique à Nicomaque* (Tome I, Première Partie: Introduction), Nauwelaerts

(1974). *Ethica Nicomachea. Praefatio* (Aristoteles Latinus XXVI, 1–3, fasciculus primus), Brill

(1975). 'Le cours sur l'*Ethica nova* d'un maître ès arts de Paris (1235–1240)', *AHDLMA* 42:71–141

Geach, P. T. (1957). *Mental Acts: Their Content and Their Objects*, Routledge & Kegan Paul

(1961). 'Aquinas' in G. E. M. Anscombe and P. T. Geach, *Three Philosophers*, Blackwell

(1962). *Reference and Generality*, Cornell University Press

(1969). 'Causality and Creation' in P. T. Geach, *God and the Soul*, Routledge & Kegan Paul

(1972). *Logic Matters*, Blackwell

Geanakopolos, D. J. (1966). *Byzantine East and Latin West, Two Worlds of Christendom in Middle Ages and Renaissance: Studies in Ecclesiastical and Cultural History*, Harper & Row

Geiger, L. (1882). *Renaissance und Humanismus in Italien und Deutschland*, Grote

(1942). *La participation dans la philosophie de saint Thomas d'Aquin*, J. Vrin

(1947). 'Abstraction et séparation d'après s. Thomas. *In de Trinitate*, q. 5, a. 3', *Revue des sciences philosophiques et théologiques* 31:3–40

Gelber, Hester Goodenough (1974). *Logic and the Trinity: A Clash of Values in Scholastic*

Thought, 1300–1335 (Unpublished Ph.D. Dissertation), University of Wisconsin
Genicot, L. (1976). 'Le *De Regno*: speculation ou realisme?' in G. Verbeke and D.
    Verhelst (eds.) *Aquinas and the Problems of His Time* (Mediaevalia Lovaniensia, Series
    1, Study 5), Nijhoff
Gerard of Odo (1482). *Expositio in Aristotelis Ethicam*, Brescia
Gerl, Hanna-Barbara (1974). *Rhetorik als Philosophie: Lorenzo Valla* (Humanistische
    Bibliothek, Reihe I: Abhandlungen, Band 13), Fink Verlag
Gerson, John, *see* John Gerson
Gewirth, Alan (1951). *Marsilius of Padua and Medieval Political Philosophy*, Vol. 1 of
    Marsilius of Padua: The Defender of Peace (Records of Civilization, Sources and
    Studies, 46), Columbia University Press
    (1961). 'Philosophy and political thought in the fourteenth century' in F. L. Utley
    (ed.) *The Forward Movement of the Fourteenth Century*, Ohio State University
Geyer, B. (1913). 'Die Stellung Abaelards in der Universalienfrage nach neuen hand-
    schriftlichen Texten' (*BGPM*, Supplementband 1), Aschendorff
    (1919–27). *Peter Abaelards Philosophische Schriften* (*BGPM*, XXI, 1–4), Aschendorff
    (1963). 'Albertus Magnus und die Entwicklung der Scholastischen Metaphysik', in
    P. Wilpert (ed.) *Die Metaphysik im Mittelalter* (Miscellanea Mediaevalia, 2), De
    Gruyter
Ghisalberti, Alessandro (1972). *Guglielmo di Ockham* (Pubblicazioni della Università
    Cattolica, Milano, scienze filosofiche, 3), Vita e Pensiero
Gibson, Strickland (1930). 'The Order of Disputations', *Bodleian Quarterly Record*
    6:107–12
    ed. (1931). *Statuta Antiqua Universitatis Oxoniensis*, Clarendon Press
Gierke, O. (1900). *Political Theories of the Middle Ages*, tr. with an introduction by F. W.
    Maitland. Cambridge University Press
    (1934). *Natural Law and the Theory of Society, 1500–1800*, tr. Ernest Barker (2 vols.),
    Cambridge University Press
    (1977). *Associations and Law: Classical and early Christian Stages*, tr. George Heiman,
    University of Toronto Press
Giesey, Ralph E. (1973). 'Medieval jurisprudence in Bodin's concept of sovereignty' in
    Horst Denzer (ed.) *Jean Bodin: Proceedings of the International Conference on Bodin in
    Munich*, Beck
Gilbert, Felix (1965). *Machiavelli and Guicciardini*, Princeton University Press
Gilbert, Neal Ward (1960). *Renaissance Concepts of Method*, Columbia University Press
    (1976). 'Richard de Bury and the "Quires of Yesterday's Sophisms"', in Edward P.
    Mahoney (ed.) *Philosophy and Humanism. Renaissance Essays in Honor of Paul Oskar
    Kristeller*, Columbia University Press
Gilbert of Poitiers (1966). *The Commentaries on Boethius by Gilbert of Poitiers*, ed. Nikolaus
    M. Häring, Pontifical Institute of Mediaeval Studies
Gilby, Thomas (1958). *Principality and Polity: Aquinas and the Rise of State Theory in the
    West*, Longmans Green
Giles of Rome (1476). *In Aristotelis De anima commentum*, Venice
    (1481). *De Corpore Christi Theoremata*, Bologna
    (1498). *De Regimine Principum*, Venice
    (1503). *Egidius Romanus de esse et essentia, de mensura angelorum, et de cognitione
    angelorum*, Venice (Reprinted Minerva 1968)
    (1521). *In Primum Sententiarum*, Venice (Reprinted Minerva 1968)
    (1550). *Aegidii Romani ... opus super authorem de causis*, Apud Iacobum Zoppinum
    (Reprinted Minerva 1968)

(1646). *Quodlibeta*, Louvain (Reprinted Minerva 1966)

(1929). *De ecclesiastica potestate*, ed. R. Scholz, H. Böhlaus Nachfolger

(1930). *Aegidii Romani Theoremata de esse et essentia. Texte précédé d'une introduction historique et critique*, ed. E. Hocedez, Museum Lessianum

(1944). *Giles of Rome: Errores philosophorum*, ed. with introduction and notes by J. Koch, tr. J. O. Riedl, Marquette University Press

Gilmore, Myron P. (1941). *Argument from Roman Law in Political Thought, 1200–1600*, (Harvard Historical Monographs, 15), Harvard University Press

Gilson, Étienne (1913). *Index Scolastico-Cartésien*, F. Alcan

(1921). 'La doctrine de la double vérité' in *Études de philosophie médiévale* (Publications de la Faculté des Lettres de l'Université de Strasbourg, No. 3), Commission des Publications de la Faculté des Lettres

(1926–7). 'Pourquoi Saint Thomas a critiqué Saint Augustin', *Archives d'histoire doctrinale et littéraire du moyen âge* 1 : 5–127

(1927). 'Avicenne et le point de départ de Duns Scot', *Archives d'histoire doctrinale et littéraire du moyen âge* 2 : 89–149

(1929–30). 'Les sources gréco-arabes de l'augustinisme avicennisant', *Archives d'Histoire Doctrinale et Littéraire du Moyen Age* 4 : 5–149

(1930). *Études sur le rôle de la pensée médiévale dans la formation du système cartésién*, J. Vrin

(1936). *The Spirit of Medieval Philosophy*, tr. A. H. C. Downes, Sheed and Ward

(1948a). *Dante the Philosopher*, Sheed and Ward

(1948b). 'L'Objet de la Métaphysique selon Duns Scot', *Mediaeval Studies* 10 : 21–92

(1950). 'La preuve du De ente et essentia', *Acta III Congressus Thomistici Internationalis: Doctor Communis* 3 : 257–60

(1952a). *Being and some Philosophers*, Pontifical Institute of Mediaeval Studies

(1952b). *Jean Duns Scot: introduction à ses positions fondamentales*, J. Vrin

(1952c). *Les métamorphoses de la Cité de Dieu*, Publications universitaires de Louvain

(1953). *La philosophie de saint Bonaventure*, J. Vrin

(1955). *History of Christian Philosophy in the Middle Ages*, Random House

(1961a). *The Christian Philosophy of St Thomas Aquinas* (With a Catalogue of St Thomas' Works by I. T. Eschmann), tr. L. K. Shook, Victor Gollancz

(1961b). 'Trois leçons sur le problème de l'existence de Dieu', *Divinitas* 5 : 22–87

(1968). 'Sur la composition fondamentale de l'être fini', in *De doctrina Ioannis Duns Scoti. Acta Congressus Scotistici Internationalis Oxonii et Edimburgi 11–17 sept. 1966 celebrati*. V. II: *Problemata Philosophica*, Cura Commissionis Scotisticae

Giorgianni, V. (1948). *Pensiero morale e politico di Bonaventura da Bagnorea*, Lupa

Giusberti, Franco (1977). 'A Treatise on Implicit Propositions from around the Turn of the Twelfth Century: An Edition with Some Introductory Notes', *CIMAGL* 21 : 45–115

Glorieux, P. (1925). 'La littérature quodlibétique de 1260 à 1320', *Revue des sciences philosophiques et théologiques* 14

(1925–35). *La littérature quodlibétique* (2 vols.) (Bibliothèque Thomiste, 5, 21), J. Vrin

(1931). 'Un recueil scolaire de Godefroid de Fontaines', *Recherches de Théologie ancienne et médiévale* 3 : 37–53

(1933). *Répertoire des maîtres en théologie de Paris au XIIIᵉ siècle* (2 vols.), Vrin

(1939). 'Notations brèves sur Godefroid de Fontaines', *Recherches de Théologie ancienne et médiévale* 11 : 168–73

(1965). 'L'oeuvre littéraire de Pierre d'Ailly', *Mélanges de sciences religieuses* 22 : 61–78

(1966). 'L'enseignement au moyen âge. Techniques et méthodes en usage à la Faculté de Théologie de Paris, au XIIIe siècle', *Archives d'histoire doctrinale et littéraire du moyen âge* 35:65–186

(1967). 'Jean de Falisca: La formation d'un maître en théologie au XIVe siècle', *Archives d'histoire doctrinale et littéraire du moyen âge* 33:23–104

Godfrey of Fontaines (1904–37). *Les Quodlibets de Godefroid de Fontaines*, ed. M. de Wulf and J. Hoffmans (Les Philosophes Belges), Institut supérieur de Philosophie de l'Université de Louvain

(1914). *Les Quodlibets V, VI, VII de Godefroid de Fontaines*, ed. M. de Wulf and J. Hoffmans (Les Philosophes Belges, 3), Institut supérieur de Philosophie de l'Université de Louvain

(1973). 'Godfrey of Fontaines: Disputed Questions 9, 10 and 12', ed. J. F. Wippel, *Franciscan Studies* 33:351–72

Goichon, A.-M. (1937). *La distinction de l'essence et de l'existence d'après îbn Sīnā*, Desclée de Brouwer

(1951). *La philosophie d'Avicenne et son influence en Europe médiévale*, 2nd ed., Adrien-Maisonneuve

Goldman, Alvin I. (1970). *A Theory of Human Action*, Prentice Hall

Golius, Theophilus (1631). *Epitome doctrinae moralis*, Argentorati (= Strasbourg)

Gollancz, Israel (1949–50). 'Strode, Ralph', *Dictionary of National Biography* (Oxford University Press), 55:57–9

Gómez Caffarena, J. (1957). 'Cronología de la "Suma" de Enrique de Gante por relación a sus "Quodlibetos"', *Gregorianum* 38:116–33

(1958). *Ser participado y ser subsistente en la metafísica de Enrique de Gante*, Apud Aedes Universitatis Gregorianae

Gómez Izquierdo, Alberto (1924). 'Valor cognoscitivo de la "intentio" en Santo Tomás de Aquino', *La Ciencia Tomista* 29:169–88

Gómez Nogales, Salvador (1976). 'Saint Thomas, Averroes, et l'averroisme' in G. Verbeke and D. Verhelst (eds.), *Aquinas and the Problems of His Time* (Mediaevalia Lovaniensia, Series I, Studia 5), Louvain, Publications Universitaires

Gonsalvus of Spain (1935). *Fr. Gonsalvi Hispani O.F.M. Quaestiones disputatae et de Quodlibet*, ed. Leo Amorós, O.F.M. (Bibliotheca Franciscana Scholastica Medii Aevi, IX), Collegium S. Bonaventurae

González, Atanasio (1958–9). 'The Theory of Assertoric Consequence in Albert of Saxony', *Franciscan Studies* 18:290–354 and 19:13–114

González-Llubera, I. (1926). *Nebrija: Gramática de la lengua castellana*, Humphrey Milford

Goudin, A. (1851). *Philosophia juxta inconcussa tutissimaque Divi Thomae dogmata*, ed. Roux Lavergne, Editores Bibliothecae Novae

(1864). *Philosophie suivant les principes de saint Thomas*. tr. Thomas Bourar, Poussielgue–Rusand

Grabmann, Martin (1909–11). *Geschichte der scholastischen Methode*, I–II, Herder

(1924a). *Neu aufgefundene Werke des Siger von Brabant und Boetius von Dacien* (Sitzungsberichte der Bayerischen Akademie der Wissenschaften, Philosophisch-historische Abteilung, 1924, No. 2)

(1924b). 'Doctrina S. Thomae de distinctione reali inter essentiam et esse ex documentis ineditis saeculi XIII illustratur', in *Acta Hebdomadae Thomisticae Romae Celebratae 19–25 Novembris 1923*, Apud Sedem Academiae S. Thomae Aquinatis

(1925). *Die Kulturphilosophie des heiligen Thomas von Aquino*, B. Filser

(1926–56). *Mittelalterliches Geistesleben* I (1926), II (1936), III (1956), Max Hueber

(1926a). 'Das Naturrecht der Scholastik von Gratian bis Thomas von Aquino', in his

Mittelalterliches Geistesleben I, M. Hueber

(1926b). 'Die Disputationes Metaphysicae der Franz Suarez in ihrer methodischen Eigenart und Fortwirkung', in his *Mittelalterliches Geistesleben* I, M. Hueber

(1926c). 'Eine ungedruckte Verteidigungsschrift der scholastischen Übersetzung der Nikomachischen Ethik gegenüber dem Humanisten Lionardo Bruni' in his *Mittelalterliches Geistesleben* I, M. Hueber

(1931). *Der lateinische Averroismus und seine Stellung zur christlichen Weltanschauung* (Sitzungsberichte der Bayerischen Akademie der Wissenschaften, Phil-hist. Abt., Heft 2)

(1931a). *Der göttliche Grund menschlicher Wahrheitserkenntnis nach Augustinus und Thomas von Aquin* (Veröffentlichungen des Katholischen Instituts für Philosophie, Albertus-Magnus-Akademie zu Köln, Band 1, Heft 4), Aschendorff

(1933). *Die Aristoteleskommentare des Simon von Faversham: Handschriftliche Mitteilungen* (Sitzungsberichte der Bayerischen Akademie der Wissenschaften, Philosophisch-historische Abteilung, Jahrgang 1933, Heft 3). Verlag der Bayerischen Akademie der Wissenschaften

(1934a). 'Eine für Examinazwecke abgefasste Quaestionensammlung der Pariser Artistenfakultät aus der ersten Hälfte des 13. Jahrhunderts', *Revue Néoscolastique de Philosophie* 36:211–26

(1934b). 'Studien über den Einfluss der aristotelischen Philosophie auf die mittelalterlichen Theorien über das Verhältnis von Kirche und Staat' (Sitzungsberichte der Bayerischen Akademie der Wissenschaften, Phil.-hist. Abt., Heft 2)

(1936a). 'Der Einfluß Alberts des Großen auf das mittelalterliche Geistesleben. Das deutsche Element in der mittelalterlichen Scholastik und Mystik' in his *Mittelalterliches Geistesleben* II, Hueber

(1937). *Bearbeitungen und Auslegungen der aristotelischen Logik aus der Zeit von Peter Abaelard bis Petrus Hispanus. Mitteilungen aus Handschriften deutscher Bibliotheken* (Abhandlungen der Preussischen Akademie der Wissenschaften, Phil.-hist. Klasse, 5)

(1938a). 'Kommentare zur aristotelischen Logik aus dem 12. und 13. Jahrhundert in Ms. lat. fol. 624 der Preussischen Staatsbibliothek in Berlin', (Sitzungsberichte der Preussischen Akademie der Wissenschaften, Phil.-hist. Klasse, 18:185–210)

(1938b). 'Ungedruckte lateinische Kommentare zur aristotelischen Topik aus dem 13. Jahrhundert', *Archiv für Kulturgeschichte* 28:210–32

(1939). *Methoden und Hilfsmittel des Aristotelesstudiums im Mittelalter* (Sitzungsberichte der Bayerischen Akademie der Wissenschaften, Philosophisch-Historische Abteilung, Heft 5).

(1940a). *Die Sophismataliteratur des 12. und 13. Jahrhunderts mit Textausgabe eines Sophisma des Boethius von Dacien* (BGPM XXXVI, 1), Aschendorff

(1940b). 'Das Studium der aristotelischen Ethik an der Artistenfakultät der Universität Paris in der ersten Hälfte des 13. Jahrhunderts', *Philosophisches Jahrbuch der Görres-Gesellschaft* 55:339–54

(1941). 'Die mittelalterlichen Kommentare zur *Politik* des Aristoteles' (Sitzungsberichte der Bayerischen Akademie der Wissenschaften, Philos.-hist. Abt., 2, Heft 10)

(1944). 'Die Aristoteleskommentare des Heinrich von Brüssel und der Einfluss Alberts des Grossen auf die mittelalterliche Aristoteleserklärung'. (Sitzungsberichte der Bayerischen Akademie der Wissenschaften, Philos.-hist. kl. 1943, Heft 10)

(1946). *Guglielmo de Moerbeke O.P., il traduttore delle opere di Aristotele* (Miscellanea Historiae Pontificiae, 11)

(1947). 'Ein Tractatus de Universalibus und andere logische Inedita aus dem 12.

Jahrhundert im Cod. lat. 2486 der Nationalbibliothek in Wien', *Mediaeval Studies* 9:56–70

(1950). 'Aristoteles im 12. Jahrhundert', *Mediaeval Studies* 12:123–62

Graeser, A. (1973). *Die logischen Fragmente des Theophrast* (Kleine Texte für Vorlesungen und Übungen, 191), De Gruyter

Grajewski, M. (1944). *The Formal Distinction of John Duns Scotus*, Catholic University of America

Grant, E. (ed.) (1974). *A Source Book in Medieval Science*, Harvard University Press

Gray, F. J. (1967). 'Peter of Candia (Alexander V, Antipope)', *New Catholic Encyclopedia* 11:213

Grech, G. M., ed. (1967). *The Commentary of Peter of Auvergne on Aristotle's Politics. The inedited part: Book III, lessons I–VI*, Pontifical University of St Thomas Aquinas

Green, Romuald (forthcoming). *The logical Treatise 'De obligationibus': An Introduction with Critical Texts of William of Sherwood and Walter Burley*, The Franciscan Institute

Green-Pedersen, N. J. (1973). 'On the Interpretation of Aristotle's Topics in the 13th Century', *CIMAGL* 9:1–46

(1974). 'William of Champeaux on Boethius' Topics according to Orleans Bibl. Mun. 266', *CIMAGL* 13:13–30

(1976). 'The Summulae of John Buridan, Tractatus VI De locis', in J. Pinborg (ed.) *The Logic of John Buridan*, Museum Tusculanum

(1977a). 'Discussions about the Status of the Loci Dialectici in Works from the Middle of the 13th Century,' *CIMAGL* 20:38–78

(1977b). 'The Doctrine of "maxima propositio" and "locus differentia" in Commentaries from the 12th Century on Boethius' "Topics"', *Studia Mediewistyczne* 18:125–63

Gregory of Rimini (1522). *Super primum et secundum Sententiarum*, Venice (Reprinted The Franciscan Institute 1955)

Grignaschi, M. (1960a). 'Nicolas Oresme et son commentaire à la *Politique* d'Aristote' in *Album Helen Maud Cam* (Études presentées à la Commission Internationale pour l'histoire des assemblées d'états, 23), Publications universitaires de Louvain

(1960b). 'Un commentaire nominaliste de la *Politique* d'Aristote: Jean Buridan', *Commission International pour l'histoire des assemblées d'états, Ancien Pays et assemblées d'états* 19:123–42

(1966). 'La définition du "civis" dans la scolastique' *Commission International pour l'histoire des assemblées d'états, Ancien pays et assemblées d'états* 35:71–100

(1972). 'Les Traductions latines des ouvrages de la logique arabe et l'abrégé d'Alfarabi' *Archives d'histoire doctrinale et littéraire du moyen âge* 39:41–107

Grisez, Germain G. (1965). 'The First Principle of Practical Reason', *Natural Law Forum* 10:168–96

(1969). 'The first principle of practical reason' (abridgement of Grisez 1965) in Anthony Kenny (ed.) *Aquinas: A Collection of Critical Essays*, Doubleday

Grosseteste, Robert, *see* Robert Grosseteste

Grotius, Hugo (1953). *De Jure Belli et Pacis*, ed. William Whewell, Parker

(1913–25). *De iure belli ac pacis libri tres*. Editio nova with translation by F. W. Kelsey (2 vols. in 4), Clarendon Press

Guelluy, R. (1947). *Philosophie et Théologie chez Guillaume d'Ockham*, Nauwelaerts

Guerault, Martial (1968). *Spinoza*, I, Aubier-Montaigne

Guerlac, Rita (1979). *Juan Luis Vives Against the Pseudodialecticians: A Humanist Attack on Medieval Logic* (Synthese Historical Library, 18), Reidel

Guillaume, Alfred (1934). *The Summa Philosophiae of al-Shahrastani*, Oxford University

Press

Guillet, J. (1927). 'La "lumière intellectuelle" d'après S. Thomas', *Archives d'histoire doctrinale et littéraire du moyen âge* 2:79–88

Gunther, Robert (1922–?). *Early Science at Oxford* (2 vols.) (Publications of the Oxford Historical Society, 77, 78), Clarendon Press

Gutiérrez, G. (1939). *De B. Iacobi Viterbiensis O.E.S.A. Vita, Operibus, et doctrina Theologica*, Analecta Augustiniana

Guy of Rimini (1937–8). *De Reprobatione Monarchiae Compositae a Dante*, ed. T. Käppeli, (*Quellen und Forschungen aus italienischen Archiven und Bibliotheken herausgegeben vom Deutschen Institut in Rom*, 27), Regenberg

Guy Terrena (1926). *Quaestio de Magisterio Infallibilis Romani Pontificis*, ed. B. F. M. Xiberta, Aschendorff

Gyekye, Kwame (1971). 'The Terms "Prima Intentio" and "Secunda Intentio" in Arabic Logic', *Speculum* 46:32–8

Hadot, Pierre (1970). 'Forma Essendi: Interprétation philologique et interprétation philosophique d'une formule de Boèce', *Les Études classiques* 38:143–56

(1971). *Marius Victorinus. Recherches sur sa vie et ses oeuvres*, Études Augustiniennes

Hain, Ludwig (1948). *Repertorium Bibliographicum in quo Libri Omnes ab Arte Typographica Inventa usque ad Annum MD* (4 vols.), G. G. Görlich

Halm, Charles, ed. (1863). *Rhetores Latini minores*, Teubner

Hamblin, C. L. (1970). *Fallacies*, Methuen

Hamilton, Bernice (1963). *Political Thought in Sixteenth-Century Spain. A Study of the political ideas of Vitoria, De Soto, Suárez, and Molina*, Clarendon Press

Hamlyn, D. W. (1968). *Aristotle's 'De anima', Books II and III (with Certain Passages from Book I), Translated with Introduction and Notes*, The Clarendon Press

Hamm, Marlis (1974). 'Engelbert von Admont als Staatstheoretiker', *Studien und Mitteilungen zur Geschichte des Benediktiner-Ordens und seiner Zweige* 85:343–495

Hamman, A. (1950). 'La doctrine de l'église et de l'état d'après le Breviloquium d'Occam', *Franziskanische Studien* 32:135–41

Harding, Alan (1976). 'The reflection of thirteenth century legal growth in Saint Thomas's writings' in G. Verbeke and D. Verhelst (eds.) *Aquinas and the Problems of His Time* (Mediaevalia Lovaniensia, Series 1, Study 5), Nijhoff

Haskins, C. H. (1927). *Studies in the History of Mediaeval Science* (Harvard Historical Studies, 27), Harvard University Press

Hayen, André (1954). *L'Intentionnel selon Saint Thomas*, 2nd ed., Desclée de Brouwer

Heath, Terrence (1971). 'Logical Grammar, Grammatical Logic, and Humanism in Three German Universities', *Studies in the Renaissance* 18:9–64

Heidingsfelder, Georg (1921). *Albert von Sachsen: Sein Lebensgang und sein Kommentar zur nikomachischen Ethik des Aristoteles* (BGPM XXII, 3–4), Aschendorff

Hendley, Brian Patrick (1967). *Wisdom and Eloquence: A New Interpretation of the Metalogicon of John of Salisbury*, University Microfilms

Henke, E. L. T. and Lindenkohn, G. S., eds. (1851). *Petri Abaelardi Sic et Non*, Librariae Academ. Elwertianae

Henry of Bracton (1968). *De Legibus et Consuetudinibus Angliae*, ed. and tr. Samuel E. Thorne, *Bracton on the Laws and Customs of England*, Harvard University Press

Henry, Desmond Paul (1958). 'Why "Grammaticus"?', *Archivum Latinitatis Medii Aevi*, 28:165–80

(1964). *The De grammatico of St Anselm: Theory of Paronymy* (Publications in Mediaeval Studies, 18), University of Notre Dame Press

(1965). 'Ockham and the Formal Distinction', *Franciscan Studies* 25:285–92

(1967). *The Logic of Saint Anselm*, Clarendon Press

(1972). *Medieval Logic and Metaphysics*, Hutchinson

(1974). *Commentary on De grammatico: The Historical-Logical Dimension of a Dialogue of St Anselm's* (Synthese Historical Library, 8), Reidel

Henry, J. (1924). 'Le traditionalisme et l'ontologisme à l'Université de Louvain 1835–1865', *Annales de l'Institut Supérieur de Philosophie de Louvain* 5

Henry of Ghent (1518). *Quodlibeta magistri Henrici Goethals a Gandavo doctoris solemnis* (2 vols.), Paris (Reprinted Bibliothèque S. J. de Louvain 1961)

(1520). *Summa quaestionum ordinariarum* (2 vols.), Paris (Reprinted Franciscan Institute 1953)

(1613). *Quodlibeta aurea*, Venice

(1974). 'The absolute and the ordained powers of the pope', ed. John Marrone, *Mediaeval Studies* 36:7–27

(1978). *Sincathegoreumata*, ed. in Braakhuis 1978

Hervaeus Natalis (1513). *Quodlibeta Hervei: subtilissimi quodlibeta undecim cum octo ipsius profundissimus tractatibus . . .* , Venice

(1647). *In Quatuor Libros Sententiarum Commentaria, Quibus adiectus est eiusdem auctoris Tractatus de Potestate Papae*, Paris (Reprinted Gregg 1967)

(1937–8). *De Paupertate Christi et Apostolorum*, ed. J. G. Sikes, *Archives d'histoire doctrinale et littéraire du moyen âge* 12–13:209–97

(1959). *De Iurisdictione*, ed. L. Hödl, Hueber

Hessen, Johannes (1960). *Augustins Metaphysik der Erkenntnis*, 2nd ed., E. J. Brill

Hexter, J. H. (1973). *The Vision of Politics on the Eve of the Reformation: More, Machiavelli and Seyssel*, Basic Books

Heynick, Valens (1950). 'Ockham-Literatur: 1919–1949', *Franziskanische Studien* 32:164–83

Heytesbury, William, *see* William Heytesbury

Hickmann, L. A. (1971). *Logical second intentions – Late Scholastic theories of higher level predicates*. Unpublished Ph.D. dissertation, University of Texas

Hill, Christopher (1965). *Intellectual Origins of the English Revolution*, Clarendon Press

Hill, W. Speed, ed. (1972). *Studies in Richard Hooker*, Case Western Reserve University Press

Hintikka, Jaakko (1973). *Time and Necessity: Studies in Aristotle's Theory of Modality*, Clarendon Press

Hintikka, Jaakko, and U. Remes (1974). *Ancient Geometrical Method*, Reidel

Hintikka, Jaakko, U. Remes, and S. Knuuttila (1977). *Aristotle on Modality and Determinism* (Acta Philosophica Fennica, 29.1), North-Holland

Hissette, R. (1976). 'La date de quelques commentaires à l'Éthique', *Bulletin de la Philosophie Médiévale* 18:79–83

(1977). *Enquête sur les 219 articles condamnés à Paris le 7 Mars 1277*, Publications Universitaires de Louvain

Hocedez, E. (1925). *Richard de Middleton. Sa vie, ses oeuvres, sa doctrine*, Spicilegium Sacrum Lovaniense

(1927). 'Gilles de Rome et Henri de Gand sur la distinction réelle (1276–1287)', *Gregorianum* 8:358–84

(1928). 'Le premier Quodlibet d'Henri de Gand (1276)', *Gregorianum* 9:92–117

(1929). 'Deux questions touchant la distinction réelle entre l'essence et l'existence', *Gregorianum* 10:365–86

(1930). *Aegidii Romani Theoremata de esse et essentia. Texte précédé d'une introduction historique et critique*, Museum Lessianum

(1932). 'La condamnation de Gilles de Rome', *Recherches de Théologie ancienne et médiévale* 4:34–58

Hoenen, P. (1945). *Cosmologia* (3rd ed.), apud aedes Universitatis Gregorianae

(1952). *Reality and Judgment According to St Thomas*, trans. Henry F. Tiblier, H. Regnery

(1967). 'Descartes' mechanicism', in W. Doney (ed.), *Descartes, a collection of critical essays*, Macmillan

Hoeres, W. (1962). *Der Wille als reine Vollkommenheit nach Duns Scotus*, Pustet

(1965). 'Wesen und Dasein bei Heinrich von Gent und Duns Scotus', *Franziskanische Studien* 47:121–86

Hoffmann, Fritz (1971). 'Der Satz als Zeichen der theologischen Aussage bei Holcot, Crathorn und Gregor von Rimini', *Miscellanea Mediaevalia*, 8:296–313

Holdsworth, Richard (1648?). *Directions for a student in the universitie*, Emmanuel College (Cambridge) MS 48 [cf. Bodleian MS Rawlinson D 200]

(1651). *The Valley of Vision*, London

(1661). *Praelectiones Theologicae, habitae in Collegio Greshamensi apud Londoninenses*, ed. Richard Pearson, London

Holmes, J. D. (1975). 'Some English reactions to the publication of *Aeterni Patris*', *Downside Review* 93:269–80

Holscher, E. E. (1932). *Die ethische Umgestaltung der römischen Individual Justitia durch die universalistische Naturrechtslehre der mittlelalterlichen Scholastik* (Görres-Gessellschaft Veröffentlichungen der Sektion für Rechts- u. Staatswissenschaft 59), Schöning

Honnefelder, L. (1975). 'Duns Scotus: Der Schritt der Philosophie zur scientia transcenden' in W. Kluxen (ed.) *Thomas von Aquin im philosophischen Gespräch*, Alber

Honoré Bouvet [Bonet] (1949). *L'Arbre des Batailles*, ed. and tr. G. W. Coopland, Liverpool University Press

Hooker, Richard (1977–81). *Of the Laws of Ecclesiastical Polity* in W. Speed Hill (ed.) *The Folger Library Edition of the Works of Richard Hooker* (3 vols.), Harvard University Press

Hopkins, Jasper (1972). *A Companion to the Study of St Anselm*, University of Minnesota Press

(1976). *Hermeneutical and textual problems in the complete treatises of St Anselm* (vol. 4 in his *St Anselm*), Edwin Mellin

Horváth, A. (1929). *Eigentumsrecht nach dem hl. Thomas von Aquin*, Moser

Hoskin, Michael, and A. G. Molland (1966). 'Swineshead on Falling Bodies: An Example of Fourteenth Century Physics', *British Journal for the History of Science* 3:150–82

Hourani, G. (1972). 'Ibn Sīnā on Necessary and Possible Existence', *The Philosophical Forum* 4:74–86

Howell, Wilbur S. (1961). *Logic and Rhetoric in England 1500–1700*, Crowell and Crowell

Hubert, M. P. (1949). 'Quelques aspects du latin philosophique aux XIIᵉ et XIIIᵉ siècles', *Revue des études latines* 27:211–33

Hubien, Hubert (1976). *Ioannis Buridani Tractatus de Consequentiis Libri iv* (Philosophes Médiévaux, 16), Publications universitaires de Louvain

Hubrecht, G. (1955). 'La "Juste Guerre" dans le Décret de Gratien', *Studia Gratiana* 3:161–77

Hugh of Saint Victor (1951). *On the Sacraments of the Christian Faith* (*De Sacramentis*), tr. Roy J. Deferrari, The Medieval Academy of America

Hunt, R. W. (1948). 'The Introductions to the Artes in the Twelfth Century', *Studia*

Mediaevalia in Honorem R. Martin, Brugge
(1949–50). 'Studies on Priscian in the Twelfth Century', *Mediaeval and Renaissance Studies* 1:194–231; 2:1–55
(1975). '*Absoluta*, The *Summa* of Petrus Hispanus on Priscianus *Minor*', *Historiographia Linguistica* 2:1–23
(1977). 'The Preface to the "Speculum Ecclesiae" of Giraldus Cambrensis', *Viator* 8:189–213
Hutchins, Robert Maynard (1949). *St Thomas and the World State*, Marquette University Press
Hyma, A. (1951). *Renaissance to Reformation*, Eerdmans
(1965). *The Christian Renaissance: a History of the 'Devotio Moderna'* (2nd edn.), Archon Books
Hyman, A., and Walsh, J. J., eds. (1967). *Philosophy in the Middle Ages*, Harper and Row

IJsewijn, J. (1971). 'Alexander Hegius (d. 1498): *Invectiva in modos significandi*', *Forum for Modern Language Studies* 7:299–318
(1975). 'The coming of humanism to the Low Countries' in H. A. Oberman and T. A. Brady (eds.) *Itinerarium Italicum*, Brill
IJsewijn-Jacobs, J. (1976). 'Magistri Anthonii Haneron (*ca.* 1400–1490) opera grammatica et rhetorica, II', *Humanistica Lovaniensia* 25:1–83
IJsewijn, J. and Paquet, J. (eds.). (1978). *The Universities in the Late Middle Ages.* (Mediaevalia Lovaniensia 6), Leuven University Press
Imle, Fanny (1930). 'Die Gemeinschaftidee in der Theologie des hl. Bonaventura', *Franziskanische Studien* 17:325–41
Incerti auctores (1977). *Quaestiones super Sophisticos Elenchos*, ed. S. Ebbesen (Corpus Philosophorum Danicorum Medii Aevi, VII), Gad
Isaac, Jean (1948). 'Sur la connaissance de la verité', *Revue des sciences philosophiques et théologiques* 32:337–50
(1963). *Le Peri hermeneias en occident de Boèce à Saint Thomas* (Bibliothèque Thomiste 29), J. Vrin
Isidore of Seville (1911). *Isidori Hispalensis episcopi Etymologiarum sive Originum libri xx*, ed. W. M. Lindsay, Clarendon Press
Iung, N. (1931). *Un franciscain théologien du pouvoir pontifical au XIVe siècle: Alvaro Pelayo, évêque et pénitencier de Jean XXII*, J. Vrin

Jacob, E. F. (1963). *Essays in the Conciliar Epoch*, revised ed., University of Notre Dame Press
Jacquin, R. (1943). *Taparelli*, Lethielleux
Jalbert, Guy (1961). *Nécessité et contingence chez saint Thomas d'Aquin et chez ses prédécesseurs*, Éditions de l'Université d'Ottawa
James of Viterbo (1926). *De Regimine Christiano* in H.-X. Arquillière (ed.) *Le plus ancien traité de l'église: Jacques de Viterbe, De Regimine Christiano (1301–2)*, G. Beauchesne
(1968). *Jacobi de Viterbio O.E.S.A. Disputatio prima de quolibet*, ed. E. Ypma, Augustinus-Verlag
(1973). *Jacobi de Viterbio O.E.S.A. Disputatio tertia de quolibet*, ed. E. Ypma, Augustinus-Verlag
Jardine, Lisa (1974). 'The Place of Dialectic Teaching in Sixteenth-Century Cambridge', *Studies in the Renaissance* 21:31–62
(1975a). *Francis Bacon: Discovery and the Art of Discourse*, Cambridge University Press
(1975b). 'Humanism and the Sixteenth-Century Cambridge Arts Course', *History of*

Education 4:16–31

(1976). 'Humanism and Dialectic in Sixteenth-Century Cambridge: A Preliminary Investigation' in R. R. Bolgar (ed.) *Classical Influences on European Culture, AD 1500–1700*, Cambridge University Press

(1977). 'Lorenzo Valla and the Intellectual Origins of Humanist Dialectic', *Journal of the History of Philosophy* 15:143–64

(forthcoming). 'Dialectic or dialectical rhetoric? Agostino Nifo's Criticism of Lorenzo Valla', *Proceedings of the First International Conference of Rhetoric (1977)*

Jeauneau, E. (1973). *Lectio Philosophorum* (Recherches sur l'École de Chartres), A. M. Hakkert

John Blund (1970). *Johannes Blund: Tractatus de anima*, ed. D. A. Callus, O. P., and R. W. Hunt (Auctores Britannici medii aevi, 2), British Academy

John Buridan (1499). *Perutile compendium totius logicae Joannis Buridani cum praeclarissima solertissimi viri Joannis Dorp expositione*, Venice (Reprinted Minerva 1965)

(after 1500?). *Sophismata Buridani*, [Paris]

(1509). *Quaestiones super octo libros Physicorum Aristotelis*, Paris

(1513). *Quaestiones super decem libros Ethicorum*, Paris (Reprinted Minerva 1968)

(1588). *In Metaphysicam Aristotelis Quaestiones*, Paris (Reprinted Minerva 1964).

(1640). *Quaestiones in octo libros Politicorum Aristotelis*, ed. G. Turner, Oxford

(1957). 'Giovanni Buridano: "Tractatus de suppositionibus"', ed. Maria Elena Reina, *Rivista critica di storia della filosofia* 12:175–208; 323–52

(1966). *Sophisms on Meaning and Truth*, tr. T. K. Scott, Appleton-Century-Crofts

(1967). *Questions on Aristotle's Metaphysics* (Book II, q. 1), tr. J. Walsh in A. Hyman and J. Walsh (eds.) *Philosophy in the Middle Ages*, Harper and Row

(1976). *Tractatus de consequentiis*, ed. H. Hubien (Philosophes médiévaux, 16), Publications universitaires de Louvain

(1977). *Johannes Buridanus: Sophismata*, ed. T. K. Scott (Grammatica Speculativa, 1), Frommann-Holzboog

John Capreolus (1900–8). *Defensiones theologiae divi Thomae Aquinatis*, ed. C. Paban and T. Pègues, Cattier (Reprinted Minerva 1967)

John of Dacia (1955). *Opera*, ed. A. Otto (Corpus Philosophorum Danicorum Medii Aevi, 1), Gad

John Damascene (1953). *Dialectica*, ed. Owen A. Colligan (Franciscan Institute Text Series, 6), The Franciscan Institute

(1955). *De Fide Orthodoxa*, ed. E. M. Buytaert, E. Nauwelaerts / F. Schöningh

John Duns Scotus (1639a). *Opera omnia*. ed. L. Wadding (12 vols.). Lyons (Reprinted Georg Olms 1968)

(1639b). *Quaestiones miscellaneae de formalitatibus* in John Duns Scotus (1639a) vol. 3

(1639c). *Quaestiones subtilissimae super libros Metaphysicorum Aristotelis* in John Duns Scotus (1639a) vol. 4

(1639d). *Reportata Parisiensia* in John Duns Scotus (1639a) vol. 11

(1891–5). *Opera omnia*. Editio nova juxta editionem Waddingi XII tomos continentem a patribus Franciscanis de observantia accurate recognita (26 vols. in 13), Vivès

(1891). *In duos libros Perihermenias, operis secundi, quod appellant, Quaestiones octo* in John Duns Scotus (1891–5) vol. I

(1895). *Quaestiones quodlibetales* in John Duns Scotus (1891–5) vol. XXV

(1950–). *Opera omnia*, ed. C. Balić et al., Vatican Scotistic Commission

(1950). *Ordinatio*, Prologus, in John Duns Scotus (1950–) vol. 1

(1950–8). *Ordinatio*, Prologus – Dist. 48, in John Duns Scotus (1950–) vols. 1–6

(1954). *Ordinatio*, Dist. 3, in John Duns Scotus (1950–) vol. 3

(1960a). *Lectura in librum primum Sententiarum*, Prologus – Dist. 7, in John Duns Scotus (1950–) vol. 16

(1960b). *Lectura in librum primum Sententiarum*, Dist. 8ff., in John Duns Scotus (1950–) vol. 17

(1966). *De Primo Principio* in A. Wolter (ed.) *A Treatise on God as First Principle*, Franciscan Herald

(1968). *Questiones Quodlibetales* in F. Alluntis (ed. and tr.) *Obras del Doctor Sutil Juan Duns Escoto*, Biblioteca de Autores Cristianos

(1975). *God and Creatures: The Quodlibetal Questions* tr. F. Alluntis and A. Wolter, Princeton University Press

John Gerson (1953). *On the unity of the Church*, tr. and ed. James K. Cameron in Matthew Spinka (ed.) *Advocates of Reform: From Wyclif to Erasmus*, Westminster Press

(1965). *De Potestate Ecclesiastica* in P. Glorieux (ed.) *Oeuvres complètes* (6:210–50), Desclée

(1978). *De Iurisdictione Spirituali et Temporali* in Posthumus Meyjes, *Jean Gerson et l'Assemblée de Vincennes* (Studies in Medieval and Reformation Thought, 26), Brill

John of La Rochelle (1882). *Summa de anima*, ed. T. Domenichelli

John of Legnano (1917). *Tractatus de bello*, ed. T. E. Holland, Oxford University Press

John le Page (1979). *Syncategoremata* (excerpted in Braakhuis 1979)

John Major (1706a). *De Potestate Papae in Temporalibus* in L. Du Pin (ed.) Jean Gerson, *Opera Omnia*, 2: cols. 1145–64, Sumptibus Societatis

(1706b). *De Statu et Potestate Ecclesiae* in L. Du Pin (ed.) Jean Gerson, *Opera Omnia*, 2: cols. 1121–30, Sumptibus Societatis

(1938). *Le traité 'De l'infini' de Jean Mair, Nouvelle édition avec traduction et annotations*, ed. and tr. H. Elie, J. Vrin

John of Paris (1941). *Le Correctorium Corruptorii 'Circa' de Jean Quidort de Paris*, ed. J. P. Muller (Studia Anselmiana, 12–13), Herder

(1968). *De Regia Potestate et Papali* in F. Bleienstein (ed.) *Johannes Quidort von Paris über königliche und päpstliche Gewalt (De Regia Potestate et Papali)* (Frankfurter Studien zur Wissenschaft von der Politik), E. Klett

(1971). *On Royal and Papal Power*, tr. with an introduction by J. A. Watt, Pontifical Institute of Mediaeval Studies

(1974). *John of Paris on Royal and Papal Power*, tr. Arthur Monahan, Columbia University Press

John Peckham (1948). *Tractatus de anima Ioannis Pecham*, ed. G. Melani, Edizioni 'Studi Francescani' s. Francesco

John Philoponus (1905). *In Aristotelis Analytica Priora Commentaria*, ed. M. Wallies (Commentaria in Aristotelem Graeca, XIII. 2), G. Reimer

(1909). *In Aristotelis Analytica Posteriora commentaria*, ed. M. Wallies (Commentaria in Aristotelem Graeca, XIII. 3), G. Reimer

John Quidort, *see* John of Paris

John of Reading (1969). 'Quaestio Ioannis de Reading de Necessitate Specierum Intelligibilium Defensio Doctrinae Scoti', ed. Gedeon Gál, *Franciscan Studies* 29:66–156

John of St Thomas (1930–7). *Cursus Philosophicus Thomisticus*, ed. B. Reiser, Marietti

(1931–53). *Cursus Theologicus*, Desclée

(1955a). *Outlines of Formal Logic*, tr. with an introduction by Francis C. Wade, Marquette University Press

(1955b). *The Material Logic of John of St Thomas*, tr. Y. R. Simon, J. J. Glanville, and

G. D. Hollenhorst, University of Chicago Press

John of Salisbury (1909). *Policraticus*, ed. C. C. J. Webb (2 vols.), Clarendon Press

(1927). *The Statesman's Book of John of Salisbury*, tr. by John Dickinson (*Policraticus* 4–6 and selections from 7–8), Knopf

(1929). *Metalogicon*, ed. C. C. J. Webb, Clarendon Press

(1938). *Frivolities of Courtiers and Footprints of Philosophers*, tr. Joseph B. Pike (*Policraticus* 1–3 and selections from 7–8), Oxford University Press

(1962). *The Metalogicon*, tr. Daniel D. McGarry, University of California Press

Johnston, Herbert (1960). 'Intellectual Abstraction in St Albert', *Philosophical Studies* (Maynooth) 10:204–12

John of Turrecremata (1489). *Summa de ecclesia*, Rome

John Versor (1495). *Quaestiones super libros Ethicorum Aristotelis*, Cologne

John Wyclif (1871). *The Church and Her Members* in Thomas Arnold (ed.) *Select English Works of John Wyclif*, vol. 3, Clarendon Press

(1885–1904). *De Civili Dominio* (4 vols.), Trübner (Reprinted Johnson Reprint Co. 1966)

(1887). *Tractatus de Officio Regis*, Trübner

(1899). *Tractatus de logica*, ed. M. H. Dziewicki (Wyclif Society, 3), Trübner

(1907). *Tractatus de Potestate Papae*, Trübner (Reprinted Johnson Reprint Co. 1966)

Jolivet, Jean (1969). *Arts du langage et théologie chez Abélard* (Études de Philosophie Médiévale, 57), J. Vrin

(1974). 'Comparaison des théories du langage chez Abélard et chez les nominalistes du XIVe siècle', in E. M. Buytaert (ed.), *Peter Abelard. Proceedings of the international conference Louvain May 10–12, 1971*, Leuven University Press and Martinus Nijhoff

(1975) 'Vues médiévales sur les paronymes', *Revue Internationale de Philosophie* 113:222–42

Joseph, H. W. B. (1916). *An Introduction to Logic* (2nd ed.), Clarendon Press

Joynson, James Turner (1975). *Ideology, Reason, and the Limitation of War: Religious and Secular Concepts, 1200–1740*, Princeton University Press

Juan de Mariana (1599). *De Rege et Regis Institutione*, P. Rodericus

(1948). *The King and the Education of the King*, tr. George Albert Moore, Country Dollar Press

Kaiser, Rudolf (1962). 'Zur Frage der eigenen Anschauung Alberts d. Gr. in seinen philosophischen Kommentaren', *Freiburger Zeitschrift für Philosophie und Theologie* 9:53–62

Kaluża, Zénon (1979). 'Le problème du "Deum non esse" chez Étienne de Chaumont, Nicolas Aston et Thomas Bradwardine', *Mediaevalia Philosophica Polonorum* 24:3–19.

Kaminsky, H. (1963). 'Wyclifism as ideology of revolution', *Church History* 32:57–74

Kantorowicz, E. H. (1955). 'Mysteries of state: an absolutist concept and its late medieval origins', *Harvard Theological Review* 48:65–91

(1957), *The King's Two Bodies. A Study in Mediaeval Political Theology*, Princeton University Press

Kasper. Franz (1967). *Das subjektive Recht–Begriffsbildung und Bedeutungsmehrheit* (Freiburger Rechts- und Staatswissenschaftliche Abhandlungen, 25). C. F. Muller

Kearney, H. (1970). *Scholars and Gentlemen*, Cornell University Press

Keckermann, Bartholomew (1613). *Systema Systematum*, Hanover

Keeler, Leo (1934). *The Problem of Error from Plato to Kant*, Gregorian University Press

Keen M. A. (1965). *The Laws of War in the Late Middle Ages*, Routledge and Kegan Paul

Keicher, Otto (1913). 'Zur Lehre der ältesten Franziskanertheologen vom "intellectus agens"' in *Abhandlungen aus dem Gebiete der Philosophie und ihrer Geschichte. Eine Festgabe zum 70. Geburtstag George Freiherrn von Hertling*, Herder

Kelley, F. E. (forthcoming) 'Some Observations on the *fictum* theory in Ockham and its Relation to Hervaeus Natalis' *Franciscan Studies*

Kennan, Elizabeth (1967). 'The *De Consideratione* of St Bernard of Clairvaux and the papacy in the mid-twelfth century: a review of scholarship', *Traditio* 23 : 73–115

Kennedy, Leonard A. (1959–60). 'The Nature of the Human Intellect According to St Albert the Great', *The Modern Schoolman* 37 : 121–37

  (1962–3). 'St Albert the Great's Doctrine of Divine Illumination', *The Modern Schoolman* 40 : 23–37

Kenny, Anthony (1969a). 'Intellect and Imagination in Aquinas' in Anthony Kenny (ed.) *Aquinas: A Collection of Critical Essays*, Doubleday

  (1969b). *The Five Ways: St Thomas Aquinas' Proofs of God's Existence*, Routledge and Kegan Paul

  ed. (1970). *Aquinas. A Collection of Critical Essays*, Macmillan

Kidd, I. G. (1978). 'Posidonius and Logic', in *Les stoïciens et leur logique. Actes du colloque de Chantilly 18–22 septembre 1976*, J. Vrin

Kilvington, Richard, *see* Richard Kilvington

Kilwardby, Robert, *see* Robert Kilwardby

Kirshner, Julius (1973). '*Civitas sibi faciat civem*: Bartolus of Sassoferrato's doctrine on the making of a citizen', *Speculum* 48 : 694–713

Kitchel, M. Jean (1974). 'The "De potentiis animae" of Walter Burley', *Mediaeval Studies* 33 : 85–113

Kleineidam, E. (1930). *Das Problem der hylomorphen Zusammensetzung der geistigen Substanzen im 13. Jahrhundert, behandelt bis Thomas von Aquin*, Breslau (Dissertation)

  (1973). 'Geschichte der Wissenschaft im mittelalterlichen Erfurt'. *Geschichte Thüringens* II 2 : 150–87, Böhlau

Kleutgen, J. (1860) *Die Philosophie der Vorzeit vertheidigt* (2 vols.), Theissing'sche Buchhandlung

Klingsford, C. L. (1949–50). 'Lavenham, or Lavynham, Richard', *Dictionary of National Biography* (reprint, Oxford University Press), 11 : 652–3

Klubertanz, George P. (1952). *The Discursive Power: Sources and Doctrine of the "Vis Cogitativa" According to St Thomas Aquinas*, The Modern Schoolman

  (1952a). 'St Thomas and the Knowledge of the Singular', *New Scholasticism* 26 : 135–66

  (1953). *The Philosophy of Human Nature*, Appleton-Century-Crofts

  (1954a). 'St Thomas on Learning Metaphysics', *Gregorianum* 35 : 3–17

  (1954b). 'The Teaching of Thomistic Metaphysics', *Gregorianum* 35 : 187–205

  (1960). *St Thomas Aquinas on Analogy*, Loyola University Press

Kluge, E. W. (1973–4). 'William of Ockham's Commentary on Porphyry. Introduction and English Translation', *Franciscan Studies* 33 (171–254) and 34 (306–82)

Kluxen, W. (1964). *Philosophische Ethik bei Thomas von Aquin*, Grünewald

  (1978). 'Glück und Glückseilhabe. Zur Rezeption der aristotelischen Glückslehre bei Thomas von Aquin' in G. Bien (ed.), *Die Frage nach dem Glück*, Frommann-Holzboog

Kneale, William and Martha (1962). *The Development of Logic*, Clarendon Press

Kneepkens, C. H. (1977). 'The Relatio simplex in the Grammatical Tracts of the Late Twelfth and Early Thirteenth Century', *Vivarium* 15 : 1–30

  (1978). 'Master Guido and his View on Government: On Twelfth Century Linguistic

Thought', *Vivarium* 16:108–41

Knudsen, Christian (1975). 'Ein ockhamkritischer Text zu Signifikation und Supposition und zum Verhältnis von erster und zweiter Intention', *CIMAGL* 14:1–26

Knuuttila, Simo (1975). *Aika Ja Modaliteetti Aristotelisessa Skolastiikassa*, Societas Missiologica et Oecumenica Fennica

(1978). 'The Statistical Interpretation of Modality in Averroes and Thomas Aquinas', *Ajatus* 37:79–98

(1981). 'Time and Modality in Scholasticism' in S. Knuuttila, ed., *Reforging the Great Chain of Being: Studies of the History of Modal Theories* (Synthese Historical Library 20), Reidel

Knuuttila, Simo, and Anja Inkeri Lehtinen (1979). 'Plato in Infinitum Remisse Incipit Esse Albus. New Texts on the Late Medieval Discussion on the Concept of Infinity in Sophismata Literature', in E. Saarinen, R. Hilpinen, I. Nüniluoto and M. Provence Hintikka (eds.) *Essays in Honour of Jaakko Hintikka*, Reidel

Koch, J. (1930). *Durandi de S. Porciano O. P. Tractatus de habitibus Quaestio Quarta*, (Opuscula et Textus, Series scolastica, 8), Aschendorff

(1944). *Giles of Rome. Errores Philosophorum*, Marquette University Press

Kölmel, W. (1962). *Wilhelm Ockham und seine kirchenpolitischen Schriften*, Ludgerus-Verlag Hubert Wingen

(1970). *Regimen Christianum: Weg und Ergebnisse des Gewaltenverhältnisses und des Gewaltenverständnisses (8–14. Jahrhundert)*, De Gruyter

König, E. (1970). 'Aristoteles' erste Philosophie als universale Wissenschaft von den ΑΡΧΑΙ', *Archiv für Geschichte der Philosophie* 52:225–46

Korolec, J. B. (1974a). 'Le commentaire de Jean Buridan sur l'Éthique à Nicomaque et l'université de Cracovie dans la première moitié du XVe siècle', *Organon* 10:187–208

(1974b). 'La philosophie de la liberté de Jean Buridan', *Studia Mediewistyczne* 15:109–52

(1975). 'Les principes de la philosophie morale de Jean Buridan', *Mediaevalia Philosophica Polonorum* 21:53–72

Kosegarten, J. G. L. (1857). *Geschichte der Universität Greifswald* I, Greifswald

Kotarbiński, T. (1967). 'Notes on the Development of Formal Logic in Poland in the Years 1900–1939' in S. McCall (ed.) *Polish Logic 1920–1939*, Clarendon Press

Kretzmann, Norman (1966). *William of Sherwood's Introduction to Logic*, University of Minnesota Press

(1967). 'History of Semantics' in P. Edwards (ed.) *Encyclopedia of Philosophy*, Macmillan

(1968). *William of Sherwood's Treatise on Syncategorematic Words*, University of Minnesota Press

(1970). 'Medieval Logicians on the Meaning of the *Propositio*', *Journal of Philosophy* 67:767–87

(1975). 'Transformationalism and the Port-Royal Grammar', in J. Rieux and B. E. Rollin (eds.), *General and Rational Grammar: the Port-Royal Grammar* (Janua Linguarum, Series Minor, 208), Mouton

(1976). 'Incipit/Desinit' in P. Machamer and R. Turnbull (eds.) *Motion and Time, Space and Matter*, Ohio State University Press

(1977). 'Socrates is Whiter than Plato Begins to be White', *Noûs* 11:3–15

(forthcoming a). 'The Culmination of the Old Logic in Peter Abelard' in R. L. Benson and G. Constable (eds.) *The Renaissance of the Twelfth Century*, Harvard University Press

ed., (forthcoming b). *Infinity and Continuity in Ancient and Medieval Thought*, Cornell University Press

(forthcoming c). 'Richard Kilvington and the Logic of Instantaneous Speed', in *Studi sul XIV secolo in memoria di Anneliese Maier*, ed. A. Maierù and A. Paravicini-Bagliani, Edizioni di Storia e Letteratura

(forthcoming d). 'Continuity, Contrariety, Contradiction, and Change', in Kretzmann (forthcoming b)

Kretzmann, Norman, John Longeway, Eleonore Stump, and John Van Dyk (1975). [Review of De Rijk 1972], *The Philosophical Review* 84:560–7

(1978). 'L. M. De Rijk on Peter of Spain', *Journal of the History of Philosophy* 16:325–33

Kristeller, Paul Oskar (1944–5). 'Humanism and scholasticism in the Italian Renaissance', *Byzantion* 17:346–74

(1952). 'Petrarch's "Averroists": A Note on the History of Aristotelianism in Venice, Padua, and Bologna', *Mélanges Augustin Renaudet, Bibliothèque d'Humanisme et Renaissance* 14:59–65

(1956). *Studies in Renaissance Thought and Letters* (Storia e letteratura: raccolta di studi e testi, 54), Edizione di storia e letteratura

(1961a). *Renaissance Thought: the Classic, Scholastic, and Humanist Strains*, Harper & Row

(1961b). 'The Moral Thought of Renaissance Humanism' in *Chapters in Western Civilization* (3rd ed.), Columbia University Press

(1964). *Eight Philosophers of the Italian Renaissance*, Stanford University Press

(1972). *Renaissance Concepts of Man*, Harper Torchbooks

(1974). *Medieval Aspects of Renaissance Learning* (Duke Monographs in Medieval and Renaissance Studies, 1), Duke University Press

Kuksewicz, Zdzislaw (1968). *De Siger de Brabant à Jacques de Plaisance – la théorie de l'intellect chez les averroïstes latins des XIIIe et XIVe s.*, Ossolineum

(1973). *Albertyzm i tomizm w XV wieku w Krakowie i Kolonii*, Wrocław

Kuttner, S (1976). 'Gratian and Plato' in C. N. L. Brooke *et al.* (eds.) *Church and Government in the Middle Ages*, Cambridge University Press

Labis, F. (1845). 'Théorie des idées selon M. Gioberti', *Revue Catholique* 3:8–19, 62–73

La Brière, Y. de (1930) 'La conception de la paix et de la guerre chez Saint Augustin' *Revue de Philosophie* 30, 557–72

LaBrosse, Olivier de (1965). *Le Pape et le concile*, Éditions du Cerf

Lachance, Louis (1933). *Le concept de Droit selon Aristote et S. Thomas*, Sirey

(1965). *L'humanisme politique de saint Thomas d'Aquin, individu et État* (rev. ed.), Sirey

Ladner, Gerhart B. (1967). '*Homo viator*: medieval ideas on alienation and order', *Speculum* 42:233–59

Lagarde, G. de (1934–46). *La naissance de l'esprit laïque au déclin du moyen âge* (6 vols.), Saint-Paul-Trois-Châteaux

(1943–5). 'La philosophie sociale d'Henri de Gand et Godefroid de Fontaines', *Archives de l'histoire doctrinale et littéraire du moyen âge* 14:73–142

(1956–70). *La naissance de l'esprit laïque au déclin du moyen âge* (3rd ed.), E. Nauwelaerts

Lakner, F. (1933). 'Kleutgen und die kirchliche Wissenschaft Deutschlands im 19. Jahrhundert', *Zeitschrift für katholische Theologie* 57:161–214

Lambert of Auxerre (1971). *Logica (Summa Lamberti)*, ed. F. Alessio (Pubblicazioni della facoltà di lettere e filosofia dell'Università di Milano, 59), La Nuova Italia Editrice

Lamennais, F. de (1819). *Essai sur l'indifférence en matière de religion* (5th ed., 4 vols.), Tourachon-Molin et H. Seguin

Landgraf, A. M. (1935). 'Quelques collections de Quaestiones de seconde moitié du XIIe siècle'. *Revue de théologie ancienne et médiévale* 7 : 124–7

Lang, A. (1937). *Heinrich Totting von Oyta* (*BGPM*, xxx, 4–5), Aschendorff
  (1962). *Die Entfaltung des apologetischen Problems in der Scholastik des Mittelalters*, Herder
  (1964). *Die theologische Prinzipienlehre der mittelalterlichen Scholastik*, Herder

Langhade, J., and Grignaschi, M., eds. (1971). *Alfarabi, deux ouvrages inédits sur la Rhétorique*, Dar el-Machreq (Beirut)

Lapparent, P. de (1940–2). 'L'oeuvre politique de François de Mayronnes', *Archives d'histoire doctrinale et littéraire du moyen âge* 15–17 : 5–151

Laso, José Alvarez (1952). *La Filosofía de las Mathemáticas en Santo Tomás*, Editorial Jus

Latham, R. E. (1965). *Revised Medieval Latin Word-List from British and Irish Sources*, Oxford University Press

La Vaissière, J. de (1925). 'Le sens du mot "verbe mental" dans les ecrits de Saint Thomas', *Archives de philosophie*, vol. 2, Cahier 2, Beauchesne

Lawrence, C. H. (1960). *St Edmund of Abingdon*, Clarendon Press

Le Bras, Gabriel, ed. (1955–). *Histoire du droit et des institutions de l'Église en Occident*, Sirey

Leclercq, J. (1931). 'Note sur les théories politiques d'Alvaro Pelayo: à propos d'une these récente', *Recherches de science religieuse* 21 : 582–9
  (1942): *Jean de Paris et l'ecclésiologie du XIIIe siècle*, J. Vrin

Leff, Gordon (1957). *Bradwardine and the Pelagians. A study of His De causa Dei and its Opponents*, Cambridge University Press
  (1961). *Gregory of Rimini: Tradition and Innovation in Fourteenth Century Thought*, Manchester University Press
  (1967a). *Heresy in the Later Middle Ages* (2 vols.), Manchester University Press
  (1967b). 'The apostolic ideal in later medieval ecclesiology', *Journal of Theological Studies, New Series* 18 : 58–82
  (1967c). 'Pierre d'Ailly' in P. Edwards (ed.) *Encyclopedia of Philosophy*, Macmillan
  (1975). *William of Ockham: The Metamorphosis of Scholastic Discourse*, Manchester University Press

Lefranc, Abel (1893). *Histoire du Collège de France*, Hachette

Le Goff, J. (1957). *Les Intellectuels au moyen âge*, Éditions du Seuil

Lerner, Ralph, and Muhsin Mahdi, eds. (1963). *Medieval Political Philosophy*, Cornell University Press

Lemay, R. (1963). 'Dans l'Espagne du XIe siècle. Les Traductions de l'arabe au latin', *Annales, Économies, Sociétés, Civilisations* 18 : 639–65

Lewis, C. J. T. (1975). *The Merton Tradition and Kinematics in late Sixteenth and Early Seventeenth Century Italy*, unpublished Ph.D. thesis, University of London
  (1976). 'The Fortunes of Richard Swineshead in the Time of Galileo', *Annals of Science* 33 : 561–84

Lewis, C. S. (1954). *English Literature in the Sixteenth Century excluding Drama*, Clarendon Press

Lewis, Ewart (1938). 'Organic tendencies in medieval political thought', *American Political Science Review* 32 : 849–76
  (1939–40). 'Natural Law and expediency', *Ethics* 1 : 144–63
  (1954). *Medieval Political Ideas*. 2 vols., Routledge & Kegan Paul
  (1963). 'The "positivism" of Marsiglio of Padua', *Speculum* 38 : 541–82

Lewry, O. (forthcoming), 'The Oxford Condemnations of 1277 in Grammar and Logic' in *Proceedings of the 4th European Symposium on Medieval Logic and Semantics*

Libera, A. de (forthcoming). 'Roger Bacon et le problème de l'appellatio univoca',
  (*Proceedings of the 4th European Symposium on Medieval Logic and Semantics*)
Liberatore, M. (1855). *Institutiones philosophicae*, Typis Propaganda Fidei
Liebeschütz, Hans (1950). *Humanism in the Life and Writings of John of Salisbury*, Warburg
  Institute
  (1967). 'Western Christian Thought from Boethius to Anselm' in A. H. Armstrong
  (ed.) *The Cambridge History of Later Greek and Early Medieval Philosophy*, Cambridge
  University Press
  (1968). 'Chartres und Bologna: Naturbegriff und Staatsidee bei Johannes von
  Salisbury', *Archiv für Kulturgeschichte* 50:3–32
Lindeboom, J. (1913). *Het bijbelsch humanisme in Nederland*, Adriani
Linhardt, R. (1932). *Die Sozialprinzipien des hl. Thomas von Aquino*, Herder
Lio, Ermengildo (1950). 'De elementis traditionalibus justitiae in primaeva schola
  Franciscana', *Franciscan Studies* 10:164–85
  (1957). *Estne obligatio justitiae subvenire miseris?: Quaestionis positio et evolutio a Petro
  Lombardo ad S. Thomam ex tribus S. Augustini textibus*, Desclée
  (1959). 'De jure ut objecto justitiae apud S. Thomam II–II, q. 57, a. 1', *Apollinaris*
  32:16–71
Little, A. (1949). *The Platonic Heritage of Thomism*, Golden Eagle Books Limited,
  Standard House
Little, A. G., and F. Pelster (1934). *Oxford Theology and Theologians c. A. D. 1282–1302*
  (publications of the Oxford Historical Society, 96), Clarendon Press
Lloyd, A. C. (1956). 'Neoplatonic logic and Aristotelian Logic', *Phronesis* 1:58–72;
  146–60
  (1967). 'Porphyry and Iamblichus' in A. H. Armstrong (ed.) *The Cambridge History of
  Later Greek and Early Medieval Philosophy*, Cambridge University
Lohr, Charles H. (1965). 'Logica Algazelis: Introduction and Critical Text', *Traditio*
  21:223–90
  (1967–74). *Medieval Latin Aristotle Commentaries* (Authors A – F in *Traditio* 23:313–
  413; Authors G – I, *ibid.* 24:149–245; Authors Jacobus – Johannes Juff, *ibid.* 26:
  135–216; Authors Johannes de Kanthi – Myngodus, *ibid.* 27:251–351; Authors
  Narcissus – Richardus, *ibid.* 28:281–396; Authors Robertus – Wilgelmus, *ibid.*
  29:93–197; Supplementary Authors, *ibid.* 30:119–44.)
  (1974–). *Renaissance Latin Aristotle Commentaries.* (Authors A – B in *Studies in the
  Renaissance* 21 (1974):228–89; Authors C in *Renaissance Quarterly* 28 (1975):689–
  741; Authors D – F, *ibid.* 29 (1976):714–45; Authors G – K, *ibid.* 30 (1977):681–
  741; Authors L – M, *ibid.* 31 (1978):532–603; Authors N – Ph, *ibid.* 32 (1979):
  529–80.)
Lombard, Peter, *see* Peter Lombard
Lonergan, B. J. F. (1957). *Insight. A Study of Human Understanding*, Longmans Green
  (1967). *Verbum: Word and Idea in Aquinas*, ed. David Burrell, University of Notre
  Dame Press
Longeway, John (1977). *Simon of Faversham's Questions on the Posterior Analytics: A
  Thirteenth-Century View of Science*, unpublished Ph. D. Dissertation, Cornell
  University
Longpré, E. (1922) 'Pietro de Trabibus, un discepolo di Pier Giovanni Olivi', *Studi
  Francescani* 19
  (1944). *The Kingship of Jesus Christ according to St Bonaventure and Blessed Duns Scotus*,
  tr. Daniel J. Barry, St Anthony Guild Press
Loserth, Johann (1918). 'Johann von Wyclif und Robert Grosseteste, Bischof von

Lincoln,' *Sitzungsberichte der Akademie der Wissenschaften Wien, phil.-hist. Kl.* 186

Lottin, O. (1925). 'La définition classique de la loi (comment. de la IaIIae, 90)', *Revue Néoscolastique de Philosophie* 26:129–45; 244–73

(1931). *Les droit naturel chez S. Thomas d'Aquin et ses prédécesseurs* (2nd ed.), E. Dillon

(1932). 'La composition hylémorphique des substances spirituelles', *Revue Néoscolastique de Philosophie* 34:21–41

(1942–60). *Psychologie et morale aux XIIᵉ et XIIIᵉ siècles* (6 vols. in 7), Abbaye du Mont César

(1948). [in Lottin 1942–60]

(1954). 'Les vertus morales acquises sont-elles de vraies vertus?', *Recherches de Théologie ancienne et médiévale* 21:101–29

(1957). *Psychologie et morale aux XIIᵉ et XIIIᵉ siècles* (2nd ed.), vol I, *Problèmes de Psychologie*

(1959). [in Lottin 1942–60]

Lotz, J. B., ed. (1955). *Kant und die Scholastik heute*, Verlag Berchmannskolleg

Loux, M. J. (1974). *Ockham's Theory of Terms. Part I of the Summa logicae*, tr. with an introduction, University of Notre Dame Press

Lovejoy, A. O. (1936). *The Great Chain of Being. A Study of the History of an Idea*, Harvard University Press

Łukasiewicz, Jan (1935). 'Zur Geschichte der Aussagenlogik', *Erkenntnis* 5:111–31

(1957). *Aristotle's Syllogistic from the Standpoint of Modern Formal Logic* (2nd ed.), Clarendon Press

Lupold of Bebenberg (1566). *De Iure Regni et Imperii Romani* in S. Schardius (ed.) *De Iurisdictione, Auctoritate et Praeeminentia Imperiali ac Potestate Ecclesiastica*, Basel

Luquet, G. H. (1901). 'Hermann l'Allemand', *Revue de l'histoire des religions* 44:407–22

Luscombe, D. E. (1969). *The School of Peter Abelard: The Influence of Abelard's Thought in the Early Scholastic Period* (Cambridge Studies in Medieval Life and Thought, 14), Cambridge University Press

(1971). *Peter Abelard's Ethics*, Clarendon Press

Lynch, J. E. (1972). *The Theory of Knowledge of Vital du Four*, The Franciscan Institute

Lynch, John Patrick (1972). *Aristotle's School*, University of California Press

Lyons, J. (1977). *Semantics* I–II, Cambridge University Press

McAlister, L., ed. (1976). *The Philosophy of Brentano*, Duckworth

McCabe, H. (1954). 'Categories', *Dominican Studies* 7: 147–79

McCall, R. S. (1963). *Aristotle's Modal Syllogisms* (Studies in Logic and the Foundations of Mathematics), North-Holland

MacClintock, Stuart (1954–5). 'Heresy and Epithet: An Approach to the Problem of Latin Averroism', *The Review of Metaphysics* 8:176–99, 342–56 and 526–45

(1956). *Perversity and Error: Studies on the "Averroist" John of Jandun* (Indiana University Publications, Humanities Series, No. 37), Indiana University Press

McConica, J. (1979). 'Humanism and Aristotle in Tudor Oxford', *The English Historical Review* 94:291–317

McCready, William D. (1973). 'Papal *plentitudo potestatis* and the source of temporal authority in late medieval papal hierocratic theory', *Speculum* 48:654–74

(1974). 'The problem of the empire in Augustinus Triumphus and late medieval papal hierocratic theory', *Traditio* 30:325–49

(1975). 'Papalists and anti-papalists: aspects of the Church – State controversy in the later middle ages', *Viator* 6:241–73

(1977). 'The papal sovereign in the ecclesiology of Augustinus Triumphus', *Mediaeval*

Studies 39:177–205.

McDermott, A. C. S. (1972). 'Notes on the Assertoric and Modal Propositional Logic of the Pseudo-Scotus', *Journal of the History of Philosophy* 10:273–306

McDonald, William Joseph (1939). *The Social Value of Property according to St Thomas Aquinas*, Catholic University of America

McDonnell, Kevin (1974). 'Does William of Ockham have a theory of natural law?', *Franciscan Studies* 34:383–92

McEvoy, James (1977). 'La connaissance intellectuelle selon Robert Grossesteste', *Revue philosophique du Louvain* 75:5–48

McFarlane, K. B. (1952). *John Wycliffe and the beginnings of English Nonconformity*, English Universities Press (Hodder & Stroughton Educational)

McGrade, A. S. (1963). 'The coherence of Hooker's *Polity*: the books on power', *Journal of the History of Ideas* 24:163–82

  (1974). *The Political Thought of William of Ockham. Personal and Institutional Principles* (Cambridge Studies in Medieval Life and Thought, third series, 7), Cambridge University Press

  (1978). 'Repentance and Spiritual Power: Book VI of Richard Hooker's *Of the Laws of Ecclesiastical Polity*', *Journal of Ecclesiastical History* 29:163–76

  (1980). 'Ockham and the birth of individual rights' in Brian Tierney and Peter Linehan (eds.), *Authority and Power: Studies on Medieval Law and Government Presented to Walter Ullmann on his Seventieth Birthday*, Cambridge University Press

McGrade, A. S. and Brian Vickers, eds. (1975). *Richard Hooker: Of the Laws of Ecclesiastical Polity: An Abridged Edition*, Sidgwick and Jackson

McIlwain, C. H. (1932). *The Growth of Political Thought in the West. From the Greeks to the End of the Middle Ages*, MacMillan

  (1940). *Constitutionalism, Ancient and Modern*, Cornell University Press

McInerny, R. (1966). *Thomism in an Age of Renewal*, Doubleday

  (1974). 'Boethius and Saint Thomas Aquinas', *Rivista di Filosofia neo-scolastica* 66: 219–45

McKeon, R. (1929–30). *Selections from Medieval Philosophers* (2 vols.), Scribners

  (1938). 'The development of the concept of property in political philosophy: a study of the background of the constitution', *Ethics* 48:297–366

McMullin, Ernan (1963). 'Matter as a Principle', with comment by W. Sellars, in E. McMullin (ed.) *The Concept of Matter*, University of Notre Dame Press

Maccarrone, Michele (1954). ' "Potestas directa" e "potestas indirècta" nei teologi del XII e XIII secolo', *Miscellanea Historiae Pontificiae* 18:27–47

Machiavelli, Niccolò (1965). *Chief Works, and Others*, tr. Allan Gilbert, Duke University Press

  (1968). *Opere*, vol. I, G. Salerno

Macken, R. (1971). 'La temporalité radicale de la crêature selon Henri de Gand', *Recherches de Theólogie ancienne et médiévale* 38:211–72

Macken, R. (1973). 'Les corrections d'Henri de Gand à ses Quodlibets'. *Recherches de théologie ancienne et médiévales* 40:5–51

  (1976a). 'Le statut de la matière première chez Bonaventure', *Franziskanische Forschungen* 28:94–103

  (1976b). 'La subsistance de la matière première selon Henri de Gand', in *San Bonaventura maestro di vita francescana e di sapienza cristiana* (Atti del Congresso internazionale per il VII centenario di san Bonaventura da Bagnoregio, Roma 19–26 settembre 1974), 3

Madkour, I. (1934). *La place d'al Farabi dans l'école philosophique musulmane*, Vrin

Mahieu, L. (1921). *François Suarez, sa philosophie et les rapports qu'elle a avec sa théologie*, Desclée

Mahoney, Edward P. (1970). 'Pier Nicola Castellani and Agostino Nifo on Averroes' Doctrine of the Agent Intellect', *Rivista critica di storia della filosofia* 25 : 387–409

(1973a). 'Themistius and the Agent Intellect in James of Viterbo and Other Thirteenth Century Philosophers (Saint Thomas, Siger of Brabant and Henry Bate)', *Augustiniana* 23 : 422–67

(1973b). Review of Marcia L. Colish, *The Mirror of Language: A Study in the Medieval Theory of Knowledge*, Yale University Press, 1968, in *Journal of the History of Philosophy* 11 : 258–62

(1974a). 'Saint Thomas and Siger of Brabant Revisited', *The Review of Metaphysics* 27 : 531–53

(1974b). 'Saint Thomas and the School of Padua at the End of the Fifteenth Century', *Proceedings of the American Catholic Philosophical Association* 48 : 277–85

(1976a). 'Agostino Nifo and Saint Thomas Aquinas', *Memorie Domenicane*, n. s. 7 : 195–226

(1976b). 'Nicoletto Vernia on the Soul and Immortality' in Edward P. Mahoney (ed.) *Philosophy and Humanism: Renaissance Essays in Honor of Paul Oskar Kristeller*, Columbia University Press and E. J. Brill

(1980a). 'Albert the Great and the *Studio Patavino* in the Late Fifteenth and Early Sixteenth Centuries' in James A. Weisheipl (ed.) *Albertus Magnus and the Sciences: Commemorative Essays 1980*, Pontifical Institute of Mediaeval Studies

(1980b). 'Metaphysical Foundations of the Hierarchy of Being according to Some Late Medieval and Renaissance Philosophers' in Parviz Morewedge (ed.), *Ancient and Medieval Philosophies of Existence*, Fordham University Press

Mahoney, Michael (1978). 'Mathematics' in D. C. Lindberg (ed.) *Science in the Middle Ages*, University of Chicago Press

Maier, Anneliese (1944). 'Ein Beitrag zur Geschichte des Italienischen Averroismus im 14. Jahrhundert', *Quellen und Forschungen aus den Italienischen Archiven und Bibliotheken* 33 : 136–57

(1944a). 'Die scholastische Wesensbestimmung der Bewegung als forma fluens oder fluxus formae und ihre Beziehung zu Albertus Magnus', *Angelicum* 21 : 97–111

(1949). *Die Vorläufer Galileis im 14. Jahrhundert* (Studien zur Naturphilosophie der Spätscholastik, vol. 1), Edizioni di Storia e Letteratura

(1951). *Zwei Grundprobleme der Scholastischen Naturwissenschaft* (Studien zur Naturphilosophie der Spätscholastik, vol. 2) (2nd ed.), Edizioni di Storia e Letteratura

(1952). *An der Grenze von Scholastik und Naturwissenschaft* (Studien zur Naturphilosophie der Spätscholastik, vol. 3) (2nd ed.), Edizioni di Storia e Letteratura

(1955). *Metaphysische Hintergründe der spätscholastischen Naturphilosophie* (Studien zur Naturphilosophie der Spätscholastik, vol. 4), Edizioni di Storia e Letteratura

(1958). *Zwischen Philosophie und Mechanik* (Studien zur Naturphilosophie der Spätscholastik, vol. 5), Edizioni di Storia e Letteratura

(1964). 'Diskussionen über das aktuell Unendliche in der ersten Hälfte des 14. Jahrhunderts' in Maier (1964–7), vol. 1

(1964–7). *Ausgehendes Mittelalter* (2 vols.), Edizioni di Storia e Letteratura

(1966). *Die Vorläufer Galileis im 14. Jahrhundert.* (Studien zur Naturphilosophie der Spätscholastik, vol. 1) (2nd. ed.), Edizioni di Storia e Letteratura

(1968). *Zwei Grundprobleme der Scholastischen Naturphilosophie* (Studien zur Naturphilosophie der Spätscholastik, vol. 2) (3rd ed.), Edizioni di Storia e Letteratura

Maier, H. (1966). 'Die Lehre der Politik an den deutschen Universitäten vornehmlich vom 16. bis 18. Jahrhundert' in D. Oberndörfer (ed.) *Wissenschaftliche Politik. Eine Einführung in Grundfragen ihrer Tradition und Theorie* (2nd ed), Wissenschaftliche Buchgesellschaft

Maierù, A. (1966). 'Il "Tractatus de sensu composito et diviso" di Guglielmo Heytesbury', *Rivista critica di Storia della Filosofia* 21:243–63

  (1969a). 'Il problema della verità nelle opere di G. Heytesbury', *Studi Medievali* 7:40–74

  (1969b). 'Lo *Speculum puerorum sive Terminus est in quem* di Riccardo Billingham' in *A Giuseppe Ermini, Studi Medievali* (Serie terza), 10.3:297–397

  (1972). *Terminologia logica della tarda scolastica* (Lessico intellettuale europeo, 8), Edizioni dell'Ateneo

Maimonides, Moses *see* Moses Maimonides

Maistre, J. de (1844). *Considerations sur la France, suivies de l'Essai sur le principe générateur des constitutions politiques . . .*, La Société Nationale pour la propagation de bons livres

Major, John *see* John Major

Makdisi, G. (1974). 'The Scholastic Method in Medieval Education: An Inquiry into its Origins in Law and Theology', *Speculum* 49:640–61

Malcolm, John (1971). 'On Grabmann's text of William of Sherwood', *Vivarium* 9:108–18

Mandonnet, P. (1908–11). *Siger de Brabant et l'averroïsme latin au XIIIᵉ siècle* (2nd ed.) (2 vols.), (Les Philosophes Belges), Institut Supérieur de Philosophie de l'Université de Louvain

  (1910). 'La carrière scolaire de Gilles de Rome', *Revue des Sciences philosophiques et théologiques* 4:480–99

  (1911). 'Autour de Siger de Brabant', *Revue thomiste* 19:314–37, 476–502

  (1928). 'Chronologie des questions disputées de saint Thomas d'Aquin'. *Revue Thomiste* 23:267–79

Manegold of Lautenbach (1880). *Liber ad Gebehardum, PL* 155

Manser, G. (1944). *Das Naturrecht in thomistischer Beleuchtung*, Verlag der Paulusdruckerei

Mansion, Augustin (1953). 'L'immortalité de l'âme et de l'intellect d'après Aristote', *Revue philosophique de Louvain* 51:457–65

Manzalaoni, Mahmoud (1977). *Secretum secretorum*, Oxford University Press

Maréchal, J. (1926). *Le Point de Départ de la Métaphysique. Leçons sur le développement historique et théorique du problème de la connaissance. Cahier V: Le Thomisme devant la Philosophie critique*, Éditions du Museum Lessianum.

Mariana, Juan de, *see* Juan de Mariana

Mariani, U. (1957). *Chiesa e stato nei teologi agostiniani del secolo XIV* (Uomini e dottrine, 5), Edizioni di storia e letteratura

Maritain, J. (1940). *Scholasticism and Politics*, tr. M. J. Adler, Macmillan

  (1959). *Degrees of Knowledge.* Translated from the 4th French edition [1946] under the supervision of G. B. Phelan, Geoffrey Bles

Markowski, Mieczsław (1968). 'Les questions de Jean Buridan sur les *Topiques* d'Aristote', *Mediaevalia Philosophica Polonorum* 13:3–7

Marlasca, Antonio (1971). 'La antropologia sigeriana en las "Quaestiones super librum de causis"', *Estudios filosóficos* 20:3–27

  (1972). *Les Quaestiones super librum de causis de Siger de Brabant*, Publications Universitaires de Louvain

  (1974). 'De nuevo. Tomás de Aquino y Siger de Brabante', *Estudios filosóficos*

23:431-9

Marsilius of Inghen (1495). *Commentum in primum et quartum tractatum Petri Hispani*, Hagenau (Reprinted Minerva 1967)

   (1501). *Questiones Marsilii super quattuor libros Sententiarum*, Strasburg (Reprinted Minerva 1966)

   (1516). *Quaestiones super libros Priorum Analyticorum*, Venice (Reprinted Minerva 1968)

Marsilius of Padua (1614a) *De Translatione imperii* in M. Goldast (ed.)*Monarchia Sancti Romani Imperii*, 2:147-53; Conrad Biermann (Reprinted Akademische Druck- und Verlagsanstalt 1960)

   (1614b). *De Iurisdictione imperatoris in causis matrimonialibus* in M. Goldast (ed.) *Monarchia Sancti Romani Imperii*, 2:1386-91; Conrad Biermann (Reprinted Akademische Druck- und Verlagsanstalt 1960)

   (1922). *Defensor minor*, ed. C. K. Brampton, Cornish Brothers

   (1928). *Defensor pacis*, ed. C. W. Previté-Orton, Cambridge University Press

   (1932-3). *Defensor pacis*, ed. R. Scholz, Hahnsche Buchhandlung

   (1956). *The Defensor Pacis*, ed. and tr. A. Gewirth, *Marsilius of Padua: The Defender of Peace*, 2 (The Records of Civilization, Sources and Studies, 46), Columbia University Press

   (1968). *Le Défenseur de la paix*, tr. with introduction and commentary by Jeannine Quillet, J. Vrin

Martin, Conor (1949). *The commentaries on the Politics of Aristotle in the late thirteenth and fourteenth centuries, with reference to the thought and political life of the time*, unpublished D. Phil. thesis, Oxford University

   (1951). 'Some medieval commentaries on Aristotle's *Politics*', *History* 36:29-44

   (1964). 'Walter Burleigh' in *Oxford Studies Presented to Daniel Callus* (Oxford Historical Society, new series, 16), Clarendon Press

Martin of Dacia (1961). *Opera*, ed. H. Roos (Corpus Philosophorum Danicorum Medii Aevi, 2), Gad

Marty, Anton (1908). *Untersuchungen zur Grundlegung der allgemeinen Grammatik und Sprachphilosophie*, Max Niemeyer

Masnovo, Amato (1945). *Da Guglielmo d'Auvergne a S. Tommaso d'Aquino*, vol. 3: *L'uomo* (Pubblicazioni dell'Università Cattolica del Sacro Cuore, n.s. vol. 10), Società Editrice 'Vita e Pensiero'

Mates, Benson (1965a). *Elementary Logic*, Oxford University Press

   (1965b). 'Pseudo-Scotus on the Soundness of *Consequentiae*' in A.-T. Tymieniecka (ed.) *Contributions to Logic and Methodology in Honor of I. M. Bocheński*, North-Holland

Matthew of Aquasparta (1903). *Quaestiones disputatae selectae*, vol. I: *Quaestiones de fide et cognitione*, Collegium s. Bonaventurae

Matthews, Gareth B. (1973). '*Suppositio* and Quantification in Ockham', *Noûs* 7:13-24

   (1977). 'Consciousness and Life', *Philosophy* 52:13-26

Mattos, Gonçalo de (1940). 'L'intellect agent personnel dans les premiers écrits d'Albert le Grand et de Thomas d'Aquin', *Revue néoscolastique de philosophie* 43:145-61

Maurer, Armand (1946). '*Esse* and *Essentia* in the Metaphysics of Siger of Brabant', *Mediaeval Studies* 8:68-86

   (1955). 'Boethius of Dacia and the Double Truth', *Mediaeval Studies* 17:233-9

   (1956). 'The State of Historical Research in Siger of Brabant', *Speculum* 31:49-56

   (1958). 'Ockham's Conception of the Unity of Science', *Mediaeval Studies* 20:98-112

   (1962). *Medieval Philosophy*, Random House

   (1967). 'A Promising new Discovery for Sigerian Studies', *Mediaeval Studies* 29:364-9

(1976). 'Some Aspects of Fourteenth-Century Philosophy', *Medievalia et Humanistica*, n.s. 7:175–88

Mazzarella, Pasquale (1974). 'La critica di San Tommaso all' "averroismo gnoseologico"', *Rivista di filosofia neo-scolastica* 66:246–83

Meersseman, Gilles M. (1931) *Introductio in opera omnia B. Alberti Magni O. P.*, C. Beyaert

(1932). 'Le droit naturel chez S. Thomas d'Aquin et ses prédécesseurs', *Angelicum* 9:63–76

(1932a). 'Die Einheit der menschlichen Seele nach Albertus Magnus', *Divus Thomas* 10:81–94

(1932b). 'Les origines parisiennes de l'albertisme', *Archives d'histoire doctrinale et littéraire du moyen âge* 7:121–42

(1933–5). *Geschichte des Albertismus*, 2 vols. (Institutum Historicum Fratrum Praedicatorum, Dissertationes historica, vols. 3 and 5), Santa Sabina

Melanchthon, Philipp (1520). *Compendiaria dialectices ratio*, Leipzig

(1555). *Erotemata dialectices* Wittenberg

(1834–60). *Opera quae supersunt omnia*, ed. C. G. Bretschneider (28 vols.), Schwetzke

(1850a). *Philosophiae moralis epitomes* [in Melanchthon 1834–60]

(1850b). *In primum librum Ethicorum Aristotelis enarratio* [in Melanchthon 1834–60]

Melani, G. (1948). *Tractatus de anima Ioannis Pecham*, Edizioni 'Studi Francescani' s. Francesco

Meller, Bernhard (1954). *Studien zur Erkenntnislehre des Peter von Ailly* (Freiburger theologischen Studien, 67), Herder

Menges, M. C. (1952). *The Concept of Univocity Regarding the Predication of God and Creature According to William Ockham*, The Franciscan Institute

Menut, Albert D. (1969). 'A Provisional Bibliography of Oresme's Writings: A Supplementary Note', *Mediaeval Studies* 31:346–7

Mercati, G. (1925). *Per la cronologia della vita e degli scritti di Niccolò Perotti, arcivescovo di Siponto* (Studi e testi, 44), Biblioteca apostolica vaticana

Mercken, H. P. F., ed. (1973). *The Greek Commentaries on the Nicomachean Ethics in the Latin Translation of Robert Grosseteste, Bishop of Lincoln (†1253)*, Vol. I (Corpus Latinum Commentariorum in Aristotelem Graecorum VI, 1), Brill

Merzbacher, F. (1956). 'Das *Somnium viridarii* von 1376 als Spiegel des gallikanischen Kirchenrechts', *Zeitschrift der Savigny-Stiftung für Rechtsgeschichte. Kanonistische Abteilung* 42:55–72

Mesnard, Pierre (1936). *L'Essor de la philosophie politique au XVIe siècle*, Ancienne librairie Furne, Boivin & cie

(1969). *L'Essor de la philosophie politique au XVIe siècle* (3rd. ed.), J. Vrin

Meulen, Jacob ter and P. J. J. Diermanse (1950). *Bibliographie des écrits imprimés de Hugo Grotius*, Martinus Nijhoff

Meynell, C. (1866). *Padre Liberatore and the Ontologists: A Review*, Burns, Oates, and Co.

Michael of Ephesus (1898). *Alexandri quod fertur in Aristotelis Sophisticos Elenchos Commentarium* (ed. M. Wallies) (Commentaria in Aristotelem Graeca II.3), G. Reimer

Michael Psellus (1926). *Chronographie*. Tome I, ed. E. Renaud, Les Belles Lettres

Michalski, K. (1922). 'Les Courants philosophiques à Oxford et à Paris pendant le XIVe siècle', *Bulletin internationale de l'Académie polonaise des sciences et des lettres*, Classe d'histoire et de philosophie, et de philologie, les années 1919, 1920, pp. 59–88

(1926). 'Le Criticisme et le scepticisme dans la philosophie du XIVe siècle', *Bulletin internationale de l'Académie polonaise des sciences et des lettres*, Classe d'histoire et de philosophie, et de philologie, l'année 1925, pp. 41–122

(1927). 'Les Courants critiques et sceptiques dans la philosophie du XIVe siècle', *Bulletin internationale de l'Académie polonaise des sciences et des lettres*, Classe d'histoire et de philosophie, et de philologie, l'année 1925, Part II, pp. 192–242

(1928). 'La Physique nouvelle et les différents courants philosophiques au XIVe siècle', *Bulletin internationale de l'Académie polonaise des sciences et des lettres*, Classe d'histoire et de philosophie, et de philologie, l'année 1927, pp. 93–164

(1937). 'Le Problème de la volonté à Oxford et à Paris au XIVe siècle', *Studia Philosophica* 2:233–365

(1969). *La philosophie au XIVe siècle*, Minerva

Michaud-Quantin, Pierre (1955). 'Albert le Grand et les puissances de l'âme', *Revue du moyen âge latin* 11:59–86

(1966). *La psychologie de l'activité chez Albert le Grand*, Vrin

Michel, Alain (1960). *Les Rapports de la rhétorique et de la philosophie dans l'oeuvre de Cicéron*, Presses universitaires de France

Michel, S. (1932). *La notion thomiste du Bien Commun: Quelques-unes de ses applications juridiques*, Vrin

Miczka, G. (1970). *Das Bild der Kirche bei Johannes von Salisbury* (Bonner historische Forschungen, 24), L. Röhrscheid

Miethke, J. (1969). *Ockhams Weg zur Sozialphilosophie*, De Gruyter

Mignucci, M. (1969). 'Albert the Great's Approach to Aristotelian Modal Syllogistic' in *Arts libéraux et philosophie au moyen âge. Actes du IVe Congrès international de philosophie médiévale*, Insitut d'études médiévales, Montréal and J. Vrin

Milburn, D. (1964). *A History of Ushaw College*, Ushaw (Durham)

Milet, A. (1945). 'Les "Cahiers" du Père Maréchal. Sources doctrinales et influences subies', *Revue néoscolastique de philosophie* 43:225–51

Miller, Robert (1954). 'An Aspect of Averroes' Influence on St. Albert', *Mediaeval Studies* 16:57–71

Minio-Paluello, L. (1952). 'Iacobus Veneticus Grecus: Canonist and Translator of Aristotle', *Traditio* 8:265–304

(1954). 'Note sull' Aristotele Latino Medievale IX: Gli Elenchi Sofistici: redazioni contaminate coll'ignota versione di Giacomo Veneto (?); frammenti dell' ignoto commento d'Alessandro d'Afrodisia tradotti in latino', *Rivista di Filosofia Neo-Scolastica* 46:223–31

(1956). 'Remigio Girolami's *De bono communi*: Florence at the time of Dante's banishment and the philosopher's answer to the crisis', *Italian Studies* 2:56–71

(1956–8). *Twelfth Century Logic: Texts and Studies* (2 vols.), Edizioni di Storia e Letteratura

(1962). 'Note sull' Aristotele Latino Medievale XIV: Frammenti del commento perduto di Alessandro d'Afrodisia ai Secondi Analitici tradotto da Giacomo Veneto in un codice di Goffredo di Fontaines, Parigi B. N. lat. 16080', *Rivista di Filosofia Neo-Scolastica* 54:131–7

(1970a). 'Aristotle: Tradition and Influence' in C. C. Gillispie (ed.), *Dictionary of Scientific Biography*, Charles Scribner's Sons

(1970b) 'Boethius' in C. C. Gillispie (ed.), *Dictionary of Scientific Biography*, Charles Scribner's sons

(1972). *Opuscula*, Hakkert

(1974). 'Moerbeke, William of' in C. C. Gillispie (ed.), *Dictionary of Scientific Biography*, Charles Scribner's Sons

Ministeri, B. (1952–3). 'De vita et operibus Augustini de Ancona, O.E.S.A. (*1328)', *Analecta Augustiniana* 31:7–56, 148–262

Mittelstrass, J. (1962). *Die Rettung der Phänomene: Ursprung und Geschichte eines antiken Forschungsprinzips*, De Gruyter

Mochi Onory, S. (1951). *Fonti canonistiche dell'idea moderna dello stato*, Vita e pensiero

Modde, A. (1949). 'Le bien commun dans la philosophie de Saint Thomas', *Revue philosophique de Louvain* 47:221–47

Modrić, Luca (1978). 'Relazione del P. Luca Modrić sui lavori della comissione Scotistica', *Acta Ordinis Fratrum Minorum* 97:82–3

Molina, Luis de (1659). *De iustitia et iure libri sex* (2 vols.), Moguntiae (= Mainz)
  (1876). *Concordia liberi arbitrii cum gratiae donis, divina praescientia, providentia, praedestinatione, et reprobatione*, Lethielleux

Molinaeus, *see* Pierre du Moulin

Molland, A. G. (1967). *The Geometria Speculativa of Thomas Bradwardine*, unpublished Ph.D. dissertation, Cambridge University
  (1968a). 'The Geometrical Background to the "Merton School"', *British Journal for the History of Science* 4:108–25
  (1968b). 'Richard Swineshead and Continuously Varying Quantities', *XIIe Congrès International d'Histoire des Sciences*, Blanchard
  (1973). 'John of Dumbleton' in C. C. Gillispie (ed.) *Dictionary of Scientific Biography*, Charles Scribner's Sons
  (1978). 'An Examination of Bradwardine's Geometry', *Archive for History of Exact Sciences* 19:113–75

Monahan, A. P. (1954). 'The Subject of Metaphysics for Peter of Auvergne', *Mediaeval Studies* 16:118–30

Monfasani, J. (1976). *George of Trebizond: a Biography and a Study of his Rhetoric and Logic* (Columbia Studies in the Classical Tradition, 1), Brill

Monfrin, J., ed. (1962). *Abelard: Historia Calamitatum*, J. Vrin

Montagnes, B. (1963). *La doctrine de l'analogie de l'être d'après saint Thomas d'Aquin*, Publications Universitaires de Louvain

Moody, Ernest A. (1935). *The Logic of William of Ockham*, Sheed & Ward
  (1942). *Iohannis Buridani Quaestiones super libros quattuor de caelo et mundo*, The Medieval Academy of America
  (1947). 'Ockham, Buridan, and Nicholas of Autrecourt', *Franciscan Studies* 7:113–46
  (1951). 'Galileo and Avempace: The Dynamics of the Leaning Tower Experiment', *Journal of the History of Ideas* 12:163–93; 375–422
  (1953). *Truth and Consequence in Mediaeval Logic* (Studies in Logic and the Foundations of Mathematics), North-Holland
  (1964). 'A quodlibetal question of Robert Holkot, O. P. on the problem of the objects of knowledge and of belief', *Speculum* 39:53–74
  (1965). *The Logic of William of Ockham* (2nd edn.), Russell & Russell
  (1966). 'The Medieval Contribution to Logic', *Studium Generale* 19:443–52
  (1967). 'Medieval Logic', under 'History of Logic', in P. Edwards (ed.) *The Encyclopedia of Philosophy*, Macmillan
  (1970). 'Buridan, Jean' in C. C. Gillispie (ed.) *Dictionary of Scientific Biography*, Charles Scribner's Sons
  (1975). *Studies in Medieval Philosophy, Science, and Logic. Collected Papers 1933–1969* (Publications of the Center for Medieval and Renaissance Studies, UCLA), University of California Press

Morán, J. G. (1951). *Cursus Philosophicus Collegii Maximi Ysletensis Societatis Iesu. Pars iv, Cosmologia*, Buena Prensa

Moraux, Paul (1973). *Der Aristotelismus bei den Griechen. Erster Band* (Peripatoi, 5), De

Gruyter

More, Thomas (1965). *Utopia* in Edward Surtz and J. H. Hexter (eds.) *The Complete Works of St Thomas More*, vol. 4, Yale University Press

Moreau, E. de (1951). Introductory memoir to *Mélanges Joseph de Ghellinck*, Duculot

Moreno, A. (1966). 'The Nature of Metaphysics', *Thomist* 30:109–35

Morewedge, P. (1972). 'Philosophical Analysis and Ibn Sīnā's "Essence-Existence" Distinction', *Journal of the American Oriental Society* 92:425–35

(1973). *The Metaphysica of Avicenna (ibn Sīnā). A critical translation-commentary and analysis of the fundamental arguments in Avicenna's Metaphysica in the Dānish Nāma-i'alā'ī (The Book of Scientific Knowledge)* (Persian Heritage Series, 13), Routledge and Kegan Paul

Morisanus, Bernard, *see* Bernard Morisan

Mornet, E. (1978). 'Pauperes scholares. Essai sur la condition matérielle des étudiants scandinaves aux XIVᵉ et XVᵉ siècle', *Le Moyen-Âge* 84:53–102

Morrall, John B. (1949). 'Some notes on a recent interpretation of William of Ockham's political philosophy', *Franciscan Studies* 9:335–69

(1958). *Political Thought in Medieval Times*, Hutchinson

(1960). *Gerson and the Great Schism*, Manchester University Press

Morris, Christopher (1953). *Political Thought in England: Tyndale to Hooker*, Oxford University Press

Morris, Colin (1972). *The Discovery of the Individual, 1050–1200*, Harper and Row

Moses Maimonides (1951). *Guide for the Perplexed*, tr. M. Friedlander, Dover

(1974). *The Guide of the Perplexed I–II*, translated with an introduction and notes by S. Pines, University of Chicago Press

Muck, O. (1968). *The transcendental method*. With a foreword by Karl Rahner, tr. William D. Seidensticker, Herder and Herder

Muckle, J. T. (1958). 'R. Holcot, "Utrum theologia sit scientia": A Quodlibet Question', *Mediaeval Studies* 20:127–53

Müller, I. von (1897). *Ueber Galens Werk vom wissenschaftlichen Beweis* (Abhandlungen der philosophisch-philologischen Classe der königlich bayerischen Akademie der Wissenschaften, XX. Band, II. Abteilung)

Mugica, Plácido (1948). *Bibliografía suareciana*, Universidad de Granada

Mullally, Joseph P. (1964). *Peter of Spain: Tractatus Syncategorematum and Selected Anonymous Treatises*, Marquette University Press

Muller-Thym, Bernard J. (1940a). 'The Common Sense, Perfection of the Order of Pure Sensibility', *The Thomist* 2:315–43

Mullick, M. (1971). 'Does Ockham Accept Material Implication?', *Notre Dame Journal of Formal Logic* 12:117–24

Mullinger, J. B. (1884). *The University of Cambridge*, Cambridge University Press

Mulvaney, Robert J. (1973). 'Political wisdom: an interpretation of *Summa Theol.* II–II, 50', *Mediaeval Studies* 35:294–305

Muñoz Delgado, V. (1964). *La Lógica Nominalista en la Universidad de Salamanca (1510–1530)* (Publicaciones del Monasterio Poyo, 11), Edita Revista 'Estudios'

Munz, Peter (1952). *The Place of Hooker in the History of Thought*, Routledge & Kegan Paul

Murdoch, John E. (1957). *Geometry and the Continuum in the Fourteenth Century: A Philosophical Analysis of Thomas Bradwardine's Tractatus de continuo*, unpublished Ph.D. dissertation, University of Wisconsin

(1962). *Rationes Mathematice: Un aspect du rapport des mathematiques et de la philosophie au Moyen Âge*, Université de Paris

(1963). 'The Medieval Language of Proportions: Elements of the Interaction with Greek Foundations and the Development of New Mathematical Techniques', in A. C. Crombie (ed.), *Scientific Change*, Heinemann

(1964). 'Superposition, Congruence and Continuity in the Middle Ages' in *Mélanges Alexandre Koyré*, Hermann

(1969). 'Mathesis in Philosophiam Scholasticam Introducta. The Rise and Development of the Application of Mathematics in Fourteenth Century Philosophy and Theology', in *Arts Libéraux et Philosophie au Moyen Age*, Actes du Quatrième Congrès International de Philosophie Médiévale, Montréal, Institut d'Études Médiévales, pp. 215–54

(1974a). 'Philosophy and the Enterprise of Science in the Later Middle Ages' in Y. Elkana (ed.) *The Interaction Between Science and Philosophy*, Humanities Press

(1974b). 'Naissance et développement de l'atomisme au bas moyen âge latin', in *La science de la nature: théories et pratiques* (Cahiers d'études médiévales, 2), Bellarmin

(1975a). 'From Social into Intellectual Factors: An Aspect of the Unitary Character of Late Medieval Learning', in J. E. Murdoch and E. D. Sylla (eds.) *The Cultural Context of Medieval Learning*, Reidel

(1975b). 'A Central Method of Analysis in Fourteenth-Century Science', *XIVth International Congress of the History of Science. Proceedings No. 2* (Tokyo), pp. 68–71

(1978a). 'The Development of a Critical Temper: New Approaches and Modes of Analysis in Fourteenth-Century Philosophy', in S. Wenzel (ed.) *Medieval and Renaissance Studies*, No. 7, Proceedings of the Southeastern Institute of Medieval and Renaissance Studies

(1978b). '*Subtilitates Anglicanae* in Fourteenth Century Paris: John of Mirecourt and Peter Ceffons' in Madeleine Pelner Cosman and Bruce Chandler (eds.) *Machaut's World. Science and Art in the Fourteenth Century* (Annals of the New York Academy of Sciences, 314)

(1979). 'Propositional Analysis in Fourteenth-Century Natural Philosophy', *Synthese* 40:117–46

(forthcoming a). 'The Analytic Character of Late Medieval Learning: Natural Philosophy without Nature', in Lawrence Roberts (ed.) *Nature in the Middle Ages*

(forthcoming b). '*Scientia mediantibus vocibus*: Metalinguistic Analysis in Late Medieval Natural Philosophy', in *Sprache und Erkenntnis im Mittelalter* (Acts of the Sixth International Congress of Medieval Philosophy, Bonn, 29 August–3 September 1977)

(forthcoming c). 'William of Ockham and the logic of infinity and continuity' in Kretzmann (forthcoming b).

Murdoch, John E. and Edith Sylla, eds. (1975). *The Cultural Context of Medieval Learning*, Reidel

(1976). 'Swineshead, Richard', in C. C. Gillispie (ed.) *Dictionary of Scientific Biography*, Charles Scribner's Sons

(1978). 'The Science of Motion' in David C. Lindberg (ed.) *Science in the Middle Ages*, University of Chicago Press

Murdoch, John E. and Edward Synan (1966). 'Two Questions on the Continuum; Walter Chatton (?), O.F.M. and Adam Wodeham, O.F.M.', *Franciscan Studies* 26:212–88

Murray, Alexander (1978). *Reason and Society in the Middle Ages*, Clarendon Press

Nagy, A. (1897). *Die philosophischen Abhandlungen des Ja'qūb ben Isḥāq Al-Kindī* (BGPM II), Aschendorff

Nardi, B. (1936). 'Il preteso tomismo di Sigieri di Brabante', *Giornale critico della filosofia italiana* 17:26–35

(1937). 'Ancora sul preteso tomismo di Sigieri di Brabante', *Giornale critico della filosofia italiana* 18:160–4

(1938). 'L'averroismo di Sigieri e Dante', *Studi Danteschi* 22:83–113

(1939). 'Una nuova monografia su Sigieri di Brabante', *Giornale critico della filosofia italiana* 20:453–71

(1940). Review of Fernand van Steenberghen, *Les oeuvres et la doctrine de Siger der Brabant*, Académie royale de Belgique, in *Studi Danteschi* 25:149–56

(1944). *Nel mondo di Dante* (Storia e letteratura, vol. 5), Edizioni di 'Storia e letteratura'

(1945). *Sigieri di Brabante nel pensiero del Rinascimento Italiano*, Edizioni Italiane

(1947). 'Introduzione' in S. *Tommaso d'Aquino: Trattato sull'unità dell intelletto contro gli Averroisti*, Sansoni

(1949). 'Note per una storia dell'averroismo latino, V: L'averroismo bolognese nel secolo XIII e Taddeo Alderotto', *Rivista critica di storia della filosofia* 4:11–22

(1950). 'L'anima umana secondo Sigieri', *Giornale critico di filosofia italiana* 29:317–325

(1960) *Studi di filosofia medievale*, Edizioni di Storia e Letteratura

(1960). 'La dottrina d'Alberto Magno sull' Inchoatio formae', in B. Nardi (ed.) *Studi di Filosofia Medievale*, Edizioni di Storia e Letteratura

Nash, P. (1950). 'Giles of Rome on Boethius' "Diversum est esse et id quod est"', *Mediaeval Studies* 12:57–91

(1950–1). 'Giles of Rome, Auditor and Critic of St. Thomas', *The Modern Schoolman* 28:1–20

(1957). 'The Accidentality of Esse According to Giles of Rome', *Gregorianum* 38:103–15

(1967). 'Giles of Rome', *New Catholic Encyclopedia* 6:484–5

Nasr, S. H. (1964). *An Introduction to Islamic Cosmological Doctrines*, Harvard University Press

Natalis, Hervaeus, *see* Hervaeus Natalis

Naus, John E. (1959). *The Nature of the Practical Intellect According to Saint Thomas Aquinas* (Analecta Gregoriana, vol. 108), Gregorian University

Nebrija, Elio Antonio de (1481). *Introductiones Latinae*, Salamanca

(1495). *Introductiones Latinae cum commento*, Salamanca

Nédoncelle, Maurice (1974). 'Remarques sur la réfutation des averroïstes par saint Thomas', *Rivista di filosofia neo-scolastica* 66:284–92

Neumann, B, (1958). *Der Mensch und die himmlische Seligkeit nach der Lehre Gottfrieds von Fontaines*, Lahn-Verlag

Newman, J. H. (1961–) *The Letters and Diaries of John Henry Newman*. Ed. C. S. Dessain et al., Nelson

Newman, William Lambert. (1887). *The Politics of Aristotle*, Clarendon Press

Nicephorus Blemmydes (1885). *Epitomes isagogicæ liber primus. Epitome logica* (P. G. 142), Brepols

Nicholas of Autrecourt (1908). *Prima epistola ad Bernardum* and *Epistola Magistri Nicolai de Autricort ad Bernardum* (BGPM VI, 2), Aschendorff

(1939). 'Tractatus universalis', ed. J. R. O'Donnell, C.S.B., *Mediaeval Studies* 1:179–280

Nicholas of Cusa (1964–8). *De Concordantia Catholica*, Felix Meiner

Nicholas of Paris. *Sincategoreumata* in Braakhuis 1979, II

Summe Metenses in De Rijk 1962–7, II (1). 449–90 (excerpts)

Nicolas, J.-H. (1948). 'Chronique de Philosophie'. *Revue Thomiste* 48:561–4

Nicole Oresme (1970). *Maistre Nicole Oresme: Le Livre de politique d'Aristote*, ed. A. D.

Menut (Transactions of the American Philosophical Society, New Series 60, Part 6), American Philosophical Society

Nielsen, L. (1976). 'On the Doctrine of Logic and Language of Gilbert Porreta and his Followers', *CIMAGL* 17:40–69

Niemeyer, Sister Mary Fredericus (1951). *The One and the Many in the Social Order according to Saint Thomas Aquinas*, Catholic University of America

Nifo, Agostino (1520). *Dialectica ludicra*, Florence
(1521). *Epitomata rethorica ludicra*, Venice

Noble, Henri-Dominique (1905). 'Note pour l'étude de la psychophysiologie d'Albert le Grand et de S. Thomas. Le cerveau et les facultés sensibles', *Revue Thomiste* 13:91–101

Normore, Calvin G. (forthcoming). 'Walter Burley on Continuity' in Kretzmann (forthcoming b)

Nuchelmans, Gabriel (1973). *Theories of the Proposition: Ancient and Medieval Conceptions of the Bearers of Truth and Falsity* (North-Holland Linguistic Series, 8), North-Holland
(1980). *Late Scholastic and Humanist Theories of the Proposition*, North-Holland

Oakley, Francis (1961). 'Medieval theories of natural law: William of Ockham and the significance of the voluntarist tradition', *Natural Law Forum* 6:65–83
(1962). 'On the road from Constance to 1688: the political thought of John Major and George Buchanan', *The Journal of British Studies* 2:1–31
(1964). *The Political Thought of Pierre d'Ailly: The Voluntarist Tradition* (Yale Historical Publications, Miscellany 81), Yale University Press
(1965). 'Almain and Major: Conciliar theory on the eve of Reformation', *The American Historical Review* 70:673–90
(1967). 'Pierre d'Ailly' in B. A. Gerrish (ed.), *Reformers in Profile*, Fortress Press
(1969). 'Figgis, Constance and the divines of Paris', *The American Historical Review* 75:368–86
(1974). *The Medieval Experience: Foundations of Western Cultural Singularity*, Charles Scribner's Sons

Oberman, H.A. (1967). *The Harvest of Medieval Theology: Gabriel Biel and Late Medieval Nominalism*, Harvard University Press

Obertello, Luca (1969). *A. M. Severino Boezio: De hypotheticis syllogismis*, testo, traduzione, introduzione e commento, Paideia editrice
(1974). *Severino Boezio* (2 vols.) (Collana di monografie, 1), Accademia Ligure di Scienze e Lettere

O'Brien, A. J. (1964). 'Duns Scotus' Teaching on the Distinction Between Essence and Existence', *The New Scholasticism* 38:61–77

O'Brien, T. C. (1960). *Metaphysics and the Existence of God*, The Thomist Press

O'Callaghan, J. J. (1955). 'The Second Question of the Prologue of Walter Catton's Commentary on the Sentences. On Intuitive and Abstractive Knowledge', in J. R. O'Donnell (ed.), *Nine Mediaeval Thinkers – A collection of Hitherto Unpublished Texts*, Pontifical Institute of Mediaeval Studies

Ockham, William. *See* William Ockham

O'Connor, Daniel John (1967). *Aquinas and Natural Law*, Macmillan

O'Donnell, J. Reginald (1939–42). 'Nicholas of Autrecourt', *Mediaeval Studies* 1:179–280; 4:97–125
ed. (1941). 'The Syncategoremata of William of Sherwood', *Mediaeval Studies* 3:46–93
(1958). 'Themistius' Paraphrase of the *Posterior Analytics* in Gerard of Cremona's

Translation', *Mediaeval Studies* 20:239–315

Oeing-Hannhoff, L. (1963). 'Die Methoden der Metaphysik im Mittelalter'. *Miscellanea Mediaevalia* 2, De Gruyter

Offler, H. S. (1977). 'The Three Modes of Natural Law in Ockham: A Revision of the Text', *Franciscan Studies* 37:207–18

Olgiati, F. (1944). *Il concetto di giuridicità in San Tommaso d'Aquino* (2nd ed.), Vita e pensiero

O'Malley, John W. (1968). *Giles of Viterbo on Church and Reform* (Studies in Medieval and Reformation Thought, 5), Brill

　(1972). 'Man's dignity, God's love, and the destiny of Rome: a text of Giles of Viterbo', *Viator* 3:389–416

Onclin, W. (1948). 'Le droit naturel selon les romanistes des XIIᵉ et XIIIᵉ siècles' in *Miscellanea moralia in honorem A. Janssen* (Bibliotheca Ephemeridum theol. Lovaniensium, I, ii), E. Nauwelaerts

Ong, Walter Jackson (1958a). *Ramus, Method, and the Decay of Dialogue*, Harvard University Press

　(1958b). *Ramus and Talon Inventory*, Harvard University Press

Opicinus de Canistris (1914). *De Praeeminentia Spirituali Imperii* in R. Scholz (ed.) *Unbekannte kirchenpolitische Streitschriften aus der Zeit Ludwigs des Bayern (1327–1354)*, vol. 2., Loescher (W. Regenberg)

Ostlender, H. (1939). *Peter Abelards Theologia 'Summi Boni'* (*BGPM* XXXV), Aschendorff

Otte, J. K. (1972). 'The Life and Writings of Alfredus Anglicus', *Viator* 3:275–91

　(1976). 'The Role of Alfred of Sareshel (Alfredus Anglicus) and his Commentary on the Metheora in the Reacquisition of Aristotle', *Viator* 7:197–209

Overbeke, P.-M. Van (1955). 'Saint Thomas et le droit', *Revue Thomiste* 55:519–64

　(1957). 'La loi naturelle et le droit naturel selon saint Thomas', *Revue Thomiste* 57:53–78; 450–95

　(1958). 'Droit et morale, essai de synthèse thomiste', *Revue Thomiste* 58:285–336; 674–94

Owen, G. E. L., ed. (1968). *Aristotle on Dialectic. Proceedings of the Third Symposium Aristotelicum*, Clarendon Press

Owens, Joseph (1948). 'Up to What Point is God Included in the Metaphysics of Duns Scotus?', *Mediaeval Studies* 10:163–77

　(1953). 'The Conclusion of the Prima Via', *The Modern Schoolman* 30:109–21

　(1965). 'Quiddity and Real Distinction in St. Thomas Aquinas', *Mediaeval Studies* 27:1–22

　(1966). 'Aquinas and the Proof from the "Physics"', *Mediaeval Studies* 28:119–50

　(1970). 'Judgment and Truth in Aquinas', *Mediaeval Studies* 32:138–58

　(1974). 'The Primacy of the External in Thomistic Noetics', *Église et Théologie* 5:189–205

　(1978). *The Doctrine of Being in the Aristotelian 'Metaphysics', A Study in the Greek Background of Mediaeval Thought*, 3rd ed., Pontifical Institute of Mediaeval Studies

Ozment, S. (1974). 'Mysticism, nominalism, and dissent' in C. Trinkaus and H. A. Oberman (eds.) *The Pursuit of Holiness in the Late Middle Ages and the Renaissance*, Brill

Padley, G. A. (1976). *Grammatical Theory in Western Europe 1500–1700: the Latin Tradition*, Cambridge University Press

Paissac, H. (1951). *Théologie du verbe: Saint Augustin et Saint Thomas*, Les Éditions du

Cerf

Pape, I. (1966). *Tradition und Transformation der Modalität I. Möglichkeit-Unmöglichkeit*, Felix Meiner

Park, Katharine (1980). 'Albert's Influence on Late Medieval Psychology' in James A. Weisheipl (ed.) *Albertus Magnus and the Sciences: Commemorative Essays 1980*, Pontifical Institute of Mediaeval Studies

Parkes, M. B. (1976). 'The Influence of the Concepts of Ordinatio and Compilatio on the Development of the Book', *Medieval Learning and Literature. Essays presented to R. W. Hunt*. Clarendon Press

Partee, C. (1960). 'Peter John Olivi: Historical and Doctrinal Study', *Franciscan Studies* 20:215–60

Pascoe, Louis B. (1973). *Jean Gerson: Principles of Church Reform* (Studies in Medieval and Reformation Thought, 7), Brill

Pasquali, G. (1952). *Storia della tradizione e critica del testo*, Felice Le Monnier

Passerin d'Entrèves, A., *see* D'Entrèves, Alessandro Passerin

Pater, Walter de (1965). *Les Topiques d'Aristote et la dialectique platonicienne; La Méthodologie de la définition*, (Études thomistiques, 10), Éditions St Paul
  (1968). 'La Fonction du lieu et de l'instrument dans les *Topiques*', in G. E. L. Owen (ed.) *Aristotle on Dialectic. Proceedings of the Third Symposium Aristotelicum*, Clarendon Press

Pattin, A. (1953). 'Gilles de Rome, O.E.S.A. (ca. 1243–1316) et la distinction réelle de l'essence et de l'existence', *Revue de l'Université d'Ottawa* 23:80–116
  (1974–5). 'Pour l'histoire du sens agent au moyen âge', *Bulletin de philosophie médiévale* 16–17:100–13

Paul of Pergula (1961). *Logica and Tractatus de sensu composito et diviso*, ed. Mary Anthony Brown (Franciscan Institute Text Series, 13) The Franciscan Institute

Paul of Venice (1472). *Logica* (= *Logica parva*), Venice. (Photoreprint Georg Olms, 1970.)
  (1493a). *Quadratura*, Venice
  (1493b). *Sophismata*, Venice
  (1499). *Logica magna*, Venice

Paulus, J. (1933). 'La théorie du Premier Moteur chez Aristote', *Revue de philosophie* n.s. 4:259–94; 394–424
  (1938). *Henri de Gand. Essai sur les tendances de sa métaphysique*, J. Vrin
  (1940–2). 'Les disputes d'Henri de Gand et de Gilles de Rome sur la distinction de l'essence et de l'existence', *Archives d'Histoire doctrinale et littéraire du Moyen Âge* 13:323–58
  (1949). 'A propos de la théorie de la connaissance d'Henri de Gand', *Revue philosophique du Louvain* 47:493–6

Payer, Pierre J. (1979). 'Prudence and the principles of natural law: a medieval development', *Speculum* 54:55–70

Pedersen, Olaf (1953). 'The Development of Natural Philosophy 1250–1350', *Classica et Mediævalia* 14:86–155

Peghaire, Julien (1936). '*Intellectus*' et '*Ratio*' selon S. Thomas d'Aquin (Publications de L'Institut d'Études Médiévales d'Ottawa, No. 6), Vrin and Institut d'Études Médiévales
  (1942–3). 'A Forgotten Sense, The Cogitative according to St Thomas Aquinas', *The Modern Schoolman* 20:123–40 and 210–29

Pegis, Anton C. (1934). *St Thomas and the Problem of the Soul in the Thirteenth Century*, St Michael's College
  (1973). 'St Thomas and the Coherence of the Aristotelian Theology', *Mediaeval*

Studies 35:67–117

(1974). 'The Separated Soul and its Nature in St Thomas' in *St Thomas Aquinas 1274–1974: Commemorative Studies*, vol. 1, Pontifical Institute of Mediaeval Studies

Peifer, John F. (1952). *The Concept in Thomism*, Bookman Associates

Pelagius, Alvarus. *See* Alvarus Pelagius

Pelster, F. (1953) 'Die indirekte Gewalt der Kirche über den Staat nach Ockham und Petrus de Palude: eine Übersicht', *Scholastik* 28:78–82

Pelzer, A. (1911). 'Les initiateurs italiens du thomisme contemporain', *Revue néo-scholastique de philosophie* 18:230–54

(1924). 'Un Traducteur inconnu: Pierre Gallego, franciscain et premier évêque de Carthagène' in *Miscellanea Francesco Ehrle* (Studi e Testi, 37), pp. 407–56

(1964). *Études d'histoire littéraire sur la scholastique médiévale* (Philosophes Médiévaux 8), Louvain Presses universitaires

(1966). *Abreviations latines médiévales* (supplement to Capelli 1961), Louvain Presses Universitaires

Percival, W. K. (1972). 'The historical sources of Guarino's *Regulae Grammaticales*: a reconsideration of Sabbadini's evidence' in *Civiltà dell' umanesimo: Atti del VI, VII, VIII convegno del Centro di studi umanistici 'Angelo Poliziano'*, Leo S. Olschki

(1975). 'The grammatical tradition and the rise of the vernaculars' in T. A. Sebeok (ed.) *Current Trends in Linguistics* (*Historiography of Linguistics*, 13) Mouton

(1976a). 'Deep and surface structure concepts in renaissance and mediaeval syntactic theory' in H. Parret (ed.) *History of Linguistic Thought and Contemporary Linguistics*, De Gruyter

(1976b). 'Renaissance grammar: rebellion or evolution?' in *Interrogativi dell'umanesimo*, Leo S. Olschki

Pertusi, A. (1962). '*Erotemata*: per la storia e le fonti delle prime grammatiche greche a stampa', *Italia medioevale e umanistica* 5:321–51

Peter Abelard (1851). *Sic et Non*, ed. Henke and Lindenkohn, Librariae Academ. Elwertianae

(1855a) *Dialogus inter Philosophum, Iudaeum et Christianum*, PL 178, Brepols

(1855b). *Theologia Christiana* PL 178, Brepols

(1859). *Introductio ad theologiam*, ed. V. Cousin in *Petri Abaelardi Opera II*, Durand

(1919–27). *Logica 'Ingredientibus'*, ed. Bernhard Geyer in *Peter Abaelards Philosophische Schriften* (*BGPM*, XXI, 1–3), Aschendorff

(1933). *Logica 'Nostrorum petitioni sociorum'*, ed. Bernhard Geyer in *Peter Abaelards Philosophische Schriften* (*BGPM*, XXI, 4), Aschendorff

(1956). *Dialectica*, ed. L. M. De Rijk (Wijsgerige teksten en studies, 1), Van Gorcum

(1969–). *Opera theologica*, ed. E. M. Buytaert (Corpus Christianorum, Continuatio mediaevalis, 11–12), Brepols

(1969a). *Editio super Aristotelem De interpretatione*, ed. Mario dal Pra in *Pietro Abelardo: Scritti di logica*, La nuova Italia Editrice

(1969b). *Super Topica glossae*, ed. Mario dal Pra in *Pietro Abelardo: Scritti di logica*, La nuova Italia Editrice

(1970a). *Dialectica*, ed. L. M. de Rijk (Wijsgerige teksten en studies, 1) (2nd ed.), Van Gorcum

(1970b). *Dialogus inter Philosophum, Iudaeum, et Christianum*, ed. Rudolph Thomas, Frommann-Holzboog

Peter of Ailly (1489). *Tractatus de arte obligandi*, Paris

(1490). *Quaestiones super libros Sententiarum cum quibusdam in fine adiunctis*, Strasburg (Reprinted Minerva 1968)

(ca. 1490–5a). *Destructiones modorum significandi*, Lyon

(ca. 1490–5b). *Conceptus et insolubilia*, Lyon

(1494). *Tractatus exponibilium*, Paris

(ca. 1495). *Conceptus et insolubilia*, Paris

(1706). *De Ecclesiae . . . et Cardinalium Auctoritate* in L. Du Pin (ed.) Jean Gerson, *Opera Omnia*, 2: cols. 925–60, Sumptibus Societatis Antwerp

(1964). *Tractatus de Materia Concilii Generalis* in Oakley 1964

(1980). *Concepts and Insolubles: An Annotated Translation*, Paul Vincent Spade (tr.) (Synthese Historical Library, vol. 19), D. Reidel

Peter Aureoli (1596–1605). *Commentarium in primum Sententiarum* (2 vols.), Vatican

(1952–6). *Petri Aureoli Scriptum super primum Sententiarum*, ed. E. M. Buytaert (2 vols.) (Franciscan Institute Text Series, 3), The Franciscan Institute

Peter of Auvergne (1951). [Continuation (from 1280ᵃ6) of Thomas Aquinas' *In octo libros Politicorum Aristotelis expositio*] in Thomas Aquinas 1951

(1967). *The commentary of Peter of Auvergne on Aristotle's Politics. The inedited part: Book III lesson i–vi*, ed. Gundisalvus M. Grech, Desclée

Peter Bertrandus (1614). *De Iurisdictione Ecclesiastica et Politica* in M. Goldast (ed.) *Monarchia Sancti Romani Imperii*, 2:1361–83, Conrad Biermann (Reprinted Akademische Druck- und Verlagsanstalt 1960)

Peter John Olivi (1922–6). *Quaestiones in secundum librum Sententiarum*, ed. B. Jansen (3 vols.), Bibliotheca Franciscana Scholastica Medii Aevi, Collegium S. Bonaventurae

Peter Lombard (1916). *Libri IV Sententiarum*, ed. A. Heysse, Editiones Collegii S. Bonaventurae ad Claras Aquas, Grottaferrata

(1971–). *Sententiae in IV libris distinctae*, Editiones Collegii S. Bonaventurae ad Claras Aquas, Grottaferrata

Peter of Poitiers (1961). *Sententiae*, ed. P. S. Moore and M. Dulong (2nd ed.) (Publications in Medieval Studies, 7), University of Notre Dame Press

Peter of Spain (1489). *Textus omnium tractatuum Petri Hispani etiam sincathegreumatum et parvorum logicalium cum copulatis secundum doctrinam divi Thome Aquinatis iuxta processum magistrorum Colonie in bursa Montis regentium*, Cologne

(1944). *Commentario al 'De anima' de Aristóteles*, ed. M. Alonso, Bolaños y Aguilar

(1945). *Summulae logicales*, ed. & tr. J. P. Mullally (Publications in Mediaeval Studies, 8), University of Notre Dame Press

(1964). *Tractatus syncategorematum and Selected Anonymous Treatises*, tr. J. P. Mullally, with an introduction by J. P. Mullally and R. Houde (Mediaeval Texts in Translation, 13), Marquette University Press

(1972). *Tractatus called afterwards Summule Logicales*, ed. L. M. De Rijk (Wijsgerige teksten en studies, 22), Van Gorcum

(1979). *Syncategoremata* excerpted in Braakhuis 1979, I

Peter of Tarantasia (1652). *In quattuor libros Sententiarum commentaria*, Toulouse (Reprinted Gregg Press 1964)

Peter Tartaretus (1497). *Quaestiones super sex libros Ethicorum Aristotelis*, Paris

(1514a). *Expositio in Summulas Petri Hispani*, Basle

(1514b). *In Perihermenias*, Basle

Peters, F. E. (1968). *Aristotle and the Arabs. The Aristotelian tradition in Islam*, New York University Press

Petrarch (1614). *Epistolae de Iuribus Imperii Romani* in M. Goldast (ed.) *Monarchia Sancti Romani Imperii*, 2:1345–1465, Conrad Biermann (Reprinted Akademische Druck- und Verlagsanstalt 1960)

Petrus da Fonseca (1577). *Commentariorum . . . in libros metaphysicorum Aristotelis*, Rome

Pfligersdorffer, G. (1953). 'Zu Boethius, De Interpr. Ed. sec. I, p. 4, 4 sqq. Meiser nebst Beobachtungen zur Geschichte der Dialektik bei den Römern', *Wiener Studien* 66:131–54

Philippe, M.-D. (1948). 'Ἀφαίρεσις, πρόσθεσις, χωρίζειν dans la philosophie d'Aristote', *Revue thomiste* 48:461–79

   (1975). 'Originalité de "l'ens rationis" dans la philosophie de saint Thomas', *Angelicum* 52:91–124

Phillipson, C. (1911) *The International Law and Custom of Ancient Greece and Rome*, Macmillan

Philoponus, John, *see* John Philoponus

Picard, Gabriel (1926). *Essai sur la connaissance sensible d'après les scolastiques* (Archives de Philosophie, vol. 4, Cahier 1), Beauchesne

Picavet, F. (1905). *Esquisse d'une histoire générale et comparée des philosophies médiévales*, F. Alcan

Piernikarczyk, E. (1930). 'Das Naturgesetz bei J. D. Scotus', *Philosophisches Jahrbuch* 43:67–91

Pierre de la Palu (1506). *De Causa Immediata Ecclesiasticae Potestatis*, fols. 24–80, J. Petit

Pierre du Moulin (1603). *Elementa logica*, Antwerp
university of Uppsala (Acta universitatis Upsalensis. Skrifter rörande Uppsala universitet, C 36), Almquist & Wicksell

Pighius, Albertus (1697–9). *Hierarchiae ecclesiasticae assertio* in J. T. Rocaberti (ed.) *Bibliotheca maxima pontificia*, 2 (21 vols.) (Reprinted Akademische Druck- und Verlagsanstalt 1969–70)

Piltz, A. (1977). *Studium Upsalense. Specimens of the oldest lecture notes taken in the medieval*

Pinborg, Jan (1967a). *Die Entwicklung der Sprachtheorie im Mittelalter* (BGPM XLII, 2), Aschendorff

   (1967b). 'Walter Burleigh on the Meaning of Propositions', *Classica et Mediaevalia* 28:394–404

   (1969). 'Topik und Syllogistik im Mittelalter' in F. Hoffman et al. (eds.) *Sapienter ordinare. Festgabe für Erich Kleineidam* (Erfurter Theologische Studien, 24), St Benno Verlag

   (1971a). 'Bezeichnung in der Logik des Mittelalters' in *Der Begriff der Repraesentatio im Mittelalter* (Miscellanea Mediaevalia, 8), De Gruyter

   (1971b). 'Simon of Faversham's *Sophisma: Universale est Intentio*: A Supplementary Note', *Mediaeval Studies* 33:360–5

   (1972). *Logik und Semantik im Mittelalter – Ein Überblick* (Problemata, 10), Frommann-Holzboog

   (1973). 'Neues zum Erfurter Schulleben des XIV. Jahrhunderts nach Handschriften der Jagiellonischen Bibliothek zu Kraków', *Bulletin de philosophie médiévale* 15:146–51

   (1973a). 'Petrus de Alvernia on Porphyry', *CIMAGL* 9:47–67

   (1973b). 'A New Ms. of the Questions on the *Post. Anal.* Attributed to Petrus de Alvernia with the Transcription of some Questions Related to Problems of Meaning', *CIMAGL* 10:48–62

   (1974). 'Zum Begriff der Intentio Secunda – Radulphus Brito, Hervaeus Natalis und Petrus Aureoli in Diskussion', *CIMAGL* 13:49–59

   (1975a). 'Die Logik der Modistae', *Studia Mediewistyczne* 16:39–97

   (1975b). 'Radulphus Brito's Sophism on Second Intentions', *Vivarium* 13:119–52

   (1975c). 'A Note on Some Theoretical Concepts of [Medieval] Logic and Grammar', 'Grabmann', *Revue Internationale de Philosophie*, 29e année, 113:286–96

   (1975d). 'Classical Antiquity: Greece' in T. A. Sebeok (ed.) *Current Trends in*

Linguistics vol. 13, Historiography of Linguistics, pp. 69–126, Mouton
(1976a). 'Some Problems of Semantic Representations in Medieval Logic' in H.
  Parrett (ed.) *History of Linguistic Thought and Contemporary Linguistics*, De Gruyter
ed. (1976b). *The Logic of John Buridan*, Acts of the 3rd European Symposium on
  Medieval Logic and Semantics (Opuscula Graecolatina, 9), Museum Tusculanum
(1976c). 'Magister Abstractionum', *CIMAGL* 18:1–4
(1976d). 'Nochmals die Erfurter Schulen im XIV. Jahrhundert', *CIMAGL* 17:76–81
(1976e). 'Diskussionen um die Wissenschaftstheorie an der Artistenfakultät',
  Miscellanea Mediaevalia 10, De Gruyter
(1979). 'The English Contribution to Logic before Ockham', *Synthese* 40:19–42
(1980). 'Radulphus Brito on Universals', *CIMAGL* 35:56–142
Pinborg, Jan, O. Lewry, K. M. Fredborg, N. J. Green-Pedersen, and L. Nielsen (1975).
  'The Commentary on "Priscianus maior" ascribed to Robert Kilwardby',
  CIMAGL 15:1–146
Pine, Martin (1973). 'Double Truth' in *Dictionary of the History of Ideas*, vol. 2, Scribner's
Piper, Paul, ed. (1882). *Die Schriften Notkers und seiner Schule*, vol. I, Akademische
  Verlagsbuchhandlung von J. C. B. Mohr
Plantinga, Alvin (1974). *The Nature of Necessity*, Clarendon Press
[Plato Latinus] (1940). I, *Meno interprete Henrico Aristippo*, ed. V. Kordeuter and
  L. Labowsky, Warburg Institute
(1950). II; *Phaedo interprete Henrico Aristippo*, ed. L. Minio-Paluello, Warburg Institute
Plotinus (1951–9). *Opera I–II*, ed. P. Henry and H.-R. Schwyzer (Museum Lessianum,
  Series philosophica, 33–4), Desclée de Brouwer
Pocock, J. G. A. (1971). *Politics, Language, and Time*, Atheneum
(1974). *The Machiavellian Moment*, Princeton University Press
Pollard, A. W. and G. R. Redgrave (1976). *A Short Title Catalogue of Books Printed in
  England, Scotland and Ireland and of English books Printed Abroad 1475–1640*. Second
  Edition, Revised and Enlarged, begun by W. A. Jackson and F. S. Ferguson.
  Completed by Katharine F. Pantzer, Volume 2, I–Z. The Bibliographical Society
Ponet, John (1942). *A Short Treatise of Politic Power* in Winthrop S. Hudson, *John Ponet
  (1516?–1556): Advocate of Limited Monarchy*, University of Chicago Press
Poppi, Antonino (1970a). *Introduzione all' Aristotelismo Padovano*, Editrice Antenore
(1970b). *Saggi sul pensiero inedito di Pietro Pomponazzi* (Centro per la Storia della
  Tradizione Aristotelica nel Veneto, Saggi e Testi, No. 8), Editrice Antenore
Porphyry (1886). *De abstinentia* in A. Nauck (ed.) *Porphyrii philosophi platonici opuscula
  selecta*, Teubner
(1887). *Isagoge et in Aristotelis Categorias commentarium*, ed. A. Busse (Commentaria in
  Aristotelem Graeca, IV. 1), Reimer
Post, Gaines (1964). *Studies in Medieval Legal Thought*, Princeton University Press
Posthumus Meyjes, Guillaume Henri Marie (1963). *Jean Gerson, zijn kerkpolitek en
  ecclesiologie*, Nijhoff
Potts, Timothy C. (1980). *Conscience in Medieval Philosophy*, Cambridge University Press
Poupard, P., ed. (1958). 'Lettre de Möhler à Bautain sur les rapports de la raison et de la
  foi', *Revue des sciences philosophiques et théologiques* 42:455–82
(1961). *L'Abbé Louis Bautain. Un essai de Philosophie Chretienne au dix-neuvième siècle*,
  Desclée
ed. (1964). *Journal Romain de l'abbé Louis Bautain, 1838*, Edizioni di Storia e Letteratura
Prantl, Carl (1855–67). *Geschichte der Logik im Abendlande* (4 vols.), S. Hirzel (Reprinted
  Akademische Druck- und Verlagsanstalt 1955)
Prentice, R. (1969). 'Univocity and Analogy according to Scotus's Super libros elen-

chorum Aristotelis', *Archives d'histoire doctrinale el littéraire du Moyen Age* 35:39–64

Preuss, James S. (1972). 'Theological legitimation for innovation in the middle ages', *Viator* 3:1–26

Prezioso, F. (1963). *La 'species' medievale e i poredromi del fenomenismo moderno*, Instituto Universitario di Magistero di Catania

Prior, A. N. (1953). 'On Some Consequentiae in Walter Burleigh', *The New Scholasticism* 27:433–46

   (1962). *Formal Logic*, Clarendon Press

   (1962a). 'Some Problems of Self-Reference in John Buridan', *Proceedings of the British Academy* 48:281–96

   (1969). 'The Possibly-True and the Possible', *Mind* 78:481–92

Priscian (1855–9). *Institutiones grammaticae*, ed. Martin Hertz (Grammatici Latini, 2–3), Teubner (Reprinted Georg Olms 1961)

Proclus (1951). 'Procli Elementatio theologica translata a Guilelmo de Moerbeke', ed. C. Vansteenkiste, *Tijdschrift voor Philosophie*, 13:263–302; 491–531

Psellus, Michael, *see* Michael Psellus

Pseudo-Albertus (1977). *Speculum astronomiae*, ed. S. Caroti, M. Periera, and S. Zamponi under the direction of Paola Zambelli, Domus Galilaeana

Pseudo-Augustinus (1961). *Anonymi paraphrasis Themistiana (Pseudo-Augustini Categoriae decem)* in Aristoteles Latinus (1961b)

Pseudo-Petrus (1489). *Tractatus exponibilium* in Peter of Spain (1489)

Pseudo-Scotus (1639). *In librum I Priorum Analyticorum Aristotelis quaestiones* in John Duns Scotus (1639), vol. I

   (1891). *Super librum I Priorum* in John Duns Scotus (1891–5), vol. II

Ptolemy of Lucca (1909a). *De Origine ac Translatione et Statu Romani Imperii*, ed. M. Krammer (Fontes Iuris Germanici Antiqui in Usum Scholarum ex Monumentis Germaniae Historicis separatim editi), Impensis Bibliopolii Hahniani

   (1909b). *Determinatio Compendiosa de Iurisdictione Imperii*, ed. M. Krammer (Fontes Iuris Germanici Antiqui in Usum Scholarum ex Monumentis Germaniae Historicis separatim editi), Impensis Bibliopolii Hahniani

   (1954). Completion of Thomas Aquinas' *De Regimine Principum* [*De Regno*] in R. M. Spiazzi (ed.) *Divi Thomae Aquinatis Opuscula Philosophica*, Marietti

Quillet, Jeannine (1970). *La philosophie politique de Marsile de Padoue*, J. Vrin

   (1977). *La Philosophie politique du 'Songe du Vergier' (1378): Sources Doctrinales*, J. Vrin

Quinn, J. F. (1972). 'Chronology of St. Bonaventure (1217–1257)', *Franciscan Studies* 32:168–86

   (1973). *The Historical Constitution of St Bonaventure's Philosophy*, Pontifical Institute of Mediaeval Studies

   (1974). 'St. Bonaventure's fundamental conception of natural law' in *S. Bonaventura 1274–1974*, 3, Collegium S. Bonaventurae, Grottaferrata

   (1974a). 'Certitude of Reason and Faith in St Bonaventure and St Thomas' in *St Thomas Aquinas 1274–1974: Commemorative Studies*, vol. 2, Pontifical Institute of Mediaeval Studies

Quintilian (1920–2). *The Institutio oratoria of Quintilian*, with an English translation by H. E. Butler (4 vols.) (Loeb Classical Library), Heinemann

Rabeau, Gaston (1938). *Species-Verbum: L'activité intellectuelle élémentaire selon S. Thomas d'Aquin* (Bibliothèque Thomiste, vol. 22), Vrin

Radetti, G. (1953). *Lorenzo Valla: Scritti filosofici e religiosi*; introduzione, traduzione e note a cura di Giorgio Radetti, Sansoni

Radulphus Brito (1978a). *Commentary on Boethius' De differentiis topicis*, ed. N. J. Green-Pedersen, *CIMAGL* 26:1–92

(1978b). 'The Sophism "Omnis homo est omnis homo"', ed. Jan Pinborg and N. J. Green-Pedersen, *CIMAGL* 26:93–114

(1980). *Quaestiones super Priscianum minorem*, ed. Heinz W. Enders and Jan Pinborg (Grammatica Speculativa, 3), Frommann-Holzboog.

Raeymaeker, L. de (1947). *Introduction à la Philosophie*, Éditions de l'Institut Supérieur de Philosophie

(1951). 'Les origines de l'Institut Supérieur de Philosophie à Louvain', *Revue Philosophique de Louvain* 49:505–633

(1952). 'Dominanten in de philosophische persoonlijkheid van Kardinaal Mercier', *Medelingen van de Koninklijke Vlaamse Academie ... Klasse der Letteren*, XIV: no. 7

(1954). *The Philosophy of Being*, Herder

Rahman, F. (1958). 'Essence and Existence in Avicenna', *Mediaeval and Renaissance Studies* 4:1–16

(1963). 'Ibn Sīna' in M. M. Sharif (ed.) *A History of Muslim Philosophy*, v. 1, Otto Harrassowitz

Ralph Strode (1493). *Consequentiae et Obligationes, cum commentis*, Venice

Ramière, H. (1861). *De l'Unité dans l'Enseignement de la Philosophie au sein des Écoles Catholiques*, Régis Ruffet

Ramírez, S. (1955). *El derecho de gentes: examen crítico de la filosofía del derecho de gentes desde Aristóteles hasta Francisco Suáres*, Ediciones Studium

Ramírez, Santiago Maria (1955). *Doctrina politica de Sto. Thomas*, Publicaciones del Instituto Social Léon XIII. 1

Rand, Edward Kennard (1946). *Cicero in the Courtroom of St Thomas Aquinas*, Marquette University Press

Randall, John Herman (1940). 'The Development of Scientific Method in the School of Padua', *Journal of the History of Ideas* 1:177–206

(1961). *The School of Padua and the Emergence of Modern Science*, Editrice Antenore

Rashdall, Hastings (1936). *The Universities of Europe in the Middle Ages* (2nd ed.), ed. F. M. Powicke and A. B. Emden (3 vols.), Clarendon Press

Raymond Lull (1744). *Logica nova*, etc., Palma de Mallorca (Reprinted Minerva 1971, with introduction by C. H. Lohr)

Reardon, John Joseph (1943). *Selfishness and the Social Order: A Study in Thomistic Social Philosophy*, Catholic University of America Press

Régis, Louis Marie (1959). *Epistemology*, trans. Imelda C. Byrne, The Macmillan Company

Reichling, D. (1893). *Das Doctrinale des Alexander de Villa-Dei* (Monumenta Germaniae Paedagogica, 12), A. Hofmann

Reilly, George Cajetan (1934). *The Psychology of Saint Albert the Great compared with that of St Thomas*, The Catholic University of America

Reilly, James P. (1968). 'Ockham Bibliography: 1950–1967', *Franciscan Studies* 28:197–214

Reina, Maria Elena (1957). 'Giovanni Buridano, Tractatus de suppositionibus', *Rivista critica di storia della filosofia* 12:175–208 and 323–52

(1959). 'Il problema del linguaggio in Buridano I: Voci e concetti', *Rivista critica di storia della filosofia* 14:367–417

(1960a). 'Il problema del linguaggio in Buridano II: Significazione e verità', *Rivista critica di storia della filosofia* 15:141–65

(1960b). 'Il problema del linguaggio in Buridano III: Il linguaggio', *Rivista critica di storia della filosofia* 15:238–64

(1970). 'La prima questione del prologo del "Commento alle Sentenze" di Walter Catton', *Rivista critica di storia della filosofia* 25:48–74; 290–314

Remigio de Girolami (1934). *Tractatus de bono communi* excerpted by R. Egenter, *Scholastik* 9:79–92 (Excepts translated in Minio-Paluello 1956)

(1959). *De bono pacis*, ed. Charles T. Davis, *Studi Danteschi* 36:123–36

Renan, E. (1975). *Souvenirs d'enfance et de jeunesse. Chronologie et introduction par Henriette Psichari. Notes et archives de l'oeuvre par Laudice Rétat*, Garnier-Flammarion

Renard, H. (1956). 'What is St Thomas' Approach to Metaphysics?' *The New Scholasticism* 30:64–83

Renard, R. G. (1930). *La théorie de l'institution: Essai d'ontologie juridique*, Sirey

(1935). 'De l'institution à la conception analogique du droit', *Archives de Philosophie du Droit* 5:81–145

Renaudet, Augustin (1953). *Préréforme et humanisme à Paris pendant les premières guerres d'Italie, 1494–1517* (2nd edn.), Librairie d'Argences

Renna, Thomas J. (1973). 'Kingship in the *Disputatio inter clericum et militem*', *Speculum* 48:675–93

(1978). 'Aristotle and the French monarchy, 1260–1303', *Viator* 9:309–24

Rescher, Nicholas (1963). *Studies in the History of Arabic Logic*, University of Pittsburgh Press

(1964). 'Aristotle's Theory of Modal Syllogisms and Its Interpretation' in M. Bunge (ed.) *The Critical Approach to Science and Philosophy. In Honor of Karl R. Popper*, The Free Press of Glencoe

Reynolds, L. D., and Wilson, N. G. (1974). *Scribes and Scholars: A Guide to the Transmission of Greek and Latin Literature* (2nd ed.), Oxford University Press

Rhabanus Maurus (1851). *De institutione clericorum*, PL 107

(1901). *De institutione clericorum libri tres*, ed. Aloisius Knoepfler, J. J. Lentner

Ricardus sophista (forthcoming). *Abstractiones*, ed. Katherine Tachau *et al.*

Richard of Campsall (1968). *Questiones super librum Priorum Analeticorum*, in Edward A. Synan (ed.), *The Works of Richard of Campsall*, vol. I; Pontifical Institute of Mediaeval Studies

Richard Fitzralph (1890). *De Pauperie Salvatoris*, Books 1–4, ed. R. Lane Poole in *Wyclif's Latin Works*, vol. 7: *De Dominio Divino*, Trübner (Reprinted Johnson Reprint Co. 1966)

Richard Kilvington (forthcoming). *Sophismata*, ed. N. Kretzmann and B. E. Kretzmann, with introduction, translation, and commentary

Richard Swineshead (1520). *Liber calculationum*, Venice

Riesenberg, P. N. (1956). *Inalienability of Sovereignty in Medieval Political Thought*, AMS Press

Riet, G. Van (1946). *L'Épistémologie thomiste. Recherches sur le problème de la connaissance dans l'école thomiste contemporaine*, Éditions de l'Institut Supérieur de Philosophie de Louvain

(1953). 'La théorie thomiste de la sensation externe', *Revue philosophique de Louvain* 51:374–408

Riet, S. Van, ed. (1968). *Avicenna Latinus: Liber De Anima IV–V*, Éditions Orientalistes/ Brill

ed., (1972). *Avicenna Latinus: Liber de anima seu sextus de naturalibus I–II–III*, E. Peeters and E. J. Brill

Rijk, L. M. de, ed. (1956). *Petrus Abaelardus: Dialectica*, Van Gorcum

ed. (1959). *Garlandus Compotista: Dialectica*, Van Gorcum

(1962–7). *Logica modernorum*: A contribution to the History of Early Terminist Logic. I: On the Twelfth Century Theories of Fallacy (1962); II, 1: The Origin and Early Development of the Theory of Supposition; II, 2: Texts and Indices (1967), Van Gorcum

(1966a) 'Some new Evidence on Twelfth-Century Logic', *Vivarium* 4:1–57

(1966b). 'Some Notes on the Mediaeval Tract *De insolubilibus* with the Edition of a Tract Dating from the End of the Twelfth Century', *Vivarium* 4:83–115

(1968a). 'On the genuine text of Peter of Spain's *Summule logicales*, I' *Vivarium* 6:1–34

(1968b). 'On the genuine text of Peter of Spain's *Summule logicales* II', *Vivarium* 6:69–101

(1969a). 'On the genuine text of Peter of Spain's *Summule logicales*, III', *Vivarium* 7:8–61

(1969b). 'On the genuine text of Peter of Spain's *Summule logicales*, IV', *Vivarium* 7:120–62

(1970). *Peter Abelard, Dialectica* (Wijsgerige teksten en Studies, 1) (2nd edn.), Van Gorcum

(1971–3). 'The Development of *Suppositio naturalis* in Mediaeval Logic', *Vivarium* 9: 71–107; 11:43–79.

(1972). *Peter of Spain (Petrus Hispanus Portugalensis) Tractatus called afterwards 'Summule Logicales'*, Van Gorcum

(1974–6). 'Some Thirteenth Century Tracts on the Game of Obligation', *Vivarium* 12:94–123; 13:22–54; 14:26–49

(1975). 'Logica Cantabrigiensis – A Fifteenth-Century Cambridge Manual of Logic', *Revue internationale de philosophie, Grabmann*, 29ᵉ année 113:297–315

(1976a). 'Some thirteenth century tracts on the game of obligation', *Vivarium* 14:26–49

(1976b). 'Richard Billingham's Works on Logic', *Vivarium* 14:121–38

(1977a). 'On Ancient and Mediaeval Semantics and Metaphysics', *Vivarium* 15:81–110

(1977b). 'Logica Oxoniensis', *Medioevo* 3:121–64

Riley-Smith, J. S. C. (1977). *What Were The Crusades?*, Macmillan

Rinaldi, M. D. (1973). 'Fortuna e diffusione del "De orthographia" di Giovanni Tortelli', *Italia medioevale e umanistica* 16:227–61

Risse, Wilhelm (1964). *Die Logik der Neuzeit (Band I: 1500–1640)*, Frommann-Holzboog

(1965). *Bibliographia Logica. Verzeichnis der Druckschriften zur Logik mit Angabe ihrer Fundorte*, (Band I. 1472–1800), Georg Olms

Rivera Recio, J. F. (1951). 'Personajes hispánicos asistentes en 1215 al IV. Concilio de Lateran', *Hispania Sacra* 4:335–55

Rivero, M. L. (1976). 'William of Sherwood on Composition and Division', *Historiographia Linguistica* 3:17–36

Rivière, J. (1926). *Le problème de l'église et de l'état au temps de Philippe le Bel*, E. Champion

Robert Bacon (?) (1978). *Sincategoreumata*, ed. H. A. G. Braakhuis in Braakhuis 1978

Robert Grosseteste (1514). *In Aristotelis Posteriorum Analyticorum libros*, Venice (Reprinted Minerva 1966)

(1912a). *De libero arbitrio*, ed. L. Baur, in Baur 1912

(1912b). *De luce seu de inchoatione formarum*, ed. L. Baur, in Baur 1912

(1912c). *De veritate*, ed. L. Baur, in Baur 1912

(1963). *Commentarius in VIII libros Physicorum Aristotelis*, ed. Richard C. Dales, University of Colorado

Robert Holkot (1518). *In quattuor libros Sententiarum quaestiones*, Lyon (Reprinted Minerva 1967)

(1518a). *Sex articuli*, in Robert Holkot (1518)

Robert Kilwardby (1935). *De natura theologiae*, ed. F. Stegmüller (Opuscula et textus, Series scholastica, 17), Aschendorff

(1975). 'The Commentary on Priscianus maior Ascribed to Robert Kilwardby', ed. J. Pinborg *et al.*, *CIMAGL* 15:1–146

(1976). *De ortu scientiarum*, ed. A. G. Judy (Auctores Britannici Medii Aevi, 4), The British Academy and The Pontifical Institute of Mediaeval Studies

Roberts, L. D. (1973). 'Indeterminism in Duns Scotus' Doctrine of Human Freedom', *The Modern Schoolman* 51:1–16

Robins, R. H. (1951). *Ancient and Mediaeval Grammatical Theory in Europe*, G. Bell

Robson, J. A. (1961). *Wyclif and the Oxford Schools* (Cambridge Studies in Medieval Life and Thought, Second Series, 8), Cambridge University Press

Roger Bacon (1897–1900). *The 'Opus majus' of Roger Bacon*, ed. J. H. Bridges (3 vols.), Clarendon Press (vols. I and II) and Williams and Norgate (vol. III)

(1902). *The Greek Grammar of Roger Bacon and a Fragment of his Hebrew Grammar*, ed. E. Nolan and S. A. Hirsch, Cambridge University Press

(1905–40). *Opera hactenus inedita Rogeri Baconi*, ed. Robert Steele (16 fascicules in 12 vols.), Clarendon Press

(1911). *Compendium studii theologiae*, ed. Hastings Rashdall (British Society of Franciscan Studies, 3), Aberdeen University Press

(1928). *The Opus Majus of Roger Bacon*, tr. Robert Belle Burke (2 vols.), Oxford University Press

(1940). *Sumule dialectices*, ed Robert Steele, in *Opera hactenus inedita Rogeri Baconi*, fasc. 15, Clarendon Press

(1978). *De signis*, ed. K. M. Fredborg *et al.*, in Fredborg *et al.* 1978

Roger Marston (1932). *Quaestiones disputatae*, ed. a pp. Collegii s. Bonaventurae ad Claras Aquas, I., Quaracchi

Rohmer, Jean (1951). 'L'intentionnalité des sensations de Platon à Ockham', *Revue des sciences religieuses* 25:5–39

Rolland-Gosselin, Bernard (1928). *La doctrine politique de saint Thomas d'Aquin*, M. Rivière

(1949). *La morale chrétienne*, Desclée, De Brouwer

Rommen, H. A. (1947). *The Natural Law. A study in legal and social history and philosophy*, tr. T. R. Hanley, B. Herder Book Co

Roos, H. (1961). *Martini de Dacia Opera* (Corpus Philosophorum Danicorum Medii Aevi, 2), Gad

(1963). 'Ein unbekanntes Sophisma des Boethius de Dacia', *Scholastik* 38:378–91

(1974). 'Zur Begriffsgeschichte des Terminus "apparens" in den logischen Schriften des ausgehenden 13. Jahrhunderts', in *Virtus Politica, Festgabe zum 75. Geburtstag von Alfons Hufnagel*, Frommann-Holzboog

(1977). 'Henrici Roos in Memoriam. Nachgelassene Papiere', *CIMAGL* 24:1–84

Rose, Paul Lawrence (1973). 'Keckermann, Bartholomew' in C. C. Gillispie (ed.) *Dictionary of Scientific Biography*, Charles Scribner's Sons

Ross, W. D. (1949). *Aristotle's Prior and Posterior Analytics*. A revised text with introduction and commentary, Clarendon Press

Rossi, G. P. (1959). *La Filosofia nel Collegio Alberoni e il Neotomismo*, Divus Thomas

Rossi, P. (1975). 'Per l'edizione del Commentarium in Posteriorum Analyticorum Libros di Roberto Grossatesta', *Rivista di Filosofia Neo-Scolastica* 67:489–515

Roure, Marie-Louise (1962). 'Le traité "Des propositions insolubles" de Jean de Celaya', *Archives d'histoire doctrinale et littéraire du moyen âge* 29:235–338

(1970). 'La problématique des propositions insolubles au xiiiᵉ siècle et au début du xivᵉ, suivie de l'édition des traités de W. Shyreswood, W. Burleigh et Th. Bradwardine', *Archives d'histoire doctrinale et littéraire du moyen âge* 37:205–326

Rouse, Richard H. and Mary A. (1967). 'John of Salisbury and the doctrine of tyrannicide', *Speculum* 42:693–709

Rubenstein, Nicolai (1965). 'Marsilius of Padua and Italian political thought of his time' in J. R. Hale, J. R. L. Highfield, and B. Smalley (eds.) *Europe in the Late Middle Ages*, Northwestern University Press

Russell, Bertrand (1910–11). 'Knowledge by Acquaintance and Knowledge by Description', *Proceedings of the Aristotelian Society*, n.s. vol. 11:108–28

Russell, Frederick H. (1975). *The Just War in the Middle Ages*, Cambridge University Press

Russell, J. C. (1933). 'The Preferments and "Adiutores" of Robert Grosseteste', *Harvard Theological Review* 26:161–72

Ruysschaert, J. (1954). 'Les manuels de grammaire latine composés par Pomponio Leto', *Scriptorium* 8:98–107

(1961). 'A propos des trois premières grammaires latines de Pomponio Leto', *Scriptorium* 15:68–75

Ryan, Edmund J. (1951). *The Role of the 'Sensus Communis' in the Psychology of St Thomas Aquinas*, Messenger Press

Rzadkiewicz, Arnold Ladislas (1949). *The Philosophical Basis of Human Liberty according to St Thomas Aquinas*, Catholic University of America Press

Sabbadini, R. (1891). *Vita di Guarino Veronese*, Tipografia del R. Istituto Sordo-Muti

(1896). *La scuola e gli studi di Guarino Guarini Veronese*, F. Galati

(1902). 'Dei metodi nell' insegnamento della sintassi latina: considerazioni didattiche e storiche', *Rivista di filologia* 30:304–14

(1905). *Le scoperte dei codici latini e greci nei secoli XIV e XV* (2 vols.; reprinted 1967), Sansoni

(1906). 'Elementi nazionali nella teoria grammaticale dei Romani', *Studi italiani di filologia classica* 14:113–25

(1914). *Le scoperte dei codici latini e greci ne' secoli XIV e XV: nuove ricerche col riassunto filologico dei due volumi*, Sansoni

(1916). 'Documenti guariniani', *Atti dell' Accademia di Verona*, 4th Series, 18:211–86

(1919). *Epistolario di Guarino Veronese*, vol. 3: *Commento* (Miscellanea di storia veneta, Ser. 3 vol. 14), A spese della Società

(1922). *Il metodo degli umanisti*, Le Monier

Sabine, George H. (1963). *A History of Political Theory* (3rd ed.), Holt, Rinehart, and Winston

Sainte-Beuve, C. A. (1854). 'Chateaubriand: anniversaire du *Génie du Christianisme*', *Causeries du Lundi* (17 April 1854)

Sajó, Géza (1958). 'Boèce de Dacie et les commentaires anonymes inédits de Munich sur la Physique et sur la Génération attribués à Siger de Brabant', *Archives d'histoire doctrinale et littéraire du moyen âge* 33:21–58

Sala, Gervasio (1957). 'Il valore obligatorio della conscienza nei primi scolastici', *Studi francescani* 54:174–98

Salamonius, Albertischus Marius (1955). *De Principatu Libri Septem* (Pubblicazioni dell' Istituto di diritto pubblico e di dottrina dello stato della Facoltà di scienza politiche dell' Università di Roma, Ser. 4, n. 5), Giuffrè

Salamucha, J. (1950). 'Die Aussagenlogik bei Wilhelm von Ockham', *Franziskanische Studien* 32:97–134

Salembier, Louis (1886). *Petrus de Alliaco*, J. Lefort
    (1931). *Le Cardinal Pierre d'Ailly*, Georges Frère

Salman, D. (1939). 'The Mediaeval Latin Translations of Alfarabi's Work', *The New Scholasticism* 13:256–61

Salmon, V. (1969). [Review of *Cartesian Linguistics* by N. Chomsky], *Journal of Linguistics* 5:165–87

Salter, H. E., ed. (1923). *Registrum Annalium Collegii Mertonensis 1483–1521*, Clarendon Press

Sambursky, S. (1959). *Physics of the Stoics*, Routledge & Kegan Paul

Sanctius Brocensis, Franciscus (1587). *Minerva*, Salamanca

Sanderson, Robert (1640). *Logicae Artis Compendium*, Oxford

Sanseverino, G. (1862). *Philosophia christiana cum antiqua et nova comparata*, Manfredi

Santeler, Josef (1939). *Der Platonismus in der Erkenntnislehre des heiligen Thomas von Aquin*, Rauch

Santonastaso, G. (1957). 'Occam e la *plenitudo potestatis*', *Rassegna di scienze filosofiche* 10:213–71

Sarton, G. (1931). *Introduction to the History of Science*, II. 1–2, Williams and Wilkins

Sarubbi, Antonio (1971). *Chiesa e stato comunale nel pensiero di Remigio de' Girolami*, Morano

Sassen, F. (1931). 'Siger de Brabant et la doctrine de la double verité', *Revue néoscolastique de philosophie* 33:170–9

Savonarola, Girolamo (1534). 'De politia et regno' in *Compendium Totius Philosophiae*, Venice

Scaliger, J. C. (1540). *De causis linguae Latinae*, Lyon

Schafer, Carl (1935). *Die Staatslehre des Johannes Gerson*, Buchdruckerei Beyer und Hansknecht

Scheibler, Christoph (1628). *Philosophia compendiosa*, Oxford

Schenk, Günther (1973). *Zur Geschichte der logische Form. Erster Band. Einige Entwicklungstendenzen von der Antike bis zum Ausgang des Mittelalters*. VEB Deutscher Verlag der Wissenschaften

Schepers, H. (1963). *Möglichkeit und Kontingenz. Zur Geschichte der philosophischen Terminologie vor Leibniz* (Studi e richerche di storia della filosofia), Edizioni di 'Filosofia'
    (1972). 'Holkot contra dicta Crathorn II: Das "significatum per propositionem". Aufbau und Kritik einer nominalistischen Theorie über den Gegenstand des Wissens', *Philosophisches Jahrbuch der Görres-Gesellschaft* 79:106–36

Schilling, O. (1930). *Die Staats- und Soziallehre des hl. Thomas von Aquin* (2nd ed.), Hüber

Schmandt, R. H. (1975). 'The Fourth Crusade and the Just-war Theory', *The Catholic Historical Review* 61:191–221

Schmaus, M. (1959). 'Leben und Werk Martin Grabmanns' in *Miscellanea Martin Grabmann* (Mitteilungen des Grabmann-Instituts der Universität München, 3), University of Munich

Schmidt, C. (1855). *La Vie et les Travaux de Jean Sturm*, Schmidt

Schmidt, R. W. (1966). *The Domain of Logic according to Saint Thomas Aquinas*, Nijhoff

Schmitt, Charles B. (1971). *A Critical Survey and Bibliography of Studies on Renaissance Aristotelianism 1958–1969*, Editrice Antenore

(1975). 'Philosophy and Science in Sixteenth-Century Universities: Some Preliminary Comments' in J. E. Murdoch and E. Sylla (1975)

Schmitt, F. S. (1936). *Ein neues unvollendetes Werk des hl. Anselm von Canterbury* (*BGPM* XXXIII, 3), Aschendorff

Schmugge, Ludwig (1966). *Johannes von Jandun (1285/89–1328): Untersuchungen zur Biographie und Sozialtheorie eines lateinischen Averroisten* (Pariser Historische Studien, No. 5), Anton Hiersemann

Schneider, Arthur (1903–6). *Die Psychologie Alberts des Grossen nach den Quellen dargestellt* (*BGPM* IV, 5–6), Aschendorff

Scholz, H. (1961). *A Concise History of Logic*, Philosophical Library

Scholz, R. (1902). *Aegidius von Rom*, Druck der Union deutsche Verlagsgesellschaft

(1911–14). *Unbekannte Kirchenpolitische Streitschriften aus der Zeit Ludwigs des Bayern (1327–1354)* (2 vols.), Loescher

(1936). 'Marsilius von Padua und die Genesis des modernen Staatsbewusstseins', *Historische Zeitschrift* 156:88–103

(1962). *Die Publizistik zur Zeit Philipps des Schönen und Bonifaz VIII*, P. Schippers [first published 1903]

Schrimpf, G. (1966). *Die Axiomenschrift des Boethius (De Hebdomadibus) als Philosophisches Lehrbuch des Mittelalters*, Brill

Schütz, Ludwig (1895). *Thomas-Lexikon* (2nd edn.), Schöningh

Schulz, F. (1945). 'Bracton on kingship', *English Historical Review* 60:136–76

Schumacher, Leo Sebastian (1949). *The Philosophy of the Equitable Distribution of Wealth*, Catholic University of America Press

Scott, T. K. (1965). 'John Buridan on the Objects of Demonstrative Science', *Speculum* 40:654–73

(1969). 'Ockham on Evidence, Necessity and Intuition', *Journal of the History of Philosophy* 7:27–49

(1971). 'Nicholas of Autrecourt, Buridan, and Ockhamism', *Journal of the History of Philosophy* 9:15–41

Serene, Eileen F. (1979) 'Robert Grosseteste on Induction and Demonstrative Science', *Synthese* 40:97–115

Seton, John (1631). *Dialectica annotationibus Petri Carteri*, Cambridge

Sextus Empiricus (1958). *Opera*, ed. H. Mutschmann, vol. I, Teubner

Shapiro, Herman (1957). *Motion, Time and Place according to William Ockham*, The Franciscan Institute

(1959). 'Walter Burley and the Intension and Remission of Forms', *Speculum* 34:413–27

Shapiro, Herman and Charlotte (1965). 'De Primo et Ultimo Instanti des Walter Burley', *Archiv für Geschichte der Philosophie* 47:157–73

Sharp, D. (1934). 'Simon of Faversham's Quaestiones super tertium *De anima*', *Archives d'histoire doctrinale et littéraire du moyen âge* 9:307–68

Sharp, E. D. (1964). *Franciscan Philosophy at Oxford in the Thirteenth Century*, Oxford University Press (first published 1930)

Sheppard, Vincent F. (1949). *Religion and the Concept of Democracy: A Thomistic Study in Social Philosophy*, Catholic University of America Press

Shields A. L., ed. (1949). *Averrois Cordubensis Compendia Librorum qui Parva Naturalia Vocantur* (Corpus Commentariorum Averrois in Aristotelem), Mediaeval Academy of America

Siematkowska, Z. K. (1960). 'Avant l'exil de Gilles de Rome: Au sujet d'une dispute sur les "Theoremata de esse et essentia" de Gilles de Rome', *Mediaevalia Philosophica*

Polonorum 7:3–67

Siewerth, G. (1954). *Die menschliche Willensfreiheit. Texte zur thomistischen Freiheitslehre*, Schwann

[Pseudo-] Siger of Brabant (1941). *Questions sur la Physique d'Aristote* ed. P. Delhaye, Louvain, Institut supérieur de philosophie

Siger of Brabant (1948). *Siger de Brabant. Questions sur la métaphysique (Quaestiones in Metaphysicam)*, ed. C. A. Graiff, Éditions de l'Institut Supérieur de Philosophie de Louvain

(1966). Die *Questiones metaphysice tres* des Siger von Brabant', ed. J. Vennebusch, *Archiv für Geschichte der Philosophie* 48:175–89

(1972a). *Quaestiones in tertium De anima, De anima intellectiva, De aeternitate mundi* ed. B. Bazán, Publications Universitaires de Louvain

(1972b). *Les Quaestiones super librum de causis de Siger de Brabant*, ed. A. Marlasca, Publications Universitaires de Louvain

(1974). *Écrits de logique, de morale et de physique* ed. B. Bazán, Publications Universitaires de Louvain

Siger of Courtrai (1913). *Ars Priorum* in G. Wallerand (ed.) *Les Oeuvres de Siger de Courtrai* (Les Philosophes Belges. Textes et Études), Louvain Institut Supérieur de Philosophie

(1978). *Summa Modorum Significandi – Sophismata*, ed. J. Pinborg (Amsterdam Studies in the Theory and History of Linguistic Science, III: Studies in the History of Linguistics, 14), Benjamins

Sigmund, Paul E. (1963). *Nicholas of Cusa and Medieval Political Thought*, Harvard University Press

(1971). *Natural Law in Political Thought*, Winthrop

Sikes, J. G. (1932). *Peter Abailard*, Cambridge University Press

(1934). 'John de Pouilli and Peter de la Palu', *English Historical Review* 49:219–40

Simon of Faversham (1957). *Opera omnia, vol. 1; Opera logica, tomus prior: Quaestiones super libro Porphyrii, Quaestiones super libro Praedicamentorum, Quaestiones super libro Perihermeneias*, ed. P. Mazzarella, Cedam

(forthcoming). *Quaestiones novae et veteres super librum Elenchorum*, ed. F. Del Punta, S. Ebbesen, T. Izbicki, J. Longeway, E. Serene, and E. Stump, Pontifical Institute of Mediaeval Studies

Simon of Tournai (1966). *Expositio super Simbolum*, ed. N. Häring in *Archives d'histoire doctrinale et littéraire du moyen âge* 41

Simonin, H. D. (1930). 'La connaissance des singuliers matériels d'après les maîtres franciscains de la fin du xiiie siècle' in *Mélanges Mandonnet. Études d'histoire littéraire et doctrinale du moyen âge* (2 vols.), J. Vrin

(1930a). 'La notion d' "intentio" dans l'oeuvre de S. Thomas d'Aquin', *Revue des sciences philosophiques et théologiques* 19:445–63

(1930b). 'La connaissance humaine des singuliers matériels d'après les maitres franciscains de la fin du XIIIe siècle' in *Mélanges Mandonnet*, vol. 2 (Bibliothèque Thomiste, vol. 14), Vrin

(1931). 'Connaissance et similitude', *Revue des sciences philosophiques et théologiques* 20:293–303

Simplicius (1907). *In Aristotelis Categorias Commentarium*, ed. C. Kalbfleisch (Commentaria in Aristotelem Graeca VIII), Reimer

(1971–5). *Commentaire sur les Catégories d'Aristote*, ed. A. Pattin (Corpus latinum commentariorum in Aristotelem Graecorum, V. 1–2), Publications universitaires de Louvain (1971); Brill (1975)

Siwek (1948). *Psychologia Metaphysica*. Pontificia Universitas Gregoriana

Skinner, Quentin (1978). *The Foundations of Modern Political Thought*. Vol. 1: *The Renaissance*. Vol. 2: *The Age of Reformation*, Cambridge University Press

Smalley, Beryl, ed. (1965). *Trends in Medieval Political Thought*, Basil Blackwell
  (1973). *The Becket Conflict and the Schools: A Study of Intellectuals in Politics*, Rowman and Littlefield

Smet, A. J., ed. (1968). *Alexandre d'Aphrodisias, Commentaire sur les Météores d'Aristote* (Corpus Latinum Commentariorum in Aristotelem Graecorum IV), Publications Universitaires de Louvain/Éditions Béatrice-Nauwelaerts

Smiglecki, Martin (1634). *Logica*, Oxford

Smith, V. (1954). 'Prime Mover, Physical and Metaphysical Considerations', *Proceedings of the American Catholic Philosophical Association* 28:78–94
  (1958). *The General Science of Nature*, Bruce

Sobociński, B. (1956). 'In memoriam Jan Łukasiewicz', *Philosophical Studies* (Maynooth) 6:3–46

Sorabji, Richard (1972). *Aristotle on Memory*, Duckworth

Soto, Domingo de (1567). *Libri decem de iustitia et iure*, Antwerp
  (1587). *In Porphyrii Isagogen, Aristotelis Categorias librosque de demonstratione commentaria*, Venice (Reprinted Minerva 1967)

Southern, R. W. (1963). *Saint Anselm and his Biographer*, Cambridge University Press
  (1970). *Medieval Humanism and other Studies*. Blackwell

Southern, R. W. and F. S. Schmitt (1969). *Memorials of St Anselm*, British Academy

Spade, Paul Vincent (1969). *An Anonymous Fourteenth-Century Treatise on Insolubles: Text and Study*, L. S. M. thesis, Pontifical Institute of Mediaeval Studies.
  (1971). 'An Anonymous Tract on *Insolubilia* from Ms Vat. lat. 674: An Edition and Analysis of the Text', *Vivarium* 9:1–18
  (1973). 'The Origins of the Mediaeval *Insolubilia*-Literature', *Franciscan Studies* 33:292–309
  (1973a). 'The Treatises *On Modal Propositions* and *On Hypothetical Propositions* by Richard Lavenham', *Mediaeval Studies* 35:49–59
  (1974a). 'Five Logical Tracts by Richard Lavenham', in J. Reginald O'Donnell (ed.), *Essays in Honour of Anton Charles Pegis*, Pontifical Institute of Mediaeval Studies
  (1974b). 'Ockham on Self-Reference', *Notre Dame Journal of Formal Logic* 15:298–300
  (1974c). 'Ockham's Rule of Supposition: Two Conflicts in His Theory', *Vivarium* 12:63–73
  (1975a). *The Mediaeval Liar: A Catalogue of the Insolubilia-Literature* (Subsidia Mediaevalia, 5), Pontifical Institute of Mediaeval Studies
  (1975b). 'Notes on Some Manuscripts of Logical and Physical Works by Richard Lavenham', *Manuscripta* 19:139–46
  (1975c). 'Ockham's Distinctions between Absolute and Connotative Terms', *Vivarium* 13:55–75
  (1975d). 'Some Epistemological Implications of the Burley-Ockham Dispute', *Franciscan Studies* 35:212–22
  (1976). 'Robert Fland's *Consequentiae*: An Edition', *Mediaeval Studies* 38:54–84
  (1977). 'Roger Swyneshed's *Obligationes*: Edition and Comments', *Archives d'histoire doctrinale et littéraire du moyen âge* 44:243–85
  (1978a). 'John Buridan on the Liar: A Study and Reconstruction', *Notre Dame Journal of Formal Logic* 19:579–90
  (1978b). 'Richard Lavenham's *Obligationes*: Edition and Comments', *Rivista critica di storia della filosofia* 33:225–242

(1978c). 'Robert Fland's *Insolubilia*: An Edition, with Comments on the Dating of Fland's Works', *Mediaeval Studies* 40: 56–80

(1979a). 'Roger Swyneshed's *Insolubilia*: Edition and Comments', *Archives d'histoire doctrinale et littéraire du moyen âge* 46: 177–220

(1979b). *William Heytesbury: On 'Insoluble' Sentences: Chapter One of His Rules for Solving Sophisms* (Mediaeval Sources in Translation, 21), Pontifical Institute of Mediaeval Studies

(1979c). 'Recent Research on Medieval Logic', *Synthese* 40: 3–18

(1980). 'Robert Fland's *Obligationes*: An Edition', *Mediaeval Studies* 42: 41–60

(1980a). 'Richard Lavenham and the Cambridge Logic', *Historiographia Linguistica* 7: 241–7

(forthcoming a). 'Notes on Richard Lavenham's So Called *Summulae logicales*, with a Partial Edition of the Text', *Franciscan Studies*

(forthcoming b). 'Quasi-Aristotelianism' in Kretzmann (forthcoming b)

Spade, Paul Vincent, and Eleonore Stump (forthcoming), 'The Treatise on Obligations Attributed to William of Sherwood'

Spettmann, H. (1923). 'Der Ethikkommentar des Johannes Peckham' in *Abhandlungen zur Geschichte der Philosophie des Mittelalters* (BGPM suppl. Bd. 2), Aschendorff

Stahl, William Harris (1971). *Martianus Capella and the Seven Liberal Arts. Volume I, The Quadrivium of Martianus Capella. Latin Traditions in the Mathematical Sciences 50 B.C.–A.D. 1250*, Columbia University Press

Starkey, Thomas (1948). *A Dialogue between Reginald Pole and Thomas Lupset*, ed. Kathleen M. Burton, Chatto and Windus

Steele, R., ed. (1920). *Secretum secretorum* (Opera hactenus inedita Rogeri Baconi, 5), Clarendon Press

ed. (1935). *Quaestiones supra librum De causis* (Opera hactenus inedita Rogeri Baconi, 12), Clarendon Press

Steenberghen, F. Van (1930). 'Siger de Brabant d'après ses oeuvres inédites', *Revue néoscolastique de philosophie* 32: 403–23

(1931). *Siger de Brabant d'après ses oeuvres inédites*, vol. 1: *Les oeuvres inédites* (Les philosophes belges, No. 12), Éditions de L'Institut Supérieur de Philosophie

(1938). *Les oeuvres et la doctrine de Siger de Brabant* (Académie royale de Belgique. Classe des lettres et des sciences morales et politiques. Mémoires, vol. 39, fasc. 3), Hayez

(1942). *Siger de Brabant d'après ses oeuvres inédites*, vol. 2: *Siger dans l'histoire de l'aristotélisme* (Les philosophes belges, No. 13), Éditions de L'Institut Supérieur de Philosophie

(1948). 'Maurice de Wulf, historien de la philosophie médiévale', *Revue Philosophique de Louvain* 46: 421–47

(1951). 'Siger of Brabant', *The Modern Schoolman* 29: 11–27

(1955). *Aristotle in the West. The Origins of Latin Aristotelianism*, tr. L. Johnston, Nauwelaerts

(1956). 'Nouvelles recherches sur Siger de Brabant et son école', *Revue philosophique de Louvain* 54: 130–47

(1966). *La Philosophie au XIIIᵉ siècle* (Philosophes médiévaux 9), Publications universitaires de Louvain Béatrice-Nauwelaerts

(1971). 'Un commentaire semi-averroïste du traité de l'âme (Oxford, Merton College 275, f. 67–84; Munich, Clm 9559, f. 74–82)' in Maurice Giele, Fernand Van Steenberghen, Bernard Bazán (eds.) *Trois commentaires anonymes sur le traité de l'âme d'Aristote* (Philosophes médiévaux, vol. 11), Publications Universitaires and

Béatrice-Nauwelaerts

(1974). *Introduction à l'étude de la philosophie médiévale* (Philosophes médiévaux, vol. 18), Publications Universitaires and Béatrice-Nauwelaerts

(1976). '"Averroïsme" et "double vérité" au siècle de saint Louis' in *Septième centenaire de la mort de saint Louis, Actes des colloques de Royaumont et de Paris (21–27 mai 1970)*, Société d'Édition 'Les Belles Lettres'

(1977). *Maître Siger de Brabant* (Philosophes médiévaux, No. 21), Publications Universitaires

(1978). 'Siger de Brabant et la condamnation de l'aristotélisme hétérodoxe le 7 mars 1277' *Bulletin de l'Académie royale de Belgique, Classes des lettres et des sciences morales et politiques*, 5th ser., Tome 44, Académie Royale de Belgique

(1979). 'Etienne Gilson, historien de la pensée médiévale'. *Revue philosophique de Louvain* 77 : 487–508

(1980). *Thomas Aquinas and Radical Aristotelianism*, Catholic University of America Press

Stegmüller, Friedrich (1935). *Geschichte der Molinismus: Neue Molinaschriften (BGPM XXXII)*, Aschendorff

Stelling-Michaud, Sven, ed. (1967). *Les Universités Européennes du XIVᵉ au XVIIIᵉ siècle: Actes du Colloque International à l'occasion du VIᵉ centenaire de l'Université Jagellonne de Cracovie*, Droz

Steneck, Nicholas H. (1974). 'Albert the Great on the Classification and Localization of the Internal Senses', *Isis* 65 : 193–211

(1980). 'Albert on the Psychology of Sense Perception' in James A. Weisheipl (ed.) *Albertus Magnus and the Sciences: Commemorative Essays 1980*, Pontifical Institute of Mediaeval Studies

Stevens, H. J. (1975). 'Lorenzo Valla and Isidore of Seville', *Traditio* 31 : 343–8

Stiegler, A. (1958). *Der kirchliche Rechtsbegriff: Elemente und Phasen seiner Erkenntnisgeschichte*, Schell Steiner

Stone, Lawrence, ed. (1975). *The University in Society* (vol. I), Princeton University Press

Stout, Harry S. (1974). 'Marsilius of Padua and the Henrician Reformation', *Church History* 43 : 308–18

Stratenwerth, G. (1951). *Die Naturrechtslehre des Johannes Duns Scotus*, Vandenhoeck und Ruprecht

Strato (1967–9). Fragments, in vol. V of Wehrli (1967–9)

Strauss, L. and J. Cropsy, eds. (1963). *A History of Political Philosophy*, Rand McNally

Strayer, Joseph R. (1970). *On the Medieval Origins of the Modern State*, Princeton University Press

Streckenbach, G. (ed.) (1972). 'Paulus Niavis, Latinum ydeoma pro novellis studentibus', *Mittellateinisches Jahrbuch* 7 : 187–251

Stump, Eleonore (1974). 'Boethius's Works on the Topics', *Vivarium* 12 : 77–93

(1978). *Boethius's De topicis differentiis. Translated, with notes and essays on the text*; Cornell University

(1980). 'Dialectic in the Eleventh and Twelfth Centuries: Garlandus Compotista', *History and Philosophy of Logic* 1 : 1–18

(1980a). 'William of Sherwood's Treatise on Obligations', *Historiographia Linguistica* 7 : 249–61

(1981). 'Boethian Theory of Topics and its Place in Early Scholastic Logic' in Proceedings of the International Boethius Conference in Pavia, ed. L. Obertello, Brill (forthcoming a). 'Dialectic in the Eleventh to the Thirteenth Centuries', in David Wagner (ed.) *The Seven Liberal Arts*, Indiana University Press

(forthcoming b). 'Peter of Spain on the Topics' in *Boethius and the Liberal Arts*, ed. Michael Masi, Verlag Peter Lang

(forthcoming c). 'Theology and Physics in *De sacramento altaris*: Ockham's Theory of Indivisibles' in Kretzmann (forthcoming b)

(forthcoming d). *Boethius's In Ciceronis Topica*

Stump, Eleonore and Paul Vincent Spade (forthcoming). 'The Treatise on Obligations Attributed to William of Sherwood'

Suárez, Francisco (1612). *Tractatus de legibus ac Deo legislatore*, Coimbra

(1856–77). *Opera omnia* (26 vols.), L. Vivès

(1944). *Selections from Three Works*, ed. James Brown Scott (2 vols.) (The Classics of International Law, 20), Clarendon Press

(1947). *On the various kinds of Distinctions*, tr. C. Vollert, Marquette University Press

(1964). *On Formal and Universal Unity*, tr. with an introduction by J. F. Ross, Marquette University Press

(1965). *Disputationes metaphysicae*, Georg Olms

(1971–7). *De Legibus*, ed. Luciano Pereña (6 vols.) (Corpus Hispanorum de Pace, 11–17), Consejo Superior de Investigaciones Cientificas, Instituto Francisco de Vitoria

Suárez, G. (1948). 'El pensamiento de Egidio Romano en torno a la distinción de esencia y existencia', *La Ciencia Tomista* 75:66–99; 230–72

Südhoff, K. (1914). 'Die kurze "Vita" und das Verzeichnis der Arbeiten Gerhards von Cremona', *Archiv für Geschichte der Medizin* 8:73–82

Sullivan, Mark W. (1967). *Apuleian Logic* (Studies in Logic and the Foundations of Mathematics), North-Holland

Susemihl, F., ed. (1872). *Aristotelis Politicorum libri octo, cum vetusta translatione Guilelmi de Moerbeke*, Teubner

Sweeney, Leo (1963). 'Existence/Essence in Thomas Aquinas's Early Writings', *Proceedings of the American Catholic Philosophical Association* 37:97–131

Sweeney, Leo and C. J. Ermatinger (1958). 'Divine Infinity according to Richard Fishacre', *The Modern Schoolman* 35:191–235

Swiezawski, S. (1934). 'Les intentions premiers et les intentions secondes chez Jean Duns Scot', *Archives d'histoire doctrinale et littéraire du moyen âge* 9:205–60

Swiniarski, John J. (1970). 'A New Presentation of Ockham's Theory of Supposition with an Evaluation of Some Contemporary Criticisms', *Franciscan Studies* 30:181–217

Sylla, Edith (1970). *The Oxford Calculators and the Mathematics of Motion, 1320–50, Physics and Measurement by Latitudes*, unpublished Ph.D. dissertation, Harvard University

(1971). 'Medieval Quantifications of Qualities: the "Merton School"', *Archive for History of Exact Sciences* 8:9–39

(1973). 'Medieval Concepts of the Latitude of Forms: The Oxford Calculators', *Archives d'histoire doctrinale et littéraire du moyen âge* 40:223–83

(1979). 'The A Posteriori Foundations of Natural Science. Some Medieval Commentaries on Aristotle's *Physics*, Book I, Chapters 1 and 2', *Synthese* 40:147–87

(forthcoming). 'Infinite Indivisibles and Continuity in Fourteenth-Century Theories of Alteration' in Kretzmann (forthcoming b)

Synan, E. A. (1962). 'Sixteen Sayings by Richard of Campsall on Contingency and Foreknowledge', *Mediaeval Studies* 24:250–62

Tachau, Katherine, Calvin Normore, Mary Sirridge, and Paul Streveler, eds. (forthcoming). *Ricardus sophista: Abstractiones*

Tacitus (1949). *Cornelii Taciti Dialogus de oratoribus*, ed. M. L. de Gubernatis (*Corpus Scriptorum Latinorum Paravianum*), G. P. Paravia

Tambuyser, R. (1958). 'L'érection de la chaire de philosophie thomiste à l'Université de Louvain (1880–1882)', *Revue philosophique de Louvain* 56:478–509

Tatnall, Edith Comfort (1965). *Church and State According to John Wyclyf*, University Microfilms

Terrero, José Riesco (1960). 'Juan de Janduno y el Gandavense' *Salmanticensis commentarius de sacris disciplinis* 7:331–43

Teufel, Waldemar (1977). *Universitas studii Tuwingensis: Die Tübinger Universitätsverfassung in vorreformatorischer Zeit (1477–1534)*, Mohr

Themistius (1900). *Analyticorum Posteriorum paraphrasis*, ed. M. Wallies (Commentaria in Aristotelem Graeca V. 1), G. Reimer

Theophrastus (1973). *Die logischen Fragmente des Theophrast*, ed. Andreas Graeser (Kleine Texte für Vorlesungen und Uebungen, 191), De Gruyter

Théry, G. (1931). 'L'Augustinisme médiéval et le problème de l'unité de la forme substantielle', in *Acta Hebdomadae Augustinianae-Thomisticae*, Marietti

Thierry of Chartres (1971). *Commentaries on Boethius by Thierry of Chartres and his School*, ed. Nikolaus M. Häring, Pontifical Institute of Mediaeval Studies

Thomas Aquinas (1874–89). *Opera omnia*, ed. S. E. Fretté and P. Maré (34 vols.), L. Vivès

(1882–). *S. Thomae Aquinatis Doctoris Angelici. Opera Omnia. Iussu impensaque Leonis XIII, P.M. edita* (Leonine ed.) Vatican Polyglot Press

(1882). *Commentaria in Aristotelis Peri Hermeneias et Posteriorum Analyticorum* in Thomas Aquinas 1882–, vol. 1

(1888–1906). *Summa theologiae* in Thomas Aquinas 1882–, vols. 4–12

(1889). *In libros Aristotelis De caelo et mundo expositio* in Thomas Aquinas 1882–, vol. 3

(1925). *Quaestiones disputatae*, ed. P. Mandonnet (3 vols.), P. Léthielleux

(1929–56). *Scriptum super Sententiis*, ed. P. Mandonnet and M. F. Moos, P. Léthielleux

(1933). *In decem libros Ethicorum Aristotelis ad Nicomachum expositio*, ed. A. M. Pirotta, Marietti

(1934a). *Summa contra Gentiles*, in Thomas Aquinas 1882–, vols. 13–15

(1948a). *In Aristotelis librum De anima commentarium*, ed. A. M. Pirotta, Marietti

(1948b). *Le 'De ente et essentia' de s. Thomas d'Aquin*, ed. M.-D. Roland-Gosselin, J. Vrin

(1948c). *In librum Boethii De Trinitate quaestiones quinta et sexta*, Société Philosophique and E. Nauwelaerts

(1948–50). *Summa theologiae*, ed. P. Caramello (from the Leonine ed.) (3 vols.), Marietti

(1949a). *Quaestiones disputatae*, ed. R. M. Spiazzi *et al.* (8th ed.) (2 vols.), Marietti

(1949b). *De veritate* in Thomas Aquinas 1949a

(1949c). *On Kingship to the King of Cyprus*, tr. Gerald B. Phelan, rev. with introd. and notes by I. T. Eschmann, Pontifical Institute of Medieval Studies

(1950a). *De principiis naturae*, Société Philosophique and E. Nauwelaerts

(1950b). *In librum beati Dionysii De divinis nominibus expositio*, ed. C. Pera, Marietti

(1950c). *Summa Theologiae: Prima Pars; Prima Secundae*, Marietti

(1951). *In octo libros Politicorum Aristotelis expositio*, ed. R. M. Spiazzi, Marietti

(1953a). *Quaestiones disputatae*, ed. R. M. Spiazzi *et al.* (9th rev. ed.) (2 vols.), Marietti

(1953b). *Quaestiones disputatae de potentia*, in Thomas Aquinas 1953a

(1953c). *Quaestio disputata de spiritualibus creaturis* in Thomas Aquinas 1953a

(1954a). *Opuscula philosophica*, ed. R. M. Spiazzi, Marietti

(1954b). *De ente et essentia* in Thomas Aquinas 1954a

(1954c). *De regimine principum ad regem Cypri* in Thomas Aquinas 1954a

(1954d). *Sancti Thomae de Aquino super Librum de Causis Expositio*, ed. H. D. Saffrey, Société Philosophique

(1954e). *In octo libros Physicorum Aristotelis expositio*, ed M. Maggiòlo, Marietti

(1954f). *Opuscula theologica*, ed. R. A. Verardo, R. M. Spiazzi, and M. Calcaterra (2 vols.), Marietti

(1954g). *Expositio super Boetium De trinitate et De hebdomadibus* in Thomas Aquinas 1954f

(1954h). *Compendium theologiae* in Thomas Aquinas 1954f

(1955). *Expositio super librum Boethii De Trinitate*, ed. B. Decker (Studien und Texte zur Geistesgeschichte des Mittelalters, 4), Brill

(1956). *Quaestiones quodlibetales*, ed. R. M. Spiazzi (9th rev. edn.), Marietti

(1957). *Tractatus de unitate intellectus contra averroistas*, ed. L. W. Keeler (Textus et Documenta, Series philosophica, 12), Pontificia Universitas Gregoriana

(1959). *In Aristotelis librum De anima commentarium*, ed. A. M. Pirotta (4th edn.), Marietti

(1961–7). *Liber de veritate Catholicae fidei contra errores infidelium, seu Summa contra gentiles*, ed. C. Pera, P. Marc, and P. Carmello (3 vols.), Marietti

(1963). *Treatise on Separate Substances* (*Tractatus de Substantiis Separatis*), ed. and tr. F. J. Lescoe, Saint Joseph College, West Hartford, Conn.

(1964a). *In Aristotelis libros Peri hermeneias et Posteriorum analyticorum expositio*, ed. R. M. Spiazzi (2nd edn.), Marietti

(1964b). *In decem libros Ethicorum Aristotelis ad Nicomachum expositio*, ed. R. M. Spiazzi (3rd edn.), Marietti

(1964c). *De veritate* in Thomas Aquinas 1964–5

(1964–5). *Quaestiones disputatae*, ed. R. M. Spiazzi *et al.* (10th edn.) (2 vols.), Marietti

(1964–76). *Summa theologiae*, Latin text and English translation, Introductions, Notes, Appendices, and Glossaries (60 vols.), Blackfriars, in conjunction with Eyre and Spottiswoode and McGraw Hill

(1969). *Sententia libri Ethicorum* in Thomas Aquinas 1882–, vol. 47, pts. 1–2

(1971a). *Sententia libri Politicorum* in Thomas Aquinas 1882–, vol. 48

(1971b). *In duodecim libros Metaphysicorum Aristotelis expositio*, ed. M. R. Cathala and R. M. Spiazzi (2nd edn.), Marietti

(1976). *De fallaciis* in Thomas Aquinas 1882–, vol. 43

Thomas Bradwardine (1503). *Geometria speculativa*, Paris

(1618). *Summa de causa dei contra Pelagium et de virtute causarum ad suos Mertonenses libri tres*, Lyon (Reprinted Minerva 1964)

(1955). *Thomas of Bradwardine His Tractatus de Proportionibus*, ed. and tr. H. L. Crosby, Jr., University of Wisconsin Press

Thomas, Ernest C., ed. and tr. (1888). *The Philobiblon of Richard de Bury*, Kegan Paul, Trench and Co

Thomas, Ivo (1953), 'Kilwardby on Conversion', *Dominican Studies* 6: 56–76

(1954). 'Maxims in Kilwardby', *Dominican Studies* 7: 129–46

(1964). 'Medieval Aftermath: Oxford Logic and Logicians of the Seventeenth Century' in *Oxford Studies Presented to Daniel Callus* (Oxford Historical Society, 16), Clarendon Press

Thomas, Rudolph, ed. (1970). *Petrus Abaelardus: Dialogus inter Philosophum, Iudaeum et Christianum*, Frommann-Holzboog

Thomson, S. Harrison (1940). *The Writings of Robert Grosseteste*, Cambridge University Press

    (1947). 'Walter Burley's commentary on the Politics of Aristotle' in *Mélanges Auguste Pelzer* (Receuil des Travaux d'histoire et de philosophie, 3rd series, 26) Université de Louvain

    (1969). *Latin Bookhands of the Later Middle Ages 1100–1500*, Cambridge University Press

Thorndike, Lynn (1934). 'Calculator and the Rise of Mathematics', in his *History of Magic and Experimental Science*, vol. 3, Columbia University Press

    (1944). *University Records and Life in the Middle Ages*, Columbia University Press (Reprint 1971, Octagon Books)

    (1959). 'John of Seville', *Speculum* 34:20–38

    (1965). *Michael Scot*, Nelson

Thurot, Charles (1868). *Extraits de divers manuscrits latins pour servir à l'histoire des doctrines grammaticales au moyen-âge*, Imprimerie impériale

Tierney, Brian (1953). 'The Canonists and the medieval state', *Review of Politics* 15:378–88

    (1954). 'Ockham, the conciliar theory and the canonists', *The Journal of the History of Ideas* 15:40–70

    (1955a). 'Grosseteste and the theory of papal sovereignty', *Journal of Ecclesiastical History* 6:1–17

    (1955b). *Foundations of the Conciliar Theory*, Cambridge University Press

    (1966). 'Medieval canon law and western constitutionalism', *The Catholic Historical Review* 52:1–17

    (1972). *Origins of Papal Infallibility, 1150–1350* (Studies in the History of Christian Thought), Brill

    (1975). '"Divided sovereignty" at Constance: a problem of medieval and early modern political theory', *Annuarium Historiae Conciliorum* 7:238–56

Tihon, P. (1966). *Foi et théologie selon Godefroid de Fontaines*, Desclée de Brouwer

Tooke, J. (1965). *The Just War in Aquinas and Grotius*, SPCK

Trapé, G. (1964). 'Il Platonismo di Egidio Romano', *Aquinas* 7:309–44

    (1966). 'Il Neoplatonismo di Egidio Romano nel commento al "De causis"', *Aquinas* 9:49–86

    (1967). 'La dottrina della partecipazione in Egidio Romano', *Aquinas* 10:170–93

    (1968). 'Caratteristiche dell' "esse" partecipato in Egidio Romano', *Lateranum* 34:351–68

    (1969). 'L' "esse" partecipato e distinzione reale in Egidio Romano', *Aquinas* 12:443–68

Trapp, Damasus (1956). 'Augustinian Theology of the Fourteenth Century', *Augustiniana* 6:146–274

    (1957). 'Peter Ceffons of Clairvaux', *Recherches de théologie ancienne at médiévale* 24:101–54

    (1958). 'Gregory of Rimini: Manuscripts, Editions, and Additions', *Augustiniana* 8:425–43

    (1962). 'New Approaches to Gregory of Rimini', *Augustinianum* 2:115–30

Trentman, J. A. (1975). 'Speculative Grammar and Transformational Grammar; A Comparison of Philosophical Presuppositions', in Herman Parret (ed.) *History of Linguistic Thought and Contemporary Linguistics*, De Gruyter

    (1976). 'The Study of Logic and Language in England in the Early 17th Century',

Historiographia Linguistica 3 : 179–201

(1978). 'Bad Names: A Linguistic Argument in Late Medieval Natural Law Theories', *Noûs* 12 : 29–39

(forthcoming). 'The Authorship of the Seventeenth-Century Cambridge *Directions for a Student in the Universitie*', *Transactions of the Cambridge Bibliographical Society*

Trinkaus, C. (1970). *In Our Image and Likeness: Humanity and Divinity in Italian Humanist Thought*, Constable

Tromp, S. (1933). 'Progressus doctrinalis in tractatibus S. Roberti Bellarmini de Praedestinatione', *Gregorianum* 14 : 313–55

Troxler, Ferdinand (1973). *Die Lehre vom Eigentum bei Thomas von Aquin und Karl Marx: Eine Konfróntation*, Imba-Verlag

Tschackert, Paul (1877). *Peter von Ailly (Petrus de Alliaco): Zur Geschichte des grossen abendländischen Schisma und der Reformconcilien von Pisa und Constanz*, Friedrich Andreas Perthes

Tuck, Richard (1977). *Natural Rights Theories before Locke*, unpublished Ph.D. dissertation, Cambridge University

Türk, Egbert (1977). *Nugae curialium: Le règne d'Henri II Plantegenêt (1145–1189) et l'éthique politique* (Publications du Centre de Recherche d'Histoire et de Philologie de la IVᵉ Section de l'École pratique des Hautes Études, Paris, V: Hautes Études Médiévales et Modernes, 28), Droz

Tusquets, J. (1923). 'El cardenal J.-T. de Boxadors i la seva influència en el renaixement del tomisme', *Anuari de la Societat Catalana de Filosofia, Institut d'Estudis Catalans* I : 243–304

Tweedale, M. M. (1976). *Abailard on Universals*, North-Holland

Tyrrell, Francis M. (1948). *The Role of Assent in Judgment, A Thomistic Study*, The Catholic University of America Press

Ubaghs, G. C. (1860). *Essai d'idéologie ontologique, ou considérations sur la nature de nos idées et sur l'ontologisme en général*, De Vanlinthout

(1861). *Du problème ontologique des universaux et de la véritable signification du réalisme*, Vanlinthout

Ullman, B. L. (1955). *Studies in the Italian Renaissance*, Edizioni di storia e letteratura

Ullmann, W. (1944). 'The influence of John of Salisbury on medieval Italian jurists', *English Historical Review* 59 : 384–92

(1949). 'The Development of the Medieval Idea of Sovereignty', *English Historical Review* 64 : 1–33

(1961). *Principles of Government and Politics in the Middle Ages*, Methuen

(1965). *A History of Political Thought: the Middle Ages*, Penguin Books Ltd

(1966a). *The Individual and Society in the Middle Ages*, Johns Hopkins University Press

(1966b). *Principles of Government and Politics in the Middle Ages* (2nd edn.), Methuen

(1970). *The Growth of Papal Government in the Middle Ages* (4th edn.), Methuen

(1975). *Law and Politics in the Middle Ages. An Introduction to the Sources of Medieval Political Ideas*, Cornell University Press

Uña Juárez, A. (1978). *La filosofía del siglo xiv. Contexto cultural de Walter Burley*. Biblioteca 'La ciudad de Dios', Real Monasterio de el Escorial

Untervintl, L. von (1955). 'Die Intuitionslehre bei Vitalis de Furno', *Collectanea Franciscana* 25 : 53–111; 225–58

Urban, Linwood (1973). 'William of Ockham's theological ethics', *Franciscan Studies* 33 : 310–50

Ushaw (1839). *St Cuthbert's College, Ushaw, Durham. The course of studies with the theses and examination papers*, Dolman

Vahlen, J. (1886). 'Lorenzo Valla über Thomas von Aquino', *Vierteljahrsschrift für Kultur und Litteratur der Renaissance* 1:384–96

Valla, Lorenzo (1540). *Opera omnia* (2 vols.), Basle (Reprinted 1962)

Valois, Noel (1903). 'Jean de Jandun et Marsile de Padoue, auteurs du Defensor Pacis' in *Histoire littéraire de la France* 33:528–623

Van Breda, H. L., *see* Breda, H. L. Van

Van den Eynde, D., *see* Eynde, D. Van den

Van Eysinga, Willem J. M. *see* Eysinga, Willem J. M. Van

Van Fraassen, Bas C. *see* Fraassen, Bas C. Van

Vanni-Rovighi, S. (1960). 'L'intenzionalità della conoscenza secondo P. Aureolo', in *Actes du premier congrès international de philosophie médiévale* 673–80

    (1971). 'Gli averroisti bolognesi' in *Oriente e occidente nel medioevo: Filosofia e scienze, Convegno internazionale 9–15 Aprile 1969* (Accademia Nazionale dei Lincei, Atti dei Convegni, vol. 13), Accademia Nazionale dei Lincei

Van Overbeke, P. M., *see* Overbeke, P. M. Van

Van Riet, G., *see* Riet, G. Van

Van Riet, S., *see* Riet, S. Van

Van Steenberghen, F., *see* Steenberghen, F. Van

Vansteenkiste, C. (1951). 'Procli Elementatio Theologica Translata a Guilelmo de Moerbeke', *Tijdschrift voor Philosophie* 13:263–302; 495–509

    (1953). 'Avicenna-citaten bij S. Thomas', *Tijdschrift voor Philosophie* 15:457–507

    (1957). 'San Tommaso d'Aquino ed Averroe', *Scritti in onore di Guiseppe Furlani: Rivista degli studi orientali* 32:585–623

    (1960). 'Autori arabi e giudei nell' opera di San Tommaso', *Angelicum* 37:336–401

Vasoli, Cesare (1954). 'Il pensiero politico di Guglielmo d'Occam', *Rivista critica di storia della filosofia* 9:232–53

    (1968a). *La dialettica e la retorica dell' umanesimo: "invenzione" e "metodo" nella cultura del XV e XVI secolo*, Feltrinelli

    (1968b). *Studi sulla cultura del Rinascimento*, Lacaita

Vásquez, Gabriel (1620). *Commentaria ac Disputationes in primam partem S. Thomae*, Antwerp

Vaux, R. de (1933). 'La Première Entrée d'Averroès chez les Latins', *Revue des Sciences Philosophiques et Théologiques* 22:193–245

Vennebusch, J. (1963). *Ein anonymer Aristoteles Kommentar des XIII. Jahrhunderts: Quaestiones in tres libros De anima*, Schöningh

    (1965). 'Die Quaestiones in tres libros De anima des Simon von Faversham', *Archiv für Geschichte der Philosophie* 47:20–39

    (1966). 'Die *Questiones metaphysice tres* des Siger von Brabant', *Archiv für Geschichte der Philosophie* 48:163–89

Ventura de Raulica, J. (1861). *La philosophie chrétienne* (3 vols.), Gaume

Verbeke, Gérard (1949). 'Le développement de la connaissance humaine d'après saint Thomas', *Revue philosophique de Louvain* 47:437–57

    (1957). 'Thémistius et le commentaire de S. Thomas au "De anima" d'Aristote' and 'Thémistius et le "De unitate intellectus" de saint Thomas' in Gérard Verbeke (ed.) *Thémistius: Commentaire sur le Traité de l'âme d'Aristote, Traduction de Guillaume de Moerbeke, Édition critique et étude sur l'utilisation du commentaire dans l'oeuvre de saint Thomas* (Corpus latinum commentariorum in Aristotelem graecorum I), Publications Universitaires de Louvain and Éditions Béatrice-Nauwelaerts

    (1960). 'L'unité de l'homme: saint Thomas contre Averroès', *Revue philosophique de Louvain* 58:220–49

    ed. (1961). *Ammonius, Commentaire sur le Peri Hermenias d'Aristote* (Corpus Latinum

Commentariorum in Aristotelem Graecorum II), Publications Universitaires de Louvain/Éditions Béatrice-Nauwelaerts

ed. (1966). *Jean Philopon, Commentaire sur le De Anima d'Aristote* (Corpus Latinum Commentariorum in Aristotelem Graecorum III), Publications Universitaires de Louvain/Éditions Béatrice-Nauwelaerts

(1968). 'Le "De anima" d'Avicenne: Une conception spiritualiste de l'homme' in S. Van Riet (ed.) *Avicenna Latinus: Liber de anima seu sextus de naturalibus IV–V*, Éditions Orientalistes and E. J. Brill

(1977). 'Introduction doctrinale' in *Avicenna Latinus: Liber de Philosophia Prima sive Scientia Divina I–IV*, E. Peeters

Vereecke, L. (1965). 'Individu et communauté selon Guillaume d'Ockham', *Studia Moralia* 3:150–77

Verger, J. (1973). *Les universités au moyen-âge*, Presses universitaires françaises

Versteegh, C. H. M. (1977). *Greek Elements in Arabic Linguistic Thinking*, Brill

Vescovini, G. F. (1965). *Studi sulla prospettiva medioevale* (Università di Torino, Pubblicazioni della Facoltà di lettere e filosofia 16.1), Giapichelli

Veuthey, L. (1951). 'Les diverse courants de la philosophie augustino-franciscaine au moyen âge', *Scholastica: Ratione Historico-critica Instauranda*, 8:627–52

Victorinus (1863). *Explanationum in Rhetoricam M. Tullii Ciceronis libri duo*, ed. C. Halm in Halm 1863

(1971). *Liber de definitionibus*, ed. Stangl, in Hadot 1971

Vier, Peter (1951). *Evidence and its Function according to John Duns Scotus* (Philosophy Series, 7), The Franciscan Institute

Vignaux, Paul (1977). 'La problématique du nominalisme médiéval peut-elle éclairer des problèmes philosophiques actuels?', *Revue philosophique de Louvain* 75:293–331

Villey, M. (1954). 'Le droit naturel chez Gratien', *Studia Gratiana* 3:83–99

(1962). *Leçons d'histoire de la philosophie du Droit*, Dalloz

(1964). 'La genèse du droit subjectif chez Guillaume d'Occam', *Archives de philosophie du droit* 9:97–127

Vincent Ferrer, (1909). *De suppositionibus dialecticis* (Oeuvres de Saint Vincent Ferrier, H. Fages (ed.), Vol. 1, pp. 3–88), A. Picard et fils

(1977). *Tractatus de suppositionibus*, J. A. Trentman (ed.) (Grammatica speculativa, 2), Frommann–Holzboog

Vital du Four (1927). 'Huit questions disputées sur le problème de la connaissance, ed. F. Delorme, *Archives d'histoire doctrinale et littéraire du moyen âge* 2:151–337

Vitoria, Francisco de (1946). *The Principles of Political and International Law in the Works of Francisco de Vitoria*, extracts, with introd. and notes by A. T. Serra, Ediciones Cultura Hispanica

(1960). *Obras*, Editorial Catolica

Vives, Juan Luis (1782–90). *Opera omnia*, ed. Majans (8 vols.), Valencia

Voigt, G. (1893). *Die Wiederbelebung des classischen Alterthums oder das erste Jahrhundert des Humanismus* (3rd edn.), G. Reimer

Wallace, William A. (1969). 'The "Calculatores" in Early Sixteenth-Century Physics', *The British Journal for the History of Science* 4:221–32

(1971). 'Mechanics from Bradwardine to Galileo', *Journal of the History of Ideas* 32:15–28

(1972–4). *Causality and Scientific Explanation* (2 vols.; vol. I, *Medieval and early modern science*; vol. II, *Classical and contemporary science*), University of Michigan Press

Wallerand, G. (1913). *Les Oeuvres de Siger de Courtrai* (Les Philosophes Belges, 8), Institut

Supérieur de Philosophie de l'Université de Louvain

Wallies, Maximilian (1878). *De fontibus Topicorum Ciceronis*, A. Haack

Walsh, James J. (1964). 'Is Buridan a Sceptic about Free Will?', *Vivarium* 2:50–61

    (1966). 'Nominalism and Ethics: Some Remarks about Buridan's Commentary', *Journal of the History of Philosophy* 4:1–13

Walter Burley (1478). *In categorias*, etc., Venice

    (1481, 1500, 1521). *Expositio super decem libros Ethicorum Aristotelis*, Venice

    (1491, 1501). *Super octo libros Physicorum*, Venice

    (1496). *De intensione et remissione formarum*, Venice

    (1497). *Expositio super artem veterem Porphyrii et Aristotelis*, Venice (Reprinted Minerva 1967)

    (1501). *In Physicam Aristotelis expositio et quaestiones*, Venice (Reprinted Georg Olms 1972)

    (1507). *Burleus Super Artem Veterem Porphyrii et Aristotelis*, n.p.

    (1955). *De Puritate Artis Logicae Tractatus Longior*, ed. P. Boehner (Franciscan Institute Publications, Text series, No. 9), The Franciscan Institute

Walter Chatton (1955). *Lecturae Chaton Anglici in Sententias*, Prol., q. 2, in O'Callaghan 1955

Walther, Helmut G. (1976). *Imperiales Königtum, Konziliarismus und Volkssouveränität: Studien zu den Grenzen des mittelalterlichen Souveränitätsgedankens*, Wilhelm Fink

Walton, D. (1976). 'Logical Form and Agency', *Philosophical Studies* 29:75–89

Walton, Izaak (1927). *The Lives of John Donne, Sir Henry Wotton, Richard Hooker, George Herbert and Robert Sanderson*, ed. with an introduction by George Saintsbury, Oxford University Press

Walz, Angelo (1962). *Saint Thomas d'Aquin*, trans. Paul Novarina (Philosophes médiévaux, No. 5), Publications universitaires françaises

Walzer, Michael (1977). *Just and Unjust Wars*, Basic Books

Watanabe, Morimichi (1963). *The political Ideas of Nicholas of Cusa: with special reference to his 'De Concordia Catholica'*, Droz

Webb, C. C. J. (1932). *John of Salisbury*, Methuen

Wéber, Édouard-Henri (1970). *La controverse de 1270 à l'Université de Paris et son retentissement sur la pensée de S. Thomas d'Aquin* (Bibliothèque thomiste, No. 40), J. Vrin

    (1974). *Dialogue et dissensions entre Saint Bonaventure et Saint Thomas d'Aquin à Paris (1252–1273)* (Bibliothèque thomiste, No. 41), J. Vrin

    (1976). 'Les discussions de 1270 à l'Université de Paris et leur influence sur la pensée philosophique de S. Thomas d'Aquin' in Albert Zimmermann (ed.) *Die Auseinandersetzungen an der Pariser Universität im XIII. Jahrhundert* (Miscellanea Mediaevalia, Band 10), De Gruyter

Webering, Damascene (1953). *Theory of Demonstration according to William Ockham* (Philosophy Series, 10), The Franciscan Institute

Wehrli, F., ed. (1967–9). *Die Schule des Aristoteles: Texte und Kommentare* (10 vols.; 2nd edn.), B. Schwabe

Weigand, R. (1967). *Die Naturrechtslehre der Legisten und Dekretisten von Irnerius bis Accursius und von Gratian bis Johannes Teutonicus* (Münchener theologische Studien, 3. Kanonistische Abteilung, XXVI), Hueber

Weinberg, Julius R. (1948). *Nicolaus of Autrecourt. A Study in 14th century Thought*, Princeton University Press

    (1964). *A Short History of Medieval Philosophy*, Princeton University Press

Weisheipl, James A. (1955). *Nature and Gravitation*, Lyceum

    (1956). *Early 14th-Century Physics and the Merton 'School' with special reference to*

Dumbleton and Heytesbury, unpublished D. Phil. thesis, Oxford University

(1959). 'The place of John Dumbleton in the Merton School', *Isis* 50:439–54

(1963). 'The Concept of Matter in Fourteenth-Century Science' in E. McMullin (ed.), *The Concept of Matter in Greek and Medieval Philosophy*, University of Notre Dame Press

(1964a). 'Curriculum of the Faculty of Arts at Oxford in the Early Fourteenth Century', *Mediaeval Studies* 26:143–85

(1964b). 'Roger Swyneshed, O.S.B., Logician, Natural Philosopher, and Theologian' in *Oxford Studies Presented to Daniel Callus* (Oxford Historical Soceity, new series, 16), Clarendon Press

(1965a). 'The Concept of Matter in Fourteenth Century Science' in E. McMullin (ed.) *The Concept of Matter in Greek and Medieval Philosophy*, University of Notre Dame Press

(1965b). 'Classification of the Sciences in Medieval Thought', *Mediaeval Studies* 27:54–90

(1966). 'Developments in the Arts Curriculum at Oxford in the Early Fourteenth Century', *Mediaeval Studies* 28:151–75

(1968). 'Ockham and Some Mertonians', *Mediaeval Studies* 30:163–213

(1969). 'Repertorium Mertonense', *Mediaeval Studies* 31:174–224

(1974a). *Friar Thomas d'Aquino: his life, thought, and work*, Blackwell

(1974b). 'Motion in a Void: Aquinas and Averroes', in *St Thomas Aquinas 1274–1974: Commemorative Studies*, Vol. I, Pontifical Institute of Mediaeval Studies

(1976). 'The Relationship of Medieval Natural Philosophy to Modern Science: The Contribution of Thomas Aquinas to its Understanding', *Manuscripta* 20:181–96

(1980). 'The Life and Works of St Albert the Great' in James A. Weisheipl (ed.) *Albertus Magnus and the Sciences: Commemorative Essays 1980*, Pontifical Institute of Mediaeval Studies

Weiss, R. (1947). *The Dawn of Humanism in Italy*, H. K. Lewis

Wey, J. C. (1949). 'The *Sermo Finalis* of Robert Holcot', *Mediaeval Studies* 11:219–24

Wieland, G. (1974). 'Ethik und Metaphysik. Bemerkungen zur Moralphilosophie Roger Bacons' in A. Möller (ed.) *Virtus politica*, Frommann-Holzboog

(forthcoming). *Ethica – scientia practica. Die Anfänge der philosophischen Ethik im 13. Jahrhundert* (*BGPM*), Aschendorff

Wieland, Wolfgang (1962). *Die aristotelische Physik*, Vandenhoeck & Ruprecht

(1970). *Die aristotelische Physik* (2nd edn.), Vandenhoeck und Ruprecht

Wilenius, Reijo (1963). *The Social and Political Theory of Francisco Suárez* (Acta Philosophica Fennica, XV), Societas Philosophica Fennica

Wilkins, John (1668). *An Essay towards a Real Character and a Philosophical Language*, London, reprinted 1974, Clearwater Press, New York (Linguistics 13th – 18th Centuries series)

Wilks, Michael (1963). *The Problem of Sovereignty in the Later Middle Ages: The Papal Monarchy with Augustinus Triumphus and the Publicists* (Cambridge Studies in Medieval Life and Thought, New Series, 9), Cambridge University Press

(1969). 'The early Oxford Wyclif', *Studies in Church History*, 5:69–98

(1972). 'Reformatio regni: Wyclif and Hus as leaders of religious protest movements' in D. Baker (ed.), *Schism, Heresy and Religious Protest* (Studies in Church History, 9), pp. 109–30. Cambridge University Press

William of Alnwick (1937). *Quaestiones disputatae de esse intelligibili*, ed. A. Ledoux, Collegium s. Bonaventurae

William of Auvergne (1674). *Opera omnia* (2 vols.), Orleans and Paris (Reprinted

Minerva 1963)

(1976). *De Trinitate*, ed. Bruno Switalski, Pontifical Institute of Mediaeval Studies

William of Auxerre (1500). *Summa aurea*, Paris (Reprinted Minerva 1964)

William Heytesbury (1494a). *Tractatus Gulielmi Hentisberi de sensu composito et diviso, Regulae eiusdem cum Sophismatibus . . .*, Venice

(1494b). *Regulae solvendi sophismata* in William Heytesbury 1494a.

(1494c). *Sophismata* in William Heytesbury 1494a.

William de la Mare (1927). 'Le Correctorium Corruptorii "Quare"', ed. P. Glorieux in *Les premières polémiques thomistes*, Kain

William Ockham (1483). *Quaestiones et decisiones in primum libarum Sententiarum*, Urach

(1491). *Quodlibeta septem*, Strasbourg (Reprinted Éditions de la Bibliothèque S. J. Louvain 1962)

(1494–6). *Opera plurima* (4 vols.), Lyon (Reprinted Gregg 1962)

(1494). *Dialogus* in William Ockham 1494–6, vol. I

(1495–6). *Super quattuor libros Sententiarum* in William Ockham 1494–6, vols. III and IV

(1496). *Expositio aurea et admodum utilis super artem veterem edita per venerabilem inceptorem fratrem Guilielmum de Occham cum quaestionibus Alberti parvi de Saxonia*, Bologna (Reprinted Gregg 1964)

(?) (1914). *De Electione Caroli Quarti*, found only in Conrad of Megenberg's *Tractatus contra Wilhelmum Occam* in R. Scholz (ed.) *Unbekannte kirchenpolitische Streitschriften aus der Zeit Ludwigs des Bayern (1327–1354)*, 2:346–63, Loescher

(1914–24). *De Imperatorum et Pontificum Potestate*, ed. R. Scholz (1914), *Unbekannte kirchenpolitische Streitschriften aus der Zeit Ludwigs des Bayern (1327–1354)*, 2:453–80, Loescher (W. Regenberg); continuation ed. W. Mulder (1923–4), *Archivum Franciscanum Historicum* 16:469–92, 17:72–97

(1930). *The De Sacramento Altaris of William of Ockham*, ed. and tr. T. B. Birch, The Lutheran Literary Board

(1944). *Tractatus de successivis*, ed. P. Boehner (Franciscan Institute Publications, 1), The Franciscan Institute

(1945). *The Tractatus de praedestinatione et de praescientia dei et de futuris contingentibus of William Ockham*, ed. Philotheus Boehner (Franciscan Institute Publications, 2), The Franciscan Institute

(1951). *Summa logicae* (in part) ed. P. Boehner (2 vols.), The Franciscan Institute

(1952). *Breviloquium de principatu tyrannico super divina et humana, specialiter autem super imperium et subiectos imperio, a quibusdam vocatis summis pontificibus usurpato*, ed. R. Scholz in *Wilhelm von Ockham als politischer Denker und sein Breviloquium de principatu tyrannico*, Anton Hiersemann [reprint of 1944 edn.]

(1956a). *Contra Benedictum*, ed. H. S. Offler, *Guillelmi de Ockham Opera Politica*, 3, Manchester University Press

(1956b). *Contra Ioannem*, ed. H. S. Offler, *Guillelmi de Ockham Opera Politica*, 3, Manchester University Press

(1957a). *Ockham: Philosophical Writings*, ed. and tr. P. Boehner, Thomas Nelson

(1957b). *Expositio super viii libros Physicorum, Prologus* in William Ockham 1957a

(1963–74). *Opus nonaginta dierum*, chapters 1–6 ed. H. S. Offler (1974), *Guillelmi de Ockham Opera Politica*, 1 (rev. edn.), Manchester University Press; chapters 7–124 ed. R. F. Bennett and H. S. Offler (1963), *Guillelmi de Ockham Opera Politica*, 2, Manchester University Press

(1964). 'The *Tractatus logicae minor* of Ockham', ed. Eligius M. Buytaert, *Franciscan Studies* 24:34–100

(1965–66). 'The *Elementarium logicae* of Ockham', ed. Eligius M. Buytaert, *Franciscan Studies* 25:151–276 and 26:66–173

(1967–). *Opera philosophica et theologica*, ed. Juvenal Lalor, Stephen Brown, Gedeon Gál, Angelo Gambatese, and Michael Meilach, The Franciscan Institute

(1967). *Opera theologica [OT]* I: *Scriptum in librum primum Sententiarum, Ordinatio, Prologus et Distinctio prima*, ed. G. Gál and S. Brown in William Ockham 1967–

(1969). *William Ockham: Predestination, God's Foreknowledge, and Future Contingents*, translated with introduction and notes by Marilyn McCord Adams and Norman Kretzmann (Century Philosophy Sourcebooks), Appleton-Century-Crofts/William Hackett

(1970). *OT* II: *Scriptum in librum primum Sententiarum, Ordinatio; Distinctiones II–III*, ed. S. Brown and G. Gál in William Ockham 1967–

(1974a). *Opera philosophica [OP]* I: *Summa logicae*, ed. P. Boehner, G. Gál, and S. Brown, in William Ockham 1967–

(1974b). *Octo quaestiones de potestate papae*, ed. H. S. Offler, *Guillelmi de Ockham Opera politica*, 1 (rev. edn.), Manchester University Press

(1974c). *Consultatio de causa matrimoniali*, ed. H. S. Offler, *Guillelmi de Ockham Opera politica*, 1 (rev. edn.), Manchester University Press

(1974d). *An princeps pro suo succursu, scilicet guerrae, possit recipere bona ecclesiarum etiam invito papa*, ed. H. S. Offler, *Guillelmi de Ockham Opera Politica*, 1 (rev. edn.), Manchester University Press

(1974e). *Ockham's Theory of Terms: Part 1 of the Summa logicae*, translated with introduction and essays by Michael J. Loux, University of Notre Dame Press

(1977a). *OT* III: *Scriptum in librum primum Sententiarum, Ordinatio; Distinctiones IV–XVII*, ed. G. I. Etzkorn in William Ockham 1967–

(1977b). *Dialogus* II, 3, vi, ed. H. S. Offler in Offler 1977

(1978). *OP* II: *Expositionis in libros artis logicae prooemium et Expositio in librum Porphyrii de praedicabilibus*, ed. E. A. Moody; *Expositio in librum Praedicamentorum Aristotelis*, ed. G. Gál; *Expositio in librum Perihermenias Aristotelis*, ed. A. Gambatese and S. Brown; *Tractatus de praedestinatione et de praescientia Dei respectu futurorum contingentium*, ed. P. Boehner and S. Brown, in William Ockham 1967–

(1979a). *OP* III: *Expositio super libros Elenchorum*, ed. F. del Punta, in William Ockham 1967–

(1979b). *OT* IV: *Scriptum in librum primum Sententiarum, Ordinatio; Distinctiones XIX–XLVIII*, ed. G. I. Etzkorn and F. E. Kelley, in William Ockham 1967–

(1980). *OT* IX: *Quodlibeta septem*, ed. Joseph C. Wey, in William Ockham 1967–

(1980a). *Ockham's Theory of Propositions: Part 2 of the Summa logicae*, tr. A. J. Freddoso and Henry Schuurman, University of Notre Dame Press

William of Sherwood (1937), *Introductiones in logicam*, ed. M. Grabmann (Sitzungsberichte der Bayerischen Akademie der Wissenschaften, Phil.-hist. Abteilung 1937, 10), Verlag der Bayerischen Akademie der Wissenschaften

(1941). *Syncategoremata*, ed. J. R. O'Donnell, *Mediaeval Studies* 3:46–93

(1966). *William of Sherwood's Introduction to Logic*, tr. with introduction and notes by Norman Kretzmann, University of Minnesota Press

(1968). *William of Sherwood's Treatise on Syncategorematic Words*, tr. with introduction and notes by Norman Kretzmann, University of Minnesota Press

Williams, G. H. (1951). *The Norman Anonymous of 1100 A.D.* (Harvard Theological Studies, No. 18), Harvard University Press

Wilpert, Paul (1931). *Das Problem der Wahrheitssicherung bei Thomas von Aquin: Ein Beitrag zur Geschichte des Evidenzproblems* BGPM XXX, 3, Aschendorff

Wilson, Curtis (1952). 'Pomponazzi's Criticism of Calculator', *Isis* 44: 355–63
  (1956). *William Heytesbury: Medieval Logic and the Rise of Mathematical Physics* (Publications in Medieval Science, 3), University of Wisconsin Press
  (1972). 'Heytesbury, William', in C. C. Gillispie (ed.) *Dictionary of Scientific Biography*, Charles Scribner's Sons
Winterbottom, M. (1967). 'Fifteenth-Century Manuscripts of Quintilian', *Classical Quarterly* 17: 339–69
Wippel, J. F. (1964). 'Godfrey of Fontaines and the Real Distinction Between Essence and Existence', *Traditio* 20: 385–410
  (1967). 'Godfrey of Fontaines', *New Catholic Encyclopedia* 6: 577–8
  (1971). 'Godfrey of Fontaines: The Date of Quodlibet 15', *Franciscan Studies* 31: 300–69
  (1973). 'Commentary on Boethius' *De trinitate*' *The Thomist* 37: 133–54
  (1974a). 'The Dating of James of Viterbo's Quodlibet I and Godfrey of Fontaines' Quodlibet VIII', *Augustiniana* 24: 348–86
  (1974b). 'Godfrey of Fontaines and Henry of Ghent's Theory of Intentional Distinction Between Essence and Existence' in T. W. Köhler (ed.) *Sapientiae Procerum Amore. Mélanges Médiévistes offerts à Dom Jean-Pierre Müller O.S.B* (*Studia Anselmiana*, 63), Herder
  (1977). 'The Condemnations of 1270 and 1277 at Paris', *The Journal of Medieval and Renaissance Studies* 7: 169–201
  (1978). 'Metaphysics and *Separatio* According to Thomas Aquinas', *The Review of Metaphysics* 31: 431–70
  (1979). 'Aquinas's Route to the Real Distinction: A Note on *De ente et essentia*', *The Thomist* 43: 279–95
  (1980). *The Metaphysical Thought of Godfrey of Fontaines: A Study in Late Thirteenth-Century Philosophy*. Catholic University of America Press
  (forthcoming). 'The Relationship Between Essence and Existence in Late Thirteenth Century Thought: Giles of Rome, Henry of Ghent, Godfrey of Fontaines, and James of Viterbo', in *Ancient and Medieval Philosophies of Existence*, Fordham University
Wolf, F. J. (1966). *Die Intellektslehre des Simon von Faversham nach seinem De Anima Kommentaren*, Inaugural Dissertation, University of Bonn
Wolfson, Harry Austryn (1935). 'The Internal Senses in Latin, Arabic, and Hebrew Philosophic Texts', *Harvard Theological Review* 28: 69–133
  (1973). *Studies in the History of Philosophy and Religion*, vol. 1, ed. I. Twersky and G. H. Williams, Harvard University Press
Wolin, Sheldon S. (1960). *Politics and Vision: Continuity and Innovation in Western Political Thought*, Little, Brown
Wolter, A. B. (1946). *The Transcendentals and their Function in the Metaphysics of Duns Scotus*, The Catholic University of America
  ed. and tr. (1962). *Duns Scotus: Philosophical Writings*, Nelson
  (1965a). 'The Ockhamist Critique' in E. McMullin (ed.) *The Concept of Matter in Greek and Medieval Philosophy*, University of Notre Dame Press
  (1965b). 'The Formal Distinction', in J. K. Ryan and B. M. Bonansea (eds.) *John Duns Scotus, 1265–1965*, The Catholic University of America
  (1967a). 'Bacon, Roger' in Paul Edwards (ed.) *The Encyclopedia of Philosophy*, Macmillan
  (1967b). 'Duns Scotus, John', in P. Edwards (ed.) *The Encyclopedia of Philosophy*, Macmillan

(1968). 'Is Existence for Scotus a Perfection, Predicate, or What?' in *De doctrina Ioannis Duns Scoti. Acta Congressus Scotistici Internationalis Oxonii et Edimburgi 11–17 sept. 1966 celebrati. V. II: Problemata Philosophica*, Cura Commissionis Scotisticae

Woodward, W. H. (1921). *Vittorino da Feltre and Other Humanist Educators*, Cambridge University Press

Woolf, C. N. S. (1913). *Bartolus of Sassoferrato*, Cambridge University Press

Workman, Herbert B. (1926). *John Wyclif: A Study of the English Medieval Church* (2 vols.), Clarendon Press

  (1966). *John Wyclif: A Study of the English Medieval Church*, Arcon Books (1st edn. 1926)

Wright, N. A. R. (1976). 'The *Tree of Battles* of Honoré Bouvet and the Laws of War', in C. T. Allmand (ed.) *War, Literature and Politics in the Late Middle Ages*, Liverpool University Press

Wrobel, Ioh. (1887). *Eberhardi Bethuniensis Graecismus*, G. Koebner

Wüsdörfer, Joseph (1917). *Erkennen und Wissen nach Gregor von Rimini. Ein Beitrag zur Geschichte der Erkenntnistheorie des Nominalismus* (BGPM, XX, 1), Aschendorff

Wulf, Maurice de (1904): *Un théologien-philosophe du XIIIᵉ siècle. Étude sur la vie, les oeuvres et l'influence de Godefroid de Fontaines*, Hayez

  (1934–7). *Histoire de la philosophie médiévale* (6th edn.), I (1934), II (1936), III (1937) Institut Supérieur de Philosophie/Vrin

Wyclif, John. *See* John Wyclif

Yates, Frances (1966). *The Art of Memory*, Routledge and Kegan Paul

Yokoyama, Tetsuo (1969). 'Simon of Faversham's Sophisma: *Universale est Intentio*', *Mediaeval Studies* 31:1–14

Ypma, E. (1974). 'Recherches sur la carrière scolaire et la bibliothèque de Jacques de Viterbe † 1308', *Augustiniana* 24:247–82

  (1975). 'Recherches sur la productivité littéraire de Jacques de Viterbe jusqu'à 1300', *Augustiniana* 25:223–82

Zabarella, Jacobus (1608). *Opera logica*, Frankfurt

Zabughin, V. (1909–12). *Giulio Pomponio Leto: saggio critico*, La vita letteraria

Zavalloni, R. (1951). *Richard de Mediavilla et la controverse sur la pluralité des formes*, Éditions de l'Institut Supérieur de Philosophie de Louvain

Zigliara, T. M. (1876) *Summa philosophiae in usum scholarum*, Beauchesne

Zimmermann, A. (1965). *Ontologie oder Metaphysik? Die Diskussion über den Gegenstand der Metaphysik im 13. und 14. Jahrhundert*, Brill

  (1967–8). 'Dante hatte doch Recht: Neue Ergebnisse der Forschung über Siger de Brabant', *Philosophisches Jahrbuch* 75:206–17

  (1973). 'Thomas von Aquin und Siger von Brabant im Licht neuer Quellentexte' in Alf Önnerfors, Johannes Rathofer and Fritz Wagner (eds.) *Literatur und Sprache im europäischen Mittelalter: Festschrift für Karl Langosch zum 70. Geburtstag*, Wissenschaftliche Buchgesellschaft

  ed. (1976). *Die Auseinandersetzungen an der Pariser Universität im XIII. Jahrhundert* (Miscellanea Mediaevalia, 10), De Gruyter

Zippel, Giuseppe (1957). 'Note sulle redazioni della "Dialectica" di Lorenzo Valla', *Archivio storico per le province parmensi* 9:301–15

Zoubov, V. P. (1959). 'Walter Catton, Gérard d'Odon et Nicolas Bonet', *Physis* 1:261–78

  (1960). 'Le traité "De continuo" de Bradwardin', *Istoriko-Matematicheskie Issledovaniya*

13:385–440

(1961). 'Jean Buridan et les concepts du point au quatorzième siècle', *Mediaeval and Renaissance Studies* 5:49–95

Zumkeller, A. (1941). *Hugolin von Orvieto und seine theologische Erkenntnislehre*, Cassiciacum. Eine Sammlung wissenschaftlicher Forschungen über den hl. Augustinus und den Augustinerorden, Band IX, 2. Reihe, 3. Band, Würzburg

(1951). 'De doctrina sociali scholae Augustinianae Aevi Medii', *Analecta Augustiniana* 22:57–84

THE INDICES

The Index Nominum covers the forty-six chapters and the Biographies; the Index Rerum covers the chapters only. Entries in the Index Nominum are unanalysed, but major entries in the Index Rerum are analysed in considerable detail, often including such subheadings as 'rights, Marsilius of Padua on'; 'psychology, Matthew of Aquasparta's'. Readers interested in a particular philosopher's treatment of some topic should consult both indices. Since the chapters are organised topically, it will also be helpful to have in mind the page numbers of the relevant chapter when consulting the Index Nominum.

INDEX NOMINUM

Page numbers divided by an en-dash (such as '72–81', '101–2') indicate either a continuous discussion or simply at least one relevant occurrence of the name on each of those pages.

Many pages referred to contain relevant material in their footnotes as well as in the body of the text, but footnotes are expressly referred to (as in '847n.' or '181nn.') only in case relevant material does not also occur in the text on those pages; and footnote references give only the number of the page on which the note referred to begins, even if the relevant material occurs in the continuation of the note on the following page.

This index is intended to include the names of all persons and places mentioned in the text of the chapters (ordinarily excluding examples) and the Biographies. The titles of anonymous works are also included. The names of modern authors whose works are cited in the footnotes are included only when the reference is more than a simple bibliographical citation – e.g., a quotation, or an appraisal of a contribution.

Ancient authors are cited under the names by which they are generally known. Medieval and Renaissance authors are cited under their first names if their careers are earlier than 1500, under their last names if their careers are later. Some such distinction is called for in an index of names covering that transitional period; the extensive cross-referencing in this index will help to avoid confusion.

References printed in italics are to the Biographies or to discussions elsewhere in the book that are particularly informative regarding the person in question.

INDEX RERUM

Page numbers divided by an en-dash (such as '72–81', '101–2') indicate either a continuous discussion or simply at least one relevant occurrence of the term on each of those pages.

Many pages referred to contain relevant material in their footnotes as well as in the body of the text, but footnotes are expressly referred to (as in '847n.' or '181nn.') only in case relevant material does not also occur in the text on those pages; and footnote references give only the number of the page on which the note referred to begins, even if the relevant material occurs in the continuation of the note on the following page.

Many Latin technical terms used in the text or notes are indexed even when their English equivalents are likewise indexed, because the many scholars contributing to this History do not all use the same terminology and because their discussions are based on Latin philosophical literature which is almost entirely untranslated. The analysed entries and cross-references should help the reader to see associations that might otherwise be obscure.

This index contains references not only to explicit discussions but also to further applications of the concept or term, enabling a reader interested in a particular topic to see something of the part it plays in medieval philosophy. Because of this book's multiple authorship and organisation by interrelated topics, it sometimes happens that a concept is employed in one chapter before being more formally introduced in a later chapter.

This index includes entries for works of Aristotle, Porphyry, and Boethius, the authors whose importance in the curriculum did so much to shape the philosophy of the later Middle Ages. The entries for Aristotle's works aim at completeness in order to provide a rough guide to the character of their enormous influence over later medieval thought.

648–9, 651; *see also* free choice *and* free will

Christ: and apostles as reflected in hierarchy, 747; as intending abolition of private property, 750; as the inner teacher, 499n.; as the model for evangelical poverty, 742–4; as the only fully realised man, 684; as the Word of God, 441, 451n.; condemned to death, 691

Christ's: commission of the Church to Peter, 747; foreknowledge, 465; precepts and natural law, 706–7; precepts as applied to war, 772; universal judicial power, 746–7

Christianity, 5, 7, 477, 521, 526, 740, 751; and Aristotelianism, 71, 90–4, 522, 600–1, 728; and other religions, 83–4, 92; and philosophy, 71, 90, 92–4, 522, 524, 530, 600–1, 660, 662–6

Christian: life, 742, 751; ministry, 742, 751

Church: as teacher, 80; councils, 89; Fathers, 80, 83, 89, 359, 642, 705, 757, 761

circumcision, 698

citizen, concept of, 725, 763

civics, 803

civilians, 764

civilitas, 749

clerics: as teachers or masters, 80, 82–3, 87; divine call of, 80; in warfare, 774

coartatio, 172

codicology, 38n.

cogitative or estimative power, 606–7, 613, 616

cognitio: propter quid and *quia*, 96; *singularis*, 461n., 463nn., 464, 476n.

cognition: abstractive (*see* abstractive cognition); accounted for in terms of (being or existence, 445–9, 450–1, 452–3, 455; light, 442–4, 448–51, 453, 455, 498–504); acts of, 487, 490, 492, 627–8; and intentions, 487–91; based on demonstration and on experience, 514; complex, 467, 509n.; evident, 466–7, 508–10, 512–14; incomplex, 467, 509n.; individuation of universal, 615, 617–18; intellective, 408–9, 442, 448, 452–3, 457, 595, 597, 620, 623–4, 627–8; intuitive (*see* intuitive cognition); manner and object of, 462, 477; mental acts in, 452, 465; of individuals, 460–78, 609, 613, 619; picture-theory of, 266; primary absolute and secondary relative, 488, 490, 513; sensitive, 595–6; undetermined by previous cognitions, 470; *see also* intellection *and* knowledge

colleges, 14, 16

comitatio, 306

commanding, 649–51, 653–4, 713, 716–17, 755–6; God's, 703; *see also under* law

Commandments, Ten, 705, 713, 718, 752

commentaries, 20–1, 25, 34, 69, 73–4, 835; and disputed questions, 26; as outgrowths of

glosses or scholia, 73, 102; literal, 29–30, 102, 125, 660, 662, 724–5, 728, 732; on Aristotle, Arabic, 45, 48–9, 52, 59–60, 71, 81, 84, 157, 184, 255, 266, 385–7, 432n., 440, 448n., 526, 617, 618n., 621, 795n.; on Aristotle, Greek, 45–6, 49, 61, 63–4, 81, 97, 103–4, 108, 122, 446, 605, 617, 618n., 659, 795n.; on Aristotle, Latin, 88, 90, 91, 96, 104, 108, 122, 390, 391n., 398, 449n., 522, 540, 657–72, 723–37, 795n., 817, 836 (*see also under individual titles*); on Aristotle, table of medieval Latin translations of Greek and Arabic, 74–9; on Boethius (*see under* Boethius' theological works); on the Bible (*see under* Bible); on the *Sentences* (*see* Sentence-commentaries); question–, 30–3, 96, 102, 125–6, 541, 660, 664, 666, 728, 732, 734; superseded by modern treatises, 835

Commentator, Averroes as the, 617

commonness, 419, 421, 423

common sense as universal human beliefs, 838; *see also* sense, common

communes rationes, 284–5

communication as the purpose of language, 189–90, 255–6

community, 739, 745, 748, 753, 759, 767, 832; natural authority of the, 764–5, 767–8, 770

comparison, 213n., 548–9

compatibility (*stans cum*), 421–2

compendia, 69

complex, what is, 319–20

complexa, 198, 202, 205–6, 368, 373, 489, 573

complexe significabile, 203–5, 794

complexio, 197–8, 200, 202, 204–5

complexum-theory of objects of belief and knowledge, 202–6; 209

composition: essence–existence, 392, 393n., 395n., 396n., 397, 399–400, 402; grammatical, 811; matter–form, 397–8, 400nn., 402, 408–10, 448, 524; of judgement, 482; or predication, 213n.; positive–privative, 406; potentiality–actuality, 400, 402, 407–8; substance–accident, 399, 400n., 406, 407n., 408

compossibility, 355, 357, 465n., 510

compounded and divided senses, 151–2, 177n., 179, 222, 370n., 378n.; and epistemic verbs, 321, 364; and obligations, 321; of modal propositions, 177n., 179, 347–8, 354–7, 363–4

compounding and dividing in judgement, 200, 207, 452n., 455n., 485n., 504n.

concedo, see under disputations

conceiving: modes of (*see modi concipiendi*); modistic analysis of, 263–4

concepts, 119–21, 207, 443–4, 625; abstract, 264n., 595–7; active, 264n.; and intentions,

713, 717 (absolute, manifested, and prescriptive, 640; as determining goodness and evil, 640, 667, 713–14, 830)

golden mountain, 438, 607

good: character of, 644–5; common or public, 675–6, 739, 761, 765, 767, 769; highest, 659, 674, 682, 706; *in communi*, 644–5; in general, 691–2; life, 643; Plato's idea of the, 658; proper or private, 739

goodness, 629; and evil as dependent on God's will, 640, 667, 713–14, 830; as will's object, 637–8, 644; God's (*see* God's goodness); intrinsic, 717–18, 830

goods: as similar to and part of supreme good, 668; spiritual and material, 750

government: as based on consent, 741–2, 745, 759–60; as consequence of sin, 757; expediency in forms of, 754; hierocratic principles of, 741, 745–6, 756, 763; in traditional grammar, 259; legal restraints on, 755; populist principles of, 763, 767; spiritual and secular, 754–5; *see also* law *and* politics *and* monarchy

grace, 87, 376, 642, 782, 688, 694, 708, 758, 829; freedom of, 631

grammar, 13, 15, 85, 493, 542, 670; ancient Latin, 254, 258, 810, 812; and logic, 109, 123, 133–4, 142–8, 156, 254–5, 268, 483–4, 810, 816; and natural science, 527; as regulatively descriptive, 198; as speculative and auxiliary science, 255–6, 261; empirical, 266; founded on classical quotations, 798, 810; Greek, 812–13; humanist (earliest, 810; fully developed, 810–11); humanist studies assimilated into course in, 806; humanists' approach to, 269, 796, 798, 802, 809–12; in early Middle Ages, 254; in late Middle Ages, 796; philosophical, 815–16; questions on, 72; scholastic, 808, 850; speculative or modistic, 254–69, 486–90, 790, 819, 833 (alleged impossibility of, 268; general nature of, 254–5; historical development of, 256–7; intentions in, 486–90; *see also* modism); traditional, 259, 813, 815; transformational, 259n.; universal, 255, 266, 268–9, 813, 815–16, 820

grammarians, 161, 163, 798; authority of classical, 261, 811–12; concerned with congruity, not truth, 261; of Port Royal, 816; proper task of, 268

grammars: vernacular, 803, 811; verse-, 815

grammatical: categories, 256–8; composition, 811; constructions, 259–61; dependency, 259–60; government, 259; semantics, Apollonian, 110–11, 123, 126

grammaticality (*congruentia*), 110–11, 126, 138,

214n., 232, 243, 261, 268n., 804

granting (*concedo*), *see under* disputations

gravia, 31

gravity, 534

Great Schism as influence on political thought, 745

greater, the, 279n., 800

Greek, 110–11, 268n.; Latin translations of Aristotle from, 45–7, 49, 52, 54, 57, 61–8, 74–9, 86; particles in Latin, 67; study of, 61, 797, 800, 809, 812–13, 836; -Latin editions, humanist, 817

growth, *see* augmentation

habitus, see under state

haecceitas or thisness, 413, 420, 456, 463–4, 823–4

handbook, 729

handwriting, 35, 728–9; *see also* paleography *and* scripts

happiness, 7, 660, 663–5; active, 663, 671, 674, 677, 679–81, 685; after death, 677–8, 680, 682, 684; Aquinas on, 678–80; Aristotelian concept of, 673–7, 679, 683, 685; as a common good, 675–6: as cognitive mental activity, 678–9, 686; as enjoyment of contemplation of God, 673, 682, 684; as God's gift, 664–5, 674; as humanly attainable, 674; as human perfection, 657–8, 673–86; as knowledge of divine essence, 682–3; as object of philosophical concern, 657; as perfect actualisation of reason, 680–2; as ultimate object of action, 674; as unattainable in this world, 673–4; as union with God, 675–7; 679, 686; Boethian concept of, 674, 684–5; Boethius of Dacia on, 680–2; Buridan on, 683–6; Christian Platonist concept of, 673–7; contemplative or theoretical, 663–4, 669, 674–5, 676n., 677, 679–86; double, 679–81; God as epitome of, 658, 675; object and activity of, 678; of philosophical life (*see* happiness, contemplative); of political or social life (*see* happiness, active); perfect and imperfect, 662, 665–6, 678–9, 682; philosophical and theological, 681–2, Scotus on, 683; uncreated and created, 675–8

health, 684

heap argument, *see* sorites

hearing, 539

heat and cold, 555, 558–60, 562, 588–90

Hebrew, study of, 813

heresy and heretics, 71, 691, 741, 743, 753

hierarchy, 747, 758; *see also under* world

hierocratic, *see under* government *and* papacy

Historia animalium (Aristotle's), 48

history, 670; of medieval philosophy, 840, 846–7

each, 620; perfections of, 582; *specialissima*, 456n.; *see also under* genus

speculative grammar, *see* modism *and under* grammar

speech: acts, 197, 199–200; figure of (*see figura dictionis*); parts of (*see* parts of speech *and partes orationis*)

speed, 533–6; *see also* velocity

Sphaera, 18

sphere soul, 390n.

spheres, celestial, 31

spirit, *see* being, spiritual *and* creatures, purely spiritual *and* substances, spiritual

spite, 831

stans cum, 421–2

'*Stans potest sedere*', 347–8

state (*habitus*), category of, 129

state of nature, 742, 757–70

state (political), 86; as natural outgrowth of smaller units, 760; man's natural dependence on, 759–61, 763; life of virtue as purpose of, 733; origin of, 757–70

states of affairs as bearers of truth-values, 204

stationarii, 36–7

statistical: interpretation of modality, 344–8; 351–4; phenomena, 505, 507, 511–13, 526

status: Abelardian doctrine of, 154–6, 165–6; *quaestionis*, 27

Stoic indemonstrables, 793

stoicism in transmission of ancient logic, 106

Stoics, 1–2, 761; on logic and language, 103, 115n., 121, 123–7, 303, 306, 345n.; on morality, 708

strength, *see* power

strife, 739

structure: deep, 820; surface, 111, 260–1, 820

students: guidebooks for, 84–7, 835–7; organisations of, 12

studia: *generalia*, 13; *humanitatis*, 808n.; *particularia*, 14

study, 445

stylistic identification of authors or translators, 54–5, 59, 62, 67–8

Suarezians, 825

subalternation, 343

subcontrariety, 343

subiective and *obiective*, 490

subject: and subject matter, 167; being in and being said of, 131; concept, 123, 199–200; terms, 110, 165–6, 188, 200, 211, 236, 485 (dummy, 211n.; taken indefinitely, 183n.); things, 207

substance: -accident composition, 399, 400n., 406, 407n., 408; and accident, 404, 428–9; as subject of discourse, 163; as the subject of metaphysics, 387; category of, 119, 129, 131,

134, 136, 138, 263, 530, 532; nature of, 163–4; not susceptible of degree, 131; varieties of, 402

substances: as significata of names, 134–5, 138, 149, 163–4, 168; and God, 387; known only by means of propositions, 435; primary, 129, 263; secondary, 129, 133, 444; spiritual, 596–9, 627

substantives, 816

subtlety, excessive, 843

successiveness, *see* res successivae

summae, 33, 89

summulist doctrines in logic, 795

superior, logical, 222, 226, 239n., 296, 430–1, 432n.

superposition, geometrical or physical, 577n., 578, 580n.

supine, 811

'*supponere*', earlier and later senses of, 164

supposita, 165, 183, 243, 289; and *subiecta*, 165, 170; determinate, 265n.

suppositing for and being truly predicable of, 192

suppositio and *subiectio*, 165–6

supposition, 123, 126, 133, 161, 165–6, 174, 185, 223, 486, 540, 557n., 591, 787, 791–2, 796, 819–21, 835; accidental, 168, 169, 177, 183–4; altered by modifiers, 433; and acceptance or acceptation, 183n., 184–5; and appellation, 178–82; and consequences, 195; and descent to singulars, 192, 194–5; and equivocation, 184–5; and exposition, 266; and signification, 188, 494, and truth-conditions, 193; and univocation, 175–7, 180; common, 196; confused (or indeterminate), 196, 550 (distributive, 176, 194, 196; merely, 176, 194–6, 458n., 583–4, 820); determinate, 194–6, 550, 583, 584n.; *de virtute sermonis*, 183; discrete, 194, 196; dispositional or habitual or virtual, 170–1, 178–80; distributive (immobile, 196; mobile, 196); divisions of, 175–6, 184–5, 192–3; equivocal; 182n., 185; formal, 196; for a proposition by one of its terms, 248; for truth's sake, 183; historical introduction of, 166, 254; improper (or metaphorical), 176, 180, 182n., 192, 196; letter-designations for types of, 792; material, 193, 196, 206, 230nn., 296; natural, 168–70, 177–8, 181, 183, 196, 820; of significata for supposita, 265n.; of subject and predicate terms, 166, 176, 179; of subject terms alone, 166, 195; personal, 185, 192–3, 196, 230n., 296, 431n., 491, 493 (modes of, 194–5); proper or literal, 192, 196; simple, 138, 185, 193, 196, 311n., 431n., 491, 493, 820; syntactical definition of, 176, 178–80; table and

'*Tu scis regem sedere*', 329–32
types and tokens, 207–9
tyrannicide, 740, 750, 768–70
tyranny, 739–40, 749–50, 752, 766, 768–70; as contradiction of kingship, 768–9

ultra, 571–2
ultramontanism, 841, 845
undergoing (passion), category of, 129, 527–8
understanding: act of, 190, 626; and significa- tion, 137–8, 168, 188; formal, 464; form of, 452; generating an, 191
unity: denominative, 413; essential or ac- cidental, 402; greater and lesser, 419, 421; numerical, 412–13, 421–2, 424–6, 428, 824; rational, 824; real, 412–13, 430n., 824; speci- fic or generic, 412, 425, 455
universal: affirmatives and conditionals and disjunctives, 305; or general concepts, 191, 432n., 434, 439, 458, 625; liberty and natural law, 706, 715
universalisation, mental acts of, 824
universality, intention of, 482, 490–1
universals: and Abelardian *status*, 154–5; and denotation, 148; and individuating principles as really distinct, 424; and particulars (dis- tinguished from individuals, 429–30; or in- dividuals, 119–20, 168–9, 423, 484); as abstracted from (sensible species, 454; sin- gulars, 444–5, 447–8, 460, 483, 604, 624); as common intentions founded on things, 484n.; as concepts only, 434, 458; as con- tributed by the intellect, 460, 462; as divided by contrary *differentiae*, 423; as first objects of human intellect, 455–7; as first subjects of some accidents, 428; as *flatus vocis*, 444; as indistinct images, 599; as metaphysical con- stituents of particulars, 411, 427; as names, 434; as natural signs, 434, 439, 458; as objects of thought, 413, 444, 455–7; as parts of particulars, 424–5, 427; as *per accidens* sub- jects of some accidents, 428; as really distinct from (one another, 425; particulars, 423–5, 432); as really identical with particulars, 430; as *sermones*, 444; as singulars confusedly conceived, 430–4; as supposita or referents, 164, 193; as *significata*, 164, 167–70; as subjects of demonstrative science, 423, 430, 445, 448n., 463; as the only (definienda, 423, 430; demonstranda, 504n., 513); as un- representable by intelligible species, 625; as words, 149, 152–3; *fictum*-theory of, 491; in Aquinas, 452–3, 457, 824; in Aristotle, 444; in Burley, 422–4, 427–9 (Ockham's and Harclay's critiques of, 424–9); in early 14th century, 411–39; in Harclay, 429–30, 432,

434 (Burley's and Ockham's critiques of, 430–4); in Ockham, 434–9, 458; *in potentia* as becoming intentions *in actu*, 482; in Scotus, 412–17, 419–26, 429, 455–7, 627, 823 (Ockham's critique of, 419–22); in Suárez, 823–5; *intellectio*-theory of, 492; problem of, 119, 123 (semantic source of, 130, 133, 191); ranked lower than individuals, 449; reduced to pure fictions, 455, 456n.; the five, 130; *see also* individuating principles *and* natures
universities, 12–13, 87–8, 174, 440; courses in, 17–19, 801; humanism in English, 788; nations in, 17n., 541n.; pedagogical tech- niques in, 16–24, 542; Protestant, 671, 802; statutes of, 18–19, 23, 73, 542n., 543n., 544n., 545, 562, 801; survival of scholasticism in, 809, 833–5, 837
univocation, 164–6, 182–4, 413, 458; and appellation, 165, 175; and signification, 164–6, 175; and supposition, 175–7, 180; division of, 175
univocity, 406n., 456–8
usage, linguistic, 135–7, 139–40, 268, 798, 803
uses, 279n.
usury, 717
usus, 650, 652
uterque, 212
utility, common or public, 762, 767–8
ut in paucioribus, *see under* contingency
ut in pluribus, *see under* consequences *and* contingency
ut nunc, *see* consequences, as-of-now *and de inesse, ut nunc*
Utopians, More's, 777n., 778, 782
utrum, 213n.
utterances (*voces*), 148–9, 209–10; *see also voces*

vacuum or void, 529, 538–9
va ... cat, 40
validity, 117, 143, 150, 156, 251, 280, 282, 286, 293, 295–6, 300, 301n.; 793; and truth, 301–2; causes of, 285–9, 293, 295; -con- ditions of consequences, 307–10, 349
variables, logical and mathematical, 112, 562
vel, 213n.; *see also aut*
velocities: comparisons of, 549, 562; propor- tions of, 34, 533, 535
velocity, 533, 536, 553, 561; considered *penes causam* and *penes effectum*, 534, 536; instan- taneous, 534–5, 541, 548n.; total or average, 534–5, 548n.; rotational, 553–4
verb: as part of speech, 123, 133, 212; -phrases, 145–7, 149, 154; substantive, 146, 165, 212n.
verbs: as determinants of reference, 165, 181 (*see also* restriction *and* ampliation); as providing completeness of sense, 144–5; as syncategore-